William Faulkner:
American Writer

Books by Frederick R. Karl

Modern and Modernism: The Sovereignty of the Artist 1885–1925 (1985)
American Fictions: 1940–80 (1983)
Joseph Conrad: The Three Lives. A Biography (1979)
The Adversary Literature (1974)
An Age of Fiction: The Nineteenth-Century British Novel (1964, revised 1972)
C. P. Snow: The Politics of Conscience (1963)
The Contemporary English Novel (1962, revised 1972)
The Quest, a novel (1961)
A Reader's Guide to Joseph Conrad (1960, revised 1969)

EDITED:

Joseph Conrad: A Collection of Criticism (1975)
The Collected Letters of Joseph Conrad: Volume I, 1861–97 (1983)
Volume II, 1898–1902 (1986), Volume II, 1903–07 (1988)
(general editor and volume coeditor—8 volumes in all)
The Mayor of Casterbridge by Thomas Hardy (1966)
The Portable Conrad (Morton Dauwen Zabel's edition, revised, 1969)
The Signet Classic Book of British Short Stories (1985)
The Secret Agent by Joseph Conrad (1983)
Chance by Joseph Conrad (1985)
The Moonstone by Wilkie Collins (1984)
The Woman in White by Wilkie Collins (1985)

COEDITED:

The Existential Imagination (1963)
Short Fiction of the Masters (1963, 1973)
The Shape of Fiction (1967, 1978)
The Radical Vision (1970)
The Naked i: Fictions for the Seventies (1971)
The Existential Mind: Documents and Fictions (1974)
The Fourth World: The Imprisoned, the Poor, the Sick, the Elderly and
Underaged in America (1976)

William Faulkner:
American Writer

A Biography

FREDERICK R. KARL

WEIDENFELD & NICOLSON
New York

Published by Weidenfeld & Nicolson, New York
A Division of Wheatland Corporation
841 Broadway
New York, New York 10003-4793

Published in Canada by General Publishing Company, Ltd.

The following photographs appear courtesy of LOUIS DANIEL BRODSKY: William Clark Falkner; William
Faulkner at Oxford Graded School; Inscribed presentation copy of *The Marble Faun*; *Mississippi Poems*
presented to Myrtle Ramey; 1932 printing of *Salmagundi*; William Faulkner in 1933, inscribed; William
Faulkner in 1951, inscribed; Albert Einstein's *Ideas and Opinions*; William Faulkner's 1957 letter to
Mrs. Jannette Tracy.
The following photographs appear courtesy of DEAN FAULKNER WELLS: Faulkner's paternal grandfather,
the "young Colonel"; John Falkner and Sallie Murry; Maud Falkner as a young woman; William
Faulkner in full regalia in 1918; William Spratling's sketch of William Faulkner; William Faulkner
with friend at Red Rock Canyon in 1932; Jill Faulkner with Caroline Barr; William Faulkner in
the Philippines; William Faulkner with his grandson; Maud Falkner at age 88; William Faulkner
in 1956.
The following photographs appear courtesy of DEAN FAULKNER WELLS and MRS. LOUISE MEADOW:
William Faulkner with two of his brothers; Dean Swift Falkner's tombstone.
The following photographs appear courtesy of the sources noted: Estelle Oldham in 1913, THE
MISSISSIPPI COLLECTION, UNIVERSITY OF MISSISSIPPI LIBRARY; William Faulkner with daughter Jill and
at the 1950 Stockholm Nobel Prize awards ceremony, JOSEPH BLOTNER; William Faulkner and daughter
Jill at her wedding, BERN KEATING; William Faulkner in Japan in 1955, GAY WILSON ALLEN; William
Faulkner with Joan Williams, JOAN WILLIAMS.

Library of Congress Cataloging-in-Publication Data
Karl, Frederick Robert, 1927–
William Faulkner, American writer : a biography / Frederick R.
Karl. — 1st ed.
p.   cm.
Bibliography: p.
Includes index.
ISBN 1-55584-088-4
1. Faulkner, William, 1897–1962—Biography. 2. Novelists,
American—20th century—Biography. I. Title.
PS3511.A86Z8588 1988
813'.52—dc19
[B]   88-13966
                                            CIP

Manufactured in the United States of America
This book is printed on acid-free paper
Designed by Irving Perkins Associates

First Edition

1 3 5 7 9 10 8 6 4 2

To the memory of Rita, and to Pat

Acknowledgments

I T IS GRATIFYING to acknowledge the help of so many individuals and institutions in the making of this biography. Two people in particular deserve special mention: Ilse Lind, professor of English at New York University, and Joseph Blotner, professor of English at the University of Michigan. Their help was decisive. Professor Lind was always available to discuss matters of Faulkner biography; her encyclopedic knowledge of his life, work, and world proved indispensable. As a colleague and consultant, she always had information or a lead to offer. From the beginning, Professor Blotner was supportive of my project and helpful whenever I went to him for clarification of points in Faulkner's life. His 1974 biography of Faulkner was a landmark study of the writer, establishing the range of materials, providing chronologies, giving us the order and organization of the life. I cannot express adequately the fullness of my gratitude.

There are several others whose support has been invaluable. In the Faulkner family, Dean Faulkner Wells, her husband, Larry, and her mother, Louise Meadow, made themselves available for my prying questions and were always receptive to my often intimate investigations. Professor Donald P. Duclos has been extremely helpful and forthcoming in matters of Faulkner family background. His researches on Faulkner's great-grandfather and grandfather are models of investigative scholarship. Among other Faulkner scholars, all researchers into the life must be grateful for the work of Carvel Collins, James B. Meriwether, Noel Polk,

Thomas McHaney, Michael Millgate, and Cleanth Brooks. My talks in Oxford with Noel Polk and Thomas McHaney proved most fruitful. My indebtedness to other Faulkner scholars and critics, living and dead, is indicated in the notes to this volume. These include: Malcolm Cowley, Murry C. Falkner, Frederick L. Gwynn, Ben Wasson, Panthea Broughton, Thadious M. Davis, Eric Sundquist, Michel Gresset, James B. Carothers, Keen Butterworth, Bruce F. Kawin, Maurice Edgar Coindreau, Judith L. Sensibar, François Pitavy, André Bleikasten, Edmond L. Volpe, David Minter, Philip Weinstein, John Cullen, Lewis M. Dabney, Doreen Fowler, John Pilkington, Jr., and Albert I. Bezzerides.

I want to single out Louis Daniel Brodsky for extraordinary support, as well as for giving me access to his vast collection of Faulkner materials through his published volumes. My talks with him in Oxford also proved helpful. Another collector, Toby Holtzman, was most kind in offering me access to his Faulkner material.

Evans Harrington, chairman of the Department of English at the University of Mississippi, and his wife, Betty, made me feel more than welcome; they extended to me the best of Southern hospitality. Evans was always available for discussion of the Faulkner landscape and took me on tours of the local landmarks.

Several members of the English faculty at the university went out of their way to welcome me to Oxford: Benjamin Franklin Fisher, Gregory Schirmer, Alan Golding, Tommy Joe Ray, Howard Bahr, Charles D. Cannon, Louis Dollarhide, Maryemma Graham, and David Holman. I also want to thank Barry Hannah and Willie Morris for showing interest in my project and providing many hours of good talk.

Square Books, the local Oxford bookstore with the national reputation, and its owner, Richard Howorth, provided a home away from home for me: fine books, good talk, authors' parties, and an open house for a stranger. The Center for the Study of Southern Culture, directed by William Ferris, with Ann J. Abadie as associate director, was another gathering place for good conversation and papers on Faulkner and other subjects.

Thomas Verich, curator of special collections at the university library, and his staff were always most accommodating and informative. At the University of Virginia, Anne Freudenberg was as helpful with Faulkner as she had been, in the past, with Conrad. Equally helpful were the staffs at other Faulkner repositories: the Berg Collection of the New York Public Library, the Princeton University Library, the Beinecke Collection of Yale University, the Humanities Research Center in Austin, Texas, and the William Wisdom Collection of Tulane University in New Orleans.

I wish to thank Jean Stein and Joan Williams for the time they spent with me in person and on the telephone. Glenn Horowitz, a rare-book dealer in New York, also provided help.

To New York University, I am grateful for two Research Challenge Fund Grants, in 1985 and in 1987; as well as for a sabbatical leave in 1986.

My colleagues at the university, besides Professor Lind, have been strong in support and information: James Tuttleton, John Kuehl, and Kenneth Silverman.

My interest in Faulkner began when my colleague and friend at the City College of New York, Edmond L. Volpe, began his work on the author in the early 1960s, when Faulkner scholarship was still rudimentary. It increased when I taught Faulkner in a graduate seminar at the City University Graduate Center and then in a colloquium on Faulkner and Conrad at New York University.

For help with the reproduction of the photographs, I am grateful to Susan Oristaglio. My agent, Melanie Jackson, was everything an agent should be: attentive, supportive, always interested; and the same adjectives should be repeated for my editor, John Herman.

No listing, however, can do justice to the vast number of individuals, institutions, and collections which made this biography possible. To those too I am indebted.

Random House, Inc. For brief excerpts from the copyrighted works of William Faulkner, published by Random House, Inc. For brief excerpts from *Selected Letters of William Faulkner*, ed. Joseph Blotner © 1977; for brief excerpts from *Faulkner: A Biography* by Joseph Blotner © 1974, and from *Faulkner: A Biography, Volume I* by Joseph Blotner © 1984.

The University Press of Virginia. For brief excerpts from *Faulkner in the University*, ed. Frederick L. Gwynn and Joseph L. Blotner © 1959 and 1977.

Viking-Penguin, Inc. For brief excerpts from *The Faulkner-Cowley File*. Copyright © 1966 by Malcolm Cowley. Copyright © 1966 by The Estate of William Faulkner. All rights reserved.

Sanford J. Greenburger. For brief excerpts from *A Loving Gentleman* by Meta Carpenter and Orin Borsten © 1976.

University Press of Mississippi. For brief excerpts from *William Faulkner: A Life on Paper* (script by A. I. Bezzerides, introduction by Carvel Collins, adapted and edited by Ann Abadie) © 1980.

University of Nebraska Press. For brief excerpts from *Lion in the Garden: Interviews with William Faulkner*, eds. James B. Meriwether and Michael Millgate © 1968.

University of South Carolina Press. For brief excerpts from *The Time of William Faulkner* by Maurice Coindreau © 1971.

Louis Daniel Brodsky. For brief excerpts from *Faulkner: A Comprehensive Guide to the Brodsky Collection*, Volume II: *The Letters*, eds. Louis Daniel Brodsky and Robert W. Hamblin © Louis Daniel Brodsky. All rights reserved. (Materials published by the University Press of Mississippi, 1984.) From Volume III: *The de Gaulle Story*, eds. Louis Daniel Brodsky and Robert W. Hamblin © Louis Daniel Brodsky. All rights reserved. From Volume IV: *Battle Cry: A Screenplay by William Faulkner*, eds. Louis Daniel Brodsky and Robert W. Hamblin © Louis Daniel Brodsky.

Contents

Foreword

THIS BOOK ATTEMPTS to integrate the latest in biographical information with Faulkner's own large body of work in fiction and poetry. It will not replace Joseph Blotner's monumental two-volume biography of Faulkner, which is an altogether different kind of book. I have not attempted to duplicate the full range of details of Faulkner's life that Professor Blotner has so ably researched and presented; but I have used the materials of Faulkner's work as biographical data in ways Professor Blotner did not attempt or intend to do. By integrating life and work, I have tried to avoid a chronicle or linear life study, which in other circumstances has its own kind of value. This study is in the deepest sense a biography: not only a presentation of the relevant facts of the subject's life, but an effort to understand and interpret that life psychologically, emotionally, and literarily. It tries to put Faulkner together—if not entirely as an understandable man then as a man who may be understood as America's greatest novelist of the twentieth century. The growth of the artist is our quest. If we are successful, then Faulkner will fit snugly into those lines of Keats's great ode, about another artist, himself:

> Ay, in the very temple of delight
> Veil'd Melancholy has her sovran shrine,

Though seen of none save him whose strenuous tongue
Can burst Joy's grape against his palate fine;
His soul shall taste the sadness of her might,
And be among her cloudy trophies hung.

Falkner Family Tree

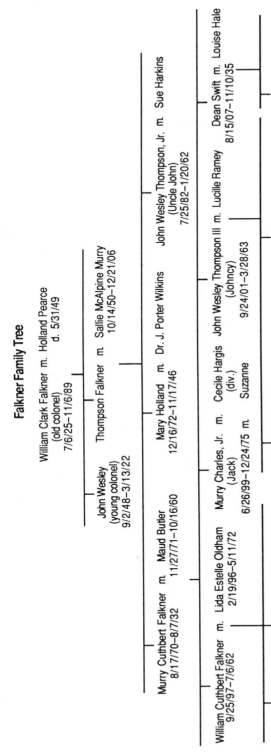

William Clark Falkner m. Holland Pearce
(old colonel)   d. 5/31/49
7/6/25–11/6/89

John Wesley
(young colonel)
9/2/48–3/13/22

Thompson Falkner m. Sallie McAlpine Murry
10/14/50–12/21/06

Mary Holland m. Dr. J. Porter Wilkins
12/16/72–11/17/46

John Wesley Thompson, Jr. m. Sue Harkins
(Uncle John)
7/25/82–1/20/62

Dean Swift m. Louise Hale
8/15/07–11/10/35

John Wesley Thompson III m. Lucille Ramey
(Johncy)
9/24/01–3/28/63

Cecile Hargis
(div.)
Suzanne

Murry Cuthbert II m. Elleine Williams
(Chooky)
2/22/28–

Dean m. Jon Mallard
(div.)
3/22/36–   m. Larry Wells

Murry Cuthbert Falkner m. Maud Butler
8/17/70–8/7/32   11/27/71–10/16/60

Murry Charles, Jr. m.
(Jack)
6/26/99–12/24/75   m.

James Murry m. Nancy Jane Watson
(Jimmy)
7/18/23–

William Cuthbert Falkner m. Lida Estelle Oldham
9/25/97–7/6/62   2/19/96–5/11/72

Jill m. Paul D. Summers, Jr.
6/24/33–

Alabama
1/11/31–1/20/31

Oldham Family Tree

Lida Allen m. Lemuel E. Oldham
8/10/73–3/10/56   2/8/70–5/6/45

Cornell Franklin
(div.)

Melvina Victoria
5/21/98–10/12/18

Dorothy Zollicoffer
(Dot)
8/15/05–12/20/68

Edward de Graffenreid
12/25/07–12/1/16

Lida Estelle m.
2/19/96–5/11/72

William Faulkner:
American Writer

Introduction

WHEN FAULKNER (Family name, Falkner) was born in New Albany, Mississippi, on September 25, 1897, there was still a mythical America; and it was still possible for an individual to wrap himself in that myth. Part of the myth had attached itself to the Falkner family well before the writer was born—its violence, its frontier qualities, its efforts to relocate itself as part of the Southern planter aristocracy—but Faulkner also created his own. Those famous silences which characterized his public pose were an essential part of the mythmaking; they seemed to locate him on some mystical or magical ground where no one else could tread. Faulkner desperately wanted to be a great writer, but he wanted just as desperately to be an epic hero. Both nature and nurture reinforced that willed sense of self.

Many factors become decisive when a man feels compelled to transcend himself, to become either a god or, in Faulkner's case, a centaur. Linked to the process were several elements, all momentous: the unresolved and ambiguous issue of Southern attitudes to modernism, chiefly its fierce opposition to modernization as a kind of foreign intrusion; its equal inability to confront white-Negro relationships on grounds not of law but of plain justice. There was, further, despite the favoritism of his mother, Faulkner's own unhappy time growing up: his small, wispy stature among big men; his father's lack of interest in what his eldest son was doing; his recognition that his father was losing ground while others were succeeding. All of these unresolved behavior patterns called for more than rebellion. Faulkner created myths in order to survive on his own terms; that is, to become someone who could work through his own sense of himself, play his destined roles as he imagined them, and do his work. Put briefly, he lied—and he lied brilliantly and wittily to make himself what he felt he was. For Faulkner, to transcend himself through artifice was the beginning of achievement.

Nevertheless, no one born in 1897 could have been more the product of his time and place. Faulkner's every fiber was shaped by his birth in the Deep South, a Mississippi birth; and it was only later, when he was a thinking, willed individual, that he was able to turn his heritage into the matter of America. Every aspect of his history fed into Faulkner, and he responded in both his personal attitudes and in his work. He represented his own heritage and that of the nation much as Balzac had reflected France in the nineteenth century. He is, in fact, the closest figure to a Balzac that America has produced.

Although his antecedents were not planters and he moved easily with rough men of another social level, Faulkner identified with the Southern patrician. One of the dilemmas he had to confront as he matured artistically was that his traditional or received ideas did not coincide with what his intelligence perceived. He became the uneasy recipient of a dialectic of elements whose center, in him, would not hold; and this dialectic, or tension, was based on everything that seemed necessary to hold a culture together or lead to its dissolution. When Faulkner dealt with social issues in his fiction, he would take on the life and/or death of a culture.

There were matters in which the very culture was at stake: racial views of every stripe, hostility to modernism and its encroachments on a basically agricultural society, industrialization and its corruption of the pastoral ideal, the consciousness of a dispossessed Eden in which the earthly paradise of the South had been subverted by injustice and racial hatred. The violence which so frequently works through Faulkner's novels and stories was a way of dealing with the rage which he felt in himself and which he interpreted as representative of the Southerner's response to what he could neither control nor resolve.

Everything converged in violence. A narrow, provincial society which could not tolerate criticism or even analysis of its situation, while insisting on a romantic, ideal view of itself, could not possibly settle anything without recourse to physical force. The latter was clear, even pure—and final. Violence was implicit in the chivalric code toward women, in racial relationships, in attempts to preserve the Southern way of life (whatever that was becoming in the face of Northern insinuation), in presenting a solid front to the North as if the war were still continuing, and even in the need to demonstrate family solidarity as a Christian virtue. The South was God-fearing and God-practicing, and force would be the means by which that message was conveyed to its people and to the rest of the nation.

Faulkner, like any serious author, had to confront a confusion of ambiguous, antagonistic attitudes and responses.

Wherever Faulkner turned—whether in his family history or in public life—he met violence as a way of preserving values. The Civil War had been, in this respect, merely the larger agent of preservation: violence writ on a historical scale, but continuing into the Reconstruction and after, well beyond the date of Faulkner's birth. To understand the South (and implicitly the frontier society which it was and wanted to remain), Faulkner needed recourse to primitive forms of response—forms that were in his own backyard, as he would discover in the family stories that saturated his childhood. Even the South's passion for politics and rhetoric was rooted in violence; language stood as a vehicle for force, as an incitement to action. Language often took the form of building a wall behind which the South's romanticism and fantasies were held hostage against Northern science and modernism, against a very different kind of rhetoric. If Faulkner waffled on racial issues, his real heroism as a writer came in his effort to penetrate that wall. It was not that he started out to crush the South's fantasies about itself; it was, rather, that he offered a different kind of rhetoric. He developed a language (or languages) which offered resistance to the South's language; for that reason he was more honored beyond its borders than within.

Despite the South's intense distaste for whatever passed for modernism, Faulkner insisted on this modernism in his fictional methods. He was, except for Dos Passos, the first of the American moderns in fiction, and the sole American novelist who, in this respect, can be discussed along with James Joyce, Joseph Conrad, Virginia Woolf, Marcel Proust, and Thomas Mann. Not coincidentally, many of these writers were ones whom Faulkner idolized, imitated, and filtered through memory and practice. But even as he worked through the moderns, the South pulled him back—and he did not resist very strongly. Faulkner remained a man of his time and place, no matter how valiantly he struggled to present conflict in more modernistic and general American terms. He was a Mississippian from Oxford, and if the matter of America did eventually become his subject, he never lost sight of his original place. He personalized his America, which is another way of saying that it remained solid, unyielding, or what the Germans call *Heimat.*

Closely linked to the antimodernism of the South and to its reliance on rhetorical modes was its insistence on fantasies. Through language, custom, tradition, and historical process, the South attempted to armor itself against reality, whatever the arena. Here Faulkner could penetrate profoundly; to understand his critique of Southern fantasizing, we must probe beneath his themes of incest, bizarre sex, and violence. Even while he compiled his own myths, he stripped away fantasies, unrealities, role-playing. Southern antagonism to his work went well beyond the sensationalism of his themes, to the real issues of his iconoclasm.

Faulkner was a dangerous commodity, a loose cannon in the mansion of tradition. Even while he honored history, he helped destroy historical process, and in this he was American, not Southern. The greatness of his fiction is predicated on Faulkner's uncanny ability to present the South sympathetically and yet suggest its death knell. Like Tolstoy, Faulkner did not so much deny tradition as present it in its self-destructive phases; there is a Chekhovian dimension here as well. The South used its incredible energies and strength of will to subvert everything which it wished to preserve; Faulkner is the cultural historian of this process.

When Faulkner was born, the South lacked a large aesthetic or cultural tradition. Its "culture" was the history and tradition of the South, but in literature, music, and art, it was deficient. W. J. Cash attributes this deficiency to an insistence on conformity, a narrow-mindedness that was necessary to present a united front against the North. It can be seen on other grounds as well. A frontier society did not have much room for aesthetics, and the Deep South up to the Civil War, and well after in many respects, remained a frontier society. The masculine control of social and political life—even in the case of an anomaly such as Faulkner's great-grandfather, the "old colonel," who both fought and wrote—preempted its values, especially when women were relegated to being flowers, madonnas, and untouchable Dianas.

Preserving an ideal of honor and chivalry was more important than the representation of real life between the sexes. Faulkner's entrance into such a world in 1897, and his subsequent development in the early years of the new century, conditioned him to a particular kind of society which clashed intensely with the modernistic culture he read about and then experienced abroad. The books which helped to change the South did not have much relevance to the South of his perceptions. Consider the following as limning regional history and a practicing culture: Joel Chandler Harris's *Uncle Remus, His Songs and His Sayings: The Folklore of the Old Plantation;* Thomas Nelson Page's *In Ole Virginia; or Marse Chan and Other Stories;* Thomas Dixon's *The Clansman, an Historical Romance of the Ku Klux Klan;* or, somewhat earlier, Augustus Baldwin Longstreet's *Georgia Scenes, Characters, Incidents, etc., in the First Half Century of the Republic.*

Matthew Arnold's warning could be applied here: a society or culture lacking a degree of mature criticism is not a society in which the arts can flourish. Arnold was speaking, evidently, of open societies, not controlled ones, in which a book or an idea becomes important only *because* all criticism has been discouraged or suppressed. Yet certain ideas and books critical of the South or its position could turn an author into an immediate outsider. Stark Young, who grew up in Oxford just before Faulkner, hewed to regional views and protected fantasies and was accepted; but Faulkner was barely tolerated when his early books were perceived as threatening a society which was, in actuality, deeply riven long before he came along.

Faulkner's courage, even heroism, in swimming upstream against the current of opinion must be stressed. His tepid and often unsatisfactory views on race, many of them based on condescension and patronization, should be perceived in the larger sense—that *any* criticism was a betrayal of Southern unity. What was necessary for the region and for the South as a whole was to retain an iron clasp on the status quo. Nothing must be allowed to slip through, for any break in harmonious accord would open up the South to Northern penetration.

Faulkner found himself caught between two highly conflicting ideas and movements: the tightly woven community of Oxford, where he grew up, which presented itself as the South, and the countering, adversarial notions of modernism, which pulled him imaginatively away from Oxford and regionality. Both his career as a writer and his personal tensions moved from one pole to the other; and this biography will, in fact, be a record of how Faulkner tried to deal privately and professionally with two radically contending elements.

Ernest Hemingway was not concerned with the region of his birth, the Chicago area; nor was F. Scott Fitzgerald torn between Princeton or New York and modernism. John Dos Passos, another Faulkner contemporary, was not committed to any particular region—his modernism did not clash with geographical or personal beliefs. Faulkner, however, lived imaginatively and emotionally in two worlds. His sense of community—the backbone of his Yoknapatawpha novels—was frayed, even tenuous, held together more by myth and tradition than by fact. He found a truly awesome opposing idea in the form of modernism—not the modernism of Northern expansionism, not simply a matter of technology and industrialization, but the modernism which swept away the past, destroyed history, and asserted defiance of society and community. It was this modernism, which his closest mentors never understood, that Faulkner assimilated, and at that level of comprehension it became both daunting and frightening.

Modernism represented a form of anarchism, whereas community represented history, custom, tradition, and myth. To take on both was to confront America at a new frontier. Faulkner spent much of his writing life trying to restore his home, Rowan Oak, to a state of grandeur; and yet he was writing, often, about a world in which a Rowan Oak—like its name—was a medieval or *Waverly* remnant, and in a language which made no contact with ideas of restoration. While laboring to restore Rowan Oak, he found his literary ideas pulling against the very ideal; moving among his fellow Oxonians, he lived in an imaginative world which not only clashed with them, but held no place for them. Staying the course in a marriage which both partners had made untenable, he limned in modern literature relationships which had no room for marriage, stability, or even sanity.

The pull of community for Faulkner was to conserve: his marriage, his traditional home, his designated place in that society at that time; it even dictated his attitude toward Negroes. The pull of modernism made him a self-destructive, subverting, adversarial individual—one who styled himself after the symbolist poets of later nineteenth-century France, who drank himself into oblivion, who fell into sudden and complete silences, and who lied about his past to create another image of himself.

Part I

History, Memories, Language

What place is besieged, and vainly tries to raise the siege?
Lo, I send to that place a commander, swift, brave, immortal,
And with him horse and foot, and parks of artillery,
And artillery-men, the deadliest that ever fired gun.
                                        —WALT WHITMAN

Chapter One

Overview

I N OCTOBER 1929, at about the time of the Wall Street panic, William Faulkner took a job in the University of Mississippi power plant, working a twelve-hour shift from 6:00 P.M. to 6:00 A.M. At this date, he could have read—if he had read reviews—notices of *The Sound and the Fury*, in which he had been compared to Dostoyevsky and Joyce. Faulkner was by this time the published author, also, of three other novels, *Soldiers' Pay*, *Mosquitoes*, and *Sartoris*, as well as numerous short pieces and two volumes of poetry.

The university power plant building consisted of boilers, furnaces, dynamo, and banks of gauges and switches—the kind of scene Ralph Ellison describes when his invisible man works briefly and disastrously deep in the bowels of Optic White Paints. Faulkner's assignment, after shoveling coal from the bunker into a wheelbarrow, was to dump the load so that the firemen could work it into the furnace and boiler. Of the twelve-hour shift, he worked perhaps five or six hours, with the heaviest part of the job falling on two Negroes who were exposed to the heat and dirt. On October 25, 1929, he began a new novel, calling it *As I Lay Dying*. It was his first extended work after *The Sound and the Fury*, and its writing almost coincided with his recent marriage to Estelle Oldham Franklin, on June 20. He composed most of it while on the power plant job. In *As I Lay Dying*, Faulkner for the first time named his mythical county and town, respectively, Yoknapatawpha and Jefferson, locations which would occupy him for virtually the rest of his writing life. On the surface, the new novel appeared simple, but its unusual, fuguelike structure contained ideas and strategies of great complexity. It was, personally and literarily, a key Faulknerian document.

The linkage of several elements was more than coincidental: Faulkner's marriage to Estelle Oldham Franklin, after she had rejected him and married another man; his taking a job which was so déclassé it was bound to be an affront to the class-conscious, rigid Republican Estelle and her family (which had opposed the marriage); his assumption of such a job after he had written and been acclaimed for *The Sound and the Fury*; and his writing of a new novel, called *As I Lay Dying*, which involves the death journey of a mother. Brought together in a mythical county are that dead mother, the incredible difficulty of burying her, a marriage and remarriage, and the openly personal title of the work. For the "I" of the title is not the mother, but Darl, a crazed would-be poet or artist. Faulkner was as close to the bone as he would ever be.

In the period of *As I Lay Dying*, we discover a tremendously productive and an equally disturbed Faulkner—using the novel to reach down into the furthest stretches of his loyalties and hostilities. For even as he honors the novel's mother, Addie, he is setting up the journey which will replace her. The husband, Anse Bundren, feels no guilt, but his son Darl does—and Darl is the registering sensibility of the journey-fiction. Darl lies on the border between sanity and insanity; he is our Orpheus, who keeps looking back, and who is, for better or for worse, seized by an artistic temperament. Darl, too, is dying, figuratively: dying to be reborn, but unable to be.

As I Lay Dying is a remarkable document of Faulkner as he moves along the major lines of his creative life, possibly the greatest sustained stretch of creative imagination in an American writer. The novel reflects him at a crossroads, in which personal and professional life confront each other. Not quite Oedipus, nor entirely Orestes, he is trying to avoid the fate of Orpheus. The personal struggles were profound, involving the deepest reaches of familial loyalty, which were expected of a Southern son and husband. And yet, in these nethermost reaches, Faulkner had to respond in his own way—with craft, cunning, silence, and rebellion, and then the drunken bouts when he could not hold it together. Yet the work evolved —for which the Bundrens were an adequate mirror. They, too, endured, even as one of them lay dead and another lay dying; they endured disasters of fire and flood. The novel is ostensibly about coming through, but it is also about loss—what is lost to the characters, and what is lost in the author as he struggles to join the disparate elements of his life.

The strikingly personal nature of the segments of *As I Lay Dying* reinforces its familial references. The segments are letters from one member to another which do not quite reach their destination. Like the letters in an epistolary novel, they are sent out as information and communication, but they speak at cross-purposes, exposing the writer while failing to reach anyone else. The letters end up in the reader's lap, for *his* response, which is the very effect of the epistolary form.

Faulkner's drinking bouts—each one a prolonged gesture of suicide— were further linked aspects of his creative imagination. What went into his writing was also part of what went into his desire for oblivion. The drinking was ordinarily not for fun or entertainment, but to intensify the quiet and silence which were already there. Everyone who knew Faulkner commented on the silences, which could be rude, embarrassing, and exclusionary. Yet those silences were an integral part of Faulkner's art—as if he needed recovery time between creative bouts. Unfitted for marriage, although he related well to children, he was a man made for perhaps three elements: writing, silences, and drinking. All else could only be withstood, not resolved.

Yet as a Southern son and husband, he was responsible for a large clan; as a man who felt that Negroes were childlike and needed tending, he became responsible for their support, too. Thus, he became intricately involved in several activities seemingly antithetical to his real drives or passions; creativity, hunting, male-bonding, farming, silences, and drinking were all somehow linked. While they seem an unlikely blend of ingredients, for Faulkner they served as elements of a reciprocating engine, each replacing the other in stroke and counterstroke.

When he married Estelle, not only did he take a woman who had rejected him, he also accepted into his home two children by her first marriage (supported by her former husband). He became a stepfather as well as a husband—a complex and pressure-ridden situation for a man who valued his time alone. Faulkner early on had molded himself in line with James Joyce's Stephen Dedalus—with isolated, lonely young men whose inner drives could not be manifested except through antisocial behavior, but which might give way to real achievement. Faulkner assumed poses and told lies; he was the "cursed poet" of the nineteenth-century *symbolistes*, the Oxford version of Rimbaud pursuing a private demon.

One of the temptations of Faulkner criticism and biography is to see him as composed of separate elements which, somehow, fail to cohere. In this view, Faulkner as writer, heavy drinker, remiss family man, hunter and horseman, even as farmer and country gentleman, all remain diverse pieces of a puzzle which resist a clean fit. This view flounders, however, because then the creative ability—especially those ten or twelve years of splendor from the late 1920s to the early 1940s—appears to derive from areas which cannot be discovered or even plumbed. Faulkner does exist as a whole; all the parts do fit. And the creative ability—to the extent we can ever recover an imaginative process—can be found where everything overlaps. The creative imagination was revealed in his work; but his drinking, his attitude toward family life, his desire to identify with hunters and farmers—these are also acts of revelation, almost on a par with the writing in their importance in his life.

For Faulkner everything had to stand still while he wrote; his desk preempted all other considerations. Just as Albert Einstein had to do physics—it possessed him and made him a man who moved in his own orbit—so Faulkner, surely more than Hemingway or any of his other contemporaries, lived to record what memory and observation were dictating to him. (William Butler Yeats and D. H. Lawrence come to mind as other priests and prophets of literature who listened to internal voices and worked constantly to record them.) Faulkner worked with intensity, even when he had to turn out movie scripts or story ideas; even to his detractors, he was one of the most productive of scriptwriters and script doctors when he worked under the director Howard Hawks. Yet while all other parts of his development as a human being are secondary, they are strongly linked in their reinforcement of the main object. Obviously, these other qualities—chiefly the drinking and the responsibility to his dependents—are significant, inasmuch as Faulkner pursued them with a single-mindedness almost equal to the intensity with which he pursued his work.

That intensity whenever it came to the written word dictated and organized his life. He had no ear for music—he forbade a radio in the house until his daughter Jill insisted on it—and while he could enjoy some painting, he had little interest in seeking it out. All his artistic energies were devoted to the word; to the written word, first as poetry, then as short story and novel. The other side of this devotion was his intense need to identify with masculine pursuits—to put away for good implications of effeminacy which had been cast upon him in his youth. Faulkner threw himself into activities normally associated with maleness: not only drinking but flying (at a time when it was still quite dangerous), annual hunting trips in rain and cold, which he continued well after he had won the Nobel Prize, and, finally, horsemanship, which was a near obsession, and which he pursued even when not up to it physically.

These activities, debilitating as some of them were, were not diversions, but the working out of a complementary side without which the creative element apparently could not function. Faulkner restored himself with what may have killed him, and, on occasion, almost did. As a flyer, he was weak on landings, and on several approaches destroyed landing gear, wing ends, or other structural parts of the plane—this at a time when the margin for safety was small indeed. He saw his brother Dean, his friend Vernon Omlie, and several others die in plane crashes, and he caught the sheer mad danger of it in his novel *Pylon* (written in 1934), as well as in short stories. As a horseman, he did not have a good seat, and yet insisted on riding large and hard-to-handle animals, evidently a test of will over physical shortcomings.

Faulkner had apparently discovered an unlikely formula: what seemed unworkable worked; what appeared irresolvable resolved itself. He married a woman for whom he felt hostility and resentment; he removed himself from his wife's caste in his dress code and in his choice of profession; he perceived himself, in that university power plant, as someone lying there dying; he drove himself into financial traps with obligations which forced him to leave Oxford for Hollywood; he drank himself into oblivion and had to be periodically saved and dried out; and he risked his neck repeatedly in planes and on horses. It doesn't seem to add up to America's greatest novelist of the twentieth century, especially if compared with Mann sitting at his desk, Proust lying in his cork-lined room, or Gide living the life of the *littérateur*. But they weren't Americans and Faulkner was—intensely; not only Southern but American, an American male finding the only way he could work and survive: an outlaw in his real work, a good old boy around the plantation.

We must locate Faulkner *there*. However much the South and his chosen few square miles became the substance of his novels and nourished his imagination, his reach was for America. Faulkner touched base with all the American themes, from the pastoral tradition and its dispossessed Eden to matters of courage and endurance, from questions of space and escape to our drive for forms of suicide, for failure. Lying behind nearly everything he wrote was the great American divide, the Civil War, the most momentous event in our history after the Revolution itself, still unresolved, surely, by the time he was born. Little can be understood in Faulkner without an awareness of that hovering presence, the shadow of courage and debacle.

He had premonitions of his role, and he would later describe it:

> . . . And now I realise for the first time what an amazing gift I had: uneducated in every formal sense, without even very literate, let alone literary, companions, yet to have made the things I made. I dont know where it came from. I dont know why God or gods or whoever it was, selected me to be the vessel. Believe me, this is not humility, false modesty: it is simply amazement. I wonder if you have ever had that thought about the work and the country man whom you know as Bill Faulkner—what little connection there seems to be between them.[1]

Nobel Laureate Faulkner wrote this at the age of fifty-five, to Joan Williams, a young student of writing more than thirty years his junior. A somewhat self-satisfied note creeps in, but in the main the statement is one of astonishment. Why me? Faulkner's choice of words is fitting: he views himself as a "maker," not as an author or a novelist, or even a writer. "Maker" is "poet" in the oldest sense. Faulkner made things—which accommodated his sense of himself as a farmer, house painter, and carpenter. He is a craftsman, also a worker, part of that vast army which "makes," not the elite which authors. When he calls himself the "country man whom you know as Bill Faulkner," he separates that "country man" from those amazing vessels which he has, somehow, filled.

Like Joseph Conrad's, William Faulkner's "real life" must be uncovered in his novels and stories. Although we have accumulated huge quantities of data about his sixty-four years, it becomes clear that the more intense existence came in those silences and withdrawals he presented to the world; for in those withdrawals he was quietly filling those "amazing vessels." In those moments, he transformed himself from farmer and sometime house craftsman to maker and poet. There, in those silences, he found the characteristic peristaltic movement of his fiction: *his* time, *his* pace, *his* sense of movement and rhythm. There, he could promote telling and retelling—and in that we have our biographical entry, the real life of William Faulkner.

It was much the same with Joseph Conrad, whose work entered so profoundly into Faulkner's imagination. Both laid traps for the biographer and for the critics of their work.* Conrad's linkage with Faulkner is uncanny. His relationship to homeland was that of a wanderer from an occupied, defeated Poland who remained what he was even as he changed. The journey to discover himself sent him around the world as seaman and ship's captain. All this, however, was merely preparation; for he, too, had an amazing vessel to fill. When he was ready, he changed his name by Anglicizing Józef Teodor Konrad Korzeniowski, became a British national, married an Englishwoman, learned another language, and stepped forth as a new person: the novelist and short story writer in English, his third language.

When we turn to Faulkner, we find the Conrad paradigm (of the artist carving out his own sense of self) confronting us at nearly every turn. Allowing for evident differences of detail and emphasis, we find a pair of writers responding to their circumstances and quality of life in greatly similar terms. Instead of a defeated Poland, Faulkner was born into a wretched South, defeated barely thirty years before, with that fiery conflict still a living phenomenon in the older generation's memory. He grew up, as did Conrad, surrounded by remnants of defeat and dimensions of desultory rebuilding; both observed society shifting radically from what they had once known. To the end of his life, Faulkner would remain drawn to the past, even as he moved out into the future as America's foremost experimental novelist.

But similarities between the two go further than a defeated Poland and a beaten-down, barely emerging South. While Conrad was an only child, Faulkner was the eldest of four sons, but so physically different from his father that he became his "mother's son." Expectation lay heavily on him, especially when the father's role became increasingly diminished because of successive business failures. As the eldest son, upon whom his mother placed her faith, Faulkner took on the quality of a unique, and only, child —tremendous pressure to be a leader was exerted on him within the family and within the culture of the South. He must be prodigal, but not adversarial. And yet, like Conrad, who fled Poland just short of his seventeenth

*Everything about Conrad was antithetical to the kind of biography which treats his life as a "chronicle." As with Faulkner, the biographer cannot be empirical or pragmatic, but someone who seeks mysteries and irrationalities.

birthday, Faulkner retreated from the family situation and family responsibility, although without overt rejection of parents or siblings.

Perhaps the greatest congruency between the two is reflected in Faulkner's enlistment in the Royal Air Force at its Canadian training ground in Toronto. For Faulkner, as for Conrad in the merchant service (first of France and then of Britian), the move was nothing less than transformational. Faulkner went from a completely marginal figure (in his own eyes) to one of heroic stature, in the way he presented himself and in the stories he related of his experiences. Faulkner cherished the transformation well into his fifties by maintaining the military falsehoods which somehow fueled his imagination. At first, he had become the subject of his own inventions, and this was the process of "lying" which was so central to his imaginative thrust; then, like Conrad in his fiction, Faulkner assimilated the idea of the "lie," or tall tale, treating memories in their expansiveness as if they had originally been true.

Perhaps more than anything else Faulkner and Conrad achieved their "filled vessels" by way of taking adversary positions on nearly everything which had nourished them. Faulkner scourged the South in his novels; later, in his notions of race relationships, he took adversary positions not only on town and region but on family. Conrad had subverted his commitment to Polish ideals by showing that such romantic ideals, in various settings, were both destructive and self-destructive. Irony was his method. Faulkner, on the other hand, used grotesque representation as his vehicle of commentary. The consequence, for both, was that they remained profoundly marginal men, deeply silent and withdrawn, force-fed by impulses and imaginative thrusts which filled *them* as much as they filled the vessels. For Faulkner, it took a lifetime to work out the conundrum of whether he filled the urn or the urn filled him.

Possibly because he seemed so marginal—an empty vessel waiting to be filled—Faulkner felt the need to play the role of imposter.[2] Intrinsic to nearly everything he did is the quality of role-playing: whether the invented heroics of his wartime bit part or even the silences, the played-down clothes, the studied early indifference to appearance, the establishment of an isolated, withdrawn persona. What made him almost impenetrable was the fact that the "real" Faulkner—whoever or whatever he was—hid himself under layers of disguise. The Faulkner who appeared was the one he revealed by choice. Playacting or imposturing became linked to his literary imagination; he was his own tale written by a self he distanced himself from. The drinking became part of this complicated apparatus, and any attempt to separate it from the creative Faulkner would split what is indivisible.

As a "war hero," Faulkner returned with a wound in his head, a limp, a flashy uniform, and related elements which speak of imposturing. There was in this the desire to be something more, to be someone else; the pose suggests a Freudian family romance. From Faulkner's point of view, if we can extrapolate, he could not remake his origins, but he could embroider a tall tale—an early filling of that amazing vessel. This was the tale of the war, and it is connected to the well-known fact that many men use war as a way of exaggerating their own feats. Faulkner went further and transformed himself, small and unimposing, into a figure and a presence, a hero by implication.

Although posing as a war hero and embroidering his exploits in the Royal Air Force, Faulkner kept his imposturing to a minimum. It did not overwhelm his life, and in a sense it did not lead to any accruing of material gain, wealth, or advantage, beyond self-aggrandizement. But it must be linked to his name change—to his addition of "u" in Falkner, which acted as differentiation from his father in particular, and in general from the entire Falkner clan. By changing his name, even so slightly, he was acting out a family romance, in which while he identified himself as belonging he distinguished himself as someone unique, the prodigal son.

The name change is of great significance, especially when taken with the role-playing as a war hero. It was an act of considerable hostility, since the Falkner name was originally connected to old Colonel Falkner and was not an ordinary name; it was distinctive, charged with history, part of the Civil War and Reconstruction. Any desire to alter that kind of name is of deep significance—it was Faulkner's way of moving outside history and establishing himself without the weight of any immediate historical past.* Yet the change was small, indicating that Faulkner was not moving far and did not intend to create waves of discontent by the alteration. By adding a "u," he could suggest his independence from history and family, but also not make a change which stressed outright defiance. It was the kind of balance which foreshadowed a good deal in Faulkner's later career: the ideological tightrope he walked on several issues, including racial ones.

Another element affecting Faulkner's sense of himself was his small stature, especially in a family of sizable men—an imposing, beefy father and two brothers taller and larger-boned than he. His physical stature was a throwback to his petite, small-boned mother, Maud, and, therefore, to the feminine side. This would in itself create uncertainties, since it was his mother who both encouraged him and reminded him of his small stature. The posing in uniform upon his return and the war tales he invented are evident ways of increasing his stature. They were ways of reinforcing his mother's admiration, in a socially and culturally acceptable arena—his posing came in ways that fitted the mores and traditions of the South. This aspect must not be neglected: his imposturing was not connected to money or personal gain but to an area of military fantasy of which the South could approve and which was, in addition, in the line of distinction derived from the Falkner historical past.

*But not out of history altogether, since it was a return to an earlier spelling.

As the son upon whom Maud doted, the eldest and potentially the most talented, Faulkner had to live up to her high expectations. This was a mother whose power over the son preempted the hold of the father. He was his mother's son rather than his father's, and, therefore, a cross-sexual linkage was established. Maud Falkner's intense devotion to her eldest son —and their similarities in size and tastes—made it difficult or impossible for Faulkner to separate himself from her. What she expected of him was what he must become.

Kind though he was, Faulkner's father, Murry, was inaccessible to the growing youngster. Even at the level of reading—Murry enjoyed pap— they parted ways when the boy was quite young; he turned to his mother's literary tastes. Murry was for the most part unavailable for identification, respect, role model possibilities, even for admiration. The sole way the young man could follow Murry was in the family male tradition of heavy drinking. The split in Faulkner came well before the writing career—by way of alcohol, he would align himself with his father, but through imposturing and role-playing he could gain his mother's affection. By that pose, Faulkner established himself in competition with his unsuccessful father, the declining member of a once-successful family. Murry had needed his father's help at every stage, whereas his son casually made it clear he needed nothing but his mother's belief in him. The family drama recalled O'Neill more than Strindberg.

The difficulties of the pursuit of a writing career for a young man in Oxford, Mississippi, after World War I cannot be overestimated. Although writing was not itself anathema, it was not considered a fully masculine endeavor; usually, it was merely an adjunct to more manly activities, as with old colonel Falkner and his literary production. The South lauded soldiers and other doers; it tolerated writers. Men who took up writing customarily had other occupations as well; Faulkner's desire to be only a writer and to pose as "the writer" with bohemian abandon led not only to outright rejection but to steady ridicule. He was early on called "the Count," "Count no 'Count," and "queer" as signs of his difference; even when he was becoming famous in the North and abroad, Oxford was slow to recognize him. The posture of the war hero gradually gave way to the role of the impecunious artist, as Faulkner carefully replaced one role with another.

Imposturing is usually perceived as some form of pathological behavior, with the imposter having an inadequate ego-ideal—he is a man out of control, so snared by the role or roles he is playing he cannot help himself; he has lost contact with reality, so that he cannot distinguish between the part he is playing and the real context. But in Faulkner's instance the role-playing gave him energies for his career as a writer. In some respects, his imposturing and his writing were indistinguishable, one leading into the other as, first, Faulkner's re-creation of himself and, then, his imaginative re-creation of his materials.

Faulkner apparently perceived the limits of his poses to the extent that he could shape and reshape them; he could limit them as other elements in his life began to take over and replace the need for the original impulses. Once Faulkner had the omnipotence of the word to sustain him, he no longer needed the omnipotence of false roles, whether war hero or bohemian. Whatever exalted ideal of his mother he wished to evoke, or whatever role he wished to take to compete with and replace his father, he sustained by way of his written work, even with those early poems he wrote and bound himself. Thus, Faulkner no longer needed the imposturing as he gained more internal security by means of his career; further, the imposturing did not really vanish, but was *absorbed into* the career, nourishing many aspects of the myths and legends which Faulkner perpetuated in his fiction. Yoknapatawpha County is a reflection of that mythmaking.

While many Faulkner myths are connected to the land and pastoral, even Edenic, visions, several of them are associated with those earlier imposturing positions and roles. Faulkner had implicit within him dozens of novels and stories which could be the verbal equivalent of the confidence man's poses. Exactly how the early role-playing was absorbed into the fictional career is impossible to describe. What we can say with more certainty is that Faulkner, by creating so profusely, was able to reinvoke powers of control and mastery: to objectify the roles and make the reader acquiesce. He was able to compete with and surpass his declining father and to satisfy, at whatever level, his mother's expectations of him. While this may be true of any male child—the imposter situation seems to be almost exclusively male—it took on special coloring for Faulkner. This is so not only because he was a "controlled" imposter but because he found ways of channeling those energies into other roles—the way an actor by going from role-playing in childhood to actual roles takes up the pathological slack, as it were. What could have been a loss of reality became a personal mechanism of creating myths and legends which the country could embrace.

It can be argued that imposter and artist are really nourished by dissimilar elements. The artist seeks control through his work; the imposter is someone out of control, under the mastery of something he cannot fathom. In this scheme, the apparent similarities soon part, and imposter and artist at the fundamental level have little in common. In fact, the line is much less clear: the imposter does not necessarily ignore reality, or decry it; he may heighten it through his role-playing, finding in his roles a creative way of responding to the environment, of manipulating the reality of his and others' expectations. He may indeed in the process lose contact with reality—but this is something that can be said of the largest and greatest artists.

We of course prefer artists to imposters, but behind both is a sense of magic and wonder, of awe and amazement. Each has discovered ways of evoking astonishment, so that we become less interested in the phenomenon of the imposter or artist than in the role or work he has created. The imposter may play his roles as a way of balancing out what he perceives as an inadequate birth—in a lower station than he deems himself fit for; or to a father whom he finds insufficient, or else to one with whom he must compete and surpass; or to a mother whose high expectations of him have created peaks which he must climb, successes which he must achieve. All of these childhood experiences make him aware of the loss of Eden, or of a possibly recoverable Eden which once existed and which no longer functions for him. A writer such as Faulkner had similar needs, however precisely or imprecisely he came to them. His entire body of work, with its explicit hatred of modern life and its attendant culture, bespeaks nostalgia for an Eden which he yearns for and yet knows can hardly be regained. In this profound way, Faulkner the artist has crossed paths with Faulkner the imposter, and whatever else we may say of them, this congruency cannot be mitigated. Whatever the imposter hopes to regain of a lost childhood, the artist hopes to regain through a redesigning of our perceptions. He seeks what has long since vanished.

If we describe an event which on its face seems bizarre here, we may indirectly move closer to Faulkner. Although the writer was to be born thirty-two years after this event, the meeting between Grant and Lee at Appomattox, Virginia, in Easter week of 1865, signaled the split within the future writer. The immediate purpose was to heal a terrible wound. Lee came to surrender, Grant to offer terms. Yet the two men would seem to represent two different countries, rather than two halves of the same nation. Lee represented the old aristocracy, with its neoclassical ideals; he personified traditional values, a chivalric way of existence which, on the surface, seemed noble and dignified, but which was, of course, contaminated by slavery. Lee spoke of an Eden, but it was in reality a dispossessed, decaying Eden. Grant reflected the new America, mainly the values associated with the West—a forward-, not backward-looking point of view. There was something of Eden in Grant's view, too, and it was untouched by slavery; however, violence, frontier roughness, and vulgarity characterized what it was and would prove to be.

Lee came dressed formally for the solemn, ceremonial occasion; Grant, in old boots and wrinkled private's coat, treated the event as inevitable, even commonplace. Lee surrendered, gave over his forces—although he could have continued to fight with guerrilla forays behind Union lines. Grant did not so much receive the surrender as acquiesce to what was a fait accompli. From the Southern viewpoint, Lee symbolized a tragic position: an older culture which no longer sufficed. Grant leveled Lee and the occasion: he met grandness with Jacksonian egalitarianism. There was no scorn in Grant's manner and method, but implicitly there was the sense that Lee's and the South's culture was now fossilized; that the new man, Grant, however vulgar and unkempt, was America's frontier.

The two men, so dissimilar in breeding, taste, manner, appearance, and deportment, were somehow prophetic of the South in which Faulkner would be born and brought up—and in an extended way of the country itself. There was something of Snopes in Grant—the man who had shifted from job to job and excelled at only one thing, winning in the killing fields. Faulkner would himself be drawn in both directions: restoring an old neoclassical mansion and living like an antebellum squire surrounded by black servants who depended on his largesse; yet sympathizing with Grant's world, with egalitarian country people, black and white alike, who were at best marginal, socially and economically dispensable.

Faulkner never resolved this split in himself—nor was there any reason to believe he should have, for the country itself had trouble doing it. What Faulkner embodied in himself as the schism of the South was in large part the schism of the country: the established, familied, and well educated who owned the wealth which the newer, coarse democratic forces were attempting to wrest away. Faulkner was fascinated by both segments, drawn to both ideologies. He saw the potential destruction in hewing to the old aristocracy, and yet he could not resist some of its attractions; he was repelled by much of the new—he personified it in waves of Snopeses—and still he saw its inevitability. It had arrived, and he attempted to wrestle with ideologies which were alien and distasteful to him. Decrying that receding wilderness was an emblem of his protest. He was, in his way, tortured by the magnitude of the dilemma, and his prose, at its most twisted and gnarled, reflected his anguish and torture. Only high rhetoric could suffice: a rhetoric beyond common speech and beyond description could raise the dilemma and the schism toward national tragedy.

To illuminate a phenomenon on such a large scale and to impart its tragic grandeur, Faulkner needed not only a language but a method or strategy. The Faulkner method is characterized by telling and retelling—the repetition of events, circumstances, sequences of actions; what comes to us appears in waves of representation. Faulkner does not merely relate, he repeats. His method is both directly and indirectly linked to his historical and imposturing sides, as well as to a profound personal dimension. Faulkner's need to lie, imposture, disguise, is reflected in the telling and retelling; the very premise of repeating is to embroider, "lying" about the original story as one adds a personal commentary. Here narrative method accommodates a private need; or, put another way, personal need finds an outlet in a narrative method which coincides with the initial drive for "lying."

In the process of retelling, Faulkner had also discovered a historical method, a means by which history could be revealed. It does not matter whether history is "true" or not. As he mentioned later in his life, there were facts, and there was the truth. Faulkner did not ignore facts; they were useful as pawns on a larger chessboard on which he sought the truth of things. This is not so different from any other novelist, except that his material was deeply historical and, therefore, connected to verifiable truth—that is, to facts. Yet Faulkner was concerned not only with writing history, but with rewriting it; this included his personal history. Embroidering the past meant more than enlarging or exaggerating it; it meant creating a sense of things sizable enough to accommodate the scale on which he wished to work: war (in the South's past) and peace (the uncertain direction of the country as a whole).

Connected, further, to telling and retelling is a view of life based on uncertainties. Faulkner's narrative method is an effort to transform internal and external uncertainties into something solid, even definite. By retelling, he was committing an act which turned an indeterminate event or ambiguous sequence into words; and words were something he could trust, perhaps the only thing he could trust. This was essential for him: to turn history, personal background, his own lies and deceptions into language; and once they were transformed, he was able to deal with them, as if language gave them the validity which they lacked as things. The internal demon which forced Faulkner into dangerous situations—the drinking, flying, horseback-riding—was the same demon which had to express itself in words. The dangers in his physical activities were dangers he confronted in his use of language: he put himself on the line, he dared all, and he sank into it, until the destructive element claimed him. His was a recklessness which carried all before it; nowhere more than in his use of language do we find that recklessness emerging, compelling him to further excesses.

The pattern was established early when Faulkner, caught up in the masculine drive for a situation which would prove his courage and fortitude, opted for the Royal Air Force. His was the eldest son's drive to replace the father, to reshape the family in his and his mother's image. Faulkner crafted his image carefully—and it dominated his middle and later life as much as it had the earlier. Image-making always took two forms: words and poses, language and role-playing. For a man seeking the truth, that obsessive quest for image may seem factitious, even hypocritical; but image-making was linked to narrative methods, and those, in turn, to nearly every aspect of Faulkner's thought, his views of history, his sense of contemporary society, his fears about the future. The images which he strove to achieve for himself were aspects of the American character which he thought were redemptive and salvational.

Faulkner was concerned with forms of behavior—he conceived his works, perhaps unconsciously, as heuristic. He differed from Hemingway greatly in this and other respects—and their slow, cautious dance around each other as mature writers competing for Number One was an emblem of that difference. Faulkner thought he saw where the country was going wrong, where it had to be restored in order to be saved. For such a formally unreligious writer, he placed remarkable emphasis on redemption and salvation. In a broad sense, he took up the role first Jefferson and then Emerson had played in the early and mid-nineteenth century, however incongruous the comparison may appear. Like Jefferson, he favored decentralization, self-reliance, and responsible individualism, and distrusted technology, urban life, and collectivism.

Faulkner began his career as a poet, propelled by the visionary, pro-phetic impulse. He had the poet's reach for the beyond, for the metaphysi-cal statement, even while he used the physical world for his narrative plan. Faulkner was a maker of myths—and he started with the myth of the self, of himself. That need for image which apparently started to develop in his youth, possibly even in his childhood, is connected, surely, to his myth-making: size, physical and otherwise, became a necessity. To speculate on how much Faulkner's relatively small stature (small in relation to his family, not necessarily small as far as the national average in the early 1900s) influenced his sense of image and mythmaking is tantalizing. We can say, with some assurance from precedents, that small men overcompensate if they feel they are special; or, they feel they are special because they must overcompensate to become seen and heard. Freud has much to say about the youth whose mother believes in him, but he has nothing to say about how maternal favoritism looked in a Southern society where displays of masculinity were historical ideals.

Faulkner—visionary, maker of self-images and myths, embroiderer of facts, small man posing as epical and heroical—came from a line of quasi-frontier figures. Although his great-grandfather, the old colonel, and his grandfather, the young colonel, were well established in business, and the old man even wrote novels, they were frontiersmen in spirit, with all that such a designation implied. The grand figures of the South, even after villages, towns, and cities were established, were still caught in a frontier cycle; and the behavior pattern of the Faulkner ancestors was that of frontier readiness for sudden violence, personal injury, and death. The first one to break with that cycle was Faulkner's father, Murry, and part of his dislocation personally and professionally was his inability to provide linkage between two very different kinds of life: the rough-and-ready existence of his father and grandfather and the subdued gentility which his own position called for. Murry fell between the two, successful at neither, and growing up with him, as we shall note, allowed Faulkner to see how the move away from the frontier and its exigencies led to deterioration.

Faulkner needed, often compulsively, the warrior's bout with death, which was merely another aspect of the poet's reach for the beyond. As we have seen, in his most intense period of creation, the late 1920s and throughout the 1930s, he grappled with forms of death: those immense, bottomless silences which filled his social life were responses, apparently, to the need to grapple with death and emerge ready for the next book. Like Hemingway in this respect, he courted disaster in order to refill whatever the books had taken from him. These two men, seemingly so different in their public attitudes—Faulkner hugged his private life, Hemingway made his into a national epic—responded similarly to inner needs. Self-destructive drinking was a phenomenon common to many American writ-ers besides Hemingway and Faulkner; their commonality went far deeper. Both needed confusion, near disaster, and a reaching for depths before they became pumped up for work.

Hemingway by the 1930s had put most of his best work behind him. He developed and peaked well before Faulkner, and the body of his achievement is far smaller as a result, although his influence was larger. Hemingway's turbulence was exhibited on a public scale. By comparison, Faulkner's turmoil was almost invisible, except to family members and friends near him. He demanded his privacy with the obsession of a man who feared to give away anything which was not in his books. But because his resources were kept so close to his chest, so dammed up inside, he was more suitable for the long haul. He could incubate ideas, techniques, and energies without dissipating them in a great public display. And he could move at his own rate of development.

Yet there is no question he thrived on turbulence. When he wrote *Absalom, Absalom!*—very possibly the greatest of twentieth-century American novels—his circumstances appeared to be the opposite of what a serious novelist needed for such a complex undertaking. Out of financial need, he was writing for Hollywood, an activity which he despised. He was drinking heavily, almost suicidally. He was watching his marriage deteriorate—a marriage whose foundation had been problematic from the beginning. He was prepared to start a serious affair with Meta Carpenter, script clerk for Howard Hawks at Twentieth Century-Fox Studios, in many ways the woman he should have married. He seemed in a literary trough, having written *Pylon* (1934), a relatively slight work, earlier and turning to *The Unvanquished* (1937), a pastiche, later. The presence of the Great Depression would itself seem to dictate its own themes and discourage historical fiction, particularly from a defeated time.[3] The considerable disruptions—added to the self-hatred and anger for even being in Hollywood—activated an inner dissatisfaction which, somehow, must have been transformed into creative energies: Faulkner resolved the turbulence with achievement.

Appearing in 1936, *Absalom, Absalom!* had, apparently, no connection with the depression years or American drift; yet if we peer deeply enough into the novel—without distorting its primary focus—we can perceive it as a response to many elements: personal, cultural, even political. For like Herman Melville with *Moby-Dick*, Faulkner was writing allegory as well as novel, a fictional representation of a certain kind of American cultural event as well as a narrative. In Thomas Sutpen, whom Faulkner had mentioned in previous fiction, the writer revealed an obsessed, monomaniacal, charmless surrogate of sorts: one who could unify the various impulses in himself and that inexorable drive toward fulfillment, however bizarre and distorted the result. It was a piece of willful America offered as a response to the drift of the 1930s; and it was a brutal, obsessive, personal response to his own demeaning of self in Hollywood, to his misstep in his marriage, to being himself a man of almost no power and less control.

We could not have predicted what kind of novel Faulkner would write in order to represent such elements; but it is clear that his greatest fiction shadows his own existence, however exaggerated and misshapen events become when touched by his creative energies. In Sutpen Faulkner saw a surrogate, as much as he sensed the Snopes in himself, or Gavin Stevens, or Joe Christmas, perhaps even as much as Quentin Compson. The greatness of *Absalom* rests on its narrative method—the strategy of telling and retelling, a device perfectly fitted to Sutpen's, and Faulkner's, need to write and rewrite history. In Sutpen, Faulkner was able to infuse much of his own duality, his own ambiguities and problems, as well as those of his Falkner heritage. The nation, represented as the South, was like a poison infecting his blood.

We return to the image of the empty vessel: it is, of course, connected to Faulkner's early devotion to John Keats. The poet's Grecian urn has within its pictorial design something of the sense of history to which Faulkner would devote his life—that tension between rest and movement, past and present, expectation and fulfillment contains much of Faulkner's, as well as Keats's, line of development. Faulkner, whatever his personal qualities, was caught by history, part of that *amor fati* Nietzsche spoke of. Life was destiny, and he made sure his own was fulfilled; but it was, he hoped, also possible to expect more, to yearn for more. He did not share Keats's morbid affliction, which meant an early death, but he did experience Keats's sense of fleeting reality. Faulkner had his own affliction, the inability to withstand certain kinds of stress for long before he went into suicidal bouts with alcohol. "I never wrote one single Line of Poetry," John Keats told John Hamilton Reynolds, "with the least Shadow of public thought."[4] The moment, the pitch of experience, the substance going into the vessel and not the vessel itself: all of these formed the matter, for both Keats and Faulkner. The latter would have agreed with Keats's lofty "I am certain of nothing but the holiness of the Heart's affections and the truth of Imagination—what the Imagination seizes as Beauty must be truth." Faulkner spoke more in terms of frontier experience, more in terms of the embattled Southerner; but if we read his early work correctly, we can see it, like Keats's early works, generating ideas and feelings for the remainder of his long career.

Chapter Two

Backgrounds

THE BABY WHO would grow up to be Quentin Compson, Thomas Sutpen, Joe Christmas, Gavin Stevens, and not a little Snopes, was christened William Cuthbert Falkner—he added the "u" later, either for the simple reasons he offered or for more complicated causes of which he may have been unaware. In 1945, as he hovered on the edge of finally gaining wider fame, he wrote to Malcolm Cowley, the critic who had much to do with Faulkner's access to a larger audience:

> The name is "Falkner." My great-grandfather, whose name I bear, was a considerable figure in his time and provincial milieu. He was prototype of John Sartoris: raised, organised, paid the expenses of and commanded the 2nd Mississippi Infantry, 1861–2, etc. . . . He built the first railroad in our county, wrote a few books, made grand European tour of his time, died in a duel and the county raised a marble effigy which still stands in Tippah County. The place of our origin shows on larger maps: a hamlet named Falkner just below Tennessee line on his railroad.
> My first recollection of the name was, no outsider seemed able to pronounce it from reading it, and when he did pronounce it, he always wrote the "u" into it. So it seemed to me that the whole outside world was trying to change it, and usually did. Maybe when I began to write, even though I thought then I was writing for fun, I secretly was

ambitious and did not want to ride on grandfather's coat-tails, and so accepted the "u," was glad of such an easy way to strike out for myself. I accept either spelling. In Oxford it has usually no "u" except on a book. The above was always my mother's and father's version of why I put back into it the "u" which my great-grandfather, himself always a little impatient of grammar and spelling both, was said to have removed.[1]

The more complicated reason, which came when Faulkner began to write, is connected to his need for rejection; a way of cutting himself adrift from a family line which was once famous and was now slowly declining. But motivation went even deeper. The name change was linked to deep hostilities within the family itself. Although there was precedent for adding the "u" in Falkner history, the additional letter coincides with Faulkner's moving out as a writer in his early twenties and suggests more than the need to correct pronunciation.

The rest of his letter to Cowley is also compelling. He speaks of having gone to the RAF—"went to RAF"—and then returning home; no mention of heroic acts or perpetuating deception about his brief service. But even more telling is the paragraph in which he speaks of having grown up in his father's livery stable. "Being the eldest of four boys, I escaped my mother's influence pretty easy, since my father thought it was fine for me to apprentice to the business." He says he would have remained, probably, in the livery-stable business if not for the coming of the motorcar. At forty-eight, Faulkner was rewriting history in one instance and retelling what he had already told in another. A childhood is, of course, made up of truth and lies, but there are two main lines which someone from outside the family must probe: to discover what happened, and then attempt to uncover what the perception of what happened was for the person experiencing it. Faulkner's perception here is that he escaped his mother's influence, when all facts from early family life indicate that he, the eldest son, was deeply under Maud's influence. Even after his marriage to Estelle, at almost thirty-two, he visited his mother every day when he was in Oxford. The relationship between the two was of utmost importance, since Maud often "protected" her eldest son against a masculine world which mocked or questioned what he was trying to do.

Of equal importance in Faulkner's letter to Cowley, however, is the soft-pedaling of his war exploits after he had so assiduously detailed them in past years. Here the Faulkner strategy of telling and retelling applied to his own life: a narrative turned inward, so that he becomes the subject of his own method. After telling and retelling what was in the beginning not only an exaggeration but a series of lies about his exploits, Faulkner now wanted to "untell" the past which he had himself constructed. As he became famous—and in 1945 he was on the edge—he needed the tales of his war exploits less. His writing career clearly fulfilled in his emotional life what the war had earlier. Now he needed to empty out history, empty out the past.

But it was not so easy. In his fiction, he could keep coming at the past until the matter was either clouded or elucidated. In real life, the matter got away from him: his lies about the past had taken on a truth of their own. In pursuing personal information for his introduction to *The Portable Faulkner*, Cowley turned to *Twentieth Century Authors*, the 1942 version edited by Stanley Kunitz and Howard Haycraft. Cowley read that Faulkner joined the Canadian Air Force (there was no such unit), was sent to France (he never left Canada), had two planes shot down under him (he never saw action, the war having ended before he was trained), and was wounded in the second shooting (impossible). Cowley knew that some of this was falsification, but, on his part, he wanted to think Faulkner was one of the "wounded writers" of his generation, like Hemingway. Although Cowley could not distinguish what the "facts" here were, he wanted to believe in them as much as Faulkner had earlier wanted people to believe in them.

Cowley, however, also had Faulkner's warning to publish as few personal details as possible; the latter had perhaps taken this new strategy because his version of the past was no longer necessary. Deep in fiction, Faulkner gets at the truth—hiding or disguising it—turning all facts into problematic matters and altering what might be the fiction's center into the very question of what a center is. Faulkner is busy deconstructing his own life to approach truth, whereas Cowley is hanging on to personal details whose veracity he questions but also whose very being Cowley wants to believe in, to justify his sense of Faulkner not only as a great writer but as a romantic, grand figure.

Cowley then went ahead in this most important document and used the material from the Kunitz edition. He writes of Faulkner having served at the front, having his plane damaged, and being shot down behind British lines. The embroidery had now become part of the record, at least as far as Cowley's draft of his introduction. Faulkner, however, who was consulted at each turn, was not happy. He insisted on Cowley's deletion of what he, Faulkner, knew was no longer needed, and insisted on the following, which is what appeared in Cowley's words. Faulkner's version: "When the war was over—the other war—William Faulkner, at home again in Oxford, Mississippi, yet at the same time was not at home, or at least not able to accept the postwar world."[2] The matter of war exploits does not arise: history as written and rewritten is effaced. Cowley now made his own revision: "When the war was over—the other war—William Faulkner went back to Oxford, Mississippi. He had served in the Royal Air Force in 1918. Now he was home again and not at home, or at least not able to accept the postwar world."

Cowley's version is precisely true: Faulkner had served in the Royal Air Force. The writer's version slides around the issue and does not even mention the part that was true, his service in the RAF. Cowley comments: "Why didn't he say flatly that he hadn't served in France during the war?"[3] His explanation is naive: "I suspect that he was adhering to his fixed principle of never correcting misstatements about himself, though at the same time he was determined not to let these particular misstatements stand at the head of my introduction to his work."[4] What Cowley misses or dismisses in this entanglement of strategies is that the author has gotten himself snared in his own method. What became his dominant way of narrating a story—its loss of fixed points as it undergoes repeated tellings —entered deeply into Faulkner's own life; so that it, too, had become a series of tellings and retellings, in which the past can then be "untold." Faulkner's desire to remain private about his personal life had within it his desire to rewrite it himself. Those early deceptions became not just the intrigues of a typical liar, but the deceptions of a man who is straining to redo all narration, history, the past, reshaping it as he saw fit.

Jumping ahead from birth to the edge of fame, the 1945 episode illustrates how Faulkner was able to turn himself into legend by tampering with truth, then making that truth or falsity the very part of the mist from which he emerges. By doing this, he links himself physically as well as spiritually with those writers with whom he first identified: Keats, the French symbolists (especially Paul Verlaine and Stéphane Mallarmé), Algernon Charles Swinburne, and a literary tradition which removed him from regionalism. Yet, at the same time, he began to create the "Oxford myth" which would become Yoknapatawpha and Jefferson; shaping it to his own life by transforming its seeming ordinariness into exploit, daring, and courage. He started the process of re-creation well before he joined the RAF—from the beginning, in fact, when he was simply the oldest son of a bizarre family whose center was falling apart.

Being eldest held its terrors, but there were others to come. Within Faulkner's perception of early events was the fact that his family had moved around a good deal; there was movement and disruption, albeit minimal. After Faulkner's birth in New Albany, the family moved to Ripley near the end of 1898, when Faulkner was a little more than a year old. Then on September 22, 1902 (Faulkner was five years old), the family moved to Oxford, where it remained. The moves occurred in his preschool years, and he was too young to have incurred any friendships. Yet his perception was of certain instabilities going back to the earliest years. A more serious form of disruption very possibly came in his perception of his role in the family when his second brother, John Wesley Thompson Falkner III (known as Johncy), was born in September of 1901 and almost died of scarlet fever—a family drama for the eldest son, who was four.

At the turn of the century and for many years thereafter, scarlet fever was a child-killer. It was severe, acute, and terrifying for both parents and patient. It mobilized and isolated an entire household. As the eldest, Faulkner would perceive the shift of maternal affection—which meant a great deal to him throughout his life—from him to his brother, if only temporarily. In addition to the dreadful intensity of the illness, there was a frightening color, the bodily redness associated with high fever. In a day before antibiotics could turn a rambunctious disease into a much milder one, there was little treatment except cooling the patient, hoping the fever would lessen, and watching the scarlet coloring return to normal with the formation of new skin. It was, then, more than an illness or a disease; it was a form of nightmarish theater.

Also, as the eldest, Faulkner could observe the household tip. Although Maud Falkner's affection would return to her eldest son—and he remained her favorite during her almost eighty-nine years—he was for this time displaced. The eldest son often has a special role, but it becomes increasingly precarious when other children come along at roughly two-year intervals. It has been found that if a family produces children every year, the eldest feels less threatened and adapts more easily. But when the interval is two years, the threat to the eldest seems far more intense. The child experiences what is called dethronement, which is simply a perception of being displaced from his rightful place. (This is, incidentally, mainly a son's, not a daughter's, predicament.) Faulkner saw a brother (Murry Charles, Jr., known as Jack) come along shortly before he was two; then a second brother, the aforementioned John Wesley, when he was four; and then a third brother, Dean Swift, when he was almost ten. By the advent of Dean, however, Faulkner's role was once again solid.

The difficulties Faulkner experienced cannot have been helped by the dynamics of the family itself. Murry, while a sometimes devoted father, was a man out of phase with himself. He kept searching for some center, but in the process seemed to lose his way even more radically. He was ill-fitted for family life, and his drinking and search for male bonding were means by which he confronted (or escaped) a profound discontent. Also, the woman he married—perhaps married her because of this—was not a Southern princess. She was domineering, and dominant, a no-nonsense, nondrinking woman who followed the principle of reality. The space between Murry and Maud was not to be breached, even as the sons kept coming.

One significant consequence of Faulkner's struggle to emerge from this welter of boys was the need to regain his self-esteem and the attention of his parents. He chose his mother as the one whose esteem he would seek. Throughout his father's relatively brief life (he died just short of his sixty-second birthday, in 1932), Faulkner felt a mixture of hostility and discomfort, along with an effort to meet Murry on his own ground, which was the family institution of heavy drinking. Despite Faulkner's benign words about growing up in his father's livery stable, the relationship was complex, hostile, reconciliatory, and lacking in mutual understanding. It was, often, the dilemma of a father who felt he had sired a son who did not seem his, and the quandary of a son observing a father ill-suited for the structured life that was forced upon him.

These early years set in motion Faulkner's need to get outside his society, even while becoming its most famous commentator. His differences as eldest son and as mediator between his mother and father created not a desire to pull together but to get out. His means of escape would be familiar: by refusing school, in the eleventh grade; by assuming the role of another person, even in another era—the doomed romantic poets of England and France; and by assuming still another persona, that of a heroic soldier who almost forfeited his life for his country. The developments which led to Faulkner's disaffection and relocation beyond the reach of Oxford started early: in the need to regain his place.

Precisely to what extent this particular childhood shaped the way Faulkner decided to shield or armor himself is difficult, perhaps impossible, to say. But it is clear that the withdrawn, reclusive writer chose a defensive life; that is, one intensely connected to the kind of family life he perceived. The significant element here is "perception": not exactly what happened—although that must be pursued—but how he viewed what happened. Each Falkner son perceived the world differently. Jack, the second, seemed a direct outgrowth of his society and culture: patriotic, an FBI agent, with traditional Southern convictions on black-white relationships. The next son, John, would also become a novelist, but to compare his body of work with his eldest brother's indicates how different a creature the latter was even from another writer in the family. Dean, the youngest, was an athlete.

The Falkner line went back to the British Isles, and particularly to Scotland.[5] The name may have been Falconer, and other family lines, as Faulkner himself indicated, were Cameron, McAlpine, and Murry or Murray (the latter providing Faulkner's father his Christian name). Although Falconer suggests Scottish background, there may also have been Welsh lineage. But whatever the precise background—English, Scottish, Welsh, or all three—the family line in America becomes demarked with William Clark Falkner, the "old colonel," on the Falkner side. The Murray line seems more clearly Scottish, both from its Murray background and from its McAlpine blood.

The Scottish connection apparently had special meaning for the novelist because when he provided the genealogy of the Compsons for *The Sound and the Fury* he gave their origin as one Quentin MacLachan Compson, who "fled to Carolina from Culloden Moor." This Quentin was the grandfather four times removed of the Quentin Compson who commits suicide in 1910, in a novel in which he is clearly one of the author's surrogates. This early Quentin also has a son whom he names Charles Stuart, part of the doomed Stuart line, which suggests the later doom of the Compson line. Ingeniously, Faulkner has intertwined the genealogy of the Compson family so that a past Quentin foreshadows the doom of the present one; as well, he crosses over this line of doomed Quentins with his own Scottish background. Moreover, this Charles Stuart, son of Quentin MacLachan, after being wounded in the Revolutionary War and abandoned by both British and Americans, becomes involved in a plot "to secede the whole Mississippi Valley from the United States and join it to Spain." When that bubble bursts, he becomes a rebel and misfit who antagonizes state (Kentucky) and country, and even his co-conspirators. Faulkner's description of him as part of the Compson genealogy is full of glee and élan; he clearly relishes this rebel and identifies at least part of himself with him.

The Sartoris family also offers clues to Faulkner's background, supplementing the tales he told of Scottish background. In a passage deleted[6] from *Flags in the Dust* (the earlier version of *Sartoris*), Faulkner writes of a Bayard and John Sartoris who served under and then followed Charles Stuart in his attempt to recover England for the Catholics. Faulkner draws lines between present-day Sartorises and those in the past, especially the one named Bayard who died at Manassas, Virginia. The import of such genealogy—in the face of a warning Colonel John Sartoris gives his son, Bayard, that these matters in America are "poppycock"—is Faulkner's own search for a romantic past.

When he wrote and then excluded such passages from *Flags in the Dust,* he was about thirty and still maintaining the romance of wartime duty. These wild, sometimes violent ingredients somehow kept the spirit of the frontier alive. As a writer, an occupation not deemed manly by his community, Faulkner needed a counterweight which was fully masculine. The counterweight he provided, in part, with the rebellious, frontier genealogies; in another, with his version of wartime exploits; in a third, with his drinking. How he thought these various elements fitted together we cannot tell, and how much they were simply part of "tall tale" storytelling, we cannot know. But the need was apparently very intense, for he repeatedly crisscrossed between fact and fiction; whenever he involved himself in a genealogical undertaking, he infused it with wildness. No bookkeepers were among those who came to these shores. Faulkner inherited a genealogical family Bible, which had passed down from his great-uncle twice removed, John Wesley Thompson, then through the colonel's son to Faulkner. He made several entries; but the factualism of the Bible tables could not inhibit his doctoring of the truth, so that we really have no clear idea of the Falkner-Murray clan before they arrived in America.

However difficult it is to separate true Falkner background from its fictional versions, the family becomes more visible beginning with the old colonel, William Clark, who was born July 6, 1825, and died violently on November 6, 1889. This was Faulkner's paternal great-grandfather. The "old colonel"—so-called to distinguish him from his son, John Wesley Thompson, the "young colonel"—would become a great influence on the apprentice writer. The old colonel was a frontiersman, a doer in the American mold, and a writer as well. Faulkner modeled old John Sartoris on him, but William Clark served a far more complicated role in Faulkner's life than as a model for an important character.

William Clark Falkner represented the family at its peak and, along with his son, John Wesley Thompson, served as part of that Falkner claim to a patrician or aristocratic background. A good deal of this was misplaced or wishful thinking, since the great-grandfather was more frontiersman than patrician, and surely not in the mold of the planter-aristocrats. (He served, as well, as partial model for Thomas Sutpen, who is a Snopes with style.)

The real importance of the influence comes in Faulkner's use of his great-grandfather as a way of restructuring the past. The young writer's familial past, beginning with William Clark, became an archetype of the Southern experience, which he would transform in his stories and longer fictions into an American experience. It was a peculiar process, for even as Faulkner defined his ambiguous relationship to this past—represented in part by the hatred Quentin Compson expresses toward it—he found in it a model or scenario for much of his fiction. This part of Faulkner's life should not be underestimated: his work derived not only from this person or that, but from the feel of the past as he sifts it through his own family. His family becomes the Southern myth and legend out of which he can carve stories and fill that amazing vessel.

But before William Clark Falkner, the old colonel, there was his father, Joseph. Joseph had married a North Carolina girl named Caroline Word, who had a brother-in-law named John Wesley Thompson. Joseph's grandson, the old colonel's son, would also carry that name, just as William Cuthbert Faulkner would carry the same middle name as his father and first name of his great-grandfather. Murry's third son was called John Wesley Thompson, and his second, Murry C. This proliferation of names, confusing even for the seasoned Faulknerian, reveals repeated duplication on genealogical charts, which then carries over into Faulkner's life as a writer. Recurring names, common in Southern families, become part of the strategy of telling and retelling. Quentin Compson, for example, repudiates not only himself in suicide but an entire line of declining, name-repeating Compsons. Faulkner biography must be found in just those seams.*

The old colonel was the eldest of three children of Joseph and Caroline, who settled in Knox County, Tennessee, in time for the birth of the child, in 1825. Once the family tired of Tennessee, they moved on and Joseph and Caroline had another son and a daughter, this time settling down across

---

*There were, for example, four John Wesley Thompsons in all, culminating in Faulkner's second brother. The name Murry comes through the young colonel's wife down to Faulkner's father, brother, cousin, two nephews, and two great-nephews. Holland is the name of the old colonel's wife and reappears as Faulkner's aunt ("Auntee") and cousin. Alabama (Aunt 'Bama) was a great-aunt and also the name of Faulkner's short-lived, first daughter. Dean, his niece, was named after his youngest brother. The name William is too widespread even to chart. In Faulkner's fiction, we need only mention the McCaslin genealogy to note duplications: Lucius Quintus Carothers McCaslin, Isaac McCaslin ("Uncle Ike"), the twins "Uncle Buck" and "Uncle Buddy," Isaac Edmonds ("Zack"), Carothers McCaslin ("Old Cass"), and a son named "Zack," Carothers (known as "Roth"), and others.

There are even overlapping acts of miscegenation: old Carothers McCaslin (with incest added), Colonel John Sartoris, Thomas Sutpen, and then (almost) Charles Bon and Judith Sutpen, also with incest.

the Mississippi River, in Ste. Genevieve, Missouri. When William Clark, Faulkner's great-grandfather, was fifteen, he left home and headed south to Mississippi. This particular journey was not unusual for a young man who either wanted to seek his own fortune or else help support his family. There is a story that he left because of a Cain-and-Abel situation: fighting with his brother, James, William Clark feared he had killed him and ran away.

The incidence of violence—the retrieval of which became so significant for Faulkner—did not end with his flight. William Clark, who would die through violence, found it early in the shape of his uncle by marriage, the John Wesley Thompson who had married W. C.'s aunt, Justiana, the sister of Caroline. When William Clark reached a point near the Tennessee-Mississippi line, where he expected to find his uncle, the latter had already been whisked away on a murder charge. The young man continued on for another forty miles, to the Pontotoc jail. His uncle was being held for a killing based on personal matters—a bizarre foreshadowing of what would recur when William Clark himself reached adulthood and killed a man. The story (sounding a little like David Copperfield's) goes that the boy was desolate and forlorn, at the end of his tether. When he had apparently given up, having no one to help him, without money, his sole future jail for debts, a little girl helped him. Some three years before his death, in 1886, the old colonel told his story:

> He came from Memphis on foot, to meet his uncle here. He was a poor, sick, ragged, barefoot, penniless boy. His cup of sorrow was filled to the brim when he learned that his uncle (Mr. Word) had left for Aberdeen the day previous. He sat down on the hotel steps and wept bitterly, as though his heart would break. A little girl came along and inquired the cause of his distress. Having learned the facts from the Colonel she promptly went and obtained the money to pay his hotel bill and gave it to him. The Colonel never forgot the little Samaritan, but married her in Pontotoc years afterwards. When alluding to this episode in his eventful history, Col. Falkner became so affected that utterance failed him, and he had to pause until his emotions had subsided.[7]

The sixty-one-year-old colonel, in 1886, is presenting a story which had by now become part of Falkner legend. Although it seems to square generally with other accounts, it has within it something of the miraculous and magical, a kind of Cinderella for males. Even the prose fits. If Faulkner was brought up on this story, or one close to it—and there is little doubt it had entered family legend by the time of Faulkner's birth in 1897—then he had an early precedent for his own sense of "family romance."

The young William Clark then and there reputedly offered to marry the seven-year-old Lizzie Vance when both of them grew up. Like Thomas Sutpen, he worked through his plan: made his fortune, married Lizzie on the death of his first wife, and had eight children by the child who had saved him. One of those children was Faulkner's beloved great-aunt 'Bama, Alabama Leroy, who died five-and-one-half years after Faulkner. Her great life span of almost ninety-four years covered the period from the old colonel's successes through his great-grandson's Nobel Prize. She was the holder of the Falkner family story. Meanwhile, W. C.'s uncle, having served as his own defense lawyer, was acquitted of murder. Self-taught, he had taken up law during imprisonment—that "self-taught" element a Falkner trademark.

Once acquitted of the murder charge, John Wesley Thompson became an American success story himself, practicing law in Ripley, in the northern part of the state. Ripley was in former Indian country, principally Choctaw and Chickasaw. On Mississippi's entrance into the Union in 1817, the southern third had been settled by whites, the upper two-thirds by Indians. About ten years before Thompson's nephew, William Clark, arrived in Ripley, the northern two-thirds had been ceded to whites by means of a treaty, and by 1835 the Indians were moving out to Oklahoma. When William Clark came, as a teenager, the northern sections of the state were frontier, barely cleared of Indians, virgin territory as far as white settlements went. All this is a bare fifty years before Faulkner's birth in nearby New Albany. What is equally meaningful is that this frontier land existed even at the birth of Faulkner's grandfather, in 1848. Few other major American writers of the twentieth century had such a close linkage with the American past of frontiers, forests, and Indians. When Faulkner's work appeared in the 1920s and 1930s, he was, in effect, bridging a period which goes back to Andrew Jackson and the thirty-odd years of settlements preceding the Civil War.

Although records are not clear on all points, it appears William Clark became the ward of his uncle, John Wesley Thompson—once the latter had argued himself out of the murder charge and set himself up as a lawyer. John Wesley Thompson, whose name would be repeated as Faulkner's grandfather, was not a genteel lawyer, but a frontiersman, a rough and tough character who passed on many of his traits to his ward. William Clark had his chance, and he took it. He began to forge the career which would impress his great-grandson; and just as he went well beyond his foster father in affluence and influence, so he would provide, through stories, impetus for the young writer after his death. Not only the model for Colonel Sartoris, William Clark fitted that myth of the South Faulkner so desperately needed for his allegiance and his agony. Without the legend of William Clark, it is doubtful if Quentin Compson could have made his anguished cry: *"I dont. I dont! I dont hate it! I dont hate it!"*[8]

W. C. followed an inner voice, apparently, as much as his more illustrious descendant would. Working in and around a jail to maintain himself, he began to seek education, through the local schoolmaster, one James Kernan. Also through Kernan, he was able to begin his study of law, which in those days did not require previous university or even secondary school preparation. The career here roughly parallels that of Lincoln, who was pursuing legal studies at about the same time in Salem, Illinois. Ripley, however, was more nearly frontier country, and William Clark was hardly Lincolnesque in his escapades. The streak of violence which would run through the entire Falkner clan was heightened by the opportunity to be the main character in what seemed Elizabethan blood dramas. Falkner found himself as notetaker for a murderer, Andrew J. McCannon, who was illiterate, and yet had a story to tell: of the murder of a doctor and four members of his family. Entrepreneurial, Falkner sold the murder notes as a pamphlet just as McCannon was to be executed—it was the kind of grisly event in which the old colonel repeatedly found himself.

William Clark's career had four basic elements: his legal activities, his commercial or financial endeavors, his military exploits, and his fiction writing. Two of those four involved violence; and it is fitting that his great-grandson should follow him in three—writing, military service, and commercial farming. The business side began with his pamphlet about the Dr. Adcock murder. It was a fine piece of quick business. Tipped the other way, the heroic great-grandfather could have qualified as a future Snopes.

After this episode, events followed rapidly. William Clark found himself involved in the military, marriage and fatherhood, and extreme violence; in the latter instance, he became the principal in two murder trials.

The military came in the form of the Mexican War, in which so many Southern officers received their training for the Civil War. On this occasion, William Clark, of the Second Mississippi Volunteer Regiment at Vicksburg, joined Jefferson Davis's First Mississippi Volunteer Regiment in Monterrey. The time was early October 1846. But even war was apparently insufficient for the twenty-one-year-old, for in mid-April he became involved in one of those bloody episodes which shaped his life. He disappeared, against orders, and was discovered with his left foot smashed and three fingers of his left hand removed, apparently by two balls. Exactly what happened is not known, but it appears he had become involved in an affair of honor and had fought it out or been ambushed. This was, however, just a ripple for him. One receives the impression that the man who would be known as the old colonel was an unstoppable force of nature; the great-grandson in his more sedate career would exert some of that same inexorable force.

William Clark recuperated and married Holland Pearce, on July 9, 1847; and she delivered a son on September 2, 1848, John Wesley Thompson, the so-called "young colonel" and William Faulkner's paternal grandfather. (This John Wesley Thompson was named after his great-uncle, the brother of his father's father and himself the man who would give William Clark his start.) Discharged from the army because of wounds—however he came by them—William Clark apprenticed to the law office of his great-uncle, passed the bar examination, and began to become a rich man. Holland Pearce's dowry had included slaves, which enabled her husband to establish himself as a planter. William Faulkner could point to his immediate predecessors as planter class, Southern aristocracy. But it also put the taint of slavery into the family, that corruption which Faulkner incorporated into Ike McCaslin in "The Bear" (1942): a desire to disown the land and the past, history itself, because slavery had turned a potential Eden into a dispossessed, contaminated one. For the writer, Eden, Nature, and America would have to struggle against each other.

William Clark, of course, could not have cared less. Like the Northern tycoons of the next generation, he was interested in setting up himself and his small family; to be a planter was the way. The trail of violence, however, continued. In the spring of 1849, at about the time his wife, Holland Pearce, was dying of tuberculosis, William Clark became involved in an altercation with one Robert Hindman, setting off a series of confrontations. Apparently the trouble came over a misunderstanding concerning Hindman's admission to the Knights of Temperance (an amusing name for the organization in the light of developments). Hindman thought, mistakenly perhaps, that Falkner had opposed his membership, and he swore to kill him. The confrontation became the American equivalent of the European duel: the request for apology, the challenge, the denial or admission of what occurred, and the following shoot-out. Infantile yet final, adolescent yet murderous, the process would continue down into the twentieth century in Faulkner's fictional version of the past: Sutpen, for one, as the agent of this violence, destruction, and infantilism. In the confrontation, Hindman disbelieved Falkner's denials, pulled a revolver, which—as so often occurred with early revolvers—misfired, twice. Falkner, relying more on home remedies, pulled out a knife and stabbed Hindman to death.

No uglier than most such affairs of misplaced honor, this episode started a series of violent events between the Hindmans and Falkner. While the latter was acquitted of murder—it was clearly self-defense, even in our terms—there is also little question William Clark was a kind of Leyden jar, drawing acts of violence to himself; or else, a lightning rod attracting violence in others to confront the wildness in himself. Even by frontier standards (if we discount those who set up outright as gunmen and bandits) he was volatile. The Hindman family memorialized the event with the tombstone inscription (so it is said, since the tombstone has disappeared), "Murdered at Ripley, Miss. / by Wm. C. Falkner." This was, however, only the beginning. Three weeks later Holland Pearce died, leaving Falkner with a small, ailing son, the future young colonel. Since he had no way of handling an infant, Falkner turned him over to his uncle and wife, Justiana, promising not to take him back if he remarried. With John Wesley Thompson Falkner now being reared by John Wesley Thompson, yet another Falkner was about to enter the family, Elizabeth Vance, the little girl who had befriended William Clark. Two years after the death of Holland Pearce, she married the frontiersman. Needless to add, her family opposed the marriage, but, like Sutpen, W. C. got what he went after.

Another series of violent events intervened between the death of his first wife and the reassignment of his infant son, and remarriage to a woman who would bear him eight children within twenty-one years: events that defy modern comprehension. Falkner found himself in an argument with a friend of the Hindmans, named Erasmus W. Morris, evidently over a rental. Words grew to red faces, red faces to threats, and Falkner shot Morris dead. Self-defense was the usual plea, only this time in court Falkner found the prosecutor to be none other than the younger brother of the man he had killed in 1848. It was now March 12, 1851, and Falkner was himself becoming a successful lawyer. He prevailed in court and was acquitted, leaving the Hindmans completely frustrated. Falkner went to eat, but the dining room was a viper's nest, and there he was confronted by Hindman's father, who aimed a pistol directly at the newly acquitted Falkner. The gun, for some reason, fell from his hand, but discharged, with the bullet harmlessly hitting the ceiling. Falkner picked up the gun, having also drawn his own pistol. This time, however, he did not shoot, letting off the elder Hindman with a warning.

One can imagine young Faulkner reveling in these stories related by his grandfather, the young colonel, and his favorite great-aunt, Aunt 'Bama, William Clark's youngest daughter (who had herself been filled with stories by her older siblings). Hardly Homeric in their import—apparently with no end, for violence bred violence—these tales were nevertheless the stuff of legend and myth. But W. C. also tried out his pen, however unlikely seeming that endeavor, and came up with a long narrative poem about his army career under Jefferson Davis called *The Siege of Monterrey*. A little later, he produced a novel called *The Spanish Heroine*, which also took place during the battle of Monterrey. This brought him up to the time of his second marriage, on October 12, 1851, when he and Lizzie Vance secretly wed. The marriage proved to be stable, with Lizzie experiencing eight pregnancies in twenty-one years.

Falkner pursued his independent way, both as family man and not, a model in this respect for his great-grandson. He helped his younger brother, James, giving him support for a university degree, but apparently fell off in his support of his son John Wesley Thompson. Whatever the circumstances, friction developed between Falkner and the uncle who had helped him get started in Ripley, initially over child support, then in earnest over an election in which the two ran against each other, with the uncle prevailing. William Clark created an aura of friction, bad feeling, and violence wherever he moved. His politics fell across the spectrum of ideological positions in midcentury: Whiggish, Know-Nothing, and then Democratic. Know-Nothingism had considerable appeal to the frontier mentality. Nativism—America first, hatred of foreigners, anti-immigration sentiment, detestation of Catholics—had made its way from the eastern seaboard to the South. One branch of the Know-Nothing party strongly supported slavery, especially after Southerners began to dictate its platform. As a slaveholder, William Clark was made to order as a supporter of the party. It is unclear what political expedience made him move to the Democrats in the 1856 presidential election, with the triumphant James Buchanan.

Violence, however, remained. Motivations once more unclear, a friend of Falkner's tried to kill Hindman, Sr., the father of the man Falkner had shot. Falkner aborted the attempt by wrestling the pistol away, but this only enraged Hindman, who seems as crazy as his attackers. He challenged William Clark to a duel; pistols at fifty yards, each one advancing and firing at will. Falkner apparently indicated he had no intention of killing Hindman unless forced to, and the matter never came to the killing ground. Yet these episodes seemed only a crease in Falkner's life. The big moments were the steady birth of children and financial success. The differences between him and his uncle were papered over, and their fortunes waxed: from legal services and slave trading to investments in land and other enterprises. As the 1850s moved into crucial stages, William Clark became more vociferously a secessionist. The slavery issue was paramount by 1855, after the passage of the Kansas-Nebraska Act (which constituted those states as territories and, in effect, permitted slavery in Kansas), and would continue to prove increasingly divisive.

Issues had now arisen which were monumental, affecting not only life in Mississippi as a slave state but the entire Western region, and beyond that the nature and makeup of America. The "united" states were being blown apart by a series of compromises within compromises. The Missouri Compromise of 1820–21, itself obviously a holding action, had permitted the entrance of Maine as a free state balanced by the entrance of Missouri as a slave state; but slavery was prohibited in territory north of the southern boundaries of Missouri. The Kansas-Nebraska Act shifted these grounds, in a further compromise. Harriet Beecher Stowe's *Uncle Tom's Cabin* (1852) only stirred matters further, followed the next year by *A Key to Uncle Tom's Cabin*: documents and testimonies against slavery.

As Congress ran out of compromises and Southerners felt their position weakening, sympathies for Southern interests increased, to the pitch of violence which was quite suited to Falkner's own tastes. We can say with some certainty that events in the latter half of the 1850s paralleled Falkner's own predilection for showdowns, confrontations, and defiances of law and order. He was, in this sense of the term and not in Emerson's, a representative man: representative of his time and place, although shrewder and more successful than most.

As events moved toward climax, toward both exhilaration and ultimate disaster, William Clark had amassed a sufficient fortune to devote himself to real military service; not the small-time stuff associated with the Mexican War, but the defense of his region, of his very home. Failing in his effort to be appointed a brigadier once Mississippi seceded, he raised his own company, called The Magnolia Rifles, and headed it as captain. He then joined it to the regular Mississippi units, at Corinth, in early May of 1861, and was elected colonel of the Mississippi Infantry Regiment, made up of a number of like units. These were raw troops whose sole aim was to preserve Mississippi's integrity and power of choice. They were led by their colonel to become part of the Army of the Shenandoah, headed by Brigadier Joseph E. Johnston. These were heady times, but the colonel's fortunes took a strange turn. He did get his promotion to brigadier, but not for the regiment he had raised, and with that, he rejected the offer, a move as foolishly impulsive as many of his previous acts.

His unit and its regiments went into action at that slim stream in Virginia which became memorialized as Bull Run, or First Manassas, so-called after Manassas Junction. Northern and Southern forces were roughly even, and the battle—the first real one of the war—had great significance. In the tremendous Southern victory, in which the Northern army was outmaneuvered and outfought, the colonel was in the thick of the fighting. He came out of it covered with glory, although his regiment had been cut to pieces by the Union batteries. W. C. was cited for outstanding behavior and became a hero. This was (although he did not know it at the time) the high point of his war career; for he spent much of the remainder of it searching for that brigadier's rank he had rejected.

The same qualities which had gone into his acts of violence against private citizens were evident in his heroic battle action: disregard for consequences, disregard for his own safety, disregard for the safety of his men. His regiment, men and officers, had been shredded. Critics asserted he had endangered his regiment through recklessness, which with victory was identified as bravery. Less than a year after his great triumph at Manassas, he was voted out as colonel; and although he protested and was upheld by his immediate command, when he was not reinstated he went home. The Civil War, which had started out for the colonel as a great event, would prove to be a deep personal disappointment.

After futilely trying to regain his former position, Falkner raised another regiment, which he claimed to have armed from captured Union weapons. It was a cavalry regiment, and it would serve as a raiding unit. After some losses here and there, Falkner had about 750 men under his command, and he used them to attack the famous Phil Sheridan, in Rienzi, Tennessee. Such hit-and-run tactics were perfectly suited to his derring-do and contempt for safety. But his triumph was again short-lived, for the men in his regiment were disbanded and sent into regular units, although he was once more allowed to reorganize his Partisan Rangers, as they were called. After a series of skirmishes, in which his losses were high, his unit was yet again split into groups who were sent into regular units. Falkner could not accept this, and spent many months of the war trying to regain his position as regimental commander, with rank as brigadier.

As he was phased out of the war—he was, very possibly, spotted as too wild and uncontrollable—it is difficult to assess what he thought his role was. While he was devoted to the Southern cause, he also saw the Civil War as providential, providing adventure and relief from the responsibilities of an ever-pregnant wife and a growing family at home. The "boy" in him found a parallel in the South's romantic ideal of the war, its struggle against far superior manpower and an industrial base which it itself lacked. Falkner's name came to be linked to that of General Bedford Forrest, himself a legend, and although the connection cannot be proven, it nevertheless gave the old colonel further distinction. At a certain point, truth or falsity about W. C.'s activities no longer mattered—the legends took over. His great-grandson would try to perpetuate comparable legends about his own exploits in the RAF.

Whatever Falkner's precise movements at this time, Forrest's forces moved in and around the Ripley area, with marked success against Sherman. But the latter was beginning his scorched-earth policy, and one of his generals started a fire which destroyed Falkner's house. Blotner reports a family story,[9] one that could only have started with Falkner himself, that the old colonel helped Forrest's men enter Memphis, with great losses suffered by the Union side. Yet these were temporary victories, for the tide was turning against the South: the Confederacy was outmanned, outgunned, and finally outmaneuvered by Grant and Sherman. Falkner, meanwhile, was not inactive. Ever the expedient capitalist, he was recouping his sagging fortunes in the final year or so of the conflict by selling contraband goods through the Union blockade: foodstuffs, liquor, cigarettes, tea, and probably coffee. The Snopes aspect of the Falkner heritage may not have been one the great-grandson cherished, but it was solidly there.

William Clark's family with Lizzie Vance had by this time grown to four children, besides John Wesley Thompson, who was seventeen when the war ended. Four more children, two of whom died in infancy, were to come. But the family was increasingly a sideline for a man interested in becoming a force. Although we know little about his psychological or emotional makeup, it is interesting to note his obsessiveness in gaining what he wanted, his juggernaut-like drive and energy. Some of this he passed on to his first son, J. W. T.; and then, like hemophilia, it jumped a generation, hopskipping Murry, but gripping Faulkner. Each man, however, chose his own means.

The old colonel was astonishing in his ability to mix modes. While he was establishing his family after the war, he sat down to write a play, a kind of broad entertainment which he titled *The Lost Diamond*, produced in 1867 with considerable success. Falkner knew his audience—as he would later in *The White Rose of Memphis*, his most famous work—and gave them not the tragedy of the war, which they saw all around them, but a mishmash of entertainment that included the battles of Manassas and Bull Run. This reminder of Southern victory at the war's beginning would balance memories of Union destruction, and the fact that Mississippi was financially devastated.* According to the Ripley *Advertiser,* the play contained a duel, a Shakespearean skit of bickering lovers, theft, false arrest, and so on. It was the kind of mélange the old colonel would offer up in his novels, all the while pursuing his particular brand of violence, trying to restore Mississippi to stability. William Clark's creative efforts were not shaped works; they projected a series of skits or tales, not dissimilar to that part of Faulkner's work based on stories, tall tales, and episodes. The oral tradition remains powerful here, even as it is caught by the written word.

While the colonel's political and ideological aim was to purify the South —to achieve a prewar condition based on white superiority—he was dogged about his law business, and he saw with considerable foresight that the future of America, even in the devastated South, was railroads. In the late 1860s, the railroad had not as yet changed the face of America, although it had caught its imagination. The railroad was a technological invasion into the heartland of the country. It was, for the American with his dreams of Eden, the quintessential machine, one that commanded visions of space and escape, even as its proliferating lines brought boundaries. Although it clashed with the American sense of space—it enclosed, bounded, and created parallel lines throughout the country—it also offered space in its speed, timetables, and establishment of a communications network. It was a dilemma for the intellectual. Emerson, for one, feared it might upset what he called the "pleached garden," but it was a windfall for those who saw it as expansionism. W. C. Falkner was one of those; he seemed not at all worried that the very mechanism he was embracing was the means by which the country he idealized in its prewar setting would be subverted and, eventually, transgressed.

The railroad was one means by which Mississippi could recover, and through a deal made to order for Falkner, he became involved in what was called the Ripley Railroad Company (altered, in 1872, to the Ship Island, Ripley & Kentucky Railroad Company). Under the original terms, the state paid $4,000 per mile to anyone who built twenty-five miles of functioning railroad within the state by the first of September 1872. The catch was that the cost of such construction was high because of outlays for labor. But the slave mentality had not died, and the state promised convict labor. Falkner, along with thirty-five others, gained a charter. The rest was a comedy of errors, none of which seemed to affect the old colonel very deeply. The railroad was built to meet the deadline, but with narrow-gauge track. The state had stipulated standard-gauge track and refused to pay its promised quarter of a million. The railroad, which did not yet even exist legally, went into default to the company which had purchased its bonds.

*One commentator indicated that one-fifth of the Mississippi budget derived from state revenues went for artificial limbs (Joseph Blotner, *Faulkner: A Biography,* 2 vols. [New York: Random House, 1974], vol. 1, p. 34).

Falkner landed on his feet, however, as did his son by his first wife, John Wesley Thompson. A curious phenomenon developed: the old colonel's son who grew up outside his orbit became a considerable success, whereas the children who came along with the second marriage, to Lizzie Vance, were either doomed to die young or else, like William Henry (the eldest), threw themselves away trying to match the old man. Only Willie Medora, Effie Dun, and Alabama Leroy ("Aunt 'Bama") survived. Of the eight children born to Lizzie Vance, five would be dead by 1878, with William Henry shot to death that year.

The railroad, meanwhile, did not lie dormant. One of the partners, R. J. Thurmond, redeemed the defaulted bond and then sold half of his two-thirds share to Falkner, who now became a major stockholder. With his acquisition of one-third of the stock, he moved into a new enterprise: the newspaper business. He was now coming into his late fifties. In order to put the Ripley *Advertiser* back on its feet after a fire, he quickly wrote a novel which he serialized in the *Advertiser*'s pages. *The White Rose of Memphis* established his reputation as a writer.

This curious mixture of narrative devices and romantic materials began to appear in August of 1880. Its basic narrative strategy was that of Boccaccio's *Decameron;* but instead of a plague bringing a group of people together, in Falkner it is a masquerade ball on a ship heading for New Orleans, where each of the costumed guests is to tell his or her story. What is interesting in the light of his great-grandson is that the multiple-narrative strategy—later abandoned in favor of a single narrator—suggests that stories, tales, and episodes are the basis of the novel. That a work can be achieved through cumulative shorter forms is a concept employed in several Faulkner works—*As I Lay Dying, Go Down, Moses, The Unvanquished, The Wild Palms,* and even more formally conceived novels like *The Sound and the Fury.*

The White Rose of Memphis was a crude pastiche of fiction, but it struck a nerve. While Falkner rolled out the story in serial, he was also occupied with railroad work; he was, in fact, moving into one of the most productive periods of his life, as he became vice-president of the reconstituted Gulf & Ship Island Railroad, with a charter that would help link north and south Mississippi. At this time, he began a second novel, *The Little Brick Church,* which also took place on a boat, an excursion steamer plying the Hudson River. Falkner tried to duplicate the success of *White Rose* by utilizing more than one narrator and playing off parallel time dimensions: the present (early 1880s) and the American Revolutionary War era. The brutal episodes of the war gave him sufficient opportunity for violence and mayhem, and also for romance.

Falkner was at the time still involved in his law firm, and he became a partner in a lumber business, once again with R. J. Thurmond. With leftover energy, he entered Democratic politics, although whatever plans he had to run for Congress came to nothing. His writing days, however, were far from over, and his next book would be of a kind his great-grandson resisted doing even when he badly needed the advance monies publishers promised. The colonel, his wife, and their daughter Effie, now fourteen, toured Europe; and Falkner, not one to waste anything, brought back sketches and commentaries of his travels, which the *Southern Sentinel* published. W. C. then collected the pieces for Lippincott, and they were issued as *Rapid Ramblings in Europe*. While not memorable, these travel sketches brought a whiff of cultural broadness to the Mississippi territory. There is no indication, however, that his experiences abroad changed him, for on his return he plunged not into the life of a leisured gentleman but into politics and business, and once again into violence.

One residue of the European trip did remain. Falkner's desire to provide for his family a residence which imitated those he had seen in Europe— châteaux, castles, palazzos. Old Colonel Falkner created his "folly" in Ripley, an attenuated, hybrid, Italianate structure of the kind constructed by Gilded Age barons on the banks of the Hudson River. Not in the European but in the antebellum Southern style, it was, nevertheless, a residence recalling greatness, success, and splendor. William Clark was a miniature of every dimension of the America of his day.

Now in his sixties—a ripe age for the time—the old colonel was settling in for the great enterprise of his life. It was also a fateful time for his son by Holland Pearce, J. W. T. Falkner. The latter, along with Sallie Murry and their three children (including the future father of William Faulkner), moved to Oxford from Ripley. Oxford was in Lafayette County about forty miles southwest of Ripley. Despite the short distance, it was in many ways a significant move. It showed independence on the younger man's part; it established the family in a permanent place. Although William Faulkner would be born in New Albany and move to Ripley, by the time he was five he could grow up in an established home in Oxford. He did not experience the transience that characterized the times, when people moved frequently as economics dictated and towns and villages were created almost overnight.

Although J. W. T. would in several respects follow in his father's footsteps, the move to Oxford signaled the coming of a new era in America itself: the passing of a representative man like the old colonel, and a gradual shutting off of frontier energies. The son would be very successful, but in areas already defined by his father; and then in his son, Murry Cuthbert, there is the final closing off of the past—not only the frontier experience as an authentic attitude, but the energies that went into individual enterprise. Murry was fifteen when the move to Oxford was completed.

A year later, W. C. Falkner owned two-thirds of the Ship Island, Ripley & Kentucky Railroad, and he and Thurmond had become bitter enemies. It proved a fateful break, for Thurmond, not a frontier type, harbored terrible resentments which he did not voice. Falkner tended to deal from the top of the deck in his negotiations with people; whereas Thurmond dealt from the bottom, and let grievances accumulate. Meanwhile, like a scene from Greek tragedy, Falkner proceeded with the railroad, laying track south with the aid of convict labor, as if he were home free.

That use of convict labor, as is known from accounts of the period, was a form of slavery more than a generation after the practice had been struck down. In Faulkner's *Old Man*, prisoners were at the disposal of the state; and what several wardens and keepers did was to hire out convicts to growers, farmers, builders, or railroad men and then pocket the fee. The other side to Falkner's frontier energy was just this: a ruthlessness in exploiting others, an expedience in his dealings with human life, and an apparent indifference to consequences. He also intimidated: not only people but entire towns and villages. If they failed to contribute—money, land, whatever he needed—he would build around them; and as railroads began to become the country's commercial canals, not to have a railroad stop nearby turned towns into ghosts. For Falkner, this was a form of extortion. Stories that were passed down about the old colonel, some legendary, some perhaps close to truth, often ignored such details.

Through deals, letting the railroad go bankrupt, then buying it back at auction, Falkner overcame a lack of ready funds and, in fact, gained monies to expand the line into the Gulf & Chicago Railroad. The line created stops which included his own name, as well as the names of characters from his books. Meanwhile, political events were favoring the colonel, and he knew that to hold state office was to grease the way for one's own enterprises. Mississippi and the Deep South in general were undergoing convulsions and, in the late 1880s, turmoil derived from the withdrawal of federal troops in 1877. White constituencies had been struggling for over two decades to break the hold of black groups, and the politics of the period were both vicious and brutal as whites attempted to re-establish their hegemony. But cutting as deep as racial lines were social and economic issues. Farming interests—farmers, yeomen, tenant farmers, and share-croppers—clashed with moneyed interests, represented by railroads, banks, corporate enterprises, the lawyers who did their bidding, and the entire commercial structure which was trying to transform the Deep South from a rural, agricultural economy to industrialization.

These struggles dictated Mississippi politics for many generations and accounted for the attractiveness to the poorer populace of the racists and rabble-rousers who ran for elective office and often won: the Vardamanns and Bilbos and their successors in state and federal positions. The complications of this political and economic mix are manifest in Faulkner's work in numerous ways. His attitudes toward nature, the yeoman farmer, cities, even toward language itself were energized by his response to the shadowy substance of Mississippi politics. Since in his background loomed a man who had attempted to turn this system to his own profit, Faulkner could write with a sense of immediacy. What another young boy growing up in Oxford might see as a classroom lesson about the past was for Faulkner part of family history: not only the war and its aftermath, but the historical development of the region. Faulkner was born into the kind of historical matrix—involving radical change and one's need to adapt—which gives rise to great literary accomplishment.

It is clear why W. C. would want to be in the state assembly. As an avatar of Snopes activities, Falkner presented himself as the candidate of the poor, representing not big commercial interests but Delta people who needed a white knight to save their fortunes against banks and corporate entities. Falkner indicated he was just such a man of integrity, and vociferously denied that he wanted political office so as to curry economic favor. He did not actively campaign, but his rhetoric apparently convinced the Democratic party officials he was the man to win over the farmers, and he remained a candidate. Railroading, however, occupied most of his time—the consolidation of his small line into the larger Gulf & Chicago Railroad—and his former partner worked just as hard to defeat Falkner in the coming election. The only explanation for Thurmond's resentment and for his unyielding desire to thwart Falkner was that the latter had somehow swindled him out of his share of the railroad, or else deceived him in some unethical way.

Yet Falkner won, by a large margin. And he won in another way, also, for he commissioned an eight-foot statue of himself carved from Carrara marble, which was to stand in Ripley, a monument to one of its "founders." With all his practical energy, the colonel had a romantic sense of himself, an egomaniacal desire to enter history on terms equal to those accommodating Lee, Stonewall Jackson, and Forrest. Carrara marble—as Robert Browning's dying bishop in Saint Praxed's remarked—would make everyone envy him.

Events then took a dark turn, and the old colonel's behavior here is somewhat difficult to understand. His great-grandson tried to comprehend the nature of the event in the final episode of *The Unvanquished.* In "An Odor of Verbena," which ends the book of stories reprocessed into the novel, Bayard is the Orestes who must avenge his father's death, but he refuses further bloodletting and allows the feud to end. In the old colonel's case, he somehow decided—why is not known—he was tired of killing. Now sixty-four, he was still in the prime of his life, and yet somehow ready to surrender; for while he knew Thurmond was set to kill him, he refused to carry a weapon. It was as though he accepted the ending. It came, predictably.

Falkner had drawn up his last will and testament. In the past there had been words, even physical violence (Thurmond had knocked him down), and more bitter words when Falkner accused Thurmond of cheating on deals.[10] On November 5, 1889, as Falkner walked toward the main square of Ripley, Thurmond advanced upon him and put a pistol to his head. The .44 pointed at his mouth, Falkner attempted to discourage his attacker with the plea "Don't shoot." The shot struck Falkner in the mouth, went through several teeth, broke his jawbone, and lodged under his ear, in his neck. The back of his head was also badly injured as he fell. The wounds were of a kind that in a later era could possibly have been treated, especially in such a good physical specimen. But for the old colonel, they proved fatal. With the bullet close to the carotid artery, surgery was out of the question; internal hemorrhaging continued. The family, including the son by Holland Pearce, J. W. T. Falkner, now dubbed the "young colonel," gathered around the deathbed. Falkner died late in the evening of November 6, thirty-six hours after having been shot.

Thurmond was charged with manslaughter and released on $10,000 bail. He had his defenders, people who had obviously also hoped for Falkner's downfall, and Thurmond was treated less as a killer than as a savior. When the trial finally took place in February of the following year, Thurmond was acquitted of all charges and allowed to go free—a peculiar kind of frontier justice, since Falkner was not armed and self-defense could not be claimed. The young colonel, for whatever reasons, did not pursue the matter, and that ended the feud. The monument Falkner had planned earlier was now completed, and the eight-foot statue was placed on a fourteen-foot pediment: in death, Falkner extended for twenty-two feet. In *Sartoris*, William Faulkner wrote of the old colonel, now turned into Colonel Sartoris, in language which recalls Conrad's description of Nostromo:

He stood on a stone pedestal, in his frock coat and bareheaded, one leg slightly advanced and one hand resting lightly on the stone pylon beside him. His head was lifted a little in that gesture of haughty pride which repeated itself generation after generation with a fateful fidelity, his back to the world and his carven eyes gazing out across the valley where his railroad ran, and the blue changeless hills beyond, and beyond that, the ramparts of infinity itself.[11]

The death of William Clark signaled several social shifts. Frontier roughness would begin that slow transformation into gentility; not the gentility of upper New York society, such as we find in Henry James and Edith Wharton, but the transforming of frontier life effectuated by an increasing identification with town and city life. The railroad Falkner had helped to build and extend was a key factor in this development. With railroads bringing speeds of fifteen to twenty miles per hour, business, friendships, movement itself focused on town and city. Urban centers began to encroach on rural areas, if not on actual land then on cultural values. The old colonel, who in so many ways had represented the frontier, with his birth in 1825 and death in 1889, was able through his own means to help destroy the frontier idea. William Faulkner, born eight years later, would find in that meeting of eras a good deal of his material. His was the fortunate fall into a time and place; an era passing even as a new one was encroaching.

Falkner's son by Holland Pearce was also on the edge of a frontier, a personal one, and he was by no means diminished under the weight of ancestral success. That fate befell *his* son, Murry, and for a while it looked as though Murry's eldest son, the novelist, was going to be the most diminished of all. J. W. T. Falkner's fortunes waxed in Oxford, as he caught this still very small community on the rise and rode with it toward expansion. He struck on several fronts, as had his father in Ripley: in legal practice; in politics, as Deputy United States Attorney for the Northern District of Mississippi; in holding together the pieces of his father's railroad; and in town affairs through the agency of his wife, Sallie Murry, who was active, amusingly enough, in the local W.C.T.U., the temperance league.

The marriage was, seemingly, one of opposites (as would be that of his eldest son, Murry, with Maud Butler in 1896). By all accounts, the young colonel was a toughened man, tall, muscular or fleshy, quite the figure for Oxford's rough-and-tumble life. Sallie McAlpine Murry was his physical and emotional opposite—arguing for temperance, a churchgoer striving for every sign of respectability. Such dualism from grandparents and parents would be Faulkner's heritage; it helps explain his own emotional-physical makeup. He inherited his small physical stature from the female side, but compensated in part with masculine pursuits: hard drinking, horsemanship, and farming.

Patterns of behavior were beginning to be established. When the old colonel was shot, Murry, his grandson, was at the University of Mississippi, but evidently unhappy there, a misfit as an undergraduate. Like his father, Murry was close to six feet tall and solidly built, even beefy. He had the Falkner nose, large and extended, and a good-natured look about him. But beneath the affable exterior simmered a good deal of violence and anger; how it had developed we have no way of knowing, but Murry liked a good brawl. The university made him uneasy, and he took every opportunity to get away (as would his son, the novelist, whose overall school attendance was sporadic). Neither Murry nor his son considered school as the central experience of growing up, although precisely what Murry wanted to do is difficult to determine. His case seemed to be one of a son unable to measure up to family expectations, or else a young man smothered by a very successful father. William Faulkner would have to move in the opposite direction. He would struggle against a weak father figure in the household and transcend the male parent.

In a curious reversal, as the young colonel moved more energetically into successful ventures, Murry found himself confused: the railroad was, evidently, his true love, as much for the male-bonding it afforded him as for the escape from university life, for which he was emotionally and intellectually unprepared. Murry was not stupid, but he entertained a romantic view of life; he tried to live the romance while eschewing the reality.

At the railroad, Murry received little preferment, except for the job itself. He shoveled coal—as his son would later help fuel a university furnace—and slowly moved up the line, to engineer and conductor. His base of operations was Pontotoc, a small village on his grandfather's line, the Gulf & Chicago, thirty miles southeast of Oxford. Apparently Murry handled the job well, as he did the heavy drinking which was his signature for much of his life. He also became involved in fisticuffs over the honor of someone he was ambiguously courting. But fisticuffs in those days did not end there, and Murry found himself in much the same situation as the old colonel: facing a shotgun barrel. And as in the previous act of this drama, the holder of the shotgun was not bashful about using it. After pumping a slug from the .12-gauge into Murry's back, the shooter, named Walker, ignored Murry's plea of ". . . you've already killed me" and shot him in the face with his pistol. Murry, more dead than alive, was carried off for treatment.[12]

The wounds were in fatal spots, middle body and face, but had missed all vital organs; the facial wound was almost identical with the one that killed the old colonel. Murry was found to have a large hole in his back, with his spinal column untouched; it was as if someone had taken a sharp knife and cut out a huge chunk of flesh. But no nerve centers or other vital parts were affected. The bullet in the face was lodged so that it blocked blood vessels which would fatally hemorrhage if freed.

As Murry lay in this state—not dying, but not really in a position to live—his father, J. W. T., came rushing in from Oxford. His own situation was curious: his father had been shot fatally, and he had been dissuaded from taking action. That feud had ended. But now he was confronted with another, in which his son had been shot in almost the same way. This time, J. W. T. did not hesitate, and while Murry lay in critical condition, he went after Walker. The proceedings took a farcical turn: when the young colonel found Walker hiding out from his vengeance, he stuck a revolver in the side of his son's would-be murderer, pulled the trigger, and nothing happened. He pulled the trigger repeatedly, and still it misfired. Meanwhile, the reprieved Walker pulled his own gun and fired, hitting Falkner in the hand. Walker then ran away, leaving Falkner to nurse a wounded hand and Murry dying from a bullet lodged in the back of his mouth.

As a desperate solution, a home remedy was tried. With a solution of gummy asafetida, Sallie Murry made her son vomit, and up came the bullet. The hemorrhage was avoided, and Murry recovered rapidly. The incident apparently ended with that; Falkner returned to Oxford, Murry returned to railroad work. J. W. T., apparently, was more concerned with furthering his career than with pursuing Walker, who disappeared from the scenario. In this crazy quilt of frontier life, William Faulkner's father, grandfather, and great-grandfather had been shot: one near dead, one slightly wounded, one dead. It was an awesome heritage, the stuff of legendary America in the making.

J. W. T. went on to scale local mountains. His legal career waxed, he was elected to the state legislature as state senator for Lafayette County, he became a trustee of the University of Mississippi, and he entered intensely into civic duties. Through it all, as part of the Falkner heritage, the young colonel was a mighty drinker, often going over the edge and being taken by his teetotaling wife to the Keeley Institute for treatment. Falkner was apparently incurable, and returned periodically to be dried out. Blotner mentions Dr. Leslie E. Keeley's *The Non-Heredity of Inebriety* (published in 1896) which tries to establish that every drinker has within himself the power to recover; that alcoholism should be treated as a disease; and that certain treatments—the use of a foul solution of double chloride of gold —can inhibit the drinker by associating alcohol with the noisome liquid. The ideas about drinking being a disease and the use of inhibitors were very advanced, but none of it worked on the Falkner clan, in which the males frequently needed treatment while the women remained sobersides. The family pattern is so pronounced as to raise the question of whether or not there was a hereditary strain, as well as individual cravings based on some inner misery.

As drinking and violence blended into a discernible scheme of continuous life in Oxford, with the young colonel pursuing his multifold activities and Murry attempting to find himself, the latter became interested in a woman who seemed his direct opposite. (It was a pattern his son would play out with Estelle Oldham: a need to gain someone who represented his opposite, a form of exogamy.) Murry's sister, two years younger, entertained one Maud Butler; the sister, Mary Holland Falkner ("Auntee"), was, in fact, quite a social butterfly, although she married a doctor and settled down. Maud came from a far less illustrious but also far less violent family. But she, too, had ghosts. Her father demonstrated a streak of wildness by running off with an octoroon woman, leaving his wife and two children without support. The female side had artistic temperaments: Maud Butler, like her mother, painted, drew, and sketched, qualities which would reappear in her novelist son, whose drawing skills early on overshadowed his fiction. To complete the description of someone directly opposite to the man she married, Maud was small-boned, very short, and slight, features which would also reappear in her son.

Maud had no means of support—her mother had kept going through a variety of jobs once Butler had vanished—but she was educated, having graduated from the Women's College in Columbus. When Maud came to Oxford as the guest of Murry's sister, the moment was there—and Murry's fortunes even seemed to take a turn for the better with a promotion which would take him to New Albany, thirty miles away. As general passenger agent, he would have a higher salary, and now at the age of twenty-six (Maud was twenty-five), Murry proposed and was accepted. They married on November 8, 1896.

This was possibly the best time of Murry Falkner's adult life. He had a job with which he could support his wife and their expected child; he had his personal affairs and emotions in check; and he had the illusion he was on his own, although he held his position through his father's favor. Murry rented a house near the center of New Albany, and he and Maud settled in with servants, awaiting the birth of their first child. When the time came, William Cuthbert Falkner was solidly encased by Falkner names in the paternal family line.

Faulkner was a small, colicky baby, possibly allergic to mother's milk. He was a fidgety infant whose small size did not inhibit otherwise good health. He had the features of both parents: the large, beaklike nose of the paternal line, a distinctive feature from his earliest years until his death; the coloring and brown eyes of the Butlers, including that hooded quality which conveyed both silence and mystery in his gaze. Faulkner's face had something of the eagle, until aging softened the lines and made him appear distinguished and elegantly handsome. Another maternal Butler quality was skin whiteness, along with the small, pursed mouth, which, together with temperament, gave him a reserved, isolated sense of himself.

Photos of the child and even of the adolescent and young man do not demonstrate character in the face. The distinctive Faulkner look did not develop until later, when the features set, the hair began to gray, and the body became straight-backed. At that point, Faulkner's temperament created the look of extreme dignity, self-control, and inwardness, tantamount to courtliness. Before that, it was, by and large, simply a pleasant face, owing the middle to Falkners, the rest to Butlers. Faulkner's small size was a reversion to the maternal line and provided uneasiness; very much aware of his small stature, he found myriad ways in which to compensate. From childhood, Faulkner tested the psychological theory that the small person achieves by overcompensating, especially important in a society where men were large-boned, women small. A certain taint of effeminacy creeps into the context, for Faulkner was not only small and dainty, but created the aura of unusualness. For rougher types, this was a sign of effeminacy, in its broadest sense. How much his drinking and association with hunters and woodsmen can be attributed to this need to overcompensate and appear masculine cannot really be measured.

With his son's birth and early months, Murry's career took on a peculiar quality. While it appeared he was advancing from passenger agent to auditor and treasurer of the railroad, as well as enjoying other responsibilities, he was falling increasingly under the thumb of his father. Murry was reaching the apogee of his career, but it is also clear he could not have reached it without being the boss's boy. Thus his very advance, in this paradox, made him even more unable to move out on his own. Murry eventually became head of the traffic and freight claim departments, which involved a move from New Albany to Ripley, twenty miles to the north. When William was only a year old, Maud was once again pregnant; the following June, she gave birth to another son, this one named Murry but called Jack. To complete the family circuitry, Jack's middle name, Charles, came from Maud's brother.

Jack proved a difficult infant, and experienced eating difficulties for about the next five years. Whatever the problem (it was not organic, since Jack lived to a ripe age) and whatever the precise circumstances, the birth of Jack disordered William's world more than most births do for the eldest. By rejecting nearly all nourishment except, apparently, biscuits, sausage, and fried eggs, Jack took over the household.[13] Under these circumstances, the first to be considered and fed was the baby, as in most households—but special care had to be taken that nothing should prove disruptive lest the baby stop eating altogether. William was displaced not only by the addition of another boy, but by one who captured center stage. It was during this early period of both William's and Jack's life that the former moved closer to his mother; for as time went on, he was clearly his mother's son, whereas Jack and the two boys who followed were more Murry's.

By the time Jack was born, Murry and Maud Falkner were relocated in Ripley, while J. W. T., waxing ever more successful, was planning to move into what came to be called "The Big Place," in Oxford. This house, and its adjoining piece of land, was near the town's central square and would prove to be a suitable residence for an affluent citizen. J. W. T. remained state senator and had been appointed county attorney for Lafayette County, some of which rubbed off on Faulkner's Gavin Stevens thirty years later. As state senator and county attorney, as well as head of the railroad, the young colonel could wield enormous financial power. For many years in Mississippi politics, as in the politics of most other rapidly developing states, elected or appointed office was pivotal in the acquisition of personal wealth, usually through fraud, bribery, insider knowledge, or embezzlement. Situated in Oxford, with his hands on everything, J. W. T. moved into real estate, telephones, and other diversified investments; the railroad, the basis of Murry's life, was becoming a marginal holding.

These business deals on the young colonel's part, while outside the inchoate world of William, his grandson, were to prove particularly crucial in the latter's development. For as the grandfather lost interest in the railroad, Faulkner's father would be displaced, to begin a gradual economic and personal decline. Not that Murry was doing poorly, given the opportunity to ride on his father's coattails: besides fathering a third boy, John Wesley Thompson III, on September 24, 1901—three sons in four years—Murry was himself diversifying. He invested in the Ripley Drug Company, and he purchased a farm, chiefly for its timber. He was also indulging what was his real love, raising bird dogs and keeping horses. For most of his adult life, Murry felt more comfortable around dogs, horses, and their handlers than he did with business affairs, townspeople, even his immediate family. Dogs and horses gave him the sense of another kind of America, which his very enterprises and those of his father would help efface. Murry was that unfortunate American whose intense personal needs clashed with his immediate financial interests.

Murry continued to expand his projects, which in the main depended on his father's role in the railroad. Family matters, of course, kept everyone busy, and William himself moved back and forth to Oxford. Then at four years old, according to the local paper, the *Eagle,* he suffered a near-fatal attack of scarlet fever. The fever spread to his brother Murry (Jack) and coincided with the birth of the third brother, Johncy. Little is known of the situation except that it was quite serious, inasmuch as scarlet fever in those days had no real cure and was considered, medically, very severe. Before the advent of penicillin, which inhibits secondary infections, scarlet fever could lead to serious complications. In Faulkner's childhood, about the only treatment was sponge baths, fluids, and waiting it out. Although somewhat frail, William recovered with no discernible complications and was rewarded by his grandfather with a Shetland pony and a hand-stitched saddle.

Murray, meanwhile, was about to receive news which would affect the next thirty years of his life, until his death in 1932. The young colonel was so involved in other business ventures that the railroad, relatively clear of debts and mortgages, was a saleable item, and he intended to unload it. At some point in late summer or September of 1902, he informed his son that his railroad position was ending, that he should seek another form of support, preferably in Oxford. This was bad news for Murry, of course, since it came at a critical time in his life, as he and his wife had three sons and he was thirty-two and not really adaptable to an indoor position. He had worked well and hard at a job on the railroad which was not quite to his taste, and it had come to an abrupt end; the new owners wanted their own managers. While the young colonel was solicitous of his eldest son, he did have two other children as well as rapidly growing business and political interests. And Murry was not easy to place. His taste in reading was James Fenimore Cooper's *The Pioneers* and *The Pathfinders* and other books more clearly aimed at ranching and roaming. But he was now a family man, caught up in a cycle of respectability from which he could not escape, except in fantasizing and drinking with his male cronies. He raised the question of buying a ranch out West—his last effort at breaking away —but Maud, the realist and practical one, refused to go. That in itself created a deep division within the family, a tension which only increased with time as Murry found himself bewildered by a world he did not accept. Tensions which had lain below the surface worked themselves out in family relationships: Maud ascending, Murry descending and becoming increasingly frustrated, moody, and alcoholic. To some extent, William would repeat this pattern in his own marriage.

Just short of his fifth birthday, William left with his family for Oxford.[14] The railroad having been sold the previous June, Murry was on his way out, and the family was preparing to move into the young colonel's former residence. While not a metropolis, Oxford, the home of the University of Mississippi, was far more advanced than Ripley had been, and even had electric lights. It was the beginning of an adventure for the boys: William already assumed command of his next brother, at three, and the baby, at one. Whatever happened to Murry in his professional life profoundly affected William; as the eldest son—the fourth and final boy would come along in five years—he was clearly the most responsive to shifts in family fortunes. And as eldest, he would be closest to family tensions as Murry's fortunes declined, whether such tensions surfaced as verbal arguments or simply in the intense movement of Maud from her husband toward her sons. Such subtle social elements are always present in the growth and development of a young person, but intensified for the eldest. For his part, William considered himself a vicarious father figure for his brothers; and this assumption of the masculine role in the family as protector and shield affected his relationship with his parents. An obvious Oedipal tension developed, and Maud, apparently, encouraged it, especially since she and Murry had disagreed firmly and permanently about a move West. Murry nursed that grievance, and used it against his wife when his fortunes faltered. The rift was broad. The eldest son is the natural one to take up the slack, to become, as William did, the man in Maud's life.

The other sons can be relatively untouched by such a situation, unless it becomes acute and nasty, which does not seem to have been the case in the Falkner household. Jack seems unaware of the tensions in this description of the family idyll:

> How kind they were, those years of long ago; how gentle the life and how pleasant the memories of it. I can almost see us now: the day is done and we are all about the fireplace in the living room—Mammy [Caroline Barr] in her rocking chair, Father with the paper, Mother sewing, and Bill, John, and I listening to Mammy telling us again and again about the War—still, as always, the only one. We were all there, each belonged, was loved, and loved in return. Mammy called us collectively "mah white folks," an affectionate and honored title as was the one we used in addressing her. To her, Father was "Mis't Murry," Mother was "Mis Maud," Bill was "Memmie," John was "Johncy," and I was "Jackie." When he came along, Dean was "Deanie."[15]

For the eldest, it was otherwise.

Those great silences for which both the young man and the adult Faulkner became noted were full of defensive maneuvering, a strategy or device he had developed to deal with what could not otherwise be managed. Such silences, or white spaces, are forms of response, and even though unverbalized, they are not negative. They seem to have been conditioned, not a spontaneous creation of the young man or of the writer; they appear to have derived from a situation in which opposing antagonists made emotional demands William could not evade, and yet could not resolve. Such is the space between brothers.

Another factor, not to be neglected, was that such growth in a troubled family occurred in a small town or village.[16] Compared with Ripley, Oxford was a thriving city, although compared with a real city, Oxford was a backwater. Northern Mississippi looked toward Memphis for urban life.

Although it was in the process of steady growth, not the least because of the old colonel's railroad, Oxford was nevertheless a self-enclosed place. If William wanted to escape family tensions, Oxford afforded few routes. Yet while Oxford's population was under two thousand—several times larger than that of Ripley—the center area extended out from the main square for several streets; it was not the usual one-street village which dotted much of northern Mississippi. There was considerable building, including the recently completed structure which housed the young colonel's law offices. In addition to law offices—lawyers were assuming a central place in the development of these near-frontier towns—were the expected institutions: the bank (of Oxford), department stores (Nielson's, founded in 1839, and Hyman Friedman's ready-made clothing for the less fashionable), hardware establishments, drugstores (whose nostrums were more cosmetic than cure-alls). And there was, of course, the courthouse.

The village houses, coming almost to the square, were of the white clapboard popular not only in the Deep South but in New England as well. They may have appeared to be comfortable and cozy, but in modern terms they were primitive. Few, if any, had indoor plumbing or running water; heating systems were rudimentary, so that in the very cold winters of northern Mississippi, the sole way to keep comfortable was to huddle before a fireplace. In the summer, insects were formidable, and sitting out meant keeping a fan handy.

Further, whenever it rained hard, the streets were quagmires, for they remained unpaved. Dust or mud were the alternatives, flung from the hooves of horses and the wheels of wagons. Even after he transformed himself from a regional writer into a more universally American one, Faulkner's rural beginnings dominated his imagination. Flowing from Thomas Jefferson and Ralph Waldo Emerson, his ideas of a city were little more than an elaborated town. Within such circumstances, people became homogeneous; Negroes were the sole "strangers" to this white, Anglo-Saxon, custom-bound community. A community became a society through strict codes, and they dictated manners and morals. Homogeneity of impulse and behavior was the sole law, since legalism favored the rights of the individual, as in the fickle justice meted out during the old colonel's life. Although religion played a huge role in Oxford life, it was not an overwhelming presence in the Falkner household. Rather it was Maud's words which counted: "Don't Complain—Don't Explain."

In Faulkner's transformation of Lafayette County into Yoknapatawpha and Oxford into Jefferson, reality ruled more than myth. Negroes made up almost an exact half of the county's population of twenty-two thousand, and despite the development being undertaken, livelihoods for nearly all depended on a single crop: cotton. Cotton was also a trap, for it exhausts the soil, and when it is a single, unrotated crop, it gives the soil no opportunity for replenishment. An unnourished soil begins to produce less and less cotton, a process which began during Faulkner's early years and led to the steady migration of Negroes to the North. It also created an even larger disparity between rural and town or city people; for the latter were attempting to move with the times, whereas cotton farmers were working at something resistant to recycling. Within this single county of perhaps twenty-five square miles, an entire culture was working itself out, for one perceptive enough to see it.

What Faulkner observed was constant struggle: not only conflicts between social classes and, especially, between races, but struggles of most people to keep their heads above water. Farmers, agricultural workers, the so-called rednecks, were locked in a struggle with the land which cotton was exhausting; those in town were setting up as entrepreneurs and merchandisers, trying to catch what little money was available once people fed themselves. Almost out of sight was the intense struggle among Negroes to work the poorest land, or to work for the poorest wages, and to avoid any incident calling attention to themselves.

For example, when payday came and people headed into Oxford to spend at the market or in one of the specialty shops, Negroes had a separate area for recreation. They created a subsociety within the many other subsocieties in and around Oxford. This layer of society Faulkner rarely penetrated—he may allude to its violence, but the ongoing life there was not all violence. How did Negroes sound when they talked among themselves, without any white people present? What did they say about white people? How did those react who were literate and felt trapped? How did their sensibility differ from that of others who were little more than beasts of burden? What plans did some of them make for escape? Who are those who did escape and what effect did this have on those who had to remain? What were the dynamics of Negro family life really like? As soon as these questions are asked, we can see that Faulkner—who repeatedly asserted only the Southerner could comprehend the Negro—evades most aspects of Negro life from which understanding could derive.

The Falkner family settled into their home, which was located about ten minutes on foot from the young colonel's establishment. In addition to Murry, Maud, and the three sons, there was Maud's mother, Lelia Butler, known as "Damuddy," who would die two months before Dean was born. She was supportive of Maud, in that she brought Butler respectability to the household and acted as a restraint on Murry's drinking, gambling, and swearing; and she also served as chief aid in getting Jack to eat, a problem which continued for several years. There was Negro help, also, but none of a sustained kind until Mammy Callie arrived and moved in. Mammy Callie was the prototypical Faulkner Negro, and she had, it is certain, a tremendous influence on his imaginative processes, especially when he matured as a writer and left behind some of his ultraromantic trappings.

Mammy Callie was almost too good to be true for a developing writer. She was intensely loyal, dictatorial, supportive of the boys, and insistent on their moral character; and yet she remained completely her own person, intractable in her ways, a woman with a varied past of husbands and children, a former slave, illiterate, doughty, and dignified. She may have weighed a hundred pounds or less, but she was the full measure of Dilsey in *The Sound and the Fury*, though less deferential, more a woman who insisted everyone play on her terms. In exchange, she gave of herself completely; in many respects she became, at least for William, another mother. She was not simply the "Mammy" of numerous Southern households, but a woman whose own life ran through the lives of the Falkner clan. She was a black Falkner, and she had almost full authority in the house, second only to Maud's. This, too, is important, since we see a pattern of William, the eldest, being brought up in a home dominated by women, in a kind of pecking order: Maud and Lelia Butler, then Maud and Mammy Callie. The strength of the female presence in the home meant Murry, although titular head, was brushed aside, with both Maud and her mother deriding his rough habits and lack of respect for the Sabbath.

Yet, withal, life was fairly easy, and very young William followed a familiar childhood. Despite the disaffection of Murry and the growing chasm between husband and wife, there was the feeling of a tightly knit family. The paternal grandparents, especially once Maud's mother died, were also a presence in the Falkner household. The young colonel would remain formidable through Faulkner's childhood, adolescence, and young manhood, living almost until his grandson was on the threshold of his career as a writer. And besides J. W. T., there were several others to turn the family into a small community: the young colonel's wife, Sallie Murry, although in eclipse next to her illustrious husband; and the colonel's own half-siblings, the children from the old colonel by Lizzie Vance. Alabama Leroy, "Aunt 'Bama," four years younger than Murry (and the aunt after whom Faulkner and Estelle would name their infant who died within days), was well loved. Also in this extended household the young boy would find Murry's sister, Mary Holland, who became "Auntee" to the boys. Although "Auntee" would marry (Dr. James Porter Wilkins), she remained devoted to the Falkner family in the manner of the unmarried sibling whose role is to fill in whenever anyone else falters. With a sickly, consumptive husband and only one daughter, who became a pal of the four boys, Mary Holland was part of that extended series of aunts who added still another female dimension to the family.

Mary Holland, however, served as more than a friend to the boys; she was a key support for Maud, all the more welcome because she understood the difficult nature of Maud's marriage to Murry. It was not that Maud was a saint and Murry was a roving, uncomfortable man—the problem lay in the nature of a marriage between two unsuitable people. As Murry increasingly faltered in his efforts to be what was expected of him—and as his dreams and fantasies became increasingly unattainable—Mary Holland's services were especially needed to keep the family resolute.

Murry's new venture was a hauling company. The young colonel had staked his son to O. O. Grady's Livery Stable on University Street: Murry had traded a railroad for a horse. It was something of a social comedown since the railroad had the glamor of the new and unexpected, and horses were considered a retreat. Yet for Murry, it was a pleasant change, for it involved both horses and dogs. With the stable, he also had his town buddies, his drink, and an outpost beyond the reach of hearth and women.

Murry had a gang of Negroes to keep the horses and a couple of other men, white, to drive the wagons. The situation, though very different in its circumstances, calls to mind that of Sutpen in *Absalom, Absalom!*: a tough, masculine world, with its wildness, Negroes on the fringes, white men closer to the inner circle, aggressive outsiders ready to cut in. Murry became involved in a brawl with a man named Dick Oliver, the kind of melee memorialized in dozens of movies where the site is pulverized as the men try to annihilate each other. Brawler Murry prevailed by throwing Oliver through a plate-glass window.

The young William, meanwhile, was on the move, as active in exploring the woods and mysteries of nature as the young colonel was in business matters. The advantage of Oxford for a curious and intelligent young child was its proximity to near-wilderness. Woods were within a brief horseback ride of the Falkner house, and William, now turning six, and his brothers, accompanied by a servant, often rode out. He was beginning that particular kind of childhood which dissociated him from all other American novelists of his generation: not only small-town life, but a woodsy experience and that separation from values linked to larger cities, immigration, corporate life, and size itself. Reading Faulkner, one recognizes how devoted he is to small things, miniatures, and minimums. As he rode in the woods exploring flora, fauna, bird life, as the boys collected eggs, there was a clear bottom line to his life, no matter what the tensions in his home. Yet that outdoor life was not necessarily connected to ideas of Eden or to deeper pastoral levels, although that might have been there, but to contrasts. Faulkner could not help but notice distinctions: between the entrepreneurial town embodied in his ever-present grandfather and the minimalist experience of woods. Faulkner did not miss the contrast; when he reached young manhood, he immediately opted for that minimal, simple form of existence, opposing not only the young colonel's interests but even Murry's lesser ambitions.

When J. W. T. diversified, it seemed as if he would tap Murry for a managerial position in a cottonseed-processing plant, part of an even larger company pattern under the umbrella of the Oxford Oil Mill Company. There is, despite differences, something of the Snopes aura to this; that dedication to advancement of personal interests through nepotism. Further, since there were a good many men as exploitative of the growing situation as J. W. T., winners needed greater guile and deceit; brains and opportunity were not sufficient. Snopesism everywhere! Blotner mentions that Falkner had probably put up the money for his son John's grocery business, as well as staking Murry—so that a pattern of dependency existed.[17] Only his daughter, Mary Holland, escaped patronage by marrying a doctor. The young colonel's interests leaped ahead, as he invested in new factories, growing businesses, another railroad line, even the purchase of the opera house. Notwithstanding the novels of William Clark, this was a new venture into culture for a family not noted for its broad cultural interests.

Meanwhile, his law practice began to falter when, in addition to the above, the young colonel entered more deeply into politics. He was now, in 1903, fifty-five years old, and approaching his most energetic and productive years—like his father at a comparable age. In contrast, Murry would be dead by sixty-one, and William at the same age would be depleted both physically and creatively. J. W. T. simultaneously took on duties as city alderman, trustee of the University of Mississippi at Oxford, and candidate for the state senate (for the second time). To relieve himself of some of his law practice, Falkner took in a young lawyer, Lee Maurice Russell, whose career proved even more amazing than his own. Russell rose from son of a poor farmer to university graduate, lawyer, and ultimately governor of Mississippi. Russell shrewdly calculated that the coming wave of power in the state would derive from the rednecks who saw themselves as beleaguered and frustrated by big-city machinations and growing industrialization. Through a consensus of interests, this group indeed became a significant force in the next generation, and Russell—along with several demagogues, racists, and opportunists—rode into the governor's seat and on to Washington, D.C.

It was a political shift of power which Faulkner caught in his Snopes trilogy and also in the life of Thomas Sutpen in *Absalom*. In this political shift, the Negro had no role, because of both racial and social attitudes. Although redneck and Negro interests often coincided, social distinctions made it impossible for coalitions to exist. A "lower-class" economic designation should not disguise large and significant differences. The young Thomas Sutpen and Lucas Beauchamp both embody lower-class interests. And even though Lucas considers himself an aristocrat of sorts with his McCaslin heritage, he is, as a Negro, relegated to a role he must play to survive; Sutpen, in contrast, has America as his oyster, however difficult success may be for him to achieve. Although Faulkner did not focus directly on this particular aspect of Mississippi life, his works as a whole convey a sense of class and caste in social and political life.

Even with the backing of the Oxford *Eagle* in his run for the state senate, the young colonel lost to the man who represented the farmers, one G. R. Hightower, in August 1903. Had he won, Murry's career and its subsequent effect on the Faulkner household might have taken quite a different course. With J. W. T. in the state senate, many preferments would have opened up, and Murry could have enjoyed political patronage. However, with the loss, the young colonel abandoned formal politics for local civic affairs. His loss was a harbinger of Mississippi politics, its isolation in that alignment of commercial interests and farmers which came to be known as Farmers' Alliances. These Alliances had some connection to populist feelings and to populist parties in other states; they would lead to the acclaim for Huey Long and his machine in Louisiana, for example. However, in Mississippi, farmers remained in the Democratic party, which became the party of the redneck, fighting to survive against town and city interests. As William grew up and began to form his detestation of such interests, it is ironic that his fabled grandfather ran as a representative of those very commercial enterprises.

William, at six, was old enough to begin assimilating more than the atmosphere of the woods. He was aware of his grandfather's loss, although not of course what it meant. As the eldest of three boys, he was maneuvering into position as the one others looked up to, and, increasingly, as the boy-man whom his mother came to favor. He must have revealed to Maud something which made her sense her eldest son was talented: her faith in him seemed to involve some special chemistry. For as William grew and developed, as he became increasingly anomalous and eccentric in the eyes of other Oxonians, he knew one thing above everything else: Maud's belief in him was complete and unbreakable. For a growing boy to know that is to make the earth his kingdom.

The past slowly faded: the Civil War (although veterans still abounded, some of them only in their late fifties or early sixties); Indians, now vanished as faces and threats; Reconstruction, with its hated invasion of Northern helpers and opportunists. The present was taking over. The young colonel was part of that present, as was Murry, who eventually moved beyond his cowboy fantasy to serve as business manager of the University of Mississippi. William was growing up in a period of intense change, change that he resisted even as it provided comfort and security.

Also part of that shift was the Oldham family, whose fortunes would interweave with the Falkners' for the next fifty-five years. Lemuel Earl Oldham, the father of Estelle, whom Faulkner would marry in 1929, was clerk of the United States Circuit Court. When he moved to Oxford in 1903, his family of three daughters and a son was complete.

The Oldhams were special. Mrs. Oldham (Lida Allen) had illustrious forebears, including Sam Houston and Brigadier Felix Zollicoffer, a Civil War hero and a founder of the Nashville *Banner*. Also, her stepfather Henry C. Niles, and the family he came from, with Northern and Republican connections, were very respectable, with lawyers, a judge, and someone who had fought for the old colonel's great rival, James R. Chalmers. Lemuel Earl Oldham was a lawyer, having obtained a law degree at the University of Mississippi (at the time Murry was a student) and launched a successful practice in Bonham, Texas, where Lida Estelle was born, on February 19, 1896—which made her nineteen months older than William. After gaining his appointment as federal court clerk, Lem Oldham moved his family into a house about a quarter-mile from the young colonel's.

When Estelle and William met as small children, the only thing they seemed to have in common was a love of reading—and a dominating mother. Estelle was very much in the shadow of her mother, also named

Lida, although Estelle used her middle name throughout her life. The elder Lida was a gentlewoman, well cared for by servants, accustomed to living in large, comfortable houses, eminently respectable, a good amateur musician on the piano, which she had studied seriously, now serving as commandant of an agreeable staff.

Superficially, Estelle's background appeared stable, without the social and personal strains evident in the Falkner home. And yet despite what seemed an ideal upbringing for a Southern belle, Estelle turned out to be dissatisfied, often wild, a heavy drinker, and in many ways self-destructive. She was certainly an unfulfilled woman who, despite her intelligence, did little with herself. In a sense, Estelle was trapped by that genteel, secure, comfortable background; it prepared her for nothing more than marriage, first to a rapidly climbing public man and then to an intensely private, but equally ambitious, writer. When both marriages, for very different reasons, proved faulty, she had no resources except drugs, drink, a suicide attempt, aggression against herself. Faulkner, deeply conflicted, did not victimize Estelle, but was caught in a similar self-destructive cycle, despite his enormous confidence as a writer. Out of his personal anguish, and Estelle's, came many of the emotional tones of his fiction.

On one occasion, when Faulkner came by on his Shetland pony, Estelle pointed at him and commented: "Nolia [Magnolia, her nurse], see that little boy? I'm going to marry him when I grow up."[18] Of course, Estelle reported this sixty years later, and it has some of the legendary quality of Joseph Conrad's assertion that when he was a boy he pointed to the map of Africa and said "I am going there," meaning the Congo. What the remark does signify, whether accurate or not, is that Estelle had taken note of William and established a pact which determined their adult lives.

Estelle was plied with the usual nineteenth-century book fare by her Niles grand-stepfather, and she did well in school. In the meanwhile, William, in the company of his brothers, led a Tom Sawyer–like existence, free of school until he was eight and able to roam the woods on his Shetland. The indifference of the Falkner clan to early schooling, despite Maud's own more formal educational background, clearly established in William attitudes he carried for the rest of his life. He read, encouraged by both Maud and the young colonel, who seemed to take an interest in everything.* But his main occupation was playing the carefree boy. His liberation also created an independence from institutions: he sensed there was life outside society's traditional forms.

*Jack Falkner lists some of the magazines and books in the house: ". . . St. Nicholas Magazine, the Saturday Evening Post, the Youth's Companion, the old Life Magazine, Collier's and the Delineator. . . . I remember James Fenimore Cooper's tales of the American Indians, Dickens's works, Treasure Island, Pepys's Diary, Amos Judd, Robinson Crusoe, Grimm's fairy tales, Uncle Remus, Mark Twain's books, The Virginian, and a number of books about the War. Later, as we advanced in school—and at the always-encouraging hands of Mother—we began a lasting acquaintance with the works of Kipling, Poe, Conrad, Shakespeare, Balzac, Hugo, Voltaire, Fielding, and many others, each of whom brought enlightenment and pleasure to three small boys in a small Mississippi town more than a half century ago" (Murry C. Falkner, The Falkners of Mississippi [Baton Rouge: Louisiana State University Press, 1967], p. 17).

William's cavalier attitude toward formal education (as apart from reading and self-education) and especially toward academics and so-called intellectuals appeared to be affected by the two or three years when he escaped confinement within the schoolhouse. The Falkners were practicing a kind of Rousseauesque education: waiting until the child was ready before forcing him into the regularizing process of schooling. But in William's case, he was never really ready for that schoolhouse. However well he did, he did not perceive that education was his means to an end; nor did he ever consider, seriously, an ongoing education. He was a picker and a selector, as he was with his reading, as he would be with his thinking. Fighting desperately against the standardization which education encouraged, he became one of his generation's most independent-minded writers.

He roamed the woods on pony and foot. He had Murry's various interests to probe: that intensely masculine world of horses, dogs, and cronies. There, he could escape the smothering world of domestic concerns. He had also his cousin Sallie Murry to play with at the "Big Place," where she lived with her mother Mary Holland, Dr. Wilkins having died. For William, she was a welcome break from brothers, in that prepuberty stage when he could be free and normal in her company. Estelle Oldham, a friend of Sallie's, often visited there too.

Further, the Big Place was a place of wonders: its very name was mythic, and it belonged to the young colonel, who carried the whiff of his legendary father. And the Big Place *was* big, with a finished attic where the children could cut themselves off from the rest of the household, and from Oxford itself. In that space within a larger space, they could let their imaginations roam, and often they would take roles—William reportedly as ship's captain, others in the pecking order of male, female, and younger children. Such activities satisfied certain of Faulkner's imaginative needs, which remained consistent: he became fascinated by houses, possibly more than any other novelist who felt compelled to defend himself from the outside world (in this he has strong affinities with Hawthorne and James); he began to enter into stories, so that it became impossible to separate the "real" William from the William of stories about him or stories of his making. The imaginative process itself developed very early and was reinforced by reading, as well as by associating with girls who read. All of these experiences in the Big Place served as necessary counterpoint to his connections with Murry's male world.

Additionally, the young colonel had bought the opera house, and thus its performances were readily available for Falkner children and adults alike. An "opera house" then was not for opera, but for performance: minstrels, puppet shows, and variety acts. Following the Oxford *Eagle* for 1904, when William was a carefree, school-free seven, the fare ranged from morality plays on the evils of liquor to musical comedy ("Buster Brown") and more serious drama, *East Lynne*, based on the enormously successful mid-Victorian novel. Further, there were performances in Memphis, only seventy-five miles north of Oxford, which, besides those for adults only, included broader fare such as *Ben Hur*. With such entertainment available to him, William became aware, as most other Southern boys did not, of worlds beyond the ordinary life of Oxford, and of life far beyond the confines of Murry's world.

Another factor entered into young William's life: his religious upbringing. Like most other major American novelists of his generation, Faulkner found in religious belief itself little to nourish his imagination, although he did find in faith those qualities of endurance and integrity which became cornerstones of his ethical system. Formal religion created a narrowness and provinciality Faulkner more often than not parodied or satirized —it was a destructive force, as in the deeply personal novel, *Light in August*. And yet the presence of the church, a mother who was a believer, and Negroes who were fervently committed to their churches all meant religious ideals and even formal belief could not be dismissed. Like his brothers, William was baptized a Methodist, even though Maud was a Baptist, that being the Butler religion.

As a Methodist, William attended Sunday school and certain summer activities in and around Oxford which were called camp meetings. How he responded to these activities is unknown, although Methodism as a formal religion came to mean little to him, and played minimal roles in his fiction. When religion did appear, it was an undifferentiated Calvinism— the hard core of Methodism, but also of several other Christian sects. The summer camp meetings may have been fun, since they had a social as well as religious purpose. They were large picnics around a tabernacle which represented the outdoor church. The tent or hut would be accompanied by groaning tables, so that salvation for the soul was intermixed with nourishment for the body. Beyond this area were playing fields, open spaces for running around and games. Some souls were saved, and if one sought salvation, this was a pleasant way to do it.

Although William's experiences here are shadowy, it is certain that Murry did not accompany the family to camp meetings. His life moved him in opposite directions to those of his wife and children. Even though his position improved with his becoming manager of the Oxford Oil Mill Company and with additional business in his transfer company, there was little integration in his life. In economic terms, he had moved well into the middle class, but in other respects Murry remained a roughneck. He hung out with hunting companions, men whom his son would turn into mythical woodsmen but who were, in reality, men who preferred masculine to genteel company, who hunted, fished, drank, told stories, cursed, and became part of that society known as "good old boys." The particular camp they favored was at the mouth of the Tippah River, northeast of the town, easily reached by horseback or wagon in less than an hour. It was rich in fish and smaller game as well as some bear and deer. The camp, however, was not always a male preserve, and accounts exist of how several generations of female Falkners went along, from the elder Sallie Murry to the younger one, William's companion, and even Mammy Callie.

These occasions afforded William a rich vein of storytelling, whether from the mouth of Mammy Callie, with her tales of the Civil War and Reconstruction, or the tales of the men, of hunting bear and deer; the setting later became so absorbed into Faulkner's imagination that he wrote about woods as if, like Sam Fathers, he had been born into them. Such experiences also meant he learned, by the time he was seven or eight, how men talked, how they related to each other, where their interests lay. As he grew older, he could absorb what they had to offer and, at the same time, measure his distance from them. For even while William took it all in, he began to perceive he was different—not in the drinking, for he drank, not in the reverence for the woods, for he revered the hunt, not in the rejection of women, for implicitly he, too, rejected women. The difference lay in a sensibility which, even by ten or eleven, was questioning that world even as he embraced aspects of it. As his desire to become a poet and then novelist intensified, he could only identify with his new role by rejection, regardless of how much of that world he integrated into his work.

Murry drank heavily, and he drank for reasons that remained quite out of sight. Ostensibly, he was better off than most—living comfortably with three healthy boys, a devoted wife, a successful and caring father—and yet he drank himself into oblivion. He had to be dried out periodically, and he resisted for many years every effort by his teetotaling wife to control him. Like his eldest son in a later decade, Murry pursued his demons. He hung in there, managing the mill, running the transfer company, trying to be a father and husband, attempting to pay homage to his ambitious father, and yet it must have all seemed unreal to him; and when it became too unreal, he drowned himself in liquor. By the time William was eight, he would be well aware of the drinking, and of a certain glamor it had; certainly more glamor than gloom. For it was manly, disturbing the womenfolk and establishing a kind of camaraderie. Part of the attraction of drinking was that it demonstrated one's independence from social values—for Murry, separating him from his father, and for William, removing him from Maud's smothering love. Drinking also connected father and son, perhaps the sole way in which they were bound.

In September 1905, the Edenic years ended, and William was inducted into formal society via school. It proved a brief and, on the whole, not very rewarding experience. Faulkner later joked about it, calling himself the oldest living sixth-grade dropout. He was nevertheless particularly fortunate, in that Oxford maintained an educationally respectable district school. With the university nearby, it was responsible for faculty children, as well. In the lower school, the homeroom teacher taught all the subjects of her particular grade—teachers were women, principals and other administrators men. At eight, already a reader, William skipped the beginning class and was enrolled in the first grade, taught by Miss Annie Chandler. Teaching was, of course, one of the few areas in which a respectable woman could work, and Chandler herself came from a very good family. But one peculiarity of her family—and William would know this because she lived nearby—was that she had a mentally defective brother, Edwin.

Edwin required constant supervision, even when he played. The Chandlers lived behind a protective fence to keep Edwin in, to keep strangers out. It is not clear if he was violent or dangerous, but he was always there, playing with his sisters, living well into his thirties. What impression he made on young William cannot be determined, but Edwin in different guise and under differing circumstances does surface in Faulkner's imagination, in his first great novel, *The Sound and the Fury*, as the idiot Benjy. Without drawing too heavily on Edwin, William caught his first glimpse of an abnormal child who had to be fenced in, who had sisters who played with him, and who lived out his years in an otherwise normal situation.

William, as noted, was a reader, and by eight he could have known the usual adventure books, *Robinson Crusoe* and *The Virginian*, the Southern classic *Uncle Remus*, and Grimm's *Fairy Tales*. He was ahead of his classmates in speed and vocabulary, but he also demonstrated proficiency in painting, drawing, and sketching—a talent which would continue through his high-school years. He proved to be an excellent student, winning one of three places on the honor roll in the first grading period, and then throughout most of the year. To achieve that, he had to obtain "Perfects" and "Excellents" in his major subjects, with little absence or tardiness. Blotner reports that Chandler, evidently fond of this young boy, gave a gift book to William in 1905: *The Clansman: An Historical Romance of the Ku Klux Klan*, by Thomas Dixon, Jr. The book had become a great success, since it caught the transitional Reconstruction period—or at least the white response to it—and would resurface as a famous motion picture, *Birth of a Nation*, directed by D. W. Griffith. Whether William read the book, then or later, is not known.

Later on, as he lost interest, absences and tardiness characterized William's school record. He became one of those rare young men who recognize that whatever talents and ambitions they have will not be fulfilled through school; that, in fact, school is somehow the enemy or antagonist of what they are and want to be. It was a little too early for Faulkner to recognize this in himself, but school took on an adversary role for him well before his plotting out his course as poet and novelist.

Life for the Oxford Falkners had begun to move in routine or regularized patterns. Maud became pregnant again, in October 1906, and gave birth to her fourth son on August 15, 1907, Dean Swift, named after his maternal grandmother, Lelia Dean Swift Butler, who had died two months before his birth. William and his brothers, when not in school, amused themselves with the baby, or roller skating, riding their ponies, picnicking with the family, or fishing at Davidson's Creek, only a three-mile walk or ride from their house. Although "Damuddy" 's death, and that of Sallie Murry, the young colonel's wife, a year earlier, would affect young William—he was in his ninth year when Sallie Murry died, almost ten when Lelia Swift passed away—what was more important was his immersion in

Confederate memorialization, Sallie's adult life's work. Despite lack of direct involvement by Maud and Murry, William was nevertheless kept informed of Civil War heroism, valor, and endurance by Falkner family interest. True to the spirit of his father, the young colonel had been the first commander of the Lamar Camp of the Sons of Confederate Veterans and active in veterans' affairs. Veterans were quite available, and memories of battles in and around Oxford, including the burning of the town, remained fresh.

These were heady times, a kind of initiation in which a boy was conditioned for life by his experiences. The feverish hatred of the North was maintained in this way; and separation of the races, with Negro inferiority cited as the reason, could be justified. The South had been dealt an uneven hand, it had suffered, it had endured. For a young boy like William, born into the midst of this brew, it would be difficult to break away; and we can perhaps understand—while not excusing—some of the bilious statements on the South and on race he later made. William eventually read and traveled his way out into an understanding of other cultures, and into a critical sense of his own.

Chapter Three

The Beginnings of Imagination

MAUD CULTIVATED HER own activities involving "culture," which rubbed off on her eldest, however much he was taken with his father's masculine world. William Faulkner's dualism was being established by 1906–7: attraction to the male world of drinking, hunting, and chewing the fat with the men; and the intense reading, immersion in language, and need to express himself. Even at this early age, the young William became immersed in alternate languages and other forms of expression as he read, whether magazines for boys, Charles Dickens, James Fenimore Cooper, or Mark Twain.

Actually, because of his reading, William would grow up with several such languages: Southern speech, the normal patterns of Oxford and Lafayette County; colloquial English from school and reading in boys' magazines; and literary languages derived from poetry and prose. Some of this would seem the likely heritage of every writer, but Faulkner's circumstance was more complex. As a Southerner, he was exposed to particular variations on English, different from and, in many instances, rhetorically richer than the standard English of the eastern seaboard or Midwest, for example. Yet measured against this rich language was the more standardized language of the school; and added to that was the language of books. In many respects, he was positioned like the sensitive, responsive young person growing up with Yiddish, Italian, or "black English" in the home, a variation of that on the streets, standard English in the classroom, and then his or her reading.

What all this means for the potential author is not confusion, but reinforcement. Patterns which develop do not weaken his hold on this or that form of the language, but strengthen sensitivity to language and its possibilities. In Faulkner, where literary influence came from the masters of contemporary language (James Joyce, T. S. Eliot, et al.), as well as from poets as dictionally dissimilar as Keats, Swinburne, and A. E. Housman, we have a reinforcement of language. Even what he read in translation— Stéphane Mallarmé, Charles Baudelaire, later Mann and Proust—had its own sense of language, its own rhythms and cadences. By nine or ten, when his reading became habitual, William was moving into that variety of languages which is the richest heritage a sensitive writer can possess. Even in the home, he would hear variations, as Maud, a college graduate, spoke correctly, whereas Murry, despite his time spent as a University of Mississippi student, spoke a rougher language that was suitably cleaned up, of course, for home consumption.

Complementing language were stories. The Oxford *Eagle* reported that the young colonel, apparently recovered from the death of his wife, Sallie Murry, had arranged a reunion of the Mississippi Brigade which had fought under Bedford Forrest, the legendary Southern general; other reunions followed, including that of his father's Partisan Rangers, many of whom boarded in his own home. Murry and the three boys were brought into these activities, giving William an opportunity to soak up the old stories and lingo of valor and, also, of defeat. For despite the victories, everyone who came to these reunions had known defeat, along with the death of friends and relatives, and the destruction of personal property. This aspect of the stories impressed William as much as episodes of valor. He was surrounded by survivors, not of victory, but of lost opportunities, romantic notions, and fantasies of heroic acts.

These were times of considerable excitement for the entire family, since they recovered from memory the glorious past. And these were not isolated, disconnected stories, but episodes which in some instances involved their own great-grandfather, and great battles fought within a horseback ride of home. What makes these experiences so indelible is that William assimilated history as part of his heritage and land, not the history of some ancient peoples whose fortunes remained distant in time and place. When Quentin Compson tries to make Shreve, the Canadian, understand what the South means, he signals that he has absorbed history and Shreve has not. The very culture he wishes to struggle against and separate himself from is part of him, flesh of his flesh. Language, pastness, and history were shaping themselves for an as yet unknown mission.

The favorable aspects of these stories related by J. W. T. turned up in *The Unvanquished* (1938), much polished and transformed into an even deeper myth. There is no question that grandfather Falkner touched up his stories so as to present his father as valorous, even instrumental in the South's defense. Virginia was here the focus of the battles, not Mississippi, but it would be easy for the boys to transform locales and to sense the proximity of the struggle. And the tales, with years, became fantastic, so that the spell of the tall tale was upon William even in his childhood—tall tales of the Civil War, bravery in the field, and maneuvers whereby Northern soldiers were turned into fools.

In 1907 the United Confederate Veterans, in an event reported by the *Eagle*, held a sham battle. North and South were once again locked in glorious combat, and the outcome was clear: the South would win the battle and, implicitly, the war. The sounds of war were made by firecrackers, but noise was not the only thing; there was spectacle, a pageant of pastness and memory ending in glory. The Northern army ran in abandon as Southern troops charged. Role-playing left little margin for reality.

What is compelling about the entire sequence of events is that cycle of life and death—Lelia died a little more than a month later, with the funeral service in Maud and Murry's front parlor; Maud was then in her seventh month of pregnancy—set against a mock battle between North and South. Here, with little embellishment, is a foreshadowing of Faulkner's later preoccupations as a writer: that solidity of detail which comes from the human cycle, from impingement of past, or of history. William observed a future episode of *As I Lay Dying*, in "Damuddy," even as Maud's pregnancy became increasingly apparent; a child will replace grandmothers. Reality and role-playing merge with each other.

The boy born on August 15, 1907, was, as noted, named Dean Swift, after the recently departed "Damuddy." Now there were four—William or Billy, almost ten; Murry or Jack, eight; John or Johncy, almost six; and the infant, Dean, born with an incompletely closed scalp which required careful treatment before the condition could pass. Joining the group of three playful boys were the two Oldham sisters. Victoria, or "Tochie," was almost two years younger than Estelle and, quite different from her more sedate sister, was one of the boys in sports ability. She was now nine, Estelle eleven and a half.*

William and Estelle were even then a "couple," separated by taste and attitude from the more rowdy antics of the others. Both were, of course, interested in books, and there was, additionally, some attraction which transcended their tender age. Also, what must be stated and even stressed was another side to Billy, not in sexual tastes, but in the desire to pass himself off as a dandy, or certainly as someone different. In terms of clothes, strut, and manner, Billy conveyed that he had chosen not to fit in, although he did in his other typical boy activities. Even at this early age, he split himself: playing the boy he was and yet eschewing that for something distinctive. Billy's clothes-mania would continue and then be glori-

---

*Other dates: Lemuel E. Oldham, b. February 8, 1870; Lida Oldham, b. August 10, 1873; Dorothy, or Dot, b. August 15, 1905; Melvina, b. May 21, 1898; Edward de Graffenreid, b. December 25, 1907.

ously repeated when he returned from military service in Canada resplendent in a uniform of his own design. William's feeling for clothes and flamboyance suggests someone who seeks roles, even at nine and ten; who, somehow, transcends his time and place and relocates himself with Charles Baudelaire, Oscar Wilde, and others like them who acted out.

Estelle, evidently, found this attractive and not at all repellent. Perhaps because she also was a reader; in her fantasies role-playing was the norm, not anomalous. That Billy could get away with it in this small-town setting can only be explained by his ability to split or divide himself between these two worlds. One was active and one was imaginative and creative, although derivative. While styling himself as the creator of panache, he was, in reality, the re-creator of platitudinous attitudes; but they worked for him, and surely acted as stimuli for his imagination. From this time, he would be a boy with one foot inside Oxford, the other elsewhere. The process of rejection was well started.

His reading continued. He may have begun to look into Conrad (in Maud's edition) at about this time, almost certainly into Shakespeare. What could he derive from Conrad? The romance, the sympathy for far-off places? The emphasis on courage and integrity even in defeat, qualities the boy would repeat forty years later in his Nobel Prize address? If so, the Conrad Billy was reading as a preteenager entered his thoughts and feelings in a way no other author could have. Shakespeare affected his cadences; Keats saturated his mind as *the* quintessential poet; Joyce and Eliot, later, would influence his mature literary style. But Conrad's characters were examples of ethical and moral men in action. *Lord Jim*, in particular, represented that fanatical romanticism which he also found in Civil War stories, although the novel might now prove too difficult for him. The stories, perhaps even more than the novels, conveyed to the boy some of that sense of fidelity and endurance which absorbed the adult Faulkner.

Other reading at this period and later included Honoré de Balzac—perhaps less meaningful at this stage—and heavy doses of Henry Fielding and Victor Hugo, although just when the boy tried this material cannot be exactly pinpointed. The precise nature of what he derived from his reading is secondary to other, more personal considerations. Reading as an act in itself had several reverberations in Billy's life. Inside the home, the stress on books, especially for an elder son, was simply another wedge between him and his father, as it had been between Maud and Murry. A son who read and played roles in a drama of his own making could not be a son whom Murry understood, even if Billy did visit his father's enterprises.

Outside the home, the situation was equally complex. Billy's heavy reading was bound to affect his schoolwork, but not in the way one would expect. The expectation was for him to prove his linguistic brilliance by moving to the front of the class because of home preparation. But the truth was he became bored by school. Although he moved easily into the fourth grade, and his achievement, even his deportment, remained high, he entered another world. If classmates are to be believed, he sat in a daze, possibly shy and unyielding, but probably more involved in home reading than in the simplistic material of the lower grades.

Still another side emerges: Billy developed into a prankster. Since Faulkner was hardly a backslapping, practical-joking adult, it can be assumed that he was passing through an aberrant phase. Pranks enabled him to gain recognition, even if it meant a chiding or punishment. They suggested he wanted to be considered leader of his little clan and indicated something of a rebelliousness which was an outgrowth of boredom or another manifestation of role-playing. His schoolwork, clearly, was accomplished without any great expenditure of energy—his teacher, May McGuire, thought Maud was carrying out the assignments in writing—and he could control his deportment. The breakout occurred in pranks, practical jokes, and other acts of temporary rebellion. In the main, the pranks were directed against his brothers, but there were elements of sadism in them, since they involved the raising of false expectations. In one, he created a false Christmas for his brother Johncy by making believe Santa Claus was coming—even to the extent of hanging up stockings with cheap presents he had himself purchased.

Billy moved on in school, into the fifth grade, made the honor roll in one of the grading periods, but was already beginning to pull away. While drawn to Maud and Mammy Callie, he needed identification with male worlds, and the livery stable provided that. In fact, Billy, now in his twelfth year, divided his time among several activities. But it is true the livery stable drew him, as well it might, with its ever-present horseflesh, stories of horses being trapped and then sent by train to north Mississippi, and the men themselves, frontiersmen and cowboys of sorts, like Boon Hogganbeck, men made for prairies or woods, trappers, hunters, and fishermen. Faulkner commented on this in his university remarks, in 1957, referring to a period when he was about twelve:

> . . . there was a big man [Buster Callicoat, model for Boon], he was six feet and a half tall, he weighed two hundred pounds, but mentally he was about ten years old, too. And I wanted one of those horses, and my father said, Well, if you and Buster can buy one for what money you've saved, you can have it. And so we went to the auction and we bought one for $4.75. We got it home, we were going to gentle it . . . and we fooled with that critter—it was a wild animal, it was a wild beast. . . . And finally Buster said that it was about ready, so we had the cart in a shed . . . and me and Buster got in the seat and Buster said, All right boys, let him go, and they snatched the sack off the horse's head. He went across the lot—there was a big gate, the lane, it turned it at a sharp angle—it hung the inside wheel on the gatepost as it turned, we were down on one hub then, and about that time Buster caught me by the back of the neck and threw me just like that and then he jumped out. And the cart was scattered up that lane, and

we found the horse a mile away, run into a dead-end street. All he had left on him was just the hames—the harness gone. But that was a pleasant experience. But we kept that horse and gentled him to what I finally rode him. But I loved that horse because that was my own horse. I bought him with my own money.[1]

The episode appears in "The Bear," Part 3, in a recollection of Ike McCaslin's.

Riding, doing chores around the stable, and playing baseball all constituted a well-rounded early childhood for Billy. The activities also gave him, despite whatever strains existed in his home, a large support system of friends and relatives. The boy had a reputation as a leader and, although small in size, was physically able to hold his own. The picture we get from those familiar with his childhood seems to point to a balanced, normal period which gives little indication of what was to come, or what Faulkner was planning for himself. Although bookishness and role-playing do not quite fit into the Tom Sawyer summers and easy school terms, they appear to be the elements tipping the balance. There was a growing disenchantment with school, a need to be different from the pack, a belief that to his mother he was special, and, finally, that mysterious element in the making of a great writer which only he or she knows about.

As part of his identification with the masculine world, he began to make hunting trips with Murry (especially for fox), trips valuable not only for hunting lore, but for tales, companionship, and the good feelings derived from common interests. All this became part of Faulkner's imaginative re-creation of America, showing how the virile America of memory was superior to anything man made of it. That mythical America stood as a challenge to man's works: yet it was not Edenic, not paradisaical, not Thoreau's vision; it was, instead, a standard against which we measure our endeavors to tame the land and the country itself.

Faulkner's re-creation of these hunts is remarkable for the quality of sadness conveyed in his narratives; their dominating characteristic, finally, is not the achievement, the trapping or killing, but the melancholy that derives from the passing of something which made us fine, even if only temporarily. How young Billy responded to these episodes we cannot tell, for when he came to write about them he transformed them into a "feeling" about America, and that feeling responded to our failures, not our successes. In another respect, hunting experiences were the other side of what was associated with the South and the Civil War; out of that, we can begin to comprehend the mature Faulkner's insistence on endurance and integrity.

Hunting passed into school, and school became a more dramatic place; at twelve, he started to draw in earnest. Twelve, incidentally, had a particular significance for rural boys of Faulkner's day. At that age, many boys ended their studies and went to work in the fields or in odd jobs. That Billy began to tire of school, then, was culturally not so significant as it would be fifty years later in more advanced, industrialized societies. For those like Billy, education was not needed for what that society deemed important: agriculture, small business, mill, or factory work in urban areas. When he left school before completing high school, he was not considered a "dropout," although the Oldhams—the social measuring rod for Oxford—found him unacceptable for that and other reasons.

A contemporary of Faulkner's, Ralph Muckenfuss, interviewed in 1967,[2] five years after the writer's death, indicated that as a sixth grader Billy was friendly but not close to anyone in school. Muckenfuss, a medical doctor, also reported that Faulkner did not seem to prepare his lessons or do any work, and generally did not appear to take much interest in class matters. As the range of subjects broadened from the usual curriculum of reading, writing, and arithmetic to geography, history, and physiology, Billy was caught up by none of these. Instead, Muckenfuss noted, he was writing and illustrating stories. The balance, apparently, had tipped, and Faulkner moved away from the rest of the class, not by outdistancing them academically, but by withdrawing. This information, if accurate, indicates Faulkner had begun to create a shell around himself, characterized then by withdrawal into his own enterprises, later by his lengthy and often unnerving silences. An internal world was taking over, and it would dominate both schoolwork and outside activities like baseball, riding, and hunting. The formation of the potential writer began here, in such routine surroundings as a schoolroom which no longer sufficed, which not only failed to fulfill but which hardly touched the boy.

The Lafayette County Fair—with its excitement of prizes and competitions—intervened, but this was an interruption of what had become an inner experience. A pattern of poor attendance at school would continue for the four years following the sixth grade; Faulkner, in effect, attended five grades faithfully and the sixth grade with patterns of absences, then continued to the second year of high school with an increasing number of absences. Even the desire to shine in Estelle's eyes did not encourage him to attend school.

Needless to say, Faulkner did not find his parents receptive to his "new" self. Maud became angry at his school absences, Murry at his lack of inclination to work. What both failed to note was that young Billy at twelve had discovered his own way, although where it would lead of course he could not know. Like Joseph Conrad, Billy moved around to relatives' homes: to Murry's younger brother (only fifteen years older than Billy), known as Uncle John; to his great-grandfather Murry, Sallie Murry's father, or to the houses of that old man's doctor sons. His relationship to his uncle John, who was studying for the state bar examination, was tenuous, especially when Billy reverted to his prankster tactics; with the Murrys he was better behaved, and even asserted he had "learned plenty from them" about the brain and its various segments. He also paid visits to the young colonel, who was at that point aging rapidly. And he continued to see the Oldhams, as he and Estelle paired off. But this was not the main arena.

Even as Billy at twelve and a half was beginning the slow recognition of who he was and what he would do, Murry seemed on the edge, in some no-man's-land of business. He was supporting his family, but he was not moving along. In some imperceptible way, the town was leaving him behind; perhaps he was faltering through inattention to his business. The livery stable was deteriorating, and other opportunities, including those with the oil mill, had gone by the wayside. In each instance, the problem was that Murry failed to grab the initiative, while others did; and his business interests slowly contracted by virtue of not expanding. Certainly his eldest son showed no interest in any of these enterprises, since it was difficult to get him to do even a minimum of chores. What exactly caused this neglect on Murry's part can be attributed to drinking, to enjoyment of hunting and the company of cronies, and, more generally, to his unsuitability as an entrepreneur. When there was little competition, Murry could thrive, but as soon as he met opposition, he showed little energy. None of this in itself was cause for tragedy, but it did affect Murry, creating even stronger bouts of drinking as well as anger and frustration. Although superficially little seemed to change, reverberations were felt in the family.

In *The Reivers* (1962), the older Faulkner, at the end of his career, looks back on the life of an eleven-year-old, Lucius Priest. There are echoes of Tom Sawyer and Huck Finn, of an Edenic America just before industrialization takes hold. Although the automobile is introduced and becomes central to the action, the area is still rural, still open to other matters besides cars and roads. Faulkner is trying to define what it was like to be a boy of eleven, and he speculates about qualities of innocence and ignorance: "The child is neither. There is no crime which a boy of eleven had not envisaged long ago. His only innocence is, he may not yet be old enough to desire the fruits of it, which is not innocence but appetite; his ignorance is, he does not know how to commit it, which is not ignorance but size."[3] What the older, wiser, now spent Faulkner wants us to know is that the Rousseauesque portrait of the boy is pure romance, that there is no such thing as remaining pure. This passage and others like it in *The Reivers* serve as a kind of summing up; often a lesser novel can provide more incisive biographical insights than a great one. Here we see Faulkner—with both wisdom of hindsight and some romance still sticking to memory—attempting to tell us about boyhood; dispelling any notions we have that the young boy is either innocent or ignorant of the entire matter before him. From this, we may infer the eleven-year-old Faulkner had insight into all the "crimes," and these included doing whatever he had to do to break away. He was, in effect, planning to rid himself of authority figures; not Oedipus on the way to killing his father in order to bed his mother, but a modern American version of that—

seeing authority as a shackling of his free spirit and planning rejection as a form of escape.

In his book about his elder brother, John Falkner (himself a novelist until his death one year after William's) tells of how storytelling began to take over Billy.[4] One of the youngster's chores was to replenish the coal supply to service the Falkner fireplaces. Billy did not like work and, like Tom Sawyer, would find ways of avoiding it. One way was through a strange friendship with one of the class bullies, Fritz McElroy, whose source of fun was fighting, wrestling, and knocking heads, including Billy's. But they became friends, and while Billy talked, Fritz moved the coal. According to John, his brother would tell a story, break it off at a suspenseful part, and promise the remainder the next day. Billy's words replaced work. The idea derives from either Scheherazade or Tom Sawyer, or both; and the stories derived from his reading or from his imagination. The episode, even if somewhat hyperbolic, suggests the splitting of Faulkner, the part that remained the boy, the part foreshadowing what the boy was to become.

Such stories, and William Faulkner's own versions of his boyhood, recall a peaceful, Edenic small-town America. In order to dispel some of the myths, Richard Lingeman wrote a book (*Small Town America*, published in 1980) on just that subject. Billy Faulkner was growing up in the period when life seemed, in the myth, to remain static. We have numerous examples of such Edenic myths, in writers as diverse as Henry Seidel Canby (writing about Wilmington, Delaware), Sherwood Anderson (well before his *Winesburg, Ohio*, stories), Thornton Wilder (who set *Our Town* in 1901 and modeled his town on Peterborough, New Hampshire, although he was born in Wisconsin), and even Sinclair Lewis (whose *Prodigal Parents* was a far cry from *Main Street* and *Arrowsmith*). The myths extended into popular magazines like the *Saturday Evening Post*, whose editor, George Horace Lorimer, lauded small-town virtues until the 1920s, when he discerned change; and *Country Gentleman*, which epitomized small towns as quintessential America even when the myth had been punctured. Modernization and industrialization, even migration to cities, were ignored; and Edenic America, as in Thoreau's *Walden*, still replaced reality. In this view, farms, pastoral elements, and agriculture itself were related to purity, perhaps because they recalled the frontier; everything that closed off the frontier or thwarted agriculture was corruptive not only of the economy but of morality.

An article published in 1949, "Values in Mass Periodical Fiction 1921–1940," captures feelings Faulkner himself helped perpetuate. What follows describes small-town life just before Snopeses take over:

> As for locale, there is no mistaking that the farm and with it the small town is exalted as representative of a whole way of life. It is significant that the typical conflict within the story is between the essential human goodness of small-town types as opposed to a metro-

politan moneyed elite; unpretentiousness against pretentiousness, and littleness versus power. In short, those values lacking in the metropolis are the ones capitalized upon in the depiction of small-town or farm life, and the latter become personifications of good while the city remains the vessel of evil. We may assume that this is gratifying not only to those who live in towns and villages, but also to those persons who have recently migrated from farm or town to city and who have sentimental associations which find fulfillment here.[5]

Country Gentleman is the target, but the application is broad. We approach a cultural divide of enormous significance.

The spoilers were, of course, Snopeses, as Faulkner was quick to note. But the problem went far deeper. In fact, the myth never had substance, and the peace which seemed to have settled over the country in the last decade of the nineteenth century and the first decade of the twentieth was no real peace at all. It was not even the lull before the storm. The small town was a seething mass of discontent, made manifest in domestic violence; a high incidence of crime based on anger and passion; epidemic-proportion alcoholism; a high rate of madness, from familial intermarriage and harsh environmental factors; disgruntled, frustrated wives and trapped husbands; rebellious children, and not only sons. Faulkner himself preserved part of the Edenic myth, as a past-present, but he also subverted it; to the extent that he did so, he was reviled by some of his Oxford contemporaries. What most Oxonians wanted as historical truth was what Thornton Wilder had demonstrated in *Our Town:* birth, love and marriage, death, and lots of neutral words in between. No violence, no alcoholism, no madness, no sexual or social kinkiness—all of which Faulkner had brought out of the closet and re-created imaginatively, and all too realistically, for his neighbors.

Young Billy's observations were of a particular kind. Even while he perceived what lay subsurface, he had decided traditional values needed support, even reinforcement; he could not destroy everything in revealing what lay veiled. The tremendous outcry over *Sanctuary* was not over sexual kinkiness alone, but over the way it illuminated people and events too close to home. What Faulkner had done was to puncture the myths, even as he suggested ethical and moral values that could replace the fantasies.

For Faulkner as a boy growing up, the entire town was home. That is, he did not need to look only to his own house; he could look to the entire community, the town, even the county, as part of what he was, what he belonged to. This was both comforting and insufferable, both secure and smothering. He was, in his way, re-creating himself, even at twelve and a half, making himself into a man who fitted and yet rebelled, someone who rejected not the town, but its values. Cities made him nervous, and whenever he left Oxford, he wanted to return, even when returning meant refitting himself into a boring, unsatisfactory life. Billy had something in him of the Murry who could dream in the livery stable.

In the latter part of the nineteenth century and in the early decades of this one, the livery stable was more than a horse motel. It was a way of life, a community, virtually a subculture. It was male, no question of that, and it was smelly, mucky, often unpleasant—and yet it carried through the idea of the country. Even after cars were introduced into village life—as Faulkner noted in *Sartoris*—horses, wagons, carriages, livery stables, and watering places formed a society of their own. And the men who tended the horses and stables were special: many of them were misfits like Boon Hogganbeck; some were young boys passing through on to better things; all were dreamers who saw in the horse the quintessential American experience. Murry was precisely this kind of dreamer, and for him the horse represented expansiveness, escape, the frontier. This was conveyed to Billy at an early age and he kept horses all his life, gave one to his daughter when she was young, and rode with the hounds almost to the day he died.

The horse, then, was more than transportation, more than a pulling animal, more than a beast of burden. It gave birth to an entire variety of careers and professions, of which keeping a livery stable was only one. The horse kept in business blacksmiths, carriage-makers, harness- and saddle-makers, feed-shops, entrepreneurs who produced and distributed feed troughs, railings, pumps, and hitching posts, those who managed depots, commissaries, and elevators; plus the cafés and restaurants where drivers and loaders congregated, the stables themselves, and various other dealers.

So the livery stable was a community of interests. On Saturday, along with the general store, it became a popular meeting place. And when the general store gave way to specialty shops during the early years of this century, the livery stable remained. The barber shop may have smelled more enticing, but the masculine quality of the stable drew "real men": crude, tough realists and dreamers. It was a wonderful education for a boy who would write, for he heard speech of all sorts—brutal language well before his time, stories, tales, and experiences of men who lived on the road. In addition, there was sex—both the sexual boasts and, more graphically, the activities of stallions and mares. One aspect of livery-stable business was mating, and a boy could learn at eight or nine how it was done. Furthermore, here drinking was validated. No puritanical wives and mothers were allowed; men drank without chiding. There is little question Billy started young.

The communal life of the livery stable helped reinforce Billy's sense of the entire town as his home; his father's business allowed into it men who considered the stable part of an extended family. Also, here class and even caste did not obtain in the same way they did in the rest of the village, as in homes or churches. While Negroes held subservient jobs in the stables, doing the lowest forms of work, nevertheless they had a presence with white men they could not have had elsewhere in small Southern towns. It was as close to a frontier, classless society as Oxford would know.

When Faulkner revolted against much of this, he was following a generation of rebels who went to the city and badmouthed the town, while retaining the ideals which the town once stood for.[6] The novels and stories associated with Yoknapatawpha County weave in and out of these rural values, catching their narrowness and hatreds, and yet embracing them as underlying a workable community. Ironically, by the time rebellion against village and town values occurred, village or town no longer reflected a clear sense of values. Only with hindsight and nostalgia did they gain their place in American fiction; and it is Faulkner's perception which enabled him both to capture that small-town vision and reject it in equal measure. The young Billy must have observed the deceptions of nostalgia; for even as he hung around waiting for his life to sort itself out, he was rejecting that life, rejecting the father at the center of it, seeking alternate forms, however inchoate and undirected.

The town was moving inexorably toward the modern values which controlled larger population areas, but not without a fight. The joinerism which characterized Oxford—so much a part of Maud's activities when she was free of household duties—was a way of holding on through exclusion: the clubs and associations for both men and women were methods of creating subcultures and subsocieties based on class and caste. The principle behind them was to keep things small, to exclude city values, to create a sense of community, to perceive the town as a subspecies of commonalities. Needless to say, class and caste excluded those who were unfortunate or misfits, as well as more obvious poor whites, Negroes, and, generally, those for one reason or another socially unacceptable.

Growing up in this atmosphere, young Billy could not escape this broad network of public opinion. Joinerism and Maud's club associations ran counter to what he saw and heard at Murry's livery stable; while the former emphasized the ability to fit in and accommodate, the latter permitted eccentricity, wildness, drunkenness, and even violence. The two worlds the boy observed were not only antithetical, they paralleled the antithesis in his parents' marriage. For just as Oxford seemed to bifurcate between genteel joinerism and crude, frontier establishments, so did Maud and Murry divide in their interests, tastes, and attitudes.

Joinerism consigned those who had failed to the discard pile. Poverty, blackness, and failure in business all meant exclusion from the town's chief social activities. As a consequence, the values stressed not only in church and school but in the very air breathed daily were bourgeois respectability and its rewards. Against this were the outcasts, or those who posed as such, in the rougher establishments. Both dimensions of Oxford life flowed into Billy's experience, and both could be assimilated. When his writing life became his way of life, he turned on everything smacking of respectability; but the impulse remained an integral part of him, and in his thirties he set up as a country gentleman. But by then not only had his sense of himself begun to shift, so had his circumstances and responsibilities. None of this could have been easy for him, for one of his abiding fictional themes is family disruption: failure of parental responsibility, mental imbalance, or outright disintegration. There are elements of Greek tragedy in Faulkner's view of family and its discontents, not only in what he observed in his parents' or his own marriages, but in the town.

Another young man who had come through Oxford several years before Faulkner and gone on to considerable national success was Stark Young, poet, playwright, and professor (at Amherst and other colleges). Young had grown up in Oxford a full generation earlier—he was seventeen years older than Faulkner. He came into Faulkner's life by way of Phil Stone, the writer's great and indispensable friend during his formative years. Young's progress is of interest since he was a role model for any young Oxonian seeking an artistic career. Ironically, it was Young's reputation which hung over Oxford and which was offered up as the respectable way, not Billy's Rimbaud-like shabbiness.

Young's drives and motivations carried him in directions different from Faulkner's. As a homosexual in a small town, he was obviously under restraints—Sherwood Anderson's *Winesburg, Ohio* demonstrates what happens to anyone different, and there is no reason to believe Oxford would prove more receptive. But Young had other drives—for academic and professional respectability, for a leader he could follow. From the latter derived his admiration for Benito Mussolini in "Il Duce" 's earliest days. Young was an Italophile, embracing not only the Italy of Dante but the Italy of Gabriele D'Annunzio. Although Faulkner would himself embrace the romanticism of Keats, Swinburne, and the French poets of the nineteenth century, he never connected his tastes to a "romantic" figure like D'Annunzio, whose poetry commingled with fascistic politics. Young evidently found here, and in Italy generally, what had been so sorely missing in Oxford: high art, purpose, and broad culture. Ezra Pound was shaping himself at about the same time.

The example of Young expresses the rebellion inevitable in every provincial youth who wants to become an artist. The paradigm of this, as Faulkner well knew, is Joyce's *A Portrait of the Artist as a Young Man* (1916). Joyce's affection for what he would have to reject and rebel against demonstrates how town or city, however hostile to one's ambitions, is necessary for working through those ambitions. Stark Young was a much more conventional writer than Faulkner, and yet his rejection of Oxford was more complete: sexually, of course, but also in terms of culture—substituting Italy, D'Annunzio, even Mussolini and fascism for homespun values. Still, Young, the real rebel, remained a favorite son, whereas Faulkner, using Oxford the way Joyce used Dublin, was deemed a traitor.

In the near background, Mississippi's racial atmosphere in the first decade of the twentieth century was not helped by the appearance of James Kimble Vardaman, one of several demagogues who poisoned the air with anti-Negro sentiment. Vardaman was cast from the same mold as the old colonel, a man who brought off successes in several areas: legal practice, newspaper work, the state legislature (rising to speaker), and, eventually, as state governor. Vardaman's "final solution" for Negroes was, within the terms of the Constitution, to return them to a slave situation. He argued from what he considered God's plan, the fundamentalist pattern which established that God intended two races, one superior, one inferior, one white, one black. God's plan was to keep the Negro in the field, not to improve his lot educationally or socially, and to sanction repeal of the fourteenth and fifteenth amendments; in all, a system similar to apartheid as practiced in South Africa. Vardaman strengthened his appeal by attacking that Easterner and New Yorker, Teddy Roosevelt, as a "coon-flavored miscegenist." Incidentally, such rhetoric was not unusual for the period, when politicians referred to "niggers," "kikes," and "dagoes." The latter designation appeared in a *New York Times* editorial in the 1920s without the quotation marks, when the *Times* became concerned about Italian immigration and the Sacco and Vanzetti case worried a lot of Americans.

Vardaman, and later Theodore Bilbo and others, were part of that group once known as "white-liners," those who gathered support for candidates who advocated white supremacy in the post–Civil War years. In the early Reconstruction era, several federal laws were passed to ensure enforcement of the thirteenth and fifteenth amendments, the former banning slavery and the latter giving the franchise to all (male) American citizens. The Fourteenth Amendment had made Negroes citizens. The laws, such as the Civil Rights Act of 1866 and the enforcement bill of May 1870, were designed not only as enforcements but as ways to prevent intimidation of black voters. The catch was that federal legislation, but not federal military muscle, was the means, and no sooner were amendments and bills passed than white-liners formed various groups, such as the Ku Klux Klan, to circumvent them.

The attractiveness of Vardaman for Faulkner's grandfather, J. W. T., was palpable. Having followed in his father's footsteps, the young colonel had never viewed the Civil War as banning slavery, but as moving it on to another stage. He became president of the local Vardaman club when Vardaman ran for senator against Leroy Percy, one of whose supporters was Lee M. Russell. Russell as a young man had appeared before J. W. T. and his board to plead for the abolition of secret societies at the University of Mississippi. He had won his plea, but this time he and Faulkner's grandfather were on opposite sides, as J. W. T. did what he could for Vardaman. Faulkner's Snopeses came from the same mold, and it is evident that Billy, growing up in the early 1900s and deeply immersed through his grandfather in state politics, could not have helped but observe the new direction. Both Vardaman and Russell derived not from planter stock but from the bottom, and both advocated reform and progressive measures except in race. Vardaman brought needed changes in school systems (separate and unequal though they remained), banks and other large institutions, and prisons. In the latter, the buddy system between prison officials and large planters had resulted in a prisoner release program, whereby the farmer gained field labor for virtually nothing. The big planter gained, while the small dirt farmer languished.

Vardaman's reforms, especially regulation of runaway businesses and industries, including railroads, had particular appeal for small farmers, down-and-out laborers, those who felt helpless confronted by big-planter prosperity. His appeal to these groups seemed to be a direct blow at someone like Faulkner's grandfather and his family's fortunes; but Vardaman seemed safer than those who promised real reform, like Leroy Percy, father of William Alexander Percy, the writer. Poor whites were on the march, and J. W. T. threw in with their leader; along the way, Vardaman picked up the support of Bilbo, whose racially inflammatory remarks later gained national attention. Bilbo proved too much for the young colonel, although he picked up Lee Russell's support.

In his fiction, Faulkner never *directly* took on these political changes, as, say, Robert Penn Warren did in *All The King's Men* (1946) with Huey Long and Louisiana; but Faulkner's fictions set in Yoknapatawpha County are saturated with the pressures and shifts political change brings. The political, in Faulkner, is assimilated into the social—into class and caste, levels of ownership and work, places where people live, the way they speak, and their backgrounds in varying kinds of poverty. It is clear he was witness, not oblivious, to these changes; that they were as much a part of his growing up as were his pony, friends, games, and schooling. As he said later, he discovered his "own little postage stamp of native soil was worth writing about" and he "would never live long enough to exhaust it." He added that his last book would be the Doomsday Book, "the Golden Book of Yoknapatawpha County."[7] He was transferring early experiences into final things.

Even as cars were slowly making their way into Oxford, Murry stuck with his horses, while J. W. T. opened a third bank in town, the First National Bank of Oxford. It would compete with the Bank of Oxford, whose president was James Stone and whose vice-president was Lem Oldham. The incestuous nature of small-town life was inevitable: the young colonel competed directly with one of the other two banks in Oxford; the vice-president of one became Billy's reluctant father-in-law, and the president's son, Phil, became extremely important in Billy's literary development. For Phil Stone took on the role, for a time, of elder brother and adviser, an avuncular, well-read counselor; and Lem Oldham was connected to Billy not only as father-in-law but as grandfather of Estelle's two children whom Faulkner brought up as his own when he and Estelle married.

Although Oxford seemed marginal to where the action was, it was touched by nearly everything occurring in the larger world. Just before World War I, cars and railroads connected villages like Oxford to nearby cities, and the connections were extended and accelerated when airplanes established their routes. Billy and his young brothers saw a confluence of modern elements in car, train, and airplane. The boys even went as far as building a model plane large enough to seat Billy, who promptly flew it into the ground. This initial adventure with paper and poles, a moment of bliss as it took to the air before falling back as wreckage, was to haunt Billy, Jack, Johncy, and Dean, all of whom learned to fly. For Billy, it became an escape: he used it as a means of avoiding Oxford during World War I and, through disguise, exaggeration, and outright deception, rediscovered in it the role-playing he had already started.

With the advent of the airplane, a head-on clash of cultures was inevitable. Past and present flowed into each other in the experiences of a young boy; but they did not fit. They were antithetical phases. What Billy learned in history class about the Civil War and about nearby battles (Vicksburg, Shiloh, and, particularly, the Union disaster at Brice's Crossroads, where Bedford Forrest routed an army twice the size of his) had its own kind of glamor, and these experiences deeply penetrated Faulkner's consciousness. The Civil War was, for him, a living thing; yet that meaningful past was being effaced rapidly by modern developments. The frontier sense, which Murry still fantasized about, no longer obtained, and yet it was in many ways still part of everyday life. While the clash of old-fashioned and new would prove destructive for some, for Billy, who moved outside it with words, it would prove a blessing.

Even as J. W. T., now in his mid-sixties, tried to adjust by playing out on a smaller scale what Eastern robber barons were doing in the larger world, he was being left behind. Billy picked out the elements which failed to fit, and he nagged them—schooling, family life, the idea of the home itself. Ferment centered on the ever-present issue of Negroes: their schooling, their right to vote, their protection under the Constitution, the subversion of federal law by states' rights. It was a time of irreconcilables and irresolutions, problems which could only be postponed for future generations.

As he turned thirteen, in 1910, experiences and events crowded out the classroom regimen. The example of Murry and his livery-stable mates showed the young boy how alternate forms of life could exist outside school. Aviation reports were filtering in, people were beginning to acquire cars, light industry was starting to make its way, the line of woods outside Oxford was receding as population increased; and Faulkner was himself reaching into adolescence and sexual awakening, with the chemical and physical changes that set him off on an entirely different course. Estelle Oldham was still there, as a playmate, but their relationship would start to become more self-conscious, as play turned to more serious things.

Destiny visited on him rounded shoulders, resulting in the need for a brace which he slipped on like a corset. While straightening his back, it made sports activities difficult to manage. He lost fluidity of movement—bending, sliding, and throwing—for the sake of better posture. With dozens of newspaper and magazine advertisements hammering at it, posture was the key word in school and at home. The idea of good posture was linked to the idea of good citizenship, to being a good American. Slouching posture indicated a lack of initiative, something vaguely subversive.

By restricting his sports activities drastically, the brace turned Billy into even more of a reader; it turned him away from the more masculine world toward that associated with traditional female concerns, acting as a refined brake on the boy. It was Maud who had insisted on straightening his back, and it was Maud who was an indirect beneficiary of his development. Somewhat like wearing glasses during adolescence, the shoulder brace "feminized" Billy by excluding him from the rough-and-tumble world of unfettered young boys. His energy was expended in the company of Estelle, and in writing, which dates from about this period. It also affected his appearance, as he lost a certain careless look and became neater. The emphasis on tidiness and cleanliness in time relaxed into a bohemian style of dress, enabling the young man to play Stephen Dedalus long before he encountered him.

The real changes, however, were occurring elsewhere. The inability to be the complete boy in sports and other rough activities affected Faulkner's sexual changes in some indeterminate way. One of the curiosities of his sexual development was a taste for a particular physical type in women: the boyish, sleek, breastless type almost indistinguishable from the male figure. In his early poetry, Faulkner made much of the word "epicene," which traditionally had meant a sexual ambiguity, denoting characteristics of both sexes, but also weakness, flaccidity, feebleness of character, as a consequence of a physical failing. It derives from Greek for "common to many," and as such connotes vagueness and ambiguity. Faulkner's tastes, early and sometimes late, ran to epicene women; but his deployment of the word was somewhat different from ours.

A good deal of Faulkner's sense of women came from an unlikely source, Aubrey Beardsley, the great satirical illustrator of the turn of the century. Faulkner drew heavily on Beardsley's work for his own early play *The Marionettes*, as well as for several illustrations he did while in high school and those for Ole Miss publications. Other sources, as his literary tastes developed, included Théophile Gautier's *Mademoiselle de Maupin*. Faulkner spoke of "epicene" as conveying "unattainability," a unique sense of the word. But it has potentialities in its application to Diana, the Chaste—a girl-figure or Kore who appears and reappears in his early work (the incomplete "Elmer", *Mosquitoes*, and elsewhere). The unattainable aspect of such a girl—with a young man's slender figure—suggests also something forbidden about the young woman, a taboo connected to her. Unattainable, she cannot be violated. She is, like Diana, to be worshiped; if observed, she condemns the viewer.

More is at stake here than the traditional Southern male placing women on pedestals and worshiping them. More is involved than a romantic boy mooning over fauns and satyrs, or other aspects of the world containing a Diana or a comparable epicene figure. Faulkner's sense of the word is significant: *unattainable*, because she should not be touched; a taboo object.

For the boy of thirteen with a back brace, to what extent did his "feminization" of activities alter his sexual direction? Can there be linkage be-

tween his abandonment of masculine activities and his devotion to a particular kind of female, in life and in fiction, both early and late? One fact is
undeniable: the bracing of his shoulders brought Billy closer to Estelle.
They worked out games together and read together, and Billy began to
write sketches and poems, as did Estelle. There is also little question that
well before his serious reading took hold, his ideal of feminine beauty
became fixed on Estelle—very possibly because she was unattainable, as
the daughter of the class- and caste-conscious Oldhams. "Epicene" again
fits here, in her lean and flat figure, and in her positioning of herself as out
of reach. When she married, in 1918, she connected herself to an upwardly
mobile young man, precisely the opposite of her childhood friend, and
made herself even more unattainable. Yet that early fixation on one type
also proved psychologically critical. Estelle was the woman he was destined to wait for, marry once she obtained her divorce, and raise children
with. His commitment to a woman he had known since boyhood was
complete, even though the marriage ultimately proved unworkable and
Faulkner craved other female attention in the years after his second daughter was born.

Billy's drive to write manifested itself once he was braced and more
constantly in Estelle's company. Her presence was not necessarily the
motivation, but it does suggest she set off in him some of that romantic
energy in which he wraps his early, epicene creations. Except for William
Carlos Williams, it is hard to find another major writer who started out
so entangled in a language he would later reject. Both Williams and
Faulkner were caught in that artificiality which resulted from dependence
on sources; Faulkner's were Keats, Swinburne, and the French symbolist
poets. These influences suggest a romantic strain, a yearning for an ideal
world. From the beginning, Faulkner was motivated to move beyond
naturalistic or realistic detail into another dimension, and the "ideal"
which resulted came from the superiority of an imagined world to a real
one. We see glimmerings of Yoknapatawpha and Jefferson.

Here lies his motivation, aided and abetted by whatever he saw in
Estelle. Whatever her precise effect on Billy, as courtly love ideal or otherwise, her physical configuration became archetypal for him; his fiction
abounds with her. In his poetry, the ever-present "La Belle Dame" is
suggested by the Estelle model. Even after their marriage crumbled—
shortly after the birth of Jill in 1933—Faulkner always looked to Oxford and
Estelle as "home," while complaining to others that his home was a shambles.

A constant in Faulkner's biography is that he was so attached to Estelle
not only because of traditional ties, not only because couples of that generation stuck it out through difficult or impossible marriages, but because she
was associated in his mind with his writing career. No matter what the
marriage had come to be, present tensions could not erase the memory of
her early role when he made his commitment to that inner life which
became his writing career. Further, as the archetypal female figure, some-

one he needed as a peg for his notions of what a woman was, Estelle could never be disentangled from the deepest reaches of his imagination. Those who observed the terrible tensions of the marriage and wondered how people so unsuited could continue failed to note that despite the external strains, there was an inner resolution defying logic and reason. Without Estelle, however objectionable she became in Faulkner's imagination, he could not have continued; she represented more than home, Oxford, or Yoknapatawpha. She represented the word itself.

Not only was Estelle the physical type he immortalized in his early poetry and fiction, she took on characteristics which helped him justify what he was and was to become. By courting, waiting for, and then marrying someone once unattainable, Faulkner could turn love-longing and marriage into an act of willfulness, into the strain that suited his literary temperament. Hardheaded realist that he could be, he nevertheless also needed a romantic pose to sustain his view of life. His attachment to Estelle included all those ingredients: even the fact that, like himself, she became a heavy drinker and turned into a destructive figure in his home—someone, he said, he could not trust his daughter with alone. However much of this sowed dire conflict, it fitted Faulkner's need. For Estelle herself took on that dualism Faulkner had explored from the first in his poetry—that ideal object man worships from a distance who is also a destructive "La belle dame," whose person proves a Venus's-flytrap for the worshiper. Whatever Estelle was precisely, Faulkner observed he could relive his imaginative wanderings in literature through a woman who took on characteristics of those women on the page.

As 1910 passed and Billy moved into his teens, we can surmise that he had gone through a critical period. For 1910 is the year Quentin Compson commits suicide in *The Sound and the Fury*, and it is the year that Flem Snopes comes to Jefferson. Why is it that that particular year survived in Faulkner's mind as crucial? No firm answers are forthcoming, and what follows is conjectural; the inner life of a thirteen-year-old is unfathomable. The year 1910, near the end, is nevertheless the time when he made his commitment, when he moved toward what his culture considered to be a feminized life.

So the year 1910 has three dimensions: it marks Billy's own movement out into new territory as writer of poems, sketches, and short stories; it is the time of Quentin's suicide; and it is the advent of Flem's career in Jefferson, the unfolding of Snopeses and Yoknapatawpha. The year seems to have had some of the impact on Billy which the blacking factory experience had on Dickens at twelve, although for the American the experiences were less traumatic. If nothing else, they rerouted his direction and regrouped his energies. That he sees Quentin as somehow parallel is clear in some senses, fuzzy in others; but there is little question that Compsons illuminate many of the intense strains Billy sensed or observed in his own family.

Nor was Faulkner's recognition of the Snopes material alien to the writer's personal experience, for all along he could observe Snopesian qualities in the Falkners. In most studies, the young colonel, who lived until 1922, is perceived as a crafty old codger, a crusty but softhearted character. In reality, J. W. T. was a brutal infighter, a ruthless, crafty, pirate-like businessman, and a person whose politics—social, political, and cultural—were based not on principle but on self-gain. He provided plenty of fodder for the Snopeses, and his arrival in Oxford, like Flem's later, was part of that process which helped destroy the world Faulkner later on celebrated.

Quentin's suicide was for Faulkner not a final thing, but the death of one kind of life and entrance into another; and Flem's appearance in Jefferson, while a beginning for the character, was the end of an era and a culture. In all three episodes, two fictional and one personal, there is the "death" of one form of self, the suggestion of another life as an outgrowth of that death. While Quentin's suicide has finality, it has symbolic import: the end of the Compsons suggests that a new era must succeed theirs; what it will be we cannot know. We do know, however, that in some inexplicable way, the year 1910 became imprinted on Faulkner's imagination. It became both need and opportunity, and it dates his movement toward what will claim his life: writing and Estelle.

Chapter Four

Estelle, Phil, and War

T HE EARLY COURTSHIP of Estelle took place over books. Billy read poetry and the novels suggested to him by Maud Falkner; Estelle favored lighter reading, but also poetry and good novels. The place was not the local ice-cream establishment but a combined bookstore and jewelry shop, Davidson's & Wardlaw's, right on the town square. The backroom area was a meeting place for those seriously interested in books and in writing. There Billy showed Estelle his own work, both verse and stories, and he even attempted to fool her by copying out "The Song of Solomon" and presenting it as his own.[1] When she selected it as the better of the two poems submitted, he praised her taste. He also took an interest in illustration, at times linking story and picture.

A pattern was established which firmed up the connection he had with women, Estelle and Maud, and loosened the tie with his father. Although Murry was still making a good living from his various enterprises at the livery stable and in the ice-and-coal business, he had been positioning himself marginally to his family and to his businesses. For whatever reasons, Murry would disappear for fairly long periods, then reappear to note that life had gone on exactly the same without him. He was in a curious situation—no one seemed resentful of him, and yet he was slowly being squeezed out of everyone's life. Now that the family was complete with four boys, his job had, he apparently felt, been done, and he was free to pursue his predilections. He seemed more than ever to have his body in one place, his head in another.

Life was not all books for the eldest Falkner boy, and surely not for the other three brothers. Outdoor shows and visiting exhibitions, as well as relatives and friends passing through, formed diversions. To these were added hunting expeditions for rabbits; on one of these Billy accidentally shot and killed one of his beagle hounds. There was also political turmoil in the air, and some of it affected the young colonel directly. In the new political alignment made by Vardaman (running for the U.S. Senate) and Bilbo (running for lieutenant governor), people like the young colonel— however much they equivocated over their support for one side or another —stood to lose. Although J. W. T. personally supported Vardaman, the latter, in order to win the redneck vote, denounced Falkner's Gulf & Ship Island Railroad Company, which of course opposed his candidacy. The old planter class and the new industrialists no longer controlled the political fortunes of candidates for state or national office. In the election of 1911, Falkner was swept out as county attorney, and Vardaman and Bilbo were elected overwhelmingly. But with that resilience and canniness which characterized the Snopeses, the young colonel became secretary of the state senate. Although not a position of commanding power, it gave him an observation post and kept him in the political boiler for the time being. He had learned how to bend with the times, while Murry seemed oblivious to what was occurring.

Billy, meanwhile, was reading. At fourteen he discovered *Moby-Dick*, and then followed it in later years with the books he read and reread throughout his life: *Don Quixote, Madame Bovary, The Brothers Karamazov*, Dickens, Conrad, and Balzac novels and, later, Joyce, Mann, Proust; and then the poets, Shakespeare early, afterwards Keats, Swinburne, Housman, Eliot. Two constants were the Old Testament and the works of Shakespeare, fair- and foul-weather friends at all periods of his life. The Old Testament saturated Faulkner's mind. In one of his Nagano (Japan) interviews in 1955, he speaks of its prevailing influence on him: ". . . the Old Testament is some of the finest, most robust and most amusing folklore I know. The New Testament is philosophy and ideas, and something of the quality of poetry. I read that too, but I read the Old Testament for the pleasure of watching what these amazing people did. . . . I read that for the fun of watching what people do."[2] Faulkner's shaping of Yoknapatawpha County has an Old Testament quality to it: the making of a community under the eyes of the artist is analogous to the Old Testament defining a culture under the eyes of God, *its* Maker. In nearly all his reading, the young and older Billy emphasized novels which "created" a world, books in which a writer shaped and reshaped a culture. And in most instances, that culture was set adrift from the main one, taking on a life of its own, as in Melville and Cervantes as well as Flaubert and Conrad.

When he discovered *Moby-Dick*, Billy was ready to enter the eighth grade, which was part of the high school. By then, he was drifting from whatever student role he was expected to play and resisting Maud's efforts to make him prepare his lessons. What *Moby-Dick* alone offered, apart from his other reading, was a view of an alternate life which tempted with liberation and independence. "It's one of the best books ever written," he told Jack, who didn't at all take to it.[3] But Jack was heading in another direction, and the separation of interests among the brothers was already becoming apparent.

Billy's reading was not the only element dissociating him from school assignments and demands; he was filling his time with other activities: the aforementioned hunting expeditions with his friend Dewey Lindner, and his avid interest in railroads—their operation, in particular, but never with the idea of becoming a railroader, as Conrad had chosen to go to sea. Billy apparently was not tempted to work his way into writing by way of other careers. He rejected school and its "normalcy" without consideration of consequences.

On January 10, 1912, J. W. T., now a grouchy and crotchety sixty-three, married Mary Kennedy, whom he had met at a reception given by his sister, Holland Wilkins. But the marriage immediately took on farcical elements which the old colonel would himself have enjoyed, and it is surprising Faulkner never made use of it. J. W. T. had clearly become infatuated with the attractive Mary, the widow of a ship's cabinetmaker, and had proposed, or been led into, a proposal. The night before the wedding, however, he wanted to renege; but threatened with legal action for breach of promise if he failed to go through with it, the young colonel found himself tied to a much younger wife. One story has him spending his wedding night in a hotel bar, in San Jose, California. Then he and Mary left for Oxford, where a reception was duly reported in the Oxford *Eagle*.

Even as his father remarried, disastrously, Murry found his life unraveling further. At the dinner table Murry was dictatorial, insisting on silence while he ate (noisily), and then permitting conversation from Maud and the four boys once he was finished. The peculiarities of this trait—for he was not monolithically dictatorial in other respects—is of interest. For it turned dinner into an especially unpleasant experience. But even further, it provides some explanation—however reductive—of where Faulkner's own heavy and dour silences might have come from. Murry, at least during dinner, controlled the family; it was his way of asserting himself as head of the family, to be deferred to at meals. For Faulkner, later, silences were also dictatorial moments; for he chilled whatever situation or conversation swirled around him by negating it, and he controlled it by creating a shield of silence. What the childhood episodes meant was that efforts at intimacy associated with mealtime were frustrated; that intimacy was itself expendable for the sake of paternal control. It meant further that Maud's assertiveness was challenged by her husband for that period, and that she must be seen as obedient to his wishes before the four boys. How Murry thought this would prove more than an illusory control cannot be fully understood, but it is possible that he had been so squeezed by strong paternal power that he needed a scapegoat.

Now that automobiles were being introduced into Oxford and its immediate environs, Murry's livery stable business started to falter.[4] Having run its course, the business had to be sold before it declined to nothing. Murry needed other outlets and tried, in succession, coal oil and a hardware store. Coal oil for lamps was a sure loser, since electricity was being introduced; for the hardware store, he needed help from J. W. T. to purchase it from Relbue Price. The store would not prove congenial to Murry, but it was almost the only thing available. He moved from one part of the town square to another, and he applied his rather weak sales talents to goods that reminded him of his livery stable business: wagons, trace chains, bits, collars, as well as the usual hardware line of nails, tools, paints, nuts, and bolts. The move, although not drastic, further removed Murry from any sense of centrality. For although he was heading into his mid-forties, he still needed money from his father; and, further, he had to move his family to another house on South Street. The adventurous life of the railroad, not to speak of the fantasies of a ranch in the West, was deep in memory.

With minor disasters swirling around, but nothing that created a real downward spiral in family fortunes, simply a gradual lowering of expectation, Billy began to settle into the process of becoming himself. Billy was becoming William Falkner, and with the war would take on his final persona as William Faulkner, the minimal name change signifying both linkage and distinction. As an eighth-grader, he had reached the age and stage at which many boys quit school, and he was himself withdrawing. Reports from classmates and teachers indicate he was not stupid but "lazy," that he was interested only in drawing and writing.[5] This would intensify as he became a marginal student in later grades, and then be reflected in his desultory attendance at the university.

In a new turn, he became a fashion plate, dressing in a high mode which called attention to himself. He began to style himself after the dandies of the late nineteenth century, or what he thought they looked like. He was of course playing roles, taking on a persona, trying out poses. A photograph of him at sixteen, in 1914, shows a high, starched collar, an expensive silk tie, and a tight-fitting jacket. The face, however, is somewhat nondescript, without the combined intelligence and dignity which later turned him into such a handsome middle-aged man. The tightly pursed lips are the characteristic Falkner look, as is the long, drooping nose; the rich hair was combed in the familiar pompadour style, unparted, giving him an additional inch or two of height. Because of his slightness, his clothes fitted him like a mannequin. Jack, two years younger, was already taller and bulkier, and Faulkner's morbid awareness of his slightness would remain with him for many years. From the face alone, one would expect a much taller person, since the forehead stretched for a long span. But the chin is not strong, so that the face ends without that clear definition we note later.

The clothes were themselves expensive, and many were paid for by the young colonel. The fact that grandfather Falkner outfitted all three boys (Dean, too, in time) suggests several elements: that Murry was not doing well enough to buy them clothes, and that J. W. T. was keeping some control over his eldest son, not only in business affairs but in family matters as well.

Patterns of young manhood in a small town set in. Social events, dances, teas, companionship with Estelle, hunting and fishing, even baseball (as the brace had done its work) became the young man's typical round. The social events eventually came to mean little to him; but the outdoors, especially scouting, remained central. There is the story of how Billy ran for president of his troop, only to lose by one vote when his brother Jack voted for the other boy. Jack's reasoning was that the other boy did not have a brother to vote for him, so that Billy had the edge. The real reason may have been embedded in family strains or simply resentment of the elder brother. Whatever it was, Billy would come to recognize that, like Murry, he too was isolated in the family—accepted for what he was, but nonetheless outside.

The Oxford *Eagle* kept up a steady barrage of information about doings in the Falkner clan, as well as the Oldhams and another important family, the Stones.[6] The tightness of the town's leading families forced young people together and created connections that rose above social events of "society." Lee Russell of the Falkner law firm, with his eye on the governor's mansion, was the subject of disbarment proceedings for his defense of a student expelled from the university for acts of violence. Of course, one part of the Oxford establishment was attempting to revenge itself on Russell for his efforts to outlaw fraternities at Ole Miss. They were themselves men who had much to gain from disbarring Russell and discrediting the firm of Falkner, Russell, and Falkner, and they included James Stone, president of the Bank of Oxford and a banking competitor with J. W. T. James Stone was the father of Phil, who would, despite conflicts in their families' business positions, become a great friend of Billy.

While the *Eagle* mounted a considerable defense of Russell, part of the attack on him, beyond the desire to draw business away from the Falkner firm, was based on class. Russell represented the "new," and was eyeing the redneck vote for future office; Stone and his cohorts represented older money and the social elite. We can observe through this suit—which was dismissed by Judge Niles, step-grandfather of Estelle—that while the attack was on Russell, the Falkner clan was perceived as not quite de rigueur socially; that J. W. T.'s association with Russell and the former's support of Vardaman and Bilbo located him somewhere below the highest levels of good Oxford society.

These little social dramas were to be played out repeatedly. Estelle would head for a select private school, then marry a young man of impeccable background who was on his way to success; and Lem Oldham, while personally fond of Billy, would dismiss him as a suitor for his daughter. How much of this located Faulkner in the position of Thomas Sutpen in *Absalom, Absalom!* is not certain. Sutpen's obsession to build his estate, acquire a wellborn wife, and raise himself in class and caste is founded on his exclusion as a child. The scene is dramatized when he appears at the door of a great house and is directed by a Negro servant to the rear. With all their illustrious background, the Falkners had a rugged, frontier quality which stuck: the young colonel, despite his father's legendary qualities, was still an *arriviste;* Murry ran a hardware shop, and the family was not moving up; on the contrary, it was slowly losing ground. Ruling families were associated with banks, law firms, or the legal process (Oldham as federal court clerk), and their incomes were high and steady. Although such a rapidly expanding place as Oxford accommodated social mobility, the sense of class was closing in, especially as large cities put pressure on smaller towns, with bankers and lawyers as the representative new aristocrats.

Estelle was groomed for Mary Baldwin College, in Staunton, Virginia, bastion of Presbyterianism, and her sister, Tochie, for Catholic Immaculata in Washington. Mrs. Oldham, an Episcopalian, seemed comfortable with the Catholic school, while Lem Oldham, himself Presbyterian, did not object to Tochie's school as long as Estelle went to one of his choosing. Such moves only further excluded Billy from the Oldham circle. No doors were closed to him, but Estelle was being sent away, and Tochie, the sister whom everyone loved, was also leaving. He was now sixteen, in the fall of 1913, Estelle one and a half years older.

Like the Oldhams, the Stones could claim an aristocratic background, but mainly on the mother's side. Whereas the Stones came from Georgia to Mississippi, Rosa Alston—Mrs. Stone—derived from well-established Lafayette County people. The couple seemed a stereotype of what outsiders perceived the upper-class Southern family was like. She was a kind of shadowy forerunner of Tennessee Williams's Blanche DuBois—frequently ill, worrisome, fretful, not quite able to deal with reality. He was outgoing, a heavy drinker—like Falkner men—and a gambler as well as a hunter and fisherman. He projected the masculine image which Faulkner's grandfather and father would demonstrate. Not so curiously, Phil Stone had many of the difficulties growing up in this household that can be traced, also, in Faulkner. While Stone was not so physically small, he was sickly, clearly not a man's man, antithetical in his tastes and ambitions to those projected by his father. Peculiar dynamics would envelop three very distinct families: the Oldhams, Stones, and Falkners, although in future generations. Because of their families' proximity in Oxford, William, Estelle, and Phil Stone would be thrown together, and we shall see how a small town can produce three people who, while friends, were as different as if they had derived from other planets.

Phil, four years Billy's senior, was educated at Yale, where in June 1914 he added a degree to his Mississippi B.A. He was an example of the bright young man who goes north for his education, but returns to his hometown to practice medicine or law—Gavin Stevens takes this route and is clearly based on Phil Stone. The consequence of this, as Stone displayed, is to play the town intellectual, to use knowledge as a form of power. That with this intellectual baggage he returned to Oxford was a circumstance coming at precisely the right time for Faulkner. For with Stone's return we have the convergence of someone who knew literature, who had tuned in to modernism and its languages, with a very young man struggling to write his way into a style, a manner, an attitude. That four-year age difference seemed, at the beginning, like forty.

They met, although not for the first time, over Billy's poems. Phil had recently returned and had dropped into the Falkner house in the summer of 1914 to see what Billy had written. In December of that same year, just three months past his seventeenth birthday, Billy dropped out of high school, in the eleventh grade. How much Stone's reading of his poems and encouragement ("Anybody could have seen that he had a real talent") led to withdrawal from school is difficult to determine, since his previous attendance had been sporadic and he evinced no interest in classroom or assignments. Yet there is little question the encouragement of a cultured young man from one of the best families in Oxford reinforced what was already present in Faulkner: Stone put into words and support what Billy had sensed all along. It was not only that writing was to be his salvation; it was also that school was not.

Faulkner did not yet have a distinctive poetic voice. The echoes of his verse, as Stone readily saw, came from diverse sources and buried any individual talent. Echoes of romantic poetry lay heavily on the young man's verse; but what Stone perceived was technical ability, adroitness in language, the ability to assimilate others' styles. Missing was the real thing, and that would only rarely flare up in Faulkner's poetic efforts. His real poetry came in his novels and stories: not only in lines, but in conception of scene, description of character and event; in the very cast of his mind as he shaped his material. Ironically, by then, Stone would retreat before the overabundance of talent, which went well beyond what he could comment upon.

The early relationship with Stone offered Billy several important links: a person still young who had traveled into the great world and read widely; the seemingly wise counsel of a guide, missing from his own father; someone like an elder brother, taking some of the pressure off Billy as the perpetual eldest; and, most of all, the sense that, whatever his future direction was, he was doing *something*, that while he might be pursuing a chimera, someone else saw value in that pursuit. In New Haven Phil had read poetry in particular, and different poetry from the kind Billy was looking at back in Oxford; the Yale student went through Yeats, the

French symbolists, and others considered avant-garde. Joyce, too, became part of his reading experience.

Stone apparently saw a good deal of Stark Young, who returned to Oxford to visit his family: Young, Oxford's favorite son, was a strong reader as well as writer. Phil, to his great credit, was interested in books for ideas, style, and technique; not information isolated from the artistry of the writer. In this, Young also was a kindred spirit. What is not clear, however, is what personal weight Young put on these meetings, how Phil responded, and to what extent this affected young Billy. For Young was homosexual, and part of his departure from Oxford was the bright young man's efforts to live independently of small-town confines. This is an extremely shaded area, in which there may have been no personal sexual interest; but an atmosphere was generated which made the two older men co-conspirators, then drew in Billy as an odd, strangely dressed bohemian and aesthetic young man. Stone, we have noted, came from a background which did not make him easy among women: a big, blustery father, two elder brothers who took after their father, and a mother prone to fantasies and disasters.* None of this suggests any more than that the three Oxford aesthetes and rebels found themselves in a shadowy, Oscar Wilde milieu, in which their literary and artistic tastes, attitudes, and assumptions set them apart. Young's homosexuality established a kind of sexual definition of rebellion; that Faulkner's early poetry and some of the men and women in his early fiction are sexually ambiguous is perhaps not happenstance.

Life in Oxford appeared to be running its course despite rumblings from abroad. As war seemed about to break out in Europe, Stone headed for a law degree at Ole Miss and Billy entered his final year of school, the eleventh grade. While surfaces seemed smooth, underneath Billy was desperately trying to reshape himself into what he wanted to be, or into what he would become, whether he consciously wanted it or not. Although he was writing poetry and reading seriously, he was treading water, so to speak; school had in reality come to an end for him, although he hung around the schoolyard to play baseball and football. At one point, at the beginning of the fall term in 1915, he was the starting quarterback, playing a game for which he was about fifty pounds too light. In a mix-up on the field, one of his own players started to run toward the Oxford goal line; Billy took off, tackled him, and broke his own nose, finishing his football career. It prefigures his later obsessional way with horses, in that he threw himself with abandon into something for which his slight stature made him unsuited, choosing mounts which he was insufficiently strong to control. With football, it was a broken nose, and some good laughs; with horses, it became damaging injuries which dog-

*Two younger contemporaries of Stone's said he had a woman friend in Memphis, presumably a prostitute; that he, also, was a gambler, a poker player who "reformed" completely when he finally married at forty-two (private source).

ged him to the grave. And yet, despite the inevitable outcome, he felt the overwhelming need to prove himself; the physical challenge had become a psychological necessity.

Embarking on a writing regimen long before he had a career in mind was another kind of stretch beyond what seemed possible. Billy was, of course, relatively uneducated, and Phil later stated he had taught the budding poet correct punctuation, grammar, and other formalities. How much of this was precise, and how much Stone's need to exaggerate his role, we cannot know; but given Billy's lack of interest in school and his inattention when he did attend, we might surmise that he was seeking some larger sense of things than grammar and punctuation. Given that, he was left with sporadic reading—books from Maud and those available from his grandfather's collection; a number of great books, but without any formal regimen of language, style, and punctuation. Writing—like football and later horsemanship—was a challenge simply because it appeared so far beyond his reach.

But Billy planned no other career. Unlike Hemingway and several other contemporaries, who could have made great careers as journalists, if Faulkner had not been a writer of poetry and fiction, he would have been nothing. The all-or-nothing quality of Faulkner's needs created for him both life situations and death contexts. His drinking took on much of the same quality: when the need to drown himself came on him, he embraced it—as he had thrown himself at the football player streaking for a wrong-way touchdown; as he threw himself into writing, when his own equipment was still only the will to do it.

Stone was particularly attached to the Greek classics—he had studied Latin and Greek at the university, and he liked to recite Greek poetry. Apparently more than a dilettante, he read the work of Sophocles, Plato, and others. In his home, he enjoyed thousands of books of all types, literary and otherwise; books whose provenance went back to Jefferson Davis. There is little question that as Billy attached himself to Stone as the older man's protégé, he was beginning to receive an education of the kind which returns us to the Renaissance: of teacher and student sitting on opposite sides of the board, that one-on-one interchange which is still the basis of the finest educations. Stone later made large claims, going well beyond teaching this country boy grammar and punctuation. He asserted he helped to turn the boy into a man, not only in the formalities of writing but in ways to confront life.

Nay, I stood upon his feet to keep them on the ground. Day after day for years—and his most formative years at that—he had drilled into him the obvious truths that the world owed no man anything; that true greatness was in creating great things and not in pretending them; that the only road to literary success was by sure, patient, hard intelligent work. . . . Most of all was drilled into him through that great weapon ridicule the idea of avoiding contemporary literary cliques with their febrile, twittering barrenness, the idea of literature growing from its own natural soil, and the dread of the easy but bottomless pit of surface technical cleverness.[7]

Slippery words, they bear examination. They define Stone, only four years older, as a Svengali, and they do so by turning the younger one into a country bumpkin. Phil suggests he showed him how to use a knife and fork and where to fix his napkin while eating. Unshaped clay, Faulkner was being molded into shape by Stone's counsel. The remarks also suggest some of Stone's own deepest problems, and his unease with the very modernism he introduced to Billy; that world of "surface technical cleverness" came to mean for Phil the ways in which Faulkner went wrong in his very greatest works. Phil never appreciated, and in some cases reviled, those Faulkner books which are most modern, most tuned in to technical excellence. His Faulkner was the talented boy from whom the country had not been removed.

The remarks further suggest Stone's desire to keep Billy under control —to have him become a Mississippi writer, not one on a national or an international scale. With all his intelligence and heavy reading, Stone remained a small-town boy. The degree from Yale gave him a certain intellectual patina, but underneath he remained attached to Oxford in ways Faulkner was not. While the latter used Oxford and Lafayette County for much of his fiction, his purview extended well beyond; for Stone, Oxford and Mississippi were the world, and he was eager to keep his friend within that world. Despite the great service he performed, a narrowness and provinciality underlay all, although Faulkner resisted. The latter said as much when he stated, later, that while he was subject to the "usual proselyting of an older person" the "strings were pulled so casually as scarcely to influence"[8] his point of view. The real question is how much inner will he could mount against the undisputed big guns of the older tutor; and how much he was his own man even before he could call himself a man.

One area in which they may have already disagreed—later it became a real gulf—was on attitudes toward Negroes. Stone remained precisely a man of his time and place, spouting all the views which would maintain Negroes as they were, in a kind of post-slavery slavery. Although Billy changed slowly, there is no question he moved to positions anathema to Stone, the Stone family, the Oldhams, and Estelle, his own immediate family, and especially his brothers. What may seem weak and diluted views to the Northern liberal were iconoclastic to the Southern Democrat, especially when rednecks—led first by Vardaman and then by Bilbo and his followers—defined Mississippi politics.

Bilbo was becoming a key figure, and played as much a central role in Mississippi political history as his type would in Faulkner's creative mind. He served twice as governor and then in the United States Senate, always on a platform of white supremacy; he was often accused of voter fraud, intimidation of Negro voters, and other corrupt acts, but his popularity rarely suffered. He died in 1947, which meant his political life spanned almost the entirety of Faulkner's mature career. It could be argued that his rise directed a good deal of Southern fiction: Robert Penn Warren, while focusing on Huey Long in *All The King's Men,* surely had in mind the broader phenomenon of the redneck's rise, but nowhere more than in Faulkner's fiction is Bilboiana revealed. The politician was a Snopes of greater magnitude than that family could have conceived; and he represented for Faulkner the embodiment of all those poisonous elements which made rational discourse impossible.

Although the Falkners were marginal to all these events, in which electoral politics reached into every town and hamlet, they were touched to the degree the young colonel was being pushed out, at the First National Bank and elsewhere. Indirectly, this would affect Murry, inasmuch as J. W. T.'s fortunes percolated down to his enterprises. Bilbo and Lee Russell barnstormed the state and came to Oxford for a rally in late summer of 1915; Bilbo running for governor and Russell for lieutenant governor in the Democratic primary. To win the primary in violently anti-Republican Mississippi was to win the election. Billy, and apparently Stone as well, took a complicated attitude toward such men, especially toward Russell. Some of this ambiguous attitude foreshadows Faulkner's handling of the Snopes family, not all of whom are cut from the same cloth. Russell represented something of that will and determination Faulkner saw as the foundation of the American character—qualities also found, although perverted, in some, but not all, of the Snopeses.

Estelle returned to Oxford in 1915, delighted to have left behind Mary Baldwin, and now a special student at the university. The contrast between her and Billy could not have been greater, and these contrasts highlight the distinctions they carried into marriage more than a decade later. As Billy moved ever more deeply into introspection—his early writing, sketchings, and his long talks with Phil Stone—Estelle was coming out. She was very much a young woman of her times: pretty, bright, sought after, well-to-do, from a high-toned family. She was being prepared for a life of little achievement outside of running a large house and caring for a husband and children (with the support of servants). All her social activities—dances, teas, flirtations with the college boys—were an apprenticeship, aimed at eventual marriage to someone as well placed as she.

The "blues," meanwhile, had become popular, and W. C. Handy of "St. Louis Blues" fame came down from Memphis to play at Gordon Hall. Billy attended the dances, probably to be around Estelle more than to dance, although he was graceful on the floor and very careful about his appearance. His bohemian phase was yet to begin. He courted Estelle, and the two young people appeared to have an agreement. But how very different were their real lives, as apart from what surfaced. In some inner region of himself, some corner of mind or imagination, Billy was transforming himself. Estelle, on the other hand, seemed to be all there in the figure she presented: the bright social butterfly the community expected a young lady like her to be. Her inner life, while rebellious, found its outlet in social activity.

One was disguised, veiled, going through social motions; the other was enjoying herself, displaying what she was, opening herself up to immediate experience. One was playing for time, although how, what, and why he probably could not tell. The other was full of life for the moment, *there*. Then Estelle accepted a proposal of marriage from a young man seven years her senior, Cornell Franklin. She was almost twenty; he was already a man, heading out to Hawaii to try his fortunes as a lawyer. Yet apparently she did not feel being pinned to Cornell meant commitment —young men gave their fraternity pins to girls as romantic acts without too much authentic feeling, and young women took the pins, playacting at courtship and marriage. For Estelle had some kind of agreement with Billy: that when they grew up, although that future was unspecified, they would marry, whatever her family felt. On her part, however, one senses a lack of gravity about feeling; Billy wanted only her, whereas she was playing a social game. There is, already, a widening distance between them: the young man intense, the young woman vain enough to play the field. Yet she was also a victim of Oldham desires for social respectability. The *Clarissa* syndrome is replicated: the young woman to be married off to someone the family accepts, her feelings not the chief consideration.

In retrospect, it all seems harmless, but for Faulkner it was a rejection which profoundly impressed him, and had an impact on his emotional life as well as his literary creations of women. Rejection fueled his imagination, while making him personally unhappy, even obsessive, just as the marriage to Cornell Franklin brought out in Estelle terrible strains which might have remained less evident in other circumstances. What seemed superficially fanciful, delightful, without too much emotional freight, would burden their lives for many years as pain, resentment, and feelings of inadequacy.

The blues and dances were balanced, for Faulkner, not only by long sessions on literature and writing with Phil Stone, but by trips into the wilderness, in the fall of 1915. It was one of the last times when hunters could still enjoy the woods in their purity, just as in the larger world, purity was coming to an end in the war's great land battles. Bloodletting at the rate of seven thousand British dead and wounded each day—when no particular battle was fought—was changing how man felt about himself and nature; and Billy Falkner experienced that sense of change when he penetrated the woods, slowly receding before him. The two worlds were not by any means congruent, but both involved the death of something; and it was that death, easily projected onto the larger world, which the young man was now assimilating and which the older Faulkner would capture in "The Bear" and several related works.

Stone told the story Faulkner later transferred to Ike McCaslin in "The Bear," of an initiation and a kill: what youth and young manhood are all about for a country boy. Taking his place on the stand at twelve, Stone fired twice at a bear which had ambled out of the woods, and it fell before him, his first kill. To complete the initiation, his father and other men of the hunt smeared the boy's face with bear blood, and with that he had entered into the deepest mysteries of the hunt. For Stone, it was almost the last; for he found a little later he did not enjoy the dance of death, however ritualistic and mysterious it was in those woods west of Oxford. Now the two young men, Billy at eighteen, Phil at twenty-two, headed into General Stone's hunting camp, and the lore which makes up the best parts of "The Bear" began to sift into Faulkner's imagination: from Stone's history, which included twin sons Theophilus and Amodeus Potts (Uncle Buck and Uncle Buddy), to the land itself, where a legendary bear, Old Reel Foot, lacking two toes on his front left paw, roamed.

Billy had himself temporarily given up hunting when he accidentally shot his dog, but now he found himself back in the magic of that mysterious and, not incidentally, male world. In stressing Faulkner's immersion in the natural world—as against towns and cities, industry and technology, and modernism itself—we should not omit that the natural world was also associated with intense maleness. Once again, we find Faulkner living through experiences analogous to Conrad's. For while the sea afforded Conrad a living, however meager, it also satisfied personal needs of isolation, removal from female company, and relief from responsibilities usually connected to marriage and family. Faulkner made no living from those magical woods, but he did have the satisfaction of fires at night, cookouts, tall tales, freely available whiskey—a kind of carefree existence which nevertheless included its own responsibilities once the hunt was on.

Although Stone knew Billy's brain was active and that his ambitions lay outside Oxford's routine world, for the rest of the community the eldest Falkner boy appeared a wastrel. He had fallen into what seemed to be passivity and, worse, idleness followed by drunkenness. By 1916, as Billy was in his nineteenth year, he was suited for no particular work, and he seemed indifferent to the alternatives a boy of his age faced: school or a job. Murry became concerned, perhaps observing in the young man some of his own indifference or self-destructive fantasies. In any event, Murry approached his father, and together they arranged for Billy to work as a bookkeeper in the First National Bank of Oxford, where J. W. T. still held large interests. This was the first of a number of jobs Faulkner tried, all of them ludicrous in the light of his interests. Whether handling money here, letters later, or coal still later, he had neither interest nor motivation to handle the job. It was not a question of doing it well or not, but a question of doing it at all.

The appearance of work was more important to his family than whatever income Billy brought in. He later said that at this time he learned "the medicinal value of his [grandfather's] liquor," good whiskey replacing what he had been drinking since he was twelve.[9] The appearance of work, however short lived—and however ill suited he was as bookkeeper—gave Billy a certain freedom to move in Oxford and within his family. It was a difficult period, these years of 1915–16. The European war was particularly bitter, and many young Americans looked forward to becoming involved, while another element sought to keep the country out. A young man found himself in a kind of limbo, like the "dangling man" Saul Bellow described during a later war. Life in a community like Oxford was untouched by any of war's realities, but young people like Billy Falkner move at a different pace from their community. The sense of limbo, of dangling, led him to drift, and one good way to drift in a place with limited resources was to drink.

Drink he did. Blotner speaks of his being seen with that small-town familiar, the village drunk, one Charlie Crouch. Billy's senseless rounds with Crouch speak of a spectacular boredom, a lack of clear direction, that very limbo the world situation seemed to dictate. Faulkner also focused on clothes: while at times favoring rags, he bought suits in Memphis, at Phil A. Halle's men's store, outfits which were, for the time, quite ostentatious —expensive in cut, made of fine materials, and styled to fit tightly. He also favored special dress suits, usually reserved for those with large incomes living in more sophisticated cities, and he wore these, his brother tells us, with grand insouciance. He was dubbed "the Count," not a term of affection, but of affectation.

Billy at this time had a good deal of imitative style—attitudes and poses associated with other people, not qualities dredged up from within: Stone, intellectually; Crouch, in the netherworld of Oxford; a dandy's role-playing, a count's manner of dress for appearance's sake. All of this suggests a very uncertain and even depressed young man struggling to find an individual voice. What was unique about him still lay far beneath the poses and attitudinizing, so far beneath he was as yet incapable of retrieving it, or perhaps even of knowing what it was.

Another area of imagination well outside his reach had to do with speed. As other young men dreamed of owning a car, and speeding it to its limits —young Bayard Sartoris, for example—so Billy dreamed of flying. Now in its earliest and most dangerous stages, aviation was the new frontier, as space would be fifty years later; and flying was even more of a challenge, since it had no built-in safety factors. It was the ultimate dare, and aviation feats and heroics were making their way into the newspapers. To see an airplane was an event and, even as late as the 1930s and 1940s, bystanders craned their necks to watch a plane cross the sky. Billy could read of the latest roll call of heroes: Billy Bishop, the great Canadian ace, Immelman, who gave his name to a particular maneuver, and others such as Georges Guynemer and Oswald Boelcke; later the Red Baron, and then William Lambert, Frank Luke, and Eddie Rickenbacker. In airplanes, one found the romance of war, especially appealing to a Southern boy already caught by a romantic past of local Civil War battles, heroic stands, and incredible forays against vastly superior forces. It was a time for decisions, and yet Billy could make none: a pedestrian bookkeeper, connected by feelings and promises to a young woman slipping away, earning a small salary (most of which went for clothes), with a personal style which involved hanging out with Stone, Crouch, or anyone who caught his fancy.

Just before Faulkner's death in 1962, Ben Wasson, Faulkner's friend and agent, wrote about his first meeting with Billy, at this time. He describes him as a "small, slight fellow." He was wearing a pair of baggy, gray flannel trousers, a rather shabby tweed jacket, and heavy brown brogans. Wasson noted that his eyes were very brown, "somewhat almond-shaped and very penetrating"; his nose "quite aquiline"; his mouth thin and straight.[10] Wasson was himself then new to the university, having entered for the fall term of 1916, and he was impressed by Faulkner's intensity and passion when he spoke of Housman's poetry. What Wasson did not as yet know was that Billy was beginning to write poetry, not only quote it. We are now on the edge of some expression from Billy's romantic, somewhat anguished, uncertain, perhaps depressed, wandering self. Strangely enough, the music of choice for young Faulkner at this time was the symphonies of Beethoven, the music of triumph, will, determination, and energy. Underneath his own seemingly languid and aimless appearance was coiled-up energy, which he recognized in Beethoven and which he was slowly releasing in poetry, however imitative and derivative.

The poetry Bill heard in his head was a compound of the mournful, sentimental, and highly aesthetic. He was, in these respects, a young man of his time and place. Modernism in poetry was as yet unknown to him —Stone would return from law school at Yale with that. Even if Billy had come across the moderns at this time, it is unlikely that he would have found them sympathetic. What is striking about his favorite poems is how he personalized them, absorbed them as part of a Southern sensibility, and insisted on the appropriateness of their language to his own linguistic needs. As he worked his way into some kind of verbal expression, he focused on Swinburne and, particularly, Housman, the latter recommended by Stone.

Housman's poetry, especially *A Shropshire Lad* (1896), was irresistible to young readers and notably to a Southerner with the weight of the Civil War in his past and World War I in his present. For nineteen-year-old Billy, Housman's economic line, his directness, his sense of world-weariness, his emphasis on the passing of youth and death's inevitability all seemed to express a timeless personal statement. "But now you may stare as you like and there's nothing to scan; / And brushing your elbow unguessed-at and not to be told / They carry back bright to the coiner the mintage of man, / The lads that will die in their glory and never be old."[11]

Swinburne may have provided a kind of rhetoric which fitted a Southerner's sensibility, but he was the poet more of Faulkner's youth than of
his manhood. Housman, although he wrote of young men, was a poet a
"man" could appreciate, whereas Swinburne churned up the language to
create passion without substance. By nineteen, Billy was seeking meaning
as well as intensity, and even the English romantics could not equal Housman's appeal. Of course, Keats would come later and dominate in ways
even Housman never achieved.

Part of the young man's choice between Swinburne and Housman was
a choice between languages. Swinburne's language created a static image
of stillness or timelessness; Housman's was quite the opposite: rapid, very
much of time past and passing, yet full of the future rushing to embrace
us in death. Even while Faulkner came to reject Swinburne's presence in
his poetry in favor of Housman and then Keats (especially the odes),
Swinburne remained a presence in his conception of fiction—not directly,
but in the way Swinburne used language to achieve silence, stillness, and
stasis. Of course, Faulkner could have gained such a sense from several
writers—Conrad among them—but it is clear that a line runs from Swinburne to Faulkner's early fictional sensibility.

While Billy's poetry is hardly first- or even second-rate in its illumination of tastes, tones, and languages in the years before he began to write
his fiction, it has considerable weight. Why did a nineteen-year-old boy
from a relatively stable family and background turn to poets of depression, death, and sadness? Faulkner's sensibility is full of examples of spatiality, search for truth, storms—elements deeply embedded in romantic
and Southern traditions. Needless to say, rural or country images dominate; there is no sense of city or city life. Pan, Bacchus, "laughing
leaves," gods and maidens, the moon and stars are the images of choice—
although it is not quite clear when Faulkner wrote these early poems. He
indicated they came in his later teens (fifteen to seventeen), although in
what form cannot always be determined. What is clear, nevertheless, is
the direction of his imagination, a kind of fruity Wordsworth, a poetry of
poses and attitudinizing, the search for a voice. The attitude is one of
terrible weariness, of truth somehow blighted, of loss, of youth passing
without an everlasting love which sustains the spirit and revives the
body. Truth has, in some measure, been subverted, victimized by change
or passing time.

Furthermore, the poetry suggests malaise, surrender to feelings before
they have even been tried out. What is significant is the nature of the drive
toward malaise, melancholy, silence, and stasis. And yet it is not strange
given Billy's romantic posturing, his sense of himself already as an outsider, and his desire to establish a persona for himself well beyond immediate family and illustrious past. Here is a young man stepping outside of
history—he repeated this in many of his protagonists (Joe Christmas,
Thomas Sutpen, Quentin Compson, Charlotte Rittenmeyer, among oth-

ers)—so it is not unusual that he was shaping himself toward this end. While this is a typically American scenario, Faulkner twists it: in his work, the outsider does not gain entrance. Like Sutpen, he is turned away at the door even when he succeeds.

Young Billy was preparing himself as a self-dramatized individual whose weapon would be defiance. Although he was still unaware of James Joyce,[12] he was following the path cut by the Irish writer, and his own situation, in several respects, was comparable. Both came from families in which the father proved a disappointing authority figure, in which the mother held the family together. The difference was one of degree: Joyce's family really declined in its position, whereas Faulkner's held even as Murry's own fortunes fluctuated. Both derived from a closely knit society in which the smallest deviation designated one as a "character," and each had to grow up against a perceived political tragedy: Joyce in Ireland's perpetual struggle against English rule, Faulkner with the background of Southern defeat in the Civil War and an ever-encroaching North. Billy, obviously, had the easier time of it—his family position held firm, even though rifts and divisions were apparent; he enjoyed what he needed in the way of comforts.

What gave him kinship with Joyce, more than social similarities, however, was the sense both had of exhaustion: the intimation that, somehow, whatever their personal situations, the comedy had been played out, and they were moving toward a frontier. There was defeat all around them. With Billy, once the teenage years were almost past, the need to forge an identity was based on rejection. Very possibly, however, in shaping a persona, he postponed adulthood; that is, maintained himself in limbo between childhood and adulthood. Pressures were enormous: three younger brothers, who were boisterous and obviously different; Murry's periodic drunken bouts, complemented by Maud's puritanical rule; the presence of Estelle, now branching out in her dates and relationships. There was also the war into which America was slowly being drawn, despite protests from Woodrow Wilson. Perhaps most of all, Faulkner had to account for profound internal changes, physically and emotionally. Photographs from this period do not show an attractive young man. Besides the small physique, the face was immature, undeveloped, unsure of itself. In his late teens, Billy was nondescript, certainly not dashing or a lady-killer.

In what was an extremely difficult period of self-definition, salvation lay in what had been the safety valve for many young men: to run away to the army or navy or to another city. The American response had always been to escape, and war offered the perfect solution. Once America declared its intention on April 6, 1917, and the draft of young men was adopted, Billy could think of a way out. The compulsory draft was for men between twenty-one and twenty-seven, unmarried, without children. Johncy tried to enlist at fifteen, but was blocked by Murry, who discovered the ploy. Yet enlistment was not the immediate escape for Billy: drawing was. The editors of the university yearbook, *Ole Miss*, asked Faulkner for a drawing, and this began a series of sketches which continued sporadically for several years, interrupted only by Faulkner's brief military service. The drawings are of considerable interest, in themselves and because they seem superficially so different from anything we would expect.

A series of three derive from 1916–18. While the work is not entirely original, it is distinctive and carefully composed. The first, called "Social Activities," and signed William Falkner, consists of a couple dancing, both figures elongated and of indeterminate age. Although this is for a university magazine, the couple could be forty as well as twenty. The completely bald man is wearing evening dress, but peculiarly cut and styled; his gloved hands seem more like claws than limbs. His shoes are much too slim to accommodate the feet of such a tall man, and end in a point. The man's face, which seems small for such an elongated body, is almost featureless. His head is twisted toward the viewer, so that only one ear is visible; but it is barely an ear; and there is, most strikingly, no nose. His eyes are brief lines, really dashes, and his mouth a small Cupid's bow.

The woman is more conventionally dressed, in a white bouffant dress, in extremely high heels on very slim dancing shoes. Across her black hair is a white band which circles her head. Her features, also, are indistinct; she is not a beauty, not even attractive. The face is barely a profile, with only the nose really visible; the mouth merely a slight pen stroke. The man has his right arm around the girl's back, and her right hand is in his left. They barely touch; only her wide dress brushes his thighs: as individuals, they are asexual; as a couple, antiseptically posed.

What has Faulkner wrought? One clear line of influence is Beardsley, although without the latter's devastating cynicism.* Another is the stylized kind of drawing which was already making its way in New York, the embodiment of the Jazz Age, of the roaring twenties—cool, articu-

---

*Ilse Dusoir Lind argues persuasively for the influence, also, of John Held, Jr., a cartoonist who, among other things, drew flappers. Held's work was known for its minimalism, his ability to catch a glance or an entire scene with a few strokes. His presence, however, may have come to Faulkner after the latter was already set in his Beardsley mode. (See Ilse Dusoir Lind, "The Effect of Painting on Faulkner's Poetic Form," in the 1978 Faulkner and Yoknapatawpha Conference, "Faulkner, Modernism, and Film"—the entire essay is recommended for suggesting how visual effects worked on Faulkner's literary imagination; also, *The Art of John Held, Jr.*, Exhibition Catalogue, Graham Gallery, New York, October 28–November 22, 1969. For Beardsley, *The Collected Drawings of Aubrey Beardsley*, ed. Bruce Harris, New York, Crescent Books, 1967.)

Using another tactic, Lothar Hönnighausen examined the artwork in the *Mississippian* and the *Ole Miss* annual for evidence of *art nouveau* that provided a context for Faulkner's graphics in *The Marionettes*. "The importance of supplementary material like that of the graphic work in *Ole Miss* is that it provides insight into the background behind *The Marionettes*. It helps us visualize the artistic milieu of the young Faulkner, demonstrating that even in the Mississippi of the 1920s, a young artist sampling means of expression would have had access to *art nouveau.*" Hönnighausen cites that as early as 1902, the Arts and Crafts movements in England, generated by Ruskin and Morris, were being introduced into America, and in time this included European *art nouveau* ("Faulkner's Graphic Work in Historical Context," in *Faulkner: International Perspectives*, eds. Doreen Fowler and Ann J. Abadie, Jackson: University Press of Mississippi, 1984, p. 148).

late, emotionless. Certainly this couple could not feel romantically for each other; they fear emotion. They are acting out a social event, a college dance, and playing roles. Their lack of touch is epitomized by the bouffant dress which keeps them separated, and by their nondescript appearance—both almost featureless, neither in communication with the other. The man's lack of a nose and the woman's lack of a mouth obviously drain out passion; if they are not grotesque, they are devoid of humanity. Furthermore, the man is leaning over slightly, so that his position is one of withdrawal, pulling away from her even as they hold on to each other.

The second drawing in this series, from 1917–18, introduces "Social Activities" for a new volume of *Ole Miss*. This far more complicated drawing demonstrates considerable technical advance in Faulkner's style. Expertly accomplished, it is a drawing of two men and a woman, as stylized as the previous "Social Activities" piece, standing before a checkerboard, which makes up the background. Both the upper and lower parts of the checkerboard are partly covered by a heavily textured material. But the material falls on the squares in such a way as to suggest a cubist conception. Lights and darks of the material against the background of the white and black checkerboard squares give the drawing a very modernized look, creating unexpected associations with movements in painting which had not as yet penetrated America. Only the center of the drawing is less modern, for here Faulkner is, while stylized, expressive and realistic. The men and woman are worldly-wise New York creatures, suitable for H. L. Mencken's *Smart Set* (1914–23). All three are in party clothes, the men in evening dress with trousers that fall like gowns; the young woman—and here she is clearly young—is wearing a see-through gown which reveals her leg line and barely covers her chest. She seems almost undressed, in contrast with the men, who are fully covered, even to the hat on the man on the right. Their poses are insouciant, haughty, and cool; arms akimbo, they eschew emotion, insist on distance. Behind them, the checkerboard suggests they are pieces which some larger force is pushing around, their will secondary to the will of the boardmaster.

The drawing suggests several forces pulling against one another, none of them resolvable. The cool creatures are caught on a number of squares, suggesting a move which must be made, or that they are being pulled by external forces. But the way they face each other—the woman turned toward the men, the men turned partially toward her, all three heads facing forward—indicates a lack of resolution characteristic of the entire frame. Just what this means for Faulkner must be speculative. A single drawing along with a few poem fragments is small evidence, but the pictorial quality here is of withdrawal, desire for distance, intermixed with a sense of inevitability, a deterministic force moving in from beyond individual will. It is no wonder Housman's melancholy was so attractive.

The third drawing in this particular series, in the same volume of *Ole Miss*, consists of a man and woman posed against a background of the large-lettered Red and Blue Club, the name of a dancing society. The woman appears to be moving away from the man, but they could be together and simply at a distance. Her costume is extraordinary: an Empire top, pulled down almost to her navel, and then a billowy bottom part drawn tight at the upper thighs. She is more naked than clothed. The man, on the other hand, is very much clothed: evening dress, with trousers so wide the bottoms appear like a dress. As a result of his clothes, the man seems almost totally black, whereas the woman, with so much flesh showing, is almost pure white; the drawing one of contrasts. She stands against the word RED, he against BLUE; yet neither, obviously, is red or blue. Once again, features are either suggested or omitted. The woman has no nose, dots for eyes, and a Cupid mouth; he has a profile, his mouth only suggested. Yet a likeness is caught, of a go-go age and a sterile couple. The scene is asexual, although the woman clearly reveals her good legs.

Is there any connection between the fragments of poetry with their clear echoes of Swinburne and Housman and the drawings, with their linkage to Beardsley and the "smart set"? Here is a provincial young man of nineteen or twenty who has not completed high school, whose sole contact with the outside world has been Phil Stone. Yet uncannily there is a response to the world at large, a sense of self-interacting, a negativism suggesting the depression of a young person whose way is uncertain. Everything has gone sour, according to drawings and verse, and yet the person for whom the souring is so evident has not yet experienced life sufficiently to feel that way. Faulkner has leapt ahead of himself, as he has leapt out of his family. From now on, no matter how devoted he may seem to his mother and brothers, he has separated himself from their world: not to attack it, not to expose it, but to express himself through it. How he will do this remains for his fiction.

Billy was living in continuing uncertainties. Drifting, he failed to hold on to Estelle, whose social life negated everything important to her young poet. Although pinned, they were establishing their differences. Cornell Franklin (now in Hawaii) was not forgotten, even while she appeared at virtually every dance. Was she, possibly, the young woman in the "Red and Blue" drawing, or in any of the others? Was Faulkner's drawing of her a form of revenge, hostility, and/or aggression for her social flightiness and partial abandonment of himself? A featureless woman is attractive to no one.

The war fever brought about by the draft was unnecessary to stir up Southern boys in general and the Falkner boys in particular. By early 1918, Billy had exhausted Oxford's resources. He played a fine game of golf, having learned the game while caddying; he was reading, as always, invigorated by Stone's summer return from New Haven; and he observed

Estelle partying. His own activities were circumscribed by waiting, his version of "dangling man." Murry was moving his hardware store and its contents, but there is no indication Billy helped. The store, now next to the Oxford *Eagle* building, was well located, but it did poorly, mainly because Murry proved a poor salesman. Perhaps he dreamed because he knew his family would not starve; and surely part of Billy's drift until he entered military service was his own sense of security.

Even while America and the world were heating up for final showdowns —in battles that made Civil War carnage seem like the work of toy soldiers —one small postage-stamp corner in Mississippi was inactive, waiting, although for what Billy could not be sure. Estelle's activities were part of that flightiness wartime brings on, engaging herself to more than one man, including Cornell Franklin three years before, while still promising herself to Billy. It was a bewildering medley of lightly held feelings, momentary gratification, and making the most of her youthful charms.

She admitted to Billy she was seriously engaged to Franklin, but also that she would run off with him if he so decided. Possibly, they consummated their youthful friendship as a sign of bonding.* Estelle was quite capable of testing the social taboos. Franklin, in the meanwhile, announced he was returning from Hawaii to marry Estelle, and the Oldham family was eager to embrace him—an ambitious, talented young man who was obviously a winner in the world's sweepstakes. No one foresaw, except perhaps Billy himself, what a mismatch it would prove. The Oldhams certainly did not understand that except for their youthful attraction Franklin and Estelle had little to bind them, surely no sense of what marriage meant.

But Billy had become something of a bystander. He cautioned Estelle that he would do nothing without the support of the fathers. On very sound grounds, both parents rejected such a union. Oldham obviously did not want for a son-in-law a young man whom he liked as a person but who had no prospects and apparently no intention of having any. Billy was the

---

*The question of any consummation between them before her marriage must remain conjectural, as must, also, the question of their becoming lovers when Estelle returned on visits from the Far East after her marriage. But the nature of their bond until Estelle's divorce seems to point to more than a deep friendship and suggests consummation. In a film script, *Country Lawyer*, which Faulkner worked on from March 20 to April 6, 1943, at Warner Brothers, we note still another shadowy replay of his involvement with Estelle, the Oldhams, and Cornell Franklin. The "country lawyer" is poor, an outsider, ridiculed, seemingly with no career. He loves a young woman whose family is town aristocracy; and she is engaged to a rich man's son. But the lawyer hangs in, vowing he will one day win the girl. On the eve of her wedding, she even offers to elope with the lawyer, but he refuses.

Faulkner's refusal to elope, incidentally, has brought many interpretations. David Minter, for example, suggests he "continued to fear deliverance" even while continuing "to need assurance" (David Minter, *William Faulkner: His Life and Work* [Baltimore: John Hopkins University Press, 1982], p. 29). Yet we could argue he rejected elopement because one part of him was already rejecting Estelle, so that he could do his work unimpeded. That rejection of her deepened as they moved, finally, toward marriage.

town drifter—golfing, drinking, writing poems, and drawing for *Ole Miss*; a school dropout; likeable, but poison for a socially conscious family. As for Murry, he knew perhaps better than anyone else how unfitted his eldest son was for a stable life; that marriage would be as unsuitable for Billy as it had been for himself. Everywhere both fathers looked, they saw only drift, and it was an immediate question as to how Billy could even support Estelle. That they would move in with one family or the other seemed inevitable; Billy even promised to work in his grandfather's bank. But such work, as he and they knew, was anathema to him.

Elopement remained as the sole outlet. If they eloped and were married by some kindly justice of the peace in another town, it would be a fait accompli, and unquestionably everyone would eventually put a good face on it. But Billy let events hold him back, and events proved too strong. Estelle became increasingly attached to the Franklin family and married Cornell on April 18, 1918. This was one of those critical times in the life of a creative person. Marriage at this juncture, whether to Estelle or anyone, would have been destructive to Faulkner's subsequent career. While we cannot predict what he would have done—working, perhaps, in J. W. T.'s bank, scribbling on the side, fathering a child, having family responsibilities, becoming against his will part of Oxford's growth—we do know he needed very badly those apprenticeship years. How he would have developed if he had married at twenty is difficult to see. Faulkner needed quite a long try-out period before he reached his maturity, almost ten years in fact, and marriage would have disallowed that.

After the marriage became set, Billy still played the fiancé. What was strange, and ultimately impenetrable about Faulkner, was that he never gave up Estelle. She recurs in his poetry and fiction for the next decade. Estelle is the woman whom he lost to another man, and this fact reinforced his sense of self as a pained romantic and anguished entity. She was "la belle dame," showing him no mercy—and this charged him. Sexual relationships in Faulkner's work, and particularly in that early poetry influenced by Swinburne, Keats, and the French symbolists, almost always had something of the sadistic and masochistic in them; masochistic for the men, sadistic for the women. It was as though young Billy had fixed in his mind, based on his rejection, what male-female relationships were like, and rather than wasting away, he turned his anguish into a literary trope; joining himself to a long literary tradition of young men whose pining after the loved one gives them sustenance. Estelle was no Beatrice and Billy no Dante, but the genre was just that. In a poem he presented to Estelle, much reworked, he wrote: "Even though she chose to ignore me, / And all love of me to deny, / There is nought then behind or before me— / I can die." In the original version, he does not die, but simply finds his heart unclaimed by the loved one. In the revision, the decision to die can suggest rebirth. This part, however, remains unstated, since it would be unflattering.

But after the marriage, Billy did become reborn. Estelle's departure seemed to nourish every part of his imagination, and drove him first to break town and family bonds in the war and then gave him perspective on his home turf. That he was aware of his situation comes in a passage from *Light in August*, if Estelle is substituted for Lena Grove and Billy for Byron Bunch. The Reverend Hightower is speaking to Byron about Lena, now almost ready to give birth to Lucas Burch's baby, trying to dissuade him from his foolish quest after this woman: "Give yourself at least the one chance in ten, Byron. If you must marry, there are single women, girls, virgins. It's not fair that you should sacrifice yourself to a woman who has chosen once and now wishes to renege on that choice. It's not right. It's not just."[13]

Writing about his brother, John Falkner says Billy, devastated by Estelle's willingness to accept Oldham opposition to him, lost all direction and fell into uncertainty. But that view of Billy lacked an awareness of his resiliency, particularly in how he was able to turn personal misfortune into literary gain. Later, when Helen Baird also rejected him, he was of course upset, but not to the extent he couldn't use Helen as a portrait for many of his fictional characters; and, further, turning rejection, anguish, and solitariness into matter for his stories and novels. What appeared to the Falkner family to be his loss of direction, and even loss of will, was nothing less than the artist-to-be collecting himself for a future which only he could understand.

Still, Billy wanted to make a fast exit from Oxford before the marriage ceremony, and the way out was through the military. He sought a commission in the air corps. But the problem was his size—both height and weight were well below standards set for pilots. Even after he tried to put on weight and to stretch himself, he was rejected. Still too young to be drafted, he was left with no apparent alternatives to staying.

Phil Stone provided the safety valve. Stone had felt all along that marriage for Billy and Estelle would thwart Billy's still embryonic writing career; that his talent, once he became a family man, would have little opportunity to develop. The law student was eager to pursue other solutions, fearful that the two might elope on the eve of the wedding, noting that Billy, having been rejected by the air force, was wandering uncertainly. He offered an out: get away from Oxford, come to New Haven, wait for his twenty-first birthday, when he would be eligible for the draft, soak up some of Yale University's atmosphere, enlarge his potentialities in an intellectual setting, and, most of all, let the Estelle and Franklin scenario play itself out.

Billy left Oxford in early April, only days before Estelle's wedding, on April 18. At the time of the wedding, he was working as a clerk or junior bookkeeper in the Winchester (Conn.) Repeating Arms Company, while Stone completed his LL.B. The move north came at one of those junctures when a creative person needs an abrupt shift, and Yale, New Haven, and the North could not have been more abrupt. But whatever New Haven involved—long discussions with Phil Stone and considerable exposure to "high culture"—Billy's chief priority was still the military. The university held little attraction for him, and obviously his position at the Winchester Repeating Arms Company, for which he was clearly unsuited, was only an interlude. On the evening of April 18, after Faulkner spent a day at his ledgers in New Haven, Estelle married Cornell Franklin in the First Presbyterian Church in Oxford. Two weeks later, her sister Tochie, one of Billy's great friends as a child, married Lieutenant Pete Allen. After a short time, Estelle and her husband left for Honolulu.

At this point, the air force intervened. Faulkner's entire "career" with the RAF (formerly the Royal Flying Corps) is wrapped in mystery, mainly because its author tried to transform his brief turn in Canada into a mythical experience. Billy treated his short stint as a dramatic poem, more metaphor than fact, more tall tale than history. That imagination which would turn event into the fabulous was already churning, the writer using himself as material for transformation. The RAF was, indeed, a kind of mythical force—men who had little chance to survive repeated flights, plane fuselages which were little more than glued together, frail engines which had no margin for safety.* For the dream, however, space itself and individual dogfights preempted danger. The very consciousness of extreme danger added to the appeal; all four Falkner brothers were brave and accommodated the flirtation with death. Perhaps it was the family heritage, steeped in violence; or else small-town boredom, the intense desire to move into the larger world and make a bang. Billy certainly threw himself against such danger repeatedly, for when the war removed that particular peril, he used drink, private flying, and horses to flirt with final things. Boredom may have provided the initial impetus, but in time it gave way to Odysseus regaling his audiences with tales of adventure. The war turned Billy into a storyteller, a fictionist, which may have been the decisive turnabout of his life.[14]

Yet it took effort for him to get into the war. Even as men married, had children, and did what they could to avoid the draft, so it took a good deal of strategy to thrust oneself, unqualified, into the fray. Faulkner thought his only hope of enlisting in the Royal Air Force was to pass himself off as an Englishman; Stone went along with this, as he had also decided to go for it, although not flying. Phil had an English friend who tutored them in a British accent, and, according to reports, Faulkner made progress. (Given his thick Mississippi accent, one wonders what his British enunciation sounded like.) Observers indicate he did well enough to pass, and on June 14, he left for New York to join the RAF. According to Stone, Billy carried forged papers, indicating that both had an address in London, and inventing a vicar who wrote made-up reference letters testifying to their status as "gentlemen." The entire hocus-pocus was presented to the RAF office on Fifth Avenue, and even though Billy was not yet twenty-one and

*The Sopwith Camel, for example, one of the glamor planes, killed more pilots in training than in combat.

was still rather short (not having grown in the interval), he was accepted as a pilot trainee. The fact is not that the disguise worked, but that the RAF was getting desperate for young men to train as pilots, since the rate of loss was becoming greater than the ability to prepare them.

Faulkner was told to report in Toronto on July 9, less than a month off. In the meanwhile, he had to cut his ties. He returned to New Haven, resigned from his Winchester gun job, and spent his remaining free time in Oxford. Home did not seem so boring now that there was direction in his life. Brother Jack was training as a marine, John was working, and Dean (eleven), was still home.

Although by the time of Faulkner's arrival in Toronto the war would last only another four months, the warring countries expected unending bloodletting. The expected German collapse did not materialize, and the Allies, therefore, had to gear up for an extended effort. Part of that effort lay in meeting the Germans in the air, where their equipment was considerably superior. In the early phases of the Pacific front in World War II, Japanese Zeroes were far superior to what the Americans could throw at them, putting American pilots at a disadvantage until a better plane came along in the campaign's later years. The chance for survival, in any event, was small for those who flew. But dying or being crippled was secondary to the adventure itself. A young man like Billy Falkner did not need American war posters to thrust him toward death to defend his country. He was transforming himself by means of a "lucky fall": the extenuation of a conflict which had killed millions and was not as yet finished.

The transformation is of great significance and in many ways parallels Conrad's. The latter, as we know, changed his name, nationality, country of residence, and, most of all, language. William Falkner, on his arrival at the Jesse Ketchum School, altered his name slightly, adding the "u" (which had been in use in earlier generations), to the spelling. That in itself was only one part of the change. He continued the British accent—thus altering his language pattern for the time being. He gave his birthplace, for the sake of consistency, as a place called Finchley, in Middlesex County, England. He made himself eight months younger, changing September 25, 1897, to May 25, 1898—his reason for this move being obscure, especially since he sought to be an officer, not an enlisted man. He cited his religion as Church of England, which did not matter as he practiced no particular faith. He gave his mother's name as Faulkner—thus altering her spelling of it, said she lived in Oxford, Mississippi, and asserted he had been a student. (Of what?—perhaps of acting out and forged documents.)

We may speculate that Faulkner (the New Man!) cut eight months from his age to account for his small stature—he was listed at five feet five-and-one-half inches, and his body build while not fragile was slight, with a chest measurement of thirty-three inches. His weight was in the range of 120–130 pounds—distinctly a boyish man, not a mannish boy. He sported a scraggly mustache. The point of appearing younger to justify his small stature seemed unnecessary; for, apparently, those who made out his Certificate of Service were uninterested in facts, but rather in a functioning, healthy, and warm body. Since the planes were ephemeral, the pilot was, also.

The transformation was completed when the RAF issued Faulkner his uniform, a heavy wool affair with a large, virtually indestructible greatcoat and a white-banded cap. Now Cadet Faulkner, he was still a small man in large clothes, but considerably altered from the Oxonian Billy who wrote romantic poetry and had felt rejected. Now part of an organization, he was tremendously impressed, and the love affair he had with things British, as well as French, remained for his entire life. Life with the cadets was, as yet, simple, without any of the complications airplanes involved. He learned how to march, swing his arms wide as he marched in cadence, work along with others in every move he made, obey orders, and remain clean and healthy. Whatever rebellion lurked in him—and it must have been considerable—was stilled, or else he would wash out before he ever came close to a plane. Insistence on military discipline was complete. This phase continued for three weeks—marching, snapping to, working with others, keeping up a meticulous appearance—and then he was posted, on July 26, to the next phase.

Having graduated from Recruits' Depot, he was now part of Cadet Wing. His serial number was 173799, his pay a little over a dollar per day —not a bad wage in 1918—and he was listed as "Cadet for Pilot," the very category he desired. His new billet was on Lake Ontario's shores, a short distance from Toronto. Here he learned certain skills (telegraphy, air force regulations, topography, and related subjects), but, perhaps most of all, that esprit de corps which made it possible for young men to go out repeatedly on suicidal missions without cracking. They were being trained to die bravely, since statistically few of them, if they reached the front as pilots, were expected to survive.

Phase 2 training was both physical and cerebral, but it also contained another dimension. The aim of the military was and is to transform the individual to a state of machine-like precision, although this was particularly tricky in the air force, where individual initiative was also called for. The air force was somehow special, since once a man entered into combat over the trenches, he was expected to be disciplined (to protect his colleagues), and yet to be sufficiently a free spirit. At this particular stage, however, hard discipline prevailed. How Billy took to this cannot be determined, although his brother John mentions in his book that Faulkner tried to throw an especially tough sergeant wrapped in a blanket into a lake. But the event never took place—it was part of a Faulkner fantasy. Still, it was an auspicious time for a person whose every nerve and muscle rebelled against orders; who insisted on being himself even when it meant extreme rudeness and aggression toward those invading his privacy.

Faulkner apparently fared well in handling wireless telegraphy and in the physical part. He kept his mother and brother John informed of his activities. In one letter to Maud, he drew a picture of himself stuffed into a shirt, with sweaters under it—"I am wearing all my sweaters and my shirts," he wrote. The mail home indicated a young man thoroughly enjoying himself, and waiting eagerly for training, flying, fighting and returning a hero. To his brother, John, he wrote in detail about routine.

Finally, on September 20, he was billetted to the next phase, No. 4 School of Military Aeronautics in Toronto. The school's name suggested proximity to what Faulkner was seeking, although first he would have to be a student, a real student. He was now connected to the University of Toronto, not to an air base, and for the time there wasn't a plane in sight. According to contemporary records, Faulkner kept up his British accent, although he was also reported to be silent, his own person. Part of that reticence was his natural manner, but part also could have been reluctance to express his artificial accent. There was, in addition to other transformational elements, the information he gave out that he had attended Yale. Since he had been in New Haven, he added Yale to his history; as, later, he added combat, crashing, and other military activities. He was reshaping himself: an Englishman of High Church birth; a Yale man with a British speech pattern; and a newly spelled name. He raised his class status in the process, since all his disguises were elevated; he even raised his caste, from American Southerner to well-born Englishman. When he left the service he retained some of these deceptions and supplemented them with a war hero's record—adding and subtracting depending on how far he could go. Oxford, after all, was far from Toronto.

One could speak of his building "a new exterior for himself,"[15] but in reality these were all interior changes. His handwritten notes, notes on lectures, his sketch of the side of the Curtiss Jenny (the JN-4), and other notes and comments reveal a meticulous person. The drawing of the Jenny had architectural precision, and the handwriting was itself unhurried, with careful, neat strokes. It had not yet become that tiny, private, and abbreviated hand which became characteristic of Faulkner's manuscripts and the bane of anyone who wishes to read him in his workshop stage. Such great care suggests obsessive neatness and defines a man hoarding whatever came his way. His manner, now and then, may have been playful, as he responded to military discipline with an occasional desire to break out, but beneath that was a very different person, missing little, retaining all he took in, and becoming completely self-contained.

The extended silences of his maturity were already implicit in what was revealed by these obsessively controlled, neat sketchbooks. Faulkner discovered the sole way he could control his inner life was by withholding, not giving. He became the most solitary of men, despite later family responsibilities, hunting expeditions, and affairs. His drinking, on one level, may be perceived as supporting the loneliness, since he did not drink in bars, but by himself—in its illogical way, also a form of control.

Faulkner's need for command went further than an eldest-son syndrome, further even than his need to contain his own space. In some area we cannot quite penetrate it became part of his imaginative process. Withholding becomes the chief characteristic of his major fiction: keeping back information, postponing essential story elements, interrupting time sequences necessary for narrative purposes. Faulkner's refusal to give up information, even at the conclusion of a fiction, was connected to an imaginative sense of incompletion: that the rest is mystery, not because God wills mysteries but because man extends only so far.

Besides sketches of soldiers and officers, he also left a fragment of a poem, called "The Ace" (1918). It must be considered within a youthful frame of reference, full as it is of heroic images, the residue of romanticism. An "ace" in Allied terms was a pilot who shot down at least five planes, and the ace was for trainees the modern centaur—a god-man. Faulkner's ace is such a god, bathed in golden light. "The sun light / Paints him as he stalks, huge through the morning / In his fleece and leather, gilds his bright / Hair and his cigarette. / Makes góld his fléece and leáther, and his bright / Hair. / Then, like a shóoting stár." (We note the affectation of accents over vowels and consonants.) The poem has rejected Housman's sadness in favor of hero worship; and yet it has a glimmer of talent, especially in its final line as a brief, ecstatic image. The poem's importance is for its mere existence as much as for its small qualities. Whatever other impressions were going through Faulkner during his training, he had not forsaken his long-range goals.

As the war wound down on French battlefields, chances of flying began to recede for the Toronto trainees. Completion of training at the School of Aeronautics led to flight training; and, in turn, to billetting at the front in an air group. The distance between Faulkner's position and the final aim was great, and becoming greater as the war reached the talking stage. Not that the savagery had ended, for Jack Falkner was badly wounded in his skull and knee less than two weeks before the Armistice. Nevertheless, it must have become evident to the trainees that opportunities for combat were ending; and, as Blotner points out, their main danger came not from enemy bullets but from Spanish influenza. Influenza, combined with the war, thinned out the Western world's population, each killing millions, and leaving the world's resources to a far smaller number of people. While less dramatic than the Black Death of the fourteenth century, the flu epidemic was equally devastating, ignoring class distinctions, being impossible to escape, as many avoided the plague, by moving outside city limits. Faulkner and other trainees remained untouched, in the main, because of quarantine. The young poet, apparently, thrived on these conditions, becoming almost chubby on exercise, discipline, and plenty of non-Southern cooking.

Once the Armistice was declared, the trainees at the School of Aeronautics were excess baggage, a disciplined group in limbo. The disappointment Faulkner felt when his attempt at adventure ended can be gleaned from what he wrote his mother about his flying activities. It is likely he invented the entire sequence of events he unfolded to her (just as earlier Conrad had deceived his uncle about losing all his gear in the sinking of a ship, the *Annie Frost,* which he probably never sailed on). Faulkner was so busy re-creating himself he needed these stories to fulfill his image of heroism. He wrote Maud of "joy rides," of flying with friends; he said he had completed ground school after the Armistice, gone on several flights —becoming so cold on one venture he had to be helped from the cockpit —and eventually soloed, with four hours to his credit by November 30. All indications are, however, that such operations had been closed down with the Armistice; that it made no sense to spend money on airplane fuel and upkeep once pilots were no longer needed. The Toronto *Star* reported the demobilization of the trainees; no flying continued, except for sporadic photography. Possibly, Faulkner hitched rides on photographic planes, but he could not have gone any further.

He was not finished, however. What he told his brother Jack was extraordinary, for it made him a postwar daredevil and adventurer, defying death long after there was any need. He was reshaping his own war. "The war quit on us before we could do anything about it. The same day they lined up the whole class, thanked us warmly for whatever it was they figured we had done to deserve it, and announced that we would be discharged the next day, which meant that we had the afternoon to celebrate the Armistice and some planes to use in doing it. I took up a rotary-motored Spad with a crock of bourbon in the cockpit, gave diligent attention to both, and executed some reasonably adroit chandelles, an Immelman or two, and part of what could easily have turned out to be a nearly perfect loop."[16] The story is so palpably false that only someone predisposed to believe it could do so.

Of course the loop was not completed, since a hangar, according to Brother Bill, got in the way, and he ended up hanging from the rafters. He does not say if he took the crock of bourbon with him when he climbed down. Johncy recollected a still different story: that Brother Bill had flown his Sopwith Camel halfway through the top of the hangar, leaving him with a limp. When Faulkner returned home with the limp,* he had numerous versions of the story. To Phil Stone, he said he and a companion began drinking right after the crash; and later to his stepson, Malcolm Franklin, he asserted his broken nose came from "landing upside down." Still another, leaner version came from Faulkner himself, a written account which purported to be the basic truth of the situation:

War came. Liked British uniform. Got commission R.F.C., pilot
Crashed. Cost British gov't 2000 pounds. Was still pilot.
Crashed. Cost British gov't 2000 pounds.
Quit. Cost British gov't $84.30. King said, "Well Done."[17]

*His limp and skull plate, which he affected later in New Orleans, precisely duplicated Jack's real wounds of a knee and skull injury.

This proliferation of stories, deceptions, and outright lies foreshadows what Faulkner would be as a novelist. He was continuous in his methods. This overlapping of stories, some of them close to the truth, some outrageous, link with his strategies of relaying information in his major novels. A tale which is told is retold in manifold ways, until the original story has vanished, and what remains is an elaboration which may or may not be close to the truth. That "elaboration" was for Faulkner in his fiction an impression, the closest we can get to truth. This was, in many respects, the strategy he devised for his own life once he decided to re-create himself. Once he activated his imagination, he discovered both a life and a fictional method which held for much of his career.

Light in August (1932) is composed of such overlapping stories, each version derived from a different quarter, each slightly distinct from the other, but basically the same story until it thickened and became the "truth." "Truth" for Faulkner involved as much rumor as fact; until they could not be disengaged. Is Joe Christmas part Negro? Others think so, he believes he is, and the novel proceeds as if he were. Yet there is no proof—it is speculative, part of the uncenteredness the novel is about.

Tip the scenario slightly: Faulkner came to believe his wartime stories. They became part of the legend and folklore he spun around himself, a mythical presence which his later withdrawals and silences helped to consolidate. A limp, a British accent, a High Church background, daring war experiences, the flying of cardboard crates without adequate training —all of these shaped him in his own eyes as well as in others'.

Although we want to know precisely what occurred, the overlay of deception was perhaps more "accurate" than the truth. Having little to celebrate, Faulkner got drunk and rued the end of the war; the deceptions substituted for a tedious reality. His demobilization documents toward the end of 1918 reveal a disconcerting bureaucratic dullness, facts, and no romance. Final discharge was indicated for January 4, 1919, and then followed in the document an assessment of Faulkner's military career. His ground work was graded at seventy percent, which indicates a mediocre class record. Billy was no student, apparently, although the quality of his notes and drawings suggests he was trying.

Then under various classifications of training and combat, the result was devastating for the man seeking heroic action. Under "Time Forfeited" in the section concerning his service in Cadet Wing and School of Aeronautics, the comment was "NIL." Under "Casualties, Wounds, Campaigns, Medals, Clasps, Decorations, Mentions, Etc.," the same word NIL appeared. The document was stamped "Discharged in consequence of being Surplus to R.A.F. requirements. (Not having suffered impairment since entry into the Service.) para. 392 (XXVa), (b), K. R.)." Not a single item appeared which Faulkner could use to justify his version of service in the Royal Air Force. He might have viewed such heroes from a distance—for example, when Billy Bishop returned to Canada from his dazzling career on the western front—but none rubbed off. The stories he told in his letters, the tales he related to his brothers, later to his stepson and to his friends, were all creations: "spotted horses" of sorts.

When Faulkner left the service, he took with him the small sum due him, $31.11, plus an officer's uniform which he had had specially made for him, and a trench coat complete with rings to hold combat equipment. At five feet five-and-one-half inches he appeared divine, even if beneath the splendor of uniform and trappings Billy Faulkner inhabited a world which neither uniform nor desire for splendor had anything to do with. What is curious about all this posing of a built-up exterior is that Faulkner had undergone tremendous internal changes pointing him in the opposite direction. Even as he stressed the heroic appearance of this small, slight, and unaccomplished youth from a Southern town, and complemented it with deceptions and outright lies, he was heading toward "a sun, a shadow of a magnitude." It was not as if he used the splendor of his new appearance to become a Dashing Dan. On the contrary, it appears he needed the splendid exterior—uniform, Royal Flying Corps shoulder patch, tall tales—in order to liberate the part that was really meaningful.

An interesting compensatory mechanism was in operation here: Faulkner transformed what people would think of him by presenting a heroic appearance behind which he could hide an interior sensibility no one would see. His method was to grasp at the sole means at his disposal: a war which had gratuitously thrust him into a position of choice and which rescued him from a stagnant routine. Even though it ended prematurely for him, the war gave him the mechanism by which he could disguise and hide himself—in somewhat the same way a sea career gave Joseph Conrad the "shield" behind which he could develop. To be a male poet in Oxford, or even a fiction writer, took a certain amount of courage; but to return a "war hero" balanced out the "feminine" stigma connected to writing. Or so Faulkner thought, as we conjecture how he eased himself into a situation difficult even in a less red-blooded context.

When Faulkner wrote to Albert Erskine, his editor at Random House, about the factual discrepancies in the Snopes Yoknapatawpha trilogy beginning with *The Hamlet*, his 1959 remarks are appropriate to his early career. He told Erskine that ". . . the essential truth of these people and their doings is the thing; the facts are not important. If we know the discrepancy, maybe, if to change the present to fit the past injures the present, we will not come right out and state the contravention, we will try to, you might say, de-clutch past it somehow." The remark was more than offhand, for Faulkner repeated to Erskine and others that truth and facts are not congruent; that his quest was for truth. Here, near the end of his career, was something he had grasped at the beginning; the supremacy he placed on art and the imagination. Even in his late teens, he was straining toward something, as yet undefined, which embodied a greater truth than fact. Faulkner did not use deceptions or lies to gain from another person or a situation; when he deceived, it was to transform banality into romantic truth as he conceived of it. He was, in this respect, in the line of those poets who influenced him, notably Keats, but also the French symbolists, whose earthly symbols shone with something "beyond"; that "beyond" was for them, as for Faulkner, the larger element.

Part II

The New Man

Chapter Five

William Faulkner of Oxford

U PON HIS RETURN from Canada, William Faulkner was a different person from Billy Falkner. Only six months had passed (he was free to leave in December of 1918), or more exactly, 179 days, but he now possessed material to change his life and fill at least two novels, *Soldiers' Pay* (1926) and *A Fable* (1954), along with several short stories. Like Hemingway, who was wounded in the Italian campaign, Faulkner gained war experience, in his case imagined, as well as time for development. Hemingway remained throughout his life enchanted with war, wounds, injuries, and killing; violence that was as much marital as martial. Faulkner used the war differently, perhaps because he experienced it differently. For Hemingway, the war had a reality of which he partook, whereas Faulkner observed it longingly from a distance, even the planes he coveted; and the war became for him observation, perception, and revered objects beyond touch. He was also able to build his major career on nonmartial elements, while Hemingway pursued war into every activity he experienced. For the latter, war was a metaphor for his own anger and hostility; for Faulkner, war was a watershed between youth and manhood, and provided, through his tales, a shield behind which he was left free to pursue his enterprises —romantic poetry, halting reviews and essays, and eventually a grand career.

In more personal terms, we must seek in Faulkner's poses some desire to establish hegemony in the family. As the eldest who was clearly not his father's favorite son, he could lose ground badly. Jack had distinguished himself in combat, was badly wounded, and was a marine hero. An eldest son's position is difficult, since he needs tangibles to make others respect him, and to maintain his place as his mother's favorite. The grand uniform he had had made gave him an edge on Murry his father could never regain, and the stories impressed his brothers.

To create an impression was the important thing; for that simultaneously held off society and permitted the inner world to move at its own pace. Faulkner obtained the recognition he sought when he returned. For his British officer's uniform, along with the overseas cap, Sam Browne belt, wings on his tunic, and swagger stick all created the impression of a man who had served overseas.[1] Furthermore, Faulkner walked with a limp, like brother Jack. The image was perfect. He was saluted by other veterans, and his limp indicated he had suffered a war-related injury. He told Johncy and others the leg injury came from his hangar crash, after the Armistice. Faulkner used the uniform as a badge: inasmuch as returnees were forbidden by army regulations to wear their uniforms except on special military occasions, he was flying in the face of decorum.

In a sense, he won on all counts. The flouting of military regulations reinforced the glamor, conveying the danger that he might be caught out, although the chances were slight. Impressive figure that he was, he wore the uniform as though he had earned it, without relenting. The Oxford *Eagle* reported that Faulkner was a star in his assortment of outfits. The various ensembles were made up of all the pieces he had accumulated: Sam Browne belt, puttees, whipcord breeches, overseas cap, garrison cap, airman's badge prominent on his chest. With his limp, he needed a rattan cane, and he smoked, so that in a characteristic pose he dangled a cigarette from his lips. He came across as a very cool fellow; for in addition to outfits and cane, he carried leather gloves—the Britisher personified. He also wore his second lieutenant's pips, which he was not authorized to do (a more serious offense than wearing the uniform on a daily basis, since until his honorary second looey came, he was impersonating an officer). A contemporary friend commented: "He cut quite a swanky figure. . . . He gave the impression that he did not have a care or worry in this world, or give a damn about anything or anybody."

Pose was all.* For if we probe what Billy Faulkner had actually returned to in Oxford, and what his own situation entailed, we find he was back where he had started. When he peeled off the uniform at night and assessed his situation, he had only his impressions left. At the very end of the year, he received his final RAF check, for $42.58. And that left him with the "empty urn" which he had attempted to fill with pomp and circumstance.

---

*Beginning with his slight name change, Faulkner fell into a pattern which Fitzgerald would limn with Jay Gatsby. It is a curious piece of Americana. Faulkner follows Gatsby's career, not in its illegalities, but in the desire to remake the past, gain the woman who rejected him (Estelle, not Daisy), even to the renaming (as Gatz made a slight alteration to Gatsby). There was, further, the need to reject the father who failed, once again with the idea of winning the girl who rejected him (i.e., re-entering Eden after the expulsion).

Now with the celebration ended, he had all the decisions yet to make and no war to save him. He had no job; he was a high-school dropout; his childhood sweetheart had married and moved away, to live stylishly and luxuriously; Murry's fortunes had not improved and the older Falkner was no happier with his situation. Oxford was relatively unchanged, although Lee M. Russell, with the redneck vote behind him, was moving inexorably toward the governor's chair. Much had changed internally in the young poet within a context of no change.

For most young men, their return from war or from peacetime military service would be a time for decision; and the choices open to them were a job, return to school, marriage, or some form of security and stability. Their slogan would be "get on with it." For Faulkner, it was none of these, since work had never held out rewards (he had contempt for ostentatious reward); nor had formal education, although the desire to read was still powerful; and marriage no longer meant anything, because some part of himself chose to wait for Estelle, and, in any event, there was no one else. What remained was the moment, the triumph of the uniform, the overseas cap, and the deference paid a returning hero.

Hemingway caught the disillusionment and uncertainty of a young man returning home, the war over, that finality, in the short story "Soldier's Home" (written in 1924 and published the following year). Faulkner wrote his own version of this in *Soldiers' Pay*, his first novel, published in 1926. A first novel is often autobiographical, although not necessarily exact in its details. Faulkner's novel can be taken as a kind of mirror image or allegory of his situation. In reading the novel as an allegory of all returning soldiers, however, we must not make equations: the wounded and impotent Donald Mahon, for example, is not Faulkner; but there are parallels in the conception of Mahon and in the depiction of Mahon's fiancée, Cecily Saunders. Here was truly a "soldier's home," and it was not heroic, or celebratory, and it smacked of deceit, lost feeling, male resentment of the female. Although Donald Mahon is the merest shell of Faulkner, a psychological evacuation, Cecily Saunders is uncomfortably close to a view of Estelle Oldham—engaged to Donald, rightly horrified at his condition, but herself lacking in substance, staying power, and solidity. She is flighty, uncomfortable with feeling itself. That a life with Donald would horrify her is justifiable, of course; but Faulkner's presentation is full of hostility, apart from whatever final decision she might make.

But overriding all particular depictions, and apart from whether Cecily is based on Estelle or Donald on Faulkner's sense of being injured, is the form of the novel, an *Odyssey* in its shaping. Donald Mahon is a contemporary Odysseus, and it is this sense of a dying, comatose veteran returning home which captures our imagination. His Penelope is a much traveled Margaret Powers, honest and loyal in her way, but not the celibate woman Odysseus returned to. If *Soldiers' Pay*, with its ambiguous title, is a contemporary retelling of the *Odyssey*, it savagely subverts heroism; it does not project what Faulkner himself displayed in his splendid uniforms. On the contrary, even as Faulkner presented one manifestation of war to Oxford, he formulated quite a different return in his imaginative life. The dual sense of Faulkner's public and private lives bolsters the idea that he used both uniform and public trappings as a shield, behind which he would be left free to pursue his own imaginings and demons.

What, then, was real when so much was unreal: disguise, shield, deception? The reality was that there was little for him in Oxford—except for his uniform, followed by a spectacular sports jacket which gave him the appearance of an English lord making the rounds of his tenants' and property. Even as he dressed for the role of lord of the manor, he was unemployed and, equal to that, Murry was slipping. Falkner contemplated a new move, and it was effected, as so much else for his stumbling son, by J. W. T. Murry was appointed secretary at Ole Miss and given a house on campus, into which the Falkners moved the following year. To a large extent, Murry would be set for almost the remainder of his life, collecting student tuition, administering odd jobs, straying far from the cowboy ideal he had once harbored. This most physical of men was harnessed to a position which was all administrative detail, as "inside" as if he had attempted banking. Yet even as Murry was bound to a position, his son resisted all connections and floated free.

The young William Faulkner who lived at home seemed at peace with both neighbors and friends, even while he was secretly moving beyond them. Even his name change, small though it was and with precedent from the past, had removed him. Murry seemed in step with his other sons, especially Dean, an excellent athlete and outdoorsman. Faulkner marched to his own drummer—refusing work, but not rejecting family, food, and shelter. We note here some arrogance: at twenty-two, he could behave as he had done at eighteen; as a school dropout, he need not take any available job, but could count on family support even as he withheld part of himself. He was preparing himself, but it is unclear even if he was aware of that. It is clear, however, he knew he was different.

Phil Stone saw a good deal of him, as did the entire Stone family, including Phil's brother, Jack, and his wife. Murry's association with the university also brought Faulkner into that setting, although he had already contributed drawings to the Ole Miss annual. Further, until his registration as a student in September 1919, he skirted the academic aspects of university life, using it as a kind of club, first for drawings, then for social activities. Only after he enrolled (for Spanish, French, and the sophomore English literature survey) did he contribute writing—reviews and poems for the Mississippian. At no time did he become academically engaged; he dropped in, and then just as suddenly dropped out.

More than twenty-five years later, when he was established as a writer, but doing badly financially, Faulkner caught some of that earlier period, writing to Bennett Cerf and Robert K. Haas of Random House: "All my writing life I have been a poet without education, who possessed only instinct and a fierce conviction and belief in the worth and truth of what he was doing, and an illimitable courage for rhetoric (personal pleasure in it too: I admit it) and who knew and cared for little else."[2] In this statement, he was feeling his mortality: the recent war and *its* end had made him feel ancient, having been rejected for service because of age; but his comments are continuous with his situation earlier, when he had nothing to show for his twenty-two years. Later on, he wrote Haas: "I have deliberately buried myself in this little lost almost illiterate town."[3] His words are affectionate, but telling; and they, too, reflect upon that much earlier time.

Both letters demonstrate how Faulkner was aware of the fragility of his condition, the frailty of his talent, of how close to the edge he was—right into the 1940s. Surveying Faulkner's situation in Oxford after World War I, the salient point is how exposed he was; how exposed he deliberately kept himself. From his family's point of view—and especially Murry's—the eldest son was caught between display (uniform) and laziness (a bum); and although they were kind, even supportive, he was certainly not achieving like other well-brought-up boys. But from Faulkner's point of view, he was chancing it all, moving to the edge, although precisely why he may not have been certain. Possibly, he did not know his feelings well, except he knew what he did not want to do; positive feelings were less apparent. He chose to drift: to be, as he wrote Random House, "a poet without education," someone who possessed "only instinct and a fierce conviction and belief in the worth and truth of what he was doing."

Not unusually, he fell into what Maud certainly considered bad company. His new set of friends were, socially, quite different—and we see here for the first time Faulkner's ability to move beyond the tight class and caste structure of his society. In a town that dictated one's friends by social and caste language, he moved to extremes. His new friends were from Clarksdale,[4] due west of Oxford, in the Delta, near the corner with Arkansas, and involved Eula Dorothy Wilcox, a beautician, and her friend, Reno (Renaud?) DeVaux. Reno was a marvelous character for a young man to know, if the friendship is fleeting, but a treacherous friend for a young man seeking a role model. Although originally destined to be a priest, Reno went from being an acolyte to gambling with dice; once he tried craps, one could say, literally, the die was cast. Phil Stone was probably the intermediary in bringing Faulkner into this circle, suggesting that Phil did not spend all his time on law and Greek and modern poetry. In fact, Phil had shown such talent at cards that Reno offered him a job in his establishment, Reno's Place, in Clarksdale. The gambler and Faulkner got on immediately, and the budding writer fitted in well with this raffish group. Faulkner became "the Poet," as Reno called him; his ability to fit in, as well as his silences and capacity for drink, made him acceptable.

The group proved useful to Faulkner in ways beyond passing his time. For one, they introduced him to New Orleans, all on Reno's bill. But, most of all, they showed him that there can be a strong commitment to life and even to each other without there being any real sense of responsibility. Distancing himself from responsibility was very important to Faulkner's development as a poet, and then as a writer of fiction. A paradox appeared, since a writer needs a strong sense of commitment, to his material, his characters, and his society. But Faulkner needed to move and stay "outside," and this group demonstrated the very opposite of what he had learned from his socially conscious family. The gamblers' responsibility and commitment extended only to themselves, sometimes to each other. Life for them was a lark—intermixed with the need to make a good living —but money accumulated effortlessly.

An interview with Albert I. Bezzerides,[5] a Hollywood writer who knew Faulkner very well in the 1940s when both were part of the Warner Brothers stable of scriptwriters, illuminates this early period. Bezzerides knew Faulkner when the latter needed help, and this circumstance may have colored his views of a man he admired greatly. But he asserted Faulkner did everything he could to avoid responsibility, even while supporting a large extended family; that he found Old Colonel Falkner so attractive because the latter demonstrated that one could break from the familial mode by becoming a writer. The ability to evade responsibility—a regular job, a commitment to family respectability, a sense of community—by being a writer nourished Faulkner's already latent talent. Bezzerides stressed that Faulkner sensed family matters were a trap—a domineering and dominant mother, and a drunken father who kept failing. Since the immediate models were weak, he turned to historical antecedents, especially the old colonel. This stepping outside the immediate family circle allowed him, even at twenty-one or twenty-two, to be different in Oxford, and gave him an angle of vision.

By extrapolating from Bezzerides, we can see that Faulkner was pursuing almost a classic "escape," and his model, once more, could have been Joseph Conrad. When Conrad left Poland just short of his seventeenth birthday, he headed for Marseilles, and fell in with a right-wing group of royalists, who supported the restoration of Carlos in Spain. He claimed to have smuggled arms, then to have been sunk; he also claimed that one Dominic Cervoni took him under his wing. (This Cervoni later turns up as Nostromo in that novel.) How much was truth, youthful romanticizing, or outright falsehood, we do not know—although many of the details are insupportable, including a youthful romance with the mistress of the pretender himself. Faulkner had an American version of this "escape" with Reno, his beautician friend, and their crowd.

Bezzerides, who was quite devoted to Faulkner during those Hollywood years, is very emphatic about the writer's failings, perhaps unduly harsh. Looking back, he notes a pattern in which Faulkner was unable to relate to others *unless* they could help him. He was emotionally hobbled to the extent he sent signals to people whom he needed; but when he was in tune with himself, he could not relate. Bezzerides felt that if you attempted to approach Faulkner when there was no need, you always felt like an intruder: ". . . his relationship to you was always very casual, as if he had other things to do and you were getting in the way."[6]

Faulkner developed such a persona long before Hollywood, and long before he leaned on Bezzerides. Such a pattern of alternating helplessness and absolute independence was beginning to be in evidence as early as this postwar period when he ran with Reno's crowd. He was clearly in need of money for transportation, clothes, and even housing and food; and for this he gave of himself. Blotner repeats the anecdote of how Faulkner took the heat when two policemen investigated an incident of some old clothes flying out of a window at New Orleans's Roosevelt Hotel.[7] The problem arose when the police saw an army uniform in the hotel closet that should have been worn by Walter Lee, still a member of the army. Faulkner volunteered that the uniform was his, and in the ensuing explanations defused a potentially nasty situation involving MPs and possible arrest for false information. This was, evidently, the side which "fitted" into the role. The other side was the silences, which were beginning, the holding back of large parts of himself, and the continued dependence on people's hospitality. He was storing up images, events, scenes, even people for later use, although at this time he was possibly unaware of final aims. Like most serious writers, Faulkner was beginning that long apprenticeship in which he "uses" people; while moving among them, he is not of them. All writers do this as part of their craft, but Faulkner's relationships were more tentative than most, and his helplessness far more pronounced.

Bezzerides argues further that Faulkner understood human associations well only when they were distant from him, and when they occurred on a large scale, like racial or social relationships which could be abstracted from the personal level.* Bezzerides says Faulkner sensed "terror" in people coming close to him. And this terror—if indeed the emotion was that strong!—would partially explain the paucity of deeper male-female relationships in his fiction. There are some rather deep commitments—one thinks of Byron Bunch's toward Lena Grove in *Light in August* as exemplary. But that commitment is never verbally or even emotionally returned by Lena; she uses indirection and body language, perhaps, but their courtship is run, mainly, through silences and withholdings. Byron's feelings are there, but hers must be inferred. She encourages him through decreasing negatives.

Even if we take Bezzerides's words with some caution, we see their import developing as early as 1919. We have further insight into Faulkner's heavy drinking, already beginning. Drinking reinforced the withdrawal, since most of it was *not* socially oriented. It was drinking for deep personal reasons, more for oblivion and negation of self than for the most usual reasons of giving the drinker pot courage. Bezzerides sees the drinking, which he observed from close up, as a form of suicide; that Faulkner used

---

*To this we might add his daughter's comments: "He didn't really care about people and he certainly didn't care what people felt about him. But he would never willingly offend anybody. He never would willingly hurt someone. But still, he didn't really care about people. I think he cared about me. But, I also think I could have gotten in his way and he would have walked on me."

alcohol with complete disregard for consequences. His drinking may not have been as final as Hemingway's shotgun blast, but it served something of the same function.

Alcoholism among American writers both current and dead is an immense topic. There is little question that American novelists, poets, and playwrights drink far more than the general population; that the percentage of drunks and alcohol-related deaths in the writing groups far exceeds that for engineers, lawyers, teachers, and others in the more educated classes, and exceeds those in working-class or laboring jobs as well. Statistics are not easy to come by in this particular area, but in a rundown of American writers who drank excessively, the figure is so impressive that if projected on the general population we would be a nation of dipsos. We are speaking here of those writers who have climbed into positions of high recognition—the Nobel and Pulitzer prize winners, the members of the National Institute and Academy. Perhaps one of the most telling statistics is that, of the eight Americans who have won the Nobel Prize in literature, five were alcoholics or excessive drinkers: Faulkner, Eugene O'Neill, and Sinclair Lewis, with John Steinbeck and Ernest Hemingway not far behind. Among those who might have been competitive for the Nobel Prize are F. Scott Fitzgerald, Thomas Wolfe, Theodore Dreiser, Jack London, John Cheever, Robert Lowell, John Berryman, Wallace Stevens (yes, Wallace Stevens), Edmund Wilson (yes, Bunny), Thornton Wilder, and others. Careers have been curtailed or destroyed by drinking: Delmore Schwartz (along with drugs and growing madness), Truman Capote (drugs, too), Dashiell Hammett, Tennessee Williams (drugs, once again), Carson McCullers, Theodore Roethke, and others.

The list is impressive and can be extended backward into the deeper past (Edgar Allan Poe, James Whitcomb Riley, Ambrose Bierce) and forward (James Jones, Irwin Shaw, Jane Bowles, William Inge, and several living writers of note). The saturation is indisputable. Theories have proliferated: for example, that drinking and writing are not antithetical but compatible, that both are part of an oral mechanism—mouth for words, mouth and digestive system for alcohol. Then, one asks, why not food, and why not a generation of fat writers instead of drunk ones? The incidence of fat writers is indeed small—Wilson, Stevens, the later Hemingway come to mind as overweight, but food does not seem to permeate the above group as much as drink. American writers drink; they do not eat to fill that oral craving.

Another theory is the manhood syndrome. This is more complicated and deserves attention. It argues that the writer has to establish his manhood while practicing what is, for an American, a "feminine" activity: writing literature in an age of science, physical accomplishment, extension of new frontiers; that drink provided continuity with the doers who opened up the country and proved their masculinity. This argument also stresses that drinking set the writer off from the general bourgeoisification of the country. It linked one with the big city, modernism, what "was going on" out there, making one part of the "smart set." Drugs played a somewhat similar role later—although drugs had a cachet to them which liquor does not, since the latter is legal and the former not. Liquor was a legal means by which one could achieve manhood and self-destruct at the same time.

There are other theories. Much of the drinking—and this characterized Faulkner's mode—was private, not social. It was desperate rather than being part of society, culture, or even community. This is particularly American, since in other countries drinking is mainly social, in cafés, among other writers or intellectuals. Jean-Paul Sartre was that kind of drinker. Silent, quiet, and solitary drinking is something we associate with the American mind-set, the cowboy on the range, the frontiersman with no one to look to except himself, the independent man or woman who eschews connections. This theory contains a good deal of what we find in our writers—not escape, not a desire to embrace a more sophisticated world, but a need to identify with the deepest sense of what is American: to self-destruct at one's own pace. Here, competition is with oneself.

The drinking, then, is part of some grand mystery: at the crossroads of the obsession to create and the compulsion to self-destruct. The question is not merely one of orality, but of life and death; but not in any simple equation of art-as-life and drink-as-death. The two are interlocked, so that drink is as necessary to life as is creation; and creation is itself part of a death act, an element of self-destruction. In this opposition of forces, we have some sense of how the brain functions once alcohol begins to work on it. Alcohol may prove stimulating, at least to one half of the brain (the right side), which has impulses for imagination, creativity, perception, or vision. But at the same time, it depresses the other side (the left), which energizes memory, history, and a moral-ethical basis for one's acts.

Liquor establishes a dialectic within the individual which nothing can resolve. The need for stimulation in order to speed up the brain is clearly present; but once that is accomplished, those tools by which creativity can be disciplined—i.e., turned into art—are depressed, muted. Many writers have spoken of how they "sailed" once they had a few drinks, and it may some day be possible to connect Faulkner's long, almost undisciplined sentences to the fact that he started drinking early in the morning as he wrote. Once the alcohol had taken effect, he felt unassailable, invulnerable, and the result could be a lack of discipline or differentiation, such as those interminable sentences. But if alcohol did unwind him to write those sentences, or think those thoughts that could be tamed only with sentences of that length, it also unfitted him for what the left side of his brain was telling him. He became, accordingly, a battleground of right and left, with liquor the joining element.

What alcohol did for Faulkner was mediate between conflicting tensions, whether those he shaped into art or those created by a mother and father who represented different cultural poles. Faulkner was pulled apart from childhood by parental tension: his father, that world of men, frontier sensibility, hard drinking, a sense of self which can never be penetrated because it is so fiercely disguised and defended; his mother, the desire to read, the support for his writing, the "feminine" world of literary endeavor which contradicted what the father represented. This is reductive, of course; but like D. H. Lawrence, Faulkner had to square two very opposing points of view, tantamount to two cultures. Liquor, which seemed to locate him in his father's world, was in actuality a means to move back and forth. It opened up worlds (mother), and it gave him stature within the male world. Furthermore, it intensified, if anything, the mystique of self behind which he could hide. Alcohol became part of the defensive position, the shield, of which silence was another element, that Faulkner used to shelter himself from whatever created "terror." It gave him control of what was "in here," without exposing him to an external world he needed to escape. Precisely how these mechanisms worked can never be penetrated; but that they were defensive mechanisms, with liquor as the primary line of defense, cannot be disputed. Take away the alcohol and, very probably, there would be no writer; and perhaps no defined person.

The drifting which led into writing was beginning. Faulkner moved from one city to another: Clarksdale, Mississippi; New Orleans; Memphis; back and forth to Oxford—dependent on people to feed him or put him up. He became close to the Oldhams, with whom he could speak of Estelle, now living like a princess in Honolulu. There is little question she remained solidly in his mind: the young woman enjoying a luxurious life, with servants for every need, while her future second husband was bumming around with a crowd the Oldhams could only have reviled. Apparently, Faulkner's openness to class and caste distinctions would later make him the point man in his family and town for desegregation. When his brother Johncy and he had radical differences on Negro rights—Johncy said that if Negroes tried to go to school with his children, he would come out shooting—Faulkner's background with friends on the social fringe gave him courage where others remained silent. On February 8, 1919, Estelle gave birth to Melvina Victoria, shortened to Victoria and known as Cho-Cho. With this, she never seemed further away.

When his brother Jack matriculated at the university, the pressure was on Faulkner, also a veteran, to attend classes, especially since Murry was assistant secretary. Instead, Faulkner wrote poems abundantly, and he indulged himself in an artificial language. His first publication, an adaptation of Mallarmé's "L'Apres-Midi d'une Faune"),* appeared in the *New Republic* for August 6, 1919; then, later, with some revisions in the *Mississip-*

---

*Also indebted, as Michael Millgate reveals, to Robert Nichols's "A Faun's Holiday," from his *Ardours and Endurances*. Faulkner adapted other Nichols's lines for Poem XXXIII of *A Green Bough* (1931) and "Magdalen," one of his New Orleans sketches in 1925.

pian. What is significant about this poem and others which preceded it is how he viewed art as completely isolated from life—quite different from the kind of novels he would write less than ten years on.

Poetry for him was disconnected from the world, its language artificial, its sentiments divorced from the mundane. No people appear; no society exists. We are drawn into a world of self-serving language which has as its thrust a melancholy, mournful, and depressed self. The unrelieved melancholy and mournfulness of the poetry goes beyond a pose: "Why am I sad? I? Why am I not content?" ending with "The whole world breathes and calls to me / Who marble-bound must ever be." There is not only Keatsian melancholy and Housman-like sadness, but real depression. Faulkner reveals more than a convention; he is using poetry to shape deep subjective feelings. The language's artificiality makes us feel he was measuring himself against a long romantic tradition, but in reality he was hardly projecting beyond the kind of musings adolescents and teenagers save for their diaries. At some points, he seems to imitate T. S. Eliot and his Prufrock, although we cannot be sure he knew Eliot at this date.

Borne out is Bezzerides's insight of the self-serving quality of the man: all caught up in himself, enraptured by his ability to put his feelings into language, disdainful of ultimate shape. Had he finished high school or gone on to the university formally, he would have put these sentiments into compositions or into early creative writing courses, where a treacherous, uncaring teacher could strike him down. What is, nevertheless, surprising in the face of these early excesses is the occasional maturity of the "Faun," which derives from about the same period of his life as other amateurish efforts. Although with no certainty, it is quite possible Phil Stone reviewed the poem, helping Faulkner to tighten it, playing Pound to his friend's Eliot. While the language of the "Faun" remains artificial and part of a false symbolist convention, we can discern shadows of discipline; and if not measured against Mallarmé or the better poetry of that tradition, it is workmanlike, if maudlin.

It is, in fact, more Pre-Raphaelite than *symboliste*. If we forget for the moment the title, we can see that the matter is Dante Gabriel Rossetti. The woman inside the poem is one of those Brotherhood models, those street women who became models for the Brotherhood painters, and often mistresses, some of them later going on to make socially grand marriages. The "I" follows through "the singing trees" a young woman with "streaming clouded hair and face"; she pauses in the "still, love-wearied air" and "shakes down her blown and vagrant hair to veil her face." The "her" has particularly active eyes, "a hot quick spark," and her kisses are a "sharp extravagance." She "whirls and dances" through the trees, a creature more preternatural than natural; perhaps "La Belle Dame sans Merci," perhaps someone even more ephemeral. She vanishes into the dusk in "silent meadows, dim and deep—In dreams of stars and dreaming dream." This ends the first section of the poem.

The second segment is the "I" once more, with his "nameless wish" to gain entrance, somehow, into the "silent midnight noon." *There,* he will join "blond limbed dancers whirling past," until their limbs become like "petals drifting on the breeze / Shed from the fingers of the boughs." Then, suddenly, a sound like "some great deep bell stroke" falls. The sentiment ending the poem is highly ambiguous—for even while Faulkner juxtaposes "falls" with "springs," the association with springs is muddled by the "earth's great heart that broke / For springs before the world grew old." The sentiment appears to be that the figures dance to the edge of the moment, and then the earth signals the end. But it is doubtful if the *New Republic* people who accepted the poem could understand the ending, no less the reader several generations later.

What did Faulkner reveal in this poem, his first published work, when he was almost twenty-two years old? We may cringe at the language, and then recall early Yeats—all affectation, artifice, full of Shelleyan excess—trying to find his own voice amidst a myriad romantic and mid-nineteenth century influences, including Pre-Raphaelites and Robert Browning. Or else, we move up to Faulkner's own time and examine segments of *The Waste Land* before surgeon Pound got his pencil going on verbosity, artificial language, lack of voice. What Faulkner revealed behind the artifice of language was someone abstracting himself from his situation; a very young man consciously removing himself from family, friends, and even region. His models here are not Mississippian or Southern, but European, from title to language. Even before he had been to France, his poetic tradition was not American—surely not Edward Arlington Robinson, or Robert Frost, or Carl Sandburg. He was not a regionalist like Edgar Lee Masters. He was like those American painters who went abroad, discovered European, especially French, styles and returned neither American nor European. At the time, Faulkner was putting on his French costume, playing with ideas of retreat, disappearance, silence, and evanescence. These are not, at least in this form, American themes. It would be difficult to predict the Yoknapatawpha novelist from these lines, and yet in less than ten years he would write *Father Abraham,* with his first Snopes, and his first Yoknapatawpha novel, *Flags in the Dust,* which he revised as *Sartoris.*

Just before writing "Faun," Faulkner composed quite different lines, for poems which eventually appeared in *The Marble Faun* (1924), his first published book. The following lines suggest another groping for a distinctive voice: "The Darkness shakes its hair / Stiffened with music, vagrant formless gleams / Like dreams to haunt our dreams, a threading of violins / And horns draw sensuously in darkness." Here there is far more control of lines and language, although the grammatical error "draw" seems less poetic than inadvertent. The influences are more clearly French, especially the poets of synesthesia—some Rimbaud, perhaps Verlaine and Mallarmé.* While the passage is still a pastiche and not distinctive, it suggests

*Faulkner translated four Verlaine poems, all of them based on Arthur Symons's translations in *Symbolist Movement in Literature,* which appeared in 1899.

that Faulkner—at the age his beloved Keats was writing masterpieces—was trying to assimilate reading into sensibility without coming to any conclusions.

Anything more should not have been expected; but what we marvel at is how rapidly he developed, so that this artificial and nondistinctive poetic style became absorbed into a distinctive prose voice within less than a decade. If we marvel at his arrival at his Yoknapatawpha material so shortly, how do we account for *The Sound and the Fury* written less than a decade after "Faun"? And yet in some strange, curious twist of the creative imagination, these early poetic stirrings, so inconclusive and often so immature, were preparation. They dared to try out a kind of stream or subterranean flow coming to the surface and being captured in a language that is, as yet, not equal to the sentiments. What they suggest, beyond the use of preconsciousness, is daring. Faulkner put himself on the edge and refused to play it safe. Such poetry was inexplicable for someone of his background and limited education—he was going all out.*

In early spring 1919 Faulkner caught sight of Estelle, who returned with her infant, Victoria Franklin, on the death of Tochie, her younger sister. Like Estelle, Tochie had married young and become pregnant, and then she suddenly died of Spanish influenza. Tochie—"bright, blonde, unforgettable"[8] as Jack Falkner called her—was the same person who, when the boys had conceived of a hockey game, appeared with her father's niblick and murdered their shins. Jack reminisced: "We stood up against her lethal charges for only a few moments, then limped off the field, leaving her the complete and total conqueror." Dead before her twenty-first birthday.

*We are all indebted to Judith Sensibar's useful discussions (in *The Origins of Faulkner's Art* [Austin: University of Texas Press, 1984]) of the early poetry and how that poetry intertwines with the language and themes of some of his fiction. Most commentators on the novelist have, obviously, emphasized the fiction and underplayed the poetry. Since Faulkner considered himself primarily as a poet during the entire early years of his apprenticeship, the serious reader of his work cannot dismiss or neglect this aspect of his career. Sensibar, however, overkills what is an acknowledged good thing. Her insistence (p. xvii, for example) that the somewhat inchoate poems can be arranged into sequences, and that these sequences invariably reflect the Pierrot figure, turns an idea into a formula. According to her reading, the Pierrot figure can be perceived in *The Marble Faun*, in the airman in "The Lilacs," in the adolescent boy figure who reappears, as well as in the young man who laments "the dead dancer." She sees Pierrot as central not only in these works but in *The Marionettes* and in *Vision in Spring*. But here and elsewhere (p. xviii), she draws too tight a net. While it is true Pierrot's narcissism is attractive for a self-conscious writer, as Faulkner was, there is more than Pierrot in his equipment; and not only that, the poems must be read not sequentially, but as individual efforts. We must be cautious when she offers her thesis: "But when they are read in sequence, we note that as each poem closes it opens out thematically, resulting in a much richer reading as one poem leads into and enlarges the meaning of the next and the whole sequence" (p. xix). It takes a much stronger poet than Faulkner to achieve this kind of alternating opening and closing so as to reveal a sequence. The strength of her readings, however, comes in her discussion of Conrad Aiken's influence on the young Faulkner, as in Chapter VI. "More important, this sequence [*Vision in Spring*, Summer 1921] shows that Aiken's chief attraction for Faulkner lay in his use of large novelistic units of poetry held together not by traditional narrative structures (plot, for example) but by patterns of language emerging in a stream of interior monologue from the minds of the narrators." Persuasive as that may be, it sounds more like an extrapolation of Faulkner's fictional methods than it does his poetic efforts.

Estelle planned to stay for a while. It was a curious time, with Estelle in the middle of what seemed a successful marriage, very prosperous and well cared for, and Faulkner writing melancholy, world-weary poems, playing golf, donning his uniform whenever he felt like posing, running around with his new Clarksdale friends, drinking, and apparently going nowhere. Except for memories, the two seemed to inhabit different universes.

Besides basic differences between them, some of the problem was that part of young Faulkner was not visible, to the extent there was little chance the relationship with Estelle could work even when they overcame the obstacle of her marriage. What was visible to her, and what she saw when she married Faulkner, was only a fraction of what was there. He deliberately held back that large fraction, which she would never see. Early on, he had decided what was his, and that part remained unrevealed. The tendency toward secrecy shielded him from some wounding process which only he was aware of; but it grasped him early, and then when he opted for writing, it solidified. By the time Estelle was becoming aware her marriage to Cornell Franklin was turning sour, Faulkner, while still offering himself, had shrunk what he had to offer. What Estelle grappled with was always far less than what was there, dooming the relationship even this early.

Mississippi, however, was not standing still. We have noted the transformation of the state's politics from favoring big planters to a redneck administration appealing to small farmers, now fully accomplished by Theodore Bilbo. Bilbo has come down in history as a vicious racist—not only in reference to Negroes, but as part of the general xenophobia prevailing in the South during and after Reconstruction. Jews were "kikes," Italians "wops" and "dagoes," and there was, of course, the ever-present use of "niggers." But Bilbo was more than merely a bigot and racist. He helped maintain a large populist tradition in the region—a tradition which spilled over into Louisiana with the better-known Huey Long, and also into Alabama and Georgia.* The strategy, in varying degree, was to represent the "little man" as the ultimate in a back-road democracy based on white supremacy.

Most of the Falkners had gone along with this, and Murry's brother John Falkner, Jr. (Uncle John in the family), was an enthusiastic part of this general movement when Bilbo's fortunes faltered because of corruption, and Lee Russell seemed like a winner in the Democratic primary. Although Faulkner seemed indifferent and found Russell and other redneck candidates unacceptable, what we have in the political arena is the idea of the Snopeses. Faulkner, we recall, touched on the Snopes clan for the first time in *Father Abraham* (in 1926 at about the time of *Flags in the Dust*). The redneck governors were ample context for Snopes prosperity

---

*George Wallace was a later beneficiary of this transformation of the South. In Georgia, Tom Watson was an earlier Wallace, adding anti-Semitism and anti-Catholicism to his Negrophobia. South Carolina had its own in Ben Tillman.

and what it represented for the state. Russell won the primary runoff, in July 1919, by some eight thousand votes and was, as a consequence, a certain winner in the November election. He succeeded Bilbo and Vardaman (who was, if anything, more vicious than Bilbo), and one of his first acts was to go after the fraternities at the university which had humiliated him during his student days. In a curious turnabout, this affected Faulkner and Jack when they became students.*

Faulkner convincingly turned his back on these heady political matters and wrote the lines which became "L'Apres-Midi d'une Faune." Phil Stone was the conduit for Faulkner's poems as they flowed to New York, using the mail from his office so as to save his friend postage and trouble. Like others, this poem went off typed by the office secretary on the back of stationery printed with "The First National Bank of Oxford, Oxford, Miss., J. W. T. Falkner, Pres." The printing in some respects foreshadows Faulkner's own "stationery," his map of "Jefferson, Yoknapatawpha Co., Mississippi, William Faulkner, Sole Owner & Proprietor." Stranger submissions have been made by poets and novelists, and the *New Republic*, the recipient of the bank stationery, paid $15 for the privilege of printing the "Faun," a considerable sum for 1919. A dozen poems a year for this kind of payment could support a man whose tastes were not too fastidious.

Both Stone and Faulkner sensed they had struck a rich lode: the *New Republic* would be the making of the Oxford poet. They retried that publication, and others, with no success, and then they submitted bogus poems, including one by John Clare and even Coleridge's "Kubla Khan," but they fooled no one, of course. What appeared to be moving fast with the acceptance of the "Faun" (and publication on August 6) suddenly dried up. "Cathay" was another early poem, which Faulkner placed in the much less prestigious *Mississippian* (November 12, 1919). That publication now became his chief outlet, but by no means were these often artificial and affected verses permitted to escape ridicule. If he chose to write this way, or couldn't help himself, there were those waiting to parody him. Not that this slowed him, for in the next few months after "Cathay" he placed eleven more poems, all of them of similar rhetorical affectation. "Cathay" is a mixture: a large dose of FitzGerald's "Rubáiyát," a soupçon of Housman's pessimism, and a bit of Swinburne's grandeur. It is a very young man's poem about time passing, death reaping, of Ozymandias-like loss: "Wanderers . . . Drift where glittering kings went through each street / Of

---

*The university was also affected in other ways when Bilbo returned to the governorship; but before he did, there was considerable talk of moving the university from Oxford, a small backwater, to Jackson, which had grown from 7,000 people in 1900 to 21,000 in 1910, and was growing as rapidly by 1920. As a result of this possibility, there was a slow disintegration at the university, culminating in the later 1920s in wholesale defections, firings, replacements of department chairmen, and dismissals by the American Association of Universities. The four state colleges were dropped by the Southern Association of Secondary Schools and Colleges, the school of engineering lost accreditation, and the medical school was placed on probation. All this came long after Faulkner had left the campus, but the assault on fraternities begun by Russell was only the opening blow in a long attack which weakened it. Murry remained an administrator through most of this.

thy white vanished cities, and the years / Have closed like walls behind them." There is still no distinctive voice, little sense of the language which would become uniquely Faulkner's.[9]

"Sapphics," which appeared two weeks later, owes much to Keats, but the Keats who was himself ridiculed for the excesses of "Hyperion." The poem is a combination of "Melancholy," "Lamia," and "La Belle Dame," intermixed with an attempt to imitate Sappho. It is an exercise in which so little of Faulkner appears that the poet seems at the beck and call of the imitational mode rather than in control of it. All the accoutrements of this genre of "cruel poetry" are there—hair, purple beaks, breasts of iron, and, inevitably, Lethean women. Moving through this is a "white Aphrodite," but she is not the Venus of pleasure, rather the cruel goddess of love. "In the purple beaks of the doves that draw her, / Beaks straight without desire, necks bent backward / Toward Lesbos and the flying feet of Loves / Weeping behind her." If the pattern seems familiar, that results from the fact that Swinburne's "Sapphics" underlies the Faulkner poem, compounded by Keatsian echoes.

It is hard to judge where a poet can go after such a poem, since he has taken such a high road. What we observe so far is a writer so tense and unrelaxed he has twisted himself into impossible shapes. His language is clearly that of a poet infatuated with the idea of writing, putting down words before he has thought them through for contemporary usage. A good deal of reading laid onto a basic intelligence and creativity led to a scattering, not an integration. Where and how the integration would come is an interesting question.

That it would come in prose, not verse, may have dimly occurred to the young writer, for intermixed with these poems for the *Mississippian* was a short story, "Landing in Luck." This appeared in a column called "Weekly Short Story." "Landing in Luck" is a very slight, breezy work revealing of the young writer. It immediately establishes Faulkner as a teller of tall tales, a vivid and significant part of his artistic imagination and a center-piece of his ludic vision. It is, also, a fantasy version of his own situation, in which World War I's end thwarted his desire to fly. In the brief story, one Thompson is not a very secure flier, but is nevertheless passed for solo by his tough instructor. In taking off, Thompson tries too quickly to climb, loses height, and shears off his landing gear on a restraining wire. Signaled this by another plane, he brings his craft in expertly. The disapproving instructor lauds him, and Thompson has the last laugh on his flying buddies who think he's a rotten aviator.

Aside from its being prophetic of Faulkner's later flying career, "Landing in Luck" has the breeziness of youth confronting a challenge and defying it. Here we have a sense of the young writer, missing out in flying school, but perceiving his early twenties with a recklessness from which there was no retreat. Its simple lines are an allegory of Faulkner's self-perception, a man not quite ready for what he is attempting, but going ahead, and then turning defeat into personal victory. He was, very consciously, living on the edge.

The story's strength as far as Faulkner's development was concerned is its partial shedding of artificial language, in favor of a more straightforward presentation. Some residue of artificiality would, nevertheless, be a lifelong preoccupation with Faulkner. Long after he was famous, reviewers complained that the sentences he put in the mouths of rustics and uneducated people were unrelated to their true capacities. But when we speak of artificiality later in his career, it is the result of a distinctive style consciously forged, used with a clear sense of context and effect. That artificial, or "high style," was Faulkner's trademark, and he worked at it as hard as Hemingway worked at an opposite effect, those simple, artless sentences of grace and rhythm. Early on, however, Faulkner's artificiality was imitational, and it provided pastiche, without grace, wit, or distinctive rhythm.

There was, also, the influence of Estelle, who did not leave Oxford for Hawaii until September 29. Faulkner circled around, and his method of capturing her attention was not through heroic deeds but through poetry. He played the role of Renaissance courtier wooing his lady through verse —a practice he followed for some time. But instead of giving her his work, he gave her something equally valuable to him, the copy of Swinburne he brought back from Toronto. It was a problematic moment, for in giving her the Swinburne, he was conveying something dear to him; but the act of getting rid of Swinburne was, also, a gesture of divestiture. He was exchanging that poet's ardent influence on his early work for other voices, chiefly Eliot and more modern sensibilities. According to Blotner,[10] Faulkner inscribed the volume so passionately that Estelle tore out the inscribed part before she took the volume with her to Hawaii. Since there seems no reason to disbelieve this—Estelle revealed it in 1966—there could also have been intimate words (and acts) between them, although here we have no evidence.

In his rambling memoir of the family, Faulkner's brother Jack indicates there was never anyone else for the writer; and even Bezzerides, in his more perceptive view, saw Faulkner and Estelle as "doomed to be together." This phrase seems more suitable for Heathcliff and Cathy than for the Oxford pair, but it bears up well in ensuing years. Estelle was his physical type, and her thin, boyish figure was the kind he seemed attracted to for much of his life; it was the image of his early drawing.

When she left at the end of September, with that inscription in the Swinburne volume, Faulkner was at another crossroads. What is striking about his early, apprentice years is how lacking in continuity they were. While the poet was biding his time, he was also groping. His activities with Reno and his group continued, with trips to Clarksdale and Charleston, Mississippi, but Faulkner found himself with considerable free time. He had become an accurate golfer, and on the course his natural meticulousness stood him in good stead, as it would later on the tennis court. What he lacked in sheer strength, he made up for in grace and care, and had he been a little beefier, he might have made a living from golf.

He found he had few choices, and returning to school was one of them. After the war, the university made special arrangements for young men who had served, and additionally Faulkner's father was part of the university administration and lived on campus. Like his father, who traded on Falkner influence, so did his son in gaining special admission and, further, in pursuing studies as he wished. We note with some amusement how Faulkner maneuvered outside of the normal sequences, how he avoided regimentation, and used the university as he saw fit; as in fact, he had "used" the RAF.

On September 19, ten days before Estelle departed, William Faulkner signed up for three language courses: English, Spanish, and French. The university, in the fall of 1919, was quite small, with about five hundred students in attendance. Although there were several major divisions— liberal arts, medicine, law, business, etc.—there were only a handful of students in each division, with about forty faculty members. The university was hardly distinguished, since it was kept by the legislature on a tight purse, and it could not attract either top faculty or students from out of state. When an adventurous, serious student like Phil Stone came along, he doubled his Mississippi degrees with those from more prestigious places. In Faulkner's fiction, Gavin Stevens, a *Wunderkind,* goes North and then abroad to complete his education.

None of this meant anything to Faulkner, since it was clear that as a special student he was not seeking a degree; nor, probably, planning to finish whatever he started. Perhaps the most distinguished faculty member in the liberal arts division was Dr. Calvin S. Brown, who was a Renaissance man in his interests and fields of study. He offered language and literature courses in German, French, and Italian, and was, as well, a professor of archeology and an ardent geologist. His avocation was music and nature studies, and he was apparently a legend on and off campus. To add to his interests, he collected sleigh bells and mortars and pestles. Faulkner remained in touch with Professor Brown long after he left Ole Miss. The English course Faulkner enrolled in was an elective in Shakespeare, taught by D. H. Bishop, who had a Ph.D. and was considered both learned and thorough. Later, the English department building became known as Bishop Hall.

What made attendance at the university more palatable for Faulkner was the presence of his brother Jack, who was enrolled as a regular student under the special dispensation given to war veterans. Jack was taking a four-year program, two years in liberal arts, two in law, preparing him for what eventually led to a successful FBI career. Jack was professionally oriented, clearly, whereas his elder brother did not care about examinations or grades. He did not volunteer answers in class and, when questioned, gave flip responses.[11] Blotner reports that when asked what

Shakespeare had in mind when he put certain words in Othello's mouth, Faulkner responded that it occurred nearly four hundred years ago and he wasn't there.[12] What is troubling about the response, if accurately reported, is not the flippancy, but the juvenile nature of it from someone who was twenty-two, not fourteen.

If this and other remarks of similar stripe were typical, they would be consistent with Faulkner's later opposition to literary talk. His letters are peppered with remarks of how he becomes ill when talk turns to literature or to literary subjects. Writing Ben Wasson: "You know that state I seem to get into when people come to see me and I begin to visualize a kind of jail corridor of literary talk. I don't know what in hell it is, except I seem to lose all perspective and do things, like a coon in a tree."[13] These remarks come several years after his short stay in the university, but are continuous with it. Faulkner was always defensive about his lack of education; but the main factor was his view of himself as a frontiersman; a manly, not a literary, man. He was an outdoorsman who wrote novels and stories, not a literary man who lived only to write.

Pertinent here is the later use of the character Ratliff as a persona, especially in the Yoknapatawpha novels. Ratliff serves something of the persona and alter ego that Charlie Marlow served in four of Conrad's works: for Conrad, Marlow played roles as intermediary, narrator, mask, but, most importantly, as a certain kind of stability. In both *Heart of Darkness* and *Lord Jim*, where his role is substantial, he is the registering consciousness, the one by whom aberrant behavior is measured. While Ratliff is not congruent with Marlow, he does serve something of a similar function. In the Yoknapatawpha trilogy, Faulkner uses Ratliff as the very center of common sense; one of the people who can, also, stand outside of people. One of the few times Ratliff's sense of proportion slips occurs when Flem Snopes deceives him and two others into believing there is buried treasure on the Old Frenchman's property. Ratliff buys in, and is of course taken by Flem, who had himself planted the coins. But beyond this, Ratliff was the persona, as a man of the people, that allowed the writer entrance into their world and, at the same time, distance on their follies. Ratliff becomes increasingly important for early and middle Faulkner, as Gavin Stevens becomes a little later. Whereas Conrad needed a stable anchor amidst a life he was not born to, Faulkner required someone who validated him as a writer, who kept him based solidly in the community he had made his little world. He may have been sole proprietor of Yoknapatawpha County, but he needed a vocal partner.

The significance of Ratliff for Faulkner suggests the latter's trepidation in identifying with a literary career. Although reading back from a period years later, it seems valid to identify Faulkner's tentative early efforts in literature as emanating from a divided self. Looking back upon a famous man's life, parts seem to fit—one element appearing to flow into the next, so that the career becomes inevitable. But if we attempt to view that career as it shapes itself, we see one false start after another; elements do not cohere. What becomes remarkable is that any career at all developed, given the chaos and uncertainty of the early years. About all that remains is that some inner drive, will, or energy has a spark which refuses to go out, perhaps unknown even to the one experiencing it.

In that mix of resolve and uncertainty, Faulkner fumbled his way toward literature, fighting himself at every stage. He set himself up so that failure at the university was inevitable; besides flippant responses, he did not appear for examinations and generally considered himself a "special student." His defiance here is astonishing, since it involved going against the grain of every aspect of a twenty-two-year-old's life. He drifted, courted failure, did nothing to gain a professional goal; in fact, he seemed to have no career ideas. Phil Stone knew he wanted to be a writer; Maud may have suspected it; but the rest of the family and community, where the Falkners were extremely well known, saw only drift, not inner resolve. What it looked like from the outside was that Murry, a university official, was protecting his son, and the son was trading on the Falkner name.

Faulkner kept up his penchant for marginal affairs, while avoiding the center. Without relaxing his poetic contributions to the *Mississippian*—dreamy, imitative poems, several of them based on Verlaine—he also agreed to contribute more drawings to the *Ole Miss* yearbook. Faulkner was kept busy in his brief sojourn at the university, but not with class work. He could, when he tried, achieve—as he did in English—but to maintain a high standard of academic work was to undermine his personal code: that anything regulated was not worth achieving.

The drawings mentioned above (five in all) appeared in 1919–20, in *Ole Miss*. Another group of four appeared in 1920–21, including one, unsigned, called "Marionettes." This drawing of a tall, female-like figure, with an inset mask, or head, coming in over her shoulder, also has a top border of several costumed figures. Under the border is the word "Marionettes," with the twisted S characteristic of Faulkner. In the year following his enrollment at the university, he joined "The Marionettes," a campus drama group, wrote a verse play for them called *Marionettes*, and withdrew from the university, on November 5. It was a sequence of events which seemed to indicate Faulkner's interest in university activities and, at the same time, suggested he used the play as a farewell.

The new set of drawings also included a contribution called "Nocturne." This is a twenty-two-line poem based on Columbine, with a sketched-in "border." Within the border are several candles burning into the very black night, with figures coming off the tip of two of the candles. They are the familiar Pierrot and Columbine, separated in the drawing by a large moon, and around them, stars. "Nocturne" was a segment of a larger group of poems which made up the volume *Vision in Spring* (eighty-eight pages, handprinted and handcrafted). Faulkner presented the volume to Estelle, who had, once more, returned. The main love poems are indebted to Eliot and the Eliotic line of cynical worldliness.

We are moving somewhat ahead, into 1920–21, when "Nocturne" and the other drawings were printed; but they allow insight into Faulkner's creative mind over a broader period of time. In assessing where he was going after his enrollment at the university, his development seemed stalled for a three- or four-year period. Unable to achieve a distinctive voice, he continued to work at more or less the same kind of thing. In that period up to his August 2, 1925, arrival in Genoa, he wrote steadily, but the results reveal little variety or sense of urgency. Some poems would later be gathered in *The Marble Faun;* there were also the poems presented to Estelle. Shortly before that, in late 1920, there was the hand-lettered play, *The Marionettes,* only six or eight copies of which were produced; and at the end of this particular period, in early 1925, there were the brief contributions to the *Double Dealer* and the New Orleans *Times-Picayune.*

Much of this production remained in the immature mode of his earliest efforts; even the work in 1925 did not show an appreciable shift in maturity or self-consciousness, despite foreshadowings of many later themes. Faulkner was writing because that was what he had decided to do, not because he had found something imperative or urgent to say. If we seek some element which curls back to the author, we are foiled repeatedly by artificiality, even affectation. In this respect, "Nocturne" is representative, as are the several Verlaine imitations immediately preceding it. By the time Faulkner arrived at the Pierrot and Columbine tale, it had been well exhausted. It had played a large role toward the end of the century in a wide variety of authors, among them Jules Laforgue, Paul Verlaine, and J. K. Huysman, in Mallarmé's adaptation of the figure and Baudelaire's foreshadowing of it in his dandy. In the early twentieth century, the Pierrot-type burst on the scene: Arnold Schönberg's 1912 *Pierrot lunaire* (based on twenty-one Pierrot poems by Albert Giraud); Pablo Picasso's clowns; in the work of Rainer Maria Rilke; Igor Stravinsky's Petrushka, Pound's Mauberly; and, most important of all for Faulkner, Eliot's Prufrock. In some of these, the Pierrot-type is absorbed into twentieth-century types, but never completely lost.

What "Nocturne" lacks is the broad use of the Pierrot-figure for social or artistic commentary. The "clown" was manipulated to stand in for several different kinds of criticism and display, as we see with Chaplin's adaptation of Pierrot into bubbling clowns for social purposes, or Picasso's to serve pure art. Faulkner has mastered the tradition, after it has been enervated, but not the substance. His individual images fail to cohere: Columbine leaning above the tapered flame, flinging a rose, then a severed hand; Pierrot spinning and whirling. Into this a "violin freezes into a blade, so bright and thin" it pierces the brain, and Pierrot is "spitted by a pin of music on the dark." Once again, Columbine flings a paper rose, and Pierrot "flits like a white moth on blue dark." Finally, both taper and sky are "stiffly frozen, bright and dark." Like so much other Faulkner verse, this was written to produce writing, without a lyrical impulse; it reads, in part, like a somewhat wooden translation.

Against the edict of Governor Russell which prohibited membership in fraternities on penalty of expulsion, Faulkner, along with Jack, joined Sigma Alpha Epsilon. This was the Falkner frat and, like drinking, it was the thing to do. For Faulkner, it was, once again, all or nothing, and the subsequent row and temporary expulsion meant little to him; he was, in any event, a special student. But for Jack, who was serious about pursuing a degree, becoming a lawyer, and moving on to a career, it could have proven fatal. What may have appealed to the elder brother was the conspiratorial aspect of the meetings, inasmuch as gatherings had to be disguised from anyone who could turn them in. They drifted to various prearranged places in small groups—the Oldham home was one such spot, as was The Big Place, where the young colonel was dragging out his final days.

A photograph—daring in the light of the threat of expulsion—shows twenty-one SAEs, with Faulkner tucked away in the back right corner. He looks like a teenager who has wandered into the group, not an older student. Having lost its original proportions but not yet settled into manhood, his face has entered an intermediary stage, so that he appears absurdly young. The mustache is gone, and without his uniform he lacks stature and bulk. Further, he is standing next to a much taller young man, coming up to the latter's chin. These physical details are worth repeating since they help explain why he wore his uniform. In the *Ole Miss* yearbook for 1920, in which he had several drawings and a poem, "To a Co-ed," he is also photographed, among other students. But here he is posed in his RAF uniform, and while the others look stiff and uninteresting, he is debonair and breezy. His hat is perched in flyboy style, and he looks his age.

Another episode linked to Faulkner's desperate effort to create a persona for himself and to appear interesting to women is quite revealing. Always a careful dresser, he ran up an excessive bill at Halle's in Memphis; the Falkners could not afford to pay it, nor could Faulkner. He had no source of income and showed no inclination to earn the money to pay off the charge. Ever the doting mother, Maud gave Sallie Murry her diamond ring and, with its sale, money was raised to pay the Halle bill. Blotner notes that Murry was infuriated,[14] but the transaction was completed. The episode reveals that Faulkner was conscious that he could count on his mother for help; but behind that awareness was a self-centeredness and a dependence on others, the beginning of a pattern.

All the pieces fit: the wearing of the uniform, the need for special clothes from a fine store, the playing of roles, often of roles within roles, the desire to impress others with his stories, the highly stylized drawings which recalled another era, the poems establishing him as "outside" his time and place. The need for a persona, or "other," recalls another young poet, William Butler Yeats. Like Yeats, Faulkner wanted to catapult himself out of his time and place; and while he avoided Yeats's use of spiritualism and ancient myths, the two paralleled each other in their need to remake themselves. In both instances, the poets leaped outside their "phase" into another: Yeats more radically, but Faulkner, also, into a romantic and heroic posture he tried to achieve vicariously through romanticized poetry and the splendors of a uniform. For Faulkner, it was not simply that he had not yet found his voice; it was that he was striving to move beyond his time. Part of the genius of the Yoknapatawpha cycle is that while it presents contemporary pressures (the Snopes family, encroaching industrialism, loss of primitive life), it creates an isolated place which in some respects stands outside of time. When Faulkner boasted he was sole proprietor of his mythical county, he was saying the writer was a kind of imperial god; not the god of creation, but of omnipresence and omnipotence. As the most modern of American novelists, Faulkner was suspicious of modernism and its works; and his various personas as a young man were ways of thrusting himself into another era. He tried to live in and outside history: inside as an Oxford man attending the university, but outside, like Yeats, as a man moving toward a reshaping of what and who he would become.

Faulkner pledged as an SAE, survived the hazing, and became a member of the Mississippi Gamma chapter. It never meant much to him; his military experience preempted fraternity life. Family fortunes, meanwhile, dipped while the eldest Falkner son indulged his fancies in clothes, the frat house, and romantic poetry. The young colonel was forced out as bank president, bought out by Joe Parks and a group of stockholders. He was played out—uninterested in business and simply holding on—and would die less than two years later. Recognizing his incompetence, the stockholders moved. One of the last holdings of the Falkner clan, the bank, passed out of the family. It seemed to have no effect on young William, whose life had taken on a superficial patina of social activities and a large number of new poems.

These poems, like those immediately before and after, were mental skimmings. The *Mississippian* was the captive audience for these efforts, and Faulkner was indeed fortunate he had an outlet for work commercially unavailing. The mixture of styles was pronounced, from Eliot to Verlaine, with Swinburne and Housman accompanying Keats. He was playing all the strings on his instrument in these years before moving with some finality to fiction. In the poem "The Lilacs," he uses as a registering consciousness a wounded or maimed soldier—foreshadowing Donald Mahon in *Soldiers' Pay* five years later. In one segment, the wounded, possibly dying soldier recalls his moments of glory, with Faulkner moving from celebration of flying to its dirty, dangerous, unglamorous side. This is not the soldier in his parade uniform, displaying splendor, but a man at the end of his tether trying to recall what, if anything, was worthwhile about his commitment.

One segment is Eliotic, an imitation which goes nowhere, since Eliot's cynical line was always located within a historical or social context. "We sit, drinking tea / Beneath the lilacs of a summer afternoon / Comfortably, at our ease / With fresh linen napkins on our knees." Faulkner has the slender line, but not the whiplash wit or context. Later, when the poem catches the central action, the shooting down of the pilot, he uses language recalling Housman: "Shot down? / Poor chap—Yes, his mind / The doctor says." The Housman sense of meaningless loss is accompanied by lines which dissipate tone: "The bullet . . . killed my little pointed eared machine. I watched it fall / The last wine in a cup." This misses altogether, and the imagery, in fact, is subversive of the poem's tone—"little pointed eared machine." What could Faulkner have been thinking of? Or how could the falling plane be compared to wine receding in a cup? Both images undermine the lines' integrity. Yet the wounded or maimed soldier clearly emerges as a forerunner of Donald Mahon; and it was the vision of the destroyed warrior returning home which begins Faulkner's journey toward a more mature vision. The poem concludes with more Eliotic lines: "I—I am not dead / I hear their voices as from a great distance . . . he isn't dead / We sit, drinking tea." Signed: W. Falkner.

When he wrote several poems for the *Mississippian*, he affixed W. Falkner. Why was he moving in and out of his own name? "L'Apres-Midi" had been signed Faulkner, and published as such; but his early drawings were signed without the "u." "After Fifty Years," published in December of 1919, used Faulkner, but the new group in 1920 was Falkner. It is tempting to speculate that the poet had split himself; that the signing of alternate names was a sign of his inability to integrate his ideas and work; that he was signaling he was wavering, unsure of direction or identity. When Conrad made his name change for professional and personal reasons, with *Almayer's Folly*, he kept to Conrad for his entire career. The decision, once made, was like stone. For Faulkner, the name change had been slight, and since it was slight, we cannot judge how meaningful it was for him to shift.

As W. Falkner, he published a number of derivative poems: "Une Ballade des Femmes Perdues," drawing on François Villon's "Ballade des dames du temps jadis"; "Naiads' Song," with its echoes of Virgilian eclogue, although Faulkner's language was more Swinburnian than the pure language of eclogue. Then came a number of Verlaine imitations, "Fantoches," "Clair de Lune," "Streets," "À Clymène."[15] Exactly how Faulkner's interests led back to Verlaine is not quite clear—from Phil Stone, possibly, or from the French class he was taking at the university, or else as the result of what seemed a commonality of poetic interests. The Verlaine line of pure language and limpid images may have appealed to Faulkner in his effort to break with his more turgid style. He was already under attack at the university for his affectations, and in one of those great ironies which characterize undergraduate university life, he was rejected by the writing society, called Scribblers of Sigma Upsilon. He was, of course, the sole writer of talent to emerge from this class, but his exclusion was probably more on personal than literary grounds. Added to the exclusion was the title hoisted upon him, "Count No 'Count"; surely more humorous than insidious, for Faulkner did need to be taken down a peg or two. He was a poseur, his language was affected, his entire manner stylized. Further, he lived under the burden of a well-known, northern Mississippi name, and his father was an official of the university. With the pieces fitted together, the picture drawn was, rightfully, the source of resentment, particularly among undergraduates more interested in style than matter. They could not care less that Faulkner was experimenting, using himself in various guises as ways of stabilizing his views and attempting to gain a distinctive voice. He was, literally and figuratively, trying on all kinds of new clothes to see which, if any, fitted.

Several nasty elements came together, but he plunged on. He received a D in English, which he proceeded to drop, keeping French (A) and Spanish (B). Parodies began to appear of his work, by one Louis Jiggitts, first of Faulkner's "Une Ballade des Femmes Perdues," with commentary; then with a parallel poem to "Fantoches," called "A Pastoral Poem," about a country bumpkin named Hiram Hayseed. We find a familiar scenario: writers with no talent insisting on a native idiom, whereas the writer of talent stumbles as he seems derivative, un-American, and affected. Criticism of him here was a slight shadow of what followed later, when Faulkner's representation of his region came under sharp attack, as un-American and subversive of real Southern values. Many thought only a Bolshevik could have written the Yoknapatawpha novels and stories. But Faulkner was armored then; now he was not. But he kept going, translating Verlaine's "Clair de Lune" into a calmed-down version. Even though the original is not Faulkner's, it has a much sounder feel for language.

Accompanying "Clair de Lune" was Faulkner's shadow, Jiggitts, with his broad parody of "Fantoches." That poem had ended with "La lune ne garde aucune rancune," which was admittedly heavy-handed in French and English translations. Jiggitts picked upon it and wrote, amusingly, "How long the old aucune racoon!" "Fantoches" appeared on February 25, 1920, "Claire de Lune" on March 3; which meant Jiggitts was writing rapidly to keep up, since he had less than a week to produce his parody. We now enter into a rivalry of sorts. The question was whether Faulkner was sufficiently piqued to respond, and if so, how he would deal with this worst of all criticisms, burlesque of what was, for him, deadly serious stuff.

He submitted two more poems for publication, both translations from Verlaine, "Streets" and "A Poplar." But along with the poems (which appeared on March 17) was commentary, directed to the parodies. Faulkner said, in effect, that the parodies were without value, merely imitations of imitations—so much at least for the first of them; as for the second, it was "a vulgarly stupid agglomeration of words," written on a "Tired Typewriter."[16] He titled his rejoinder "The Ivory Tower," intending possibly some satirical effect. But his answer as a whole, while relaxed, was not incisive, and he made little effort either to justify himself or to attack the parodists. He could have indicated he was trying to break from the provincialisms implicit in their criticism. Or else, he was still so uncertain he could not muster a full attack on his attackers. A pattern was beginning, in which Faulkner did not respond to those who disliked his work; although his letters to editors and publishers indicate his disdain for those who judged him by standards other than what he was trying to accomplish. The attacks continued, apparently fueled by Faulkner's response. How could they not continue! Here was an Oxonian from a well-known family with antebellum roots, a young man whose great-grandfather had become something of a legend, and what did this person do? He wrote imitations and translations of French poets, he carried a cane, and he wore his air force uniform to impress people and to pose for photographs. Such a young man was courting parody. The parallel with Stephen Dedalus cannot be missed—the man who would be an artist even if role-playing alienated everyone. Faulkner represented a *fin de siècle* voice of foreignness, and foreignness was indistinguishable from decadence; and what the satirists stood for—Jiggitts, now joined by W. H. Drane Lester (the name a bit affected)—was Mississippi homespun. Jiggitts, incidentally, was everything Faulkner was not, and disdained: sportsman (football, track), debater, sharpshooter (with a pistol), and musician—a young man clearly out to make it in the great world once his university career ended. In one of his ripostes, after a parody called "Cane De Looney," Jiggitts drove home his real point, that his work was "homemade," whereas the Count No 'Count's was borrowed. This expressed not only the provincialism of the region, but the sentiment of the country. Large cities were undergoing a series of witchhunts conceived chauvinistically to drive out all foreign influences. These were the Palmer raids, and while Oxford was spared, we get some of the flavor in Jiggitts's distaste for the unfamiliar.

The rivalry continued with a response from Faulkner to the latest parody. We could, if we wished, see this back and forth as something, albeit on a small scale, with considerable ramifications: the struggle, in this Oxford backwater, between those who represented traditional literary values and resisted anything smacking of modernism, and the single, heroic individual who understands that, with changing sensibilities, poetic expression must change. This sounds grand and perhaps disproportionate to a small dispute between students. But in a way all such conflicts are part of the larger struggle. What Faulkner did not know, not at least until he went abroad, was that the very forces of modernism which he had perceived and put into practice were on broad display in that larger world. He was fighting the battle not only of modernism but of internationalism, and in only eight years he would assimilate some of the furthest reaches of that movement in his *The Sound and the Fury*.

The immediate scene, however, was alternately riposting and defending. Faulkner cannot have been too deeply moved by this public attack, which Jiggitts and crew kept up, since he continued with the poems. Besides "À Clymène" on April 14, there were "Study" on April 21 and

"Alma Mater" on May 12. At the same time he was contributing drawings and poems to the *Ole Miss* yearbook and would follow up with several book reviews in the *Mississippian* toward the end of 1920 and on into 1921. These efforts do not appear to be those of a man struck down by criticism, or even touched by it, although Faulkner continued to respond. Polemics, however, were not his forte, and his reply on April 7 is a weak effort at wit. "I could, with your forbearance, fill some space in endeavoring to bite the author with his own dog; but I shall content myself by asking him, through the columns of your paper, where did he learn English construction?" Far sharper was a letter in defense of Faulkner, signed "F" (possibly Faulkner, possibly not), calling him "The Mushroom Muse" and citing Liggitts as the "Hayseed Hoodlum." This was a far superior form of polemics, and if Faulkner did write it, then he had risen fittingly to the occasion. The defense is full of good sense, but its bite comes not from slam-bang thrusts, but from its identification of Faulkner with a funny kind of pastoral and Jiggitts with another kind, the country bumpkin with some gangster in him. Blotner feels it is not Faulkner's voice, but someone who was wittily having a go at Jiggitts. Yet the following comment is so perceptive, it tends to lead back to Faulkner himself: "Poets don't sprout in every garden of learning, and how can they grow and bloom into a genius when they are continually surrounded by bitterweeds?"[17] Since this was precisely Faulkner's dilemma, who could have known it better than the "Mushroom Poet" himself!*

"Alma Mater," the May 12 entry, and the final one for that academic year, is far more subdued—a farewell to the school year in the more stately cadences of a Shakespearean sonnet. Lackluster, it demonstrates that Faulkner's sense of language fell flat and dead when he dropped the stylization. It is safe to say that at this time he had to thread his way between two styles: the high, artificial, stilted style identified with his symbolist efforts, and the flattened-out manner characterizing his more realistic poems. Since neither was adequate for what he wanted to do, 1919–20 is noteworthy for him as a period when he moved between two styles neither of which was fulfilling. No poem can survive this beginning: "All our eyes and hearts look up to thee / For here all our voiceless dreams are spun / Between thy walls." The reader can only ask for a return to the Verlaine imitations.

When we try to characterize Faulkner at this time, in 1920, we find little reliable evidence. Comments from his brothers are inadequate—they had little or no understanding of what a serious writer was going through; and outsiders knew even less. Perhaps Maud Falkner had a glimmer, but she left no comments on her eldest son. We must go to Faulkner himself, although letters in this period are nonexistent. We do have an incomplete manuscript dating to five years later, the almost incoherent "Elmer,"

---

*Unless "F" was Phil Stone.

which Faulkner refers to in a letter to Maud, on August 23, 1925: "I am in the middle of another novel, a grand one. This is new altogether [he had put aside the one that became *Mosquitoes*]." He holds that he doesn't feel quite old enough to write *Mosquitoes* as "it should be written."[18]

"Elmer" never came close to completion, but Faulkner carved several elements from it—his usual practice with both published and unpublished books. Out of "Elmer," in varying degrees, came some spillover into *Mosquitoes*, "Divorce in Naples" (which appeared in *These 13*), "A Portrait of Elmer" (unpublished), "Equinox" (lost), and even *The Wild Palms* (1939). "Elmer" material, then, ran through a good part of Faulkner's early and middle career, and, therefore, we can assume it had considerable significance for him. For the biographer, it suggests a kind of shadow existence of the younger Faulkner: we move back from the composition of "Elmer" when he was turning twenty-eight to a period five years earlier. The incomplete "Elmer" is a replication of the portrait of the artist as a young man, although it has none of the artistry of Joyce's novel, or even of *Stephen Hero*. It does, however, have considerable unrealized meaning for the writer.

In the letters to his mother, saved from this period, in 1925, Faulkner repeatedly remarked on his progress; and he clearly had great hopes for the novel. It would reveal who he was, how he felt, and the pain and wounds he suffered. It is, like most bildungsromans, barely disguised autobiography. In a particularly revealing letter (September 6), he mixed "Elmer" and what would be a segment of *Sanctuary*, fully six years before that novel was published. "I have over 20,000 words on my novel," he writes. But before that, he is ecstatic: "I have just written such a beautiful thing that I am about to bust—2,000 words about the Luxembourg gardens and death.[19] It has a thin thread of plot about a young woman [Temple Drake, at the end of *Sanctuary*], and it is poetry though written in prose form." Four days later, he can report "The novel ["Elmer"] is going elegantly well—about 27,500 words now. Perhaps more."[20] In a very lengthy letter to Maud, on September 22, he reveals some of his ideas for the novel —now half done and "put away temporarily to begin a new one." This is his description: "Elmer is quite a boy. He is tall and almost handsome and he wants to paint pictures. He gets everything a man could want—money, a European title, marries the girl he wants—and she gives away his paint box. So Elmer never gets to paint at all." Most of this description of Elmer is not in the extant manuscript of the novel; Faulkner was projecting much further than what he achieved. But if we align what he projected and what he accomplished before putting the novel aside, we have a shadowy sense of the young writer moving toward his art.

The ultimate Elmer, described as tall and almost handsome, is quite different from the Elmer found in the fragment. This young man is fat and ungainly, although masculine, at a young age. He is hardly attractive, more an ugly duckling until he is old enough to go to Europe. Growing up is painful, since he seems to move in the circle of his own waddle. He is traumatized when young by a fire, and after that the color red becomes for him a signal to panic. If we match the young Elmer against Faulkner's description of him later, we see considerable wish-fulfillment. This is not the young man who will get the girl, money, and a European title, but a klutz. Yet with paints and painting there is some continuity. Even at this young age Faulkner feared that the development of his art, however dimly perceived, could be blocked by circumstance or wrong choice.

Without reading too much into this split, but taking it into consideration, we can see Faulkner measuring out his enchantment with Estelle against the kind of career he was planning. "Elmer" was, like *Mosquitoes*, a semiautobiographical novel, based on conflicting themes of sex and art: from his earliest days, Faulkner set these in opposition, as they were themselves opposed in his twenties. Elmer Hodge's failure to achieve his painting career—in the unfinished part of the projected novel—is connected to his marriage and acceptance of bourgeois pleasures. Sex is diverted to security.

Nevertheless, sex does play a large part in Elmer's life, although Faulkner is circumspect. Early on, Elmer fondles his tubes of paint, caressing them, feeling their weight, letting them dangle from his hands in their heaviness, and feeling the swell of the tubes as paint exerts pressure to escape. "To finger lasciviously several dull silver tubes virgin yet at the same time pregnant, comfortably heavy at the palm—such an immaculate meeting of bulk and weight that it were a shame to violate them. . . ." The tubes are "thick-bodied and female and at the same time phallic: hermaphroditic."[21] The language here is so unmistakable we are obligated to carry away insistent images of masturbation. Yet Elmer plans to sublimate his sexual desires to artistic achievement; that is his choice, until his plans collapse. If we move back to the time when Faulkner was still at the university, writing those imitative poems and doing those derivative drawings, we can see some of the tensions. They become extraordinary by the terms of Faulkner's covenant with his talent: that in posing such a conflict, so that paint and semen are equated, he recognized in himself, as later with Elmer, that inevitable conflict was present. Even if the feeling going into Elmer is merely a shadow of his sense of himself, then Estelle and his career are on a collision course.

Yet this is only the beginning if we assume "Elmer" is a shadow fiction of Faulkner's own inner life. Another aspect of Elmer's psyche is just as significant as the fondling of the tubes, with their troubling sexuality. That is the strong suggestion of unconscious incestuous feelings Elmer has for his elder sister, Jo-Addie. Incest will prove a compelling theme in Faulkner's later work, with Caddy and Quentin in *The Sound and the Fury* only the most obvious and most important. Elmer loves to sleep beside his sister, touching her whenever she permits it. She undresses in front of him, and this gives him great, relaxing pleasure—before he is old enough to masturbate. What intensifies this entire relationship, however, is that Jo-Addie is no fine figure of a woman; on the contrary, she is as lean as a whippet, boyish, no breasts, lean hips and belly. She is, in many ways, Faulkner's own ideal—certainly Estelle and, a little later, Helen Baird fell into this pattern. The prepuberty female body caught his eye, so that the mature woman who retains her boyish figure becomes attractive. Further, the boyish sister has an ambiguous name, Jo, so that there is an androgynous quality to it, besides the strong incest pattern. Still further, the "sex" of the relationship is based on a voyeur's pleasure, and it is two-sided: Jo-Addie likes to be observed, apparently, as much as Elmer enjoys peering.

Elmer's sexual tastes are further complicated when he observes an older boy, "tall and beautiful as a young god." He finds himself in "blind adoration of this boy slender and beautiful as any god and as cruel." Faulkner writes that Elmer "dreamed of the boy's splendor at night: and by day went out of his way to see him." If Elmer were only older, the description of his adoration recalls Aschenbach and Tadzio in Mann's *Death in Venice*, a linkage based on cruelty, passivity, and voyeurism, all connected to a debased form of art, or an art which, unlike the real thing, crumbles. The older boy stands for a kind of cruelty, although observed from a distance; and so do those breastless, thin-hipped, bellyless young women whom Elmer and Faulkner so admire. There is here, as in the symbolist and decadent literature young Faulkner so admired, a sexuality of masochism, although on a smaller scale; one based on denial and pain as dimensions of pleasure.

Reading back almost five years from a fictional effort to the life itself is a dangerous procedure, and any conclusions we draw must be treated skeptically. But since Faulkner's fiction has proved to be so intensely autobiographical, we are tempted to look everywhere. The advice a much older Faulkner gave the young Joan Williams—who was twenty when she caught his eye and imagination—reveals how the young Faulkner felt. Here is the older novelist's suggestion: "The grasp of that middle-class Southern background" is unshakable. "It won't let you go easily. No one can really break away completely: you can only keep trying." He stresses: "An artist ought to be free."[22]

We can perhaps see further signs of uneasiness or uncertainty in his signature, which included the "u" for the drawings in *Ole Miss*, and used the old spelling for the poem "To a Co-ed." As W. Falkner, he was listed as one of the art editors. Keeping both spellings suggests he perceived himself as two people, Janus-faced: Falkner, the self facing to the past, and Faulkner, looking to his new life, whatever shape it took. Or perhaps the two signatures meant relatively little, at least consciously. In any event, as the academic year closed, Faulkner was well represented. Also represented was Estelle, but in the background—the subject was a visit to Honolulu by all the Oldhams except for her father, Lem. And in one of those torturing yet irresistible situations, Faulkner accepted Oldham's invitation to stay with him in the now empty house. The poet moved in for a week amidst all the memories and memorabilia of the woman who had rejected him and the family that considered him not good enough. The context for Thomas Sutpen was, in part at least, established fifteen years prior to Sutpen's humiliation. What the week's experience conveyed to Faulkner was that while he was liked by Oldham as a person, he simply wasn't solid enough to be a son-in-law, and nothing would change that. As school ended, Calvin Brown, the Renaissance man, gave a prize of ten dollars to William Faulkner for best poem.[23] The poem was not stipulated, but this was one notch up on Jiggitts.

Chapter Six

Where To?

W ITH THE ACADEMIC year over, Faulkner was thinking of withdrawing from formal studies—he had gained little from them. Yet he was living in the university community. Murry had moved family and goods to the campus, the former Delta Psi house. This was a commodious, three-story house, and it featured a round tower; here Faulkner settled in, in a small tower room. Barely large enough to accommodate his bed, dresser, and desk, it was, nevertheless, rich in charm. It was a perfect setting for a young poet. (A tower as study and retreat had been considered a romantic place ever since Montaigne wrote so lovingly about it. Stephen Dedalus also cherished his.) Faulkner could write, drink, come and go in privacy, or be part of the family if he chose. Further, his selection of the secluded tower room indicates he thought of himself as marginal or special, not only as a writer but as a family member.

Faulkner had few earnings of consequence, and yet he could live very well. In a curious replay of patterns, just as Murry Falkner depended almost entirely on the largesse of the young colonel, so Murry's son depended on the fortunes of *his* father. However much they may have circled each other, they were living off others: Murry because of an inability to make his way in an increasingly commercial society, his son because of his uncertainty about what direction his life would take, if indeed it took any. Yet even while the house appeared to bring them together, in fact it separated them even more. Faulkner lived in the house without being part of it; and Murry kept his family in good circumstances by surrendering his fantasies.

In the summer of 1920, Faulkner literally played away his time, on the golf links and tennis court. On the surface, he was doing nothing, painting a house here or there, doing odds and ends to make pocket money, most of which went for drink. As he moved toward his twenty-fourth birthday —a decisive age for a Southern boy from a traditional family—he seemed in no better position than the previous year or the one before that. To the outsider, except for a few drawings and some imitative poems based on the remote Verlaine, he was standing still; a parasite of sorts and a poseur, already a man of rude silences. He also tagged along, on cookouts, woodsy games, trailing the hounds—activities for either the very young or the very old. It must have been an extremely difficult time; he had no longer work on hand to sustain him, simply those short poems. For whatever it was worth, he was moving from the Swinburne orbit into other influences. The moderns were beginning to take over.

We know Swinburne was receding because on November 10, 1920, he published in the *Mississippian* a review of W. A. Percy's *In April Once.* William Alexander Percy was a distinguished native son, a man whose political ideas did not match those of the older Falkners, a severe critic of the rise of the redneck politicians, especially Vardaman and Bilbo, and a member of what was once known as the planter aristocracy. Author in later life of the now classic *Lanterns on the Levee,* he graciously adopted Walker Percy, the contemporary novelist; like Faulkner's Gavin Stevens, he was the graduate of a Northern law school, Harvard. Faulkner's review, which is respectful, is also chiding of Percy's old-fashioned muse—a curious response from someone whose own first book of poetry would be *The Marble Faun* and whose poems in the *Mississippian* were hardly models of contemporary style. After a brief description of Percy's illustrious career, Faulkner moves to the heart of his commentary: that the poet has "suffered the misfortune of having been born out of his time. He should have lived in Victorian England and gone to Italy with Swinburne." Faulkner then moves gently to the attack: ". . . he is like a little boy closing his eyes against the dark of modernity which threatens the bright simplicity and the colorful romantic pageantry of the middle ages with which his eyes are full." After praising his Browningesque "Epistle from Corinth," he says that it "would have been better except for the fact that Mr. Percy, like every man who has ever lived, is the victim of the age." In the final paragraph, the reviewer both giveth and taketh away: Percy on one hand has not written a "great book," because there "is too much music in it for that, he is a violinist with an inferior instrument"; but on the other hand "the gold outweighs the dross." Finally, Faulkner says he finds it difficult to judge, for, like Swinburne, Percy "obscures the whole mental horizon, one either likes him passionately or one remains forever cold to him."

Like most reviews by young men, the critique becomes a means by which the reviewer can sort out his own priorities. Faulkner is working through what should be meaningful to him in poetry, and, by implication, in literature as a whole. The key phrase comes in his chiding of Percy for closing his eyes against the "dark of modernity," which is somehow a threat. Significantly, Swinburne is dismissed except as a nostalgic item. Also of importance, apart from the opinions, is the note of condescension Faulkner allows to creep in. Given the frail nature of his own accomplishments to date, he had not yet earned either forceful judgment or even a strict, personal point of view. Apparently, Percy did not take it amiss, or if he did he kept it to himself; when Faulkner was in New York, in 1921, working as a bookstore clerk, Percy helped him with introductions.

After that uneventful summer, Faulkner reenrolled as a special student at the university, in the fall of 1920. On the advice of Professor Brown, he tried mathematics, but gave it up shortly afterward. But he did join The Marionettes, and later that fall wrote his play of the same name. It proved to be minor stuff, although it contains certain daring forays: strategies bearing on narrative, on denial of linear telling, on that need to reveal the created work in the act of being created that characterizes many of Faulkner's mature works. We also see his continuing interest in Pierrot, Columbine, Harlequin, and others from the world of mime and commedia dell'arte.* Their appeal, as The Marionettes makes clear, was to a make-believe world which, nevertheless, reflects the world of art. We should not make too much of a minor effort like the play, but it does display Faulkner's attraction to a never-never land, which serves as a mirror of reality: in such slight, unlikely beginnings, we have glimmers of his later proprietorship of Yoknapatawpha County.

Other rumblings at the university came not from Faulkner but from Governor Russell. Russell was an interesting politician in that many of his acts, and especially those directed at the university, were based on vengeance. Having been slighted in his youth, he waited until he gained power and then moved for purposes of retribution. His obsession was connected to secret, arcane, and clannish societies which could exclude someone like him—uncouth and untutored; a diamond in the rough. Having capitalized on the redneck thrust for power which began with Vardaman and continued with Bilbo, Russell now expressed his dislike for anything smacking of planter aristocracy. He insisted on democracy at the university level, although *his* kind of democracy—for whites like himself. It was an interesting development, inasmuch as the phenomenon became part of Faulkner's thought as well. Russell and his followers are not Flem Snopes and those

---

*Obvious parallels, or influences, were H. Granville Barker's *Prunella,* a Harlequin play known in America; Oscar Wilde's *Salomé;* Ernest Dowson's *Pierrot of the Minute,* a play as well as a book (illustrated by Aubrey Beardsley). In the background, besides the presence of many Pierrot plays and books, was a large dramatic literature of the dream play: Maeterlinck, Strindberg, and even Ibsen's *Peer Gynt;* also, Mallarmé's "Igitur," the early plays of Yeats and those of Synge, and others. Faulkner apparently wrote another play, before *The Marionettes,* which he gave to Ben Wasson for a reading. It has not survived. (See Ilse Dusoir Lind, "Faulkner's Uses of Poetic Drama," 1978 Faulkner and Yoknapatawpha Conference, *Faulkner, Modernism, and Film.*)

like him; but they are part of that critique of an older culture which Faulkner could put to use, and which he shared. We must always remember in reading Faulkner on the Snopeses that the world they were wearing down and replacing was not a gentle or kind one; Faulkner did not vaunt the Varners so as to attack the Snopeses. Both Varners and Snopeses were signs of decadence and decline; they were both the end of the line, a sign of loss.

Russell represented not the growth of democracy in Mississippi, but the use of democracy for personal ends, quite a different thing. He wanted equity, but on his terms. Fraternities, dissolute weekends, excessive partying, drinking and smoking on campus, lavish dances were all anathema;[1] and Russell promised to appear in person at each campus to make enforcement certain. The students responded by burning him in effigy. At the investigation, Russell was insulted even more, when he was told that if he applied for the Red and Blue Club, the dancing club of Ole Miss, he would not be admitted, just as he was excluded when he was a student. This was a red rag drawn before a bull, and expulsions followed. Furthermore, all students were required to list any organizations to which they belonged, or else face dismissal, as would anyone filing false information. Before the deadline, William Faulkner departed, silently. His brother Jack withdrew at the same time, on November 5, 1920. Faulkner's withdrawal did not cause even a personal ripple, inasmuch as there is no record of his attendance for this school year, nor of any participation except in marginal activities connected to The Marionettes and the *Mississippian*. True to his manner of doing things, he simply slipped away. Jack was later readmitted under a general amnesty for all those forced out during that semester. Faulkner ignored this sign of Governor Russell's tolerance.

Nevertheless, he continued his marginal university activities. Besides his interest in The Marionettes, he did another group of drawings for the *Ole Miss* yearbook, wrote the aforementioned commentary on Percy's poems, reviewed Aiken's *Turns and Movies* (poems), and turned out the slight "Co-Education at Ole Miss." These were stretched out over the entire school year.

The drift became pronounced, the time when he picked up Oxford's designation as "town bum." Very possibly, Phil Stone was providing him with pocket money. Although direct evidence is lacking, some of the language Phil used later and Faulkner's lack of work point to this. It also fitted into the lawyer's sense he was "making" Faulkner into something, not only with books but with occasional financial aid. Another possible source was Maud, although, while the family lived comfortably, little money was available, and this seems unlikely. Still another possible source is Reno DeVaux, one of his Clarksdale friends and owner of the gambling establishment. The marginal Reno was just the kind of man who would be taken with the waif-like poet, a drinker, a man whose everyday clothes looked well worn, even ragged. The image Faulkner presented to the world was one of the romantic poet giving his all for literature, self-destructive in a way, and uncaring about personal needs. He had abandoned himself to his muse. Such a creature called out for help, and it is possible Reno tucked money in Faulkner's pocket. But the most likely steady source is Stone—for if this is so, then Stone's later hostility toward his friend has an even stronger basis. Lending books and providing intellectual support are not nearly the basis for hostility that lending money is. Further, if Stone had given Faulkner regular sums, it helps explain the latter's alacrity in putting up, much later, a large amount for Stone when the lawyer's fortunes were sinking.

Even as Faulkner was encouraging the waif-like look—alternating rags with splendors of uniform and other outfits—he received in the mail something very grand, a parchment scroll indicating "he had been gazetted Honorary 2nd Lieutenant" from the date of his mobilization. The accompanying comments were very firm about his use of uniform, as though someone from London had been peeking into Oxford. It forbade the wearing of the uniform except on military business (he had none) or on special occasions (parades). The British wording was extraordinary: "Given at Our Court at Saint James's the First Day of January 1920"; the grantor: "George, by the Grace of God, King of the United Kingdom, Defender of the Faith, Emperor of India, & c." The document was addressed to William Faulkner, in script, with greetings from his majesty: with all due respect, and believing in his trust and confidence, did "Constitute and Appoint him to the Honorary Rank of Second Lieutenant in His Royal Air Force."[2] The ragged, penniless, romantic poet framed the document and hung it in his tower room. It was a fitting conclusion to the last bit of glamor in his life for several decades. The next awards were Pulitzers, the Nobel Prize, the National Book Award, and the Gold Medal for Fiction.

Faulkner illuminated his literary stance in the fall and winter of 1920–21 when he reviewed Conrad Aiken's *Turns and Movies*.[3] It is far more revealing than his comments on Percy's work, and it demonstrates Faulkner has made a considerable intellectual leap in those few months. The Aiken review demonstrates an authority, and also announces he is questioning his own fuzziness. He is concerned with clarity and mocks those still caught in writing "inferior Keats," or "sobbing over the middle west." He attacks Vachel Lindsay, with "his tin pan and iron spoon," Alfred Kreymborg, with "his lithographic water coloring," and Carl Sandburg, with "his sentimental Chicago propaganda"; all of them as "so many puppets fumbling in windy darkness."[4] Into this haze comes Conrad Aiken, who has learned to keep silent instead of trying to fill "every space religious, physical, mental and moral."[5] We note Faulkner's recognition of spareness, his suggestion that the moderns, and especially Eliot and Aiken, had remodeled verse and one had better listen. Fail to hear new sounds and pay the price of being left behind.

The review, however, suggests more than that. Faulkner has grabbed hold of one of the most significant points in modern poetry: its impersonality. Eliot's presence is indisputable. He praises Aiken's "clear impersonality," and after quoting from "Discordants," comments that it is one of the "most beautifully, impersonally sincere poems of all time." The language he uses for criticism is crude, but the idea is there: that deeply personal feelings must be given aesthetic distance; that spareness, which seems to suggest lack of feeling, can be more passionate than expressions of passion; that leanness of line expresses more through image and symbol than can more direct, more emotive statement. Faulkner was not able to embody these precepts in his own poetry, nor in his early fiction; but the lesson was well learned when he came to the end of the decade.

What also pokes through in the review is an assumption of authority, even if somewhat forced. Faulkner at twenty-three has taken the high road, as though he were sure of his own mind. As with the Percy review, he is using criticism to give himself guidance and direction. He praises Aiken's experiments with "an abstract three dimensional verse patterned on polyphonic music form." Faulkner says Amy Lowell had tried to do this—although precisely what it is and how it works he does not say—but the results, despite some successes, are "literary flatuency." Faulkner notes that the French symbolists influenced Aiken's verse, and adds that when this era of "aesthetic sterility which is slowly engulfing us" finally ebbs, Aiken may be left as our "first great poet." This is said for the sake of a review, but Faulkner was prescient: Aiken became a considerable literary force, although overshadowed by contemporaries like Yeats, Eliot, and Stevens.

The review appeared on February 16, 1921, but we have jumped ahead since the ideas informing the piece return Faulkner to the fall of 1920 when he dropped out of the university. His mind was racing along even as his body seemed sunk in lethargy or apathy. The lethargy, however, was not defined by lack of movement but by lack of purpose. Faulkner was often on the move, taking advantage of whatever the situation offered in order to travel, whether to other parts of Mississippi or to Memphis. Physically, he let himself be led by the needs of others; intellectually, he was now his own man, not even deferring to Phil Stone. He finally resolved this lack of direction when he found ways of linking his physical movements with his mental activity: using his travels as sources for his ideas, and connecting them in prose fictions. But that was still distant.

Phil Stone's brother, Jack, and Mr. Oldham were engaged in a lumber company which had fallen on hard times. Jack was appointed receiver and Lem was an investor. Although this did not affect Faulkner's fortunes, he was apparently moved by what he saw occurring. In nearby Charleston, southwest of Oxford, the Lamb-Fish Lumber Company was leveling the trees; in effect, deforesting the area and turning new wilderness into potential farmland. Although General Stone had a hunting lodge in the vicinity of Charleston, his family would no longer be able to hunt there, since the game was forced out. When Phil and Jack Stone traveled to collect company debts, Faulkner tagged along for lack of anything else to do. But what he saw and stored up provided one of those momentous insights a writer sometimes experiences. He surely knew of what was going on, but to see it and experience it as happening to people he knew was a great moment. The loss of wilderness land, the retreat of wild game, the need to travel ever greater distances in order to return to what once was: all had enormous impact on the young man.

For in this, he had one of his great themes, perhaps his greatest; and his hatred of the modern world and of commercialism and industrialization would either begin here or be reinforced. When his publisher, Random House, put together a volume called *Big Woods*, in 1955, he wrote a prelude for each of the four stories and an epilogue. The stories included his most famous hunting pieces, "The Bear" and "A Bear Hunt" (as well as "The Old People" and "Race at Morning"). He collected the woodsy lore of Sam Fathers and old Ike, the entire cast of those fading into the past as America changed and the wilderness receded. America was now a country where "profit plus regimen equals security," as Faulkner put it in the first prelude. But the epilogue was really his epitaph. He knew, surely by 1955, that it was all gone, that there was no going back, although in his final fictions, *The Mansions* and *The Reivers*, he did attempt some linkage with the past, with his past. The epilogue should be bracketed with his Nobel Prize speech about enduring, for the two pieces play off against each other. Each displays a somewhat simplistic Faulkner, but bracketed they reveal a deeply divided and uncertain man.

Because this is my land. I can feel it, tremendous, still primeval, looming, musing downward upon the tent, the camp—this whole puny evanescent clutter of human sojourn which after our two weeks will vanish, and in another week will be completely healed, traceless in this unmarked solitude.

It ends:

This land, said the old hunter. No wonder the ruined woods I used to know don't cry for retribution. The very people who destroyed them will accomplish their revenge.[6]

Here are acclaim and lamentation, laudation and bitterness. It had occurred in his lifetime, as Oxford and every town and village spread out, aided in this respect by the need not only for housing but for farmland. Jack Stone and Lem Oldham had helped to make it possible, especially the latter; and Faulkner had gone along with it, having no alternative but to follow. He had been present, when young, at the creation; when middle-aged, at the embalming.

The young man of twenty-three did not appear to weep over the loss of what he called "the old brave innocent tumultuous eupeptic tomorrowless days." He may not even have been conscious he was in the presence of his great theme; for he was interested, mainly, in having a good time, drinking, and, of course, writing his way into writing. He apparently squired any young lady who was available, not flirting so much as overloading her with his sense of himself as an embryo writer, someone who would become important. He did this with Dot Oldham, Estelle's sister, and with Florrie Friedman, daughter of Hyman Friedman, a local merchant. With all, he practiced drinking and driving at the same time; so that he suffered a series of car mishaps.

It is, also, very possible Faulkner's other major theme—the "fall of the House of Atreus" motif—was connected to this sense of the receding, destroyed wilderness. For if we seek linkages between his perceptions and his imagination, we note the interrelatedness of "loss" and "decline," one connected to the land, the other to the people living on it. His overriding concern was the "fall of"—whether land or people; so that modernism and its twin evils, commercialism and security, are corruptors of the human spirit. Man had to endure against these onslaughts. The mythical kernel in Faulkner's thought was the tragic decline of the House of Atreus, parent against child, brother against brother, the curse carrying into every cranny of family life and destroying all semblance of relationship. The Civil War was, of course, the primary struggle illustrating that fall, when the house divided against itself and brother fought brother. That this condition would persist in America was a fear Faulkner voiced throughout his mature life, in fiction and in public statements.

He connected loss of the land to loss of values and ethical systems which lead to decline and fall. To link these themes was not to reduce them, for each in its way was a mighty topic, his *American* topic. By reacting so strongly to the inroads of the new and by attaching that to the fall of the South, Faulkner had far more than a regional theme. This was not some mythical nation he wrote about, but a nation caught by class, caste, political and economic issues; all of it linked to land and people.

Yet as twenty-three began to move toward twenty-four, the footloose life more than ever indicated a young man without bearings. His appearance, pathetic and hostile in its implications, was less that of a down-and-out poet than of a bum or jerk. Worn clothing, stuffing coming from seams, mismatched shoes and socks, and a tongue thickened by liquor—he seemed to be sinking into a manhood which would horrify not only his family but Oxford. Named after his great-grandfather, he had taken on a persona the precise opposite of that energetic, go-for-the-jugular man; he was a symbol of walking antisuccess, the very principle of opposition and rejection. He insisted he wanted only to write, but his activities suggested all he wanted to do was carouse. At twenty-three, he was drinking heavily, although to assuage what pain or to nourish what vision it is difficult to say. The pain of losing Estelle was there, but everything he was doing justified the Oldhams' decision. At one point, as he later told Cowley,[7] he was prepared to go to Cuba, to serve as an interpreter (in a language he did not speak or read); and then on a venture in which (he writes in "Mississippi") he would be a French interpreter for a company intending to operate in

Europe. Nothing came of this—apparently the company ended up in a Memphis hotel, where, if any part of the story is valid, Faulkner was a secretary signing chits. The chief business of this outfit seemed to be bootlegging.

Withal his air of the tramp, Faulkner was not idle, apparently; for he turned out *The Marionettes*, "A Play in One Act" by W. Faulkner. It was intended for production, and was an outgrowth of his brief stint with The Marionettes at Ole Miss. It was, however, as Ben Wasson recognized, not playable—a stillborn poem with strong visual effects, really a closet drama in the nineteenth-century mode. The play was completed and in Wasson's hands by December 1920, although actual writing occurred in the fall. Faulkner said he created six copies, doing all aspects of the production, lettering, drawings (ten in all), and even the binding. Of these probable six (but possibly eight or more), four remain. This early work is striking in its insistence on totality, what in Europe had developed as the *Gesamtkunstwerk*, or "total artwork." In this conception, the total artwork cuts across genres to create the impression of "performance." Once staged, something like *The Marionettes* could be choreographed as well as acted out, with musical background and perhaps scenic designs such as Faulkner provided for the book contributing to the whole. We associate this with *Parade*, of May 1917, the collaboration among Jean Cocteau, Erik Satie, and Pablo Picasso, in which intermingling of genres creates a synesthesia of effects. What is striking as we move along Faulkner's creation of the play is how well he was paralleling European movements in the arts before he had any direct acquaintanceship with them.

The *Gesamtkunstwerk* as a shadowy presence in *The Marionettes* is significant for other reasons as well. Besides implying new strategies and a more sophisticated break with genres than we associate with American writers, Faulkner's effort at the "complete work" suggests the fullness of subject matter he would later treat, as well as technical subtleties he would attempt. Not the least, the relationship of his play to the more sophisticated efforts of his European contemporaries implies that in his reading he had discerned a modernistic way of doing things; that he had already begun the break with the naturalism and realism of his contemporaries: Anderson, Dreiser, and Lewis. Further, the effort indicates he had decided this early a serious writer could not be a popular one; for implicit in the *Gesamtkunstwerk* is the sense of playing to an elite, eschewing popularity, even acceptance.

Most of all, Faulkner was creating on a broad scale, moving beyond the brief poems he had published in the *Mississippian* and aiming at a larger vision of what art could be. *The Marionettes* is in that familiar genre of the artwork describing or delineating the process by which art is made, and thus it has that self-consciousness of "making" and putting together which distinguishes Faulkner's more mature art. It may seem a random act to compare this early, inchoate exercise with something as well-formed as *Absalom, Absalom!*; and yet if we make the analogy, we see the later work as growing out of certain daring forays in the young man's play: strategies bearing on narrative, on denial of linear telling, on that need to reveal the created work in the act of being created. This effort to make the sum greater than the parts characterizes many of his mature works.

Equally compelling is how Faulkner was able to expand his idea of the puppet, so central to *The Marionettes,* into his later sense of men as puppets moving on a broad social scale. In his mature work, puppets are connected not to fairy tales but to terrible moments of class, caste, repression, and race. In *Light in August,* Joe Christmas is described in puppetlike terms, and his fate is as predictable as that of a puppet hanging on strings. In *Absalom,* people are described (by Judith Sutpen) as moving their limbs with strings, only to discover their strings are connected to the limbs of others. In *The Wild Palms,* Harry is a puppet controlled by Charlotte, and he is unable to break free of entanglements; and in *Sanctuary,* the repulsive Popeye is himself little more than a puppet, responding to a background which could produce only a Popeye. The puppet image appealed so strongly to Faulkner because it supported his fatalism; but even more, it forced him to respond to that determinism and fatalism with some countering idea which made life more than mere holding on.

The Marionettes has about it the stillnesses associated with the French symbolists. The stage directions include a peacock "silhouetted against the moon," motionless, and the key figure of Pierrot, who "does not change his position during the play." Pierrot himself "appears to be in a drunken sleep," so that any voices, when they enter, will speak in soft, muted tones. The first figure to enter, in fact, comments on how "still it is!" The stillness provides a "setting" against which sound can serve as contrast; sound is not something itself, but the result of contrasts in textures, here voices. There is also, in keeping with the poetic tradition Faulkner is following, a painterly aspect to the setting—soft colors played off against blacks and whites. The poet we think of most immediately is Mallarmé: both for the stillness and for the use of color imagery, especially the Mallarmé of the faun poem (already imitated by Faulkner) and to some extent *Hérodiade.* Just as Faulkner's Pierrot is depicted as a "shade of Pierrot," so Hérodiade, in the nurse's opening words, is a "shadow of a princess." What strengthens the relationship is that emphasis on mirrors and reflections characterizing both pieces: the essential Mallarmé strategy by which reality is reflected and questioned; the Faulkner ploy to create fairy-tale incandescence.

Although *The Marionettes* seems relatively simple and straightforward, the struggle takes on several dimensions. It is deliberately ambiguous. Marietta may seem victimized, for example, but it is also possible she seduced Pierrot and then abandoned him; it is also possible she is linked to those lamia-like women who populated nineteenth-century poetry and fiction, beginning with Keats's Lamia and his *La Belle Dame sans Merci.* But the larger and more important structural element concerns the garden, and what it implies for the moral argument of the play. Since Faulkner has deliberately cast *The Marionettes* in archaic language—and his hand printing, with the reversed S, emphasizes the archaic dimensions—we find ourselves deep into the pastoral, with intimations of Andrew Marvell's *The Garden* and like poems using nature and the pastoral to make moral/ideological points. As the action of the play moves forward and Marietta seduces or is seduced by Pierrot, and he is then abandoned, or else abandons her, nature is constantly changing: from blooming to dying, from garden to wasteland. The formalized aspect of nature, roses, lilacs, carefully located elements, suggests restrictions on what should run wild; yet the wasteland which develops—"how my garden is changed," Marietta comments, with dead leaves "like sorrowing faces"—is the obverse of unrestricted nature. Marietta represents the lack of limitation or restriction, as does the comatose Pierrot; and together they come to manifest something of the artistic spirit which strains against formality and limitation. But when that artistic spirit breaks free, it can be destructive and, as well, self-destructive. It is as though Faulkner on the threshold of his own development into a modern artist saw the dangers implicit in modernism: its lack of moral center, its failure to take responsibility for itself, and its inability to find normalizing elements within its avant-gardes.

Marietta is of interest as a virginal being (she enters dressed in white) who turns herself into a palimpsest of desires. But of equal interest is the Pierrot figure, physically present as a comatose body in a drunken stupor, and yet also listed as a "Shade of Pierrot," a voice and a moving body. There are two, possibly three Pierrots—so we can speculate that, like the faun, the drunken Pierrot is dreaming, or on the threshold of dream and waking. We can further speculate Pierrot has fantasized the entire episode, that it never occurred, and the entire play is a dream sequence. Or else, the episode has occurred, and the sleeping Pierrot is replaying it like a film, either in expiation of what he has done or in exultation at the evil emanating from his actions. That such possibilities have some validity is in itself of interest in Faulkner's development, since, once again, we note a technique he honed in his mature work.

We return to that dead garden: an astonishing forerunner of Eliot's "waste land" and in itself an image of waste and stagnation which characterized Faulkner's early novels: *Soldiers' Pay* and *Mosquitoes,* even *Flags in the Dust (Sartoris).* As against that dead nature, the spirit of autumn, is the moon image of Pierrot. As in most Pierrot literature, the moon dominates, not as eeriness but as exemplary of "the other": the other side of routine life, as art, as creation and imagination, but not always as a good. The moon allows Pierrot to move outside controls impressed on man, and thus it grants him a superhuman dimension, which he uses to gratify personal desires. Art enlarges, but excess follows.

Any reader of *The Marionettes* must agree Faulkner demonstrated in his lines as well as in his illustrations a deep indebtedness to decadence: those poets (and novelists) associated with a movement which played to extravagance, sensory satisfaction, sensuality, individual gratification, abhorrence of social aims or the common good, disdain for the bourgeoisie; an early phase of what has become known as narcissism in its nonpathological manifestations. The roster of poets in the service of decadence can be huge, depending on how far we cast the net; but for beginners: Swinburne, of course, Oscar Wilde, Walter Pater, Ernest Dowson, Lionel Johnson, and the French: Baudelaire, Verlaine, Rimbaud. Although not a decadent in any narrow sense, Mallarmé has often been associated with the movement and, loosely, with the group.

If these poets filled his imagination, apparently Aubrey Beardsley was their representative illustrator, or the representative artist of the period: self-destructive (as most of the poets were), a defier of orthodoxy, a "terrible" artist in his immoral or amoral implications, an artist of whimsy and hyperbole, a dabbler in forbidden tastes (homosexuality? bestiality? unstated sexual perversions?). His drawings combine eroticism with grotesqueness, innocence with knowingness, naiveté with sophistication of line, figure, and scene.

What is compelling for us is Faulkner's need, at twenty-three and twenty-four, to create his Pierrot. What was there in the figure which drew him, a young man from Oxford, Mississippi, only a generation or two removed from the frontier, a young writer whose father dreamed of running a ranch, the scion of a once illustrious family now slowly in decline? It was, perhaps, all of these which made the Pierrot tradition attractive: the bourgeoisification of the Falkner clan, loss of eminence and brilliance, the settling into ordinariness, a desire to find some literary equivalent of dream, fantasy, imagination, creativity itself. For the young Faulkner, Pierrot becomes the embodiment of those aspects of life, his life, which were slipping away in the growth of community, at the expense of art. Pierrot becomes the representative artist figure, but whom could Faulkner explain this to? Only in a play, a fantasy, could he reveal that he saw himself as a Pierrot or a dandy of the imagination.

Behind the Pierrot figure is Baudelaire's dandy, and here Faulkner's identification is secure; for the dandy, as the French poet perceived him, provided "the last gleam of heroism in times of decadence. . . . Dandyism is a setting sun. Like a great sinking star, it is superb, cold and melancholy." Yet the dandy, in his heroic challenge to a dying society, feels and shows no emotion. He subverts emotion to project it in style. Style here means aesthetics, and Pierrot's dedication to aesthetic principles preempts direct social and political matter. One twentieth-century manifestation of the Pierrot figure, adapted for modern tastes, is Eliot's Prufrock, and known to Faulkner. Prufrock embodies the Pierrot concept of outsider status, observer, someone dying in himself and in that way becoming a witness to the death of community, society, civilization. Pierrot-Dandy-Prufrock: Oxford had spawned a bizarre son.

The Marionettes was the first of several longer works in verse Faulkner produced before turning to longer fiction. Although the language of the play is arranged like prose, it is clearly in the vein of his earlier poems, with his typical diction and rhythms. Also, the manner of production, hand-lettered and bound—a kind of Hogarth Press without typefaces—was characteristic of all these books leading up to his novels. After *The Marionettes*, the next such production, and one far more personal, was *Vision in Spring*, presented to Estelle in the summer of 1921. Estelle was still married to Cornell Franklin, and yet Faulkner pursued her with intimate poems, including several Pierrot verses. *Vision in Spring*, rearranged, revised, and retitled "Orpheus, and Other Poems," was submitted to the Four Seas Company in 1923, the first submission of a Faulkner volume for publication. Four Seas would not publish without a subsidy, and Faulkner, unable to raise the money, subsequently withdrew the volume.

The next year, in 1924, the Four Seas Company published *The Marble Faun*, with an introduction by Phil Stone, and dedicated to Maud Falkner. It, too, was strongly influenced by the Pierrot figure, with pastoral motifs which recalled Keats, Housman, Swinburne, and others. Faulkner inscribed a copy to Myrtle Ramey, a classmate of his since the third grade, and also the recipient of another group, of twelve poems, subsequently published as *Mississippi Poems*. Of the twelve, eight can be placed in the last three months or so of 1924. In this group, he continued his affection for earlier influences, Keats, Spenser, the Elizabethans, and Housman. Then to complete the cycle of poems dedicated to young women, Faulkner presented Helen Baird, with whom he was deeply taken, with *Helen: A Courtship*, in 1926. In the earlier part of that year, in January, he had already presented her with *Mayday*, still another hand-lettered and hand-bound volume, this of fiction in the medieval mode of a knight questing for his lady love. *Helen: A Courtship* is a fifteen-sonnet cycle, all dating from June to September of 1925. But the poems display little of the modernistic tone which crept shortly into his fiction—they are traditional poems in the style of the masters he imitated. Helen remained as a kind of Elizabethan inspiration, for Faulkner dedicated his second novel, *Mosquitoes*, to her, and created a character in that novel whom she recalls. As late as 1939, he still was not finished with Helen—who rejected his marriage proposal, for another man—for in *The Wild Palms*, she turns up in Charlotte Rittenmeyer, and there are even intimations of her husband in Harry.

This five-year outburst of creativity in verse, here overlaps with Faulkner's first fictional effort, in *Soldiers' Pay*. (On July 7, 1925, Horace Liveright gave him a $200 advance for the novel, enabling him to sail for Europe.) The significance of the early verse cannot be overestimated, for it, along with reviews and occasional pieces, gave Faulkner the sense he was a writer; and while the verse only indirectly leads into the fiction—Faulkner had several voices—there is sufficient overlap for one to see the poetry writer in the writer of fiction. Also, his method of presentation of various volumes, to Estelle, Myrtle Ramey, and then Helen Baird, suggests a kind of gallantry and courtliness which, inevitably, bled over into his fiction. Yet Faulkner was very much an American writer in his use of gallantry as a cover for a confused sense of women and their roles, and this, too, we find in the poetry. As his considerable and memorable list of female characters begins to mount, we should keep in mind those early dedications of volumes: his pursuit of romance by way of the book, his need to cast literature itself in a romantic mold by presenting it to a woman, his use of the "gift" as somehow justification for the writing itself. A pattern such as the one forming in the early volumes of the 1920s cannot be ignored or dismissed.

One factor emerging from this period is that the young writer's development is not linear, nor does it seem to have a particular goal. What we noted earlier, that Faulkner was writing his way into writing, seems still to hold; and even after he had crafted his first two novels, *Soldiers' Pay* and *Mosquitoes*, the way forward was not linear. What becomes apparent alongside the need simply to write was the equal need to find not a voice but voices, to aim not at a single goal but at several. The one constant is a quality we discover in the early volumes of verse: a dedication to what he knew, and then an ability to move slowly to another stage of imagination. We can see the books as stepping-stones to that achievement.

We can glean some indication of how different the literary voices could be from the catalogue of Faulkner's library, in which we learn he was reading deeply in the realists—Hardy, Tolstoy, and Balzac—at the time he was finishing *The Marionettes*, a fantasy with medieval overtones. Yet in poetry, Faulkner was vaunting Conrad Aiken, as the man in whom various American poetic voices had joined to create a unique poet. Aiken has a "plastic mind," which is a favorable metaphor, not an oxymoron, and means he is not single-minded, that he "uses variation." Faulkner also praises his impersonality which "will never permit him to write poor poetry."[8] He uses Aiken in order to whip himself, while fortifying his mind with solid realists.

Faulkner and Stone cemented their friendship with common reading tastes, although the younger man began to pull away to assert his independence as a person and his liberation as a unique artist. Nevertheless, in the fall and winter of 1920–21, the two did more than read. At about this time Faulkner doused himself in the demimonde life of Memphis, and along with Stone visited the whorehouses on Mulberry Street along the river and on Gayoso Street, the very heart of Memphis "fun town." On Gayoso Street, one found the classier white whores, although there was an extensive pecking order; on Mulberry Street, one came upon the cheaper white houses and the Negro brothels. It is unclear where the Stone and Faulkner taste lay, although money, especially for the poet, was a consideration. Since Oxford afforded few instances of pleasure, except for local stills, Memphis, drenched in marginal activities, including gambling, which Faulkner loved, was an obvious outlet for many young men.

That spring, learning that Estelle was to return from the Far East in May, Faulkner interrupted what seemed idleness to others to produce the eighty-eight-page volume of verse called *Vision in Spring*, completed during the summer of 1921. The volume is of considerable interest, for itself and as part of a larger, longer voyage into art it heralded for its maker. For with it not only did he pursue Estelle (who had two-year-old Victoria or Cho-Cho with her), he consolidated certain themes in his poetry which were of evident concern to him; and, later in the year, he broke with Oxford once more and journeyed to New York to take a job as a book salesman, aided and abetted by Stark Young, then the most famous Oxford son. Still later in 1921, he returned to Oxford to become postmaster of the university post office, a position he held for about two and a half years, finally resigning when he was almost indicted for tampering with the mail and failing to carry out his duties.

Recurring tropes in *Vision in Spring* concern the faun, the Pierrot figure, Yeatsian and Eliotic voices, and especially Prufrock. That poem made an overwhelming impression on Faulkner, as it had on an entire generation of poets waiting for a new and fresh language. The most obvious Eliot imitation comes in "Love Song," which is Roman numeral IX, and follows several untitled sections. "Love Song," a slightly abbreviated "Prufrock," calls to our attention that Faulkner felt kinship with more than the Eliotic voice. Prufrock was himself someone Faulkner perceived as a persona— the marginal, fearful, uncertain, frustrated, hovering, passive impotent Prufrock somehow connected with this young man from Oxford. In this poem, Faulkner attempted to get inside the skin of the Eliot antihero as well as into his own skin. Although he was wooing Estelle with the volume, if she read carefully she would perceive how unfitted he was for her; that if his persona was Prufrock, he was no Orpheus pursuing his Eurydice —more like Hamlet turning Ophelia mad.

"Shall I walk, then, through a corridor of profundities / Carefully erect (I am taller than I look) / To a certain door - - - and shall I dare / To open it?"[9] This is not an Elizabethan love song, nor a Shakespearean sonnet on the permanence of beauty in a sea of temporality. It is a challenge to the reader, here Estelle, to see a very dubious suitor. We must also keep in mind the type of book this volume presented—it was, clearly, quite different from a printed volume dedicated to a loved one, or a published volume with contents expressing only barely disguised love for a woman. Yeats's love poems to Maud Gonne come to mind: thinly veiled and set into printed volumes which also contain other matter. Faulkner had completely personalized his collection, and there was only one original, delivered to the loved one. This establishes an intimate context, a declaration, or a proposal, or a statement of intentions. By breaching every custom and tradition in this act, his offering was so personal she could not refuse it; yet by accepting it, she in effect made a declaration of herself as still interested in "Billy," although married, a mother, and planning to return to her husband. The circumstances of the volume dictate certain ways in which we must read. "Love Song" is a peculiar kind of beckoning; it is, given the conditions, a negative love song, discouraging the loved one even as, overall, the volume seduces.

Another consideration lying somewhat outside the poem is that as a pastiche of Eliot the Faulkner poem seems particularly artificial and forced. But that occurs only because "Prufrock" has become such a central poem in our consciousness that we are attuned to any imitation. When Faulkner wrote his pastiche, Eliot was still very new, and "Prufrock" had not entered the modern sensibility. And since this was a unique copy presented not to a connoisseur of poetry but to a general reader, the poverty of invention would not be obvious; nor would the context itself. The hesitation, impotence, and inability to act—the Hamletic qualities which so appealed to the mature Faulkner as well—were all shadowy ideas, not yet the received notions of modernity. Thus the reader in 1920 was quite different from one fifty or sixty years later. From our point of view, the sole Faulkner line of any worth is "The world revolves behind a painted smile"; whereas for the earlier reader, the diction was itself revelatory, as were the energies and rhythms of the poem. There was a distinct voice, although the discerning reader would know it was not Faulkner's, but Eliot's; but the less discerning reader heard a conversational voice, and very possibly did not even recognize what Prufrock or his surrogate stood for.

Halfway through, Faulkner circles around to what Eliot wrote at the beginning of his poem: "And now, while evening lies embalmed upon the west / And a last faint pulse of life fades down the sky, / We will go alone, my soul and I." The cadences are all wrong, and the language almost farcical. Caught up in imitation, Faulkner did not develop the ear he had for the rhythms and cadences of prose. Yet the poverty of invention when measured against Eliot's poem is far less significant for us than the placement of the poem in Faulkner's imagination. In that respect, it disturbs the flow of artificial love poetry, turning the collection into something else; the use of a unique volume carefully wrought and presented to the beloved as, in actuality, an expression of the poet's self.

At just twenty-four, Faulkner presented a collection which displayed a prancing, romantic, narcissistic young man. "I should have been a priest in floorless halls / Whose hand, worn thin by turning endless pages, / Lifts, and strokes his face, and falls / And stirs a dust of time heaped grain on grain, / Then gropes the book, and turns it through again; / Who turns the pages through, who turns again, / While darkness lays soft fingers on his eyes / And strokes the lamplight from his brow, to wake him, and he dies." What we discern is that the young writer could not find in this form what he was seeking imaginatively, although he retained the wasteland image. His quest for self-expression was bound to be frustrated in these areas; for the language is all wrong. "Gropes" in this passage is altogether an infelicitous word; and the pose itself, a priest turning and groping pages and books, has little significance, inasmuch as Faulkner did not plan to be a scholar and was not a bookworm. To be a priest of the imagination, like Joyce and Mann, was something else. That would come not through posing, but through a clearer, more cogent selection of experiences and a better understanding of himself.

Had Estelle measured the volume correctly—but could any young woman have whose life had been soft and caught by frippery?—she would have observed the unsuitability of the two. Faulkner was as wrong for her in one direction as Cornell Franklin was turning out to be in the other; not through her fault, but as the result of her background and conditioning. While the young man from Oxford had possibly been Romeo to her Juliet, she was now an experienced woman, and yet there was no clear path through the poems to the author. With better understanding, she would have perceived, no matter what her personal needs, that this young man playing at being a "priest" had a life in which she had no place.

Untitled Section VI starts out like a pastiche of a Yeats poem directed at Maud Gonne, and then heads directly into Eliot territory, "Prufrock" once again. "Let us go, then, you and I, while evening grows / And a delicate violet thins the rose / That stains the sky; / We will go alone there, you and I, / And watch the trees step naked from the shadow / Like women shrugging upward from their gowns."[10] Then the poem resettles into Yeatsian language: "silver star grow pale and brown," "the ripples of its fall," and some flaccid imitational Verlaine images of Faulkner's own: "the shadow of your smile" trembles in eyes "like rain upon two pools" and "dreams like lilacs on your hair." Once again, if Estelle had read correctly, her "Billy" perceived her not as a loved object, but as a literary embodiment of that object. She is embedded not in his imagination but in his reading, and he can retrieve her solely by way of that reading; without such language and context, she has little reality. It was a difficult role for a woman to play in an ongoing romance, for she had to compete against the roll call of literary characters, who, inevitably, must overwhelm her.

Faulkner is all role-playing. He disguises himself with one persona after another, none of them really close to definitive. All are roles he can put on and shuffle off. Everything is a trying-out, not a reality, or part of his ongoing feeling. In the titular poem, "Vision in Spring," he is the faun awakening ("with a sudden vagueness of pain"); then he is "old and weary and lonely,— / Too weary to alone set forth again?"[11] In "Interlude," the faun is suggested, as is a persona from Keats's Grecian urn. Dominating all, however, is Pierrot, a standard character from his earlier poetry and evidently very important for Faulkner's sense of himself as, somehow, polymorphous, sensual, a clown of sorts; a man in whiteface and balloon costume moving marginally, pantomiming while others must speak. *Vision in Spring* is most effective in its Pierrot lines, although the poet's straining after effects subverts several passages: "Pierrot spins and whirls . . . / The dark sea on a dark cliff silverly hurls / And freezes like teeth laid on the throat of the sky."[12] What begins well ends in incongruity.

Pierrot fits well into the "Count No 'Count" tag rather affectionately attached to Faulkner at the university. If he is all role-playing, all dramatic turns, all disguises, then at this stage Pierrot is the archetypical "folie" for him. The mask is continuous, in its way, with his presentation of himself upon returning from the war. The grandness of the uniform, the tall tales of exploits, the false dangers he experienced were all early stages of the Pierrot role-playing, of that mythmaking young Billy and then William Faulkner found so necessary for both life and art. We know that when Hemingway returned to Oak Park, Illinois, at the end of the war, this all-American boy was wearing a knee-length officer's cape lined in red satin, a Bersaglieri hat with a cockfeather, and a British tunic decorated with medals and ribbons. He, too, walked with a cane, and even went so far as to sign up with a lecture agency to retell his heroic exploits to civic groups. Hemingway had been close to action, the wounds were real; the pose was there, but also the actuality. For Faulkner, there was only role-playing. Pierrot was the perfect blend of these tendencies and needs: naive and mad, innocent and lacking ability to live in the real world; but, foremost, the distancing of oneself from that world so as to narrate a different kind of truth. Here, with hindsight, we perceive the beginnings of Faulkner's main career.

Faulkner even cautions himself in "The World and Pierrot: A Nocturne." "But you are young, Pierrot, you do not know / That we are souls prisoned between a night and a night; / That we are voiceless pilgrims here alone / Who were once as arrogant in youth as you are, / But now with our spent dreams are overblown."[13] The cautionary remarks are directed to Pierrot so that he does not make the same errors mere mortals have made; and yet since Pierrot is a mask, the remarks are addressed to Faulkner's "other half." He conceives of himself as dual, and the mortal half must warn the immortal (literary) half of the dangers the world offers —even though Pierrot thinks he is outside, beyond the pale. Pierrot may spin and whirl in what seems a Tennyson cosmos ("The darkness is a world of lesser worlds / Swiftly spinning in soundless rings of light"), but the waste land is always there to claim him, body and soul. "His soul is a paper lantern / Hung sadly in a garden of dead trees. / His soul, that he once carried so carefully before him / Now gutters and drips." Near the end of this meditation on escape, capture, flight, Faulkner turns Pierrot into Prufrock: "Shall I stay alone, / Shall I stay alone to watch a dead man pass, / Gibbering at the moon and twisting a paper rose petal by petal apart,—— / Or do I see my own face in a glass?" He ends by growing "faint upon a wall."

Pierrot and Prufrock weave their way through the remaining eleven sections of *Vision in Spring* (fourteen in all, roman numeraled). Some exceptions exist, such as the poem Estelle herself gave the title "A Symphony," number VII. Here the intimations are Keatsian: timbrels, pipes, stars, beauty. Faulkner runs together imagery from *Urn, Nightingale, Melancholy,* and even introduces some Matthew Arnold: "We beat our hands on walls of blind despair. . . . We cannot know, we only grope and stare / At restless lights reflected in the sea." Then comes the "Love Song," which is the most Prufrockian of the poems in the volume, followed by "The Dancer," which is Yeatsian in its attempt to interweave art and artist, maker and object made. "She plays, and softly playing, sees the room / Dissolve, and like a dream the grey walls fade / And sink."[14] Mallarmé's favorite word, azure, appears, although without the density of meaning he conveyed.

Following this, "Orpheus" is inevitable, not only for the forward movement of the volume but as a metaphor of Faulkner's yearning for the life of the artist. He re-creates himself as Orpheus, throws himself after a lost Estelle-Eurydice, and loses his life with a last glance as she is, for the moment, liberated from a living hell. Could Estelle have read this brief segment as a foreshadowing of her own life, as another role which Faulkner had marked out for her as well as for himself? Here he trespasses on the myth. He remakes himself into a dreamlike figure in which faun and Prufrock are replaced by something more substantial, and yet the dream in which transformation occurs is the perfect symbolist dream: "heavy with budded flowers that never die," a "voice ever calling, ever calling," all this among "the smooth green buds." Beyond this is the yearning Eurydice, and before us Orpheus who "stands and sings." If Faulkner, like Keats, had only been able to freeze time, he would have achieved ecstasy.

Although Faulkner is a deeply introspective poet, and a gloomy one at that, he is not completely static. There is a good deal of walking, running, whirling and swirling, even journeying. Nearly all of the poems fit into that preoccupation with voyage characteristic of French symbolist poetry. Such voyages were interior journeys, opening up the soul, and leading to revelations which both liberated and saddened the subject. Except for the Prufrock passages and poems, which are interior voices without much movement, the others are like "Orpheus," involved in moving, following, chasing, stirring, singing. The movement, however, is rarely pure; it is almost always played off against a static, dreamlike sense; movement grudgingly gained, not movement associated with delight, no Matisse figures celebrating life. In this, we find the tensions in early Faulkner; working his way through a dream or fantasy world into a breaking out, in many respects a metaphor for himself and his immediate future. For the remainder of the year, he moved very distantly from the world of *Vision in Spring* to places as dissimilar as a New York City bookstore and then a university post office as a fourth-class postmaster.

Since *Vision in Spring* is only a thinly veiled assertion of his continuing affection for Estelle, we might look ahead to what would be marriage and even pregnancy. In other contexts, Faulkner wrote such poems. Although "Pregnancy" came first, we should analyze "Marriage" before it. "Marriage" was the original name he gave to the second poem which appeared in his volume *A Green Bough*, in 1933. In that volume, it was roman numeral II,[15] although in a draft version it was, clearly, "Marriage." What quality or response did the partners have to each other? The relationship, like Faulkner's marriage to Estelle when it did come in 1929, lacked communication; the partners seemed to move on different planets, not showing conscious cruelty or neglect, but creating tensions which sent sparks into the air. The man watches, "laxly"—a key word, with a multiplicity of potentialities—as she sits, "her plastic shadow on the wall," the firelight making it appear as if she were playing on piano keys. The atmosphere is "gloom" turned into "a palpable substance," an oppressive weight he feels heavily: "Until his brain, stretched and tautened, suddenly cracks."

She plays, and in playing becomes unearthly: "like a dream the still walls fade / And sink." He thinks of her as a flower "lightly cast / Upon a river flowing, dimly going / Between two silent shores where willows lean." He wishes he could fix her in this dream or fantasy—like a Keatsian vision of permanence amidst flux. But he returns to the reality, in which his brain is "hissing from him, a spark, a spark." His eyes like fingers fumble at her throat, and we sense a desire to strangle, not embrace, her. His brain continues to disintegrate, shooting off sparks into space. She mounts the stairs, and the mood turns sensual with her suppleness and "nervous strength." He feels he must follow, and while she trembles, he mounts— the image of sexual upward movement.

The poem enjoys a cohesion many earlier poems failed to achieve, and while lines reach for significance the poet cannot deliver, the overall effect is a mixture of amateurism and strengths. "That nervous strength" the wife displays is an excellent description of Estelle, but, overall, we are caught not by individual images or lines, but by the image of marriage close to a living hell: the ever-present fire as the background of Hades, and the partners as caught in Jean-Paul Sartre's *No Exit*, doomed to be with each other.

"Pregnancy" (turned into "Pregnacy" by a typographical error) was part of a small group of poems Faulkner presented to a grade-school class-mate, Myrtle Ramey, whom he met in the third grade in 1906. In late 1924, he presented her with an inscribed copy of *The Marble Faun*, his first published volume, in the presence of Stone, and also with the group of twelve poems later published as *Mississippi Poems*.[16] What he gave her were copies, autographed, along with a carbon typescript of an essay called "Verse, Old and Nascent: A Pilgrimage," which appeared in the *Double Dealer* in April of 1925. "Pregnancy" turns up, also, in *A Green Bough*, untitled, as roman numeral XXIX. The group which became the *Mississippi Poems* is generally gloomy, and reflective of Faulkner in and around 1924. Those we can date all fall within the autumn of 1924, which is also the date of the essay.

Yet "Pregnancy," like "Marriage," is associated with Faulkner three years previously when he presented Estelle Franklin with *Vision in Spring*. What makes the two later poems important is their suggestion of Faulkner's views on marriage and pregnancy even as he made himself available to Estelle with that presentation copy. The brief poem speaks more of anguish than of joy, more of sorrow than pleasure. Everything in the poetry argues against marriage and family even as Faulkner threw himself at Estelle, was rejected, threw himself at Helen Baird, was rejected, and perhaps flirted with Myrtle Ramey by way of presenting poems to her; she, too, soon married. The first stanza of "Pregnancy" juxtaposes strong contrasting elements: the seed "huddled dark," and yet warm, with three "cold stars" standing for "rain and fire and death." The seeded woman feels her "harried body wrung to a strange and bitter lyre," which was once "pure strings simply married." The third stanza, in shadowy Keatsian terms, offers the ravages of time which allow past pleasures to deteriorate. The final stanza locates the three cold stars in her heart, even as "spring's rumor shakes," and the grain in her loins is preparing itself to blossom.

The poems making up *Vision in Spring* (Estelle's copy was noted as "Manuscript Edition," 1921) were dispatched to various publications, but kept coming back. Faulkner used Stone's office and his secretary for this tedious job of mailing, keeping track of submissions and rejections, filing away returned poems. (Later when he moved to short-fiction writing as a means of supporting his family, he kept this record himself, meticulously so, and handled most aspects without outside aid.) When the poems continued to be returned, his sole outlet for his work was *Ole Miss*. The summer of 1921 was a curiously otiose one for a young man who was fermenting as much as Faulkner was. As before, he idled, painted (houses, not canvases), golfed, and generally seemed a young man going nowhere. At twenty-four he was still living off his family. We marvel at his ability to hold himself together under community and family pressures to get on with his life. Usually, in the folklore of the incubating, misunderstood genius, the young man (or woman) leaves home and acts out his development beyond the reach of community and familial pressure, most likely in the big city or secluded in a cabin. But Faulkner went through it in the heart of his country where he could expect little but disapproval.

Furthermore, others were moving up the scale. The most famous of them all, Stark Young, then a professor (at Amherst, Mass.), returned to Oxford in September 1921, after a year in Italy. Young was glamorous, well known, well traveled, an "authority," and was to become even more famous as a theater critic. Given his sexual preferences, Oxford was clearly not the territory for him. He needed large cities and travel abroad, where he could blend into the landscape and escape unnoticed. Whether Faulkner ever recognized Young's homosexuality is not known; and how this sexual preference affected what became a threesome—Young, Faulkner, and Stone—is also not known. What is known is that Young's aestheticism would surely preempt any other consideration in Faulkner's eyes; and the fact that Young had encouraged him from the time of their first meeting in the summer of 1914 was a significant factor. Furthermore, although he strove throughout his life to maintain a supermasculine image, Faulkner was not a homosexual-baiting, hate-filled male, such as Hemingway or other "red-blooded" American authors. Given his background close to the frontier and his family ancestry of bloody revenge, Faulkner was curiously passive about those with different sexual preferences, just as he was the most sensitive of anyone in his family toward Negroes. Even in his relationships to Jews, he was rarely anti-Semitic (*Pylon* demonstrates a notable exception to this), and surely far less anti-Semitic than could be expected from a small-town man suspicious of anything Northern and Eastern; that is, Jews or those linked to them.

Stone, also, was outside the usual homosexual-baiting, although some suspicions must have been directed his way, with his late marriage, bookishness, and preference for male company. Yet from all evidence, he liked a Memphis whore as much as any good old boy and had a "frontier" side to him. Stone was enjoying a burst of careerism, for he had been appointed Assistant United States District Attorney for Mississippi's Northern District, at twenty-eight. Such success was good news for Stone, but it tightened the screws for Faulkner to have his friend move so rapidly into public favor while he dallied as alternately Count No 'Count and the local tramp.*

In this threesome, Faulkner was the youngest by four years, a full sixteen years junior to Young; and his prospects seemed dim. Stone was moving up the ladder the community recognized as the rightful climb for a wellborn young man, and Young had made his name in the wider world. He talked to Faulkner of Italy, and his enthusiasms, paralleling Pound's, included fascism, Mussolini, and D'Annunzio. Neither Faulkner nor Stone shared in this and, in fact, laughed at such pretentious nonsense. But Young was a man of many predilections and tastes. Worshiping at the altar of fascism, he was, clearly, an incomplete man who, like Pound, needed proximity to power and authority to make him feel whole. But in other ways he was exemplary: a man of wide learning, a local who had stepped out into the larger world and conquered it, and someone who was kind to developing talent, although his literary tastes were far more conservative than Stone's or Faulkner's.

The young poet saw a good deal of Young that summer of 1921 and showed him his latest work, which meant the poems in *Vision in Spring*. Both the poems and the life, in Young's eyes, seemed to be wasting on the vine, and he suggested that Faulkner go to New York and stay with him until he found a position. There is something ambiguous in Young's invitation, in that Faulkner may have seemed sufficiently bohemian to be open to anything; but, on the other hand, there also appeared to be a genuine desire to help an aspiring writer. Young was a friend of Elizabeth Prall (later to become Sherwood Anderson's second wife), who managed a Doubleday bookstore in Lord & Taylor; and with her connections, Young assured Faulkner, he would be able to find a position. There was little to hold Faulkner in Oxford, as the older man realized. And there was the

---

*Phil was not simply a success in a little pond, for he had been asked by former president William Howard Taft to join his law firm after Stone had distinguished himself at the Yale Law School (Joseph Blotner, *Faulkner: A Biography*, 2 vols. [New York: Random House, 1974], vol. 1, pp. 313–14).

talent, which Young felt needed nourishing in more sophisticated surroundings. "It seemed more and more futile that anyone so remarkable as
he was should be thus bruised and wasted."[17] What Young failed to recognize was that Faulkner needed Oxford and Lafayette County far more than
they needed him; that wherever he went, he carried that "little postage
stamp" of territory which he would shape and reshape, even in novels and
stories not located in Yoknapatawpha County. Young failed to perceive
this, and perhaps Faulkner himself: that even though he was not set, or
hardly even started, his world was *there*, already fixed in his imagination.

At the immediate level, Oxford was suddenly an inhospitable place.
Young's visit was over; Stone was immersed in his work; and Estelle was
occupied with the arrival of Cornell Franklin, with whom she would leave
soon for Honolulu and Shanghai. However her marriage was going, it
seemed exciting and adventurous, as she moved with the highly ambitious
and successful Franklin from one exotic place to another. Now a federal
judge, Franklin was more than a coming man; he had arrived. Estelle
became accustomed to living in splendor, with house servants and help for
young Victoria. She dressed well and entertained lavishly. The contrast
with Faulkner could not have been more glaring, and yet she felt the tug
from childhood years; for she accepted, with pleasure apparently, the copy
of *Vision in Spring* and welcomed Faulkner's visits before her husband
arrived. As their closest childhood friends suggested, Estelle and Faulkner
were destined for each other, despite their unsuitability. A woman whom
Faulkner was soon to meet, Helen Baird, a completely different kind of
person from Estelle, was perhaps closer to him than anyone he knew and
would know; and yet marriage to Helen would probably have proven
disastrous. Faulkner liked women, but it is problematic whether he had
anything to give them.

With forty dollars in his pocket, he ventured out from Oxford for the
second time in his life, taking the train to New York.* But instead of
joining a glamorous outfit during wartime, he was leaving to find work,
at a time the economy was booming for young men very different from
him. After a week on his own, in which the money he had earned painting
began to disappear, he moved into Stark Young's one-bedroom apartment,
with a front room where Faulkner slept on a sofa. Until Young returned,
the young poet knocked around, claiming to have worked as a dishwasher
in a Greek restaurant—which sounded romantic and fitted well into a
New York story. Young brought Faulkner together with Elizabeth Prall,
manager of the Doubleday bookstore, at Lord & Taylor. With the holiday
rush coming, she took on Faulkner, and he suddenly found himself in the
middle of smart New York: a well-known bookstore, a classy department

---

*One idea, never realized, was to study art on this 1921 trip. Although not a regular
museum-goer or connoisseur of painting, Faulkner revealed an interest in art from the time
of his own early illustrations through his trip to Europe in 1925 with William Spratling, a
painter and architect. We have no reason to believe Faulkner's talent as a visual artist lay in
any direction except cartoons and illustrations, although his Elmer Hodge plans a grand
career in painting.

store, and well-to-do patrons, mainly women. He turned out to be an excellent book salesman, low-key, sincere, charming, exactly what was needed to sell books to people who hadn't originally wanted them.

Elizabeth Prall (Anderson) wrote about this episode in her autobiography, *Miss Elizabeth* (which is how Faulkner addressed her). "All the customers fell for him like a ton of bricks. He sold armfuls of books."[18] But she also noted that Faulkner "drank himself to sleep every night." He established his routine: meaningless work, which supplied his immediate needs; drinking, which enabled him to keep going; and writing, which he worked at the rest of the time. As soon as he had a steady income from bookselling, he moved from Young's small apartment and found a room of his own, near Miss Elizabeth's. Young had found him a difficult boarder, what with his incessant drinking, his strange hours, and his inability to adjust to a more normal routine. Further, Faulkner had insomnia and was accustomed to rising at all hours of the night, to sit at his desk, where he drank and wrote. His new room, a rathole, was in Greenwich Village, and he was there at the time the Village began to boom literarily. He preferred, however, to drink and write.

Exactly what he wrote at this time is difficult to establish accurately. Little of it was meaningful in terms of later development, although his reading of one book, according to Stone, was critical. But whether Faulkner actually read it or assimilated some of it through Stone is unclear. The book was *The Creative Will: Studies in the Philosophy and the Syntax of Aesthetics* by Willard Huntington Wright (S. S. Van Dine of the Philo Vance detective tales). The poems he possibly wrote during this tentative period were "Two Puppets in a Fifth Avenue Window" and "On Seeing the Winged Victory for the First Time," which he saw at the Metropolitan Museum of Art in a plaster cast model (of the Nike of Samothrace). But the book is what Stone stressed, asserting with typical hyperbole that all of Faulkner can be clarified if one understands the Wright book. Precisely when this book or its ideas came into Faulkner's purview we cannot tell, but its stress on innovation, its depreciation of simplistic realism, and its emphasis on achieving new forms found an appreciative audience in the young poet. Strikingly, even before Faulkner met Anderson and was befriended by the older writer, he had assimilated literary ideas which would set him against Anderson, leading, finally, to an unpleasant break.

In Wright's book, the tension is between Balzac and Zola, two realists of sorts. Already one of Faulkner's favorite authors, Balzac is praised as providing more than fact or detail; he is lauded for his ability to create context, what Wright describes as an "environmental climate." Zola, on the other hand, in his pursuit of realism has not been realistic enough— precisely the same criticism Conrad had of Arnold Bennett's work. It was a lesson Faulkner took to heart: too much realism subverts the realistic mode.

But Wright stressed other matters as well, both within and outside literature. He perceived the artist as essentially alone, a solitary figure apart from schools, movements, milieu. His ideal was a priestly writer, a dedicated worker, whose fidelity is to the written word. Wright's treatise adapts many ideas from Conrad's preface to *The Nigger of the "Narcissus"* and Henry James's *The Art of Fiction*, along with Walter Pater's essay on "Style." James and Pater fed into Conrad, and he in turn seems a shadowy presence in the Wright book. That the artist struggles with his conscience in a moral and aesthetic battle is a given of all three essays, as well as of Wright's study. He says: "In all great and profound aesthetic creation, the artist is an omnipotent god who moulds and fashions the destiny of a new world, and leads it to an inevitable completion where it can stand alone, self-moving, independent. . . . In the fabrication of this cosmos the creator finds his exaltation."[19]

Although precise dating cannot be made, Blotner assigns two prose pieces to this period: "Moonlight," which exists in a sixteen-page typescript and was never published and never used; and the long, incomplete "Love," also unpublished and unused. What is noteworthy about "Moonlight" is not literary or conceptual quality, but its hardness of prose, similar to Hemingway's style, although without the latter's ability to make a tough, hard, short line sing. It demonstrates, in fact, how poverty-stricken Faulkner's prose was before he found his own voice. "Now he could not be seen as he went swiftly now across the dappled and dew-drenched lawn on his rubber soles and reached the sanctuary of the inky and vine-screened veranda." Or: "But he gained the porch without having been seen." "There was a French door here, giving into the dark house, locked. From his pocket he produced the broken blade of the kitchen knife, fruit and symbol of the interminable afternoon's waiting—the periodic dissolution of his entrails into salty water while he waited for dark to come and so anneal the trailed dumb flesh with the bright sweet fires of hope." There is clearly no personal voice—the shorter sentences are Hemingwayesque, the longer sentences dead matter of Swinburneian excess. The modern line Faulkner learned from poetry could not transfer to prose; language here is all artifice. The story is itself about a young man's efforts to seduce a girl, her resistance to the idea, then her consent, then his change of mind. The inconclusive piece ends, with a Hemingway pose: "He felt nothing at all now, no despair, no regret, not even surprise. He was thinking of himself and Skeet in the country, lying on a hill somewhere under the moon with the bottle between them, not even talking."[20]

The twist of the story is of interest; for it places control in the hands of the young man, not the girl, and he finally rejects her. The subject suggests some sexual malfunction, or some psychological maladjustment, since the young man desires not the sexual act itself but the fulfillment of the need "just to seduce somebody." We note in this almost a fantasy revenge on Estelle: that is, getting the girl into the right frame of mind, then turning her into an object to be repulsed. Slight as it is, the story displays considerable hostility toward women. If Faulkner did indeed write this in the fall of 1921, when he was just past twenty-four, the story memorializes a young man building defenses against rejection: soon after he had presented Estelle with a volume indicating his devotion, and very shortly after she was reclaimed by her successful husband to return to a life of splendor in the Far East. The tangle of psychological meanings here is difficult to unwind, for so much depends on speculation, including the precise dating of the story; but it must have been early, since its poverty of invention and language does not characterize later Faulkner. If so, then despite its unfulfilled qualities, "Moonlight" demonstrates the writer on a rack; so that the steady drinking reported by Elizabeth Prall is profoundly connected to a very depressed young man.

While working in New York, he was befriended by William Alexander Percy (whose *In April Once* Faulkner had so condescendingly reviewed), who introduced him to a couple, the John K. Joices. The brief friendship is of little concern except that Mrs. Joice told Blotner that Faulkner arrived with his story of a wounded war hero: walking with a cane because of a limp, telling her he had recently been released from a hospital with a metal disc near his hip, and dressed in a dashing and heroic-looking mackintosh. It was, clearly, all artifice and role-playing, what with the pipe, the carefully placed dark hat, the limp and cane. Too bad the Joices did not have a metal detector. At one point, Faulkner asked for a loan, claiming he came from a Southern plantation; and this alerted the kind couple they were being taken for fools by this aspiring writer.[21]

The brief episode, which depends on Mrs. Joice's reliability, demonstrates Faulkner's creation of a "family romance." In such a romance, which he had previously created when he enlisted, the individual "removes" himself from his own life and lives as if he were a different person, with another, more exalted birth.

Since his track record with women—apart from Memphis whores—was mainly one of rejection, the family romance was one way he could deceive himself. Estelle's rejection was engineered, mainly, by her family, which liked him but saw him as a loser. We learn of still another young woman (Gertrude Stegbauer), whom Faulkner met in Phil Stone's Charleston law office. He apparently fell in love with her and was rejected, in what terms or in what degree of seriousness we do not know.* According to Carvel Collins, Faulkner felt considerable emotional distress. He cured himself, he told Stone, by fantasizing her in an ugly daily routine: i.e., on the john. How deep this "love" went we cannot tell, but its ending with the "fantasy" related to Stone smacks somewhat of a tall tale.

*To Gertrude Stegbauer, we can add several others: Helen Baird, who was the most serious; Shirley Kirkwood; Elise Huntington; and Mary Victoria Mills.

Chapter Seven

The Center of Indifference

WHAT DID FAULKNER make of his brief stay in New York? He returned to Oxford on December 10, just as the book business was peaking for the Christmas season. He returned to take the examination for what he called a "fourth-class postmaster," for the University of Mississippi post office. But what went into that rather dismal decision? Primarily, he could not function well in a large city, and except for the New York Public Library and an occasional play, he made relatively little use of its great opportunities. His job as book salesman was not attractive, and in any event it was not permanent; nor was he qualified for any other position. Most probably he found it difficult to write: we must always interpret Faulkner's decision-making in terms of his ability to function in that situation as a writer.

When Faulkner took the post office examination on December 10, his appointment had already been fixed behind the scenes by Mr. Oldham. Such positions might seem to be available through civil service examination, but were in actuality part of a vast patronage system—here the siphoning agent was M. J. Mulvehill. Faulkner surely knew that if he returned and took the examination—there were two other candidates—the job was his. The station was itself a small operation on campus, and it proved to be a handy meeting place for cronies and, in time, less than useful for people wanting their mail or stamps. However bizarre the job seems for a future Nobel Prize winner, it was not at all a bad interim position, giving the postmaster free time to think, read, dream, and even write. Faulkner had few duties in managing such a small operation, chief of which was to sort mail into suitable categories and man the stamp window. He proved incapable of doing either, but otherwise used the time well.

In this period, until the end of October 1924, when he was forced from the position and fortunate to escape punishment, he quarried many significant aspects of his career. He published regularly, in the *Mississippian*, reviews of drama (Millay, O'Neill, a general article called "American Drama: Inhibitions," in two segments); wrote for the same publication "The Hill," a prose-poem which appears to be located in what he later called Yoknapatawpha County; began to publish in the *Double Dealer*, a New Orleans literary magazine of considerable importance in his developing career; published a harsh, judgmental review of three Joseph Hergesheimer novels; revised segments of *Vision in Spring* under a new title, "Orpheus and Other Poems," and submitted it to the Four Seas Company; wrote his earliest stories, two of them noted above, "Love" and "Moonlight," also "Adolescence"; submitted to the Four Seas Company, with Phil Stone's help, *The Marble Faun*, and had this, his first book, accepted with authorial subvention; wrote or at least signed a poem which made up his second, and last, volume of poetry in 1933, *A Green Bough*; and met Sherwood Anderson in New Orleans shortly after he was asked to leave his position as university postmaster.

Little of this activity produced work of lasting worth; most of it, admittedly, of interest simply because Faulkner became Faulkner. But few writers start from so little as he did, and few achieve important work from the start, unless, like Conrad, they begin at a much older age. He had several disadvantages to get through: his lack of formal education; an environment which did not promote or nourish literary activity; few active supporters except for Stone and, to a lesser degree, Stark Young; a recalcitrant disposition which often led him to lose his way; and uncertainty whether he wanted to concentrate on poetry or prose.

The period bears close examination: Faulkner playing dual roles as postmaster and as writer-in-residence at the Ole Miss post office. It was not the last time he played such curious roles. On March 10, 1922, he published in the *Mississippian* the brief prose work "The Hill." Like several other short pieces, it is an exercise, an unlimbering—what a tone poem might mean to a symphonist. It has several similarities to the prose-poems we find in French symbolist poets, especially Baudelaire, Rimbaud, and Mallarmé. It was not, nor has it become, an American mode. What catches our attention in this somewhat overwrought bit of writing is the third paragraph (of five, in under one thousand words). In some clairvoyant way, Faulkner had stumbled on what would be one of his major themes. Further, the passage provides an entry point into Lafayette County and, by implication, into Yoknapatawpha, Faulkner's mythical kingdom. As we see the material through the eyes of the viewer, we experience a kind of Shangri-la stretched out before us:

From the hilltop the valley was a motionless mosaic of tree and house; from the hilltop were to be seen no cluttered barren lots sodden with spring rain and churned and torn by hoof of horse and cattle, no piles of winter ashes and rusting tin cans, no dingy hoardings covered with tattered insanities of posted salicites and advertisements. There was no suggestion of striving, of whipped vanities, of ambition and lusts, of the drying spittle of religious controversy; he could not see that the sonorous simplicity of the court house columns was discolored and stained with casual tobacco. In the valley there was no movement save the thin spiralling of smoke and the heart-tightening grace of the poplars, no sound save the measured faint reverberations of an anvil.[1]

The theme is that contrast between what nature has provided and what man has wrought; between the primitive and the contamination of it. The detritus of the culture is hidden for the moment, and we recall Wordsworth on Westminster Bridge in the stillness of the early morning gazing over London before it awakes to its degradation.

Faulkner's consolidation of his "view from the hill" came in a two-piece article he wrote for the *Mississippian* on March 17 and 24, called "American Drama: Inhibitions." Here he picks up, knowingly or not, on Henry James's point in his little book on Hawthorne about the paucity of material available to the American writer. Faulkner charts those who have departed either physically or imaginatively so as to create: O'Neill writing not of America but of the sea; Marsden Hartley, the painter, running for France; Alfred Kreymborg to Italy; Pound in London. Faulkner has observed and foreshadowed the American exodus to Europe, the 1920s of Hemingway, Fitzgerald, Stein, Dos Passos, and many others, what Cowley called a generation of exiles. But although Faulkner would follow with a walking tour through southern and central Europe, he argues a point different from physical exile. This, too, could be something he gained from James, who had wisely cautioned the writer to be "one of the people on whom nothing is lost." The mind of genius, James reminds us, takes "to itself the faintest hints of life," converting "the very pulses of the air into revelations."

Instead of running away, Faulkner warns, the artist should look around, gauge what is there. "Sound art, however, does not depend on the quality or quantity of available material; a man with real ability finds sufficient what he has to hand." America is chock full of material, experience, rich life, if one only opens oneself to it. For the lesser writer, material "does aid that person who does not possess quite enough driving force to create living figures out of his own brain; wealth of material does enable him to build better than he otherwise could."[2] And this links with some remarks about language which he made on O'Neill on February 3. There he writes of an American glory, which is "our language." A national literature, he insists, can come "from the strength of imaginative idiom. . . . nowhere today, saving in parts of Ireland, is the English language spoken with the same earthy strength as it is in the United States; though we are, as a nation, still inarticulate."[3]

In these three distinct pieces, from February through March 1922, he presented a coherent point of view, really for the first time. As if to test his own ideas, Faulkner wrote an inchoate version of such everyday material in a story called "Adolescence." Although it cannot be precisely dated, Faulkner did speak of it as deriving from the early 1920s. It remained unpublished, but it was surely submitted for publication and returned. "Adolescence" not only links several of the ideas in Faulkner's articles but foreshadows several characters and themes in later works. Without relenting on his poetry, he had with this story a good many things going for him —including his initial vision of the future. Part of his problem, however, as we note with its ending, is his inability to find a language. He was, as yet, caught between poetry and prose, trying too hard to infuse poetry into his prose, and unable to reach a distinctive balance.

Even though "Adolescence" is full of uncertain touches, it brings its author a little closer to integration of his talents. The first element we note, in the second paragraph, is a foreshadowing of *As I Lay Dying*.* The basic ingredients, but not the poetry, are present: a woman married to a man culturally inferior to her, her death, his remarriage to a "tall, angular shrew," the similarity of names, here Bunden, later Bundren. Just a glimmer, the elements lack wit and irony, qualities which raise the later work from pedestrian to achievement. There is, also, a reflection of the kind of marriage Faulkner's mother made, Maud Butler to Murry Cuthbert Falkner, in which cultural imbalances were clear to their eldest. Mrs. Bunden's desire to have twins and name them Romeo and Juliet is an intimation of Maud's literary bent, her desire to add a cultural dimension to a rowdy home.

But the story is not the older generation's. It centers on a Huck Finn– type of young girl, the Juliet or Jule who was the firstborn. Now a tomboy, she is sent to live with her paternal grandmother, and her life takes on shapes she can handle: chores, swimming naked in a pool in the woods, sunning herself—the life of the body which for Faulkner often meant peace with oneself. She also meets a rough boy, named Lee, whose young body is similar to hers. He is, in some ways, the twin Romeo her mother never had. Then suddenly one day while they are huddled naked in a rough blanket, the grandmother comes upon them. In a scene of recrimination, she drives Lee away, as the white trash son of a white trash father.

---

*Commentators on the story (Blotner, and Hans H. Skei, Margaret Yonce, Dianne Anderson Cox, for example) see rough foreshadowings in "Adolescence" of *Soldiers' Pay* in particular, as well as *Mosquitoes* and *The Wild Palms*. Some stretching of the material is necessary for the latter two.

Juliet's adolescence, as such, ends with his departure. She is now locked into a hated relationship with her grandmother, an inescapable situation, since she cannot return home because of her stepmother. Juliet the outcast now becomes Juliet the victim.

In scenes of verbal vituperation and near-physical violence, Faulkner tries to capture how adolescence flees in the face of adult confrontations. Youth is connected to the primitive life: woods, water, nakedness, lean, hard bodies, asexual companionship. Juliet is horrified at the idea her grandmother stresses, that Lee has victimized her; that she be unconscious of sexual contact is essential to Faulkner's presentation of the girl's condition. Caught in a compromising situation, she has remained innocent, in mind as well as body. And yet she must pay the price of the world.

The story is all yearning and little completion. Juliet and grandmother spar, argue, come close to murder. They split, rejoin; and then when the father dies, one of the sons, Bud, appears, ready to go on the road. Juliet helps to outfit him with food and some change, and then sees him leave. We have been told, unlikely as it sounds, that later in life he becomes a professor of Latin with a penchant for Catullus. This is simply one of the several anomalies in the story. Once Bud trudges off, Juliet feels truly alone. And here Faulkner, in his own relative youth, falters, confusing what he wants with the thrust of the character. He seeks a poetic end, a poetry of loneliness. Juliet stands motionless observing Bud's back recede, then descends the hill, and puts her ear to the wind. She picks up the distant mellow sound of a horn, which she attributes to possum-hunters. She remains quiet, sorrowful, and despairing. The language lifts: "Here at her feet lay the pool: shadows, then repeated motionless trees, the sky again; and she sat down and stared into the water in a sensuous, smooth despair. This was the world below her and above her head, eternal and empty and limitless. The horn sounded again all around her, in water and trees and sky; then died slowly away, draining from sky and trees and water into her body, leaving a warm salty taste in her mouth."[4]

Of considerable interest to the reader is the expression of sexuality. We are initially struck by the chasteness of the point of view: the virginal young girl is pitted against a grandmother who accuses her of having lost her virginity. The point of view of "Adolescence" reinforces Juliet's position, so that sexuality is made to seem a transgression; i.e., part of the adult world which dirties things. As practiced by Juliet and Lee, in the form of exposure and bundling, physicality is more that of brother and sister than man and woman. Despite intimations of incest, this level of sexuality supports Faulkner's view that the primitive life—swimming nude, bundling, woodsy experiences, isolation of two young people from civilization—is presexual, chaste, innocent, and Edenic. The sexual innocence of the two is an obvious replay of Adam and Eve in a temporary Garden, dispossessed and driven from the earthly paradise by the grandmotherly snake with her intrusion of knowledge.

At another level, Juliet is not built for sex—she is at first described as having a flat body, virtually indistinguishable from the boy's. Such bodies are the source of chasteness. A duality lies here, whereby Faulkner transforms an attractive "flat gleaming body" into an object of purity and innocence, as far removed from sex as the woods themselves. Implied is a deeply ingrained prudery interfused with a sexuality that spills over; and yet innocence must be preserved to maintain the vision of the innocent woods. Faulkner establishes a major tension between the demands of the flesh which intrude on innocence and the need to reaffirm innocence as the very voice of forest and pond, as heart and soul of a primitive life which saves.

Faulkner comes at this theme in several ways. In her fourteenth year, Juliet is beginning to alter—her once graceful, boyish figure is reaching the "gawky stage"; and in contrast to Lee's "smooth ivory symmetry" her "thin arms and shoulders and little bony hips made her appear almost ugly."[5] Here, her barely developing womanliness is an intrusion upon the perfection of their idyll—the twinning pattern is broken, and because of physical changes she is no longer the perfect mate. As long as she remains adolescent and, therefore, boyishly slim, she is a sprite of the woods, indistinguishable from what primitive life reveals; but when her body begins to turn gawky in its initial stages of filling out, she traduces the covenant innocent man has made with the woods. She prefigures the transgression which will drive her and Lee from the Garden; and the fault, clearly, lies with her. Lee's body remains true to itself and the spirit of the woods: his slim hips and graceful bearing at one with primitivism. But she breaks the cycle, even before her grandmother discovers them bundling and throws Lee off the property into what will become, outside of the story, his decline from splendor.

Of considerable interest is that Faulkner has prefigured the dispossessed Garden in the physical development of the female. The sibling incest pattern is broken; movement toward man/woman sexuality bespeaks the idyll's end. Sex in this guise not only reinforces our sense of Faulkner's prudery, but reveals his hostility toward the female, as the breaker of a holy icon, the disrupter of an ancient ceremony. In the temple of the forest, man is the priest at the ceremony of the gods; and woman is clearly revealed as playing her Christian role as Eve, the disrupter of the covenant with a woodsy god. Once this break with the covenant occurs, the grandmother intrudes, and Juliet is thrown back into her family with the appearance of her brother Bud. At the end, she feels despair and loss, but in his peculiar way Faulkner blames her.

On another level, not at all sexual, Faulkner's work on "Adolescence" finds him moving forward. For that early presentation of the Bunden family foreshadows not only *As I Lay Dying* but, on a broader scale, the coming of the Snopeses. Note the similarity of the names—Jeff Davis, for example; but there is also the sense of children being pressed out of a birth machine—in an unending procession. Like the Snopeses, they are simply thrust out into the world and left to themselves, becoming everything from a criminal and a state senator to a professor of Latin. There are in this brief period glimmers of an entire career.

The post office position gave Faulkner plenty of free time, especially as, it became apparent, he was doing little work. He wrote steadily on the job and resented interruptions. He ignored patrons who wanted stamps or other services, and only when they tapped repeatedly with a coin on the window did he serve them. According to one informant, Faulkner read the magazines which came in, distributed them to his friends, and when they were finished put them in the mailboxes. What he didn't know was that several people, including university faculty, were keeping a file on him, an informal file which led, eventually, to his dismissal. What they didn't know was that he would not have cared if he had known, since the job, like the mail, meant nothing to him.

The young colonel, John Wesley Thompson, Faulkner's grandfather, died on March 13, 1922. The once grand figure was of course a personage from another era: he had been, in effect, dying for some time, through deafness, disaffection from family business, withdrawal into his own world. At seventy-three, he passed on from a heart attack, leaving everything to his three children, Murry, Mary Holland ("Auntee"), and John Wesley Thompson, Jr. ("Uncle John"), willing nothing to his second wife, Mary Kennedy. His death in a real sense cut off the four Falkner brothers, and especially William, from the past. If they mourned him, it was as a link with his father, Colonel Falkner, and with the Civil War itself. The young colonel was seventeen when the war ended and, therefore, a witness; he had been a witness to his father's success and, finally, murder. The nineteenth century shut down with him; his increasing deafness as he aged was a symbolic as well as physical condition. The new age whose dissolution and disillusion his grandson would do so much to chart meant little to the man born in 1848, in another time and another America. Although he and his father in their business dealings had not been much better than the Snopeses, they did cut flamboyant figures; they became in the mind of William Faulkner that aspect of the old the Snopeses were replacing for the worse. In other respects, the death of the young colonel "liberated" his grandson, freeing him to see the new age more clearly without remnants of the past to block his view.

At the same time as Faulkner did a good deal of reading in magazines (belonging to other people), he also read books acquired by Phil Stone from a New Haven bookstore. This was a varied collection of poetry, fiction, plays, and philosophy: from Edgar Lee Masters, Conrad Aiken, Hilda Doolittle, and Swinburne to Catullus, Euripides, Plato, and Sophocles, on to Havelock Ellis, Henry Adams, Edna Ferber, and Melville. Much of this material, coming from so many cultural directions and historical eras, proved nourishing for Faulkner's imagination. Edgar Lee Masters's *Spoon River Anthology* (1915), with its community of dead souls, was a rich source for Faulkner's conception of his own county with its collection of souls, living and dead; it was as important a source as *Winesburg, Ohio,* proved to be. *Moby-Dick* was another book which provided a community, plus that tension between outcast and belonging so essential to Faulkner's conception of America. Yet no single book, or even group of books, influenced him; he absorbed, as any autodidact does, what was important to him, discarding along the way what fails to fit. In his juvenile piece "Adolescence," he had mentioned Catullus, and yet it is difficult to see what meaning Catullus could have for him. On the other hand, Faulkner might have gained a sense of a mature writer completely in command of his material, and that confidence in self and material would have sufficed. Influence, as such, can be as fleeting as that.

What is equally striking is that as politics once more heated up in Mississippi, including activity on the part of "Uncle John" Falkner for a judgeship, his nephew remained aloof—so aloof, in fact, his life and work seemed to have no relationship to these bitter, factional campaigns. Of course, if he had had to admit it, Faulkner would have recognized he owed his position to good old Democratic party patronage; but in terms of his work, attitudes, reading, and time spent, he appeared as distant from Mississippi machinations as from Tibetan campaigns. And yet he must have been observing, and assimilating, for the Bilbo-Vardaman-Russell jockeying for position appears much later in the Snopes cycle, in the political atmosphere of the later novels, in the sensibilities of Yoknapatawpha County life.

Accompanying the political maneuvering was family activity: Johncy got married to Lucille "Dolly" Ramey, and Jack four days later married Cecile Hargis, whom he would later divorce. The youngest, Dean, was still a schoolboy. What this latest flurry of family activity meant was that younger brothers were beginning to settle into their lives—Johncy returned to the university, in the engineering school; Jack was a graduate in law. As though in a Jane Austen novel, this left the unmarried elder brother a little farther "out" as far as the community was concerned, not to speak of subtle family pressures to settle down. None of this appears to have moved Faulkner outwardly, as he continued with his poetry and inchoate efforts at prose. If anything, his brothers' marriages and career paths strengthened his own sense of self; for however close the brothers were—and they considered themselves an insulated group—he recognized early how different he was. They shared many activities: some wrote, they all drank, and they flew airplanes, but they had completely different sensibilities—attitudes which emerged when segregation and civil rights activities turned them into a house divided against itself; to the degree they maintained peace only through silence.

While Governor Lee M. Russell was being brought to trial for seducing and alienating the affections of his former secretary, Frances Birkhead—a suit brought with the possible connivance of Bilbo for purposes of revenge—Faulkner was reviewing three Hergesheimer novels in the *Missis-*

sippian. In a brief review, signed "W. F.," Faulkner was probably responding to the political stench of the trial and ensuing charges and counter-
charges when he opened the review with an attack on the age. He accused
Hergesheimer, rather excessively, of a "deliberate pandering to the emotions"; he spoke of the age as having degenerated, of a "strange case of sex
crucifixion turned backward upon itself."[6] The three novels under consideration *(Linda Condon, Cythera, The Bright Shawl),* however, were not shredded in a political meat-grinder. Faulkner quickly moved into aesthetic
considerations—questions of genre and of art and life—and demonstrated
that his younger affection for Hergesheimer had now passed into a more
mature consideration.

The year 1923 was a holding period. Faulkner himself later commented
on the time as one in which he was "just writing the books for the sake
of writing the books."[7] As he revised *Vision in Spring* and possibly wrote
one or two of the short stories noted above (which may have come from
an even earlier time), he was in a curious pattern. He had only odds and
ends to show for his efforts at writing for close to ten years. Maud Falkner
still believed strongly in her eldest son, but Estelle was pregnant again,
with her second child (Malcolm, born December 3), and certainly out of
reach. There had been the rejection by the young woman in Phil Stone's
Charleston office. Stone was himself slowly moving from small-time to
bigger things, although he was still very supportive of his writer friend.

Nothing had really changed in Faulkner's life. He had not as yet broken
out of the small circle of local publications; and while he still played the
role of genius, he had not proven anything—only Maud and Phil believed
in him. The year was a cruelly indifferent one, not at all helped by the offer
of the Four Seas Company to publish the revised *Vision in Spring* if the
author could provide a subvention. Four Seas was aptly called a vanity
press. Faulkner did not have the money. His submission and covering
letter went out on June 20, 1923: "I am sending you today under separate
cover a manuscript entitled 'Orpheus and Other Poems.' Enclosed find
postage for its return if the manuscript be not accepted."[8] He signed
William Faulkner, using the "u."

The letter's brevity somehow communicates the hopelessness of the
submission, as if he were protecting himself from the inevitable rejection.
A return letter outlining terms was sent on June 26, which Faulkner
apparently did not receive or failed to open, or else it fell prey to his
cavalier attitude toward mail. He wrote again in November, and Four Seas
sent a copy of its June 26 letter, indicating that while the volume contained
several good things, the company would require a subvention: ". . . if you
were in a position to stand solely the manufacturing cost of the first edition
we might be willing to co-operate with you in trying to bring out this book,
paying you a royalty on each copy sufficient to bring back the return of
your original investment out of the sale of the first edition." Faulkner
replied: "As I have no money, I cannot very well guarantee the initial cost
of publishing this mss."[9] Next year, however, with Phil Stone's help, he

came up with sufficient subvention to publish *The Marble Faun* with Four
Seas. What he added to his letter in November suggests he did not believe
in *Orpheus;* for to the note about lack of money he admitted that, upon
rereading the manuscript, he could see some of the things "aren't particularly significant." The depreciation of his own work may have been merely
a defensive act, but it could also have been a hardheaded assessment that
what he had put together for presentation to Estelle was an inferior product; and his sense, a year later, that *The Marble Faun* was of sufficient quality
to justify the subvention, that is, a loan from Phil.

Four Seas promised November 1, 1924, publication, with $200 due on
signing and another $200 with proofs. What is remarkable is that with this,
his first book, Faulkner let Phil Stone handle all the details. Stone attended
to the correspondence, sent on the first check for $200, wrote a brief preface
and biographical sketch, and arranged for photographs, which Faulkner
never liked to pose for. Stone also handled the business end, providing a
list of people who might review *The Marble Faun* and a description of the
volume for publicity purposes. The Faulkner collections at the University
of Virginia and at the Humanities Research Center in Texas have files on
this matter, and astonishing is the degree to which Stone, with a law
business to run, took the time to handle Faulkner's affairs, while the writer
was not at all busy with his post office position. The two sides of the
arrangement are of considerable interest, since Stone would come to feel
he "owned" Faulkner. For his part, Faulkner relegated his friend to the
role of business manager, in which, while he would write the poems, his
manager would take care of them thereafter. The rift between the two
seems implicit in a situation where they appear more linked than ever.
Resentment was bound to surface, since Stone was acting out of great
benevolence, whereas Faulkner was role-playing the poet who eschewed
business matters.

Certainly *The Marble Faun,* with its title unconsciously borrowed from
Hawthorne, was not distinctive. When we examine these poems as correla-
tives of Faulkner's mind as he read and sought new ground, we find
synapses uncoordinated, connectives misdirected, linkages lost in excesses
of verbiage, and muddled thinking. Although these poems cannot be
definitively dated[10]—the dates April, May, and June 1919 indicated in the
volume may be those of conception, not revision and final versions—we
should nevertheless judge them as part of Faulkner's imagination in the
early 1920s.* Also, since he did submit the volume in 1924, we should view
it as something he considered and approved of before sending on. As an
example of revision between 1920 and 1924, "The Flowers That Died"
underwent nine rewritings (there are nine extant typescripts, all somewhat different from one another); and "I Will Not Weep for Youth"
experienced ten rewritings. Another, "Knew I Love Once," appeared in

*In an earlier typescript of *The Marble Faun* (at the University of Texas Humanities
Research Center), three of the sheets are dated 1920; also, there are titles to individual sections
or divisions: Prologue, Spring, Summer, Noon, Autumn, Winter, and Epilogue.

The Marble Faun in sonnet form, and then metamorphosed into the ten-line Poem XXXIII of *A Green Bough,* nine years later. As far as his early poetry was concerned, Faulkner was truly a man in motion: roaming back and forth, tinkering, altering, rarely satisfied, all indicating a writer who, while very much in his experimental stages, was meticulous.

Most strikingly, *The Marble Faun* reveals Faulkner's inability to deliver on first lines which promise a good deal: "The hills are resonant with soft humming," or "All day I run before a wind," or "The world stands without move or sound." Once the line ends, the poem falls into either stereotype (in language and thought) or a straining for significance. The language quickly breaks down or exhausts itself. "The world stands without move or sound / In this white silence gathered round / It like a hood." Followed by "It is so still / That earth lies without wish or will / To breathe." Or: "All day I run before a wind, / Keen and blue and without end, / Like a fox before the hounds." Or, finally: "The hills are resonant with soft humming; / It is a breeze that pauses, strumming / On the golden-wired stars / The deep full music to which was / The song of life through ages sung; . . ." "Golden-wired stars" on which the breeze is strumming destroys the initial impulse, for we have little sense of image or effect, or even what the makeup is of "golden-wired stars."

Several of the poems in their beginning have intimations of Shakespeare and Keats: that large, generalized effort to draw in with grandness, before later lines individualized. But such a method requires an epigrammatic or succinct quality Faulkner cannot deliver; so that his beginning generalization flattens out into discourse, losing the impulse in explanation, not gaining through development. Such observations are obvious, and they occurred to Faulkner, who came to recognize he had no vocation as a poet.

Yet *The Marble Faun* in several ways does give meaning to the career. We can start with the preface by Phil Stone, which is notable for its diminution of the work he was himself funding. Stone realized his friend was not a poet for the ages, and that he, Stone, had been caught between supporting a volume and publicizing his taste. By denigrating the collection, he decided not to look bad himself. "They are the poems of youth," he wrote. "One has to be at a certain age to write poems like these. They belong inevitably to that period of uncertainty and illusion. . . . They also have the defects of youth—youth's impatience, unsophistication and immaturity." He does state that the poems show promise: the work of a man "steeped in the soil of his native land, a Southerner by every instinct, and, more than that, a Mississippian."[11]

The collection is itself arbitrary—that is, while all the poems have natural settings and are clearly pastoral (as the title suggests), they have no inevitable sequencing, nor do they create any overall quality. Although one typescript does indicate division headings of seasonal change, the poems could easily be replaced by others without altering the volume. There is so little inevitability one senses an uncontrolled verbal frenzy. The first poem after the prologue, for example: "If I were free, then I would go / Where the first chill spring winds blow, / Wrapping a light shocked mountain brow / With shrilling tongues and swirling snow, / And fiery upward flaming, leap / From craggy teeth above each deep / Cold and wet with silence." This is spring, and it has dim intimations of "The Rite of Spring," but despite the craggy images without distinct rhythms or sufficient passion. Stereotypically, Pan is ever there, with his "shrill pipes," his foreshadowing of spring, his "sharp hoofed feet," and sense of danger in suggesting an alternate, sensual life.

In these poems of seasonal change and rioting of nature, Faulkner is nevertheless on the edge of discovery; so that the volume is valuable as a guided tour through his imagination in his middle twenties. *The Marble Faun* indicates that nature has assumed a sacred place in his life; that while within the natural world there is of course change, it is timeless: change within temporal stasis is one of Faulkner's great themes. Further, the poems indicate there is a profound inner life; and even though his body is elsewhere, in apparent waste, his real life lies in language. That "real life" is impervious to what the world thinks and to what is occurring to him temporally. *It* is eternal, it must be preserved, and it is salvation. Still further, it is a dangerous world; nature is not benign, nor is it fully accommodating. It is a testing of oneself, and Pan is ever there to create havoc. If man settles himself and his emotions in the temporal world, in nature he must move to a different set of coordinates. It is that wild, primitive, heathlike force which Faulkner sees as something he must flee to, away from city and town. In that respect, *The Marble Faun* offers us considerable insight into a very closefisted man.

In the lesser world, Faulkner, who did have an income from the post office, acquired a roadster which he painted white, and he became active in the Boy Scouts. As scoutmaster, he was a natural: interested in young people, knowledgeable about nature and woods, convivial when he was not being pushed socially. Faulkner took the troop to Waterford, a summer camp north of Oxford, where they lived in tents, learned woodlore, and played baseball. On other occasions, they went to Warren Lakes, in the vicinity of Holly Springs, with Dean Falkner, now sixteen, as one of the scouts. In the evenings, Faulkner told stories, usually of the horror kind which kept the boys strung out and interested. Several boys later commented that in the field Faulkner was like another person: giving, helpful, and yet an authority figure. The "Count No 'Count" aspect vanished once he felt the pressure of town and vocation relieved. The disparity between his forbidding and often unapproachable behavior in town and his behavior in camp, as everyone's uncle, suggests not two sides to his personality, but, rather, the extreme tension under which he was operating as a writer. True, he drank heavily while with the scouts—he was eventually dismissed for "moral reasons," i.e., drinking—but he seemed relieved of the burdens of life once he could describe trees, flowers, and animal tracks to the boys. It is very possible he continued to write while in camp, in the privacy of his tent, although we cannot accurately date any story from this time.

Meanwhile, as a diversion, he and Louis Jiggitts (his earlier tormentor) concocted an insurance scam, with the so-called Blue Bird Insurance Company; the company would offer insurance to students against failing courses on an elaborate scale worked out with a deliberately foggy formula. Two notices of the scale appeared in the *Mississippian* as large advertisements. "The professor's knowledge and experience plus the size of the class divided by the ignorance of his students. For example, where the ignorance of the class is predominant, the rate is low, as in the pharmacy department. On the other hand, the knowledge of the professor may off-set the ignorance, as in the freshman English classes, where the rate is very high."[12]

Several faculty members took the ploy seriously, replied, and that ended the scheme; as had an earlier one involving oil, signed by Count Wilhelm von Faulkner, Marquis de Lafayette (county), Postmaster-General (retired). Since these hijinks involved not a college freshman but a man in his twenty-sixth year, they cannot simply be dismissed. They suggest an overwhelming boredom, a personal sense of stagnation, a continued hostility toward authority, here focused not on family but on university, and a good many unresolved attitudes. These scams are not simply the work of a practical jokester, for once Faulkner got his mind in order, he did not make a practice of this. It indicates a young man who has, so far, fallen between desire and achievement.

The outward signs of Faulkner's life seemed to have changed little, and if someone had said he was the town eccentric with a penchant for liquor, who wrote a little poetry on the side, the report would be right. In few American writers have the internal world and external appearance been so far apart. But much of this was deliberate, role playing Faulkner insisted on to give him the opportunity to ripen out of sight. All the roles led into this one overriding fact: that whatever was going on had to occur behind disguises and veils, beyond the eyes of even his family. Stone would himself be completely fooled by what was happening in his friend, so successful was Faulkner in hiding himself. Those long silences, that indifference to what people thought, that ragged failure-oriented exterior were means by which he cultivated a persona, not to assert himself, but to wall himself behind.

But if the persona worked for the artist, it failed for the clerk. Prominent people complained about nondelivery of their mail or found their periodicals in the garbage can. Indeed, patrons of the post office, instead of asking for their mail at the window, went directly to the garbage to sift through for what they were expecting. Faulkner's days as postmaster were numbered, as were his days as a leader of the scouts. But the loss of salary in October 1924 did not seem to make much difference to him, even though he was indebted to Stone for $200, and, eventually, for $400, in connection with publication of *The Marble Faun*.

Faulkner agreed to pose for photographs, in Memphis. In one pose he is holding a pipe in his mouth, while his eyes are turned downward, in a pensive, contemplative gaze. The chin has firmed, and the nose, while fleshy, is well-shaped. His hair is suitably tousled, but not in disarray, an effort to capture the romantic role without looking effeminate or a social outcast. In the other photograph, his eyes are in an upward gaze, as if he were mesmerized by the Muse. Here one can see the slightness of the man from just above the waist, although he is not skimpy or shrunken.

These two photos he sent to the Four Seas Company for his first book. For the biographical sketch, the details are of interest, for the deception about his war service becomes more subtle, and he uses the "u" in the spelling of the old colonel's name, as follows:

> Born in Mississippi in 1897. Great-grandson of Col. W. C. Faulkner, C. S. A., author of "The White Rose of Memphis," "Rapid Ramblings in Europe," etc. Boyhood and youth were spent in Mississippi, since then has been (1) undergraduate (2) house painter (3) tramp, day laborer, dishwasher in various New England cities (4) Clerk in Lord and Taylor's book shop in New York City (5) bank- and postal clerk. Served during the war in the British Royal Air Force. A member of Sigma Alpha Epsilon Fraternity. Present temporary address, Oxford, Miss. "The Marble Faun" was written in the spring of 1919.[13]

Faulkner was now ready to move on, and the vehicle of his movement would be Sherwood Anderson. Before publication of *The Marble Faun,* on December 15, Faulkner met Anderson in New Orleans, where the older writer was now married to Elizabeth Prall. She had given Faulkner his job at the Lord & Taylor bookstore, through the intercession of Stark Young. In a sense, Faulkner was being passed along the network, from Young, an Oxonian, to Prall, now to Sherwood Anderson, perhaps the single most important contact of his literary life. Anderson was almost the perfect figure for a young writer to encounter early on. He would not be an influence but a presence: a good writer who was not so good so as to overwhelm a beginning novelist; not overbearing, but sympathetic, generous, and on most occasions, forgiving. Considering that Hemingway turned viciously on him and that Faulkner (and his friend, Spratling) gently mocked him, Anderson bore up with dignity. On a small scale, he did with Hemingway and Faulkner what Pound and Ford Madox Ford were doing on the continent for other poets and novelists. They were, more formally, impresarios; but then they had more varied material than Anderson had to work with, from Yeats and Eliot to Joyce and Lawrence. Before meeting him in New Orleans, Faulkner had been reading Anderson's stories, and he came to think *I'm a Fool* the second-best short fiction he had ever read, after *Heart of Darkness.* He read aloud some of the Anderson pieces to his friend Ben Wasson, whose home in Greenville he often visited.

Faulkner was infatuated with *I'm a Fool.* In some uncanny way, Anderson had come close to Faulkner's own youth, his use of deceptions and lies, his tendency toward disguises. The story is of a young man hiding himself in a skin he does not own; in presenting himself falsely; in losing what he desires because of his lie. It is about an America of class and caste, and someone who wants to break through in one forward shove, without the years of application it takes to gain a toehold. It uses horses as a source of upward mobility, but also as a means of depicting lowlife, America's margins: the class extremes of the country and its aspirations. But there is more to the story than that. It employs a language, a vernacular Faulkner was himself groping for. In late 1924, he needed still, as we have noted, a personal or distinctive voice. In *I'm a Fool*, he found that voice. The vernacular Mark Twain idiom and use of a narrator meant so much to Faulkner because they afforded him distance and, at the same time, intimacy. Further, the idiom illuminated that mixture of naiveté and sophistication he would himself soon cultivate.

On the more personal level, *I'm a Fool* plays in and out of Faulkner's own relationship to Estelle. The narrator has class and caste problems with the girl he meets at the race track, and he assumes a false name and past to bring himself up. Yet even as he does this, he recognizes that she accepts him as is—but his sense of inferiority forces him back on lies and deceptions to overcome feelings of failure. He must try to transform himself into another person to become acceptable. Faulkner could not have missed how the story bites into a kind of America he himself knew intimately, foreshadowing not only *Absalom, Absalom!* but *An American Tragedy* and *The Great Gatsby*.

I'm a Fool was a story for Faulkner's youth, the shadowy retelling of his problems, his dilemmas, his disguises. *Heart of Darkness*, the far greater work, was a story for his maturity. Conrad's novella conveyed to Faulkner moral and psychological weight and a mature narrator in ways few other fictional works provided. But *Heart of Darkness* could not be a large presence now—it was for a writer who had begun to find himself, not for one still flailing around.

Anderson became the most important figure in Faulkner's still very young career. Anderson was solid, not "arty," and his attitude toward America was similar to Faulkner's, even at this time: their mutual suspicion of urban values, their dislike of technological progress and industrial riches, their detestation of standardization or conformity in behavior and expectation. As he had demonstrated in *Winesburg, Ohio*, Anderson was a rebel, or at least a man who sympathized with underdogs and outsiders. "The Book of the Grotesque," at the beginning of that collection of Winesburg stories, describes Anderson's fascination with what he calls "grotesques." "The grotesques were not all horrible. Some were amusing, some almost beautiful, and one, a woman, all drawn out of shape."[14] Anderson's conception of this "race" was quite appealing: "It was his [the old writer-narrator's] notion that the moment one of the people took one of the truths to himself, called it his truth, and tried to live by it, he became a grotesque and the truth he embraced a falsehood."[15] This inversion of values, in which the man of faith is deemed a grotesque by a society reversing truth and falsehood, accommodated Faulkner's growing sense of irony, his own use of "grotesques" to carry his sense of society's reversal of values. In this, progress is retrograde, success is failure, advancement an aspect of decline, and high position a sign of bad faith. Such ideas are commonplace now, but in the first quarter of the century, though while not new, they were still fresh; and they were the stuff of fiction, as also seen in Hemingway, Dreiser, and parts of Fitzgerald. The denizens of Winesburg become hostages to this value system. Anderson perceived that the small town and village were being pushed aside by the metropolis; that values developed in the small place were traduced in the larger.

When Faulkner swam into the older writer's life, Anderson was newly remarried and only recently settled into New Orleans. Faulkner had casually visited New Orleans before, but this time, in 1924, it would be a major move, an alternative to what he saw as stagnation in Oxford. The city was proving a magnet for talent, and much of that talent was gathered in the *Double Dealer*, which had already published his poem *Portrait* in 1922. But while the *Double Dealer* was an exciting new magazine (started in January 1921), there were other attractions in New Orleans: the sense of a Southern literary revival in general, the presence of many literary personages, the growth of the city as a cultural center, such as has been associated with New York's Greenwich Village, and, much later, with San Francisco in the 1950s. The environment and what it promised a young writer could not have been more different from Oxford.

The focus was the *Double Dealer*. It had the same influence on Southern culture that the *Egoist* in England and the *Dial* in northeastern America would have. It was established, in part, as a response to H. L. Mencken's ill-tempered remark that the South represented, culturally, a wasteland. The periodical would, eventually, gain recognition from Mencken that it was rescuing the South from a backwater existence. Founded by Julius Weis Friend and Albert Goldstein, with help from Basil Thompson and John McClure (who reviewed *The Marble Faun* favorably, saying "Mr. Faulkner promises fine things"), it became a weekly with an illustrious list of contributors: Faulkner (beginning in January–February 1925), Anderson, Pound, Crane, Wilder, Wilson, Hemingway, Ransom, Cowley, Djuna Barnes, Allen Tate, Robert Penn Warren, and several others of almost equal stature. Some careers, like Faulkner's, were just beginning; while others, like Anderson's and Pound's, were already well launched. Southern writers joined with those from other parts of the country, principally the northeast, to fill the pages.

The title of the magazine came, of course, from William Congreve's 1693 play, *The Double Dealer;* and the line on the masthead also derived from Congreve: "I can deceive them both by speaking the truth." The magazine was less interested in the ironies generated by the seventeenth-century playwright than it was in presenting something of the revolt in the arts slowly entering the country from abroad. Contemporary heroes were

Pound and Joyce, as well as Yeats, Eliot, Lawrence, and to a lesser extent Conrad and Ford. The directive of the publishers and editors requested their authors to speak to the nature of the new. "We mean to deal double, to show the other side, to throw open the back windows stuck in their sills and disuse, smutted over long since against even a dim beam's penetration."[16] Not very elegant prose to introduce a publication of some considerable elegance, but the editors and publishers were businessmen, not poets or fiction writers. Their prose may have been muddy, but their aim was true: to hit the target of modernism from all directions. The magazine lasted six years.

While it is an exaggeration to say Faulkner came to New Orleans to join the *Double Dealer* circle, or to bend himself to the wishes of Sherwood Anderson, there is little question this cultural ferment had special meaning for him. He had planned to go abroad, but the New Orleans artistic milieu caused him to postpone those plans until he sailed on July 7, 1925. Faulkner had already been at the quarters of the *Double Dealer* during the winter of 1921, and had announced—according to James K. Feibleman—"I could write a play like *Hamlet* if I wanted to."[17] Since everyone in the office was drinking, we can assume Faulkner was not quite sober when he made that statement. At the very end of 1924, he finally did meet Sherwood Anderson: the forty-eight-year-old, well-regarded writer and the twenty-seven-year-old novice. Within seven months, Faulkner had completed the manuscript of *Soldiers' Pay* and was under contract, but now he was still the author only of bits and pieces, and one volume of poetry (published December 15).

The Andersons lived in the Vieux Carré, in the Pontalba Building, located on the south side of Jackson Square. The immediate area was an artists' quarter set within a larger, bohemian section. The location is worth mentioning because it surely contributed to the entire experience—meeting Anderson, of course, but meeting him in what looked like a writer's paradise. In a fictional sketch called "A Meeting South," published in 1925 in the *Dial*, Anderson wrote of his encounter with a young writer, Faulkner; and Faulkner himself commented later on the experience. There was considerable drama, inasmuch as Anderson met and helped the two foremost fiction writers of the period—Hemingway and Faulkner—and was repaid by a savage attack by Hemingway and a milder one by Faulkner. Something about the older writer made him vulnerable to ridicule, and yet it was his qualities of openness, generosity, and willingness to help that attracted younger writers to him.

In the series of question-and-answer sessions he conducted at the University of Virginia (in 1958), Faulkner commented on Anderson. He spoke of happening to be in New Orleans in November and making a chance call on Prall. ". . . I wasn't going to bust in on Mr. Anderson without an invitation from him. I didn't think that I would see him at all, that he would probably be in his study working, but it happened that he was in the room at the time, and we talked and we liked one another from the start, and it was just the chance that I had gone to call on Miss Prall."[18] In the same sequence of questions, Faulkner indicates he had not gone originally to New Orleans to join an artists' group but to "get a job in a ship and go to Europe . . . it was no pull to be a part of a literary group, no." He then elaborates on how comfortable it is to be with people who share an artist's concerns, and how problematic it is to be a writer in America. What emerges is Faulkner's early recognition of the difficulties ahead in attempting to be a writer in a culture so inimical to artists. He compares Anderson with Balzac and Dickens in this respect: the American writer has to be much tougher than his French or English counterpart. "It may be it took somebody a little tougher than Anderson to cope with America." In the France and England of the earlier novelists, "you could carry your tender edges around without getting them bruised."[19]

Continuing with comments about Anderson, Faulkner gives us a glimpse of what may have been growing contempt for the man who was so generous to him: ". . . he didn't have the ruthlessness to, well, to rob from any [and] every source he wanted." Faulkner caught the particular attitude an important writer needs, ruthless toward others, ruthless toward himself, his art first. "He probably didn't have a concept of a cosmos in miniature which Balzac and Dickens had, that all he knew was this single man who was humble and ignorant and dreamed better than he was afraid he might ever reach." Faulkner attributes this lessening of achievement (after *Winesburg*) to Anderson's lack of interest in people, the fact that "he knew too little about people, he wasn't interested in people in the way a writer's got to be. . . . he don't have to like people at all, he can loathe people, but he's got to be interested in them, and Anderson didn't know people, he was afraid of people."[20]

Faulkner picked up the contradictions: the burly man of the people who presented sympathetically the marginal losers he had known in the Midwest and in his travels. That one kind of person he repeated and repeated. Anderson came from a personal background with a very different set of assumptions from Faulkner's. Whereas the latter had grown up with belles lettres, Anderson was part of a tradition which dealt more with history and philosophy, with ideas of progress, technology, social advancement, and retrogression. Anderson derived from a tradition which had listened to Emerson and Thoreau, and now to Robert Ingersoll. These writers, and especially Ingersoll, looked forward to a transformed man, to a new order based on labor; and Ingersoll himself became a prophet of progress which, while denying utopias, was founded on labor and the laboring man. Ingersoll believed in invention (which dominates several of Anderson's fictions); but he also believed fiercely in individual independence and liberation, the self emerging stronger than ever after adversity and struggle: ". . . we enslave the winds and waves," he wrote at one point.[21] He turned Emerson's sense of man transforming himself into a paean for American democracy, and it was especially appealing to Midwestern writers and thinkers: heartland people. Anderson was part of a group of writers familiar not only with Robert Ingersoll, Emerson, and Thoreau, but with Henry George and his single-tax theory, Herbert Spencer and his theories of progressive evolution, Edward Bellamy and his utopia. Their political hero was the "great commoner" William Jennings Bryan. Besides Anderson, in this grouping we have other "rough writers," Edgar Lee Masters, Carl Sandburg, Vachel Lindsay, and Theodore Dreiser. These were writers with little or no linkage to the East and Northeast, and their material remained small towns, small people, the legacy of Abraham Lincoln. When Sandburg wrote his monumental life of Lincoln, he was, in a sense, summing it up for entire generations of middle-American writers.

Anderson had little of Faulkner's feel for belletristic material. The older man would go not to the French symbolists but to Twain and Emerson and theories of progress buried deep in America's sense of itself. The world of foreign writers was alien to him; whereas Faulkner, from his beginnings as a poet, had imitated international writers. Although the two seemed congenial, there was little common ground. Faulkner became an American novelist, overcoming both regionalism and tutelage to foreign literatures, but his Americanism was of a completely different kind from Anderson's. His was not only the larger talent, it was a talent which absorbed others' strategies and devices and made them his own—the mark of the major writer. Anderson, on the contrary, could look only to himself. He was impervious to the winds of modernism and to what it meant in artistic terms; and when he peered into himself, he saw much the same at every stage of his career.

What did Anderson see when he met Faulkner and began to have dinner with him fairly regularly, at that Pontalba Building apartment? In "A Meeting South," Anderson wrote his impression of the poet; it is close to the way Faulkner chose to present himself to the more famous writer. The portrait Anderson draws is very revealing, for it shows Faulkner romanticizing himself, a *poète maudit* in the tradition of Keats and the French symbolists. He is all roles and disguises: the limp, the war record, the uninhibited drinking, the inability to sleep, the losing of himself in art ("all for poetry"). Faulkner plays the Southerner to the hilt, and, most of all, plays the artist who drinks himself into oblivion because of a pain beyond pain. Much of it was a put-on, of course, a source of personal need and a source of amusement; but Anderson presents it seriously, as something the South, not the Midwest, produces.

Faulkner is described physically as being gentlemanly, with "sensitive, rather thin, lips, which produce a little smile." Anderson presents him as a "cripple," which is then translated as a "slight limp," accompanying the look of pain "that occasionally drifted across his face." The "little laugh" was intended to be jolly, "but did not quite achieve its purpose."[22] Faulkner is "small and delicately built," and the limp is the result of both legs having been broken in a crash, one of them in three places; additionally, his scalp had been "badly torn" and some facial bones "had been splintered."[23] The sum of these injuries has led to almost constant pain, relieved only by whiskey. Further, injuries added to a sensitive spirit have resulted in stretched, taut nerves which prevent sleeping and make peace of mind possible only by drinking. All roads lead back to alcohol. And Anderson does describe the famous Faulkner overcoat, whose pockets held huge containers of whiskey, made, according to Faulkner, by a Negro who worked for the family and did nothing but run a still. The social side of this implies a planter background, a family and an estate of some substance. At one point in the story, Anderson says the young poet reveals that his father is down to his last few hundred acres, heavily mortgaged, because Negro labor is no longer available.

In all, the story fed by David, the young writer, to Anderson, the narrator, is not that of a real person, but of a Southern myth or legend. All the odds and ends of the Southern experience are dovetailed into this young poet's brief existence, and he relives the last seventy-five years of Southern history and culture. And that sad, bright little smile on the thin lips is his recognition of the tragedy of it all, somehow embodied in himself—after all, Anderson has called it "A Meeting South." The story, while not much in itself, was prophetic, since Faulkner's pose would, inevitably, be transformed into Faulkner's achievement; and while that thin smile conveyed to Anderson in late 1924 the pain of war injuries, it would later convey the tortured anguish of the South.

This romantic figure caught the eye of Anderson: the pose, the roleplaying, the limp, the head wound, the hard drinking; all of them adding up to a personage of some interest. Faulkner on this particular trip to New Orleans, in November, did not stay long, and returned to Oxford for Christmas with his family; but by January 4, 1925, he was back in New Orleans, accompanied by Phil Stone. The New Orleans atmosphere served as a release, because in a brief time, Faulkner began to publish with some consistency in three areas: short fictional sketches, more poetry, and further criticism. He also announced the publication of a second volume of poetry, to be called "A Greening Bough," which was eventually *A Green Bough* (1933). But, most important, he was to begin his first novel, *Soldiers' Pay*. Everything in his imagination had been in place, and either New Orleans was the catalyst or merely escaping Oxford for a place receptive to artistic endeavor renewed him. Further, we cannot overestimate what it meant to him to have in hand his first volume, *The Marble Faun*, in its edition of one thousand copies. For someone who had created so many legends about himself, the reality of the book was essential to keep him from sinking into romantic sentiment; or into a condition in which he could not himself differentiate between reality and role-playing.

The *Double Dealer* (for January–February 1925) became the recipient of some of this barrage. "Dying Gladiator" is an aptly titled poem in that issue of the magazine. It is appropriate in that it foreshadows Faulkner's first longer fiction, *Soldiers' Pay*, with its images of death and dying, and its dying gladiator in the shape of Donald Mahon, brought home a vegetable and a burden on others. Further, the poem, like the novel, which he completed in May, maintains the level of romantic pose and reinforces that sad view of life which became his under the influence of Housman.

The same issue of the *Double Dealer* contained his essay called "On Criticism" and eleven brief sketches of life in New Orleans titled, appropriately, "New Orleans." The essay is of considerable interest because it suggests Faulkner, in an Arnoldian tradition, recognized that a great (and new) literature required a great (and new) audience for it. Critics and reviewers in periodicals and magazines should educate the neophyte reader in taste so as to make him ready for the great writers. Faulkner wrote, "The American critic blinds, not only the audience but himself as well, to the prime essential. His trade becomes mental gymnastics: he becomes a reincarnation of the sideshow spellbinder of happy memory, holding the yokelry enravished not with what he says, but how he says it."[24] Faulkner has grasped one of the cultural difficulties in any democratic society: the very openness of the society permits anyone to be a critic, and educated taste (an Arnoldian criterion) is minimized.

Arnold, of course, foresaw all this a good sixty to seventy years earlier; but now, in America, Faulkner prophesies what would be his own reception. As he published one masterpiece after another in the 1930s, critics like Clifton Fadiman (in the *New Yorker*) trashed each effort as unintelligible drivel. To be modern, Faulkner foresaw, was to become marginal, a cultural outcast. When critics of taste do exist in America, they "have no status: the magazines which set the standard ignore them." The chief accusation: "The English review criticises the book, the American the author." The writer is always at a disadvantage; he cannot compete with the critic: "he is too busy writing and also he is organically unfitted for the contest." Even worse, the critic, once accepted, is judged infallible by his readers; and since he has frequent contact, he has the last word. Writing this even as he is writing *Soldiers' Pay*, Faulkner has foreseen his own critical reception.

Perhaps the most significant part of his output was the eleven fictional sketches entitled "New Orleans," none much more than a page. And at almost the same time he was publishing these sketches, he was writing sixteen short fictions for the *Times-Picayune* of New Orleans, this work paralleling the beginning of his first novel. The "New Orleans" group are like Czerny exercises for pianists, to keep fingers supple and minds agile. They bear out the title: brief vignettes of New Orleans life, but none too raw for the pages of the magazine. Perhaps the most compelling is the first, called "Wealthy Jew," since it has lines which carry through Faulkner's career: "I love three things: gold; marble and purple; splendor, solidity, color." While the start may seem to have a slight anti-Semitic tinge—in the stereotypical identity of the Jew with wealth and gold—the sketch opens up into a sympathetic view of the "wealthy Jew." In Faulkner's hands, he becomes a kind of wise man of the ages, the man who has outlasted all efforts to extinguish him. "But I am old, all the pain and passion and sorrow of the human race are in this breast."²⁵

In a sense, by their ability to survive, Jews have been triumphant. And here we sense Faulkner's sympathy for those who endure and survive, whatever the historical odds against them. "No soil is foreign to my people, for have we not conquered all lands with the story of your Nativity?"²⁶ Or: "The seas of Destiny foam by. Let them! My people will crest them." This identification with the Jew which opens the group of sketches was the first public statement in what became Faulkner's problematic feelings about Jews. He had, of course, known the Friedman family in Oxford, but his response to Jews was often intertwined with his feelings about cities and urban values; as, for example, in *Pylon*. There, the "wealthy Jew," Feinman, represents all the stereotypes of the race, and his value system, to make a buck, is juxtaposed with the aviators and jumpers, who place little value on money. In more general terms, Faulkner never shared the virulent anti-Semitism which surfaced in many of his contemporaries: Hemingway, Wolfe, and Pound in particular; but also in Masters, James Branch Cabell, O'Neill, Lindsay, George Jean Nathan, E. E. Cummings, and Dreiser.* Of course, the *Double Dealer* was itself financed and supported by Jews, and along the way in later years Faulkner would be helped by Jewish editors and publishers. By the time of World War II, his earlier uncertain attitudes toward Jews had definitely shifted from stereotyping them to deep sympathy and understanding.

Possibly more than any other early work, the sketches for the *Double Dealer* and the *Times-Picayune* serve as a transition in Faulkner's career: bridging the writing exercises and poetry going nowhere (however important they were for him personally) and his more considered work, which led into his masterpieces of the late 1920s and the 1930s. That he was writing these *Times-Picayune* selections at about the same time he was beginning *Soldiers' Pay* must be stressed; not so much because the novel owed anything directly to the short stories, but because he had snapped the cycle of trying to express himself in poetry. Whatever was in him, and it was apparently varied, broad, and deep, would now increasingly emerge as fiction. Poetry was relegated to a secondary position. Since Faulkner had not in the eight or so years of writing poetry forged a distinctive voice, or displaced his obvious influences, the decision he made to pursue expression in prose must be viewed as exactly the right one. The meeting with Anderson did not trigger the decision to write fiction—those brief vi-

---

*Writing to Mencken, another anti-Semite, Dreiser gave his view of New York: "New York to me is a scream—a Kike's dream of a Ghetto. The lost tribe has taken the island." In another place, he commented: "Don't care for it. Too many Jews." (Quoted by W. A. Swanberg, *Dreiser* [New York: Scribner's, 1965], p. 167).

gnettes for the *Double Dealer* came when Anderson was away; but the encounter and association with Anderson certainly strengthened his resolve to emerge as a fiction writer. The dedication of *Sartoris,* his third novel, would acknowledge his debt to Anderson.*

Further, there was a feeling in the South that a literary renaissance was in the offing, and that it needed a leader around whom critics and creative people could rally. In 1921, a *Double Dealer* editorial by Basil Thompson, one of the founders and now an editor, announced that the South was looking for "some doughty, clear-visioned penman to emerge from the sodden marshes of Southern literature." This editorial was reprinted in the 1924 memorial number, at almost the time Faulkner was swimming into view; and it would seem to him, if not to the magazine, he was the man being called for. Thompson is firm that the Southern potboiler must vanish, along with the "little Eva" stuff, the "lynching-bee" material, the Kentucky colonel and "beautiful Quadroon stuff." He prophesies: ". . . a surer, saner, more virile, less sentimental literature must come in. By all the symptoms the reaction is near at hand."[27]

Faulkner's postponement of his trip to Europe was not chance; something indicated to him that there was a juncture of his talent, place, and time: that privileged moment, spot of time, or epiphany writers since Wordsworth have spoken of as the "magical moment." After the new year (1925), Faulkner had returned to New Orleans, but instead of seeking a boat for England, he stayed with Elizabeth Prall while Anderson was away lecturing, and then, after another brief visit to Oxford, moved into his own place until July, when he finally did sail to Italy. His tiny apartment, where he remained for four months (from March through July), was at 624 Orleans Alley, now called Pirates Alley; and his neighbor was the artist William Spratling. Faulkner's "apartment" was in reality a room on another floor; they apparently shared a bathroom. Although Spratling was clearly homosexual, he and Faulkner became drinking and carousing partners, and the artist assumed no small place in the writer's life. Spratling at this time was only twenty-four, an orphan from childhood, with a strong professional drive, but socially an outsider. It seemed like a perfect arrangement, especially as Faulkner needed privacy in order to work on *Soldiers' Pay.* In those four months, he brought the novel near completion.**

Both the *Double Dealer* and the *Times-Picayune* paid very small fees—twenty dollars for five sketches sold to the newspaper—but payment of

---

*Faulkner's long review of Anderson's work appeared in the Dallas *Morning News* (Sunday, April 26, 1925). He is certain Anderson's stories in *Winesburg* and *Horses and Men* are his most considerable work. As noted above, Faulkner felt *I'm a Fool* was the finest of American short stories, and not the least because of its juxtaposition of men and horses. Anderson's sympathy for horses created a strong attraction between the two men; horses would become a sizable element in Faulkner's work, identified with a world he lamented as disappearing. Their history and the "history of man are intermingled beyond any unraveling; separate both are mortal, as one body they partake of the immortality of the gods" (*William Faulkner: New Orleans Sketches,* ed. Carvel Collins [New York: Random House, 1958], p. 136).

**The plaque outside the apartment on Pirates Alley mispunctuates *Soldiers' Pay* as *Soldier's Pay.*

any kind encouraged Faulkner to believe he could support himself in Europe by writing. All of this took place without the actual presence of Anderson; but even without the leading figure in New Orleans, the atmosphere was exciting. The rejuvenation of the Southern cultural scene was in the making, and he had the opportunity to be near the center.

In several ways, the *Times-Picayune* stories served as a quarry for Faulkner. But even when they don't foreshadow later work—although several do—they provide a good indicator of the slippery nature of his imagination as it began to grapple with new materials and new ways of representing them. Some intimations are slight indeed. Yet others are remarkably prescient of an imagination awakening to its own possibilities. "The Kingdom of God," in the April 26, 1925, issue, for example, merely sketches in an idiot boy with a narcissus in his fist; but the idiot clearly will become Benjy in *The Sound and the Fury*, and the brother protecting him in the sketch prefigures a brother in the novel, although not specifically Quentin. "Yet always in his slobbering, vacuous face were his two eyes of a heartbreaking blue, and gripped tightly in one fist was a narcissus." The centerpiece of the story is the idiot and his need for the narcissus; for when the flower becomes broken, he sets up a bellowing which can be stopped only by its repair. *The Sound and the Fury*, four years later, reads on its final page: "The broken flower drooped over Ben's fist and his eyes were empty and blue and serene again as cornice and façade flowed smoothly once more from left to right." Flower, blue eyes, empty expression in a vacuous face: the shaping of Benjy is unmistakable.

Less vivid is the intimation of Lena Grove* in *Light in August*, foreshadowed dimly in "Out of Nazareth," in the issue for April 12, 1925. Here the entrance of a young boy named David sets up, first, a brief meditation on the beauty of men ("beautiful as gods, as no woman can ever be"); second, the presence of Spratling, whose "hand has been shaped to a brush as mine has (alas!) not" and, third, how David "reminded one of a pregnant woman in his calm belief that nature, the earth which had spawned him would care for him," that he "now need only wait." Even more than this brief intimation of Lena and her patience, her expectations, we have David's movement over the landscape, living from moment to moment, prefiguring Lena's journey from Alabama to Mississippi in search of her still unborn child's father. David's physical beauty, however, sets up other considerations, inasmuch as Spratling's insistence that he model for him establishes a sexual context for the boy which Lena defuses by her condition.

"Yo Ho and Two Bottles of Rum," which appeared on September 27, 1925, well after Faulkner had departed for Europe, looks both forward and backward. There is the conception of a dead body decaying in the heat, here a Chinese cabin boy killed by mistake: " 'He won't keep long in this latitude.' "[28] The remainder of the story is made up of efforts to bury the servant among his own people, on an island off Cambodia point, near the

---

*Named after a small town in Mississippi, Lena Grove (I am indebted to Professor Ilse Lind for pointing this out to me).

mainland of Siam. The journey into the interior, with drunken white sailors accompanied by large numbers of Orientals, has early glimmers of *As I Lay Dying*. What links this story and the later novel of journey and death is Faulkner's sense of a death carrying forward into the lives of those around the dead person; further, his recognition that death has strange consequences in the ceremonies which follow, and his awareness that even when the death is ignominiously that of a servant and the procession unruly and drunken, there is still ritual, ceremony, something holy.

But the story looks backward as much as forward. The hand of Conrad and Maugham lies heavily here, and it demonstrates how poorly Faulkner imitates when he is under other writers' direct influence. The situations are Conradian, the sentiments Maugham's: that reaching for meaning which lies beyond what the author can achieve recalls the latter. The language is inflated, vague adjectives and nouns striving for wonder and awe: implacable and implacability, inscrutable, eternal, wallowing (for the ship), impenetrable. Only later, when he had matured, did Faulkner assimilate Conrad, and then the latter is represented not by particular scenes or language but by a method of perceiving and a moral/psychological dimension linking the two authors. But by then, Faulkner had written himself into the equal of Conrad.

In "The Liar," we have ambience rather than specifics, although the beginning of the story does have intimations of Murry Falkner's livery stable; and the overall setting of store and railroad recalls Oxford when Faulkner was growing up. The casual opening, with townsmen relaxing at the store, the owner himself laid-back, has that country setting we find in the Snopes trilogy. The owner, Will, prefigures Will Varner of *The Hamlet* (1940), and one of the men, the liar Ek, has a name that could be a Snopes's. The incident, rapidly passed over, of the horse that gets free and runs through Miss Harmon's house foreshadows the wild horses episode of *The Hamlet*, and Faulkner's use of horses in more general terms— as the untamed and unmastered symbol of nature. The story itself, however, lacks center; little more than a joke on a liar telling the truth.

Other stories which appeared in the *Times-Picayune* have less direct linkage to later work; but there is the sense that these pieces act as connective tissue. They were bringing Faulkner out into the open, making him reveal a little more of his hand as a writer. In his poetry, he hid behind influences and borrowed voices; but in the fictions, he was forced to forgo artificiality and emerge. That is their chief value, as revelation. They serve something of the same function as the brief stories of *in our time* did in Hemingway's early career: as establishing a mode which permitted the writer to break through. In Hemingway's case, the vignettes were almost the voice; in Faulkner's, there was still some way to go.

"Sunset," for example, in the May 24 issue, starts with a news bulletin about the killing of a Negro ("Black Desperado Slain"). Although this Negro has little relationship to Joe Christmas, the idea of a black man on the run, trapped by the sheriff, and then shot to bits, resonates in

Faulkner's work and surfaces in *Light in August*. The black in "Sunset" is seeking Africa, and he is willing to pay his way; but he is misled, relieved of his money, and when he feels threatened by a "wild animal" in what he thinks is Africa, he shoots—until he is trapped and is himself shot to death. Yet while the story is simplistic—a kind of tragic one-joke tale—the prose begins to raise itself, especially near the end.

> Here was the wind coming up; the branches and bushes about him whipped suddenly to a gale fiercer than any yet; flattened and screamed, and melted away under it. And he, too, was a tree caught in that same wind: he felt the dull blows of it, and the rivening of himself into tattered and broken leaves. The gale died away, and all broken things were still. His black, kind, dull, once-cheerful face was turned up to the sky and the cold, cold stars. Africa or Louisiana: what care they?[29]

This story, too, looks back to Conrad, with intimations of his "Amy Foster" running through: the misunderstood, linguistically confused foreigner who cannot be accepted anywhere. "Sunset" is full of glimmers, and with hindsight we can catch the real Faulkner lurking in its shadows.

"The Cobbler" in the *Times-Picayune* was an expanded version of "The Cobbler" sketch (1925) in the *Double Dealer*, and no more adaptable to Faulkner's talent than was the earlier form. "The Kid Learns" is also an expanded version of an earlier piece in the *Double Dealer*, "Frankie and Johnny." In this latter instance, we can trace some changes which have fictional resonance. The early version is a one-dimensional, one-page description of a tough guy and his girl compared to two ferryboats: ships passing in the dark, before they sight each other. The expanded version, "The Kid Learns," is full of perceptive materials, especially if we read it as a shadowy suggestion of Faulkner's own life. As Johnny, the Kid is, once again, a young tough, waiting for his moves to get to the top, where the "Wop" is now king. "Gimme five years, though, and it'll be Johnny Gray." He must learn his apprenticeship, while the "Wop" remains on top; and then, once he's learned "to be good," he can move. He recognizes that "They ain't anybody good from the jump."[30] The line of development may be from young tough to smart hood, but it also parallels Faulkner's own sense of what will catapult him to the top as a writer, a position now precariously held by Anderson.

Crossing Johnny's path just as he prepares himself to wait for his turn to rule is a young girl, one of Faulkner's characteristic "flat young" bodies. When Johnny sees her, he enters another level of desire: not only for power but for her. And when the "Wop" begins to manhandle the girl, Johnny must act—although he knows his plans for the future will be disrupted or destroyed. He beats up the mobster, whisks the girl away to a safe place, and now must face the showdown, a kind of frontier shootout in which the older mobster holds all the trumps. At the end of the story, Johnny finds his hand taken by "Little Sister Death." The action is melodramatic, as it should be for Frankie and Johnny, but more than that it raises questions of Faulkner's perception of Estelle. For if his preparation for a career is revealed by Johnny's destructive choice, then the latter's relationship to the girl—physically like Estelle—also has personal resonance. Still several years before he married the divorced Estelle, Faulkner saw the doom in it, and yet, like Johnny, could not help himself.

Though the difference in writing was only a few months, the later story is revealing, whereas the earlier one is simply an exercise. One reason for the greater revelation of the *Times-Picayune* story may have been Faulkner was moving along on his novel, and that extended piece of writing forced him to re-examine his personal impulses, his reasons for writing, the line of development of every aspect of his life. In that meditation on self, career and personal life suddenly crossed; his career was not linear, but intermixed with other needs or desires, and the two could not be reconciled.

Finally, we should not forget the entire series was introduced by the title "Mirrors of Chartres Street," which appeared on February 8. The mirrors here are not only held up to Chartres Street in the French Quarter, but to Faulkner himself. Mirrors played a huge role in the poetry he had cherished as a very young man, and surely he had in mind Mallarmé's frequent use of the mirror image. In Mallarmé and other French symbolists, the image is the very standard-bearer of creation; for the mirror not only reflects, it creates the dualism so necessary for the making of art. Faulkner had that in mind, and also the fact that every time he held a mirror up to nature he was holding it up to himself.

Chapter Eight

The Wasteland

NOT ALL STIRRINGS in Faulkner's imagination, however, were literary; nor were they linked to words. Amidst the welter of young women who passed through his life, most of them fleetingly, while he waited for Estelle, was one who more than caught his fancy; she captured his imagination. Marriage to her—and Faulkner proposed and was rejected, probably several times—might have been interesting, but would have proved, ultimately, disastrous. For she had such deep emotional problems of her own that Faulkner would have had to console her when he was prepared to think only of himself. But the attraction held, and it superseded the others: Gertrude Stegbauer, from Ben Wasson's Charleston office; one Shirley Kirkwood in Oxford, herself recipient of a barrage of love letters and even poems—she married and left Oxford; a coed from Natchez, named Elise Huntington—how deep Faulkner's involvement, if any, went, we cannot tell, but she married a medical student. Faulkner even showed interest in Lida Oldham's niece, sending her letters, sketches, other writings; and he would be attracted by Margery Kalom Gumble, wife of another *Double Dealer* contributor. What is striking about these "attachments"—some superficial, some less so—is how firmly these young women were connected to another world from Faulkner's. They married into an active, often professional world; and their rejection of the poet— if it was indeed rejection—only reinforced his marginality. We get the feel of the Mann story "Tonio Kröger," in which Tonio prowls the margins of life while others dance and enjoy themselves: the artist must suffer his isolation. Faulkner played that romantic stereotype to the hilt in the months before he left for Europe.

One woman, however, could not be that easily shuffled out of his imagination. Her name was Helen Baird, and superficially she seemed an unlikely candidate for Faulkner's interest. She did have the right figure, boyishly slim, very small (four feet eleven inches or so), almost wispy. When he saw her in a bathing suit, he noted the deep scars she had suffered from burns in her childhood. Profoundly flawed as a physical specimen, emotionally and psychologically she hardly seemed at peace with herself. She was, as Faulkner wrote much later, "a sullen-jawed yellow-eyed belligerent humorless gal in a linen dress and sunburned bare legs sitting on Spratling's balcony and not thinking even a hell of a little bit of me that afternoon, maybe already decided not to."[1]

There was, in fact, little to think much of. Faulkner was this little fellow with a mustache whose bedraggled look was the reverse of his good opinion of himself. Helen reached well beyond all the poses and role-playing to get at the real man, and she wasn't impressed. Unless one was predisposed to accept Faulkner on his own terms, that he was doing everything for the sake of art, there was little reason to find him prepossessing, or even socially acceptable. Further, Helen was so full of her own needs, which made her not only sullen but sarcastic, caustic, witty, defensive, that she was, at twenty-one, hardly in a position to respond sympathetically to a not so budding poet of twenty-seven. Still further, under all her defensiveness, Helen had a hard, practical streak, and Faulkner's type of existence did not appeal to her wifely or motherly instincts. She looked for a decent, equitable, moderate life, and what he brought to the relationship was little but an edgy peril. While living at the edge was suitable for him—*he* was the artist—it was, she perceived quickly, the opposite for her.

Yet withal, she was attracted to him, but as an opposite; whereas he saw in her something very different: high spirits, a painful existence, a human being capable of considerable depth of feeling. What he apparently missed, or else chose to ignore, was her practicality and deeper longing for a secure life. In his fullest portrait of Helen, as Charlotte Rittenmeyer in *The Wild Palms*, she is quite different from what she actually was, although Faulkner caught some wildness in her character. Charlotte is possessed, and yet practical—the little dolls she makes indicate her ability to work in small matters even while her temperament carries her into a passionate but self-destructive attachment. If we project Helen forward into Charlotte, as well as into the several other fictional roles Faulkner wrote for her, we note his perception of her was as ambivalent as hers was of him. Each perceived more than either was going to admit; and while she eluded Faulkner by making a safe marriage with another, he translated his sense of her into ambiguous literary roles.

In the spring of 1925, when Faulkner met Helen, we run up against an even more complicated and textured circumstance. The meeting took place through James R. Baird, a reporter whom Spratling knew and invited to his parties. Spratling said Helen was originally "his girl," and that Faulkner stole her; but since Spratling was homosexual, the story served, probably, as a cover. But whatever the checkered meeting and linkages of Helen to both Spratling and Faulkner, we come to something else: that Faulkner at this time was shaping *Soldiers' Pay* in deeply autobiographical terms, and not more so than in his relationship to women rejecting him. Beneath the situation of a returning soldier/hero in the novel is a personal scenario which reveals a good deal about Faulkner and the women who had in the last few years slipped through his life.

Not only did Faulkner in the scenario between Donald Mahon and Cecily Saunders work out his own relationship with Estelle, he tried out nearly every one of his roles. In several respects, *Soldiers' Pay* is a personal memoir of Faulkner's efforts to establish a relationship; but how curious the terms are. In the novel, he has as protagonist a dying soldier, an unacceptable, crippled human being who tests the loyalty of the woman he intended to marry. Faulkner has located the relationship in a crucible in which the woman has no chance of surviving. Given the nature of the soldier's condition and what she is herself, she *must fail.* The implications of this equation are enormous. For they demonstrate within the workings of the novel a profound hostility not only toward *that* woman, but toward women. Margaret, who finally marries the dying Mahon, is outside the circle, but she is not so much a wifely figure as she is mother, nurse; the "real" wife, meanwhile, recoils.

Other curious elements surface. Although *Soldiers' Pay* and *The Sun Also Rises* are ultimately very different books, the Hemingway novel far more sophisticated and refined, they share overlapping material by their contemporary authors. Each has a wounded protagonist who has lost his sexual function, and, thus, his manhood—Faulkner names his soldier "Mahon" to make certain we do not lose his point. Each is working over the "sick king" popularized by Eliot in *The Waste Land,* and each is, also, turning the war and its wounded into a mythical occurrence, an archetype of young men sacrificed to hungry gods. Faulkner's Mahon is completely passive, far more than Hemingway's Jake; passive to the extent any woman who associates with him must be not wife but nurse and mother. When Cecily recoils from this situation, she recoils from something abnormal into a relationship with George Farr, which is, at least sexually, normal.

As a wounded warrior, Mahon is a not too disguised version of Faulkner in one of his poses. The association with Cecily has within it Faulkner's deeper feelings toward Estelle: her betrayal of him when she married Franklin; but even more than that, a trapping of her in alternatives neither of which is viable. She is not only a deceiving, traitorous Eve; she is a woman whom the author has chosen not to give even a chance. He has offered her several possibilities, but each is a trap, and yet she is expected to make an honest, loyal decision. When she cannot, and no woman rightly could, she is condemned as unfaithful.

Once we see that Cecily's role is to walk into a mine field from which there is no escape, then we can measure the depth of Faulkner's hostility. For even if she had decided to marry Donald, even if she had chosen to see it through, she would have fallen into the trap: marrying a Mahon who is not a man. It is all right for Margaret Powers to marry Donald because she is a widow, she has tried out a brief marriage, found it wanting, broken it off just as her husband is killed overseas; and now, as she enters this new situation, she is drained. A washed-out woman who cannot put the pieces of her life together can make a minor adjustment in *her* life; what would be for Cecily a major and lasting choice.

Furthermore, the portrait Faulkner draws of Cecily is immensely hostile in itself. Apart from her role in Donald's life, she is an unappetizing young woman—except for those who find her physically attractive. Faulkner is, apparently, fascinated by her—by her unsuitability for marriage, for companionship, for decency itself. She represents the "new woman," but at her worst: she is chic without being clever, fashionable without being smart. She is full of tease, wears revealing clothes, seems sensual, but, in actuality, lacks feeling. She promises far more than she delivers. But she is, somehow, the prototypical young woman for Faulkner, at least in this phase of his manhood: the boyish, breastless figure, skittish, and, in the codes of the day, sexually frigid. She telegraphs that by her behavior—offering much, but giving little, an avatar of Temple Drake. A consumer, not a producer, she is self-centered, vain, aimless. One could, if Faulkner permitted it, feel sorry for her, as one feels sympathy for the plight of Zelda Fitzgerald, all bottled up in herself and lacking sufficient outlet. Under different circumstances, that trapped quality in a woman evokes a different response; but in Faulkner's terms, Cecily seems entwined only in her own needs, incapable of giving.

A sense of payback, retribution, even revenge, is suggested. Faulkner is getting even with Estelle not only for her rejection but for all rejections, even when his own response had been slight or without depth. We perceive his revenge in the kind of alliance Cecily makes, marrying George Farr in order to avoid Donald Mahon. George's surname is also indicative —he is far from anything a woman would want, unless that woman sought a blob she could lead around. When they return from their honeymoon, he looks desperately unhappy, and Cecily is herself on the verge of breaking down. He is in sexual thrall to her—she has, after all, promised so much; but she is no sexual kitten. On the contrary, asexual: that boyish body contains little passion. This completes the cycle of revenge, since the man who yearns after Cecily gains little. It is a savage portrait, indicting her at every level. And yet she is the woman for Faulkner—fascinating because of the pain and anguish she causes him; part of a childhood fantasy even reason and deep feeling are unable to vanquish.

Soldiers' Pay not only says something significant about "a woman," it suggests something serious about women. Although we are of course interested in Faulkner's feelings about Estelle, via his literary re-creation of her, we are equally concerned with his attitudes toward women generally. Basically, Faulkner was caught in the clash of two types, and not unusually this conflict remained as he matured. Whatever the later sophistication of his vision, he saw women as dualistic: the whore and madonna opposites defined by Freud. The madonna is not virginal, but she is sacrificial, able to get beyond her own self, and is motherly. She cossets her man or her family—thus, several Negro women, like Dilsey in *The Sound and the Fury*, fit the madonna image. The whore is not quite a whore, but her values derive from Babylon, here represented by Cecily. She is a kind of dry run for Temple Drake and Charlotte Rittenmeyer, and, more immediately, Patricia of *Mosquitoes*, Faulkner's next novel. The woman as whore is not necessarily unsympathetic, as we see with Charlotte; but most of the time, she displays little beyond her own self. Margaret Power, however, who seems "loose," in reality plays the madonna role. In these thickets of alternating hostility and sympathy, we perceive how Faulkner's shaping of the female image was fixed by his early rejections, and by his close attachment to Maud Falkner.

Strengthening this dualistic positioning of the women is his definition of the men, and particularly of his protagonist. Once again, overlapping with Hemingway occurs—a remarkably similar reading of a postwar phenomenon and, as well, the sense of authorial narcissism that would characterize 1920s fiction. Faulkner has shaped his protagonist into a dying king or god; in this small town, Charleston, his dying commands the stage. As a dying god whose name is Mahon, Donald, with intimations of a Jesus figure, "forces" everyone near him either to become infertile and stale or else to demonstrate inner reserves and blossom. His condition determines how people will live, how they will love, how they will relate to themselves and to each other. The war has turned Mahon into a shell or hulk, a helpless warrior, a Parsifal who awaits some miracle, and especially a miracle in the shape of a saintly, angelic woman.

The sense of the "dying god" is something Faulkner could have obtained not only from Eliot but from Conrad's *The Nigger of the "Narcissus."* There the god is an ambiguous figure, James Wait, a dying black man, but he becomes a god to the extent he puts everyone on hold until he dies. His very feebleness adds to his power, since he must be cared for as if a child; and that ability to nurse and cosset attracts the men. Similarly, Faulkner can structure his sense of an ironic world by way of Mahon's helplessness —so that each person reveals himself or herself by way of how he relates to the dying soldier. Faulkner has his hero, but reduces him to incapacity, surrounding him with people who define themselves through his powerlessness.

This sense of the dying god (or goddess) became standard in Faulkner's fiction, culminating in *A Fable*, his last fully wrought work. What is symbolized is not only the sacrifice of the young—Wilfred Owen's or Housman's themes—but a celebration of the victim. In this respect, the victim gains power by virtue of his feebleness, the reverse of Eliot's waste land king or ruler. In this zigzagging fashion, Faulkner somehow continued the image of himself martyred to the war—even though he missed the war and came out of it with only assumed injuries. That limp identified him with an imperfect god, Vulcan; floating around in Faulkner's mind was an ego-ideal that rose beyond man. On one hand, he identified with the returning hero, the crux of his pose; but on the other, he saw the dying god as a sacrifice, as a passive victim who loses out on life. Strung out along this thread from hero to passive victim is Faulkner himself: the "hero" role cast into doubt by the truth; the "victim" role as the way he can see himself, rejected, marginal, isolated.

But there is more to this role-playing as victim and sacrifice. Even by this time, all of Faulkner's friends spoke of his immense silences: not clear acts of hostility, but sudden assumptions of passivity; as if he were a board wiped clean waiting for someone to write, to make him respond. When he withdrew, he became untouchable and unreachable, defining his own space so completely it was as though he were a deaf-mute. In effect, Faulkner was working through this role with Donald Mahon. Donald commands his own space by virtue of his "as I lay dying" passivity; becoming unreachable through withdrawal, he becomes the litmus test for everyone else. Withdrawal is a will to power; but power of a particular kind, essential to Faulkner and his way of "seeing." He has given Donald a kind of wandering speech, virtually a free-associational voice, but the soldier remains, most likely, incapable of hearing or understanding what is said to him. As a consequence of lacking communication, he lacks a personal "story"; whatever he may have said about himself is lost. All narrative derives from the fact that others must speak for him, put words into his mouth—although they are not his words. Because he makes others respond with words or ideas which may or may not be valid or viable, Donald remains the only possible source of truth *because* he is silent, *because* he bottles it all up within himself, whatever *it* is.

Faulkner found it essential, in following Conrad, Eliot, and Housman, that he begin with the "death of ———." The crucial context is death, not life, perhaps a strange start for a young novelist. By way of death, Faulkner undercut sentimentalism—implicit in his heroic view of war—in the process leaching out his romanticism. At the same time, he established terms by which the victim (himself in one scenario) is able to gain revenge on his fiancée (Estelle in the same scenario). If this seems stretched out or bizarre, we can cite numerous other Faulkner novels and poems which are disguised versions of such personal injuries; novels which took not a few months to write, but several years.

How much of Helen Baird actually went into Margaret Powers we cannot tell, since Faulkner began the novel before he got to know her. But he didn't really need Helen here, or even Estelle, since he reached so deeply into a personal core unconnected to special models. Faulknerians have often overreached in trying to find models for everything and everyone in his work; such procedures, even while they do seek accuracy, create a mistaken impression of how he thought and created. A reliance on one-to-one relationships in Faulkner discounts how absolutely set he was in his attitudes: how little, for example, the particular women he met did anything to change the intense terms of acceptance and rejection. A good deal of his outlook—on women, mainly, but also on the uses of power and ways of responding—undoubtedly came from Maud Falkner's influence over him. Essentially a very cold person, somewhat immobilized by a marriage which was desperately unhappy, she tried to turn her eldest into a surrogate for her attitudes and desires.

In his own coldness, withdrawal, and desire to immobilize himself within an inner core, untouchable and unreachable by others, he was, in part at least, playing out Maud's influence. Naturally enough, she helped form in him—however consciously or not—a sense of women, the mother as ultimate arbiter of female values. Once shaped, his attitudes resisted to some extent the evidence of his senses, even when he was touched by a particular young woman, as he was by Helen. Further, the set attitudes help explain the fixity of his purpose in waiting for Estelle, even when everything told him she was as unsuitable for him as he was for her. A pact was drawn that somehow went beyond individual control, superseding whatever else their senses or intelligence told them. And yet this was extremely significant for Faulkner: the pact simply reinforced that fixity of purpose, those unchangeable basic assumptions Maud had instilled and from which he would never really break.

He remained faithful to a code which divided women into two untouchable halves.* No matter how he seemed to strain traditional Southern ideas of womanhood in *Sanctuary* and elsewhere, he remained basically loyal to a nonproductive view of women, fitting them into categories which allowed them little air to breathe. When his marriage to Estelle was proving as disastrous as anyone could have predicted, Faulkner turned his young women friends into angelic creatures, into madonna-like figures, while he was having affairs with them, and against them was this witch-like wife —from whom he could never break. Part of Jill Faulkner's disenchantment with her parents—perhaps on an equal par with her distaste for their alcoholic bouts—was the tension created by Faulkner's attachment to Estelle even while he found her a witch, someone draining him of joy. This tension he subtly conveys in his fiction, well before his marriage, demonstrating the fixity of his sense of women, much of which remained even later when he saw women with more sympathy. Perhaps our best example

---

*Caddy in *The Sound and the Fury* exemplifies both halves, never breaking through Faulkner's imposition of dualism. Alternately whore and madonna, she has no narrated segment of her own because she cannot live beyond those imposed coordinates.

comes in *Light in August* with the pairing of Lena and Joanna—one "saved" by her pregnancy and inviolability, the other "damned" by her profligacy and nonproductiveness as a woman.

Accordingly, Faulkner's attachment to Helen Baird, which seemed so extraordinary because of his persistence in pursuing her in books, was his pursuance of a female ideal. He maintained the medieval tradition of romance in idealizing a woman, so that she could be worthy of his literary devotion. His early, romantic pact with Estelle, then, would also be part of this: no matter how tired they were of each other even before they married, they had to come together.

The conflicts in Faulkner's creative and personal life at this time are keen, as he finds himself on the edge of creative breakthrough. To derive these tensions in his life appears to be at least as significant as any literary effort to trace linkages between his earlier poetry or poetic sequences and his later career as a fictionalist. In the latter, literary view, *The Marble Faun*, *Vision in Spring*, *The Marionettes*, and the poem "The Lilacs" are perceived as leading into Faulkner's early novels. Thus, they allegedly give us insights into his fiction, and provide us with what can be called "new forms for consciousness."[2] Yet that argument, seeking linkages between early poetic work and early novels, especially *Soldiers' Pay*, neglects the lived context in which such transformations took place. Faulkner was working through several shadowy aspects of his life which came to be revealed in his literary output: both in quality and in type. Literary linkages are reinforced by lived experiences: the early desire to be his own man—which meant slowly separating himself from Stone, who was associated with his poetic production; dealing with Maud Falkner to whom he dedicated *Faun*, and her ever-present influence on his life and, inevitably, his work; his relationship with women—based mainly on seeking out women who would reject him; his holding himself for Estelle—even though she formed something in his mind which was more medievally romantic than realistic. Most of all, however, he needed to find his center—the most difficult thing of all for a creative person; that is, locating the nature of his talent and then mining it as if nothing else mattered.

When Faulkner returned to New Orleans on January 4, 1925, he entered into an "artistic milieu." Such an environment is a special dimension of an artist's life—the best example is Paris at the turn of the century—when the artistic life encompasses everything. It is isolated from outside activities, especially from the quotidian working world. Its values are generally shared, and the chief ingredient is that artistic considerations preempt any others. It is a complete world, for the writer in an artistic milieu eats, breathes, and lives for his work. There was, of course, no chance for Faulkner to enter such a world back in Oxford or in Memphis: New Orleans was the "Paris of the South." Only New York's Greenwich Village could rival it.

This world was not something Faulkner stuck with—by early July, he and Spratling sailed for Europe. And once he found his voice, he avoided anything that smacked of an artistic milieu, in New Orleans or anywhere else. Ultimately, he saw himself as an isolated artist, a priest of the word and imagination, marginal even when famous and sought after. But for this brief time, his association with others like him was extremely important for building his confidence in himself and his values. We notice how rapidly his output increased, and how he pushed himself into different genres.

In "Verse Old and Nascent" (April 1925), he even provides us with a rare piece of autobiography. Subtitling that work "A Pilgrimage," Faulkner takes us on a journey from the excesses of Swinburne, through the polished *A Shropshire Lad,* and on to the giants, Shakespeare, Spenser, Shelley, and Keats. He tells us of how he was part of the "pack belling loudly after contemporary poets," even though he could not always tell "what it was all about."[3] But then, he says, he achieved some balance within himself, making order out of internal chaos, and he moved on to those poets whose effect on him was permanent. In that latter confession, he mentions that young Keats wrote "Endymion" trying to "gain enough silver to marry Fannie Brawne and set up an apothecary shop." The identification here with Keats is compelling, especially in the light of the Oldham family's original rejection of Faulkner as a husband for Estelle because he lacked "silver." This admission is of course a romantic one—that the poet uses his precious career in order to win the beloved's hand. But more than any single statement in this essay, or anywhere else, is the fact of Faulkner's diversity of interests: he was not only writing himself into writing, he was publishing virtually everything that came from his pen, and he was living his craft, breathing its very air.

Equally important is still another dimension to his stay in New Orleans, a six-month stretch, along with a brief return to Oxford in late February and early March. This was, clearly, his first extended stay away from his family since his military service; and it became his first leave-taking as a mature adult. Its significance cannot be overestimated. Faulkner had gotten out from under the direct influence of his mother, supportive as she had been; and this was important for him, for along with her love she was commanding and imperious. He had taken leave of his father, who, while generous, simply could not understand his eldest son, and was himself increasingly caught up in his own efforts to survive. He had even escaped brothers whom he was close to, but whose demands on life were inevitably different from his own.

Most of all, he had escaped from an Oxford environment where he was a strange character, a failed son of a well-known family, a defeated suitor of one of the town's best catches, a young man who seemed destined for drifting. He had in reality gotten away from the reputation he had himself cultivated. But he was changing, and that role-playing fitted less: now he was moving into a more intense writing career, and as such he had substance as well as manner. Put another way, Oxford had been a place of defeat for him—personally and professionally. Like Joyce with Dublin, he had to escape it periodically so as to preserve it in his imagination. Deceptions had kept him going in his own world; but once in New Orleans, he could let go. What he did with his pen was much more important to him than what he continued to do publicly with uniform, cap, limp, and cane. He still maintained the wounded pose, and very possibly he needed to maintain that pose while he wrote of Donald Mahon in *Soldiers' Pay*. But being away from a no-win family situation, a domineering mother, and the scene of many defeats allowed him to blossom.

We get some sense of what Faulkner felt about Oxford if we look at the several introductions he wrote to *The Sound and the Fury*. In one version, he said, "Art, which is no part at all of modern Southern life, is almost the complete sum of the Southern artist." In another, he was even more insistent: "Art is no part of Southern life. . . . in the South art must become a ceremony, a spectacle: something between a gypsy encampment and a church bazaar held by a handful of alien mummers who must waste themselves in protest and actual self defense until there is nothing left with which to speak." This strong condemnation continues that the old South is dead, killed by the Civil War. "There is a new south," he adds, "but it is not the South." The New South, as he calls it, is indistinguishable from the North. The import of these remarks is that to survive the artist must recognize the superfluous nature of his achievement and, if possible, distance himself from those who denigrate or ignore him. Or else, he can become a circus performer, part of a ceremony, someone performing in an arena. If we can extrapolate from these later remarks, they suggest he needed that distance from Oxford to expand; that while New Orleans *was* the South, its structured artistic milieu and intellectual atmosphere marked it as a friendly host for what the young writer wanted to become.

The larger world of Southern thought and literature was also awakening there. Only five years after Faulkner spent his months in New Orleans, the Southern Manifesto was issued. It came to be identified as an agrarian statement, *I'll Take My Stand*,* and it was a cry of rebellion. It seems curious reading now, but it is a document of considerable historical significance not only in Southern culture but nationally, since it described attitudes which penetrated from reactionary and conservative to liberal and radical. One of the signatories was Stark Young, but others included Robert Penn Warren (who later disowned the manifesto), Allen Tate, John Crowe Ransom, Andrew Lytle, and Donald Davidson. It was the protest of a certain kind of rebel: the man who saw the South as still potentially an agrarian paradise, and who reviled industrialism and the machine. It is full of the "master race" 's sense that the South occupies a superior position in the nation because of its moral, social, and religious superiority.

***I'll Take My Stand: The South and the Agrarian Tradition*, Twelve Southerners (Baton Rouge: Louisiana State University Press, pap., 1977). The villainous Mencken had already called the South "The Sahara of the Bozart."

It is, essentially, a religious and economic manifesto; but because the Negro is virtually omitted, it becomes a racial one also, and a venomous one at that. The ideal community is a foreshadowing of Eliot's Christian society, and, accordingly, it is a kind of club of white Christian gentlemen dedicated to holding back noisome progress. Their idea is not the status quo, but to roll life back to a pre–Civil War existence, although the signatories deny this represents their emphasis. Theirs seems to be a Jeffersonian agrarianism, but without any awareness of Jefferson's intense democracy of ideas. Their stress on pastoral values, however, is what holds the manifesto together; their assumption being that America is an Eden defiled by the machine. Its import is nostalgia for a South which is, we recognize, the South of fantasy and legend.

Although Faulkner did not sign and would not have signed such a document, it does illuminate what would become of many of his ideas. First of all, however, unless drunk and pressed by someone particularly vulgar, Faulkner would not have recognized the South as superior because of moral, social, and religious considerations. If anything, his fiction demonstrates that major tensions exist between what the South thinks of itself and the reality of life there. As far as Jeffersonian agrarianism, he agreed the backbone of the South was the small farmer (Jefferson's image of democracy at work), and he certainly deplored the encroachment of an industrial complex. But he hardly glorified the small farmer, nor saw in him the salvation of America. Neither did he glorify the agrarian ideal. For him, agrarianism went well beyond farming, back to the wilderness and the primitive, the "big woods" of Sam Fathers and young Ike McCaslin. He looked for deeper values in a man, and farming, while commendable, did not in itself create or reinforce those values, however often he later referred to himself as a farmer.

Yet behind the vague ideas of the manifesto was the sense America still had Edenic potentiality. If one could reach beyond current developments, beyond Northern value systems, to the "real South," then it would be retrievable. But the signatories ignored not only the current situation of the Negro; they also ignored that the sense of America as Edenic had been sullied; it was a dispossessed Eden they glorified. The atmosphere had been poisoned by slavery—this was a corrupted Eden, and the Civil War had not cleansed it, since men like the signatories were for the most part unregenerated. Faulkner caught all this in the second part of "The Bear." They did not seem to be cognizant that their agrarian ideal, or utopia, had proven a terrible prison for millions of people, and that by ignoring these people in 1930—in effect, creating a potential society in which they played no role—their efforts at community were merely fantasies.

In this area, Faulkner disagreed sharply. For even though he might have occasionally played the Southern aristocrat in his treatment of Negroes, personally as well as literarily, he was profoundly aware of what slavery and the condition of the Negro in this century meant. In *Soldiers' Pay*, for example, he might seek a laugh by addressing the train porter, a very dignified and caring man, as "Othello"; but he *also* demonstrates that the porter is more humanized than the drunken white soldiers around Mahon. Faulkner slipped into traditional roles, but in the larger sense, he knew that no society could operate on the principles of *I'll Take My Stand* and endure. Such a society was corrupted from the start, agrarian or industrial. In such knowledge, Faulkner found the tensions and counterpoints which conveyed such gravity to his fiction. Fiction based on the manifesto—and such fiction had thrived in post–Civil War years—would have little relevance to contemporary life.

Although by the time of *The Sound and the Fury* Faulkner moved to the "art novel," he never lost his realistic, social, and communal footing. Thomas Jefferson may have been one of his ideological heroes, but it was Jefferson updated; and as far as a Christian society goes, few writers went further than Faulkner to demonstrate that Christian values played a small role in either the traditional world or the new developing societies. What is notably absent from his community life (except for blacks) is the Christian base. The God-fearing and churchgoing connive, deceive, and cheat as much as those who profess no faith, or who are indifferent. Christian values, for Faulkner, were meaningful only as moral and ethical values. In speaking of his "communities," one must be very careful to note how minute a role Christianity as such plays. What matters is life and how man organizes his moral responses.

It takes a document like the 1930 agrarian statement to underline how clearly Faulkner, both before and after it, was not part of any organic Southern view of itself. The signatories here sought an "organic South," the South as a distinct unit of thought, ideology, religion, economic system, and, we can assume, color; as much untouched by outside influence as was possible. Yet despite all its obvious shortcomings, *I'll Take My Stand* heralded an enormous contribution of Southern literature to American culture, and Faulkner was in the vanguard of that renaissance.

The artistic milieu in New Orleans that Faulkner entered included, besides Anderson (perhaps its dominant figure), the very young Hamilton Basso, the artist Spratling, and hordes of other writers and artists. The time was auspicious for a Southern revival, although nothing could have been further from Faulkner's mind than a joint enterprise intended to refute Mencken's disparaging comments on Southern culture.* Faulkner was himself able to break with the kind of fiction small towns took for granted; by satirizing certain types and yet not destroying their effectiveness, he was, unlike Anderson, able to take regionalism up a notch into a national literature. Indications of this in his first novel are slim, but they are nevertheless there, in the rector, Donald's father; in Januarius Jones; in Cecily Saunders, at the least. Also, like the Compsons

---

*"South has not only lost its old capacity for producing ideas; it has also taken on the worst intolerance of ignorance and stupidity."

later, the family is a disruptive force, not at all a unit, not harmonious, quite different from the public image of the "Southern family." He drew, of course, on his own sense of a disrupted family scene, and one, incidentally, which he would re-create when he and Estelle made home life so difficult for their daughter.

In liberating himself from clichés and stereotypes, Faulkner was taking literature out into the open—part of a massive effort in the 1920s with Theodore Dreiser, Sinclair Lewis, H. L. Mencken and others to show the small-town American family differently, often scathingly. In theater, O'Neill was working the same ground. We normally do not think of Faulkner in this light, or in this company. But in his way, he was revealing the rifts and seams in family life, aided and abetted by his first real removal from Oxford after military service. The evidence of his success is not the particular quality of any single work, but the multiplicity of works and the variety of genres he attempted.

The Marble Faun, meanwhile, was a fact. Stone worked mightily to see it did not die the natural death of a first volume of poems by an unknown young man from the Deep South. He knew that volumes of poetry unconnected to large urban areas went unrecognized. Frost, for example, had to go to England and publish to become known in America. He requested Four Seas to send copies to people as different as Estelle, the Andersons, the Mississippi governor, and former president William Howard Taft. For publicity, he used Young as much as he could, and he tried to sell the *New Republic* and Four Seas on Faulkner doing a collection of overseas articles, first in magazine, then in book form. Stone was trying to blow everyone away with his friend's genius—and it was surely here, in his frantic work on behalf of the volume, that he gained the proprietary air he took with the writer. Faulkner had, in effect, a secretary, an agent, a man confident even with famous people he did not know. Trying to raise money for Faulkner's forthcoming European jaunt, Stone asked Four Seas to buy out the contract for *The Marble Faun* as well as to contract for the yet-to-be-written articles.

Stone plugged away with extreme urgency. He reports that Faulkner's departure is imminent, now scheduled for just past mid-November (he didn't leave until early July, and with the money from *Soldiers' Pay*, not Four Seas); the fault, if they lose him, will be theirs. Possibly, Stone's sense of urgency with Faulkner was simply that of a friend who wanted the writer to get a fair shake; or, possibly, it was a desire—and this is a real point—Stone needed coattails on which to ride, and Faulkner was his entrance into a literary world a lot larger than Oxford or Mississippi. Possibly, Stone—unmarried, uncertain about himself, not fully committed to law practice—used Faulkner as a surrogate for the kind of life he wanted to lead. He may even have wanted Faulkner to leave Oxford and New Orleans before Estelle Franklin returned from the Far East, scheduled for the time *The Marble Faun* was due to appear.

In Stone's urgency, we have many motivations. If we are correct in suggesting his proprietary sense of Faulkner had already taken hold by then, Estelle's return with her two children in early December of 1924 was an auspicious event for both men. Although evidence depends almost solely on Stone's labors, the unmarried, somewhat divided lawyer saw Faulkner as his and would be, under ordinary expectations, unsettled by Estelle's continuing hold on the young poet. Although she was still married and remained so for another five years, her marriage was coming apart, despite Victoria (Cho-Cho), almost five, and Malcolm Argyle, one. Her life was a steady round of social events in an alien environment, Shanghai, and she was for the most part isolated—this for a woman accustomed to support systems. Her husband, Cornell, may or may not have been unfaithful,* but he was absent a good deal; and even if things had gone differently, it is doubtful if she could have sustained life in such foreign surroundings without severe deterioration.

If we are correct that Stone needed to "own" the young poet whom he "had made," then inevitably he had to perceive Estelle as a serious rival. For not only might she take Faulkner away from him, she would stress values and needs antithetical to the writer's tasks: turn him toward bourgeois pursuits that might frustrate or even end his still-young career. Stone feared for the future if and when the two met and reexchanged vows. Yet little did he understand Faulkner, for the latter could not be diverted from writing, which meant more to him than anything else in his life except possibly alcohol; more than Estelle, home and family, even his own welfare. What Stone the lawyer and reader of great books could not comprehend was the obsession of a man possessed by words. Stone measured by his own needs and failed to perceive his friend could take Estelle and family in stride without breaking an internal rhythm.

Faulkner did not allow Estelle's return to alter his plans radically. He stayed in Oxford only a short time before returning to New Orleans on January 4, as noted, accompanied by Stone. That act is in itself suspicious, since it lends itself to the possibility that Stone accompanied Faulkner to ensure he went. Yet we have no indication Faulkner intended to dally in Venus's bower: the attractions of an alternate life drew him back to New Orleans. Before he left, he finally had copies of *The Marble Faun* in hand, with dedication copies going to the usual people: Estelle, his mother, and the Oldhams. And he was beginning what would be for him a long apprenticeship to the big magazines: sending out stories and poems, receiving them back, keeping track of them, and resending until he either found a publisher or else worked the piece into something else. Sometimes he did both, publishing a story, then reusing it in a novel.

*The entire question of faithfulness, on both sides, is a thorny one, and will be taken up later, when Estelle and Faulkner come together, in 1929. At stake is the possibility that Malcolm may not have been Cornell's son. Against the latter supposition is the fact that Malcolm does seem to resemble Cornell Franklin in some photographs.

Responses and reviews began to come in even before Faulkner had left Oxford for New Orleans.* We learn that Major Oldham complained at Faulkner's title, telling him Hawthorne had used it for a novel. "Who's Hawthorne? The title is original with me," Faulkner responded.[4] Oldham seemed convinced. Yet it was a typical Faulkner answer, part of his tall-tale mentality. We have no conclusive proof of how well he knew Hawthorne or the title, but even if he did not, Stone surely would. They may have exchanged remarks on this, but Faulkner with characteristic stubbornness held to his view: titles were anyone's property, as legally they were. It is, nonetheless, a lovely title, and it does indicate, perhaps more than any he might have invented, the peculiar quality of his volume: that tension between softness and solidity, or among fleetness, evanescence, impermanence, and resistance to change, wedding Mallarmé, Hawthorne, and Keats. And if Faulkner heard that anyone asking for *The Marble Faun* got Hawthorne, not himself, he might think that a coup, not an error. After all, his first novel was called "Mayday" (not *Soldiers' Pay*) in manuscript, not exactly a word or title original with him. When he finally hit his stride, his titles were brilliant, but, once again, many of them came from "sources," Biblical, Shakespearean, and folk literature.

Even as he was entering the lists with *The Marble Faun*, he was preparing a second volume or at least a tentative collection. What later became *Mississippi Poems* was presented in the form of a sheaf of twelve poems to Myrtle Ramey. Whether Faulkner intended this as the volume to succeed *The Marble Faun* or simply as an act of giving, we cannot tell; Stone had intimated a succeeding volume in his preface to the just published volume. As noted above, the poems were themselves concerned with death, full of melancholic posturing, moon poems of a kind Faulkner outgrew. But despite their continued immaturity of pose and subject matter, there is a consistency between the poetry and the novel which became *Soldiers' Pay*. That consistency is not all in Faulkner's favor, since it suggests some considerable immaturity of both purpose and execution. Death remains a constant, of course, as does the "loss of," characteristic of both the poetry and fiction. But the despair is attenuated—one poem begins "Moon of death, moon of bright despair"; so that death, despair, death wounds are not part of the cycle of existence, but aspects of role-playing and posturing. The poems and novel demonstrate Faulkner had not reached beyond the rather superficial personal pain he felt—for whatever reasons—into a historical or universalized pain he could convey.

*Most of the reviews were from the South. John McClure, in the *Times-Picayune*, was the most sympathetic, calling Faulkner a "born poet," someone trying to be another Keats. Admitting deficiencies in the poetry, McClure nevertheless indicated: "Mr. Faulkner possesses to an exceptional degree imagination, emotion, a creative impulse in diction and a keen sense of rhythm and form." In the Memphis *Commercial Appeal*, the anonymous reviewer was less enthusiastic, but supportive, labeling Faulkner "splendidly atavistic" and seeing his derivation from Swinburne, not Keats. He said that many lines ring "with a silvery daintiness that evokes the image of a kitten stepping fastidiously through wet leaves." But he did condemn the profusion of mixed metaphors, a disregard for meaning, "stumbling lines, devoid of distinction and of grace."

Except for the artistic milieu in New Orleans, Faulkner went his own way, remaining also on his own in Europe, and, most certainly, once he returned to America. The aspects of childhood development leading to his feelings of marginality persisted into mature life and became a cornerstone of his literary philosophy: the writer working very early in the morning, whiskey at his elbow, pen in hand, or at the typewriter, and not much else. In 1923, he wrote later, he discovered the major thing about himself, and it created a pattern not even the sojourn in Europe would alter. "It was in 1923 and I wrote a book and discovered that my doom, fate, was to keep on writing books: not for any exterior or ulterior purpose: just writing the books for the sake of writing the books."[5] He wrote that in 1953, and for twenty years after *The Marble Faun* little changed: the writer possessed by demons, and so preoccupied with himself for the sake of writing that the demons left him little time for anything else. By 1925, just two years after he said he felt possessed, he was, if anything, more driven by the need to get it out, to find catharsis by turning what was inside into words.

Faulkner's movements among the people around the *Double Dealer* and his own contributions to the publication gave him access to persons he could not have met otherwise. They were a diverse lot, including several Jews around the magazine: editor Julius Weis Friend; Julius's sister, Lillian Friend Marcus; their uncle, Sam Weis, who owned the building at 204 Baronne Street where they ran the bimonthly. There was also Albert Goldstein, a journalist on the *Times-Picayune,* and friend of John McClure, poet, critic, and part-time editor of the *Double Dealer.* Such a concentration of Jews—Faulkner had known only the Friedmans in Oxford—established another dimension both for his personal experience and for his use of Jews in his fiction. For the first time, he met Jews who were not merchants (the peddling background associated with those who settled in the South), but were connected to the arts, either as backers of a financially losing proposition or as editors and publishers. But the people in New Orleans were not all Jews, of course. By the time Faulkner caught up with the *Double Dealer* and entered its pages in the January–February 1925 issue, the bimonthly had touched, as noted, on many young careers: from Hemingway and Wilder to many of those who would sign the *I'll Take My Stand* manifesto —Warren, Tate, Ransom, Davidson—to other beginners such as Wilson and Crane, as well as the more established Anderson, Pound, Arthur Symons, and Amy Lowell. Although Faulkner met very few of these writers, by publishing so extensively in the January–February number, he entered the lists.

Besides the fact that he had entered the front door of literature was his domination of that winter issue, virtually a Faulkner monopoly. He had three segments to himself: the essay "On Criticism," mentioned above; the poem "Dying Gladiator," also mentioned above; and the eleven sketches called "New Orleans." In his domination of the issue, he also displayed versatility; for while none of the pieces is particularly distinguished, they are startling for their variety.

Yet even though in New Orleans he did not have to impress anyone with appearance, in the contributors' notes for the January–February issue, he repeated he had been "severely wounded." He also spoke of his "brilliant record" in the RAF, apparently to maintain his manly pose. Interestingly enough, he mentions that having lately published *The Marble Faun*, he "is about to publish another 'The Greening Bough.' " What is striking is he had the title at hand, but even more striking is the continuation of lies about his war record.

The lies or deceptions indicate he still needed that reinforcement of himself, despite the literary achievement he knew he was capable of. The silences Faulkner was beginning to make his signature were perhaps indicative of a very unsure person; one who had learned to control himself by means of nonverbal communication. Linkages between silences and drinking are revealing: both methods to control fears, sense of inferiority, marginality, or whatever was seething within. The Faulkner we see in 1925, however bolstered by the heady company he was keeping, in person and in print, still needed propping up: wartime service, wounds, deep and long silences, accompanied by alcohol. Beneath the writer moving inexorably into his career and seemingly fearless of privations and losses was a man still uncertain of himself, unwilling to let the truth of events prevail without doctoring. But what is more significant is he had discovered a way that worked for him. He began to drop the lies later on, but the accompanying elements of silence, alcohol, and deep introspection were fixed.

The Faulkner of 1925 was now, essentially, the writer moving into his major career, although, evidently, as literary quality deepened, later books lost the gaucheness of *Soldiers' Pay* and *Mosquitoes*. The discovery of Housman's poetry, the influence of Eliot and Joyce, the need to distance himself from his contemporaries (especially Dreiser, Lewis, and Hemingway), the willingness to take on the slings and arrows of public disapproval on sexual, moral, and literary grounds, were all shaping themselves into distinct forms of consciousness.

The pieces Faulkner wrote for the *Times-Picayune*, begun on February 8, 1925, are slighter than the sketches for the *Double Dealer*. Yet he was attempting different things, trying to write a kind of anthropological study of New Orleans people and places. He was starting to distance himself from his material and perceive his subject matter as a researcher might view another culture. In this respect, he was seeking subjects which filled out the landscape; imagining a place, time, and people cocooned from the outside world. He was neither a fantasist nor a realist: he was moving toward a form of abstraction, different from painterly abstraction and yet not unconnected to that relatively new development. His would be a unique abstraction: sketches or stories which lie between the conscious and preconscious, in a realm just beyond reach and yet distanced from the unconscious.

What Faulkner emphasized in these early New Orleans pieces is the quasi-abstracting of a culture viewed with an objective eye. He had looked into, possibly read large chunks of, Frazer's great study, *The Golden Bough*. Its effect upon him, if we project, was to give him distance on his subjects even when they became close to him; to provide him with a mechanism for viewing which blended in with his own experience and his personal angle of view. Even when he used models for his fictional characters, he had learned how to distance himself: through interior monologue (suggested already in *Soldiers' Pay*), switching back and forth from third to first person, making narrative leaps and jumps, interrupting plot elements, looping, and other such strategies. These are the devices of modernism, and Faulkner made them part of the American novel as his way of "seeing." Among contemporaries, only Dos Passos similarly mined modernism.

The work Faulkner did before a brief return to Oxford in February derived from that period when he lived, really, off the generosity of Anderson's wife. That is why his attitude toward Anderson when he returned to New Orleans on March 3 is so difficult to understand. Anderson had himself returned the previous day, but Faulkner indicated he did not intend to see his benefactor; he wanted to sail to Europe without delay. Although he changed his mind and did visit the Andersons, with the idea of staying there again, Anderson was tired and wanted his privacy.

The entire matter concerns us because Faulkner was demonstrating several conflicting attitudes toward Anderson. We begin to notice a ruthlessness toward people who could help him, and then a lack of gratitude for their support. Even after being turned away, he asked to leave his things there—mainly large bottles of liquor. There is a pattern here Faulkner repeated throughout his life: his use of people and their advantages (connections, property, or whatever) as it suited him, and then a dropping away from them when they had served their purpose. Phil Stone began to feel this, although the writer continued to pay him verbal praise. Anderson had been straightforward and generous, but Faulkner saw the older writer as someone he could handle with charm and then discard as a man of inferior talent. His comments on Anderson in the review cited above revealed that ambiguity; and then the unnecessary parody in *Sherwood Anderson and Other Famous Creoles*, done with William Spratling, itself coming on Hemingway's sophomorically cruel *Torrents of Spring*, suggests a wellspring of self-serving and ingratitude.

There also appears to be more than a little hostility. If we are correct, hostility could spring from several sources: Anderson's ability to negotiate in the literary waters and live well; his settled condition personally and his relatively high literary reputation; and, most of all, Faulkner's basic contempt for nearly everything Anderson had done except *Winesburg* and a few stories. There is always an unknown factor in hostility, and here it may have derived from Faulkner's resentment of Anderson as a father figure. Faulkner found himself in a typical Oedipal conflict. He needed to eliminate the father to establish himself, and yet, like his own father, Anderson was a substantial, large-sized figure for the small, almost runty younger writer. And yet it may not have been Anderson himself, but what he represented: the man making a success of it on inferior work, or on work Faulkner, at least, could not appreciate. If any of this is valid, it meant Faulkner found himself in a double bind: ruthlessly trying to put this man down at the same time he was dependent upon him. Every move he made, except his actual writing, had been helped by Anderson and his wife; she, before their marriage, and now the two of them. There is also the murky question of whether or not Faulkner had any interest in her as a woman, or perhaps felt she was available—although we have no evidence for this; or else saw her as a symbol of women available to writers like Anderson, who could afford to move from one wife to another and still live well.

Once settled into his tiny quarters near Spratling's apartment, Faulkner reinsinuated himself into Anderson's life. The older man always seemed ready to accommodate the young writer, even though it must have dawned on him he was being used. One thing besides literature that kept them together was a mutual liking for the bottle. Also, both did like to tell stories. The tales Anderson related to Faulkner seemed straight out of *Winesburg*, but what Faulkner specialized in was the tall tale. Out of this grew the "Al Jackson letters"—a series of tall tales in which each attempted to outdo the other in the realm of the fantastic, all based on the character known as Al Jackson. The name derived from the last descendant of Andrew "Old Hickory" Jackson, whose place Faulkner claimed to have seen on a boating trip on Lake Pontchartrain. The Al Jackson exchange was carried on at a cordial level of writer confronting writer, a country version of the inner city game of "dozens," another form of verbal competition. The best of the lot is Faulkner's piece about Al's sheep which, raised in the swamp, begin to transform themselves into alligators; and about Al's second son, Claude, who also is transformed, eventually into a shark who bothers the blonde lady bathers: " 'That's Claude,' said old man Jackson, 'he always was hell to blondes.' "[6]

Yet the exchange, while light and pleasant, was a form of competition. Faulkner was measuring himself against Anderson, the up-and-coming writer against the one everyone in New Orleans literary circles knew and deferred to. Anderson was clearly the father figure, and only the first of many writers Faulkner would measure himself against. Later, he angered Hemingway by his ranking of contemporary novelists, putting Thomas Wolfe at the head because of his courage and degrading Hemingway for having settled for less than his talent called for. While all this ranking might have seemed an amusing sidelight, it was really part of the competition Faulkner established for himself: bolstering an ego less than commanding, or asserting his birthright as the eldest son, in whom the mother believes completely.

Anderson seems to have entered into the exchange of the "Al Jackson letters" innocently enough, without realizing he had anything to win or lose. He was a far more open man than Faulkner, less caught, apparently, in the treacherous waters of literary ambition, and, of course, the lesser writer—within three or four years, Faulkner had raced past anything Anderson could hope to accomplish. In 1925, as they exchanged tall tales, the trajectory of both was approaching a juncture: Anderson probably at the peak of his reputation, Faulkner moving upward in an arc that would in a brief time carry him out of the older man's sight. It was auspicious they should vie with each other, for the exchange probably meant far more to Faulkner than to Anderson.

Phil Stone was delighted by what he took to mean a collaboration. Little did he realize Faulkner would not collaborate with anyone on a serious fictional project—the Al Jackson lark was just that, a lark, although it did prove to him he could hold his own in direct confrontation with a far more experienced writer. Stone missed the nuances of the exchange, and he wrote Four Seas—ever the huckster for Faulkner's products—that the two were jointly writing a novel. The only novel Faulkner was writing was "Mayday." And that was well along, if the sketches for it are any indication. But Anderson also warned him not to burn himself out with too rapid an output, telling his young protégé, "You've got too much talent. You can do it too easy, in too many different ways. If you're not careful, you'll never write anything."[7] Anderson's remarks, while well meant, indicate how little he knew of Faulkner, or how little the latter revealed of himself. Anderson was judging by ordinary standards, perhaps his own: go slowly, contemplate, conserve your forces, don't dissipate your energies. Faulkner was planning the opposite: write like a demon until he reached the words which defined something uniquely his, and then keep going obsessively.

If we judge by the undated notes for "Mayday," that early title for *Soldiers' Pay*, it was all planned out, apparently, at the time the pieces in the *Double Dealer* and the *Times-Picayune* were appearing. As the notes indicate, the novel was a hodgepodge of Faulkner's experience, some fantasies about the war, and a plundering of his own very early work.* One sheet of notes summarized in synopsis form the narrative line through part 3 of the novel. The other sheet was more of an outline, moving in its four paragraphs from details to bare statement of characters' names. It was

---

*The notes at the Berg Collection of the New York Public Library suggest that *Soldiers' Pay* may well have been conceived as a series of sketches or short stories, lengthier versions of what Faulkner was writing for the *Double Dealer*. It is also possible the notes came after he had begun the project and served as reminders. A large influence on the novel was James Branch Cabell, mainly *Jurgen*, although critics tend to overstate the Cabell presence. The completion date was May 1925 (not May 25), on the typescript at the Alderman Library.

clearly a check-off list more than a summary or even an outline; and, in fact, all the elements in the first paragraph are checked off.

Following the notes through, we see Faulkner's mind at work: the novel all in his head, and yet shaky in manuscript, needing revision and another typed version before final revisions. The process underwent several stages which suited his way of working: the sketchy notes or checklist of items to include; the almost illegible manuscript, written in a hand so tiny one often needs magnification to read, as if some hieroglyphic; then revision of this handwritten copy—cutting, looping, inserting, interpolating, as needed; then a typescript, which he prepared himself; revision of the typescript, which often involved further looping and inserting; final copy —taken from the revised typescript. Since all of this took considerable time, we must take into account how much effort went into Faulkner's novels once he had shaped the idea in his mind. Unlike Henry James, who sat down and in the main wrote out his novels, Faulkner directed a battle between the idea and final page. But manuscript copy itself flowed easily, apparently because he knew he would have to revise heavily and there was no reason to dawdle early on. In any event, he put in long hours, something we might forget because of his drinking and his relatively heavy visibility in New Orleans. Spratling does mention how Faulkner rose very early— insomnia brought him to his desk at 4:00 or 4:30 A.M., farmers' hours; and we know that after he married and settled into Rowan Oak, he rose well before the servants and went to his typewriter.

The "outline" note starts with Cecily, "engaged to an aviator reported as dead," with some further comments on her which don't seem particularly applicable to the development of the novel. Then follow lists of characters, Rector, Jones, Saunders, Mahon—crossed out, but then mentioned several times in this second paragraph. Part 4 of this segment lists "Death of Mahon," with reference to stories by Rector and Gilligan. Once again, we see this as a checklist, not an outline, since words and phrases are reminders rather than guides; mental jottings Faulkner apparently needed to jog his memory or keep the ideas flowing. The third paragraph stresses Jones, and one of his epigrams; and the final paragraph Jones again, characterized as "Boldness" and then something that looks like "stupidly." This page closes with what will be on the final page of the novel, the phrase: "Feed thy sheep, O Jesus," adding "into the moonless world of space, beyond despair." "Boldness" and "Stupidly" are both checked off. At the very bottom of this first sheet is scrawled: "Scribners / 597 Fifth Ave.," suggesting he had the famous New York publishing firm in mind, the house to be associated with Fitzgerald, Hemingway, and Wolfe.

Later, in the typescript, Faulkner numbered the words in each chapter, precisely, not estimating. All this is in keeping with distinct personality traits. In this one area, he was compulsively neat, careful, and accurate— his handwriting suggests a completely hermetic individual, and the numbering as well as care in his manuscripts and typescripts indicate a person who hates to give anything of himself, very close to what Freud defined as the classic anal personality. Such a harboring of the self and even of its products fits well with the silences. Further, Faulkner's use of every shred of his own experience and the stories he heard reinforces our assumption he could let nothing go. If it left his memory, it was not wasted, for it went into his books, which sealed it off from loss. Faulkner was a retaining creature, a self-contained individual of such intensity that had Estelle observed any of this and absorbed it, she would have known he was unmarriageable. He called his first novel "his mistress," and that designation remained true for all his work, for his career.

While Estelle remained behind in Oxford, caught between a marriage not working and a man who had found another "mistress," Faulkner was writing her, in large part, into the novel as Cecily Saunders. But whether she replicates Estelle or not, Cecily is a thoroughly unpleasant young woman; and her situation, as we have noted, is a shadowy one of Estelle's with Faulkner's. Full of the vanity of her own worth, this self-serving twirp, neurotic and flighty, lacked even the pretense of decency. Opposed to her—and Faulkner was careful to provide a woman with the right stuff —is Margaret Powers, the good woman despite a reputation for indecency. Had Faulkner wished to dramatize Cecily rather than gain literary revenge, there were alternatives for his presentation. One weakness of the novel is, evidently, the predictability of the characters—Cecily acts like a yo-yo among different men, even offering herself to the now blind Donald. Her relationship with Januarius Jones makes little sense, since he is presented as a repulsive male with sweaty palms. Thus, in turning Cecily into an object of derision, Faulkner undercut his own novel: she declares herself from the first and then is made to squirm at each turn of the screw. His hatred of her was so intense, so full of anger and hurt, that even in a literary dramatization he could not let go.

As we try to reconstruct the young Faulkner from his first novel, we note several autobiographical elements. As a psychological portrait, he has, in effect, divided himself into three men: first, the young, amateurish Julian Lowe, based broadly on Cadet Thompson from Faulkner's 1919 piece in the *Mississippian*, "Landing in Luck." Julian is gauche, unknowing, and a hayseed. The war, however, has ended for him, and in this respect his situation recalls not only Cadet Thompson's but Faulkner. He desperately wants to be a hero, to be given a chance, but now he must invent a bravura pose, which fools nobody. His letters to Margaret about his love for her and his conquests are documents of self-parody: Faulkner mocking himself as hayseed and poseur, as the young man rejected by the woman he wants.

But he is also Donald Mahon, Donald the man. Donald has gone through the baptism of fire Julian Lowe so wanted for himself, what Faulkner coveted and lied about. The terrible injuries and shock he has suffered draw some of the glamor out of war and battle, but they also give him an aura. In his comatose, near-silent, near-catatonic state, Donald becomes the focus of attention. Once he returns home with the help of Margaret and Joe Gilligan, another soldier, Lieutenant Mahon silently directs all the action. Thus, while the wound—whether psychic or physical—will kill him, at the same time it makes him a magnet. The great scar on his forehead becomes a circus attraction—everyone wants to see it even while everyone wants to make believe it is not there. Playing in and out of Donald is Faulkner's fantasy of himself, the uniform, the limp and cane, the head wound, the stories, all embodied in the sacred body of Donald.

His presence as a dying god—as much from Eliot and Frazer as intrinsically Faulkner's own image—sacralizes nearly all existence around him. Thus, if anyone profanes him, as Cecily and Jones do, then their worth is measured by their opposition to his sacred presence. As a god, he confers a certain dignity on those who defer to him. Both Margaret and Joe raise themselves as human beings because of their devotion to his welfare; and even the foolish old rector gains a certain dignity in his deep grief at his son's misfortune. If Donald were to speak, he would break the sacramental aura which silence makes possible; and here, as in other respects, Faulkner found a way of transferring his own personality into his character, or using a character to reveal himself.

The third young man is Joe Gilligan, and he further represents some part of Faulkner. Commonsensical, yet sappy over Margaret Powers, willing to pick up crumbs, softhearted and generous beneath a gruff exterior, a soft man posing as a man of the world, Gilligan is another side of the author—not symbolical or part of a fantasy, but the man as he is. Gilligan, later, is revealed in several Faulkner characters, the most conspicuous being Ratliff, but also some of the men at deer camp in the hunting stories. Such a man is Faulkner's presentation of "the salt of the earth type," and he is juxtaposed with someone like Januarius Jones. The latter spouts knowledge and witticisms far beyond the range of a Joe Gilligan, but Jones is artificial, self-serving, fundamentally a parasite with his fat, his love of food, his attempt to move on every young girl he meets. Gilligan's virtues are endurance, integrity, silence, qualities Faulkner admired and respected; such virtues, strong in themselves, are highlighted when opposed by Jones's greediness.

Of the three, however, Faulkner's strongest identification came with Mahon. Something in the idea of the dying god particularly suited Faulkner's outlook: his personal attraction to the phenomenon evidenced by its strong presence in his first novel; and his use of it, later, as a means of viewing the South when he writes his Yoknapatawpha novels and stories. Donald Mahon imposes himself in several forms: as the wounded Sartoris of *Flags in the Dust*, then in the novel carved from that and named after its protagonist; as Benjy of *The Sound and the Fury*, but also as Quentin Compson—a perfect blend of characteristics which make up a dying god without any physical or visible wound; to the basic situation in *As I Lay Dying*, where the entire situation reinforces the idea, with Addie Bundren commanding the scene as much as Donald does.

The application of the "dying god" to the South more generally comes in that famous manifesto, mentioned above, *I'll Take My Stand*. As Ransom wrote: ". . . the latter day societies have been seized—not quite so violently as our American one—with the strange idea that the human destiny is not to secure an honorable place with nature, but to wage an unrelenting war on nature."[8] By severing that link with nature, modern society has lost its association with mystery and with supernal life; thus, what was once the immanence of god or even his actuality is now a regression to a society whose gods are dying or dead. The enemies of a true god are everywhere: industrialization, modernization, progress, loss of community life, uncertainties in the individual.

These ideas play in and out of Faulkner. His attitudes toward community became more ambiguous and conflicted than those of the signatories of the agrarian statement, but community will play a stabilizing role in his conception of a society. His is almost always the microcosm, which in social terms is the community; although in many instances the community idea can be detrimental as well as supportive. But if we project Ransom's expression of outrage back onto Faulkner, we can see how he wanted to penetrate into mysteries, and how he shaped the dying god—Sartoris, Benjy, Quentin, Addie—into expressions of those mysteries.

Withal, *Soldiers' Pay* is, nevertheless, a young man's work. Near the end of his life, Faulkner stated the writer needed three tools: experience, observation, and imagination. As of 1925, they were pulling against each other, with imagination and observation subservient to experience. Poor habits appear abundantly in *Soldiers' Pay* and, even worse, in the aborted manuscript he worked on mainly in Paris, the uncompleted and ill-fated "Elmer." Those who know the "Elmer" material only through the thirty-page story Faulkner carved from it, "A Portrait of Elmer," a product of the early to mid-1930s, have little idea of how ill-planned a venture it was. "Elmer," which exists in several versions, derives from the same period as *Soldiers' Pay* and repeats many of the least creditable aspects of that novel. It had reached well over 30,000 words when Faulkner discarded it, apparently convinced the material was unsalvageable. "Elmer" is full of autobiographical touches, so that as a personal document it is significant, perhaps the single most significant material we have about Faulkner's attitudes and feelings in this critical period of his development. His decision to abort was a decision based on his recognition he was outgrowing the material even as he wrote it; that the mode in which he was working was ill-suited to his talent. He later told the Faulkner scholar James Meriwether that while "Elmer" was funny, it was not funny enough.

But before we come to "Elmer"—Faulkner's novel of "exile, cunning, and youth"—we can see poor habits already developing. The idea of the returning soldier was becoming quite common. Fitzgerald had already done it in a story called "Mayday," which was the working title of *Soldiers' Pay.* Hemingway wrote "Soldier's Home." But more than using a common theme, Faulkner echoed other writers' attitudes, tones, and voices, unassimilated into his own imagination. Eliotic lines appear straining for the rhythms of *Prufrock:* that intermingling of physical movement with internalized dialogue. "Women come and go . . ." There is an attempt to be arty, a kind of mock Henry James: ". . . Jones a fat Mirandola in a chaste Platonic nympholepsy, a religio-sentimental orgy in gray tweed, escaping an insincere, fleeting articulation of damp clay to an old imperishable desire, building himself a papier maché Virgin."[9] Margaret Powers is presented not in herself but as if Beardsley had seen her: "Had Gilligan and Lowe ever seen an Aubrey Beardsley, they would have known that Beardsley would have sickened for her: he had drawn her so often dressed in peacock hues, white and slim and depraved among meretricious trees and impossible marble fountains."[10] There is the usual youth's slap at James: "Jones grew up in a Catholic orphanage, but like Henry James, he attained verisimilitude by means of tediousness."[11]

These passages tell us little; they yearn for cleverness while blocking perception. The James quip seems like a gag waiting for a scenario; and the Beardsley is quite misleading, since Margaret is not at all a Beardsley character. Anderson, who saw part of the typescript, was alarmed by Faulkner's borrowings and cautioned him to write his own book, not to read others. Yet in one regard, it was necessary for him to mar his own work, so that he could purge it from his system. His first two novels and the incomplete "Elmer" were great learning experiences. The latter, for example, taught him that, unlike Hemingway, he could not write about Americans abroad, or about life in foreign countries. The only sense of place he had was that little postage stamp of territory, which early on extended to New Orleans.

Soldiers' Pay remains, nevertheless, as a sequence of meaningful scenarios of Faulkner's life, not only past and present but future. In that division of Faulkner into three men, he foresaw his own fall from grace; and in a fourth, George Farr, who marries Cecily, he predicted how his own honeymoon would work out—a foreshadowing of the miserable marriage to come. The dying god dies—having briefly obtained the woman, Margaret, who marries doomed men. She is, in one respect, a lamia: as she reminds Joe when he suggests marriage, the men she touches die. Julian Lowe, the amateur, continues to write letters and then vanishes, as if Faulkner were predicting he no longer represents him. And Joe, faithful Joe, gets on and off a train, missing Margaret who has remained aboard to say goodbye to him on the platform. He loses her in a Marx Brothers routine. He stays in the house of death, as Cecily and Farr return, themselves figures of doom in their unhappiness.

One dead, one disappeared, the other frustrated; and a fourth—not the main event—miserable. But the novel is not only male-female scenarios.

It presents views of marriage, of older couples who have lived through it, despite each other. Cecily's parents bicker, disagree, turn one another into opposites of the other. Mr. Saunders is under his wife's thumb; she lives to domineer. The marriage is made up of two people who have survived; yet there is no closeness, no compatibility, no sharing of interests. Maud and Murry come to mind. The rector, Mahon, is a widower, grown silly and unrealistic in his life alone, the person who has survived marriage to become a self-deceived old man. Perhaps Faulkner's grandfather was a partial model, the young colonel who had retreated into himself and memories before his death in 1922. Certainly Murry, big, bluff, dreamy, drifting off, full of unresolved fantasies, was a model, too. Emmy, the ill-fortuned young servant in the rector's household who longs after Donald, is marginal to everyone—yet lurking beneath her irritability is a solidity of love and loyalty to the young man's memory. Faulkner catches in her a certain realistic doggedness, a holding on—that endurance he was to make his trademark. Like Dilsey, she will endure. If we really wanted to divide Faulkner into even smaller slices, we could see him, also, in Emmy. Her very marginality gives her substance he comprehended. Finally, Donald, on his return as a vegetable, is cared for by his Mammy, as Faulkner was by his Mammy Callie (Caroline Barr). This alone is not a big point, except it demonstrates how the writer has so identified with his character's situation—so very different from his own in reality—that he has moved real people into a circumstance which is itself a fantasy of his own self.

The perception of men in the novel reveals an eye for weakness, not strength. Januarius Jones, with his spouting of information, his display of arcane references, may recall some aspect of Stone; and the sexual play Jones forces on all women may be a thin disguise for a total disdain for the sex. Lowe, for his part, moves offstage, represented only by fatuous letters. Farr, Cecily's "escape" from Donald, yearns after someone who will make him miserable. Margaret may find men who will die when she touches them, but Cecily "kills" in other ways. Faulkner spends a good deal of descriptive space on her clothes and figure, indicating how closely he has observed her—as would be the case with Estelle Oldham. He is very graphic about her figure. It is a "Twenties" shape: boyish, angular, with limbs that seem desirable because she is a tease, not because of any intrinsic attractiveness. She is constructed for displeasure, and even the diaphanous clothes she wears reveal not an enticing dish but a body which rejects. Such is the woman the men, except for Joe, flock to. In his depiction of the male figures and some of the female, Faulkner reveals his adversarial position to both society and community. As he seeks his own distinctive voice, he is the conscious rebel against authority and discipline, seeking values in the individual and not in any community. His "community" is, in fact, represented by poor marriages and shoddy relationships; his society, made up mainly of matrons circling the town with gossip, is insubstantial, hateful, full of self-pity and little, or no, self-knowledge.

His world beyond the rector and the dying god is one peopled by ghosts or phantoms: no one works or accomplishes anything; no active world, only one of words. This is true, also, of the "Elmer" material and *Mosquitoes*, his second published novel. With all his rootedness in Oxford and Lafayette County, with all his knowledge of Charleston, to the west of Oxford, he perceived society as drained of active life, will-less, caught up in cycles of failure and depression. The Faulkner of this period, despite his constant activity at his desk, must have experienced extreme uncertainty—if what passes for community is an indicator of personal feelings.

In another personal sketch, which combines some Sherwood Anderson and the Falkner family history, Faulkner writes of both the old and young colonels in surprisingly open terms. It is called "And Now What's to Do," and it remained unpublished, incomplete because it apparently became adrift in a sea of words. Faulkner tells of an ancestor who killed a man and was himself shot, but over cards, not business; and of a grandfather who retreated into himself, deaf, defeated politically. The protagonist's father is clearly a portrait of Murry, a man who runs a livery stable and cherishes horses and the outdoors.

Another, "Nympholepsy," is a hyped-up piece of prose, a graft on "The Hill," published in 1922 in the *Mississippian*. Like the earlier piece, it is an exercise in writing, about a worker making his way across country and suffering (enjoying?) a kind of hallucinatory experience. It is a valuable exercise in that it enabled Faulkner to move in and out of conscious and preconscious: between reality and dream, between the hardship of the worker's condition and gratifying fantasy.

He was not, however, forgetting "his" women. At a somewhat later date, he made up another one of his hand-decorated and hand-printed volumes for Estelle,* presenting it to her on October 29, 1926. Called *Royal Street* and comprising ten of the pieces he had published as "New Orleans" in the *Double Dealer*, it was carefully conceived and wrought. He omitted, for whatever reason, "The Tourist" and replaced it with "Hong Li."[12] The little volume was dedicated "To Estelle, a / Lady, with / Respectful Admiration." This dedication and declaration comes only shortly after he has completed the cycle of poems called *Helen: A Courtship* (in June of 1926), a declaration of love for Helen Baird, and a book he worked on while abroad. But that is not all. The title "Mayday," having been removed from *Soldiers' Pay*, is now connected to a brief allegorical piece and dedicated to the same Helen. And then when he completed his second novel, *Mosquitoes* (September 1, 1926), he dedicated that to Helen as well. There he calls her "beautiful and wise," making her

---

*By this time, Estelle had tried her own hand, with a story (unpublished) called "Star-Spangled Banner Stuff."

only part kin to the Trojan Helen, who was indeed beautiful, but whose wisdom Homer did not stress. What all this demonstrates is that in a period of about a year, Faulkner was rhapsodizing about fantasy women in his fiction and fantasizing rhapsodically about the real women in his life. He was, apparently, still seeking a center.

There now was a routine in New Orleans. Although the Andersons did not want him living with them, he continued to visit, and he had long sessions with Anderson. Faulkner listened carefully even as he was pulling away; and he took some advice to heart, even as he struggled to become his own man. Anderson was a focused writer, with a limited literary outlook; he recognized *Winesburg* was his signature piece, and he was eager to continue that sense of America, shaped as he had shaped it. He saw those sketches of American grotesques as symptomatic of the country. Having become an American writer with that material, he was, in effect, saying to the younger man: "Be an American writer." And the way to do it was to build on what he knew. Faulkner paraphrased the counsel: "You're a country boy; all you know is that little patch up there in Mississippi where you started from. But that's all right too. It's America too; pull it out, as little and unknown as it is, and the whole thing will collapse, like when you prize a brick out of a wall."[13]

Yet we have seen what Faulkner thought of Anderson in his mixed review of the man's career to date; and Anderson himself could not have understood how Faulkner would turn to European methods to help him deal with that "little patch" of Mississippi. Like Phil Stone, Anderson had little idea of what was stirring in the talent of a far greater writer, one capable of tremendous growth. It was the classic case of the father figure who does not understand what is stirring in the son, tries to lead, gives good advice, only to find it irrelevant. Then he senses betrayal.

Faulkner was embarrassed by Anderson's sentimentality,* his lack of dimensionality, his linear development of character and narrative. Anderson's situations were static. He always moved forward, lacking the memory, recall, retelling quality Faulkner was already experimenting with in *Soldiers' Pay*, however rudimentarily. Retelling, as opposed to telling, was so significant to Faulkner because it brought him into conflict with temporal modes. Time, memory, and historical sense became manifest through retelling: that accrual of past detail in present circumstances, that accretion of present fact injected into the past. Lacking the facility, or even the ability, to develop, Anderson bulldozed ahead, with honesty and integrity, but open to every young writer who decided to step on him. Faulkner and Hemingway were the first of that breed.

The innocent outings with Anderson continued until Faulkner par-

---

*Faulkner called Anderson "a lusty corn field in his native Ohio." He spoke of *Marching Men* and *Windy McPherson's Son* as lacking humor, "but then growing corn has little time for humor." The corn metaphor reappears in the comments on *Poor White*, and the remarks on *Many Marriages* are outright disapproving (in his Dallas *Morning News* review of Anderson).

ticipated, with Spratling, in the satiric presentation of the older writer which cooled the relationship.* Meanwhile, Faulkner moved ever deeper into New Orleans artistic and reportorial circles. Through Josh Baird, a young, junior reporter on the *Times Picayune,* Spratling met the former's sister, Helen; and then at one of Spratling's parties, Faulkner also met her. Like Faulkner, Helen Baird "presented" herself, her role-playing almost as insistent as his. Yet while she appeared to penetrate his role-playing rapidly, he had difficulty figuring out hers. She was planning to sail to Europe shortly and she became for him an obsession. Eventually, he portrayed her as Charlotte Rittenmeyer in *The Wild Palms,* more than a decade later; but even in that complicated portrait, he still did not grasp the real Helen Baird. What seems to have occurred is that Faulkner turned Helen into something he wanted her to be, or obsessively needed, and then refused to see her as she was, a profoundly troubled young woman whose unconventional manner disguised a deep desire for a conventional, even bourgeois marriage.

Another way of looking at it, which takes us beyond evidence, is that Faulkner continued to pursue her *because* she so forcefully rejected him: that in her rejection, he found something necessary, such as the ability to remain faithful to Estelle without being completely tied to her. By pursuing Helen well beyond the time when he knew he was rejected, he could break out of the Estelle net and yet somehow save himself for her because he knew Helen would say no. To pursue that argument even further, we could say Faulkner was moving within cycles of rejection, choosing women who would not only turn him down, but who would, if married to him, prove absolutely wrong.

Helen was a marvelous idea of the woman who got away, but who, if netted, would have proved intractable. As they circled each other, they were playing a dangerous game, although Helen proved the more realistic. Yet the game remained dangerous for Faulkner because it identified him with romantic pursuit doomed to failure. When he and Estelle finally came together, each brought a particular kind of freight to the union: she, the

---

*By the next year, 1926, Anderson's comments were full of ambiguities. In one letter to the publisher Horace Liveright, he asks him to help Faulkner, although he, Anderson, does not like the writer. In another, he tells Liveright: "He is modern enough and not too modern; also he is smart. If I were you, I would do what I could to encourage him to keep at work. If you want to do so, why don't you write him a letter telling him some of the things I have said about him, as it may buck him up, particularly if this first novel does not have much sale?" He also says, "I do not like the man personally very much . . ." and then adds: "He was so nasty to me personally that I don't want to write him myself . . ." (*Selected Letters of William Faulkner,* ed. Joseph Blotner [New York: Vintage Books, 1978; orig. publ. 1977], p. 155).

What Faulkner and Spratling did to Anderson's son, Bob, may have contributed to the disenchantment. In his *File on Spratling: An Autobiography,* the painter says that when Spratling and Faulkner couldn't get rid of the boy, they grabbed him one day, "took his pants off, painted his peter green," and then pushed him out into the street, locking the door behind him. Faulkner's role in this seems debatable, since he was usually quite kind to young people, but he and Spratling may have been carried away by heavy drinking into uncharacteristic sadism. The suggestion here of some homoerotic byplay must remain precisely that, a suggestion.

many years of dislocation and unhappiness in marriage; and he, an attitude toward women already distorted by expectations of rejection and failure. They were both, in effect, exhausted.

The Faulkner Helen met, as he moved in this most productive year of his young life, was still role-playing. He limped, carried a cane, affected a British accent, apparently, spoke of the head plate—as ever the war-weary, wounded warrior, now seven years after the war. This went beyond role-playing as a put-on or joke. It had become part of Faulkner, a shield, or response to deep feelings of inferiority: his sense that if he presented himself unadorned, he would not be taken seriously. This is strange behavior for a boy whose mother believed in him so strongly, but he was marked by some kind of trauma which dictated deception and which would only dissipate itself when he was famous. Helen became the prime recipient of that internal conflict, and she responded as she was expected to: with rejection. She became, as a result, a cause for Faulkner. When he could not have her (although the relationship may well have been consummated), he turned her into a literary convention, the knight dedicating a joust or kill to his lady.

Apparently, Helen was not the only one he carried on his role-playing with. It extended to other members of the group and even to those on its fringes. One such acquaintance was Harold Levy, a businessman with musical interests, who reported that Faulkner maintained both his British accent and the fact of his wound. Levy said he had the impression Faulkner had been pensioned off by the air force and had suffered or was still suffering from his affliction. The maintenance of the British accent, if true, is remarkable. Faulkner's normal speech was a deep Mississippi accent, often so softly produced and slurred he was unintelligible to those only a few feet away. The fake accent—unlike the wound, limp, cane—involved words; and the words he was accenting were very different from the words he was writing. The British accent deserves separate consideration, inasmuch as it involved communication, not simply appearance. Faulkner was altering the sound of himself, even while his writing reflected a very different cultural stance. To write about the South as in *Soldiers' Pay*, *Mosquitoes*, and *Flags in the Dust*, while speaking in an accent which belied the "accent" of what he was writing, was for him to assume a split, even a schizoid personality. Apparently, one side of him needed that pose, while the other, protected by that shield and disguise, could be activated to do his real work. Such was the complicated human being Faulkner presented to his New Orleans friends, impenetrable even to the shrewdest of them.

This intense role-playing paralleled his writing about his pilgrimage from Swinburne to Housman, in the essay already referred to, "Verse Old and Nascent: A Pilgrimage," in the April *Double Dealer*. This piece was a freeing force for Faulkner, much as the preface to *The Nigger of the "Narcissus"* had been for Conrad in 1897. The drift to Housman, by way of other moderns (Frost, Aiken, Robinson), is perhaps linked to that continued role-playing. By writing unyieldingly of young men and their inevitable doom, Housman added a toughness to his lyric voice. With his "splendor of fortitude," Housman foreshadows Faulkner's own sense of endurance, and with his "beautiful in sadness" suggests both men's bleakness without bitterness. Housman perhaps reinforced Faulkner's dissembling: to hold back the doom of youth, the passing of beauty, to unravel the paradox of splendor and bleakness.

The manuscript of *Soldiers' Pay* is dated March 1925, its writing placed in New Orleans; the typescript is 473 pages long, in Faulkner's own typing. In fact, he completed the novel toward the end of May, between the twentieth and twenty-fifth, most likely. The typescript at Virginia shows relatively few revisions, and those of an insignificant nature—Faulkner had a solid grasp of his novel from the beginning and seemed satisfied with the result. In later work, revisions were numerous and extensive.

In *Faulkner in the University*, a collection of his informal lectures and responses to questions, the writer reported Sherwood Anderson's words repeated by his wife to the young writer: "He said he will make a trade with you. If he don't have to read it, he will tell his publisher to take it." Faulkner responded, "Done."[14] Blotner then reports that in a letter from Estelle, he learned the exchange went something like this: Anderson said, "I'll do anything for him so long as I don't have to read his damn manuscript." Estelle said Faulkner was hurt by the hostility implicit in that, in so far as Anderson had previously been supportive on the manuscript. But the older writer was true to his word and put Faulkner in touch with Boni & Liveright, who accepted the novel.

In either version, the story has something apocryphal about it, something of the hostility Faulkner would like to transfer to Anderson, but which Faulkner was himself feeling, as he was forced to depend on his friend for a publisher. In this scenario, as long as he depended on Anderson—here, for Boni & Liveright's services—he, Faulkner, would need some way to displace his hostility, and what could be more effective as a defensive act than to have Anderson taketh away even as he giveth. In that way, Faulkner could justify to himself his further use of Anderson without giving up his self-containment—the rudeness of the remark made him suffer for the sake of his art. That he mentioned it to Estelle Franklin and then himself repeated it several years later only supports that it had become part of his emotional life; but less as a wound than as a way of telling a good tale.

With *Soldiers' Pay*, the year 1925 was only half over for Faulkner; the second half was to prove just as remarkable. 1925 would not equal 1929 in quality of manuscript produced—1929 was truly an *annus mirabilis* for him—but 1925 was nevertheless a year of variety, abundance, and engagement. It brought together, furthermore, several strands of Faulkner's life, pleasant as well as unpleasant, but nearly all of them leading to development and maturation of talent.

After nearly six months in New Orleans, Faulkner returned to Mississippi in June, for less than a month, prior to his sailing for Europe on July 7 with William Spratling. Immediately after his departure from New Orleans—which he left without saying goodbye to Anderson—he spent a good deal of time at the Gulf resort of Pascagoula, where Jack Stone, Phil's brother, had a modest place. When we elaborate on Faulkner's dependence on Phil, we should not neglect how he used all of his friend's resources: office, typist, brother's place, friends and contacts, family home and hunting camp. In a real sense, the Stone experience enveloped Faulkner, and it was surely this dependence on the part of one, the act of patronage on the other, that finally got under their skin when the agreed-upon roles began to fall apart. Yet at this time, when Faulkner had nothing of his own, he depended completely on Phil's considerable largesse. With or without Helen Baird, Pascagoula was a perfect retreat for the writer. The area lay in the farthest southeastern tip of the state, almost on the Alabama border, nestling up against the Gulf and only a few miles from Mobile Bay. It was not only a perfect retreat, it was a way of remaining away from Estelle, who with her children remained in Oxford in semipermanent separation from her husband. It would appear that with his imagination boiling away on so many different projects, Faulkner had decided to spend little time in Oxford; needless to add, the occasional presence of Helen Baird helped.

Although Pascagoula recalled a time when industrialization had brought great prosperity, industry had receded, and the city was a sleepy place, with beach and waterfront dominating. The Stone house—nicknamed "The Camp"—was simplicity itself, precisely what would appeal to the writer. Faulkner's sleeping arrangements were located on the side porch, and his work area was on the grounds, his desk a board on which he placed his typewriter. Faulkner worked at all hours of the day and night, although he congenially entered into house activities. In most respects, he was the perfect guest: compliant, splendid with the children, never voluble. But the outward display of compliance could not disguise his obsessional need to put words on paper. Despite the casual atmosphere, the partying, the encounters with new people, the drinking, Faulkner pecked away at his typewriter.

Yet even in the middle of his most productive year to date, he was still relatively undefined in his own mind about direction. Despite certain overtures to Eliot and Joyce in techniques, his material was traditional in narration and scenic development. The forthcoming "Elmer" would move him a little more toward a convoluted narrative, but was itself so unfocused and so unclearly organized in its various drafts that it self-aborted. The poetry he directed at Helen was conventional, also, although he spoke of having broken free. In prose work after "Elmer" had been set aside, *Mosquitoes* and *Father Abraham,* he was still caught up in traditional and conventional modes, virtually up to the time he was thirty—with only occasional breakouts. The assimilation of modernist techniques which finally came toward the end of the 1920s reveals how profoundly Faulkner had to work into his talent to discover what lay beneath conventional modes; and how, inevitably, his career would be a struggle not only between community and individual but between the conventional and the modern in technique. He did not come by such matters easily, or acquiesce simply because everyone of moment in Europe was becoming modern.

The people around him in Pascagoula could not have had any hints of what was going on in him, and the struggles may have themselves been blurred to him. It is hard to imagine a man who looked like a beachcomber, and was, in effect, that, planning out works which would catch the attention of the world and bring the deep reaches of modernism to American fiction. He was certainly not the European image of the man of letters. Helen Baird, for her part, didn't think he looked like much at all. After she married Guy Lyman, she wrote that he reminded her of a "fuzzy little animal."[15] She also referred to him as one of her "screwballs."

She was herself no great apparition, since she cared little about her appearance and showed a good deal of her body in outfits revealing deep burns from childhood. She wore the scars as badges of pride and dared anyone to feel sorry for her. Faulkner simply fell in deeper and deeper. He was a conservative man with a flair for extremism: modernism was one aspect of it, Helen another. Life with her would have been a circus, as she must have recognized when she repulsed his offers. Her mother, also, did not think much of Faulkner, calling him a "wild man." What made him "wild" was not behavior, but appearance: unshaven, bare feet, trousers held up by a string or rope, mustache (although usually neatly trimmed), pipe in mouth—he was not anyone's dream of a son-in-law or fiancé.

Apart from Helen herself, Faulkner saw nearly everyone around him marrying, and he had no one—Estelle was part of that nether world of attraction and dismissal. Helen herself seemed like an original: her cynical, indifferent manner; her boyish figure, barely beyond a child's stature; her ability to stare down anyone who might question her scars; her artistic tendencies, as a painter. Most of all, Faulkner was taken with her façade. She was all defenses, having developed a manner or pose which was the equivalent of a persona. Her straightforwardness about her disfigured body was part of that persona, and this was something Faulkner could understand and appreciate. He thought she was like him, carrying on with a wound—his psychological, emotional, pseudo-physical; hers of both worlds. This made them, he felt, secret sharers. He read into her shielded, defensive manner someone who was indifferent to what the world thought, even as she arranged in her own favor what it did think. He misread her almost entirely: the defensiveness was certainly there, but she was not an extremist, not ready to flaunt her indifference to society, unprepared to oppose her mother's wishes and tastes.

After Helen departed for Europe, Faulkner prepared for his own trip. *Soldiers' Pay* was still being put into shape for mailing in Phil Stone's office.

While his office typed, corrected, and tidied up Faulkner's own accidental errors, Phil began to write letters of introduction for his friend to the top-drawer modernists, Eliot, Joyce, and Pound. He was, in effect, creating an aura of fame around himself by becoming a Ford- or Pound-like impresario of letters. Since he did not know these writers, there was a grandeur to his gesture, and, also, a delusion of grandeur. He meant well for Faulkner, but such acts made the small-town lawyer, the Oxford man with the big Northern education, appear like a worldly man of letters. Meanwhile, once the manuscript was ready, Faulkner mailed it to Boni & Liveright and returned to New Orleans, ready to leave. He hoped to support himself in Europe by writing articles, stories, and sketches, such as those for the *Times-Picayune.* * Hemingway had done it, and there was considerable interest in America for European vignettes. The great travel boom was still in its infancy, but growing in the 1920s. Faulkner became part of that literary pilgrimage abroad. He would carry with him a piece of Helen—the first seven poems in the cycle dedicated to her, *Helen: A Courtship.*

It was a crazy mix of elements: an apparent understanding with Estelle; a new love in the shape of Helen, who rejected him and left before he did; a sheaf of poems dedicated to the person who rejected him; a desire to work his way across, with Spratling, in a freighter or some such ship; a lack of money, but a desire to write pieces to support himself; a novel he had sent to Boni & Liveright, for which he later received a $200 advance. He said he had $50 for expenses, plus an additional $20 from his Aunt 'Bama, the old colonel's daughter. She was later described as someone "pickled in martinis"—but she liked her grandnephew and chose to help.

When the time came, he and Spratling ended up crossing in style, on the *West Ivis.* After several stops in the South, the last in Savannah on July 14, the *West Ivis* steamed toward Genoa, Italy, with Spratling and Faulkner enjoying their own staterooms and living as well as the captain. Faulkner apparently wrote "The Liar" for the *Times-Picayune* during the first stages of the voyage. "The Liar" was the beginning of the cracker-barrel, rural material which became his stock-in-trade, but in itself is a shabby piece of fiction, using an O. Henry surprise ending. It was a regression on Faulkner's part, and he possibly considered it a throwaway; or, more likely, the price he would have to pay to gain funds for Europe.

"Elmer," also written at this time, has elements which can be transferred to Faulkner's trip, since that manuscript is a shadow version of his own journey, both psychologically and physically. Elmer Hodge takes some heavy reading with him, Clive Bell, for example, and Elie Faure's *History of Art,* also Ludwig Lewisohn's *A Modern Book of Criticism.* Although he would later play the semiliterate farmer with reporters and critics, Faulkner made periodic efforts to educate himself in a broadly

*Two of them from around this period are "Episode," which appeared on August 16, and "Peter," unpublished. Spratling is in both; in the latter the narrator is a mulatto child who relates his mother's experiences in a brothel.

humanistic way; while he read haphazardly, he did go beyond novels and poetry, into history, art, and even criticism. "Elmer" is essentially Faulkner's portrait of the artist as a young man, although inconclusive and inchoate. Spratling reports his friend threw over the side of the *West Ivis*, just two days out of New Orleans, a bundle of manuscript, confirmed by Faulkner as some sonnets. In the same way, although without the actual dumping, Faulkner used "Elmer" as a throwaway, emptying into it a variety of personal elements, as well as a shadowy version of his own *Wanderjahr* into the heartland of modernism. "Elmer," however, was more than shadowy Faulkner. Piecemeal, disguised, reshaped, it found itself in later work. We see aspects of it in *Mosquitoes*, Faulkner's novel following *Soldiers' Pay*, and then in his third novel, *Sartoris*, which was carved from *Flags in the Dust*, itself a quarry. If we look forward into the ripest part of Faulkner's career, we note the Elmer-Ethel relationship assimilated into Harry and Charlotte in *The Wild Palms*. As for stories, the best-known piece carved from the incomplete novel is "Portrait of Elmer" in the 1930s; earlier, "Growing Pains," from the 1920s and itself incomplete, and then "Divorce in Naples," either the late 1920s or very early 1930s.

Bits and pieces of "Elmer" exist in the Virginia and Mississippi collections, including possible other beginnings for the novel, or else incomplete versions of stories carved from the original material. Virginia, for example, has "Elmer and Myrtle" and "Portrait of Elmer Hodge," either the start of the novel or, more likely, another version of a story snipped from the novel. The Rowan Oak papers at Mississippi have further inconclusive bits, either of the novel or of a story to be carved from it, the "Growing Pains" mentioned above. The proliferation of materials from a manuscript itself considered inchoate creates an interesting psychological situation. We ask: if Faulkner after tinkering with the novel to the tune of well over 30,000 words evidently found it was unworkable and had to be abandoned at a time he needed money, what was there about that material which made him return to it with such assiduity? This and many other related questions about "Elmer" must be addressed.

Faulkner and Spratling reached Genoa on August 2—almost a month out of New Orleans. Their trouble with Italian money has become a famous story, and while Faulkner transferred it to himself, it was really Spratling's problem. It turned up in "Elmer" and became the way to introduce Elmer to the Italian Angelo, thus setting off one of the many subthemes of that work. In a cabaret visited by prostitutes, Faulkner and Spratling were enjoying their introduction to Italian low life, when Spratling was suddenly seized and whisked off to the police station. He was charged with a crime against the Italian royal family—committed when he accidentally stepped on some Italian money with the king's portrait. He spent one night in the local jail, and the future was presented as dire. Italian nationalistic fervor was high since Mussolini's march on Rome in 1922. Through the intervention of the American consul and a Genoese official, however, Spratling was released—informed how lucky he was to get off. With that he left on his own jaunt, to view architectural structures. Faulkner was now on his own. From Italy, he would travel through Switzerland (which he disliked) and then head for Paris. He was turning twenty-eight, having been writing for ten years, five of them seriously. As he journeyed to Rapallo, where Pound now lived, he was part of that world which included Pound, Eliot, Joyce, Yeats, Mann, Proust, and the other modernists he so admired.

Chapter Nine

Into the Den

FAULKNER'S TRAVELS IN Europe did not put him in direct touch with modernist writers or with their ideas; but he was, through books lent him by Phil Stone, already acquainted with many phases of modernism. And it was not necessary to know everyone to become touched by the new; one could read a few—Eliot, Joyce, Mann perhaps— and from that extrapolate what was innovative, what was being discarded. Never a systematic reader, Faulkner intuited what fitted his own temperament. He could not actually imitate Proust, for example, or even Joyce to any large degree and still accommodate the materials of his own experience. He was not the kind of writer who could invent his material far from the region of his own grounding.

How, then, would Faulkner join them? To be modern, he could not continue along the lines of "Elmer" or *Soldiers' Pay*. He would have to shift his literary stance radically. In Rapallo, Pound was writing cantos that were deeply filmic in nature, utilizing techniques borrowed from the still-infant motion-picture industry. Pound touched virtually every aspect of modernism. His experiments with language coincided with those Faulkner found in *Ulysses* and *The Waste Land*. They brought home to him the advantages of indirect narration in both poetry and prose, the drama of rapid changes, the benefits of introducing material obliquely. Further, both Eliot and Joyce conveyed to him a new sense of history: not the linear history of traditional literary modes, but history collapsed, telescoped, reshaped—modes which went into his own particular brand of telling and retelling, culminating in *Absalom.*

But Faulkner's use of modernism went further, even when he was resistant to such developments or relatively ignorant of them. "Elmer" is full of very carefully planted Freudian images tracing Elmer's adolescent, regressive sexuality. It is not, however, very carefully nuanced. To begin with, there is his horror at the color red, signifying fear of the vagina; his fondling of paint tubes, so that touch, color, and shape connect his yearning for art with masturbatory sexuality; his fascination with cigars and cigar stubs; his collection of whips; his obsession with phallic shapes of all kinds. Much of this is obvious and unsophisticated Freudianism, but Faulkner's linkage of art and sexuality is somewhat less immature, more on target. Just a few years after "Elmer," Faulkner began deep Freudian journeys in his fiction, influenced partially by Joyce's explorations, but equally by Freud's own innovative analyses of what lay disguised under the conscious mind. Faulkner had in fact much earlier become a "Freudian case" by using uniform, wound, limp, and cane as ways of transforming himself, as a means of disguising whatever trauma he had suffered.

Yet this was still only the beginning of his response to modernism. In his use of time, Faulkner showed responsiveness to modernism's major achievement: that assimilation of Einstein and, before him, Bergson, into literary narrative. Here is, perhaps, Faulkner's largest contribution to modernism. No other American novelist of his generation responded to this degree—only Dos Passos seemed to be aware of the potentialities of different temporal modes for fiction, what we find in Woolf, Joyce, Ford, Hermann Broch, Robert Musil, and, of course, Proust. Modes based on relativities and uncertainties, modes founded on the inexorable forces of irrational elements pushing out and challenging rationalities, modes in which motivations, behavioral matters, and incentives are all scrambled— such temporal modes involved new types of narrative, since the writer could not express this pull from the irrational without finding new ways of expressing it. Here, still early in his career, Faulkner was most responsive with *The Sound and the Fury* and *As I Lay Dying.*

Yet temporal modes, the uses of the unconscious, and the awareness of new languages were still only part of modernism's radicalism. What Faulkner had to respond to was the introduction of new forms of seeing and hearing. By 1925 the move toward nonrepresentation and abstraction had not only taken over painting, it had spread significantly into all areas of creativity from writing to architecture. The basis for abstraction was the attack on objects, on what is routinely perceived and taken for granted. The object (as well as person, scene, specified element) was the enemy, in a complex movement away from representational art toward line, plane, and color—what Kandinsky identified and defined as a spiritual mode. The theorizing of this vast movement was beyond Faulkner's interest, but the import of it was not. The assault on objects as the enemy of creativity became part of his weaponry as a writer, in his emphasis on the withholding of information, in the distribution of facts so that they never seem collected or resolved, in his collapsing of historical detail so that it appears and reappears differently shaped at different times. While this is not quite "abstractionism"—impossible to achieve in a verbal medium—it is an approximation of what cubists and then nonrepresentational painters were attempting to do on canvas. Joyce in *Finnegans Wake* is the furthest remove from representation in fiction, and obviously Faulkner did not travel that route. But in his work beginning at the end of the 1920s, he tried it all; and in *Sound* and *Absalom* he found equivalent vehicles, where every aspect of his use of modernism found its place.

The new music, while less obvious as an influence on writers, also had its place. By 1910, Arnold Schönberg with his introduction of atonality was attempting to change the way we hear and listen. Music was "different sounds." And chamber music and even symphonic works structured without a dominant tonic were vehicles of reordering sounds, in some ways paralleling the cubists' reordering of our ways of perceiving. Then when Schönberg in 1922 moved to twelve-tone or serial music, there was further development, whereby musical notation paralleled painterly abstraction (although dimensions in different genres can never be more than approximate). What Schönberg and the second Viennese group (including Alban Berg and Anton von Webern) wrought was nothing less than a reordering of aural experience. It found its place among experiments with prose and in the avant-garde painting of Kandinsky and Mondrian and their epigones.

Where does Faulkner come into this? Unlike Broch or Musil or Joyce, he was not a knowledgeable experimenter, but a visceral innovator responding to his sense of what was now possible. His emphasis on interior monologue derived from his reading in Joyce and Eliot, but also from his awareness of art as internalized in irrational areas. His stress on verbal disharmonies which coalesce somewhere beyond rational meaning suggests he was responding to the new sense of sound and sight. And his attempt through sophisticated symbols (no longer cigar stubs and fat tubes of paint) to reveal a disordered, unsettled, and uncertain world suggests he keyed in to virtually everything occurring on the Continent.

Faulkner's method of telling and retelling, if viewed imaginatively, has within it the same kernel of "unfolding" Pound was employing in his *Cantos* of the 1920s and 1930s. The method is to give only as much information as is necessary, in order to undercut any sense of traditional narrative; the plan is to fold in material, not to expose it unless absolutely necessary.* Pound's method is filmic, montage-oriented; and while Faulkner is

---

*Faulkner modulated the "telling and retelling" dimension of his work. *Absalom* fits into that mode, in which language does not refer to things but to other forms of language. As structuralist critic Gerard Genette says, "The notion of showing in narrative, is, therefore, an illusion. Words are signifiers bearing meanings, they cannot imitate actions, the only things they can imitate are other words." In *Sound*, telling exists, but "showing" dominates, so that referentiality is more significant than in *Absalom*. For an excellent discussion of this matter, see Sonja Bašić's "Faulkner's Narrative Discourse: Mediation and Mimesis," *New Directions in Faulkner Studies* (Jackson: University Press of Mississippi, 1983).

less attuned to motion-picture techniques, his withholding of material creates the impression of interior montage.

In still another area—what we may call "spiritual autobiography"— Faulkner entered deeply into the modernist experience. A large body of Faulkner's work fits into this very broad category of fiction. The bildungsroman, the novel of formation or development in which a young person comes to maturity, had been an extremely popular form in the nineteenth century, revealing the deepest needs of the period and demonstrating how youth may rise from small beginnings to positions of affluence and power. With the modern movement, the ideology evidently changed, so that a representative of the lower or marginal classes eventually finding his or her niche in society became secondary to other considerations.

By the turn of the twentieth century, the bildungsroman began to undergo mutations. It responded to the same elements that nourished the modern movement in general. The previous form of the novel, with its assumption that a mature individual will be a social asset, finds its focus shifting from individual and social well-being to matters of spirit, soul, and self. The traditional bildungsroman, which was nearly always a form of disguised autobiography, now becomes far less disguised as matter shifts to spirit. The shift is from physical well-being, happiness, and stability to intangibles like mental health, sexual discovery (or uncertainty, even rejection), and, chiefly, spiritual needs located outside formal religion. The protagonist, now a mere shadow figure for the author, no longer shapes himself into a social unit, but exists solely for himself, a cell without reference to any group or person responsive to his needs. Narrative itself, as we see with Faulkner, reflects the change, with linear becoming convoluted, incidents recurring simultaneously or in memory, present tense giving way to indistinct pasts, ends implicit in beginnings.

Spiritual autobiography called for new tactics, new narrative strategies such as interior monologue and stream of consciousness, or, as in Faulkner's case, a middle ground between preconscious and unconscious —*there*, but not quite either. Such spiritual self-display appears, in primitive form, in "Elmer," then somewhat more assuredly in *Flags in the Dust*, and then reaches its fulfillment two years later. In fact Faulkner's first two novels could be added to this list, except their relative conventionality conflicts with the fact that spiritual autobiography requires new strategies to become itself. What characterizes the form is a secession from nearly everything naturalism/realism purports to reflect. As Faulkner moved into this form in the late 1920s, his break with Sherwood Anderson's own thinly disguised naturalistic autobiographies was complete.

Faulkner was reaching for the "new man" (Benjy, Quentin, Darl, Joe Christmas, Sutpen, even Popeye) who is disaffected, outside social coordinates, or else a juncture of emptiness, what Sartre called "Faulknerian man." He is a person for whom the outside world, however defined, has ceased to function, for whom it has become a dark place. Joyce's *A Portrait of the Artist as a Young Man* comes to mind immediately as one of the most accessible novels of this new breed. Joyce's progression from *Dubliners* through *Stephen Hero* and *A Portrait* can be seen as an increasingly intense movement toward spiritual autobiography. In Faulkner's career, we have, very roughly, something of the same passage: from *Soldiers' Pay* and *Mosquitoes* through "Elmer" and *Flags* to *Sound*, *As I Lay Dying*, *Light in August*, and *Absalom*. Since the materials for each author were so different, the comparison is somewhat crude, but the significant element is the passage they take: from realist/naturalistic works, through something more indeterminate, unformed, and incomplete, into fully realized works of disguised spiritual autobiography.

In these respects, Faulkner's predecessors had been, besides Joyce, such obvious figures as Proust (in *Jean Santeuil* as well as *Remembrance of Things Past*); Hesse's several turn-of-the-century fictions, prototypes of spiritualized quests; Gide, especially in *The Immoralist;* Conrad, in part, in *Lord Jim;* and writers Faulkner did not know, Franz Kafka and Robert Musil. Behind this transformation of the genre are Nietzsche and Freud. Freud influenced the entire movement with his *The Interpretation of Dreams* (1900) and his theory of the unconscious; and Nietzsche wrote an early form of spiritual autobiography in *Ecce Homo*, which signifies a new man for our times. Jesus uses these words, and He meant a holy man for a parlous, material era. On the edge of madness—no small commodity in this developing form of autobiography—Nietzsche saw himself as this "new man," portrayed as heading into the unknown, where "the 'great nothing' lies." Nietzsche contrasted "world-weariness" with "becoming": the twin terms of spiritual autobiography and, of course, terms perfectly suited to Faulkner's post–Civil War and post–World War I protagonists.

As he moved into the den of modernity, his correspondence gives us a sense of his trip. He passed through Rapallo, missing (or not attempting to see) Pound. He was on his way to Paris, by foot. He saw Milan, Pavia, and Stresa, above Lake Maggiore; then moved on to Switzerland, where he felt uncomfortable.* In a postcard to Maud Falkner (postmarked August 13) from Domodossola-Milano, he expressed his feelings about Switzerland: "Full of Americans—terrible. . . . The people eat and sleep and sit on the sides of mountains, watching the world pass, and that's all." He found it, in a word, dull. Even after he arrived in Paris, his feelings about Switzerland remained sour, although as he expresses his sentiments to Aunt 'Bama, his distaste seems more for Americans than for Swiss. "I didn't like Switzerland. Switzerland is a big country club with a membership principally American. And I am quite disgusted with my own nationality in Europe. Imagine a stranger coming in your home, spitting on your floor and flinging you a dollar. That's the way they act." He then contrasts this with life in France. The logic here is somewhat skewed: "But France, poor beautiful France. So innately kind, despite their racial lack of natural

*One poem, "Nostalgia," has "Capri" at the end, although there is no evidence of Faulkner's making a visit to that island; also, another island is indicated, without proof of a visit.

courtesy, so palpably keeping a stiff upper lip."[1] His perceptions of people and races are predisposed by what he wanted to see: vulgar Americans, dull Swiss, and French whom he liked from his reading.

In the same letter, he speaks of spending long hours in the Luxembourg Gardens. "I write there, and play with the children, help them sail their boats, etc." Describing an old man he has noticed who sails a toy boat on the pool, he says he will himself one day pass his time like that: "I shall have a weathered derby hat like his and spend my days sailing a toy boat in the Luxembourg Gardens." Earlier in the letter, he spoke of his stay in Sommariva, a dot of a village above Stresa, where he lived and worked with the peasants: ". . . going out with them in the morning to cut grass, eating bread and cheese and drinking wine from a leather bottle at noon beneath a faded shrine with a poor little bunch of flowers in it, and then coming down the mountain at sunset, hearing the bells on the mule jingle and seeing half the world turning lilac with evening." Supper was outdoors, followed by drinking with the people, and communicating with "those kind quite happy people by signs."[2] The young Faulkner sounds like the young Hemingway.

We can sense a liberation as Faulkner embraced new experiences. He preferred the simple things; one possible reason he was put off by his Swiss experience was the pretense and ostentation of Americans there, whereas the Italians and French he met were simply themselves. Going back to August 13, he writes to Maud of reaching Paris in the same vein of happy liberation from the past and from himself. The tone of this and other letters is quite different from the heavy tone and weight of his fiction— perhaps for the first time in his life he felt distance from himself; enough so that he could open up. He tells his mother that he and Spratling have found a pleasant hotel in Montparnasse, on "the left bank of the Seine, where the painters live." He indicates he is waiting to hear about his novel and planning to write some travel pieces.

The letters which follow, separated often by only two or three days, are all upbeat and forward-looking. Although Faulkner began to write "Elmer" shortly after he came to Paris, his letters do not suggest the difficulties the novel was causing him; from the beginning he could not get a handle on it. The letter of August 18, also to Maud, has the tone of a kid with a grin on his face, as Faulkner recounts what he has seen: the Seine, Notre Dame, the Champs Élysées, the Luxembourg Gardens. Two days later, he writes of his exposure to the Louvre, the visit combining a view of the Winged Victory and the Venus de Milo ("the real ones"), the Mona Lisa, the "more-or-less moderns," Edgar Degas, Edouard Manet, Puvis de Chavannes. These "moderns" were by 1925 old hat, having been replaced by several waves of avant-garde painting. By then, even cubism in its various phases was ancient history, and dada had been displaced by surrealism.

Five days later (August 23), he writes exuberantly of "Elmer": "I am in the middle of another novel, a grand one." He indicates he has put *Mos-*

quitoes aside for the moment, and that work on "Elmer" was the result of a thought the "day before yesterday."³ He fears he doesn't know enough to write *Mosquitoes*, a strange assessment inasmuch as he had his entire cast from his New Orleans experience. On August 26 he is full of "Elmer," writing as fast as he can because his head is so full of it, "so clear in my mind." But writing is not everything, as he reports what he eats, how he breaks up his day into reading and sitting in the Luxembourg Gardens, and writing letters home regularly. Four days later, he tells his mother, as he would tell Aunt 'Bama, of the old man who sails his boat in the pool of the Luxembourg Gardens—apparently a scene which has so impressed him he will use part of it for the ironic ending of *Sanctuary* more than four years later. On September 6 he foreshadows that particular scene with Temple Drake, "2000 words about the Luxembourg gardens and death." "It has a thin thread of plot, about a young woman, and it is poetry though written in prose form." He calls it a beautiful and perfect thing, a jewel.

"Elmer" moved along quite rapidly, with 20,000 words reported by September 6, also a poem "so modern that I don't know myself what it means."⁴ But while there was euphoria—the pleasure of both life and work going well—in the background there was a shadow: *Soldiers' Pay* perhaps being rejected by Boni & Liveright after one of three readers failed to recommend publication. The recipient of this news was Phil Stone, not Faulkner, who remained oblivious to what might have undermined his extended holiday. By this date, Spratling had left, and Faulkner was alone in Paris, but not at all eager to take advantage of the introductions established by Stone. In his ignorance, he told Aunt 'Bama he expected a fall publication date.

He wrote to Maud (September 13) the first indication "Elmer" was faltering. "I have put the novel away" in order to start another one, "a sort of fairy tale that has been buzzing in my head."⁵ He says this "will be the book of my youth," and he will spend two years on it, finishing it by his thirtieth birthday. The book which comes to mind as a "fairy tale" is *Mayday*, a novella in the form of an allegory and itself the original title of *Soldiers' Pay*. He hardly spent two years on that work, however, for the date on the manuscript indicates January 27, 1926. What all this means in the larger sense is an extremely active, imaginative effort, even though the work derived from this period was not memorable. Faulkner's manner of working indicates a considerable overlapping: putting aside *Mosquitoes* to write "Elmer"; suggesting a scene for *Sanctuary*, several years off; then putting aside "Elmer" to write another prose work, which he sees as a two-year job, but which is completed within a few months, if the dated manuscript is any indication; followed by a return to *Mosquitoes*. To add to the dipping in and out, *Mayday* has some intimations of *Sound*.⁶

The difficulty with "Elmer" suggests a certain blockage because of the personal nature of the material. That is, Faulkner's inability to find some way of making it coherent, of associating various strands of art, sex, and scenes of upper-class England, was not only artistic but personal. He returned to "Elmer," but this initial stoppage—what ultimately resulted in an aborted effort—reveals that Elmer's own troubled sexuality and his divided family background may have been coming very close. By way of parallelism, Elmer, like Faulkner, is one of four siblings (two brothers and a sister), strikingly like the Compson family situation also. The incestuous feeling Elmer has for his sister, Jo-Addie, is full of resonance; Faulkner repeated it in the near future with Quentin and Caddy, the sister's names similar and overlapping. Precisely what this meant for Faulkner we cannot tell, but he was re-creating an extremely troubling family situation—one based on deep trauma (the fire when Elmer felt abandoned by his parents), the relationship with his sister (fantasized, of course), and the disintegration of the family as one member after another drifts away.

The letter of September 22, also to Maud, continues the gossip he knew his mother expected. Vannye, his cousin by his great-aunt, Willie Medora, 'Bama's elder sister, arrived in Paris, and Faulkner apparently saw a good deal of her, with enjoyment. His letter, which runs on for several pages, announces he is moving on by bicycle. This almost two-week trip suggests Faulkner found his novel drifting, and a break might enable him to regain his creative energies. He tells his mother of the music he has heard, the bands playing Jules Massenet, Frédéric Chopin, Hector Berlioz, and Richard Wagner. He mentions the Moulin Rouge, "the last word in sin and iniquity,"[7] and uses the occasion to comment on how sex for the Latin people is far healthier than it is for Americans, who sweep it under the table. He mentions painting once again, Henri Matisse, Pablo Picasso, the Rodin Museum, and Paul Cézanne: "That man dipped his pen in light." He enjoys his newly acquired beard, and then re-creates a scene in a restaurant which is an excellent parody of Hemingway dialogue.

Once he leaves Paris for Rouen, Amiens, the war zones and trenches, and Chantilly, he regularly sends postcards to his mother to indicate his location. He is the dutiful son, for his letters and cards indicate pleasure in reporting back to her what he did; he becomes her surrogate European trip. He writes on October 3 of going to various places not too far from Paris: Compiègne, Pont Sainte-Maxence, Senlis; then further trips to Brittany, Normandy, and so on. His October 7 letter indicates London, which he finds so expensive he plans to leave the next day. But before departing, he does the usual tourist bit: Buckingham Palace, Westminster, the Tower, the old coffeehouses redolent of Shakespeare's crowd (Ben Jonson, Christopher Marlowe, Joseph Addison), some of Dickens's areas, Bloomsbury, Piccadilly, St. Paul's, Trafalgar, and Mayfair.

A letter postmarked October 9 indicates he is tramping through Kent and suitably impressed with the countryside. "Quietest most restful country under the sun." And he adds: "No wonder Joseph Conrad could write fine books here."[8] Once again, he is surprised at costs, but despite that he has purchased, secondhand, a Harris tweed jacket, "cut by the swellest West-End tailor." By October 15 he is back in France, writing from the port city of Dieppe, on his way to Paris. He indicates he has been writing, but now a "queer short story" about a case of reincarnation; "The Leg" comes close to that description. He still hasn't heard from Liveright, and we can speculate he possibly stopped writing longer fiction—putting aside both *Mosquitoes* and "Elmer"—because of uncertainty over *Soldiers' Pay.*

Faulkner avoided meeting all major (or minor) writers—he saw Joyce in Paris, but did not speak to him; he avoided Pound in Rapallo; he did not seek out French or English writers or other Americans. He stayed self-contained, visiting the usual tourist sites, turning them into words in his letters back home. Was he impressed by what he saw? He certainly cemented his sympathy for things French, and he opened an interest in Italy. When he returned in December of 1925, he brought back with him a certain confidence about the reality of art and artists. This was possibly his most important discovery: in Europe, art, the artist, and artistic effort counted; in fact, they counted a good deal, intermixed as they were with the very streets one walked. Just as New Orleans had been a step in breaking free of a comfortable, secure place where art had no significance, so now in Paris and elsewhere he had seen for himself how small New Orleans was in comparison. This trip forced him apart from Sherwood Anderson, as it forced Hemingway: once they had assimilated some of Europe, they could never return to being solely "American writers," as Anderson had chosen to do.

Important distinctions must be made about Faulkner as a literary artist, as a man using his imagination as much as his powers of perception. We do not quarrel with the regionalists' and Americanists' emphasis that Faulkner's function as a writer was "to make you see," as Conrad once phrased it. In this view, Faulkner re-created what was already there, heightened or intensified it, and staged it. This view of Faulkner, however, is only partial, tending to downplay his importance as a modernist. It ignores the fact that he differs from his other major contemporaries— Hemingway, Fitzgerald, Wolfe, Lewis, Dreiser, Anderson—in his ability to modulate his world through innovative strategies and technical means. There is really no radical contradiction here between the group which wants to see him as representative of particular Southern views of community and the individual and that other group which sees him as an avatar of modernism and beneficiary of modernist methods. Faulkner clearly chose to stage his world in unorthodox terms to intensify individual, family, and community. Stream, interior monologue, withholding of information, long, intense silences, extraordinary attention to language, free association of sentences and entire passages, revelation of character through language, burial of authorial voice, creation of a multiplicity of voices in a given text—all become inseparable from Faulkner's desire to make you see in particular ways. Without modernist temporal designs, he would be a strong regionalist; without strategies involving convolutions of narrative and experimentation with words, he would be a traditional

Southern storyteller. The modernist mode was essential to his imagination, not a separable item, not something grafted on.

What Faulkner brought back was an awareness of art and what it could do. We can argue that *Mosquitoes*, completed in the summer of 1926, was his farewell to a particular kind of novel; that with this book, he worked through his ideas about what art was, what being an artist entailed, how one went about turning the man into the artist. The world of *Mosquitoes*, in this respect, becomes a stepped-down version of the artistic milieu he viewed in New Orleans and Paris: a group of writers or painters who sealed themselves off ideologically from the rest of society, and using that solidarity emphasized values of significance to the group rather than the society at large. With its "ship of fools" notion, *Mosquitoes* is such a mix. Through this, Faulkner developed his sense of artistic ideas fermenting (or being contaminated) within a contained frame of reference: those inside, like Gordon Fairchild, the poet Mark, and those within their orbit, the Semitic man (Julius), the niece's brother (Josh); as against those well outside, Mrs. Maurier, Jenny, Pete, and the niece. In this line of reasoning, the novel is constructed of concentric circles of meaning, with the "artistic meaning" (however demeaned) as the inner core.

Faulkner warmed up for *Mosquitoes* by trying out "Elmer." In this period, while he was undergoing intense change into a professional writer and under the influence of his European jaunt, he was writing novels about the act of writing novels. He turned personal experience of the deepest kind into fictions, in the act interpreting the very nature of what fiction or art can mean. Although he was not yet in full command of a distinctive voice, this early work becomes clearly oriented toward the theoretical questions of how art is produced, how it comes into the world, and how its ingredients are shaped. For these reasons, the journey to Europe, and especially to Paris, carried great significance in Faulkner's developing sense of himself as a writer.

"Elmer" becomes pivotal here, simultaneously pushing Faulkner into deeply personal material and yet permitting him to gain distance on himself. As noted above, Elmer has three siblings, in his case two brothers and a sister, all older than he. Unlike the Falkners, who held together physically, the Hodges disintegrate, but in ways that contain significant psychological ambiguity. When Elmer is five, his house burns down—one of several flashbacks which enter his mind as he sails for Paris. His father and mother are ill-suited, the father described as "that inverted Io with hookworm and a passionate ambitious wife for gad-fly."*[9] Two people pull against each other—a silent war, in which one dreams while the other

---

*Besides the works derived from "Elmer," it reverberates nearly everywhere in Faulkner's later work: the "inverted Io," for example, describing the schoolmaster in *The Hamlet*. For an excellent essay on this and related matters, see Thomas L. McHaney's "The Elmer Papers: Faulkner's Comic Portraits of the Artist," originally in the *Mississippi Quarterly*, 26 (Summer 1973), but more readily available in *A Faulkner Miscellany*, ed. James B. Meriwether (Jackson, Miss.: University Press of Mississippi, 1974), 37–69. Anyone writing on "Elmer" is deeply indebted to Professor McHaney.

dominates. Then a series of traumas begins: the fire,* coinciding broadly with Faulkner's removal from Ripley and the family move to Oxford. Coincidentally or not, Faulkner relates Elmer's fear of the color red to feelings of abandonment; Elmer, in fact, temporarily "loses" his family. This fear of red recurs throughout his young life, and in one of its manifestations is sexual. It prevents Elmer from developing along natural lines early on, leading, among other things, to his infatuation with his sister and, while in the fourth grade, with a boy "tall and beautiful as a young god," an older boy who ultimately tricks and humiliates him.

The sexual development of Elmer is not part of the comic sense of the fragmented novel; and one could seriously argue this is not a comic quest or a comic portrait. The underlying psychological elements are too obsessive for one to feel secure with comedy or even satire. Elmer is eleven when Jo-Addie, the beloved sister, "sleeps" with him for the last time—she feels no shame undressing before him and getting into bed with him, allowing the boy one touch. She then disappears, and is glimpsed only once more, when Elmer is seventeen, and thinks he sees her, probably now a prostitute (like Caddy Compson later). He is devastated by her departure, although the description of her as bony, all shanks, flat hips, and breastless suggests an undeveloped sexual taste on the part of any boy desiring her. Elmer is presented as ambiguous in his desire to "possess" her: for not only is she his sister, she is physically more boy than girl. Elmer's fear of red also suggests a rejection of the female, since red is associated with the vagina and vaginal discharge, with the female organ as a gigantic maw set to chew up the man. All this is typical psychological speculation, but more compelling is the patterning Faulkner establishes, of trauma, fear, and rejection.

Elmer's trauma with red is transferred, in part, to his love of paint tubes —fat, bulging, erectile tubes, phallic in design and in his pleasure at stroking them. Emphasis on the tubes displaces sexual fear—the red, the female —to masturbatory images, which are private and self-contained. Elmer as masturbator—and it is difficult to perceive the tubes any other way—is in keeping with the author's obsession with self-containment, his need not to give, his saving nature. The masturbator can accommodate rejection because he has himself; rejection, in fact, only feeds his sense of abandonment and justifies his dependence on himself.

In other areas the incestuous pattern of Jo-Addie and Elmer is repeated in *Mosquitoes,* part of a pattern of incest which recurs in *Sound.* Such a

*"But on that scarlet loud night when their house had burned, when his mother had seemed bitter and strange and Jo unearthly, immortal as a dark flame herself in the glare— Elmer could close his eyes feeling again that stark terror when he found that his mother had forsaken him little and naked, could smell again that unfamiliar woman holding him . . . could see against his eyelids his father nightshirted and hopping on one leg that was nimbused with light like a miniature grass fire . . ." (the Garland edition of "Elmer," edited by Thomas L. McHaney [New York, 1987], is the most accessible edition—although not all quotations are exact; cf. page 6 of Garland with typescript at University of Mississippi). With their ambiguous maternal roles, Elmer's mother and Jo-Addie foreshadow another Addie, Addie Bundren in *As I Lay Dying.* Her segment is full of her fears that, as Cora Tull has said, she is not "a true mother."

concentration of incestuous potential within a period of less than five years suggests some sexual ambiguity or imbalance, or else an emotional and sexual immaturity, a return to a preadolescent state. In *Mosquitoes* the incestuous pattern is accompanied by a kind of ritual as well. The niece and nephew of Mrs. Maurier—Patricia and Josh—are in their own quarters when she insists, after showering, on joining him in his room. Wearing only pajamas, she enters the dark room against his wishes and gets into his bed, against his even stronger wishes. He grudgingly allows her to remain if she will lie still. But she insists on talking and moving around, as he falls in and out of sleep. Then she makes a request which specifically repeats the scene in "Elmer" when the latter asks Jo-Addie if he can touch her—and she agrees, but only once. It is that sense of touch which satisfies him and makes it possible for him to sleep. When Josh indicates Pat should be quick about it—"He turned his face away and she leaned down and took his ear between her teeth, biting it just a little, making a kind of meaningless maternal sound against his ear"[10]—he immediately says that that is enough and orders her out. This is clearly a ritual, having been repeated numerous times, and it signals some kind of understanding between the two. Despite his protests, he permits it both to settle and get rid of her. When she returns to her room she removes her pajamas and falls into a deep sleep. By describing it as a "maternal" act of love and possession, Faulkner has attempted to neutralize it, to make it seem less specifically sexual than something familial, something ambiguously incestuous.

Elmer's preadolescent fixations, his lack of adequate sexual development, his inability to relate maturely to women later are part of a deep problem Faulkner experienced in 1925–26, possibly associated with the immediate rejections and beyond that the more serious difficulty of early trauma and profound suspicion of women. To skip to *Mosquitoes* once again: he picked up from *Soldiers' Pay* and "Elmer" in this respect for the crux of Talliaferro's problem in the 1926 novel. One way to read *Mosquitoes*, apart from its shaping of the artist and statements about artists, is its insistence on rejection: it is a dialectic of moves and countermoves, nearly all of them stressing failure. Talliaferro comes away frustrated with Jenny Steinbauer; Mrs. Wiseman is frustrated by both men and women; Miss Jameson is caught in a cycle of her own spinsterhood and unable to attract a man. Nearly all forays into companionship and possible sex underline the characters' foolhardiness and frustration. Those who manage social/sexual affairs are mindless; those who give thought to them fail miserably.

Faulkner has established a pattern. He repeats his dictum that women are unfathomable: that the man who gains a woman only does so because he happens to be around at the right time. Why a woman chooses him and not another is circumstance. "You never have but one chance with a woman, you know. If you fail her then, she's done with you—the next man that comes along gets her without a struggle. It ain't the man a woman cares for that reaps the harvest of passion, you know: it's the next man that comes along after she's lost the other one." This is fraternity-house or hunting-camp talk—where women become mechanical objects who respond without differentiation.

The advice here, to Talliaferro, returns us to "Elmer" and looks back a little further to *Soldiers' Pay*. Faulkner has turned personal rejection and perhaps deeper problems into such an undeveloped perception of women that we marvel at the strategies he deployed later to avoid repeating this self-defeating view. Yet it is not so much the view itself which changes, as the sophisticated methods he employs later to disguise and thicken it. "Elmer," however, lacked the benefit of later strategies. Elmer is himself fixated on his own genital functions, suggesting masturbatory satisfaction as his chief or dominant sexual pleasure. Masturbation as a stage is one thing, masturbation as fixation another. One is tempted to say that what Faulkner saw as a child in the relationship of his parents—their lack of sexual or emotional feeling for each other, despite four children—profoundly affected him. Several commentators stress the "comic" aspect of his presentation of Elmer,[11] and especially the sexual components; but we should, rather, read behind any possible comedy to personal needs that will imprint his later work.

To the infatuation with paint tubes, fear of red, and other obsessions (cigar stubs, whips), can be added Elmer's deep infatuation with a handsome schoolboy—an attachment he repeats in "A Portrait of Elmer," one of the stories Faulkner carved from the original manuscript of the incomplete novel. The handsome boy is older, presented as a cruel god. So in addition to the themes of incest and obsessive masturbation, we also have the theme of homosexual longing, presented with masochistic dimensions. The infatuation is a "blind and timeless adoration," which ends when the sadistic god trips Elmer and sends the humiliated younger boy flying. Elmer is fourteen, just forming, and if the godlike boy had shown interest or made overtures, it is quite possible Elmer would have responded and become less sexually ambiguous.

Although still in the fourth grade at fourteen—Elmer's lack of success in school suggests Faulkner's own growing lack of interest by that age— he moves from this rejection to something safe: his sexless affair with his teacher (herself a refugee from *Winesburg, Ohio*). While maternal in certain aspects, she is so profoundly frustrated that she becomes interested in the youthful but already developed Elmer. The scene is one of tremendous pain, although here the boy has the upper hand. The shifting of roles is compelling for several reasons. Even though Elmer has transferred his interest from the beautiful boy to a female figure, he has moved on to a woman who is clearly a victim of any show of feeling. Her response to Elmer's large, lethargic, rather dumb physicality gives him the opportunity to inflict pain, by running from her house. He is also devoted at about this time to a picture of Joan of Arc—another ambiguous transference of sexual energy. Here he worships someone who is a religious icon, a Holy Mary figure, who also has sisterly and motherly connotations (since the very point about Joan was her sexlessness). His ideal is in fact a Diana-like girl who somehow lies outside time, a Keatsian urn figure.

This hodgepodge of sexual longings and fantasies, added to the cigar stubs and other phallic objects, shows Elmer in a sexual quandary, experiencing an entire range of feelings before forming a heterosexual pattern by making a girl pregnant and then departing for military service. How much of this was Faulkner's own sense of uncertainty, which he honestly tried to explore in Elmer's quest for manhood and the artistic life? There can be no equation, of course; but since Elmer does experience some of the rejection trauma we associate with the writer, we can posit a shadowy author-protagonist kinship. Of interest is the intermingling of homosexual figures in Faulkner's life up to this time. Did the trip he made to Europe with the overtly homosexual Spratling trigger a desire on Faulkner's part to illuminate ambiguous attitudes by way of Elmer's revelations? Stark Young, who had helped Faulkner along the way with introductions and encouragements, was also homosexual, and Phil Stone, a bachelor until he was forty-two, who was carried along by the Greek idea of friendship, harbored deep resentment toward Faulkner after having supported him both intellectually and financially, and then later in fits of jealousy and petulance undermined Faulkner's reputation even as that reputation rose.* His behavior has many qualities of a lovers' quarrel; Faulkner tried to deal with it by slowly withdrawing, cutting his friend off with some cruelty.

If nothing else, "Elmer" forces the reader to rummage through Faulkner's past for the shadows revealed in the novel.[12] The shaded existence presented in "Elmer" leaches out into *The Wild Palms* and several other books shaped by a male drawn into a web by women who distract him from his artistic goals, profession, or security. There is an attitude toward women, already reinforced by *Soldiers' Pay* and *Mosquitoes*, of a man destined to make poor choices because women represent extremes of behavior. Elmer himself moves from easy marks to Myrtle, a tease and unattainable: once again the Estelle syndrome.

There is reason to imply Faulkner was unable to break through his desire for revenge on Estelle for her rejection, and also on Maud, whom he appeared to love dearly, for having squeezed Murry out of their marriage. His inability to deal with females is not the traditional American male's superficial inability. It goes deeply into personal causes, suggesting the generalized sense of a marriage that was no real marriage, a relationship which faltered before it began. Faulkner did more than reject an unworkable situation; "Elmer" was an effort to work out some of the

---

*Stone appeared at early Faulkner conferences once the writer was dead and displayed his checkbooks, going back to the 1920s, demonstrating that it was his money which made it possible for Faulkner to survive. He loved to show these checkbooks and canceled checks to newcomers to the Faulkner scene, thus establishing himself as the power behind the throne. Such behavior was aberrant, and Stone was, inevitably, institutionalized preceding his death.

trauma, but it proved incomplete, aborted, a frustrating experience, not least because it touched on matters Faulkner proved unable to resolve. Out of that internal conflict, which surely made him the unhappy man he was,* he formed and re-formed his fiction. The conflict, however, remained.

Another dimension of "Elmer" is particularly revealing of Faulkner working through material as a form of therapy. Noticeable in the aborted novel are the names of the two women who figure in Elmer's life —Ethel and Myrtle, both names recalling Estelle. Elmer's response to Ethel is almost a direct consequence of Estelle's rejection and Faulkner's form of retribution. In "Elmer," the protagonist, not Ethel's husband-to-be, fathers her child. The situation is full of real-life drama transferred to Faulknerian fantasy: in this, the still-single Estelle gets pregnant by him, then marries Cornell Franklin, telling Faulkner that marriage to him would be like wedding her own brother. Thus, literarily, he gains revenge on Estelle, as he had already done in his portrait of her as Cecily Saunders.

The complications are enormous, for intermixed with this fantasy of Elmer's winning the woman before she gives herself to someone else is the dimension of brother-sister incest—Ethel's feeling she and Elmer are so alike marriage would be incestuous. Here, too, using both fantasy and real history, Faulkner has perceived his relationship to Estelle as "twinning," or as a sibling linkage in order to justify their parting of the ways. In reality, as we have seen, they had paired off as adolescents, with Faulkner a frequent visitor to the Oldham house; more like a son, while unacceptable as a son-in-law. This has given him a sense of ownership: Estelle was his, even as it became apparent they were ill-suited. That early relationship blinded them to their vast differences of sensibility and outlook, and helped create their doomed marriage—doomed before they married. In the fantasy version Elmer walks away from Ethel, but by making her pregnant he has established his "ownership" of her body; thus, by working through fact and fiction, Faulkner already owns Estelle well before her divorce comes through. Further, the fantasy allows Elmer to triumph—he wins over Ethel and then leaves for war before learning she will have his child. The triumph in the fantasy version is dual: Ethel becomes his for the time being, and he does not have to keep her.

The fantasy version grows. For Faulkner told Elizabeth Prall (now Mrs. Sherwood Anderson) that his girlfriend had married another man but had borne his baby.** The fantasy here is another form of ego-boosting;

*Unlike most subjects in photographs, the typical Faulkner pose is one of extreme sobriety. He may look at the camera directly, or even slightly downward, but there is no give in the face for the sake of accommodation. One photograph in 1950 shows Faulkner laughing heartily, but the overwhelming majority reveal him as deadly serious, tucked in upon himself, a circuitry no one will penetrate. Photographs usually reveal—and in Faulkner's case, they do: what they illuminate is a man who refuses to reveal anything beyond the tensions implicit in his fictions.

**Dating Estelle's pregnancy makes this impossible (unless by artificial insemination).

Faulkner simply could not sustain defeat. While "Elmer" was written in the latter half of 1925, the events go back to the period near the end of the war, when Faulkner had found rejection everywhere: his marriage proposals, enlistment in the Royal Air Force, need to be a hero. All this was in the past, but as Faulkner recognized in both life and fiction, there was no past—it was all present. And when he wrote "Elmer" those past events became present, a continuum.

Structurally, the novel was supposed to concern Elmer and his fortunes in parts 1 and 2. Book 3 was to shift to the Monsons and their ridiculous associations with English gentry and lower royalty. But in renumbering or rethinking the book, Faulkner moved the Monsons into book 2, pushed Elmer back from 2 to 3. Thus, the Monsons divide the Elmer material, in ways that possibly led Faulkner to feel the material as a whole was recalcitrant. The Monson episodes are in themselves inflexible material—wooden, without any grace or particular insight, unconsciously amusing in their unfocused presentation. Faulkner was not only in over his head, he was writing himself into an awareness of his own impasse. One can sense in the presentation of the English lords a kind of desperation or hope that something would rise out of the words; and nothing does—the material is a total loss. That none of it could be retained for future use is in itself an indication of how desperate Faulkner's condition had become. Abandonment was the sole recourse, although other parts of "Elmer" became a quarry.

In book 2, as renumbered and rethought, Myrtle Monson appears. And a dreary creature she is—one more young woman in the Faulkner stable of revengeful portraiture. She is, not unexpectedly, part Estelle—and here, Faulkner even makes her run to heaviness, a kind of physical burlesquing of Estelle's extreme leanness. Ethel rejects Elmer with the words ". . . you are much younger than I am: like a brother," and then proceeds to marry Grover—Myrtle is just out of reach, in the way Estelle was. This combination establishes the two young women into a projection of Estelle; and even the growing fatness of Myrtle becomes a sign of disaffection, inasmuch as Elmer has indicated sylphs as his sexual ideal. Beyond this, it is difficult to make any definite statements about renumbered part 2. The material is so incoherent, so lacking in specific insight as to the English upper classes, that the segment disintegrates as we read.

Remaining of interest, and several critics have commented on this, is Faulkner's attempt to interpolate or loop temporal elements. Flashback, looping to past events, recapitulating, convolutions of narrative are all part of the temporal flow of "Elmer." In terms purely of technique, it demonstrates his willingness to venture innovation in telling a story—a move onward from *Soldiers' Pay*, surely. Here his temporal master is in the Bergsonian tradition; from Bergson to Joyce and Woolf; it is also something Faulkner might have learned from a careful reading of Eliot, where temporal looping and telescoping of time and historical events are apparent.*

Although "Elmer" seems an unlikely place to look for technical "progress," we find there some of the fruits of Faulkner's immersion in the New Orleans artistic milieu. It carries him beyond *Mosquitoes,* which he had put aside to write "Elmer," then leapfrogging that novel to relate to the beginning of *Flags (Sartoris).* The early pages of that ill-fated novel (later carved up by Faulkner's friend, Ben Wasson, to make it publishable) are a crisscrossing of historical and present events, so that the narrative, without any recourse to the stream or to free association, nevertheless zigzags through events and memory.

As we know, Faulkner did return to write *Mosquitoes.* But in that return, he was in a real sense forgoing his movement toward his major development. At its best an imperfect work, *Mosquitoes* demonstrates his "old style," hindering him for the time; whereas "Elmer," rightfully aborted, looks forward toward parts of *Flags,* ** especially the early pages, and then to the breakthrough itself, in *Sound* and *As I Lay Dying.*

On a more deeply intimate note, Faulkner wrote in "Elmer": "We are always shocked to discover that people whose lives we once filled can not only get along quite well without us, but that we seem to have left no impression whatever on their lives." Put in Elmer's mouth, these words leave little impression, since Elmer lacks gravity or weight. But as expressive of Faulkner's own feelings, we can empathize to a greater degree, especially as we see him moving ambiguously among his various rejections. The negative value of such a statement given to Elmer is that it pinpoints Faulkner's recognition of something about art as well as about life. For if we project the sentence, we can see he has moved into a traditional view of what art can do: it creates memory, it encodes the artist on history, it brings to him some historical role, whereas the purely personal

*Thomas L. McHaney writes persuasively of Bergson in Faulkner's background, citing in particular Bergson's *An Introduction to Metaphysics,* a kind of primer contrasting solid objects and the fluidity of memory. According to McHaney, Faulkner's use of time and memory owes a great deal to the French philosopher's sense of "continuous flux" or continuous flow and "successive states," which characterize our response to things (Thomas L. McHaney, "The Elmer Papers: Faulkner's Comic Portraits of the Artist," *Mississippi Quarterly,* 26 [Summer 1973]). Bergson stresses the inner life, where temporal modes are durational, and the self develops through intuition. While much of this can be applied to Faulkner's methods in "Elmer," as noted, Eliot could have brought him around to similar practices. Eliot was himself of course familiar with Bergson, and Eliot's influential friend, T. E. Hulme, had translated this very book. Through Stone's help, Faulkner had picked up from Eliot early on.

**It seems preferable to write primarily of *Flags,* which is the novel Faulkner did write, than of *Sartoris,* which is the novel Ben Wasson produced from the longer, earlier form. To choose here is tricky, because Faulkner did approve the deletions and shaping under Wasson's hand; but it is not the novel he wrote, not the novel he thought so highly of, and not the novel whose failure to find a publisher brought him low and impelled him to write *Sound* for his "personal enjoyment." It was *Flags* into which he poured his family history, his sense of the Falkners, his view of the historical mold into which he had been born; fact, legend, and myth all intertwined in the doomed lives of the Sartoris clan.

element is ephemeral, a vanishing point. That "impression" on other people's lives which Elmer wants to make can come only through the agency of art, if at all.

Faulkner left "Elmer" at 30,000–40,000 words, although he would carve away at it, as part of his economy of expression. We have noted some reappearances of the "Elmer" material*: "Divorce in Naples" (known as "Equinox" in 1930), published in 1931, and mainly "A Portrait of Elmer" in the early to mid-1930s—although it remained unpublished even after Faulkner reshaped it.

"A Portrait of Elmer" is a thirty-page version of the original, beginning not with memory, history, or looping recall, as in the original, but with Elmer sitting with his Italian savior, Angelo, in the Dôme in Paris, enjoying the life of the Left Bank. After that, it moves in a fairly linear way, although after the initial introduction, it does contain some uncomplicated flashbacks. Part 3 communicates the key personal material, taken without much alteration from "Elmer": the fire, the boy's response to Jo-Addie, the infatuation with the beautiful, cruel boy, Elmer's humiliation, followed by the episode with the teacher with her "unmistakable odor of middle-aged virgin female flesh,"[13] his fleeing her house when she puts her hand on him. Then follows a brief Joycean paragraph, a rhapsodical passage on young girls in Montparnasse. Faulkner returns to Elmer and his first fling, with "pinksoftcurved plump sixteen" Velma, somewhat slow or retarded. Section 3 ends with Elmer losing his virginity. As in the original work, Elmer's father is presented unfavorably, as having lost reality for Elmer; the father, in turn, seems to have moved beyond reality into "a kind of smug unemphatic cheeriness." Ethel enters basically as before, with her announcement she will marry Grover when Elmer proposes—recalling what happened with Helen Baird, who announced her upcoming marriage even while Faulkner importuned her more intensely.

In "Portrait," with its intimations of Joyce's *Portrait*, Elmer is a struggling figure who does the usual tramp bit that we expect from 1930s fiction. He sleeps, however, not only in railroad stations but in picture galleries; then works in a lumber camp where he draws portraits of the rough men: loggers, sawyers, axmen. This is American "on the road," Hemingway, Dos Passos country: the making of a man, or the end of the road for some. Faulkner returned to this type of site in *The Wild Palms*, when Harry and Charlotte find themselves seemingly at the end of the world in a mining camp. If Elmer is to survive as an artist, he will have to come through a

---

*And some of the foreshadowings, including a brief beginning of "Elmer" called "Growing Pains," one brief part at Virginia and another in the Rowan Oak papers at Mississippi. The Virginia segment begins with the naming of "Jefferson," and if that brief segment dates from this period of "Elmer" then it is the first mention of Faulkner's mythical town; if it belongs with the reworking of "Elmer" in the 1930s, then the mention of Jefferson here has been superseded by its use in *Flags*. It is impossible to date these two-page false starts. In another area the Englishman George Bleyth foreshadows Horace Benbow, almost to parallel passages (see Stephen Dennis, "The Making of *Sartoris*: A Description and Discussion of the Manuscript and Complete Typescript," unpublished Ph.D. dissertation, Cornell University, 1969).

welter of experience sufficient to frustrate him, or strengthen him for the task ahead.

If we read "Elmer" in all its manifestations, it is not a wasted effort. Its varied content goes well beyond simply providing drab revelations of personality and character. It is not only a personal document and a source for later work, but has professional properties of the greatest significance for the writer. Every serious novelist needs a book which becomes, as it were, his laboratory—where early experiments can be tested, out of sight of his readers' expectations. In some undefined, shadowy way, the questing, yearning, fear- and anxiety-ridden Elmer, the young man divided between desire and artistic achievement, is a prototypical Faulkner protagonist, no less than Stephen Hero of Joyce's earliest fiction evolves into the protagonists of his mature novels.

Faulkner returned to work on *Mosquitoes* a wiser man. He left France on December 9, 1925, to return home. Besides the experiences stored up, his sympathies for France were set for the rest of his life, as was his antipathy for whatever was German, whether its literature (except for Thomas Mann) or its war-making potential. He had read Ludwig Lewisohn's anthology of essays, *A Modern Book of Criticism* (1919), and, as Blotner points out, underlined several key passages.[14] If the underlinings mean anything, Faulkner forged a conscious personal aesthetic. But fortunately for his more profound work, it proved inadequate. What he insisted on more than anything else, as evidenced by what we see in his reading of essays by Jules Lemaître and Wilhelm Dilthey (the latter on Goethe), is the need to write out of personal experience. Faulkner felt one must love something to understand it well, and as in the Dilthey, he agreed a writer must interpret life based on his own experience. He mocks those critics who try to develop other scenarios, for in his view all poets—Shakespeare, Shelley, Keats, Verlaine, Swinburne—became poets through accident. He reviled the Germans for always seeking some determining factor within the psyche of the writer, whereas the French know better and downgrade the importance of ideas.

Luckily for him and for us, Faulkner only half-believed what he thought should be his credo. Later he added "imagination" to this credo, complementing observation and experience. His main fault was in his ignorant dismissal of unconscious motives, needs, and desires—what worked so significantly in his own work. His reading of these essays derives from an old-fashioned, antipsychological sense of man and his creative work. He parodies the idea that poets could have been aware of greater complications, and he dismisses any sense of subsurface developments in the individual which may direct his imagination.

We need only compare Faulkner's assessment of art here with Conrad's preface to *The Nigger of the "Narcissus,"* where he outlines early on a mature statement of what art can do, and what he intends to do. Faulkner's attempt to define what was important for him does stress observation and experience, the givens of every major writer. But he dismisses what was really significant: the reaching down well beyond "chance" or "accident" to what is unique in the writer; the ability to scrutinize all the old traumas, wounds, deceptions by way of the work at hand. Faulkner had that ability, and to reveal himself in that way drove him to write greater books—it was not accident, and surely not what he calls here "observation and experience." He accomplished the very thing he labeled here "bunk."

Faulkner returned to America on December 19,* disembarking from the SS *Republic* in Hoboken, New Jersey. Stopping off at the Liveright office, he found out Anderson had been instrumental in the acceptance of "Mayday," whose title was changed in the publisher's office to *Soldiers' Pay*. This prolonged his indebtedness to the older writer at almost the exact moment he needed to break away from nearly everything Anderson represented so as to achieve his own ends. This proved a typical situation for Faulkner: depending on those (Anderson, Stone, Murry) from whom he had to cut himself off. Long after Faulkner's death, his friend from Hollywood, A. I. Bezzerides, saw Faulkner as parasitical; but what Bezzerides lost sight of —and he was one of those abandoned friends—was that Faulkner at every turn found himself moving on from people who, while they helped him, were themselves standing still.

Returning to Oxford the now-bearded, unkempt, unwashed Faulkner faced a mixed and conflicted situation. Everyone in the immediate family except Murry came to greet him at the train station; Maud confirmed that he smelled. He was caught between the familiar and unfamiliar, which distanced him—the beard, the look of the bum, the marginality he so carefully cultivated all set him off even as he returned home. He was just in time for Christmas. He chose to live in several places, including the university dormitories. With Murry as comptroller of the university, his son the writer had the run of the place, and such a life fitted his romantic sense of the drifting, rootless artist.

John Falkner (in *My Brother Bill*) dates at about this period, or shortly after, two stories, "Divorce in Naples" and "Mistral," clearly derivative of Faulkner's stay in Europe.[15] The stories, which may date from somewhat later, are among his weakest published work, and indicate how easy it was for him to regress even as he moved toward more mature work. The first story** draws on the episode in which Spratling had stepped on the banknote with the king's likeness and gone to jail, until the Angelo of "Elmer"

---

*During his stay in Paris, he possibly wrote an Eliotic-Cummingsesque poem which appeared as number IV in *A Green Bough*, a surprisingly jaunty turn: "and let / within the antiseptic atmosphere / of russel square grown brisk and purified / the ymca (the american express for this sole purpose too) / let lean march teasing the breasts of spring / horned like reluctant snails within / pinkeintervals / a brother there / so many do somanydo." The poem, at least, relieved the self-consciousness which made "Elmer" so gassy.

**"Divorce in Naples" ("Equinox" was once the manuscript title) was rejected by four magazines (*Forum*—as "Equinox," *Scribner's, American Mercury, Blues*) and appeared in *These 13* (1931).

got word to the consul. But the story is interesting for another reason: Faulkner makes the two men homosexual lovers—George, the Greek, and Carl, from Philadelphia. One is dark, the other fair. The dark George is much older, the fair Carl only eighteen. Although George is possessive on the ocean crossing, Carl has heterosexual interests. The break and reconciliation between them forms the inconclusive plot. How much of this should be taken seriously, however, is another matter; Faulkner re-created his crossing with the homosexual Spratling in terms which flirt with, but do not describe, forbidden subjects.

The second story, "Mistral," is also sexually shadowy. Two men, most likely Faulkner (the "I") and Spratling (Don), walk with backpacks through Alpine villages and countryside. The approach is elliptical, and it is possible Faulkner was experimenting with narrative methods, delaying information, and throwing in some lurid details (murder, guilty love, et al.) without fleshing them out. The story runs on and on, like several he wrote in this general period (possibly 1926 or a little later). Another is "Evangeline," in which he mentions a Colonel Sutpen—a remarkable evocation of the *Absalom* Sutpen—a man who thought he could control every line of his adult life and who instead headed into personal and familial doom. These stories, together with the novel he had written, the one he could not complete, and the one he had temporarily put aside, indicate on how wide a front his imagination was racing.

As part of this looking ahead—to Sutpen, Snopes (in *Father Abraham*), the use of the title "As I Lay Dying" for part of the spotted-horses episode—Faulkner is hearing for the first time a character who would help him become both famous and notorious. This information appeared in "The Big Shot," a curious story he wrote very probably in the mid-1920s, at about the same time as "Divorce in Naples" and "Mistral." The only way to date this story is by way of the character Don, who seems a creation of this general period.* Here we encounter not only a foreshadowed Sutpen, Wash Jones, and Temple Drake, not only the episode in which the child Sutpen is turned away at the big house in *Absalom,* but Popeye himself.

The story nevertheless lacks the inevitability of the characters, something the mature Faulkner never faulted on; and we become caught in coils of unshaped talk instead of that narrative race to an inexorable end. "The Big Shot" is so structured, in fact, that it can end only with an O. Henry punchline, which turns the story into a kind of amusement for which we are unprepared. Faulkner was reaching for a commercial success of sorts, but this leaden piece never found a publisher (it was rejected by the

---

*And so do passages like the following: "There was nothing he could do with his money save give it away, you see. That's our American tragedy: we have to give away so much of our money, and there's nobody to give it to save the poets and painters. And if we gave it to them, they would probably stop being poets and painters" ("The Big Shot," *Uncollected Stories of William Faulkner*, ed. Joseph Blotner [New York: Vintage Books, 1981; orig. publ. 1979], p. 504). The passage sounds like something caught between "Elmer" and *Mosquitoes,* when Faulkner was coming to less than flattering conclusions in his assessment of the artist and his function.

American Mercury and at least four other magazines). At nearly every stage, the story falls into stereotype, and the "big shot" seems formed by those stories of gangsters which found their way into the pulps, or a little later into Hollywood movies with James Cagney, Edward G. Robinson, George Raft, and then Humphrey Bogart. Faulkner is clearly out of his depth, trying to write tough-guy fiction with a sentence structure suited to other materials.

Certainly the most dramatic character is Popeye, whose description opens the story. Faulkner based Popeye on one Neal Kerens Pumphrey, known as Popeye Pumphrey, a Memphis racketeer and punk gangster. Popeye's reputation was that of a ladykiller who was impotent. Faulkner learned from his informant (a young woman he did not see again) that Popeye was a sexual deviant who got his kicks from raping young women with various objects—in *Sanctuary,* he uses a corncob on Temple Drake—and kept one girl in a brothel. None of these details, however, ended up in "The Big Shot."

Yet in the story Popeye is described, prophetically, as "a little, dead-looking bird in a tight black suit . . . with a savage falsetto voice like a choir-boy." He is a "slight man with a dead face and dead black hair and eyes and a delicate hooked little nose and no chin." Withal, when he cleared out he left "more than one palpitant heart among the night-blooming sisterhood of DeSoto Street."[16] What is striking about Popeye, besides his repulsiveness, is how Faulkner built into him some of his own appearance: the slightness, of course, dominates. But Faulkner also adds the receding chin, his own characteristic in early photographs; the hooked nose—although Faulkner's was hooked without being particularly delicate; the "dead face," a quality he assumed when he became silent; and even the dead eyes, which he took on when he sought privacy. He may have been writing about a petty Southern gangster, as part of that 1920s fascination with the underworld, but he saw in the gangster some of his own marginality. Even Popeye's devotion to his mother—he is described as visiting her each summer in Pensacola—parallels Faulkner's own.

"The Big Shot," then, despite its focus on Dal Martin (the big shot, a pre-Sutpen "force") and his Temple Drake–like daughter, has something very personal in it. And although Faulkner does not describe Popeye's sexual deviance here, saving it for *Sanctuary,* he suggests in the story something of Popeye's epicene quality. How much this mirrored Faulkner's sense of himself we cannot tell; but we do know that Popeye's bizarre sexuality played an important role in the sexual patterns in Faulkner's work for the next ten years.

The publication of his first novel (February 25, 1926) found Faulkner moving into that rather seedy, morbid treatment of material which put him at odds with family and fellow townspeople. Even as he became known locally as author of something as substantial as a novel, he found himself living amidst hostile witnesses. Murry—the Murry of the livery stable and cracker-barrel—refused to read the book because he deemed it dirty. So did the true believer, Maud. It was too sexy, too full of innuendo and byplay for her, insufficiently reverent about subjects better left undeclared.

What *Soldiers' Pay* revealed was the hypocrisy or uncertainty in those closest to Faulkner. But the frostiness extended further: the University of Mississippi Library refused the novel when tendered it by Phil Stone. Apparently Faulkner expected fallout, for he was already in New Orleans, where he moved in with Spratling at 632 St. Peter Street. Although Maud later relented because she wanted to believe in her eldest son, the reception was monitory: it meant Faulkner would from now on have to maneuver in a hostile environment, even as he began to rival Stark Young as Oxford's most famous son. Those early depictions of Faulkner as fitting into Oxford and Lafayette County as if into a glove, or those commentaries suggesting he was part of the world he described in such detail,* were all misplaced.

Faulkner was located like Sisyphus—he could climb, but as far as Oxford was concerned he was being readied for a big fall. His depiction of town and county as Jefferson and Yoknapatawpha did not create awe or respect but distaste, even revilement. Stark Young was the prodigal son—he could be honored from a distance. Faulkner, however, was there, part of a very well-known family—and he was seen by many as a bad seed, the descendant of an opportunistic, violent, uncouth line in the family. Like Thomas Wolfe, with his close portrayal of family and town, Faulkner was caught in a bind: if he idealized the town, he would, of course, have been untrue to his way of seeing and feeling; if he was true to the latter, then town and county were bound to resent what he had done. Writing novels which family and townspeople could embrace would have betrayed not only himself but that artistic circle from which he had gained strength. But by being loyal to the ideas of the artistic milieu experienced in New Orleans and sensed in Paris, he only solidified his marginality as an Oxonian.

Furthermore, his personal life was topsy-turvy, a mix of loyalties, abandonments, rejections, and frustrations. By January 27 he had completed the manuscript of *Mayday*, which he dedicated to Helen Baird. By June he completed his cycle of poems and dedicated those to Helen. In September he finished *Mosquitoes* and dedicated that to Helen. In late October he dedicated to Estelle in chivalric terms a manuscript, hand-sewn, called *Royal Street*, part of the *New Orleans Sketches* (January–February 1925). In December he and Spratling published *Sherwood Anderson and Other Famous Creoles*, notable mainly for Faulkner's parody of Anderson's style. The year that began with his abandonment of "Elmer" ends with his completion of *Mosquitoes*, but his intimate emotions are stretched between two very different women: an infatuation with the completely unsuitable Helen, and a long-term promise to Estelle, now moving toward freedom and also

---

*John Cullen's *Old Times in the Faulkner Country* was one of those. Cullen marvels how Faulkner recalled every detail, every story, every facet of the past; and he reminisces as if Faulkner was at heart just a good old boy who hunted with the men and never spoke of his calling or his successes.

completely unsuitable. She was by now drinking, although how heavily is unclear; but by the time Estelle gained her divorce in 1929 and married Faulkner, she had become an alcoholic.

It is possible that feelings of scorn and disregard for himself fueled Faulkner's resolve. He often wrote best under conditions which might have hobbled another writer—personal distress seemed to force him into depths he might not have plumbed had his personal life been more serene. By saddling himself with personal baggage that should have sunk him—acts as well as ideas—he drew from these personal wounds and traumas revelations of man, time, and history.

Back in New Orleans he gained sustenance from artistic activity. Anderson's name comes up in Faulkner's own correspondence, and Faulkner's in Anderson's. The latter's attitude was clear: "I do not like the man personally very much. He was so nasty to me personally that I don't want to write him myself."[17] This was written well before the Faulkner-Spratling parody in December of that year—yet Faulkner seemed unaware of how deeply he had hurt the older writer, his mentor. In a letter to Anita Loos, he mentions having seen the Andersons in February, and that there is no indication of the latter feeling "sick of people," meaning him. Yet when Anderson wrote how sick he was of people in New Orleans and needed a change (he and his wife headed for California), he clearly had Faulkner in mind; from his point of view, there had been a betrayal of trust, an act of disloyalty. What seems plausible is that Faulkner needed to make the break with the older man in order to prove himself, to free himself for his own work, which so differed from Anderson's. The assassin son had to sever all ties to those elders who rejected change. If Anderson could have taken any solace from the fact, he should have known that Faulkner had done the same with his family, his town, his county. If he had seemed ruthless with a generous friend, then the only explanation was that the rift, which remained, was artistically necessary.

The handwriting of the rift is on the wall in *Mosquitoes,* where Anderson as Dawson Fairchild mouths a lot of nonsense about art and Faulkner simply gives him the reins. Faulkner was heading in quite a different direction, with quite different goals which he could not articulate except in his writing. Anderson would not have understood or felt sympathetic; and Faulkner forestalled the confrontation by cutting himself away with his oft-used brusqueness, rudeness, and self-serving attitude. The situation was not a pretty one. Faulkner did not have much good fortune in his "coupling" with others; the association with Anderson was only one of many that ended badly.

The breach can also be attributed to the fact Faulkner presented himself as he was not—a war-wounded victim with a plate in his head, a limp, a cane, a combat record. The "real" Faulkner, whoever he thought he was at this time, was hidden from Anderson even under intimate circumstances. Anderson opened up, and Faulkner, characteristically, closed down or deceived, establishing his need to create a persona. Yet once the persona was created and lived out, no one could get close to the real thing. Anderson thought he had, but like everyone else, he missed the mark. This was a circumstance Faulkner wanted and needed: to have people relate not to him but to the persona; to force people into maneuvering his shadow, not his substance. If we guess such a pose is based on unresolved traumas, deep personal wounds, conflicts lying below the surface, the answer is that he functioned well this way. Anderson needed openness and directness, whereas his young friend required the opposite.

By spring Faulkner was preparing to resume work on *Mosquitoes.* The allegorical *Mayday* (only the title was taken from *Soldiers' Pay*) was completed, and he was, possibly, working on short stories, written as it were in the interstices of novels. The forward movement of his career, in his own eyes, depended on the frequent appearance of novels. But stories, he hoped, would make him money. By 1926 that pattern could be discerned. Somewhere in the lull before he completed *Mosquitoes,* he may have written "Carcassonne," "Once Aboard the Lugger" (which was never reprinted), and "Black Music." While none of these stories moved Faulkner toward larger goals, they are notable for containing characters who reappear in his longer fiction.

Our dating, in fact, derives from this overlapping of characters. Mrs. Maurier, the disagreeable rich patroness of *Mosquitoes,* appears in the manuscript of "Carcassonne," as does David, the steward of that novel. In "Once Aboard the Lugger" (both stories of that name) we encounter Pete, from *Mosquitoes.* Faulkner also made use of what he claimed was his experience working with Italians as a bootlegger, in New Orleans in 1925. All three stories eventually found publishers, but were left-handed works, valuable perhaps for giving him practice in the use of narrators and modes of telling.

Faulkner returned from New Orleans to see his brother Dean graduate from the local high school—the youngest brother had gone much further than the eldest. Also, Estelle had returned once more, with Malcolm and Cho-Cho in tow. The marriage was obviously not working, and her own condition was beginning to deteriorate with her effort to keep up appearances—she recognized the union with Cornell Franklin was winding down. Estelle's position is a delicate and difficult one to determine, especially since Faulkner commentators have tended to see the relationship from the novelist's point of view. In many respects, however, she is the classic female victim. She worked out her situation by hiding from its realities with drugs and drink. Faulkner's own drinking was, really, of a very different kind.

In becoming a heavy drinker, and alcoholic by the time of her remarriage, Estelle was flouting the social mores of the South. It was socially acceptable for men to drink, indeed to need periodic drying out—an essential element of the frontier, masculine tradition. But women were expected to be antibooze, and for them to tipple was to gain a bad reputation. As a married woman, Estelle never picked up this reputation; but her drinking was certainly not part of the family tradition, as it was with Faulkner and the other males. It was a strictly personal response to a victimizing situation. It was tragic that her son, Malcolm, growing up with a heavy-drinking mother and stepfather, witness to many boozy domestic battles, himself became an alcoholic. Estelle was conditioned from childhood to be a certain kind of woman within a heavily paternalistic society. Without much more than a fragile prettiness and a good background, she was expected to make a respectable, solid marriage which brought honor to her and to the well-placed Oldhams. She was the female sacrifice to their sense of position; and she fitted herself into that role. It would have been almost impossible for Estelle to avoid her situation; she was neither highly talented nor endowed with a strong will. She was a typical "daughter" of the time, moving into an essentially arranged marriage with a man she did not love.* Although Cornell Franklin was good-looking, career-oriented, and successful, he was remote after marriage, a seeker after good times, probably a philanderer, and a man who was happier separated from his family than with it. Estelle could have hung on under these circumstances, but the marriage was effectively over only a few years into it. The rest of the time was spent in trying to make it work.

Although Estelle had few outlets except drinking, well before she remarried, Faulkner made good use of his childhood friend, fiancée, and "betrayer" of his belief in her. She became a prototypical female for him —he couldn't marry her, but he could portray her. Another dimension of the relationship emerges: even as Faulkner was finally moving toward marriage with Estelle, he had already portrayed her so unsympathetically, and hostilely, that it would be difficult for him to "see" her as she was. His literary portraits of her as Cecily, Pat, and others in his early fiction gave him a fantasy or imaginative view of her which was devastatingly negative; dealings, then, with the live Estelle would be colored by the women he had portrayed as shadow versions of her. It was a curious situation, for unlike many other writers—Keats, for example—he did not glorify his intended; on the contrary, he vilified her in his imaginative work before he married her. The flesh-and-blood Estelle had already been turned into part witch, part flirt or whore, and denied her dignity as a woman.

Here we enter very tentative areas in this triangle of Estelle, Faulkner, and Franklin. According to a manuscript in private hands whose source may not be divulged, Estelle Franklin became pregnant by a man not her husband.[18] Cornell Franklin subsequently sued her for divorce (a procedure highly unusual for a Southern gentleman since the stigma of divorce instigated against a woman was very strong) although he, the husband, was also guilty of adultery. Apparently they had tolerated each other's adul-

---

*Purely speculative, although likely, is that Faulkner and Estelle sexually consummated their relationship before she married Franklin, turning "brother and sister" into "man and wife." All reports indicate Estelle was unconventional and wild (Temple Drake?); for her to have broken the taboo on unmarried sex would help explain the intense bond between her and Faulkner during her first marriage.

tery; but when Estelle became pregnant, it was too much for Franklin. There is, however, no evidence that she was pregnant by Faulkner—none of her return visits to Oxford coincides with Malcolm's conception date. Indications are that sexual activity between Franklin and Estelle ceased at about this time; this is of more than passing interest inasmuch as Estelle and Faulkner also ceased sexual activity after the birth of Jill, according to Faulkner. One goes this deeply into Estelle's first marriage because so much of it presages the second: there was in her a wild, uncontrollable streak which put her outside conventional behavior—and this is what had originally appealed to Faulkner and possibly led to their prenuptial consummation.

The possibility that Malcolm was illegitimate makes Faulkner's handling of him and attitude toward him clearer. Malcolm was not a "legitimate" stepchild, although Faulkner took him into the home as Estelle's and Franklin's son. Faulkner's resentment of him can be explained by Malcolm being such a weak link; there was a cruel streak in the writer which made him go after weakness—either directly with a savage and cruel tongue or else indirectly by venting his anger in letters. His rage and hostility directed at Estelle herself were palpable—the drunken binges were as much ways of controlling her as they were means by which he could withdraw and reshape himself. But he saw in Malcolm someone relatively defenseless. Jill Faulkner seems to have had animosity toward Malcolm as well, measured by the fact she returned to Oxford for her half-sister's funeral, but not for Malcolm's.

In all, this is a family caught up in self-destructive tension over past actions and present responses to that personal history. These tensions added to the strain of insufficient money to sustain a high-spending household, and the level of steady drinking which brought a chaotic quality to the home routine. Buried well out of sight were the angers, hostilities, and resentments—perhaps not verbalized until both parties were drunk and beyond restraint. Drunken family scenes, many of which Jill witnessed, were forms of bloodletting, exacerbated by the sexual disunion between the principals. There was no making up and heading for bed. There was no pillow talk—there was, apparently, only the maintenance of appearances (and barely that), the upholding of conventions.

In the meantime *Soldiers' Pay* had appeared, in an edition of 2,500 copies. For a first novel, and not a particularly strong effort, it generated considerable reviews. Nearly every reviewer agreed with what Anderson wrote Liveright about the book and Faulkner's talent: that whatever its specific faults, the novel showed energy, intelligence, vividness, fervor, and other striking qualities. The novel obtained the full range of reviews, in the *New York Times* and the New York *Herald Tribune*, the *Literary Review*, the *New Republic*, and elsewhere.[19] Anderson had written, in what are now famous words: "I have a hunch on that he is a man who will write the kind of novels that will sell. He is modern enough and not too modern; also he is smart. If I were you I would encourage him to keep at work. . . . He may be a little bit like a thoroughbred colt who needs a race or two before he can do his best." Anderson's words were prophetic, since after two novels, Faulkner hit his stride and moved beyond anything his older friend could have predicted. Especially prescient was Donald Davidson's review, in which he placed Faulkner above Dreiser, Lewis, and Dos Passos. Dreiser in the same year published *An American Tragedy*, which, despite patches of poor, uncritical prose, became one of the great American novels of the century. Lewis was in his major phase, with *Main Street, Babbitt, Arrowsmith,* and *Elmer Gantry* (in 1927). Davidson does not mention the very young Hemingway here, but Dos Passos with *Three Soldiers* and *Manhattan Transfer* was moving into a major career which almost rivaled Faulkner's in ambition and scope.

Mosquitoes both enhanced and undermined that sudden reputation. Even such a sophisticated reviewer as Louis Kronenberger had predicted great things for Faulkner, as a man who could create his own world. *Mosquitoes* was another such world, and it was populated by many of the people who had befriended Faulkner in New Orleans.[20] They had helped him, and he would skewer them. Hardly anyone comes away looking whole or sympathetic, except Gordon, the sculptor, and he remains silent through most of the novel.

The impetus to start up again on *Mosquitoes* came in the form of another visit to the Pascagoula, home of Phil Stone's brother. There, Faulkner could see Helen Baird, who was intimately involved in everything he was doing. In this respect, she was something like the "lady" to the medieval knight: his source of inspiration, his way of dedicating himself, and the support (in his mind) of his deeds. Faulkner was ready to set forth. This was the period when he smothered her with poems, dedications, and characterizations (not always favorable).

Faulkner came to Pascagoula bearing gifts—for Helen, mainly. *Mayday* was one of those curious presents, and it demonstrated that Faulkner did perceive himself as a medieval knight, in some kind of *Faerie Queene* quest. Here he is not Donald Mahon, the mortally wounded soldier of World War I, but Sir Galwyn of Arthgyl, perhaps from deep in Faulkner's Scottish past. Sir Galwyn (an acronym of several Tennysonian idyllic figures) is accompanied on his journey by Hunger and Pain, from which he must liberate himself. But his quest proves doomed. Together with a maiden called Little Sister Death (a refugee from a Hardy novel), he drowns—a suicide, apparently.* The brief allegory of life and death in the name of love was accompanied by colored drawings—Faulkner had produced the entire book and bound it, hand-sewn. Just how this was expected to appeal

---

*"Little sister Death" had come up at the end of Faulkner's short sketch "The Kid Learns" in the *Times-Picayune* (May 31, 1925), where the doomed Johnny has thrown everything away for his "Mary." She offers her real name: " 'Little Sister Death,' corrected the shining one, taking his hand" (*William Faulkner: Early Prose and Poetry*, ed. Carvel Collins [Boston: Little, Brown, 1962], p. 91).

to the hardheaded Helen cannot be fathomed. Her interest was in sculpture, not literary work. Yet Faulkner came bearing gifts, rather ludicrously in the form of a medieval tale of love and death, a Wagnerian weltschmerz, an allegory of a lovesick knight. What, then, did Faulkner have in mind? He presented her with an attractive little book he had obviously taken trouble with, but from her point of view, it was something unreadable, and from his a confession of pain, anguish, suffering. One possibility is that Faulkner wanted to encourage ridicule, rejection, or rebuttal—whatever Helen was capable of. Another is that he simply misread her—he thought he could appeal with a thinly disguised tale of pain and suffering, a display of himself on a platter. A third, more likely, possibility is he was caught in the grip of a romantic idea—that, like the Romantic poets he imitated, he needed an object of love for a focus. In this sense, Helen becomes the equivalent of Dante's Beatrice, Petrarch's Laura, and Keats's Fanny Brawne. There would be, in this kind of offering, some of the Southern gallant, the courtier, the knight and his lady.

A fourth response might be that Faulkner was carrying through on something he thoroughly believed: that, as he told it later, the writer "is a congenital liar incapable of telling the truth."[21] This was his credo, based as it was on his sense of the imagination taking over from both observation and experience; part of that transformational quality characterizing nearly all of his work. It was his way of explaining to himself how he could break out of simplistic realism and naturalism. If this was indeed at play in his presentation to Helen, then the little book existed *independently* of the person for whom it was intended. Helen was a bystander in a process Faulkner had set into motion years earlier; he meant less by his devotion than dedication, presentation, sentiments would seem to mean.

Nearly every Faulkner act has comparable complications. In few areas can we say unequivocally that he did something for this or that reason. The desire on his part to be rejected should never be discounted. His selection of women, his approach to them, his comments on their mysterious ways, all suggest that rejection reinforced his sense of women and his idea of their sensibilities. Accordingly, he pursued Helen in Pascagoula while playing a role even a mother might not love—as before, he looked dirty, he smelled (if witnesses can be believed), and appeared like a beachcomber at the end of his tether. Unshaven a good part of the time, his hair uncombed and beginning to shade here and there into gray, barefoot, his clothes mismatched, he was hardly a suitor for a young woman with less of the bohemian in her than met the eye.

Whatever Helen was, however, and whatever the circumstances, she did serve one function: Faulkner was energized into picking up *Mosquitoes.* He had put it aside because he felt he wasn't sufficiently experienced to write that novel; now he felt ready, and he wrote steadily through the summer of 1926, dedicating the book to Helen even as he prepared *Royal Street* (from *New Orleans Sketches*) in a hand-bound version as a presentation to Estelle. The pain of rejection kept him busy. As he moved toward his twenty-ninth birthday, *Mosquitoes* would prove to be a recapitulation: it looked back, not ahead, and even the discussions of art and the artist applied to the passing Faulkner, not the future writer.

He handwrote *Mosquitoes* segment by segment and then typed each part on his portable. Although his personal affairs were in disarray—no job, rejections by women, dependence on family for roof and support, use of the Stones' place for his "office," few prospects except his own sense of himself—he retained a sharp view of what he wanted to do. The references for *Mosquitoes* were not Faulkner's great loves—Dickens, Balzac, Conrad —but rather Aldous Huxley's *Crome Yellow* and *Antic Hay*, Eliot's *Prufrock*, some Joyce. Like Huxley's books, this was to be a 1920s novel, full of glitter and superficial dialogue which would, however, be counterpointed by serious discussions of art and the artist. It was a mix of Faulkner's sense of the times, his own experiences and observations, and his efforts to locate the artist in all this. About half of the men on the boat are artist figures —writer, poet, sculptor, carver. And those who don't make art talk about it.

A second novel is always a strange object for the writer. The first usually displays the self in the most abandoned way—and we have noted how Faulkner divided himself into three in *Soldiers' Pay* in order to reveal (or disguise) who and what he was from several angles. By the time of *Mosquitoes*, however, he was personal, even autobiographical, in a different way: instead of revealing the self as split among three men, he divulged his sense of himself as artist. The second novel displays a transformation: intimate pain, deceptions, lies, disguises have given way to assessment of position, his place in the scheme of things. In that New Orleans artistic milieu, his world had opened out; *Mosquitoes* would be the beneficiary of that liberation. In hindsight, we can see that the novel served a considerable function in Faulkner's artistic and personal development, moving him, finally, from the weltschmerz of the war, wounds, et al., into a more objective world, where observation has taken over from purely personal need.

With *Mosquitoes* Faulkner got away from the war which had dominated his first novel, but not so far away he did not return to it in *Flags*. Even "Elmer" had its military scenes. We see in this fascination Faulkner's use of contemporary war as an approximation of the South's great conflict. As in Eliot, all wars fuse into one; all war is contemporary. Intermixed with Faulkner's early war novels, one completed, one unfinished, is an essay, a brief piece of writing called "Literature and War." This is a very carefully crafted and prepared typescript of five paragraphs, indicating some of Faulkner's war reading and his comments thereupon.[22] While nothing he says of these war writers is momentous, the significance of the brief essay, which we can date in late 1924 or early 1925, derives from Faulkner's awareness of a war literature.

In the five paragraphs, he mentions Siegfried Sassoon (his poetry); Henri Barbusse *(Le Feu* or *Under Fire: The Story of a Squad)*, whose famous novel would be reflected much later in *A Fable*, as well as in several earlier stories; Rupert Brooke (his war poems); R. H. Mottram (a forgotten classic, *The Spanish Farm*); and Stephen Crane (his *Red Badge of Courage*). While this is not an exhaustive list of reading, it demonstrates how war and the military persisted in Faulkner's imagination, reinforced by reading among those who stretched the Civil War (Crane) into World War I (Sassoon, Brooke, Barbusse, and Mottram). Faulkner would then himself extend the First World War into the Second, writing *A Fable* about the former while suggesting its application to the latter—in fact, to all wars.

Although *Mosquitoes* forgoes direct war references, it contains sufficient hostility and personal aggression within a shipboard situation to suggest a war. The group on board the *Nausikaa* (from Joyce? Homer?) is like an army company, a little bit of this or that, isolated or cut off from the main group. Once the boat is stranded when Josh, the "carver," removes a key wire from the steering, it is like those army companies which must go it alone. Under these circumstances, each person will reveal what he or she really is—unsupported, the individual must come forward. While heroism here is muted, one's sense of self is illuminated. Such is Faulkner's method of working—in the broadest sense, *Mosquitoes* is structured as a shadowy war novel.

The hostility is between characters and directed by the author toward certain characters—Dawson Fairchild, who stands in many ways for Sherwood Anderson; Patricia Robyn, whose boyish, lean, breastless figure recalls both Estelle and Helen; the "Semitic man," who seems based on Julius Weis Friend, who had brought together the group around the *Double Dealer* and whose designations (including "fat Jew") suggest a not-too-subtle anti-Semitism. Faulkner was revealing not virulence but small-town provincialism, intermixed with derogatory references to Negroes and Italians.

But not all characters in the novel are based on acquaintances from Faulkner's New Orleans life; some are literary references, and equally scornful. Ernest Talliaferro, already met in the unpublished "Don Giovanni" as the hapless Herbie, is a composite Eliotic creation, with some overtones of Faulkner himself. Nearly all commentators have noted the resemblance of Talliaferro to Prufrock and to the other undersexed, hapless men who appear in Eliot's poetry; but none has remarked on how the character's inability to make headway with women is a not-too-shaded version of Faulkner's own frustrations and rejections. In *Soldiers' Pay* Faulkner caricatured his own failure in the overbearing, strikingly unsuccessful Januarius Jones; and while he did not identify with Jones's methods of approach, he found in that loathsome creature the means of expressing a man's failure with women.

Faulkner made this a striking point in his fiction of the mid-1920s—that unsuccessful quest for the woman which leads either to outright rebuff, mockery, or, in the case of the knight in *Mayday*, suicide. It is a meaningful pattern: the mismatch between male and female, usually physical opposite, so that the man has no chance. Cecily Saunders, lean and physically slight, and fat, sloppy Jones; in *Mosquitoes*, curvaceous, fleshy Jenny and awkward, stumbling Talliaferro. The women as a whole are unappetizing creatures, either mother hens like Mrs. Maurier, or spinsterly eager Miss Jameson, or loose and mindless Jenny, or footloose and equally mindless Pat Robyn.

In fact, except for the sculptor, Gordon, not a single figure is sympathetically presented, with the further possible exception of Mrs. Eva Wiseman, the sister of "the Semitic man." She frequently rises above the group, although her interest in Jenny creates an ambiguous sexuality in the novel. If the major characters are unpleasant, minor ones are even less appetizing. Faulkner, too, appears in an unfavorable light. He is offstage, used as commentary by Jenny when she is speaking to Pat. Faulkner caught his own image as he must have seemed to Helen Baird and her mother: "kind of shabby dressed," a "liar by profession." Jenny feels he is not dangerous, "just crazy." The two fumble over his name, in an apparent stunt to come up, eventually, with Faulkner. " 'Faulkner,' the niece pondered in turn. 'Never heard of him' she said at last with finality."

The potentialities of this brief episode are compelling. Why, we wonder, did he present himself so unfavorably, through the eyes of those who had already rejected him? In this episode, he is in effect experiencing the rejection of two women who represent distinct aspects of the women who rejected him. It is a curious use of parallelism to substantiate his own existence, and we can perceive it as a kind of assertion of him, even if negative. The need to introduce his name and presence becomes, then, far more affirmative than negative. For he refuses to go away, and finds in those very rejections ways of mocking the two women for not taking him more seriously. He is, as it were, saying it is to the detriment of the two young women that they have treated him so lightly; and his use of his own name and person is his way of evening out a score, however briefly, however superficially. "Faulkner" does not arise again. The "little kind of black man" merges with the forward movement of the book, and is gone. Faulkner's triumph in this curious passage is in his refusal to change what others perceive him to be, and to use that image as his moment of splendor, a target. The episode is part of a general mix of everything he has experienced not only in New Orleans but in himself. Like *Soldiers' Pay* and "Elmer," *Mosquitoes* is part of his use of the novel as a cover for personal feelings he cannot quite objectify.

The focus is ostensibly on the artist—how undependable he really is as an alternative to life—and yet the focus in the novel's subtext is on Faulkner himself. Every aspect of *Mosquitoes* radiates out from him: his women, his dislike of hangers-on, his ridicule of Anderson's views of life and art, his own sense of the artist in the sculptor, Gordon, his curiosity about outsiders and even criminals, his ambiguities about sex, his desire to suggest and titillate. Many of these negative factors in *Mosquitoes* become positive factors later on. The sexual ambiguities of this novel become profundities in *Sound*, even in *Flags (Sartoris)* and *Light in August*. Yet in his views concerning the role of the artist and art, Faulkner is often contradictory, full of sarcasm at his own sense of things. He is unclear in his own mind because this novel is antipathetic to his talents—it is a stage on the way to something which, since it has not as yet appeared, cannot be achieved. This also explains why his poetry and shorter fiction in this period are so uneven, so lacking in what we consider the Faulknerian touch and manner.

Where is he artistically? He is almost entirely negative: eager to demonstrate artistic prowess as part of a negative response to the world. Although the sculptor, Gordon, represents the furthest reaches of the artistic temperament, he does not reveal any ideas or theories which make him an artist; instead, he demonstrates a temperament Faulkner identifies as artistic because it is based on withdrawal and silence.* Talk about art seems an antithesis of the process, and Faulkner has grounded his sense of art in temperament and personality rather than in ideas or even proven achievement. The same people who so admire Gordon's sculpture in the making are those whose views of art Faulkner parodies or exaggerates. A curious process is at work, for he demonstrates a deep suspicion of the very thing his novel is about—how the artist might survive on a ship of fools. Faulkner, apparently, has not seen his way clear of the debris of art to the thing itself—that came only when he forwent all talk about its creation and simply did it. He works very hard in *Mosquitoes* to display knowledge of that inner artistic milieu, but in so doing he demonstrates how much of a trap he felt it could be. The true artist, he would soon agree, removes himself, and in cunning, silence, and withdrawal enters into the depths and stages of his own talent.

Whenever Fairchild, the superficial cover for Anderson, tries to explain what he means, he falls far short, and his explanations read like parodies: ". . . let it [language] be historically or grammatically incorrect or physically impossible; let it even be trite: there comes a time when it will be invested with a something not of this life, this world, at all. It's a kind of fire, you know." Then Fairchild gives his theory of why someone writes, a pseudo-Freudian argument: "I believe that every word a writing man

---

*There seems little question that Faulkner transposed his own silences and withdrawals into similar qualities in his characters; so that, at least here, people who talk too much—like Fairchild—are fools. Yet even Fairchild shifts his ground, from finite (things) to infinite (art). Much of this foreshadows Richard Chase's later point, about *Light in August*, that linear in Faulkner is rational and curves are aesthetic (an equation which Faulkner himself mocked). But any attempt to make this formulaic must fail. Like Fairchild, whom he parodies, Faulkner was himself inconsistent. (See Panthea Reid Broughton's *William Faulkner: The Abstract and the Actual* [Baton Rouge: Louisiana State University Press, 1974], esp. pp. 29, 31, 81.)

The recent discovery of forty-five handwritten pages of *Mosquitoes* reveals a rearrangement of comments on art from what we find in the typescript, but no appreciable differences in what Faulkner has to say about either art or creativity. The interesting point about the discovery of the holograph material is that Faulkner handwrote at a time when we believed he composed the novel, as he did *Soldiers' Pay*, on the typewriter.

writes is put down with the ultimate intention of impressing some woman that probably don't care anything at all for literature, as is the nature of women."[23]

A good deal of the discussion about art is masculine bluster. The "Semitic man" challenges Fairchild's belief in words, language, rhetoric. As the child of an ancient race, he argues "one who spends his days trying to forget time is like one who spends his time forgetting death or digestion. That's another instance of your unshakable faith in words. It's like morphine, language is. A fearful habit to form: you become a bore to all who would otherwise cherish you."[24] The "fat Jew" argues for life—that those who are not artists "get along quite well with . . . [their] sleeping and eating, procreating." He says the chief function of art is to "keep the artists themselves occupied." But Fairchild cannot of course accept this—he tries to see art as, somehow, a masculine challenge. Once again, he downgrades women's responses: "Women can do without art—old biology takes care of that. But men, men . . ." A woman conceives without caring whose seed it is, "and all the rest of her life . . . is filled." But a man must create, for when he does, it is all his, only his.

The continuing hostility to women in the novel, and the dismissal of any aspirations beyond their female destiny, is already foreshadowed by *Mayday*, completed earlier in 1926. The progress of Sir Galwyn's journey is structured on the women he encounters. Each is lovely. The tale is itself based on a kind of destiny, but a happy one: on the legend that one who looks in the stream on May Day will observe his love, whom he will marry. After a succession of beautiful women (Yseult, Elys, and Aelia), Sir Galwyn insists on gazing into the stream, and on the second look he finds Little Sister Death. By insisting on that second look, he has in effect chosen suicide, like Quentin Compson a little down the road. Death is implicit in choice. Women fit comparably into the parable of nature Fairchild relates: "There is a kind of spider or something. The female is the larger, and when the male goes to her he goes to death: she devours him during the act of conception."[25] Fairchild voices the fear of the *vagina dentata*, carrying it from fear of castration to actual death. Woman becomes the Medusa—gaze on her, and man perishes.

Fairchild plays a mixed role in *Mosquitoes*. He fills the air with words and masculine bluster; he undermines and destroys the female as little more than an animal for purposes of reproduction. And yet his plea for the artist as someone special—as against the "Semitic man" 's argument that life is separate and more significant—is for something ennobling, transcendent. Some of Faulkner's confusion can be located in the novel here: in his inability to tunnel his way out of a self-imposed trap. He has posed a life which is somewhat demeaning, yet he is unable to find a voice for an art which offers something else. This confusion of aims and voices—in which someone who argues some of his own points is a windbag—makes the novel teeter on the edge of parody even as it attempts to move into serious territory.

Faulkner has created a form, a philosophical voyage of a ship of fools, which he constantly undermines. A large amount of material remains unmalleable; folded in, it cannot be made to fit. And the reason for this goes beyond Faulkner's still-immature sense of craft or his inability to get beyond personal needs. The helter-skelter achievement of *Mosquitoes,* its sense of a scattered and unfocused imagination, derives from Faulkner's failure to measure method against substance. Although he would show he could be the master of the journey idea in *As I Lay Dying,* in *Mosquitoes* the journey fails because method pulls away from subject.

Faulkner attempts both scene and panorama, which clash. By scene, we mean concentration on individual episode; by panorama, something which moves that individual episode onto the grand scale of novel-making. In one sizable segment, Faulkner tries to convey huge import to a scene which remains paltry; he is reaching for Conradian significance with an insufficient episode to achieve it. Pat Robyn, Mrs. Maurier's niece, and David, the steward of the *Nausikaa,* sneak off to have an adventure, the jaunt starting off as a kind of Huck Finn–and-Jim search for the pure life. In this, Pat is Huck, David is Jim. Their aim is to make shore from the grounded boat and to work their way inland—an extended picnic with flirtation at its base, and perhaps consummation at some point, although Pat is both epicene and indeterminate. She seems to enjoy stroking Jenny's flank as much as drawing David's attention; her relationship with the young man depends less on sexual attraction than on his worshipful, lower-class deference toward her. The class and caste difference is as great as with Twain's characters—David her slave, she his white goddess. The inequality of the mating already undermines their sense of an Edenic experience.

The crux of their effort to experience bliss together is to re-create an Edenic picnic, a return to the Garden. They leave the boat with a picnic basket and high expectations for a time of good cheer and solace, with an undercurrent of sexual indulgence. When at first they cannot find the road to Mandeville, the excursion begins to take on qualities of an anti-Eden, which intensifies. Faulkner intends them as people whose expectations of the "land beyond" has no quality of reason or logic. They have a false sense of what the world offers. Like the hopes of Heyst and Lena in Conrad's *Victory,* their plans for an idyll must be smashed, and their fate becomes nightmarish, almost disastrous. Faulkner exposes them to the trials of Job: nature rises up against them, and they suffer ignominy. Their physical and psychological mechanisms are worn down, so that Pat becomes hysterical and David is unable to control the situation. The insects which attack and nip them are like vengeful furies, relentless in their attack. Mosquitoes indeed become furies. The heat becomes the hell of their situation, and their great thirst suggests that their Edenic ploy has turned into a wasteland.

Faulkner tries to project a great universal scene with huge implications, yet both characters and method trivialize it. Their great thirst on land, for example, is paralleled by the shipboard disgust with ever-present grape-fruit, which everyone rejects. Their jaunt is also juxtaposed to trivial talk about life and art: while their quest for life intensifies, the others sink back into idle comments. The novel at this point is structured on parodic point-counterpoint, which Faulkner may have picked up from Huxley or Eliot or Joyce. Faulkner's method, however, is frivolous, and even the use of hourly designations each day fails to break through reductive narrative forms. Talk goes on like a barrage: "Talk, talk, talk: the utter and heart-breaking stupidity of words. It seemed endless, as though it might go on forever. Ideas, thoughts, became mere sounds to be bandied about until they were dead."*[26] Meanwhile, the noon sun becomes oppressive, and while words heat up the *Nausikaa,* real heat is beginning to drive Pat crazy with thirst. Counterpointing only reveals the inability of narrative tech-nique to illuminate a large scene with Garden potential.

With life and death being played out on shore, Fairchild continues the barrage. He asserts that words do not have a life of their own, that "words brought into a happy conjunction produce something that lives, just as soil and climate and an acorn in proper conjunction will produce a tree. Words are like acorns, you know. Every one of 'em won't make a tree, but if you have enough of 'em, you're bound to get a tree sooner or later." To this inanity, Julius responds that if you "just talk enough, you're bound to say the right thing some day."[27] Fairchild is coming close to the monkey who taps at a typewriter and produces a novel.

The method, obviously based on juxtaposition and contraries, has a serious negative effect. Instead of each part enhancing the other, which justifies such a method, each part undermines the other. Although he is imitating the satirical mode of Huxley, Faulkner lacks one essential ele-ment of satire or burlesque, which is consistency. He is earnest on some occasions, caustic on others. While making fun of the artistic life on board, both its setting and language, Faulkner misjudges the couple on shore. It is true they have pursued an Edenic idea and discovered a veritable anti-Eden, a wasteland of sorts, but they are not worthy of satire or burlesque, nor of farce or tragedy. They have misconceived the nature of life, but their error is not so great as to have produced such travail. By cutting back and forth to them, Faulkner indicates a greater weight and gravity than they achieve. These are faults common to his two early novels, but by *Flags,* that cutting back and forth—so essential in all his work—achieves a higher level of integration and a more cogent sense of people.

*Sexual frustration in the novel—among the adult figures only the sculptor, Gordon, acts on a sexual urge and visits a whorehouse—is connected mysteriously to frustration with language. If the characters could free up language to express themselves, the implication is, they could liberate themselves sexually. To what extent Faulkner saw this as a metaphor of his own condition we can only speculate. For interesting comments on these numerous subtexts in Faulkner's work, see Michel Gresset, *Faulkner ou la fascination I: Poétique du regard* (Paris: Klincksieck, 1982). Gresset posits a grounding of some of the work in what he calls "Faulknérie" (the land of Faulkner), a temporal-spatial area which lies beyond earth or fact. The study, overall, demonstrates the value of applying poststructuralist ideas (especially Barthes's) to Faulkner's intricate texts.

Another relationship carrying considerable freight for Faulkner, although not essential to the novel, is the doggish devotion Pat feels for her brother, Theodore, whom she calls Josh. Brother-sister reverberations are so significant in Faulkner's later fiction that the reader is tempted to seek all kinds of meaning even in a relationship as superficially developed as this. Although the sister often dominates in Faulkner—Jo-Addie in "Elmer," Caddy in *Sound*—here she tags along and lets herself be ruled by Josh. We could argue that her use of David the steward to do her bidding, jeopardizing his job by making him run off with her, is simply a way of gaining attention from her brother; whereas he, without any sense of Pat's presence, goes after Jenny, whose flesh everyone wants to fondle. Brother and sister are drawn together in *Mosquitoes* not out of any particular novelistic need, but out of a personal one—as if Faulkner felt he needed a dry run for more important sibling relationships to come. Self-absorbed, uninterested in the boat's welfare as he steals a piece of wire from the steering mechanism, narcissistic about his own activities, Josh is incompletely drawn, unintegrated into the novel.

What remains is Faulkner's need to create a young couple in which one, the girl, follows the other with doglike devotion. A psychological mechanism seems at work here which, while somehow defying precise definition, does imply an incestuous pattern that generated real literary originality in his later work. We cannot ignore the pattern even in his journeyman work, however, but the danger is to look for it everywhere. The incestuous pattern is only one of many Faulknerian ploys; in some instances it does not function meaningfully. Here it is merely part of the narrative and rarely part of the meaning.

It does serve, nevertheless, as part of the general deterioration of heterosexual relationships in the novel. While no pattern of male homosexual activity is visible, there is a strong sense of male-bonding. Repeatedly, Faulkner speaks of how the men break off from the women, disappear on them, seek their own company to discuss weightier matters than they think women are capable of. Male-bonding preempts any serious dialogue with the opposite sex; and when such bonding does break down, it is not for lack of company but for purposes of flirtation and fondling. The women, however, definitely show a potential lesbian-bonding—Mrs. Wiseman with Jenny, and Pat Robyn with Jenny. Jenny is, in fact, a Nana figure, with her flesh worshiped by both men and women. She is otherwise presented as a birdbrain, lacking both grammar and sense—in many ways, a far less appealing Eula Varner. We must locate the incestuous couple, Pat and Josh, within this frame of reference, in which the usual sexual alignments are put to test and certain undeclared tastes are experimented with.

We may wonder about the title—insects seem to bother most people, and they drive Pat and David almost insane. Yet the title seems to carry us beyond the insects, although they are not to be discounted as destroyers of an Edenic experience. If we so consider them, mosquitoes are almost the sole source of movement, since the *Nausikaa* is marooned on high ground and the situation, with its endless talk, is static. The germ of a real idea is here: that while the boat remains static, the couple on shore is tortured almost to craziness by buzzing, attacking, zooming mosquitoes. That couple has something of the Faulkner–Helen Baird quality to it, inasmuch as Pat Robyn is described in terms recalling both Helen and Estelle, and David is a kind of wandering jack-of-all-trades suggesting Faulkner himself. The mosquitoes become more than simple annoyances. Like furies, they are harbingers. They are the means by which the "picnic" and flirtation between the young people become nightmarish—part of the heat and thirst which almost bring them down. In his prescient way, Faulkner is foretelling the present and future: seeking relationships doomed by circumstance.

The presence of Helen in the Pat Robyn portrait is strengthened by a letter Faulkner scribbled to her on the back of a page of *Mosquitoes,* but never sent.[28] What is curious about the lines which are legible is that Faulkner was writing down to her, as if she were a bad child he had to treat with special care. It is not quite a love letter, nor is it one addressed to an equal in age and intelligence. Instead, he speaks of her name as "a little golden bell" hung in his heart; of the people in the novel as being "nice," which they certainly are not; of having made "another book" for her—as if he were holding out some goody as a present. The letter is "cute," and he demonstrates—if such small evidence can be cited—that their relationship was not on any mature level, but part of a childish give-and-take, at the level of baby talk.

The epilogue of *Mosquitoes,* which takes up over forty pages, is an awkward affair—an indication of how Faulkner was reaching here and there to construct his novel. He apparently felt the epilogue would balance the beginning segment on shore, the prologue, with the *Nausikaa* episode itself as the large middle. But an epilogue suggests a certain dramatic finality which is lacking in this piece, and Faulkner was, in fact, unable to find suitable coordinates. The switch to Pete, Jenny's boyfriend, is especially vapid, since to begin with he is not a character of any interest. We sense Faulkner had material left over—memories of tales of his bootlegging days —and he grafted these onto Pete. The Italian milieu intended to give the character context is off the mark, an indication of how wobbly Faulkner became when he did not know his subject. His effort at tough Italian talk turns the language flat, and his description of an Italian restaurant is cliché-ridden and pedestrian.

From these, he circles around via Fairchild and the unfocused Englishman, Major Ayers (who has concocted a remedy to relieve American constipation), to Talliaferro. Here, as above, Faulkner had leftover material, the story "Don Giovanni," reproduced in its essentials. While he seems to be marginally fey, Talliaferro is obsessed with his pursuit of women. He is markedly unsuccessful, and Faulkner seems to feel his relentless quest here and shipboard is amusing. A Prufrock with a will, Talliaferro, whose line is women's clothes, cannot get hold of the woman. In the prologue, his somewhat effeminate manner is juxtaposed with the hard masculinity of Gordon. But Faulkner has his switch, really a chiasmus: Gordon is very manly, but has little interest in pursuing women. Art is his line, and he has suppressed love, sex, romance for sculpture. Talliaferro, in this switch, is less than manly, and yet he is the one who defines himself in pursuit of women.

In fact, nearly all sexual roles in the novel are either reversed or distorted —and Gordon's potential sexuality is wasted, whereas Talliaferro's impotence is celebrated. But since Faulkner is not finished with leftover material, he creates an overall sense of segments grafted onto each other without inevitability or momentum. We return, still in the epilogue, to Pat and her brother, Josh—the siblings who have lost sexual distinctions by referring to each other as "Gus," indeterminately male and female. As we have already noted, Pat insists on lying next to Josh in bed; but while Elmer wanted to touch Jo-Addie, Pat insists on taking her brother's ear between her teeth, biting it, and then making "a kind of maternal sound against his ear."[29]

The epilogue drives home the sexual and relational aberrations which have occurred on the boat, and which become even more extreme on shore. Why Faulkner should have wished to emphasize these is unclear, since he has already satirized everyone connected to the world of art and creativity, even the silent, withdrawn Gordon. The point being made, no more was needed. Returning once again to Fairchild, we encounter more talk—the buzzing mosquitoes here as sounds and words. Fairchild also tells us something about Mrs. Maurier, who married a much older, and rich, man when she was young and pretty. But this information does not enhance our sense of her—it is disconnected from the mother hen trying to push grapefruit on her guests. We learn, furthermore, that "the Semitic man"'s background and name derive from Julius Kauffman, his grandfather, who was involved in a raw land deal. This information also fails to enhance our sense of "the Semitic man," although it does make us wonder why Faulkner failed to name him sooner. Mark Frost then heaves into view, the poet who finds it difficult to write, and a young man so effete he is out of touch with his feelings. The scene asks Miss Jameson to try to seduce Frost, but his name bespeaks his attitude. While she disrobes and makes herself as attractive as she can be, he worries about missing his trolley and suddenly bolts. Another missed assignation, another heterosexual rendezvous thwarted.

Then in a reprise of the Nightown ("Circe") episode of *Ulysses*, Faulkner has Fairchild, Gordon, and Julius enter a Joycean world of molten language and boisterous street activity. Once again, the scene appears grafted on, lacking inevitability. Coming as it does after the previous brief episodes, it moves us still further from resolution or meaningful openness. Borrowings from "Elmer" appear once again, in which Elmer has a hallucinatory street experience with a prostitute in Genoa. Some of the street life is pulled from Faulkner's own New Orleans sketches, especially from

"The Wealthy Jew." There is finally some heterosexual activity as Gordon decides to join a prostitute and, borrowing some money, he goes in—the sole connection made in the novel between a man and a woman.

The final episode of the epilogue returns to the "Don Giovanni" material—Talliaferro in yet another attempt, this time with Jenny, the fleshy tease from the boat. Once more he is frightened off, on this occasion by a tough man who has picked Jenny up while Talliaferro gets a cab. The wording of his dismissal is precisely the same as in the short story, and with that Talliaferro assesses his failure: ". . . he had never had the power to stir women."[30] He telephones Fairchild and announces his latest strategy: bully them, push them around, dominate them, that's what women want. *Mosquitoes* pivots on rejection.

Faulkner brought the novel to an end at Pascagoula on September 1, 1926 —he was clearly a very rapid worker. One reason for his rapidity here and elsewhere was surely his decision early on that either manuscript or typescript, once established, should become the beachhead for repeated invasions, those extensive revisions which often became almost rewritings of the original. Characters' names were altered, lines rewritten, emphases changed, descriptive passages added—all of these characterized his later dissatisfaction and desire to get matters right. Throughout his entire career, Faulkner retained an obsessive attention to detail.

When Faulkner returned temporarily to Oxford, with little changed from the tramp look he had cultivated several years before, his marital destiny was at hand. Estelle had returned to Shanghai to see if anything remained of the relationship with Franklin, but there was finally open talk of divorce. Faulkner shortly returned again to New Orleans, near the end of September (1926) and moved back in with Spratling. With the completion of the *Mosquitoes* typescript on September 1, his production slowed for the time being. He did produce for Estelle the hand-bound *Royal Street*, less than two months after dedicating *Mosquitoes* to "beautiful and wise" Helen. His sole other work during this period was on the sketches and burlesques by Spratling known as *Sherwood Anderson and Other Famous Creoles.*

This little volume appeared in a limited edition of four hundred copies, privately printed and published by the Pelican Bookshop Press in Royal Street, the heart of New Orleans' French Quarter. It was, Spratling said, a parody which took its methods from Miguel Covarrubias's *The Prince of Wales and Other Famous Americans.* The plan was to present Spratling's drawings of various New Orleans figures. Lyle Saxon, their friend from the *Times-Picayune,* is depicted as a decadent, effete fellow with an imperious look. Anderson, in a cartoon that opens the book, is drawn by Spratling in an unusual pose, sitting like a pupil in a very low easy chair, hands holding his knees. The book *Tar* is on the floor just behind him. Anderson is wearing spats, and a cane is on the floor under his drawn-up legs. His face is set, with a look of either arrogance or boredom. Overall, the effect is halfway between portraiture and parody.

The book opens with Faulkner's foreword, four paragraphs which gently mock Anderson's style. Only the final paragraph on American humor hits home. What Faulkner attempts is to turn Anderson's dogged, earnest prose into something so limpid it becomes juvenile.* But the sense of real bite is missing—there is a kind of fraternity-house fun involved, as there is in the Spratling drawing. Yet if we see it from Anderson's side, he has been put upon. There was really no reason for such a parody except that beneath the bonhomie with Faulkner there lay real hostility toward a lesser writer who had become successful. There was a venomous streak which later emerged in Faulkner in different ways depending on circumstances. It begins to surface here, albeit without the sheer nastiness Hemingway exhibited in *Torrents of Spring.* Faulkner's, fortunately, was brief.

Biographically, the chief interest in such a piece is evidence of a festering need to cut himself adrift. By rejecting Anderson, with Spratling's connivance, Faulkner helped establish himself, in his own eyes, as more important. He needed bolstering, and the venom alluded to above would almost always be forthcoming when he felt he had to assert himself, or felt smothered. A good deal of that sharp tongue and desire to destroy opposition emerged in his marriage; it was present even in his relationship with his daughter, Jill. It was an almost uncontrollable need, and the entire enterprise with Spratling seems unworthy of a writer who was himself poised in his work to pass Anderson without further need for denigration.

Meanwhile, *Mosquitoes* was accepted by Liveright on the enthusiastic recommendation of its reader, Lillian Hellman. But Liveright insisted on several deletions, chiefly the sexual byplay between Jenny and Pat as they kiss after Pat strokes her side. A remark by Mrs. Wiseman on women making love with each other was also excised, along with certain speculations on the right kind of sexual intercourse. Little did Liveright know that Faulkner was only warming up, saving his heavy arsenal for the future.

---

*"We have one priceless universal trait, we Americans. That trait is our humor. What a pity it is that it is not more prevalent in our art. . . . Our trouble with us American artists is that we take our art and ourselves too seriously. And perhaps seeing ourselves in the eyes of our fellow artists will enable those who have strayed to establish anew a sound contact with the fountainhead of our American life."

Chapter Ten

Perceiving Himself

A S FAULKNER MOVED toward work which would prove pivotal in his career—the fragmentary *Father Abraham* and the well-fleshed-out *Flags in the Dust*—he became immersed in his family in a new way: as an observer as well as participant. For with these books, he needed every detail and bit of observation to produce what he had in mind. Phil Stone always claimed he had introduced Faulkner to the Snopes material, or at least insinuated the theme of a redneck family infiltrating the community and eventually taking it over. But the Snopes idea was a natural outgrowth of Faulkner's own observations: his use of such material, perhaps reinforced by Stone's suggestion, came from his own experience of Oxford and the South. It is implicit in his early novels, especially in *Mosquitoes*, where Snopes potential lurks around the edges of the well-heeled crowd at the novel's center, and even in *Soldiers' Pay*, where a Snopes atmosphere is also potential.

Faulkner's observations of his family—his now dead grandfather, his younger brother Dean, his other two brothers, Jack in the FBI, John an engineer—gave him both location and history for *Flags*. Minor characters could also be found in long-term Oxford residents. Even the Negro servants in the novel appear to be based on those close to Faulkner, with Simon corresponding in some ways to Ned Barnett, a long-time Faulkner family retainer. One could elaborate extensively on possible models,* but it is a huge mistake to see either *Father Abraham* or *Flags* as distinctly based on his family. Faulkner carefully selected certain details, but he also invented, deceived, fudged, and crafted. His "secretive art" was already at work, and that conspiratorial sense entered deeply into his work, even as it was beginning to intensify in his own life.

Estelle reentered, returning to Oxford in early 1927 with finality. Her return, everyone understood, meant that, with divorce depositions taken, she would be divorced in two years—the actual date April 29, 1929. Now as she came back to Oxford in January, the issue was forced: Faulkner's offer of almost a decade earlier would be taken up. She also returned with a novel in manuscript, called "White Beeches." Faulkner wrote Liveright on February 18, 1927, asking him to look at it for publication. But nothing came of that, and it was never published.[1]

But even as Estelle returned, knowing she had someone in the wings, Faulkner had moved so far from her that their worlds, in Oxford, were completely different. Faulkner was voyaging into an intensive period of creativity, not quite as frenzied as when he and Estelle married, but almost as significant in his career. *Flags* would carry him back into his own family, to stories he had heard and reheard as a child and young man, and to his need to re-create them in his own way. He was to be involved in himself to such a degree that no one, even someone as deeply embedded in memory and young allegiances as Estelle, could throw him off course. It was Estelle's misfortune to hang on to these memories and promises even as the man who made them was drifting away into his own deeply felt life.

Within this frame of reference, Faulkner wrote *The Wishing Tree*, a fairy tale he typed and bound himself, and presented to Victoria (Cho-Cho) Franklin on her eighth birthday, from "Bill he made this Book." The tale is fittingly slight, with some bows to *Alice in Wonderland*—a tale of children shrinking and then returning to size, and a wishing tree which promises good things in life. At the end, Faulkner makes a switch and indicates that if children are kind, a wishing tree is not necessary "to make things come true." Only one passage need detain us, and that is the association of Dulcie in the story with Victoria and the further identification of Dulcie's mother with Estelle. Faulkner writes of Dulcie's mother in strange colors: "Dulcie's mother was beautiful, so slim and tall, with her grave unhappy eyes changeable as seawater and her slender hands that came so softly about you when you were sick."[2] The description indicates Faulkner's old attachment is still present, but also reveals he has picked up something so insistent he must intrude with it into a passage where it doesn't fit. Those

---

*Blotner cites Stark Young's father for Lucius Peabody, Dr. Ashford Little for young Dr. Alford, and two local residents for Will Falls (Joseph Blotner, *Faulkner: A Biography*, 2 vols. [New York: Random House, 1974], vol. 1, p. 537). More apparent are old Bayard, based on Faulkner's grandfather, and Aunt Jenny, modeled on "Auntee," Murry's sister, Mary Holland.

"grave unhappy eyes changeable as seawater" jar us with the reality of the situation; Estelle was not only unhappy, she was unwell, beginning the decline which continued right into the period when she married Faulkner two years later.

As he made his way around Oxford in the winter and spring of 1927, Faulkner did not seem like marriageable material. In his head was an entire world, but in his activities he seemed little more than a man going nowhere, despite two novels and numerous poems. None of it had brought him nearly enough money to live on, and he depended still on family and friends, chiefly loans from Phil Stone which were tantamount to handouts. Only writing offered a way out of this financial dilemma, and yet what Faulkner was writing appeared uncommercial; and as his imagination intensified, his work would become progressively less commercial until he wrote *Sanctuary*. Stone for his part was still enormously supportive—telling one and all that some day Faulkner would be famous, adding that *The Marble Faun* would become a very valuable item. He was right—first editions of the volume became collectors' items in later years. But Stone's way of putting it to Dot Wilcox was compelling: someday, he said, "this tramp will be famous,"[3] perhaps confusing Faulkner with Chaplin.

As part of his visualization of his new work, Faulkner not only noted members of his family and their servants, but Oxford itself. He had begun to imagine Oxford into Jefferson, and Lafayette County into Yoknapatawpha. This transformation of what appeared on the surface a rather low-keyed place into a beehive of rancor, hatred, and violence, intermingled with routine life, was a great act of imagination, and Faulkner's greatest contribution to American fiction. But even as we praise his act of transformation, we should not hold him too closely to it; Oxford joins with a more generalized sense of the state and of the South to make up his "little postage stamp" of an imaginary county. Further, we must not neglect Faulkner's birthplace, New Albany, nor the background of his ancestors in Ripley— just as we should not forget the entire history of what was occurring as old and new South met. And finally, in discussing convergences, we should not assume that equal amounts of real life went into equal amounts of imagined life.

But even before Faulkner completed his first version of *Flags*, with its intimate connections to his own family, reviews of *Mosquitoes* were arriving in June. The reviews came from figures who were on their way to large careers of their own. Lillian Hellman praised the brilliance of the novel in the New York *Herald Tribune*; Conrad Aiken lauded the novel's style and wit in the *New York Evening Post*. Other reviews by Ruth Suckow, Donald Davidson, and the like were unfavorable—with most of the poor reviews focusing on the tiredness of the material, the recognizability of the characters and situations—criticisms for which the novel, with its heavy Eliot borrowings, provides considerable foundation. All things considered,

Faulkner had come out about as well as he could have expected, once we get behind the hype provided by both Hellman and Aiken. Far more disappointing was the marriage on May 4 of Helen Baird, after *Mosquitoes* had been dedicated to her as both beautiful and wise—the adjectives were mysteriously removed from the first edition. As Faulkner moved closer to marriage with Estelle, the dedication became, simply, "To Helen," and then she was gone, married to Guy Lyman.*

Money was apparently very short, if we can believe Faulkner's letters to William Stanley Braithwaite about collecting his royalties for *The Marble Faun*. In the fall of 1925, he was owed eighty-one dollars, and he wanted to collect it. In fact, the Four Seas Company was playing some of Faulkner's own game—not responding to letters or inquiries. Knowing this ploy well, Faulkner had even sent a registered letter, only to receive an acknowledgment from the post office, but nothing from Four Seas. He threatened legal action—which would have involved Phil Stone. "It never occurred to me," he wrote, "that anyone would rob a poet. It's like robbing a whore or a child."[4] In the same letter, Faulkner thanks Braithwaite for including "The Lilacs" in his *Anthology of Magazine Verse for 1925.*

Faulkner followed this up with another letter on February 25, saying he understood Four Seas was financially troubled and not attempting to wait out the two years which would, according to the contract, void his claim. He says: "I shall feel easy about getting the money some day." He never received it, and in fact a good part of the edition was destroyed in a warehouse fire. Nor did the volume sell well, although it would later become a very valuable collectible. Faulkner's fortunes with Four Seas were somewhat typical of what occurred with poetry volumes: poor sales to start with, and then some disaster, so that royalties, small though they would be, were not forthcoming. When we speak of shifts in Faulkner's imagination which took him from poetry to fiction, we should not neglect the financial dimension. It had become clear to him, no matter how much he wished to be known as a poet, that he could not survive that way.

Exactly when Faulkner started to write *Father Abraham* is difficult to determine; perhaps it was in the lull when lovesickness did not take up all his time. That would place the beginning of *Father Abraham*—incomplete and briefer than the versions of "Elmer"—sometime after September 1926. Intermixed with the writing of this was his start on *Flags*, probably also the product of this lull in time. By the early winter of 1927, both books were moving along, although *Father Abraham* proved a sourcebook rather than

---

*Margery Gumbel, Faulkner's friend from *Double Dealer* days (in a 1965 letter to Blotner), recalled that he confided in her, saying he had declared to Helen his love. Her memory of this spans some forty years, and we have no way of knowing the context. Faulkner may have been using Margery as a sympathetic audience for a romantic scenario (Joseph Blotner, *Faulkner: A Biography*, 2 vols. [New York: Random House, 1974], vol. 1, p. 526).

a fleshed-out manuscript. The latter is a curious work, probably titled ironically, with Flem Snopes as the local patriarch.* (In *Flags* Flem is referred to as Abraham.) Coming from "a small settlement known as Frenchman's Bend," Flem "had appeared unheralded one day" and had found a position in a small restaurant. "With this foothold and like Abraham of old, he led his family piece by piece into town."⁵ In addition to the connection of Flem to Abraham, we note how Faulkner is mythmaking; turning the "unheralded" appearance into an event which transcends history. With *Father Abraham* he was apparently on the threshold of a great transcendent event.

Caveat lector: not all Snopeses in Faulkner's depiction of them are venomous; Flem is, but others (Eck, Wall) have a variety of qualities. Flem has not a single redeeming feature (unless one counts tenacity)—he is indeed slimy in every act he commits, in every thought he has. But even the people Flem is struggling to supplant are rapacious and amoral. The Varners, Will and Jody, have little to recommend them, except that they have been around for a long time and are integrated into the Jefferson way of life. What they represent, however, Faulkner cannot offer as an alternative to Snopesism. Neither name calls up either delicacy or elegance. Many commentators neglect to note that both sides have crawled out of the swamp. In their own way, the Varners have cheated and deceived for generations, and now they find more than a match: these are opposing forces of equal negative moral weight.

With *Father Abraham* Faulkner begins his devastating examination of class and caste in the South, by implication in America—and he does so in purely literary terms. Thus this incomplete work, in itself little more than stories linked together, takes on considerable freight; it suggests for the first time Faulkner's major mode of working. In Flem he has his Snopes —the triumph of the redneck, as a later writer called it. But however sleazy the redneck, Faulkner demonstrates little sympathy for those he was attempting to replace. As we have noted earlier, when Faulkner was growing up politics were in the hands of Vardaman and Bilbo, opportunistic, expedient, underhanded men. Bilbo was perhaps the vilest man ever to achieve high office (as governor and senator) in any state, although Tom Watson of Georgia runs him a close race for the distinction. Yet even Bilbo left a legacy of achievement; intermixed with his racism and personal corruption were a series of reforms in prisons, highways, and other areas. Faulkner could see that this man who represented the very worst in politics (and whom several Falkners supported wholeheartedly) could also put into place needed reforms. The point is that the redneck interests Bilbo courted to gain office gave him leverage against past interests which had left the state in miserable economic and political order. Faulkner drew on

---

*A lesser possibility: Faulkner borrowed the title from Anderson, who was using it for a biography of Lincoln. Whether Faulkner considered the irony of substituting Snopes for Lincoln we cannot determine. Given Southern attitudes toward Lincoln, he may have.

just such oppositions in using the Snopes family against those they were supplanting.

In addition to Flem, Faulkner has his location:[6] the Yocona River* and Frenchman's Bend, the latter coming close to present-day Tula. He has Will Varner, the old Frenchman's Place, and Will's ripening daughter, Eula—the first of Faulkner's women to break free of the hipless, boyishly figured Diana type. Eula is pregnant, and Flem marries her, carrying her off to Texas; she returns with a baby, the daughter Linda, who will become one of Faulkner's most interesting females, and Flem returns with a herd of wild ponies held together with barbed wire. The horses become the centerpiece of the fragment. Their wildness and desire for freedom is juxtaposed with the Jefferson men's desire to own them cheaply and to tame them. Here we have vintage Faulkner: the opposites which dominate his fiction. The horses represent quintessential primitive life, the spirit of the wilderness and range; they are violent to the point of self-destruction, and their teeth and hooves are lethal weapons. Untamable creatures, they do whatever they can to resist man's control of them. This rampage of horses represents Faulkner's unleashed Edenic vision—something that cannot be controlled *because it should not be.* Man's efforts at taming the horses only reveal what fools men are, and how vicious some can be. That they fail to make the horses defer is, for Faulkner, the mark of the mystique of the animal—its ungovernable nature.

It is in their relationship to the horses that the men in the story reveal themselves. The herder, Buck, is a confidence man who is able to make money for himself and Flem Snopes by seeming to offer useful ponies at low prices. But the offer is never commensurate with the goods, which are not bankable. The goods prove vapid because the men hope to turn into a cash crop what lies beyond man's control. They are tampering, unconsciously, with the mysteries of nature; and their lack of success suggests that man's efforts to tame the wild are undermined by nature itself, which provides the "wild" with an escape.

Henry Armstid, who returns in *As I Lay Dying*, reveals himself as the worst—forgoing his wife's hard-saved five dollars for a pony. But Armstid is only an excess of what exists in the others, that inability to pass up what seems a bargain even if it goes against nature. *Father Abraham* encompasses a profound Faulknerian "presence": the discord that results when human wildness, based on greed or acquisitiveness, runs up against real wildness. But not everyone is avaricious. One Snopes, the blacksmith Eck, shows consideration and restraint, a foil for Flem. And Faulkner introduces an extremely important character, one reminiscent

---

*Yocona is now on the maps, but once Yoknapatawpha was on both maps and county records. One translation of Yoknapatawpha (a Chickasaw word) is "furrowed ground." For a close examination of how Lafayette County parallels Yoknapatawpha, as well as how the reality differed from Faulkner's "little postage stamp," see Elizabeth M. Kerr, *Yoknapatawpha: Faulkner's "Little Postage Stamp of Native Soil"* (New York: Fordham University Press, 1969).

of Conrad's Marlow, in V. K. Suratt (at one time June, and later on V. K. Ratliff). The conception of Suratt-Ratliff gave Faulkner (as Marlow gave Conrad) a point of view within the narrative; furthermore, it provided him with a voice of reason, set within the text. Through this mechanism, Faulkner could remain distanced from his narrative and yet enter into it. It afforded him a dual strategy: personal, intimate entrance into his novel, and impersonality, which is one of the lessons he learned from the moderns.

Suratt-Ratliff does not function like Stephen Dedalus in Joyce. Suratt gives the author not so much a directing intelligence in the text as a disciplined way of perceiving the material. His insights into human motives allow Faulkner to keep his sights on the normal world, so that no matter how egregious Flem or someone else becomes, we are presented with a measure of moderation. It would be a huge mistake to say that Suratt represents Faulkner (any more than Marlow represents Conrad). Both surrogates represent an inquiring mind which the author can utilize in the way the Greek chorus once operated: an external element brought into the text as commentator, moderator, voice of reason (usually), and balance against extremism. Suratt-Ratliff increasingly takes on large proportions within Faulkner's way of working—a necessity for a writer so involved with his vision he needs someone not a visionary.

Not by chance, Faulkner interrupted the manuscript of *Father Abraham* to work seriously on *Flags*. *Father Abraham* appeared to open up an entire vein of imagination: area, place, location, reinvented characters. This opening up of material in a relatively brief manuscript then extended, with *Flags*, into an opening up of the author's own background, with its wealth of detail which could be reinvented for the sake of fiction. With *Father Abraham* and *Flags*, Faulkner had that dualism his work called for: a tensing of materials stretched between geographical area (town and country) and historical background, so that the Civil War in the latter overlaps and merges with World War I. The tensing and blending of materials is extremely important, since history is no less a Faulknerian substance than is geography.

All this appeared to be a freeing process for him. By late 1926 or 1927 he moved across manuscripts, going from lateral to vertical, from geographical area to historical backgrounding. He did not alter his mode of perceiving; he simply switched it onto a different track. In both cases he was adumbrating the South, using the South as a means of saying something about America. Whether working geographically or historically, Faulkner was positioning himself as an American novelist.

At the Beinecke at Yale, there is a curiously aborted document, coming about two years after Faulkner had switched to *Flags*. In this brief manuscript, he writes of his fear of losing the world he knew; of feeling himself growing into decrepitude, and hastening to capture his world before it drifted away. He says that to preserve this disappearing world, he invented characters and created others out of tales he had heard ". . . thus I improved on God who, dramatic though He be, has no sense, no feeling for, theatre."[7] This brief document reveals Faulkner's profound interest in salvaging the past; but it also illuminates something about the workings of his imagination. He needed a sense of history, and what better place to seek it than in his own background? As we have seen, the Falkners were archetypal, intrinsically part of the land; but then, with Snopes-like tenacity, they helped open up the South to the new era of modernization. To a large extent, Faulkner had to recognize the line between earlier Falkners and Snopeses was not that broad; that the old and young colonels had extended their fortunes with methods that would, probably, not stand close scrutiny.

Father Abraham and *Flags* cross geographically and historically. Byron Snopes provides the unlikely crossover. Part of the Snopes clan in *Father Abraham*, Byron writes obscene letters to Narcissa Benbow in *Flags*; and she, while somehow cherishing them, marries young Bayard Sartoris. The point is not simply the tentative nature of the Snopes family reaching into the Sartoris family, but the fact the two overlapped in Faulkner's imagination. They were not there as opposites (as Marion O'Donnell's early interpretation put it, pitting Snopes animalism against Sartoris humanism) but as overlapping entities. The poisoned missives Byron directs at Narcissa are the work of a marginal man. Yet against him in the competition, as it were, for Narcissa's hand, Bayard Sartoris has his own furtive, uncontrollable agenda: his sense of doom, his almost catatonic curling back upon self, his inability to feel anything except for his dead twin (and thus for himself). As the menu is presented, neither is an appetizing morsel. They do not oppose or counterpoint; they overlap.

Faulkner's sense of history here is of a gigantic kaleidoscope of people and events interweaving with each other. To view these elements as opposing each other is to lose sight of Faulkner's vertical or historical sense. The difference between Snopes and Sartoris comes in what each claims for itself. The Sartoris clan is still operating at the Edenic moment in American mythical history. The early years, both the Mexican and Civil wars, to which we might add the Spanish-American, were part of that myth, despite the terrible defeat the South suffered in the Civil War. Faulkner's use of the war is to stress its Edenic qualities, those of gallantry, fearlessness, courage; traits one associates with the Bayard not only of that war but of medieval legends, where his name as the Chevalier Bayard became renowned. The myth of Eden has transformed the war into a time of such gallantry that killing and carnage are secondary matters: what does matter is the recollection of the South's brave resistance and moments of superb courage, even to the point of foolhardiness.

The Edenic moment, however, cannot last. It is only immortal in memory, in historical re-creation. What ends it is World War I, in which young Bayard's brother, John, is killed. Although John dies in a gallant action in the skies, outnumbered by German planes, his death breaks the cycle of Edenic wars. But up to his death, and then the useless, wasteful death of young Bayard himself in a willed crash, the Sartorises were responding to historical moments. They were those people for that time; just as the Snopeses, in their very different way, were to be people for another time.

If it was Sartoris for pre–World War I, it was Snopes for post–. In both instances, we have people responding to differing historical moments, although neither—Sartoris nor Snopes—has provided the South with direction or leadership. If we speak of the "aristocratic" Sartoris clan, we assume some degree of leadership, but the Sartoris name was connected to bravery on one hand and commercialism on the other. Old Bayard is not productive, not a leader; he is a relict, a piece of history. His life is made up, chiefly, of memories—lost causes, his son (also John) lost from fever and wounds garnered in the Spanish-American War, reaching back in time and place to the Mexican War when his father (also John) had fought, before getting rich slowly during the years before the Civil War.

The Sartoris clan fought gallantly in its wars, but the elder John's main preoccupation was acquisition of property: land, slaves, goods, railroad, bank. On a much smaller scale, and without the gallant moments, of course, the Snopeses begin their assault on the goods of the world. Since the historical moment has altered, with the Edenic myth no longer viable, they must grub, whereas the others expanded. The Sartorises were outside people—part of the expansiveness of the South and the nation; they acted as if they were themselves the moving frontier. The Snopeses evidently march to a different drummer, because America is different; expansiveness has given way to enclosure, to work and inside acquisition. The Snopeses in their acquisitiveness are grubby and deceitful because they make their gains on a small scale; the Sartorises seem grand and gallant because their gains had been writ large. It is not so much that Sartoris is replaced by Snopes, or that they are antithetical to each other, but that the historical moment for each has defined a different response. Even if a Snopes wished to be gallant—and they can be an uneven lot—the smaller scale necessitated by the shift in the country would not permit it.

But there is more to Faulkner's historical memory and re-creation of the past. The historical moment is clouded considerably by the interpenetration of names—there is deliberate obfuscation for the reader who attempts to keep the Sartoris clan straight. In the interweaving and doubling of brothers, sons, grandsons, we see Faulkner's awareness of the historical moment and how it dictates actions. Old Bayard's father and uncle, respectively John and Bayard, are two aspects of the old colonel, William Clark Falkner: by dividing his great-grandfather into two, Faulkner was able to achieve that doubling and overlapping of parents, children, and grandchildren which fulfill his sense of history as a sequence of interwoven events. Old Bayard's father, John, has acted bravely, fighting in the Mexican War, then in the war between the states, eventually losing his command, though regrouping his forces when he could fight a guerrilla war against Grant (around Vicksburg). His commitment to the war seems total, but he also appears not to be quite as headstrong as his brother, Bayard. Both the John and Bayard lines are doomed by history and character, but this Bayard is foolhardy rather than simply brave. In this older generation, Bayard Sartoris throws his life away trying to get hold of some anchovies in the Union camp, where he is shot by an irate cook hiding behind a table. So ends Bayard and his effort to emulate his commander, Jeb Stuart.

As modeled after the old colonel, John Sartoris comes out of the war and achieves his career in railroading and politics. But his career is not at all Edenic: he uses his power for white supremacy, harasses and even murders carpetbaggers, and makes certain that Negroes lose the vote. He is part of that movement to roll back Reconstruction, such as it was, and to pave the way for the Klan in its later, racist years. Working within the Southern power base, John Sartoris is not just a wild young man—he is a power-hungry, politically obsessed individual whose will is law. He establishes a dynasty, and its elements, while high and grand, are little different from the dynasties at the middle level established by Will Varner and at the lower levels by the Snopeses. In *Flags* and *Sartoris* the Sartoris clan is presented with a certain reflected glory; but overall, Faulkner understands that this family, too, has helped destroy the Edenic myth.

Faulkner should not be read reductively, as establishing oppositions and antipathies; in fact, he reveals how history dooms one generation after another. In his public statements, he may have spoken of coming through, endurance, et al., but the fabric of his fiction makes another point: the dingdong of history, circumstances, the moment. In the structuring of the generations, we get some sense of Faulkner's use of history—which is not at all liberating or enduring, but part of a vast destiny which gathers in the individual and shapes him. Defining this outreach of history will become Faulkner's task for the next ten years, culminating with *Absalom* where all simplistic notions of history and the individual go up in contradictions. *Flags*, for example, is populated by alternating, often contradictory Bayards and Johns. The oldest generation consists of these two, with John coming through and establishing himself and the Sartoris line, even as Bayard gets himself killed in a caper over anchovies. So much for ideology. John fathers old Bayard, whose career suggests that of the young colonel, just as John's suggests that of the old colonel. This intermingling of names strategically intermingles events of the novel with Faulkner's personal links to the past; it also sets up ideological and historical contradictions.

Old Bayard, son of John, has his own son, whom he names John: generations alternate as Bayard and John. This latter John, the grandson of a John and the son of a Bayard, has twin sons, and names them Bayard and John. John, like his great-uncle, Bayard, is killed in the war—only now the war has passed to World War I, from the Mexican struggle which engaged old John, to the Civil War which had engaged both Bayard and John, and killed Bayard, to the Spanish-American conflict, from whose effects another John has died. When old Bayard dies of a heart attack during a car crash brought on by young Bayard, only the latter survives, the sole Sartoris for the moment. Deaths pass in and out of each other, the clan almost a killing field. Young Bayard has married, and his wife, Narcissa Benbow, gives birth to a son, whom everyone expects to be named Bayard. But she attempts to break the doom of history and calls him Benbow Sartoris, as if that will make any difference.

The baby will be all that remains of the line. But as Jenny Du Pre, the sister of the original Sartoris brothers, comments: what does a name mean, when the blood is still Sartoris blood? But except for Jenny, this is primarily a tale of male history. The women are given short shrift both by Faulkner and by life. In the immediate foreground, young Bayard's wife has died before the novel opens; in the more immediate past, his mother has died about the time her husband, John, passed away. Old Bayard is a long-time widower; and the older generation of Bayard and John had little time for women. Only Jenny carries on the female tradition, which is one of commentary, rebuke, nagging, and civilized pressure. Her role is to try to transform tribal savages into civilized human beings, an enterprise which is self-defeating. She witnesses generation after generation of death —and, true to Faulkner's early philosophy about women, at least one survives to keep the race going. What is curious is that Faulkner kept the older woman alive, but killed off the younger. Until Narcissa marries young Bayard, no current wives in the Sartoris line call attention to themselves: the men have walked all over them. Only the elderly Jenny remains, and her role is not really to do anything but to prevent anything from being done. She is herself a kind of transformation of Faulkner's mother and great-aunt " 'Bama."

What are we to make of the name-change in the manuscript of the younger John, originally called Evelyn? Although Evelyn can function as a male name in England, it is also the name for a woman. Normally such gender ambiguity could be overlooked, but Faulkner was still immersed in dual role-playing, and we are tempted to view "Evelyn" as suggesting brother-sister as much as fraternal bonding. The manuscript of *Flags* opens with Evelyn with the RAF in France, then moves to old Bayard in his study at home, with his old relics. That opening with Evelyn indicates that the sibling relationship preempts everything—even in the altered version of the novel. This scene was itself removed, and *Sartoris* opens with old man Falls bringing "John Sartoris into the room with him"—but this "John" is old Bayard's father, not his dead son or grandson, also named John. In the manuscript, however, the presence of Evelyn (John) so early points up Faulkner's emphasis upon not a vertical descent of Bayards and Johns but a lateral one—the preeminent relationship is sibling. In point of fact, young Bayard misses his brother far more than he does his wife; flesh-and-blood is a closer linkage than marriage. As "Evelyn," John would be sweetheart as well as brother—the female, considerate, caring side of Bayard, now suddenly killed. How far Faulkner would carry this is unclear, but the shift from Evelyn, with its dual nature, to John, suggests some conceptual ambiguity. The shift to the repetitious John also shows how Faulkner was moving into complicated history, because with the Sartorises, a family of doomed "Johns," the youngest becomes simply the beneficiary of history.

The death of John-figures in the Sartoris line obviously subverts the Edenic nature of their quest for self-fulfillment and makes quite problematic the nature of every belief and direction. Only in his public speeches and letters to editors, or in his responses to interviewers' questions, did Faulkner simplify on matters of race and his attitudes toward the South and America. In his fiction he was aware of how the Edenic myth was contravened at every turn by historical doom. Every garden was despoiled, dispossessed, invaded by corruption. This was true of *the* Garden, America, most of all, with the South as its metaphor.

It is important to see *Father Abraham* moving parallel to *Flags*, just as later we should see *Sound, Sanctuary,* and *As I Lay Dying* as a unit of thought, although very different fictions. Phil Stone helped contribute to the supposed dichotomy between Snopes and Sartoris. In connection with both *Father* and Flags, Stone spoke of the chivalrous, aristocratic Sartoris family in opposition to the "poor white trash"[8] Snopeses. The South, however, is an overlapping, intertwining, interconnected sequence of scenes and people. The Sartoris clan is destroyed by the twentieth century, whereas the Snopeses are a post-Reconstruction phenomenon, developing aspects of the South which the Sartorises—with planter disdain—are too haughty to touch. Still, they work not against each other but in tandem, to make the South into the doomed, destined place Quentin Compson can decry even as he states his love for it. When he repeats at the end of *Absalom* that he does not hate the South—a phrase, incidentally, far more significant for Faulkner than the rather glib words of his Nobel Prize acceptance speech—his assertion has profound meaning only if we correctly assess those cycles of Southern doom. Quentin's own family is, in actuality, more central to the genteel tradition which is being displaced than is the Sartoris clan, which, like Faulkner's own family, had something violent and disreputable associated with it.

Faulkner caricatures Sartorises as much as he detests Snopeses. The tragedy of the South is it was caught in the grip of succeeding cycles neither of which offered it respite from its travail—each only intensified and deepened existing dilemmas. Aunt Jenny, for example, may be the surviving Sartoris, reaching back into another era, but her presence and her verbal admonitions are futile. Her main purpose is to stop history, to fix the South and its culture in a past epoch. Her function has nothing to offer. Her views on race are antebellum, and her sense of Southern culture as a whole has been untouched by circumstance. Through her, Faulkner shows the courage of the older generation, yet at the same time her presence implies its impotence. She hems and haws and intimidates—especially the Negro servants—but she has no effect; with her death, the dam breaks.*

If we agree that in this respect Sartoris and Snopes are both emblematic of Southern destiny and doom rather than opposing forces, we can take into account another major symbolism in *Flags*: glassblowing. This is such an unusual twist in Faulkner, so out of keeping with his usual pursuits, that we must see it as fulfilling a very complicated need. Horace Benbow, whose sister Narcissa will marry Bayard and have a child by him, comes home from World War I with a glassblowing set. Like Bayard, he has been in the war, but, unlike that doomed young man, he has been behind the lines with a YMCA unit. Horace and Bayard are paralleled throughout, and in fact compete for Narcissa's heart. Although he is infatuated with Belle Mitchell and eventually steals her from her husband and marries her, Horace comes across as sexually ambiguous. A lawyer by profession but also a frustrated artist, Horace appears caught between several inchoate urges, some of them sexual. Even as he plays a spotty incestuous game with Narcissa and pursues Belle, he tries through glassblowing to withdraw from everything associated with his personal-sexual life. Horace seems to have in him something of Phil Stone, but also amounts of Faulkner himself —especially in his weak war role, as contrasted with Bayard's heroics. We can see Faulkner replaying the war in his ridicule of Horace's safe activities, his inability to get near the front. Since both Bayard and Horace are competitors for Narcissa, we can also see in this a replay of Faulkner's own personal history, in which Estelle finally goes not to the artist but to the man of action.

These shadows of a Faulknerian pattern are richly textured. The glassblowing, in itself so unusual for the writer, has within it as many layers of personal meaning as the broad social and historical aspects of Snopes and Sartoris. Faulkner later referred to himself as an empty vessel waiting to be filled, and the image is here. Besides blowing glass, Horace is waiting for something to happen; passive, lax, withdrawn, he lets himself be filled by others. Belle Mitchell, before and after their marriage, seems to call the turns, and her demands are met by Horace without question—even to his regularly hauling a stinking package of frozen shrimp for her. But the glassblowing commands our attention. It suggests a vacuum, an empty space, something which must be filled with air. Its expansion is made against nearly all laws of nature: its creation is based not on the solidity of lines, words, or even musical notes, but on the insubstantiality of breath filling an ever-thinning lining of glass matter. It is transparent, a bubble, a matter of deceiving what nature seems to intend. As the glass expands, it becomes ever thinner, and the art of blowing is to find the tensile

---

*The novel, written when the levee of the Mississippi River was destroyed so as to save New Orleans from a rampaging flood, may have taken some of its impetus from that event, on April 22, 1927. At one level, we may read *Flags* as a novel of a society breaking open and exploding, being riven; if we add to it the emblem of water pouring through, we are not far from the truth. In *The Wild Palms*, the break in the levee is moved up to May 3.

strength of the glass at the moment of the object's peak beauty, a perfect balance. This balance is of course missing in Horace; and the glass—this particular dimension of artistic activity—replaces in him an inability to live.

We can also see the blowing of glass as part of Horace's dissatisfaction with himself and the guidelines of his culture; despite (in his own culture's terms) the effeminate nature of his pursuit, he must attempt this liberation of self. He becomes, in this act, curiously epicene, androgynous, beyond social expectation. The blowing of glass locates him so far outside it frees him to be brother-husband-lover of Narcissa. Since their relationship is one of Faulkner's "incestuous" ones, we must see Horace's activities as devoted to his apartness from regular pursuits, his commitment to Narcissa, despite his dismal marriage to Belle.

In the novel's structure, Faulkner makes evident contrasts between Horace and Bayard Sartoris. Bayard is all doomed masculinity, grieving over his brother but most of all grieving over himself in ways we cannot understand. One of the evident weaknesses of *Flags* is Faulkner's inability to find in Bayard the coordinates for his nihilism—the war experience explains only part of it. As if Faulkner had recognized how insufficient Bayard is, he created Horace as an opposite. A simplistic reading of the novel, however, is to see the two men as reverse sides of the author. In that view, Horace represents the artistic, sensitive side, whereas Bayard reveals the heroic role Faulkner yearned after but which was denied him. In this reductive view, Horace's career is a thinly disguised one for Faulkner's, especially in their mutual attachment to an unsuitable woman. To complete this picture, Bayard is so war-doomed he has passed beyond normal activities; he must drive himself into one death situation after another—the romantic, even nihilistic side of Faulkner.

But to view the novel's design in those terms is to lose sight of what makes it, despite its flaws, a strong effort. While personal in several aspects, *Flags* is foremost a meditation on history, an act of retrieval, the first of the author's many retrievals which emanate from *Father Abraham*. The personal dimensions of *Flags* occur not in places where Faulkner has located himself in this or that character or this or that situation, but in the way he has presented history and its meanings. For hovering over the entire novel, almost from the first with the introduction of old man Falls, is the awareness of historical destiny claiming its due. Faulkner is trying to understand the South—not solely as a collection of people but as a collective, historical, cultural idea. None of this deemphasizes the importance of the people, or what they represent; but it does suggest that this is the first extended work in which patterns, cycle, history, and cultural matrix preempt individual representation.

In its inchoate way, the novel is as much about history as the far greater and more sophisticated *Absalom*. Faulkner was seduced by history, and his reading of Eliot, among others, further reinforced his insight into historical process as ever-present. In *Flags* Faulkner reaches back fleetingly to the

Mexican War; but the reality of struggle comes preeminently with the conflict between the states, and then in World War I. In the fall of 1927, when Faulkner was thirty, the Civil War was a living monument, providing a comparison between its veterans and those of the world war. Whatever achievements a man gained in the larger war provided sources of comparison with the deeds and legends of the Civil War. Veterans of the latter conflict were still in abundance throughout the nation—men now in their seventies and eighties vying with younger veterans, those in their late twenties or early thirties. In *Flags* a generational conflict is working its way out by way of the war one fought in. When we meet old Bayard, he has lost his son John and grandson John, so that with his father John reaching back deep into the previous century, he becomes a measure of war's continuity.

The opening of the novel stresses this historical proximity. When the pauper Falls enters the prosperous old Bayard's office, the presence of a third person is palpable. "As usual, old man Falls had brought John Sartoris into the room with him." Faulkner repeats: the presence of "the spirit of the dead man," the presence of the "dead man's son," the "company of him who had passed beyond death and then returned." Faulkner has his motif here for the entire novel, and it is the permeation of the historical sense. Like Conrad in *Nostromo*, Faulkner makes every move a historical maneuver. Even young Bayard, who parallels so many of Faulkner's own preoccupations, cannot be approached except in terms of his war history, and beyond that, the history which has doomed the South.

Horace's glassblowing, then, is a means of rejecting that time and place, *that* history. As a noncombatant who labored in the YMCA unit, far from action and danger, he has broken from the dingdong of historical doom; and his strange "effeminate" activities are a means of stepping outside socially—though at the expense of his masculine side. Faulkner is very clear that Horace is an incomplete man, a Prufrockian, somewhat effeminate type, hanging on to women in general and his sister in particular for what they can do for him. As Aunt Jenny points out, wherever Horace goes, women will attempt to help him. His passiveness becomes a way by which he attracts attention, his helplessness one of his positive features. Narcissa, who has difficulty reflecting anyone but herself, relates only to Horace. The two become a kind of hermetic enclosure, breathing air not unlike the breath Horace blows into his expanding glassworks.

These activities and this side of Horace are part of what Ben Wasson, Faulkner's friend and later agent, excised to carve out *Sartoris*. Whatever the precise need of the material, Faulkner was using *Flags* as a serious trying-out, although it did not satisfy his publisher Liveright, who rejected the work. Relationships as a whole in *Flags* concern us, since they seem to be telling us a good deal about Faulkner's sense of family patterns. The central doom is, of course, the death of young John Sartoris in a dogfight with German planes, and the guilt his surviving elder twin, Bayard, feels —that somehow he was at fault in permitting the impetuous John (direct descendant in this respect of the Bayard who died for anchovies in the Civil War) to go up against overwhelming odds and better planes. In Bayard's wash of guilt, his inability to feel, his own desire for romantic death, we sense Faulkner working out some of his own feelings for his brothers. But just *what* he was working through we cannot tell, and speculation leads nearly anywhere: hostility, aggressiveness, competition, feelings of inferiority, even a displacement of fraternal feeling to a desire for the death of the father. Any of these may be true, or all of them false.*

The paralysis or ineffectuality of the older generation in *Flags* and other novels of this period seems to point to a personal attitude toward fathers. But it could also be a more generalized point about the culture itself: the generational conflict absorbed into cultural and historical elements. Yet even here we are uncertain, for "movement" in the novel is curiously arranged. While young Bayard is associated with speed, with flying and with reckless, abandoned car driving, old Bayard is linked to sleep, rest, smoking, drinking; a role which leads him gradually toward death. All signs point toward a peaceful death, not a violent one, and the imagery linked to his physical being is associated with passivity, memories, winding down toward nothing. Yet young Bayard's speed, such as it is, is always self-defeating—he moves rapidly to get nowhere; movement is not "toward," but circular. However fast he drives, he ends up being himself. He speeds to drive out demons, but unsuccessfully. In a way, his abandoned driving is little different in resolution of inner demons than is Horace's glassblowing. Speed as an alternative to comatose elders solves nothing.

All movement ends up as figures on a frieze, the frieze of the Grecian urn. Although they suggest frenzy and desire, they go nowhere. The expression of terrible grief and of generational conflict winds down to a rejection of all movement: *Flags* becomes in this respect Faulkner's expression of a denial of action, a reflection of a personality grinding to a halt. In creative terms, we can see *Flags* as Faulkner's expression of hitting bottom emotionally and psychologically, the lull before he entered into a great creative strike. In this suggestion of meaning, *Flags* is a reaching toward his nihilism, but also preparation for the move out. He was readying himself, surely not consciously, with the means by which he could retrieve, coast, descend, and then return with his full creative force. Conrad's means were similar—as he once remarked to his agent, Pinker, he lost a tooth each time he made a major effort. The toothache and ensuing loss

---

*One danger of Faulkner biography is to view events in Faulkner's novels as transcriptions of attitudes in his own life. According to this misreading, which vets the creative enterprise and turns fictions into documentaries, *Flags* is a hotbed of sibling rivalry; and Faulkner in his handling of young Bayard and his relationship to his brother is expressing a kind of forward-looking guilt. If we follow this, Faulkner was foreshadowing in his work what would actually occur—Dean was killed in a plane Faulkner gave him; and the guilt foreshadowed here became a reality. Such a reading, while ingenious, stresses that sibling hostility is a constant which reappears in Faulkner's work regardless of the creative disguises. It turns Faulkner into little more than a collection of anxieties, guilt feelings, hostilities, and aggressions, and denies he had the power to transcend them.

were his means of reaching into himself so intensely his bodily functions were affected. Faulkner's teeth remained intact, but he descended into elements which remained unresolved except through a turning of all effort, whether activity or passivity, into destructive behavior which went nowhere.

Such a resolution, in the destruction of all movement, is of considerable importance in assessing how Faulkner dealt with the various strands of his own life. By turning young Bayard's desire for movement into circles of frustration, by letting old Bayard's passivity decline toward death, Faulkner was making a large cultural statement as well as a personal one. In cultural terms, he was putting the South or his region on a threshold: in this precarious positioning of itself, the old ways no longer functioned, but were sunk into memories, passivity, history which no longer applied. In the younger generation, we have equal ineffectuality. The climactic scene of movement is the car accident which kills old Bayard and sends the young man careening off to Christmas dinner with a dirt-poor black family. It proves to be the finest scene in the novel—revealing Faulkner's overwhelming sympathy with the black dirt farmer—and yet what it demonstrates in the larger sense is the futility of movement. Here activity and passivity come together in the end of both main characters. Generations meet: old Bayard gets buried here and now, and young Bayard's doom is foretold.

The other side of this triangle is Horace and his glassblowing. This, too, is movement which is contained and, inevitably, denied by the nature of the materials. Horace is literally blowing bubbles—breathing into an enclosure, which contains his expression of movement. The Faulkner imagery is based on a negation of motion as much as on motion itself. Such tension between movement and stasis is not confined to *Flags*, although this novel becomes the first full display of this motif. It also affords a way of reading the novels clustered in the next few years—*As I Lay Dying*, *Sound*, even *Sanctuary*. Linking these books, perhaps more than any other quality, is that authorial awareness of where stasis meets motion. For Faulkner that precise point was the meeting ground of greatest tension— when he could work most imaginatively and least deterministically. One quality he had to overcome throughout his career was his overwhelming sense of destiny, which blurred over into a deterministic sense of historical process, the result of background, Civil War, sense of place. But Faulkner fought against pure destiny, even as he absorbed its inexorable force.

One way he offered resistance was in the workings of art and the artistic process—something he had learned very early from Keats, whose urn and its frieze are precisely that meeting ground of destiny and creative imagination. Faulkner did not have that urn or frieze, but he did have that creative sense of the moment, very close to Joyce's epiphany, Proust's privileged moment, or Wordsworth's spots of time. All of these "moments" enable the writer to break out, to leap from historical process into a "beyond."

Flags was a huge quarry for Faulkner. *Father Abraham* may have pointed the way to the Snopes trilogy and to the Yoknapatawpha cycle, but *Flags* pointed the way ahead to Faulkner. The meeting of motion and stasis, however, was not the only auspicious moment. The novel contained nearly everything Faulkner would embrace: the woods and hunt in the scenes with the MacCallums—where Faulkner already shows a mature mastery; the scenes with Negro servants—part of an evolving portrayal of the Negro from comic to dignified; the evocation of despair and loneliness—conveyed in Bayard's sense of himself once old Bayard has died; the Christmas scene with the Negro dirt farmer and his family—demonstrating Faulkner's ability to catch nuances of feeling and behavior lying deep beneath language. There are scenes still lacking full potential—for example between Horace and Narcissa, which are inchoate beginnings of major developments in his ideas and art. The eventual cutting of *Flags* by Ben Wasson may have eliminated longueurs, but it also eliminated characteristic Faulkner—turning a daring piece of fiction into a more ordered, safer one.

Horace Benbow is also part of that inchoate Faulkner which *Flags* represents. As we have suggested, Horace is based to some extent on Phil Stone, but also with elements, possibly, of Ben Wasson. Wasson partially replaced Stone; as the latter receded in Faulkner's life, Wasson loomed larger, until they also had a serious falling-out. Wasson's portrayal of Faulkner in *Count No 'Count* is by no means flattering—it cites lies, Estelle's flirtatious nature, and Faulkner's sodden drunkenness. How much of this was Wasson's response to Faulkner's partial portrait of him in Horace we cannot tell; but we do know there was a good deal of backbiting in Faulkner's use of friends for portraits and their response in speech and the written word.

Horace presents an interesting conflict in Faulkner: the male henpecked by a woman he does not even like. The temptation is to see Belle Mitchell as still another portrait of Estelle; but Belle also takes on qualities of a distinct Faulkner type—the "whore" figure not made for mothering or home, the Temple Drake archetype. Belle has no decent qualities; yet it is a mistake to see her as unsuited for the reticent Horace. Narcissa cannot understand how he can be attracted to a woman who seems physically and morally dirty. But Horace needs precisely this kind of woman, someone who can twist, bend, humiliate him, turn him into a weasel, into something less than masculine. Faulkner knew exactly what he was doing: Belle embodies what he thought of women who were not the cows of the world —like the later Lena Grove. They are discontented, disenchanted, seductive, morally ambiguous creatures lying in wait for men who need their type.

The racking tensions Faulkner threads through young Bayard are familiar to us in the author, although disguised and redrawn imaginatively. Bayard's movement in and out of marriage, for example, has certain familiar coordinates. With his first wife dead in the background of the novel, Bayard marries Narcissa to replace the child, also dead. But marriage is otherwise for him a nonbinding element—he flees from it, as if wife and home were contaminated. The demons which drive him make any kind of domestic arrangement impossible, as if he has no choice in the matter. Men among men: even this proves difficult for Bayard, when he stays with the MacCallums, in a marvelously evocative scene, although this is after his car accident in which old Bayard dies of a heart attack. Even here Bayard feels demon-driven, alternately emblazoned and chilled. One thinks of the great Flannery O'Connor image of "an enduring chill" which strikes Asbury, and applies here to Bayard as well—a chill which enters into him and is the sign, despite its cold, of a living hell.

So insistent and unrelenting is the depiction of Bayard that there is a suggestion of something emotionally or psychologically disturbing in his creator. There was, of course, the doom in Faulkner which emerged in dangerous behavior—there was on occasion rock-bottom despair, and several friends attest to seeing him bottom out. Was this the attitude he grafted onto Bayard, using the death of his twin brother as the legitimate means for displaying himself in this way? This is speculative, but there is little question *Flags* revealed a dark vision, and it is seductive to speculate further that this dark vision coincided with the proximity of Estelle's divorce and her coming marriage to Faulkner. All of these incidents seem to be linked, but the first half of 1927 when he was writing *Flags* was by no means a time of despair.

Rather the opposite. A good deal of his work at this time is humorous, broadly amusing, full of Faulknerian tall-tale matter. In December 1926, for example, he was involved in that collection of sketches which so annoyed Anderson, characterizing him as a famous Creole. Shortly after (in winter of 1927), Faulkner wrote the wild horses episode which fills *Father Abraham*, once again a work which suggests anything but despair. This work, which foreshadows so much of the Snopes trilogy, bespeaks a light heart, a sense of fun. Faulkner was discovering himself here, as he enters Snopes territory even while preparing to mine Sartoris history—each complementing the other. And yet there is despair in young Bayard, severe, concentrated, destructive.

Faulkner's personal life might be a source, for he was storing resentment against the slings and arrows of women. Rejection rankled him, especially Helen's coolness; and Estelle was looming large. Young Bayard is drawn to Narcissa as someone who may fill his life, but he also suspects she will become part of its emptiness rather than its fullness. The sexual atmosphere of *Flags* is clouded by ambiguity, hostility, and plain confusion. Bayard's response to Narcissa is one aspect, Horace and Belle another, Horace and Narcissa a third. What is compelling is how despairingly Faulkner has arranged the love and sexual experience of his main characters—and as subtext he has the Narcissa-Byron "courtship" bleed through as secret letters bordering on the pornographic. When we link these lines of relationships, we do not get one complete or satisfactory one; they run from pathological to unpleasant to indifferent to self-destructive. Even Narcissa's capitulation to Bayard is based on a certain fascination with disaster which overpowers her when she feels his extreme masculine energy. The only satisfactory sexual arrangement comes in Horace's vicarious glassblowing.

The secretive elements of *Flags* are not to be neglected: those "love letters" written by Byron to Narcissa, and somehow cherished by her even while she reviles them. Narcissa is one of Faulkner's unpleasant young women; as her name implies, she has little to give, unless it is with her brother. The letters, in whose writing Byron employs the Beard boy, are a form of emotional blackmail—but they also function, curiously, to make Narcissa feel wanted. Aunt Jenny locates the ambiguity by suggesting that in some way Narcissa encourages them. The young woman denies this, but she does keep them, bundled like love letters. She desires the attention, especially since the terms of endearment cannot be carried out. She can remain pristine, untouched, even while being made love to; her narcissism is reinforced by a secret admirer, however illiterate he seems. Although in Jenny's presence she tears up the latest letter, in actuality the correspondence is part of her hope chest. The episodes with the letters become part of the sexual play of the novel, which is nasty, lacking in reciprocity, and demeaning. Little good feeling exists where men and women are involved.

It is tempting to read the entire novel metaphorically, to see Faulkner revealing his own ambiguous response to sexuality and using Horace's glassblowing as his means of sublimating sex for the sake of art. In this view, Faulkner was himself trapped in a sea of change which he could not personally deal with or resolve; accordingly, he flagged the various elements symbolically, and used the novel as a way of framing his tentative response. The analogue of his own problems comes with Horace's glassblowing, an artistic element itself ambiguous in its results. Played out by life itself, Horace has thrown himself—as will Faulkner with Estelle—into the maelstrom of unsatisfactory sexual arrangements and derives his sole pleasure from his form of art. Horace's use of this medium reveals his dissatisfaction not only with sexual arrangements but with modern life as a whole—inasmuch as glassblowing is an ancient art derived from an ancient city. His antimodernism, then, is illuminated in his choice of a dubious art for an American male. Played off against this frail, somewhat effeminate activity is another male who has competed for Belle and lost— her husband, Harry. Coarse, rough, uncultured, he is the "typical" male, the symbolic modern man caught in a bad marriage to which he is strangely devoted. Horace strives to avoid this with his "art," but succumbs to the sexual destiny which, in early Faulkner, seems the lot of all men.

Read this way, *Flags* suggests a good deal of Faulkner's sense of himself and his inability as yet to fight his way out. It reveals, most of all, how tentative his grasp was, that he was unable to find the right vehicle for his distinct manner of thinking. For all its foreshadowing and accomplishment, *Flags* is journeyman work, insofar as it did not give Faulkner the leeway he needed to spread, develop, experiment. He was still so wrapped up in his own problems and dilemmas that his art reflected rather than transcended him. To that extent, *Flags* is autobiography.

That is a tempting way to read the novel and its cutdown version (shaved by about 20,000 words in *Sartoris*); but it may be delusive to think we can read Faulkner so close to the bone of his work. *Flags* is important only in part for its personal message; more significant is its role as both closing out the past and foreshadowing what was to come. It is Faulkner reaching for new material—that interpretation which pits aristocratic Sartorises against sleazy Snopeses, making this the novel's major movement. *Flags* closed down one phase of Faulkner's career in terms of failure to innovate and draw upon the implications of modernism. Even the fact Faulkner let Ben Wasson handle nearly all revisions of *Flags* and turn it into *Sartoris* demonstrates he was ready to let go. For an author as fastidious as he about his manuscripts and even galleys, Faulkner was strangely neglectful about the shaving of *Flags*, and this could have occurred only if his interest had shifted not only to new works, but to new methods—to an entirely different way of looking at fiction.

The real internal struggle in *Flags* derives from Faulkner, for possession of his creative imagination. Nothing less than daring the ruling literary gods in America (regional, naturalistic, and otherwise) was at stake when he broke with his previous work to write *Sound*. That work he began early in 1928, as a short story called "Twilight," based on the Compson family, with some early intimations of it as early as 1925. This move was the true dramatic event of his still-early creative life; it is at this point that the conflict between class and caste in the South becomes secondary to Faulkner's decisions about the "how" of presentation. Even *Sanctuary*, which seems oddly placed between *Sound* and *As I Lay Dying*, is notable for extremely sharp cutting; in the original, uncut version, it is so sharply angled that the uninitiated reader has difficulty in knowing which characters are involved.* The sister Narcissa is unnamed, also the marriage to Bayard—events described in *Flags* and *Sartoris*, but presented here as a brief interruption in a discussion with Belle. The pronominal use, characteristic of later Faulkner, was already a factor in jumbling names and situations, creating that confusion, through shifting pronouns and references, which suggests montage in film.

Another new factor in *Flags* is Faulkner's use of narrative. In *Sound* he buried narrative in voice; he made narrative not a matter of revelation but a matter of hiding, either through a confusion of voice (who is speaking) or through deliberate language obfuscation. *Flags* is in this respect the first of his novels to work through concealment, withdrawal, withholding,

---

*Early on, a scene is presented through Horace Benbow's eyes, where he comments on Harry Mitchell and his wife, Belle, whom Horace is stealing away. Belle has remarked that Horace is in love with his sister, and has some kind of complex. He picks up the word "complex" and denies that anything could be complex with a woman who (who?) "married a man (who?) whom anyone could have known was doomed . . ." (*Sanctuary* [the Original Text], ed. with an afterword and notes by Noel Polk [New York: Random House, 1981], p. 16).

silences—although not to the intense degree of later works. The best example comes in the submerged material, which is revealed only through hints and intimations. The past is a deep mystery, since it demands some knowledge of early references—to Redlaw (Thurmond in the old colonel's life); John Sartoris, the father of old Bayard, as well as his son, along with his grandson killed in the war; to the Sartoris who killed two carpetbaggers, and the Sartoris killed in his quest for Yankee anchovies.

None of these references, all part of the past, is clear, and in fact they become part of the rush of names, events, and situations which charge the historical past. Faulkner proceeded to dole out information, but without any clear statement of how the information fitted. He did not transform information into clear narrative; in fact, most of the information has little or nothing to do with plot. It has a great deal to do with meaning, with pressure and impingement; the matter from the past is turned mainly into voices; the retrieval of history, of the South and the Sartoris clan, is eked out, so that narrative line really turns to vocal line, as if in some extended operatic aria.

If we look temporarily at *Sartoris*, whose revision Faulkner may or may not have taken seriously, we note in part 4 (chapter 4) a sharp shift after the accident in which Bayard drives off the road and old Bayard dies of a heart attack. One of the pivotal scenes in the novel, it closes young Bayard off from life and points him inexorably toward death. Here his antics have resulted not only in *his* accident but in working out some ancient fate or prophecy. He has killed another, intensifying his guilt over the death of his twin brother in the war. Although John's fatal flight was his own doing, not Bayard's, he assumes blame for the death of two members of his family. The Cain analogue becomes Oedipal as well.

Within this circumstance, where the novel turns from even minimal life to death itself, Faulkner's radical shift leaves the reader with little sense of where he is. There is only the awareness of something occurring. The consequence is "process," neither plot nor narrative nor progression. Plot has been replaced by process: a presentation of life proceeding without apparently going in any particular direction. In this method is a kinship with books surrounding *Sartoris*—*Sound* and *As I Lay Dying*. The development of this method is significant, for it indicates Faulkner was perceiving differently, advancing from his earlier novels. And from this we can see, once again, how earlier work like *Flags* ended one phase and began to blend in with his great middle achievement.

Part III

The Transformation
of William Faulkner

Chapter Eleven

The Sound and the Fury

THE FINANCIAL HARDSHIPS Faulkner indicated in February, when he attempted to collect his *Marble Faun* royalties, continued with Horace Liveright in the summer of 1927. In one letter, Faulkner speaks of gambling away some money and drawing a $200 draft on Liveright—saying the publisher can either reject it or else charge it off against his next advance. Liveright, whom Faulkner characterized as not being a white man (i.e., a Jew), paid up, but told Faulkner to give him future warning about such actions. The latter in his thank-you letter (of later July) tells Liveright a yarn which seems right out of his Snopes material. He had buried twenty-five gallons of whiskey, gone to Memphis and blown $300 on a wheel, returned to see his whiskey had been tampered with and lost to the authorities. This being Prohibition, he had thought he could sell the twenty-five gallons and recoup his losses, but all was gone. Thus, he needed the draft to meet gambling losses. He says he is working on *Flags* and collecting enough verse to make up a new volume, "A Greening Bough," published in 1933 as *A Green Bough.*

His high spirits with Liveright continued with his letter of October 16, 1927, in which he announces he is ready to send on "THE BOOK of which those other things were but foals. I believe it is the damndest best book you'll look at this year, and any other publisher. It goes forward to you by mail Monday."[1] Faulkner's high spirits make him sound out of tune, someone like Hemingway; but he evidently felt he had achieved something. He was correct in his assessment of his new novel, clumsy though it was in parts, because it is clearly an advance over his first two books and foreshadows an entire career. His elation, so unusual for this self-contained man, allows us to see how passionate he was about his work. In a month and a half, Liveright responded by rejecting *Flags*, and Faulkner, showing no disappointment in his letter, wonders if the publisher is planning to hold it against the $200 draft he drew in the summer. If not, he wants the book returned so he can "try it on someone else." He adds: "I still believe it is the book which will make my name for me as a writer."[2]

In the same letter he indicates he is working "on a book which will take three or four years to do," by which he may mean *Father Abraham*, and still another "which I shall finish by spring, I believe." This one is less identifiable, and may mean some stories or even "Twilight," the working title of *The Sound and the Fury*. In a follow-up letter in February of 1928, Faulkner indicates he has put aside the unnamed *Father Abraham* volume to get on with some short stories. He is still trying to find out if Liveright plans to hold *Flags* against repayment, and some of his hurt does emerge. "I have just sent some short stories to an agent; perhaps I shall derive something from them with which to pay you. Otherwise I dont know what we'll do about it, as I have a belly full of writing, now, since you folks in the publishing business claim that a book like that last one I sent you is blah. I think now that I'll sell my typewriter and go to work—though God knows, it's sacrilege to waste that talent for idleness which I possess."[3]

Faulkner's attempt at humor cannot disguise that he was bewildered; for even as his work improved, he was suffering rejection. He even alludes to money problems, not only for him but for the entire South, which lives without cash. He adds once again that if he can place the manuscript he will pay up the advance and have the incentive "to bang you out a book to suit you—though it'll never be one as youngly glamorous as 'Soldiers' Pay' nor as trashily smart as 'Mosquitoes.' "[4] Early the next month (March 1928) he indicates he has "got going on a novel, which, if it continues as I am going now, I will finish within eight weeks. Maybe it'll please you."[5] Faulkner's casualness in speaking of his new book, which was almost certainly *Sound*, is remarkable, since this ushers in his great period of creative work. Possibly, his casual approach is a form of disguise: in this view, Faulkner's dismissal of his two early novels as "youngly glamorous" and "trashily smart" suggests that only his current work mattered to him; that he was, in fact, so deeply immersed in his imaginative work all else had become secondary. He could trivialize not only Liveright but his own work—later on, to his Aunt 'Bama, he referred to *Sound* as "the damndest book I ever read."[6]

As he moved into books which deepened his world with each one, he also found himself losing publishers who could not or would not follow him into the thickets of language and innovation. Liveright's rejection of *Flags* brought him to Harcourt Brace & Company, when he had extensively revised the manuscript and retitled it *Sartoris*.* But Harcourt did not last long, for it found *Sound* undigestible and rejected it. Harrison Smith, who was about to leave Harcourt, however, believed in the book and in Faulkner and offered to publish it with his new firm, Jonathan Cape and Harrison Smith.

In 1928 *Sound* was not the same book as it seems to the reader fifty or so years later. It was, in its way, as challenging as Joyce's *Ulysses* and Woolf's *The Waves*, and it took a special publisher to chance its acceptance. If Faulkner had not found a publisher for *Sound*, after the rejection of the more traditional *Flags*, it is hard to predict what turn his work would have taken. He might have gone on, for he had tremendous tenacity and belief in himself; but as the showdown with Estelle and marriage approached, he might have turned from innovative work to lesser stuff, as he thought he was doing with *Sanctuary*. Smith touched Faulkner's life at exactly the right moment, a publisher who saw beyond sales to something extraordinary.

When Faulkner left Smith, in time, he found an equally devoted group of publishers at Random House, where Bennett Cerf, Robert Haas, and Saxe Commins, among others, were completely committed to his work, whatever shape or direction it took. Faulkner's words to Harcourt, to return to that period, in a letter of February 18, 1929, are poignant, concerning the *Sound* manuscript: "I did not believe that anyone would publish it. I had no definite plan to submit it to anyone. I told Hal [Harrison Smith] about it once and he dared me to bring it to him. And so it really was to him that I submitted it, more as a curiosity than aught else. I am sorry it did not go over with you all, but I will not say I did not expect that result."

Although we are jumping ahead to 1929, when Faulkner had several irons in the fire besides *Sound*—he had started to write and send out short stories—we must try to reconstruct his state of mind as his last two books were rejected, one a traditional novel and one quite innovative and daring,

---

*Every publisher who saw *Flags* in its original shape rejected it—and yet it is far more interesting than what Faulkner and Wasson carved out of it for eventual publication. Liveright's rejection of *Flags* on November 25, with the publisher's recommendation that "we don't believe that you should offer it for publication," was devastating. Liveright could not leave the rejection alone, but poured on reasons for it and seemed in the process to destroy Faulkner's entire career. As we read these lines, we wonder at the author's resilience in returning with persiflage from such a personal disaster. After stating that even *Mosquitoes* showed a creative decline from *Soldiers' Pay*, the publisher states that *Flags* "is diffuse and nonintegral with neither very much plot development nor character development. We think it lacks plot, dimension and projection. The story really doesn't get anywhere and has a thousand loose ends. If the book had plot and structure, we might suggest shortening and revisions but it is so diffuse that I don't think this would be any use. My chief objection is that you don't seem to have any story to tell and I contend that a novel should tell a story and tell it well" (Joseph Blotner, *Faulkner: A Biography*, 2 vols. [New York: Random House, 1974], vol. 1, pp. 559, 560). While Liveright was writing so devastatingly to Faulkner, the Oxford *Eagle* kept up with a steady barrage of the changes taking place in Oxford, so-called "improvements" which further depressed the writer.

indeed the "damndest book" anyone ever saw. Defeats and rejections continued. As usual, there was no money. He apparently hoped to pick up amounts here and there by selling bootlegged liquor, if we can believe his letter to Horace Liveright. He was still living mainly at home and depended on Phil Stone and others for handouts. He saw his next two brothers flourishing with legitimate jobs, steady incomes, and opportunities for promotion. He also saw, if he chose to look, that his youngest brother, Dean, had become the favorite of Murry Falkner.

These are all substantial negatives which are sufficient to create depression, blockage, even inability to function. If we had to predict, we would not expect him to write *Sound* at this time, with its innovative methods. In fact, the wonder of it all is that he apparently turned his back on what should have floored him, and let his imagination dictate completely the kind of book he would write. It seems that his creative talent was stimulated by adversity, or by self-pity, or whatever name we give to the condition in which personal complaint appeared to overwhelm him. In 1927–28, as he embarked on his greatest period of achievement, the personal dimension was near its worst; and prospects for the future, with so many responsibilities piling up, were even worse.

As Faulkner confronted the rejections, the lack of money, the indifference of a reading public to what he already considered lesser works, we would predict, if not a breakdown, then some weakening of purpose. Instead he gathered his forces like a general heading a troop of men faced with certain disaster who chooses to counterattack. Premonitions of disaster simply strengthened Faulkner's resolve. Where did this complete and utter belief in himself come from? His mother's faith in him—as Freud had predicted for all men who enjoyed their mother's belief—certainly helped support him. But the inner resolve was more like a compulsion, and he went to his desk as if programmed to write the novels he did, regardless of intrusions on his emotional life. Yet he paid, and paid heavily. As noted, his fictional outlook is far darker than his pronouncements or even his letters. "Twilight" was the working title of *Sound,* and later "The Dark House" served for several fictions. There is not another major American novelist in the twentieth century—and only Hawthorne and Melville come to mind in the nineteenth—who sustained over a long period of time such a devastatingly dark vision, as Faulkner did from *Sound* through *Absalom.* Even *Light in August,* which has the leavening of the counterpointed Lena Grove episodes, is in its fullest sense a very dark book about a man's lack of identity and the tragedy it creates for him.

As Faulkner flourished in the later 1920s, he either gained strength from adversity or deadened part of himself and let his imagination take over; most likely, both. Examples in literary history abound of writers who create their greatest works during their most difficult situation. Balzac (one of Faulkner's favorite novelists), deeply in debt, living penuriously, comes to mind; so do Joyce and Conrad, as well as an entirely new generation who live in totalitarian countries and write their best work under conditions which should silence them. Faulkner did not have such a repressive atmosphere, but he did have an area which was hostile to his kind of fiction and remained hostile well after he had received the Nobel Prize for literature. Nearly any area might be hostile to books such as *Sanctuary*—but in nearly everything he wrote he had few advocates in his own town and county.

Faulkner found the means to transmute most personal problems into fiction. Rejection becomes one of his themes and subtexts. Estelle herself becomes transformed into many of his fictional portraits, as Fitzgerald used and reused Zelda. His growing family responsibilities become interwoven into his novels, which despite their often sensational scenes are deeply moralistic and ethical. His own sense of personal inadequacy becomes submerged in characters like Quentin and Darl, sensitive figures for whom life is too much. In nearly every respect, Faulkner found the means to use personal pressures as part of his professional life and, in the act, transform them into creative materials. We are present at that creation.

By mid-1927 changes in Oxford were portending changes Faulkner would transmute into the "death of the old," his sense that life in being transformed was lost. As the Oxford *Eagle* reports, the inner town was being paved over, a civilized way of controlling street muck and mud, but also making the town accessible to the automobile. Horses disappeared as the mode of transportation—as Faulkner himself already revealed in *Flags* with Bayard's frenetic car-driving. Building was also increasing, and Oxford was slowly being altered from a sleepy backwater, frontier village, into a twentieth-century town with amenities and advanced means of transportation. Another improvement was the arrival of electric lights.

Faulkner's father became part of this transformation of Oxford. Through a transaction with Uncle John, the executor of the John Wesley Thompson Falkner estate, Murry got hold of some of the property on which the Big Place sat. Developing the land meant he could parcel out the property, and he created one lot which became the Standard Oil Company, another which was developed into a service station. A third development involved altering the house so that it became a number of apartments, "The University Apartments," so named because they fronted on University Avenue, the main thoroughfare connecting Oxford to the University of Mississippi. This change in itself would portend for Faulkner such a sharp shift in history and tradition he could associate it with the "fall of," his adaptation of Greek tragedy to this small village and county in northern Mississippi.

Other events impinged. As Faulkner moved toward *Sound* his life was a mixture of dashed hopes, rejections, disappointments, and plans for the future. Although his response to Liveright's rejection of *Flags* was brief and measured, the wound went deep, since *Flags* had delved into Faulkner's emotional and personal as well as professional life.* The writer's internal world was turbulent, but he was still willing to walk the edge. Outwardly, his life in Oxford or on short trips remained much the same: seemingly directionless, odd jobs, drinking. He saw Estelle when she came home, but in a peculiar way—he drove her to Columbus, Mississippi, to see the parents of the husband she was divorcing. The Franklins were fond of her, and also of Faulkner. Estelle's younger child, Malcolm, left a rapturous evocation of those trips to Columbus, how magical they seemed in the old Model T, with Faulkner driving, picnics along the way, snow falling, and then the big celebrations when they arrived— all this both before the marriage and after. Yet these trips could not have been so idyllic as they are made to seem because Malcolm had a hard childhood and turned into an extremely troubled man.

That spring, in 1928, Faulkner made the move which determined the future course of his career, with the first pages (really intended as a short story) related to Sound. As Blotner suggests, very possibly the early work was the material that grew later into "That Evening Sun Go Down" (or "That Evening Sun"), which was a beefed-up version of "Never Done No Weeping When You Wanted to Laugh." In those early pages, we are introduced to the Compsons; to Nancy, who works for the family; to Quentin, the narrator; and, marginally, to Candace and Jason. There is as yet no Benjy. Nancy is fearful of her male friend, Jesus, for she is pregnant with a white man's child, and Jesus has threatened to kill her with a razor. She foresees her death. Even as Nancy becomes more certain, the older Compsons downplay the chance of violence. Faulkner developed the story subsequently to contrast the older Compsons' lack of concern with the younger ones' more immediate involvement in a kind of violence which will eventually envelop them. What is remarkable about the early version is how Faulkner wrote something he saw only dimly, but which would, with incremental developments, work its way through his imagination to emerge as one of his masterpieces. Although the original idea may have derived from an actual killing in which a black man virtually severed his wife's head, Faulkner saw that the killing itself was secondary to other more dynamic novelistic factors.

Within this frame of stories,[7] two others appear in the same cluster which Faulkner wrote for magazine sale through Ben Wasson. One was

*In what was probably intended as a preface or an introduction to Sartoris, in manuscript at the Beinecke Library of Yale University, the following is the fourth of six paragraphs: "... for the first publisher to whom I submitted six-hundred-odd pages of manuscript refused it on the ground that it was chaotic, without head or tail. I was shocked; my first emotion was blind protest, then I became objective for an instant, like a parent who is told that its child is a thief or an idiot or a leper. For a dreadful moment I contemplated it with consternation and despair; then like the parent I hid my own eyes in the fury of denial. I clung stubbornly to my illusion; I showed the manuscript to a number of friends, who told me the same general thing—that the book lacked any form whatever. At last one of them took it to another publisher, who proposed to edit it enough to see just what was there."

The perceived formlessness of Flags very possibly derived from its beginnings as a short story, after which it just grew. Fragments of manuscript in the Alderman Library of the University of Virginia suggest a short-story etiology, which may even have been written before the Father Abraham segment.

"A Justice" and the other "Twilight," the story which began as ten pages and ended up as *Sound*. In "A Justice," Quentin Compson recalls at a later date a visit he made with Caddy and Jason to hear Sam Fathers tell of how he obtained his name, of his being the child of a Negro slave and an Indian father. Sam Fathers, like so many other figures Faulkner touched upon early, will return, as if acting out an extended, sequential drama. He will become in *Go Down, Moses* and, particularly, "The Bear" a summation of an era—coming as he does early in a period which closes with the end of the big woods. Sam Fathers fathers no one, but becomes the last son of the wilderness.

Faulkner stated in an interview that "Twilight" was based on the funeral of his maternal grandmother, Damuddy (Lelia Swift Butler), an episode, caught in medias res, of "some children being sent away from the house" as they were too young to be informed what was going on and because "they saw things only incidentally to the childish games they were playing, which was the lugubrious matter of removing the corpse from the house, etc."[8] Interestingly, that ten-page "episode" was the beginning of Faulkner's more experimental mode, in that it did not have a story's shape but the flow of an experience or a stretch of consciousness. Although the story was to become the novel, we see the germ of the technique, in that need not to capture events or activities but to describe consciousness.

Just when Faulkner moved from the story idea to the novel we cannot precisely pinpoint, but it was sometime in February or March of 1928—the first part of *Sound* is dated April 7, and we know that once Faulkner got hold of his idea, he worked with great rapidity and fluency.* Faulkner later related how he slid from story into novel:

> I did not realise then that I was trying to manufacture the sister which I did not have and the daughter which I was to lose, though the former might have been apparent from the fact that Caddy had three brothers almost before I wrote her name on paper. I just began to write about a brother and a sister splashing one another in the brook and the sister fell and wet her clothing and the smallest brother cried, thinking that the sister was conquered or perhaps hurt. Or perhaps he knew that he was the baby and that she would quit whatever water battles to comfort him. When she did so, when she quit the water fight and stooped in her wet garments above him, the entire story, which is all told by that same little brother in the first section, seemed to explode on the paper before me.[9]

But Faulkner was not finished with his conception. We have already cited that foreshadowing of the crucial element in *Sound,* the figure of

*The April 7 dating could mean Faulkner began the novel then, or else he dated that section April 7 after having completed part or all of it. An educated guess is he dated April 7 after having written some or all of the first segment.

complete innocence in the shape of an idiot.* Faulkner did not lack for such a figure from his reading, such as Conrad's *The Secret Agent* or Dostoyevsky's novels and Russian fiction as a whole. Faulkner sought such a figure of innocence—with his inevitable linkage to Jesus and to a period preceding the expulsion from the Garden. In his brief vignette "The Kingdom of God," published in the *Times-Picayune* in 1925, he had described an idiot: ". . . vague and dull and loose-lipped, and his eyes were clear and blue as cornflowers, and utterly vacant of thought. . . . always in his slobbering, vacuous face were his two eyes of a heart-shaking blue." In his hand was a narcissus, his own gesture toward the funeral he was attending.

Faulkner, who may have drawn physically on an idiot boy and man living nearby in Oxford, suddenly saw in this figure the missing element. He said later: "I became interested in the relationship of the idiot to the world."[10] This became crucial, for as soon as he perceived the relationship, he needed someone to shield the idiot "in his tenderness" from that world. For this, he decided on a sister who protected Benjy, and with that, Faulkner asserts, "the whole shape and meaning of the story started to change."

Although many of his later statements about his books are suspect, either deceptions or exaggerations, this rings absolutely true, part of the very process of creation. In the same interview, he speaks of how the idea "struck me to see how much more I could have got out of the idea of the blind, self-centeredness of innocence, typified by children, if one of those children had been truly innocent, that is, an idiot." But the idea could also be connected to his desire for new techniques, to his development of interior monologue and free-associational material. The creation of an idiot, accordingly, while functioning at the level of "story," was also a means to a new method. Since an idiot is basically nonverbal, or minimally verbal, Faulkner was forced back on an interior mode. With *Flags*, he had withdrawn into himself, his family, his background; the interiority of *Sound* was a more radical stage of that withdrawal into self. Benjy thus functions within methodological terms as well as in counterpoint to the destructive family. The enlargement of the idea from his own "The Kingdom of God," with its title so close to Tolstoy's "The Kingdom of God is within You," shows how he could take an ephemeral portrait and intensify it into a whole.

As Faulkner moved toward his first major effort, the question of how much he drew on family portraits for characters becomes more significant. Undeniably, the Faulkner clan of four brothers was transformed into aspects of the Compson children: four brothers slimmed down to three, one of them an idiot. For Caddy, the fourth sibling, the desire to cite

*According to Carvel Collins, Faulkner told William C. Odiorne in 1925, in Paris, that he was writing a novel about a declining family with a girl and three brothers, one of them an idiot, another nasty, mean, and grasping. Odiorne, a friend of Spratling's, was a photographer who did a series of portraits of Faulkner; they met briefly again in West Hollywood in 1951.

Estelle as model, however partial, is tempting. She did not materialize from nothing, and we know that Faulkner's method, already operating, was to work from real-life models and transform them. The binding of Quentin to his sister would relive on a family level the binding of Faulkner to Estelle, especially if their relationship had been consummated before she married Cornell Franklin. The Quentin-Caddy linkage is so obsessive we must seek some analogue for it in Faulkner's life, and the sole place we can locate it is in his relationship with Estelle, now herself back in Oxford, with all their memories of the romantic idyll they once enjoyed.* As we read in the following passages Faulkner's words about the genesis of the novel, we glimpse how much *Sound* depended on childhood images, on childhood binding.

Faulkner later told of a kind of dreamlike state and desperation which took over when he wrote the novel. Speaking of the coming together of Caddy, the funeral, and the children's innocence faced with something overwhelming, he stated that he experienced ecstasy when he started to write, saying this combination of events was the sole thing in literature which could move him very much: ". . . Caddy climbing the pear tree to look in the window at her grandmother's funeral while Quentin and Jason and Benjy and the negroes looked up at the muddy seat of her drawers." He added: "I loved her so much I couldn't decide to give her life just for the duration of a short story. She deserved more than that. So my novel was created, almost in spite of myself."[11]

Earlier, he had spoken of the branch, the "peaceful glinting of that branch [which] was to become the dark, harsh flowing of time sweeping her to where she could not return to comfort him, but that just separation, division, would not be enough, not far enough." She must be swept "into dishonor and shame too." Yet Benjy must remain fixed at this point; for him, "all knowing must begin and end with that fierce, panting, paused and stooping wet figure which smelled like trees." Benjy "must never grow up to where the grief of bereavement could be leavened with understanding and hence the alleviation of rage as in the case of Jason, and of oblivion as in the case of Quentin."[12] The fixedness of that image of Caddy on the branch argues for Faulkner's recognition of how inexorably linked he was to Estelle—if we accept that form of speculation about their relationship. We find him here acting out something very deep within him; and perhaps the novel's passion, despite the coolness of the technique, derives from these overheated moments: life becomes fixed for Benjy, but so did the youthful romance of Estelle and Billy. That it was all doomed only reinforces the images of obsession.

---

*Blotner mentions Sallie Murry as a possible source for Caddy, and there is something to say for this good pal of Faulkner's childhood, who was almost a sister. But the relationship with Sallie Murry lacked the obsessional qualities of that with Estelle, and simple brother-sister images recede to images of incestuous longing, of possessing the other person. All this argues for Estelle, not Sallie Murry.

Faulkner wrote a long explanation which deserves quotation in full, this also from a draft of the introduction to the novel:

> I saw that they [the children] had been sent to the pasture to spend the afternoon to get them away from the house during the grandmother's funeral in order that the three brothers and the nigger children could look up at the muddy seat of Caddy's drawers as she climbed the tree to look in the window at the funeral, without then realising the symbology of the soiled drawers, for here again hers was the courage which was to face later with honor the shame which she was to engender, which Quentin and Jason could not face: the one taking refuge in suicide, the other in vindictive rage which drove him to rob his bastard niece of the meager sums which Caddy could send her. For I had already gone on to night and the bedroom and Dilsey with the mudstained drawers scrubbing the naked backside of the doomed little girl—trying to cleanse with the sorry byblow of its soiling that body, flesh, whose shame they symbolised and prophesied, as though she already saw the dark future part she was to play in it trying to hold that crumbling household together.[13]

This, then, would become the fiction which turned Faulkner, in his own eyes, away from traditional novel-making, saying that here he had "shut a door" between himself and all publishers. He added: "I said to myself. Now I can write. Now I can make myself a vase like that which the old Roman kept at his bedside and wore the rim away with kissing it. So I, who never had a sister and was fated to lose my daughter in infancy, set out to make myself a beautiful and tragic little girl." We are interested, however, not only in the progression of ideas which nourished the novel, but in Faulkner's state of mind as he wrote it: that "ecstasy" which recurs in his comments. He said that each morning as he sat down to write he felt "that emotion definite and physical and yet nebulous to describe: that ecstasy, that eager and joyous faith and anticipation of surprise which the yet unmarred sheet beneath my hand held inviolate and unfailing, waiting for release."[14]

The rhetoric is high, but it communicates a rare experience. Faulkner had entered something close to Proust's "privileged moment," when time is suspended and a kind of ecstasy possesses one. His description of the state when he wrote has within it qualities usually associated with a religious or spiritual experience. Possessed by something, he moved beyond himself—thus "ecstasy," which suggests standing outside oneself. One reason we should stress this "beyond" is that it carried over for several years, and coincided precisely with his marriage to Estelle and their honeymoon, when she attempted suicide. If he was indeed in such a state of ecstasy, then little could reach him—only that blank page with its need to be filled. And if the experience is almost religious, akin to a privileged moment or Joyce's epiphanic state, then Faulkner had removed himself even as he entered a situation in which someone needed to reach him. He had, as it were, abstracted himself from routine life and become a moving pen sitting before a blank sheet of paper.

But we should not judge Faulkner's remarks to mean *Sound* was a kind of automatic writing, or composed under a spell and therefore outside his conscious control. He may well have felt that ecstasy, and it may well have taken him over; yet at the same time, he was very much the conscious artist in the novel. It is nonsense that, as some commentators have suggested, he just "let it wing." A novel as tightly organized and thought through as this does not flow uncontrolled from the unconscious or preconscious. Faulkner felt himself transported, and part of that feeling surely came from his recognition he had put together personal emotions with family history. After three novels of trying out, he had found the combination for himself, as Melville had in *Moby-Dick*. But none of this mitigates against the conscious, careful control of the materials. He made decisions at every stage.*

In the manuscript, we note very careful consideration of artistic problems. In the early part, as he thought he would write a short story, not a novel, he began to reconsider—and then what he thought would be complete was incomplete, still the raw material of a much larger effort. His later comment that "the story was complete, finished" with the Benjy segment is belied by notes which begin to appear on the manuscript by page 20. Faulkner may have meant that that part of the story was complete —but alone it was incomprehensible, as he later admitted. He said: "There was Dilsey to be the future, to stand above the fallen ruins of the family like a ruined chimney, gaunt, patient and indomitable, and Benjy to be the past. He had to be an idiot so that, like Dilsey, he could be impervious to the future, though unlike her by refusing to accept it all."** Faulkner

---

*Faulkner later told Maurice Coindreau, his faithful French translator, he was under severe strain from personal problems. The latter cannot be completely disentangled, but the developing situation with Estelle was surely part of them.

Another example of personal problems comes in an enigmatic passage in a letter to his Aunt 'Bama, in early 1928 (at the Alderman Library). He writes of her coming down to see a woman he wants to show her, someone he describes as possessing both "utter charm" and "utter shallowness," like a "lovely vase." The description seems to fit Estelle, but since Aunt 'Bama already knew her and had seen her several times, another woman may have been meant.

**Dilsey is always cited as an example of Faulkner's great compassion, and his feeling that the Negro (woman) held the Compson family together, or at least attempted to. But there are several dimensions to his reliance on Dilsey, who devotes her life to a crumbling white family—and one of them is Faulkner's sense of the Negro as enduring and having great integrity within the framework of service. This is a complicated subject, and only some of its intricacy derives from Faulkner's own Caroline Barr, who served his family for several generations. What Dilsey means will come up later, more extensively.

For the moment, we might consider the contrast between Dilsey's treatment of the Compson children and the harsh, almost cruel handling of Luster, her grandson. As Darwin T. Turner once commented, possibly she was so worn out by her white charges, she had neither energy nor patience for her own. Such a view reinforces a reading that asserts Dilsey's segment is not a clear affirmation—that the novel as a whole cannot be "resolved" as affirmative or negative; that, in fact, the novel never closes since human life remains in motion whatever time tells us. Even innovative language fails, for it solidifies what must remain fluid. This is Bergsonian, not Joycean.

recognized that this idiot, "shapeless, neuter, like something eyeless and voiceless," existed "merely because of its ability to suffer" and because it [he] carried with him "that fierce, courageous being [Caddy] who was to him but a touch and a sound that may be heard on any golf links and a smell like trees."[15]

Part 2 of the novel contains more extensive notes,[16] a kind of working outline of the novel and something rather rare for Faulkner. At what stage he wrote these reminders—whether when he began part 2 or later—we cannot tell. But they telegraph a good deal of what will follow and demonstrate that by part 2 he knew he was embarked on a novel-length project. Most of the jottings take the form of a list of people, dates, and events:

Quentin born	1890	
Caddy	1892	
Jason	1894	
Maury—Benjy [written in]		1897
Damuddy dies	1900	
~~Reskus dies~~		
Caddy marries	1910—age 18	
Quentin dies	1910—age 20	
Father dies	1912	
born		
Quentin ~~arrives~~------------ ~~1913~~ 1911		
~~Quentin~~		
Roskus dies	1915	
Quentin runs off	1928—age 17	
Benjy's nurses.		
Versh—	—5	
T. P.₅————————18		
Luster 18————————————		

Show resemblances between Jason and Uncle Maury. [at top left of page] Father said because of the fine sound of it. 40 acres of land little enough to pay for a fine sound.

The carefully wrought manuscript hardly supports the notion that Faulkner was feeling his way. He began part 2 at least twice, and then used the discarded first effort at a later stage, interspersing it as a disruptive element in the narrative. The initially discarded material—headed June 2, 1910—starts with Quentin's memory of Benjy's dependence on Caddy and then shifts to Quentin's own obsession with her, and his suggestion they make a suicide pact. She is about to meet her lover, Dalton Ames, and this encounter makes Quentin realize he would prefer to die with her rather than permit her violation by someone outside the family. That Faulkner treated this explosive material so early in the novel indicates it lay heavily on his mind. He viewed the Compson family disruption as having created a terrible sexual problem for Quentin; lacking a strong parental figure, he had displaced sexual feelings onto his sister, as if she were all women to him in lieu of a functioning mother-figure. It is a moment of great significance, especially since Faulkner saw *that*, initially, as the direction the novel should take—although how much weight it had in his life is unclear. We are tempted to judge the Compsons as replicas of the Faulkners, but that would be inaccurate. That the failure of Murry Falkner to provide strong leadership in the home, that Maud Falkner dominated, that all four sons were beholden to her and not to their father must have played a strong role in Faulkner's development of Quentin and the Compson scene. But the Falkners produced four sons who went on to some achievement, and Maud was indomitable, not at all like the neurasthenic Caroline Compson. Yet beneath the surface, Faulkner may have sensed the corrosion in it, the need to realign sentiments, the recognition that Maud had provided Murry with a poor, loveless marriage, as he had failed her, and that this emotionally crippled some of the sons. Out of this could come Quentin, Jason, and Caddy, as well as young Quentin.

Whatever the precise significance in personal terms of this early and critical scene, we do know Faulkner moved it around in the manuscript. Putting aside these seven pages—really an enclosed episode in itself—he started part 2 again. This time he shifted more closely to the finished novel by locating Quentin at Harvard on the day he will commit suicide. He then tried to insert the original seven pages here, on page 43 of the second part. But he later removed them, so that they turned up as 44–50 and then as 70–76. Finally, they were moved much further along, to the three-quarter mark of the episode, as Quentin approaches his suicidal gesture.

Faulkner demonstrated an author fully in control, carefully shaping the sense of the material as he perceived it artistically. Death persists in part 2, which belongs to Quentin and to his awareness of final things. This, too, is an interesting development in Faulkner—for while his work contains a good deal of violence, cruelty, and brutality, Quentin is his only significant suicide. We are tempted, once again, to read into Faulkner's own life some of the meaning he is projecting in his work; but his life seems full of projects, plans, and hopes for the future. It is not at all that of a man contemplating final things. But we must be careful, since Faulkner held everything in, and there are always two or three levels of experience within him.

What comes through at the personal level of *Sound* is Compson coldness. Those who knew the Faulkner atmosphere testify that despite Maud's possessive love for her four sons, the household was cold, even frigid, a pattern Faulkner himself repeated after he married and fathered a daughter. This coldness, plus Mr. Compson's pattern of drinking and Mrs. Compson's fantasies of superior family background and persistent hypochondria, upset the entire sexual nature of the siblings. One other consideration: we cannot tell what weight to place on Benjy's idiocy as an explanation of the Compsons' dissolution. In any event the four are dislocated—Caddy is promiscuous, doomed by sexuality; Quentin is obsessed, also doomed; Jason is asexual (except with prostitutes) in his drive to set things "right"; and Benjy must be gelded because of sudden and violent sexual desires. Faulkner evidently perceived how a disruptive family pattern could erupt in sexual malfunctions.

Although we are speculating, it is quite possible Quentin's "malfunction" for Faulkner is a shadowy homosexuality which is displaced onto Caddy. In Faulkner's eyes, the incest pattern is less personally and socially unacceptable than the homosexual one, and perhaps without full consciousness of Quentin's depth of feeling, he turned to brother-sister love as a shield. In any event, their attachment for each other, which seems to exclude all others except Benjy, recalls that of the doomed lovers in *Wuthering Heights*. Hovering above a good deal of Faulkner's thought, in fact, is that scenario—of a marriage that cannot take place because of family opposition, but whose relationship transcends normal love, even sex. Emily Brontë also understood something about obsessions. Most analysis of *Sound* sees the relationship solely from Quentin's point of view, since he is in the forefront, and Caddy's activities are in the shadows or on the margins. But if we see the situation from her vantage point—if we invent for her an episode—we note the unnaturalism of her own feelings. The two siblings, like Horace and Narcissa, or brothers and sisters in "Elmer" and *Mosquitoes*, are caught in spirals of uncontrollable fixation.

Quentin is doomed by a variety of elements, as Faulkner recognized working through the manuscript. He moves toward the experience of twilight, the working title of the book, and the dominant image in Quentin's imagination. As Caddy becomes increasingly promiscuous and then pregnant, Quentin retreats more and more into his fantasies of how love was lost. From Caddy's point of view, which we must infer, she acts out her own ideas of "twilight," which means throwing herself on a succession of lovers, each relationship by its very nature doomed. Yet sex with these lovers, Dalton Ames being the most noticeable, is no substitute for the connection to Quentin—and once more we return to the assumption their linkage transcends sex, like Cathy's and Heathcliff's. Behind the doomed, obsessive quality of the relationship is a romantic idea of love, one permeated by innocence, naiveté, and childhood dreams. We find ourselves reminded of Faulkner's linkage to Estelle, a linkage that promises not release, but a form of bondage for both.

Having written the Quentin section, Faulkner was now caught in the spiraling of a novel which demanded further counterpoint. In the interview already cited, reprinted in *Lion in the Garden*, he speaks of the need for "the other brother, Jason," to counterpoint Quentin.[17] Thus he went on to the Jason section, which he dated April 6, 1928. As the manuscript seems to support, Faulkner wrote rapidly here—with little of the hesitation and shifting around of materials which the Quentin segment dictated. The reasons are obvious: Jason is being perceived from without, and is relatively uncomplicated in his desires and needs. He is a Snopes of sorts, and Faulkner could depict him without false starts or much insertion material. Further, his world is the visible one, not the shaded, hooded domain in which Quentin moves, one inaccessible to facile description. Quentin's world was so complicated—and so much more sympathetic to Faulkner—that the writer was possessed by the need to include everything.

Still further in the Jason episode, Faulkner could deal with the "real" events of the Compson family, subsequent to Quentin's and Mr. Compson's deaths, the events of Caddy's divorce, and her stealthy visits to see her daughter, Quentin. This is the conventional stuff of fiction without that intense inner probing which required inventive distinctions between past and present. In Jason's segment the past arises, but it is easily demarked from the present—no need here for italics and roman type to distinguish between inner and outer, or past and present. Stream of consciousness in Quentin is replaced by a relatively clean, free-associational method in Jason: a free association almost equivalent to routine novelistic narrative. We marvel in this breakthrough novel at the multiplicity of narrative devices Faulkner was able to put together—an indication that, unlike his contemporaries, he could fit method to content, thus breaking completely from the realist-naturalistic mold of the dominant American novel.

With the Jason segment completed—a straight run—Faulkner was confronted by several choices. We assume he immediately foresaw he needed an outside voice because, much later, he made that comment. "But I saw that I was merely temporising; that I should have to get completely out of the book. I realised that there would be compensations, that in a sense I could then give a final turn to the screw and extract some ultimate distillation. Yet it took me better than a month to take pen and write *The day dawned bleak and chill* before I did so." Followed by: ". . . and then I had to write another section from the outside with an outsider, which was the writer, tell what had happened on that particular day."[18]

These statements, however, do not deal with all the choices before Faulkner, whether for purposes of clarification or obfuscation. He could have, had he wished, remained *within* the novel and continued to reveal material through the stream—thus creating the kinds of difficulties Joyce brought to *Ulysses.* Or he could have, to change tactics, given the final segment over to Caddy, who was in a position to be an objective narrator —since she had survived from the pastness which makes up much of the novel. The argument against his using Caddy was that Jason had already covered some of that ground and her objective report might be repetitious; also, Faulkner may have felt unequal to the task of getting inside Caddy's head—simply a question of what he felt he could do creatively.* On the other hand, a segment on Caddy does seem called for, at least at the level of trying to understand the situation from the other obsessed half. Still

---

*Even later on, as in *The Town,* when he wanted to personalize Eula Snopes and her daughter, Linda, he did it through shifting, external narrators. The method with Caddy carries over to the Snopes women.

another choice was to remain both within and without by the creation of a character who slides in and out—as later with Ratliff in the Snopes trilogy and *Light in August;* but this method might have presented logistical difficulties.

As one critic has made clear,[19] what Faulkner seemed set upon was to draw parallels—rather distant ones, admittedly—between his tale of sound and fury and the Passion of Jesus Christ.* Why he did this is difficult to understand, since the idea of a Christian Passion does not readily enhance the novel. In any event, the final segment is dated "April 8, 1928, Easter Sunday," after Jason's Good Friday two days earlier, and Benjy's Holy Saturday. A "passion" is not apparent in any of this, unless it is Quentin's guilt, which can be redeemed only through self-sacrifice—but that does not appear to be the central meaning of the novel. He is not redeemed, and his particular passion is one of an obsessive fixation destroying his life. Quentin neither injures nor helps others, except perhaps the little Italian girl he befriends in the back streets of Cambridge.

His "passion" is of another kind, and all his efforts are directed not outwardly but toward himself. Quentin is one of Faulkner's most narcissistic characters; and even his passion for Caddy is the fulfillment of his own need. He cannot tolerate her behavior with other men and rarely comprehends her life: he measures her against his desires, sees himself reflected in her eyes and behavior, and kills himself because he cannot snap the circuitry of self. Quentin has been the most damaged of the "normal" Compson children, although all have been crippled. That is why it is so tempting to see him as possibly acting out Faulkner's sense of himself in his own family atmosphere, and also so misleading. For no matter what possible analogies may be drawn between them, Faulkner, unlike Quentin, was a man of enormous drive, will, determination, and, of course, accomplishment. He could turn all his depression, pessimism, and self-destructiveness into creative work, into stories and novels.

If we do not belabor the Passion theme, we can speculate Faulkner perceived Quentin as the ultimate sacrifice—not a Christ figure but one who is nevertheless crucified. This theme Faulkner pursued far more dramatically and intensely in a later work, *A Fable;* it is not very distant from his sense of endurance and determination of purpose. He judged the

*Carvel Collins has firmly established this parallel (see his "The Pairing of *The Sound and the Fury* and *As I Lay Dying,*" *The Princeton University Library Chronicle* [Spring 1957], pp. 115–19, and the segment called "Christian and Freudian Structures," in *Twentieth Century Interpretations of The Sound and the Fury,* ed. Michael H. Cowan, pp. 71–74). The question, however, is not merely the technical one that Faulkner worked out a series of Christian analogues in the novel, but why. The novel functions at its most significant *without* such parallels, and while they are undeniably there, we feel they enhance far less than do the broadly psychological, Freudian elements. Father and son is less Christian than Oedipal, for example. (Also, see Sumner C. Powell, "William Faulkner Celebrates Easter, 1928," *Perspective* [Summer 1949], 195–218.)

In another area, particularly useful are the scene shifts in sections 1 and 2 charted by Edmond L. Volpe, in *A Reader's Guide to William Faulkner* (New York: Farrar, Straus, 1964), pp. 353–77. Volpe's careful work returns us to a central consideration in the novel, its determined technical mastery of difficult temporal and psychological dimensions.

crucified man as someone who subverts hypocrisy and reveals a kind of ultimate truth about himself and his world. Self-sacrifice is, obviously, a desperate gesture, but for Faulkner it had integrity.

The final segment is notable for Dilsey, who is apparently based on his own Mammy Callie.* Dilsey has always been cited—and will long continue to be referred to—as the devoted servant who tries to hold a crumbling family together; she becomes, in this view, Faulkner's woman of good faith in a household of little faith. If we pursue this view, Dilsey becomes Faulkner's example of loyalty, fidelity, and support. From this, readers have extrapolated that his view of the Negro is of Dilsey. But this Edenic view of Dilsey must become part of the Negro's role in a dispossessed Garden, a Garden despoiled by slavery and its aftermath. Faulkner's sense of her is of a person who retains the traditional role: serving a white family, supporting others, maintaining a life dependent on noblesse oblige. Without taking anything away from Dilsey, we can see her in a long line of Faulkner Negroes who also stand and serve—until Lucas Beauchamp of *Intruder in the Dust* catches the winds of change. But before we deify Dilsey, we must recognize her position. For it is as the result of that position—subservient, powerless, taking orders from people who cannot control themselves, sacrificing herself for them—that Dilsey emerges and sparkles.

Dilsey has submerged her life in the lives of others, and she has no other horizons. We must consider her class and caste role when we judge her—too much commentary turns her into a goddess and, therefore, "a credit to her race." That she plays her role loyally is undeniable; but that Faulkner sees her idealistically cannot be disentangled from the fact she is in the traditional servant's role, a woman submerged, her body a Compson possession. The implications of Faulkner's handling of Dilsey can be quite different from what the usual commentaries make of her. That he admired and respected her is undeniable. But that he viewed her in conventional terms of the illiterate Negro finding her role is also undeniable. She is indeed heroic if the race is judged solely as serving, as having no aspirations beyond those she has. These considerations should not destroy our sense of Dilsey, but they do undermine efforts to applaud Faulkner for making her so important in the Compson household. She should be lauded for that. Yet if she is the "moral center," she is also the "sacrifice" to the Compson household; she becomes a "moral center" only because Faulkner sees no other role for the Negro woman.

Dilsey is an extraordinary creation; she hovers over the novel, although her major role comes near the end. She is the bellwether of the family, in that she seems to be the role model—although, unfortunately, no one can

*Blotner suggests Della, a Negro maid Faulkner had sketched in his notes for "The Devil Beats His Wife," an incomplete story which goes back to late 1925. Della has the advantage over Mammy Callie of being close to Dilsey's physical type. In Faulkner's several attempts to get the story right, Della intervenes in the arguments between husband and wife. Ben Wasson later published a book called *The Devil Beats His Wife.*

follow her. She maintains a routine and an organizing power within a centerless atmosphere. Like Cassandra she has powers of prophecy even though she does not verbalize clearly. Dilsey is, in fact, all we have by the end of *Sound*—for except for her the Compsons disintegrate. The image of Benjy clutching his withered narcissus cannot mitigate the facts of the novel—among these self-oriented and self-destructive people, only Dilsey can express humanity. With this, Faulkner let go, later admitting that his effort on the novel had emptied him out—"written my guts" into it. The title of course came from Shakespeare, via Faulkner's unconscious, and is well-suited to his "dark story of madness and hatred."[20] Faulkner added he had stopped thinking in publishing terms, which brings us to some of the larger implications of the novel: as something approaching final things not only for the Compsons but also for the author.

Beginning with *Sound*, Faulkner's work can be characterized in the next decade as part of his "twilight imagination."[21] But even more than distinguishing the declining Compsons, twilight is associated with shadows; here is the dominant coloring of the book. Faulkner has shaded the novel with a consistency and homogeneity of imagery which reaches back to *Flags* and ahead to *Light in August* and *Absalom*. The narcissus which Benjy clutches at the end of the novel is symbolic of that twilight mentality, since the flower is always linked to death. Twilight imagery, however, is also associated with honeysuckle, with the repetition of water images (need for cleansing, for redemption, for death as a release). But even more than this —and here the linkage to *Flags* is firmed—it suggests man's inability to grasp the truth of any situation, his inability to perceive where accident/ fate crosses with human will and desire. That incapacity to cross over between the accidentals of existence and the needs of individual will places man in a twilight zone. There, the condition of being itself underlies Faulkner's sense of will in its constant struggle with accident.

Probing this theme, we see how it has become the dominant one of his mature period; but it also loops back into his earlier career, even into his poetry. The theme is not a simple one. But its presence in his work almost from the beginning suggests how he moved from "region" to America, from regional writer to American author. In most regional literature which takes this theme into account, the emphasis is on the ability to make the crossover, or else such complete impotence that breakdown and decline are inevitable. Faulkner probes the incapacity, but does so without naturalistic stress on decline—he internalizes it, so that as fate and will meet, we have something of the gradual change we sense in Greek drama, or in Nietzsche's sense of *amor fati*, love of fate. The human will may be baffled, but the individual's ability to maintain himself in the face of accident (or fate) leads not to a naturalistic end but into a twilight of existence. That twilight area is our immediate arena for the Faulkner of *Flags*, *Sound*, *As I Lay Dying*, even *Sanctuary*.

Holding together the work of this period, then, is a deep concern with ultimate questions. How does the individual handle his own needs in the face of an adversarial destiny? how does a person deal with present life when impingement of history and pastness burdens him at every stage? How does one respond to internal needs which defy social constrictions, which break taboos? Further, how does the individual deal with illuminations (from within) when darkness (from without) seems the dominant shade? And the converse is also germane: how does that individual respond to possible illuminations from without when everything internal seems dark? These ultimate, and unanswerable, questions have keen biographical dimensions, and nowhere more than in *Sound*, which, Faulkner said, was his "favorite novel" because it gave him such difficulty.

In part 2 of the novel, Faulkner's extensive revisions in manuscript, while varied, primarily concern the nature of Mr. Compson and Quentin's relationship to him. These revisions shift some of the significance of *Sound* and demonstrate that in the deadly struggle between individual will and the play of fate, the family was critical. What this meant exactly in terms of Faulkner's feelings about Murry Falkner or, more generally, his family, we cannot tell. However, there is a pattern of family concern, based in the main on decline, ineffectiveness, disregard of parent for child, coldness, the problem of the parent living in a past beyond recall. The general tenor of the pattern suggests—and we repeat "suggests"—that Faulkner was writing about the only son-father relationship he was familiar with. Whether he was writing out of some personal trauma or from a desire to understand his and Murry's situation, the family drama indeed stresses paternal passivity and lack of focus. The reverberations of this, as Faulkner demonstrates, can be deadly: Jason is a deceptive, hateful human being; Candace becomes a whore; Quentin commits suicide; and Benjy, as if fate were lurking somewhere, is born an idiot. As though in a Dickens scenario, the children become hostages to parental indifference, and, particularly, to the father's incapacity to take command of his household, especially in the face of a fantasy-ridden mother. Mrs. Compson does not seem drawn from Maud Falkner, who loved and protected her sons. Her apparent favoritism toward her eldest resulted from his being most under attack, as fitting least into the community and needing her support. More generally, however, she was derisive of her husband and a domineering, unbending figure. As we shall see, she had very mixed responses to her daughters-in-law, resenting all but Dean's widow.

Deriving as he does from an old family, with a general (not a colonel) in his background, Mr. Compson is incapable of crossing over between historical destiny and individual desire. Whatever he wanted from life remains ambiguous, since his excessive drinking disguises whatever he was or wished to become. He is a desolate figure, perhaps close to the bone of the author, possibly a perception of him which lay only in the eye of the beholder. Whatever the derivation, we have a worked-over segment which suggests a family trauma—the self-destructive family Faulkner would himself enter when he married Estelle, took in her two children, and had one of his own. The pattern did not create an idiot, a whore, a suicide, and a Snopes; but it did generate extreme ill feeling, a drunken stepson, an unfocused stepdaughter, an alienated daughter, and a miserably unhappy marriage.

Sound projects Faulkner biography in other ways as well. The lack of a section on Caddy is suggestive. She was, after all, the author's "heart's darling." The little girl with muddy drawers becomes the basic image of the novel; the girl and woman a tragic figure, a sacrifice to Compson ineffectuality; a fleeting mother, daughter, and sister—the one who fails to galvanize the family into positive action in the face of pathological parents. Rather than lead, she helps draw the family into obsessive decline. As female "sacrifice" (an Iphigenia to an ineffectual Agamemnon), she sees it all: the neurasthenic mother, the alcoholic father, the troubled brothers. Yet she is denied her own segment, which even the idiot Benjy has.

A standard argument is that Faulkner failed to give her her own section because, as viewed through the eyes of her three brothers, each differently, she becomes their fantasy figure. But biographically more is at stake. It is not only a question of Faulkner feeling more comfortable with the male point of view. The question is one of what can be revealed, and that leads in turn back to Faulkner's own sensibility and protective attitude about himself. By keeping her "hidden" in the interstices of the novel, Faulkner created the others through her reflected light. She is more image than reality, more metaphor than actuality.

The material is viewed from four points of view, each of which "creates" a Caddy far more significant than she could possibly be by herself. Faulkner revealed a mother-figure (through Benjy), a lover-sister (through Quentin), and a caddish sister (through Jason)—how much she is any or all of these depends on perception, not reality. Faulkner wished to make this a novel of viewing. Realities derive not from actuality, but from perceptions. By the time of *Sound* he had become a phenomenological novelist. This is the major shift in his creative abilities—from a depictive novelist to one concerned with manifesting phenomenologically internalized worlds. *As I Lay Dying* fits perfectly into this development, and *Absalom* is the culmination.

If we assume perception counts more than actuality, then Caddy becomes a ghost or phantom, the unachievable woman: goddess, virginal, maternal, as well as whore—the whole range of Faulknerian possibilities. This is deep psychological biography for Faulkner, indicating that elusiveness was his key insight into women and suggesting he compensated for the lack of a sister with a young child and woman (also, Caddy's daughter, Quentin) who plays all roles: woman as someone chameleonlike and undefined. In the novel's twilight imagery, everything is bathed in a northern light—not light in August, but light in December, when days are short, light contracts, and perceptions are illusory.

The component of literary narrative here is a highly creative biographical impulse, a biographical process absorbed into a creative one. Thus we find a curious shifting back and forth of values. In pursuing Faulkner's development and growth—*his* biography—we come up against his deceptive, disguised, creative biographies of families and individuals who recur in his life in an abundance unknown in any other American writer except, possibly, Thomas Wolfe. *Sound* and the following novels tell us his biography is layered deeply within the biographies of those families: layered so deeply and deceptively we would be presumptuous to assert this is positively *his*. Yet we would be neglectful to pass over what those fictional biographies signify, for in them, however precariously, we have Faulkner, as much as anyone will ever have him.

In the novel, Jason, along with the older Compsons, usually receives the weight of negative criticism. He is viewed as ruthless, interested only in material welfare, isolated from feelings for others, driven by feelings of anger and revenge. Yet it is incorrect to see Jason as more isolated than any other Compson. Faulkner has drawn a self-destructive family, the point being that they have ceased to function as a subgroup. To argue Faulkner was pitting individual against community or society is belied by the novel: there is no community to begin with. Faulkner discerns only breakdown and self-destructiveness. There is nothing to measure Jason or any of the other siblings against. There is no ideal, no possible structure, no suitable role model. Coming in as we do *in medias res*, we sense the timeless continuity of disintegration. Compson isolation and familial alienation are outside history.

Some siblings, admittedly, are more generous than others—Jason is obviously the meanest. But Jason has the most reason for anger and isolation, inasmuch as he is the sole sibling functioning within a regularized society. The others range from idiocy to promiscuity to obsessional suicidal depression, against a background of withdrawn, impotent parents. Everyone except Jason has backed off into his or her own place, and however contemptible his inner thoughts and actions, he has to carry the family. We must attempt to determine how much of Jason's attitude Faulkner himself felt as eldest son, with the weight of the family pressing on him. The tendency is to see Faulkner as placed somewhere in Quentin —the artist in disguise trying to emerge in Quentin and reflecting Faulkner's own dilemmas as an artist. But this is in part a false trail, since Quentin lacks the ability to transcend his obsessions so as to reorder them into an art form. More accurately, he is the opposite of the artist, or else the artist manqué, caught up by forces he is unable to re-create.

What has helped support this false trail is Quentin's obsession with Candace, which appears as part of a pattern in Faulkner going back to that all-important "Elmer" manuscript. But this is only one course, not the entire menu. Faulkner did have a keen interest in brother-sister relationships, and this interest did take on taboo-breaking potentialities; but it was never acted upon, and for all its sensationalism, it remained subsurface.

What seems more likely is Faulkner's resentment at being the eldest sibling and his resistance to being something of a surrogate parent in his developing years, especially since Murry had abdicated close paternal ties when the boys (except Dean) were small. Also, the domineering mother tinged Faulkner's role as son, creating in him the expectation he would have to act as a responsible husband-peer.

It is difficult to see *Sound* as socially real or even realistic. This is, after all, "a tale told by an idiot full of . . ." and it appears *that* is the determinant, not routine realism. We must seek a montagelike experience, a filmic sense of panning and crosscutting. The intense subjectivity of the first section, Benjy's, is counterpointed by the objectivity of the last section, the novelist's; this arrangement turns the two inset sections belonging to Quentin and Jason into an internal drama, with Candace in the seams. The internalized drama occurs among Jason, Quentin, and Candace, with the latter's daughter, Quentin, as a further dimension.

Apart from the Quentin-Candace obsessional material, the real struggle in the household occurs between Jason and young Quentin. With Mr. Compson dead, Jason becomes nominal head of the household, and she threatens his hegemony. Is Faulkner shadowing his own sense of things, prematurely killing off the father so he can assay nominal rule? The temptation is great to divine an internal authorial drama projected onto the page; but *caveat lector,* Faulkner is more deceptive than this, more disguised, defensive, and shielded. He remains out of sight. In the familial war, Jason represents order, however nastily; Quentin denotes disorder, as befitting her background. She is chaotic, unplanned, destructive, and self-destructive—a true daughter of Candace. She becomes a threat simply because of who she is and what she represents. To Jason, she suggests everything he cannot handle—not only a threat to his kingship, but to his sense of how the world holds together. A throwback to another era, she symbolizes everything Jason has hated in the family while growing up. This is a possible personal touch for Faulkner: the use of a second generation as mirror of everything Jason detested in the earlier generation. In a sense, we have childhood hatreds not lived but relived. Her theft of the $3,000 which Jason has systematically stolen from her mother's checks is indicative of the way elements are reprogrammed: he sees the $3,000 as rightfully his, and she steals it. The scenario of retelling and redoing is a familiar one in Faulkner: Jason saves, holds on, puts away, does not spend—a typically anal personality—whereas she spends, wastes, gives it away—a typical orality. Money is merely another way of representing a sexual conflict at the deepest levels. The struggle is between withholding and wasting, sexual continence and promiscuity. In such tensions, Faulkner is caught in the interstices of the Compson struggle, not identified with a particular person.

If we assume the conflict over money is fundamentally sexual, what does this suggest for Faulkner as he entered his early thirties? Modern psychological developments suggest that beneath familial, social, and community tensions lies the real conflict, a sexual one. In this respect, Quentin, Jason, Candace, even Benjy and the older Compsons, are locked in some generational, lateral, sibling combat. Sexuality makes family life disruptive, disorderly, uncontrollable; and it reveals another dimension to the Jason–daughter Quentin hatred. As her uncle, Jason must deal with her as his brother Quentin had to deal with her mother, his sister. While the two struggles are not congruent, the names are, and in each there are strong elements going beyond either attraction or dislike, into areas of sexual obsession.

If we begin to locate the tensions here rather than in individual and family, another pattern emerges. Each male is pursuing the sister—not only Quentin, as the conventional view has it. And they are fighting among themselves, each in his different way, for command of the family, for the male role which will dominate. One way to achieve that is to "gain" the sister, by whatever means. Benjy goes wild whenever he hears the word "caddie" on the golf course because it recalls Caddy. The idiot's response is almost orgasmic, with his "fit" possessing a sexual dimension, especially before he is gelded for making a purported sexual attack on two passersby. If even Benjy is sexually involved, we can certainly say the same for Quentin and Jason—and then find it repeated as part of Jason's vendetta against Caddy's daughter. *That* Quentin recalls everything from the first generation, as Faulkner intended it by naming her after her uncle.

The sexual obsessions and dilemmas revealed in the family unit are linked to another large thematic presence, that of the quest for Eden. Quentin is the Compson most linked to Edenic visions: seeking that perfect moment with Caddy when inner and outer are unified. Since he discovers no such moment because of sexual taboos, his quest becomes a form of foolish idealism which ultimately proves self-destructive.

Eden becomes a replacement, even while Faulkner recognizes it fosters a false idealism—and this realization makes him reach back to Southern idealism, the basis of both the region's glory and self-destruction. He was working through ideas he held precariously in tension: *his recognition of familial failure projected onto a wider screen, where it becomes the basis of a false idealism.* When in the final segment Quentin wanders the back streets of Cambridge and encounters the Italian child, the message he receives is a complicated one. He is moving through an urban landscape which negates Eden, which disproves Eden can be either recalled or rediscovered; and yet he seeks some semblance of it in the little girl. On one hand, his quest in Cambridge refutes the search; on the other, there is an obsessive need to continue the quest to discover some remedy. Quentin seeks that perfect moment when Caddy showed her muddy drawers at the top of the tree, and he felt a revelation—that epiphanic moment which can be personally apocalyptic. It was as though he had glimpsed some distant Eden in those muddy drawers—a mixture of sexual arousal, dirt or excrement, and voyeurism, all of which transform a sister into a perfect, loved object. That Keatsian urn is not distant.

By transforming his confusing vision into an Edenic vision which *must* fail him, Quentin has sought out his own doom: a frustration and psychopathology which permit no resolution. Leading his main character into a dead end soon after Quentin has stated so vociferously to Shreve in *Absalom* that he does not hate the South,* Faulkner has opened up the tensions of his own life, however indirectly. The Edenic quest, so essential to Quentin's outlook, nevertheless overwhelmingly frustrates him. He seeks another perfect moment, that Garden where a little sister reveals herself vulnerable and desirable. He will preserve her as Eve, mate to his Adam; but in the real world, that becomes a destructive ideal. When the police run Quentin in for questioning on a possible morals charge, they are in general correct, although off base in the particular instance. Quentin, in fact, has a precedent in his father, who cynically admits he saved his life for an Edenic discovery, but it all came to nought. The sad demise of Mr. Compson sufficiently exemplifies how Edens turn to swamps; but Quentin cannot learn, or even pay attention.

Deeply involved with the Edenic myth in Faulkner is conflict between father and son. The older man has had ideals, which now have soured; the younger still seeks the Edenic. One's cynicism crosses with the other's search. Yet both are suicides: Mr. Compson through drink, the son through drowning. Both are identified with a liquid which destroys—an apt choice for Faulkner, who grew up with drinking all around him. Neither can live a reasonable, orderly life. Like a classical Greek family, the Compsons have somehow ingested sufficient hubris so that they must live out their own doom; they are, in this respect, the creators of destiny. This, too, is Faulkner biography, at the level of ideas, if not actual experience: a way of perceiving family life.

This is also in its way a means of judging the South, a way of perceiving a larger piece of history in terms of a malfunctioning unit. Extending Faulkner's historical metaphor, we can place in perspective Quentin's divided self and his loyalty to the South coexistent with his desire to break from it, as well as the author's own sense of time and place. Although Faulkner remained deeply faithful to both Mississippi and Oxford, he did

---

*A suicide in *Sound*, Quentin is resurrected in *Absalom*, where his words to Shreve precede his own death only shortly. His anguish in the later novel suggests another reason, besides Caddy, for his sense of doom. Nevertheless, Quentin's agony here, based on himself, Caddy, and Dalton Ames, is paralleled, in *Absalom*, by the trio of Henry Sutpen, Judith, and Charles Bon. In his brilliant study *Doubling and Incest/Repetition and Revenge*, John Irwin sees these overlapping "triangles" as part of the fear of castration, which "lies at the core of narcissistic doubling." Quentin and Henry are linked in their common fear of being castrated by their sisters, who become here substitutes for the avenging father. By immobilizing Caddy with his own impotent importuning, Quentin hopes to restrain her; analogously, Henry "keeps" Judith by killing Bon. The Irwin argument is particularly rich for *Sound* and *Absalom*. For further doubling and revenge, see Hawthorne's *The House of Seven Gables*, the "Alice Pyncheon" chapter.

enjoy his greatest growth when he left. With caution, we see in Quentin's divisiveness many of the divisions tearing at Faulkner himself.

Unquestionably, the effectiveness of *Sound* depends on how the Compson lives are presented. While ostensibly about the South, a particular Southern region, a fantasized county, the novel is also about language, voices, speech, expression, temporal relationships. It is concerned not only with how things appear to three very different brothers and their creator, but with how they express themselves. Four tellings—which involve considerable retelling—mean four different voices: the meandering moanings of Benjy, the stream of Quentin, the more logical telling of Jason, the overall "objectivity" of the author in the final segment. This use of voices and its reliance on individual languages is Faulkner's major breakthrough in his middle-period fiction.

This, too, has obvious biographical implications. His innovation reinforced his escape from a regional or sectional mentality; it isolated, even alienated, him psychologically from a particular place; it offered him reentry into that milieu where artistic (not social or community) standards obtained; it gave him self-confidence to confront the major Europeans on their own ground—stream, linguistic experimentation, use of voices, free-associational material; it separated him from his predecessors like Anderson or the naturalists-realists; it divided him, further, from those like Phil Stone who were unsympathetic to experimentation; it made him a novelist who declined a popular readership at the very time he needed money for marriage and family; it isolated him from his Oxford background, where such a book could not possibly be interpreted in 1929; it separated him from all traditions of contemporary American fiction—only Dos Passos proved competitive at this level; it nourished his desire for adventure and daring —what had failed in his military career, he compensated for in the derring-do of literary innovation; and, finally, it justified in his own eyes his sense of specialness, something he had cultivated in manner and dress before he could do it in print.

In still another sense, *Sound* moved deeply into biography. In his depiction of a self-destructive family, Faulkner contrasted two views which always warred within him: the nature of constituted society (historical tradition) as against the new (disorder and disruption, metahistory). The Compsons are a family incapable of responding to the demands of a new society; only Jason can compete, but at the expense of his humanity. He loses soul as he attempts to keep abreast of the new spirit of the age. This is a surmounting theme for Faulkner, and in his middle career it supersedes any struggle between individual and community. The matter is nothing less than a Faustian effort to salvage one's own soul in a society which has sold itself to the new. But Faulkner is not purely antimodern, or else he would sound like a nag. He is in fact able to see how modern ideas are necessary for some way out of the morass. But how far one should go he does not know. His attitudes toward modernism and modernizing are, in many respects, like those he applied to race: he wanted change, and yet he profoundly feared change. He wanted the Negro's position to improve, but feared for the community's stability if the Negro moved too fast. He relied on organic change—and of course was proved wrong repeatedly. In his fiction, his sense of tradition and history in their struggle against the modern world has overtones of race, how he perceived race within a segregationist, Negro-baiting, hostile atmosphere.

By revealing his ambiguous fear of modernism—already illustrated in *Flags*—Faulkner critiques both history and the past. He was essentially trapped; and that was why, we can posit, he decided to tell his story in *Sound* from four points of view: his own, finally, but first supported by the three brothers' responses. If we follow his remarks in 1955 at Nagano, Japan, we perhaps have some clues as to his thinking more than twenty-five years before. At Nagano he related how he wanted to plumb the "blind self-centeredness of innocence, typified by children, if one of those children had been truly innocent, that is, an idiot."[22] After that, Faulkner recognized he needed a protagonist to tell the story, and thus Quentin appeared. By this time, there was no containing everything in a short story, and novel length became necessary. As Faulkner details his work on *Sound*, he makes it seem as if he stumbled upon everything. After Quentin's narrative, he felt he needed counterpoint, and from that came Jason's version—he later characterized Jason as the "most vicious character" he ever invented. When he had the three narratives, he needed another to draw things together "from the outside with an outsider." That role was filled by the writer, the omniscient, godlike author. "And that's how that book grew. That is, I wrote that same story four times." He goes on to speak of his original plan to print the first section in different colors, "so that anyone reading it could keep up with who was talking and who was thinking this, and what time, what moment in time, it was. To that idiot, time was not a continuation, it was an instant, there was no yesterday and no tomorrow, it all is this moment, it all is [now] to him." Since color is prohibitive in cost, italics are used in modern editions.

Without accepting all aspects of Faulkner's explanation of the book's derivation,* we still find his remarks suggestive. By stressing in the first segment Benjy's innocence, Faulkner suggests how his own dream of Eden and of Adamic man is linked with his recognition of blind forces which make Eden unachievable. If anyone could grasp the Garden experience, it should be the idiot, the holy saint of premodern verities. Implicitly, Faulkner is looking back; and yet even in his fantasy of an idiot's innocence (the past, antebellum, premodern certainly), he recognizes that in some

---

*He spoke (in the Jean Stein interview) of writing "five separate times" to tell the story. By that, he meant not only the four published in the original version, but the appendix he prepared for Malcolm Cowley's *Portable Faulkner*. According to him, the book was not finished until fifteen years later, when he made "the final effort to get the story told and off my mind." Linked to this, surely, are the five versions of an introduction to *Sound*.

uncontrollable way the Garden is contaminated: the innocent figure *is* an idiot. The balancing of segments—two for this world, two for the other (Quentin's added to Benjy's)—suggests his dilemma about modernism and the world preceding it. Further, even as he questioned the values of that encroaching modernism, he used its most advanced techniques to plumb Benjy's psyche. With a daring that can be compared only to Joyce's, Faulkner adapted the Irish writer's stream and free-associational technique, and carried them beyond their use in *Ulysses*. While modernism is questioned, it provides the method for questioning it.

In his revealing interview with Jean Stein early in 1956, Faulkner shifted his focus somewhat for the beginning of *Sound*. Here he stressed a "mental picture," the "muddy seat of a little girl's drawers in a pear tree,"[23] Caddy's drawers revealed as she strains to see through a window where her grandmother's funeral is taking place. Even with the muddy pants as the guiding idea or symbol, however, the dilemma in Faulkner's thinking remains the same. For the muddy drawers are several things, part of that unresolved attitude we find in his response to modernism. They are not white, pure, unsullied, pristine, not part of Thoreau's vision, but closer to Emerson's and Melville's awareness that nothing remains untouched.

The muddy drawers reveal a good deal about the author and the South. While they remain part of the love-longing of Quentin, the mother fixation of Benjy, and are repeated in Caddy's daughter Quentin climbing down the drainpipe to the consternation of Jason, the drawers also bring together the dilemmas and conflicts the novel takes on. In this respect, the tensions of the novel are not "resolved" until Quentin's final words at the end of *Absalom*, that brief hymn to love and hate for the South. Those muddy drawers, which Faulkner recognized as a symbolic "mental picture," are a polluted vision of an Edenic existence, a dispossessed Garden, part of what Emerson called a "pleached garden." They reflect an existence Faulkner could not resolve in his own thinking, encompassing not only the sullying of an Edenic fantasy, but that clash between indolent stability and corrosive, active modernism. Yet Faulkner also perceived that while the new and innovative may be corruptive, the old is stagnant, indolent, passive, a historical backwater.

The biographical revelations of a novel like *Sound* are almost infinite. But especially the use of language: its twisted, gnarled forms of syntax or, really, "asyntax," reinforce the dilemmas at the book's heart. At almost the midpoint, Quentin in his section is seeking his shadow in Cambridge, when he meets three boys who are fishing. His search for his shadow is his attempt somehow to unify his life: he feels separated not only from a self but from a shadow. He walks upon the belly of his shadow as a way of asserting his existence, which his mind doubts. The three boys, in contrast, know themselves; they represent life. The contrast is clear. As he moves amidst their fun-and-games attitude (in a replication of Stephen Dedalus's "dedication" scene), Quentin zeroes in on his sense of doom, focused on him and Caddy when they were children. Her insistence on marriage, which occurs in this passage, dooms her brother, even as he responds to the playful questions of the three boys. Shortly after, he will befriend the child who is indeed the shadow of Caddy—the scene the present evocation of a historical relationship which thrust Quentin from the Garden.

Language for this difficult and critical scene is twisted, no straightforward stream or free association. In italics, we read: "Caddy that blackguard can you think of Benjy and Father and do it not of me." The tortured syntax, with the "not of me" at the end, is Faulkner's emphasis upon how past and present cannot meet, how they cannot be resolved. The "not of me" belongs with Benjy and Father, and yet the syntax locates it with "do it," meaning do it with Dalton Ames. Yet even as we relocate the crucial "not of me," we see it does not quite fit after Father—there, too, the syntax is gnarled. In this one sentence, Faulkner is suggesting, through language, Quentin's condition; and suggesting, further, how he views himself as sexually replaced by Ames: the juxtapositioning of "do it" and "me" leave no other reading. Even in this distraught condition, Quentin can answer the boys. But his response bleeds off into more italics, in which he suggests he and Candace run off together, taking Benjy with them. Interspersed in the same sequence are guilt feelings about the family's selling of pasture land so that he can go to Harvard and his father's drinking (which he says will kill him within a year). The scene then moves directly into the bakeshop, the tinkling of the bell, the appearance of the Italian child.

The quest for the historical Caddy paralleled by the sequence with the small Italian child reinforces the theme of a search for a lost Eden. Eden is appropriately centered on childhood experiences, and when Quentin follows the child through the back streets of Cambridge he is doing little more than seeking salvation through some form of innocence. But once again Faulkner has contaminated or polluted that innocence; for behind Quentin's pursuit of the child is a sexual shadow, transferred from the innocent little girl to Candace. That sexual shadow involves Adam and Eve, but with the Garden traduced so that there are shame, embarrassment, need to redeem oneself—by no means pure, pristine innocence. The imagery here is quite complex, fittingly so for a social vision which cannot be reduced to simplistic equations of individual versus community, or even past versus present. The vision has within it the contradictory nature of tragedy, of events which occur somewhere beyond the choices of men, in acts which they see as part of their social tradition, but which turn out to be self-destructive. Punishment exists "out there," in excess of what anyone does or even thinks of doing. Quentin is punished far in excess of what he has thought or felt; he is a sacrifice to something existing beyond, whether fate, destiny, or the curve of Southern history. Whatever the cause, it lies deep in the country's collective unconscious, and someone must pay. Quentin, unredeemed, is the victim. Chased by Furies, he will have no favorite god allay them.

Sucked into this vision of a great dramatic stage is a particular language and a particular way of arranging the material. Even as the little girl eyes the buns, Faulkner modulates wildly: "The little girl watched them with still unwinking eyes like two currants floating motionless in a cup of weak coffee Land of the kike home of the wop."[24] The shifting of perspective from little girl to saleslady is brilliant, since it occurs in the space between "coffee" and "Land." This sentiment, which seems to derive from Quentin, is projected as if from a ventriloquist onto someone who is at this juncture disembodied. Introduced in the previous paragraph, the saleslady has vanished from the paragraph in which her thought is pitched. If we read carelessly, we seem to feel the sentence is from Quentin, or from Faulkner, but it is the sentiment of the bakery woman—set off by the apparition of the little Italian child. Brilliantly handled, besides the sudden transition, is the disparity in worlds Faulkner creates through juxtaposing Quentin and the saleslady to the child. He will buy her a bun and become involved, eventually, with the police; she will castigate foreigners and come off with the upper hand. There is no justice, only human feeling.

Yet the passage, in addition to the modulations of tone and content, keeps pointing back to the Italian child as surrogate for Caddy. This was powerful stuff in 1928–29, since it does have a whiff of perversion. That Faulkner would go on to write *Sanctuary* soon after *Sound* was not chance —the presence of sexual perversion is intrinsic to both novels. Faulkner's attitude toward sexuality here is somehow connected, unconsciously or otherwise, to a broad range of women: Maud, grandmother(s), Mammy Callie as surrogate mother, Aunt 'Bama and similar maternal figures, as well as Estelle, Helen Baird, and others. Exactly how he transformed such feelings into fictional attitudes we cannot follow, but the fact remains that the Compson brothers fight over a sister who is obsessively loved by two, and the third is "involved" with her daughter. Quentin repeatedly refers to the Italian child as "sister," and the language of certain passages supports this blending: "You live a long way, dont you. You're mighty smart to go this far to town by yourself." This is addressed to the child, followed by the internal monologue: *"It's like dancing, sitting down did you ever dance sitting down? We could hear the rain, a rat in the crib, the empty barn vacant with horses. How do you hold to dance do you hold like this / Oh."*[25]

Without the italics, one part blends with the other, although the difficulty of Faulkner's pronominal usage remains—essential for his kind of conscious confusion of images. *"She turned her back I went around in front of her. . . . I was hugging her I tell you."* The "I" is Quentin, the "she" and first "her" is Caddy, just mentioned on the previous page; incidentally, the second "her" is Natalie, but the "you" is Caddy. Then follows a succession of "I" and "you" and "she," all of them related to Caddy and Quentin. The "her" is Natalie, but the "she" is Caddy—and the immediate focus the small girl. The effect is that of montage, of deliberate merging and blending of elements; so that as far as is possible in language past and present are telescoped. The pronominal confusion is definitely linked to the interior method: a grammatical way, as Faulkner had discovered, of getting into and remaining in the interior seams of narration. In *As I Lay Dying*, there is a comparable use of interiors, and that book, it seems, is a natural outgrowth of method in *Sound*.

Another related method is Faulkner's ability to bury matters—reading him here is like observing an archaeologist trying to uncover layers of the past. In Quentin's segment, at the middle of the novel, we have a scene of considerable density. Several people are speaking, including the Canadian Shreve, and interspersed with their talk in roman type are the italics of Quentin's inner monologue. He has abstracted himself from the conversation and journeyed back into his own obsessive need. There he confesses to Mr. Compson his incest with Caddy—a mental incest, not an actual act. The moment has a Joycean dimension since, as if in the confessional, he is admitting crimes to a priestlike father. "*. . . there was something terrible in me terrible in me Father I have committed Have you ever done that We didnt we didnt that did we do that.*" Intermixed with that "confession" is an interchange between Quentin and Caddy about how far she went with her lovers. "*. . . did you love them Caddy did you love them When they touched me I died.*"

At this point, the past is thrown into roman type because it now lies outside Quentin's mind in some intermediate range of narration neither authorial nor interior monologue. This is a unique place Faulkner has established in his fiction: a scene with no witnesses (performed with even greater sophistication in *Absalom*), narrated from no fixed point, coming to us as part of history created by the whirlwind. This scene, which is now all in roman type, culminates in Quentin's holding a knife to his sister's throat in what will be a murder-and-suicide pact. Yet Faulkner seems less interested in the actuality of the unsuccessful pact than in the method of narrating this material. All is past, and yet it is not memory, not internalized. It is dramatized as if present, though set in as part of flashback. Who is narrating it? Faulkner is obviously the omniscient novelist, however disguised; but he shields himself against direct presentation by means of this intermediate area, in which the suicide pact is distanced and Quentin questions Caddy about Dalton Ames. Then, just as suddenly, the narrative returns, without change of typeface, to the present.[26]

The key ingredient is disguise, defense, withdrawal, hiding. All of Faulkner's literary methods have a biographical dimension if we seek how he secreted himself in his narratives, peeking out here or there, withholding, retreating, then emerging. The patterns are unmistakable. As he entered his thirties, his work became significant to the extent he could impose a particular method of narration upon it: for example, from *Sound* through *Absalom*. Despite wide distinctions in content, this work holds together because of particular technical achievements. And that accomplishment was precisely Faulkner's ability to find seams and intermediate areas in his narrative to create a voice no one else in fiction had achieved.

The method, if we read back into the life, appears to mirror a person who has already decided to withdraw from his commitment to Estelle, even as he is being propelled to it by Dot Oldham, her sister, and by his own vows. It suggests, further, he has moved almost entirely into an artistic milieu, beyond the reach imaginatively and intellectually of those around him, whether friends or relatives. It indicates, still further, he had become such a loner he needed to develop a voice which would be uniquely his, something original in fiction; and this voice, once developed, would enable him to break away even from that artistic milieu.

Finally, it suggests he had taken an imaginative leap into the unknown, that area which separates the mere literary worker from the artist, which distinguishes the minor writer from the major figure. He took chances in *Sound*, but also for the next ten years, which redrew the map of American literary history. Not only did he forge a unique personal style with those voices, he provided a way of judging his contemporaries; and they all failed in one way or another when perceived through the lens of his work. His life in these years is linked mainly to imaginative activity, internalized, a captive to his work. Faulkner became both subject and object, part of the cycle of creation which used and then absorbed him, becoming more than he was without forsaking what he was.

We can read back the literary method to illuminate a man who was imaginatively rejecting nearly everything in order to preserve his disguise, *at almost precisely the time* he was reaching out to marry a deeply troubled woman with two children, acquire a home which needed extensive renovation, and become benefactor for a large number of people, including his mother when Murry died in 1932. As Faulkner approached the 1930s, he was moving on two distinct levels: one, demonstrated by the literary advancement he had made, which subsumed the artist, created disappearance; and the other, revealed by a personal life which involved reaching out to increasingly large numbers of people who became dependent upon him. The two halves could not possibly fit. The artistic and personal sides warred against each other, without resolution of their conflicting ends.

What this meant in personal terms was that Faulkner became in many respects an impossible person to live with; that he could, when he needed to, create an atmosphere of sheer destruction; and that his behavior severely masked the inner life, which he considered paramount and which he revealed to no one. When people in Oxford say to this day (late 1980s) that no one really knew Mr. Bill, they mean something like this. All writers hide, but Faulkner hid more. All writers play roles, but Faulkner played a greater variety of them.

Back in *Sound*, of considerable importance is the gradual accommodation of language to Quentin's developing desperation. Near the end of the segment, the modified stream has given way to the actual stream—and the water imagery, first for Caddy and then for Quentin, is unmistakable, not the least also for Benjy in his segment. The second section of the novel is as a whole a kind of "running-on," since Faulkner's original conception appears to have been the Dalton Ames affair with Caddy as perceived through Quentin's fuzzy, guilt-ridden consciousness.* He then became caught up in Quentin's adventure with the Italian child—which does fit well and is not anomalous—and introduces several characters who play only a collateral or marginal role.

When the modified stream becomes the stream, language indicates Quentin is losing control of himself. In these passages, he will work himself up to death by water. All the bits and pieces of the past float through his consciousness, and he is in thrall to memory, helpless before the onrush of events which are tearing him apart. As he loses control of himself, key images of his life pour in: gasoline, watch, time, Caddy, Maury-Benjy, other family members in various states of disintegration. He denies himself in Latin: *"Non fui. Sum. Fui. Non sum."*[27] "I wasn't. I am. I was. I am not." Hostile recollections of Mr. Compson follow: ". . . she [Mother] couldn't see that Father was teaching us that all men are just accumulations dolls stuffed with sawdust swept up from the trash heaps where all previous dolls had been thrown away the sawdust flowing from what wound in what side that not for me died not." The passage recalls once more the Elder Heyst's burden on his son, Axel, in Conrad's *Victory*, a relationship which also leads to suicide.

As Quentin experiences these memories, several of them clash with Faulkner's own outspoken statements on man's endurance. Here we have a much more modified sense of endurance, a very qualified free will. Faulkner was working through what was for him a delicate and critical point: that life dices with man. The endurance he publicly pronounced came with full recognition that a bad throw of the dice compromised will. Man must face that "every breath is a fresh cast with dice already loaded against him."

Even as he contemplates final things, Quentin wonders if she, Caddy, is worth despair. Faulkner is on the edge—not the existential edge, but the edge where belief in oneself and the sanctity of life confront the accidentals of existence which make one question everything. This is a profound American dilemma: that choice which every American protagonist ponders, whether individual effort is worthwhile in the face of chance, accidentals, fate. The classic Faulkner moment has arrived. Quentin sits poised on the edge of existence: his own, society's, perhaps America's—Ahab choosing whether to go on in the face of doom. The Emersonian moment confronts the Dreiserian, with Melville and Hawthorne not far distant. There is little of Hemingway's retreat into those few great moments which make it all worthwhile, pristine and marvelous as such moments are in early Hemingway. This is much harder stuff. It has elements of that doom-struck country D. H. Lawrence found characteristic of our fiction; and even time must pay attention. Time dominates the final passages of

---

*The holograph manuscript at the University of Virginia's Alderman Library suggests this —although it is a revision of the working manuscript, not itself the original.

Quentin's segment: ". . . and i temporary and he was the saddest word of all there is nothing else in the world its not despair until time its not even time until it was / The last note sounded."[28]

Does time have personal dimensions here? Time, Bergsonian time, supports the irrationality of all three brothers. Benjy's April 7, 1928; Quentin's June 2, 1910; Jason's April 6, 1928; the novelist's April 8, 1928—three days clustered, the other almost exactly eighteen years earlier. What does it mean? Why those dates? Why the shift of almost eighteen years between Benjy-Maury's segment and Quentin's; then the leap back to the eighteen-year gap for Jason's and the novelist's segments? Is there indeed a holy week implied in the 1928 dates? If so, what does that mean in terms of Faulkner's own life, a man who had withdrawn from almost all formal religion? Does the very arrangement of the novel have implications, as, for example, the arrangement of *As I Lay Dying* definitely does? If so, what do these arrangements imply about Faulkner the man manipulating the material? Or, contrariwise, had the material perhaps gone so far out of control, become so personalized, that even the "maker" could not handle it? We do know Ben Wasson felt the novel had lost control or was incoherent, for he made changes, introducing italics and inserting breaks to indicate temporal shifts. Faulkner felt Wasson had overstepped boundaries and chewed him out. The author did not consider the novel impossible to follow and restored the original text in most places.

By making time so central in the novel Faulkner was taking on the strategies of the great moderns, Joyce and Proust primarily. The religious references to Holy Week are less apparent, but very possibly exist as an effort to create his own ironic sense of a holy family, a mockery by means of the fatigued, pathological Compsons. It is also possible that religious ramifications are not distinct from temporal considerations, intrinsic to them. Faulkner's reasoning: the incoherence of the Compson family was so enormous, so unyielding, that the sole way to give it the semblance of cohesion was, first, by a quasi-religious patterning, and, second, by finding a temporal method for perceiving them obliquely. The interiority of the segment for Benjy becomes apparent—here Faulkner can brilliantly improvise on time in someone for whom time is meaningless; and in the Quentin segment, he needed a temporal sequencing which turned Quentin's anguished world into a combined past and presentness. Although Faulkner inveighed against Freud, we find here a sophisticated awareness of the unconscious, with its seamless time. To catch the unconscious of the four Compson siblings, Faulkner provides a story which, as Sartre suggested, does not unfold, but which we discover under each word. A linear, sequential mode would not have conveyed their basic incoherence, irrationality, self-destructiveness.

On a more personal level, we can see Faulkner's use of time as a possible distancing device for dealing with a family. Faulkner had distinct feelings about family, and devised some way of capturing deeply personal attitudes within a literary mode; using the methods of the moderns to abstract family from realistic-naturalistic references, as in Lewis and Dreiser. In *Look Homeward, Angel,* Wolfe was moving in a similar direction, and Faulkner later praised Wolfe for attempting so much even while failing. The precise use of calendar time in each of the segments, clearly demarked, is one way of maintaining a hold on reality; so that by the time we reach the final section, narrated by the omniscient novelist, we still have an anchor in the external world. Sartre's comment on Faulkner's "present" is significant here:

> What is revealed to us is the present, and not the ideal limit whose place is neatly marked out between past and future. Faulkner's present is essentially catastrophic. It is the event which creeps up on us like a thief, huge, unthinkable—which creeps up on us and then disappears. Beyond this present time there is nothing, since the future does not exist. The present rises up from sources unknown to us and drives away another present; it is forever beginning anew.[29]

In a compelling sequence, Quentin goes from meditation on watches and time to reflections on the Negro; from plans for his own death to ideas which govern him and the South. He recognizes that ". . . a nigger is not a person so much as a form of behavior; a sort of obverse reflection of the white people he lives among." He realizes that the sole way to understand people, black or white, "is to take them for what they think they are, then leave them alone."[30] Even as he slides closer to suicide, Quentin's stream of reflections maintains Faulkner's effort to make sense of the conflicts one has toward a family he or she may even love. Shortly afterward, Quentin undergoes an intense stretch of free association, in which Mrs. Compson, mothers in general, sin, morality, poisoning of one's mind, hostility toward siblings, all such grave matters of family life, well up. The passage leads directly to considerations of Mrs. Compson, as lacking tenderness and qualities of embracement, as missing those warm qualities found not in mothers but in grandmothers, aunts, older relatives. The shifts in time, from past (Mother) to present (Caddy and Herbert Read, her fiancé) become more sharply angled, more intense and insistent. Quentin's attitude toward women is affected not only by his mother and by Caddy, but by his father as well, who sees them as sewers: "Delicate equilibrium of periodical filth between two moons balanced. Moons he said full and yellow as harvest moons her hips thighs."[31] Every dimension of family is raked over, and the overall effect is one of distaste, hostility, inflexible attachment, and, in some instances, obsessive love.

It is hard to avoid emphasizing that with its temporal modes of shadowing family pastness as well as presentness, *Sound* is a deeply personal document. Not so much for the content, but for the strategical method— which made it possible for Faulkner to express himself so intimately in an impersonal mode. What is striking is how Maud Falkner made her eldest son feel like Jacob; but when Faulkner came to draw the family, Jason became Esau, and Jacob, for whom property has been sold so he can attend Harvard, has been vanquished. The rough brother survives; the artistic one—like Darl among the Bundrens—declines and destroys himself. The patterning is unmistakable: Faulkner is not only reproducing aspects of his own family, he is foreseeing a form of ending. The artistic, sensitive brother clearly does not fit; the realistic one takes over, and the poet among the savages has no alternative but to do away with himself.* Had Faulkner not utilized a complicated temporal method, it is doubtful he could have revealed himself and his sense of family this intensely, this obsessively.

If we link all of the above matters, we can see time strategies, Mother, Caddy, and Quentin's incestuous longings as all connected not only to the fall of the house of Compson but to the Fall. Quentin's response to his incestuous feelings, which are a deflection from mother to sister, can only occur because he has been expelled from the Garden. The Eden of expectation has turned into an exiled existence; and for *that*—an emblem of the South?—he responds by destroying himself, an unfilled vessel. This novel, clearly, foreshadows all of Faulkner's longer work through Go Down, Moses.

While Faulkner was going through the final stages of *Sound*, he put *Flags* in Ben Wasson's hands, and his agent got an agreement from Alfred Harcourt on September 20 (1928) that he would publish the book if severely cut. Harcourt considered the manuscript overwritten. With this arrangement, Faulkner also had a reading from Harrison Smith, who became a heroic figure at this stage of the writer's fortunes, for it was Smith—breaking off from Harcourt, Brace—who had sufficient belief in *Sound* to publish it after Harcourt rejected it. What created the professional crisis was Faulkner's movement in new directions at the very moment he was being at least partially rejected in his old direction, on *Flags*. Ben Wasson agreed to make the cuts on *Flags* for $50 plus an additional $300 advance against royalties. Wasson sent part or all of the money to Faulkner, who used it to come to New York, for him a journey into the heart of darkness itself. Faulkner agreed to allow the cuts, and very possibly his compromise was motivated not only by his desire to see it published after so many rejections, but also because it was in a style he was no longer attached to. Finally, he harbored the hope that if he agreed and created no difficulties here, Harcourt might entertain publishing his latest manuscript, which he took with him to New York. It was indeed a critical moment, when all his decisions focused on his professional, not personal, life; decisions which, as it proved, were critical for the kind of fiction he planned to write in the next decade or so. Whatever other feelings he had about *Flags*, it was an offer he had to accept. He left for New York in September of 1928, with a contract for *Sartoris* which called for cutting about 25,000 words of *Flags* within 17 days: a novel of 110,000 words, contracted for on September 20,

---

*Sartre comments: ". . . Faulkner's entire art aims at suggesting to us that Quentin's monologues and his last walk *are already* his suicide. This, I think, explains the following curious paradox: Quentin thinks of his last day in the past, like someone who is remembering" (*Literary and Philosophical Essays*, Annette Michelson, tr. [London: Rider, 1955], p. 91).

due date on October 17. With *Sound* in his possession now, unrevised, he must have thought it was a funny way to make a living: with the help of his agent, to strip a novel within a little more than two weeks.

At the time Faulkner moved in with Wasson at the latter's Greenwich Village apartment (at 146 MacDougal Street), New York was full of fellow Mississippians, going back to Oxford and New Orleans days. Stark Young was building his reputation as a drama critic; Bill Spratling was, as usual, bustling around with art and architectural projects; and Lyle Saxon, a friend from New Orleans, where he had written for the *Times-Picayune,* served as local hosteler. Saxon came from a well-to-do family, with a plantation background, and had a rather ostentatious, voluble manner. Unlike Faulkner and most of the writers who came to New Orleans, Saxon could afford a large, three-story house on Royal Street, in the French Quarter, even before he became a best-selling author with *Father Missis-sippi,* the story of the same spring flood Faulkner wrote about in *Old Man.* A bachelor, like Young and Spratling, Saxon lived well in New York, on Christopher Street in Greenwich Village. Faulkner, among others, stayed with him. Saxon's apartment became a kind of clearinghouse for Southern young men coming to the city, what came to be called the Southern Protective Association.

Saxon deserves a place in Faulkner's life for several reasons. He was part of that crowd of single men, bachelors for life, who aided Faulkner at critical points when he was about to make a decision. His accommodation of Faulkner in New York demonstrates how close the writer stayed to his beginnings—how when he ventured outside of Oxford, he felt most comfortable with fellow Southerners, most of all, fellow Mississippians, to the exclusion of a broader literary crowd. Finally, the presence of Saxon, Young, and Spratling here indicates Faulkner feared to venture much beyond defined territory, and that the world of New York became for him forbidden turf. In time New York nourished his idea that cities were necropolises, the literal end of those things he defined as enduring values.

As a matter of principle and because he was working on *Sound* and also revising it, Faulkner did not want to involve himself in the cutting of *Flags.* Wasson found the book moving in several directions, precisely Liveright's response in his rejection. Our tendency in reading *Flags* before it became *Sartoris* is to excuse Faulkner's digressions because we know where they were leading: we know how *Flags* served as quarry for later exploration. We read it with hindsight, whereas for the contemporary reader only the book itself existed. Nearly everything having to do with Horace Benbow is slimmed down—his early years, his relationship to Belle (so significant to Faulkner in personal terms), his brief affair with her sister, the strong incest motif between him and Narcissa. Wasson's cuts reflect a sharper focusing on the Sartoris themes, deemphasizing how Horace is counterpointed to Bayard Sartoris. That fatal dalliance with Belle, now revised, has in it some of Faulkner's feelings about Estelle, his recognition he was entering into a doomed relationship with his eyes wide open. Just as

Sartoris is one dimension of Faulkner—mainly the romantic, doomed, wish-fulfilled war hero—so is Horace an unflattering portrait of the artist. The latter also has other mysterious personal resonance, since his strange attachment to Narcissa comes just before the appearance of Quentin and Caddy, and not long after Elmer and Jo-Addie, the brother and sister in *Mosquitoes.*

By the time *Sartoris* was given its title by someone at Harcourt, Brace, it had taken on such a different character from the original it ceased to reflect Faulkner and came, rather, to represent what the market demanded of a novel: something with simple lines, well-organized, and heading toward a particular, defined end. *Flags* had been the earliest stage of Faulkner's decision that he would write only for himself; but *Sartoris* emerged as an artifact for the marketplace, even as Faulkner was revising a book he felt no one would publish.

Further, he dedicated the revised *Flags* to Anderson, granting Anderson's encouragement with his first book; but the dedication came at a time when Faulkner was moving literarily as far from someone like Anderson as a writer could go. The dedication was compensatory for the parodic view of the author Faulkner had taken with Spratling—which seemed to Anderson to lack either wit or charity. Faulkner was reaching back into a now nearly dead past even as he stepped out into what would be a glorious future, literarily. And he was effacing some of the most troubling personal elements, in the Horace Benbow material, even as he moved toward the stormy reconciliation of those elements in his own life. The literary statement and the personal life seemed not in harmony, but something like the idea of convergence in Hardy's great poem, "The Convergence of the Twain," in which both ship and iceberg are headed toward a destiny which will rip apart the ship. How much of this Faulkner was consciously aware of we cannot tell, since his letters for this period are spare, and even if more abundant would not reveal much: we recall his joyous phrasing of his honeymoon days even while Estelle attempted suicide.

Chapter Twelve

The Depths of Yoknapatawpha

F AULKNER WAS NOT idle while he visited with Mississippi and other Southern visitors to the city. Finding his own place in Greenwich Village, he worked steadily trying to get *Sound* right, a display of his concentration on an extremely difficult manuscript while diversions existed all around him. This ability to concentrate amidst turmoil (or anguish) continued through the middle part of his career, when film work in Hollywood was accompanied by some of his most creative fiction. Part of the problem with *Sound,* as Faulkner realized, was to make it intelligible to the reader and to bring greater consistency to it. Revisions in this instance did not mean a word here and there, or polishing phrases. It meant considerable rewriting for two purposes: clarification on one hand and deepening the meaning. He emphasized the "religious" nature of the text, by making Benjy thirty-three, although precisely what he hoped to gain from the comparison with Jesus Christ is unclear. We suspect a certain pretentiousness, as, later, with the Jesus parallels of *A Fable.* In addition, Benjy's role was refined, one way through additional phrases and lines and another through intensification of italicized passages.

The typescript revisions reveal refinements as well as addition of entire pages, an effort to link the first (Benjy), third (Jason), and fourth (novelist) segments. Faulkner was completely dedicated to this, his first breakthrough novel, aware he was trying to create a masterwork. In the second section, he worked back and forth with italics and regular type, penetrating as deeply as he could into Quentin's obsession with water, with self-destructive acts. In the revisions, Quentin is far more out of control than in the original manuscript; a change which shifts some of the novel's meaning, since it signifies that not only Benjy but still another son was close to mental unbalance. Before killing himself, Quentin takes great care with his toilet, then weights himself with two flatirons, and seeks death by water. The water motif throughout illustrates forms of obsession and death—very possibly an idea Faulkner obtained from his reading of Joyce, and especially *A Portrait of the Artist as a Young Man*. But whatever the borrowings, Faulkner made the motif his own, turning unlikely water images into all-embracing metaphors for the novel.

Blotner indicates that when Faulkner completed his major revisions of the typescript, he became monumentally drunk, one of his typical binges when he stopped eating and drank himself into oblivion.[1] These were virtually acts of self-destruction, since he needed to be saved by others, who, fortunately, always came along in time. Two friends, Jim Devine and Leon Scales, entered Faulkner's apartment in the Village and found him unconscious, malnourished, and too weak to walk. The pattern became a familiar one, especially after a particularly long and difficult pull on a book.

While there was a suicidal component in some of these binges, since they involved almost a complete stoppage of the body's normal needs, Faulkner consciously did not intend to die—the writing urge was too powerful for him to forsake that most significant part of his life. But that survival urge, manifest in writing, had to confront the desire to throw himself away, and then be saved by one good samaritan or another. Since the pattern repeated itself numerous times, we must note how Faulkner depended almost completely on men who mothered him. More often than not, his binges took place in circumstances whereby only men could help him—so that we have the curious situation of his turning men, even drinking companions, into maternal figures and nurses. A superficial psychological view would see him as crying out for a parental figure, perhaps a father, perhaps a mother; but, in fact, we have no way of defining this pattern. The one constant, however, is that unconsciously he had discovered a way to make people do his bidding.

Alcohol was a source of great disturbance to Maud, however, as she saw her eldest son following in Murry's footsteps in this respect. She also saw there was no way to prevent it—it was a fact of life. But she did try to keep it from getting completely out of hand; so that when Faulkner in Oxford went on for days in a certain pattern, she intervened. His pattern was to drink himself into sleep, then awake, drink enough to get back to sleep, and maintain that alternation of drink and sleep until the binge ran its course; or else he had to be dried out in Byhalia or elsewhere. Strikingly enough, contemporary witnesses indicate Estelle did not object to this; on the contrary, she wanted her husband to stay drunk—in that interlocking of mutual interests alcoholics have. Drunk, he belonged to her; drunk, he needed her, as well.

But Maud Falkner took a different tack. She wanted to keep her son alive, and some of the binges were suicidal in their intensity. To prevent him from maintaining that murderous cycle of alcohol and sleep, Maud gave him sleeping pills, which put him out without further drinking. In that way, she hoped he would sleep off a binge and get the alcohol out of his system, without recurring bouts that could continue for days or more.[2] What she didn't know, since it had not been established medically, was that she could have killed him. With the pills, she could have induced a coma, by mixing barbiturates and alcohol. We don't know what success she had, and, as it turned out, much of Faulkner's heavy drinking took place outside her reach.

With *Sound* essentially completed—and the manuscript turned over to Ben Wasson—Faulkner began to enter more fully into Village life, the parties, the talk, the binges. He was now, in mid-fall, staying with Jim Devine, in the latter's apartment on 111th Street, near Columbia University, and was apparently fully recovered. At Lyle Saxon's, where a succession of Southern young men appeared, Faulkner met Owen Crump, a struggling artist, and moved in with him in his MacDougal Street apartment. In this rather unsettled place, where there was little privacy, with Crump and his paint materials spread out, Faulkner set himself to write short stories. He had told Liveright he planned a volume of shorter works, and with Wasson's connections to editors, he felt he could start to make a living. At this time, Fitzgerald was receiving over $3,000 for a *Saturday Evening Post* story, and claimed that he had gone to $4,000. The enterprise was potentially lucrative, of course, but also very dangerous for a writer like Faulkner. Once he had made the turn into his career with *Sound*, working for magazine editors could be, in one sense, contrary to his best interests, or so it appeared. To earn the money he needed to return to Oxford with some capital, he would have to find a formula—as Fitzgerald discovered when he began to raise his sights and rates. How Faulkner met this new situation would prove a test of his seriousness.

One of the first editors he encountered was Alfred Dashiell, of *Scribner's Magazine*, a man who knew his own mind and, however much he liked Faulkner's stuff, was not to be pushed into acceptance on personal grounds. The best of all worlds for Faulkner was to publish stories in magazines which paid well, then republish the stories in a collection, for which he would receive an advance, and all the while continue to work on serious longer fiction, which would remain the main arena of his career. However chancy all that looked, and however discouraging it would become as 1928 moved into 1929, with the Great Depression looming, this is exactly what Faulkner was able to do. His prices did not approach Fitzgerald's, but, unlike his contemporary, he did not permit himself to get caught in an equivalent spiral of needs which made serious novel-writing

dislocation, of a society running off-balance. The focus is lack of focus, lack of order. Faulkner was revealing more intensely his theme—not the clash of old and new, not tensions between civilized behavior and animalism, but the struggle between order and disorder, between balance and extreme, what he foresaw in *Sound*. Here in *Sanctuary* we find continuity with his next decade of work, Faulkner deciding to go for it all: to limn a world bent by disorder into barely recognizable shapes. That head ready to topple off its stem, its blood gurgling and bubbling, foreshadows not the action of the novel but the tone it will take: disharmony, disorder, imbalance. Negro spirituals in the background, Horace's viewing of the murderer, the latter's imminent execution, the crossover to Goodwin, imprisoned for a murder Popeye committed, Goodwin, further, expecting Popeye to get him with sniper fire: truly a world out of kilter, bleeding over into barbarism, atavism, something far deeper than Snopes' animalism.

Yet images alone, even these, do not create a fictional tone. The author needs to slant in: touching the material from off base, askew, angling toward the shape of things. Faulkner developed a "verbal cubism," by which he tried to capture the matter through angles, slants, edges, indirectly, surely not through pure representation. He was interested in the geometry of fiction here, as he would be in *As I Lay Dying*. Verbal cubism implies that beyond the descriptive matter of the scene is the conception of angles, planes, edges. This is the effect of the original beginning of *Sanctuary*, but lost in part in the revision. In the first form, Faulkner achieved distancing; perhaps what André Bleikasten has called Faulkner's final transcendence of his "narcissistic self-involvement." Put more accessibly: he is still within, still there, but less evidently so, scrutinizing as well as immersing.

In the revision Horace and Popeye are immediately brought together at the still in Frenchman's Bend; the theme of imprisonment is temporarily lost. Yet it is that theme which makes the idea of "sanctuary" so meaningful. The idea is worth exploration, in as much as Faulkner chose to rewrite the beginning and shift the emphasis. Sanctuary signifies a holy place, a sacred retreat, an untouchable spot (with its obvious sexual connotation); but also suggests a place where criminals have immunity from arrest, a refuge from the hunt or chase. There is, even, an Edenic intimation. Its use creates a "spiritual" or at least moral tone, and reverberates throughout Faulkner.

He explores many potentialities of the word—the paradox that while sanctuaries exist, no one has a claim to one. The individual can be sought out anywhere; all refuges are false, artificial, a snare. Even the criminal, who would seem to have the ultimate sanctuary, is unprotected—Goodwin is lynched; and Horace himself is almost lynched. Even Temple Drake, *the* temple, cannot find sanctuary when, after the car accident in Frenchman's Bend, she seeks refuge with the Goodwins. She is an uncaring, thoughtless young woman who takes it for granted someone like herself, the daughter of Judge Drake, will always enjoy sanctuaries—they will materialize wherever she is because of who she is.* One of her desperate tactics is to assert she is the daughter of Judge Drake, himself a sanctuary for her, but one which fails. She cannot enter the temple of salvation. With everything aslant, she becomes the temple of doom.

The opening of the novel evokes a shadowy world, in which the "ragged shadow of the heaven-tree" acts as a snood on the street lamp, so that it fails to illuminate the "overwhelming and symbolic darkness." From the start, we seem back in Conrad's *Heart of Darkness*, where light barely penetrates, and all sanctuaries there prove unprotective. This is Faulkner's jungle novel. Frenchman's Bend, Memphis, the prison, whatever, are presented as barbaric, savage, or atavistic; there are few or no amenities. If we judge *Sanctuary* apart from Faulkner's later inflammatory words about it, we perceive it as a terrible vision—a perfect novel for the Great Depression. Not unlikely, it would influence another Great Depression writer, Nathanael West, whose own novels—especially *Miss Lonelyhearts* and *The Day of the Locust*—owe a great deal to Faulkner, and especially to *Sanctuary*. What gives this novel its expressive power, as well as its symbolic importance to the 1930s, is that quality of "aslant" writing, that hitting off-key Faulkner developed. We began to see it in *Sound* and will note it again in *As I Lay Dying*, but in those novels off-key qualities are submerged in internalized monologues, or absorbed into other techniques. In *Sanctuary* the aslant writing, as in the opening scene, has its own life.

Another element in the original opening has a strong biographical flavor. Horace is involved with a woman, however indirectly, by way of the Negro who murdered his wife; leading to Goodwin, with his woman, Ruby. That look-in, as so much else, is aslant, but it suggests what will be a major development in the novel, Horace's relationship with women. His life is a swirl of women—Narcissa from *Flags*, the sister who would be wife and mother; Belle in past and present, and her daughter, Little Belle— unattainable but tantalizing and an analogue to Temple Drake; Ruby Lamar, Goodwin's woman, who fascinates Horace with her dogged loyalty, her qualities of sheer survival. Temple is herself part of Horace's life through Ruby and reflected by Little Belle. One theme of the novel (its subtext, as it were) has to do with women at the very point in Faulkner's life where his sense of female swirl has narrowed down to Estelle Franklin.

The theme uncovers Horace's inability to handle the women in his life —what has already been suggested in *Flags*. The persistence of the theme is what compels us, since Horace is himself an uncommanding character. Faulkner's continuing interest in him appears to be in the weakness of his personality or character, rather than in developing his sensibility. His inability to cope with women in his life, according to Faulkner, is a sign of his failure as a man and as a person. There is more here than a male-female polarization, although that is surely present; more than Orpheus

---

*As we read *Sanctuary*, our melancholy conclusion is that Temple Drake reflects the very young Estelle Oldham.

and the Maenads; more than the artistic (glassblowing) Horace and voracious females seeking to devour him.

Impossible to ignore is Faulkner's devastatingly hostile view of women, except for Ruby. If we perceive women through Horace's eyes and situation, we observe a man trapped in a fog or miasma because women have painted a cloud around him. There are several box images in the novel—the earliest, one of Ruby's child lying in the box to protect it against rats —and they proliferate because they exemplify Horace's own life. He is, figuratively, boxed in. Tommy lies dead in a box; Van, also. Boxes are coffins, enclosures, prison images—boxed-in prisoners; the way Faulkner emblematizes claustrophobia. Houses are not places where people live—for example, the house Temple wanders into with Gowan Stevens—but enclosed space, spatially suffocating. This house is ultimately linked with the one in Memphis and Temple's room, another prison.* Her name suggests something expansive; but she comes to represent a closing down of possibility, not an opening up. Horace's difficulty with his women, which imprisons him, is paralleled, and intensified, by her relationships with men.

In biographical terms, we cannot be explicit about what all this meant for Faulkner. We do know that *Sanctuary* was being written at a time when it was certain Estelle would divorce Cornell Franklin (effective April 29, 1929); that *Sanctuary* was completed in its initial phases in May (rejected by May 25 by Cape and Smith even while plans for *Sound* went ahead). Faulkner's work on the novel was interwoven with his interest in Estelle's proceedings to get free so as to marry him. Yet his way of portraying male-female relationships in his fiction is hardly that of a suitor eager for her hand. On the contrary, he sees such connections as nightmarish; at best, as obsessions which surely almost destroy the man. There are no happy or even pleasant marriages in the world of white men and women; and in the black world, Faulkner had no sense of how marriage worked, or how power was divided between male and female. Even the book he wrote immediately after his marriage (on June 20, 1929), *As I Lay Dying*, does not have a propitious title for a newly married man. He, in fact, entered one of his darkest periods.

As if life were imitating art, Faulkner's honeymoon proved the culmination of what he was suggesting in his fiction: that the female entraps the male in her silken web and then proceeds to seek his destruction, possibly along with her own. Writing to Ben Wasson in late June or early July, Faulkner says: "We have a very pleasant place on the beach here. I swim and fish and we row a little. Estelle sends love."[5] The words sound idyllic. But the truth of the matter is that, according to reliable sources, Estelle

---

*Houses here (including rooms, pens, cribs)—as in *Light in August* and *Absalom*—take on lives of their own, what we might call "creative architecture." A house, which is supposed to be holy and sacred, a sanctuary, becomes a trap. It is an "imaginative space" which contains its own kind of energy and doom. Every Faulkner-enclosed space is as much metaphor and emblem as reality. Only the "big woods" offer an alternative.

tried to commit suicide by walking into the waters of the Gulf to the point where the shelf dropped off and she could not have made her way back. What precipitated this precise act, which we must judge as a serious suicide effort, we cannot tell. She did enter the marriage much shaken, having been drinking heavily and often uncontrollably, with her physical and emotional life a shambles and her dependence on Faulkner almost complete.

It is worth noting, once again, there had been quite a turnabout for this woman who had wanted to dance through the night with a succession of beaux. Her experiences in the Far East disabused her of her privileged sense of herself, and made her, in this new relationship, a woman without a center—coming to her former suitor with two children from a previous marriage and herself in physical and emotional disrepair. What occurred between her and the sharp-tongued, intensely private Faulkner now he had fulfilled his childhood destiny with the woman of his choice may have driven home to her the futility of her position, the impotence of her role.

We have to keep in mind she officially entered Faulkner's life as he embarked on the most intense creative effort of his life; as he entered, in fact, one of the most rewarding and intensive periods of imaginative work of any American novelist, past or present. She did not come into a life that was opening wide for her. It was, indeed, a life which was closing down to outside intrusions so as to allow itself the fullest possible internal play. Faulkner was a man gripped by the books he had to write, not by the life he had to live. Like Conrad from 1900 to 1910, Faulkner existed to write his books, and where could Estelle and her two children—and even their daughter, Jill—find a place? This realization may have struck her on the beach at Pascagoula as early as the honeymoon. Worn down as she was physically and psychologically, she could not have found much consolation in Faulkner's immersion in his "other" life, which for him superseded all else.

Most certainly, Estelle wanted this marriage to be a success, after the unhappy period with Cornell Franklin; but the reality was already clearly different. As her life moved toward its unhappy termination with Franklin, she had little sense of the overwhelming changes in Faulkner during these eleven years. Although she had returned to Oxford for several months at a time, Faulkner was often away—and his interests were already sliding away from her toward his work. By the time of *Father Abraham* and *Flags*, his career was beginning to extend before him.

But even if she had followed his career—and indications are she was interested—she could not have comprehended the enormous changes in personality and character that type of career brought. He was not simply any author, but was entering a period of his life when he became possessed by the need to express himself uniquely. He had apprenticed himself to every aspect of his craft before attempting these large, experimental works. He had been a poet, which Estelle and his other friends could understand; he had written essays, drawn cartoons, and even published a couple of accessible novels to establish his credentials. But as he pivoted on *Father Abraham* and *Flags*, he moved toward works which took over his inner life to the exclusion of everything else. Despite the considerable intelligence of both women, Estelle could have no idea what went into such a complex, intricately woven, innovative type of fiction as *Sound*; just as Zelda Fitzgerald could have had no idea what her husband was doing in *The Great Gatsby*.

Yet Estelle's position, while similar to Zelda's, contained different expectations. She wanted, in some way, a marriage which compensated for her previous failure, which united her with a memory or romantic idea of two very young people separated by a bad marriage made with her parents' blessings. The very expectation she brought to her second marriage would throw her into depression and frustration when fantasy failed to meet reality. Despite Faulkner's jaunty description of his honeymoon, in the above letter to Wasson, it must have been clear to both that the pre-1918 "romance" could not be retrieved—in fact, Faulkner had moved so far outside of their arrangement that he was a stranger entering into a union with someone he felt obligated to marry. If they still loved each other, their love must be viewed in such a context.

This moves us well ahead of the writing of *Sanctuary*, into Faulkner's further pre-publication revisions of *Sound*. In that same letter to Wasson, Faulkner makes some remarkable comments on *Sound*. His comments indicate his immersion in something so far distant from his honeymoon that Estelle must have picked up his removal from her and her interests. Wasson had altered Faulkner's original typescript in what amounted to major revisions, inasmuch as they would have altered meaning by altering tempos. In this interchange, which suggests Faulkner's anger, however tamped down by the circumstances of the letter, we see how insistent he was on *his* meaning, perhaps implicitly taking out some anger at Wasson's changes in *Flags*. Although Faulkner approved the changes, the idea of anyone tampering with his work, for whatever purpose, nearly always resulted in his feeling of being taken over.

In his effort to clarify an extremely difficult book, Wasson had removed Faulkner's italics from the Benjy segment—replacing italics with spaces to point up time shifts. His theory was the fallacious one that italics only differentiated between past and present, and failed to distinguish among several temporal shifts: he felt Faulkner's system was binary, when, in fact, it suggested multiplicity. Wasson's was an honest response to a manuscript which presented immediate difficulties and seemed at first unfinished, or else completely antagonistic to the reader. Faulkner immediately indicated he wanted the italics returned and the spaces closed up. He is quite clear the Benjy segment involves at least eight time shifts, including events which occur when he is three, five, fourteen, fifteen, eighteen, and thirty-three, plus his age when Quentin commits suicide and Mr. Compson dies. Wasson's spaces do not account for such multiple time changes, not even for the four he mentions.

Faulkner's reasoning, however, goes even more deeply into his aims. "But the main reason," he says, "is a break indicates an objective change in tempo, while the objective picture here should be a continuous whole, since the thought transference is subjective, i.e., in Ben's mind and not in the reader's eye. I think italics are necessary to establish for the reader Benjy's confusion, that unbroken-surfaced confusion of an idiot which is outwardly a dynamic and logical coherence."[6] Faulkner here is focusing on something well beyond *Sound:* his adherence to notions of time which, communicating an inner state, must be distinguished from external, clock, or calendar time. In this, he is following a European tradition, established with Bergson and continuing through Woolf, Joyce, and Proust; it has little to do with American traditions of time, especially those associated with the naturalistic-realistic novel. Faulkner suggests a kind of impressionism, with temporal dimensions here being the broad equivalent of the use of light in impressionist paintings: both methods as ways of shifting the focus from the object or the objective event to a subjective state of mind, to dynamics and away from things.

The argument was, accordingly, more than a question of Wasson's alterations, but involved a misreading of Faulkner's deepest intentions in this novel and in his mature fiction in general. Faulkner says spaces present "a most dull and poorly articulated picture to my eye." He suggests that rewriting the entire segment from the third person (objective) point of view might be a solution, but since Wasson has rejected that idea also, there is no other recourse except to leave it as is, with italics.

Faulkner then becomes acerbic as he repeats that all the italics must be restored, along with the original punctuation. "You'd better see to that, since you're all for coherence. And don't make any more additions to the script, bud. I know you mean well, but so do I." Remarks on the idyllic honeymoon follow, with still another paragraph on the changes Wasson made. The final paragraph circles back: "Your reason above disproves itself. I purposely used italics for both actual scenes and remembered scenes for the reason, not to indicate the different dates of happenings, but merely to permit the reader to anticipate a thought-transference, letting the recollection postulate its own date." We see from this remark Faulkner had moved closer to Proust's method than to Joyce's; for in that final statement—letting "the recollection postulate its own date"—we have Proustian memory, Proustian privileged moments, Proustian temporal fluidity, in which event and memory of it are indistinguishable. That Ben Wasson had not grasped this point in 1929, despite his intelligence as a reader, only indicates how far out in front Faulkner was in his fiction, and how removed his mind-set was from that of a man on a honeymoon.

As we move back and forth in Faulkner's mind between *Sanctuary* and the revisions of *Sound,* we cannot miss how exclusionary he was and was becoming. The demands of writing a "popular work" and getting right a work he felt nobody would read were the two extremes of his imagination; and there appeared to be little social center. His depreciation of *Sanctuary* as a book intended solely to make money was an effort, we can surmise, to disguise his own artistic guilt at having tried something less ambitious than *Sound*. Listen to the snobbish cynicism. "I took a little time out, and speculated what a person in Mississippi would believe to be current trends, chose what I thought was the right answer and invented the most horrific tale I could imagine and wrote it in about three weeks and sent it to Smith . . . who wrote me immediately, 'Good God, I can't publish this. We'd both be in jail.' "[7] Smith, of course, later published a revised *Sanctuary*. By depreciating *Sanctuary*, Faulkner could publicly exorcise a private demon: which was, that his every effort should be of the innovative, daring, adventurous kind indicated by *Sound*, that anything else was a sellout whose writing he could deal with only by open admission. But by throwing *Sanctuary* to the wolves in this manner, Faulkner led his readers on a false trail; for *in its way* it involves some radical changes in Faulkner's art and in the very nature of where American fiction might head. But in an intense, personal way, *Sound* and only *Sound* became his measure of his greatness. His later remarks on that novel indicate the delicacy of his feelings: ". . . the writing of it as it now stands taught me both how to write and how to read, and even more: It taught me what I had already read" —the Flauberts, Conrads, and Turgenevs he "had consumed whole" as much as ten years before. With those words, and the following, he shielded himself against whatever else he was doing, especially when it was for money. He continued in the same vein: ". . . that ecstasy, that eager and joyous faith and anticipation of surprise . . . will not return."[8]

When we observe Faulkner's defensiveness about *any* retreat from innovation and daring, then we can better understand his trashing of *Sanctuary*. Further, we can even find in this same introduction something of the frame of mind which went into *Sanctuary*. "But in the South art, to become visible at all, must become a ceremony, a spectacle; something between a gypsy encampment and a church bazaar given by a handful of alien mummers who must waste themselves in protest and active self-defense until there is nothing left with which to speak."[9] A "ceremony, a spectacle . . . a gypsy encampment"—how well these words of a circus atmosphere describe the road show of Popeye, Horace, and Temple Drake.

Many features of the original *Sanctuary* were later downplayed or altogether deleted in the published version of 1931. The considerable deletion of material limning the Horace-Narcissa relationship reverses Faulkner's insistence on the Quentin-Caddy linkage in *Sound*. In the ur-*Sanctuary*, we note a definite incestuous theme playing through Faulkner's imagination as he moved closer to marriage with Estelle. With the downplaying of that motif in the revision, the complementary theme of Temple and her entourage becomes more insistent. Gowan Stevens and Temple become more prominent, as doomed in their relationship as brother-sister connections. What all this means in biographical terms is nothing less than Faulkner's failure of nerve in his attitudes toward male-female associations, whatever shape they took. His effort to label that first version "base and cheap"—

in a Japanese interview in 1955—was one way of hiding real feeling about sexual matters behind commercial necessity. This dimension of Faulkner's emotional needs is worth examining, even repeating. In shifting the weight of *Sanctuary* from Horace and Narcissa, a quasi-incestuous affair, to Temple Drake and Gowan and then Temple and Popeye, Faulkner was traveling the byways of male-female relationships, far from the arena of adult or mature connections.

Even as Faulkner excised Horace from *Flags* in order to shape *Sartoris*, so he reintroduced Horace into the original *Sanctuary* as some sort of compensation.[10] The lawyer becomes the very centerpiece of infantile male-female linkage. The reversal of chapters 3 and 4 in the *Sanctuary* manuscript, while not conclusive, suggests Faulkner was seeking a way of relating the story through overlapping information about Horace. He has left his wife, the unacceptable Belle, just as Faulkner was preparing to embrace his own; and his emotional straying is that of a man directionless. Yet Faulkner was right to stress Horace in that early conception. He is, in many respects, something of a replay of Quentin Compson almost twenty-five years later (Horace is forty-three), unable to face life, immune to real change, jaded by his situation, and fading rapidly from mature human involvement. To Horace and Quentin, add Darl Bundren—three basket cases who are expressing something of consummate importance to Faulkner at this time.

Horace seems so antithetical to the author that we must wonder at the considerable weight placed on this aging, ineffectual, and uninteresting man. The fauns and passive Pierrot-figures of the early poems now come full circle in the energyless, fading Horace Benbow. It is insufficient to say Faulkner was seduced by Eliot's Prufrock or saw in Horace some kind of Frazerian dying god, however ironical the portrait. The personal need transcended the literary. Faulkner sought nothing less than a way of dealing with a self so involved with itself that it had little or nothing to give. Horace connects only to his sister, herself the twin of his narcissistic self, because she is part of himself. He has nothing else to give or offer.

With Quentin Compson, Faulkner had made his first serious effort to deal with self-involvement, although his earlier novels suggested some grappling with self. Quentin, however, begins that quest for the obverse of energy and success, the side associated with American failure. Through this period of his development, Faulkner evidently found in failure a somewhat deeper, personal meaning than he found in success: the latter became associated with Snopes and Sutpen types; but the former, the failures, were more introspective and even narcissistic. Faulkner did not exorcise the narcissistic demons from himself; he learned how, through technical means, to plumb the depths of those demons. Quentin leads from and into Horace, and the emphasis on the latter in a novel where he is really unnecessary indicates authorial need. Further, narcissistic involvement transcended to some degree by technical expertise is an essential ingredient of Faulkner's creative powers. He did not relieve himself of self-involvement; instead, he learned how to harness these negative energies and utilize or exploit them.

He seized upon failure as a means of structuring his sense of passivity and helplessness in the grip of circumstance. Horace repeatedly turns to circumstance as his means of explaining himself and his situation—he rarely looks within to find the coordinates of his passivity and failure.* Revisions of the novel undoubtedly permitted Faulkner to get "outside" of Horace; to break from his, the author's, obsession with the middle-aged lawyer's sense of failure. But revising did not mitigate failure; it simply allowed Faulkner to gain distance. In the original version, nearly everything is filtered through Horace's mind in a modified stream of consciousness. Here, we see the effect of that technique from parts 1 and 2 of *Sound*, distinctly a carryover in Faulkner's mastery of his material. What we learn of various situations comes mainly through Horace's memories of them, in bits and pieces. The plot unfolds largely through a series of flashbacks —initially from Horace's memory, then tunneling from Ruby's and Temple's tales, arriving achronologically and requiring the reader to make linear sense of them. In the revision such events become action or narrative, linear matter, without Horace's memory working on them. The original definitely carries us back into *Sound*, an internal novel; whereas the revision carries us outside, into an externalization.

Internal matters are rarely better illuminated than in a scene in chapter 12. Horace, on his way back from Oxford, where he has checked into Temple's whereabouts, meets State Senator Clarence Snopes on the train. The passage in question occurs completely within Horace's memory (free association without stream difficulties). Horace recalls Snopes as a "dull youth" ten years ago, son of a restaurant owner, part of a family large enough to have elected him without "recourse to a public polling."[11] From this, Horace wanders to the jail window, and the woman, unnamed, who is Ruby. "Tell me again about that girl," he says, as if Ruby were present. She then recalls to Horace what she has seen of Temple and a "He" going fast on the road. The "She" is Temple, but we do not know who the "He" is, whether Gowan, Popeye, or someone else. The paragraph is signature Faulkner, in that all references are pronominal—a flourish of "She," "He," "me," "Her," "I," "he," "she," and "it." It is a brilliant touch, since pro-

*He tells Ruby: " 'You see . . . I lack courage: that was left out of me. The machinery is here, but it won't run . . .' " (*Sanctuary* [the Original Text], ed. with an afterword and notes by Noel Polk [New York: Random House, 1981], p. 56). The critique Horace offers seems to be a commentary on another person. When Ruby asks why he left his wife, he responds: " 'Because she ate shrimp.' " He explains he had to pick up the box of shrimp at the train station, and carry it home while the frozen mess slowly melted. It was so heavy he frequently had to change hands, after each hundred steps. He has been turned into a servant carrying out a lowly, humiliating chore; but his perception of it is of something *happening to him*, not of something he did himself. " 'But I have done it for ten years. . . . All the way home it drips and drips, until after a while I follow myself to the station, stand aside and watch Horace Benbow take that box off the car and start home with it, changing hands every hundred steps, and I following him, thinking Here lies Horace Benbow in a fading series of small stinking spots on a Mississippi sidewalk.' " In his eyes, he is an object manipulated by external forms; he has lost center, acting out self-involvement without a self.

nouns give the text the right sense of abstraction: no people, only reference to them, and the abrupt shift itself, which further abstracts the encounter by locating it in memory. By removing the meeting of Horace and Ruby from actuality and relocating it in past time, Faulkner has given it a timeless quality, in the Bergson-Proust sense of mental time as fluid and infinite. Further, the containment of the scene in memory, brief though it is, reinforces the idea of a scrim placed over events: that we must perceive through another medium, since events are dreamlike or part of nightmare.

The presence of several such instances in *Sanctuary* indicates the degree of artistry in this "throwaway" novel, and negates Faulkner's avowal of it as the product of "three weeks" of work. Some of this is lost in the revision, so that the finished product seems glossier and more commercial than the original ever was. In turn, this affected the reputation of the novel, and the unquestioned acceptance for many years of Faulkner's designation of it as a potboiler. An examination of the original shows how indebted Faulkner was to his own developing technique, to revisions he was already making on *Sound,* and looks ahead to *As I Lay Dying.* His creative ability during this period was coming in bunches; not as isolated efforts, but as a rapid acceleration of his ability to manage his material in ways no American novelist had done before.

Other differences between original and revised versions illuminate Faulkner's thought processes at this time.* While the original is rougher in texture, because of more daring techniques, it was in actuality less violent than the revised book. In the first, Goodwin's lynching is intimated; in the final version, it is described. Part of the greater violence in the later version resulted from Faulkner's having transformed raw experience once trapped in memory into narrative and story line. Another factor is the greater social dimension of the revised book; this, too, is the consequence of the need to provide narrative line for earlier presentation of consciousness or sensibility. The first version is much more literary, more concerned with edging in, angling; whereas later, corruption and its ramifications become more apparent.

Further, as part of this earlier literary quality, the relationship of Horace and Ruby, bizarre as it is, recalls another "literary relationship," that between Axel Heyst and Lena in Conrad's *Victory,* a novel well known to Faulkner. In both instances figures of excessive civilization encounter women from other worlds: Lena and Ruby are women living on the edge,

---

*The most significant document in this comparison becomes the unrevised galleys of the novel in the Linton Massy Collection at the University of Virginia's Alderman Library. Also at the Alderman Library are a 138-page complete manuscript of the original version, and a bound carbon typescript of this same version. The University of Texas Humanities Research Center has still another set of the unrevised galleys Faulkner prepared for the printer. The text of the original *Sanctuary* is based on the original ribbon typescript (in Special Collections at the University of Mississippi), which was itself used as a printer's copy by Cape and Smith; it was these galleys Faulkner revised so carefully.

both having sold their bodies, and both caught in a life of roughness and brutality unknown to their respective admirers. Heyst and Lena are, eventually, isolated, and in a way so are Horace and Ruby—isolated by some attraction which develops beyond their obvious unsuitability for each other. In Conrad, the Heyst-Lena coupling determines the outcome of their respective fates, as well as the resolution of the novel. In Faulkner, Horace and Ruby remain just outside the main arena, their byplay only occasionally on center stage. Nevertheless, in both books are instances of Hamletic figures rising to the occasion when confronted with women from worlds beyond not only their comprehension but what even their fantasies could conjure up.

Another aspect of the shift from original to revision involves the displacement of Horace by Popeye—both of them sexually troubled, one simply passive, the other pathological. Common to both is impotence—permeating Horace's entire life except in his defense of Lee Goodwin; in Popeye's, connected to his rape of Temple with a corncob and his whinnying cry as he witnesses Red's intercourse with her. The two dimensions seem widely separated, but are in reality part of the same psychological fix: Faulkner's choice to avoid adult life/sex; to present, instead, regression to childish passivity or to perverted pleasure. With Popeye, we get a whiff of evil; with Horace, we sense waste, little more. They are extremes which meet, and they say something about Faulkner in 1929, pivoting as he was between self-indulgence and social responsibility.

A second pair of coordinates, Horace and Temple, is compelling for other reasons, but equally revealing of Faulkner's attitudes in this period. Both the middle-aged lawyer and the seventeen-year-old university student need extreme situations to move them: Horace must flirt with Ruby and roam in Lee Goodwin's world to relieve his lethargy. Without that, having left Belle, he will regress into his shell, without even his glassblowing to sustain him. Temple must walk the line; and we can understand her, it appears, only if we perceive that her very being demands danger. Sexually, she comes alive if the act is close to death—she uses Red sexually, indirectly causing his death, and then testifies against Goodwin in the killing of Tommy. All of this is sexually connected, inasmuch as she protects Popeye, the agent of her perverse sexual experience.

We may find it surprising that the middle-aged lawyer and the young university girl meet on such strange ground; yet for Horace, Ruby represents forbidden fruit, the Eve who finally does offer herself in payment. Horace refuses, putting his refusal on high moral grounds, that a man "might do something just because he knew it was right";[12] but his real reason for involvement has been fascination with the ex-hooker, masochistic, loyal Ruby. She represents the extreme from the women he has known. Similarly, Temple, with her judge father and respectable law-abiding family, breaks free; and while we find her reprehensible and even repellent,

Faulkner is getting at something: her need to tempt herself with forbidden games, given the dull nature of things.

Another potential sexual connection occurs between Horace and Little Belle, Belle's daughter by Harry Mitchell. This relationship, replayed in Horace's longing for her photograph, combines the pathology of Popeye, the extremism of Temple, and Horace's own ambiguous sexuality. Confronted by women he fears, or is unable to achieve satisfactory intercourse with, Horace finds Little Belle an Edenic version of perfect sexuality because she is unattainable. She is always the child, now ten years after her first appearance in *Flags*, appearing in a "small white dress . . . the delicate and urgent mammalian whisper of that curious small flesh in which was vatted delicately a seething sympathy of the blossoming grape."*[13] What Horace means is that, like Humbert Humbert, he hungers after his own Lolita. She becomes his "sweet, veiled enigma." Later, he ponders her photograph: ". . . the face appeared to breathe in his palms in a shallow bath of highlight, beneath the slow, smokelike tongues of invisible honey-suckle. Almost palpable enough to be seen, the scent filled the room and the small face seemed to swoon in a voluptuous languor, blurring still more, fading, leaving upon his eye a soft and fading aftermath of invitation and voluptuous promise and secret affirmation like a scent itself."[14]

Even more compelling, however, is Horace's association of Little Belle with Temple (also described as a child-woman). The "innocence" of the first is besmirched by the evil of the latter; but, even further, Horace wishes, somehow, to link in both the combined innocence and evil implicit in woman. His ambiguity about his desires, whether he wants daughter or mother Belle, whether he finds Temple's evil attractive, makes him vomit moments after he puts the photograph down. But even as he vomits, his vision is of Temple lying on the corn shucks in the crib, followed by an image of the bound and naked Temple roaring out of sight on a flatcar. The proliferation of images resolves the connection in Horace of the doubling, causing us to question the author's own sexual positioning of himself as he prepared to marry a divorced woman with a young daughter.

Confusion over pronouns in this particular passage reinforces sexual ambiguities. No one is named, and yet Faulkner moves confidently from "he" (Horace) with the photograph, presumably "she" or "her," into a sequence of female pronouns which are not Little Belle but Temple. Even as he vomits, "the shucks set up a terrific uproar beneath her thighs." The "her" grammatically should refer to Little Belle, but connects, instead, to Temple; so that through pronominal confusion, Faulkner achieves what would be montage in film.

This pairing of opposites who meet fits perfectly into another aspect of Faulkner's mind: his presentation of the *Sanctuary* world as an anti-Eden,

*This and other masturbatory fantasies for Horace are repeated, later, in Gavin Stevens's love-longing first for Eula Varner and then, openly, for her teenage daughter, Linda. More generally, Faulkner places young women in a scenario suitable for male masturbatory fantasies.

an antipastoral. As we have seen, Faulkner's use of the Edenic, pastoral myth is not simple. He never equated pastoral with perfection and antipastoral with pure evil, but he did seek a vision of pastoral as part of that myth of America he was limning. The golf course in *Sound,* carrying "caddie" back and forth, is intermixed with an idiot's sense of his sister, Caddy. The pastoral aspect of the golf course is, thus, intermixed with an innocent but deeply flawed element—so that "caddie" carries with it intimations not only of an Edenic existence but dimensions of abnormality. This is mainstream Faulkner, although as his reaction to the inroads of technology intensified, he did find in nature and the pastoral something innately aristocratic and redemptive.

The anti-Edenic images are the jail, coffin, Frenchman's Bend, corncob (as sexual instrument, not feed), and shucks. The latter two are particularly revealing, since corncobs and shucks are deeply connected to that pastoral ideal, agriculture as only one step removed from Eden. But Faulkner's use of such images is to demonstrate malevolence—we can never again think quite the same of a corncob after the bloodstained one is offered in evidence in Goodwin's trial; and shucks, which shift with Temple's weight in the crib or in Horace's nightmare of her experience, have been transformed into emblems of death. Similarly, the jail and coffin also dominate—in actuality and in dream; but, even further, as part of that enclosed geography characterizing the novel. We are made aware of contained places, and even in the greater expansiveness of Frenchman's Bend we experience enclosures—the house and crib, the doors opening and locking. Faulkner's purpose was to create suffocation, to close down on spatial and temporal arrangements in favor of containment. We enter an airless, weatherless world where anything is possible. Since he is presenting the nature of evil, he must foreclose all aspects of life which allow a breath, an escape, or alternatives. One advantage of the revised version is that from the beginning it reveals Horace's entrapment at the Old Frenchman's Place, when Popeye asks him if he wants to run, and he answers he doesn't. If he runs, he fears being shot; if he stays, he enters into some strange ritual.

Faulkner has caught this with his aslant prose, the sense of place which is not quite place, the sense of time which is not quite time. In his previous novel, he had done this with language and narrative strategies; here, he does it by containment. That airless, weatherless spot where bootleggers hang out and boil their brew is described as just the place where evil potions are conjured. *Sound* may have appropriated words from *Macbeth,*[15] but *Sanctuary is* Faulkner's *Macbeth.* While most of the people are men, they are closer to witches of nightmare; as one after another appears—the blind man, the crippled and the halt, the pathological, the wasted matter of society—they seem conjured from some witches' tale, some medieval morality play. And yet they represent Faulkner's sense of Southern evil, by implication evil everywhere. The idea was to create a place so antithetical to bourgeois morality and bourgeois behavior as to make it seem another country.

Yet that "other country" complements and reinforces the one accepted as respectable. Gowan Stevens, the man who learned to drink at the University of Virginia, needs whiskey from this crowd, and becomes intertwined in their fortunes; Horace is on his way to Jefferson when he stops by a spring for water, and gets caught up in the old Frenchman's household. Temple, with Gowan while he gets drunker, becomes encoiled in the house. It is like a web waiting for victims; one by one, they enter the circle of entrapment. Once within, they are fascinated by it, and in Temple's case indistinguishable from it.

There is little moral stability in either world. If we were to point to one nontechnical change Faulkner made in this period, beginning with *Sound*, it would be his recognition that moral extremes meet; which is another way of saying morality and immorality under test become indistinguishable. Faulkner did not persist in this attitude, nor did it ever harden into doctrine. *Light in August* demonstrates a break, and his Hollywood years sharpened his moral stance. But before that novel, in the period of his marriage, Faulkner found himself as creator of a moral vacuum. Not that he countenanced immorality, but he found respectability—Horace, Clarence Snopes (the state senator), Temple, the Drakes, Gowan—ready and willing to accommodate corruption, stink, or evil itself. Horace fights against it, but is drawn to it through Ruby. He is led as before by a woman, whatever his stated intentions; and this for Faulkner is a kind of moral suicide.

Here death is the handmaiden of an immoral society, and there can be no escape. Nearly every character either meets death or faces a deathlike situation. Even Narcissa is in a death-cycle: having married Bayard Sartoris ten years before, she courted death through his sense of doom. Horace is confronted by the death of his marriage to Belle, and the dingdong of his attachment to Little Belle. Temple Drake courts death in her desire for experience which will, somehow, distance her from her judge father and lawyer brothers. Having lost her mother when young, she has had no female role model, and her male relatives have only reinforced her bid to blot out her former existence. If she were more sympathetic, we could elaborate on Faulkner's sense of what it was like for a girl to grow up in a family of strong, purposeful men. Ruby seeks death in her loyalty to Goodwin, who repays her with a brutal form of loyalty, a life in crime, on the edge of doom.

Popeye is, of course, Mr. Death himself. That Faulkner needed the epilogue in which Popeye is hanged for a murder he did not commit, while free of the two he did commit, indicates how he wanted to pull Popeye into death situations wherever he went, whatever he did. He follows death, and it follows him. The crowd around Popeye eventually dies—Tommy, shot by Popeye, also Red, similarly shot, and Lee Goodwin, who is lynched (in the revised version) for a killing and rape he did not commit. If we move above the violence to the structuring of the novel, we sense how Faulkner has created a puppetmaster named Death, an avatar of Bergman's *The Seventh Seal.* There is almost a mechanical movement toward doom, as if people were playing roles they could not resist.

This sense they are acting out roles is connected to their emptiness. The hollowed-out include the so-called respectable as well as contemptible people. Temple parallels Popeye in this respect: neither is approachable through normal means; each has gone beyond the point of return. There is no inside to Temple. As an empty vessel, a negative place of worship, she is lacking, missing faith and morality. If we attempt to justify her lies about Goodwin's complicity as a way of protecting her father and brothers, we must recognize she has put herself beyond such family feeling. She is a temple without altar, a body without soul.

Only when we view it this way does the title become clarified. If we see it as emblematic of the woman's virginity—her "inner sanctuary" protected against violence and rape—then we observe the inner temple violated. As in Greek tragedy, this uncovers a multitude of connected crimes and retributions. Once this begins, there is no stopping it, for the Furies delight in raging and ripping. Another related sense of sanctuary is to see, as a result of the virgin's rape, a violation of all value systems. The very "inner being" of things is violated, pierced, traduced, and trespassed upon. The meeting of the vaginal wall with the corncob, furthermore, is the confrontation of what is human with an ungiving object: a situation spelling doom. If we accept Temple as setting off a chain of events which become uncontrollable, leading only to death, then we can add that her relationship with Popeye has something of the Oedipal in it. If he becomes her father violating her—with Faulkner pursuing a crooked path from Greek tragedy*—then we can make some sense of her response. Her own father, Judge Drake, has remained outside her needs, as male power broker, keyed into his sons and success. In a kind of inversion of the Freudian family romance, she has repudiated her high birth and sought out a lower, more satisfactory one; and Popeye becomes the father-lover replacement, with a vengeance. In this respect, he satisfies her desires for revenge on a family and background which, evidently, provided little sustenance, or failed to perceive who and what she was growing into. Only in Popeye's hands, or under Red's body, does she find her center—however perversely, they fill her emptiness; and once more we are returned to the idea of a sanctuary which serves none of its moral functions.

A scene of disturbing ramifications occurs when Temple tries to seduce Popeye and interchanges him with "Daddy." Popeye cradles a pistol in his right armpit holster and Temple begs for it. " 'Give it to me,' she whispered, 'Daddy, Daddy.' " She leans her thigh against his shoulder, caressing his arm with her flank. " 'Give it to me, Daddy,' she whispered.

---

*André Malraux, on other grounds, interpreted the book as demonstrating the intrusion of Greek tragedy into the detective story.

Suddenly her hand began to steal down his body in a swift, covert movement; then it snapped away in a movement of revulsion. 'I forgot,' she whispered; 'I didn't mean . . . I didn't . . .' "[16] Faulkner is picking into corners Freud had made popular: the gun as phallic, the confusion of brutal man with father, the desire to be violated in some kind of perverse desire to get closer to the father figure.

Faulkner repeats this scene exactly in the revised book, a scene of particular daring for the time, since the sexuality is not disguised or muffled in ambiguities. It suggests that Temple, brought up in a household of males, lacking a mother figure, has not straightened out her sexual priorities when young and, therefore, focuses on the dominating male, whether lover or not, whether suitable or not, as a father figure. The drunken Stevens cannot fill the bill, inasmuch as his alcoholism disallows masculine domination. In the face of such weakness, Temple invites violation as the sole way she can relate to her father, either to seduce him or else to create a circumstance in which he must pay attention to her. She, of course, achieves her goal; for Judge Drake will dramatically enter the courtroom after her false testimony to take her away and spend time with her in the Luxembourg Gardens.

With Popeye as father figure, she obeys his commands, defers to his perverse wishes, enjoys her thralldom. As her father's slave, the greater the perversity the greater his hold on her; she now has a role. We are dealing here with situations where all value systems are reversed. Instead of the routine paternal figure, we have the malevolent male taking over the father role; and instead of the demure daughter, we have an agent, literally, of destruction: get in her way and she will see to your demise. A curious touch is Temple's ability, with her name suggesting a sanctuary, to become an agent of death. The avenging father passes on his hatred and rage to the daughter, who carries it out; at the same time, he can violate as he wishes and in ways which please him. All this can occur because Temple intends to trample her respectable name and background. Strikingly, Faulkner has supplied her with four brothers—the Falkner four, one more than Caddy in the Compson household.

Through use of Horace's memory, Faulkner could forsake linear narrative and proceed on the principle of a reciprocating engine, with jumps back and forth at about twenty-five-page intervals. In the early parts, these are often characterized by the recurring expression, " 'You see, I've just left my wife.' " This phrase, so pointedly repeated by Horace, counterpoints Temple's insistence that " 'Something terrible is about to happen.' " Horace's words suggest that he is, finally, a man, his attempt to define himself after years of slavishness; also, a plaint that he is a man who is now alone, open to new experiences.

Movement back and forth in the original provides a roughness which blends with content. It is like matte, or a rough surface, which modern painters often insisted upon—the very type of art Faulkner would have noted in his 1925 trip to France. This roughness was smoothed out in the revision, and inevitably the question arises why Faulkner produced such a rough book as the original *Sanctuary.* We can understand his need to revise, so as to find a publisher; but what is difficult to comprehend is why he moved to such sensational material—unless we take his 1931 preface to *Sanctuary* literally—that he wrote it to make money. Yet even if we do, the same question arises of why this material, this perverse sexuality; after all, to make money one presented a more palatable sexuality. Popeye is not exactly "well hung," nor is Temple described in ways to make her appetizing. Corncobs are not privileged sexual tools.

Perhaps there is some biographical runoff, in the description of Temple. Repeatedly, in both original and revision, Faulkner writes of her as a child-woman, "a small childish figure, no longer quite a child, not yet quite a woman."[17] She is slat-thin, hipless, straight up and down, with long legs. Her childish quality permits Horace to identify her with Little Belle: to blend them together as objects of his own desires. This emphasis on Temple's thinness, the frailty of her figure, the fact it has not developed into womanhood cannot but remind us of Estelle Franklin. Even in her early thirties, after two children, she was wraith-thin, almost anorexic in appearance; not least with that thin, wasted quality which comes with physical deterioration, as if during or right after a serious illness. Estelle is, of course, not Temple, but the curious attraction and repulsion the young woman elicits in both author and reader appears to have a personal foundation.

We have a further, telling point beyond physical description: Estelle's energies as a young woman were all mobilized toward social activity. She was, if the description fits anyone, a social butterfly—becoming alive, all witnesses tell us, at gatherings, parties, and dances in particular. She lived for dressing up, cosmetics, mingling with people, at times trying to outrage them with unpredictable behavior. Part of her attraction for the young Faulkner, we can assume, was her "off-the-wall" qualities, which fitted in with his own sense of marginal behavior. He sensed in her a rebel of sorts, a rebel, however, within the structure and framework of what her society demanded of her. While Estelle Oldham moved to the extremes of what was permissible, she made the marriage expected of her. But she fought against the Oldham traces—those self-righteous, Republican, seemingly upstanding people—and she would go rather far, in drinking, sexual activity, general behavior that needed toning down. Further, Faulkner makes a good deal of Temple's father as a judge, and Lem Oldham, also, was a judge.

There is an even more engaging dimension. In juxtaposing Ruby Lamar with Temple, Faulkner has, as suggested before, implied something insidious about female behavior. In every way, Ruby, the ex-hooker, is presented as superior: in her loyalty and steadfast nature, her attention to her child, her realism about the role she must play, her acceptance of who and what she is. Ruby is everything Temple is not, all to the younger woman's disadvantage. The sharp contrast moves the reader to more than a condemnation of Temple's flightiness and hauteur. It forces us to reconsider Faulkner's values, since for us, also, Ruby is a far more attractive human being—yet, at the same time, she is caught in the slough of despondency, tied to a brute, lacking the simplest amenities, a slave for a household of subhuman men, without aspirations or hope for herself or her son. All she still has is some raw attractiveness which she poignantly offers to Horace as a payoff.

And yet she has something, in Faulkner's presentation of her, which goes beyond the masochistic, debasing role she has decided to play. In her loyalty to Lee Goodwin, she transcends her debasement, something which enables her to haul water (one mile, six times a day), cook for men who come and go, suspect Goodwin of disloyalty, and "jazz" when necessary to pay for legal fees. Once her act is cleaned up, she becomes Lena Grove in *Light in August*: that embodiment of a female principle which transcends the circumstances of her life. This was essential for Faulkner—to plumb the depths of the female so as to get behind the surface of her social presentation of herself, to the very needs, he felt, of the woman. In offering Ruby as an alternative to Temple Drake, Faulkner revealed how much he hated the type Estelle Franklin represented on the eve of their marriage.*

In the original version, the last lines describe Popeye's final moment as the trap is sprung. These lines appear italicized, for emphasis, and they are particularly ironic. Popeye is, as we know, hanged for a murder he did not commit, while someone else is implicated in the one he did; and, further, he is concerned about his hair even as the sheriff releases the trap. In the revision, the end is all Temple's. The two paragraphs about her in the Luxembourg Gardens end the book, on a deeply ironic note. After her testimony which dooms Goodwin to what will be a lynching, she sits bored with her father in the loveliness of the Parisian garden. In the original version, these two paragraphs appear, but *before* the final two lines on Popeye. The question is why Faulkner reversed the order, giving Temple final say in the revision, and Popeye final say, as it were, in the original.

Aside from narrative smoothness in the revision, the reversal of order of these materials gives the book back to Temple and takes it away from Popeye. This is done subtly, and it suggests Faulkner was already looking ahead to doing something further with Temple; whereas Popeye was fin-

---

*Other physical aspects of Temple indicate Faulkner's extreme distaste: repeated descriptions of her mouth "painted into a savage and perfect bow," and the "two spots of rouge" on her cheeks. Here the two spots of rouge are "like paper discs pasted on her cheek bones," and the bow mouth is "like something both symbolical and cryptic cut carefully from purple pear and pasted there" (*Sanctuary* [the Original Text], ed. with an afterword and notes by Noel Polk [New York: Random House, 1981], p. 275). The descriptions here and elsewhere are toward the inhuman, toward a magic rite where femaleness becomes completely artificial and even mechanical, or else clownish, like those harlequins Faulkner drew and wrote about early in his career. Whatever the precise nature of the analogies, she is dehumanized, her womanness decentered.

ished and hanged. The original has a deeper ironic bite to it, inasmuch as Popeye and Temple are presented in alternating segments: Popeye moving toward execution, then Temple in the Gardens, and, finally, Popeye hanged. Since Faulkner was insisting on this kind of irony, the original gives him more of what he wanted. The revised book is indeed smoother, but also dissipates irony. Faulkner was overreaching himself in making his final statement about Temple, bored amidst Parisian splendor, and perhaps even in tidying up Popeye's career with that twist of his dying for what he hasn't done. Both of these scenes are displacements of the real movement of the book; sideshows, as it were. They provide a *frisson* of cynicism, but at the expense of deeper commitment to the material.

In such scenes Faulkner is faltering, perhaps, or miscalculating. Certainly *Sound* and *As I Lay Dying*, which surround *Sanctuary* like bookends, do not contain miscalculations, nor do they indicate faltering. They are organic inventions. Critical opinion has swung around on *Sanctuary*, from taking it at Faulkner's dim evaluation in his 1932 introduction to the Modern Library edition to seeing it as fitting in the august company of the books surrounding it. Yet even as we agree he was moving on to new ground, we must cite areas which create soft spots in the book. We note those passages cited above with their reaching toward obvious ironies; the scene with Fonzo and Virgil Snopes, finding themselves, two country bumpkins, in a brothel—a tired story even by the time Faulkner got to it; some scenes in Miss Reba's brothel—the emphasis on dogs, Mr. Binford, on her meeting with her genteel friends, and, finally, the exchange of letters, in the original version, between Horace and Narcissa, preceding the final chapter on Popeye.

The letters, in particular, are difficult to justify literarily or aesthetically. They simply seem a miscalculation, as though Faulkner had tired of trying to cast the final material in more suitable form and took this old-fashioned way out. The novel sputters. Perhaps he wanted some ironic effect, to contrast the exchange of letters between the "bourgeois" elements with passages on Popeye and his execution. But little of it works on any level either of irony, contrast, or social statement. Possibly one reason the letters fail artistically is that the movement back to Horace's missive (chapter 25) returns us to material we have put behind us. Horace writes of his return home in Kingston to Belle and of Little Belle's polite indifference to him on the telephone. Given the nature of the excesses which have recently occurred and their consequences, Horace's problems vis-à-vis his young stepdaughter are trivialized. His words come as a plaint from a weak, uninteresting man; the book's energies lie elsewhere. Even the dramatic final segment on Popeye—much punchier and more pointed in the original—flattens rather than leavens the novel.

Sanctuary falls into several literary genres, and, in fact, subsumes several modes Faulkner would explore throughout his career. Primarily, it slices into the detective-novel genre and adds to that the gangster theme, which would become so popular in both fiction and film. In the detective mode, which is less emphatic here than it would be in *Intruder in the Dust* and, even, *A Fable*, we have what has become familiar, the courtroom scene, in which there is some desultory effort to discover the killer. But this is not the strength of the novel, inasmuch as Goodwin's defender, Horace Benbow, is not a strong lawyer, and he relies on Temple's telling the truth without determining if she will, or is even capable of it. The gangster dimension is more apparent. Popeye Pumphrey was the model, not quite a gangster as much as a punk and hood, not a killer but a burglar and robber, and, of course, bootlegger.

Faulkner, clearly, changed nearly every aspect of the model's life to fit his own Popeye, who becomes the embodiment of crawling, sleazy evil. The original Popeye was possibly homosexual, whereas Faulkner's version has so perverted the sexual experience he fits no category. Further, Faulkner's Popeye, whatever the original, has no redeeming qualities; and even the effort to give him some "body" in the final chapter does not create either sympathy or understanding. Popeye has been created as too mechanical, as too unfeeling; there is no give, no entrance into humanity. He exists as less than Flannery O'Connor's Misfit or Camus's Meursault, someone so far outside normal society as to become unreachable, or the ultimate terrorist. He is both triumph and incomplete—the kind of person Faulkner wanted to create, but also someone who remains beyond what we can encompass. He is programmed for evil. When we come to Joe Christmas, another man programmed for evil, we can see how Faulkner has progressed, since Joe's background and struggle for identity make him human, even though he becomes a grisly killer.

How much of this Faulkner observed when he was hanging around Reno DeVaux we cannot tell, although his friend went through all the twists and turns associated with private clubs which sold bootlegged liquor and ran girls on the side. Another factor is Memphis itself, notorious for its criminal activity, for its reputation as a tough but "fun" place, for its burglaries and murders, and for its police and politicians with their hands in the till. Miss Reba often mentions how she takes care of the police while she caters to judges and other high officials in Memphis city government. Prohibition, of course, added another dimension of illegality, making the importation of whiskey in a large, fun-oriented city a hugely lucrative business. As such, it attracted the dregs of society—the way drugs would later do for coastal cities like Miami or smuggling for the border cities and towns in Texas. Memphis became known as the "Murder Capital of the U.S.A.," although it is doubtful if it could compete with Chicago in this respect. In Chicago, deaths were spread out from the murder of innocent people to criminals killing other criminals, especially when Alfonso Capone took over from the Torrio gang. The federal government estimated that Capone had taken in over one hundred million dollars in the year 1927, a great year, as well, for Babe Ruth, Charles Lindbergh, Gene Tunney, and Bobby Jones. Memphis had no one of that originality, and most of the killings were of the seedy rather than flashy, gang-war variety. All Faulkner had to do was to keep his ear to the ground in Oxford, or occasionally read a Memphis newspaper, to pick up the vicious side of "fun city." It is also possible the Capone gang reached down into Memphis itself, since such lucrative pickings could not be ignored by a man who vied with J. P. Morgan and John D. Rockefeller as the richest man in America.

Blotner relates a series of crimes committed in Faulkner's own Lafayette County, although most of them—shootings, killing of children, axe murders—are marginal to *Sanctuary* and its particular world of evil. But the listing of such crimes, most of them sudden and violent, brings to mind Michael Lesey's *Wisconsin Death Trip:* not the tranquil small-town atmosphere a chamber of commerce stresses, but small-town violence where alcoholism and long-smoldering rage lead to terrible crimes against innocent adults, children, and even farm animals. Madness, drunkenness, perversions of every type characterize these isolated towns and villages, as Lesey reveals in his showpiece Wisconsin town—one of those small, dairy-farm places presented as idyllic, a wonderful spot to raise children in. Faulkner, however, was not interested in simple killing or even lesser crimes. He departs from the classic, detective-gangster mold by emphasizing social backgrounds, casting his novel deeply within his still-new Yoknapatawpha County and making the matrix of that society his focus.

The *Sanctuary* manuscript at the University of Virginia reveals Faulkner did not quite know how to enter into this novel—but that whatever method he used, it would be indirect and have dimensions of the mystery genre. He first tried out the idea of having Judge Drake enter the courtroom to gather up Temple. This method would have shifted the novel into indirect narration requiring immense flashbacks. It would have removed the story line from Horace's memory into authorially inspired flashback and changed the nature of consciousness in the novel overall. The second attempt at a beginning has Temple running to get into a car driven by an escort. How this would have worked is difficult to determine, for if Faulkner had begun with Temple, he would, once again, have needed considerable authorial flashback to locate her in the narrative where consciousness could take over; or else, he would have forsaken consciousness (memory) altogether. The two abandoned starts suggest more of a detective-mystery methodology than Faulkner eventually used, more of a winding narrative.

In the version he decided on (in the original of the novel), he used, as we have noted, the prison image, of a doomed black prisoner. This image is of an enclosure which will dominate the novel, moving from Temple's enclosures in a corncrib to another kind of crib in the Memphis brothel. The abandoned other two starts, each little more than a dozen or so lines, would not have been disastrous, although we cannot foretell consequences. However, both indicate Faulkner was dissatisfied with a straightforward beginning; that whatever method he chose, he would carry over from

Sound his sense of a diminishing story line in favor of inner consciousness and memory.

If we compare this novel once again with *Light in August*, begun only six months after the revised *Sanctuary* was published, we note how Popeye has been transformed into Joe Christmas; only here, the qualities missing earlier which allow for understanding and perception are present from the beginning. In the later novel Faulkner in a kind of bildungsroman incorporates Joe's childhood and development into his character—not leaving it for the odds and ends of a conclusion. Even the sexual perversity—Joe's hatred of women, of sex, and especially of mothers—is given extended explanation; so his responses are fitted into contexts missing for Popeye and also for Temple Drake.

Working on *Sanctuary* and waiting for word from Harcourt on *Sound,* Faulkner found himself responding to reviews of *Sartoris.* That book had appeared on the last day of January 1929. The exact sequence was: publication of the book, writing *Sanctuary*, rejection of *The Sound and the Fury*, contracting for the book with Smith—intermixed with Estelle's divorce, his own forthcoming marriage, and the writing and submission of numerous short stories. Writing to Harcourt, Brace, Faulkner indicated a desire to see reviews, pointing out he lives "in a complete dearth of print save in its most innocent form."[18] He mentions that the local pharmacy owned by Mac Reed (the Gathright-Reed Drug Company, which is still operating in Oxford) handles *Sartoris*, but only out of friendship for Faulkner. Everything else, he says, is a drug here. This letter, moreover, belies the idea Faulkner was completely indifferent to his reviews—we also see indications of his interest with *Soldiers' Pay* and *Mosquitoes.*

Faulkner assumed indifference so as to make him seem superior to reviewers and reviews, part of the mass media apparatus he detested in every form. He perceived reviewers as parasites, since few of them did little more than review, and thus became "gods" of criticism who could not be criticized in turn. But it wasn't only reviewers to whom Faulkner felt superior; he detested radio, he rarely went to motion pictures, and he closed out nearly everything except local newspapers. He may have railed against the isolation of Oxford, but he gloried in its separation from and rejection of the buzzing, humming America he associated with a Northeast culture.

The reviews were not promising.* They stressed the looseness and lack of command in the novel—even after *Sartoris* had become a tighter version of *Flags.* Donald Davidson, one of those who would help put together *I'll Take My Stand* in 1930, found Faulkner a stylist, but lacking a suitable theme

---

*The anonymous reviewer for the *New York Times* noted the dedication to Anderson ". . . with the belief that this book will give him no reason to regret the fact," but called the novel a work of "uneven texture, confused sentiment, and loose articulation" (O. B. Emerson, *Faulkner's Early Literary Reputation in America* [Ann Arbor, Mich.: UMI Research Press]). The *Bookman* critic called Faulkner immature.

or character. Davidson's point is shrewd and yet still not on the mark. Clash of class and caste, sense of defeat, the collapse of all wars into one give order and organization to the novel. More telling in Davidson's review, however, is his remark that Faulkner's style is perhaps excessive for the story conveyed. He needed more, and this "more" is precisely what he was providing in *Sound* and *Sanctuary*.

Contracts for *Sanctuary* were signed in May—as yet it was called "A Novel"—and Faulkner received the obligatory $200 and the same royalty-rate. He had not advanced, and he soon recognized his short stories could earn him far more than novels, even while he wanted to define himself with longer fiction. The date he placed on the typescript was 25 May 1929. After mailing the ribbon copy to Hal Smith, he gave Estelle the carbon to read, once their marriage plans were fixed. She is reported to have said it was horrible, and he is reported to have responded it was meant to be horrible, but it would sell. This is Estelle's memory of the event more than thirty-five years later, and it seems too pat, too fixed into the pattern *Sanctuary* had established for itself by 1965, when she had the interview with Joseph Blotner. The book, by then, was considered pornographic, Southern Gothic, perverse. In any event, when people in Hal Smith's office read the typescript, they agreed that in its present form it was unpublishable; but there is no direct evidence Smith had read it when he told Faulkner: " Good God, I can't publish this."[19] Smith's response may have been based on his readers' reports, which included those of Lenore Marshall, Louise Bonino, and Evelyn Harter. Smith would, as noted above, publish a revised manuscript, on February 9, 1931.

Faulkner's reception of the news was, of course, one of disappointment. But it went beyond that, into the very nature of his imagination and his efforts as a writer to express a complex vision of man and society. After having attempted what he considered to be his complex vision of man in *Sound*, he had tried to simplify, without selling himself to the marketplace, despite his comments to the contrary. *Sanctuary* was, nevertheless, concessionary, and it, too, had failed—at the very period in his life when he needed not only money but some stability. With added responsibilities looming, he was apparently little better off now, in mid-1929, than he had been a decade before when he had offered himself to the Oldhams as Estelle's husband.

While the Oldhams continued to disapprove of his marriage, Faulkner's future sister-in-law, Dot, urged it. In time this pressuring led to bad feeling between Faulkner and Dot, and, most of all, between the Falkner family and the Oldhams. Just below the surface, feelings seethed, a low-level feud. Maud had never forgiven the Oldhams for their condescending treatment of her eldest son, and the Oldhams themselves with their Bourbon posturing and class-consciousness were not exactly beloved in Oxford. Not that Faulkner himself was unaware of the potential abyss in this marriage. In a letter to Harrison Smith requesting $500 for marriage,* he let go. "Both want to and have to. THIS PART IS CON-FIDENTIAL, UTTERLY. For my honor and sanctity—I believe life—of a woman. This is not bunk; neither am I being sucked in. We grew up together and I don't think she could fool me in this way; that is, make me believe that her mental condition, her nerves, are this far gone."[20] Faulkner indicates he could no more be fooled than if she were pregnant. "Neither is it a matter of a promise on my part; we have known one another long enough to pay no attention to our promises. It's a situation which I engendered and permitted to ripen which has become unbearable, and I am tired of running from devilment."

Only after Faulkner and Estelle had decided to marry—Faulkner obtained a marriage license on June 24—did he, perfunctorily, ask for permission and once again was given the back of Lem Oldham's hand. At the time Oldham repeated his original objections the couple was already dressed for the wedding, which took place on that day just outside Oxford proper, in the old Presbyterian church of College Hill. Because of her divorce, Estelle had been refused a service at her own Episcopal church, and so they settled on the Reverend Winn David Hedleston, D.D., who taught at the university. The College Hill Presbyterian church was, and is, a distinct building, with its Corinthian columns, its slave gallery in the back, its main-floor area containing private entrances to each aisle of pews. Although it was a traditional wedding, neither family was pleased with it. Faulkner had to borrow money for the honeymoon (in Pascagoula, where he had pursued Helen Baird); Estelle was in a state of deterioration, neither mentally nor physically well; there were the two children from her previous marriage; and, most important perhaps, the bridegroom was so caught up by a boiling imagination that all else was secondary to his need to put words on paper.

That last development, as we observed above, from the beginning puts its mark on the marriage. Faulkner would convey to Estelle on their honeymoon that his writing came first; whatever was left included her. His immersion in his work, in his creative ideas, and in himself was complete. Perceiving he had a gift no one else in America had, he had to protect it with any means at his disposal. Witnesses in the Faulkner household indicate he had a sharp, wounding tongue, a manner which cut and pierced. Since he could be a considerate man, such a wounding manner—which he displayed to both Estelle and their daughter—seems a shield or defensive gesture to protect himself. Remaining loyal to the dictates of his inner voice, he allowed little to pierce it and he became entrenched in his own needs. Yet Estelle had her own expectations. Even as they spent their wedding night in Aberdeen before heading for Pascagoula, they were pursuing different dictates, pulling against each other. While they honeymooned in a most casual place—Faulkner had rented a house on the beach

*Apparently, Smith did not come through, and it is possible Sallie Murry's husband lent Faulkner money for the honeymoon.

from Frank Lewis, a friend—Estelle insisted on dressing as if she were the lady of the manor. There is an almost incipient madness in her obsession with looking grand—Madwoman of Chaillot velvets and other fine materials in a beach house—and this may well have been her way of insisting on her own identity, no matter how ludicrous she appeared. All this is of great weight in trying to understand her suicide attempt on the honeymoon, because if we see her struggling to assert herself, we can recognize the pressures on her not to be "lost." There is, also, the fact she was a person so conditioned to grandeur she had to carry it through whatever the circumstances. We must not forget she was in poor condition, and heavy drinking on the honeymoon only exacerbated her physical decline.

Faulkner had *Sound* in his head, further revising proofs for an October 7 publication by Cape and Smith. On his honeymoon he was revising a book whose theme is nothing less than cosmic dislocation, and insisting in a letter to Ben Wasson on his way of handling time sequences through italicized passages which represented "thought-transference," not different dates of happenings. Yet this is also the letter which contains brief comments about what a pleasant time he and Estelle were having on the beach at Pascagoula.

Her suicide attempt, about which we have already speculated, seems something out of *Sound*; as if she, and not Faulkner, were revising the book and identifying with Quentin's death by water. There is an eerie quality to this particular juxtaposition. For even as Quentin recoils from his sister Caddy's affairs and marriage, and finding himself alone, seeks the only way out for him, so Estelle appears to have found herself in a circumstance from which there was no recoil. Unless we see her suicide attempt as an acute response to an argument or flare-up, we must view her act as part of a much broader scenario. We must, as we have already done in part, focus on her expectations and match those against the results.

According to available evidence, Estelle walked from the beach into the water dressed in one of her outlandish outfits after she had been drinking heavily. Both she and Faulkner were drunk or close to drunk every night, although such activities did not seem to interfere with his writing. Curiously, she walked down the beach in her finery. Was it a fully conscious decision, or an aberration? A moment of alcoholic depression? How much did her physical decline contribute to her state of mind? Was the depression the result of drinking and taking drugs, or was she in a cycle of depression and need which only suicide could end? Was she simply dead drunk and seeking attention? The evidence comes from a neighbor, Mrs. Martin Shepherd, who heard Faulkner call out to her husband that Estelle was "going to drown herself."[21] Shepherd pulled her out before she stepped into deep water.

Faulkner spent time with her, as his letter to Wasson indicates, but he was abstracted. Manuscript alterations indicate how many times he had faltered and on how many occasions he returned to certain material to shift and adjust it. The same thing occurred in proofs: they had to be put right while his life (and wife) waited.* Faulkner had the ability to hold himself in suspended animation, to close out the world, when he felt the pressure of a particular work. Those often terrible silences were forms of creativity; he kept himself for himself even in social situations which called for giving.

It was this shell her husband had created around himself which Estelle encountered on the honeymoon—not the callow young man who read and wrote poetry a decade earlier, or even the man who courted her with presentation copies of his work. Faulkner had honored a commitment which he kept until his death; but hers was not a "happy fall" into a suitable marriage for someone in poor shape. It was a situation which she could ease only by heavy drinking and drug-taking. Apparently even death seemed better.

Another aspect of the honeymoon was that Faulkner remained busy. Not only was his mind elsewhere, but his time was elsewhere as well. Yet there were activities together, and even some group festivities when friends showed up—Tom Kell, for example, from a much earlier time. In an interview with Blotner, Kell, in fact, repeated something Faulkner reputedly said to him: " 'Tom, they don't think we're gonna stick, but it is gonna stick.' "22 Like most such remembrances, this one came thirty-six years after the event, and we must take it as having been sifted through a lot of other mental debris. On one hand, it rings true—Faulkner recognizing the delicacy of the relationship; on the other, it seems doubtful he would be so confessional, even to an old friend. A third possibility is that, like Estelle, he felt desperate and had to say something to someone to

*One reason Faulkner referred to his novel as a "magnificent failure" was that it underwent such drastic revisions he was never certain he had gotten it right. He was a compulsive tidier and rearranger. A real problem was where and how to set in episodes which do not directly affect the fate of the Compsons or the thrust of the novel. For example: Uncle Maury (after whom Benjy is first named) and Mrs. Patterson, a married neighbor, carry on a disagreeable affair—where was Faulkner to place it, since its location is somewhat arbitrary, ending in 1908, just two years before Quentin's suicide? Another problem came with Faulkner's hesitation about *Father Abraham* material. There are illusions to "Spotted Horses" which are not carried through.

Some of these placement problems became acute in the Quentin section, as the manuscript numbering of this section demonstrates. Of particular difficulty was the Dalton Ames material—Ames is the bounder with whom Caddy has an affair in the summer of 1909. The material is thematically important because it communicates to Quentin the futility of his attachment to his sister, and the promiscuity he can expect from her is now established. All the female qualities he had heaped upon her in his fantasies are now to be denied when she gives herself to a man who cannot appreciate her. The Ames story is pushed back into the novel, into a flashback or memory journey Quentin takes when unconscious. It appears as if in a dream, in a flow, as though temporal considerations were stilled. Inner and outer become molded to the same temporal frame in some intermediate area between conscious and unconscious, in that undefined area where interior monologue is often located.

Faulkner was moving so drastically into internalization that no one, without the thread Ariadne supplied Theseus, could follow or emerge. Very possibly, as some critics have commented, he gave up the internal method of narration in this section for the more direct methods of parts 3 and 4 because he became lost in the entanglements of his own creation. Even the method of Quentin's suicide seems incidental, for references to his use of flatirons come in marginal notations and not as central images.

relieve himself, if only temporarily. In a real boost to his morale, he received a splendid prepublication review of *Sound* from the novelist Evelyn Scott. Scott was a writer of prodigious talent who by her mid-thirties seemed on the verge of a major career; but subsequently she faltered, and her later life became sad. But at this time she provided Faulkner, by way of Ben Wasson, with a sympathetic, understanding, and percipient reading of this difficult novel; and considering it was 1929, it is a remarkable reading. She compares Faulkner in his creation of Benjy to Dostoyevsky and his idiot, and she suggests that the American writer was able to gain the kind of distance from and involvement in his characters associated with Joyce. In all, Scott gave Faulkner a reading that novelists dream of getting —a reading, incidentally, few established critics and reviewers would provide.

Stories continued to go out regularly to Dashiell, and were promptly returned. But Faulkner's mind was an engine right now, and while rejection was disappointing, it did not slow his forward progress. In a short time, even as he looked back to *Flags* for "An Empress Passed" with Narcissa and Aunt Jenny, he was working on *Sound* proofs, had *Sanctuary* still in mind, was preparing other short pieces for magazine publication, and was readying himself for another major fictional effort, *As I Lay Dying*.

But before he started *As I Lay Dying* in October of 1929, he had several other matters to get through. His ability to compartmentalize his activities and keep his mind on essentials was remarkable. Only a man as neat in his habits as Faulkner could have kept his personal and professional life so clearly demarked. That clipped manner and pared-down style of living, that promptness in all but answering his mail carried over into arrangements of his professional life. After Estelle's suicide attempt and her subsequent recovery from the ordeal, the Faulkners prepared to leave Pascagoula for Oxford, where they intended to set up house. In all his arrangements for living in Oxford, Faulkner made sure he was within walking distance of his mother's, when she lived in the old Delta Psi house and then when she moved to S. Lamar, just off the square. The Faulkners rented the ground floor of a very pleasant Oxford house, owned by Elma Meek, at 803 University Avenue, just a short walk from the Ole Miss campus. Very possibly the genteel arrangement, and the use of four, good-sized rooms plus kitchen and bath gave Faulkner the desire to own his own home, for within the year he signed the deed which gave him possession of what he called Rowan Oak.

With all his literary properties in some stage of publication or revision, and stories going out and coming back, Faulkner in the fall of 1929 had plenty to keep him busy. But none of this earned a living. Estelle's two children, Victoria (Cho-Cho) and Malcolm, were being supported by their father;* but nevertheless Faulkner felt pressure to hold up his end. Also, whether he liked to admit it or not, the Oldham shadow was present: their

*We examine later the possibility Malcolm was not Cornell Franklin's son, although there was some physical resemblance.

rejection of him had been on grounds he could not support their daughter, and now they lived only a short distance away.

But there was an even heavier presence, although she was a small, slight, even demure woman in appearance. That was Maud Falkner, the matriarchal presence. Murry had by this time faded into the background as the boys were grown—only Dean seemed close to his father. Maud had won the marital battles—Murry had even given up drinking—and winning in this respect meant her hold over the hearts of her sons. According to witnesses of the Falkner household, the daughters-in-law were never welcomed, and only Louise Hale, who was married briefly to Dean before his death in 1935, at twenty-eight, became accepted into her household. Maud did not like Estelle because she drank, and, more generally, because the Oldhams were no one's favorites—with their airs and pretensions to Bourbon aristocracy, their Republican sympathies, and their rejection of Billy over a decade before. Further, Maud felt Faulkner could have done better; marrying a woman who drank heavily, was evidently in poor physical condition, and brought two children to the marriage was not a mother's idea of an ideal wife.

Once Faulkner moved back to Oxford, first at 803 University Avenue, then at Rowan Oak, Maud played a central role in his life; and he apparently discussed things with her he passed up with Estelle. Maud became his confidante, to the extent he talked to anyone; and, to her credit, she remained his staunchest supporter even when he fell under attack for *Sanctuary* and, generally, for writing disparagingly of Oxonians and Lafayette County. Maud never gave up on her sons, although Johncy was not well motivated and went from one activity to another; and Faulkner himself was barely able to support his family for many years to come. The situation, however, went beyond Freud's dictum that the son with his mother's love can go all the way. Maud gave love, but she expected deference and obedience in return. She tried to be the central woman in all her sons' lives. One question is how much this warped Faulkner in his relationships with women: Mammy Callie, on one hand, treating him like a potentate, and his own mother, believing from the beginning in her son's genius. What outsider could live up to these devoted, slavish twin mothers?

Even while Faulkner and Estelle established themselves in Oxford, seemingly like any married couple, the marriage seemed under a curse. Except for Maud's presence, Estelle remained the central woman in Faulkner's life, as she had been since their teens; but he came to need her the way Fitzgerald needed Zelda: chiefly, as the standard by which other women could be measured. His fiction reveals that almost lifelong battle to understand women by way of Estelle. An Estelle-figure pops up in nearly every novel, either thinly disguised, or openly there. She was a shadow on every move Faulkner had made for over a decade and would continue to make for the remainder of his life. The obsession with Estelle, and hers with him, comes in a story called "Selvage," mentioned above as

Estelle's work which Faulkner revised. This story as such never appeared in print—rejected by *Scribner's*, where it was titled "Salvage," a very different meaning, then by *Forum* and by *Liberty*. It turns up four years after these submissions, once more heavily revised, as "Elly." Almost certainly, "Selvage" and "Elly" are the same, although Faulkner heavily reworked the latter for publication. Of primary interest is its shadowing of the Estelle–Faulkner–Cornell Franklin triangle.

The main thrust is of a flighty young woman, Elly, who is connected by an obsessive need to Paul de Montigny. The latter will not marry her, but is also unacceptable to her family, especially to her grandmother, who believes he has Negro blood—an avatar of Joe Christmas. When thwarted here, Elly takes up with one of many beaux, the solid and stolid Philip, an assistant cashier in the bank who was, people said, slated one day to be bank president. But Elly finds nothing of interest in Philip beyond his respectability, and on the eve of marriage—the trousseau is being readied —she flees with Paul, who continues to insist he will not marry her, or as he puts it, " 'I don't marry them.' " With this, Elly, who is driving with Paul and her hated grandmother, pulls the steering wheel sharply, throwing herself clear while the car is demolished. She survives hurt; the others apparently die.

Elly is eighteen and is much sought after. She apparently flirts to the final degree of teasing, but then pulls back, since she states she is still a virgin. The triangle is familiar from the time when Estelle was eighteen, Faulkner a little younger, and the families were displeased with the possible union. The introduction of "Negro blood" in Paul here has its counterpart in the unacceptability of the Falkner clan as socially beneath the Oldhams, and Faulkner's own lack of class and caste standing to vie with Estelle's. Elly is presented as unable to settle down, caught by a need to explore, seek danger, find her own way; all this a frank admission on Estelle's part. Paul, however, remains dim. We have no sense of him, and except as a figure in the triangle he has no weight; nor does Philip, who is present simply as the man with a sound future, a respectable figure to counterpoint Paul and represent the bourgeois principle Elly is struggling against. As personal revelation, the story is compelling; as fiction, dismal.

Along with a rush of stories going out came reviews of *Sound;* reviews of a book Faulkner had now put behind him. When his books required revision, or when there was delay as he moved from publisher to publisher, we find all kinds of time warps. For even as he moved on to other projects, earlier ones came back in the form of proofs and then of reviews; the overlap often involved several properties, as they did here. For the reviews of *Sound* came in while he had *Sanctuary* on hold and was preparing to write *As I Lay Dying* and a number of shorter pieces. The reviews were favorable, which in itself is remarkable given the nature of the novel—but fewer than two thousand copies were printed, and there was no way he could make money on that. A friend, Lyle Saxon, wrote most enthusiastically, for the New York *Herald Tribune,* a review which was so full of favorable comments it must be viewed as *parti pris.* Saxon called it a "great book," and his other comments went on from there. But the *New York Times* critic also found it a daring experiment which worked, and others in the leading magazines recognized something was happening in American fiction that warranted watching.[23]

Also, at this time, the linkage between Faulkner and Joyce became apparent. Several reviews commented on it, including Saxon, who had some insight into what the novelist had read and thought about. But some critics (Harry Hansen, among them) felt the Joyce connection only made Faulkner as incoherent as the Irish writer—so that in this view the attachment was disadvantageous. The significant aspect of the reviews, however, apart from whether they were favorable or not, is that they hailed a new, innovative talent in American writing. The book had made its impact in that respect, although sales and popularity were not deeply affected. Of course, the stock market crash did not help the book market, coming as it did in the same month reviews began appearing.

Faulkner was purring along like a well-oiled motor. Outside intrusions —wife, family, visits, rejections by Dashiell and others, good or poor reviews—could not sidetrack him. Even the visit of Cornell Franklin, Estelle's former husband, and his new wife did not seem to disturb him, although he took off for Memphis for some of that time. He had reached the point where his imagination was unfolding as if under its own energies, and he would write anywhere, under any conditions. Thus, his ability to turn out *As I Lay Dying* while working at the power plant—an easy job, but so boring it might have turned him into a mummy, not a working author.

A major question arises why Faulkner wrote a book like *As I Lay Dying* at this time. With its array of speakers who replace a standard narrative and its thematic emphasis on death and disaster, what possible connection did this novel have with his life which seemed diametrically opposite the Bundrens's and their burden of burying the dead? To ask this question is not to assume there is necessarily a direct linkage between a novelist's work and his life when he writes that work; but what it suggests is that in an author as autobiographical as Faulkner, there must be leads or threads which circle back from life to work and from work to life. It is insufficient to say that putting in time in a buried occupation, during the night shift, keeping the fires going, Faulkner was naturally drawn to some mythical event to match his own Vulcan-like position. It is also inadequate to say his own circumstance recalled a long journey of death and burial, that he felt himself somehow buried in this job, perhaps in this marriage. None of this works, although some of it may be applicable. A much more complicated, imaginative maneuver is involved.

Faulkner wanted to achieve a book which derived from that region between consciousness and unconsciousness that he had explored in *Sound.*

He spoke of having written *As I Lay Dying* deliberately: "Before I began I said, I am going to write a book by which, at a pinch, I can stand or fall if I never touch ink again."[24] He denied the novel (which he dedicated to Hal Smith) was written with the same "ecstasy, that eager and joyous faith and anticipation of surprise which the yet unmarred sheet beneath my hand held inviolate and unfailing, waiting for release" he had experienced with *Sound*. And yet, despite denials of eagerness and ecstasy, these are the characteristics we associate with *As I Lay Dying*. He was carried along by an obsessional need to get under the surface of things, into that world represented by an interiorized monologue, a hidden but spoken language. Through this means—and it is technique as much as content—he explored that process of telling and retelling which characterized his major work; for nothing is so apparent in *As I Lay Dying* as overlap, repetition, circling back and forth.

Furthermore, *As I Lay Dying* recalled his use of that title for the spotted horses episode of *Father Abraham*, and that latter work seems to have taken over his imagination as if some form of salvation for himself and his career. It was a discovery on his part of what would weave in and out of his whole creative effort. Yet the significance of *As I Lay Dying* in his life went even beyond that, toward some mythical re-creation, in which fire, water, flood, a bridge, a road, all come together. These elements and man-made objects were in reality the essential part of the Faulknerian world; add to that horses, mules, wagons, and we have the writer fixed in his country setting. *His* world, *his* people, *his* nature and objects. There was an elemental quality to Faulkner, one often forgotten or neglected in our rush to view him as a sophisticated novelist. He was that, also; but beyond the sophistication, there were the simple matters spread out before him, as in this novel. All of these considerations bring *As I Lay Dying* into focus in his life at this time—perhaps more than ever a desire to get back to elemental matters as his personal life was becoming increasingly complicated.

Even the locale of his "study" was important: in the guts of a power plant on a night shift, the silence overpowering except for the motors in the background. He sought almost a denial of the entire world of things here, except for the monotony of humming and running. In that setting, an anti-Eden on the surface, but almost Edenic in other respects, away from family and responsibility, Faulkner conjured up something timeless. There is a kind of ironic Eden to the Bundrens and their quest to bury Addie, the dead mother: their journey certainly seems a mockery of the Edenic journey; and New Hope, one of their destinations, only increases that mockery. There is, nevertheless, a united action, a desire to please the mother—not the least, that!—and a pulling together in adversity, even on the part of the father, the villain of the piece. One is tempted to read further and suggest that even as Faulkner's marriage was, somehow, a betrayal of his mother, he wrote a book paying homage to the sons' love for *their* mother. There was redemption in that, if such a feeling existed.

One commentator quotes Allen Tate as having heard Faulkner say the entire book grew out of Anse Bundren's feeling that the road has ruined his life and livelihood; that it brought nothing but bad luck.[25] If true, this would be in keeping with Faulkner's feeling about simple things; for the road would be an inroad, a trespasser on what should be kept inviolate. If this sounds simplistic, we must recall the rural, frontier nature of small towns at the turn of the century: the sense that whatever their problems, they were somehow connected to Eden, and that any interruption of their natural flow was the work of Satan. Faulkner soaked up this attitude as a boy and saw the automobile as intruder, as well as anything which brought technological advances to the area. While this kept the South poor and agricultural, it fitted an ideology of less is more: that the quality of life (for whites) was more important than quantity of goods.*

It is possible to see *As I Lay Dying* as fitting into Faulkner's sense of this South in its final stages: this novel initiates a phase in which he will write about the passing of that South, first in *As I Lay Dying*, then in *Light in August* and *Absalom*, ending with "The Bear" and *Go Down, Moses*. Here we find the real inner need, that desire to fix the outward sense of things even as his own life was moving into a complex, inexorable phase. What Faulkner could not control personally he hoped to put forth in his fiction as conservation. *As I Lay Dying* is the first phase of that "conservative" element: a disagreeable family which is like the first people on earth in their determination to struggle against flood and fire. He felt this was rock-bottom humanity.

Our view of *As I Lay Dying* as a vehicle for Faulkner's fear and hatred of the new is reinforced if we see the novel as his first "play," his first effort at a theatrical event. In this respect, the characters step forth and utter their soliloquies, or else they pair, but rarely more than two of them on stage at the same time. The use of the monologue here—all acts pursued by way of inner voices—strengthens the idea of a theatrical event. If we accept this, the Bundrens are a traveling family troupe. Instead of moving on to the next engagement, however, to play new roles, they are involved in their own internal drama—not only to bury their mother and wife, but to work out relationships among themselves. These relationships have developed and festered; and each, as in any traditional soliloquy, must

*Jackson Lears's important study of antimodernism in turn-of-the-century America, *No Place of Grace*, demonstrates the complexity of this response throughout small towns. "Groping for alternatives to modern unreality, they [Lears's 'educated bourgeoisie'] sometimes clung to the shreds and patches of republican tradition, but they also turned to other cultural resources as well: the literary romantic's rejection of urban artifice in the name of rustic or childlike 'simple life'; the philosophical vitalist's rejection of all static systems in the name of the flux of 'pure experience'; the avant-garde artist's rejection of bourgeois respectability in the name of primal irrationality." Further: "The internalized morality of self-control and autonomous achievement, the basis of modern culture, seemed at the end of its tether; the chief source of that morality, the bourgeois family, seemed a hothouse of suffocating repression and insoluble personal conflict" (Jackson Lears, *No Place of Grace* [New York: Pantheon, 1981], pp. 5, 6).

reveal the past even as he moves along into the present. As theater, as role-players and characters in a drama, the Bundrens can posture, and the events can be sensational. We permit a kind of excess in theater which would be suspect in fiction.

Is this development so exceptional on Faulkner's part? Not if we see in hindsight that *Sound* has a good deal of theatrical potential in it—that those somewhat staged interior monologues which make up the bulk of the novel are like speeches made by actors stepping to the side or to the front of the stage. One of the ironies of Faulkner's career is that when he turned to the theater for *Requiem for a Nun*, he faltered badly (*pace* Camus, Sartre, and his other French admirers). But when he wrote fiction, he entered into a theatrical, melodramatic prose which carries some of his novels close to stage presentations. The heroism of a typical dirt farmer family in *As I Lay Dying* gains credence if we can see it as acting out. The initial scene, with Darl as our incipient Hamlet, has within it a "chuck, chuck, chuck" of the adze which would be equally effective as background sound in a dramatic presentation. Anton Chekhov discovered this in *A Cherry Orchard.*

As I Lay Dying is theater, although it isn't only theater. Darl is Hamletic, deteriorating throughout the "play" the way Hamlet does; he is our mad poet, the voice carrying the literary sensibility of the author. Darl can step outside the family, as necessary, and see the futility, obsession, self-destructiveness of the Bundrens. He is matched against Jewel, his half-sibling, the illegitimate son of Addie and the Reverend Whitfield. Together they are like bookends: one the retreating poet, the other the possessed doer, the man who will half kill himself with work to buy one of the descendants of the spotted horses in *Father Abraham*. By complementing each other, they help establish a view of the family which also has personal overtones for the maker of the book.

The Bundren family: the father who is lazy and indolent works his wife to death, and the rest, mainly sons, help to bury her. Here, if we wish to pursue it, is a scenario of the Falkner family, allowing for facts screened out or distorted. It must be stressed that Faulkner is writing this as he breaks with *his* family in order to establish one of his own, the novel his first longer work since his marriage and acquisition of two stepchildren. There is a fantasy here: an extreme hostility to the father who, indolent and catered to, is the true survivor. He gains his teeth at the end, and that is equivalent to his being reborn: he can now eat normal food, remarry, be rejuvenated, gain a second life as a man. Yet in the background is the ceremony of death, the celebration of the death of someone who really held the family together. The main action is getting her into the ground where she wants to be buried.

Yet before we become too grim about the family, we must view the journey as a celebration, a ceremonial and an acted-out event. It is a celebration of death, a staged funeral which goes wrong. Nature botches it, just as the marriage and upbringing of the children were botched because of an unresponsive father. The novel has deep ritualistic significance, indebted to Frazer and his *Golden Bough*, among other influences.* The coffin, an obvious enclosed place, is one of the key symbolic presences; it dominates the early narrative, as, later, Addie's putrefying body dominates the latter parts. Coffin and body: the making of one, the decay of the other are twin coordinates for the novel's progression. Even as the family acts out its journey, the object of its activity is already returning to earth in decaying flesh and tissue, a primitive ritual. In death, Addie assumes a more central role in everyone's consciousness than she had in life. In life, she was buried, so to speak, whereas in death, she is resurrected, incapable of being ignored.

As we know, Faulkner derived his title from the *Odyssey*, the eleventh book, Agamemnon's speech to Odysseus: "As I lay dying the woman with the dog's eyes would not close my eyelids for me as I descended into Hades." Agamemnon's hatred for women is palpable in these lines, but the feeling is reciprocal. He himself brought on Clytemnestra's enmity and desire for revenge for his sacrifice of Iphigenia so he could achieve his male destiny as warrior and hero. The title has reverberations, since with some transposition it can serve many purposes. It can be the plaint of a man who feels betrayed—some application here to Murry Faulkner; it serves as a curse on women—a signal of hostility to the mother who dominated the Falkner household; it can suggest identity between writer and speaker of words: Faulkner as "dying" in his new situation, waiting for the coffin lid to be nailed shut. It can fit none of these, also, since Faulkner's precise state of mind was an ever-widening pool of conflicts; but as a shadow, or scrimmed, version of an attitude, a feeling, a state of mind, it can be some or all of these.

What compels us about the work of a man just married is how much this novel becomes the obverse of an epithalamion, the traditional song or lyric in honor of a bride. Faulkner's "epithalamion" is a celebration of death, a journey to a funeral, a voyage back to nature via flood and fire. One point not to be neglected is that Addie is alive at the beginning of the proceedings, listening to the steady "chuck" of Cash's adze. She slides into death while listening to the preparation of her final container. Just as her marriage has been a kind of slow death, so now in actuality she sinks into that

---

*Including Joyce's *Ulysses* and Eliot's *The Waste Land*. The ritualistic and mythical elements dominate, as we see from André Bleikasten's comment (in *Faulkner's "As I Lay Dying"*): What assures Faulkner "a place among the great mythopoeic novelists is not the occasional reference to mythological figures found in his books, or even the parallels to mythical patterns discernible there, but precisely the way in which—from the heterogeneous variety of sources to the organic unity of the finished novel—his creative work is accomplished. Neither invention *ex nihilo* nor servile submission to earlier models, Faulkner creation goes in search of its own structures through a careful and complex reordering of all the debris and residues it finds on its way" (André Bleikasten, *Faulkner's "As I Lay Dying,"* trans. Roger Little [Bloomington: Indiana University Press, 1973], p. 20)—what Claude Lévi-Strauss suggests by "intellectual bricolage." Bleikasten overreaches, however, in yoking Faulkner's novel to Hawthorne's *The Scarlet Letter*: Addie is *not* Hester Prynne, and Jewel is *not* Pearl, despite superficial similarities, nor is Whitfield like Dimmesdale. When differences become greater than likenesses, one must forgo an analogue.

terminal condition. Faulkner has very carefully not let her die prior to the making of her coffin, but during. This signifies a development which goes beyond mere ceremony or celebration, into a view based on endurance of the worst that life can bring. Addie "endures" her fate without quibble, waits for it, is gathered up by it. As Cora says: "She lived, a lonely woman, lonely with her pride, trying to make folks believe different, hiding the fact that they just suffered her, because she was not cold in the coffin before they were carting her forty miles away to bury her, flouting the will of God to do it. Refusing to let her lie in the same earth with those Bundrens."[26]

Some of Faulkner's finest passages focus on Addie's dying moments, then her death. In one segment, labeled "Darl," he achieves a breathtaking tour de force. Although the segment is Darl's, he is not at the bedside, and the entire passage of Addie toward death comes not through him but through what he senses. Darl is himself off with Jewel to make that additional three dollars so important to Anse, and at the bedside is Dewey Dell, Darl's only sister: "She looks down at the face. It is like a casting of fading bronze upon the pillow, the hands alone still with any semblance of life: a curled, gnarled inertness; a spent yet alert quality which weariness, exhaustion, travail has not yet departed, as though they doubted even yet the actuality of rest, guarding with horned and penurious alertness the cessation which they know cannot last."[27]

Then in italics, in the same segment, Darl's voice enters, commenting on the dying Addie; the young man imagining a scene, like some mad poet creating lines for himself. What makes the sequence of passages so remarkable is that Faulkner, utilizing interior monologue, in the italicized passages creates another dimension altogether. Through a kind of extrasensory perception, without revealing authorial presence, he moves in and out of the character's consciousness. This is an innovative technique, since it relies on internality at the same time it allows for something more external than interior monologue: the voice coming from a middle ground which is neither completely inside nor outside, but in that intermediate region Faulkner has uniquely established. This partial obfuscation of the mental process, this moving in and out, is linked to Faulkner's deliberate confusion of pronoun references here and in several other sections.

That kind of confusion was, in turn, connected to his desire to blur partially an issue or draw a scrim over routine action: to defamiliarize the familiar. Like the great abstract painters, he also intended to deny narrative line (representation) in favor of form, attitude, and sensibility. Relocating matter was, for Faulkner, a dimension of the new, and evidently part of his reliance on interior monologue. For if voices emanate from someone, somewhere, then those voices must not be clarified by naming them. The reader struggles through pronouns, but the struggle intensifies his identification with the passage; putting him, the reader, in the position of a translator working his way through an unfamiliar language. In more personal terms, this obfuscation—the *he* and *she* and *hers* and *his* which proliferate in a Faulkner passage—is connected to his desire for secrecy, deception, and distortion. Although the original military deceptions he perpetuated about himself gradually lessened, he maintained artifice by way of obscure prose, hiding his traces, camouflaging himself. Like the hunter he was, Faulkner insisted on stealth: pronouns rather than names create stealthy reading.

We are tempted to shape other dimensions of *As I Lay Dying* into personal terms. The disparities between Darl and Jewel are clear. Although they are half-brothers, they do not know this, and in their respective roles Faulkner seems to be playing out his own differences from *his* brothers—although to what extent this parallelism is valid we cannot be certain. Nevertheless, like Faulkner and his three brothers, Darl and Jewel are polarized, antipodes: the one sensitive and going mad, the other visceral, physical, ready for violence, an active man getting the job done. Jewel saves the coffin from the flooding river, also from burning. He is the man who dooms himself by his devotion to tasks with no ostensible reward, only for themselves; whereas Darl is sinking ever deeper into madness. Both identify with water, Jewel to master it, Darl to become submerged in it, like Quentin. It is not coincidence that the journey of death really begins in Darl's segment: "The wagon moves; the mules' ears begin to bob. Behind us, above the house, motionless in tall and soaring circles, they diminish and disappear."[28] Anse then follows, the man who has the most to gain from Addie's death, with his disapproval of Jewel's new horse; but, most of all, Darl's laughing: ". . . but we hadn't no more than passed Tull's lane when Darl began to laugh. Setting back there on the plank seat with Cash, with his dead ma laying in her coffin at his feet, laughing. How many times I told him it's doing such things as that makes folks talk about him, I don't know."[29]

We have here in miniature the personal embodiment of the situation. Jewel prancing, active, showing off his horse, while Darl, seemingly unaffected, laughs, a form of hysteria. Anse disapproves, fails to understand Darl's laughter is not disregard but a sensibility too tightly wired. Darl demonstrates exactly the opposite of his feeling, while Jewel is what Jewel is: not caring what Anse thinks because he is not Bundren's son. And Anse: he worries about neighbors, full of disappointment his boys are not exactly like him; or else they touch some other deep disapproval in him, as Faulkner touched Murry.

Seeking selective passages for biographical import while ignoring others can be misleading, unless there is a pattern of events, images, situations, and circumstances. *As I Lay Dying* has a sufficient number of such passages, mainly in fraternal polarities, so that we can offer, however tentatively, some parallels. Darl has the most statements of the fifty-nine segments, and Cora Tull describes him as "the one that folks say is queer, lazy, pottering about the place no better than Anse"[30]—adjectives applied to the young Faulkner whenever he appeared in Oxford, and especially applicable in the years after he returned from military service. The description of Darl also fits that of a poet or maker, someone who seems to have endless time on his hands, and who earns nothing—much is made by Cora of the fact Cash is a good carpenter and Jewel was "always doing something which made him some money."

Another suggestive element: the Tulls, Vernon and Cora, with their five daughters, are functioning well, working together as a team and getting by; whereas the Bundrens, pulling apart because Addie considers Anse dead in her life, are going under, the result of family disunity. What works with the Tulls fails with the Bundrens: Vernon has shelter, mules, horses, wagons; Anse is slowly losing everything, his wagon, Cash's tools, and even the coffin with Addie inside when they attempt to ford the swollen river. Anse is marked for failure, and to a large extent he carries the family with him, especially since Addie has given up on him, even conceived a child not his, Jewel. Addie's confession, a kind of centerpiece, is the sole segment devoted to her, and she's already dead when she speaks out in her defense. Her motif is rejection of Anse—she relates how he entered her life and remained a stranger in it: "Sometimes I would lie by him in the dark, hearing the land that was now of my blood and flesh, and I would think: Anse. Why Anse. Why are you Anse. I would think about his name until after a while I could see the word as a shape, a vessel, and I would watch him liquefy."[31] Addie does no less than nullify Anse in her mind as she lies in the dark—a remarkable sequence of images in which she creates a "not-Anse." She says, "I gave Anse children. I did not ask for them. I did not even ask him for what he could have given me: not-Anse."*[32] Jewel is the sole child she considers hers, because she conceived beyond Anse, with the Reverend Whitfield. "I gave Anse Dewey Dell to negative Jewel. Then I gave him Vardaman to replace the child I had robbed him of. And now he has three children that are his and not mine."[33]

Addie's confession of feeling is all negative, even to the children because she conceived them with Anse. Most of all, however, she denies him, the scenario of Faulkner's sense of Maud and Murry. Something more than Maud's domination of the household, this is an outright rejection of Murry until their somewhat later years when he finally stopped drinking. In the boys' childhood years, however, Faulkner was privy to the atmosphere of "not-Murry," some of it abetted by the father, some of it generated by the mother's dislike of the man she married. Besides the general atmosphere of the Falkner home, there are many specific incidents. A key one occurred when Lelia Butler, Maud's mother, moved in with the Falkners and Murry was displaced from his own bedroom. Maud literally put him out, while she shared with her mother—an act of such direct hostility the children could not help but be silent witnesses.

---

*We recall that in "Elmer" Mrs. Hodge rejects her husband, a drunk; all he had "given his children was lightish hair, and he hadn't been able to do this for Jo [Jo-Addie]." Elmer labels his father "an inverted Io with hookworm." "Addie" recurs, as family dislocation moves from Hodges to Compsons and Bundrens.

As shadow images, both Compsons and Bundrens live with a lack of reality. However they differ from each other, they maintain a fantasy life which profoundly affects the children, leading to madness, violent acts, and self-destruction. Darl matches up with Quentin; Dewey Dell, pregnant by Lafe, has parallels with Caddy; Vardaman seems retarded and recalls Benjy; and Cash has some characteristics in common with Jason. Only Jewel evades the family doom, and he is not Anse's son.

However shaded, it appears Faulkner was writing a version of his own life as a palimpsest; so that if we rub the surface sufficiently, we can perceive the lineaments of another world beneath it. The early stages came with the Sartoris background, with its obvious linkages to Faulkner's past; then came the Compson family, with some further reference to his own situation; but now appeared the more obvious representation, however much he changed class, caste, and aspirations. The revelations come in descending order: from Sartoris upper-class posturing through Compson genteel posing to dirt-farmer Bundren deterioration.

The decaying, stinking Addie is smelled by everyone except the Bundrens, who either consciously ignore the rot or miss it altogether. The circumstance is of more than casual interest, since it comes in a context of watching the mother die, death itself, followed by the main part of the novel which is to get her into the right piece of ground, near Jefferson. Faulkner's description of her putrid decay is not the usual way in which a mother's funeral is presented: the purity and sainthood normally associated with mother are lacking. Addie has committed adultery, borne an illegitimate son, and now she lies putrefying in water and sun. This is the presentation of a mother with a vengeance!—making Mrs. Compson seem saintly in comparison. Further, Vardaman, who thinks of his dead mother and her coffin as simply another fish, bores holes in the coffin top with Cash's augur, two holes right into Addie's face. Once again, the desecration of the dead body, and a mother at that, suggests that the ceremony of death has special dimensions to it. Although we have come to sympathize with her and see Anse as a brutal, nonfeeling, self-oriented man, we must take account of these authorial touches in which a great deal of hostility is poured down on Addie. We see that "mother" passes over into object. She is a piece of body lugged hither and yon in a wooden box; as though some object which must be delivered to a given place, regardless of her condition. There is little reverence for her body, little indeed for her spirit. The sole consideration is to get the package delivered, as if the family were a parcel post delivery service. Their ability to endure the worst of nature is in the tradition of "the mail must go through."

Related to this need to deliver the goods, as it were, is the stress made on the dreamlike nature of the journey; as though there is a journey in every man he must make, and a mother's death is simply a good reason for making this particular journey. As in so many other key segments, Darl stresses this aspect: "We go on, with a motion so soporific, so dreamlike as to be uninferant of progress, as though time and not space were decreasing between us and it."[34] With that, the sign for "New Hope Church 3 mi." looms up. "It wheels up like a motionless hand lifted above the profound desolation of the ocean; beyond it the red road lies like a spoke of which Addie Bundren is the rim."[35] All journeys are in a sense oneiric because they partake of the mythical or archetypal journey we associate with human life: the birth of the fetus, the expulsion of Adam and Eve, the voyage from ignorance to knowledge associated with growth.

Yet this particular journey seems both more and less; for it is only on this journey the family gets to know itself. It is dreamlike because it involves an unconscious or preconscious acquisition of self-knowledge, as well as knowledge of "the other." Despite the particularities of the experience, there is something quite abstract about Faulkner's telling of it, a good deal of that attributable to his working from the inside out; from using characters as forms of commentary on others while also expressing their own point of view. Before the journey, the family is a discrete number of individuals—each, as Addie says in her monologue, unknown to anyone else; each, perhaps, "killed" by the other, as Addie has "killed" Anse. But on the journey, they must function as a family, however lacking in unity, or else they cannot accomplish their primary task.

Faulkner never experienced situations binding the family together in this way. He sensed apartness, between husband and wife, himself and father, his brothers and himself, but not the overriding moment which would force them together to survive. There was no hardscrabble existence, no scratching of the land, no time when they were really up against it. Survival was never the issue, although shaping an identity and holding to it was. Faulkner did not have to worry about his next meal or shelter as he tried to carve out of himself what he wanted to become. He could become. The Bundrens, however, only achieve whatever they do achieve by acting under the gun. As the journey is winding down, we get a glimpse of what they look like. The wagon has pulled up in front of Grummet's hardware store in Mottson: "They came from some place in Yoknapatawpha County, trying to get to Jefferson with it. It must have been like a piece of rotten cheese coming into an anthill, in that ramshackle wagon that Albert said folks were scared would fall all to pieces before they could get it out of town, with that home-made box and another fellow with a broken leg lying on a quilt on top of it, and the father and a little boy sitting on the seat and the marshall trying to make them get out of town."[36] Suddenly, the hamlet of Mottson appears like order itself, the Garden, against which the intrusion resembles an apparition from another planet, not another part of Mississippi.

The image is of complete disunity, things falling apart; and yet it is Faulkner's point that even as the Bundrens create this appearance of disintegration, they are pulling together. Part of the unity Faulkner gains, however disguised to the mere observer in Mottson or elsewhere, derives from the Christian elements he is able to infuse into the story. Although Dewey Dell wishes to abort her fetus, she is pregnant at the very time her mother dies—the rise and fall of human existence is implicit here, and it is cast within the pessimistic aspect of Christianity, the world of Ecclesiastes.

Other dimensions suggest a Christian motif—a motif present, as we have observed, in *Sound* and which will appear notably in *Light in August*—such as the emphasis on bridges. The lack of bridges, the fact that the bridges are down, that the flood has destroyed the bridges, this fact leading to the recurrence of "New Hope 3 mi." all suggest the breakdown of human communication curable only by family unity in the face of spiritual poverty. The key is the "lack of"—means of getting around are removed or made almost impossible, access to and from is blocked, people must go over or around or through, obstacles are located nearly everywhere, the familiar transformed into the unfamiliar, all these part of a Christian testing-out. Within that setting, people are dwarfed: the familiar Christian motif in which people are presented against a background which miniaturizes them, so that when pride and vanity are confronted, enormity of place and circumstance brings man back to the small thing he is. Once again in Darl's segment, we have a recognition, in some of Faulkner's most rhapsodic prose.

> The river itself is not a hundred yards across, and pa and Vernon and Vardaman and Dewey Dell are the only things in sight not of that single monotony of desolation leaning with that terrific quality a little from right to left, as though we had reached the place where the motion of the wasted world accelerates just before the final precipice. Yet they appear dwarfed. It is as though the space between us were time: an irrevocable quality. It is as though time, no longer running straight before us in a diminishing line, now runs parallel between us like a looping string, the distance being the doubling accretion of the thread and not the interval between.[37]

Faulkner has invented a language for Darl's vision.

The mules have a premonition of the fate in store for them: ". . . their gaze sweeps across us with in their eyes a wild, sad, profound and despairing quality as though they had already seen in the thick water the shape of the disaster which they could not speak and we could not see."[38] In this tragedy shifting back and forth from Christian to classical Greek, the mules are Cassandras—but, as Faulkner implies, even forewarned the Bundrens will continue on. This scene just cited has something of a Hardy landscape in it, the amphitheater which dwarfs Henchard in *The Mayor of Casterbridge* as he tries to work out the increasingly involved aspects of a life suddenly out of control.

The log, an aspect of man's destiny, bears down inexorably on the wagon, as if an arrow shot from the bow of some despairing god. Faulkner is straining for significance on a broad front: the evident Christian symbolism of journey, unity, testing, redemption through work accomplished; the

Greek sense of fate or destiny—the log, the mules as Cassandra; and the literary—the place in and out of Hardy landscapes, Conradian ideology, even some Housman irony. The log which winds its way toward the wagon—drowning the mules, breaking Cash's leg once again, throwing Addie's coffin into the river—is a particularly telling part of Faulkner's hidden agenda. While he speaks of unity, of the family pulling together in its graceless, ignorant way, he is also describing events which go beyond human control, which seem part of some scheme man can never penetrate. The log calls up many kinds of mystery—the presence of the unexpected, the bizarre nature of circumstance, the puniness of man's work in comparison with nature's plan, the very question whether there is any plan at all, or only a discrete number of circumstances and conditions.

Implicit in this book, more than in any previous one, including *Sound*, is Faulkner's sense of man's placement in the universe. With such archetypal images as flood, fire, an anti-Eden, a journey, it is not unusual he should be questioning the universe. What he finds when he asks relevant questions is not-something, but also not-nothing. There is everything and nothing, balancing each other. The nothing is generated by nature, as part of some universal plan which exists whatever man does for or against it; the everything includes man's contribution, although it may seem to be all for naught, or of little moment. Faulkner arranges and rearranges, perhaps seeking more than the "nothing" which is nature's plan, but finding only individual acts, moves, scenes. The point of *As I Lay Dying* is neither pessimistic nor optimistic. Readers have made too much of uplift in Faulkner; he can be deadeningly down. But here he is neither; he is full of challenge and response, but the consequence is not triumph. It is part of the cycle. This is, in a sense, the beginning of a new maturity. Often it is not the better book which becomes the mature work—*Sound* is a far more startling novel. But in *As I Lay Dying*, Faulkner confronted, as he had in his personal life, a stage beyond which he recognized no man can go. There are limits to human response, and there is the inexorable plan of nature, unknowable, ineffable as the Christian God Himself.

The use of multiple points of view—with some segments complicated by other voices besides the one stipulated—reinforces and strengthens our sense of Faulkner coming to terms with a personal philosophy. There are, in all, fifteen different voices, comprising fifty-nine segments or minichapters. Of the fifty-nine, Darl, with nineteen, has the most. The multiplicity of voices—and here the literary influence seems Browning, especially the techniques of *The Ring and the Book*—established Faulkner's sense of the world as relativistic, fluid, and lacking in center. Joycean and beyond that Bergsonian time helps us understand how Faulkner was questioning objects, deconstructing them. If both people and events lack center, then centering on this or that character as in the traditional novel is no longer viable. By decentering and moving the narrative energy into several voices, Faulkner could express that everything and nothing existed in equal dosages. Truth is, of course, elusive, as we already knew from his earlier fiction; but here he has found a means of expressing the softness of truth, the possibilities of a deobjectified, decentered world.

That new maturity we have cited in his outlook, involving neither solutions nor sliding into nihilism, gains breadth through multiplicity. He had looked as far as he could look and discovered through his method that truth exists in the mind of the speaker: deception, self-deception, and truth are intermixed. Validation of point of view comes through the speaker, in keeping with a theatrical and dramatic method. Multiplicity does not mean Faulkner fragmented a point of view, but that by focusing less on certitudes he came closer to that world of "not-nothing" and "not-everything." Unlike Hemingway, who was sinking toward nihilism, Faulkner halted: voices in this innovative work provided an anchor.

The "I" is Darl, not Addie, and Darl is carried off to Jackson, mad, laughing all the way. Faulkner is suggesting that in this quest for "not-nothing" and "not-everything" one cannot be too sensitive, nor too anomalous. Darl does not fit; he is not quite intellectual, but for a family like the Bundrens he is a dangerous spirit, and he must, therefore, fail. More commentator and observer than doer, he sinks—he replaces Addie as the one dying. He is dying into life; she has died into death. Her life was a living death, his a deathlike life. In the title, and in the implied ambiguity, they join: she is "not-Anse," and he is "not-Bundren." We can read into this whatever personal validation we wish. *As I Lay Dying* would appear on October 6, 1930, published by Cape and Smith, and dedicated to Hal Smith.

Chapter Thirteen

Annus Mirabilis and Thereafter

T HE YEAR 1929 was not only supercharged for Faulkner. It was, as one critic called it, an *annus mirabilis* for the South as a whole, and indeed for the nation if we take into account the stock market crash and the beginning of the Great Depression. The year following saw the significant statement of twelve Southerners, *I'll Take My Stand*, a manifesto with which Faulkner's own views overlapped. In 1929, besides *The Sound and the Fury* and his writing of *As I Lay Dying* (while *Sanctuary* was on hold), Thomas Wolfe published *Look Homeward, Angel*. Wolfe was the writer whom Faulkner cited as the most daring of his contemporaries, the means by which he could depreciate Hemingway's achievement while vaunting a Southerner. But Wolfe was only one of many in what was a true literary renaissance, a mix of established authors with young writers publishing their first books: James Branch Cabell, Ellen Glasgow, T. S. Stribling (whose trilogy of *The Forge*, 1931; *The Store*, 1932; and *The Unfinished Cathedral*, 1934, foreruns Faulkner's Snopes trilogy, especially *The Store*), Robert Penn Warren (just starting out, but included in the *I'll Take My Stand* group), Stark Young (also in the group), Allen Tate (another agrarian voice in the statement), DuBose Heyward (whose *Porgy* became the basis of George and Ira Gershwin's *Porgy and Bess*), Hamilton Basso (whom Faulkner had met in New Orleans), Merrill Moore (the psychiatrist who wrote perhaps fifty thousand sonnets during his lifetime), and others.

The *annus mirabilis* was foreshadowed and even foreshaped by a group of writers who came to be known as "the Fugitives" and who appeared in an influential publication called, appropriately, the *Fugitive*. By the time it ceased to appear in December of 1925, it had laid the groundwork for a concerted literary movement: a loose association of Southern writers who had a common heritage, a more or less common ideology, and a more or less common perception of the future as agrarian, not industrial. *Fugitives: An Anthology of Verse* appeared in 1928, with contributions by Tate, Warren, Donald Davidson, and Ransom, among others. These are the voices which reappeared in the *Stand* manifesto.

Faulkner never belonged to any group. An essential fact about him was his independence from groups, organizations, clubs, and any other kind of literary-social activity. But when *I'll Take My Stand* appeared in 1930, it echoed much of what we have already observed in Faulkner's thinking. Whereas the Fugitives had been a clearly defined group, with regular meetings and a common outlook on the need for a resurgence in Southern letters, the agrarian statement of 1930 was not the result of a preconceived plan. Each writer went off on his own, held together with the group only by the "Introduction: A Statement of Principles." The agrarians (Ransom, Herman Clarence Nixon, Andrew Nelson Lytle, Warren, John Donald Wade, Henry Blue Kline, and Young) did agree that the South, as they perceived it, was unique: sharing a common tradition and common interests. "The South is a minority section that has hitherto been jealous of its minority right to live its own kind of life. The South scarcely hopes to determine the other sections, but it does propose to determine itself, within the utmost limits of legal action."[1] Their assumption is that the South (the white South, since blacks are ignored, and segregation is taken for granted) has an organic quality to it which makes it an entity; and that common interests are sufficiently strong so it can negotiate the modern world on its own. "The members of the present group"—and, by implication, the Southern-white constituency which they represent—"would be happy to be counted as members of a national agrarian movement."[2]

Faulkner's vision of a unique South was far thicker and more textured than that of the twelve spokesmen—mainly because he was a far greater artist than any of them. Unlike them, he did not ignore the rot lying in the interstices of any society cut off and ingrown. As early as *Father Abraham*, where he began to develop the Snopes family as a piece of social history, he perceived how an agrarian society could be subverted by its own kind. Despite their denials, the twelve were nostalgic for antebellum times, whereas Faulkner recognized a historical development was under way which could not be denied with memories of an Edenic past. By the time of *Flags* or its revision, *Sartoris*, Faulkner had posited the meeting of at least two Souths; and his treatment of the Sartoris clan does not bode well for nostalgia and fond memories. They may have been heroic warriors, but they self-destructed and destroyed anyone near them. They were doomed, and they doomed themselves, as though acting out a classical

Greek tragedy. In the 1930 symposium the past is so linked to agrarianism that social history is made to appear Edenic.

This manifesto proscribing postagrarian life contains nostalgic yearning for an older, organic period: "Turning to consumption, as the grand end which justifies the evil of modern labor, we find we have been deceived." As we complete this passage, we recognize that (though it would horrify the essayists) we could fit their critique of modern industrialization into a Marxist diatribe against the evils of capitalism. Extremes meet, agrarians and Marxists, when each tries to quantify something as complex as society. "We have more time in which to consume, and many more products to be consumed. But the tempo of our labors communicates itself to our satisfactions, and these also become brutal and hurried. The constitution of the natural man probably does not permit him to shorten his labor-time and enlarge his consuming-time indefinitely. He has to pay the penalty in satiety and aimlessness. The modern man has lost his sense of vocation."[3]

Faulkner treads the margins of this statement, surely agreeing that "modern man has lost his sense of vocation," but less certain the past offered an unalloyed Edenic memory. He was too aware of injustice, lack of fair play, Negro subservience, divisiveness in community and society, the destructiveness of empire builders like Sutpen, even of men like Colonel Sartoris—who once ordered any Negro woman appearing on Jefferson's streets to wear an apron. While the essayists ignore this side of an agrarian culture, Faulkner as a novelist could not. He warned against the loss of values accompanying modern life, but was fully aware of the hardship, deprivation, ignorance, and injustice the land enforces on those who work it. In *As I Lay Dying* the confrontation between country and town comes when the Bundrens arrive in Jefferson: Dewey Dell is cheated in the exchange of her body for pills which will abort the fetus in her belly. In Jefferson there is medical attention for Cash's leg, whereas country treatment (concrete) could lead to death. Country kills, town saves; whereas with Dewey Dell, town deceives. Bundren life is hardly idyllic: both town and country can be antilife.

Worried about the role of religion in society, the symposium writers perceived religion as being man's submission to "the general intention of a nature that is fairly inscrutable; it is the sense of our role as creatures within it."[4] If we redefine "nature" as the big woods, Faulkner would agree: inscrutable nature contains if not a religious message then at least a spiritual one. In the big woods, there is a transcendence of the petty and trivial in human character, a vaunting of man's potential to enter into and possibly understand his surroundings. This occurs somewhat later in Faulkner's hunt stories, although we find it contemporaneously in "Red Leaves" and "A Justice" in *These 13* (1931), with "Red Leaves" written for 1930 publication.

This story is a massive indictment of a little-known development in Southern history: that Indians acquired and owned slaves, in fact raised slaves to sell them to the white man. Faulkner had written to *Scribner's* (late

1929 to early 1930) that "Few people know that Miss. Indians owned slaves; that's why I suggest you all buy it. Not because it is a good story; you can find lots of good stories. It's because I need the money."[5] (*Scribner's* rejected it; the *Saturday Evening Post* took it.) Faulkner then invents the fact that he sold one of these Indian stories to *Blackwood's* in England for 125 guineas. "Red Leaves" is not a particularly strong story—its focus is diffuse, and it wanders aimlessly—but it is a revealing one. It demonstrates Indians utterly corrupted by slaveowning. They are slothful, lazy, fat, declining in their own way as the Sartoris tribe declines in its. The founder of the clan, Doom (mislabeled "*du homme*"), fathers a declining race, ending with Moketubbe, who is maybe an inch over five feet tall and weighs 250 pounds. The Indians have lost their traditional skills, and now, like planters, they sit around while slaves work for them and become their capital. Yet for Faulkner, the Indian in his incorruptible state was a noble savage of sorts. Sam Fathers carries with him a wisdom of the woods which transcends any other kind of wisdom: it is the very historical destiny of the races Sam Fathers carries in his blood, what he passes on to those who will listen. The aged warrior of mixed black and Indian blood is the ultimate sage for Faulkner. But his type has become corrupted, and the land itself contaminated by slavery, a form of degraded capitalism.

Faulkner was obsessed with other forms of background, race, mixtures, and he gave his own genealogy in terms *Scribner's* could never use. "I was born in 1826 of a negro slave and an alligator—both named Gladys Rock. I have two brothers. One is Dr. Walter E. Traprock and the other is Eaglerock—an airplane."[6] This turned up in an interview in 1931, in the Memphis *Press-Scimitar* with much the same wordage Faulkner had written to *Scribner's* the previous year, and then again in the *Bookman* version of the same interview. Faulkner's mockery of his background locates him in this chosen, spiritualized past, where the dichotomy is not only between town and country but between trivialized and spiritualized man.

The symposium continues, on how religion is subverted by modern life: "But nature industrialized, transformed into cities and artificial habitations, manufactured into commodities, is no longer nature but a highly simplified picture of nature. We receive the illusion of having power over nature, and lose the sense of nature as something mysterious and contingent. The God of nature under these conditions is merely an amiable expression, a superfluity, and the philosophical understanding ordinarily carried in the religious experience is not there for us to have."[7] The other side of that argument, ignored in the symposium, is that the kind of survival labor represented by the Bundrens (or, later, Mink Snopes) leaves little opportunity for religion or for communion with the inscrutable qualities of nature. We recall Coleridge's response to Wordsworth's preface to the second edition of the *Lyrical Ballads* in 1800, in which Wordsworth rhapsodized about the wisdom gained from living close to the land. Coleridge would have none of that sentimentality about the "wise farmer" or the "percipient peasant." He argued instead that unrelieved work on the land deadened all responses and made the individual insensitive to anything except work itself; men turned into little more than beasts of burden.

Faulkner's fictional response to the agrarians has something of the same quality. If we want to see the Bundrens as superior to the world represented by roads and bridges we must find qualities of superiority in them; and yet Anse and Addie, those twin beasts of burden, have little to acclaim. She dies unfulfilled, bitter, and full of self-pity; and he, in turn, is full of self-pity for a poor sexual life, his lack of teeth, and the failure of his children to respect him enough. The Bundrens have hardly been transformed by proximity to nature into spiritualized people; they have been worn down to survival level by excessive hard work and poor fortune. They represented, in fact, that redneck faction in society which supported the Vardamans and Bilbos and got almost nothing from it. Implied in nearly everything Faulkner wrote was a critique of the land as fulfilling; what was fulfilling was nature as some abstract principle, a vision of nature, the idea of the Edenic myth extending into the hunt and into man's relationship to nature. But the "land," as apart from nature, was doom-filled: doomed as people left it, doom for those staying with it.

Faulkner would agree with the symposium definition of humanism as an entire culture: ". . . the whole way in which we live, act, think, and feel. It is a kind of imaginatively balanced life lived out in a definite social tradition." The essayists say they believe this humanistic tradition "was rooted in the agrarian life of the older South and of other parts of the country that shared such a tradition." It did not derive, they add, from the classics or from the top, but from a way of life itself, "its tables, chairs, portraits, festivals, laws, marriage customs." This humanistic life contrasts with existence under industrialism: "a system that has so little regard for individual wants." Men, they say, "are prepared to sacrifice their private dignity and happiness to an abstract social ideal, and without asking whether the social ideal produces the welfare of any individual man whatsoever. . . . The responsibility of men is for their own welfare and that of their neighbors; not for the hypothetical welfare of some fabulous creature called society."[8]

These twelve men (the number for a jury, all white men, a representative Southern jury) were presumably Democrats whose sympathies were conservative; in contemporary terms, they would be neoconservatives or part of the Moral Majority in their fear of social change. Their social philosophy, if it could be adjudicated, would be represented by the most conservative members of the United States Supreme Court as presently constituted, and earlier by those calling themselves "states' righters." There is, here, almost paranoia about the effects of industrialization, even after the depression had brought agrarianism down to mere subsistence. Behind their intransigence about change was their fear that modern life would bring disorder, even chaos, to family hierarchies and traditional values rooted in village life. Where did Faulkner fit? He was prepared to go part of the way: he saw industrialization as a necessary evil, but as something unsuitable for him.

For the most part, Faulkner finessed this argument. As we have seen, he evaded the country-versus-city controversy. His allegiance was to nature, not to the land; his feelings were not directed to hatred of industrialization but to love of what nature could bring the individual. He deferred to the idea of individual man, but he was not indifferent to society, especially not in later years when he observed the South driving blindly toward disaster over racial issues. His loyalty to the individual, however, did not shield him from man's frailty, from the distortions nostalgia brought, from the weakness of memory as a means to preserve. Each hypothesis about man he tested out, and he found no overall formula. The essayists in the symposium were seeking permanent formulas for life, some way for the South to define or redefine itself. They cut through all problems, romanticized what they thought the South had been, perceived it as a Garden—when, in fact, it had been a dispossessed garden, riven by torment and injustice, lacking fair play, with intimidation its chief weapon as a means of maintaining majority control. The agrarians felt decisive thought and action could prove meaningful for the South when the country was itself failing and declining, and industry seemed on the run. Since the main body of America was faltering, the desire to cut themselves off was enormously attractive. Faulkner, however, did not accept this—no major Southern writer did. The major ones looked further, beyond the agrarians and their enticing ideology for a provincial, organic society, toward the country as a whole. Had Faulkner fallen into the agrarian camp at this time, he never could have become an "American novelist."

Manuscript changes in *As I Lay Dying* reveal several efforts on Faulkner's part to adjust temporal notions within the interior monologue. One of the problems with this mode of telling is that the present tense is called for, and yet such is reader expectation that too much present tense begins to sound artificial. Faulkner shifted to past tense when he could, to adjust to reader expectation, although against the grain of a monologue's thrust. Similarly, he needed to create a dialect which was close to the way the Bundrens spoke and yet would be comprehensible to an audience beyond Mississippi hill country. While there is high rhetoric in the novel which obviously does not fit a particular speaker, Faulkner did try to be true to country speech.[9] Dialect appears, but it is accessible, not the kind of regional speech which turns the reader away with faithful reproduction. We become aware of Faulkner's effort to create a new language, between the demands of the semiliterate people he is depicting and the sophisticated audience at whom the novel is really aimed.

Sound was gaining for him something of a following, and while sales were small, he was being noticed. The serious reputation he was gaining with this novel would compensate for *Sanctuary* when it appeared in 1931. Meanwhile he was preparing the typescript of *As I Lay Dying*, doing his own typing and making further corrections as he went along, finally dating the ribbon copy January 12, 1930. It was an auspicious follow-up to his previous novel, which had found a British publisher in Chatto & Windus through the efforts of the novelist Richard Hughes. His fiction was also catching the attention of a French professor and translator, Maurice Coindreau, whose presence in Faulkner's career would prove considerable.

Faulkner was spewing forth short stories as if programmed, and sending them out on a regular schedule; dates of submission, acceptance or rejection, and place where sent were duly registered. What characterizes the short fiction of this period—much of which ended up in *These 13*, dedicated to Estelle and the short-lived Alabama—is their unevenness. While certain masterly stories were submitted and accepted, others are amateurish and tedious; they are miscalculations of the worst sort. It is as though Faulkner were leaving the matter of taste up to the editors to whom he submitted his work, and had himself forsaken responsibility for what he had written. The schedule itself indicates a kind of mechanical approach to writing, for it was strictly a business proposition. Perhaps we should reverse the question of taste and authorial responsibility and say that what Faulkner achieved was remarkable considering the volume of short fiction he produced at this time. Not that he wrote so many bad stories, but that he wrote so many good ones, given the pressures on him personally and professionally, given the need to make money rapidly. Shortly after this, he moved into a home of his own, a home which was itself a production, inasmuch as it was a shambles and virtually unlivable without renovation. But little of this seemed to distract him from his main goal, which was to churn out stories and submit them like pellets from a shotgun. His gun was aimed at New York outlets, where the competition was his major contemporaries, Fitzgerald and Hemingway, among dozens of lesser but quite able writers all trying the same markets.

The sending schedule is a record of two years of submissions, acceptances, and rejections. It begins with a submission on January 23, 1930, and ends with one for January 9, 1932. There are 129 entries, of which twenty-nine are undated. Faulkner kept track on a sheet of paper with lines drawn to form columns; on the left were the names of stories submitted. The *Saturday Evening Post* was a veritable revolving door, but Faulkner persisted because of the high rates.

Up to the time of these submissions, he had published no stories (unless we count those early prose pieces published in the *Mississippian*), in itself a curious fact for so obsessive a writer now over thirty-two years old. Nevertheless, his plan was a good one: to write stories as rapidly as he could and to hope that proceeds from short fiction would eventually give him time to write novels, which had higher priority. The plan worked only partially. While he earned more from the *Post* for his four stories accepted there than he did from his first four novels, it was *Sanctuary* which pushed him into commercial success. It was also *Sanctuary* which gave him the opportunity to go to Hollywood, and it was studio money which enabled him to write his novels. As we shall see, none of these interruptions— neither the saturated writing of short stories nor the trips to Hollywood —affected his work on longer fiction in the 1930s. When his quality did decline in the 1940s, it was attributable to more complex reasons than merely outside activities. The old saw that Hollywood, which he hated, put him in the position of a man painting himself into a corner—writing scripts so he could write seriously, but unable to write seriously because he was preoccupied with scripts—does not hold up. Hollywood caught Faulkner on the rise into his career, not in the middle or at the tag end. He was a motor in the early 1930s, and nothing was going to shut down his acceleration.

Of the 129 entries on the list sent to twelve publications,* we count forty-four different titles, but since two titles were alternates of other stories on the sending list, we are dealing with a total of forty-two stories. Of these forty-two, thirty were eventually published; twenty within the period of the sending schedule itself, the other ten somewhat later. In the period before *Sanctuary* appeared, on February 9, 1931, Faulkner had four stories accepted, beginning with "A Rose for Emily" in the April 1930 *Forum*. Of the remaining twelve of the original forty-two, there are several complications. Six were unpublished and have vanished, at least in their original form. Two ("Dead Pilots" and "Point of Honor") have either disappeared or else been absorbed under other titles, as "All the Dead Pilots" and "Honor," respectively. Two others are unpublished but available in manuscript at Virginia, and two more underwent a strange schedule. "Peasant" was not circled as accepted, but may have appeared under the title "Spotted Horses" (*Scribner's*, August 25, 1930), and "Aria con Amore," which was circled to indicate acceptance by *Scribner's*, was not published by them or anyone else under this title. "Peasants," incidentally, was most likely connected to the revised title, "Spotted Horses," inasmuch as the two titles come together in *The Hamlet*, where the section on spotted horses appears in the segment titled "Peasants."

What is clear from the sending schedule is how Faulkner favored the *Post* and *Scribner's*. The latter had first look at "A Rose for Emily" and rejected it, although *Scribner's* did accept "Dry September" ("Drouth" in manuscript, title changed on publication) after the *American Mercury* rejected it. *Harper's*, not one of the magazines listed at the top of the sending schedule, received a large number of stories from Ben Wasson and published several, whereas the *American Mercury* received sixteen stories and accepted only four. By the time of the publication of *Sanctuary*, besides having had five stories published, Faulkner saw eight accepted for future

---

*The sending schedule looks like this: *Forum*—9 submissions; the *American Mercury*—15; the *Saturday Evening Post*—32 (5 acceptances); *Scribner's*—26 (3 accepted by October 1931, 9 in all); *Miscellany*—3; *Liberty*—6; *College Humor*—3; *American Caravan*—1; *Cosmopolitan*—1; the *Southwest Review*—1; *Blues*—1; *Woman's Home Companion*—10; also 8 sent to Hal Smith and 13 to Ben Wasson. This accounts for 129 entries.

publication. He noted the amount received for each story, and we see how lucrative this market was for the successful author: $750 each for "Thrift" and "Red Leaves," although only $200 from *Scribner's* for "Dry September," a finer story.

Even while rejecting stories, editors generally recognized that a very talented writer was knocking at their door. We note that editors and publishers throughout the 1930s embraced Faulkner's work far more warmly than did the general run of critics. While reviewers such as Clifton Fadiman in the *New Yorker* regularly trashed each Faulkner novel, Faulkner found editors who believed in him, even when sales were poor. Kyle S. Crichton, an assistant editor at *Scribner's*, for example, wrote to Faulkner in 1930: "We consider you one of the greatest writers alive and want to use everything of yours that is humanly possible."[10] Within six months (July 23, 1931), he wrote again to Faulkner that he wanted all stories with Flem Snopes: "He is our character and we think that in your hands he will become one of the great characters of literature." He offered to take any Flem stories rejected by the *Saturday Evening Post*. Even Dashiell, who catered to a particular audience quite different from Faulkner's, was sympathetic and encouraged the author, while rejecting five for every one accepted. Dashiell, for instance, at first criticized Ginsfarb in "Death Drag" as a caricature, although the story ended up eventually in *Scribner's*. The latter could also be recalcitrant—trying to fit Faulkner to its audience, it returned "The Hound" and "Indians Built a Fence" (disappeared) as "horror stories" unacceptable to their readers. "The Hound," under the title "Hound," was taken by Harper's when submitted by Ben Wasson after going the rounds of the *Saturday Evening Post, Scribner's*, and *American Mercury*.

This type of sending schedule took a good deal of resilience in the author. He had to face almost daily or weekly rejection, then continue to write more stories, sending out those and the ones already returned. He was at the time the author of four novels, and had two more being prepared for publication—not a beginner, but a professional writer who knew, even if the world at large did not, he had written at least one masterpiece in *Sound*. Faulkner's belief in himself was complete. Except for the drinking, which was constant during most of his adult life, there was no hesitation, no need for visible support. He did receive encouragement, however, from his friend and agent, Ben Wasson. Wasson stayed with Faulkner through this period of almost circuslike submission and rejection of manuscripts, rewritings, retitlings, going back repeatedly to magazines which seemed intractable in what they demanded from their authors. Later on, Wasson's injured feelings led him to tell several unpleasant stories about Faulkner, but during this period he was steady and supportive. Another great support was Harrison Smith, who had come along to publish *Sound, As I Lay Dying*, and the revised *Sanctuary*. He was the right man at the right time, when Faulkner might have faltered for lack of a publisher who believed in him.

In the years from 1930 to 1932, Faulkner's activities seem overwhelming, and we can only account for them by his ability to concentrate amidst turmoil. With the typescript of *As I Lay Dying* completed (January 12, 1930), the sending schedule was made up, on January 23. On April 12, to continue this turbulent odyssey, Faulkner and Estelle bought a run-down antebellum house which required considerable renovation. On April 30 *Forum* became the first national magazine to publish one of his stories. As we shall observe below, *As I Lay Dying* was published on October 6, and Faulkner sent Cape and Smith further revisions of *Sanctuary*, under contract and due for publication on February 9, 1931. In addition to the *Forum* publication of "A Rose for Emily," three other stories appeared in 1930: "Honor," which turned up later in *Doctor Martino and Other Stories* (1934); "Thrift," which remained uncollected; "Red Leaves," which, like "A Rose for Emily," ended up in *These 13*. All except "Thrift" were later published in *Collected Stories of William Faulkner*.

But other things were happening out of sight. At Princeton Maurice Coindreau was becoming interested in Faulkner stories and would translate "A Rose for Emily" and "Dry September" into French before asking Faulkner if he could also translate *Sanctuary*. The significance of this cannot be overestimated; Faulkner's reputation in France soared well before it began to gain momentum in America with Malcolm Cowley's 1946 *Portable Faulkner*. The French intelligentsia embraced Faulkner early—Sartre, Camus, Beauvoir, especially Malraux—while their American counterparts remained undecided. In another development, Sinclair Lewis in his Nobel Prize acceptance speech in Stockholm on December 12, 1930, spoke warmly of a new generation of writers whose work was so authentic and passionate he had himself been left behind. Among them, he singled out William Faulkner "who has freed the South from hoop skirts."[11] Lewis may have been drawn to Faulkner for the latter's ability to penetrate hypocrisy and sham, as Lewis had so successfully done. But whatever his motives, it took a good deal of courage to cite those who would become the next generation, among them Hemingway, Wolfe, Dos Passos, Wilder, and, strangely, Michael Gold. Fitzgerald is, unaccountably, missing.

Faulkner felt that if he kept up the pressure he would become more broadly noticed. This he did despite a terrible setback when his and Estelle's infant daughter Alabama, named after Faulkner's great-aunt Alabama Leroy McLean, died on January 20, 1931. Hard on this unexpected and unsettling event, the sharply revised version of *Sanctuary* appeared on February 9. Its sales moved to over six thousand within a month and a half, eventually being surpassed only by *The Wild Palms*. On August 17, 1931, Faulkner began a novel called "Dark House," which became *Light in August*. The title "Dark House" goes back to "Twilight" as the governing title of *Sound*, and "Dark House" would recur as the working title of *Absalom*. Faulkner now found himself also courted, in the fall of 1931, by other publishers, namely Knopf, Harold Guinzberg of Viking Press, and Cerf and Klopfer of Random House.

But 1931 was not over. Besides making several trips outside Oxford, Faulkner published sixteen stories during the year, including *Idyll in the Desert*, which Random House published in a limited edition of four hundred copies. Metro-Goldwyn-Mayer also became interested in acquiring him as an author, and Sam Marx invited him out to Hollywood as a scriptwriter. Of those sixteen stories published in 1931, a few became classics of the genre: "Dry September" and "That Evening Sun Go Down." Another one, "Spotted Horses," served the important function of bridging the period between *Father Abraham* and *The Hamlet*, the first in the Snopes trilogy.

After a year which went from the low of his infant's death to the successful publication of *Sanctuary* and the start of *Light in August*, Faulkner kept up the pressure for 1932. It was as if he knew he had to race along to get it all down before it vanished. In those two years he established himself as a writer both for the marketplace (the stories) and for the more serious reader (the novels). As we have seen, despite its notoriety—no little fueled by Faulkner himself—*Sanctuary* is a very serious work.

He completed *Light in August* by February 19, 1932, an incredible six months after beginning it. The notoriety surrounding *Sanctuary* following its publication led Paramount to take an option on it, and in the meanwhile Faulkner had left for Hollywood, under a six-week contract with MGM, at $500 per week, from May 7 to June 16. Those six weeks earned him almost as much money as he had made in ten years of writing. *Contempo*, a small literary magazine published in Chapel Hill, devoted almost its entire February 1, 1932, issue to Faulkner's work: the story "Once Aboard the Lugger," nine poems, a review of *These 13* and *Idyll in the Desert*, plus an assessment of his work against that of his contemporaries, Hemingway, Cather, Lewis, Anderson, Dreiser, Dos Passos, and Evelyn Scott (who had so passionately reviewed *Sound*). The result was that he was estimated to be "the most creative of contemporary American writers."

As *Light in August* was being prepared for publication (which occurred on October 6), Faulkner extended his stay in Hollywood, now at $250 per week, getting acquainted with Howard Hawks, then at MGM. Back in Oxford, Murry Falkner died suddenly at the age of sixty-one, leaving Maud with little money and making her almost entirely dependent on her eldest son. Even while returning to Oxford, Faulkner continued to work for Hollywood, now earning $600 per week because of the largesse of Hawks. He prepared his second volume of poetry, *A Green Bough*, which appeared the next year. And, in this year of herculean activity, he managed to publish eight more stories, although few of them can be considered of top quality. In the meanwhile, renovations were continuing on his house, now called Rowan Oak, with Faulkner doing much of the handiwork when he was in Oxford.

This two-year period, even in summary form, suggests Faulkner worked best when under the gun—needing money, distraught because of his infant daughter's death, unsettled in a new home which was hardly livable, dealing with a difficult Estelle, with her drinking, her own grief, her poor physical condition generally, travelling extensively to New York and then to Hollywood, which he thoroughly disliked, pressed for time in everything he did. By the end of 1932 he had published a total of twenty-four stories, some written before 1930; he had written an entire novel, *Light in August;* he saw the publication of two other novels, *As I Lay Dying* and *Sanctuary.* He saw his reputation begin to spread through the good auspices of Maurice Coindreau with his translations into French and his important article on Faulkner in *La Nouvelle Revue Française.* He had to deal with contracts, options, the possibilities of his story "Turnabout" being adapted for a film, through Hawks's brother, William.* It was a two-year period almost unmatched by any other major writer—we can think only of the pitch of activity of Melville, who thundered his way into *Moby-Dick* by the time he was thirty-one. But whereas Melville seemed exhausted and played out after that masterwork, Faulkner kept going for another decade at virtually the same speed, finally slackening off in the early 1940s for a variety of reasons, personal and professional.

"Idyll in the Desert," like "Selvage" (Estelle's story turned into "Elly"), was probably written in late 1929 or early 1930. It was rejected by *American Mercury, Liberty, Forum,* the *Saturday Evening Post, Scribner's, Harper's,* and *Woman's Home Companion.* It also went out through Ben Wasson, who may have submitted to other magazines as well. It was finally published, probably as a way of gaining and holding an author, by Random House, in a limited edition on December 10, 1931. The story is slight, in a style which did not serve Faulkner well, but it contains, once again, that shadow world of his relationship to Estelle.** It is, however, better disguised than "Elly."

*Hemingway, later, included the story in his anthology *Men at War.*

**"A Dangerous Man," which remained unpublished although submitted to both *Forum* and the *American Mercury,* also had a curious series of personal transformations, until Faulkner gave up on it. It was originally an idea of Estelle's, perhaps even a partial manuscript by her, called at one time "A Letter" and then retitled "A Letter to Grandmamma." Her name appears on the title page of a manuscript fragment. Faulkner himself tried two versions of the story, both of them with some personal dimension. In the more fully fashioned version, in the Rowan Oak Papers at the University of Mississippi, the "dangerous man," Bowman, has the build, temperament, and potential violence identified with Murry Falkner. Yet despite his fierceness and readiness for a fight, with fists or pistol, he passively allows his equally fierce wife to run his household and his life. She even cheats on him with a "dapper little man" who sells "insurance or something," and Bowman, we are led to assume, countenances the relationship. The inconclusiveness of the story, really a fragment, suggests Faulkner was touching on a deeply passive element in his bluff, gruff father—and then retreated, unable to shape such explosive material. In the other fragment, another hard man and a tough wife live uneasily, and when he leaves her he is afraid his mother will stop their support money. The personal dimension here is that familiar triangle in Faulkner, of husband, wife, and his mother; but, once again, the piece is fragmentary.

As well as shadowing Faulkner's own life with Estelle, the story foreshadows *The Wild Palms*. The inner story has altered several aspects of Faulkner's "romance" with his wife, but it portrays the woman as having abandoned her husband and two children for the love of a younger (thus, forbidden) man, and he repays her with abandonment in return. It develops an idea Faulkner would return to repeatedly: that in most instances women's sacrifices are not borne out by subsequent experience; that those who throw precious things away get only the moment, not any permanent reward. He felt a certain chill at a woman who abandoned her traditional role in order to live on the edge, even with him.

That puritanical strain Coindreau and others identified as running through Faulkner* becomes very clear here: the wages of sin are literally death, the moment of experience must be paid for with a lifetime of regret, and for everything gained one must lose considerably. Nothing comes freely, which is another way of saying salvation comes only from a life lived righteously. Faulkner may have fudged this view—but even in *Sanctuary*, and perhaps *especially* there, he would have it no other way.

Faulkner was also looking ahead, often using his stories to foreshadow later work of much greater magnitude. In a slight piece called "Smoke," written in very early 1930 but not published until April of 1932 (by *Harper's*, after three submissions to the *Post* and one to *Scribner's*), Faulkner introduced a new character, Gavin Stevens, the county attorney. Superficially, Gavin—Harvard and Heidelberg educated—seems a misfit in the town, someone on the order of Phil Stone. More likely, Faulkner once again was drawing a shadow of himself: the man who, having perceived wider worlds, is drawn back to his region. Gavin reappears in various roles in *Knight's Gambit*, in 1949, one of Faulkner's weakest collections of stories, but he is quite compelling in the Snopes trilogy, with his obsessive feelings about Eula Varner and her daughter, Linda.

"Smoke" also features a glimpse[12] of someone akin to Popeye, a hired hit man. But the story becomes neat and strategic, Faulkner's deference to the detective genre which was becoming so popular. It has little life of its own outside the coordinates of the murder and the need to straighten out the facts. The county attorney, who can discuss Einstein with college professors and squat on his heels talking to country people, does not live beyond his fact-finding ability.

*In his April 14, 1932, letter to Coindreau, Faulkner commented on the professor's article in *La Nouvelle Revue Française*, affirming "I see now that I have a quite decided strain of puritanism (in its proper sense, of course, not our American one) regarding sex. I was not aware of it. But now, in casting back and rereading now and then or here and there of my own work, I can see it plainly. I have found it quite interesting." (*Selected Letters of William Faulkner*, ed. Joseph Blotner [New York: Vintage Books, 1978; orig. publ. 1977] pp. 63–64). More later on whether his puritanism was "in its proper sense, not our American one."

Written at about the same time as "Smoke," "Dry September" is another level of fiction.* This story, titled "Drouth" in manuscript, also made the rounds, inexplicably when we consider its consummate artistry. The *American Mercury, Forum,* and *Scribner's* rejected it before *Scribner's* finally accepted it on a resubmission; it appeared in January 1931. Here Faulkner pulled everything together: exact sense of place, sure grasp of atmosphere, sharp characterization, and a situation of immediate moment to him and to the South—the lynching of an innocent Negro for the alleged rape of a white woman. It also introduces a tremendous sympathy for the Negro, Will Mayes, in a different way from Faulkner's attitude toward Dilsey, a house servant. Will Mayes exists as an independent man caught up in a brutal victimization which says a great deal about the South.

The World War I veteran, McLendon, who raises the mob against Mayes, is presented sharply, forerunning Percy Grimm in *Light in August.* McLendon cannot assimilate into civilian life after the "high" of the war; he needs violence, even killing, to hold his life together. Like a Hemingway character, he finds domestic life insufficient, and this show of male supremacy—against Mayes first and then against his wife, whom he strikes—compensates for his lackluster civilian or sexual life. As for the alleged crime, Faulkner dug deep into Southern folklore, in which it is assumed the Negro's greatest need is to rape a white woman, and the white woman's greatest fantasy is being raped by a Negro. Minnie Cooper is the female counterpart of McLendon. Having been rejected, now growing old alone, she needs excitement to hold herself together. Sexually hysterical in Faulkner's presentation of her, she must create a situation in which she seems desirable. Since no white man finds her attractive, she conjures up the Negro Will Mayes as her attacker, knowing that her accusation or rumor of a Negro attack will turn the entire town into defense of her.

But Faulkner twisted the story much further. By stressing the weather —the unrelieved drought, the dry heat—he was able to present the townspeople as bored, on edge, waiting for something to happen, rain or otherwise. "Through the bloody September twilight, aftermath of sixty-two rainless days, it had gone like fire in dry grass—the rumor, the story, whatever it was."[13] The rumor becomes like a fire which eventuates because of the drought and the town's boredom. A lynching will relieve the tension, the "dryness." The image is striking. Against this is presented the "cool" of the barber shop, where we meet a barber, Hawkshaw, who doesn't believe Mayes did it. Faulkner then turns the screw, so that the

*"Dry September," "A Rose for Emily," and "Miss Zilphia Gant" (written in 1928, accepted by the *Southwest Review* and published by the Book Club of Texas in 1932) form a "spinster group." In the first two, a spinster's condition leads to violence, and in the third, a mother and daughter, although briefly married, are deserted and lead spinsters' lives. For the mother, also, there is violence. The interest of the grouping is twofold: in its revelations of sexual repression and how such repression leads to its own kind of explosion; and in Faulkner's view of four women who are trapped and/or consumed by the male world. Max Putzel (in *Genius of Place: William Faulkner's Triumphant Beginnings*) sees Faulkner's 1925 sketch "Frankie and Johnny" as a predecessor, but that piece in the New Orleans *Times-Picayune* is little more than a vignette.

sympathetic Hawkshaw becomes, initially, part of the lynch party—the good man caught up by the fire, who cannot protest if he wants to remain in town. It is striking how Faulkner, by 1930, was shaping one of his most significant racial themes: that in the face of injustice, the good man is silenced by intimidation. The worst may lack all conviction, but the good go along or leave.

This story was joined by another type—the war story, a whole group of them, few of them particularly compelling or enduring. In some instances they do give us insight into Faulkner's need to maintain his war memories well over a decade after his discharge from the RAF. "Ad Astra," "Victory," "Crevasse," and "All the Dead Pilots" derive from this period of furious story-writing, and all were published in *These 13*. "Ad Astra" and "All the Dead Pilots" went through the sending schedule, with "Ad Astra" finding a place in the annual *American Caravan* (March 25, 1930) and "All the Dead Pilots" (under the title "Dead Pilots") coming to rest in *Woman's Home Companion* (April 23, 1931). Of them all, only "All the Dead Pilots"— with its proximity to Faulkner's own sense of himself—comes close to realization.

"Ad Astra" is an attempt to romanticize the tragic death rate among RAF pilots—a way, perhaps, for Faulkner to dramatize the risk he had been in, if people accepted his deceptions about his military service. But whatever his precise motives, Faulkner had a lingering affection for those doomed fliers—as he would also show in "Honor," "Death Drag," and finally in *Pylon*, his homage to those who rejected the ground for almost inevitable death in the air. One of the fliers in "Ad Astra" is Bayard Sartoris, and another familiar face is Gerald Bland from *Sound*. Among them is a kind of honor, embodied in the act of Comyn, a belligerent Irishman who insists on bringing a "defeated" German into the bar full of French soldiers. Comyn had himself shot the German down the previous day, and he keeps him around as a kind of trophy, a sign of Irish superiority. The story comes to us almost as a whine.

"All the Dead Pilots," however, attempts and achieves more. It has a superb beginning:

In the pictures, the snapshots hurriedly made, a little faded, a little dog-eared with the thirteen years, they swagger a little. Lean, hard, in their brass-and-leather martial harness, posed standing beside or leaning upon the esoteric shapes of wire and wood and canvas in which they flew without parachutes, they too have an esoteric look; a look not exactly human, like that of some dim and threatful apotheosis of the race seen for an instant in the glare of a thunderclap and then forever gone.

Because they are dead, all the old pilots, dead on the eleventh of November, 1918. When you see modern photographs of them, the recent pictures made beside the recent shapes of steel and canvas with the new cowlings and engines and slotted wings, they look a little outlandish: the lean young men who once swaggered. They look lost, baffled.

They are, in fact, lost in "this saxophone age of flying."[14]

They are all dead now because they are no longer lean or hungry. They have thickened about the waist, they sit in important jobs behind desks, they have wives and children and suburban homes, they have gardens and they putter around when they get home in the evening. There is more than mortality here, although there is that. These "dead pilots" have passed through a rite of passage, but with the war gone, they have reverted to facelessness. There is a great deal of Housman in this: the lads who gave their lives for the moment of glory and now are gone. In Housman they are dead; in Faulkner, as in Eliot, they are among the living dead. The end of the story is in perfect harmony with the beginning—only the middle cannot maintain the tone. John Sartoris has died in a plane crash fighting against the enemy in the skies. It was, as we know from *Sartoris,* a brief life, and it was snuffed out even as Aunt Jenny writes him to come home, that enough is enough. And then Faulkner comments:

And that's all. That's it. The courage, the recklessness, call it what you will, is the flash, the instant of sublimation; then flick! the old darkness again. That's why. It's too strong for steady diet. And if it were a steady diet, it would not be a flash, a glare. And so, being momentary, it can be preserved and prolonged only on paper: a picture, a few written words that any match, a minute and harmless flame that any child can engender, can obliterate in an instant. A one-inch sliver of sulphur-tipped wood is longer than memory or grief; a flame no larger than a sixpence is fiercer than courage or despair.[15]

The piece emerges as a reverie, a fantasy world of Faulkner's own making, in which he is both puppet and puppet-maker. He uses an omniscient narrator, a person uninvolved in the story itself, an "I," and the tone is personalized, with direct references repeatedly made to the reader. This conveys a double remove for the author, as Faulkner had learned from Conrad. It put him behind the "I," and, further, made the "I" seem responsible for the entire production. It also gave him freedom to roam free of both "I" and internal story. Unfortunately, the piece as a whole does not hold to the splendors of the beginning and end.

If "All the Dead Pilots" has moments of greatness in it, another war story of a somewhat earlier period, "Victory," was the working out of an idea with only marginal interest for Faulkner. It too has something of the "dead pilot" in it. Alec Gray, a Scotsman, passes through a terrible rite of passage in the war, becoming a great hero, but also a murderer, of the sergeant-major who persecuted him on the parade grounds. We note the shadowy presence of a typical Conradian conflict. After the war Gray tries to trade on his distinguished appearance, his uniform, and credentials. But once demobilized, he falls into the abyss awaiting those who cannot distinguish between what marks success in war and in peace. Instead of returning to work in the Scottish shipyards, as his father recommends, Alec tries to make a go of it in London. But there he is just another "dead pilot," a man attempting to trade his past for the future. Although a man who maintains his appearance to the end, shabby but distinguished, he ends up selling matches.

The presentation of Alec here, Sartoris elsewhere, and several others who cannot communicate, was apparently an integral part of Faulkner's plan. Self-contained like himself, these men experience moments which do not translate into words. When the time for action comes, they act brutally and effectively, and kill or are killed. Is this only a macho pose, or is Faulkner digging for something deeper? Part of it is a masculine reticence to express feeling, to remain bottled up; but some of it is Faulkner's sense of life as lived in privileged moments, in epiphanies of feeling, or in revelations. None of these lend themselves to talk. While it is true all of these moments here belong to men, Lena Grove will shortly enter into his plans. She has little to say, and communicates by body language, gesture, nods, and facial expressions. She *is*. These men *are*. What this signifies for Faulkner is that specialty which gives life meaning. If turned into language, this speciality is diluted; telling and retelling may become forms of dimunition. The idea is to catch the pitch.

On the whole, these stories are slight—especially "Crevasse," but less so "Turnabout" (or "Turn About" when Wasson placed it in the *Post*, March 5, 1932). "Crevasse," incidentally, was carved out of the original manuscript which was called "Victory," This title served as overall label for all four war stories in this cluster—"Ad Astra," "All the Dead Pilots," "Victory," and (a segment pulled from the latter story) "Crevasse." These four, plus "Turnabout," then appeared in the *Collected Stories* under the title of "The Wasteland." This designation is unfortunate, since it connects to Eliot's poem and misjudges where the weight of the stories lies. The label loses altogether that splash, that flare or glare which for Faulkner heightened all experience and made sudden death bearable. It loses sight of that romantic heroism which tinges so much of his thought and work, and makes him appear as an undiluted pessimist.

"Crevasse" is itself a throwaway, an effort to portray war as hell. The chief image of the story is, in fact, hellish, for the men are thrown by the heaving earth into a crevasse, with almost half of the party lost, buried alive. "Turn About," which interested Howard Hawks as a film property, is more ambitious. As we read it, we can see why Hawks, who directed *Dawn Patrol* with Errol Flynn in 1930, would visualize it in scenario terms. It is not a throwaway, but another clear statement of Faulkner's sense of the moment: the sheer exhilaration that comes when an act of bravery cuts across a potential moment of death. So intense is this feeling here and elsewhere that it can be likened to an act of artistic creation, when the imagination spurts and wraps itself around an idea. Faulkner found it in war, later in hunting, as Hemingway did in blood sports. For both, such moments became increasingly important as civilization closed in.

Using a story related by Robert A. Lovett about the Royal Naval Air Service and the Coastal Motor Boats, Faulkner forged a fiction in which he combined the two with wit and dash. What he did was to sneak up on the main idea and spring it as one does in a tall tale. The fliers think they are the bravest, the most courageous men in the military, *la crème de la crème*. Faulkner's aim is to demonstrate to them that flying is for children compared with the dangers experienced by the Coastal Motor Boat patrols. The job of these young men is to penetrate mine fields in razor-thin and speedy motor boats, launch torpedoes at German shipping, dodge the torpedo so that it doesn't blow them sky-high, and then try to return through enemy fire. One airman, Captain Bogard, accompanies them.

This is a very long story (thirty-four pages in the *Collected Stories*), but it is carefully planned. It has twists and turns, beginning with the discovery of a drunken young man, Claude Hope (clawed hope?), sleeping on the docks. The location is Dunkirk, and the American MPs who find the drunk have no idea what to make of him. The young men in the story are seventeen or eighteen and "run those little boats that are always dashing in and out."[16] The American captain, Bogard, starts to learn what the boys do, and he becomes interested enough to see what kind of stuff they are made of. We have the shaping of what will be "moments" when Bogard offers Hope a chance to fly with him as gunner. The young man is predictably cool, so resigned to death he has come through to the other side of indifference. His life is completely subsumed to the task at hand, and flying is a lark for him. On a bombing run, one bomb becomes stuck to the plane, suspended by its tail, and while Bogard and his copilot McGinnis are larking around, Hope keeps leaning out to observe the bomb. When they land, it trails in the sand, of course ready to go at any time. The English boy: "Frightened myself. Tried to tell you. But realized you know your business better than I. Skill. Marvelous. Oh, I say, I shan't forget it.' "

Courage under grace: Hemingway's statement becomes an understatement. In turn, Bogard goes out with Hope and his copilot Ronnie, who is all of twenty but already an old man of the sea, who looks "like someone's grandmother hung, say, for a witch."[17] The main part of the story now comes with Bogard's realization of what these men actually do. Once they have penetrated the mine fields by making the slender boat skim the water's surface, they must aim the boat at their target, release the torpedo, and then swing back to avoid being struck by their own missile. But sometimes the torpedo, once loaded and ready to blow, fails to function, and they have to use a windlass to re-aim it in the tube. This part of the job involves playing with a live bomb, but Hope handles it with his characteristic cool. He keeps remarking that compared with flying it must seem quite tame, while Bogard begins to feel ill. While Hope's airsickness in the plane had been just that, Bogard becomes sick from fear. Yet his sickness goes further: it reaches into the heart of a darkness which for the first time he has understood. Up to now, he has perceived his own role as flier as the most dangerous, but failed to comprehend what war might involve. Now he perceives another dimension, so that his sickness involves a revelation as deep as an artistic moment. He experiences an epiphany.

Sections 9 and 10 are anticlimactic. Once the moment of perception has occurred, the story is effectively completed. In the penultimate segment, Bogard sends a case of Scotch, the "best we've got," to the "child about six feet long" sleeping in the street. In the final section, the English *Gazette* carries a notice of the missing torpedo boat with the crew, Hope, Ronnie, and their assistant. Although "Turn About" does not have the pithiness and succinctness of Faulkner's finer efforts at this time—inevitably we compare it with "Dry September" or "A Rose for Emily"—it is a considerable contribution to war fiction and deserves to be resurrected. Further, it has something only Faulkner's finest fiction has—the "moment," the recognition or revelation. In "Turn About," Bogard's so-called seasickness is a fictional moment, saying something about soldiers and war. And the final statement—that if we could kill all the leaders, we could end the slaughter—became Faulkner's great theme for *A Fable* twenty years later. The best we have is a young man such as Hope or Ronnie, and they are human sacrifices. Wilfred Owen said it more succinctly:

> And there, there overhead, there hung over
> Those thousands of white faces, those dazed eyes,
> There in the starless dark the poise, the hover,
> There with vast wings across the cancelled skies,
> There in the sudden blackness the black pall
> Of nothing, nothing, nothing—nothing at all.[18]

Faulkner redeems the "nothing" by locating it in the memory of Bogard and his deed of attempting sacrifice for sacrifice. But that too will recede into nothingness, for Bogard is doomed. He gets away with this latest bit of bravura despite enemy aircraft pursuit, but like the torpedo crew, his days are numbered. And then the memory is lost, and they become like the men in still another Owen poem, "those who die as cattle" without even "passing-bells"[19] commemorating them.

There is great depth of feeling here, as though Faulkner had finally recognized that his wearing of the uniform and his deceptions about his military service were charades compared with the real thing. That he was a fake, a poseur, a deceiver are potential in this work of great compassion. Behind it all, although we have no direct evidence of it, is the sense of the young Confederate dead in the Civil War, those young men given monuments in every small Southern town; "in memorial to the Confederate dead," they read, as does the one in the Oxford square.

Having purchased the old Shegog house and adjoining property on April 12, 1930, Faulkner and Estelle moved in in June of that year. Ever since the Shegogs put up the house in 1844, it had been allowed to deteriorate. It went through the hands of the Baileys, who gave their name to the adjacent woods where the Falkner boys had played as children. It then belonged to the Bryants, Mrs. Sallie Bailey Bryant and her husband, Will. They rented it out, even as the house fell into increasing disrepair. It was a typical antebellum specimen, built on a small scale, designed in the colonial style by an English architect, William Turner. Before entering, one was confronted originally by four wooden columns, then a wide entrance with parlorlike rooms on each side leading to a dining room and kitchen. Three bedrooms upstairs completed the arrangement, with a small balcony set above the Georgian front. The house gives the sense of symmetry, designed as it was to provide space for a small family and yet make an original statement. The grounds leading up to it permitted a view, with flower beds and brick walks, turning the woods into a gentle place. When one views the house now, it creates an aura of stability, something well set into the community and culture of the region.

Faulkner had worked out an advantageous deal with Will Bryant. Since the writer had no money in hand, Bryant asked for no down payment: purchase price for the house and four acres (only a fraction of what was available) was set at $6,000, with monthly payments of $75 and interest at six percent. The numbers now may seem low, but this was 1930, the early part of the Great Depression, and $75 per month was not a small sum, nor was interest of six percent. The attractive part was Faulkner did not need a down payment, and that he could acquire more acreage as his finances permitted. In time he acquired another twenty-seven acres. What the purchase of the house and property and subsequent renovation over the years meant for Faulkner was stability. Despite his romanticism, such as we see in his war stories of this period, at thirty-three he had reached the point in life in which the footloose, tramplike poet was giving way to the country squire. The establishment of his small family in its own place indicates a bourgeois side to Faulkner which should not be ignored. He wanted it all: the sense of life on the edge as well as the stability the house gave him.

Estelle was not suited to this kind of rough living. What occurred between them as they tried to make do in the early years before the house became livable could not have helped what was already a touchy relationship. There was a lot of living on nerves; and while Faulkner balked at Hollywood and hated it once he arrived, there is little doubt it served as a safety valve. Whatever waste of time it involved, it also gave him breathing space; and although we might deplore the loss of masterpieces, we might also consider that the masterpieces he wrote occurred because he could breathe away from Oxford. Those who argue Faulkner depended heavily on community for the tensions of his major work lose sight of the fact that he needed something close to "anti-community," a situation in which he was all nerves, so taut and caught in himself nothing beyond mattered.

The old Shegog place, set deep back from a country road with Bailey's Woods alongside, became his home for the rest of his life. He only wavered from it when he and Estelle considered moving permanently to Virginia, near Charlottesville and the university that had made him feel welcome in the late 1950s. While he was involved in the move from the Meek apartment into his own house, the sending schedule was kept going. To the above stories, we add "Lizards," which became "Lizards in Jamshyd's Court-yard" when it appeared in the *Post* and then was incorporated into *The Hamlet*; "Selvage," which went out again, this time to *Forum*, was rejected, and ended up as "Elly" in *Story*, four years later.

By the time the Faulkners moved into what came to be known as Rowan Oak, Estelle was pregnant, and one necessity was to get the house in livable condition for the coming child. Further, Malcolm and Victoria were still small and needed attention. The question was where to begin, for the house needed every renovation possible: strengthening of the very beams on which it rested, repair and painting of walls, installation of indoor plumbing and electricity. The entire house needed to be replumbed before even the kitchen functioned. In the meanwhile, the Faulkners used oil lamps and water from an old wellhouse. The roof leaked, and windows let in not only air but insects, requiring adequate screens. Step by step, Faulkner undertook the renovation, with a helper in whatever specialty was required. A staff was assembled, a staff which seemed more underfoot than useful, but functioned loyally and would have marched with the author into cannon fire.

Ned Barnett acted as a kind of Figaro—majordomo, horse trainer, milker, waiter, and butler. He was a man of considerable dignity who demanded as much respect as he gave. He was a voice of sanity in a household which had a good many volatile temperaments ready to blow. Mammy Callie was there as maid for the two children and part-time cook. Estelle was herself a fine cook and baker, but others generally controlled the kitchen. By assembling this staff, Faulkner took upon himself an extended family for which he was liable not only for food and shelter, but medical expenses, clothing, and incidentals. Later, he complained of the financial burden he had placed on himself, and this becomes an important part of the story. For even as he willingly entered into these arrangements, and continued to honor them, they evidently ate away at him and made those intermittent releases from home welcome.

As a short story writer, Faulkner's progress in just a year or two was enormous, whatever other diversionary arrangements he had made in his life. *Contempo* published "Once Aboard the Lugger" (the one marked "I") in February 1932, after *Scribner's* had rejected it. That story derives from a period just before or around November of 1928. A twin story by the same name (marked "II") comes from a slightly later date, perhaps December

1928, and it too was rejected by *Scribner's* and remained unpublished.[20] Neither one has a voice or signature, Faulknerian or otherwise—in fact, both stories seem little but hard-boiled detective fiction, without the trenchant quality good detective writers give to their language.

The writer had yet to learn not only economy and grace, but accuracy. Even the title of the two pieces, "Once Aboard the Lugger," is lacking—the words suggest "Once upon a time" but are jarred by the unpleasant sound of the word "lugger," the small boat which carries contraband liquor. The titles two years later have a rightness to them, "A Rose for Emily," "Death Drag," "Dry September" (much improved from the original "Drouth"). We can see that just as the novels became more supple, more accommodating to his distinct voice, so too the short stories began to take on a Faulknerian quality. Unlike Hemingway, who had his voice from the beginning, Faulkner had to work through novels and thousands of words of short fiction to reach that sense of himself we consider distinctive.

As stories underwent changes of title as they passed through various revisions, so did the Shegog place need naming. Faulkner found a passage in *The Golden Bough* to the effect that if pieces of rowan-tree were placed over a door, they would negate witches' bad spells. The name Rowanoak or Rowan Oak came to indicate a secure place. Once inside Rowan Oak, no witches' brew or prediction could touch one. How American! Faulkner's very home was rooted in the Edenic tradition, allowing for the transformation of Scottish legend to American soil. Also, how ironic that the desire for Edenic security should produce a household whose disaffection began almost with its naming, with the death of Alabama. Drinking, self-destructive acts, and monumental personal struggles were to be fought out—all in contrast to the Adam and Eve who hoped to close themselves off in their own personal Garden.

Just as life in 1930 was beginning to solidify for Faulkner—marriage, family, home, reputation, a succession of published stories and books—it was falling apart for his father. It almost seemed a Freudian scenario in which, as the son gained in strength, the father faltered and declined. Murry's position as secretary and business manager of Ole Miss was essentially a political appointment, for he served at the pleasure of the chancellor, the latter in turn responsible to the trustees, who were themselves more or less controlled by the governor. Governor Bilbo saw the university as simply another part of his fiefdom, and did what he could to control the majority of the trustees, and through them the chancellor. When a large "volunteer" political contribution was requested—in Murry's case $500—he declined as he could not afford it, and resigned, which is precisely what Bilbo wanted. The post could then go to someone loyal to the governor. Since the appointment had not prepared Murry, now sixty years old, for any other position in life, he was a man without a role. He and Maud had earlier made peace, especially since she had gotten him to stop drinking; but he was in the main isolated from his sons, except possibly for Dean.

The eldest son, of course, had resources denied the father, and they were immense. He had a fantasy world, which he had already created in the shape of Yoknapatawpha and Jefferson; and whatever the personal demons, unresolved conflicts, family tensions, he had the intensity of his work. In the summer of 1930, he sent out still more stories: "Red Leaves," which the *Post* accepted and published on October 25, 1930; "Was a Queen," a revision of "The Window," which *Scribner's* published in January 1933 as "There Was a Queen"; "Per Ardua" (not to be confused with "Ad Astra"), which remained unpublished after making the rounds of the *Post, Scribner's,* and *Liberty* twice; and "The Peasants," which may have been "Spotted Horses," and in any case found its way into *The Hamlet.* As for prices, Faulkner was generally receiving in the range of $200 to $750, the latter from the *Post,* which was paying Fitzgerald $3,000 or more.

The tastes of the magazines were hard to judge, since the *Post* had rejected many more compelling stories than the one it accepted, "Red Leaves." The latter, nevertheless, is of interest to those studying the historical Faulkner—especially his sympathy toward Negro slaves and the fact that Indians themselves were slaveholders—but as fiction it is long and strung-out.* Yet the *Post* editor may have been impressed by Faulkner's seeming knowledge of Indian life and lore and his stress on ritual burial, among other details. But a good deal is pure fantasy, especially the Parisian background of Issetibbeha. What is compelling is the cycle: the Negro servant's flight when his master dies, and then his almost passive acceptance of his fate in ritualized death which will complete the cycle. In this portrayal of a culture, there is as much of *The Golden Bough* as there is of Indian culture.

Shining through is Faulkner's high regard for ritualistic acts: his compassion for the Negro is equaled by his sense that the Indians need to carry through their ceremonies in order to survive, however much slavery has diminished old customs. The most incisive part of "Red Leaves" occurs with the chase, a kind of scene that was to become a hallmark of his fiction. The chase here prefigures that of the French architect by Sutpen and his slaves in *Absalom,* that of the escaped convict in *Old Man,* and, more immediately, that of Joe Christmas once he has murdered Joanna Burden.

The death of the servant after Issetibbeha's death is full of significance for master-and-servant relationships—indeed for the entire question of slavery, whether the masters are white or Indian. The Indians may own the slaves, but the medium by which they acquired them was a white New

*Lewis M. Dabney, in *The Indians of Yoknapatawpha: A Study in Literature and History,* points out that the Chickasaws were considerable slaveholders. Slavery among the Chickasaws, as Faulkner suggests, is part of the deterioration of Indian culture, brought on in large part by the Indians' emulating a white culture of farming and trading. The "red leaves" in Faulkner's title refer to Indians.

England captain—so that Faulkner is implying the whole country conspires to create a slave culture. As the slave makes his passage in degradation from his African village to the slave markets of the South, systemic poison is spread across the country. Nature itself, in fact, somehow conspires to complete the cycle, for "red leaves" suggest late autumn, the death of nature and the Indian in preparation for the long sleep before resurrection.

"A Justice," while introducing the extremely important character Sam Fathers, is linked to "Red Leaves" by the theme of Indian and Negro relationships. Here the issue is not slavery but coexistence—as Sam Fathers narrates his past to Quentin Compson; in *Go Down, Moses*, he will relate it to Isaac McCaslin. In both narratives the idea of color dignifies the two races. Sam Fathers's grandfather works and plays with Doom *("D'homme")*, and the Indian passes on his lore, so that Sam eventually becomes like an Indian when he takes to the woods. He is the son of two fathers, Negro and Indian, and this is the lesson he passes on to the young Quentin Compson.* This meeting changes Quentin, but when Mr. Compson comes to get him and asks what he was doing, he says: " 'Nothing, sir . . . we were just talking.' "[21] Here slavery is transcended, indeed transformed into a racial composite which ennobles members of both races. "A Justice" should be read with "Red Leaves" and other stories on this theme, "A Courtship" and "Lo!," both from a much later time.

"A Courtship" (from the early 1940s) is significant less for itself than for what it demonstrates about Faulkner as he worked his Indian material. Critical for him is the re-creation of a vanishing world, which, despite its cruelties and excesses, has the whiff of an Edenic past. In their adherence to nature and to historical tribal rites, the Chickasaws have preserved a way of life, up to the encroachment of slavery into their culture. Faulkner is touching on one of his most romantic ideas, his Wordsworthian belief —perhaps laced by Jefferson—that in "lower life" a viable, livable culture can be found, and that this culture is somehow superior to the more sophisticated works of man.

In "A Courtship," Faulkner goes back into the early life of Ikkemotubbe, before he becomes Doom (the man, the chief) and develops his imperious ways. Here he is the playful supplicant for the hand of the lovely sister of Herman Basket. His chief rival for her is the white man of gargantuan size and appetites, David Hogganback. The right way for them to fight their duel for possession of the girl is with knives, but neither wishes to kill the other. The story unfolds as they show their love for each other as much as they do for Basket's sister. In fact, the tie that binds them becomes stronger than any desire for her hand. The competition becomes a series of tall-tale contests: eating, running, eventually saving each other when a cave, which was to bring death to one of them, collapses on them. In the

---

*This is the beginning in tentative terms of an impossible idea which grasped Faulkner's imagination: that the South eventually would become one race; that racial issues would dissolve because everyone would be black-and-white.

days when Ikkemotubbe could respond like a man and not like the corrupt person he would become, the two men, Indian and white, were brothers. This is for Faulkner the purest form of friendship, cemented by honorable competition and, by implication, a criterion of human behavior. It is, of course, a vanishing world. The Chickasaws will become invisible parts of Mississippi culture, another aspect of the disappearance of the Edenic ideal, however foolhardy and unachievable that ideal may be.*

"Lo!," one of Faulkner's least impressive stories, also fits into this panoramic sense of history, in which the uses of the past cannot be permitted to vanish. The entire tale (dating from 1934) is wrapped like a tall tale. It concerns an Indian march on Washington, a camping-out on the lawn of the White House, and an importuning of the president to redress certain rights. Faulkner was surely responding to the march on Washington of the Bonus Expeditionary Force to seek relief from unemployment. They too camped out in tents; but they were routed, with several deaths, by Patton, MacArthur, and Eisenhower, the heroes of the war in the next decade. For Faulkner, however, the march on Washington was to be a success, and the poor Indian would outsmart the white man and triumph.

The title comes with ironical intention from Pope's "Essay on Man": "Lo, the poor Indian! whose untutored mind / Sees God in clouds, or hears him in the wind / . . . Yet simple nature to his hope has giv'n / Behind the cold-topt hill, an humbler Heav'n." Pope's "poor Indian" becomes a wily horse trader.** The Chickasaws with their pertinacity win out over Washington sophisticates. Faulkner is in one sense replaying the Civil War; only here Indians are the counters, and Yankees are outflanked. The Indians specifically have come to seek a ritualistic or ceremonial acquittal for the nephew of a lace-covered chief for the murder of a white man who tried to maneuver a valuable piece of land from them. All the president wants is to get rid of the Indians, since they have infiltrated even his White House bedroom. They have made his life miserable; as is the way of the white man, he wants the Indians to become invisible. Until they get the

---

*Lest we think the Edenic vision of the Indian has disappeared from our literature: in the 1960s, when so much of our past and so many of our myths were being reexamined, the Indian reemerged. Several nonfiction studies of Indians include Vine Deloria, Jr.'s *Custer Died for Our Sins*, Alice Marriott and Carol K. Rachin's *The American Epic: The Story of the American Indian*, and Leslie Fiedler's *The Vanishing American*; in fiction, Ken Kesey's Chief Bromden in *One Flew Over the Cuckoo's Nest*, Joseph Heller's Chief White Halfoat in *Catch-22*, Thomas Berger's *Little Big Man*, Peter Matthiessen's Meriwether Lewis Moon in *At Play in the Fields of the Lord*, and numerous others. In one way or another, these books circle around to Indian forms of existence as ways of responding to the very qualities civilization is proud of silencing. The "savage Indian," in this reversal of values, becomes the purest form of civilization.

**Professor Calvin S. Brown, of the University of Mississippi, wrote to Lewis M. Dabney, author of *The Indians of Yoknapatawpha*, that his, Brown's, mother once asked Faulkner where he got his Indians from, since "she knew of no real sources, and he answered matter-of-factly, 'Mrs. Brown, I made them up'" (Lewis M. Dabney, *The Indians of Yoknapatawpha* [Baton Rouge: Louisiana State University Press, 1974], p. 11, n. 15). And to Cowley, Faulkner wrote: "I never made a general genealogical or chronological chart perhaps because I knew I would take liberties with both" (Malcolm Cowley, *The Faulkner-Cowley File: Letters and Memories, 1944–1962* [New York: Viking, 1966], p. 55). Faulkner's are mythical Indians with real values.

ceremony they came for, they refuse, and when they threaten to return after a second white man is murdered, the president offers them ownership in perpetuity of the land they claim, provided they do not cross the eastern side of the river. The president very much resembles Andrew Jackson—he is tall and lean, renowned as a general, and given to action. In fact, Jackson was known for his open house for Indians who came to Washington.

"Mountain Victory," submitted to the *Post* on October 4, 1930, and accepted for the December 3, 1932, issue, has some marginal connections to the other Indian stories. Although it is more closely associated with the Civil War than with Indian material in "Lo!," it links to that story because the Confederate major here is the son of a Choctaw chief named Francis Weddel, the Weddel-Vidal of "Lo!" The story deals with several of Faulkner's early and continuing interests, particularly miscegenation, racial identity, and questions of master-slave relationships. The major looks Negro and is taken to be Negro by the Tennessee-mountain family where he stops for shelter; the family is not sympathetic to the Confederate or to the Negro aide with him. The son of the mountain family has fought with the Union Army and wants to kill the major, Saucier Weddel, and the Negro. The misidentification of Weddel as Negro, part or full, looks ahead to *Light in August*, where questions of Joe Christmas's racial background determine his fate; and it looks still further ahead to Sam Fathers in *Go Down, Moses*, a suggestion of which already came in "A Justice." Faulkner was very much alive to an Indian-white mix which created a white man (Weddel is three-quarters white, Choctaw only on his paternal grandmother's side) who because of dark skin might look Negro.

But identification becomes more complicated because Weddel refuses to leave the Negro behind, and while the black man protests he is protecting his master, it is the master who protects the servant. Faulkner's sense of noblesse oblige between blacks and whites is clear: without the white man's shield, the black servant stands no chance of surviving. This, too, was an attitude which died hard; Faulkner never really let go of the traditional idea that the white man was the black's best friend and would not desert him. Faulkner himself did not desert his black servants and was deeply devoted to them, but failed to perceive that in the larger sense there were areas of the relationship that were destructive of black interests and dignity. Noblesse oblige was a form of intimidation.

"There Was a Queen" (variously called "Was a Queen" and before that "Through the Window," then "An Empress Passed") was probably written in the month before Faulkner bought the old Shegog place; that is, in March 1930. The story returns to the Sartoris clan, specifically to details in *Flags in the Dust*, and it may have been triggered by Faulkner's plans to settle into his own place. "There Was a Queen" has several unpleasant overtones, established by the specialness of the Sartoris family, of which old Aunt Jenny is now the sole direct survivor. The story focuses on what kills her. Narcissa is still living with Aunt Jenny, who is now ninety and confined to a wheelchair. Just prior to going away to Memphis for two days, the younger woman brings a man to dinner, and Aunt Jenny turns on him when she recognizes he is a Jew and a Yankee. ". . . but she knew at once that he was a Jew, and when he spoke to her her outrage became fury."²² She leaves the table in a rage and refuses all food. When Narcissa returns from Memphis, she tells Aunt Jenny she has lied about the pornographic letters from Byron Snopes—that there was not one, but eleven in all; that they were stolen by the man who robbed Colonel Satoris's bank; that the federal government was on the trail of the bank robber; that the Jew at the dinner table was a federal agent who had the letters. Then she drops the blow which will kill her aunt: in order to obtain the letters before letting anyone else read them, she has slept with him. For lack of money, she had no other recourse. She then burned the letters, returned, and washed herself clean in the creek behind the house. Aunt Jenny asks for her hat and awaits the end. The most unpleasant aspect of the story is its palpable anti-Semitism. We could argue that as a matter of course Aunt Jenny is anti-Semitic, just as she is anti-Yankee; but Faulkner presents her as someone not only caught up in the past and unable to escape but as someone redeemed by her relationship to the past. She speaks for values, standards, a superior way of life; he even has her die when she learns of what the younger generation will do—sleep with the enemy. Thus, her expression of anti-Semitism becomes more than the voice of the character. It carries the weight of the author's approval, and the Yankee Jew becomes an instrument of the new world, a reincarnation of the evil Reconstruction foisted on the South. The agent of debasement is clearly a Jew without honor, juxtaposed with the honorable Sartoris men in Aunt Jenny's memory and, by implication, in Faulkner's own value system.

Lost in the historical past, meandering among the Snopeses and Indians of his imagination, creating a vanishing culture from his own mind, Faulkner was repeatedly called back to the present by events in his personal life. Estelle—anemic, physically run-down, almost anorexic in appearance—was pregnant. But the money from short stories, chiefly from "Red Leaves" ($750), allowed them to introduce electricity to Rowan Oak, one of the first upgradings of the new acquisition. Faulkner agreed to act in an Oxford Chamber of Commerce production of *Corporal Eagen*, playing Izzy Goldstein, the Jewish sidekick of Red Eagen. Why he did this we can only speculate—perhaps it was the need for relief from work, the desire to get outside the house, the growing commitment he felt to community affairs. Except for Estelle's pregnancy, the most important event of this period was the October 6 publication of *As I Lay Dying*, in a printing of 2,522 copies.

The importance of this book went beyond the question only of sales and potential income. It had to do with Faulkner's effort to follow up something as innovative as *Sound* with another novel of almost equal daring.

As I Lay Dying would indicate whether he could continue as an experimental, innovative writer, or whether he would have to write more traditional narrative in order to survive with all his personal responsibilities. This novel was pivotal in what it told him about his career. His position recalls that of all serious writers who seek to develop along their own lines, but feel the pull from the marketplace because of familial, personal, or other commitments. But Faulkner's position was not quite theirs. His work was far more daring than that of his contemporaries; his penchant for experimental narrative and other innovation went to the very heart of his imagination; and his vision of American fiction differed from Wolfe's, Hemingway's, or Fitzgerald's. He put himself closer to the edge than anyone else. He was more clearly ready to fall off if he could not find critical and financial support for his experimental work. Further, his career was peaking, his imaginative powers ascending to their highest level, just as he came under the burdens of family responsibilities. None of his contemporaries moved so rapidly into two seemingly conflicting circumstances—even as his imagination was intense with new ideas, as his desire for creativity was apparently cutting him off from everything else, at that moment he was becoming involved in responsibilities which seemed to jeopardize the entire creative process.

Unfortunately, Faulkner did not receive any clear signs. Although he hoped for a strong marketplace response to his innovative work, it was mixed and diluted. He was still on his own. The reviews for *As I Lay Dying* fell into that area which respects the writer but hesitates about the book. The consensus was that while the novel was the product of a unique mind —even Clifton Fadiman agreed to that in his *Nation* review—there was too much obscurity. The reviewers felt uncertain about an aspect of modernism which had already been twenty-five or more years in the making when they faulted Faulkner's lack of a clear narrative. *As I Lay Dying* is, in fact, a central modernist document, with its betrayal of narrative, its decentering of material from one voice to another, its emphasis upon consciousness as the chief form of data. The reviewers had not caught up with the important modernist works of the twentieth century—those of Joyce, Kafka, Woolf, Conrad, Proust, Ford, and others—and their ignorance of these books, or their rejection of them (as with Fadiman), caused them to read Faulkner in self-defeating ways.*

---

*The *New York Times Book Review* (October 19, 1930), for example, castigated Faulkner for writing "in fluid Joycean terms." The reviewer placed the novel "in a high place in an inferior category," because of the author's unfortunate selection of material, his use of people of such low mind. Only a Dostoyevsky could rescue such material and "put it into literary channels whereby it can be handled by human intellect." Some reviewers, however, tried to understand. In the New York *Herald Tribune Books*, Margaret Cheney Dawson wrote favorably of Faulkner's "photographic mysticism." She says his "strength mounts when he externalizes his subject matters" and suggests his method can "be very exciting" (October 30). Similarly, the *New Republic* reviewer (October 19), Kenneth White, found it "an uncommonly forceful novel" and admired the ingenuity with which Faulkner kept "his various strands tightly knit" and contrived "the steadily increasing horror."

There were always exceptions. When a young Oxford schoolteacher came to pay homage to Faulkner, she was full of praise for the more difficult works.[23] She came out to Rowan Oak in a tour of admirers led by John Falkner, the third brother. But Faulkner was completely unresponsive and went into his act about his RAF service, including the well-worn tale of the hangar crash. Emily Whitehurst, the schoolteacher, was the kind of admirer whom later on Faulkner would cultivate, and with some he would have affairs—deferential, lovely-looking young Southern women who came offering gifts. Instead, Emily later married Phil Stone when the lawyer was forty-two; by then, as she came to recognize, Phil was already burned out, heading downward on his descent into rage, resentment, finally instability.

Between novels—Faulkner did not begin *Light in August* until August of 1931, still nine to ten months away—he ground away at short stories and tried to ingratiate himself with his stepchildren by telling them ghost stories, while watching carefully the progress of Estelle's pregnancy. Despite his ability to compartmentalize himself, he had arranged his life and held to it. As he and Estelle awaited the birth of their first child—in March or April of 1931—he wrote new stories, rewrote old ones, entertained the children on holidays, and reworked *Sanctuary*, which he found "just a bad book."

In another area, Faulkner was working with intractable material when he returned to "The Big Shot" for material, with Dr. Gavin Blount, the reclusive but socially well-placed doctor of that tale as the connecting link. He tried two more stories with Blount, not a particularly interesting character, in "Rose of Lebanon" and "Dull Tale." "Rose of Lebanon" was rejected by the *Post* on November 7, *Woman's Home Companion* on January 10, 1931, and *Scribner's* on July 23, 1931, and remained unpublished. Faulkner chose not to include it in his *Collected Stories* of 1950. "Dull Tale" suffered a briefer but similar fate, being rejected by the *Post* on November 14, 1930, and remaining unpublished and uncollected.

Unfinished and available only in manuscript, "Rose of Lebanon" is of interest only because its development in the existing nine pages follows the interior consciousness techniques of *As I Lay Dying*, using different people to present the material from their own points of view, then cutting back and forth until the whole is represented. The material in the brief excerpt concerns Blount's background, and explains why he is so dedicated to the Chickasaw Guards' Ball, for which he chooses the debutantes who will appear.

Faulkner picked up Blount and the situation again in "Dull Tale," clearly a reworking of "The Big Shot" from about five years earlier. Blount here and then has the resonance of a character who will appear as a major figure in the Snopes trilogy and in the several stories which make up *The Unvanquished*, Gavin Stevens. Blount also has a whiff of Horace Benbow and, behind him, Phil Stone. As a member of a fading aristocracy, he has little left to hang on to except his chairmanship of the Guards committee, which gives him the power of selection. As in "The Big Shot," he is visited by Val Martin, who wants his flighty daughter to be invited as one of the debutantes introduced at the ball.

Although *Absalom* is still four years away, a pivotal situation of that novel is foreshadowed by Martin's humiliation, which makes him vow "that some day he too would be rich, with a horse, saddled and unsaddled by niggers, to ride, and a hammock to lie in during the hot hours, with his shoes off."[24] From such humble beginnings, the big shot emerges. In another respect, the later story differs from the earlier version by dropping all references to Popeye and other mobsters.

It concentrates instead on the confrontation between Martin and Blount, and on Blount's personal background. Here too we are drawn to some details. For Blount can recall only a humiliating domestic situation, in which he moved fearfully, afraid of his father's wrath. The intensity of these scenes seems to suggest a personal resonance, or else a reflection of Faulkner's fantasy in which he perceived Murry Falkner as such a person. Blount is completely emasculated by these encounters—he goes on to become a doctor and to inherit his father's practice, but remains reclusive, a bachelor at forty, and unreachable except through his class and caste sense of himself. The domestic dread built up here cannot be ignored; in some ironic and terrible way, Faulkner re-created it for his own daughter Jill, using a caustic tongue as a way of making the domestic scene untenable for her.

"Dull Tale" unfortunately fulfills the promise of its title. It has biographical interest and little else. That Faulkner decided not to publish it in his *Collected Stories* was wise. Not so wise was his decision to publish "The Brooch," which he wrote late in 1930 or early in 1931. The story was originally submitted to *Forum* and *College Humor* and rejected by both on January 29, 1931, and February 13, 1931, respectively. A story of this name was finally accepted by *Scribner's*—of all places!—in January of 1936.

The story is a curious one for Faulkner, and one is once again tempted to see in it personal dimensions. Howard Boyd is tied to his mother so tightly no one can break through. While he hates her to such a degree he marries someone calculated to make her resist, he also is devoted to the older woman, especially after she suffers a debilitating stroke. Once married, he and his flighty wife—a clone of Temple Drake—live in her house, in a room on the floor above hers. He has been brought up to be nonsexual or homosexual: to eschew other women in favor of his mother, to show devotion to no one else. The intensity of this upbringing cannot help but remind us of Faulkner's closeness to Maud and to the fact that after he married he visited her, without Estelle, on every day he was in Oxford. He also supported his mother once Murry died, and she herself died only two years before her eldest son, so that she was with him during his entire married life.

"The Brooch" of the title is the means by which Howard recognizes Amy has been cheating on him—not only going out to dance while he remains home with his mother, but going further. The brooch, which she misplaces or loses, is the family heirloom, given to her by Mrs. Boyd in a kind of truce. When Amy is finally ordered by the mother from her house, she pleads with Howard to go with her, to assert his masculinity. But he refuses and takes upon himself the responsibility for the mess he is in. The last scene reveals him in the bathroom, the muzzle of his pistol "between his teeth like a pipe."[25] But even while planning his death, he is considerate of his mother, having padded the bathroom to muffle the shot. The story fails to cohere on many levels, chiefly because it has no distinctive voice. Dialogue is awkward; the handling of the scenes between Howard and Amy is clumsy, even gauche. Faulkner could deal with such material only when he could sharply angle it, or strike it obliquely or marginally.

Shortly after, "The Hound"—which would be incorporated into *The Hamlet* with Ernest Cotton of the story transformed into Mink Snopes—started to make the rounds; after an initial submission to the *Post* on November 17, it went on to *American Mercury*, ending up through Wasson's intervention as "Hound" in *Harper's* (August 1931). Like Mink Snopes later, Cotton shoots and kills a neighbor named Houston, who, he felt, had wronged him; the body is discovered and Cotton is sent off to the penitentiary. But the story differs considerably from its later incarnation in *The Hamlet*. The demands of a short piece dictated a more immediate approach. "The Hound" is in the grand guignol tradition: first the shooting, then the hiding of the body in a tree stump, with Cotton jumping up and down on the body to make it sink deeper into the stump; when the corpse is dragged out of its hiding place, an arm is left behind, and Cotton finally returns to retrieve the missing arm.

What is curious is that Faulkner seems coiled with hate, rage, hostility, and anger. The story is like a rattler's venom, and even the hound is no longer a "dog," but an agent of retribution. It suffers hideous wounds in order to destroy Cotton, and he takes palpable chances to kill the avenging hound. The story lacks give or relief, as if a fatal destiny had descended on everyone involved. Only the inevitability of fate remains. Faulkner struck and was gone. That *Harper's* took it is unusual.

He completed his revisions of the *Sanctuary* galleys at Thanksgiving of 1930, so that they arrived at Cape and Smith's about two weeks before Christmas. The stories kept coming, especially as he and Estelle expected the added expense of an infant within the next few months. "Built a Fence" went out to the *Post* as "Built Fence," an awkward title, then headed to *Scribner's* and *American Mercury* on November 29, December 20, and January 29, 1931, respectively. No one would take it, and in that form it remained unpublished. But there is a section in part 5 of "A Justice" which concerns the building of a fence by Indians under the order of

Doom. ". . . they worked on the fence all that winter and all the next summer until after the whisky trader had come and gone."[26] Probably an outgrowth of "Built a Fence," "A Justice" never found magazine publication either. Faulkner selected it to appear in *These 13*.

The Depression was deepening, and Faulkner, with all his responsibilities, was not making ends meet. The nature of his stories was dark, brooding, without relief. Like "The Hound," "Death Drag" (published as "Death-Drag" in *Scribner's*, January 1932) is grim and unrelenting, an example of inexorable fate challenging the wild antics of already doomed men. What gives "Death Drag" some of its additional interest, apart from tone and attitude, is the consideration of Faulkner's use of himself. He has taken the story of three men on an almost hysterical quest to find their doom and located himself at various points in the narrative. If the piece is any indication of his feeling at this time in late 1930, the Great Depression was getting to him, not only as economic loss* but as a frame of mind gripping America and taking something as glamorous as aviation and stunt flying and transforming it into a death wish. For Faulkner, in some of these stories as well as in aspects of his novels, these few years had changed America from a Garden into a wasteland. Nothing less than that image underlies "Death Drag," as it does the revised *Sanctuary;* and this image or metaphor recurs in the novel Faulkner would begin in a few months, *Light in August*, whose stronger half was little but desert.

"Death Drag" moves along several aspects of Faulkner's life and attitudes, and its manner of telling has several of his new techniques. One narrator is a townsperson, of "our field" and "our town." The field and town seem clearly to be Oxford, with its barely adequate landing strip carved from a cotton field lying in the hills. Everything connected with this operation—in which a man dangles from a ladder over a moving car, drops onto the car, and then swings back up to the plane on the ladder—is flawed. He is himself crippled by a physical defect, lack of money, inadequate equipment (plane, car), torn and ripped clothing. The three-man team is hardly a level above bums in their appearance and their demands on the town.

Another dimension of the story involves Faulkner's designation of two of the three-man crew as Jews: the jumper, Ginsfarb, who is the dominant figure in the interior story, and the driver of the car, Jake. Every stereotype is played upon by Faulkner—the Jew interested only in payment, not the art or the act itself; Ginsfarb as possessing a nose which makes Pinocchio's seem snub by comparison: "He had a nose which would have been out of proportion to a man six feet tall." This is repeated: "As shaped by his close helmet, the entire upper half of his head down to the end of his nose would

---

*Blotner writes of the general economic downfall in Oxford, with the failure of General Stone's Bank of Oxford (Joseph Blotner, *Faulkner: A Biography*, 2 vols. [New York: Random House, 1974], vol. 1, p. 678). Stone had fallen behind with his creditors to the tune of $50,000, a huge sum for those days. It was this amount Phil Stone vowed to pay off after his father's death, and which kept Phil himself bitterly in debt. At one point, Faulkner had to bail him out.

have fitted a six-foot body." His jaw makes him look like a shark: "His jaw was a long flat line clapping-to beneath his nose like the jaw of a shark."*[27] The Jew represented for Faulkner that part of the world which made everything part of the cash nexus; which took the glamor out of all acts because he exacted a price. The Jew, then, commercializes all heroical potentialities in life, encroaching in his way on our fantasy life, turning the dream of the Garden into an urban nightmare. This act is replayed in *Pylon*.

"Death Drag" made the rounds, *Scribner's* on December 16, the *Post* on January 5, 1931, *American Mercury*, February 1, *Collier's* and/or *Woman's Home Companion*, dated April 5; it was returned by all, and then placed in Ben Wasson's hands after a second submission to *Scribner's* failed in the early fall of 1931, until Wasson finally placed it with *Scribner's*. The complicated route the story took indicates how Faulkner was an agent's nightmare. Although he retained Wasson to handle his affairs, Faulkner was sending these stories out on his own, exhausting the possibilities, as it were. Only after he was ready to give up did he put the story in his agent's hands, and often Wasson had little choice but to make the same rounds with the piece. In this instance, he placed "Death Drag" with *Scribner's* on what appears to be the third try.

Another story making the rounds at about the same time was "Fox Hunt," which was apparently written the previous spring or late winter, and then titled "The Fox," recalling D. H. Lawrence's (much stronger) story of that name. "Fox Hunt" made just about every round it could, as Faulkner entered markets he normally eschewed: *Forum*, *Miscellany*, and *Liberty* in early winter of 1930; then the *Post* on December 29, followed by *College Humor* on January 9, 1931, *Woman's Home Companion* on March 11, *Harper's*, undated; and even through Wasson on April 7. The story kept changing titles, suggesting Faulkner's dissatisfaction with it: "The Fox," "A Fox," just "Fox," "Foxhunt," and, finally "Fox-Hunt," in *Harper's* for September 1931. It was placed there by Wasson—Faulkner added his name on the sending schedule after circling the story in the *Harper's* column. The pertinacity Faulkner demonstrated in trying to publish a story of little merit suggests how desperate he was for money at this time, although we note that he skipped *Scribner's* this time around, perhaps saving that valuable outlet for better stuff. In any event, he did try the *Post*—inevitably, since it offered the best rates. Surprisingly, we note no effort to break into the *New Yorker*.

In this sending, with its inevitable rejections outnumbering acceptances by three or four to one, Faulkner must have felt humiliation. In terms of the magazine market, he was still marginal, submitting stories as if he were a novice trying to break in, an unknown out to make a marketplace name for himself. We have no direct statements from him, although the face of the sending schedule itself suggests a flippant, cynical attitude toward

---

*In the manuscript of the story, Jewish accents are stressed—an anti-Semitic emphasis deleted from the published version.

what he was doing. His response to rejection after rejection is a blank page in Faulkner's life. One thing we do know: that his resolve to support his extended family on magazine earnings did not waver, and the sending only flagged when he found that he could earn more in Hollywood, while still continuing his serious work.

While not one of Faulkner's more successful efforts, "Fox Hunt" utilizes an interesting technique. The inner story is all that really counts—the fox hunt as metaphor for another kind of hunt—and yet that inner core is related to us almost completely from the outside. We never get close to the people involved, Harrison Blair and his young wife, because their story circulates through several kinds of narrator. It is a modernist technique, Conradian and Fordian in many respects; but, unlike them, Faulkner could not generate interest or intensity from the method. It is a technique in search of a more compelling subject.

Depending on where the point of observation is, the fox hunt is divided into several segments. The first vantage point comes from three Negro stable boys who set up the situation of the upcoming fox hunt. Controlling them is an omniscient narrator, who moves outside of the other narrators in order to hold everything together. Thus we have an overall teller, plus numerous other tellers, and within it all, the core story, the drama of Blair and his vixen wife. From the stable boys, the narrator moves the reader to eleven poor hill men, later joined by a twelfth, who watch the proceedings, ready with envious, angry, contemptuous comments on the rich Blair. The final narration comes from Blair's valet, speaking to his chauffeur. As the saying goes, no man is hero to his valet, nor to his chauffeur. The valet fills in that Blair has married a wealthy young woman, whose grandmother insisted on the marriage.

Three other stories which appeared in *These 13*, in 1931, were written in early 1926, around the period of "Elmer." As we have seen, "Mistral" is a tale of passion and murder, a Verdi opera played back in low key. "Divorce in Naples" has to do with the relationship of two men; Faulkner used his own journey to Italy with William Spratling as partial content. "Carcassonne" is the most problematical, the most adventurous, and almost completely unexpected. Although we have noted these stories earlier, they come up again because Faulkner resurrected them for this, his first volume of short stories. Further, a comparison of stories going back five years with the stories of 1930 to 1931 affords several insights into the developing writer. Those early stories came just on the edge of Faulkner's shift from poet to fiction writer, but apparently he thought well enough of two to circulate them on his sending schedule. "Mistral" went to the *Post* (June 19, 1930) and *Scribner's* (July 12, 1930), remaining unpublished until *These 13*. "Divorce in Naples," certainly one of Faulkner's less substantial pieces, went to *Forum* (as "Equinox" on May 21, 1930), *Scribner's* (June 20, 1930), *American Mercury* (June 30, 1930), *Blues* (October 1, 1930), and then to Wasson (on April 7, 1931) in a last, desperate effort to place it. It too was unpublished until it appeared in *These 13*.

With a story like "Divorce in Naples" on the sending schedule, we recognize a certain desperation to obtain money, since it could only muddy the waters with publications which had been taking him seriously. Unless Faulkner misjudged his work entirely, which is unlikely, "Divorce in Naples" submitted to Mencken's *American Mercury* is as unlikely as *Sanctuary* being sent on to a Boston publisher. The sending schedule seems to have established a rhythmic or organic function of its own, so that it took over, and whatever Faulkner could find in his drawer was fodder for its maw. It is hard to resist the notion he was so utterly contemptuous of what he was doing, and what magazine editors were up to, he saw his stories as a barrage or as scattered shot, of which something had to get through.

"Carcassonne," however, was not submitted. It was connected in some ways to another piece of quasi-experimental fiction he had written in this earlier period, called "Black Music." The latter story returns us to Faulkner's stress on the faun, and relates a fantasy in which Pan appears and becomes a "farn," perhaps half-faun, half-farmer. When we meet him, he is, like the protagonist-poet of "Carcassonne," sleeping at night in a roll of tarpaper, under the auspices of a Mrs. Widdrington, a forerunner perhaps of Mrs. Maurier, the mother-hen of *Mosquitoes.* "Carcassonne" is itself a poetical vision, virtually unreadable except for our interest in Faulkner's attempt at a stream technique as early as 1926. The story seems cut from a much later period, and its inclusion in *These 13* mirrors the Faulkner of *Sound* and *As I Lay Dying.*

"Carcassonne" is like no other short fiction in Faulkner, whether of the 1926 period or the time of *These 13.* His inclusion of it in that volume and then in *Collected Stories* demonstrates his affection for it.* More than twenty-five years later, on February 25, 1957, in an undergraduate class at the University of Virginia, an astute student asked Faulkner about his viewpoint when he wrote it. Faulkner replied, "That was—I was still writing about a young man in conflict with his environment. It seemed to me that fantasy was the best way to tell that story. To have told it in terms of simple realism would have lost something, in my opinion. To use fantasy was the best, and that's a piece I've always liked because there was the poet again. I wanted to be a poet and I think of myself now as a failed poet, not as a novelist at all but a failed poet who had to take up what he could do."

Faulkner in these *anni mirabiles* (1929–31), perhaps as never again in his body of work, was caught up in the Bergsonian flow, however much he fudged on the method. He would simply transfer his own description of things to the inner world of the character, a process of shifting from the outer to the inner world. The interior would not become uniquely different from its outward manifestations; with this method Faulkner was merely re-adapting a realistic mode. In "Carcassonne," however, as in *Sound* and *As I Lay Dying,* there was a real effort to plug into another world,

---

*In *These 13,* "Carcassonne," with its emblem of the dying or dead man as the failed poet, may well have been intended to anchor the collection.

that area Mallarmé caught in his faun poem, or, even more ambitiously, in "Un Coup de Dés" ("A Throw of the Dice Will Never Abolish Chance"). As Faulkner recognized in these works, the stream, always more than "inner fact," derives from Bergson's sense of "pure memory." The latter is intensive and powerless, beyond movement or sensation. Memory can never be equated to cerebration. The latter seeks reference points, divisions, artificial distinctions; memory seeks an intuitive linkage with objects, something written in water. Abstract art is the pictorial equivalent.

Chapter Fourteen

Into the Mouth of Cannon

ESTELLE TOLD JOSEPH Blotner[1] that within a year of their marriage, she and Faulkner were regularly attending Episcopalian services (the Reverend William McCready's Episcopal Church); that Faulkner not only had in hand a Book of Common Prayer, but joined in hymn-singing with the congregation. Christmas Eve services saw them at church, and Estelle indicated they returned in later years. There is no reason to doubt Estelle's report of these events, however surprising, but they must be kept in perspective. Faulkner's "religious views" had never been part of any organized religion, no less the Episcopalian service, although in his work he increasingly stressed spiritual values. Manual labor, the land itself, the link between work and duty, the ability to identify one's needs and hew to them were all aspects of his "religious" impulse. But they were the stock-in-trade of nearly every American novelist who found himself in opposition to the mechanical-technological development of the United States.

Faulkner also believed in certain kinds of men—those who were heroes in the shaping of their lives, although to the outside world they were hardly heroes, hardly recognizable. Such men preserved personal integrity and conserved a value system which the larger world was set upon destroying.* And in memory itself, Faulkner found a spiritual, even religious,

*Those who recur: Ratliff, Ike McCaslin, Sam Fathers, Gavin Stevens; more singularly: Lucas Beauchamp, Lena Grove.

function—for memory preserved who and what a man was. Once he forgot, he was isolated, without bearings, virtually deracinated. Place, locale, and region were so significant for Faulkner because they indicated where memory and the past could be located. Lose them and man loses his spiritual dimension. These were his religious values. It is difficult to think of him attending formal services, singing with the congregation, and making notations in the Book of Common Prayer. Only if he was playing at being the correct husband while Estelle was pregnant, or else attempting to enter a community which deemed him marginal, or if he experienced some sudden need to formalize a feeling—these are possible reasons for such a series of episodes in his religious life. Faulkner was "Christ-saturated," but that was a very different thing from formal worship. With all his focus on spiritual and Christly values, he was indifferent to church, priest, and formal worship.

None of this, of course, produced the money he needed. The Great Depression had also struck the magazine market, and he suddenly found it difficult to place stories. Although several were slated to appear in the first half of 1931 ("Dry September," "That Evening Sun Go Down," "Ad Astra," "Hair," and "Spotted Horses," carrying through June), he had been paid for them and the money had been spent on living expenses and house repairs. *Scribner's* was still returning stories as rapidly as he sent them on, the latest casualties being "The Hound" and "Indians Built a Fence." Stories and books, however, were not to dominate his mind for the next month or so. It was the birth and death of his first child.

Alabama, named after Aunt 'Bama, was born on Sunday, January 11, 1931. According to Faulkner's own notation in the John Wesley Thompson Bible, the baby died five days later. It was nine days later, according to a telegram Aunt 'Bama received from Auntee (Mary Holland, Murry's sister). Alabama was born more than two months prematurely, and her early death appeared to be of natural causes. But given the premature delivery, the run-down condition of Estelle to begin with, including her anemia during pregnancy, and her persistent drinking, Alabama may have been born without much chance.* All of these negatives could have resulted in an infant whose physical welfare was jeopardized even without the premature birth. No incubator was available, and premature deliveries were generally not something doctors and hospitals were prepared for. Alabama was taken home, in the care of a trained nurse; in poor condition herself, Estelle needed personal care. Faulkner attempted to get an incubator when the infant began to decline, but very possibly nothing could have saved her. She was buried in St. Peter's Cemetery, in

---

*It is possible, although not provable with hospital or medical records, that Alabama was an alcohol-drug infant, a condition which could not have been diagnosed in 1931. Estelle was of course a heavy drinker, and, according to some members of the family, a user of heavy drugs, a habit she started in the Far East. In later years she broke the habit, but remained on Seconal, a habituating barbiturate.

a plot lined with three other infants, the sons of Aunt Sue and Uncle John, Murry's younger brother.

Faulkner spread the tale he would not take the death lying down, that Dr. (John) Culley was somehow responsible for not being prepared, or possibly for not having treated Estelle more firmly so as to improve her physical condition during pregnancy. In any event, Faulkner spread the rumor—he said it was a fact—that he had shot the doctor in the shoulder, an act of revenge for Dr. Culley's failure to respond to telephone calls when it was apparent Alabama was sinking. Faulkner told various versions of the story, including one in which he shot at the doctor, but missed. His response to the death of the infant in this respect is of interest. Since obviously he did not shoot anyone, he apparently needed the story, one of masculine retribution which fitted in well with earlier stories of his RAF feats. Expenses, of course, piled up—nurses, burial costs, doctors' fees, and hospital bills. The sending schedule was reactivated, with the addition of "Death Drag," "The Hound," "Indians Built a Fence," and "The Brooch,"* none of them top quality, but many of them personally revealing. They suggest anger, resentment, desire for revenge, and feelings of impotence—an entire garden variety of subterranean feelings operating under the smooth surface of a man confronting his future and working his way toward it.

Sanctuary was published on February 19. With this, he began to attract that larger audience which led, temporarily, to increased sales, work in Hollywood, and even an international reputation through Maurice Coindreau's translation of it into French. *Sanctuary* did sell, moving to over six thousand copies within less than two months of publication. Reviews began to connect Faulkner to Dostoyevsky, whom he claimed not to have read. But even reviewers who gagged at the novel's morbid view of mankind were struck by the power of its language and its overall impact. Even Clifton Fadiman in the *Nation* found Faulkner to be an original; but Fadiman's shift in attitude was surely connected to the book's readability —it created no difficulties for him. Still, even while rating Faulkner with the first rank of American novelists, Fadiman was disturbed by the sadism and nihilism. The sadism tag became a popular one, but it wasn't helped by the publisher's advertisements. One ad: ". . . *Sanctuary* is a mosaic of furious evil, of cold brutality, of human viciousness, and human hopelessness." It goes on to speak of "blackest sin and crime," of the novel as "hideous and terrifically . . . great."[2] What reviewer could argue against this, that the novel was really a mosaic of moral points, that brutality and so-called Gothic elements were corollaries of an ethical point of view, and that society was viewed ironically, not in purely realistic terms? To obtain his success, Faulkner had to accept widespread misreadings.

*The sending schedule indicates a story called "Fire and Clock" (more likely "The Fire and the Clock"), submitted to four magazines, rejected, and then probably absorbed into "The Brooch," or else simply renamed "The Brooch." The original vanished.

In time, more considered reviewers began to see the novel in terms not of sensational details, but as a design. One noted that it had grandeur, which may be going too far. In the New Orleans *Times-Picayune*, Julia K. Wetherill Baker placed *Sanctuary* in the perspective of Faulkner's greater works, *Sound* and *As I Lay Dying*, but handled it without condescension. She called it "both sensitive and intense" and said he was dealing with the same "dark and malevolent impulses in human nature" which we find in Euripides and John Webster. All things considered, Mrs. Baker ranked Faulkner as America's best living novelist, a position which contrasted with that of a Memphis reviewer who called *Sanctuary* a monstrosity, labeled it as repulsive, and graphically described it as having been "vomited."[3] This local notice held the field much more than did Mrs. Baker's sympathetic and praiseworthy review.

Religious considerations affected the way people viewed the novel. It seemed a blasphemy in a Christian society—in fact, to exist outside anything a Christian society could have created. It was clearly an aberration, shaped and brought forth by a man who fell into no recognizable religious community: Baptist, Episcopalian, or Methodist. It was as if the devil or Satan himself had entered into the writer's consciousness, and what emanated was putridity, foulness, and sheer ugliness. Sexuality was more than besmirched; it was turned into something so ugly it was unrecognizable as a Christian practice. In several ways, this book fixed Faulkner's attitudes in the mind of Oxford and the general area for years to come. When people railed against his presentation of their community, or charged him with making money from New York publishers at their expense, they meant *Sanctuary*. Even if they missed the perverse use of the corncob—and many readers early and later did miss it—there was sufficient other activity in the book to label it the work of an ugly imagination. What price fame? several asked, and their response was Faulkner had placed himself beyond the pale. Maud Falkner, however, supported him, as did Phil Stone, which was almost the last time the two friends agreed on anything.

The notoriety and ensuing sales of *Sanctuary* meant Faulkner became a "hot property." It meant that short stories which had been rejected would become acceptable, that his prices for stories could rise exponentially. It meant, further, that he was a saleable commodity in the Hollywood markets. As for the South, he was a marked man, although his celebrity in Oxford was not of the kind he appreciated. Like Erskine Caldwell, who weighed in with *Tobacco Road* in 1933 and *God's Little Acre* shortly after that, he had made the South a laughingstock in the eyes of the North. No matter that the South thought of itself cut off from Northern values—it always had one eye on what the North would think. It wanted respectability, economic progress, and a sense of its own civilized way of life. Yet Faulkner's book could only increase Northern scorn. He not only revealed low life outside Oxford and in Memphis, but reviled a Southern judge and the judge's daughter, showing her to be as depraved as those who lived in the gutter. Southern womanhood, whose transcendental position was a mark of this civilization, had come under attack; and yet the protection of Southern womanhood was the very cornerstone of Negro-white relationships, the justification for keeping Negroes down, for occasional lynchings and continuous intimidation. Yet here Faulkner had turned a college virgin into a depraved whore, someone who actually enjoyed her stay in a Memphis brothel.

How was Faulkner able to ride out the storm, maintain an even keel, and continue to work on serious subjects? Even as he tried to put *Sanctuary* behind him, the stories which had suddenly become marketable were precisely those which were weak, amateurish, and inferior—like "Divorce in Naples" or "The Leg" from 1925. Some of these had already been submitted and rejected, but now he saw his lesser work grabbed up—sixteen stories in 1931, some of them, of course, accepted before *Sanctuary* appeared. *These 13*, coming in September, contained much inferior work.

Two new stories began to make the rounds in late winter of 1931, but even the notoriety of *Sanctuary* could not help him with the *Post.* "Doctor Martino" went to the *Post* on March 5, and as it was being returned he sent on "Artist at Home," which was also rejected. A third story, "Black Music," began to make the rounds in July, starting with the *Post.* This story, as we have seen, returns to early 1926, the time of "Carcassonne," among others. Of them all, "Doctor Martino" is the most interesting; also, its sending schedule is the most tortured. After rejection by the *Post* (March 5, titled "Martino"), it went to *Woman's Home Companion* (March 16), then to Ben Wasson (June 5), back to the *Post* (September 1), back to Wasson, and was finally accepted by *Harper's* (published November 1931).

Like so many other Faulkner stories, "Doctor Martino" has a shadow existence in his own life. The narrator, Hubert Jarrod, may be from Oklahoma, he may have oil wells and be a student at Yale (a Phil Stone transposition), but he has qualities of a Faulkner type. The young woman he yearns after, Louise King, has strong elements of Helen Baird, and even Estelle, as if Faulkner had merged them into a common experience. Louise is described as a "thin, tense, dark girl," then as "a little on the epicene" —qualities which recall Faulkner's youthful taste in women, harking back to his earliest writing and drawing. But she is in thrall to Dr. Jules Martino, who tries to save her from a bourgeois, conventional experience as a child and as a young woman.

Here is one of Faulkner's most familiar statements about women, especially young women: the area in them which makes them incomprehensible, the great mystery of femalehood no man can enter into, and which makes woman something apart. Faulkner does not always mean this to be commendatory. Often, such views locate woman beyond good and evil, and while man strives for good within a moral universe, woman—like the archetypal Lilith and Eve—strides outside any known coordinates. When-

ever Faulkner starts to re-create the Garden, he comes up against a recalcitrant Eve, with Satan never far behind. What is remarkable about this
unremarkable story is how Faulkner could play himself back: bits of himself in Jarrod, aspects of Phil Stone, and of the character Gavin Stevens;
pieces of Helen Baird and Estelle in Louise King; something of the Oldhams in Mrs. King; something further of himself in the enigmatic Dr. Jules
Martino, the magical figure of the artist who turns his bench into a throne.
Like a palimpsest, those old patterns lie just beneath Faulkner's surface,
ready to reshape themselves into fictions, really little pieces of his life, his
feelings, his repressed attitudes.

"Artist at Home" also made the rounds after *Sanctuary* was published.
It was sent to the *Saturday Evening Post* (March 16), rejected, as noted above,
submitted to *Scribner's* (June 6), rejected there, and sent on to Ben Wasson,
who apparently placed it in *Story* (August 1933), not one of the higher-
paying publications. It does a curious turn on Joyce's short story in *Dubliners*, "The Dead," along with intimations of Shaw's *Candida.* In the Joyce,
Gretta Conroy, as she sits in the warm comfort of Dublin's Gresham
Hotel, recalls to her husband, Gabriel, how a young man once waited
outside her window and eventually died of consumption, aggravated by
standing in the rain for the love of her. Gabriel is aware of the distance
between himself, comfortable, complacent, well-fed, and young men who
martyr themselves for a romantic ideal—as he had realized earlier at an
evening party when Miss Ivy chided him for not spending his vacations
in the west of Ireland, where patriots went.

A good deal of Faulkner's writing is awkward: artists who are "those
gaunt and eager and carnivorous tymbesteres of Art."[4] "Tymbesteres" (a
pseudo-archaic form of a female tympanist) indeed! But of considerable
interest is how this story fits in with other short fiction to help us understand Faulkner's thoughts during this frantic period of his life. Like "Doctor Martino," "Artist at Home" reestablishes the conflict between the
settled existence of the successful writer and the "real" life of the poet: the
first is seeking return, the other new forms of expression. While the formulation of the idea is naive and disingenuous, it was a real conflict for
Faulkner—so much of a struggle he allowed a clearly inferior piece of
work to go to the *Post,* and finally to be included in *Collected Stories.*

One other story was being circulated, although it derives from early 1926:
"Black Music." It went to the *Post* (July 27, 1931), then to *Woman's Home
Companion* (August 7) and *Scribner's* (September 1), finally to Ben Wasson,
who could not place it. Faulkner used it in *Doctor Martino and Other Stories,*
published in 1934. Only his desperate need for money could make him
circulate this crude piece now that his work was so much more polished.
As mentioned above, it has some frail linkage to "Carcassonne," carrying
the author back to his days when fauns (what his protagonist, Wilfred
Midgleston, calls a "farn") dominated. The story begins with an affected,
pseudo-Joycean prose: "For fifty-six years, a clotting of the old gutful

compulsions and circumscriptions of clocks and bells, he met walking the walking image of a small, snuffy, nondescript man whom neither man nor woman had ever turned to look at twice, in the monotonous shopwindows of monotonous hard streets. Then his apotheosis soared, glaring."[5]

One story merits attention as a preview of things to come. Although "Beyond the Gate" falls into a slightly earlier period of composition—it was submitted to the *Post* on April 22, 1930—Faulkner picked it up later, revised it, and shortened the title to "Beyond." It was published in *Harper's*, in September 1933, and the revisions probably occurred earlier that year. It seems, however, to fit loosely into the group of stories he was shaping in the general 1929-to-1932 period. Although the story is otherwise pretentious and unsuccessful, we are thrust back toward *Sound* and ahead to *Light in August*. In the version which included Faulkner's rewriting for resubmission, the protagonist, an unnamed judge, goes from his deathbed examination by Lucius Peabody—the huge, old doctor from *Sartoris*—into his afterlife. Here, in the afterlife, Faulkner spreads his net to regroup in a kind of heaven a number of his own former characters and people from his life. The judge is searching for his dead son—paralleling Lem Oldham's loss of his nine-year-old son, Edward DeGraffenreid. Faulkner even uses the touching words on Edward's gravestone: *"Auf Wiedersehen, Little Boy."* The judge's boy is killed at ten by a fall from a pony; Edward died of a mysterious malady.

But while the judge searches for his dead boy, the piece becomes a quest for God. The chief adult figure to whom the judge speaks is Ingersoll, who is apparently the well-known orator, lawyer, and agnostic Robert Green Ingersoll. Ingersoll became known as the "great agnostic" and wrote a book called *Why I Am an Agnostic* (1896) and died in 1899. Faulkner's use of such a figure as part of his story is unusual in itself, and we can only read "Beyond" as both an allegory of the human quest for truth and as a gloss on Faulkner's own vacillation or desire for clear direction. However we read the story—objectively, subjectively, or both —we do have a lengthy explanation. Faulkner wrote Wasson in the summer of 1933, annoyed that *Harper's* editor, Lee Hartman, had apparently questioned its direction and meaning. He tells Wasson a writer tries "to explain a story and some characters by writing it down." If that doesn't work, then the writer must explain by deletion or by a footnote. The explanation he supplies: "The agnostic progresses far enough into heaven to find one whom his intelligence, if not his logic, could accept as Christ, and who even offers him an actual sight and meeting with his dead son in exchange for the surrender of his logic-agnosticism. But he naturally and humanly prefers the sorrow with which he has lived so long that it not only does not hurt anyone, but is perhaps even a pleasure, to the uncertainty of change, even when it means that he may gain his son again." Faulkner admits that the story is a "tour de force in esoterica," but that he has employed the best method he knows to say this. "I have mulled over it for two days now, without yet seeing just how I can operate on it and insert a gland."[6]

What Faulkner actually wrote and what he explained to Wasson differ, and the story does indeed become, not a tour de force, but an exercise in "esoterica." But there is also a glimmer of *A Fable*, which did not begin to occupy him for almost another fifteen years. As we read back to his mind and imagination, we learn not to be surprised at how far ahead his ideas ranged. Works that do not emerge for a decade or more are foreshadowed, as *Father Abraham* presaged an entire career of writing. Faulkner's explanation of the story to Wasson, rather than the story itself, suggests the linkage to *A Fable*: that search for Christ by the agnostic, who cannot believe and who yet wants some proof there is reason to believe. Perhaps Estelle's comment that Faulkner was attending church and reading the Book of Common Prayer indicates his temporary desire for a real religious experience. More likely, he had entered realms of the imagination through his experimental novels, and the story is an attempt to bring a particular technique—that of a freely associative, dying, half-conscious, half-preconscious mind—to the sleeping-waking state we once saw in his faun pieces.

One strong reason for linking the judge's "moment" to *Sound* is that he describes himself in ways paralleling Quentin Compson. The passage when he denies Ingersoll his identity because the latter lacks certainty about God's existence contains the judge's own summing-up of himself. Having dismissed Ingersoll as a fraud, he says: "Anyway, there is a certain integral consistency which, whether it be right or wrong, a man must cherish because it alone will ever permit him to die. So what I have I am; what I am, I shall be until that instant comes when I am not. And then I shall have never been. How does it go? *Non fui. Sum. Fui. Non sum.*"[7] That statement of conflicting existence and nonexistence which Quentin expresses in *Sound* is Faulkner's expression of "faith." What he is writing here, if we can disentangle the allegories, is something like Albert Camus's later exploration of being and nonbeing in *The Fall*. That novel uses distinct Christian imagery and Christian quest for redemption to question the entire frame of Christian reference. His unreliable narrator subverts as much as he asserts; and the end result is deliberate confusion of both certainties and uncertainties. On a much smaller scale and with far less artistry, Faulkner has forged a statement which is itself a nonstatement, a blurring of the line between belief and agnosticism. In treading that line, he was himself quite comfortable.

Still another inferior story circulating at this time was "The Leg," also a product of the "Elmer" period, in 1925. "The Leg" went to the *Post* (December 14, 1930), was then submitted to *Scribner's* (June 8, 1931), given to Ben Wasson, and finally published as "Leg" in *Doctor Martino and Other Stories*, in 1934. In *Collected Stories* it became "The Leg." Only an author desperate for income would intrude with such a journeyman piece about a severed leg which jeers at the victim. It carries Faulkner back to World

War I, and duplicates some of the personal baggage he carried from the war, such as his limp from a leg injury. The story attempts a mystery-supernatural effect, possibly in the style of H. G. Wells, or the ghost-story genre of James's *The Turn of the Screw.* Needless to say, Faulkner's primary markets found it unacceptable. In a letter to Wasson, which does not concern "The Leg" specifically, Faulkner nevertheless seems troubled by what he has been doing: submitting inferior stories without his agent's knowledge, and then using Wasson when it suited him. His promise to send on his mailing schedule for recent pieces is surely connected to his uncertainty about what he had been dredging up. Wasson was apparently sufficiently in awe of Faulkner not to warn him that by saturating the *Post*, *Scribner's*, and *Woman's Home Companion* with inferior submissions, he was undermining his best markets.

Of the stories submitted at this time, we have already mentioned the strong "All the Dead Pilots," which, rejected by *Woman's Home Companion* and/or *Collier's*, ended up in *These 13*. That collection only took shape in May of 1931, when Faulkner signed a contract with Cape and Smith for *A Rose for Emily and Other Stories*, which evolved into *These 13*, published on September 21. It took this shape:

Group of Four: Ad Astra
All the Dead Pilots
Victory
Crevasse

Yoknapatawpha Group: Red Leaves
A Rose for Emily
A Justice
Hair
That Evening Sun
Dry September

Final Group: Mistral
Divorce in Naples
Carcassonne

The problem with the collection is that it exists only as discrete stories, some of them Faulkner's best, some among his worst. It gives away the fact that superb as Faulkner could be in individual stories, he was not thinking, primarily, in short-fiction terms; that such stories were the product of a supplementary or subsidiary need: to generate income so he could write novels. In this respect, Conrad was a clear precursor.

Other foreshadowings occur at this time. Even before starting *Light in August*, Faulkner had a vision of material which became the basis of *Absalom*—"Evangeline," written sometime in June or early July of 1931 and submitted to the *Post* on July 17. It was rejected and sent on to *Woman's Home Companion* (July 26), which also rejected it. The story would remain unpublished, although heavy revision led into various aspects of *Absalom*. This inchoate story, with the great novel implicit in it, reveals a degree of supernatural dimension to his imagination. His creative mind appeared to have stored away all the materials he wanted to use, and as he moved along, this material did not have to be invented, but reinvented. It was all *there*, ready to be tapped. If we assume some such working, then we can connect it to his need to tell and retell; for reinventing is a form of retelling for his own use. It was not so much that he was a natural-born storyteller— he was a retriever of what was somehow implanted in his imagination and which could be recalled only through a complicated method of narrative repetition. The enemy of his imagination was apparently the simple line, the straightforward story. As though he were in thrall of something he could not quite control, he had to let his emanations evolve in the only way they could—through looping, overlapping, and repeated telling. This was true in his early career, even as soon as "Elmer" and *Father Abraham*, but it becomes clearer as we move through these miraculous years of 1929–32. By now, he has foretold his future. Like some Biblical Joseph prophesying the ways of the land, Faulkner was reading his own career for the next twenty years.

"Evangeline," the name of Burden's wife in *Light in August*, the name of his daughter, also, was just such a seed. As a title, "Evangeline" recalls Longfellow's poem of two lovers separated by a destiny they cannot control—which is the very point of Faulkner's story and, more intensely, of *Absalom*. A great deal was coming together, for in this story of a "dark house" in which terrible secrets reside and have to be burned out at the end, there is also the dim beginning of *Light in August*, titled "Dark House" in manuscript. Terrible secrets which must be torched to the ground, a house which contains lovers who strain against each other, tremendous forces of fate or destiny which disallow human achievement: Faulkner was on his way in this long story. It is almost novelistic in its implications; in fact, it needed far more space for its development than was suitable for magazine publication.

"Evangeline" begins innocuously enough, with a lighthearted get-together between the narrator ("I") and Don, who is clearly the Spratling-figure in the New Orleans sketches and several stories. In "Evangeline" Faulkner shortly changed the narration of Don and "I" to that of Chisholm and Burke, and those two, in turn, to Quentin Compson and Shreve. The latter two take up the narrative function of *Absalom*, when "Evangeline" became submerged in that novel. All of this indicates that Don-Spratling was merely a narrative device, and that Faulkner had not worked out any real function for him. He was part of an evolutionary phase in the writer's development, not at all like Conrad's Marlow, who appeared fully shaped at the turn of the century in "Youth," *Heart of Darkness*, and *Lord Jim*.

Unlike Marlow, Don is merely a name, a face, a body, someone to bounce words off.

Very quickly in "Evangeline," he becomes secondary. What character-izes the story is its tone of persiflage: *Absalom* started out as something of a comic routine. Don and the "I" go through a kind of vaudeville act, in which each tries to top the other, played out for an audience waiting to be amused. The story which emerges, though, is not very amusing, since it involves incest, murder, miscegenation, desperate people in desperate situations, and a society of Sutpens closed to everyone. Don is now back in Mississippi, and he and the "I" can no longer play off against Italians; the world they inhabit is intense, and while they may joke, the story that unfolds belies their tone. When Faulkner rewrote the material for the novel, he eliminated the persiflage and went right to the heart of an American tragedy: the conflicts generated by the Civil War and by race that permeated every part of contemporary Southern history—and, by implication, American history.

But "Evangeline" is not to be dismissed as merely the ur-version of a greater work; while not fully satisfactory, it establishes its own terms. The pivotal character is Colonel Sutpen, although he is dead when the story begins. His shadow, however, falls over everything: to be a Sutpen is to be something special, fenced off. As Don begins to tell his "ghost story," the "I" fills in, as though the story belongs, in a sense, to everyone.

In the first section we meet Sutpen's son and daughter, Henry and Judith, and Henry's friend from the University of Mississippi, Charles Bon. After a visit to New Orleans with Bon, Henry insists Charles and Judith cannot marry. When the couple refuses to accept Henry's prohibi-tion, he and Bon fight an aborted duel, broken up by Sutpen and Judith. As opposed to the novel, this story has Charles and Judith marry, and then he and Henry go off to fight the Union army for four years. Henry assumes that the war will kill Bon and thus end the marriage and the profound problem it entails, but when this does not occur, he fires the last shot of the war, killing his friend. Charles is laid out on the bed in the room Judith has kept ready for four years. As she becomes obsessively involved in Charles's death, we recognize that we have entered the obverse of "A Rose for Emily": the room, the dead body, the vigil over the lost one all bring together the two stories. Once again, Faulkner's overlapping imagination becomes apparent: that grinding-out of stories, many of which become part of a repeating, overlapping sensibility.

Still in the second section of the story—the first is merely the setting for Don and the I-figure—Judith survives, putters around the Sutpen grounds, then dies; but her ghost is believed to haunt the house. Another touch, perhaps with Conan Doyle in mind, is the presence of a large German shepherd. This dog never seems to die: as soon as one grows old, a younger one replaces it. The dog haunts the house: "A haunted house that bears police dogs like plums on a bush,"[8] the narrator says. Here Faulkner seriously miscalculates, for he skews the intensity of the inner story with diversionary tactics.

The old Negro woman who still lives in the house is also a Sutpen. And so, at the end of section 2, the mystery remains. Don has sent for the narrator to discover what lies behind the ghost story: the figure seen when she was supposed to be dead, the dog which never seems to die off, the person living in the house, and the identity of that Negro woman, also a Sutpen. Faulkner had the seed of his development not only in the Sutpen family and its situation but in the withholding of critical pieces of information. It is that information we receive directly before the story ends, in section 7.

The narrator goes to the house and speaks to the old, wizened Negro. Although dark-skinned, she is a true Sutpen, still "as granite and as cold." Faulkner, as always, is excellent on eyes. Like a painter, he observed eyes perhaps more intensely than he did any other organ:[9] ". . . she nursing the pipe and watching me with eyes that had no whites at all; from a short distance away she appeared to have no eyes at all. Her whole face was perfectly blank, like a mask in which the eyesockets had been savagely thumbed and the eyes themselves forgotten." After she tests the narrator (he must pass by the dog), she takes him up the stairs, and there the "ghost" of Sutpen's body lies on a bed, in a state of such disrepair that death is very close. It is Henry Sutpen, lying there for forty years, "lying in a foul, yellowish nightshirt on foul, yellowish sheets. . . . He lay with closed eyelids so thin that they looked like patches of dampened tissue paper pasted over the balls."

With this Faulkner has entered deeply into his distinctive world: the dedication to an idea which is itself destructive, the foulness of an existence which is single-minded, the obsessiveness of particular ideas, the destructiveness of racial ideas which honor insists upon, the ability of the human being to endure the unendurable. Once the dog is forgotten and Don has disappeared, Faulkner can move along, secure in material he has possessed by his own immersion in its ruinous force.

The old Negro woman—Raby here, Clytie in *Absalom*—unfolds the story in her own way, as part of that unrolling of facts intermixed with the way the facts have been lived. They have been so digested, so interwoven with tragedy and daily life that she cannot relate them in any consecutive way: she must deal with them as Faulkner's literary sensibility dictated, through telling and retelling, recapitulation, digression, and withholding piecemeal revelation. Even though there is no interior monologue, Raby's method of telling has some of the strung-out quality of freely associated interior monologue. Words emanating from her are approximations of a thought process beyond reason and logic.

She informs the narrator that Bon already had a wife, and that seemed to be the reason for Henry's insistence that the marriage to Judith could not take place. But the narrator suspects more: ". . . something she hadn't told me and had told me she was not going to tell and which I knew she would not tell out of some sense of honor or of pride."[10] There is a good chance, the narrator says, even as details pour out, that we may never learn what is missing in her tale. Judith invited the woman, who came with a child—and the presence of the nine-year-old boy is also offered as the reason for Henry's insistence. Raby tells of the New Orleans woman's departure and of Judith's sending her a monthly stipend. Henry returned when Judith felt death creeping up on her, and he stayed, hermetically sealed in the room, a murderer who is slowly rotting away with only memories, as Henry, brother of Raby.

The narrator leaves the house in section 5, but returns to sit on the porch, his back against a column, fantasizing what may have occurred. His reverie takes the form of a sudden dialogue among himself, Henry, and Charles. The scene is hallucinatory: "Soon the sighing cedars, the insects and the birds became one peaceful sound bowled inside the skull in monotonous miniature, as if all the earth were contracted and reduced to the dimensions of a baseball, into and out of which shapes, fading, emerged fading and faded emerging." The narrator and Charles try to find out from Henry why he did it—the implication being he had shot Charles, that that had been the last shot of the war. But the dialogue is still inconclusive as to why Henry responded with murder, even with the woman and child. The narrator gets close to the truth: "What was it that Judith knew and Raby knew as soon as they saw her?" In the reverie Henry answers "Yes."[11] The mystery is pushed on to a further section.

In section 6 the house is torched, apparently set by Raby to entomb the last of the Sutpens in a kind of fiery purification rite. This is Raby's final act of protecting Henry—to prevent anything from emerging which could change her story or allow a stranger access to the Sutpens' closed world. The revelation comes in section 7. Raby's daughter finds a metal case with, she thinks, the picture of Judith in it—Charles Bon's own picture. But it is not of Judith; it is of the New Orleans wife, and her features are unmistakably Negroid: "I looked quietly at the face: the smooth, oval, unblemished face, the mouth rich, full, a little loose, the hot, slumbrous, secretive eyes, the inklike hair with its faint but unmistakable wiriness—all the ineradicable and tragic stamp of negro blood." The inscription, in French: "*A mon mari. Toujours. 12 Aout, 1860.*" With that, the narrator knows why "Charles Bon's guardian had sent him all the way to North Mississippi to attend school, and what to a Henry Sutpen born, created by long time, with what he was and what he believed and thought, would be worse than the marriage and which compounded the bigamy to where the pistol was not only justified, but inescapable."

Faulkner had the subject for his greatest work. But in the development of this story for the novel, he made many critical changes. Not only did Henry recognize that Charles had Negro blood; there is also the factor—a lesser one—that Thomas Sutpen is their father. They are half-brothers, and Charles is half-brother to Judith. Incest, however, takes a secondary role to miscegenation. In another equally necessary change, Faulkner gave the narrator a real character and made the story emanate from someone for whom this tale, which flows from his lips to Shreve, the Canadian student, was one of personal doom as well. Faulkner moved even beyond a Conradian Marlow-figure in Quentin; the consciousness of a responsible, sensitive South flows through this young student at Harvard. And when he tells the story of Thomas Sutpen and his family, he tells of his own history, his heritage, his awareness of how doomed he is, the South is, and how race is part of that history and that doom, interwoven with every facet of it.

Other stories making the rounds at this time were considerably inferior, although one of them, "Centaur in Brass," became part of the Flem Snopes legend in the Yoknapatawpha trilogy. "Rose of Lebanon" remained unpublished in separate collections and did not even appear in the *Collected Stories.* *

Like "Evangeline," which presaged *Absalom*, "Centaur" demonstrates how Faulkner was shaping his Snopes material almost a decade before *The Hamlet* appeared. When we examine his stories during this period, we see he had at least a decade's work lined up; and if we recall some earlier work in New Orleans, we recognize he had intimations of his future career even in those sketches and brief pieces.

"Centaur in Brass" gives a quick run-through of Flem Snopes's background, from his beginnings as a country clerk (for Varner), as half-owner of a restaurant (traded from Suratt, the later Ratliff), his marriage to Varner's daughter, the pregnant Eula, their disappearance to Texas, Eula's return a year later with a well-grown baby, Flem's own return a month after that with the wild mustang horses described in "Spotted Horses." Briefly outlined is Snopes's gaining of Suratt's half of the restaurant in a land scam, and then his desire to build on that. With a friendly mayor in town, Major Hoxey (later De Spain), who is sleeping with Eula, Flem becomes the superintendent of the municipal power plant. While there, he strips it slowly of the brass and replaces it with cheap plugs, which put the entire plant in jeopardy of blowing. He tries to con two Negroes working for him, Tom-Tom and Turl, to take the blame, but he ends up trapped by the Negroes and forced to repay the town for brass he couldn't keep.

When Crichton at *Scribner's* rejected it for publication—with regret, but firmly—he could not foresee that the piece meant more to Faulkner as a foreshadowing of later work than as a story in itself. As we read through several of these less-than-compelling short pieces, we must always be aware that while Faulkner was seeking a market for them he

---

*Nine pages of unnumbered manuscript remain, at the Alderman Library of the University of Virginia. Even with growing fame, Faulkner could not, or had decided not to, place it.

was also using shorter fiction as a means of working through, or toward, larger ideas.

Faulkner was now ready to begin *Light in August.* * All the rest had been marginal. On August 17, 1931, "Dark House" was on his writing table at Rowan Oak. This was a momentous occasion for him, since he had been spending his time since *As I Lay Dying,* completed about one and a half years earlier, on short stories. We might see his career as stalled, or side-tracked significantly. Although Faulkner's sensibility was essentially that of a novelist, it looked as if he could not afford to spend the long months a novel required, especially a novel of considerable complexity. *Light in August,* therefore, has to be seen as a new thrust in fiction for Faulkner, connected to his other major work for the next decade: tied closely to *Absalom* and *Go, Down, Moses,* more loosely to *The Wild Palms* and *The Hamlet.*

During his work on *Light in August,* his life was frequently turbulent. In October, he attended a conference of Southern writers in Charlottesville, Virginia; he went to New York for a celebration of *Sanctuary;* and, most notably, he was offered and accepted a job in Hollywood. The main arena, however, was clearly the novel, which he worked on steadily, whatever the interruptions, until completing it eleven months later, on July 21, 1932. His ability to work with such regularity on a complicated work bears comment, since the interruptions were major ones, including several drinking bouts which incapacitated him.

The romantic poets believed that drugs or alcohol was a necessary fuel, and so did the symbolists in France, those poets Faulkner had embraced early in his life. Faulkner could have taken his text from Baudelaire and Rimbaud. The latter's "drunken boat" is the life of the poet, as is Mallarmé's "A Throw of the Dice Will Never Abolish Chance." All those great symbolist poems of journey beginning with Baudelaire are linked to the way the poet separates himself from the man in order to achieve his work. Rimbaud spoke of a dream journey entered by way of alcohol and drugs, and through these methods he could explore new languages. There

*With this novel, Faulkner was in the middle of his examination of father-son relationships: the weak Compson father, the survivor and destructive Anse Bundren; now the other extreme of what Jacques Lacan called the Law, in McEachern and later Thomas Sutpen. In each case the father (or Father) is too little or too much, either an Abraham who fails his son or else one who carries through the sacrifice. (See chapter 4 of André Bleikasten's *The Most Splendid Failure: Faulkner's The Sound and the Fury,* Indianapolis: Indiana University Press, 1976, and Lacan's *Ecrits,* Paris: Seuil, 1966.)

Very possibly, the problems of father and son carried over into Faulkner's difficulty with the beginning of the novel. The present chapter 3 on Hightower originally began the novel, as chapter 1, in the manuscript at the University of Texas.

In *Faulkner's Un-Christian Christians: Biblical Allusions in the Novels* (UMI Research Press, 1971, 1983), Jessie McGuire Coffee includes a useful chart on "Patriarchs, Sons, and Siblings: Patrimony, Sacrifice and Salvation" (pp. 132–33). The chart reveals unmistakably Faulkner's themes based on God-Christ-sons (or daughters—Candace, Joanna, Judith Sutpen, Eula), sin, and sacrifice.

was no other way in, except by that detachment of artistic self from ordinary self achieved by external stimulants which led to the separation. One becomes a Prometheus of the imagination or mind, ready to bring fire, but at the expense of oneself.

What made this particularly appealing to Faulkner was that he could, as he wished, reshape himself in the effort, and reshaping of self had always been one of his goals. After the war, he had returned to Oxford, reshaped by physical appearance and clothes. As a poet, he reshaped himself into a bum or tramp, his notion then of what the poet should appear to be. He further reshaped himself when he went to New Orleans and assumed a persona, which Sherwood Anderson and others commented upon. His final reshaping occurred when he took on family responsibilities, when the reshaping began to blend with actuality. But then the reshaping moved inward, where he was untouched by events or others, even family. It was here that the real reshaping of his life took place, and where alcohol became the principal fuel. It not only kept the fire going, it provided nourishment—without it, Faulkner somehow feared, the flame would become extinguished. It was a fearful vision, a fearful quest, a "drunken boat" in its way. Rimbaud, Verlaine, and Baudelaire had destroyed themselves on their journeys. But in that internal, untouchable self, Faulkner spent more than a season in hell; he had completion, satisfaction, and final achievement. His drinking may have been suicidal for the man, but it was joy and delight for the writer. Like Rimbaud on his journey, Faulkner discovered another god.

Light in August was written in pursuit of one of those gods. Beginning with its title, it takes the reader on a metaphysical, almost supernatural, journey. Although much of the novel concerns mundane affairs—pregnancy, a birth, growing up, routine work—Faulkner saturates such matters with a supernatural light, or with a brush of many colors. Most of all, he makes the novel an internal affair, so that, despite the presence of many externalities, it is basically a novel which remains out of the light—indeed a dark house, as the original manuscript title indicated. Faulkner was working from within out, not from without in, as he had done in his earliest fictions. Although less obviously internalized than *Sound* and *As I Lay Dying*, *Light in August*—like its successor *Absalom*—limns interiors.

In discussion with his class at the University of Virginia on April 13, 1957, Faulkner tried to settle the meaning of his title. Asked whether it was a "colloquialism for the completion of pregnancy," he responded: "No, used it because in my country in August there's a peculiar quality to light, and that's what that title means. It has in a sense nothing to do with the book at all, the story at all."*[12] Faulkner probably meant the particular light had

---

*Shortly after writing the words "Dark House," Faulkner crossed them out and supplied "Light in August." There is the Southern saying a pregnant woman would look ahead to term as being "light in August." But, according to Blotner, Estelle suggested that the light in August is different from any other times, and with that Faulkner changed the title (Joseph Blotner, *Faulkner: A Biography*, 2 vols. [New York: Random House, 1974], vol. 1, p. 702).

nothing to do with the meaning. The story is one of lights, darks, and twilights. It has to do with "dark houses," and houses which are less dark, even those which are light.

Some of that quality derives from a stress on pagan dimensions, the fauns and satyrs Faulkner also mentioned in 1957. He speaks of a luminosity "older than our Christian civilization. Maybe the connection was with Lena Grove, who had something of that pagan quality of being able to assume everything."[13] She has the calmness or certainty of a woman impregnated not by Lucas Burch, but by Jupiter, the king of the gods. She treats her pregnancy as if it were something extraordinary, as if Lucas had come to her in a shower of gold, and the resultant infant would be a prince or god. Faulkner was able to convey just that.* And it impregnates the entire novel, even those brutal sections devoted to Joe Christmas. His name, of course, helps to shape the ceremonial dimension close to rite, ritual, and sacrifice. Other names nourish the idea: Joanna Burden and the Reverend Hightower as obvious examples of naming to suggest further dimensions.

Names, in fact, play a significant role, so that the proliferation of the letter "B" takes on almost a ritualistic effect: Lucas Burch, who runs out on Lena; Byron Bunch, who wants to take her in; Joanne Burden, for whom life seems a little too much; Mrs. Beard, a minor player who puts up Byron; Brown, the name Burch takes when running. Those "B" names join to other significant Bs: birth and burning. Lena's birth rite parallels Joanna's burning ritual. Lena Grove (named after a Mississippi village) suggests an Eden or Garden, surely a pastoral life; and Joe Christmas, her opposite, has a name which derives from Jesus born in a manger, for him an anti-Eden, but nevertheless a whiff of the Garden. The Reverend Hightower has a name which locates him above others; but his life is twisted, perhaps influenced by the ambiguity of his full name, Gail Hightower, which sexually could go either way.

The use of name-destiny or doom is reinforced by the novel's time-sequencing. When Lena reaches the outskirts of Jefferson and sees smoke rising from a house, a main part of the novel has already occurred. While Lena was spending the night at Armstid's, Joanna was being murdered, the climax of a long development, nearly all of which is past action. Most of

---

*Lena's pregnancy isolates her, makes of her an "other" who remains beyond the mundane events of the world. She is a "Faulknerian woman," moved by her femaleness from routine and given speciality by pregnancy, sexuality, or simply otherness. Charlotte, Laverne, and Eula are obvious examples of this type in his 1930s fiction, ushered in by Lena.

If we could date a three-page manuscript segment devoted to Hightower, called "Light in August," at the Humanities Research Center in Austin, we could better tell if Hightower or Lena provided initial impetus to the novel. But the brief fragment, whether intended as an outline of Hightower's background or as the plan for a short story, remains undatable. James B. Meriwether (in *William Faulkner: An Exhibition of Manuscripts*, Austin, 1959) reproduced the first page of the manuscript. Regina K. Fadiman (*Faulkner's "Light in August": A Description and Interpretation of the Revisions*, 1975) and Carl Frederick Wilhelm Ficken (*A Critical and Textual Study of William Faulkner's "Light in August,"* unpublished dissertation, 1972) have written the fullest analyses of the novel's development.

the novel involves catching up, a Conradian mode. The historical method of *Nostromo* lies heavily over the novel, whether Faulkner consciously drew on it or not. We can in fact establish a structural consistency: as Lena Grove's episodes move forward toward birth, the rest of the novel must be gathered up from the past. For Lena to see the smoke rising from the burning house as she approaches Jefferson, Faulkner has had to backtrack to recapture Joe, Burch-Brown, Joanna, the Reverend Hightower, altogether a good part of the novel and its meaning. That meaning is historical, and it reinforces the sense of doom hanging over characters with B-names. Only Byron (whatever his misnomer) escapes.

The sole part that goes forward, after the burning of the house, is the act of vengeance meted out to Joe by Percy Grimm; and this occurs when Lena gives birth, on the ninth day after her arrival in Jefferson. Although we have the feeling a good deal of time is covered in *Light in August*, the temporal scheme depends on recapitulation. The main ingedient is a structural method, which becomes part of the contents, although not antithetic to the above: Lena arrives and Joanna dies, she births and Joe dies. That counterpointing of cyclical life and death is linked to a historical play of events and also to a sense of doom. Nowhere else in Faulkner up to this novel do we find such suggestions of a doom-filled society; that is probably because nowhere else has he met the racial question at such a profound level.

Despite his later public statements about race, which were contradictory and even inflammatory, embarrassing for a major writer to make, Faulkner's views on race *in his fiction* were highly sophisticated, not easily summarized or tidied up. While we must be very careful not to simplify his views, we must also be equally careful not to let him establish his own terms. The familiar line that the Negro was a Southern issue is one Faulkner often repeated, but it is false: false to the idea of race, unjust to the Negro, and blind to the extent of the issue itself. As we probe into Faulkner's sense of race here and in the next decade, we enter a very dramatic moment in American cultural history. For what is at stake is not only the South, not only the Negro, but the country. We can find some of this dramatic awareness in Faulkner, although he remains very much a Southerner and a man of his time. But in his best work, he becomes an American and there race bursts all boundaries and becomes part of American themes.

Complications begin in *Light in August*. It does not ultimately matter whether or not Joe Christmas has Negro blood—as people in the novel assume, and as many critics have taken for granted.* There is no firm proof he does, for the novel deliberately blurs that point. What does matter is his

---

*Nor whether he was suggested by the Negro Nelse Patton, victim of a lynch mob after his razor-slaying of a white woman. Both Blotner and John Cullen (*Old Times in the Faulkner Country*, 1961) cite Patton—Cullen as a teenager helped in his capture—but Faulkner shifts the contexts for Christmas to very different racial terms from those in the earlier murder. Early on, Faulkner thought of explicitly giving him Negro blood, but when he made the background deliberately ambiguous, he moved completely from any model.

perception of it, and others' perception of him. If he believes, as he does, that he is part Negro, then his life is totally affected; and if others have come to the same assessment, they will treat him accordingly. Faulkner's point here is surely Joe's lack of identity, but not only that: we must add *his* perception of what may or may not be true of his background. There is a double action consuming him and the direction of the novel. It is a question of identity: who is he? what is his background? what is uniquely his? Certain assumptions he must make are based on purely circumstantial evidence.

With this, Faulkner has cut directly across a profound American theme of identity—who am I? what role do I play? how do I find myself? But he has crossed this with another factor, creating a hybrid of the American theme: the search for identity become part of a racial curse. A pivotal scene both for Joe and the reader comes when he tells Bobbie, the grubby prostitute he takes up with: " 'I got some nigger blood in me.' 'You're what?' she asks. 'I think I got some nigger blood in me,' he responds. 'I don't know. I believe I have.' 'You're lying,' she retorts. 'All right,' he said. 'I don't believe it,'[14] her voice said in the darkness."

The next pivotal scene of Joe's racial makeup comes with another woman, Joanna Burden. Joanna is recounting to him her background, her grandfather and half-brother murdered by Colonel Sartoris because they tried to register blacks for the vote. Then she tells of what it means to be white and to see blacks as a shadow. We take her words as describing a shadow Joe is part of, a racial background which has "shadowed" him:

> But after that I seemed to see them for the first time not as people, but as a thing, a shadow in which I lived, we lived, all white people, all other people. I thought of all the children coming forever and ever into the world, white with the black shadow, already falling upon them before they drew breath. And I seemed to see the black shadow in the shape of a cross. And it seemed like the white babies were struggling, even before they drew breath, to escape from the shadow that was not only upon them but beneath them too, flung out like their arms were flung out, as if they were nailed to the cross. I saw all the little babies that would ever be in the world, the ones not yet even born—a long line of them with their arms spread, on the black crosses.[15]

Enfolding Joe in this dream or fantasy, Joanna sees him as her reclamation project. The beginning of the end of their relationship is implicit in her desire to "raise" him. " 'You must struggle, rise,' she says. 'But in order to rise, you must raise the shadow with you. But you can never lift it to your level. I see that now, which I did not see until I came down here. But escape it you cannot. The curse of the black race is God's curse. But the curse of the white race is the black man who will be forever God's chosen own because He once cursed him.'" But Joe is not paying any attention to this wild, apocalyptic talk. He wants to know if Joanna's father ever killed "that fellow—what's his name? Sartoris." She moves back to his parents. "You don't have any idea who your parents were?" His response, brooding, sullen: "Except that one of them was part nigger. Like I told you before."[16]

Playing before us is a great American drama. For when Joanna asks Joe, "How do you know that?", he answers with the sole possible response: "I don't know it." But he is already tiring of the history lesson and personal probe. He slides away, saying he has already "wasted a lot of time." The question remains: who is he? how does he respond? and most of all, what can he know? The American question of identity ends with the racial shadow and curse. He is not Jesus but Cain, his mark a tinged skin some think is foreign, others think is Negroid. What Joe thinks is what others perceive him to be—he takes on their "coloring" of him. He becomes—is —a man whose destiny is determined by the context in which his identity is presented to him; he is beyond choice. Choice was made in his "I don't know it." He accepts that position on the edge as his identification, and with that accepts his doom.

The sense of the novel is set. As Lena moves into Mississippi from Alabama pursuing Lucas, she is trying to establish a family; her journey is the quest for a unit—father, mother, child, the holy family which she has imprinted in her mind and has made her difficult trip possible. To find Lucas and make him honor his commitment is for her to make the past, her past, a meaningful time. If she cannot find Lucas, she has in a sense thrown away the past, allowed history to defeat her. Her dogged pursuit of him, her implacable, undisturbed sense of her rightness, is predicated on her desire to make history work for her. For Joe the quest is opposite. For him history and the past are forms of the shadow Joanna has described. To allow history to overtake him is to court disaster. Like Lena, Joe keeps running, but while she runs to embrace her destiny, he runs to escape his. Both characters, so different in motive and quest, are part of the vast movement which defines the country: movement toward for the woman, movement away for the man.

To change the metaphor: Lena is running to find the "grove," the Arcadia or Garden she is certain will complete her cycle of the family unit. Cast out by an event in which she has been tricked, she refuses to accept the deception. She sees her America as just, providential—she is white, stable, implacable. Joe, however, sees America obliquely, angled, and therefore as a distorted place. The Garden for him is dispossessed. She moves smoothly—her pacing is always described as deliberate, slow, part of the rhythms we associate with the movement of the earth itself. Joe's movements, however, are jerky, full of spurts, without any rhythmic accord with his surroundings. She blends in; he never does. They differ so in pacing because their Americas are different. She can experience the "light" of August; he must never experience it, for his is the world of perpetual shadow.

Faulkner worked all this deliberately into the novel. In its deepest sense, it is among his most profound commentaries on race, and there is no solution here. There are none of the resolutions he would later offer, some of them demeaning of the Negro in their condescension, some of them laudatory in their desire to give the Negro his due against a fanatical white foe. Racial matters are interwoven with elements seemingly as distant as "pacing." Lena's walk from Alabama, mixed in with occasional rides, suggests a snail's pace: it is keyed in to her pregnancy, and therefore it is a walk full of expectation. Unshadowed by the racial curse, she lives outside time, space, and history itself. Her journey and the growth of the fetus are reciprocal, and the entire novel as it is presented to us occurs within the final stages of the fetus's development. Faulkner has written a novel in which whores, murder, a racial curse, matters of history are all encapsulated within the final stages of pregnancy—dependent, all, on the birth of a baby.

While this is a comment on women—that in their function as potential mothers or potential wives they have removed themselves from any other history—it goes beyond mother worship or a perverse misogyny. The deeper point is that while the woman can reach for the Edenic moment, the giving of life, the man, and especially the man under the shadow of a curse, has no such quest. His desire for survival is at a much more dire level. Everyone helps Lena, even other women who know there is no husband. Her condition and her implacable belief in her own quest make her everyone's ward. But Joe is precisely the opposite—no one helps him; he must create his own terms, since he is so marginal. His self-help comes first at the lumber mill and then as a bootlegger. His sex is with a whore, as is Lena's, in its way, with Lucas. But their experiences so differ not only because one is a pregnant woman and the other a man, but because their relationship to race is so obviously different.

Black and white occupy a different spatial world. Lena carries a certain mental picture of space in her mind, as practical, realistic, and linear. If she walks from Alabama to Mississippi and follows what people tell her, she will arrive at the place where Lucas is working. Her belief in this is unshatterable because she has assimilated the sense that space belongs to her by right of her being what she is. She is full of focal points, directions, and perimeters. The boundaries she defers to are only the boundaries of what her body can take her to; she has no mental boundaries or sense of spatial limitations. America is hers if she can walk it.

For Joe quite the opposite holds true. There is for him no clearly defined space. His use of space is conspiratorial. He occupies a different kind of space, i.e., a different kind of America. Whereas Lena is clear-eyed about her objectives, Joe has blurred vision because the space he must move in is without clear definition. At any point it may turn hostile. He cannot even count on space as neutral. He must assume something that never enters his mind, that the boundaries for spatial relationships in his world are enclosures, even traps. The eye that meets Lena on her journey is the eye which Joe must avoid on his.

If we shift the terms somewhat, it is evident Joanna and Joe must be linked either as the obverse of each other, or be in some way symbiotic, since their names are variations of each other. Jo is short for Joanna and, furthermore, her family name is "Burden," just as "Christmas" is a burden. When Joe first comes to the lumber mill, one of the workers comments that no white man is named Christmas. Since Christ was lily-white, the remark is rich in irony; but in the racial mix of Mississippi and America, the irony becomes fact: Joe is condemned by a name which should be a celebration.

But they are burdened in more subtle ways than by naming alone. Both can survive in their own ways by being reborn. Joanna carries the burden of Burden only to be able to throw it off in prayer and the seeking of salvation. She hopes to achieve this new condition through aiding the Negro, trying to balance out the residue of slavery which exists after slavery has ended. Joe too must be reborn, or else he will perish; his name forces that. Yet he insists he was only born, and not reborn. He fights off any effort on her part to re-create him with a regular job and education. He is appalled by her because he insists on his history as his way of survival. But his way is a form of self-destruction; yet so is hers. Whenever Joanna prays as a means of seeking redemption for history, it replays nightmarish history for Joe (his experience with the praying McEachern). Her sense of history and his mesh, but in the deeper sense they inevitably clash. Both are trapped in history which will destroy them—so is the Reverend Hightower—but each responds to his or her entrapment differently. Yet so symbiotic are they that despite the evident differences in response, they are mutually self-destructive. Joanna's desire for rebirth miscalculates at every turn, and Joe's insistence he was born once and only once is for him the road to personal doom. When Joe kills her he kills himself, of course; but the murder goes deeper. He tries to cut off her head, for that head was her means of manipulating him and the past, her attempt to alter a history which he insists on as the sole one he can embrace. It is a curious Laocoön pattern, for the coils which strangle are historical, racial, and of a determinate past.

If we understand the novel as structured on spatial principles which are also elements of content, then the two halves, Lena and Joe, are not so dissimilar. Joe is eternally escaping whoever tries to help him as well as those who reject him. Lena is eternally embracing and being embraced, and that, literally, is her fate. Even as Lucas slips away, she finds another in Byron, who miraculously appears as the would-be father. Joe's run is to find some identity amidst the ruins, an escapade which is, of course, impossible given the racial perception which haunts him. Lena's journey never involves a moment of doubt of who she is and what she wants. Lena

Grove suggests solidity, fruitfulness; his name is a joke, a displacement of reality.

Their entrances are synecdochical: the element indicating the larger sense. Entrances are important for Faulkner, in any case—how the Reverend Hightower enters the novel, as the ruined "high tower" of the Christian Church, as a part which has fallen, decayed, rotted, not fulfilling his name, but mocking it. Entrances of all four main characters suggest their marginality, their having fallen. Even Hightower's history, with his celebrated grandfather in the Civil War, indicates a fall, past exploits he cannot possibly duplicate. He, like Joe and Joanna, is a victim of history.

If space creates distinctions between Joe and Lena, so do qualities of language. They speak at different levels of communication. Lena's speech is as brief as Joe's, but while his is laconic and rejecting, hers is open and accepting. He hugs speech to himself, as if it is a commodity he must conserve, as if the supply is limited. Her attitude toward speech and language is that it is available to her whenever she needs it—but she needs little. Her demands on life do not include too much talk; her distended body speaks for her, or else her implacable certainty and good nature. Joe, however, must withhold words, because language does not function for him, any more than does space. He has in fact discovered no medium of expression: he must simply be, and when being fails, he must move on or self-destruct. Lucas talks all the time, until Joe slaps his face or warns him to be silent. Joe has found that in his world, words make no sense. Words are literally for the rest of the world, if it chooses to use them; he can only hug himself, not language. In this formulation of a character, there is a good deal of Faulkner's personal sense of language, that laconic withholding, for example.

In another setting the Reverend Hightower uses language as if it could give him an identity he has suddenly lost.[17] He tries to talk himself into a role, and his performance in church is so extraordinary because of the barrage of words he insists upon. But the words represent nothing. They do not even represent him; they become a wall behind which he remains unidentified. His aim ultimately is not to express himself, but to create a shield or smokescreen behind which he can hide. His is the language of a madman, or one almost mad; and his words are a futile effort to bring together elements which cannot cohere. "Then Sunday," Faulkner writes, "he would be again in the pulpit, with his wild hands and his wild rapt eager voice in which like phantoms God and salvation and the galloping horses and his dead grandfather thundered, while below him the elders sat, and the congregation, puzzled and outraged."[18]

While Joanna Burden's use of language is closer to the bone, it also draws in events and memories which are not agents of reality; therefore her frantic language cannot relate to a real world. Instead, she tries to make words (advice, requests, and demands) adhere to an idea in her head which is a kind of theater. She plays out the drama in her head and uses words to express it, but it does not link to what exists outside. That is perhaps why Faulkner has her lose her head so early,[19] barely one-sixth of the way through the novel. He lavishes attention on that grotesque head, turned opposite to her body. Her words and body are disconnected, in death as in life.

The point of language here is that it serves no communicative function. It begins to have a role of its own, disembodied. What is a sign of civilized behavior has ceased to function that way. With Joe and Lena, the two polarities of the novel, the use of language keys in to racial distinctions: she as white able to use language as she wishes, he, suspected of black blood, using language so protectively that we barely recall his ever speaking by the end of the novel. He is almost silenced by his role, whereas Lena is inhibited only by intellectual or emotional limitations.

These 13 appeared on September 21, and its reception, as was fitting for such an uneven collection, was uneven. The unsigned *New York Times* review said it revealed a writer of "significant fiction" and recommended it unreservedly; but Granville Hicks in the *Herald Tribune* made a more correct judgment, which was that Faulkner was more at home in the novel than in shorter fiction.*

In an unusual move, he agreed to attend the aforementioned conference of Southern writers held in Charlottesville, on October 23–24. The acceptance was unexpected on several grounds. It interrupted his work on *Light in August*; it meant meeting other writers in an academic setting; and it would make him leave Rowan Oak when it was still in disrepair and Estelle had not fully recovered from anemia and the pregnancy. Or put another way, the conference offered a welcome respite from both work and home. In a witty response to James Southal Wilson, of the University of Virginia, Faulkner put his acceptance in frontier terms: "You have seen a country wagon," he wrote, "come into town, with a hound dog under the wagon. It stops on the Square and the folks get out, but that hound never gets very far from that wagon. He might be cajoled or scared out for a short distance, but first thing you know he has scuttled back under the wagon; maybe he growls at you a little. Well, that's me."[20] He says he will be there on October 23. With this, Faulkner initiated a number of acceptances to diverse events which, he discovered, he could only bear if he stayed drunk. This began a pattern.

The conference was a worthy idea, initiated by Ellen Glasgow, a well-established Virginia novelist who had written her way out of the regional novel. With the support of the University of Virginia, the plan was to give Southern writers an opportunity to mingle and talk; from this, it was hoped, the interchange of ideas would energize individual writers and create a sense of mutual sympathy, replacing isolation with a sense of community. A committee was formed of white writers such as Glasgow

---

*In a 1933 review in the *New Statesman and Nation*, David Garnett trashed the entire volume except for "Red Leaves," the work, he said, of a great creative artist. Most other reviewers preferred "That Evening Sun" and "Dry September."

herself, Wolfe, Young, Paul Green, Cabell, DuBose Heyward, and Archibald Henderson. In addition, Sherwood Anderson, Allen Tate, Donald Davidson and others had been invited and indicated they would attend. There would be a mix of established writers, newcomers, and agrarians, some from the recently published *I'll Take My Stand.* That manifesto, in fact, may have served for some of the impetus behind the conference: to present a solid front of creative talent against the North. At the outset, while the conference looked promising on paper, there were so many volatile or alien spirits invited it was hard not to have dark forebodings of the outcome.

Faulkner had barely arrived, on the twenty-first, when his drinking began. He expected Harrison Smith on the twenty-second. Smith was interested in making sure Faulkner felt secure with Cape and Smith and would not skitter off to another publisher if an attractive offer were made to him. There is little question he was becoming an attractive property; and there is also little question that, despite several, well-established figures at the conference, he was considered the main attraction. Had he wished, he could have starred; instead, he chose to withdraw.

His withdrawal began with his first night there. Rather than face the group of writers already arriving, Faulkner preferred to drink away the evening in the local SAE house with a congenial reporter. He dutifully wrote to Estelle the next morning, and his language seems as if he had recovered completely. "The people here are mighty nice to me. When I arrived last night I found waiting for me guest cards to a country club and to the faculty club [neither of which he attended]. I wired Mrs. Sherwood Anderson . . . from the train at Bristol yesterday, but got no answer. Maybe she is still mad at me [the result of his and Spratling's satire of Sherwood]. I'll find out within the next day or so."[21]

Faulkner seemed to hit it off with Paul Green, the playwright, just before the conference started. But the first day was everything that he could not bear, with Ellen Glasgow giving an earnest talk on relationships between fictional and historical truths. He must have withdrawn by then, for reports indicate that he was beyond her words, jabbering, "I agree, I agree." She finished and talk went on and on, all meaningless to the apparently drunk Faulkner. Despite the grand reputation of the conferees, it was a typical conference, which meant that people took seriously what they said and closed their ears to whatever anyone else said. Agrarians pitched in, Tate and Donaldson among them, to defend an agricultural society against those who found a technological age acceptable or inevitable. Clashes occurred on these grounds with people talking at each other, since no one, evidently, was prepared to change his mind. In this pitch of voices, Faulkner was lost, and he fortified himself accordingly. He vanished on a trip to Castle Hill, and when that became apparent, someone stayed by his side to prevent a recurrence. At dinner, where he became the center of attention, he went into his act, silence and withdrawal, while remaining affable. He drank steadily and finally went to sleep.

He also gave interviews, including one at midnight to a reporter from *College Topics*. In one earlier interview, he stressed his military service in France, his work as a reporter on the *Times-Picayune*, and the writing of a novel (never discovered) while he was working on the newspaper. To the reporter who showed up at midnight, he was more coherent and less defensive. Although he continued with deceptions about his war service —he repeated his story about action in France, this time with the British, not the Canadians—he did focus on literary matters. He cited his favorite books as *The Nigger of the "Narcissus"* and *Moby-Dick*, and mentioned Alexandre Dumas as a favorite novelist. He emphasized that he left school at seven, an exaggeration downward, but perhaps an indication that while he attended, his head was elsewhere. Since he was presently engaged in writing *Light in August*, his comments on writing are of interest. "A story usually makes its own plot, works itself out as you go"—which is untrue for him, since he worked out the shape well ahead of time. He insists "the novel form as we know [it] . . . will break down completely"; but then he complicates this by saying one works because of the money and "the demand of one's publishers, who not only set the deadline, but suggest the topic and length of your story." Despite his attendance at a conference of literary luminaries, his assessment of significant contemporary American fiction is dim: "Mr. Faulkner said very decidedly that there is none being produced." When asked about the South, he responded: "Nothing of any real value is likely to come out of it in the next twenty-five years at least. The outstanding Southern authors of today are only the pioneers: their own work is setting the pace, but not very significant in itself."*[22]

These remarks, however facetious, seem to subvert the claims of the agrarians; they imply that out of the clash between ideas a significant fiction will arise. They were of course correct, since their very premises would be confronted by Faulkner's own fiction. After some disparaging

---

*Writing in *Green Hills of Africa*, Hemingway apparently agreed at least in part. Although Faulkner had praised Wolfe, Hemingway thought he was the Primo Carnera of writing and in his letters referred to Wolfe as the "over-bloated Lil Abner of literature," a "glandular giant with the brains and the guts of three mice" (*Selected Letters, 1917–1961*, ed. Carlos Baker [New York: Scribners, 1981], pp. 681, 726). The relationship among the three is a compelling subject in itself. Although there is no evidence on the Faulkner side of meeting Wolfe, the latter noted he had met both Hemingway and Faulkner once, possibly twice. I am grateful to Professor David Herbert Donald of the Harvard University history department for this information. The sources: in the William B. Wisdom collection of Wolfe manuscripts at the Houghton Library, Folder 1188, Wolfe notes writers he has met once or twice; and in May Cameron's *Press Time* (1936), pp. 1247–48, in an interview with Wolfe which he wrote himself, he says: "I have met both Hemingway and Faulkner and my own deep feeling is that neither has begun to reach full maturity and that both will do much better books than they have yet done."

For a description of Faulkner's role in the conference, besides Blotner (vol. I, pp. 707–716), see Dorothy Scura, "Glasgow and the Southern Renaissance," in M. Thomas Inge, ed., *Ellen Glasgow: Centennial Essays* (Charlottesville: University Press of Virginia, 1976), pp. 46–61. For a more general placement of Faulkner among Southern writers, see Louis D. Rubin, Jr., "The Dixie Special: William Faulkner and the Southern Literary Renascence," in *Faulkner and the Southern Renaissance*, eds. Doreen Fowler and Ann J. Abadie (Jackson: University Press of Mississippi, 1982), pp. 63–92; also, in the same volume, Floyd Watkins, "The Hound Under the Wagon: Faulkner and the Southern Literati," pp. 93–119.

remarks on women made idle by modern America, Faulkner offers some cogent observations on fiction. "In the future novel or fiction . . . there will be no straight exposition, but instead, objective presentation by means of soliloquies or speeches of the characters, those of each character printed in a different colored ink [his plan for *Sound*]." He continues: "Something of the play technique will thus eliminate much of the author from the story."[23]

This is clearly a defense of his own methods. Only the story itself counts —the author's personality is deadweight. "What is interesting in Dickens is not the way he takes things, but," as Faulkner says, "those people he wrote about and what they did." If we remember these remarks are being made at midnight by a sleepy, somewhat hung-over Faulkner, we may not take them too seriously; yet at the same time, they suggest how influenced he was by modernist impersonality, by the removal of the author from the text in Eliot's poetry or Conrad's and Joyce's prose. His remarks and practices also point up the difficulties and dangers of trying to extrapolate what he "means" or where he stands. If the author is, as he says, dead-weight, then we cannot find substantive meaning in any kind of authorial statement but only in fictional seams, structures, and shapings.

For Faulkner the conference went by in a haze of congenial people—a big party from which he could extract abundant whiskey. On October 25, he rode up to New York in a car with Paul Green, Milton Abernathy, and Harrison Smith. As we know, Smith was along to protect his valuable property, and he was right in his assessment; for publishers in New York were hovering like buzzards, waiting for Cape and Smith to fail so they could get their claws into the author of *Sanctuary*. Reciting Joyce's poetry and drinking heavily along the way, Faulkner arrived in New York to real attention. By November 4, he wrote Estelle that a movie agent told him he could go to Hollywood and earn $500 or $750 per week. "We could live like counts at least on that, and you could dance and go about. . . . if all that money is out there, I might as well hack a little on the side and put the novel off." He describes himself as "some strange and valuable beast"[24] besieged by people all day. Although shy, withdrawn, very much his own counsel, there is in this and a successive letter (postmarked November 13) a certain enjoyment in the attention. Even Faulkner could not resist the advances of the rich and famous, and the country boy had his head partially turned.

His sending schedule was winding down. "Smoke" had gone out to *Scribner's*, and come back. *Harper's* finally took it. "Idyll in the Desert" was still kicking around, rejected by all of Faulkner's usual magazines and only published in a limited edition by Random House on December 10, 1931. Bennett Cerf, now reorganizing Random House, was eager to get Faulkner, and his publication of the story was one means. With few submissions and that source of income drying up, with no end in sight for his long novel, Faulkner was ripe for offers. The heavy drinking was certainly one manifestation of his anxiety in which he could avoid the problem. Yet even when he drank heavily to forget, he wrote continually. He had brought the manuscript of *Light in August* along.

In New York he found Alfred A. Knopf, Harold Guinzburg of Viking, and Bennett Cerf of Modern Library (purchased by Cerf and Donald Klopfer from Boni & Liveright) and Random House eager to sign him on. With his usual inventiveness, Cerf had more to offer: the publication of *Sanctuary* in the Modern Library edition (which later drew Faulkner's notorious introduction) and a limited printing of *Idyll in the Desert*, one of his least successful stories, a real piece of corn pone. Such belief in an author was bound to impress Faulkner despite his loyalty to Smith. The latter tried to protect his client by having the writer wafted away by Abernathy on a cruise to Jacksonville, Florida. Faulkner used the trip mainly for drinking and pulling pranks, such as hiring an airplane and pilot and flying upside down. At the end of October, he and Abernathy ended up in Chapel Hill, where *Contempo*, the small magazine edited by Abernathy and Anthony Buttitta, was located. The latter two wanted to do a Faulkner issue and make the writer a contributing editor, which he agreed to. What degree of sobriety or drunkenness he was in is impossible to tell, but he also agreed to leave a chunk of the *Light in August* manuscript with them for publication, and promised them a pile of other stuff stored at Rowan Oak. In the meanwhile, as Harrison Smith resigned from Cape and Smith, Faulkner returned to New York to face the onslaught of publishers eager for an acquisition.

He had taken in sufficient money to pay his debts, especially the back rent to the Bryants, a total of seven months in arrears and current rent. *Contempo* was going ahead with publication plans, although this would, in time, foul copyright matters for Faulkner. Still in early November, Smith conveyed to Faulkner his intention to set up for himself and his need for the writer to stay. But now Smith would have to compete with publishers who could offer real advances, perhaps as much as $10,000 (Depression money). What both would have to decide when money was offered was whether Faulkner would remain with a man whose belief in his experimental work was critical, or whether he would deal himself out in order to balance his checkbook. The ostensible issue may have been money, but tremendous career choices were in the offing.

In the letter to Estelle postmarked November 13, as matters were heating up in New York—and the country man was being exposed to the seductions of big-city financial clout—Faulkner seemed manic in his elation at the money he could make. As we read these remarks and reports about him, we must keep in mind that his "high" was literally that: he was high much of the time, maintaining himself in alien territory on whiskey, day and night, eating little, and saying whatever came into his head. It was as though he had come to New York to enjoy a manic situation he could sustain only by way of drinking; and as Estelle interpreted the letter, correctly, he was going off his head, letting himself be carried by people and events; that is, he was not himself.

I am writing a movie for Tallulah Bankhead. How's that for high? The contract to be signed today, for about $10,000. Like this: yesterday I wrote the outline, the synopsis, for which I am to get $500.00. Next I will elaborate the outline and put the action in, and I get $2500.00. Then I write the dialogue and get the rest of it. And then likely we will go out to the Coast, to Hollywood. I will let you know as soon as I can.[25]

He continues: "I have created quite a sensation . . . luncheons in my honor by magazine editors every day for a week now, besides evening parties, or people who want to see what I look like. I have learned with astonishment that I am now the most important figure in American letters. That is, I have the best future. Even Sinclair Lewis and Dreiser make engagements to see me, and Mencken is coming all the way up from Baltimore to see me on Wednesday." He adds: "I'm glad I'm level-headed, not very vain. But I don't think it has gone to my head. Anyway, I am writing. Working on the novel."

Faulkner also writes of sitting next to Jack Oakie, the actor, in a restaurant, meeting Pauline Lord, the actress, at a party, and waiting for rehearsals of a play based on *Sanctuary* to begin the following week. Nothing came of that, nor has the script survived. We can see, however, in the script and "rehearsal" portents of the later work, *Requiem for a Nun*, which was to prove so fascinating especially to European writers and theater people. What Faulkner may or may not have recognized is that it was the author of *Sanctuary* who was being lionized, not the creator of *The Sound and the Fury* or *As I Lay Dying*. The publicity mills had gone into high gear to capitalize on what was increasingly seen as a daring and sensational novel, the *Peyton Place* of its day. But the really innovative work was not in the minds of the publishers (except Harrison Smith), surely not in the plans of the publicists and Hollywood people.

A week before this "high" letter to Estelle, Faulkner met Maurice Coindreau. Unlike the publicity people, Coindreau was interested in vintage Faulkner, *Sound* and *As I Lay Dying*, and he suggested to Gallimard that he be commissioned to translate them. This was the beginning of a long and fruitful relationship for both men—a curious one, for while Faulkner's respect for academics was slight, his feeling for Coindreau was strong, both for the man and the French linkage. As for the publishers, Smith had the inside track. Faulkner in fact contracted with the new firm Smith had established with Robert Haas, and it was assumed that *Light in August* would be published by the man who had had faith in *Sound*. Apparently, other publishers did not accept Faulkner's commitment to Smith, and they hovered, especially Cerf and Guinzburg. Both were also part of recently organized firms, but they stood on far firmer financial ground than Smith.

Faulkner was partying and even spent a weekend in Connecticut, where he met Dorothy Parker, who took a maternal interest in him. Faulkner offered himself as the cool, courteous individual who was self-sufficient, and yet projected a helplessness—Parker called it vulnerability—which made people, especially women, feel protective. But even without the helpless persona he presented when drunk, he regressed to the small boy —whether with Maud, Elizabeth Prall (Anderson), Estelle herself, Dorothy Parker (in her own words), or later with the Random House people (Cerf, Haas, Commins). The need created a curious split in his personality between the frontier, fiercely independent individual and the "little boy," who needed everyone. It was part of his charm.

Faulkner also fell in with the Algonquin wits, whose centerpieces included Alexander Woollcott, Robert Sherwood, Marc Connelly, Franklin P. Adams, and several others such as John O'Hara,* Philip Barry, Joel Sayre, and Dorothy Parker. Joining them was Robert A. Lovett, a Yale man and a World War I hero, in his way everything Faulkner had wanted to be. Lovett had served with the RNAS (Royal Naval Air Service) and flown countless missions. It was Lovett[26] who told anecdotes of the Coastal Motor Boats Faulkner used for his ambitious story "Turn About," which the *Post* published on March 5, 1932. The Algonquin wits were about the last people we would expect Faulkner to find attractive; but they were careful of his feelings, did not push him, and seemed genuinely fond of him. They were, however, the essence of New York City sophistication and cosmopolitanism. Harold Ross of the *New Yorker* often joined them, and Faulkner met Ross, apparently. It is strange that despite his connection to this group, and by extension to Ross, he never submitted work to the *New Yorker*, which from the beginning was a prestigious outlet for fiction. Whatever the inner workings of this crossplay of meetings and people, Faulkner felt cheered by these associations, and he may have realized his acceptance went well beyond his notoriety as author of *Sanctuary*.

He found it congenial to work in Ben Wasson's apartment, and he apparently started immediate work on the material suggested by Lovett. As we have seen, his fictional treatment created a morbid but witty counterpoint between two doomed groups, the men in the torpedo boats and the fliers. Lovett and his story touched just the right nerve in Faulkner and made him interrupt work on *Light in August* to get it down. His immersion in the story at this exciting and disorienting time in his life indicates how the torpedo men reached deeply into his sense of a frontier

---

*For a man who felt left out and who resented others' success, John O'Hara's comments on Faulkner suggest the latter had made a good impression. Writing to John Steinbeck in 1949 (June 2 or 3), O'Hara lauds Faulkner (while not forgetting himself). "Writing. You and Ernest and Faulkner only. Me, of course. But room for all of us. You and I are the only ones who come out and get our whops. You know that the one is Faulkner, the genius. You are closer to him than Ern or I. Fitzgerald was a better just plain writer than all of us put together. Just words writing. But he dade. The working men are you and I. Faulkner, there is nobody like little Willie. Ern has become the modern syno-something for writing and knows it. Has taken a Christ-awful beating because of a funny name. But what a good decent writer. When I think of all of you I want to crawl except when I think of what an honest writer I am" (*Selected Letters of John O'Hara*, ed. Matthew J. Bruccoli [New York: Random House, 1978], p. 224).

world. The men riding death-boats are on the edge of something very meaningful, which only they, and he as author, could capture. In this respect, he found himself as more than a short story writer trying to crack the New York marketplace; here he was historian of a particular sensibility which would otherwise be lost amidst traditional heroics. There was also the quiet of their activity, the fact so few people seemed aware of these men's sacrifice, and the further fact that their work consumed their lives—they died or barely survived by day and then drank themselves into oblivion at night. It was a cycle Faulkner recognized. As author—isolated, secluded, unknown—he poured himself into his books, and then had to find solace in alcohol in order to keep going. Whatever the exact range of emotions this story touched upon, it cut profoundly into the Faulkner psyche.

"Turn About," the product of this piercing experience, took Faulkner until January of 1932 to complete, since it was not submitted to Wasson until the ninth; from there, it went to the *Post*. This is, incidentally, a sign of how the *Post* came to respond to him that it even accepted "Turn About," which was not only very long but not quite their kind of short story. One could, in fact, examine how these vastly popular magazines altered their standards and their perception of their readers' tastes to accommodate a writer like Faulkner. There can be little question he "educated" their editors and forced a greater flexibility so they could publish him. Even at his most mediocre, he was presenting a kind of fiction the *Post*, *Collier's*, and *Woman's Home Companion* rarely published.

Faulkner moved among several places—the Algonquin, a Tudor City apartment, Stark Young's, and Ben Wasson's. At the latter's apartment, he gave an interview to a reporter from the New York *Herald Tribune*, which turned out to be one of his most notorious. The chemistry between writer and interviewer was apparently terribly wrong, or quite possibly Faulkner was so soused he said whatever he thought would be outrageous. He was quite capable, when pushed or when feeling self-pity, to say what was calculated to offend and outrage, and what better whipping boy for a liberal Northern interviewer than the Negro and his place in Southern society! It is difficult to judge how seriously we should take Faulkner's comments, since much of the interview was a put-on, and the interviewer apparently fell into every possible trap. In the first place, Faulkner pointed out that in Oxford he is not thought to be a great man, but "merely lazy." "A lot of them don't know I write books, and they think I don't do anything at all." Then follow his comments on Southern Negroes, who he thinks would be better off under slavery, in a "benevolent autocracy." He adds: "The Negroes would be better off because they'd have some one to look after them. I don't think it would be as good for the white people as for the Negroes to have slavery come back—theoretically, anyhow." The reporter says Faulkner stated Negroes "are like children in many of their reactions." When he asked about Negro artists, Faulkner responded: " 'Well, most artists are children, too.' "[27]

This begins to sound like typical perversity, since Faulkner did not at all believe the artist was a child. Quite the contrary, he held an exalted view of the artist as a maker and poet, and his favorite writers were priests of the imagination. A little further on, after some incomprehensible remarks about Negro-white relationships in the South, he mentioned he never read his reviews, which was only a partial truth. He was not deeply influenced by reviews, nor was he devastated by poor reviews, but with Ben Wasson sending them on he could not avoid them.

On book matters, Faulkner was equally misleading. When asked about the influence of Hemingway on some of the stories in *These 13,* he categorically denied what seems to be an obvious stylistic presence, if not influence. He said that the stories in question were not published in any form until *These 13* appeared and that in fact he had never read any of Hemingway's work "until two years ago."[28] Faulkner may not have read Hemingway until two years ago, as he says, but the Hemingway style had penetrated into short fiction even for those who had not read him closely; and the war stories in *These 13* demonstrate an apparent awareness of Hemingway's kind of language and sentence.

Still another interview occurred on this trip,* a neutral one for the *New Yorker,* which appeared on November 28 in the "Talk of the Town" section. It is a tissue of misinformation, erring on everything from Faulkner's own life to even the date when Rowan Oak was built. It repeats the familiar exaggerations of war service, reporting that Faulkner crashed behind his own lines, broke both legs, was considered dead, recovered, transferred to the American air force, now holds a pilot's license and flies a "rather wobbly plane owned by a friend in Oxford."[29] He says, according to the interview, that he writes when he feels like it, fishes, hunts, and "bosses the plantation"; everyone, he repeats, thinks he's lazy, including his father, who thinks his son is wasting his time. His mother, however, reads his every line.

The lies, deceptions, tall tales, and exaggerations are evident; leading us to believe the interview about Negroes and slavery in the *Herald Tribune* —while devastating when coming from a white Mississippian—was simply talk. However, one cannot avoid the view that what comes from the mouth of someone drinking deeply is often what sits in that person's subconscious. We must conclude that while Faulkner's public statements about race would continue to create outrage, they would not at all coincide with the way he presented race fictionally. In *Light in August,* his ongoing project, race enters into the novel as a curse on white as well as black.

---

*Even Estelle got into the act, giving an interview to Marshall J. Smith of the Memphis *Press-Scimitar* on her way to join Faulkner in New York. Her mission was one of salvation: " 'The reason I'm going to New York is to keep people away from him' " (*Lion in the Garden: Interviews with William Faulkner,* eds. James B. Meriwether and Michael Millgate [Lincoln: University of Nebraska Press, 1968], p. 26). She indicates her favorite novel of Faulkner's is *As I Lay Dying,* but doesn't think much of his short stories. She also complains that being married to an author is not all fun; that Faulkner disappears into his room for hours at a time, taking the doorknob with him so no one can enter.

Faulkner stayed on in New York for almost eight weeks, extending to a week before Christmas. The partying continued unabated, as did the drinking, the bar- and saloon-hopping. He also fitted in writing of *Light in August*, because the manuscript is dated February 19, 1932, a bare two months after he returned from New York. He also indicated to Paul Green[30] he was doing a dramatization of *Sanctuary*, in which he would act the role of the corncob. Just when he found time for this (unless such a dramatization was a fantasy) we cannot tell; it is even difficult to account for his progress on *Light in August*, a long, complicated book. *August* required a sharp, clear mind in its organization of time sequences. Withal the drinking and conviviality, he was plugging along, probably in the early morning hours when insomnia brought him to his desk.

He met several people he liked. Lillian Hellman, one of his earliest supporters, and Dashiell Hammett, a Marylander and already the author of *The Maltese Falcon*, proved congenial. In addition to being knowledgeable and laid back, Hammett was a considerable drinker, good for the immediate bout or for the binge, and Faulkner found in him a kindred fellow. They argued, however improbably, over books, particularly over Thomas Mann's *The Magic Mountain*, for Faulkner one of the touchstones of literary greatness. Hammett attacked it as untruthful, possibly because he found it politically flabby. There were potential fireworks here, for while Faulkner was politically moderate or even apolitical in ideological terms, Hammett was a confirmed Marxist and radical, and not at all afraid of applying ideological interpretations to whatever he read. Another congenial fellow was Nathanael West, the author of the recently published *The Dream Life of Balso Snell*. West was an original in every sense, a Jew who was profoundly in love with guns and hunting; a satirist and fantasist who lived in and around the Hotel Sutton. West took to Faulkner, liked his books, and was influenced by *Sanctuary* in the remainder of his brief life.

Never before had Faulkner worked on a long novel while staying away from home for more than a few days. What we find remarkable is how internalized *Light in August* remains even while its author is projecting himself with friends, at parties, in saloons.

If we separate *Light in August*'s basic elements from the overall narrative, it consists of a number of stories which must be told. Once we get past the thrust of the narrative to the subtext, we discover that the stories as related are intact in themselves. There are four basic ones: Lena's, Joe's, Joanna's, and Hightower's. Everything else is subsidiary, and even the connections among them are secondary to the stories. The characters are parallel, discrete individuals; to make their stories touch is of course the novelist's task. But these stories remain short fictions in themselves, as if Faulkner had blended four pieces into a longer work. Joe and Joanna become complementary figures, as suggested; in different ways, so do Joanna and Hightower. Lena touches Hightower by way of Byron Bunch, who serves as connective tissue with all of the characters, whether in physical terms, as with Lena and Hightower, or with tales, as with Joe and Joanna. Joe and

Hightower touch by way of events—they, too, complement each other as men who no longer have an identity, only memories. Joe and Lena touch only in their counterpointing possibilities, he as escaping, she as seeking. Only Lena and Joanna have no actual contact, since the latter is dead when Lena comes to the outskirts of Jefferson. Nevertheless, as women they represent the whore-madonna dichotomy characteristic of so many Faulkner females.

In chapter 10, Faulkner dug in, and the internalized line of the novel associated with Joe is revealed in language which comes from the outside but is presented as interior monologue freely associated. The technique is uniquely Faulkner's, but it is more than technique: it suggests how Faulkner was seeking seamlessness in temporal matters to blur distinctions between actual and internal. The chapter begins: "Knowing not grieving remembers a thousand savage and lonely streets."*³¹ Italicized material further down the page presents a form of commentary spoken by someone else (Max, a pimp) but assimilated into Joe's sensibility as interior monologue, even stream:

> *Here bobbie* [the whore Joe has been sleeping with] *here kid heres your comb you forgot it heres romeos chicken feed too jesus he must have tapped the sunday school till on the way out its bobbies now didnt you see him give it to her didn't you see old bighearted thats right pick it up kid you can keep it as an installment or a souvenir or something what dont she want it well say thats too bad now thats tough but we cant leave it lay here on the floor itll rot a hole in the floor.*

As they leave, the blonde woman with Max leaves a banknote for Joe, and then the reader enters his life as he begins to run: "he entered the street which was to run for fifteen years."³² In true Great Depression terms, Joe hits the rails, hitches rides on trucks and country wagons, sleeps in the open, joins the army for four months, deserts, wanders cities, beds down with prostitutes, and then tells them he is a Negro, at times being beaten unconscious by other cathouse patrons. In Chicago he lives in the black neighborhood, for a time bedding down with a "woman who resembled an ebony carving." As he lies beside her, he tries to expel from himself "the

*The worked-over manuscript reveals several dilemmas facing Faulkner, nearly all involving time sequences. Beginning with chapter 6, the novel moves deep into Joe's past when he crosses the dietician in the orphanage. From this point, his past is picked up in his years with the McEacherns, running through chapters 7–10. In chapter 10, Joe starts to run. It is here, in this chapter grouping, that Faulkner tried out several temporal sequences, including moving 7 to positions 8, 9, 10, and 11, before putting it back. He also shifted around later chapters, trying to break through temporal sequencing, before restoring them to a more linear narrative. Eventually, the original chapter 19 was moved to 17, where Lena gives birth, with Hightower's help. The enormous revisions of *Light in August*, the shifting and renumbering of pages and entire chapters, plus the thousands of verbal alterations, imply Faulkner was trying to impress an internal method on a basically external narrative; making pastness into content.

white blood and the white thinking and the being. And all the while his nostrils at the odor which he was trying to make his own would whiten and tauten, his whole being writhe and strain with physical outrage and spiritual denial."[33]

Then, found on Christmas Eve and now "coming out" at thirty-three, Joe is in Mississippi. Joanna's "dark house" is there, as is the planing mill where he goes to work, where Lucas Burch (Brown) joins him, where Byron Bunch has been a loyal worker, taking off only on Sunday to sing in a church choir. With this passage, in the middle of the novel, the narrative begins to catch up the present: we are in the immediate past before Lena comes to Jefferson and sees the smoke from the burning house.

Joe remains a wraith, a ghostly presence, a phantom. In chapter 6, Faulkner begins to chart his background, which he does in far greater detail than for Joanna and Hightower, or even for Lena. But in the piecemeal background we do get about Lena, there is also repression, a line drawn around her, doors and windows closed to the outside world. She too escapes from a "dark house." That shadow of darkness—as house, life lived, race—dominates. We first meet Joe in a dark house of sorts, a closet where he hides in the orphanage, and where he is caught when the dietician and a doctor enter her room to enjoy a quickie. In that dark closet, the bewildered child cannot contain himself, and the toothpaste he has been eating makes him sick; he vomits, and that vomiting is in a sense his signature for life. He will vomit, and life will vomit him. From that point, he is not a child or person; all directive will is taken from him. He is manipulated by the orphanage, by the janitor who is his grandfather, by the McEacherns who adopt him, by Mr. McEachern, who abuses him in the name of God.

Before we meet Joe as a child, we see him after he has murdered Joanna. Faulkner achieves interiority by way of stepping back after the fact; and by this time, Joe is a ghost: "Yet though he was not large, not tall, he contrived somehow to look more lonely than a lone telephone pole in the middle of a desert. In the wide, empty, shadow-brooded street he looked like a phantom, a spirit, strayed out of its own world, and lost."[34] Joe is introduced in chapter 6 by way of a Joycean passage in which his surroundings suggest the anomie which will characterize his life.

Knows remembers believes a corridor in a big long garbled cold echoing building of dark red brick soot-bleakened by more chimneys than its own, set in a grassless cinderstrewnpacked compound surrounded by smoking purlieus and enclosed by a ten foot steel-and-wire fence like a penitentiary or a zoo, where in random erratic surges, with sparrowlike childtrebling, orphans in identical and uniform blue denim in and out remembering but in knowing constant as the bleak walls, the bleak windows where in rain soot from the yearly adjacenting chimneys streaked like black tears.[35]

For the first time, in this novel there is a distinctive Faulkner prose. It breaks free of syntax and grammar; it combines words as Joyce did, but it has little of Joyce's softening rhythms. It is deliberately jagged, not mellifluous; it is a savage language in its hatred of the orphanage as a city nightmare or trap, full of urban images of bleakness. Faulkner's daring was in bringing to a novel with crime-detective aspects a prose expressive rather than descriptive. He refused a straightforward approach to his narrative and insisted, along with temporal manipulations, on a language which establishes words as if for the first time. The brutality of the jagged, edgy language is a perfect medium for expressing Joe's initiation into life. There is no give to it. While we are not induced to sympathize with Joe in any ordinary sense, we do recognize his identity has been taken away from him. Faulkner understood what it was to fall outside of all social mechanisms, first as a foundling, then as a child taunted as "nigger," discovered by the dietician in a situation which baffles him, and finally adopted by a religious fanatic and sadist, McEachern. Once all this is accomplished, there is no way he can reach into himself—the self has been deleted before he has a chance to explore it.

The scenes with McEachern have Dickensian touches, even to the name. But in Dickens, the main character is never permanently damaged by his experience, whether in a school, orphanage, or home. Repression may destroy a minor character, but the main one (Oliver, David, etc.) bounces back as soon as he or she is shown tenderness, identity intact. For Faulkner, the experience is scarring and permanent; Joe loses all feeling, and in fact identifies with the oppressor, which is psychologically quite astute. When Mrs. McEachern shows tenderness and kindness, Joe rejects her utterly. Rather than responding to her gesture, he sees her as weak, and his hatred of women is formed here.

The McEachern experience is critical for Joe, for it occurs at the very time he should expand, and instead he is compressed. He loses all feeling, rather than withholding feeling, as in Dickens, until the right time comes for its expression.* It is tempting, once again, to see a biographical dimension for Faulkner here. For although Murry did not of course treat his eldest son this way—he was kind but indifferent, indulgent but distant—Faulkner's perception of the withholding of feeling as the result of an outsider father is palpable in his view of Joe. And his attitude toward Maud Falkner, while on the surface devoted, would seem to have colored his sense of women as lying outside "principles," however brutal those principles prove to be. All this is speculative, but the hermetic quality of the McEachern experience for Joe appears to probe deeply into the very nature of family relationships, where the boy is marginal, outside, adopted,

---

*In the revision of *Sanctuary*, which directly preceded the early stages of *Light in August*, there was the effort to humanize Popeye in the epilogue, where his anomie is given some circumstantial basis. Joe Christmas, in one respect, is an extension of Popeye, a less automatic, less reptilian being, but one nevertheless caught in the same spiral of destruction and self-destruction, even to the indifference with which he meets his end.

not considered part of the family process. This is Faulkner's perception, not fact.

There are other biographical dimensions. Faulkner stresses Joe's small size, as against McEachern's large, solid body. The foster-father is eerily built like Murry, large, creaky, bulky. But there is another aspect, and this is the repeated trauma in Faulkner's work of a small boy losing a sister, or sister-substitute. Here, Joe is three, and he dimly recalls Alice, twelve, who wakes him up one night to say goodbye. Her disappearance is dream-like, between sleeping and waking, and when he fully awakens her bed is occupied by a new boy. The scene is brilliantly conceived, for it is a crucial one in Joe's development. Had Alice remained she might have made a difference, as friend and as female, and yet she leaves when the boy is not even fully conscious. The great loss of his early life is only a blur in his memory, as the boy, now five, struggles to remember what has happened to him. The disappearance of Alice brings us back to Quentin's loss of Caddy, and then further back to Elmer's loss of Jo-Addie, who steals out of his life in much the same way that Alice does in Joe's. The recurring image of the lost "sister" is like the loss of Eden, the expulsion from the Garden. It obviously had tremendous meaning for Faulkner and would seem to be interwoven with the loss of childhood, the surrender to despair, the first step in a path to destruction. Two of the three young boys are doomed, utterly—Quentin to suicide, Joe to murder and then to his own ritual death. Elmer escapes such finality, but his artistic career ends, and perhaps that too must be viewed as a form of death.

There is another critical parallel. Like Temple Drake in *Sanctuary*, Joe repeats, *"Something is going to happen. Something is going to happen to me,"* earlier *"Something is going to happen to me.* I am going to do something."*[36] The significance of this repeated passage is that it serves as a kind of logo for the entire novel, as it did for *Sanctuary*. It functions not only for Joe, but for Joanna and Hightower, and in a more positive way for Lena. Its intrinsic interest is not in its sense of doom or fate but in its congruence with internal stories. For each character, it becomes the motto of his/her own story, and Joe verbalizes it because his is the most desperate, the most outside personal control. The passage reveals that the individual is about

*It also appears exactly in "Miss Zilphia Gant," a story from the first *Sanctuary* writing period. This slight story of obsession and madness has curious parallels to Faulkner's inner life. Written before mid-December of 1928, although published in 1932, "Miss Zilphia Gant" has fictional affinities to "A Rose for Emily," but its more direct appeal is its personal side. It is about a woman's desertion by her husband and her assumption of an obsessively domineering role in bringing up her daughter, Zilphia; then the repetition of the mother's narrow, hate-filled life by the daughter. It involves, in turn, the daughter's rejection of her husband after a three-day marriage and her decision to return to her mother's control. But after her mother's death, Zilphia peruses the news columns for word of her husband's remarriage, in which she substitutes her name for the new bride's while seeking the name of the husband. Inconclusive in itself except as a piece of domestic Grand Guignol, the story plays upon several Faulknerian family tensions: the crushingly domineering, destructive mother, the mate who drifts away to someone else (Estelle to Cornell Franklin?), the daughter who cannot say no to her parent (Estelle and the Oldhams?), the hatred which men and women alternately feel for each other—all this on the eve of Faulkner's own marriage.

to be manipulated by "something"; he has lost control to make his life happen. The phrasing of the passage suggests the motif of the novel: that race, history, pastness, circumstance make and subvert the individual.

These great middle novels of Faulkner's, from *Sanctuary* through *Go Down, Moses,* demonstrate a fatalism: the individual—whether Popeye, Ike McCaslin, Thomas Sutpen, from low to high—goes through stages which seem predestined for him. And even when he rides the highs of power, he is becoming subservient to a dooming historical process. The Greeks called it hubris; Faulkner called it, in the words of Quentin in *Absalom,* the curse of the South. If not the curse, then history itself, race, the presentness of the past: there was no escape. That is why, to return to an earlier topic, it is so misleading to accept Faulkner's views on race in his public statements: race is part of this very doom, white and black alike in a common destiny.

Even as Estelle represented her husband as attending church, he was writing a book in which his chief character moves outside the Fall. If the Fall is the means by which Jesus can redeem man's sin, Faulkner has created a character for whom the Fall, Jesus, redemption, and salvation lie on another planet. As a Christmas, Joe provides an alternative to Jesus; an anti-Christ, perhaps, or, more likely, a non-Christ. As a nihilist, he has tried to reach out—the episode with Bobbie, the prostitute—but even this feeble attempt to make contact is denied him. For not only is Joe amoral, and outside society; society itself has no mechanism to contain him. He is programmed from the moment he tastes the dietician's toothpaste, *his* "forbidden fruit."

We do not know just where Faulkner was in *Light in August* when he attended a November party at the home of Alfred and Blanche Knopf, a dress affair which he and Hammett arrived at already drunk. Hammett promptly passed out, Faulkner following shortly afterward. Faulkner in fact appeared to return from the dead: seating himself, standing up, and passing out again. Wasson helped him out. Blotner speaks of another occasion when Cerf invited Faulkner and Knopf, who asked the writer to inscribe some of his out-of-print books for him. Faulkner refused, saying signed editions were a source of income for him. When Cerf interceded in what was becoming a typical Faulkner ploy, he agreed to sign one book.

He somehow continued to work on *Light in August,* and by late November had also finished his notorious introduction to the Modern Library edition of *Sanctuary,* with his "confession" that it was written for commercial purposes with no regard for the audience's intelligence. While it showed contempt for readers, the introduction also revealed a self-destructiveness about Faulkner. For its 750 words suggest not only a hatred of those seeking thrills in *Sanctuary,* but self-hatred. Possibly because of his heavy drinking or the separation from Estelle and recent memories of Alabama's death, possibly out of feelings of guilt generated by his association with a chic New York crowd, possibly because he was committing adultery or considering it, he used the Modern Library introduction to work through some of his self-hatred.

When such an act reveals itself—where an author trashes his own by no means negligible work—the motives are more complex than the outside world can penetrate. He may also have been responding to Cerf's overtures for him to come to Random House and abandon loyal Harrison Smith with a verbal act of contempt for Random House's product, more directly aimed at himself for being involved. Perhaps we can never discover what came over him. Perhaps it was little more than writing done in a drunken haze, striking out at a life which, while glittering in parts, was unsatisfactory, full of responsibilities (Rowan Oak, wife, stepchildren) from which he saw no surcease. One final line of reasoning is that Faulkner felt contempt for the revision, for having had to revise a book he originally believed in.* Cerf paid him $100 for the introduction; in a sense, he was throwing in his lot with Random House with this contribution to their line. The Modern Library edition of the revised *Sanctuary* appeared in March of 1932.

Faulkner had been thinking of a second volume of poetry which he wanted Smith to publish. Smith later agreed, with *A Green Bough* appearing on April 20, 1933, in both a limited edition of 360 copies and a regular trade edition. At the end of November Estelle left for Memphis on her way to New York. As she suspected, Faulkner was heading into a collapse from overdrinking, and she was coming to collect him—a reclamation job she was undertaking while still in poor shape herself. Once in New York, she went to the Algonquin where Faulkner was staying; but her efforts to make some sense of her days in New York came to little in a pattern of appointments, missed engagements, heavy drinking, general testiness when they were together, and disappearances by Faulkner.

A sense of collapse characterized everything. Faulkner could not handle the social scene, and his inability to relate to it emotionally and intellectually led to bizarre and self-destructive behavior. His marriage at this point was already tenuous, since he was moving wildly in a world where he was constantly courted, while also uneasy in his own world. The Algonquin was a perpetual party scene, an artificial society whose center was the "Round Table," where Woollcott as King Arthur presided over his knights. By 1931 steady attrition had lessened its luster, but the Round Table knights still made informal appearances, including Dorothy Parker, Robert Benchley, Frank Sullivan, and now Faulkner.

With Estelle's appearance, the trip was winding down for Faulkner. Her rescue effort was well calculated: he needed retrieving both from his friends and from himself. He had gone into high gear for almost two months, and now he required drying out. Cerf gave a farewell party—still

---

*In the light of Faulkner's care with *Sanctuary*, we must discount his hyperbole that he "speculated what a person in Mississippi would believe to be current trends, chose what I thought was the right answer and invented the most horrific tale I could imagine and wrote it in about three weeks and sent it to Smith." When he saw the galleys, "it was so terrible that there were but two things to do: tear it up or rewrite it. . . . So I tore the galleys down and rewrote the book" (Library of America, *Sanctuary*, p. 1030).

courting Faulkner, of course, but also generous and warm. The Cerf who comes down to us has something of the clown about him, with his appearances on television and his "joke books"; but he was a serious publisher and for those he liked and wanted he was a most accommodating, understanding man. When Faulkner finally did go with Random House, Cerf made him feel that its New York offices and the apartments and houses of its top editors were a home away from home for him. Given the twists and turns of Faulkner's personality, his bouts of drinking, his growing adulteries, he needed someone as understanding as Cerf proved to be. It was, as we shall see, a perfect meeting of a difficult but brilliant author and the publisher who knew how to indulge him.

On the way back to Memphis and Oxford, the couple stopped in Baltimore, where Faulkner and Mencken, after dinner, went out for the evening. While part of Faulkner's intention was to secure Mencken for future submissions to *American Mercury,* the more immediate reason was to gain a heavy, steady drinker for a companion. Once home, Faulkner received a pre-Christmas gift from Sam Marx of MGM, requesting the services of Faulkner in Hollywood. After asking about his availability, Marx inquired "how much?" The "how much?" was to be a dramatic moment, since in the height of the Great Depression the pinch was on, not only for Faulkner and his efforts at story sales, but for his friends in Oxford and the region as a whole. The economy was reaching its nadir, and the poor South was becoming steadily poorer. Banks were closing, businesses were defaulting, and individuals were heading into bankruptcy. Hollywood would prove to be a "happy fall." That revision of *Sanctuary,* which brought fame, should perhaps not be viewed entirely in personal terms but in the context of the South's worsening economic condition. The revision which made it palatable for a larger audience, and which Faulkner saw as pandering, becomes linked to larger economic and fiscal questions that Faulkner—any more than Phil Stone, the banks, farms, and businesses—could not evade. MGM wanted the man who wrote *Sanctuary.*

Chapter Fifteen

Anti-Eden

SETBACKS CONTINUED—AS noted, *Scribner's* rejected "Smoke"—but Faulkner was an engine chugging along, set in his ways, working out the pattern he had established and would keep to for many years. The intrusion of Hollywood into this pattern was not a waste of time, but an opportunity for release and relief from a domesticity he both needed and rejected. Louis Cochran, an acquaintance from Ole Miss days, tried to interview Faulkner, but was referred to Phil Stone. Cochran described Faulkner, however, as having the "delicate step and waist line of a girl," eyes that were "a soft, luminous brown," and hair of the same tint, but thick "and more often tousled than otherwise." He continues: "A thin face, wide forehead and high cheek bones complete a countenance that is at once remotely aloof and sensitive to every living thing."[1] The description is apt, and the comment about the face as aloof and yet sensitive is incisive. Cochran believed fully in Faulkner and predicted he would become a classic, studied at universities and a source of pride for Oxford.

Cochran went to Stone, as Faulkner had suggested he do, and from Stone's responses we see resentment building in the older man in direct proportion to Faulkner's growing reputation. He emphasized that Faulkner was his creation, trained by him, as if a pet dog. He considered Faulkner sane and normal, but what he meant by that is difficult to ascertain. Probably he wanted to indicate that Faulkner was not extraordinary

—just your everyday Oxonian who happened to write. The mentor then went into the main part of his act, which was to question whether his former student would ever become articulate in prose, stressing Faulkner's weaknesses and shortcomings, his lapses of literary taste. He suggested that the author of *The Sound and the Fury* and *As I Lay Dying* had remained in his "adolescent groove," the implication being this was the result of his neglect of Stone's advice. Nearly every aspect of Stone's response was built on assumptions that Faulkner had failed or gone wrong, with the further implication that it occurred because he drifted away from a man of breeding and taste. The mentor was striking back. But Stone was beginning a long process of deterioration and dissatisfaction. The high energy which had characterized his early career had led into burnout and loss of direction; he was going through the motions as a lawyer, meanwhile becoming emotionally unstable and deeply unhappy. Stone had seen Faulkner, in the classical-Greek sense, as the student he would tutor; and that relationship was implicitly a man-to-man linkage he could not forgo. He was full of contradictory impulses, and it is possible that his uncertainties and dissatisfactions had a buried sexual etiology to them.

In early 1932 Faulkner wrote Harrison Smith about the book of poetry he had in mind, originally titled "A Greening Bough," which became *A Green Bough*. Since Smith and Haas (Robert Haas, who later joined Random House and became deeply attached to Faulkner, as Faulkner to him) were to publish *Light in August*, Faulkner may have found it expeditious to submit a volume of poems while he had leverage with Smith. He comments that the stuff "does not seem so bad on rereading . . . worse has been published." His characterization of his work contained a good deal of truth; worse had been published, but so had much better. This was journeyman work of a man who had long since graduated from being a derivative poet into an original novelist. While knowing this, he could not resist using Smith's firm as a last hurrah. He tells him to call it "Poems," and reports what Smith really wanted to hear, that he was accomplishing "about 1000 or 1500 words every day, sometimes more. Did 3000 Thursday [on *Light in August*]."[2]

As 1932 began, where was Faulkner? In professional and personal terms, it was to prove another eventful year. He would demonstrate an astonishing run of energy. In March, the Modern Library edition of *Sanctuary* appeared, but money was not forthcoming, since Smith and Cape were being liquidated and royalties were withheld. The need for money was desperate, and this would explain his readiness to go to Hollywood. On February 19, Faulkner completed the first draft of *Light in August*, and read proof on it in July. It was published on October 6. He also published eight stories.

Early in the year, on February 1, *Contempo* (published in Chapel Hill) signaled a new event in Faulkner's life: an issue devoted to his work. It included nine poems (which Smith wanted held back) and "Once Aboard the Lugger," which had been sitting around after magazine rejections.

That issue of the magazine, the first, included reviews of *These 13* and *Idyll in the Desert*, which Random House had published in a limited edition. Further, there was an assessment of Faulkner, already noted, as the "most creative of contemporary American writers." While Smith rightfully fumed, Faulkner could not have helped but be pleased. In a parallel action, he permitted the Casanova Book Shop in Milwaukee to reprint in the literary journal, *Salmagundi*, some of his pieces written for New Orleans magazines in 1925. Smith thought Faulkner was giving material away which should be held together carefully for purposes of volume publication and copyright. Faulkner half agreed, but argued—after trying unsuccessfully to retrieve the verse from Buttitta at *Contempo*—that he had made commitments and needed publicity.

While Smith's fears were surely justified, Faulkner desperately wanted attention. We think of him as laid back, indifferent to the reception of his work, but the record shows otherwise. While he often said he wanted publicity for the sake of sales—the brunt of his Modern Library introduction—he also sought attention; he needed reinforcement of his own estimation of himself.

Within this context, the visits to Hollywood in 1932 take on the quality of salvation. Faulkner went to Hollywood from May 7 to June 16 as a scriptwriter with Metro-Goldwyn-Mayer at $500 per week; at the end of that period, Paramount took out an option on *Sanctuary*. Faulkner returned to MGM in July, when he met Howard Hawks, the director, an encounter which affected his entire future in Hollywood. Hawks's brother recommended a film adaptation of "Turn About," which Faulkner helped to turn into *Today We Live*, with Joan Crawford and Gary Cooper. At MGM until August 10, Faulkner was doing the same work as before but now for $250 per week. In early October he returned to Hollywood, this time with Maud and his brother Dean, who was twenty-five. He was in Hollywood when *Light in August* was published, on October 6. On October 22, Faulkner returned to Oxford, and from November through May of 1933 was able to remain at home while working for MGM, now at $600 per week, this through the intercession of Hawks. With this kind of income, he could afford to support his extended family, make renovations on Rowan Oak, which was still in disrepair, and indulge in certain luxuries.

Hollywood took its toll. Although Faulkner finished important work while shuttling back and forth in early 1932, by 1933 he was unable to settle in to a new novel. Not until early 1934 did he begin to work on a long fiction, what became his masterpiece, *Absalom, Absalom!* The Hollywood stints nevertheless served many functions and cannot be dismissed merely as work in a very minor mode of a major writer. In terms of Faulkner's greater talent, it was of course journeyman work, even less than that in the case of some films he worked on. But it fulfilled him in other ways. It fitted well into the emotional pattern he needed, which was to escape periodically, even from those to whom he felt attached. It was part of that process of rejection we cited in 1925: without utterly rejecting those close to him, he nevertheless had to deny them. And in that feeling of guilt at the abandonment, in that desire to be alone and without encumbrance, in that self-pity at having to do it all, he found the correct ingredients for his imagination to function. In this respect, he was curiously like Murry—both carried in their heads the desire to escape, to roam their own territory. In his way, Faulkner became as much a part-time father and husband as Murry had been.

But there was another area in which Hollywood fulfilled him. Despite his constant pleas of poverty, Faulkner had a large need for luxury items, extending to objects well beyond his means. In 1933, at a time when he was barely getting on his feet financially, he indulged himself in areas which took a good deal of money, such as flying and owning an airplane. He continued to seek such indulgences—better planes and cars, a farm—even when money was tight. Later, when his finances were still shaky, he bought horses. And he spent a good deal on maintaining them, although he never became a sure rider, as he never became a good pilot.

Hollywood became a necessity in still a third area. Although Faulkner grew up in the 1910s, he was a man who had to come through the Great Depression just as he was trying to get on his feet. Because of his long apprenticeship as a poet and then as a struggling novelist, he was thirty-five before he could earn a decent living. His earning years had been postponed to a time when the country went dry; and thus Hollywood became for him, with all its hated glitter and disadvantages for serious writers, a true part of the American dream. Hollywood was littered with the bodies of writers trying to maintain stability in the Depression years; and it was controlled by men who enjoyed having important authors reduced to lackeys, working on trivial scripts for their studios. Producers and directors were crass and crude, and writers were frequently humiliated in order to earn their money. There is this part of it; but, withal, Hollywood represented a way out, and we cannot neglect this aspect of it for Faulkner. He wanted what Hollywood offered. Much as he might sneer at its values and its handling of him and others, it offered a piece of the American dream. He had already recognized in his novels and stories how tarnished that dream was, but when it presented itself as a reality, he could not resist.

There was a final, very personal factor. Hollywood gave him access to pretty young women and afforded him the opportunity to enjoy a sexual life which he could not find with Estelle in Oxford. This is a thorny, circuitous part of Faulkner's Hollywood career—and it extended for years, for example in his long-term affair with Howard Hawks's script clerk Meta Carpenter—but it is an essential part. He apparently needed affection as well as sex, or at least the sense that after so many rejections in his twenties, he was able to find young women who liked him. Part of his attraction may have been his growing power as a nationally known novelist; but whatever the reason, women could be his—this for a man who had found himself either directly denied or ridiculed.

The year 1932 becomes important not only for the work Faulkner was completing, but because it gave him some nourishment for a part of himself he had been forced to keep hidden or disguised because of financial limitations. There was the Faulkner who sought expansion, even though he recognized his material lay in Oxford and surrounding areas, that is, Jefferson and Yoknapatawpha. There was real tension between the need to hold tight to what he knew and the equally strong and urgent need to slip away. The drinking was one aspect of this need to break through to another level of existence, even if it proved destructive; the flying would become another way, the affairs with young women still another. The year 1932 gave him a glimpse, during a low time in terms of morale and finances, of this new, somewhat promising land. Hollywood glamor could be ridiculed, but it was still there. The other side of this—as Fitzgerald discovered—is that the studio experience was the ultimate marketplace lure, the whore of Babylon. It became a burial ground for many of those once serious talents; and even for those like Faulkner who resisted its death-dealing forces, the seduction could be destructive. The following year became an indifferent one for Faulkner; and while it could be argued that after the long haul on *Light in August* and the production of several major works in just five years he needed a mental rest, nevertheless it came at just the time he went to Hollywood.

Such reflections recall the period in 1932 when he was working on *Light in August*. It is possible to see in Joe Christmas elements of particular concern to Faulkner: aspects which are a metaphor of the writer, however disguised and enfolded in other dimensions. The lack of identity, whereby Joe moves in and out of the black and white worlds, unsure of where he belongs, or of which he wants to enter into, using his potentiality (or liability) as Negro or white as the situation demands—such an identityless person recalls the isolation of the artist employed by Faulkner's earliest influences, the French poets of the nineteenth century. These influences never quite abated: the writer as outside, isolated, martyred; the poet as lacking any social identity; the albatross in Baudelaire's great poem, the drunken boat in Rimbaud's. These are extremely powerful images of the writer's drift from one world to another, or of his rejection by any world which he tries to enter. The metaphor is drift, journey, directionless movement; the personal element is confusion of realms so that the poet, from the social point of view, is anomic, useless. This was a role Faulkner imitated in the 1920s, when he walked around Oxford as town tramp. He assumed the roles of his poetic heroes and became a part of theater. Yet even when the physical elements in his life changed, the mental and emotional stance remained. Joe is that metaphor.

None of this vitiates the fact Faulkner saw his protagonist as a vicious punk. Given the nature of his conditioning, he is unredeemable. The turning point comes in his affair with Bobbie Mason, the prostitute—had she responded differently, he might have maintained some balance; but he deliberately destroys even that by telling her he has Negro blood, and that, as he knows, she cannot accept: " 'He told me himself he was a nigger! The son of a bitch! Me f---ing a nigger son of a bitch that would get me in a jam with clodhopper police. At a clodhopper dance!' "³ There is nothing romantic or sentimentalized about this; but it does occur at a point in Joe's life when he might have been stabilized. Faulkner, however, will have none of this, no salvation through the love of a whore—that was Steinbeck territory. Joe is doomed to his fate. But we must not forget that in Faulkner's view it was the fate of every serious writer: isolation, martyrdom to the page, society's taunts. If this in itself sounds romantic and overly dramatic, we recall it was the 1930s, and writers who did not go to Hollywood were having a hard time indeed.

Faulkner opened 1932 in controversy: Harrison Smith's fear he was cutting his own throat by permitting the *Contempo* and *Salmagundi* publications. Faulkner did try to retrieve the poems Smith hoped to publish in the new volume,* but *Contempo* had already gone to press. So he wrote Smith in mid-January. "Goddam the paper and goddam me for getting mixed up with it and goddam you for sending me off . . . in the shape I was in."⁴ As his letter written at the same time to Ben Wasson indicates, he was more upset at Smith's reaction than at what he had done. He mentions he had given Buttitta "a bum short story, and then I gave him a batch of verse and told him to take what he wanted." He asserts that he gets into a state "when people come to see me and I begin to visualize a kind of jail corridor of literary talk. I don't know what in hell it is, except I seem to lose all perspective and do things, like a coon in a tree." He speaks of having "a howl from Hal." He admits things have gone wrong, but wonders if "Hal is just jealous?" He speaks of wasting "ten novel chapters of energy and worry" over the matter. He starts to blame everyone for letting him go on in the shape he was in—intoxicated for several days and willing to accommodate any request. At the end, he feels it is not so serious as Smith says.

There was still the question of a limited edition. *Contempo* was one thing, but a limited edition, Smith warned, could really undermine future contractual arrangements. The *Salmagundi* business, which appeared to involve two limited editions, would have to be blocked. Faulkner tried to placate Smith by saying that before gaining his reputation with *Sanctuary*, he had agreed to the publication of some New Orleans material written before *Soldiers' Pay*. What eventually appeared in *Salmagundi* (April 30, 1932) were two essays, "On Criticism" and "Verse Old and Nascent: A Pilgrimage," and six poems, "New Orleans," "The Faun," "Dying Gladiator," "Portrait," "The Lilacs," and "L'Apres-Midi d'un Faune." The republication of the two essays was actually a good idea, since, as we have observed, they expressed a good deal of Faulkner's aesthetic direction. He reassures

---

Contempo published the following poems, none of them masterpieces: "April," "Vision in Spring," "My Epitaph," "Spring," "Twilight," "I Will Not Weep for Youth," "Knew I Love Once," "To a Virgin," "Winter Is Gone," "A Child Looks from His Window."

Smith, who had been loyal and trustworthy: "I will never make any agreements about my stuff hereafter without letting you know. But at that time, like the *Contempo* business, I didn't realize that I had a commercial value, since it was stuff which I had been starving to write for several years. But I have learned my lesson now, and these two instances are all my mistakes."[5] He repeats to Smith what he had already told Wasson, that the *Contempo* stuff was "pretty poor." The matter blew over, at least as far as it concerned Faulkner, for within ten days or so he was writing Wasson about progress on *Light in August*, which moved along very rapidly in manuscript. He was so eager to continue he tells Wasson he does not want to break his concentration by making a typed copy.

Occupied on several fronts, Faulkner was not eager to go to Hollywood just yet. He arranged matters so he could conclude *Light in August* in manuscript before taking up scriptwriting duties. Also, he wanted to prepare his volume of poems, and wrote to Wasson to get what he could: "I am going cold-blooded Yankee now; I am not young enough anymore to hell around and earn money at other things as I could once."[6] His choice of language is revealing, since by associating moneymaking with the North he was purifying himself and, by implication, the South of grubbing around. He hugged the stereotype, although his fiction revealed something quite different: that the more established South, represented by Varners, could be as moneygrubbing as newcomers and rednecks, represented by Snopeses. His off-the-cuff stereotypes become complexities in the fiction.

He was, in addition, calculating the future, and wrote to his agent that he was worried to what extent Smith and Haas, the new firm, had him tied up on options. He hoped his contract called only for two books, one of them *Light in August*, the other the volume of poems. Writing sometime in the winter, when he had both books set on paper, he was evidently thinking of switching publishers. He mentions Harold Guinzburg, but does not want to act behind Smith's back: "When I get ready to swap horses, I will tell him." Although he wanted to be honorable with Smith, he was beginning to calculate his career in terms of financial return. The setting-up of the sending schedule was an initial step in that process, but with *Sanctuary* making people come to him and another major book completed, he saw himself differently. The "cold-blooded Yankee" had been assimilated into the calculating Southerner.

About the same time, Henry Nash Smith, then in the early part of his career as a distinguished student of American culture and literature, came to interview Faulkner. The interview was linked to the publication of *Miss Zilphia Gant* for the Book Club of Texas (in June), for a limited membership subscription and to be introduced by Smith. He came to Oxford at the end of January, finding Faulkner "a small man in a blue shirt and carpet slippers, standing before a coal fire in a front room of his delightful old house."[7] When the questions came, Faulkner went into his peek-a-boo stance even with the knowledgeable Smith. He spoke of the laziness of Negro help, of "how hard it was to get any work out of a colored boy and girl employed around the place"; he denied ever having read *Ulysses* before writing *Sound,* indicating that until recently he had never seen a copy; he offered up his technique in that novel as if a bee had transferred "a sort of pollen of ideas" from Joyce to him; he refused to speak of his war experiences, but repeated he had smashed up a couple of planes. All in all, he gave away nothing, and in fact perpetuated some of the myths.

He did tell Smith he gets to work early in the morning, writes with a fountain pen, types and binds his manuscripts himself, and can write at almost any time, although he is usually finished by late morning. He misled Smith by saying the "stories seem to shape themselves," since many of them were worked and reworked. Of interest is his statement he was "working on two novels now, and it may take me two years to finish one of them."[8] One was *Light in August,* ready in manuscript; but the other remains a mystery. Most likely, it was some form of a Snopes novel, of which he had written a part by way of short stories submitted over the last two years. He also admitted he liked *As I Lay Dying* best, although on other occasions he cited *Sound.* Finally, he insisted he had mellowed, saying he had passed through three stages in his attitude toward his characters: first, when you believe everyone is good; second, when you believe the opposite, that no one is; and third, when "you come to realize that everyone is capable of almost anything—heroism or cowardice, tenderness or cruelty." This may have been the most important residue of the interview. It explains a good deal about *Light in August,* where four very different experiences are related sympathetically.

As Faulkner progressed with *Light in August* and completed the manuscript, he began to type it. Writing to Wasson, probably at the end of March, he indicated he was making changes as he typed. He asked his agent to try to find a serialization for him, but not for less than $5,000; that amount and no editing. He is quite insistent, saying he can get along if his conditions are not met. Meanwhile, Paul Romaine of the Casanova Book Shop in Milwaukee asked Faulkner to autograph copies of *Salmagundi,* and Faulkner gave his standard answer: he would do a few, but autographs were his bread and butter. Too many depreciate their value. Romaine also passed on Hemingway's compliments: he called Faulkner "a good skate"[9] and was glad to hear he was doing well. This was just one of many efforts Hemingway made to get closer to Faulkner, and in nearly all cases the latter fought him off, or made disparaging remarks involving Hemingway's stature as a writer. While Hemingway has the reputation of ruthlessness toward those around him, and Faulkner the reputation for courtesy with occasional rudeness, when the two were involved, roles were reversed. Hemingway could not come near without being rejected or maligned; and in time, Faulkner spent some energy apologizing for remarks he said he never meant, but which he had nevertheless made.

In the spring, he wrote again to Wasson and this time included the manuscript of *Light in August*. Balancing movie work against serialization of the novel, he said that if the $5,000 asking price was not met, "the movie offer is still open," this from Marx of MGM. If serialization was not forthcoming, then he would give the novel directly to Smith for October publication. With *Light in August* off his desk, Faulkner was already looking ahead to his Hollywood stint, which was only weeks away.

What changes was Faulkner making in the manuscript as he transformed it into typescript to send on to Wasson? As we know, he used his own typing version as a way of revising, sometimes extensively, at other times merely lines, phrases, and sentences. One of the most significant alterations came in the change of a line in which Joe Christmas is thinking about his parents. He knows little about them, but says with some certainty in the manuscript, "one of them was a nigger." This becomes in the typing, "one of them was part nigger." Faulkner has altered Joe's fraction from half to quarter or something less, but left it speculative. In both versions, Joe accepts the common view of his parentage which made him part Negro. The minor change, however, suggests how Faulkner wanted to keep the racial matter open to speculation, making Joe's lack of identity the source of his self-destructive attitudes. Faulkner also changed Joe's age from thirty, when he reached Joanna's and his job in Jefferson, to thirty-three. In the revision, he dies at thirty-six, not at Jesus' thirty-three—but the parallelism remains.

The manuscript further reveals changes in tense, with many transformations from present into past, although the reverse is also true. Here Faulkner was working his distinctive mode: the structural coherence of *Light in August*, he recognized, depended on a temporal sequencing which brought past up to present during the time of Lena's nine-day stay in Jefferson, during her search for Lucas and her coming to term. The manuscript also reveals—and the typed version confirms—that Joe Christmas will take over the major thrust of the novel, despite the powerful and witty opening with Lena. While Lena conveys the life-giving part of the novel, relieving the heaviness of the "dark house" metaphor, it is Joe who bears the weight of Faulkner's point. Those who see a balance between Lena's life-giving role and Joe's death orientation miss the point that the balance never really works: Lena serves as leavening, whereas Joe's "dark house" dominates.

Sexually, Lena is normal—but normalcy in a novel can never carry the author very far. Sexually, Joe is interesting—far more so than Popeye, whom he superficially recalls—and Joe's displacement of normal sexual attitudes provides a good deal of the impetus to the novel. Since the murder of Joanna comes early in the novel, it apparently was the episode to which Faulkner would return throughout most of the narrative; that murder, as we discover, is part of a sexual pathology of both characters. Joe's psychosexual problems warrant comment, but Joanna's are even more ambiguous.

Her sexual history is already star-crossed when she is born. Faulkner, very carefully and with typical ambiguity, crisscrosses present and past families. Her father has brought back a Mexican wife, along with a son, Calvin; but Calvin and his grandfather are killed by Colonel Sartoris when the grandfather tries to register Negro voters during Reconstruction. The father, having also lost his wife, writes a New Hampshire cousin to send him a marriageable woman, any woman who is a good housekeeper and at least thirty-five. Joanna is the product of that union, but Faulkner so conflates the two marriages that they seem indistinguishable. For just as the new woman arrives and is married on that day, so the first marriage —twelve years in the making—finally takes place at the grandfather's spread. The timing device, which blends both marriages for Joanna's father and makes her part of that ambiguous Reconstruction time, conditions her to what she is. Furthermore, Joanna is named after her father's first wife, the Mexican, and thus is associated with the dead Calvin, her half-brother, and with his murder by someone vehemently opposed to Negro rights. Her life is twisted and turned by her background, so that her vision of mankind is of white and black cursed by the "black shadow already falling upon them before they drew breath."[10] She sees white babies, even before they draw breath, "flung out like their arms were flung out, as if they were nailed to the cross."

Just as black and white are cursed, so too is Joanna sexually tainted. With that background, her sexual life becomes one of atonement and withdrawal. Cold by day, she becomes insatiable by night; and she is drawn to Negroes. Faulkner suggests that her fantasy is to be seized, treated sadistically; whereas her appearance is one of severity and propriety. One part is plain, folksy, the other abandoned. A woman of extremes, she is in turn frigid and passionate; and she somehow has to redeem the men in her life, the murdered half-brother and grandfather. As a consequence, she reveals both the desire to help men and tremendous hostility to them. She needs to diminish them even as she tries to help; such is Joe's entanglement. She exists beyond actuality, in her own vision of what her life should be and, by implication, of what her sexuality can be. In this respect, like Joe, she has fallen outside society and community. Her aggression is both outward and toward herself. She punishes and yet abandons herself; rejecting the male, she also makes him seek her out, naked, in dark places, hidden, with intimations of rape.

Faulkner is never as precise with her as he is with Joe. Joe is the product of females for whom he has only contempt. The dietician at the orphanage, Miss Atkins, is the archetype of woman for him, and she is associated with gagging, hiding, vomiting, being punished and banished. The etiology of his sexual pathology is quite clear. Joe's first experience of a woman is not of a mother, but of a woman fearful of her position and therefore vindictive and hateful. Further, his first subliminal experience of sex is of something which must be disguised, hidden, treated as a hated secret. It is also associated with something he puts in his mouth and which sticks to his throat. Whatever goes in and is in turn vomited is linked with what becomes the great sexual secret of the dietician.

This hatred of all bodily functions is then reinforced by the maniacal religious fervor of McEachern. Joe comes to applaud strength even when it works against him. He views the beating as a male test, and has nothing but contempt for Mrs. McEachern's efforts at sympathy and help. What she offers frequently is food, something McEachern ignores. But the food she brings Joe is poisoned by his association of it with his own weakness, gagging and vomiting; so he hurls it away—as later he will hurl it away when Joanna prepares and leaves it for him. His mouth and throat are emblems of his ongoing sexual pathology, long before he can't tolerate Joanna's pressures. Further, food is connected to prayer: McEachern's insistence on prayer becomes Joanna's death warrant, when she also insists upon it.

Faulkner has created a series of coordinates which add up to pathological responses: food, sex, and religion. Even Joe's introduction to Bobbie Mason, the large-knuckled, small-bodied prostitute, comes with food, when he cannot pay for both coffee and pie. Here, too, eating is associated with humiliation, rejection, and mockery. It takes little imagination to see food is linked to women, since they provide food in the home; and the two become associated with weakness, which Joe cannot bear. His treatment of Lucas Burch, in fact, can be attributed to the fact he views Lucas as womanly, as lacking masculine strength; and Joe dominates him physically as a husband would brutalize a wife. Their sharing of a cabin on Joanna's property is in fact a kind of marriage, with Joe as dominant, Lucas as subservient.

Joe's sexual pathology has several ingredients which do not necessarily mesh with each other. That Joanna is pregnant just before Joe murders her is a point which both fits and does not. In one respect, her pregnancy creates a symmetry with Lena's more advanced condition, bringing together the two stories; in another sense, it is an arbitrary parallel. It is clear the pregnancy is a deadly trap for Joe, just as Lena's condition is the "happy fall" for Byron. For the first, it is the closing of the gates around him, for the other the opening of doors into a better world. Joe avoids a dominating woman who is pregnant; Byron seeks to embrace a dominating woman who is pregnant. In both instances, the woman tries to or actually does call the turns. Joe must flee; Byron wants to get into her bed. The parallels are there, but not structurally coherent. But there is another factor which does matter. Joe cannot bear the reproduction of himself. He is so filled with self-hatred he cannot consider a small Christmas male or female. For him to have impregnated a woman, for Joanna to have that hold on him, is for him to have surrendered to that negative force of weakness represented by women.

Here is something of a Faulkner shadow life, the sense that woman denotes the trap or snare; the Venus's-flytrap, waiting for a victim.

Faulkner had impregnated a woman, and the baby had died; he would impregnate her again, and the child would live. And that would in effect end his active sexual life with his wife. It cannot escape us that even *before* this finality occurred, sexual relationships could not have been satisfactory for him—not in the aftermath of their disaster, not with Estelle's anemia and other physical ailments, not with both of them drinking heavily. The presentation of food and women in Joe has something of a counterpart in Faulkner, with alcohol, his wife, and his mother. Joe moves in out of Faulkner's shadow in this respect: the aggression and hostility toward sex is so great it cannot be ignored.

Some readers see a continuity between Popeye and Joe, and there are parallels, extending from the role Memphis plays in both novels (Bobbie is from a Memphis house), to the bootlegging in common, to the anomic attitude each displays toward society and his own welfare. But Faulkner is at pains to distinguish them. Popeye is perverted, sexually impotent, profoundly pathological, and, until the epilogue of the revision, unexplained. Joe's brand of pathology is explained in great detail, and we can understand the formation of his twisted mind and personality. But curiously, in most ways Joe is "normal." As Faulkner writes, in comparing Joe to the corrupted Joanna after six months: "His own life, for all its anonymous promiscuity, had been conventional enough, as a life of healthy and normal sin usually is."[11] Until his raging outburst in which he slits Joanna's throat, Joe has led the normal life of a marginal American. His response has been to survive, and while he has displayed violence here and there, it is violence fitted to its context—as his slapping of Bobbie, or his striking out in wild anger at McEachern. The murder is a different order of behavior, but Faulkner is careful to explain its etiology and to make it meaningful within the context, even given its horror and brutality. With Popeye, there is no explanation of what and who he is: he simply is (until the revised ending elaborates). The distinction between the two is significant, for it marks the difference between *Sanctuary* and *Light in August*.

The need for money was pressing. Funds from *Sanctuary* were withheld as Cape & Ballou (the new company Cape formed with Robert Ballou when Smith pulled out) was going bankrupt. Faulkner told Wasson he was sending on a manuscript—some bottom-drawer piece—to *Harper's*, after rejection by *Scribner's*, as an act of desperation. He wrote Maurice Coindreau he was pleased with the French translations of "Dry September" and "A Rose for Emily," as well as for a commendatory article in *La Nouvelle Revue Française*. All of this was welcome, but it did not pay dunning notices. What would pay bills and even provide extra was work in Hollywood. Through Leland Hayward's agency where Wasson worked, Faulkner was offered a contract with MGM, to begin May 1 at $500 per week. The terms called for Faulkner to write original stories and dialogue, to do adaptations and treatments, and to be loaned out when required to other producers.[12]

The resident genius at MGM was Irving Thalberg, and he had declared good movies result from having good writers. As a result, he tried to grab up the best writers in America and bring them to Hollywood.* While the best survived, he helped to destroy many middle-range novelists who might have had substantial, although not major, careers. Faulkner not only survived but thrived, some of his best work coming out during his early Hollywood years. There was in fact little choice, since not only was there no money, he was overdrawn. The difference between what was in his head—*Light in August*—and what he would be writing in Hollywood could not have been missed by an author soon to turn thirty-five and very possessive of his career. Aside from the literary dimensions of his work, the move meant going from relative isolation to a vast moviemaking machine. The young man who controlled Culver City, Irving Thalberg, presided over a veritable empire of directors, writers, producers and associate producers, and vice-presidents. MGM was not only heavy with talent—its string of movies in the 1930s was extraordinary—but top-heavy with brass. There was clearly a pecking order, and Faulkner could be certain of one thing: the writer was at the bottom, regardless of salary. But all was not negative. There was a great deal of excitement, not only because of Thalberg, the boy genius who would make great movies, but because talkies had just begun to come into their own. An entire new era was at hand—actors who could speak (and the phasing out of voices too high or too reedy) and new directors who could coordinate all the new techniques of sight and sound. Previously unimaginable movies were produced, and a whole new order of actors would become famous—many of them, like Gable and Bogart, becoming Faulkner's friends. Faulkner may have been entering a dream factory, but it was one generating high energy, especially considering that he was signing on during the depths of the depression. To be making $500 per week at this time was like having a rich benevolent uncle.

Faulkner appeared on May 7, in somewhat typical fashion, with his head bleeding from a gash.[13] According to Sam Marx, the MGM executive, Faulkner claimed to have gotten it from a taxicab; more likely it was the result of a drinking episode. Confronted by a new situation, or one alien to his temperament, he drank himself into oblivion. It was as simple, or complicated, as that; for while drinking was a destructive act, it was also one of survival. It enabled him to get through. But quite often, when in this kind of binge situation, he injured himself, sometimes with cuts and abrasions, gashes, or, more seriously, deep burns. Like many heavy drinkers who lose all sense of caution, Faulkner was injury-prone. Over the years, he suffered a series of bodily injuries from which his rapid recovery was nothing short of miraculous. He was clearly programmed to live as long as his mother if he had not abused himself so as to bring on a much earlier death. Sam Marx may or may not have believed the taxicab story,

---

*Wolfe and O'Neill turned Thalberg and Samuel Marx down, but the studio catch still included Fitzgerald, P. G. Wodehouse, Anita Loos, Ben Hecht, and, as reader, Lillian Hellman.

but the reputation for drinking dogged Faulkner during his entire Hollywood career.

It is unlikely a writer of Faulkner's stature could be found who knew less about motion pictures than he did. He had no idea what MGM did, nor did he know the movie stars by name. When a remake of *The Champ* was contemplated, Faulkner had never heard of Wallace Beery. At one point he suddenly disappeared, a recurring event in all aspects of his career. His contract was canceled, although he could keep the advance. Just as suddenly he returned, offering up a cock-and-bull story about having been wandering in Death Valley. Marx was beginning to smell the truth: that his famous writer had been holed up somewhere seeking oblivion against the demands made upon him. The contract was reinstated, through the good offices of Marx. In the *New York Times* at the end of the year, Faulkner as much as admitted he had gone on a binge, saying he was frightened at the whole enterprise, "scared by the hullabaloo over my arrival, and when they took me into a projection room to see a picture and kept assuring me it was all going to be very very easy, I got flustered." "Flustered" was another name for panicked, and panic was always a prelude to oblivion. He had alerted the studio to the fact he had to be watched, that he was not only eccentric but unreliable.

Under the direct supervision of Marx himself, Faulkner was put to work on a diverse group of enterprises. Until Howard Hawks appeared, Marx protected him. Remarkably, the pattern kept repeating itself: Faulkner, the seeming waif with a temperament of steel beneath a vulnerable exterior, found someone like Phil Stone to keep and protect him. After Hawks came Cerf and the Random House contingent, before him Smith. No matter what their age, they all became father figures, men who nursed him when he needed help. For a brief time, Sam Marx fitted this unlikely role, generously protecting Faulkner against very suspicious producers— mainly nondrinking Jews—who feared they had still another drunk on their hands.

One of his first adaptations, tantamount to an original script, was his own story "Love," which went back to 1921; the film was to be called "Manservant." The story features Das, an Indochinese manservant, who out of gratitude to the major becomes his valet. The major is pursued by an Italian maid, whom Das suspects of such passionate jealousy she will eventually poison his master. When she does, Das drinks the brandy with the poisonous potion in it and dies. Another branch of the story, somewhat disconnected in tone and feeling from this one, concerns one Bob Jeyfus, a pilot suspected of lying about his flying record in the war. But unlike Faulkner, Jeyfus was telling the truth—he had been shot down, had lost his nerve, and had become a cook. The connection between the major and Jeyfus comes through a young woman named Beth, who loves the major but marries Jeyfus out of pity, then leaves him. The one who survives well is the impeccable major—the cool father figure Faulkner continued to admire.

Needless to add, "Manservant" was intractable material, even after Faulkner provided treatment and dialogue, boiled down to twenty-one pages. All who saw it dismissed it. He went on to other equally meaningless scripts, one called "The College Widow" (earlier title "Night Bird"), the kind of thing Tennessee Williams might have done. The reader of the extended treatment was immediately put off by the *Sanctuary* parallels: "It is an evil, slimy thing, absolutely unfit for screen production, in the face of current censorship."[14] Faulkner had succeeded in *Sanctuary* even more than he had calculated; for if a sophisticated Hollywood reader reacted this way, then the novel had struck home. At the same time, a treatment based on details of the Sartoris background and on his own work in "All the Dead Pilots" went through the reader's mill. This was called "Absolution," and it presented two men whose relationship with each other is destroyed by the presence of a woman not worthy of them. The film was not made.

The return to the war apparently brought forth still another conception, the problematic Faulkner story "With Caution and Dispatch." The history of this piece is tortuous, but it seems to derive from the time of Faulkner's immersion in "Turn About," published on the preceding March 5, but before he worked on the script for "Manservant." Although "With Caution and Dispatch" is of little literary interest, it brings back John Sartoris. Here is a detailed look into his life as a flier, in the period between his early service and his death in both *Sartoris* and "All the Dead Pilots." If, as Faulkner asserted, the idea of the story came from early 1932, it did not end then, for he tinkered with it extensively. It became the basis of another film script for Hawks, "A Ghost Story," for which Faulkner added Sartoris's romances. There were also descriptions of the young man gadding about England, a country for which Faulkner had little feel. This detailed material was part of a version he wrote on the back of the ribbon copy of *The Hamlet.* All of it proved intractable and unacceptable.

The story suggests once again that tremendous romanticization of war and military service Faulkner was capable of—war as purification. Sartoris wrecks three Camels in his headlong abandon to be a dashing, fearless pilot. As his squadron leader, Britt, tells him: "It cost the government the equivalent of three enemy aircraft to train you and get you here. And now you have washed out three of ours before you have seen the front lines. Dont you see? you will have to shoot down six huns before you can even start counting." Sartoris's most sensational exploit is in crashing his Camel on a ship in the English Channel which is operating in the most hush-hush way; and he is whisked away by a destroyer, as if he were high brass. Until he is vouched for, he is suspected of being a spy.

The exploits of John Sartoris are those of a Tom Sawyer with airplanes. Although we and Faulkner know he will die—he has already died, long before, in *Flags in the Dust*—he is resurrected to become the typical American boy, an antidote to Great Depression woes, a return to a purer, cleaner version. Death here is a pure act of volition. Sartoris is clearly seeking how to die in order to justify his life; or, put another way, his life takes on significance only to the extent he can control it by way of making death imminent. Surely, some or all of this is the other side to Faulkner's personal sense of embourgeoisization. He has become like one of those "dead pilots" in that story, a man who was once photographed in the glory of his aviator role, but who is now thickening around the waist while he accumulates goods. Sartoris finally becomes one way that Faulkner hoped to remain young.

The significant part of these scripts, which came to nothing, was how Faulkner resisted imagining new material, how closely he stayed to his own work, or to some shadowy replica of it. Yet money started to come in; his rent was only $30 per month at 4024 Jackson Street, near the studio, and his expenses otherwise remained low. Marx still believed in him, although Faulkner had not generated any material the studio could use. Enclosing $100 from his second paycheck, Faulkner wrote Estelle (postmarked June 2) that if she needs more to tell him; otherwise, he will apply the money to outstanding bills. He mentions he is now writing a scenario for Wallace Beery (whom he has heard of by this time) and Robert Montgomery, in collaboration with an actor-author named Ralph Graves. Marx had provided Graves, an experienced writer, to work with Faulkner in the hope of getting some return on MGM's investment. He also mentions having met Laurence Stallings, of *What Price Glory* fame.

Shortly before, Faulkner had met Meta Doherty (later, Meta Carpenter and Meta Carpenter Wilde), who worked as script clerk for Howard Hawks at Twentieth Century-Fox. Their intimate relationship was to develop somewhat later, when Faulkner worked exclusively for Hawks on *The Road to Glory*, and the affair was to prove intense and of considerable significance in both their lives. Meta was almost a perfect young woman for Faulkner, who liked his females to be compliant and emotionally uncomplicated. She had been married briefly (to Billy Carpenter) in the early 1930s, and now was separated. Faulkner was feeling sorry for himself, separated from his Oxford home, however tension-filled it could become; later, the self-pity would derive from being away from his baby daughter, Jill. His sexual life with Estelle had not been satisfactory, either before the birth of Jill (as we can speculate) or after, as we learn from what he told Meta. Whatever his plaint to the woman he wanted to bed down, it would be difficult to see him as fulfilled sexually. For a man like Faulkner, such satisfaction or fulfillment could probably not occur in marriage. The women he had thought of marrying, like the one he did marry, were all unsuitable; and he was hardly a model husband, considering his heavy drinking, his periodic need to escape, his self-absorption, his desire for isolation and withdrawal. Such a man is a heavy weight on any woman, and Estelle was herself something of a frail reed. But even aside from Faulkner's dissatisfaction at home, encountering an unencumbered pretty young woman in a distant place is the male fantasy. Add to this the young woman impressed by the older man's accomplishments and we have the making of a fantasy romance. When Faulkner pressed his suit, Meta initially rejected his offers of companionship because he was married, but the relationship eventually developed.

Meanwhile Faulkner was beginning to get caught in the coils of studio contracts. Eventually he found himself working for less than when he started out, and far less than was being paid to writers of far less distinction. One problem was that he was not an effective screenwriter. His dialogue read like novel dialogue and, worse, like Faulkner talk—great for fiction, ponderous for a script. Despite a well-developed visual sense in his novels, he had little or no visual sense in a motion picture. He rarely mastered blending of word and camera eye, and could not foresee how a director shaped a scene through camera work in ways alien to the printed page. Offered $250 per week to stay on, he felt MGM was treating him cheaply. What prolonged his stay, finally, was the intervention of Howard Hawks, who was alerted to the screen possibilities of "Turn About" by his brother, William.[15] In this instance, the story did have considerable film potential. Hawks was a sophisticated man who remained laid back and cool, and he won Faulkner's confidence. Also, he had made a film close to Faulkner's heart, *Dawn Patrol*, with Errol Flynn as part of a group of daredevil, doomed fliers living for the moment before the fiery crash.

The meeting with Hawks turned out to be most fortunate. The director became for Faulkner in those days in Hollywood what Cerf would later become for him in book publishing. Faulkner offered to do Hawks's script in five days, and indicated to his agent he would do it for nothing. But as of July 26, he went back on the payroll at the aforementioned $250 per week, half of what he had been making when he first went out to Hollywood. Faulkner submitted the treatment, and both Hawks and Thalberg were enthusiastic. With this, his fortunes seemed to have turned. He could look forward to the publication of *Light in August* in October and to *A Green Bough* early in 1933. While he did not have any major novel on the table—although he may have been mapping out piecemeal that early version of *The Hamlet* called "The Peasants"—he had enough going for him so that he did not lose self-respect. For a writer still not settled into his reputation —and Faulkner had not quite achieved that—one important part of making his career is to keep his name before the public. Faulkner's letters reveal that despite his display of insouciance, he was quite aware of his reputation and of his current standings in the literary pennant race. He was always setting up rankings featuring himself, Hemingway, Wolfe, Dos Passos, sometimes including Lewis, Dreiser, and Cather. He definitely wanted to be first.

Murry Falkner died suddenly on August 6, and Faulkner was informed on the seventh in Culver City—he had been away hunting on Catalina Island. When he heard the news, he made plans to return immediately, and the studio, at Marx's urging, permitted him to work on "Turn About" while he remained in Oxford.

Murry's life was in several ways the obverse of the American success story. He was not quite an example of American failure, but its neutered product. Faulkner himself felt his father simply gave up, or at least this is what he told Blotner many years later.[16] Estelle also corroborated this, speaking of his boredom, even his sense of desperation. Although what finally killed him was a heart condition, surely abetted by poor diet, drinking, and internal stress, he seemed to have faded well before that. Just short of his sixty-second birthday, he died, and was buried in St. Peter's Cemetery in Oxford in his father's plot, with the obituary as M. C. Faulkner. The "u" which the son had added to the name, but which Murry had not, now became, at least in the notice, his. He left everything to Maud, which amounted to a year's living. Her support would devolve on Faulkner, who found "Turn About" at least acceptable enough to have the option picked up. For the time being, Hollywood money could cover all the outlays. There Faulkner's recovery from Murry's death appeared rapid, whatever the emotional scars or guilt feelings. He was reading proof on *Light in August*, leading him into a profoundly troubled relationship, and into material running parallel to his father's death. One dimension of Joe's "passion" in the wilderness has to do with parentage: the question not only of paternal black blood but his linkage to his living relatives, Doc Hines and his wife, his maternal grandparents. When Joe is caught, Doc Hines only wants to strike him, screaming he should be killed. Hines is the same man who as janitor of the orphanage monitored Joe and whisked him away before McEachern took over. Hines's hatred of Joe is complete. When, at the end of chapter 14, Joe circles around close to where he started, he also circles around in time; so that he is returned after his stay in the wilderness to the proximity of a relative, who, like everyone in the past, rejects him.

The ostensible reason for Hines's hatred and rejection is race, but an even greater hatred seems behind it, based on the idea of rejection itself. Once again we come up to the frontiers of a personal sense in the fiction, an acting-out of a feeling about fathers. There is nothing definitive here, simply an impression Faulkner created repeatedly: the failure of the family in providing community or society. The family is sown with dissension, with underlying currents of distaste, rage, and violence. It is a savage place, fathers and sons struggling against each other, throwing off all restraints in their desire to seek destruction if not of the other then of themselves.

After six weeks in Oxford, Faulkner was due to return to Hollywood at the end of September, taking with him Maud and Dean. The latter, at twenty-five, was having some difficulty finding himself and was footloose. Bright, a good athlete, in many ways the family favorite, somewhat taller than Faulkner (by two and one half inches) but slightly built, Dean was engaging, but somewhat submerged in a family which, despite surface cohesiveness, was pulling apart. Murry had lavished attention and affection on the boy as he grew up, the one area in which the older man displayed his feelings. But Dean was in a difficult situation—too slight for serious athletics except of the sandlot variety (although he excelled as a golfer); something of his father and eldest brother in his desire for something beyond a bourgeois life; not overly engaged by his studies at Ole Miss, where he had graduated in engineering. He had also tried law, even attempted to write and to paint. Full of ability, he had not found what would interest him, and he was drifting. He was also drinking to fill in his time. Faulkner was concerned about him, and that explains why he asked him to come out to Hollywood with Maud.

Estelle was herself entering the first stages of pregnancy. It is of interest that Faulkner returned to Hollywood, arriving October 3, just when Estelle became pregnant; certainly, after the experience with Alabama, it was a period of considerable anxiety for both of them. While it is true their finances necessitated his return—he could no longer stay on the studio payroll while remaining in Oxford—the coincidence of his departure cannot be ignored. He would be gone less than a month. On October 17, he signed the contract for the film version of *Sanctuary*, clearing over $6,000 on the option. With that money, he had no need to hang around, despite Hawks's offer that he stay.*

Faulkner was back in Oxford by the end of October 1932, a strange year coming toward its close: *Light in August* measured against memories of Culver City and MGM. He had assumed many roles and faces. Family man, serious writer, author of negligible stories, Hollywood writer, a man with an interior life no one could penetrate, drinker, self-destructive individual, anxiety-ridden, demon-ridden human being—all of these existed side by side. Faulkner lived a balancing act, at the center of a circle he had drawn around himself and which periodically he had to break out of. The drinking helped, but it was only temporary death. When life reintruded, he got back into harness, meeting his obligations to his creditors and, most of all, obligations to himself. The serious work did not falter—he still had a decade of some of the greatest work any American writer ever produced. He was a man of infinite complications: an unfit husband who met his obligations; in many ways unprepared to be a father for the child whom he wanted badly and would love dearly. All roads pointed inward, and yet he tried to relate to others, however badly he faltered. But that dot in the middle of the circle beckoned, and more often than not, he felt obligated to retreat, draw up the bridge and let the moat discourage anyone from entering.

Light in August reveals that desire to dip out of sight. Although Faulkner had used pronouns before as ways of introducing verisimilitude—that is, people talk as if everyone already knows the pronominal reference—here he has extended his repertory. The ambiguity or blurring of such refer-

---

*Faulkner met the famous and, as the following oft-told story indicates, could more than hold his own. Out hunting in the Imperial Valley with Hawks and Clark Gable, he was asked by Gable who he thought the best living writers were. Gable, who was usually as silent and withdrawn as the writer, did not read. But Faulkner responded and gave his usual list— Mann, Hemingway, Cather, Dos Passos, *and* William Faulkner. Gable: "Oh, do you write?" Faulkner: "Yes, Mr. Gable. What do you do?" (Joseph Blotner, *Faulkner: A Biography*, 2 vols. [New York: Random House, 1974], vol. 1, p. 751.)

ences is, of course, an excellent ingredient in a novel whose protagonist lacks identity. The following passage, as an example, labels not only Joe but nearly all the principals as referential points in a drama which has proceeded beyond their control. "Except that I have kept it from her that it was the man she is hunting for that told on the murderer and that he is in jail now except when he is out running with dogs the man that took him up and befriended him. I have kept that from her."[17] The speaker is Byron, his listener Hightower. I=Byron; it=the situation generally, but also particulars like Joe fleeing, Brown's friendship with Joe; it=an expletive to start the clause; man=Brown, who is really Burch; she=Lena; murderer=Joe; he=Brown or Burch; he=Brown or Burch; man=Joe; him=Brown or Burch; him=Brown or Burch; I=Byron; her=Lena.

Faulkner told Smith he liked the look of *Light in August*, and well he might. For Smith and his new company, the book represented their major publication. Reviews began to appear, and while Faulkner appeared to turn away from them, it is difficult to believe he was as indifferent as the pose made it seem. The big reviewers were, predictably, disturbed by what they read.* Dorothy Van Doren (in the *Nation*) inexplicably wrote of the book as undisciplined and attacked Faulkner's understatement, as well as the mindlessness of his characters. Henry Seidel Canby in the *Saturday Review of Literature*, while praising the book's power, judged it as turgid, obscure, and sloppy, demonstrating an alarming descent toward morbidity. He granted "extraordinary force and insight," a novel "incredibly rich in character studies, intensely vivid, rising sometimes to poetry, and filled with the spirit of compassion which saves those who look at life too closely from hardness and despair." Margaret Cheney Dawson in the New York *Herald Tribune Books*, while judging the end after Joe's mutilation anticlimactic, found the book "rich, sinister, and furious," with abundant details and considerable insights into its characters. Fanny Butcher in the *Chicago Tribune* commented that Faulkner had eliminated his "most glaring idiosyncrasies in writing [apparently in *The Sound and the Fury* and *As I Lay Dying*]." Nevertheless, the book lacks form: "it hops about on its toes, but the point is that it is on its toes *all* the time" and demonstrates considerable activity which will increase his popularity with both the knowing reader and the general public.[18]

Faulkner showed indifference and seemed wrapped up in his next book, "Poems Miscellaneous," or *A Green Bough*. By November, he was dickering again with the idea of going to Hollywood, although he really wanted to remain in Oxford. But as he told Wasson, he was unhappy with the terms set by intermediaries Joyce and Selznick in their negotiations with Marx. They wanted him to sign on at $250 per week for six months—which in Hollywood terms meant peon's wages. Writers of far less distinction were drawing $750 or $1,000, or more. Faulkner says he worked on "Turn

Time, in fact, was so disturbed it titled its review "Nigger in the Woodpile" (October 17, 1932).

About" without any contract and arranged with Marx for the same amount without committing himself to an agent's fee on top of the low amount. His anger is real, and it reveals how he moved to racial stereotypes: ". . . I myself arranged with Marx to have $250.00 a week without any signed contract at all, to work on "Turn About" alone and no interference from any Jew in California, with the privilege of returning to Oxford to do the work—thus accomplishing an arrangement which my so-called agents either could not or would not attempt. Yet I paid them ten percent of this. . . . the only communication I ever had with them would be when they would send me bills, one of which was for money I had already paid them."[19]

By identifying the Jew with shady business tactics, Faulkner appeared to forget that everyone he dealt with in Hollywood except Hawks was Jewish, including Marx, who was trying to make things as easy as possible for him; that most of these people had accepted him despite severe misgivings about his ability to stay sober or to produce meaningful treatments, no less workable scripts. As a movie writer, Faulkner was hardly distinctive, and yet people like Marx now, others later, supported him because of his reputation as a writer. He says disparagingly that he is probably "too small potatoes for them to bother with, I imagine, except to bleed at ten percent. So I want to get loose from them, and as long as it is Hawks who gets me the jack, I am going to let his brother handle any business that requires an agent out there." Then maintaining his full press about money, he asks about the *Sanctuary* check, which he needs for bills and repairs at Rowan Oak.

On his return from Oxford, Faulkner's imagination was going full blast with new ideas, not about movies either, and the most likely source of his interest was his own past, the already well-used John Sartoris, modeled on the old colonel. Following Faulkner through his latest venture, one marvels at the cohesiveness of his ideas and plans, how each book is struck off a central core, as though his imagination contained all the work for a ten- or twelve-year period he could draw upon at will. He had been working on a script of "Turn About," which in turn led to "All the Dead Pilots," and those two works paralleled the early version of "With Caution and Dispatch," all of which returned to parts of *Sartoris*, itself an adaptation and revision of *Flags in the Dust*. The latest piece on Sartoris was a seven-hundred-word biographical sketch of the man, the old colonel, shot by his onetime partner. Faulkner called it "The Golden Book of Jefferson & Yoknapatawpha County in Mississippi as compiled by William Faulkner of Rowanoak." It is dated MCMXXXII and located in Rowanoak. But this brief biographical sketch did not complete the cycle. For in *Light in August*, Joanna Burden relates to Joe her background, which includes the shooting of her grandfather and her young half-brother, Calvin, by "an ex-slaveholder and Confederate soldier named Sartoris over a question of Negro voting." She comments further: " 'So I suppose that Colonel Sartoris was a town hero because he killed with two shots from the same pistol an old one-armed man and a boy who had never even cast his first vote.' "[20]

There was even more to this "moving core" of memories he could draw upon and turn into material for sketches, stories, and novels.* Although more than a year passed (between late October of 1932 and early winter of 1934) before he publicly announced he was working on still another "Dark House," what became *Absalom*, there is the germ of it here. Searching out memories, recycling material going back to *Flags*, creating continuity with his own ancestral past, Faulkner was setting himself for his single greatest historical effort.

In the final two months of 1932, Faulkner moved from large projects to a kind of holding action. At the end of November, Hawks allowed him to remain in Oxford and yet collect $600 per week from MGM, for which he was to script still another war story, this one based on *War Birds: Diary of an Unknown Aviator* by John McGabrock Grider and "treated" by Elliot White Springs. Under a little studio pressure, Faulkner tried to use some of his old material from "All the Dead Pilots" and "Ad Astra." Also, he did some halfhearted sending out of stories, including the aforementioned "There Was a Queen," which *Scribner's*, having once rejected, now accepted for January 1933. He was less successful with "Black Music" and "The Leg," both of which ended up in *Doctor Martino and Other Stories*.

When Bennett Cerf asked Faulkner to write an introduction, for $500, for a limited Random House edition of *Sound*, he refused. Since he was earning Hollywood money, he could tell Cerf $500 was insufficient, although in depression terms most families could live on it for months. In a follow-up letter, indicating Estelle was sick, he said he hoped "that some day we can agree"[21] on a higher fee. But the larger news he mentioned to Harrison Smith either in late December or early January of 1933. "Estelle and the children have been sick in rotation since the middle of November, and the day after Xmas Estelle succeeded in falling down stairs (no one would have been surprised if it had been me now, on Dec. 26) and she has been in bed ever since. She is getting up today, though."[22] The context suggests Estelle was drunk, since Faulkner indicates people would expect him to fall down the stairs after a day of Christmas celebrating. She was now three months pregnant, and if she was drinking so heavily, she was repeating the pattern with Alabama. The letter does not suggest any particular anxiety, but it does reveal a household on the edge, with both drinking heavily and the relationship maintained only by a succession of binges.

Nevertheless, he was now William Faulkner: the name was established, the style was recognized, his material was sought after by several publish-

---

*Still another connection to the Sartoris clan had come a little earlier in "There Was a Queen" (originally called "Thru the Window" and submitted as "Was a Queen"), which is, as we saw, about "Miss Jenny" (old John Sartoris's ninety-year-old sister) and Narcissa Benbow.

ers, there was a small public waiting to read him, critics were beginning to view him in his own terms. He was doing what every major novelist eventually achieves—beginning to dictate the ways in which people would read him. Except for recalcitrants like Clifton Fadiman, who rejected most aspects of modernism, Faulkner was establishing the terms on which he would be reviewed and criticized. He would not have a large reading public, and his books generally sold poorly and went out of print by the mid-1940s. But with little·question, he was Faulkner, he had arrived, and other writers paid homage and respect.

Where was he intellectually? What supported him besides liquor, Hollywood money, recognition, and family ties? Was the inner man any different from his various fictional personas? Or, conversely, can we discover in those fictional personas some area Faulkner was defining for himself as well as for his characters? We wonder at the attention he pays Hightower. The Reverend is not in structural terms a major player in the novel, and yet in its working out, he touches on everyone and everything. Furthermore, segments, long ones, are devoted to meditations on what it means to be a Hightower in a community where everyone else seems to fit. He is not the outsider poet, but he has the sensibility of the poet, and his identification comes as he mediates ideologically between community and someone like Joe. Additionally, Hightower's past involves a figure like Bayard Sartoris, just as Joanna refers to the old colonel. Hightower represents the transitional figure, his past defined by a war which no longer makes any sense and is, merely, a piece of romantic history. He is, in many respects, in Faulkner's own situation: the man who must make a transition to another kind of America.

Faulkner at thirty-five, in the middle of the journey, was trying for the first time to put it all in perspective. It is hard to exclude him from his probe into meaning for Hightower. The shift from Joe's shooting and castration to Hightower is deliberate in terms of giving additional dimensionality to the novel. Not the least, Hightower's segment, chapter 20, comes right after the Reverend has tried to save Christmas by claiming they were together the night of the murder. Even after being struck down by the latter, he lies to protect Joe. With this, Hightower's meditation becomes intermixed with the peculiar light which gives the novel its title: "The wheels whirls on. It is going fast and smooth now, because it is freed now of burden, of vehicle, axle, all. In the lambent suspension of August into which night is about to fully come, it seems to engender and surround itself with a faint glow like a halo."[23]

This part of the drama Faulkner left unresolved. As he knew, the ghosts will remain; as he demonstrated in his next novel, they remained for him. But he needed to identify his material, to reveal where the ghosts were. *Absalom*, also, would be a novel about ghosts, phantoms, apparitions, even more than *Light in August*. And race would lie at the heart of the ghosts, as would the Civil War in its fantasy dimensions. The past was no longer history, Faulkner assumed, but an apparition which called itself history. Events and people were long ago transformed, so that the Civil War, Reconstruction, history itself had become legends and myths which subverted everyone who accepted them; and yet they could not be rejected. It seems apparent that in Hightower's meditation Faulkner felt obligated to reveal the nub, what lay deep within him as a person and an artist.

Faulkner's paternal great-grandfather, the "old colonel," William Clark Falkner, near the time of his death, in 1889.

Faulkner's paternal grandfather, the "young colonel," in his Masonic uniform.

LEFT: John Wesley Thompson Falkner and his wife Sallie Murry, Faulkner's paternal grandparents, in 1910, when Falkner became president of the First National Bank of Oxford.

RIGHT: Maud Falkner, Faulkner's mother, as a young woman.

Faulkner at eleven, with schoolmates, Oxford Graded School, 1908 (second from left in middle row and inset).

Faulkner (center) with his brothers Jack (right) and Johncy (Dean, the fourth brother, was too young to be included).

Estelle Oldham, Faulkner's future wife, in 1913, when she was seventeen.

Faulkner in 1918, in full regalia at the end of World War I.

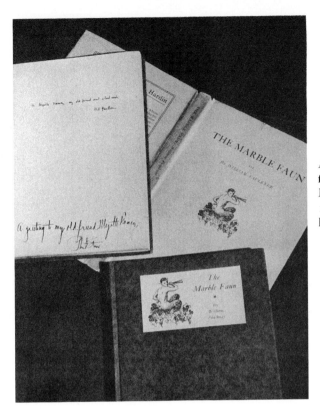

A presentation copy of Faulkner's first book, *The Marble Faun*, to Myrtle Ramey, an old friend, in 1924, inscribed by Faulkner and Phil Stone.

A further collection of Faulkner's poems, *Mississippi Poems*, in carbon typescript, was presented to Myrtle Ramey, at the same time as *The Marble Faun*, December 30, 1924.

William Spratling's sketch of
Faulkner in 1925. Spratling, an
architect and artist, was the
writer's close friend in New
Orleans; they sailed for Europe
together in July 1925.

Faulkner with a friend at Red Rock Canyon,
1932, on the novelist's first trip to Hollywood
as a film scriptwriter.

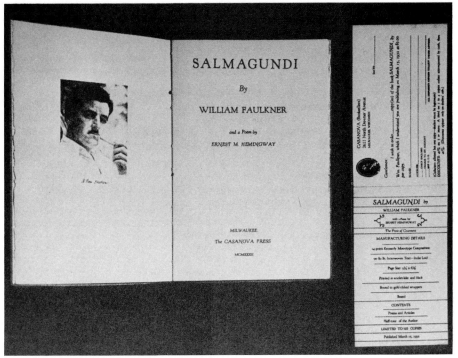

Six poems and two essays by Faulkner appeared in this 1932 printing of *Salmagundi*, which also included a poem by Ernest Hemingway.

Faulkner in 1933, the photograph inscribed to his great-aunt 'Bama McLean.

Faulkner with Jill at Rowan Oak, when she was about six months old.

Dean Swift Falkner's tombstone, with the inscription from Faulkner's novel *Sartoris:* "I bare him on Eagle's wings and brought him unto me." Dean died in 1935 in a plane crash.

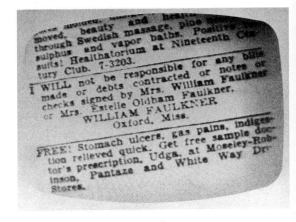

The notice Faulkner placed in the Memphis *Commercial Appeal* and the Oxford *Eagle* on June 22, 1936, that he would no longer be responsible for Estelle Faulkner's bills.

Jill Faulkner at age four with Caroline Barr, "Mammy Callie," then ninety-six or ninety-seven.

At the 1950 Stockholm
Nobel Prize awards
ceremony, Faulkner sits
next to Bertrand Russell
(first from right).

Faulkner and daughter
Jill at her wedding to
Paul Summers, August
21, 1954.

Faulkner in a 1951 photograph inscribed to Saxe Commins, his Random House
editor and friend.

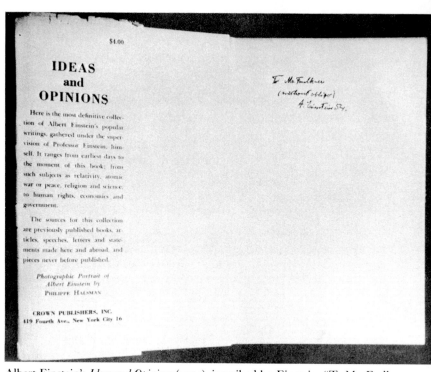

Albert Einstein's *Ideas and Opinions* (1954), inscribed by Einstein: "To Mr. Faulkner (without obligo) A. Einstein 54."

Faulkner eating at an inn in Nagano, Japan, in 1955.

Faulkner and the young writer from Memphis, Joan Williams.

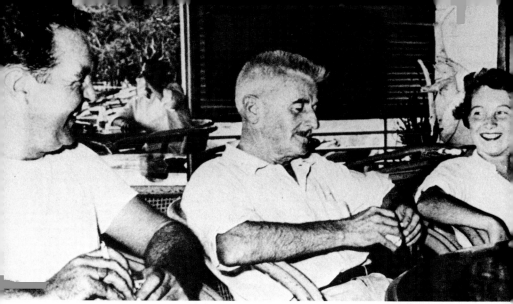

Faulkner relaxing in the Philippines with his stepdaughter's husband, Bill Fielden, and the Fieldens' daughter, Vicki, after his three-week visit to Japan in 1955.

Faulkner's December 4, 1957 letter to Mrs. Jannette Tracy, clarifying a situation in which it was thought Faulkner had written an anonymous letter to his stepson, Malcolm. The misunderstanding created considerable family disharmony.

paved with good intentions—but the wisest man on earth would find it practically impossible to do do anything for him now after he has supposedly heard from his family that he's a disgrace to their honor.

Sincerely,

Jannette Tracy

Dec. 4, 1957

Dear Mrs Tracy:

His aunt, Dorothy Oldham, wrote the letter. She failed to sign it simply because she showed it to Estelle and me for approval, and Estelle added a postscript and sealed it before she realised Dorothy had not signed it. We all took it for granted that Malcolm would know who it was from, since he knows me better and longer than to think I would write him that sort of letter myself.

Whether the idea in the letter is justified or not, I dont know. But I felt and still feel that his aunt, who loves him and who has been hurt very much by the fact that something went in in this business that none of us knew about apparently. Decency demanded that Gloria should have told Malcolm as soon as the thought occurred to her, that she planned to marry Lamar as soon as she was divorced. Simply gratitude should have compelled her to tell him at least an hour before the wedding, that she was going to. we have all watched for years the ruthless way in which she took advantage of Malcolm's innate gentleness and decency, and I think his aunt had every right to blow her top. I also think in the end it will help Malcolm. He has been babied too much in his life. That's why he got himself into the mess he did.

Thank you for your letter. I hope you will see Malcolm and assure him that I did not and would not have written him such a letter myself, but that if his aunt Dot felt she must, I felt she had that right.

William Faulkner

Faulkner with his grandson, Paul D. Summers III, in Charlottesville, Virginia.

Maud Faulkner near the end of her life, at age eighty-eight.

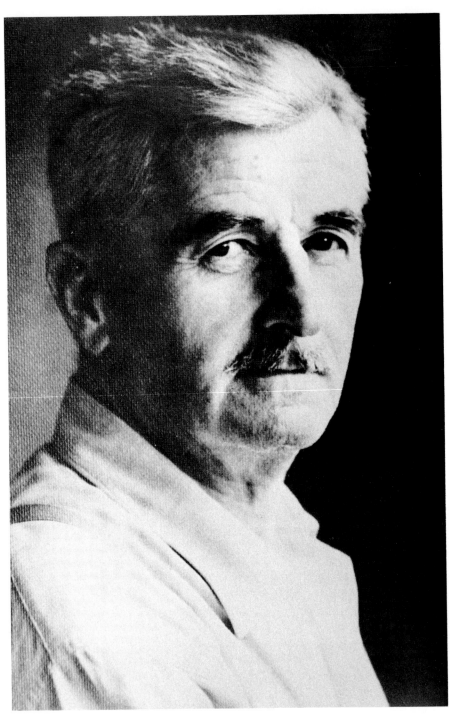

Faulkner, six years before his death in 1962.

Chapter Sixteen

Air and Airless

THE YEAR 1933, which began with Faulkner rejecting Cerf's offer
of $500, then $750, to write an introduction for a limited edition of
Sound was more dramatic in personal than in professional terms. He was
not idle, but it was not a year filled with important projects. He did tell
Harrison Smith in the fall of 1933 that he was plugging along "at the Snopes
book" and that he had "another bee now, and a good title, I think: *Requiem
for a Nun*. It will be about a nigger woman. It will be a little on the esoteric
side, like *As I Lay Dying*." But it was also the year in which the sole book
he published was *A Green Bough*—forty-four rather undistinguished poems
—along with three short stories: "There Was a Queen," in *Scribner's* (January); "Artist at Home," in *Story* (August); and "Beyond," in *Harper's* (September).

The period was one of consolidation. He had made sufficient money in
Hollywood so that he could rest; and it was the year his daughter, Jill, was
born, on June 24. It was also the year when he fulfilled his long-held dream
to fly. In early spring he began to take flying lessons, soloed, went on to
get his pilot's license, and in the month before Jill was born splurged by
buying a Waco-210 monoplane. Flying fulfilled many aspects of his life: the
need for danger (and flying then had its share of dangers, since instrumentation was rudimentary); the need to get away where no one could touch
him; the desire to identify with those he had been describing in "Turn
About" and other stories. Perhaps most important of all, it helped him

balance out the deceptions he was still perpetuating about his military service. Later, when he stopped flying, big, powerful horses fulfilled something of the same need.

The best way to see 1933 in his life is as a year of preparation. His imagination had been working intensely; he had produced within a five-year period several novels of the highest order, as well as half a dozen stories which would enter into the permanent canon. There was no burnout or blockage, simply the need to stop and take account. According to his letters, he was not slackening, with the Snopes novel and *Requiem* in mind and on paper; but in reality, he was priming the pump for future action.

Faulkner's script of "War Story" (the work he had done on *War Birds*) was completed and sent off to MGM, and early in 1933 he mailed in his "list dialogue script," which revealed a good deal of unfilmable writing.* Clearly he had not mastered screen language and was writing phrases and sentences only the printed page could accommodate. He also sent the printing copy of *A Green Bough* to Smith and Haas in New York, where it would appear April 20. Best of all, MGM continued payments while he doctored the script of "War Story" and remained in Oxford. He wrote Wasson on February 12 that he was adding another bedroom and bath to Rowan Oak, putting in heat, and painting. But the bulk of the letter concerns business, his agent having suggested he try to sell his stories to the movies, mainly to Hawks. But then, Faulkner says, he would be obligated to two agents: Hawks's brother, William, and Wasson himself. He found himself in a dilemma about agenting: much of what he sold he did through his own "shopping for prices," as he put it, and yet if he followed through on Wasson's suggestion, he would be paying two agents. He liked being under no contractual arrangement with anyone, and yet he appealed to his agent "to protect me from myself, but how to do it?"[1]

All this immersion in military and flying bore other results. In working on his story "Honor," he wrote his way into the life of barnstorming aviators living on the edge; even more than that, he had the triangle which became the genesis of *Pylon*. One leads directly into the other: the pilot, his wife, and the wing-walker, who become the two men and the woman in the novel completed the next year. Further, as if to complete this part of the creative cycle, the film of "Turn About" premiered in Memphis on April 12, called *Today We Live*, directed by Hawks, and with an all-star cast of Gary Cooper, Joan Crawford, and Franchot Tone. Faulkner took the seventy-five-mile drive to Memphis along with several relatives to see the film, which apparently made a good impression on him and the audience. Hawks was still able to convince Louis B. Mayer to continue Faulkner on the payroll, although with a halving of salary after March 6. Nevertheless, the deal was too good to reject: remain in Oxford, tinker with movie

---

*Even though he revised passages from *Flags* and *Sartoris* as well as material from the stories "Ad Astra," "All the Dead Pilots," and "With Caution and Dispatch."

scripts, work on his own material, and start up an entirely new enterprise: flying.

Flying was to become a Falkner family occupation and preoccupation. All four brothers came to take flying lessons and gain pilot's licenses, an extraordinary outcome given the scarcity of money in the 1930s. What is even more extraordinary is how Murry's fantasy of living freely in the spatial West was carried through by his four sons, who found it in the air. Faulkner's instructor at the Memphis airport, Vernon Omlie, further served as inspiration for the fliers in *Pylon*, and the woman he married was a veteran aerial acrobat, a model for Laverne in *Pylon*. According to Omlie, Faulkner was not a natural pilot, unlike Dean, who took to it as if made for the cockpit. Faulkner needed a good deal of instruction, trying to recall what he had never really known, and being slow to recognize that instrumentation, however rudimentary, had changed the old rules. Usually the eight hours of dual instruction were followed by soloing, but in his case, it took seventeen hours of instruction.

Soloing was itself an adventure. With a parachute strapped on his back, the new pilot was on his own in a quite insubstantial plane. The single engine was all that stood between him and disaster. Taking off was relatively easy, but circling the airport and making the approach to land was daunting. For a man of thirty-five, with all his responsibilities, soloing was particularly daunting. But on April 20, Faulkner did it, on the day Smith and Haas published *A Green Bough*. Faulkner was a careful pilot, having been inculcated with aerial safety by Omlie. The writer apparently did not take well to acrobatic flying, nor to stunts, although his admiration for those who did becomes evident in *Pylon*.

Following that busy April, on May 12 *Sanctuary* went into production at Paramount Studios, with Miriam Hopkins as Temple Drake and Jack La Rue, the heavy from crime movies, as Popeye. George Raft had turned down the Popeye role as too perverse even for someone known on screen as a professional killer. The casting ensured that the movie, in which Faulkner played no role, would be poorly done. Not a single major Faulkner novel, in fact, ever made it to the screen in an acceptable fashion. Only the weak *Intruder in the Dust* made a passable motion picture, perhaps because most of its thrust is action, not subtextual complication.

Earlier on, he became involved in still another motion-picture venture. Because he was on the payroll at Hawks's request—the director thought he could use Faulkner to adapt his own stories—he felt obligated to come up with ideas. One was called, bizarrely, *Mythical Latin-American Kingdom Story*, which seems to have had a shadowy relationship to Conrad's *Nostromo*. The protagonist would be "a Christ-like young man" leading a "revolt against tyranny," set in a mythical kingdom Faulkner called Rincon, a name already used in two of his stories.[2] It was a patchwork affair, with a flier somewhat reminiscent of John Sartoris as one of the main characters. None of this could hold together, but he persevered because he wanted the money to continue;

and he felt obligated to Hawks, who believed in him and served as intermediary with a wary MGM front office.

Events, however, were reaching an impasse. Hawks did have certain expectations, what with Faulkner collecting his salary while remaining in Oxford, but not producing anything screenworthy. "War Birds" was stalled, and the "Mythical Kingdom" script was unsatisfactory. It was clear even to someone as loyal as Hawks that Faulkner was not concentrating, or else needed supervision to write acceptable dialogue and narrative for the screen. The studio assessment of Faulkner was unfortunately correct: as great a genius as he may have been on the printed page—and not everyone even agreed on that—he could not write a film script unless someone experienced was at his elbow. Faulkner now confronted a dilemma: with Estelle well along in pregnancy—we are speaking of April 1933—he did not want to return to Hollywood, which was one option, nor did he want to go off salary, which was the other.

All of these events, including the flying, were pulling him away from serious work; which explains his relatively low production for 1933. Decisions meant tension, and tension meant drinking bouts, oblivion as preferable to Hobson's choice. With the dilemma whether to return to Hollywood or forgo salary, he chose to remain behind for Estelle's final two months of pregnancy and, perhaps, to get on with his purchase of an airplane. But Faulkner perpetuated his own version of what occurred, turning simple fact into embroidered tall tale. In the revealing 1955 interview with Jean Stein, he turned what must have been an anxiety-ridden interlude into a caper. He tells of receiving a long-distance call from the studio ordering him to report to director Tod Browning in New Orleans. Browning was an original filmmaker, best known for the frightening *Freaks*, which he made after gaining the confidence of circus freaks and then drawing from them truly professional acting. His other famous motion picture was *Dracula*. Now he was working on another eccentric film, called "Louisiana Lou," or "Bride of the Bayou." Since Faulkner's reputation rested on *Sanctuary*, what better author to request for dialogue, atmosphere, or creative ideas? Browning was a serious director, but his planned use of Faulkner was hardly at a high level.

Faulkner recalled that the studio told him to go to New Orleans by plane, although he was only eight hours away by train. Instead, a plane meant Memphis, where, according to his story, he waited three days to catch a flight to New Orleans. He reported there on April 26 to Tod Browning. Those three days in Memphis are unaccounted for, although we can assume a three-day bender. Browning told him to get a night's rest, but first Faulkner was to see the continuity writer. The latter reportedly said: " 'When you have written the dialogue I'll let you see the story.' " Back to Browning, who told Faulkner to sleep off the night. The next morning, the saga continues, the author and Browning sailed in a rented launch to Grand Isle, where the picture was to be shot. No continuity writer was as yet in sight, and the one-hundred-mile trip itself barely allowed them to lunch and return before dark. After three weeks of such activity with nothing to show, Faulkner became worried, but Browning reassured him, telling him to get a good night's sleep. Then one evening, Browning showed Faulkner a telegram telling him he was fired. "Faulkner is fired. MGM Studio." Browning still reassured him, saying he would get him back on the payroll. A few minutes later, another telegram arrived, firing Browning. "So I came back home. I presume Browning went somewhere too. I imagine that continuity writer is still sitting in a room somewhere with his weekly salary check clutched tightly in his hand. They never did finish the film. But they did build a shrimp village—a long platform on piles in the water with sheds built on it something like a wharf. The studio could have bought dozens of them for forty or fifty dollars a piece."[3]

The story is clearly intended for the interviewer and serves many purposes. It demonstrates to the attractive and rich Jean Stein the difference between serious writing and writing for the screen; and indicates, further, that Faulkner was one cool fellow, moving easily among people who clearly had no sense of reality. The truth was that Browning did complete his films, studios did turn out some creditable work, and salaries were high simply because talent had to be bought. Behind the scenes, in the real world, Browning had told Marx that Faulkner wrote unsatisfactory dialogue,* which was true, and also had refused to return to Culver City until after his child was born in June. Marx then sent Faulkner a long, apologetic telegram giving perfectly valid reasons why he could not be retained on salary as long as he remained in Oxford, holding out future employment if he came to California. Faulkner did not return until July of the following year, when his salary went to $1,000 per week and his boss was Howard Hawks, now at Universal Studios.

He was back in Oxford probably by the end of the first week in May and went off the MGM payroll a week later. Intermixed with the flying—solo and dual with Omlie—was a strong bourgeois desire to possess property and build an estate. We see in Faulkner some of the need he would soon describe in Thomas Sutpen and his "Hundred." In Faulkner's case, the estate-building came when he purchased three more lots, giving his Rowan Oak property greater expansiveness. In all, he invested $3,300 in land, an enormous sum for 1933. While it is very possible the acquisition was intended to give him great privacy by protecting the house against trespassers and the curious, the other, acquisitive side cannot be ignored. While Faulkner continued to display anger against a materialistic world and railed against the comforts of the age, he desired it all—house, extensive grounds, airplane, automobile, indoor plumbing, wife, and child.

There were the two, radically divided Faulkners, as we see dramatized in his next completed novel, *Pylon.* The visiting aviators and their troupe represent a frontier world which had really disappeared. They could exist

---

*"Louisiana Lou," based loosely on Lea David Freeman's play *Ruby*—also titled *Dance Hall Daisy*—was released on March 7, 1934, as *Lazy River*, with no sign of Faulkner's work on it.

only at the behest of someone like Feinman—the stereotypical Jew who constructs a new airport, dedicates it with an air show lasting several days, and then sweeps away the scum which has served his purpose. The fliers, the wing-walkers (Omlie's wife had been a wing-walker), the jumpers, even the mechanics represent a world of ghosts. Remnants of a past, they are the cowboys of the air, although Faulkner tries not to sentimentalize them. They are, merely, the "other," the world which is as different from Feinman and his crowd as if people on another planet.

The purchase of an airplane had to wait while he brought Rowan Oak toward the state he wanted. It was quite a different house from the one he had moved into three years earlier: now there was indoor plumbing, electricity, heat, the main parts were painted, the floors restored. When Jill was born on June 24, 1933, with a perfectly normal delivery and the baby herself perfect, the house was livable. Jill was tiny at birth, a little over five pounds, which was not unusual for a woman of Estelle's size, especially given the small stature of her father. Delivering the baby was Dr. Eugene Bramlett, to whom Faulkner had donated the incubator he thought might have saved Alabama's life. Jill did not need it, and she returned home on time in the care of a nurse. All this of course incurred considerable expense —hospital stay for Estelle, doctor for delivery, nurse, plus baby clothes and related incidentals. Even in the depreciated currency of 1933, the sums needed were high.

Because of that, Faulkner could not afford to turn down offers, including Cerf's generous reoffer of $750 for an introduction to *Sound*, now to be produced in different colors. This was how Faulkner originally wanted the novel to appear: with different colors indicating levels of time rather than italics distinguishing between past and present. All this he put to Wasson (received June 27): "How many colors shall I be limited to? Just what does he want in the introduction? I'm ready to start right away."[4] The edition, incidentally, never appeared, and Faulkner's marked copy has disappeared. The principal coloring was to have come in Benjy's section where the time shifts are the most radical and perhaps confusing. Another letter, to Harrison Smith on July 20, suggests he is deeply immersed in the Snopes book, and he was receiving advance money from Smith for it. But that novel, if indeed that was the project he said he was working on, was like most other projects for 1933—either strung out for much longer than foreseen or aborted.

The year kept bringing him back not to his work, but to himself. Estelle's physical condition, which at its best was never good, the aftermath, or aftershock, of Murry's death, the birth of Jill, his additional responsibilities, the sudden access to Hollywood gold—all of these could not be easily resolved. Faulkner's head was turned one way or another, and his emotions were spread thin. Under it all, he was not satisfied sexually, nor would he be until he gained a succession of compliant younger women. We should not underestimate his dissatisfaction in this area. Sexually, Estelle seemed burned out, brought down by one bout of poor health after another or simply depressed, which she tried to relieve with alcohol and heavy medication. She was caught in a familiar cycle. If we can believe Faulkner, his role now was to live a celibate life at Rowan Oak. Despite his cold exterior, his curt and sometimes rude manner, he craved affection. His women friends later all testified to how he desired female understanding, affection, sympathy—but, of course, on his terms.

Throughout the year, Faulkner was battling to control his life, regain direction. This showed itself in many ways, including his use of Morton Goldman as his new agent, and his movement away from Wasson, especially when Wasson went to another agency. Although he did not hold his friend responsible for the way his properties were being handled, he was dissatisfied and decided to try a new agent, as well as his own wiles. When Sam Marx, for example, asked for rights to certain stories ("Ad Astra," "Honor," and "All the Dead Pilots"), Faulkner demanded payment in advance.[5] Even in his letter to Smith, already cited, he says he will hold the check until Smith agrees to raise his royalty rates from fifteen percent to twenty percent on the first printing. But he sought control in other ways as well. He liked an idea Wasson raised during the summer about a book on the Mississippi River. It would be something of an updating of Mark Twain's classic book, not about riverboating but about the transformation of the river into the waterway it had become, a commercial lifeline. But Faulkner, while tempted, finally rejected the book as well as even an article on the subject. He was trying to clear time and mental energy for a new book which, he told Wasson, Smith was going to publish in the fall of 1934. Although no such book materialized, we have the sense Faulkner had given enough time to marginal projects; that if he needed money, he would return to shorter fiction: ". . . a short story now and then is about all I had better undertake."[6] Some of this attention to short fiction would definitely pay off in 1934, when he published eleven stories. Some of those stories went into *The Unvanquished* at the end of the decade.

The sending schedule was reactivated. Most of the stories were old material, some revised and rerouted. *Scribner's* returned whatever was sent except for "There Was a Queen." But Faulkner's heart was not in it; he was trying to direct his career back on track. It is very possible his interest in writing the introduction to *Sound* was related to his need for linkages in his career—that is, to reconnect 1933 with 1928. If so, the introduction got him into the mood, both historical and personal, which made *Absalom* possible.

We have already cited parts of this introduction, important in itself, but especially significant as revealing aspects of Faulkner's mind and concerns just before he tackled his most ambitious project to date, *Absalom.** As mentioned, he speaks of the difficulty of creating art in the South, where

---

*The introduction has many lives in manuscript and typescript, so that part of the problem in quoting from it is the choice of texts. One version was published in the *Southern Review* (Autumn 1972), but there is no reason to believe other versions are less valid or "authentic."

to succeed it must become "a ceremony, a spectacle; something between a gypsy encampment and a church bazaar."[7] This would, in part, be an apology for his sensationalism, or a response to charges made against *Sanctuary.* The old South no longer exists, he says, "killed by the Civil War," and the new South is not the South but the North trying to remake the region along Northern lines. Here we have the plight of the Southern artist, finding himself in a transitional society, hanging on to the ghostly past, rejecting the present, which is actuality, but alien. We have here not so much a delineation of the mind-set for *Sound* as for *Absalom.* In that book, Sutpen represents the ghosts of the old South, brutal and uncouth, whereas Quentin represents the new South, which cannot sustain him. We already know an anguished Quentin has committed suicide in the book for which Faulkner was writing the introduction; but we also see how that anguish will nourish his role in the later novel. Faulkner was curling back on himself.

From this doleful portrait, Faulkner returns to how necessary art (words, oratory, rhetoric) is to the Southern writer and, indirectly, to the Southerner. With this, he winds back to *Sound,* with comments already cited. He stresses the fury, anger, rancor which go into a Southern novel and a Southern novelist. It was in fact this anger and fury he needed to call upon in order to write his next two novels. The function of this introduction was to rev up the motor, move him from a certain temporary complacency and self-satisfaction, goad him into doing the one thing he knew he could do well. He would never be a first-rate flier, nor a good horseback rider, he was spotty as a father and husband, and, according to some witnesses, not an exceptional lover. But in one area he was supreme, and he knew it. Cerf, who judged precisely when to tap Faulkner, when to be flexible, when to offer friendship and his home, had come at just the right moment with the right project. Faulkner wrote to Wasson: "I have worked on it a good deal, like on a poem almost."[8] He sent it on, sometime in the middle of August. On August 24, Faulkner followed up the introduction with the color-marked copy of *Sound,* telling Cerf to be careful with it as it is his only copy. It vanished. Also at this time, Faulkner shifted from Wasson to Goldman.* He was now $500 richer, the first installment on the $750 promised by Cerf; the remainder was to come after he went over and signed the sheets of the new edition.

With Jill born, some of the diverse aspects of his life began to fall into place. He went ever further into flying, piloting with Omlie the Waco-210

---

*Ben Wasson, in *Count No 'Count* (1983), offered his side of events. While Wasson was loyal and devoted to Faulkner, his comments must be taken lightly. His claim that Estelle and he embraced and kissed at the Oldham home, until Cho-Cho entered, is somewhat dubious. Wasson was known to all as homosexual and seemed an unlikely object of Estelle's flirtation. In other areas, his stories of Faulkner fleeing a Harlem night spot when the songs and glances got rough are also suspect; as are some of his assertions of his own centrality in the writer's life. Once Faulkner became famous everyone wanted or claimed a piece of him. None of this in any way diminished Wasson's years of fine service to his friend.

—a large, powerful, and sound airplane. Increasingly Faulkner would take up children from the family, including his two nephews, Johncy's sons, but also Jill and Maud. Even though he avoided acrobatics and approached flying with respect for both plane and elements, he was not a natural pilot, and on one approach to a landing, he cracked up the Waco. It was not a serious accident, with the plane far more damaged than Faulkner—he crawled out unhurt. The plane suffered top wing damage and a bent propeller when it nosed over. But the accident was the first of several with planes and, later, with horses.

In October he indicated he was working more steadily. He wrote Harrison Smith that the Snopes novel would not be ready for spring, but he had another idea, *Requiem for a Nun.* Smith had asked for a volume of short stories, but Faulkner was uncertain of what he had. "It has been almost 16 months since I have written anything original or even thought in such terms." He promises to look into it and "see if we can get a book we won't be ashamed of."*[9] This activated Faulkner into resending some new writing and a good deal of revised older manuscripts, going back to the time of "Elmer" and his trip to Italy, France, and England. In this period, we can place "Wash," "A Bear Hunt," perhaps revision of what he described as the "Christmas Tree" story. The first two were prophetic—for "Wash" foreruns the latter details of *Absalom,* and "A Bear Hunt" is a trying out for the later "The Bear," in *Go Down, Moses.*

Meanwhile, Faulkner and Estelle had Jill baptized at St. Peter's Episcopal Church, with Jack Falkner and Sallie Murry Williams as godparents. Harrison Smith came down from New York, with the plan of spending some time at Rowan Oak. What he saw could not have been encouraging. Faulkner was the mainstay of his firm, the linchpin of a very financially shaky operation, and yet Smith saw Faulkner drinking heavily in the aftermath of the baptism. And he also could not have been encouraged by Faulkner's new enterprise, flying. Smith had no way of knowing if the writer was sober when he went up, and even if sober how careful he would be; and even if sober and careful, how safe it was in those primitive planes which depended completely on adequate mechanical upkeep, luck, and flier attention to details and warnings.

Faulkner was planning to fly with Omlie to New York, to look over his various projects, meet with Robert Haas, talk to Smith about the new volume of stories. Yet while his mind was percolating with new ideas, he was also considering his brother Dean. What eventuated became a powerful force in Faulkner's life, for not only did it affect Dean, his wife, and his still unborn daughter (also named Dean), it deeply affected Faulkner's

---

*That book became *Doctor Martino and Other Stories,* which Smith and Haas published in April of 1934. It contained the following stories, of which only "The Leg" and "Black Music" had been previously unpublished: "Elly," "Wash," "There Was a Queen," "Beyond," "Death Drag," "Turn About," "Smoke," "A Mountain Victory," "The Hound," "Fox Hunt," "Doctor Martino," "Honor."

own future life. And since it did all that, it ultimately affected Faulkner's work. In some strange way, John Sartoris and Dean began to merge, although his brother was a far more reasonable and rational human being than Sartoris. But Dean had not found himself, and at twenty-six, he was still footloose. He was seeing a young woman, Louise Hale, who had graduated from Mississippi State, and he still threw himself with abandon into sports and other activities. But he was drifting, not for lack of talent, not for lack of intelligence, but as the youngest son with three older, bustling brothers. Faulkner had always been particularly fond of the baby brother, as had Murry; and now he thought Dean needed some direction. What better profession for this athletic and intelligent young man than flying? Commercial piloting was still in its infancy, and all of Faulkner's instincts about a future career for his brother were correct. He could eventually obtain a commercial license and then be able to fly mail and passengers. In a short time, Faulkner put the plan into motion.

But other things came first: the work on "Wash" and the trip to New York to gain control over his immediate future. The New York trip was carefully orchestrated by Cerf to give Faulkner a maximum of exposure to old friends (Dorothy Parker, Frank Sullivan, the Guinzburgs, among others) and to allow the publisher to keep his eye on what he hoped would be a future property. But if we can borrow the title of the story Faulkner was completing at this time, it didn't wash. Faulkner turned up drunk at Cerf's cocktail party and apparently was under the weather for the remainder of the eight-day stay (from November 3 to 11). He did meet Haas and liked him immensely—Haas acted as a father figure to Faulkner when the latter came over to Random House. A Yale man, a World War I hero, and a founder of the Book-of-the-Month Club, Haas combined urbanity and intelligence with extreme discretion and tact. One quality which must have impressed Faulkner was his silence, reserve, almost withdrawal. Later, during World War II, when Haas's son, a Navy pilot, was lost at sea, Faulkner made one of his strongest statements about Jews, only this time indicating he'd like some American Legion–type to make an anti-Semitic remark so he could smash him. This was in fact a real turning point in Faulkner's fictional handling of Jews, and he dropped the innuendoes and other remarks from his letters.

"Wash" is about the murder of a patriarch, Wash Jones slicing up with a scythe Thomas Sutpen, the king or emperor brought down by his vassal. It is a strange story Faulkner carved from his expanding idea of the South before and after the Civil War. The death of a patriarch, coming so soon after Murry's death; the murder, also by Wash, of the granddaughter bearing Sutpen's child, coming so shortly after the birth of Faulkner's own child; the burning of the house by Wash, with his granddaughter's and great-granddaughter's bodies in it, coming as the writer was renovating Rowan Oak—all kinds of glints and glimmers play in and out of this early conception of *Absalom*. Further, Faulkner would soon start to write the novel in which still another daughter, Judith Sutpen, is caught in the coils of her father's making—he too virtually ends her life by having her brother kill her suitor. Daughters and granddaughters are trapped—either killed or have their lives subverted—by patriarchs.

"Wash" offers several entries into Faulkner's complicated emotional life. Its insistence on the patriarch, the role Faulkner had assumed on the death of Murry, and then the decline of the patriarch through hubris and moral decadence form a cautionary tale. But the psychological ramifications go much further; Faulkner was measuring the very nature of patriarchal rule, the struggles which must be fought with the son(s) and daughter. Beyond the immediacy of his own emotional needs, he was introducing racial illness into the equation and pitting patriarchal power against all these other forces. If we must label *Absalom*, it would be America's classical Greek tragedy, really paralleling only one other similar venture in the country's literature, Eugene O'Neill's *Long Day's Journey into Night* or his trilogy about Agamemnon and Clytemnestra in *Mourning Becomes Electra*—the metaphorical use of a family to suggest final things, final deteriorations.

The trip to New York and then home, with Omlie piloting, was the beginning of a drinking bout for Faulkner. When he went to hunting camp after Thanksgiving of 1933, out of which came the story "A Bear Hunt," he suffered from a severe bout of hiccups, for which he tried his usual remedy, whiskey. Hiccups were, apparently, a common affliction for him, and they left him exhausted after several days of unending jerks and spasms. Unable to hunt, he hiccuped and drank, and finally left camp, came home, drank some more. Finally the condition passed, leaving him weak and dispirited. A doctor told him his health was deteriorating, his insides ruined by alcohol on an empty stomach. It was indeed a false alarm, for Faulkner continued to drink abusively, and his stomach did not rebel —his heart did. The hiccup condition, however, earned him $900 (he'd hoped for $1,000) when the *Post* paid him that sum for the story (published February 10, 1934) based on the episode, "A Bear Hunt." He turned it into a comic gambit, the joke played on him.

Connected to these seemingly self-destructive bouts, which often proved restorative, was his laxity in dealing with editors and publishers who made demands on him. He accepted many offers outside his agent's purview, and Goldman did not know how to handle deals in which he had played no role. On the surface, Faulkner undercut his agent, even displayed hostility to anyone handling his work, but the situation seems more complicated. It is true he liked control. Dealing directly with an editor made him seem like the farmer growing his own crops, rather than depending on others. But Faulkner also nourished a deeper sense of uncertainty about his market value, and that need to sell his own work, dispensing with his agent, was linked not to pride but to feelings of inferiority. He also suspected anything that smacked of "deals," and an agent, by profession and nature, is involved in dealing. Faulkner liked the straight connection between buyer and seller: it fitted his notion of how things were done in the South, not in the North.

Money was a continuing problem. The influx of Hollywood money had made Faulkner gear up his living expenses, and now without Hollywood work, he was short of cash—a familiar cycle until he gained the Nobel Prize in 1950. This meant short stories, and his letters to Morton Goldman sound desperate.* He combed his files, this in the month or two before he began "Dark House," the early version of *Absalom*. On the eve of his greatest effort, he sounds like a man lost in debt. "Bench for Two" was taken from his drawer and remodeled into "Pennsylvania Station," for which *American Mercury* paid $200. "A Christmas Tree" was resurrected, remodeled, and rewritten, but nothing happened to it until its publication, as "Two Dollar Wife," in *College Life* in 1936. "A Portrait of Elmer" may have been carved out of the original "Elmer" manuscript, but probably derives from a somewhat later date. A further sign of Faulkner's desperation was that the stories submitted were in the main inferior work, even while he was writing one important novel after another. It becomes clear he did not consider his short stories, except in a few cases, a significant part of his career.

Between September and February, he had no magazine publications. In February of the new year, he had four ("Elly," "Pennsylvania Station," "Wash," and "A Bear Hunt"); then in April of 1934 two more ("Black Music" and "Leg," in the volume *Doctor Martino*). But before the end of 1933, on December 17, he began what was distinctly *Requiem for a Nun*, not only with the title but with material suggesting the later work, including a jail and a "nekkid razor." He was, according to his January 31 letter to Smith, writing a Snopes novel; this manuscript reveals the dim beginnings of *Requiem*, but was laid aside. He shortly began "Dark House," early in 1934; he was writing new stories and recycling old ones. And his flying interests intensified. He now owned the Waco-210 and had taken his test for pilot and passed. All this activity suggested that Faulkner's "cure" had worked. He was revving up.

Those stories came from all directions on the eve of *Absalom*. Was there some common factor or revelation in work that seems so discrete, so distinct from the longer fiction boiling up in Faulkner's imagination? "Wash," "A Bear Hunt," "Pennsylvania Station," "Two Dollar Wife," plus several other stories brought back from the dead and recycled, all pointed to a writer heading in several directions, scattering his shot until he finds his focus. Where, in brief, was he? Where was he going?

*He wrote in late 1933 or early 1934: "Let me know as soon as you sell any thing. I am living on credit and and trying to write a novel at the same time" (Alderman Library, University of Virginia; *Selected Letters of William Faulkner*, ed. Joseph Blotner [New York: Vintage Books, 1978], p.77). The novel was probably the Snopes project, which he then told Harrison Smith on January 31, 1934, was fully two years off. That letter is full of money concerns as well.

"Pennsylvania Station" (a recycling of "Bench for Two") finds Faulkner so distant from his characteristic material we wonder at his desperation in resurrecting it. A group of street people have gathered in the warmth of Penn Station, as a refuge from the snow outside. An old man begins to tell his story to a younger man, the entire group dressed in motley and waiting for the railroad policemen to chase them. The story he relates is overwhelmingly about death. That image dominates in the old man himself who has alone survived among eight siblings, a sister (called Sister) who saves fifty cents a week to pay for a coffin when she dies, the terminal itself as a final place on a snowy death-oriented day in New York City. Death is present as metaphor as well as in the story's images. Sister believes in her son, Danny, and while he skips from one bout of trouble to another, the old man tells us, she protects him—even to the extent of letting him draw out her coffin money and then lying that she has approved his theft. Danny is involved in grand larceny and the murder of a policeman, of which he may or may not have been guilty. The old narrator works to protect Sister against such knowledge of her son, but she discovers all and dies within the confines of the inner story. At that point, the street people are moved out of Penn Station by the uniformed guard and drift away to the warmth of Grand Central Station.

Faulkner tried *Scribner's* with this piece, but was turned down. It showed up in the section of *Collected Stories* called "Middle Ground," a kind of dumping ground in the volume. One element which makes sense in terms of Faulkner's larger career is the story's emphasis upon images and metaphors of death. Here it connects with a much more mainstream story, "Wash." That is altogether another order of business: tight, controlled, directed, firm. But it gains much of its power from the linkage to the larger work which followed, and it is in fact difficult to read the story without putting it within the context of *Absalom*. It is part of the central Faulkner vision, which is one of decline, deterioration, holding on, ultimately death. These values dominate in the period preceding the Snopes trilogy. *Sound* foreshadows it, *As I Lay Dying* and *Sanctuary* solidify it, *Light in August* gives it further resonance and weight, and now many of the shorter fictions serve as pilot fish leading to the most powerful statement of all about decline, fall, and death.

The strange configurations of patriarch and daughter in "Wash" have shadowy parallels to Faulkner's own situation sixty years later. But images of death command our attention. Everything is declining. Since the South's defeat in the war, all direction is lost; houses as well as people begin to collapse. A hero of the war, Sutpen, is now reduced to running a small store: ". . . a frame shelved room where, with Wash for clerk and porter, he dispensed kerosene and staple foodstuffs and stale gaudy candy and cheap beads and ribbons to Negroes or poor whites of Wash's own kind."[10] When they haggle "for dimes and quarters," Sutpen closes up. But Wash feels broken and meditates it were better if his kind *"be blasted*

508 | WILLIAM FAULKNER: AMERICAN WRITER

from the face of earth than that another Wash Jones should see his whole life shredded from him and shrivel away like a dried shuck thrown into the fire."[11] But even in the utter defeat of his kind, he has refused to run. "If he ran he would merely be fleeing one set of bragging and evil shadows for another just like them, since they were all of a kind throughout all the earth which he knew."

The story line enables Faulkner to express his sense of the South as defeat and death. While Wash Jones, Sutpen's "white trash" factotum, devotes himself to the patriarch, his granddaughter of fifteen becomes entangled with Sutpen and bears his child. Sutpen, visiting her, is more interested in a mare of his which foaled at the same time, a "fine colt," in contrast to the daughter from Milly. Wash overhears Sutpen's disregard for her new daughter and his favorable comments on his horse. It is unclear if Wash expects marriage to legitimize this relationship, but he faces down Sutpen: the latter's whip against the servant's scythe. With Sutpen dead, Wash ministers to Milly and, when the sheriff closes in, burns the shack to the ground and rushes the lawmen with his scythe upraised: ". . . it bore down upon them, upon the wild glaring eyes of the horses and the swinging glints of gun barrels without any cry, any sound."[12]

The story is highly concentrated, the prose reaching toward Faulkner's best. The principals are enervated, but with enough nastiness left that murder and disregard are quite possible. The real part of "Wash" is the subtext of complete, total defeat, of both the old and the transitional South. The Sutpen who raised himself by sheer willpower is now dissolute, as brutish as ever, defeated except in his disregard for his own death. He and Wash are two drunken stumblebums, with only memories which belong to the servant. Judith, Sutpen's daughter, is still around, but his "son had been killed in action the same winter in which his wife had died." More than forty years Milly's senior, Sutpen gets her with child and abandons her for a horse, a moral failure tantamount to a form of death. Amid his brutishness, Sutpen once had a kind of personal honor, but even this has deteriorated. When he falls beneath Wash's murderous scythe—as Milly will fall beneath his butcher knife—the cutting of necks is like a general execution. As Wash advances on the lawmen with his scythe to cut their necks or to be cut down, he is ending an era.

"A Bear Hunt" is a different form of death. Although the shape of the story is a version of the tall tale, the introductory matter is one of "the death of." The narrator is Ratliff, the emergence of one of Faulkner's favorite characters, a standby in his repertory—a mixture of folksiness, common sense, and country acumen, the perfect voice for himself. Before Ratliff gets to the inner story of the hiccuping Faulkner, he tells of one Lucius (Luke) Provine and of the others on the hunting trip. What characterizes all is decline: they are onetime toughs who now have abandoned families and direction for wandering lives as salesmen of meaningless objects: like all the dead pilots. Duke is typical: "There are other men among us now whose families are in want; men who, perhaps, would not work anyway, but who now, since the last few years, cannot find work. These all attain and hold to a certain respectability by acting as agents for the manufacturers of minor articles like soap and men's toilet accessories and kitchen objects, being seen constantly about the square and the streets carrying small black sample cases."[13]

Now pitiful, in their prime they terrorized the town square, and particularly terrorized Negroes, as the Provine gang. On one occasion, they broke into a Negro picnic at a nearby church and burned off the celluloid collars of the men—not harming them, but intimidating and demeaning them, knowing the Negroes could not protest or fight back. These small-town men are the substance of the hunting camp, headed by Major de Spain. Hardly glamorizing them as hunters, Faulkner presents them as figures barely this side of death. Well before we arrive at Ratliff's tale, we have entered a soggy, misshapen piece of human life. Ratliff tells of Luke's hiccuping which cannot be stopped by any normal means. The narrator suggests he consult a local Chickasaw named John Basket on the Indian mounds about five miles from camp. Before Luke arrives, Major de Spain's Negro servant slips out, tells the Indians Luke is a revenue agent, and suggests they frighten him with a burning at the stake. They do, and Luke returns without the hiccups. As it turns out, the Negro servant was one of the men whose celluloid collar Luke had burned twenty years ago. The latter accuses Ratliff of setting him up, but by now the story is part of legend. While the inner tale is mildly amusing, what sticks is the makeup of the camp and the figures of death living on memory.

It is unclear when Faulkner made the revisions in "Two Dollar Wife" which led to its publication in *College Life* (January 1936). But since he wrote Morton Goldman about it probably in the winter of 1933–34—when it was called "Christmas Tree"*—we can assume he was working on it in the period just before he began "Dark House." The story went through several incarnations, but it proved intractable. It shares, however, one aspect of the death motif we see in this period: the characters so involved in trivia and in dissolute lives (dicing, a forged marriage license, a country-club party, drinking, racing cars on narrow roads) they are close to death-in-life. Writing about people of exquisite inconsequence, Faulkner became inconsequential. The lack of dimension in these characters, middle- and upper-middle-class equivalents of the hunting-camp companions in "A Bear Hunt," is a sign of their death. Implied in this is Faulkner's distaste

---

*Faulkner wanted Goldman to show an editor a piece of the story, and if it was approved, he would write the rest, estimated at twenty thousand words. The story comes closer to five thousand, and padded at that. Faulkner indicates he would rather not finish it at the present time as he was "trying to write a novel." But he followed with another letter asking whether "XMAS TREE [was] . . . still hanging fire." (Both letters are winter 1933–34. Alderman Library, University of Virginia, *Selected Letters of William Faulkner*, ed. Joseph Blotner [New York: Vintage Books, 1978], p 77.) "Two Dollar Wife" goes back in Faulkner's career, perhaps to around 1930, with a three-page version called "The Devil Beats His Wife." He even tried to do a treatment for MGM in 1932, and he later supplied several versions, all of which proved intractable.

at their waste of advantages, but the story so lacks distinction it is difficult to locate conviction.

The year 1934 was another *annus mirabilis* for Faulkner, as a contrast with the country, still sunk into the deepest reaches of the depression despite several New Deal policies to help out. Although Roosevelt had restored some measure of confidence, especially in the banking system, his various proposals to invigorate a capitalist economy which Faulkner both supported and distrusted were unavailing. Situated in Oxford, Faulkner was outside some, but not all, of the political events occurring in the country at large. One area to which he could not remain oblivious was the fact that agriculture, which occupied fully twenty-five percent of the American population and a far greater proportion in Mississippi, was slipping badly. Farm after farm went under as loans were called in or as markets for products dried up. Negroes had already begun the long trek north for jobs. In the larger political sense, fellow writers were voting in patterns which would have made no sense to the staunchly Democratic Faulkner. In 1932, when America still perceived herself as a pastoral or agricultural society, the Communist party here, already under thrall to Soviet communism, enlisted the support of the following writers for its candidate for president: Hemingway, Dos Passos, Dreiser, Richard Wright, Langston Hughes, James Farrell, Katherine Anne Porter, Edmund Wilson, Malcolm Cowley, Lincoln Steffens, Nathanael West, and Erskine Caldwell (a good old boy from Georgia).

Amusingly, the newly formed Book-of-the-Month Club offered *New Russia's Primer* as a selection, a book which favorably compared Russian order with American disorder. The point of the book, which struck home to America in the early years of the depression, was that everyone worked in the Soviet Union. In Mississippi the demagogue Theodore G. Bilbo saw virtues in the Soviet system and said: " 'I'm getting a little pink myself.' " If some fantasy of communism seemed attractive, so did Fascist groups, like the one formed in Atlanta called The American Facist [sic] Association and Order of Black shirts, modeled on Mussolini's Blackshirts. The depression was creating a struggle for men's minds, and extremes of both right and left were active in this pursuit. The military in fact had pockets of discontent, especially in the reserves, waiting to see if Roosevelt could get a grip on the country. The great fear was twofold: chaos in general, but socialism/communism in particular. Totalitarian governments were perceived as more efficient, and a good deal of the support for Mussolini and then Hitler derived from what seemed to be their more efficient way of doing things. The desire to extend central power was great. Claire Booth Brokaw (later Luce) offered this piece of wisdom: "Appoint a dictator!" and Congressman Hamilton Fish, Jr., a House member to the right of the Count of Paris, said that if dictatorship is not given to the people, the people will themselves change the system. Others on the right weighed in, including Alf Landon, who would become Roosevelt's opponent in the 1936 presidential election.

This rhetoric did penetrate the South, and it did lead to men like Bilbo —an unlikely voice in support of communism—making extreme political and racial statements. Faulkner seemed well outside of all this, as he would remain outside Hollywood political activity. Guarded by his Jeffersonian-Emersonian beliefs, he hardly ventured into more ambiguous waters. Yet he recognized his ideals were fantasies, that he had to transform history and the past into allegories to make them seem valid. Faulkner was a man who resisted all extremes—as he would try to do in racial areas also —and yet he realized his own moderate positions were unavailing, incapable of bringing resolution. As a novelist Faulkner did not have to resolve such political and ideological matters; but as a man writing those novels he had to work through some forms of belief he could transform into his fictions. His dilemma bears pursuing. He played a balancing game. He could not settle any of it in his mind; that his fictions derived from a man as close to Keats's sense of "negative capability" as we could have in fiction, a mind open to possibility, closed to resolution of individual and society working together.

Mississippi fell just outside most of the developing New Deal policies. The Civilian Conservation Corps was designed to put slum youths on projects in rural areas, and this hardly touched Faulkner's state. Banks were bailed out, and that helped to some small degree in increasing confidence in the country's institutions. But as the Stone family experience showed, bankruptcy was always close. Farmers were helped with outreach programs, and the Tennessee Valley Authority would generate power. But the main business of America was industry, and here Mississippi was bypassed. The National Recovery Act (NRA) had virtually no effect on the state's fortunes, since it affected chiefly states with strong unions. While the country came back from the brink, Mississippi maintained its flirtation with demagogues whose populist fervor gave birth to a new word in the English lexicon: Snopes.

The desire to preserve an agrarian society, expressed most recently in the *I'll Take My Stand* manifesto of 1930, became increasingly a fantasy. For if anything appeared to be the salvation of America it would be industrial production to take up the slack, eventually, of a failing agricultural product. Recovery on one hand and agrarianism on the other seemed oxymoronic. While the machine might be a hateful thing, it provided employment in the larger population centers—the coming of the war almost a decade later proved just this point. Much of the manifesto was based on nostalgia, if not for antebellum days then for something exclusive in the Southern soul or spirit which recalled the antebellum period.

Implicit in the agrarian ideal was Jeffersonianism, a pastoral dream now undermined by Northern socialists. Agrarians envisaged a purer form of capitalism, although how it would work is unclear. While continuous with Jeffersonian agrarianism, their dream or fantasy lacked Jefferson's great doubts, his play of ideas and sense of the individual's worth—that is, Jeffersonian without Jefferson's idea of democracy. He held that farmers with interests entirely agricultural are the real representatives of great American interests, and they alone are to be relied upon for expressing correct American sentiments. And if God had a chosen people, it is those "who labor in the earth," small landholders as the most precious part of a state. What mattered was soul, not matter. But Jefferson was distant indeed from the agrarians. For him, reliance on the individual was foremost; for them, it was the nature of an organic society which dominated. Although Jeffersonianism superficially seemed to be at the core of agrarianism, the two could not be more different. Further, once his warnings were clear, Jefferson did not oppose the machine or technology, but incorporated it into his organic society. He railed against excesses: science became a mixed blessing, a source of strength and an impersonal giant to be attacked. Jefferson feared privilege more than he did the machine, but he preached against both. He cherished the Edenic past, the Garden as a perfect place, a prelapsarian vision as a guide for the future.

What did all this mean in the depression? Faulkner, who was more Jeffersonian than agrarian, was confronted by a withering society; and if not withering, then changing so rapidly as to become unrecognizable. More than woods were receding and more than Snopeses were taking over: the very sense of an organic community was being altered, rent in fact. In order to recover that society, it was necessary to write allegory; realism or naturalism was no longer possible. Therefore, when Faulkner moved to the past, as he did in *Absalom* or in the stories making up *The Unvanquished*, he was on the edge between realism and allegory. He had to develop a literary style which took into account that what he believed in profoundly was no longer viable; that what he held to be the values of his region during the Great Depression were themselves self-defeating. Like Jefferson, Faulkner came to hope that there would be no change even while change occurred; that recovery could come without the alteration of certain fundamental forms of life. Pastoral, Eden, the good life, the simple life, and "virtue and talent" became intermixed, even sentimentalized. The hope was for continuity within discontinuity, even while the mind said otherwise. Although not a traditional believer, Faulkner left a good deal to Providence.

It is impossible to understand Faulkner in the 1930s without seeing how deeply immersed he was in a pastoral tradition, which was itself an allegory of St. Augustine's formulation of the City of Man struggling against the City of God. *Absalom*, which is about so many things, is also about the land, about carving an empire out of the wilderness, turning a purely pastoral setting into an estate, into a state, Sutpen's Hundred as a place unto itself. What Sutpen lacks, however, is that inner possibility or poetic imagination which would join with the pastoral experience to produce the Jeffersonian and Emersonian ideals. Sutpen is in fact quite the opposite: once the empire is established, he wants only to be emperor. The deeper values that should come after the City of God emerges are missing.

Emerson had warned that the individual can destroy himself outside a context; he foresaw the dangers of ego-worship and self-indulgence. Even a brief story like "Wash," an avatar of the larger work, makes this clear. Yet intermixed with this is Faulkner's awareness we must pay a price for the individual's right of freedom from the limitations of the past. Yet even while he understands how destructive ego-worship is, Faulkner has a sneaking admiration for Sutpen and his will to power. Like Conrad's Kurtz, Sutpen lacks balance between self and history. A Nietzschean figure, he attempts to break from history, to destroy the past, to embody in himself the sense of the new. Faulkner perceives the seductiveness of this, and also the consequences—the rising up of the servant to destroy the emperor, who is suddenly seen in all his seedy nakedness. The farm as "holy emblem" for Emerson is now a desolate place. The 1930s were, in the Biblical sense, the years of drought, literally in the dust bowls of the Midwest, symbolically in the lives of the people. In the Deep South, foreclosure was the order of the day. Marches on Washington proved ineffective.

Faulkner wrote "Mule in the Yard," which he intended for the *Post*,[14] but was taken by *Scribner's* (August 1934) after probable rejection by *Cosmopolitan*. Since he was engaged, as he told Smith, in writing a Snopes novel, it was a natural outgrowth. But even as he wrote it, he was turning away from both the Snopes novel and the *Requiem* idea. Writing to Smith on January 31, 1934, Faulkner noted: "About the novel, I still think that SNOPES will take about two years of steady work. I could finish the other one [*Requiem*] in good time, if only the Snopes stuff would lie quiet, which it wont do." He indicates that after he pays off his taxes and insurance with stories, he intends to settle down on it by March 1. If the stories do not earn what he needs, then he will have to draw on Smith as per their agreement, either $1,000 or $500. He lists some of his burdens, which are impressive in their total weight: ". . . I have my own taxes and my mother's, and the possibility that Estelle's people [the Oldhams, now in need and coming to the man they rejected] will call on me before Feb. 1, and also my mother's and Dean's support, and occasional demands from my other two brothers which I can never anticipate."[15] He adds that his insurance for $700 and income tax of about $1,500 complete the financial picture. An alternative he presents to Smith is that he, Faulkner, draw upon the full amount of their agreement and concentrate only on the Snopes novel, perhaps for a late fall printing.

Yet so quickly did his imagination change directions and demand its own way of doing things, Faulkner wrote Smith within weeks of the last letter that he has put aside both the Snopes and Nun novels. "The one I am writing now will be called DARK HOUSE [the same name he gave in manuscript to *Light in August*] or something of that nature. It is the more or less violent breakup of a household or family from 1860 to about 1910."

He continues: "Roughly, the theme is a man who outraged the land, and the land then turned and destroyed the man's family. Quentin Compson, of the Sound & Fury tells it, or ties it together; he is the protagonist so that it is not complete apocrypha. I use him because it is just before he is to commit suicide because of his sister, and I use his bitterness which he has projected on the South in the form of hatred of it and its people to get more out of the story itself than a historical novel would be. To keep the hoop skirts and plug hats out, you might say. I believe I can promise it for fall."[16] The rest of the letter concerns his need for an advance of $1,500, since his two short stories have not as yet sold.

All this seems straightforward enough, but it became a winding trail of other projects which intruded into the writing of "Dark House." The year 1934 was in fact a kaleidoscope. But even before that, "Mule in the Yard" seems something out of a pastoral idyll. I. O. Snopes may be pulling his devious tricks, but he is outsmarted by Mannie Hait, just as he had tried to outsmart the railroad. Snopes has worked a scam on the railroad by driving mules onto the tracks at a particularly bad curve, and then collecting when the train hits them. It also hits Mr. Hait one night, and Mannie picks up $8,500 from the railroad as a settlement. Then she and Snopes struggle over a mule which has terrorized her property and kicked over a scuttle into her basement, causing the house to burn down. She gives Snopes $10 for the mule, and when he comes to plead for more—he had asked for $150—she takes back the $10 and offers him the mule back. But it is dead, shot by Mannie. So she bests Snopes, and things return to normal. It was the kind of story Faulkner wrote with his left hand, but it demonstrates how deeply committed he was to the pastoral, imperfect as it was, with Snopeses and their scams.

Then the complications increased. A brief run-through of the year 1934 for Faulkner suggests how overwhelmingly complicated his life was, and how his work, nevertheless, seemed to pour out of a writing machine programmed to scatter its material in several directions. In 1934 he published no fewer than eleven stories, three of which, revised, appeared in *The Unvanquished* (1938): "Ambuscade" (*Post*, September 29); "Retreat" (*Post*, October 13); and "Raid" (*Post*, November 3). The eight others: "Elly" (*Story*, February 4); "Pennsylvania Station" (*American Mercury*, February); "Wash" (*Harper's*, February); "A Bear Hunt" (*Post*, February 10); "Black Music" (*Doctor Martino*, April 16); "Leg" (*Doctor Martino*, April 16); "Mule in the Yard" (*Scribner's*, August); "Lo!" (*Story*, November 5). "Black Music" and "Leg" (reprinted as "The Leg") were the two original stories in *Doctor Martino and Other Stories;* all others in the collection had been published in magazines.

Faulkner had five larger works to occupy him in 1934. The Snopes novel, now put aside; the work on *Requiem,* now also put aside; six stories for *The Unvanquished;* early work on "Dark House"; and the seven segments of *Pylon.* What is even more remarkable, however, is that the styles for many of these are varied. *Pylon* may look ahead to *Absalom*, moving along as both were on parallel lines. But the *Unvanquished* stories are a different kind of rhetoric, in a different mode; and the Snopes material created still another style or voice, in itself distinctive.

As we take up the year in more sequential order, Faulkner contemplates still another project. "I have a plan," he told Goldman, "a series to be called 'A Child's Garden of Motion Picture Scripts.' They will be burlesque of the sure-fire movies and plays, or say a burlesque of how the movies would treat standard plays and classic plays and novels, written in a modified form of a movie script."[17] We can be grateful nothing came of this idea. Yet what about "Dark House"? On the verso of page 9 of the manuscript, Faulkner had drawn a little sketch showing the round-robin of information as it moves in a circle from one principal to another, Sutpen to someone deleted, to Mr. Compson to Quentin to Rosa, with Quentin marked as "central." Off to the right is "French," probably the architect of Sutpen's house. Faulkner already had a start on "Dark House" with the stories "Wash" and, before that, "Evangeline," in 1931. That latter story seems the most direct source for the novel, despite the closeness of "Wash" to the final scenes. In "Evangeline" Faulkner had discovered the way the novel eventually would be narrated, in the "I" and Don character (Spratling). The "I" and Don had appeared elsewhere (in "Mistral" and "Snow"), but here they move right into Sutpen material. When Faulkner came to turn this volatile and brutish matter into a longer fiction, he transformed "I" and Don into Chisholm and Burke, using the opening material from "Evangeline." But clearly this was not the way to do it, and Faulkner's letter to Morton Goldman naming Quentin Compson as the central narrator, the one who "ties it together," is critical. Chisholm and Burke are themselves eventually transformed into Quentin and Shreve, the Canadian student. The triumph of the method came when Faulkner discovered it had to be Quentin, now resurrected from *Sound*.

Faulkner went through several stages of fragmentary manuscript trying to catch the telling of Sutpen's story. "Telling" had become for him the key element. He had planned on keeping it a dialogue between two rather colorless characters, until, on February 11, he hit upon his method. He started not with Shreve but with a letter from Mr. Compson to Quentin; not yet his true beginning, but coming close to a solution. The problem was the letter proved unwieldy. It did, however, bring forth from Quentin, while responding to his father's news Miss Rosa Coldfield had been buried yesterday, January 10, 1910, that he was a young man preparing for Harvard and yet too young to be buried with the other ghosts who make up the South. Faulkner was homing in on his great theme: the South as ghosts, phantoms, specters, and the story to derive from a dualistic Quentin, the young man with one foot in the modern world, the other in the ghost-ridden South of his history. The next and final stage was to remove the letter and to put Quentin directly into contact with the very old, but still vocal, Rosa Coldfield. At this point, with these strategies having settled the matter of "voice," Faulkner describes the scene between young Quentin, trying to move forward, and Miss Rosa, interested only in telling about the past, trying to make the new generation understand the history of the South. The language here is very close to what it would be in the printed book.

It was these beginnings which made Faulkner write to Smith he had a novel which would "keep the hoop skirts and plug hats out," and which he promised for the fall. "Dark House" metamorphosed into *Absalom* and was ready only in early 1936, for publication on October 26, 1936, his publisher Random House. The first copy was inscribed for "Meta Carpenter, wherever she may be."

His letters up to his return to Hollywood, from July 1 through July 24, are filled with developments on the stories which make up *The Unvanquished*. They are concerned with prices from the *Post*, almost never sufficient, and with his own difficulties in creating a sense of continuity between the first three stories and the Reconstruction group. He writes repeatedly to Goldman about these stories even while "Dark House" lies inchoate on his desk; the Snopes novel is gathering dust, as is the *Requiem* project. Extraordinarily, he is within a short time of hatching *Pylon*. ". . . I seem to have more material than I can compress. I have just now decided that the trouble is this: The Reconstruction stories do not come next. In order to write them, I shall have to postulate a background with the characters which they embrace. Therefore, there must be one or two stories still between the War-Silver-Mule business and the Reconstruction. I am just starting one ["The Unvanquished," which became, in the volume, "Riposte in Tertio"] which will be a direct continuation of the return home with the mules, which should be included in the series of three which are done[18] ["Ambuscade," "Retreat," "Raid"]." With this, he hopes to get into the Reconstruction stories. Along with "The Unvanquished," he used "Vendée" as a transitional piece, and then ended with "Skirmish at Sartoris" (called "Drusilla" in manuscript) and "An Odor of Verbena."

Writing again to Goldman on July 29, after a three-and-a-half-week stint in Hollywood, Faulkner said he couldn't get enough money out of the *Post*, so he "got lined up with a moon pitcher script."[19] He indicates, now back in Oxford, he is working on it at present and does not know when he will get back to the stories or return to the novel—presumably, "Dark House": ". . . it all depends on how much or badly I need money at the time. That is, I would like to keep the Post hot for a while longer, so if, when I finish the script, I need more cash I can write the other stories." Then to Harrison Smith, in August, he wrote about "Dark House," which he would eventually publish with Random House:

> The only definite news I can tell you is, that I still do not know when it will be ready. I believe that the book is not quite ripe yet; that I have not gone my nine months, you might say. I do have to put it aside and

make a nickel every so often, but I think there must be more than that. I have a mass of stuff, but only one chapter that suits me; I am considering putting it aside and going back to REQUIEM FOR A NUN, which will be a short one, like AS I LAY DYING, while the present one will probably be longer than LIGHT IN AUGUST. I have a title for it which I like, by the way: ABSALOM, ABSALOM; the story is of a man who wanted a son through pride, and got too many of them and they destroyed him.[20]

After these twists and turns, the letters to Goldman stress the need for funds; Faulkner has returned to the *Unvanquished* stories. But in the midst of this, he announces (October 18, 1934) a story called "Courage," out of which he is writing the novel which became *Pylon*. His work on that would be phenomenally rapid, even for him, with its seven chapters sent on to Smith in the five weeks between November 11 and December 15, with galleys ready by January 9 of 1935. While by no means a forgettable work, *Pylon* was clearly "filler" material, while *Absalom* simmered on the back burner. It was, however, in its own way, a statement.

Right up to mid-December of 1934, when Faulkner tells Goldman that the "forced draft" of *Pylon* is finished, he is also pushing the stories, "Drusilla," in particular. He additionally feels the *Pylon* manuscript might have film possibilities, and he sends on a copy to Hawks in California. And in the final letter to Goldman for 1934, he encloses "Lo!" (which *Story* published in November), asks about the "Drusilla" piece, and announces: "I can use money right now to beat hell."[21]

Other events in 1934, not directly related to money-making—although eventually transformed into that—were equally important in Faulkner's life. Some of them affected him profoundly, and not only literarily. On February 14, which also happened to be Ash Wednesday, during an air show at the inauguration of the Colonel A. L. Shushan Airport in New Orleans, Captain Merle Nelson was killed. A seemingly isolated event, tragic in itself but unconnected, reached Faulkner, but not only to inspire his conception of *Pylon*, which grew out of this. If Estelle had infinite perception into her husband—and perhaps she did, drinking to hide what she saw in him or in herself—she would have noted how unsatisfactory he found his home and family life. They did not fulfill him: wife, daughter, two stepchildren now reaching an age where they could tune in to everything taking place at Rowan Oak. He was discontented, perhaps not with specifics, but with "being there," with the lack of communication he had with Estelle, with the frigid atmosphere (to which he contributed), with responsibilities, with his stepchildren, on whom he had begun to lean, sometimes cruelly. His one solace was his daughter, Jill, but apparently that was not sufficient.

If Estelle had infinite wisdom, she would see he had drifted into two kinds of worlds: one, where he had been for some time, in his imagination as a writer; the other, into reliving the adventures and fantasies he had recounted as disguises and lies. He had found, now past his mid-thirties, a means by which he could validate what had been deceptions. Although he could not be an RAF hero downing enemy craft and limping home on a sputtering craft, he could enter into something fitting for peacetime, the life of aviators as they barnstormed and risked their lives. This phase of his life also coincided with his going off alcohol, something he bragged of to Smith in the February 1934 letter about "Dark House": "On the wagon since November." This continued, apparently, perhaps creating another source of friction with Estelle, who did not follow. Faulkner reveled in the fact he was now one of the boys, a licensed airplane pilot; he liked to chew the fat in hangars and airport lounges, much as Murry had done at the livery stable and hardware store. Faulkner did not himself like acrobatics and tricks—he was not a good enough pilot, and he had a degree of caution —but he liked to be around those who did.

The new airport in New Orleans—which becomes the Feinman Airport in New Valois in *Pylon*—gave him and Omlie an opportunity to be present at an exciting event: the gathering together of some of the leading barnstormers in the country. Airports became Faulkner's "baseball," a metaphor for the way he linked himself to a national pastime, a pastoral with frail machines. His devotion to the air in the 1930s was the fantasy wish of many young men or boys, for airplanes gripped the imagination. Still in their infancy, they seemed flimsy and immaterial, hardly a machine, and surely not part of the military-industrial complex which they later became. They seemed far indeed from being killers, although they had functioned militarily in the first war. Rather, they were romantic, becoming with automobiles the "spaceships" of a still slow-moving America.

Flying—and, by implication, airplanes and their pilots—were part of a pastoral tradition. Forget the machine and see the setting: extensive fields, surrounded usually by trees and further space; urban area distant, the world of commerce far; the pilots amateurs, money rewards minimal. Aviators were a throwback to an earlier time. Jiggs, the mechanic in *Pylon*, is described repeatedly as an ape, his short legs barely visible as he scuttles along. The women in this setting are antibourgeois, little different from the men, disconnected from home and kitchen, somewhat epicene. Laverne is dressed indifferently as male/female, and she is serviced by two men. She has taken on the qualities of this male world, falling well outside the defined role expected by society. The people, female as well as male, lie beyond, and it is this which makes them romantic, even when they are being desperately practical about bus fare or food money.

Faulkner was captivated. Flying joined with war at this time to occupy his imagination. Stories that, revised, ended up in *The Unvanquished*, *Pylon*, and *Absalom* all have forms of violence in common—male pursuits, in the main. Even the women, Laverne, Drusilla, and Judith Sutpen, act like men and are defined by flying or the Civil War. Coequal with this world of "beyond" is Faulkner's need to break out, suggested by his immersion in the male camaraderie of flying and hangar talk. The Hollywood venture in July reinforced this; and we can see all these activities as revealing his need for rejection of what he also wanted to keep. He was deep into that cycle of rejection of family and home, although he needed them as anchor. If Estelle had been aware of this—and she may have been—then she could have expected that when her husband went to Hollywood he would playact another role and seek out young women. In fact, one way to assess flying and planes in Faulkner's life is to see them as compensation for sexual dissatisfaction, although that might be a simplistic way of judging his complex delight in aviation.

The Shushan Airport and its dedication festivities would become embedded in *Pylon*. The dedication was to "Conquest of the Air," and it featured the coming together of professional fliers in a series of dangerous events. There were acrobatics, upside-down flying, pylon flying, jumping with parachutes, wing-walking, and all the rest, including a woman parachute jumper. The festivities were due to begin on Wednesday, February 14, and continue for three days, after delays due to poor weather. Faulkner arrived on the fifteenth, accompanied by Omlie. The events which had occurred the previous day, opening day, and those which continued through the dedication activities found their place in *Pylon* with only minor alterations. Besides a parachutist (Jack Monahan) being blown off course into a seawall, there was the failed stunt of Merle Nelson leading to his fiery death, the Frank Burnham crash of the novel. More was to come. Faulkner was in his milieu, far from the madding crowd of publishers, editors, and parties, deeply immersed in the lives of men he had already limned in "All the Dead Pilots." In his mind he had lived through their experiences dozens of times and written about them long before he ever saw them.

The hero of the day was Jimmy Weddell. He was a speed champion, winner of numerous races, a daredevil, nonpareil as a flier, but careful of himself and his plane. Faulkner had teamed up with a reporter from the New Orleans *Item*, Hermann B. Deutsch—thus the idea for the reporter in Pylon, although unnamed—who introduced him to Weddell. The latter had already set the land plane record of 306.33 m.p.h., once held by the equally famous Colonel Roscoe Turner.* Here was a turning point for Faulkner. Confronted by the larger-than-life Weddell, Faulkner could only think of how to put his experiences of the man and meeting into fiction. Weddell was himself a self-contained man, intent on his records, making a precarious living from exhibitions, lessons, charter flights, and fees from airports like Shushan. Faulkner could see a good deal of himself in such enterprises, if he transferred exhibitions and lessons into his own world of short stories, Hollywood scripts, and other endeavors to make a

---

*As a marginal comment, the present writer while a very young boy had heard of these fliers, Turner and Weddell, much as young boys began to hear of Joe DiMaggio and Ted Williams a little later. There were no chewing gum cards for aviators, but so splendid were their achievements they broke through into name recognition for those completely outside aviation.

living. As for Weddell's main goal, his concern with speed, that too could be translated into Faulkner's sense of the novel, which was all that really mattered to him. Meeting Weddell was like meeting his other half. He was hooked, not only into flying but into writing about it.

After Omlie left, Faulkner moved in with another old acquaintance from New Orleans, Roark Bradford. On Saturday, during the extended fete, another mishap occurred when a chutist became entangled in the tail area of the plane, and both chutist and pilot plunged toward the lake. Both were killed; the chutist (Ben Grew) was found, but the barnstorming Charles N. Kenily was never recovered from the water. After this, Faulkner got caught up in a fog of reverie, accidents, and drinking bouts with Bradford and others who hung around his apartment. Faulkner also met up with the Lymans, Guy and the former Helen Baird, now living in New Orleans. He eventually disentangled himself from the drinking bouts and storytelling episodes, returned to Batesville, and then was on his way to Memphis for more personal flying.

His experience had shaken him in several ways. He commented much later that these men "were a fantastic and bizarre phenomenon on the face of a contemporary scene, of our culture at a particular time. I wrote that book [*Pylon*] because I'd got into trouble with *Absalom, Absalom!* and I had to get away from it for a while so I thought a good way to get away from it was to write another book.[22] . . . They were ephemera and phenomena on the face of a contemporary scene. That is, there was really no place for them in the culture, in the economy, yet they were there." Even twenty-three years later, Faulkner was still awed by the experience, and that is because it shook what he believed. As a man who felt the pull of the pastoral and thought that urban life was destructive of individual values, he believed deeply in enduring, despite long stretches of pessimism about both individual and society. In the final analysis, Faulkner was for life, and yet in the pastoral of an airfield with men who profoundly attracted him, he perceived a disregard for life.

He was torn. His admiration for these men who had no fit in society —he had himself experienced this earlier, as a youthful poet in Oxford— had to confront the fact that they themselves had little respect for life, only for derring-do, feats, performances. If they represented something of what he believed—that need to step outside society and community to reassert oneself as an individual—then how could he accept their ruthless undercutting of their own existence in order to keep this kind of life going? He saw them as men and women eager only to get "just enough money to live, to get to the next place to race again." They traduced life itself in order to assert their way of life, and they seemed to do it unconsciously, as part of a performance in which only the act, not themselves, mattered.

Here was something he had not figured on, and when he came to write *Pylon*, he tried to create a breathless run-on prose which departs from grammar and syntax in order to simulate the rush of their lives. But emotionally and psychologically he was twisted. For in his fantasies of bravery and courage, he had not, except in the brief "Turn About," figured on this disregard for life. When he perpetuated deceptions about his own military service, he had not factored in this dimension; his lies had all focused on the creation of the hero, on suggesting the indescribable bravery of the young. None of it had the nihilism he now confronted, and which he would write about. It was as though the very pastoral he so desperately wanted to retrieve and embrace were now betraying him.

Because of its airport, Memphis became of importance in Faulkner's life —he went often, and stayed. On occasion Estelle accompanied him, and Blotner reports[23] that one time she asked to see Miss Reba's brothel, the "home" of Temple Drake in *Sanctuary*. Faulkner took her, and she was disappointed, for Miss Reba seemed like a respectable woman running a business. Blotner reports Miss Reba appeared to have no idea Faulkner was a writer, or that he had written a book which would make her establishment famous throughout the world. *Sanctuary* simply had not entered her mind. This interlude aside, the flying continued, and it included Dean, who was now apprenticing with Vernon Omlie. Faulkner was paying expenses, hoping the talented Dean would stick to something he could make a living at. The letters to Morton Goldman pleading poverty continued. Before his July trip to Hollywood, Faulkner had only the stories from which he could eke out an uncertain income. Book royalties were small, and the publication of *Doctor Martino and Other Stories* on April 16 was not going to make much financial difference. Since he knew the volume was a catchall, including stories going back to the early days of the sending schedule, he could not have been surprised the reviews were mixed, some citing work of better quality while others went after the potboilers. It was not a distinguished volume, even though it included "Wash" and "Honor," which looked ahead, respectively, to *Absalom* and *Pylon*.

Yet even as Faulkner was reaching a wider audience—and *Doctor Martino* did not hurt him with those who read his best work sympathetically —he was being torn down locally. Part of his poor reputation in Oxford and the region generally, for those who were even aware of him, was that his presentation of the South (and of Jefferson and Yoknapatawpha in particular) was considered cruel, unjust, and vilifying. His characters were nothing but vile, whereas other writers such as Stark Young in *So Red the Rose* created the fantasies people wanted. Faulkner offered a grim South, one populated by unpleasant creatures, some violent (Popeye, Tommy, Joe Christmas), some effete and useless (the Compsons, Gavin Stevens), some at the lower end of the scale (Lena Grove, Byron Bunch, the Bundrens), some just stumblebums (Lucas Burch), at least one an idiot (Benjy), some polluted young women raffish in their moves (Caddy, Temple Drake), and places which ranged from stills to brothels to jails. No great houses, no splendid living, no vision of a happy, adjusted South, no drawing upon memory to perpetuate fantasies. Faulkner was ungiving, unrelenting, and he kept coming on.

Philip "Moon" Mullen of the Oxford *Eagle* got into the interstices of Faulkner's reputation. Posing as the writer's friend, he seemed to provide Faulkner with publicity in the local newspapers; but in point of fact, Mullen took away more than he gave. He was suspicious of Faulkner's reputation among the sophisticates, and, playing the country bumpkin, kept bringing the writer back to his roots—not unlike Phil Stone in some respects. Mullen thought of Faulkner as "one of ours," and rarely failed to suggest he was betraying his origins. Faulkner's continuing reputation as the "town drunk," which carried well into his years of international fame, resulted from the way his career was presented in the *Eagle*.

Stone did not help. He was beginning that slide into discontent which would devour his later years; and while still stable in the 1930s, his feeling of exclusion from Faulkner's growing fame brought out the worst in him. Using Mullen's facilities on the *Eagle*, Stone began to publish comments in the *Oxford Magazine*, first in the initial issue of the magazine on April 1 and then in two succeeding articles, on June 1 and November 1. They are the remarks of a man who feels betrayed, or, more likely, unloved. The relationship of Phil to Faulkner ("Billy," in the early days) was that of master to apprentice. Given this advantage, Stone, now just over forty, attempted in his comments to hang on to memories—those moments of glory when he had a bright, talented youth under his tutelage. It was a kind of power he was never to have again, and as he drifted into resentment, even early stages of paranoia, he struck back. Stone married within a year of his November 1 piece on Faulkner, and it is tempting to observe that his loss of the writer had to be compensated for; by October of 1935, it was clear to him the master-apprentice relationship was sundered, that the apprentice was an ingrate.

In his comments Stone established he knew Faulkner better than anyone else, that this knowledge gave him the opportunity to "record of him many things that no one else knows." In order to protect his original investment, Stone argued that the simple country boy whose education had been furthered by his friend was now writing little more than "little black marks." He granted Faulkner was an exponent of modern technique, even that he was talented, but with "no trace of genius."[24] He indicated he doubts if he will ever show genius, that he has gone as far as he will ever go. In the June 1 installment on the "biography" of Faulkner, Stone draws a portrait of the family background, labeling part "the Rise of the Redneck." Although the portrait of the involvement of the grandfather and uncle in Vardaman politics is accurate, it is presented as distasteful, making the immediate Faulkner background approximate to "the rise of the Snopeses." And it emphasized Stone's more elegant family tree, his removal from the dirty, lower-class side of Mississippi politics. Yet Stone is respectful of the old colonel, and he notes that if Faulkner can capture the social and political upheaval implicit in the Snopes saga, then he can do something great. But even here he is misreading his friend's literary purpose, which was not to capture "social and political upheaval," but to limn a geography of the imagination.

In the November 1 episode, continuing with family background, Stone —in what was expected to be another part of a six-part biographical memoir—sketched the past of Oxford. He indicated Oxford was Faulkner's sole milieu, and that if he departed from it, his art would suffer. Stone here repeats that it was he who made Faulkner into Faulkner, kept his feet upon the ground, "drilled into him the obvious truths that the world owed no man anything." We can assume that the next episodes would be much the same, but the *Oxford Magazine* folded with this issue. It was somehow fitting. For Stone was attempting to put a cap on Faulkner's career, cautioning what was best for him, coming down as a harsh parent on a prodigal son. We conjure up the image of fisherman and fish, with the former struggling to land his catch, and the fish managing to stay out of reach. Stone could see how close his catch was, but to no avail; and Faulkner—who helped his friend financially at a later date—did stay beyond reach. What had cooled beyond redemption was everything except memory, and Faulkner did not forget the memories, although he knew he had to remain outside Stone's net.

While Stone was beginning his extended biographical comments, Faulkner was flying. He tried another story on fliers called "This Kind of Courage," but *Scribner's* turned it down and nothing came of it. His main enterprise was putting in hours on the Waco and getting involved in an air circus underwritten by Oxford merchants, on March 31 and April 1. In charge was Dean Falkner, and Omlie was to provide the stunts. There was also parachute jumping, many of the ingredients to be absorbed into *Pylon*. The circular for the next big event, on April 28 and 29, cited WILLIAM FAULKNER'S (Famous Author) AIR CIRCUS; it listed STUNT FLYING by William Faulkner and Capt. V.C. Omlie, and mentioned a parachute jump as well as passenger rides. The latter, taking up local people, provided Dean with a living. At the end of the circular: "These Ships will burn That GOOD GULF GAS."

Strange doings for a man who has on his desk one of the greatest novels of the twentieth century! But this was glorious release—it removed him from Oxford and from Rowan Oak; financial matters were left behind on earth, and he could buddy around with men whose exploits he admired. He even brought into his circle the brother of Jill's mammy, a young man named George McEwen, later known as the "Black Eagle." He apparently took McEwen through the early stages of flying, and McEwen eventually became a pilot. With all this going on, the publication of *Doctor Martino* on April 16 appeared to roll over Faulkner, an inconsequential publication inasmuch as it meant little or no additional revenue.

In May of 1934, Faulkner began to contemplate still another project, not linked in any direct way to what was already on his table: the stories that would make up *The Unvanquished*. When he began, he did not conceive of them as a volume, but of a few stories on interrelated themes of two boys coming through the final years of the Civil War and then dealing with the realities of Reconstruction. The two boys, we can assume, were to be of the Huck Finn–Tom Sawyer variety, although their lives fell into a far grimmer social and political context. Instead of Huck's destructive father, there would be war and Reconstruction. The plan, if it worked out, was to pit the courage of the young against the increasing hopelessness of the South's decline and deterioration under the onslaughts of superior Union strength. Further—and here we can see some spillover from the intense racial situation of *Absalom*—the two boys would represent the South as Faulkner saw it, one white, one black. The white was Bayard Sartoris, son of the legendary Colonel Sartoris, grandfather of the doomed Bayard and John, whom Faulkner had been writing about in his stories of fliers. The black youth was Ringo, who was indeed seen as a brother. We observe once again the shadowy presence of *Absalom*, with Henry Sutpen and Charles Bon as brothers in arms and spirit, only divided by Bon's insistence on marrying Judith Sutpen.

By late spring Faulkner had already produced two of the stories, was prepared to write the third, and foresaw all six. All were destined for the *Post*, which paid the highest prices, and his letters to Morton Goldman at this time indicate how essential these sales were for him. They also posed problems, chiefly his need to tie together the Civil War pieces with the Reconstruction ones. Yet despite Faulkner's strategies, the failings of the *Unvanquished* stories (except for "An Odor of Verbena") are apparent. No matter how well they fit as "filler" between major enterprises, they must be viewed as toying with the story form. There is little resonance; they are tricky, based on fictional deceits; and their movement is frequently solely along the line of narrative development, a method Faulkner had already abandoned in his longer fiction. The first story starts with a specious idea: to make Ringo, the black youth, a fountain of perceptive sayings, a street-wise kid, full of smarts;* and Granny, a crafty old geezer who with lies and deceit can beat the Yankees. These are soap-opera formulations; to complete the cliché, the Yankees are so courteous they court Granny's deceptions.

These and other frailties of conception and development do not undermine one point—that is, how these stories act as a hinge in Faulkner's career. If we view the stories as part of the volume published in 1938, the idea of a hinge no longer works; but if we see them as deriving from 1934, when they were written, then they do. What they connect is earlier and later Faulkner, past and future work. They move him, strikingly enough,

*The Negro Ringo, moreover, is completely devoted to the white cause, a fervent supporter of the South against the Yankees. Everyone, including Bayard, calls him "nigger," which he fully accepts, although he is playing an equal role with his white friend. Here "nigger" is less race than it is a distinction of class—the "lower" Ringo allied with the aristocratic Bayard, the son of a war hero. Even so, Ringo's acceptance of his role and his loyalty to a cause which would keep him a slave puts Faulkner on dubious racial grounds.

into family matters. The Sartoris family, which he had described before in several works, now becomes part of a bildungsroman, one of Faulkner's few works in that mode of the development of a young person. By the final story, Bayard Sartoris is twenty-four; by linking past and present and limning youthful development, the stories lead into *Absalom* and the Snopes trilogy, all of them family novels.

But the stories have other, equally important resonances. In some uncanny way, Faulkner, now passing thirty-five, had created a vicarious self for himself in young Bayard, at twenty-four. The way in here is tortuous, but he is pursuing a shadowy self. In this vicarious use of Bayard, the writer finds someone in the past who can involve himself in heroics no longer possible for the now-aging writer. In Bayard, who responds to his father, the Colonel Falkner of Faulkner's own family, *his* great-grandfather, we have a fantasy of Faulkner himself, showing loyalty and bravery but pulling back from the cycle of killing that the old colonel had perpetuated. In this immersion, Faulkner finds an ideal duality, enabling him to establish family ties and at the same time allowing him to escape domesticity and family burdens. The cycle of "war and peace" characteristic of the seven stories has resonances of tragedy amidst play, a kind of sporting Eumenides. By refusing to kill his father's killer, Bayard halts the work of the Furies; peace is restored, society can go on. We have put the Civil War and its aftermath to rest.

The series, then, served several functions in terms of Faulkner's personal needs, besides providing that hinge connecting work before 1934 with *Absalom*. It supplied Faulkner with a fantasy life, giving the writer an arena, in addition to the *Pylon* flying, in which a vicarious creation tests his manhood, not by killing but by quieting the Furies. It gave him entrance into Mark Twain territory, Bayard and Ringo acting out Huck and Tom. It afforded Faulkner historical contexts, displacing the contemporary world in which flying was preoccupying him and moving him into the pastness he needed for the work on his desk. It allowed him to re-create the myth of the war and Reconstruction, using his great-grandfather once again; but this time, by using boys, he demonstrated that the myths, legends, and fantasies so beloved by his contemporaries are finished and must become "play" to gain reality. Once again, he was preparing himself emotionally and psychologically for *Absalom*, giving himself the right perspective for the South's only great story, the Civil War. Not least, he has turned the war into an entertainment or sport. The fighting is in the distance, the legends come down to us as reported, John Sartoris and his feats recede into the background. The foreground, however, is tricks and strategies: selling the Yankees back their own mules, re-creating Vicksburg with chips, trench, and water, hiding the house silver from the enemy.

Faulkner appears to accept fully the legends of Reconstruction, but not the main truth of it. The truth was that despite the excesses of carpetbaggers, vultures who descended on a dying South to draw out final blood, the major thrust of Reconstruction was not bloodsucking but an effort, however faulty, to redress terrible injustices. Ringo himself abjures the tag of "nigger": " 'I ain't a nigger any more. I done been abolished.' " His uncle Cash is running for marshal of Jefferson. " 'They ain't no more niggers, in Jefferson nor nowhere else.' " He mentions the Burdens from Missouri, " 'with a patent from Washington to organize the niggers into Republicans.' "[25]

But even with the twisting sense of race and violence in the stories, they are concerned with making peace. In this area Faulkner reveals he is settling in, using Bayard to demonstrate that the war and wars are over, that the time has come to take account and put the past behind him. Bayard has himself been an avenging Orestes, revenging the death of Granny, a vicarious parent for him and Ringo. The two track Granny's killer, a man named Grumby; after killing him in a kind of ritual, they cut off his right hand as proof and leave Grumby pinned to the door of the compress. But this is as far as Bayard will go. When his father, John, is murdered, he refuses to kill the killer, and his discussion with Drusilla in "An Odor of Verbena" suggests Faulkner wanted to put an era to rest.

Faulkner left Oxford on July 1, to stay in Hollywood until the twenty-fourth. On the twentieth, he gave Estelle a reprise of events, and we cannot tell if he was being intentionally amusing, for his remarks reveal Hollywood at its most characteristic. The writer is left in the dark by the studio, by Hawks himself; and Faulkner says he has no idea what is happening to the properties he has worked on or what is expected of him. One property was to feature Margaret Sullavan, and there was no word on the other, a Mary of Scotland job, which in an earlier letter had seemed pressing.

Hawks, meanwhile, although still incommunicado, was trying to get Faulkner his money, and the writer was planning to be in Memphis on the following Tuesday, the twenty-fourth. What a brief visit like this amounted to—while not posed in these terms—was that Hawks supported Faulkner's writing career by periodically giving him Hollywood jobs which might amount to nothing in terms of treatments and scripts. So far, for all the money he had made, Faulkner was recipient of one screen credit, for *Today We Live,* released on April 28, 1933, based on his "Turn About." Faulkner did the original treatment and was listed as having provided story and dialogue. The screenplay, however, was by Edith Fitzgerald and Dwight Taylor. Another Hawks film, *Road to Glory,* would be released on September 4, 1936, with screenplay by Faulkner and Joel Sayre and featuring Fredric March, Warner Baxter, and Lionel Barrymore. It was produced at Twentieth Century-Fox, whereas the first had been an MGM release. But except for those, although Faulkner may have done bits of dialogue here and there or worked over a script, in these first ventures into Hollywood his hand was not apparent. Hawks was quietly providing him with a kind of stipend. In his letter to Estelle, Faulkner indicates: "I am getting nervous and a little jumpy to get home, at the fingernail chewing stage [i.e., drinking]. I wasted a whole week doing nothing at all; that's what frets me about this business."

On the home front, Estelle and Jill presented an unchanged situation. The house was still full of servants who had to be supported, as well as Faulkner's mother in her own home. Dean was moving toward a career in aviation. His brother Jack was doing well as an FBI agent, having been involved in a very important case, the John Dillinger trapping at the Biograph Theater in Chicago. The setting for the deadly outcome, in which Dillinger was shot to death by waiting FBI agents, is worth attention, since the "Biograph Theater" derives from the studio established by D. W. Griffith, whose films *The Birth of a Nation* and *Intolerance* had great meaning to the South. Jack Falkner, however, was not interested in film, but in forging himself a career as important in the FBI as his brother's was in writing. What also had not changed was Maud Falkner's dislike of her daughters-in-law, and her refusal to welcome them in her house; if, like Estelle, they occasionally showed up, they received a cold reception.

Yet the stability Faulkner periodically sought was there. The bad feeling, the hard drinking, the resentments, all became part of what he came to take for granted as his anchor. Further, there was the full desk, something he had to get away from, on occasion, but which, after a week or weeks in Hollywood, he willingly returned to. Although he was not prepared to start writing, *Pylon* was incubating, reverberating. The spending also had not ended. Faulkner purchased a Chevrolet coupe and became friendly with a local mechanic, E. O. Champion, or Champ. When they went flying together, Faulkner dug up his old stories about the Sopwith Camels and how dangerous they were; in fact, he had never flown one. He flew in Champion's biplane and in his own Waco, often taking his stepchildren with him, or else Johncy's son Jimmy. In September he sponsored another barnstorming air circus, slated for September 15 and 16, including passenger rides and stunts. Blotner reports[26] the various accidents Faulkner experienced in flying: a wing almost came off, his engine cut out and he barely landed, Champ's plane with Faulkner aboard lost power, Faulkner himself miscalculated on landing, losing a tire, on occasion smashing a wing. He was cautious, but played Russian roulette with frail planes.

He continued work on the fourth and fifth stories of the series in September, but Lorimer, of the *Saturday Evening Post* editorial staff, asked him to rewrite parts of the fifth, "Vendée," not objecting to the ending but to Grumby's falling out of character. Faulkner made the changes because the *Post* was a market he could not afford to jeopardize. He followed swiftly with the sixth story, "Drusilla." In October he told Goldman about an air story called "Courage." This was on October 18 and indicated he had, between the completion of "Drusilla" and this date, begun what would become *Pylon*. So compacted and intense had the story become in Faulkner's imagination that within two months he wrote Goldman that he had "worked forced draft on the novel and finished it yesterday."²⁷ He still had to finish revisions on the "Drusilla" story, which he did toward the end of December. But in the latter half of 1934, he had in effect written two full books: the stories which became *The Unvanquished* (with the addition of "An Odor of Verbena") and the seven chapters making up *Pylon*. Those chapters began to arrive at Smith's office on November 5 and ended on December 15. If we check the dates of receipt or of sending, some show less than a week of composition.* Faulkner had worked this rapidly with *As I Lay Dying*, but here his intent was not only book publication but also possible adaptation as a film. He sent a copy of the novel manuscript to Hawks in Hollywood.

Although not a major work, *Pylon* brought together in Faulkner's real and imaginative life many significant aspects. Flying and, by suggestion, writing about flying, served both therapeutic and imaginative needs. The dedication of the Shushan Airport near New Orleans was the catalyst, as were the encounters with famous fliers. In his letter to Smith, Faulkner tried to demonstrate the fictional dimensions of the novel: ". . . the incidents in Pylon are all fiction and Feinman is fiction so far as I know; the only more or less deliberate copying of fact, or the nearest to it, is the character of 'Matt Ord,' who is Jimmy Weddell. . . . But as I said, the story and incidents and the characters as they perform in the story are all fictional."²⁸ He admits that New Valois "is a thickly disguised New Orleans," or some people will take it to be—it surely is not Cheyenne, Wyoming. And the "Feinman Airport" is the "Shushan Airport of that place named for a politician."

Fascination with fliers becomes part of Faulkner's fascination with death—his themes, his drinking, his living on the edge. But then he recoils. They are throwing it all away in their headlong desire for destruction, their defiance of all rules, in the air as well as on the ground. The danger in validating Faulkner's performance in this novel is to romanticize the fliers beyond the self-contained way in which he presents them. Despite their defiance of bourgeois respectability, of space, of life itself, they are defined by their machines. The planes are both romantic objects and vehicles of death. They move outside the mechanical world in their ethereal, almost incorporeal fragility; and yet they are part of that world of machines. They are the "other," and therefore praiseworthy; but as the

*In his late-December letter to Smith, Faulkner listed the chapters, and someone in the New York office added the dates they were received. For the final two chapters, Faulkner indicated he mailed them on December 18 (Alderman Library, University of Virginia, late December 1934; *Selected Letters of William Faulkner*, ed. Joseph Blotner [New York, Vintage Books, 1978], p. 87); so the receipt date of "12/15" must be in error, or else he miscalculated the date. "Dedication of an Airport" (received 11/5); "An Evening in New Valois" (received 11/23); "Night in the Vieux Carre" (received 11/30); "Tomorrow" (received 12/5); "And Tomorrow" (received 12/10); "Lovesong of J. A. Prufrock" (received 12/15); "The Scavengers" (received 12/15). In the manuscript of *Pylon* at the University of Mississippi Library, the year 1935 is superimposed over 1934, which is the year Faulkner needed to make the dated events fit into the calendar.

"other" they can be overly seductive. The entire fantasy world Faulkner had created about himself from the war divides him here.

That is why he had to tell the story from the reporter's point of view, and it also explains why he made the reporter so physically defiant of space. Repeated references cite the reporter's nearly incorporeal presence: skeletal, an "etherized patient in a charity ward," in a suit "as though made of air and doped like an aeroplane wing with the incrusted excretion of all articulate life's contact with the passing earth." They emphasize Faulkner's desire to get "beyond" into some realm in which body is minimalized. The reporter is never observed in a routine setting: he lives in taxis, eats on the run or not at all, barely sleeps. He lives off his needs and anxieties, and that explains in part why he is so thin— "better than six feet tall and . . . [weighing] about ninety-five pounds."[29] He is beyond anorexic. Weightlessness has not affected his energy level, or his sexual desire. *Pylon* and *Absalom* are "narrated" novels—the reporter here, Quentin Compson there—and for each the problem is to find anyone to believe their observations. They rant and rave, they bemoan, and yet the story defies true telling. Quentin, of course, has far the greater story to tell Shreve than the reporter has to tell Hagood, his editor, but the effect is similar. Whereas the reporter's story involves people who defy space, Quentin's is about a man who defies time; the two novels neatly etch a temporal-spatial dimension which encompasses the country.

The matter of *Pylon* is highly literary, the result of Faulkner's decision to cast his novel in Eliotic terms. As the chapter titles indicate, *Prufrock* and *The Waste Land* are everywhere. Even more pervasive, perhaps, is a death motif which seems to go beyond Eliot, represented by the reporter as an emissary of final things. In *Pylon* death is negation only, unlike its function in *As I Lay Dying*, where Addie Bundren's death is an occasion for spiritual renewal or regeneration of other Bundrens. In the later novel, it exists not only in the activities of the fliers and in the physical embodiment of the reporter, but in the way sexual symbols are manipulated. The pylon, an obvious emblem of sex, can kill or mean more money. But its reverberations go far deeper—into the relationship the two men, Roger and Jack, have with Laverne, whom they share. As the jumper, Jack brings in little money, $25 or so, whereas Roger as the pilot can win hundreds. Thus their survival depends on him, and his relationship to the pylon, shaving it ever closer, is critical to the fortunes of the entire crew. Death and sex are interwoven. It is a curious combination, not so much because it is artistically extraordinary, but because Faulkner is so insistent on it in this period of his life. How deeply is it linked to the breaking off of sexual relations with Estelle after the birth of Jill? How profoundly is it associated with his trips to Hollywood where he saw hitherto unimaginable opportunities to bed young, pretty women? How is it connected to his own deepening depression, manifest in his need to fly, his heavy drinking, his uncertainty about money matters as he passed his mid-thirties? Certainly all of these personal elements are potentially present.

In another area, the novel reveals Faulkner's deep conflict over civilization, modern culture, urban values. The record is by no means clear. The world of fliers is pitted against the world represented by Colonel Feinman, whom the reporter refers to as "the Jew" or "the kike." The withholding of two and one-half percent of the barnstormers' money to defray costs of the circulars is a "Jewish plot" against those who risk their lives. The barnstormers themselves are admirable defiers of convention, but death-oriented in their activities and proclivities. They do not stand for pastoral values; their lives are not Edenic. Their world of space and air is not of the Garden variety.

What makes all this ideologically unsettling is that both parts of the equation seem antilife. The defiers of convention are deracinated, disconnected from all that would give them substance, while the exploiters of convention, the businessman, are plungers of a different sort. Both elements have subscribed to a kind of mechanical universe which has different faces for each. Feinman is the stereotypical Jew—fat head and neck, ruby in a gold clamp on a finger, fat cigar, a gangster-type from a Jack Levine painting, a George Grosz drawing, Eliot's Bleistein. But the fliers are also freaks of sorts—Jiggs with his short legs, Roger with his life on the edge, their uncertain positioning of young Jack, who at the end must be shuffled off to grandparents who might not even be his.

Faulkner has fallen into gross stereotyping in order to create an opposing force to the fliers' world. Feinman is connected to the sewage system —Chairman, Sewage Board, and, therefore, pegged as shit. He is not only the Jew as exploiter, but the carpetbagger, a "colonel" of something or other. He remains safe while Burnham and then Roger crash to their deaths, the jumper suffers a leg injury, and Laverne must give up young Jack.

The novel ultimately is about waste: human waste mainly, waste of energy, waste of meaningful life, waste of what should be the best. Here it moves in and out of Eliot. Even including the fliers, Faulkner's world is a wasted land. New Valois belies its name. The dedication of the airport becomes a hymn to death. The Mardi Gras on Grandlieu Street preceding Lent is a *danse macabre*. We are interested in Faulkner's angle of vision, for while flying had come to mean personal release for him, in two months of compacted writing he had created a world of wasted beings, a land dedicated to death. Endurance, patience, and his other attributes do not amount to survival. Depleted by loss, the crew moves on to another encounter with disaster, their lives. There is no increase, no reward, no yield, none of the usual Faulkner qualities.

Two elements suggest how powerfully this novel gripped Faulkner's imagination: his method of relating it, through the unnamed reporter, so that he obtained distance on the material; and the prose itself, angled, oblique, dense, and often almost incomprehensible in its rush of nonsyntactical, nongrammatical language. We get one of our first views of the planes, through Jiggs's eyes, as those "waspwaisted, wasplight, still trim, vicious, small and immobile" objects. Seen on the ground, they are pieces of metal, whereas in the air they achieve grace man cannot achieve alone. On the ground: "Unbonneted, its spareentrails revealed as serrated top-and-bottomlines of delicate rockerarms and rods inferential in their very myriad delicacy of a weightless and terrific speed any momentary faltering of which would be the irreparable difference between motion and mere matter, it appeared more profoundly derelict than the halfeaten carcass of a deer come suddenly upon in a forest."[30] The juxtaposition of Faulkner's two worlds in this passage reveals how his point of reference was the woods, deer, pastoral; and against this the plane brings home to him death in the forest, the rib cage of the half-eaten deer analogous to the opened-up cowling of the plane. Within this world of planes, vicious and entrailed until they take flight, the world of humans is equally dubious, or mixed. Laverne appears as epicene: ". . . a woman not tall and not thin, looking almost like a man in the greasy coverall, with the pale strong rough ragged hair actually darker where it was sunburned, a tanned heavyjawed face in which the eyes looked like pieces of china."[31]

The use of the reporter gave Faulkner distance on what was ultimately an incomprehensible experience. But he also gave the writer an opportunity to express a good many personal feelings. The slurring emphasis on Jewish financial interests and on a certain type of Jew can be attributed to Faulkner's recent stay in Hollywood, linked to his need to defer to those interested only in commercial return. A good deal of the self-hatred Faulkner felt for the weeks and months spent in Hollywood—most recently in July of that year—went into the reporter's castigation of "kikes" at the heart of it all. The release implicit in the celebration before Lent is juxtaposed with the astringent, ascetic life of the fliers and their crews; that in turn is somehow equaled to marketplace Jews on one hand and an artist like Faulkner on the other. None of this is symmetrical, but the acidulous stereotyping appears to be Faulkner's way of striking back at a "type" which remained mainly invisible and yet paid him the money he needed to live on.

This is also the first novel in which Faulkner tried to get inside the world of booze—where drinking, heavily and steadily, becomes part of the story line. Alcohol inevitably destroys Roger because Jiggs was drinking so heavily he was incapable of working, making it impossible for the valve job to be done properly on time.* As a result, Roger takes up a faulty plane, which crashes. Although he isn't hurt, with its loss he arranges to buy a more powerful plane from Ord which is clearly unsafe

---

*Jiggs seems to carry over from the aborted "Mythical Latin-American Kingdom," with *its* airplane mechanic. Simian in his shortness of leg, he is a curious creation, more devoted to drink than to anything else. He has deserted a wife and two children, but seems uninterested in Laverne or any woman. His loyalty is to the group, like some friendly pet, but his affinity for the bottle makes him unreliable.

and which Ord does not want to part with. But the reporter intervenes and works out a deal convincing the airport authorities. When this plane fails, Roger is killed—drowned. All the references to Noyades Street ("Drowning Street") are met in Roger's upside-down death in water—and his demise is directly linked to other liquid images, including Jiggs's drunkenness. The sequences are clear, with the reporter himself stumbling around much of the time dead drunk, helpless, a new corpse in his doorway.

In the Eliot section, the reporter rushes to and fro, all movement, in counterpoint to the watery burial of Roger, stuck fast somewhere, undiscoverable in the muck and debris of the lake. The moment of truth has arrived. For Jiggs, it means selling his beloved boots, that sole reward for a life on the run. For the reporter, the segment means the end of all his plans, even the wildest hope of all, that he might share Laverne with the barnstormers. To describe the scene, Faulkner uses Joycean language, with Eliotic images:

> He [the reporter] was not escaping it [the city]; symbolic and encompassing, it outlay all gasolinespanned distances and all clock- or sun-stipulated destinations. It would be there—the eternal smell of the coffee the sugar the hemp sweating slow iron plates above the forked deliberate brown water and lost lost lost all ultimate blue of latitude and horizon; the hot rain gutterfull plaiting the eaten heads of shrimp; the ten thousand inescapable mornings wherein ten thousand swinging airplants stippleprop the soft scrofulous soaring of sweating brick and ten thousand pairs of splayed brown haired Leonorafeet tigerbarred by jaloused armistice with the invincible sun: the thin black coffee, the myriad fish stewed in a myriad oil—tomorrow and tomorrow and tomorrow; not only not to hope, not even to wait: just to endure.[32]

The swiftness with which Faulkner turned out *Pylon* suggests he saw it as a kind of extended poem—that he felt such pressure from the material he could not wait to find the right context for it. The rapidity with which he wrote the book, however, should not blind us to the struggle that took place between him and his publishers over the text itself when it was set in galleys. But even before that, Faulkner played with the beginning, where he juxtaposed three elements in the same time frame: the dedication plaque, the program of events, and the view of Mardi Gras. From this, he moved to a minor character, then revised and opened with a third-person narrative. Once he finished, having sent off the novel chapter by chapter before completing it as a whole, he then had to resist publisher's changes. What disturbed Smith and Haas was the syntax. The galleys reveal how they simplified sentences, altered syntax, shortened paragraphs, all toward readability. It was for Faulkner a familiar struggle: to preserve the integrity of his text over the publisher's need to sell books.

There was, however, a sense of impending disaster implicit in the lines of the book, original and revision. What Faulkner sensed was the sheer doom of this kind of life, even as he pursued it himself and encouraged his brother. The foreshadowing here is part of the depression hanging over him even while he was still in his mid-thirties. The clotted language, the excessive verbiage, the attempts to reach beyond syntax and grammar all suggest the mad headlong rush of ideas which make the page into a form of therapy. It had to come out to clear the decks, so that *Absalom* could be brought forth. In a sense, *Pylon* emptied out his personal life, so that he could reach the greater book based in history. He needed to move beyond himself in order to interpret the South and ultimately the country.

Part IV

From War
to Shining War

Chapter Seventeen

The Death of Absalom

O N SEPTEMBER 30, 1934, Dean Faulkner married Louise Hale, whom he had known for the last year. The marriage took place amidst the young man's barnstorming, sometimes with Vernon Omlie, sometimes without. There was little question Dean had found a vocation, working in the main for Omlie in Memphis. Not only had he found a vocation, he was excellent at it, a more natural flier than his eldest brother. The two brothers seemed close, and Dean even added the "u" to his name in deference to the man who brought him into aviation. Yet the two were pursuing similar roles only on the surface. For while Dean was getting married and barnstorming, Faulkner was burrowing in, moving toward the writing of *Pylon*: catching on paper what Dean and his crews were doing in the air.

Pylon was part retrieval system, returning Faulkner to older days. When the reporter stops to buy some absinthe, he enters a speakeasy where the character Pete from *Mosquitoes* and "Once Aboard the Lugger" sells him what passes for absinthe. And the liquor is itself prepared by the old lady who was the mother of the bootleggers in those earlier pieces. We have here not only a reminiscence of past days in New Orleans, but also the sense Faulkner's entire literary production was massed in his head and came out not in sequential pieces but in overlapping, interconnected elements. With his neat habits, he hated to waste anything, or to give anything up.

Another example of holding on comes in titles. The "Tomorrow" of the fourth and fifth segments derives from *Macbeth* and from the same passage in the play that provided the title for *The Sound and the Fury*. That sentiment from Shakespeare fits well with the generally depressive atmosphere of *Pylon* and Faulkner's grim sense of a brewing tragedy. When Macbeth speaks these lines, in act 5, he is beyond the reach of normal feelings: "I have almost forgot the taste of fears. / The time has been, my senses would have cool'd / To hear a night-shriek, and my fell of hair / Would at a dismal treatise rouse and stir as life were in't."[1] His next speech is so famous we have diluted its pessimism, and as it has become part of the language, piece by piece, we have forgotten what a dire prediction it means. "Tomorrow, and tomorrow, and tomorrow, / Creeps in this petty pace from day to day, / To the last syllable of recorded time; / And all our yesterdays have lighted fools / The way to dusty death. Out, out, brief candle! / Life's but a walking shadow, a poor player / That struts and frets his hour upon the stage, / And then is heard no more. It is a tale / Told by an idiot, full of sound and fury, / Signifying nothing." Faulkner has reached into the bottom of the human pit for this: loss, grief, personal tragedy, disaster, the very abysses of human feeling.

Yet *Pylon* comes in what would appear to be a relatively calm period in Faulkner's life, belying the reliance on Macbeth's shriek of despair which finds its echo in Conrad's Kurtz and his "The horror, the horror." In some way, beyond the perceiver's eye, Faulkner was entering the valley in the shadow of death; and perhaps his depression and pessimism were not for "nothing," but his way of getting back into harness for *Absalom*.

The early part of 1935 was full of business schemes: the usual need to drum up income from one source or another, including loans. Smith arrived at Rowan Oak bearing gifts and corrected galleys to read over with his author. They also went over Faulkner's new story, "Golden Land." After Smith left, Faulkner told Goldman he felt he should diversify his sending out of stories, Smith having suggested *Cosmopolitan*: "As it is," he wrote, "I sell either to Scribners and Harpers for pittances [$200–300], or to the *Post* [$500–700, up to $900]." He says he has a line to *Cosmopolitan*: "I want to try it and see what comes of it. So suppose you recall Golden Land and give it to Smith and let him try his idea, as a test case. As you say, with its flavor of perversion, possibly the only magazine which will consider it and which will or can pay well, will be Cosmopolitan. . . . I want to see if I can establish a wellpaying alternative to the Post." "Golden Land," as we have seen, went not to *Cosmopolitan* but to Mencken's journal. In the same letter, however, Faulkner indicates he is "going to dope out another series for the *Post* and work on it right away."[2] Faulkner did not carry out this latter plan, unless "Lion" was part of that plan of a series of stories, somewhat like those for *The Unvanquished*, which would become *Go Down, Moses and Other Stories* (before he dropped the "stories" part and treated the interrelated parts as a novel).

"Golden Land" would never win any awards, and he was fortunate Mencken even took it; Faulkner also reprinted it in his *Collected Stories*. It is one of those second- or third-rate pieces which prove revelatory, not only for showing Hollywood as a golden wasteland, but for the shadowy way in which Faulkner illuminated a good deal about himself. The protagonist, Ira Ewing, is a real-estate man whose ego and personal needs have destroyed his family. His wife is completely alienated by his drinking and women, his son is a homosexual and unpleasant to boot, and his daughter, to further her film career, has become involved in sex orgies, and is currently on trial. Ewing retreats from the family mess which he has created by visiting his old mother every day. She wants to return to Nebraska where her roots are, but she is not permitted to go, since Ewing withholds money from her. While Ewing escapes to his forty-year-old mistress and fantasizes about much younger female bodies, his mother counts her coins, hoping to save enough for a return to Nebraska, the land of cold, away from Beverly Hills, the golden wasteland.

One of Ewing's ploys is to use his daughter's trial as a means of gaining publicity and business for himself. He "sells" the story of her scandal to a newspaper in exchange for thirty percent of the front page with his photograph, and a legend identifying him as president of the Ewing Realty Company, with its address. Ewing does not demonstrate one saving grace: he is a drunk, an adulterer, a man capitalizing on human misery, an enslaver of his wife and mother, a man who controls everything in the lives of those around him. A good deal of the story's weakness is linked to the sustained unpleasantness of the protagonist, and the lack of any redeeming force which would create contrast or opposition. Faulkner's perception of Beverly Hills—by analogy, Hollywood—is of inexorable corruption.

But if we move behind the Beverly Hills/Hollywood locale to the human issues implicit in the social context, we see outlines of Faulkner's own fears, anxieties, and assessment of himself. The story is a screed of self-hatred. He is taking himself apart for his work in Hollywood; going further, he is measuring the corruption implied in every step which is not creative. His self-hatred for his Hollywood role goes further than a man seeking redemption for having sinned; he is fighting off the sense he has entered a death situation. Hollywood or Beverly Hills is a wasteland, a citadel of death.

The impermanence of the place, its ability to be washed away, is juxtaposed with the Nebraska of the Ewings' origins. In Southern California, the very sun, heat, and light are forms of death; in Nebraska, in contrast, the numbing cold and snow are aspects of life. All values are based on paradox, all lives exist on the edge of deception. At the beach, Ewing observes the bronzed, unselfconscious bodies of the young girls, and he perceives how the world is organized:

Lying so [the young bodies], they seemed to him to walk along the rim of the world as though they and their kind alone inhabited it, and he with his forty-eight years [Faulkner was a decade younger] were the forgotten last survivor of another race and kind, and they in turn precursors of a new race not yet seen on earth: of men and women without age, beautiful as gods and goddesses, and with the minds of infants.[3]

This passage illuminates Faulkner's revilement of himself for going there, and how self-hatred welled up at the thought that he, a heavy drinker, a deserter of wife and daughter, a man approaching middle age but attracted to young women and soon to start a liaison with one, a serious writer selling his wares at a far lesser value—that in all this, he was approaching Ira Ewing.

There is another dimension only touched upon. With the mother not too different from Maud Falkner (who came out to California and then yearned to return to Oxford) and with Ewing's wife bitter and distant (as Estelle could be)—with these considerations, we must evaluate the extreme hostility Ewing shows toward his children. The young son and young daughter bring us back not to Jill but to Faulkner's stepchildren, Malcolm and Victoria (Cho-Cho). They were still developing—Victoria would be sixteen in 1935, Malcolm or Mac eleven going on twelve by the end of the year. Ewing demonstrates considerable anger and hostility toward his offspring, who became monsters through his treatment of them—supporting them lavishly, but providing no moral guidance, remaining distant through drink, work, and womanizing.

In February successive letters to Smith and Goldman are full of plans and strategies for making money to gain "two months to work at the novel before ... [he has] to boil the pot again." "Golden Land" will be his partial salvation, for he hopes Goldman "can gouge somebody for a thousand...."[4] He strongly opposes a facsimile publication of The Marionettes, his one-act play from 1920, something Centaur Press was interested in doing. He also declined to do a nonfiction piece on the Mississippi River, although later he wrote a very moving piece on Mississippi. His argument against the river book was that he was a novelist, "people first, where second." He says doing a book like that would be a sort of holiday, and when he takes a holiday he "damned sure wont spend it writing." He plans an "air story" for Cosmopolitan, or else he will try to "hang something" on the Post. Vanity Fair wrote him for a "lynching article," but he says he "never saw a lynching and so couldn't describe one." These February letters indicate that if he had wanted to, there were a dozen ways he could pick up extra money, but by postponing his novels. Although Hollywood created a sidetracking, it was a self-contained unit; he went out, worked on more-or-less meaningless projects, made his money, and returned home. Also, Hollywood gave him that break with Oxford and family he needed. It was almost the perfect alternative, whereas journalistic ventures writing about the Old Man or a lynching had no quality of release or escape; more of the same, only on a lower level of intensity.

The Falkner family gained another writer in Johncy, who was knocking about without too much to do and without any clear goals. Johncy was a hard-drinking man, someone trying to catch up to two hard-driving elder brothers. He had written some stories for his son Chooky, then seven, and he asked Maud Falkner to help him enlist the aid of his writing brother to get them in shape. The collection of stories, *Chooky*, which did not find a publisher until 1950, was not Faulkner's kind of thing. But on reading them over he offered to sign his name also—although, on reflection, he said that would do John's career no good. The stories were submitted to the *Post* and promptly rejected as unsuitable; the angry Faulkner then withdrew and put his brother in touch with Goldman. Johncy's first novel, *Men Working*, appeared six years later.

During a letter of explanation to Goldman (on March 9), in which Faulkner distinguished between what his agent should handle (stories and "magazine stuff") and what he and Smith should handle (novels and film rights), he indicated he was at work on "another novel now."[5] This was, apparently, not "another novel," but *Absalom*; for just three weeks later he placed the date (March 30) on the first page of the final manuscript and started to send the novel chapter by chapter to Smith. It is also possible his composition of "Lion" was, in his mind, the beginning of still another novel, what eventually became *Go Down, Moses*. In the previous month, Smith and Haas had given Faulkner an advance of $2,000 on *Absalom*, a pitiful sum in contemporary terms, but not negligible in 1935.

Faulkner also told Goldman he was dissatisfied with Smith. ". . . I do believe I can make more money through someone else. That is, I am not exactly satisfied. This in absolute confidence, of course. I am coming East in the fall and get myself straightened out." He says he will try to get an offer elsewhere and then see if Smith can match it, but only after he tells the latter what he is doing. ". . . I cannot and will not go on like this. I believe I have got enough fair literature in me yet to deserve reasonable freedom from bourgeoise [sic] material petty impediments and compulsion, without having to quit writing and go to the moving pictures every two years." He adds: "The trouble about the movies is not so much the time I waste there but the time it takes me to recover and settle down again; I am 37 now and of course not as supple and impervious as I once was."[6]

But in thinking of skipping to another publisher even in the face of Smith's loyalty, Faulkner was not demonstrating ingratitude, but survival. The literary landscape was littered with serious authors abandoned by publishers for marketplace reasons. As an overpowering talent, Faulkner was a bankable commodity for reasons of prestige and as a hedge on the future. He was literature itself, as both Smith and Cerf recognized. But other authors who were not so exalted were abandoned; publishers could be as brutal as sports teams which drop or sell players when they falter. A few editors, like Maxwell Perkins at Charles Scribner's Sons, gained intense loyalty from their authors; but in most cases, editors shifted positions, and an author who started a book with one could see two or three materialize before the book was published. In these circumstances, loyalty was foolhardy. Faulkner, then, was not abandoning Smith, nor showing ingratitude: he was merely playing the publishing game, and he was being honorable in informing Smith what he planned to do before doing it.

Faulkner's financial needs were huge measured in depression terms. As he wrote Goldman in April, he wanted $10,000 to settle debts, insurance, bills, and peace of mind. He did not mention he had an opportunity to buy more land, Bailey's Woods, which lay just outside the Rowan Oak grounds. If he had failed to purchase this acreage—for $500 down in cash and another $1,000 at five percent, payable at $100 plus interest annually—then Rowan Oak would have on its borders, hunters, picnickers, passersby. He found himself in a bind, since his very conception of Rowan Oak had been to obtain privacy.

Several short stories derive from this March–April period: "Lion," "That Will Be Fine," and "Uncle Willy." He also brushed off several oldies, "Moonlight," from his earliest days, and "The Brooch," which would only appear in his *Collected Stories*. As he told Goldman in April (or so), he was "writing two stories a week now. I don't know how long I can keep it up. This makes six or seven." As we shall see, this did not relieve the financial pressure, and later in July he informed his agent he would have to sell his manuscripts to avoid bankruptcy, with loss of home and insurance. It was becoming clear, even in the spring, when he had hopes the stories could save him, that salvation would come only from that corrupt golden land, offering a total of $8,000, almost precisely the sum he needed to get by.

"Lion," an avatar of "The Bear" in *Go Down, Moses*, was perhaps the furthest extreme in Faulkner's world from "Golden Land." These two stories stand at opposite ends, each denying the efficacy of the other. But it is a mistake to interpret "Lion" as representing his ideal world, and "Golden Land" as representing his revelation of hell. "Lion" and all stories like it do represent one validation of Faulkner; but "Golden Land," despite its nightmarish qualities, also represents something: that bourgeois acquisition of property and goods which he condemns in the story but which was a necessary part of his own life. In one respect, "Lion" reveals the fantasy of a little boy and young man (of sixteen), a world generated by James Fenimore Cooper and Faulkner's own early years with a gun in the woods. This is, despite discomforts, dirt, bad odors, poor food, an Edenic world—the Garden, untouched by man, part of the original plan God or nature had for man. But it is a fantasy, a specter—it begins to vanish as a reality once one grows up; and the reality or what passes for it blends into the adult fantasy which keeps it alive. Against that is the traducing of all civilized behavior in "Golden Land," and yet reality lies there, only exaggerated, a noisome image of what man can become. Faulkner had a horror of extremes, disorder, personal disorganization, although in his drinking he paid periodic homage to that wild world. Nevertheless, he was able to generate such self-hatred in his California story because he recognized so much of that world in himself, or at least its potential.

"Lion" is part of that classic hunting world Faulkner could periodically bring forth. A strong piece in itself, it became classic in the revisions of "The Bear." Here the emphasis is on two forces, the part mastiff Lion, and the part Chickasaw Boon Hogganbeck. Each is massive, each has eyes which are depthless. They are simply instruments for seeing, neither generous nor mean; each creature moves through time as though it had no more meaning than air. The story focuses on how a sixteen-year-old boy grows up in deer camp, how he responds to the tales of Old Ben, the great bear which has eluded generations of hunters, how he reacts to men intent on trapping Old Ben this one day of the year when Major de Spain has them out to his hunting camp.

In the center of this "recognition" scene are Boon and Lion. Both of these are "beyond." As their physical description indicates, they have moved into a world of their own making, the man and animal in a kinship of dedicated purpose. Lion's goal is to hold Old Ben at bay while the hunters shoot him, and Boon's function is to make sure Lion does his job without getting killed. Boon is one of Faulkner's half-man, half-animal creations. A giant of a man (six feet four inches), he has a face which only a walnut approximates: ". . . as if somebody had found a walnut a little smaller than a basket ball and with a machinist's hammer had shaped the features of the face and then painted it, mostly red."[7] Part of the red comes from Indian, but most from whiskey and from a violent and vigorous out-of-doors life. Except for his loyalty to Major de Spain, his is an unfathomable character. Lion is also unfathomable, a huge dog whom nobody owned. "Lion was like the chiefs of Aztec and Polynesian tribes who were looked upon as being not men but both more and less than men." The dog is pure hunter, which becomes in Faulkner's hands a designation somewhere outside man or animal. The entire story strains for some metaphysical level, an analogy to the hunt. Old Ben is a legendary bear, Boon a fathomless man, Lion a dog shaped only for the hunt, the men at the camp having reached beyond themselves as hunters. In the stands, waiting for Old Ben, or seeking the bear in the woods, the men achieve what Lion stands for, "an immeasurable capacity not only for courage and skill and will to pursue and kill, but for endurance, the will to endure beyond any imaginable limit."

The boy is assigned a stand and given a gun. "I could smell the solitude, the loneliness, something breathing out of this place which human beings had merely passed through without altering it, where no axe or plow had left a scar, which looked exactly as it had when the first Indian crept into it and looked around, arrow poised and ready." This time and place reaches back to join *that* time and place, the era Edenic, the moment epiphanic and revelatory. A boy grows up in this situation, the experience an awakening *to what the world can be because of what it once was.* The moment holds, and it becomes an experience that remains for a lifetime. The romantic Faulkner is reaching beyond here, going much further than he had in "A Bear Hunt," where the woods were a backdrop for an amusing tale. Here we have entered the hunt as a shaping experience which reaches deeply into magical moments. Boon is badly injured by Old Ben as he drives his knife deep into the bear's chest, and Lion is raked so badly his entrails are opened up. The wounded Boon will not let himself be nursed until he can try to save Lion, but the dog dies silently, uncomplaining.

The next summer the boy returns, but change has already occurred. "They [the woods] were changed, different," and when he thinks it is only seasonal change, he perceives he is wrong: ". . . they would never again be as I remembered them, as any of us remembered them."[8] Now he knows why Major de Spain will never return. The experience is unique, and since one cannot reachieve it, as de Spain knows, then everything else is diminished. This, too, the boy must learn. The final image is of Boon smashing his gun into fragments, his face wild, his helpless fury gripping every part of him. For the story, Faulkner had reached deep into his own sense of woods, the hunting trips into General Stone's camp, and re-creation of legendary tales, this one with Old Ben, missing three toes on one paw, indestructible, with dozens of bullets in him. Old Ben is the very spirit of the woods, the quarry who cannot be cornered and finished off; and Lion represents the perfect hunter, greater than man and perhaps only approached by Boon.

There is less ambiguity about civilization here than in *Pylon*. In the novel Faulkner found himself representing several ambiguities; but in "Lion," it is the immutable moment in the woods which represents the deepest reaches of man's achievement. Faulkner of course realized how transitory it was; but if one had the experience just once, it served as a measure for the rest of one's life. The hunt becomes, then, like the creative revelation of the artist, that moment when everything coheres and makes sense; in that deep reach, the artist finds the means to forge his tools.

"Lion" recalls Hemingway at his finest, in those "pure" early stories where everything is clarified by the pristine moment. But the other stories Faulkner wrote at about this time—"That Will Be Fine," "Uncle Willy," and "The Brooch"—are journeyman work, without the dense intrusion of self which makes "Lion" so intense.

Continuing with another short fiction, Faulkner produced the undistinguished "Uncle Willy," which he was also fortunate to have accepted by the *American Mercury* (for October). Once again we have an attempt at humor with a ne'er-do-well, a fourteen-year-old's beloved Uncle Willy. Alongside "That Will Be Fine," this story can be labeled country corn, something below a tall tale, which has the virtue of concision and compactness. As if Faulkner calculated that his market needed twenty pages, "Uncle Willy" is drawn out. The idea is a sound one: how a boy is affected by an older man who has chosen to live completely outside the limits of his community, first by injecting dope into himself for forty years, then turning to liquor, and finally by getting hold of an airplane and crashing it rather than conforming to social and religious standards.

These short fictions were nostalgic trips for Faulkner, and they suggest, by turning them out rapidly in order to generate income, that he was running out of material. The imaginative component in the stories is small, the invention flaccid, and the development busy rather than trenchant. Except for "Lion," there is no density, and no sense of a story welling up; only a sense of fictions growing out of a professional writer's need of production.

Another story from this period was "Moonlight," which goes back to Faulkner's earliest efforts, perhaps, in short fiction: 1919–20. The story had several lives before he rewrote it and sent it on to Goldman for sale, he hoped, to the *Post* or *Scribner's*. Even though rewritten after rejection at least twice (at *Scribner's*, in the later 1920s), "Moonlight" is flimsy stuff indeed, and a clear sign of Faulkner's monetary desperation. It remained unpublished, not even included in his *Collected Stories*. It does fit, however, into the general pattern of stories coming forward in the spring of 1935. For it too works with the theme of escape—that intense need to escape conventional behavior in a return to youth, or in activities which defy bourgeois life.

One more story derives from this time, "Fool About a Horse," which *Scribner's* took (for August 1936), after the *Post* rejected it. The story has a long and involved history inasmuch as it exists in several stages of development. The typescript at the University of Virginia indicates a piece of work far more intricately wrought than the story Faulkner eventually published in *Scribner's*. Then the *Scribner's* version was itself further revised for inclusion in *The Hamlet* (book 1, chapter 2, part 2). One of the major differences between typescript and magazine and book versions comes in the use of narrators. Faulkner originally wrote a far more self-consciously told story than the one *Scribner's* accepted and published. Then for *The Hamlet*, he shifted characters' names and accommodated the piece to the Snopeses, as befitting the trilogy.[9] The story in *Scribner's* has as its center the legendary trading powers of Pat Stamper and the deception of Suratt, the father of the Suratt who becomes Ratliff in *The Hamlet*. The story is related by an unnamed narrator, who must have gotten it from the Suratt boy, then twelve, when the transactions between his father and Pat Stamper took place. In all, the short fiction works as a kind of "down home" work, part tall tale, part country-bumpkin comedy, part rural wisdom, and part masculine foolhardiness.

Just on the eve of publication of *Pylon* (March 25), Faulkner found his center was not holding. He had worked hard to find his way financially and had apparently failed, as he was bound to with a series of substandard short fictions. He began to drink, and his mother became worried. A long bout meant that he could not work and that he would need recovery time. Yet his drinking was part of an obvious sequence, surely part of that escape motif we have already noted and linked to his need for a periodic rejection. With his career on the edge of greatness, he was a man gratified by writing, but requiring diversion from what seemed insurmountable problems. He stopped short, however, of a long-term binge.

This apparently did not prevent him from trying to fly, although we have no evidence he ever went up while drinking heavily. Dean Faulkner and Omlie were still barnstorming in the Memphis area, even as reviews which memorialized their existence started to come in. Most reviews from Southerners indicated distaste for the novel, with John Crowe Ransom predicting "Faulkner is spent"—this on the eve of *Absalom*, followed by *The Wild Palms* and *Go Down, Moses*. Hemingway, on the other hand, always a generous reader when it came to Faulkner, extolled *Pylon* in the June *Esquire*. The local pundit, Moon Mullen, who did so much to undermine Faulkner's Oxford reputation, weighed in with his folksy admission that Faulkner's new novel was unintelligible to him and added nothing to his literary stature.[10]

But the appearance of *Pylon* on his desk, the reviews, even the very world of aviation and barnstorming all became secondary matters as Faulkner moved into the writing, rewriting, and run to the finish of *Absalom*. On March 30 he wrote the title on the manuscript piled before him. It came from Second Samuel, and he says that as soon "as I thought of the idea of the man who wanted sons and the sons destroyed him, then I thought of the title."[11] Many of Faulkner's problems with *Absalom*—and probably the reason why he put it aside so frequently—were connected to methods of telling. He had to devise a means by which the transmission of information about Sutpen and his enterprise became not only a matter of narration but the story itself; the novel became so dense and complex because Faulkner wanted to embed the narrative means, the act of transmission, into the narrative itself. Although he did not use Joycean techniques of interior monologue, his purpose was often the same: to make monologue or telling indistinguishable from what is told. He had started out with Quentin receiving a letter from Mr. Compson describing Rosa Coldfield's final days; this letter was sent to Cambridge, Massachusetts, where Quentin is rooming with Shreve, the Canadian. But Faulkner realized the letter created an interiority to the story which had not been established by any context. Also, he came to recognize he had to establish the terms so that Quentin could relate the material to Shreve: "Shreve was the commentator that held the thing to something of reality. If Quentin had been let alone to tell it, it would have become completely unreal. It had to have a solvent to keep it real, keep it believable, creditable, otherwise it would have vanished into smoke and fury."

In the papers from Rowan Oak at the University of Mississippi John Davis Williams Library is a rough working draft of the novel as it evolved. The sketch is quite rudimentary, but it apparently provided Faulkner with the basic directions he needed. In the same lecture in which he commented on Shreve, he says he put the rough draft down because he didn't feel "passionate enough or pure enough" about it, but that when he took it up again "I almost rewrote the whole thing. I think that what I put down were inchoate fragments that wouldn't coalesce and then when I took it up again, as I remember, I rewrote it." The brief sketch helped, for it shows a clear line of transmission of material; what remained for Faulkner was to latch onto his method of telling so that it included the major elements of the interior story. Faulkner was struggling to achieve, in this his own war and peace, a blending of technical means, race, and dimensions of pastness and history.

The sketch is a circuit of information, with a Charles (not Thomas) Sutpen at the top of a double-headed arrow pointing between him and General Compson. Then lines come down both sides, from Charles Sutpen to Rosa Coldfield and from General Compson to Mr. Compson. At the bottom between Rosa Coldfield and Mr. Compson are lines connecting both to Quentin Compson. The sketch reveals an interesting development in that Sutpen and Quentin are both hooked up, as if by lifelines, to those around them, so that we can see a linkage which makes them secret sharers of sorts, one demonic and historical, the other humanistic and contemporary. Although the sketch is very crude, Faulkner has reached into his sense of pastness. Next to Sutpen is the comment that he had come to Jefferson, married Ellen, fathered two children, ruined their lives; that Rosa is sixty, an old maid, and "tells" Quentin, twenty-one, who becomes the thread. Mr. Compson's role is to tell Quentin, and General Compson's role before that had been to tell his son, Mr. Compson. A tale of fathers and sons recalls Faulkner's archetype, the Biblical story of David and his sons, Amnon and Absalom. Amnon becomes Bon; Tamar, with whom he has committed incest, is Judith; Absalom is Henry. The sketch illustrates that the problem was transmission and communication, a point Faulkner had to emphasize if his historical sense was to be established.

Absalom was to be nothing less than Faulkner's great historical novel, coming at about the same time as Margaret Mitchell's *Gone With the Wind*, a vastly more popular attempt to illuminate the past. It was not at all unusual that two such different writers should approach the Civil War, since the years of the Great Depression had turned American society in general and Southern society in particular back upon himself. The Mitchell novel proved immensely popular because it turned history into spectacle, and into romantic emblems of the past—attractive to a country which had fallen on bad days. Its function was heuristic. It made the war seem gallant, and it bypassed all the insidious aspects of slavery, race, and injustice that preceded the war and went into its making. By sidestepping the real issues and turning the past into Scarlett O'Hara, Rhett Butler, and Tara, Mitchell had the equivalent of the great musical comedies which were captivating audiences on the screen. Her settings were no less appealing than the Busby Berkeley settings for Fred Astaire and Ginger Rogers's extravaganzas: she provided escape, romantic fantasy, release from the ordinary.

Faulkner's sense of the past was precisely the opposite, although also heuristic. The past was not romantic—not when it could be embodied in a man like Thomas Sutpen. The issues were race and history, and the South was not only defeated, but morally corrupt. The Union victory, moreover, was a hollow one, and all one could point to as the resolution of the struggle between the states was deterioration, decline, collapse, disaster.* Faulkner's aim was not to present this as fact, but to have it become the consciousness of Quentin, a young man attempting in 1909 to understand the past, *his* past. The distinction is crucial. To present it as a fact, as a given, would mean a one-dimensional appraisal of what had happened; to incorporate the events into consciousness by making Sutpen and then Quentin half a century later into secret sharers was to create a sense of history, a theory of the past. Quentin can share in Sutpen's quest for respectability, his role in building a certain kind of South, his yearning to make something of himself, and his destruction of himself through pride and selfishness. In that area of Quentin's consciousness, Faulkner could find his perception of the conscience of the South; and in Quentin's inability to know whether he loves or hates the South, Faulkner could find the sole way in which one could relate to the region, indeed to the country. The combinations and permutations of these views involved a literary effort as complex as the views themselves. Faulkner set himself nothing less than a refutation of all those views which appeared in a novel like *Gone With the Wind*: hoopskirts, balls, flouncing, and romance. He headed in the opposite direction: not Scarlett O'Hara preserving Tara through strength of will, but Judith

---

*In "A Return," a 1938 rewriting of a story started in 1930, Faulkner writes of a South caught between reality and fantasy, one theme of *Absalom:*

> It [what happened to the Gordon family in the war] was just one of the thousand repetitions through the South during that year and the next two, not of actual suffering yet but merely that attenuation of hardship, that unceasing demand upon endurance without hope or even despair—that excruciating repetition which is Tragedy's tragedy, as if Tragedy had a childlike faith in the efficacy of the plot simply because it had worked once—an economic system which had outlived its place in time, a land empty of men who rode out of it not to engage a mortal enemy as they believed but to batter themselves to pieces against a force with which they were unequipped by both heredity and inclination to cope and of which those whom they charged and counter-charged were not champions as much as victims too; armed with convictions and beliefs a thousand years out of date they galloped gallantly behind the bright bunting of a day and vanished, not in battle-smoke but beyond the irrevocable curtain-fall of an era. . . . Some of them returned to be sure, but they were shadows, dazed, bewildered and impotent, creeping back onto the darkened stage where the old tale had had its way and surfeited . . . (*Uncollected Stories of William Faulkner*, ed. Joseph Blotner [New York: Vintage Books, 1981, orig. pub. 1979], pp. 551–52).

"A Return" has a tortuous history of its own, as a revision of material in "Rose of Lebanon," itself rejected for publication in 1930 and 1931. It plays in and out of 1930s events, even recalling the death of the Reverend Gail Hightower's grandfather in *Light in August*. In 1938 Faulkner had no better luck in trying to publish the much reworked material as "A Return." Various versions and fragments exist in the Rowan Oak papers at the University of Mississippi and at the University of Virginia Faulkner collections.

Sutpen overseeing the downfall of Sutpen's Hundreds, hostage to her father's mad plans for himself and for the South.

By the time Faulkner came to the novel, he had Wash Jones in place; in that story, he had also fixed upon Sutpen. He had the pivotal motive in Sutpen, his having gone to the big house and been turned away by the Negro servant. In a 1957 questioning from the English Club at the University of Virginia, as to whether Sutpen lost his individuality or gained respectability, Faulkner replied at length:

He wanted more than that. He wanted revenge as he saw it, but also he wanted to establish the fact that man is immortal, that man, if he is man, cannot be inferior to another man through artificial standards or circumstances. What he was trying to do—when he was a boy, he had gone to the front door of a big house and somebody, a servant, said, Go around to the back door. He said, I'm going to be the one that lives in the big house, I'm going to establish a dynasty, I don't care how, and he violated all the rules of decency and honor and pity and compassion, and the fates took revenge on him. That's what the story was. But he was trying to say in his blundering way that, why should a man be better than me because he's richer than me, that if I had the chance I might be just as good as he thinks he is, so I'll make myself as good as he thinks he is by getting the same outward trappings which he has, which was a big house and servants in it. He didn't say, I'm going to be braver or more compassionate or more honest than he— he just said, I'm going to be as rich as he was, as big as he was on the outside.[12]

Faulkner's way of interpreting the novel on these grounds is compelling; for he simplified the lines of the book in order to stress the revenge motif, the sense of injury in Sutpen which leads to his actions. So much of this winds back to Faulkner himself—not in any definitive way, but in the way he was turned away from the Oldham house, in the way he spent all those years in penury and oblivion while he honed his talents, while he buried himself and his talent and waited for it to grow. There is in this explanation an attempt to resolve personal problems: to see in the acquisition of goods the effort to revenge oneself on the past, and yet to perceive in that the way in which the self is destroyed. Faulkner is exalting pride and yet demonstrating how destructive it can be; and he is revealing how that aspect of the South—and, by implication, the country —is destructive on the larger scale. The South's situation—fantasizing the past, distorting history to apologize for itself, using emblems of victory to disguise defeat—are all part of Sutpen's spirit of revenge. By simplifying what the novel was to become, Faulkner drove home the personal dimension, what was meaningful to him in this quest for historical truth.

The chief factor which determines the outcome of the narrative is race.* Of what are usually deemed Faulkner's three key novels, *Sound, Light in August,* and *Absalom,* all have strong racial overtones, and the latter two dominantly so. *Absalom* moves in and out of racial issues from pre–Civil War days to 1909, when Quentin is relating his story—thus it bridges one of the most significant eras in American history. As its core, the novel focuses on attitudes toward race which themselves determine the outcome of the book, which fuel and nourish narrative. Further, the chief narrator is himself shredded by race, although not exclusively by that; and his desire to make his college roommate, Shreve, understand the South is in part the need to explain something about race which cannot quite be explained.

This much can be granted. Yet while *Absalom* moves on several levels —social, historical, and personal—it comes at race through secret passageways, by means of hiding necessary information and by using divulgence as a psychological weapon. As a detective story of sorts, it is also a tone poem, employing colors and shadings as a vehicle for thematic material; this is for Faulkner a way of both presenting and commenting on race. What we must consider is not the obvious point that racial matters are the stuff of this novel, but that such matters are buried in dark rooms, attics, enclosures, and most of all in words. To extrapolate race we must extract virtually the entire metaphorical meaning of the novel. In one sense, we can say race *has been absorbed into technique.* But the matter is even more complicated, for Faulkner has also absorbed race into history, and into a particular view of history. History, in this respect, becomes part of technique; it is "created history," process more than fact. Race lies in *there,* in the creative process itself.

The method of narrating the novel, as a modified stream of consciousness, underlies racial matters. For by turning everything into subjective, personalized data—the data of the novel remain buried in commentaries which may or may not be accurate—the novelist has provided a strategical commentary on race itself. It becomes an element which can be approached only from a private point of view, having no substantial qualities beyond those perceived by the holder or speaker. Race is, in a sense, held hostage to the perception of the beholder. It is the great hidden metaphor, the secret god at the center of totem and taboo.

*Eric Sundquist makes the suggestive comment that, on matters of race, "there is an analogy between Lincoln and Sutpen, each of whom labors heroically to build or preserve a magnificent 'house' symbolic of his national and personal dream, and both of whom, at about the same time, face a crisis in the house and try desperately to postpone it. . . . It is not by any means an analogy in which they or their designs are exactly duplicated but, rather, one in which they are mirror images in the sense that a mirror image reverses the figure to which it corresponds. . . . In remarkable counterpoint to his prominent statements of white supremacy, Lincoln's troubled devotion to equality is everywhere evident in his speeches, and his rise from humble origins to heroic magnificence, like Sutpen's rise, dramatizes the dream denied to an entire race of Americans for close to a century after the signing of those documents—a dream redeemed into a promise by Lincoln and others but broken and betrayed, for nearly another century, by those judiciously read in the thought of the fathers and devoted to perpetuating their visionary design" (Eric Sundquist, *Faulkner: The House Divided* [Baltimore: Johns Hopkins University Press, 1983], pp. 105–6).

Absalom moves toward forbidden areas by way of a method which disallows divulgation. The narrative transforms what has occurred into a totem, and it transmogrifies Sutpen into a mythical figure who challenges explanation in ordinary language. History, Sutpen, events—all of these have something of the qualities Faulkner associated with racial resonances between black and white, a Caravaggio canvas. Race arises out of shadows, caves, labyrinths. It is part of Sutpen's past, and it brings Charles Bon into the family not only as future member but as the racial "other half." Yet the physical presence of Bon is not so important as is the textured shadow of the young man, the past as racial avatar. He is the forbidden, the tabooed object, the nasty myths turned into flesh; and his presence begins to dominate the novel less than one-quarter through, although we barely see him. His figure then hovers over the entire novel, which while it doesn't seem to be about him is, in actuality, almost always about him.* If Faulkner is re-creating the felt texture of Greek drama or an Elizabethan revenge play, then the "American ingredient," so to speak, is race: race and family intertwined, all cast into shadows and depths and enclosures, the contemporary equivalent of the early myths.

History moves through the novel in similar twists. As Faulkner comes at race by way of metaphors of disguise and enclosure, so he comes at history; and the two, race and history, cannot be disentangled. While history in *Absalom* is as real as race, it is presented not in its reality, but in its literary dimension as metaphor, as image. Everything appears in the form of something else, as if the novel were itself a gigantic syntactical litotes. When Henry and Bon go to New Orleans for the first time, Bon preparing him for what New Orleans means to a young man with a mistress-wife and child, Faulkner presents a brief history lesson in terms of sex, class, caste, and race. In speaking of Bon's octoroon mistress and child, he meanders into what kind of women are available to a Southern gentleman; and here history, social status, sex, and race become intermixed. There are the virgins one marries; there are the courtesans one visits when in cities; and there are the slave girls—field hands and housemaids, who are accessible and cannot say no. Everything is here, and it is presented as a very complex subculture, which is history as shaped by sexual need, by racial presence, by class and caste considerations. Behind it all is even economics, since marriage to a virgin ensures one's lines of descent; and it is also political, inasmuch as such a vision preserves white supremacy in all major areas: sexual, racial, social, economic.

---

*Race also mixes with manhood. Bon uses his race as a way of forcing Sutpen to recognize his manhood. It is only by insisting on marriage to Judith, which Sutpen cannot permit because of Bon's part-Negro blood, that the latter can "gain" his father's acknowledgment. That this acknowledgment means the young man's death only intensifies his need for recognition. A parallel situation comes in Quentin's "confession" to *his* father that he has committed incest with Candace. In both instances, incest is intertwined with father-son relationships and the need for some recognition. (John T. Irwin's *Doubling and Incest/Repetition and Revenge* [Baltimore: The Johns Hopkins University Press, 1975] provides a superb reading of analogous and interrelated elements.)

Almost in the center of the book, as a kind of archstone, Faulkner presents one of the many "returns" or duplications which display history as both accretion and flow. Incidentally, many of the points established here had already been made in *Light in August*, where Joe Christmas has foreshadowed the son of Charles Bon. Clytie goes to seek the twelve-year-old boy, finds him in New Orleans, and returns with him on a steamboat. The boy is part-Negro, the result of an octoroon mother (one-eighth Negro) and a part-Negro father, Charles Bon, and is, of course, considered Negro. On the boat, Clytie (half-white) and the light-skinned, almost white boy sleep on deck with the Negroes. When they arrive at Sutpen's Hundred, Judith tells him to call her "Aunt Judith," while he is put under the care of Clytie, who has herself shared in the household as half-sister. Clytie is Sutpen's daughter, the boy is Sutpen's grandson and Judith's nephew; Judith is half-sister to Clytie and the bereaved of the part-Negro Charles Bon, who was the best friend and potential brother-in-law of his murderer, Henry Sutpen, who is put up to the killing by their joint father, Sutpen. All these crosscurrents of relationships are apparent to anyone who reads the book, but if we examine them in the light of race, we note that Faulkner approached the subject as much by blending as by distinctions.

When the boy grows up, as an act of scorn, mockery, self-hatred, or whatever, he marries a coal-black Negro, and has a part-white, dark son. This son is brought up at Sutpen's Hundred, chiefly by half-white Clytie. To add to the racial dimension, the grown boy, Charles Etienne, contracts yellow fever which he transmits to his great-aunt Judith, who nurses him in the big house; she dies before he does from the jointly held fever. Thus it is indirectly race which kills Bon (murdered by Henry when he learns his friend is part-Negro and plans to marry Judith), which is then counterbalanced, as it were, when Bon's son kills "Aunt Judith" with contagious fever. If the play of events is perceived as tragic and not as melodramatic, then the tragic ingredient is not Sutpen's hubris, but race itself: race as embedded in historical practice.

Race comes to us so formed by other forces that it cannot be disentangled. Further pressing them together so that elements are indistinguishable from each other is narrative, presented as a kind of modified stream. The stream is in itself a form of history, since it suggests a flow which makes past and present into elements of a single experience. One of the themes of *Absalom* is, of course, that past and present join, flow, remain intertwined. History is not simply past for Faulkner; therefore, the substance of history—sexual matters, class, caste, race—has no clear beginning in time or demarcation one from the other. What we are claiming for the novel here is that while such a momentous question as race is affected by Faulkner's sense of history, it is influenced even more by his method of presenting that history with particular narrative strategies. Accordingly, we have not only the modified stream, we have that stream influenced by the use of speakers, who direct and redirect the words which make the stream flow.

If history is subjective, as much speculation as fact, then race is part of that same mind-set, all of it intensified by the particularities of transmission. Racial matters, then, are indistinguishable from narrative sequences, for each transmission of information derives from someone with a racial view different from the one receiving it. General Compson and Mr. Compson appear to have standard racial views as men of their day; but the information they receive from Sutpen and dispense is not representative. Since nothing about Sutpen is standardized, we wonder how much has been distorted. Similarly, information about Sutpen also comes from Rosa Coldfield, who is herself traditional in every respect. Faulkner depicts her as the epitome of the Southern lady, disgusted by the close living of white and black in the Sutpen household. While the material she funnels to Quentin comes with traditional racial attitudes, he is already of a generation breaking from tradition and history, or at least caught on the edge of that break—it becomes his dilemma. The transmission of what is for him an archetypal Southern story, with its tragic racial consequences, involves the very memories and historical sense he cannot deal with—he shivers, he cries out, he must, like the Ancient Mariner, tell his story. Shreve, who is the final recipient of information in this complicated daisy chain, is not even an American, and as such has no connection to slavery, racial questions, or even the historical matrix in which race is presented.

For Faulkner, in this mélange of information and speculation, history remains outside definition, in the seams between subjective experience and objective phenomena. *Absalom* consists of several historical texts, whose primary momentum depends on the subjective use of words to understand one's relationship to past and present. Wherever history lies, it is driven by individualized narrative transmission; and embedded in all is race. In the primary text, Quentin's grandfather, father, Rosa Coldfield, and Bon's letter are forms of information funneled into Quentin, then into Shreve, and they tell the reader what happened. Yet what happened is always secondary to what it all means; words as well as narrators fail. What it means—history—is associated with Sutpen, and that aspect is part of the secondary text, in the seams of the primary, as it were. What Quentin is trying to explain to Shreve is nothing less than what the South is, and yet significance goes well beyond any of the details or events as described by relaying narrators; the true explanation, unachieved, lies in what Quentin cannot retrieve from all the words funneled into him. Meaning or history—and indirectly race—should be the culmination of language, but turns out to be embedded in silences between words, in spaces between lines, in seams between narrators.

Race, then, like history, becomes inseparable from telling. Faulkner achieved what the stream intends: that reflection of levels of consciousness which cannot be quite defined. Unlike other forms of interior monologue, the stream derives from an undiscriminated area, somewhere between unconscious and conscious. It is therefore an approximation in language of what is unreachable, and therefore a perfect transmitter of ideas of race as they rush from one generation to another. Before the Civil War, Southern history seemed to have moved slowly, with all generations bunched together; but after the war, the time scheme changed, and generations became demarked and moved in smaller time periods—not the twenty years assumed by the Bible, but in five- and ten-year spans. This speeding up was connected in part to race, and what could be a better means of catching this than use of the stream?

Yet even as Faulkner recognizes the irretrievability of what he is gathering and reflecting, he uses its indeterminacy to present information which, because of the transmission, must be suspect even as it is presented as fact. History becomes so untrustworthy in its transmission that Faulkner after only three pages of *Absalom* locates *his* voice just outside the voices of the narrators. He will be, we suspect, the "voice of truth," but it does not work that way at all, inasmuch as the Faulknerian voice becomes simply another form of dubious history. He cannot disentangle elements, and in that recognition of hopeless confusion, of straying thoughts, of motivations lying beyond explanation, of objectives which go beyond life itself—in all this, race, like history, resists language.

The two Quentins, the one in the past (the Quentin identified with Henry or with Bon), the one in the present (the Quentin "modernizing" himself at Harvard with Shreve), recall the two Marcels in Proust's novel; or else the two (or more) Jims in Conrad's *Lord Jim*: young men who live in multiple time frames and upset our very notions of time and history, of information received, of factual bases for anything. Such men and their voices decenter all data. Later we see how whole numbers and fractions in the text reinforce the idea of a nonverbal history and a decentered universe. These two Quentins move along with Faulkner's "over" voice and Rosa's different set of details. First, the interior narrative establishes the two Quentins, then Quentin takes over and in surges of italicized comments counterpoints Faulkner's voice; inserted into this is Rosa Coldfield's narrative of events, which nourishes Quentin's narrative and parallels Faulkner's. There is still another dimension, for Quentin responds to Rosa's remarks even as (in italics) he answers Shreve.

Narrative strategies in the revised text of the novel centralized the key sensibility in Quentin, and that is precisely where Faulkner has located the racial dilemma of *Absalom.* For the others, race is not so difficult to work through: for Sutpen, it counts mainly as something which cannot upset his grand design to establish himself; for Judith Sutpen, it does not seem a dominant factor—she lives with Clytie, would probably marry Bon whatever the makeup of his genes, and dies nursing Bon's son; for Henry, race becomes significant only when Bon insists on marrying Judith—otherwise, he accepts a half-Negro sister in Clytie and he embraces Bon as a friend. Only for Rosa Coldfield are Negroes still slaves, inferior creatures at the service of whites.

Henry's dilemma brings him into Quentin's orbit and makes them, historically, "brothers." They must confront the dilemma of how to respond to what the South demands when it runs counter to what they feel. Even more than Henry, however, Quentin is the one to embrace the full racial dilemma: the knowledge that the Negro should be equal and yet the feeling that for the white Southerner things are more complicated than that. His tirade at the end of the novel that he doesn't hate the South—"I dont. I dont! I dont hate it! I dont hate it!"—is a display of self-hatred, the result of his inability to link what his mind tells him with what his feelings are saying.

But there is more to it than this. One of the major themes, an offshoot of race, is lack of recognition: Sutpen goes unrecognized when he calls at the "big house" and is turned away by a Negro servant; Bon, according to Quentin's and Shreve's speculation, would give up marriage to Judith if only Sutpen recognized him, however slightly; Sutpen cannot recognize his first wife once he discovers she has some Negro blood; Bon does not recognize his first marriage when he considers bigamy. Yet even when this theme is traced out, which comes at every crucial turn, we see that such "lacks," whatever form they take, are linked to race and are part of a narrative which accentuates absence. The novel gains its intensity from a negative of contraries—a litotes which is best served by a technique which omits, skips, holds back, bottles up, and withdraws.

Faulkner may squirrel away, but the narrative method he employs to bring this about is all words, talk, and dialogue—what seems to be the very opposite of withholding. Yet words in this use of stream serve to disguise and shield—not as in detective fiction, where such disguises are connected to plot sequences, but as in more serious fiction where disguise is linked to character and to understanding. Once this occurs then all information coming through this method has a different life from what it would be in a more objectively framed fiction. On closer examination the verbal stream is revealed to also be a temporal stream; voices are divided into subtexts —the way information in an epistolary novel is divided among letter writers. That division means all significance will lie in secondary texts: those areas cutting between voices, not in the voices themselves. For the latter represent persons—whether Compsons or Rosa Coldfield—who play little or no role except as recipients of information. As characters (even Rosa as Sutpen's potential third wife), they serve to pass on what is necessary for our understanding; whereas the active arena lies elsewhere, beyond their words or action.

What is of consequence in *Absalom* lies in seams—not in what speakers say, not in the stream itself, but in what remains unsaid, what must be left to speculation. An entire area of Faulkner scholarship has grown up around trying to determine who knew what, and when, and how. What Faulkner has done is to bury the intense racial theme (and, by implication, the Southern theme) deep within those seams. He has bypassed questions of fairness, justice, and equality in favor of the historical and traditional role race played in a region which fought and died to preserve a way of life that cannot be glamorized because it included slavery. Faulkner's point, then, is not to present a balanced view, not to argue this advocacy or that, but to freeze a *possible* social and cultural context that created the condition. If we argue over who told whom what and when he did it or how he did it, we perform a valuable service, but also deny a method which presents history as ahistorical; which describes a society as asocial; and which defines a subculture as having its own frontiers.

In fact, there is still another stream, a nonverbal mathematical stream, and this form of narrative is also connected to matters of race. For example, at the beginning of part 3, the numbers intensify, even as the voices come at us. Their tale is of time. Rosa moves out to Sutpen's Hundred in 1864 (as embedded in Quentin's relaying, in 1909); Rosa was then twenty, four years younger than Judith, her niece; Rosa had been born in 1845 (which is, incidentally, sixty-four years before 1909, coinciding with the 1864 of her move to Sutpen's Hundred, itself ten by ten); when she was born, her sister had already been married for seven years, with two children; her mother was "at least" forty. So we have one level, the ages of twenty, four, seven, forty; then the level of dates, 1909 (the present), 1864, 1845; finally, the inferred ages, sixty-four for Rosa, unlisted for the children; and, overall, Sutpen's Hundred (ten by ten the original design).

Similarly, at the beginning of part 5, Rosa's grasp of fact becomes shaky, and her mind wanders in terms of numbers: the twelve miles she travels to Sutpen's Hundred, the two years since Ellen died, or was it four after Henry vanished? or nineteen since "I saw light and breathed?" Numbers are repeated: the reappearance of Henry after four years, the twelve miles Rosa rode, etc. This numerology is then associated, both directly and indirectly, with purely racial matters, when we begin to figure fractions of what makes one a Negro. Sutpen has married a woman whose family has deceived him about her background—as Bertha's family deceived Rochester in *Jane Eyre*—only here it is racial, some small fractional part of her which is not Spanish, but Negro.

Fractions serve as a kind of nonverbal history—a stream of its own making which, like so much else in the novel, moves beyond language. The diluted part, that fraction, dooms her son, Bon, when he seeks acceptance as a Sutpen. That same Bon marries an octoroon, one-eighth Negro, and has a son who is that fraction of Negro which derives from one-eighth Negro plus whatever fraction of Negro Bon is, if indeed he is. Further, Sutpen has Clytie by a Negro slave, which makes her half Negro; she is, also, half-sister to Henry and Judith, and, we may forget, half-sister to Bon, but a much greater fraction of black than he is. At issue when Bon wants to marry Judith is less that they are half-siblings than that diluted fraction of Negro blood. In many respects, as Shreve and Quentin reconstruct the confrontation scene between Henry and Bon, the life and death of the characters depend on fractions. It is ultimately fractions which destroy Sutpen's grand design. As Sutpen tells General Compson, he can let matters stand—let Bon marry Judith—but *he* will know his plan has been turned into mockery.

This fraction, then, will lead to Sutpen's own death, inasmuch as once he tells Henry about Bon—in the reconstruction of events in that Harvard dormitory—his first and second family will be destroyed and he will still need a viable heir. When he attempts this, his own death is foreshadowed, at Wash Jones's hands. The circumambient narrative, the secrecy of withholding of evidence, the squirreling away of fact, the use of a verbal and nonverbal numerological stream, all wind back to the racial theme, itself based on fractions; but internally, subjectively posed, without any substantial basis in actuality—nearly all speculation, reconstruction, a mental set. The question of race becomes a question of destruction. If we seek Faulkner's point about racial matters in the novel, we must conclude that he perceived race as heading toward suicide, murder, and doom. Sutpen, the man of will, the man of destiny in the American mold, has been doomed by race: that fractional element which has evaded his design. His desire to mold his adult life after the rebuff at the great house is collapsed by forces that he cannot comprehend or foresee, much less control.

One further point on the interlocking of race and method, of doom and withholding. Although about one-third through *Absalom* we possess all the facts we need to understand the dramatic situation, the problem is *we do not know* we have all the facts. A by-product of the narrative method and all the numbers and dates is our insecurity about what we already know, what we still have to learn, what later may be revealed. Information manipulates the reader until he is uncertain about what he controls, and experiences in this respect an inverted detective story: not too many details, but an insufficiency. This uncertainty is of course a correlative of the question of race, since the characters' apprehension is linked to what they know or do not know about the racial makeup of Bon, Sutpen's first wife, and others. If the characters settle for the surface information and seek no further, they preserve the amenities the culture demands; but if they probe in order to work out the puzzle, then they will discover the very elements of race which will destroy the surface, the design, the family itself.

In the pivotal scene in which when Henry shoots Bon, the action takes place in the deepest regions of the novel. It comes as reconstruction, as speculation, and it is cast almost entirely in pauses, what is left unsaid. It is a scene communicable only by silence. Yet everything meets here— history, personal experience, the quintessential Southern confrontation— and it comes to the reader from some primal region of consciousness. Faulkner has layered it between the conscious and the preconscious, so that it is history lying outside history, experience forming beyond experience.

Yet even as that terrible event is to take place, the narrative shifts from deep interiority to the external frame of Quentin and Shreve in their room at Harvard. The shot that kills Bon occurs not in this frame, but in the segment associated with the two college students, in the words of Shreve and the speculations of Quentin. Faulkner has refracted the event at least three times: first, as an event at which no witness was present; then to Quentin through a means which is never validated; finally, his words repeated and interpreted by Shreve, a foreigner. A Canadian, for whom the words have least meaning, is the messenger of this information; so that Faulkner has achieved filters, relayers within relayers. History comes to us as a deflected stream.

Quentin's sole response is "Yes," which superficially seems to acknowledge Shreve's view of why Bon switched Judith's picture in the metal case to that of the octoroon and their child. But the "Yes" is a more generalized response to the madness of the situation, to the lunatic history of the South, and, of course, directly to the racial issues underlying that madness. Yet it is all inevitable. One of the by-products of a stream technique is its quality of inevitability; since the stream is subjective, it is final. There can be no external evidence to deflect it. It becomes history, inasmuch as it cannot be argued with. The historical dilemma of race seems finalized by the method Faulkner has chosen to narrate it. If history is transformed into stream, there is no redress from it, even as we attempt to disentangle history from subjectivity, emotional response, feelings of guilt, qualities which relate more to race than to anything else. Further articulation is impossible.

If we add our speculation to Quentin's and Shreve's, we find Faulkner moving toward his most radical statement on race, the furthest he would ever go. It was possible only in fiction, and it clashes directly with nearly everything he said in his public statements. Here he appears on the edge of suggesting that the resolution of the South's (and the nation's) racial dilemma was in a single race, one that would transcend black and white by becoming black-and-white. The play on fractions, which amounts to a mockery of "octoroon," "quadroon," "mixed blood," is only meaningful if Faulkner saw the South as monoracial. This too could be part of Quentin's perception, that what he believes and what he knows is politically and socially untenable.*

It is important *not* to see Quentin as a young man who hates the South. At first, Faulkner conceived of Quentin as someone who transfers his bitterness over his sister (from *Sound*) to a hatred of the South and its people. But in a later phase of the novel, Faulkner came to distinguish between the Quentin of the earlier novel and the Quentin of this one; once he did that, he could make the college student more perceptive. The young man understands that Sutpen was not merely an object of his hatred, but a figure who revealed a good deal about the South; and his own ambiva-

---

*Yet even as he recognized this impossible vision, Faulkner became obsessed with the idea, which becomes apparent in *Go Down, Moses*. There the racial mix is ennobling, as it also becomes in Lucas Beauchamp in *Intruder in the Dust*. The more racially "mongrelized" the race, Faulkner posits, the more representative it becomes: of the South, of America, of a passing, transitory culture. The racial mix, rather than weakening the culture, as the politicians warned, created strength, resistance, and endurance. This racial oneness after *Absalom* becomes indistinguishable from father-and-son patterns.

lence about Sutpen and his achievement would become a more generalized ambivalence about the South. This is not to downplay the incest theme which runs through *Sound* and makes a self-destructive figure of Quentin, out of his doomed love for Caddy. Some of this is transferred to *Absalom*, of course, to an already morbid Quentin and in the implied obsessional feeling between Judith and Charles; but that incestuous, doomed love does not overpower the novel. Quentin rightly emphasizes it in its place, but he moves beyond it to larger considerations of Sutpen and his role in race and history.

Incest itself in *Absalom* takes on a wider role: not only the relationship between Bon and Judith but between the Sutpen men in their desire to hold on to their sister and daughter. In this pattern, Henry fights Bon for Judith, and then obtains his father's sanction to kill Bon as the way father and son can keep her indentured to them. All of these motives have at their base an incestuous pattern—Judith shall be theirs or no one's. Further, incestuous motives are indistinguishable from self-destruction. The Fall is implicit in the desire to hold Judith within the family fold. Incestuous drives become no less than historical patterns.

What makes *Absalom* such an astonishing performance is Faulkner's ability to keep so many elements in balance. Too much sympathy for Sutpen's dilemma or else too much antipathy to what he had wrought could have simplified the novel. Any effort to turn the war and its aftermath into a romance, or a fantasy, as in *Gone With the Wind*, would have undermined both racial and historical factors. Somewhere in the making of the novel, Faulkner recognized the Civil War was not a matter of contingencies; it was not what the South had claimed it to be, the right of a group of states to express their independence, their rights as states. He recognized, and built into the novel, the sense that there was a determinacy to the Union and a determinacy to what had occurred—the result of Sutpen's hubris and the South's combined hubris and injustice, the consequence of human affairs which do not hold to personal design. There was in Faulkner enough of a fatalist or believer in destiny to comprehend that elements fell beyond the control of man; the sense that history is made, as Tolstoy had said in *War and Peace*, by unplanned incidents, uncontrollable events, predetermined factors which remain invisible until they come into play.

As Faulkner reached the apex of his talent, the greatest moment of his creative career, he seemed fully conscious of where he was and what he was doing. The successive revisions in order to get the telling of it straight indicate one level of consciousness and care. Manipulation of the prose style—heated, rhetorical, often transcendent in its ability to create mounting tensions—also suggests full awareness. As he later commented, there is a period when a writer's craftsmanship (a matter of age) and energy (a matter of imagination) come together, and then the writer moves beyond or outside himself. Some of this sense of how it comes about Faulkner carried over from his reading of the French symbolists almost twenty years before: their reaching for the perfect blend of imaginative or creative energy with the craftsmanship gained from experience.* With the publication of *Absalom* on October 26, 1936—in one of the worst years of the depression—Faulkner found himself on his own Everest. Although he was still capable of compelling work, he would never again reach so high or so far; he would never set himself so many problems and overcome them, although in *A Fable* he tried once more to reach beyond himself. But *A Fable* becomes a cautionary tale for both reader and writer: that while the novelist may have all the craft, once he loses the energy he forgoes the blend. While *Absalom* is triumphant, *A Fable*, despite nine years of attention lavished on it, did not cohere. It was a noble effort of spectacular parts, but overall the signal of a dim farewell.

Once he had grasped the novel, Faulkner began to send it on to Smith chapter by chapter; the first going out at the end of March, the second the end of June, the third received on July 22, the fourth received on August 19, the remainder after Dean's death on November 10.

Within this pitch of excitement generated by a novel he suspected was his major work, Faulkner took time out for flying, and he transferred his Waco to Dean, who had acquired a transport license. The transferral was a sale which put Dean under small obligation, something like the negotiation Faulkner had made with the Bryants over Rowan Oak. On the weekend of April 27 and 28, he, Dean, and Vernon Omlie staged an air show in Oxford, complete with aerobatics, formation flying, and a Negro wing-walker and parachute jumper. More and more, Faulkner depended on Dean for company, using the now-proficient and able young flier as an alternative to family life. Measuring the time Faulkner spent flying with Dean at airports, along with the time spent at his desk, now on *Absalom*, one concludes that he had withdrawn effectively from family life at Rowan Oak. He was there, and not there; and he found as many reasons for not being there as he could. Louise Meadow, Dean's wife, told this writer Faulkner asked Dean to accompany him on several flights, some overnight,

---

Absalom comes close to what Roland Barthes called an "infinite text," and its method is characterized by what Mikhail Bakhtin called "the dialogical imagination." In that, the dominant voice is influenced by the presence of other voices; so that we have a polyphonic novel of real and implied voices. Critically, Bakhtin (not overused) provides an excellent way of reading Faulkner as a whole and *Absalom* in particular. (See Stephen M. Ross's "Oratory and the Dialogical in *Absalom, Absalom!*" in *Intertextuality in Faulkner*, Michael Gresset and Noel Polk, eds. (Jackson: University Press of Mississippi, 1985), pp. 73–86.

Like so much of Faulkner, *Absalom* resists any ideological reading—i.e., one based on a continuous, coherent value system. André Bleikasten puts it well in implying Faulkner's deconstruction of the novel form: ". . . the demystification of the Southern past is closely related to the subversion of the novel as an established genre." Questions of form bring us "close again to Faulkner's modernity: to his singular, almost perversely playful relationship to the realist tradition of *mimesis*, to his dismantling of narrative sequence, to his uses of polyvocal and polymodal narration, and to all the other procedures he used to revitalize the language of fiction" ("For/Against an Ideological Reading," *Faulkner & Idealism: Perspectives from Paris*, eds. Michael Gresset and Patrick S. Samway. [Jackson: University Press of Mississippi, 1983], p. 47).

but Dean bowed out, saying he was newly married and wanted to remain home when not barnstorming.

Faulkner's reliance on his brother for company when he could obtain it fits well into the pattern of rejection. He wanted that base at Rowan Oak, and Estelle and Jill meant a good deal to him; but at another level, he could not bear the steady routine of it, nor of Oxford. The liaison with Meta Carpenter, which began in December, a little more than a month after Dean's death, suggests that once in Hollywood Faulkner sought out company with her as he had with his brother—with the important addition she gave him, of the sexual satisfaction or warmth he missed at home.

Meanwhile, Smith's comments on chapter 1 of *Absalom* were returned, and the publisher said he found the beginning confusing. Faulkner heeded his publisher's comments and removed one inconsistency, the reference to 1910, which was the year Quentin committed suicide in *Sound* and moved the dialogue between him and Shreve to 1909, which made more sense. He further got his pronouns more under control. As noted, a good part of the Faulknerian technique depended on pronominal confusion, a deliberate blending of "he" and "him" and "his" (or their feminine counterparts) so as to approximate actual dialogue and situation rather than the artificial identifications which occur in writing. By confusing pronoun references, Faulkner hoped to draw the reader (the struggling reader!) into the actual scene where references can be gleaned from gesture, look, body language. Even after revision, *Absalom* is still full of such confusions, deliberately so, and often to the advantage of greater intensity. But Smith felt the beginning at least should be clarified.

Faulkner was then involved in a dual activity, making the corrections Smith suggested, while moving along on the manuscript, getting chapter 2 ready by the end of June. What the novel required was steady application. Faulkner had to balance several elements: the basic line of what happened as against the manifold variations he had deliberately intruded so as to create narrative withholdings and retrievals. In chapter 4, which he sent on in mid-August, much of this comes together. The relationships are established, and Bon's body is brought into the house: the tragedy of the House of Atreus, Southern-style, has been worked through. But then Faulkner backs up and gives the context for Bon and further context for Henry's attitude toward Judith. He pulls in the Biblical story of Absalom in Second Samuel (13ff.), where Amnon forces Tamar to lie with him.

Henry was provincial, the clown almost given to instinctive and violent action rather than to thinking who may have been conscious that his fierce provincial's pride in his sister's virginity was a false quantity which must incorporate in itself an inability to endure in order to be precious, to exist, and so must depend upon its loss, absence, to have existed at all. In fact, perhaps this is the pure and perfect incest: the brother realizing that the sister's virginity must be destroyed in order to have existed at all, taking that virginity in the person of the brother-in-law, the man whom he would be if he could become, metamorphose into, the lover, the husband.[13]

With this and similar passages, *Absalom* echoes what we have already observed in the incomplete "Elmer" and the more recent *Sound*: that obsession with incest. Faulkner suggests strongly Henry killed Bon to prevent him from possessing Judith: that race was the façade behind which Henry could protect his more intimate feelings toward his sister. " 'Yes, it was Henry who seduced Judith: not Bon, as witness the queerly placid course of Bon's and Judith's courtship—an engagement, if engagement it ever was, lasting for a whole year yet comprising two holiday visits as her brother's guest which Bon seems to have spent either in riding and hunting with Henry or as acting as an elegant and indolent esoteric hothouse bloom."[14]

The suggestion goes further—that the real attachment is between Henry and Bon, that they are the true engaged couple, and Judith is the means by which they can come together. There is implicit in the incestuous obsession something of a homoerotic impulse: the need to draw close to Judith so as to prevent her from ever gaining Bon; the reciprocal need to draw close to Bon to prevent him from ever possessing Judith. The third dimension in this triangular obsession is Judith's loyalty to both, as if they were all meeting as a result of her presence: her need to remain loyal to each one's feelings, whether that of lover or of brother. This point is reinforced by a passage in which Judith assumes the shape of what is now a commonplace Faulkner image, the empty vessel. "She was just the blank shape, the empty vessel in which each of them strove to preserve, not the illusion of himself nor his illusion of the other but what each conceived the other to believe him to be—the man and the youth, seducer and seduced, who had known one another, seduced and been seduced, victimized in turn each by the other."[15]

As all this comes together in chapter 4 in the summer of 1935, one wonders what instigated such a powerful motif at this time. Not that it was new, simply more intense and searching. As we know, Faulkner had long been fascinated by tabooed linkages. Temple Drake had called Popeye "Daddy." Even as recently as *Pylon*, he had an unusual triangle in the relationship of Laverne to two men, Roger Shumann and the jumper, Jack Holmes. Having her child with one of them, her present pregnancy with Jack, the sharing of beds and floors create a triangle that is both heterosexual in its overt forms and homoerotic in its subtextual implications. Later, in the final story of *The Unvanquished*, "An Odor of Verbena," written in the summer of 1937, Faulkner introduced a shadowy incestuous theme.* The wife of John Sartoris, Drusilla, plays with a seduction of his son, Bayard, kissing him, forcing him to tell his father of her advance, testing out the father's attitude toward young wife and young son. The triangle

---

*Nor should we ignore Darl's incestuous feelings toward Dewey Dell in *As I Lay Dying*.

was a constant in Faulkner, with its incestuous pattern, its homoerotic subtext; in *Sound,* Quentin, Caddy, and Ames. Polymorphous behavior was both a constant in his work and an intensification in and around *Absalom.* In some way, it was linked to dissatisfaction with his marriage, surely his response to an inadequate or nonexistent sexual life with Estelle. Perhaps it was his effort to test out in fiction what would soon become part of his life, his first long-term affair, with Meta Carpenter. There was certainly the need to try out limitations of behavior, befitting a novel which reaches toward racial boundaries and everything that implies.

At this time he wrote Goldman[16] his financial situation was so poor he was prepared to sell his manuscripts of *The Sound and the Fury, As I Lay Dying, Sanctuary, Light in August,* and *Pylon,* as well as short stories. He felt bankruptcy was imminent, although we know he wanted money to expand Rowan Oak's property line to include Bailey's Woods. As he moved into August of 1935, he was setting himself for more short stories, including a retread of "Christmas Tree," which now became "Two Dollar Wife." It is a dismal piece of writing, and he was fortunate that even such a low-level publication as *College Life* took it (for January of 1936). Blotner thinks Faulkner submitted it as part of a contest worth $500 to the winner (he did not win); but more likely he was willing to settle for anything he could get with work for which he had no appetite. We must not underestimate the tensions created in him as he recycled distinctly inferior work while he was trying to concentrate on the complexities of *Absalom.* Living in those two very differentiated worlds was like experiencing two distinct existences, without meeting or resolution. Each need was as great as the other: to produce what he knew he was capable of doing, while keeping the extended family and property together with steady income. The alternative, as ever, was Hollywood.

Yet even as he prepared that critical chapter 4 of *Absalom* for Smith in New York, he found time for flying in Memphis. Although he was cutting down on flying time, the need was strong. Perhaps he wished to measure himself against Dean, who was in every respect a more effective pilot, with a more sensitive touch on the wheel and better overall skills. For the first half of August, he balanced *Absalom* against flying, along with sporadic attempts to sell stories or come up with ways to settle his affairs. Then with the sending of chapter 4, he slackened, possibly because the tension was building toward a binge. He needed to go to the source of his financial problems, New York. His salvation, if he could think in such exalted terms, lay with *Absalom,* both book and magazine rights.

It is hard to imagine *Absalom* as a serialized novel. He could not possibly break it at the indicated chapter headings, since they were far too long for magazine publication. Nor could he separate the novel at other places, since it is written like a mosaic, without clear points of interruption. Several of his other novels might have been serialized if he had tried, but *Absalom* was a unit. The *American Mercury* turned it down as too long, he wrote Estelle from New York (September 27), and now, he says, Goldman is trying *Scribner's* and *Harper's.* "If that will not work, I have told Hal that I am coming down on him for money. . . . I will wait until I hear from the 2 magazines, then I will put it to the test."[17]

He mentions his "headache is gone now, and I feel better"—an indication he may have binged and has now recovered. "I feel good and ready and 'hard-boiled' now, enough to cope with Shylock himself." That refers to dealing with Cerf, Klopfer, Guinzburg (of Viking), and others seeking their pound of flesh. He lists some of the people he knows who are now in California: Frank Sullivan, Corey Ford, Dorothy Parker. In a follow-up letter to Estelle, on October 5, Faulkner's return address is the Murray Hill Hotel, a sedate, rather posh and high-toned place on Park Avenue, well east of Times Square. Here he announces he has worked out a deal to improve their financial situation, eight weeks in Hollywood if Smith can arrange a contract. With that, he can pay back the advance money, $3,400. "It will pay all bills, taxes, insurance, etc. and I included in it a sum for winter clothes for you and the children. We will shop carefully and pay cash, and it will do." His words suggest a mild warning that perhaps Estelle was spending above their means, that she will have to show more care—a warning that he repeated later in stronger and shameful terms.

The rest of the letter is a potpourri of social and business engagements: an upcoming appointment with Lorimer of the *Post,* a visit with Harold and Alice Guinzburg (whom he could hold over both Smith's and Cerf's heads as a possible future publisher),* a story in the typewriter for *Scribner's* ("The Brooch"). He had, also, met Harold Ober of the Ober Agency, a fateful meeting in that the loyal, helpful Ober would become Faulkner's agent and help him over his worst periods. For the time being, Goldman still handled his short stories. Faulkner made a trip to Connecticut, where Smith had a place in Farmington, saw Lorimer (on October 10), who was publishing the stories that would make up *The Unvanquished,* and returned to Memphis on October 13. The trip was a success. In the main he had stayed sober and had concluded some important business, although his affairs were far from settled. And he had met Ober.

He returned to flying, then settled back in Oxford, to find Phil Stone, at forty-two, planning to marry twenty-six-year-old Emily Whitehurst. Once married, the couple moved in with General and Mrs. Stone. The marriage was curious. Stone was in decline, as his wife came to recognize; part of his decision to marry at this late date was a response to Faulkner's slipping away. Emily wanted to write, so that in marrying her Stone was taking on, as it were, another pupil. But he was played out, as she later told Blotner:[18] "Phil Stone was burned out. His life was over when I married him, but I didn't know it." Stone was full of eccentricities, one of them being extreme shame at his baldness; but other flaws of anger and resent-

---

*Guinzburg gave Faulkner a copy of Humphrey Cobb's brief novel *Paths of Glory,* which turned out to have considerable meaning in the background of *A Fable.* That book, which germinated and evolved over a nine-year period in Faulkner, and whose handwritten outline adorned his study walls, surely had some of its origins in the Cobb book.

ment intensified, leading to a mental decline and increasingly bitter attacks on the writer who got away.

Faulkner's effort to build a financial wall came in his attempt to sell "A Portrait of Elmer" to Cerf for a limited edition. Like many of the stories he was writing for the *Post* and other magazines—and which Smith deplored as a waste of talent—"Portrait," while of personal interest, was not something Faulkner could be proud of. It was, like so much else, an effort to cash in, here on a Christmas limited edition. Cerf evidently felt that in its present shape it was not ready for publication, although he told Faulkner of its stretches of fine writing. Much of this was a publisher buttering up an author that he wanted on his list, for the piece has little to recommend publication, except as the oddity of an established author. Cerf did tell Faulkner he wanted him on his list more than "any other fiction writer living in America" and indicated he could write his own ticket. But Cerf was aboveboard, not devious, adding that none of this could be arranged until Faulkner settled his next book, with Smith and Haas still very much in the picture.

By October 15, Faulkner was back working on chapter 5 of *Absalom*. He fell into his routine, writing, seeing Dean and Louise, trying to pile up as much manuscript as he could before the call came from Hollywood. As he worked his way more deeply into the manuscript, with chapter 5 and then the first glimmerings of chapter 6, he found himself increasingly in the world of "telling." Blotner is surely correct in saying that the shadow of Conrad was becoming of considerable importance. The introduction of Shreve McCannon (the Shreve MacKenzie of *Sound*) brought in a Marlow-like character; someone steadier and less involved than Quentin, but nevertheless someone drawn into Quentin's tale, the way Marlow is drawn into Jim's in *Lord Jim* or Kurtz's in *Heart of Darkness*.

Faulkner gleaned from Conrad's narrative strategies the sense a story had to be "told" in order to be presented adequately. Quentin by himself would have flattened it out, as Faulkner recognized; but Shreve as the recipient of this turbulent, upsetting, maddening story, even while remaining outside, becomes an adequate participant. There is a touch of Henry James here in the use of a central intelligence; but Faulkner parts with James, since Quentin's centrality is insufficient. He must share what he knows and feels with someone completely alien; and here the Conrad analogy becomes apparent. With the insistent pressure of "telling" now becoming established, Faulkner was in the very middle of his effort, creating a gigantic puppet show for the South and for the nation as well. One can read the novel as a farewell to a purer form of individualism or a condemnation of individual behavior which brings down not only the principals but the region itself. In a way, *The Great Gatsby* is a kind of palimpsest for *Absalom*. Yet such a reading forgoes the narrative entanglements and views the novel more limpidly as a depression-years product, as an assault on the country's worship of the individual, and the consequences of that worship in misery, poverty, and disability for the majority.

Faulkner kept picking away at Quentin, entering ever deeper into him, while continuing occasional episodes of flying. But he was rocked to his deepest reaches on November 10 when Dean crashed in the plane Faulkner had sold him. Dean was working at an air show, at Pontotoc, on the weekend before Armistice Day, November 9 and 10. According to reports in both Memphis and Oxford newspapers, he had taken up three young farmers, who wanted to see their property from the air. As part of the air show, with its stunt flying and aerobatics, pilots took up the curious—most of them people who had never flown before. The young man sitting beside Dean in the Waco was Lamon Graham, well known to him. Graham's cousin and a friend sat in the back. It was part of a routine completely familiar to Dean.

What occurred next is in dispute. After taking off, the Waco disappeared and then, according to two witnesses, seemed to come apart in the air, with the top wing fluttering away from the fuselage. The Waco then nose-dived and smashed into small pieces. Another report had the plane come out of a loop and keep going into the ground. An examination of the wreckage revealed that the control wheel had passed from the pilot's to the passenger's side, leading to the theory Graham had frozen at the wheel and Dean, a small man, had been unable to wrestle it from him. At exactly what point in this episode the wing ripped off is unclear. Out of control, with Graham possibly terror-stricken, the plane and its occupants disintegrated on impact.

Faulkner was devastated. He felt responsible, for having sold Dean the plane and having encouraged him to fly, even for providing the money for the early lessons. Already possessed by several demons, since the death of Dean occurred even as he was burrowing into the psyche of Henry and Bon, he entered the valley of death. We can only speculate how Faulkner felt as he wrote intensely, passionately about brother killing brother, grieving for his own brother killed in the plane he had sold him. And delving into Quentin, he was really writing about a dead man not much younger than Dean; Quentin would commit suicide the next year, but was already a suicide from *Sound*. Just as Faulkner was putting together what would doom Quentin's emotional and psychological life, he found himself with an equally grisly job of helping the undertaker to put Dean together. The body and face were smashed beyond recognition, and Faulkner did not wish Maud to see her youngest in this condition. He provided the undertaker with a photograph, and possibly stayed to help. Those close to Faulkner say he suffered nightmares and feelings of horror for years afterward. The job on Dean was apparently not satisfactory, and he was buried in St. Peter's Cemetery without Maud's viewing him.

The grief was real, as was the guilt. To put it all behind him, Faulkner could have binged, but the family need for some stabilizing element was so powerful he remained sober and ministered to both Maud and Louise, now four months pregnant. She would give birth to a daughter on March 22, 1936, and Faulkner would take complete financial care of her and her daughter for as long as they needed help. In a controversial move, opposed by the family, he had written on the headstone over Dean's grave words that commemorated John Sartoris in *Sartoris*: "I bare him on Eagles' wings and brought him unto me."

Another form of relief for Faulkner, since he postponed binging, was to throw himself into work. As the family extended itself, he now had additional financial obligations. In a rush of activity in the next two and a half months, he headed for Hollywood to work on a film, moved along on *Absalom*, completing the manuscript by January 31 in a feat of sustained writing, and began the liaison with Meta Carpenter. On one hand, Dean's death depressed him; on the other, it pushed him into a tremendous burst of professional and personal activity. Of course, the inevitable was waiting: at the end of this spurt, he needed hospitalization, the first of several such stays after heavy, sustained, virtually suicidal drinking.

The remaining work on *Absalom* took place mainly at his mother's house on South Lamar, where Dean's widow was also living. By December 4, he could announce to Goldman he was "working like hell now. The novel is pretty good and I think another month will see it done."[19] He adds he has written no short stories, nor contemplates doing any until the novel is completed. He still hoped to sell "Elmer" to Cerf, although nothing came of that. He was working solely on the novel with advance money from Smith and awaiting the call to Hollywood. His words to Goldman sound a note of inevitability. "My feeling about the movie contract is, as you know, that I don't particularly want to go at all but I am doing so as a part of my agreement with Smith; so let them find the way to farm me out, if that's what they want." Despite disclaimers, a trip to Hollywood would be in the main a good move, removing him from the scene of his grief. Of course, it interrupted that intense involvement *Absalom* demanded, forcing once more that clash of career and personal life. Faulkner felt the Hollywood venture was so inevitable that if Smith and Haas could not get him good terms, he decided he would work around them through Goldman. When he left for the coast on December 10, to begin on a contract starting six days later, he was making only the first of several trips in 1935 and 1936.

There were three dimensions to his life in Hollywood thereafter. First, he worked with scriptwriter Joel Sayre, an experienced craftsman, producing vast amounts of material for *The Road to Glory*,* a film based on the novel *Wooden Crosses* by Roland Dorgeles. Rising early, he also worked steadily on *Absalom*, chapters 8 and 9 of which were completed within a month of his return to Oxford in early 1936.

Finally, the third dimension of Faulkner's life at this time was personal but far-reaching. It probably helped to keep him sane, although it had in it some of the seediness secret liaisons usually have. The woman was Meta Doherty (Carpenter), gofer and script clerk for Hawks, a lovely young

---

*Screenplay by Joel Sayre and William Faulkner, directed by Howard Hawks, with Fredric March, Warner Baxter, Lionel Barrymore, June Lang, and Gregory Ratoff; released on June 2, 1936.

woman from Tunica, in the Delta, and the kind who was immediately appealing to Faulkner: pretty, compliant, a Southerner, bright and well spoken, unthreatening and low-keyed. He wanted solace, sex, and companionship without serious challenge—a purely romantic liaison in which he could play the courtly gentleman. *A Loving Gentleman* is the title Meta Carpenter gave to the book-length description of their relationship, which went on for several years. Meta had been married briefly to Billy Carpenter, but had moved on from that into a position of considerable responsibility under the loyal Hawks. Actually, she and Faulkner had met much earlier—in 1922, when she attended the East Ball in Oxford. At that time, the writer was, as she put it, "the town scapegrace, who wrote stories hardly suitable for the scrutiny of decent folks, rode horseback recklessly, hunted with riffraff and darkies, and didn't give one boot for Oxford's opinion of him."[20]

The next time she saw him was at the studio; two days later she encountered him obviously drunk, unsteady on his legs, his speech slurred. She was not impressed, although she was taken with his dignity, his good manners, and courtliness. But once they began to work together, her manner changed. The fact both were Southerners was a considerable factor. Meta describes herself as pretty, with blonde hair that fell straight to her shoulders, possessing a lithe ninety-two-pound body (about the same size as Estelle or Helen Baird), and a gentle, pleasant smile. Photographs show an extremely attractive young woman, with a good deal of sensitivity and intelligence in the expression. She also describes Faulkner as he takes her in worshipfully:

> The bones in his face were fine, the cheekbones high and prominent, the chin strong and thrusting. His moustache concealed a small, sensitive mouth somewhat out of keeping with the strong facial planes. The brown springy hair was freshly barbered and the smell of the barber's talcum was still faint on the nape of his neck. Nothing in his likeness at thirty-eight suggested the face that was to overtake his young visage as he grew older—proud, hawklike, forceful, austerely handsome.

Faulkner's looks did, in fact, improve considerably. The man at fifty had an appearance of dignified courtliness that made him, small and compact as he was, a presence; earlier, until age put its mark of character on them, his features seemed caught in an indistinct phase, somehow unshaped.

In a short time the meetings and working sessions evolved into dating, dinners, and then an affair. The meeting with Meta Carpenter strongly influenced Faulkner's life, directly affecting his career at several turns. It was not simply a hit-or-miss event in his life; she made a profound impression, and he arranged aspects of his life—even to their discussion of whether or not he would leave Estelle—as the consequence of their mutual devotion to each other. Faulkner's dislike of Hollywood remained a constant, but he made efforts to return because of Meta's presence there; added to Hollywood's infusion of sizable checks into his finances, she gave him incentive to go on.

There is also the highly speculative question of whether his affair with Meta weakened or strengthened his marriage. On the surface, it appeared to open up all the seams in the marriage, but on another level, his relationship to Estelle had worsened to such a degree only the presence of another woman could make him decide to keep his vows. If what he told Meta was true—that he and Estelle had ceased sexual contact since Jill's birth—then the affair with the young woman was his way of keeping his balance in an area where he had definite needs. His hostility toward Estelle, which became manifest in several ways (as in his making her meet Meta later), was kept under control by his having an outlet which provided at the beginning few or no problems. The relationship with Meta far from Oxford, away from prying eyes, and in the Hollywood playland where anything went, had the quality of Adam and Eve finding their way back into the Garden after the expulsion. Much of Meta's book on the liaison has the quality of a playland, or Garden, especially in the earlier stages.

There is one other factor in this brief digression. Late in her book,[21] Meta speaks of certain mental failings in Faulkner, as if he were suffering from what we now identify as incipient Alzheimer's disease, or something akin to it. There is the possibility that part of the faltering in his creative powers, as well as in his memory itself, resulted from the steady heavy drinking. Faulkner did suffer from spells of "almost amnesia," causing him to say things repeatedly, or to forget. Falls from horses may have contributed, but the largest unknown factor is the effect of alcohol. His body amazingly seemed relatively untouched by a lifetime of whiskey, although his heart may have been weakened. His other bodily functions were working well just before he died; but the effect on the brain—particularly on the brain of someone as finely honed as Faulkner—must remain speculative.

Meanwhile, on the last day of 1935, Sayre and Faulkner had completed a working script of *The Road to Glory*.* After the celebration, in which Faulkner indulged, but not disastrously, he continued on *Absalom*, through chapter 9 (which he finished at the end of January, back in Rowan Oak). According to Blotner,[22] he showed the manuscript to David Hempstead, an admirer of his work, and asked him to read it, adding, " 'I think it's the best novel yet written by an American.' " He gave Hempstead his only copy, but clearly his words and the act itself were the result of heavy drinking. If sober, he would not have risked his sole copy of the novel. Now that the pressure of completing the script and the novel wore off, he was in fact drinking himself out of a job. As of January 7, he was off the payroll, so incapacitated by heavy boozing he needed nursing, which Hawks provided. On January 17, he was in shape to return home.

*The finished script, in typical Hollywood fashion, had to go through three very tough bosses before it was considered completed: producer, Darryl Zanuck; associate producer, Nunnally Johnson; and director, Howard Hawks.

He now went into a strange syndrome of parting. He had become so absorbed with *Absalom* he disliked putting it down. The end of the manuscript indicates "31 Jany 1936," with three other notations: "Mississippi, 1935," "California, 1936, Mississippi, 1936," and then "Rowan Oak" added. He had worked his way so deeply into the book and penetrated so far into the various identifications that he suffered from ailments associated with saying farewell. There were of course other factors: the interruption of his relationship with Meta, and the fact of the return to Oxford, which had become the place for which he felt what Quentin indicated about the South at the end of the novel: *"I dont hate it! I don't hate it!"* He didn't hate it, but there were many times when he couldn't bear it—the life at Rowan Oak, the responsibilities, and a marriage which had soured.

There was also the delayed response to Dean's death, reactivated when he returned to see Louise, now coming close to term, and Maud; his own sense of loss, guilt, and related emotions were stirred. He knew, further, that he had not earned enough to carry on for any length of time—that Hollywood was still his fate. Most of all, there was the ending of the deeply felt novel. Once home, he shaped and reshaped it in small ways, revising and coddling the manuscript. And he drank and drank. He became helpless, so that Maud and his stepson Malcolm (who would himself develop into an alcoholic) had to care for him. Finally he was taken to a sanitarium to dry out, at Byhalia, north of Oxford, about halfway between Holly Springs and Memphis, a familiar place for Falkners. He was dehydrated and malnourished; for when he drank he stopped eating, and had not had a normal meal for several weeks. Dried out, force-fed, his constitution once again reinforced—and he was a tremendously healthy man—he left after a stay of several days. He returned, however, to everything which contributed to his chronic alcoholism, that of a man who would control the daily drinking but not the periodic binges when life became too intense and complicated.

He had entered 1936 in Hollywood, and was now picking up the pieces in Oxford. His stay in Byhalia was in its way a consequence of the end of 1935, with Dean's death and mounting debts. The new year saw him in Hollywood for longer periods of time than ever before. He also published five stories, all of which had been written earlier: "The Brooch" (January, *Scribner's,* reprinted in *Collected Stories*); "Two Dollar Wife" (January, *College Life,* reprinted in *Collected Stories*); "Fool About a Horse" (August, *Scribner's,* revised for *The Hamlet,* 1940); "The Unvanquished" (November 14, *Post,* revised and retitled "Riposte in Tertio" for *The Unvanquished*); and "Vendée" (December 5, *Post,* revised for *The Unvanquished*). At the very end of the year, he moved to arrange for publication of the *Post* stories with Cerf, his new publisher. Except for work on revisions of *Absalom,* brought out by Random House on Oct. 26, the year 1936 was not very productive for Faulkner professionally—we see Hollywood eating deeply into his time and taking up his working hours; and the affair with Meta was slowing his production of new material. Except for the latter two stories which ended up in *The Unvanquished,* he had stopped writing short fiction for the time being, and the stories he was writing were not top drawer. In family matters, his niece Dean was born on March 22, and he was committed to her support until she gained her majority. In even more personal terms, he was to eschew all bills run up by his wife, by taking out a notice in the Memphis *Commercial Appeal,* on June 22, that he was no longer responsible for any debts or bills incurred by Mrs. William Faulkner or Mrs. Estelle Oldham Faulkner. Such an action reveals a profound tension in the household over money, probably a reflection, on a deeper level, of the sexual desert the marriage had become.

The year 1936, then, becomes the period when his greatest novel is published, which he unsuccessfully tries to sell to Hollywood for $50,000. But it is also a year when his work grinds almost to a halt; he is definitely in a holding pattern, forced for the first time by economic necessity to put everything serious aside and concentrate on scripts. Yet while his professional inactivity can be explained by his monetary and personal involvement in Hollywood, it can also be attributed to his need to recoup imaginatively after years of a creative whirlwind.

In what was a stroke of good fortune for Faulkner, Random House under Cerf and Klopfer acquired the sinking firm of Smith and Haas. The latter had already cofounded the Book-of-the-Month Club, although it was far from the huge success it would later become. Haas was a splendid mixture of business acumen and taste, and he proved to be a generous and sympathetic support for Faulkner through the remainder of his career. Smith and Haas had themselves been no slouches as publishers, having acquired besides Faulkner distinguished writers such as Isak Dinesen and André Malraux; but in their quest for excellence, they were defeated by the depression and perhaps by a little too much gentlemanliness in a highly competitive business. Cerf believed fervently in Faulkner—believed that whatever the commercial potentialities of his work, he was an adornment, and he vowed to keep him afloat financially. He was true to his word, and having Cerf as publisher was like having a believing mother. The entire Random House staff mobilized around its new writer. Faulkner had a home in New York whenever he wanted to make use of it.

Back in Oxford he fell into his familiar patterns, drinking heavily and seeing his mother every morning in her home. Faulkner was doing little, sinking into himself, heading for trouble with alcohol, commiserating with himself over Dean's death, talking to Maud about Dean and his own life. We do not know to what extent, if at all, Faulkner revealed to Maud his domestic unhappiness. But considering the closeness of mother and son, and if we take into account Maud's acceptance of and defense of whatever her eldest son did, it is not unlikely that the usually tight-lipped Faulkner used her as the one person he could express himself to.

By February 26, Faulkner was back at work on films, helping to develop a script for *Banjo on My Knee.* This story of bargemen underwent several revisions, so that Faulkner's contribution was buried under Nunnally Johnson's final script. The movie was released on December 4, 1936, with actors Barbara Stanwyck and Joel McCrea, directed by John Cromwell. Moving through Faulkner's film work, we see that most of the time his words did not appear in the final script—that he was rewritten out. Nevertheless, he worked on films with stellar casts and first-rate directors, and his name was connected to, among others, *Gunga Din, Drums Along the Mohawk, The Southerner,* and *The Left Hand of God.* As for films which used enough of his work to give him a credit, we have popular releases such as *To Have and Have Not* and *The Big Sleep,* on whose sets he came to know Humphrey Bogart, who became a good drinking companion.

But back in late February and March of 1936, his assignment was *Banjo on My Knee,* a strange interlude for a man whose newest novel was *Absalom.* His scripts were usually unacceptable inasmuch as he wrote unspeakable dialogue. Although he gradually became more adept, his skills in movie dialogue never fully developed, and his value was more in the area of atmosphere, ideas, possible developments of plot or story line. He wrote home to Estelle on successive weeks, March 2 and 9, that everything was "coming along fine." He says he wishes he were at Rowan Oak, "still in the kitchen with my family around me and my hand full of Old Maid cards."[23] And he tells her not to count on an immediate New Orleans meeting since he is looking toward a "long contract" once the present script is finished. He stayed in Hollywood until May.

His life on the West Coast was a round of inconsequentials, intermixed with his evenings with Meta. He gave the impression to people who knew him—Blotner reports this—of being vulnerable and incapable of taking care of himself. We know that much of this was pose, that except when he was drinking very heavily, he knew what he was doing. The assumed vulnerability, however, made people protective of him; he turned both men and women into mothering figures. Although this would seem a weakness, it served Faulkner well: it helped him to retreat and isolate himself within the walls of his own making, while others hovered around. Also, when he was binging and defenseless, it made others protect him against himself. What might seem regressively immature was in fact another kind of defensive position Faulkner had perfected, consciously or not, to allow him his own kind of life, his own way of creating or re-creating it. His accidents became legion, and while some of them could have had serious consequences, there were always rescuers.

He went to parties, where he chiefly drank. He played poker, and he met celebrities (S. J. Perelman, Marc Connolly, well-known actors and actresses), but he passed evenings mainly with a glass in his hand. Since he was not writing anything except scripts, time lay heavy. Living in the Beverly Hills Hotel as a permanent guest, he had a stable residence. He made friends with Jo Pagano and his wife, Jean—Jo was a writer of short stories—and he felt very warmly toward them. They, like others, helped to protect him. His work on *Banjo on My Knee* did not meet Darryl Zanuck's standards, however, and Faulkner seemed out of a job after March 28. He was offered a new deal beginning August 1, at $750 per week, with a raise of $250 every six months if his option was picked up. He wrote Goldman he was taking it, and then added (in late March) that he was "going to try to make some money without having to borrow it."[24] He says he intends to send on a short story from time to time, but admits he has nothing now.

In the meanwhile, before that contract went into effect, Faulkner moved over to RKO at $1,000 per week, for a month to five weeks, to work on *Gunga Din*. How much work Faulkner did on the film is unclear—it did not appear for almost three years, and the final script was by Ben Hecht, Charles MacArthur, Joel Sayre, and Fred Guiol. With a cast of Douglas Fairbanks, Jr., Cary Grant, Joan Fontaine, Sam Jaffe, and Victor McLaglen, it went on to become a film classic. He began at RKO on April 9, which gave him time to touch up *Absalom*. He also became friendly at this time with Nathanael West, whom he had met in New York five years before. An obsessive hunter—West preferred talking guns to talking literature—he found a friendly colleague in Faulkner. The two went boar hunting together on Catalina Island, a rather dangerous venture which both relished. In West, Faulkner had a good, offbeat companion, and West in turn was probably influenced by at least *Sanctuary* in his own writing, especially *The Day of the Locust*. An uncertain and forgetful driver, and a man with a self-destructive strain, he died in an automobile accident four years later.

Faulkner's stint at RKO was uneventful; he seemed to have himself under control, and the presence of his brother Jack on a visit steadied him. In mid-May he returned to Oxford for Jill's third birthday and his seventh wedding anniversary. Except for revisions on *Absalom*, which continued almost up to publication in October, he did little work.* He was biding his time, mailing revisions and corrections to Smith, who remained his editor at Random House, all the while building up considerable resentment at Estelle and her ways. He had wanted to return, surely, for Jill's birthday, but the Oxford pressure cooker was beginning to create familiar tensions.

Strains with Estelle took several forms. As he compared his wife—a drinker, physically in poor shape, showing her age (now over forty)—with

---

*One such enterprise for *Absalom* involved clarifying chronology with a genealogy of characters and dating of events which appeared at the end of the novel. He listed in all seventeen characters, establishing the relationships among them. Of particular use are the Bon linkages and those related to Wash Jones. He also provided the now famous map of "Jefferson, Yoknapatawpha Co., Mississippi, Area 2400 Square Miles—Population, Whites 6298; Negroes 9313; William Faulkner, Sole Owner and Proprietor." The map went well beyond reference to Sutpen's Hundred and to the fishing camp where Wash Jones killed Sutpen; it extended to incidents in *Sanctuary, Sound*, the Snopes stories, *As I Lay Dying, Sartoris*, and *Light in August*. It was in its way a road map to Faulkner's imagination as of 1936. Matching himself against Sutpen's Hundred was Faulkner's 2,400; against Sutpen's mansion was Faulkner's town and county. As he expanded Rowan Oak, he expanded in his imagination to an empire.

Meta—still young, lithe, fresh—the inevitable happened. His dissatisfaction with his marriage, even as he celebrated his seventh anniversary, could only increase. Also, his sexual predicament was clarified: denied at home, he was welcomed elsewhere. He inscribed the first copy of *Absalom* to Meta, and that alone displays a great buildup of hostility toward his wife during this stay. It was at this time he wrote Goldman he had gotten out of the habit of writing trash—that although he was out of touch "with the Kotex Age," he would try to come up with something suitable for *Cosmopolitan* or some other magazine. In the midst of this, thinking of stories, missing Meta, polishing *Absalom*, and creating the map and chronologies, he blew up at Estelle. What followed was a particularly ugly episode, but one with a solid background.

It had been a developing situation: Faulkner's hostility to his wife, her disregard of their money problems. Blotner puts it well[25] when he says that basically the principals had grown up under different assumptions: Faulkner in a home marked by frugality and niggardliness, Estelle in a home where money was more abundant and she was treated like a princess being conditioned to make a lavish marriage. During her marriage to Cornell Franklin, money was also abundant, and she had been accustomed to servants, rich clothes and jewelry, the ability to indulge herself. Although she may seem spoiled and indifferent to Faulkner's plight, we must not lose sight of the fact her entire conditioning had been to marry someone quite different from her second husband. She had received the typical "Southern belle" upbringing, which gave her only superficial accomplishments and intended her to live with servants whom she would oversee. The husband for such a woman was not intended to be a writer, one who wanted to be a great writer at that. The marriage itself was at fault, not Estelle or Faulkner. The pact they made when young was romantic and blissful; the actuality when they came to carry it out had moved to other grounds, and their efforts to achieve stability based on nostalgia and memories were inevitably futile.

On June 22, Faulkner took out a signed advertisement in the Memphis *Commercial Appeal*, which was to run for three additional weeks; it was also reprinted in the Oxford *Eagle* on June 25. It read: "I will not be responsible for any debt incurred or bills made, or notes or checks signed by Mrs. William Faulkner or Mrs. Estelle Oldham Faulkner." Particularly telling was the inclusion of Estelle's family name of Oldham, and the fact the *Eagle* picked it up and brought it into the backyard of both Oldhams and Faulkners. When Faulkner took out these ads, he had discovered Estelle was funneling household funds and any other monies she could get her hands on to support her father and mother. The Oldhams had fallen on hard times, and contemporary witnesses suggest Lem Oldham had lost any interest in making a living, that he sat in his office and did nothing. Estelle, meanwhile, became their source of support; and inevitably it was Faulkner—whom they had rejected twice as their son-in-law—who was unknowingly supplying their money.* Faulkner's rage is indicated by the ads which humiliated not only Estelle but the man who placed them. Within the Southern ethic, Faulkner should not have revealed rifts in his marriage; he should have preserved proprieties and most of all protected Estelle's reputation whatever his personal sentiments. Instead he went public, and the Faulkner name was dragged through the mud, even as he was reaching toward respectability. The act demonstrates such a desire for revenge it went well beyond a financial necessity. Faulkner, after all, spent a good deal on flying and had even purchased a plane.

Connected to his rage was the fact that Estelle periodically moved out with Jill to her parents' home, especially when Faulkner entered a period of heavy drinking; or else as the result of arguments which might lead to Estelle going after her husband with her nails. These comings and goings to her house were particularly galling given the nature of the Oldham resistance to the marriage, and given, further, the Oldham attempt to lord it over the Falkners. There was a caste difference which cut much more deeply than would a class one. Both families belonged to the upwardly mobile bourgeoisie; but the nature of the Oldham money at one time gave them a caste advantage over the Falkners, whose money came from business ventures. Apart from all else, the Oldhams considered themselves superior. The fact that almost alone in Oxford they voted Republican suggests they looked down at the Democratic rabble while they identified with a more conservative, more respectable tradition.

The advertisement climaxed a running disagreement. More than that, it indicates the degree of strain existing in Faulkner as the result of his efforts to support his and Estelle's lifestyle. Some of his resentment must be attributed to the sacrifices he felt he was making while she appeared to be making none. He and only he knew to what extent he had forgone part of his serious career in order to write short stories he knew were destined for the "Kotex Age" and film scripts which ended up trashed. There is not only anger at Estelle in his public statement, but tremendous resentment at his own role, feelings of sacrifice intermixed with a kind of helplessness. There was additionally the fact that in 1936 he was not producing anything new: that his literary work consisted of marginal polishing of *Absalom,* ** the drawing up of a chronology of events and a map outlining his career to date. Even work on the map could have contributed to his feelings of self-pity, since the map, while indicating how much he had produced, revealed how much he was giving up.

*One type of "support" was in the form of Cornell Franklin's child-support payments which Oldham kept. Resenting Faulkner's support of so many members of his own family, Estelle felt this was a suitable quid pro quo.

**A revised form of chapter 1 of *Absalom* was published by the *American Mercury*, where it appeared with the excerpted work of Dos Passos and Wolfe. Also, Faulkner's short story "That Will Be Fine," the undistinguished story of childhood memories which ends with Uncle Rodney's sudden death, was included in *Best Short Stories of 1936*, edited by Edward J. O'Brien.

It was, withal, a critical point in his personal life, especially with the compliant, self-supporting Meta waiting for him in Hollywood. She provided no problems, financial or otherwise, and was a willing sexual partner. To her he was the great man, the infamous but courteous author of *Sanctuary*, the successful writer brought to Hollywood who moved as he wished with celebrities and stars. In Oxford he was remembered by Estelle and the Oldhams as the town bum, the man no woman would accept, a reject except for the iron determination contained within himself.

Blotner reports the events[26] that followed, based on a communication from Taylor McElroy, who overheard Lem Oldham chewing Faulkner out for the disgrace. Oldham even called McElroy into the room, speaking of his son-in-law (and future Nobel Prize winner) as "this lowdown so-and-so." McElroy tried to back away, but the major insisted he stay and continued to rail against the writer. According to this report, Faulkner did not respond, but stood tight-lipped, and exited when Oldham finished. The notoriety brought in reporters, and even *Time*, ever on the lookout for gossip (before *People* magazine took over this area), nosed in. Faulkner explained he was trying to protect his credit until he could pay his debts. But the nature of the public appeal went deep into the nature of his relationship not only to Estelle but to Oxford. His resentment against the Oldhams, reinforced by the hatred his mother felt toward that family, is implicit in his use of Estelle's family name. One thing Faulkner knew: he had the complete and sympathetic backing of Maud in whatever he did, most of all here.

On July 15, Faulkner left for Hollywood again, only this time with Estelle and Jill. The latter two would be driven out, while Faulkner went ahead to locate living quarters. He was to report to work, as per contract, on August 1. Victoria (Cho-Cho) stayed behind, to get married in September. Driving out was Jack Oliver, a black man with thoughts of writing, and Narcissus McEwen, as servant. Faulkner and Estelle settled near Santa Monica, at 620 El Cerco, Huntington Palisades, in a two-story house, a ten-minute drive from the studio. On August 7, he began work on an adaptation of the novel *The Last Slaver* by George S. King (1933), called "The Last Slaver" in early form and released in 1937 by Twentieth Century-Fox as *Slave Ship*, with Warner Baxter, Mickey Rooney, George Sanders, and Wallace Beery. Faulkner received a screen credit, but it is doubtful if anything he might have contributed to the script remained in the final shooting version. There is, further, some question whether or not he was ever assigned to this project.

While the setting in Santa Monica was lovely with ocean and mountains in the distance and the house itself was commodious, personal relationships outside the servants' ears could not have been pleasant. The studio work was aimless, and then Faulkner received word Vernon Omlie, his ideal pilot and a cautious man in the air, had crashed while trying to land in a fog. Omlie's death came only nine months after Dean's. The cast was being whittled down, although Johncy had taken up aviation and was also flying. With Estelle present, Faulkner's movements with Meta were inhibited, although he began to take enormous chances and no longer seemed to care what his wife thought, or what course of action she might take when she found out. He was deliberately moving toward the outer limits of his marriage, testing out Estelle's tolerance.

The strains were all there: no real work, inability to see Meta regularly, Omlie's unexpected death, and presence of a wife who was unhappy in California and consequently drinking heavily. Estelle was now an alcoholic, unable to get through the day without support. Faulkner also drank heavily, so that the household was held together not by the principals but by the servants, as though in some melodrama where downstairs keeps upstairs from disintegrating. The conflict, verbal at most times, could become physical, as both, drunk and unhappy with each other and their situations, went at each other. Estelle struck out, scratched and even attacked with objects, intending to wound and disable. It is difficult to believe Jill was not witness to some of this, as she would witness similar episodes back in Oxford; and here we have the very earliest stages of her withdrawal from the Faulkner clan. The very love Faulkner truly felt for her could not obliterate her memories of misery which made her home almost incoherent, in which only servants offered a measure of stability and security.

Faulkner brought home a few of his friends, although he never knew what to expect. Clark Gable, a hunting companion, came by, as did Joel Sayre, sometimes accompanied by Ronald Coleman and his wife. Although there were diversions such as these, also parties and some excursions, Estelle was unhappy, not the least because she was an appendage. At the studio, Faulkner felt the futility of it all, as he was moved into a property called *Four Men and a Prayer*, then to *Splinter Fleet*. Whatever his contribution to these, if any, no trace remains. He wrote Goldman he expected to be in Hollywood for a year, "up to my neck in moving pictures."[27] He then announced he was going to sell *Absalom* for no less than $100,000, accepting nothing less. He offered it to Nunnally Johnson for $50,000, saying it was about miscegenation. His offer was not taken up. *Absalom* was destined to remain only in book form, except for the segment of chapter 1 in the *Mercury*.

But another development in his personal life opened up. He began to take chances, those of a man who no longer cared what happened. He sneaked in time with Meta—a lunch here, part of an evening there—and, according to her, they resumed sexual relations. Meta also wanted to see Jill. Faulkner decided that Estelle was so lost in drink or sick while recovering from it that he could take out Jill with Meta. They sneaked in such visits. In her book, Meta said it was the first of "many mornings and afternoons with Jill," when Faulkner called to indicate he did not want his daughter to see her mother ill or indisposed. But this apparently was not dangerous enough: Faulkner insisted Meta come to the house to meet Estelle in a social situation. The intermediary was Ben Wasson, who knew what Faulkner was up to and agreed to play his part in this edgy, unpleas-

578 | WILLIAM FAULKNER: AMERICAN WRITER

ant drama. Meta in her account says she was unaware of what was happening, of how she was being manipulated, caught up in the hostility Faulkner was displaying toward Estelle.

> Dressing for my first meeting with Estelle Faulkner in her temporary home, it did not once occur to me that what I was about to do was shoddy and contemptible. Bill had asked it of me and therefore it was right. He was the superior being and I, in my blundering artlessness, my incapacity for self-defense, the lesser one. Bill, who loved me deeply, who was wiser in the ways of men and women and their murkier passions than any writer of his time, would never ask me to do anything that was questionable or degrading.[28]

This sounds disingenuous, but also rings true: the younger woman (by more than a decade) in thralldom to the famous writer, caught up in her own sense of herself and her relationship to the man who had rejected his wife for her.

> It was only in later years [Meta writes] that I came to realize what I, her husband's lover, had done to Estelle Faulkner by invading her home. That mindless imposture still has the power, forty years later, Estelle dead and buried, to chill me to the marrow when I remember it. Why Bill really wanted it—was it to feel a morbidity in his nature that even he could not fully understand?—was it to compare the two women?—was it to experience a sexual thrill by playing a dangerous game?—I have never decided. But along with my own mean participation in the charade, I am also aware of the enormity of Bill's punitive act against his wife. I cannot exempt Ben Wasson from fault either.

Her appraisal of him: that of a man performing "a service to a client and friend, something that one man will unhesitatingly do for another when deception will help him bed a woman or deflect a wife's mistrust." The homosexual Ben was to present Meta as his lady friend; they would address each other as "dear," but would not overdo it. Of course, there was the danger Jill was still awake and would recognize Meta from their outings; but that was part of the *frisson*. Meta meets Estelle: "She was a small, gray wren of a woman in a nondescript dress. If she had ever been pretty —and she must have possessed some beauty to have attracted her first husband—she showed little trace of it now. Of the first impressions swirling in my mind, the discovery that she was a pale, sad, wasted creature [at forty] was the most startling."[29] The evening proves nightmarish for Meta, as perhaps it was intended to. Everyone tried to behave normally, and Meta, despite the mundane conversation, attempted "to project ease and charm from every pore to please my lover." Faulkner kept drinking, glass after glass, at the same time preventing Estelle from getting drunk. As Meta was about to leave, Estelle said she hoped they would see a lot of each other "and become good friends." Meta mumbled something and retreated to Ben's car. "The full force and import of the evening's shameful dissemblance would not hit me for years to come, but it left me at the time with an enemy shrunken in size, foreshortened, no longer the commanding, baleful woman whom I had constructed from the clay of imagination. My hatred had been taken from me and without my consent. But friend I would not be to her."*

Meta had not figured on Estelle being pitiful, the forsaken wife of the great man. If she had at least proven a worthy adversary, she could have dealt with the situation; but Estelle proved no adversary. Instead, she appeared like a sick woman, avid to drink herself into oblivion, an insignificant appendage. Home life for her was a wasteland, as it was for Faulkner; but he had proved that by shaming everyone present. The situation was as complicated as any in a Faulkner novel; and if a protagonist had done what Faulkner did, the writer would have disapproved. The first and chief way to perceive his strategy here is to see his need to take the marriage to its outer limits, to test it so as to reestablish the terms on which he could live with Estelle. The latter was, apparently, not fooled, and a subsequent meeting with Meta at a get-together (the Crowns' Sunday musical) solidified her perception of the situation. From Faulkner's point of view, without anything being said, Estelle was to accept the direction of their marriage.

But beyond that we perceive his terrible hatred of Estelle. Bringing Meta to meet her at a small dinner party was a kind of rape; an invasion of his wife's home, a male ploy for which she had no possible defense. He had penetrated any attempt at self-respect. But the action also shows immense hostility to Meta—something she appears not to have felt, or else sublimates, as the result of her obvious superiority to Estelle.** Yet the situation tests her, under the most stressful circumstances, so as to prove

---

*With this book coming many years later (1976) and written in soap opera language, we must remain on guard: how much is accurate, how much wistful nostalgia, how much resentment that Estelle won the war while she, Meta, won all the battles.

**On that subsequent meeting at the concert, Meta's comments are even more devastating —she hates Estelle for being the wife of the great man. "In spite of the years she had spent in the Orient, the stamp of a small Mississippi town was upon her—dress lacking in distinction, hair stringy and uncontrollable, the splotch of rouge and layering of powder on her face giving her a pasty look." When they see each other, Estelle makes the expected pleasantries. As Faulkner was introduced around, *the* celebrity, "She was talking loudly to gain Bill's attention and there was a strident insistence in everything she said, as if it were a life-and-death matter that Bill recognize her own powers to compel an audience. She was not, I made the judgment, an interesting person." She did not even appear to know much about music. Meta hears: " 'Billy is going to teach me to write, aren't you, Billy?' " She adds her own observation: "The narrow face fevered suddenly with the audacity of what she had said and entreated her husband to say yes, to grant her the miracle that would transform the dross of herself. Zelda Fitzgerald had written stories and a novel; so then would Estelle Oldham Faulkner in her desperation to achieve parity with the man to whom she was wed. . . . I caught the suffering on Bill's face before he turned his head from her, chagrined, pretending not to have understood, not to have heard at all" (Meta Carpenter Wilde and Orin Borsten, *A Loving Gentleman: The Love Story of William Faulkner and Meta Carpenter* [New York: Simon & Schuster, 1976], pp. 178, 179). The observations suggest Meta had herself turned on Estelle, hating the older woman for having "all pride drowned in whiskey and lovelessness," for being such a weak fool. If Faulkner had wanted everyone to reveal the worst, he had succeeded.

to Faulkner he controls her completely. By agreeing to his terms, she agrees to being possessed and to suffering humiliation for his sake. There is a considerable overlay of sadism in Faulkner's desire for the situation, as though his novelistic eye demanded such a confrontation, while ignoring the personal humiliation created.

Another dimension of this encounter involves Faulkner's relationship to women: to know he was all that counted. Now that he was becoming famous, a celebrity, sought after, there was in Faulkner's response to women a form of revenge for the early years of rejection. As he played back the sequence of refusals—marriage, affairs, even dates—he became increasingly imperious in his need to control those who accepted him. Part of this is a natural response: the little man of unprepossessing appearance who was considered a poor catch; now with fame and attendant power, he had returned, re-created himself, as it were, and he wanted everything he had missed. But part of it was sadistic as well. To build himself up, he had chosen humiliation of others; to observe his ability to control a situation, he had demeaned Meta, Estelle, and Ben.

And of course he had demeaned himself. Not only had he humiliated the two women (and also turned Ben into a court jester), he had lacerated himself. The implications here are complex, and conjectural. He needed, in some deep part of himself, not only to punish his wife, not only to punish Meta, but to punish himself. He found it necessary to put himself in the impossible, squirming "spot" when a man's wife and mistress meet in the same room, the wife so far ignorant of the true state of affairs, the mistress carrying off the deception with the help of a faithful friend (the panderer of older literature). There is here—we cannot avoid saying it— a novelistic situation irresistible to the writer, a scenario, even a film script; and to achieve it, he sacrifices decency, compassion, even self-respect.

It is possible to see his laceration of self here as having its counterpart in the lies about his war experiences he repeated to Meta early in their relationship. She says he spoke of his training with the "Canadian Royal Air Force" (which she probably misheard), but also of overseas combat missions. He spoke of flying a mission in France and crashing, which resulted in "a silver plate in my skull. . . . The sterling in my head is worth more than I am down at the Oxford bank." Meta says that until after Faulkner's death she believed he had been shot down over France. She adds, somewhat ingenuously: "It was an inconsistency in the life of a man otherwise given wholly to truth, the utterance of which sometimes hurt those around him."[30] It was also at about this time he told Meta he and Estelle had ceased having sex after Jill's birth, that they slept in separate beds.

We observe the older man patronizing the younger woman willing to accept and believe him at every turn. The lack of sex with Estelle may well have been true, especially with both of them drinking so heavily. But the wartime tales made him into a world-weary Hemingway character, something that delved into personal terms where she could only nod in awe and admiration. So much of his life with Meta was compensatory for earlier slights by women and for his years as the "town tramp" that we must judge his behavior now in that light. The encounter between Meta and Estelle was part of Faulkner's need to *orchestrate* his life: to pull reality into line with his fantasies; to draw out his fantasies by trying to create a scenario for them.

Or else we must come around to see that his hatred of Estelle was so great—and for himself equally great for having married her—he could not help himself. Jill was too young to understand anything of the situation, but using her also showed a disregard of others' needs. What he required, perhaps more than anything else, was self-punishment: to bring home to himself how unappealing his wife was in comparison to the lithe, healthy and fresh-looking mistress, introduced into his home. He needed, in some part of himself, to highlight his mistake.

This turn in Hollywood, which was to last for almost another year (until September 1, 1937), brought him down. According to Meta, who received her information from Faulkner, he had come to feel his marriage could not continue. We are dealing here with information from two people who had ample reason to qualify it with their own needs: Faulkner as the distressed husband seeking pity and compassion, Meta as the "other woman" seeking to find some permanent place in the married man's life. Faulkner asked Estelle for a final separation and divorce, but he wanted custody of Jill. The description that follows must be taken with all the cautions noted above:

> She must realize [Meta writes], as he did, that their life together was empty, meaningless and without substance. It was (probably) then that he saw fit to tell her about me. . . . he vouchsafed for me to know for myself how he had finally phrased and spoken the words that he had not been able to say before, and how at first she had stood there, inert, paltry, superable, and then, learning that the other woman was I, who had been a guest in her home, who she had hoped would be a friend, became a wraith of iron, transformed by outrage into a screaming, frenzied woman, venting all the compacted meanness within her on this man who would sunder all that held her together, take away her child, give his name to a younger woman. He held her off from him while she, with the unnatural strength of the deranged, struck out at him, fought him, cursed him, then ran up the stairway threatening to ruin him.[31]

The description of the confrontation depends on Faulkner's presentation of it to Meta. In turn, her response is mean-spirited, since she must have observed how Estelle was being squeezed from the scene. But there is another possibility: that Faulkner related this story so as to make it seem impossible for him ever to seek a divorce, since that meant the loss of Jill. By presenting Estelle as implacable and hysterical, Faulkner had an "out" in his relationship to Meta; for he could always claim—as he did on several occasions—he could not relinquish Jill. Subsequent passages in Meta's book bring up the question of Jill's custody, and also Faulkner's martyrdom to a marriage which was, he made it seem, destroying him. Another dimension to Faulkner's argument was that he could not leave Jill in the custody of an alcoholic mother, although he did not explain what custody in a binging father would mean. Separation, still further, would mean a further strain on his finances, and that would dictate his remaining a movie-studio hack; for that, he would have to forsake serious writing. *That* was a meaningful argument, while the others were ways in which he could justify the status quo with Meta.*

The levels of Faulkner's life in September–October of 1936, on the eve of the publication of *Absalom*, defy simplification. Moved from "The Last Slaver" to *Splinter Fleet*, which was being produced by the ex-writer Gene Markey, he found himself working on a script which was at best banal. Faulkner appeared to Markey always well-dressed, "neatly-tailored tweed jackets and grey flannel trousers," with the "grave air of a High Court justice."[32] Although he was drinking heavily, Faulkner was trying to maintain appearances. His dialogue was deemed useless, with virtually no reference to the naval story he was assigned to. Markey liked the writer and did not want to see him fired; so he, too, protected an obviously unhappy man.

With studio work a waste of his time, and his domestic life a shambles, the only level of Faulkner's life holding out hope was the publication of *Absalom*. His serious career had otherwise been stalled for most of the year, and if he peered into the future, he could see more of the same wastage. The novel appeared (on October 26) in a regular edition of six thousand copies, with a limited edition of three hundred copies. Bennett Cerf and the entire Random House staff were excited, and the jacket of the first edition indicated it was Faulkner's most "important and ambitious contribution to American literature."

Absalom is the peak of Faulkner's fictional achievement. It is unquestionably the greatest American novel since the turn-of-the-century publication of Henry James's *The Ambassadors*, *The Wings of the Dove*, and *The Golden Bowl*. Its sole competitors among contemporary American novels are Dreiser's *An American Tragedy* and Fitzgerald's *The Great Gatsby*, neither of which approaches Faulkner's innovative daring. When we speak of the great novels of modernism, Faulkner's is the sole American fiction which can be discussed with those by Proust, Mann, Kafka, Conrad, Musil, Broch, Woolf, and Joyce. He was pursuing modernist techniques at a time when the movement was being exhausted in Europe, but had barely entered into the American fictional imagination. Except for Dos Passos, he was the only American novelist to be aware that fiction had undergone

---

*Whatever the truth or falsity of the above arguments, there is little question Faulkner was anguished. Meta reports he was impotent: "The indignities heaped upon him by his wife had leached him of passion and he wanted only to hold me quietly in his arms" (Meta Carpenter Wilde and Orin Borslen, *A Loving Gentleman: The Love Story of William Faulkner and Meta Carpenter* [New York; Simon & Schuster, 1976], p. 186).

shifts in narrative which would permanently alter the way serious writers had to write and serious readers had to read. *Absalom* is a truly original work of modernism, indebted to Joyce and Proust, but very much a product of the American imagination. Except perhaps in details, it cannot be faulted, a sustained work which links all the great American themes. If Melville as a way of pursuing a great theme wrote about whales, Faulkner had, if anything, a greater theme in the American Civil War and its aftermath. In the depths of the depression, he had caught the full glory of American failure.

Cerf and the jacket copy were correct. Clifton Fadiman, in his review, however, represented everything a serious author must somehow live with. Writing in the *New Yorker*, Fadiman weighed in with his usual commentary, that *Absalom* was consistently boring, that he could not see why it had been written, that he did not know what it was about. One wonders why, if this was the case—and there is no reason he *had* to like the book, or know what it was about—he did not pass it on to another reviewer. The sole answer is that it was quite reputable in the 1930s to use Faulkner as a whipping boy in the popular press. The *New York Times*, *Time*, and the *Saturday Review of Literature* all weighed in with negative criticism, although with some occasional praise as well. *Time* considered it, when all was said and done, Faulkner's most impressive novel. Even in the South, the book received less than enthusiastic praise.*

Absalom was, and is, admittedly, a difficult novel to read. But Faulkner had been for years, since *Sound*, educating reviewers with his books. Something of the same thing had occurred with Conrad: early incomprehension of his more difficult novels gave way to gradual understanding because English reviewers became educated in the way Conrad worked. One hoped for the same result in America, but reviewers here seemed set in their ways and unable to make the leap into another dimension which Faulkner's more difficult novels called for. Even as I write in the 1980s, reviewers who are clones of Fadiman continue to gripe and rail against innovative writing. Despite some reviewer perception of his greatness, Faulkner was paying the price of being an avatar of the new. In *Absalom* he had blended the strategies of high modernism—language derived from Joyce and Eliot, uses of memory and the historical past from Conrad, Bergson, and Proust. But that process of telling and retelling, that assimilation of overlapping narratives as they march their way to reach Quentin and Shreve at Harvard, that method was his own. It created repetition, which the reviewers cited; it created some boredom, which the reviewers latched onto; and it

---

*A broad sampling (O. B. Emerson, *Faulkner's Early Literary Reputation in America* [Ann Arbor, Mich.: UMI Research Press, 1984]).: Harold Strauss in the *New York Times Book Review* titled his piece "Mr. Faulkner Is Ambushed in Words," saying that its unreadable prose should be left to those who like puzzles. Malcolm Cowley in the *New Republic* felt Faulkner failed to find a "satisfactory relationship between the horror story in the foreground and the vaster theme that it conceals," concluding that it was style which finally failed the author. The anonymous reviewer in *Newsweek* said Faulkner "bulks larger in American fiction as a technician than as a creator."

created difficulties in locating where the voice was coming from, and there also the reviewers were disturbed. The novel took careful reading, which is not conducive to routine reviewing; and even those whose labors were more leisurely could not easily adapt to the rigorous close reading Faulkner called for.

What the reviewers could not possibly understand was Faulkner had reached so deeply within himself for this novel they had to accept it completely on his terms, or not at all. In his comments on Cézanne, Rainer Maria Rilke, the German poet, speaks of art resulting from the artist having been in danger, "of having gone through an experience all the way to the end, where no one can go any further." The further in the artist goes, the more private and personal the experience, ". . . and the thing one is making is finally the necessary, irrepressible, and, as nearly as possible, definitive utterance of this singularity," which no one "would or even should understand, and which must enter into the work as such, as our personal madness, so to speak . . . like an inborn drawing that is invisible until it emerges."[33] Once the artist accomplishes this, there is no middle ground. To follow Faulkner into the work means picking up the thread which went into the making of the novel. The artistic process has so transformed the material that it cannot be "read" in the usual way; it needs, like all great art, a different set of faculties. It can be understood, but not summarized; it can be experienced, but not rerelated. The reviewers and even more serious readers were confronted by a phenomenon relatively new in American fiction; they failed to see it as such.

Faulkner's personal lifeline was clearly Meta, although she would begin to drift away and eventually marry Wolfgang Rebner, a serious musician, the following April. With the publication of *Absalom*, which went into a second and third edition within a month, Faulkner had nothing new on the drawing board. He did plan to put together the Civil War stories into a volume, what became with the addition of "An Odor of Verbena" *The Unvanquished*. He would rewrite and revise for the volume, but that was not fresh material. He told Goldman he had "no stuff now," but planned some short stories; he "also had another novel in my bean."[34]

He was no longer on assignment at Twentieth Century-Fox, for even the sympathetic and helpful Markey could not disguise the fact Faulkner was not producing usable copy. He drank and did some flying. He was marking time, waiting for something to happen, sitting it out while he wrote checks, still supporting a large establishment in both California and Mississippi. The letter to Cerf outlining his plan for the book of Civil War stories seemed a relief, giving him a chance to work at something. As he and his family celebrated Christmas of 1936 in Pacific Palisades, changes were occurring beyond his reach. Victoria, Estelle's daughter, had married; Harrison Smith was no longer with Random House (Faulkner received this news right after Christmas); Phil Stone's father was dead of a heart attack, and the hunting lodge over which he presided would have to take a different turn; and Meta was soon to begin the move toward another man so as to gain stability in her own life.

The consolation: there was money, more than $19,000 from the Fox studio alone, an enormous sum for the depression years, but barely sufficient to maintain the fairly lavish Faulkner life-style. He had two sets of everything—houses, cars, servants, children, even wife and mistress; and he wanted to expand into Bailey's Woods as well. Reviling himself for the work he did on meaningless scripts, he nevertheless wanted to own property, almost a Frenchman's sense of the need to possess the land. He argued it would protect his privacy, but there was more to it than that: there was the desire to have it, to become a large landowner, as he would demonstrate later when he purchased a farm and let it bleed him. He needed an identification with land as a way of giving himself substance. Perhaps a man who spent so much time at his desk, or contemplating his work, needed land and earth to convey reality. Absalom was dead, and he needed to move on.

Chapter Eighteen

Anguish

THE YEAR 1937 proved to be a diluted mixture of nearly everything in Faulkner's life to date. He continued in Hollywood, at Fox, until very late summer. But he also returned to serious work, since he had free time while on the Fox payroll. At $1,000 per week, up from $750 (as of March 18), he was well paid for doing his own work. He published only one story this year, "Monk" (which appeared in *Scribner's* in May), but the story, like "Smoke" (published in *Harper's* in 1932), was becoming part of a larger plan. He turned this and subsequent stories into a volume, *Knight's Gambit*. Stories aside, however, he began work on *The Wild Palms*, that interwoven tale of two men adrift, one pursuing the happiness he never had, the other trying to stay alive on the raging waters of the flooding Mississippi. Plans also went ahead for the collection of Civil War stories, including the writing of "An Odor of Verbena" to complete the volume.

Except for beginning work on *The Wild Palms*, probably the most significant incident in the year was the marriage of Meta Carpenter to Wolfgang Rebner. She was for the time lost to Faulkner, although their relationship would take an on-again, off-again character. His life emptied out, what with her marriage in April and Estelle's leaving, with Jill, in May. Moreover, his inability to do serious work in 1936 resulted in no publishing activity to speak of now. *Absalom* had already receded, and in writing to

Cerf at the end of 1936, Faulkner acknowledged a certain slackening of effort. He was, in his way, revealing that something had gone out, although his words indicate he means speed of production.

His efforts in the new year were also directed to putting his finances in shape so that when the present contract expired he could leave Hollywood for good. His letter to Goldman on January 21 speaks of Cerf's plan to tie him up with a long-term contract of three or more novels. He indicates he wants an advance, to repay the balance of the Smith and Haas loan. He adds he may produce some stories, also that he has a novel in mind, which may have been *The Wild Palms*. At the end of February, however, he was back on assignment. He was moving from one project to another, from *Gunga Din*, on to *Slave Ship*, then to *Splinter Fleet*, when Markey had him dropped, to something called *Dance Hall*, and on to a real film, *Drums Along the Mohawk*, directed by John Ford. On none of these, apparently, was his dialogue or treatment used; we can assume that whatever his role was, his work was discarded. He received no screen credits. As his letters indicate, the waste was apparent to him. But the money was good, $1,000 per week. In this long stay in Hollywood, Faulkner becomes possibly the best example of an American writer brought out for his reputation, but who had little or nothing to contribute. On further visits, he seems to have been more useful, especially on the Bogart movies of 1945–46, but in this year-long stint, he served neither himself nor the studio very well.

Maurice Coindreau, the French professor and translator, provided a bright spot, with his translation into French of *As I Lay Dying*. Faulkner was particularly pleased that Coindreau—who remained a faithful translator of his work and became a good friend—was planning to undertake *Sound*. "I want to see this translation, indeed, because I feel that it will probably be a damned poor book, but it may be a damned good one (in French, I mean, of course), but in either case, particularly in the latter, it will be Coindreau and not Faulkner." He adds he will be glad to "draw up a chronology and genealogy and explanation, etc. if you need it, or anything else."[1]

The importance of Coindreau's many translations cannot be overestimated; Faulkner's reputation in France—and by implication in Europe—became solidified well before American critics saw him for what he was. The hold he had on the minds of French intellectuals was awesome, moving deeply into the consciousness of such disparate figures as André Malraux, Camus, Sartre, and Simone de Beauvoir, among others. What appealed to the French was almost precisely what had made American reviewers turn away: the use he made of modernist techniques, the fact he had broken with American naturalism/realism in order to penetrate into an area between conscious and preconscious, the additional fact he had a sense of place and history and was not all movement. Hemingway may have been an influence, but Faulkner was an abiding presence. Influence means something temporary, which a writer feels and then passes through to his own style; but presence remains, even after the writer has moved on to his own distinctive voice. The Faulkner voice entered French and European consciousness as a presence, in large part thanks to Coindreau.

By late February or early March, Faulkner and Estelle moved to Beverly Hills, 129 North Le Doux. This more or less coincided with his return to heavy script work, for *Drums Along the Mohawk* (based on the Walter Edmonds novel, with Henry Fonda and Claudette Colbert among an all-star cast). But an event of much larger size surfaced: the climax of Meta Carpenter's relationship to Wolfgang Rebner. Rebner was a talented pianist from a distinguished Jewish family, a refugee from Germany who had lived in London. He was a good talker, witty, highly sensitive, and intelligent; he served as accompanist for many major virtuosi, including Emmanuel Feuermann, the cellist. His own career as a soloist, however, never seemed to take shape. His relationship with Meta somehow defies definition, although he was probably drawn to the same qualities in her which attracted Faulkner: her softness as a well-bred Southerner, her compliance, her intelligence. Culturally and intellectually, they were worlds apart, and his marriage to her would prove as disastrous in its ways as Faulkner's with Estelle.

As Meta began to see the age of thirty not too distant, she apparently pressed Faulkner for some decision. She reports several intense discussions about a breakup with Estelle; but Faulkner warns her she would be named as corespondent in the ensuing scandal. " 'Among other threats and maledictions, she said she would have my Miss Carpenter's name dragged in the mud from here to Memphis.' "[2] Faulkner was playing a double game. Although there is no question he was miserable with Estelle and happy with Meta and in the best of worlds wanted the split, there is also little question he could not make the break, although Maud would have supported him. He did feel an obligation to Jill, and there is some justification to his fear the child would be living with an alcoholic mother, who in her desire for vengeance might possibly prove unsuitable.

But there was more: Rowan Oak, Bailey's Woods, all the material things he had acquired. To marry Meta meant that, at close to forty, he would have to begin all over again. He would be supporting three households (including Maud's) and starting from scratch. Rowan Oak would go to Estelle, as would everything else. He would be in an even deeper financial hole, and Meta would probably expect to have children of their own. The proliferation of responsibilities seemed to have no end, and in the meanwhile he had gotten accustomed to a certain style of life. Part of the price he paid for that style—cars, servants, a comfortable home with spacious grounds—was to continue living with Estelle and having affairs on the sly. In putting his situation this way, we make it sound more clear-cut than it was—yet the heavy and near-suicidal drinking which followed later in the year indicates how Faulkner paid emotionally for whatever decision he made.

Meta shrank from the idea of being named corespondent. She sensed not only the lack of the killer instinct in Faulkner which would have forced the divorce, but also her own inability to sustain the scandal. She feared what her family would think; but she also misjudged Faulkner in believing he "did not care what other people thought of him." She envisages what it would be like, waiting ten years or so for Jill to choose which parent to live with, moving into her middle or late thirties with no children of her own, pretending she did not care what Faulkner's friends really thought of her. "Bill's closest friends would pretend to accept me in Oxford, but I would be an object of disdain for the general community, particularly people sympathetic to Estelle and partial to the Oldham family." She decided: "We had exhausted our options, Bill and I."

She sees her withdrawal from Faulkner as lifting "from his shoulders my dependence on him that he bore so manfully." She views the entire situation from Faulkner's position, which may have been one reason she so attracted him. She sees him as "bruised and bloodied," and apparently she believes every story he tells her—she was the maiden, he the hero. In Meta's framing of her thoughts, there is something of an old-fashioned romance in which her job was to serve, his to direct. They meet and she announces her engagement to Rebner. Faulkner asks her for the final time to wait it out with him, but she pleads that soon she'll be thirty. The biological clock for the woman puts her into a different time frame from that of the man. Faulkner, she says, asked for "one last time," but she insists there can be no more sex between them now that she is engaged. That too, she says, is part of her Southern upbringing, to behave honorably toward the man she planned to marry. Dismissed as a lover, Faulkner asks if they can remain friends, and she agrees.

The entire scene as she shapes it in her book—our sole source of information for this extended and important episode—has echoes of the movie *Casablanca*, in which she plays the Bergman role; Faulkner is Bogart, and Rebner is Paul Henreid. When she wrote the book in 1976, *Casablanca* had become a classic, and it appears to have informed her scenes with Faulkner and even the lines, with Hollywood providing the glamorous backdrop. There is a clichéd quality to everything, as if it were run through a movie script before she could envisage it on paper. We must accept it all warily, especially since by 1976, forty years after the event, Meta saw this as a central episode in her life. Looking back as a woman moving toward seventy, she turned it into legend.

In the final scene before her wedding, Faulkner turned up at Meta's place, "haggard in the weak light, livid gashes caked with blood disfiguring his face."[3] According to his story, he had informed Estelle it was all over between him and Meta, since she was getting married; and Estelle responded by throwing an expensive compact out of the car window, then raking her fingernails down his face while he was driving. " 'I think she wanted to kill me, if not herself.' " The scene seems almost staged: the rejected lover showing up as the victim of his wife's anger, and the compliant bride-to-be comforting her wounded hero. Meta's description of how she eased his suffering, with his head against her breast, has something of the wounded Siegfried in it, or a dozen fadeout scenes in movies. Faulkner vows he will not let her out of his life. On April 5, Meta was married, and she reports she heard Faulkner went on a nonstop drinking binge on the day, leading to an acute alcoholism which required medical care for six weeks and a stay in a Los Angeles hospital. The chapter ends with Faulkner "skin and bones," and hardly recognizable.

At least some of this is true. Faulkner went on sick leave from the studio in mid-April (the fourteenth). William Spratling, his traveling companion from earlier days, turned up, and he observed that after a few drinks Faulkner passed out, indicating his system was saturated. Spratling could see the couple was miserable, and reported that Estelle displayed arm bruises.[4] Faulkner was brought to the Good Samaritan Hospital for nourishment and drying out, but whatever care he received was only for the short term. Seeing a psychiatrist, suggested to him by Joel Sayre, was out of the question. He not only distrusted all psychological probing, but had little faith in medical science as a whole. Further, he had to avoid medical expenses or else remain a slave to Hollywood indefinitely. Two weeks after Meta's marriage (not the six weeks she suggests), Faulkner returned to the Fox payroll. Before his crack-up, he had produced a treatment of *Drums Along the Mohawk*, plus descriptions of the characters—apparently this was a more congenial assignment. The completed movie, which erased all discernible traces of Faulkner's contribution, turned out to be excellent.

By late May, Estelle and Jill returned to Oxford, and Faulkner was left with Narcissus Ewen to take care of him and the house. Back at the studio, he had little to do, and was fortunate he had not been dropped for drinking. He had once more been well shielded from the studio heads, who were adamant about drunken writers; and he could thank intermediaries for disguising his condition. It was a limbo-like existence, as late spring and early summer appeared to hold little for him. On June 20, Maurice Coindreau arrived for a week's stay, with a list of questions about *Sound*. Faulkner gave him the sketch "Afternoon of a Cow" by Ernest V. Trueblood when he left for Mills College.

"Afternoon of a Cow" is less a creative achievement than a retrieval of a memory. It reaches deep into Faulkner's past, back to the days when he published in the *Mississippian*. His imitation of François Villon, "Une Ballad des Femmes Perdues" had appeared on January 28, 1920. Those two wags at the university, Jiggitts and Lester, who saw in Faulkner a perfect object for their mockery, wrote their own version, for the May 20 issue, "Une Ballade d'une Vache Perdue." Whatever the effect upon him of this mocking piece about a lost cow, Faulkner retrieved the title fully seventeen years later and produced his own "Afternoon of a Cow." And not only did he produce this story which he read to Coindreau, and presented to him afterward; he introduced another version of it into *The Hamlet,* where Ike Snopes scandalizes the town by falling in love with Jack Houston's cow. The story and its inclusion in *The Hamlet* indicate Faulkner could wildly miscalculate his effects.

The story takes an unusual form: a writer, the priggish Trueblood, has "Mr. Faulkner" as a character in his tale. And he is the butt of the joke —which focuses on a frightened cow shitting all over Mr. Faulkner while he tries to drive the cow from a raging fire. The story purports to show said Faulkner in various ridiculous roles: trying to move rapidly, which he does well for someone of his "shape and figure"; as a man who curses easily and often in language which cannot be repeated in print; as someone whose silences have within them what he calls "static violence which was his familiar character." The cow is rescued, the boys appear who started the fire, Mr. Faulkner is cleansed of the cow shit, and order is restored with a calming drink or two. The writer insists he has the prerogative to write the story his way, "in my own diction and style and not yours."[5] End of tale, until, reshaped, it appears in *The Hamlet.* There is, withal, one good phrase, "static violence," to describe the silence and withdrawal character-istic of "Mr. Faulkner." The phrase captures the man as a quiescent vol-cano, at any time ready to blow, but on the surface settled and resolved.

Coinciding with Coindreau's stay, Faulkner received a go-ahead for the revision of Civil War stories to make up a volume. The stories had been conceived to stand on their own. To put them in a volume where they are interconnected, as a "novel of stories," was to work them over with the novelist's, not the short story writer's, skill. Faulkner had here an experi-mental mode: sequential stories as the basis for a novelistic treatment of the material. Although *The Unvanquished* remained unfulfilled, a collection without real coherence, in his next effort at this intermediate genre, *Go Down, Moses,* Faulkner conceived of the stories as linked into a novel. Bringing his work around to this new mode depended on foreshadowing, recasting, inserting dialogue, and preparing the reader. While the stories have their own shape, for the collection they had to seem like chapters in a longer work. This was not to be a volume such as *These 13, Doctor Martino and Other Stories,* or even *Knight's Gambit.*

Faulkner moved back from Thomas Sutpen to John Sartoris, and inter-polated material in the first story which more finely fixes Sartoris, the father of young Bayard. That thickening of the older man's affairs becomes apparent throughout; so that we have the buildup for "An Odor of Ver-bena," which Faulkner was about to write. In order for young Bayard's potential vengeance to have a suitable context, Faulkner needed to inten-sify the lines holding father and son together. When Bayard decides to end the killing by not killing, by exposing himself to the bullets of his father's murderer, he does so after Faulkner has provided him with every motive for continuing the feud. The Civil War John Sartoris is a legendary crea-ture, on his legendary horse, Jupiter. Faulkner was reaching for some dimension which placed the older warrior outside of time and place, and yet brought him back in as father, head of family, protector of his house, and, finally, husband to Drusilla.

We note how Faulkner was carrying over ideas from *Absalom* into his revisions of the *Unvanquished* segments. In *Absalom* he had been able to turn Sutpen into legend and back again into man/devil because he had provided a large context. In the stories, he wanted something of the same with Sartoris, the legendary warrior overlapping with Sutpen, the legendary empire builder; but with stories in hand, he had insufficient scope. To create what he really had in mind for the volume, he would have needed to put the stories aside and then redo them.

There is another factor, and an important one, in this transition from one form to another. While Faulkner had to keep John Sartoris in view until he is murdered, he also had to remind us of the other equally important theme, the growth and development of a young boy into manhood. Yet the Tom Sawyer–Huck Finn parts of the stories do not work very clearly with the Sartoris element. They pull against each other as much as they overlap; for to grow and develop, young Bayard must be involved in many activities which are marginal to those of his father. He develops in the main while his father is away; and his means of development are connected to activities having nothing to do with Sartoris. The sole connecting link is the war itself, but that can be shown, equally, as in the revisions of "Raid," as an element separating rather than linking them.

On July 24, when he wrote Goldman that Random House was collecting the Civil War stories, he announced he had just finished "An Odor of Verbena." He hoped the *Post* would buy it, and since time was important he sent the story directly there. There was, however, no sale, either to the *Post* or anywhere else. "An Odor of Verbena" is possibly the strongest of the pieces, explained by the fact it was freshly written for the book and did not need to fit into the *Post*. It is a true cap to the collection, and it brings together a good deal of Faulkner's feelings about the war, Reconstruction, the equality of the races, and the need to reconcile, if not forgive. The final growth and development of young Bayard comes in his refusal to commit the obvious: to seek vengeance on his father's killer. Redmond waits for the young man of twenty-four, fully expecting to kill or be killed, but Bayard tries the braver route, and his steady walk, unarmed, into the barrel of Redmond's pistol, satisfies everyone except Drusilla, John Sartoris's young widow. Her response is to go mad, but in her various rages before that she had already been moving there.

Drusilla was an interesting experiment for Faulkner: the young woman more man than the men, more of a warrior than most soldiers. Her dedication to Southern victory is so overwhelming she cannot see beyond killing. Her view of history is that the South can do no wrong; whereas Bayard recognizes that his father was violent and ruthless, in his dealings during the War, after, and in his railroad business with Redmond. Faulkner's evaluation of the old colonel has now changed considerably from what it was in *Flags in the Dust* and *Sartoris*, perceiving how ruthlessness and violence bring on their own self-destruction.

But Drusilla goes beyond being an advocate of killing. She has some of the qualities Faulkner associated with an attractive female: an epicene, androgynous quality, lean, hipless, thoroughly disguised as a woman when in a soldier's outfit. She goes either way, and she is apparently seductive to young Bayard. At one point, when she insists he kiss her, body to body, we have a familiar incest theme—she is now John Sartoris's second wife, Bayard's stepmother, only eight years older. Bayard feels obliged to tell his father what has occurred, but John Sartoris does not respond to it; he only says, as the old colonel was supposed to have said, " 'I am tired of killing men, no matter what the necessity nor the end. Tomorrow, when I go to town and meet Ben Redmond, I shall be unarmed.' "[6] He dies, Bayard lives, and Drusilla laughs madly.

The final story in the volume creates the impression the entire work is stronger than it is. Rather than seeking literary excellence, however, we should see it as a guide to Faulkner's ideas about the war and about America. His presentation of the war is that of a conflict composed of several individual efforts. There is no sense of a "war effort" or of a concerted attack or defense by Southern forces. The war results from innumerable individual acts. When John Sartoris feels like it, he fights; when he feels otherwise, he returns home, builds a pen with his son, and then goes back to fighting—something like Faulkner with Hollywood. What this suggests is that Faulkner saw the war, at least in his literary representation of it, as a kind of medieval joust, in which men paired off, fought, then returned to their more or less normal lives. Or else he saw it in terms of hand-to-hand combat, part of the golden age of fighting when warriors were like gladiators, unorganized into units or groups. Faulkner's presentation of the war fits into his overall sense of the individual: even war can be scaled down to individual effort. His hatred and distrust of all government action, of any centralized control, is epitomized in his representation of war. Part of it could be attributed to his own area of choice: flying. He had tried to be a combat pilot in World War I, and when that ended, he eventually went into piloting his own plane. In some way, flying emblematized war for him, or the way war should be fought: not under a centralized command, but as the sum total of individual actions. When he returned to war on an ambitious scale in *A Fable*, he would, once again, demonstrate that the individual is supreme, or should be. Man in his plane or the writer at his desk, alone, became the measure of all things.

Coindreau's visit of June 20–26 was a pleasant interlude. Although a quite different spirit from Faulkner, Coindreau found common ground with the writer, and they charmed each other. With Faulkner drinking steadily, they spent several hours working on difficult passages in *Sound*, and apparently the intake of alcohol did not affect Faulkner's precise memory of passages. He told Coindreau he drank while writing. When Coindreau asked him about the use of "La Vendée" as the title of one of the stories, inasmuch as he came from that section of France, Faulkner said that from his reading of Balzac's *Les Chouans* he felt Southerners and people from La Vendée had much in common. The remark becomes prophetic, for Faulkner was preparing to start on a book about the Snopes family, his "Vendée peasants." The following year, on November 19, he sent "Barn Burning" to Harold Ober, and that, heavily revised, became the first chapter of *The Hamlet*. By December 15 of the same year, he sent Robert Haas a letter detailing the Snopes project, a trilogy to be called "The Peasants," "Rus in Urbe," and "Ilium Falling"—that is, *The Hamlet*, *The Town*, and *The Mansion*, adding that he is halfway through volume I.

We observe a familiar pattern: well before a particular book has shaped itself in his mind, he was already preparing himself to write it—in this instance, an entire trilogy. In his remark that the peasants of La Vendée and the South had a good deal in common, Faulkner was revealing how his early and deep reading in Balzac colored his imagination. Ultimately, Southern conditions in the post-Reconstruction era dictated a different kind of novel from that which Balzac wrote; but that particular recognition of the people, present also in the Russian novel, was sufficient for Faulkner's glimmer.

The end of the visit came with the reading of "The Afternoon of a Cow," which seemed to have puzzled everyone except Coindreau, who ended up with the typescript of the story. Faulkner later told Harold Ober he wrote it one afternoon when he "felt rotten with a terrible hangover, with no thought of publication, since the story is a ribald one."[7] Reed Whittemore of *Furioso* obtained it and wanted to publish it (it finally appeared in the summer of 1947), and Faulkner could not ignore the $75 to $100 fee offered.

The emptying-out process continued when Coindreau left, since the studio also left him in limbo. As he was by himself a good deal, he felt mellow toward Rowan Oak, and even toward reunion with his family. He missed Jill's fourth birthday, on June 24, but sent a telegram. With his contract not taken up, he told Estelle he would be home sometime after August 15. "It's hot here and I dont feel very good, but I think it's most being tired of movies, worn out with them." He added: "Bless Pappy's girl."[8]

When Faulkner drove back to Oxford, with Ben Wasson accompanying him, he had achieved a curious victory and suffered a familiar defeat. Although he had made over $21,000 in Hollywood in half a year, he had few prospects for income. *Absalom* was not going to carry his burden, and he had nothing specific on his desk, no short stories, nothing except what he carried in his head. On one hand, he was liberated from a chore he disliked; on the other, he was heading back to more financial problems, to a wife deeply estranged from him, and to a general situation which, if anything, was worse than the one he had left. Meta Carpenter was off in Europe, out of sight but not out of mind.

Faulkner's return was marked by almost a full-page map in the Oxford *Eagle* captioned "Mississippi in Literature and Legend," and listing Oxford's six outstanding features. The *Eagle* notice was like a miniature of Faulkner's life, reducing his privacy by extolling him as a "tourist attraction," one of Oxford's six, but providing publicity as a town boy who had made good. His life had oscillated between those two elements: the obsessive, driven need to keep his life private and yet the equally driven need to prove himself and prove others' opinions of him wrong. He was becoming an American, not simply an Oxfordian, celebrity—mentioned in gossip columns, his career charted and followed, his personal life aired, especially since his advertisement about Estelle's charge accounts. The editor of the *Eagle*, Moon Mullen, had an uncanny way of getting under Faulkner's skin—providing him with the publicity which demonstrated to everyone he had made good, yet undermining his desire to hide at Rowan Oak behind the acreage he was purchasing for that purpose.

What is remarkable—and as yet unnoted—is how insulated Faulkner was from what was occurring in Europe and Asia, what would engage America in a few years. Although he went up to New York occasionally and mingled with a heavily Jewish crowd, the situation in Germany did not seem to have penetrated. Blotner does report[9] Faulkner predicted a war was imminent, but the actuality of it was not to become part of his work. The Spanish civil war, which many saw as the first round of the coming larger war, did not appear to have penetrated deeply into his imagination. He did, however, respond to a request to register his opposition to Franco and fascism.* Although later Faulkner became politicized with the racial question and responded to the poor leadership Mississippi's governors and senators provided, he nevertheless lacked an acute sense of what was occurring in the larger world.

One reason, perhaps, is that embedded in a rural, agricultural community, in a poor state with few if any industries capable of producing arms, he was insulated from events in a large world. But Faulkner had just spent over a year in Hollywood, where refugees from Europe were pouring in, unmistakably so. He was not simply someone bedding down in Oxford. In Hollywood he could not have been ignorant of the influx of very famous people. Directors, writers, composers were turning Southern California into a "new Weimar." Those who settled in included Fritz Lang, Luis Buñuel, Alfred Hitchcock, among directors; Stravinsky, Schönberg, and Korngold, among composers; Aldous Huxley, Thomas Mann and his brother, Heinrich, Franz Werfel, Bertolt Brecht, Christopher Isherwood, and Antoine de Saint-Exupéry, among writers. These were only the most famous; there was a flood of lesser figures in all areas of the arts. Not all of them had arrived when Faulkner was there, but even though he dealt mainly with Hawks and Markey, he could not have avoided the in-gathering of talent in the studios and the general community. Similarly, in New York, on his several trips, the talk was of a coming disaster. Jews were becoming aware of the fate of Jews

---

*Which we see in May of 1938.

in Germany, and the Spanish civil war had engaged the imagination of an entire generation of writers.

Yet Faulkner let all this go by. This is not to insist he should have written fiction mirroring political events. Quite the contrary. What it points to is his removal from large-scale politics. In "Monk," which ended up as the second story in *Knight's Gambit,* Faulkner does touch on local politics. The governor who speaks without regard for justice or principles, only for votes in the next election, is clearly Bilbo, governor from 1916 to 1920 and again from 1928 to 1932, before his election to the Senate. "At that time we had for Governor a man without ancestry and with little more divulged background than Monk had; a politician, a shrewd man who (some of us feared, Uncle Gavin and others about the state) would go far if he lived."[10] With the pardon board completely under his control, he decides to issue pardons so as to pick up the votes of the released prisoners in the upcoming election. When Gavin Stevens argues with him that he is releasing murderers, he says he knows he is, that they will probably murder again, but there is a place for them to return to if they do.

Faulkner's image of America was basically apolitical in any committed sense; but deeply political in the cultural sense that he absorbed into his work what the region and country were becoming. In his pursuit of this "culture" or body politic, Faulkner had no time for political action, political commitment, or political loyalties. He voted for the Democratic party, although as an intense individualist, he opposed many, if not most, of Roosevelt's New Deal efforts to get the country going again. He saw life, politics, and human experience in atomistic terms: not as part of state or government, but closer to frontier terms, each man in his Jeffersonian armor doing battle with life on his and its terms.

Not until *A Fable* (1954) can we say Faulkner became politicized, and yet even here he has transformed a political and military situation into a Christian parable, making individuals count far more than concerted action. Mixing Job, Jesus, suffering, martyrdom, and repentance, he trod on Dantean territory. Yet ironically, he responded to America's victory by stressing not conquerors, but victims and victimizing. Thus when he finally came to write a "political novel," he turned politics into philosophy and religion, making the conflict in the novel hinge on a religious struggle between Jesus and God; as if rewriting Dostoyevsky's Grand Inquisitor scene in terms of World War I conflicts.

On September 15, he apparently had his subject for his new novel, for he put that date on the first page of the holograph manuscript of *The Wild Palms.* His line of thought here is very interesting, very much in keeping with his characteristic way of working. The female figure in *The Wild Palms,* Charlotte Rittenmeyer, is unmistakably based on memories of Helen Baird. Physically, she is closely patterned, even to the burns both suffered; and emotionally, both are severely independent women given to extremes of behavior.

Now ten years after Helen married Guy Lyman, Faulkner begins a novel in which a "Helen figure"—even to the name symbolism—figures largely. But that is only half of the story. The other half is that the Helen connection was surely evoked by the loss of Meta to Wolfgang Rebner. Back from Hollywood, settled in Oxford, Faulkner still felt the "heartbreak" which he told Meta he suffered; and that significant wrench of his emotional life led him back to another heartbreak he had suffered, rejection by Helen, leading to her marriage shortly afterward. The parallel lines of two situations creating patterns of heartbreak ten years apart could only be resolved by fictionalizing them. In the light of the parallelism, it seems likely Faulkner and Helen had sexually consummated their affair.

With initial work started on *The Wild Palms*, Faulkner in mid-October made another trip to New York, to meet his new editor at Random House, Saxe Commins, and to work over further revisions of the *Unvanquished* stories. That volume appeared on February 15, 1938, with illustrations by Edward Shenton. Random House had high hopes for the volume, less for sales alone than to solidify Faulkner's position with them. Beginning with this visit, Random House became for him a home away from home. Saxe Commins was an ideal editor for Faulkner: low-keyed, hardworking, accommodating, familiar with the quirks of difficult authors. When he had been a dentist, one of his patients was Eugene O'Neill, and Commins had come into publishing by way of his own book, *Psychology: A Simplification*. In her little study of her husband, *What Is an Editor? Saxe Commins at Work*, Dorothy Commins tells of how Commins waited for the six copies of his book to arrive from Liveright. When the package did arrive—this was in 1927—there were six copies of *Mosquitoes*. That was his introduction to Faulkner. When the latter came to Random House, Commins took over the editing of his books from 1936, with *Absalom*, to 1958, with joint work on *The Mansion*. In effect, he was present during Faulkner's entire mature career, capping the role Harrison Smith had filled before.

Space was cleared away at Random House, and Faulkner had his work area for as long as he wished. But he had come for more than work: he needed to negotiate advances, and to turn Random House into his personal banker. In effect, the publishing house controlled his finances for many years to come, the way Conrad had done with his agent, James Brand Pinker. To prevent unnecessary expenditures, Faulkner asked Random House to hold his Hollywood earnings and to send on a stipend at intervals. He hoped this way to budget himself; but the clearer indication was that his income could be hidden from his wife. Since their estrangement emotionally and psychologically was so intense, there seemed little reason to him why he should maintain a financial partnership. What he was doing, of course, was turning Estelle even more into a Zelda-like creature: completely on his string and unable to make any of the decisions which affected them both. Within the framework of the marriage, he was, in actuality, divorced from his wife.

The stay in New York, up to a certain point, was congenial enough. He saw old friends, including Smith, who went on to make a career for himself at the *Saturday Review;* he became chummy with Cerf and Robert Haas, who entertained him. Wherever he went he was a celebrity, a single man much sought after at dinner parties. On one occasion, he met Sherwood Anderson after all those years of estrangement. Anderson was now in eclipse, and his onetime pupil or apprentice was, with Hemingway, the man of the hour. In his *Memoirs,* Anderson speaks of seeing Faulkner, but avoiding him, until the latter tugged at his coat sleeve. Faulkner: " 'Sherwood, what the hell is the matter with you? Do you think that I am also a Hemy?' "[11] The remark was snide, of course, and referred to Hemingway's method of cutting away everyone who had tried to help him, as if now that he was a giant, he could pose as self-made. Later, in retrospect, Faulkner felt nostalgic, calling Anderson a giant in *Winesburg, Ohio; The Triumph of the Egg;* and some of the pieces in *Horses and Men*—but he also recognized how uneven his onetime idol was. Yet in the land of pygmies, he was a giant, "even if he did make but two or perhaps three gestures commensurate with gianthood."[12]

Faulkner was drinking heavily, not the least because Meta Rebner's return from Europe with her husband deeply depressed him. He wanted to take them to dinner, so he could see her, but before he did, another event intervened. When Faulkner's phone at the Algonquin did not answer and he had not turned up, his New York friend, Jim Devine, went to the room, where the writer in his undershorts, window open, had fallen against the radiator, and was lying there, oblivious to the burning of his back near his left kidney. The pipe had penetrated to the third degree of burn, and could possibly have killed him if not for Devine's interruption. His condition was serious, not only because of the severe burn but because of his malnourished condition. Only his exceptionally strong constitution kept him from permanent damage.

This time Faulkner needed immediate and extensive treatment. The burn required surgery and his dependence on alcohol was complete: he had slid perhaps further than ever before. Paraldehyde took the place of alcohol, to help him withdraw; and he needed nourishment—thick malteds with eggs beaten in. Recovery except from the burn was rapid: some sleep, some nourishment, a quick withdrawal on the paraldehyde, and he was up and around. His recovery powers were phenomenal. Interestingly enough, he asked to see Sherwood Anderson at his bedside, as it were a father figure. The older writer was himself a heavy drinker and could speak to Faulkner without admonition. Anderson comprehended that what might appear self-destructive to outsiders was, in reality, a way of arranging one's life so as to be able to write: it was that exchange of one's personal well-being for immersion in a process which transformed it.

Although the back burn required skin grafts—and would continue to bother Faulkner for almost the rest of his life—he made the trip back to Oxford, via Memphis. There Estelle took care of him, although herself in need of attention. He was interviewed in Memphis by one Harold Burson, an interview which appeared in the Memphis *Commercial Appeal* on November 18. Faulkner said he did not intend to return to Hollywood, which he characterized as a "very wealthy, over-grown country town." He added: "I don't like scenario writing because I don't know enough about it. I feel as though I can't do myself justice in that type of work, and I don't contemplate any more of it in the near future." He says he has not read *Gone With the Wind* or *Anthony Adverse* because they are too long: ". . . no story takes 1000 pages to tell."[13] What he neglects to add is that to read the four-hundred-odd pages of *Absalom* takes far longer than the one thousand of the Mitchell or Allen novel. Faulkner admits "he hasn't written his 'best novel,' that it is yet to come"; that his method is always to write his first draft in longhand, then make revisions, finally to rewrite when typing out his manuscript for the publisher. It was a breezy interview in which Faulkner revealed nothing of himself, little of his career except what was already known.

Writing Haas[14] on November 19, he assures him he is better, although his back is painful. The rest of the letter is concerned with financial considerations. He asks for a better royalty rate than fifteen percent first printing, twenty percent second, twenty-five percent thereafter, although these were generous terms. Mainly, however, he wants to put his finances with Random House on a stable, realistic basis, so that what he has is his and does not result from a juggling of the books. By November 29, Faulkner has ironed out all problems with the accommodating Haas, and he writes he has gotten "into the novel," called in manuscript "If I Forget Thee, Jerusalem"—*The Wild Palms*. He feels he will have it ready by May 1 (1938), although he cannot be sure, as work is going slowly. He was not far off, for the typescript was mailed in June. Once he got into it, he moved as rapidly as ever.

There was the semblance of order now in his life, and the emptiness he felt in Hollywood receded as he moved more intensely into a new novel, especially one with as much personal freight as *The Wild Palms*. The memory of Meta, however, was present and strong. Fifteen years later, he wrote to Joan Williams, another young woman with whom he had a liaison, that he worked on *The Wild Palms* "in order to stave off what I thought was heartbreak too. And it didn't break then and so maybe it won't now, maybe it wont even have to break for a while yet, since the heart is a very tough and durable substance or thing or what you want to call it."[15] An incurable romantic about young women, Faulkner went after them only to see them, in time, marry young men, and then he could indulge his sense of loss, accompanied by feelings of uselessness and aging. The affair with Meta, followed by her defection, sent him back to Helen Baird, whom he had also lost; and then drove the engine which made *The Wild Palms* an intense adventure of gain and loss.

What is further remarkable is his intertwining of the *Wild Palms* story of two errant lovers with the Mississippi background of "Old Man." It was

as if the novel were a sandwich made of the two slices of his own experience: the errant romance in Hollywood linked with the familiar home
scene, the protagonist as prisoner. The emblems seem almost too personal,
too congruent with his sense of his own life. The prisoner is entrapped by
the river, as Faulkner by his domestic situation; but played out in the
contrasting corollary story is the adventure of a doomed love. In one, he
aborts the pregnancy which has tied him down; in the other, he goes ahead
with it. The two elements complement each other so perfectly Faulkner
could indeed write rapidly, certain of the transformation of his own feelings in the two parts of the novel.

Much speculation has followed on why Faulkner wrote alternating
chapters of *The Wild Palms*: one on the errant lovers, one on the prisoner
and his attempt to deliver the pregnant woman and to surrender, back and
forth. Some have asserted the two halves are happenstance or haphazard,
others that there is a counterpointing, still others that the resultant book
should be divided and published as two separate stories, as it has been in
some editions. Faulkner presented his own ideas about the novel in his
comments to Jean Stein some eighteen years later; but before we get to
those remarks, we should mention that the "Old Man" segments of the
book depend heavily on the *Wild Palms* chapters. Although they are interwoven, the latter is the dominant tale, "Old Man" the lesser one. Both are
imaginatively necessary, inasmuch as Faulkner was putting together two
sides of his own recent experience: straying in a doomed affair, returning
to be a prisoner of sorts.

In that important *Paris Review* interview he gave Jean Stein in 1956,
Faulkner said he started with one story—"the story of Charlotte Rittenmeyer and Harry Wilbourne, who sacrificed everything for love, and then
lost that." But once he started the book, he saw it had to be two separate
stories—very possibly to relieve the strong personal element in the tale of
two errant lovers.

> When I reached the end of what is now the first section of *The Wild
> Palms*, I realized suddenly that something was missing, it needed
> emphasis, something to lift it like counterpoint in music. So I wrote
> on the "Old Man" story until the "Wild Palms" story rose back to
> pitch. Then I stopped the "Old Man" story at what is now its first
> section, and took up the "Wild Palms" story until it began to sag.
> Then I raised it to pitch again with another section of its antithesis,
> which is the story of a man who got his love and spent the rest of the
> book fleeing from it, even to the extent of voluntarily going back to
> jail where he would be safe. They are only two stories by chance,
> perhaps necessity. The story is that of Charlotte and Wilbourne.[16]

When Stein asks how personal this is, Faulkner is evasive, and speaks of
what the writer needs in general terms: experience, observation, imagina-

tion; and denies inspiration as something he knows nothing about. What is clear about both halves of the book is the theme of alternating imprisonment and liberation.

In late fall and early winter, Faulkner was getting well into it. To Haas, on December 21: "The novel is coming pretty well; I found less trouble than I anticipated in getting back into the habit of writing, though I find that at forty I dont write quite as fast as I used to."[17] He still promises it by May 1. Writing a week later to Jim Devine: "I have about a third of it done, should come in under the wire May first with my tail up and my eyes flashing."[18] He adds his back is so painful he cannot sleep, so he writes at night, hunts quail by day.

Yet beneath the cheerful remarks is a work which moves at the extremes of behavior. In both stories, the male protagonists have lost their freedom: Harry in liberating himself becomes a prisoner of a different kind; the prisoner in getting free of his jailors has become a prisoner of greater intensity during the flood. For each, release from their existing conditions creates more pressure. The prisoner wishes to be back in the safety of jail —which becomes an Edenic vision once he finds himself at the mercy of the Old Man. Harry may not wish himself back, but he suffers intensely during his release and finds himself sliding toward destruction. When he performs the first abortion in the Utah mining camp, he recognizes how far he has declined; a passionate love affair is destroying, not strengthening, him.

Even as Faulkner is writing the novel in remorse at loss of Meta and before that Helen Baird, we cannot mistake the hostility toward women the book reveals. He may have been profoundly hurt by Helen's rejection, but in building his novel around a Helen-type, he demonstrates how disastrous any long-term relationship with her would have been. In her needs, she consumes men; she is not only Helen of Troy, but the Venus's-fly trap embodied. Although his presentation of Charlotte is sympathetic to her kind of energy and leadership, she is the Biblical Lilith or Eve. General comments on women, which include her, are obviously unfavorable. Such remarks that begin *The Wild Palms*, section 3, seem directed at Estelle and her type, women who find ways to bring about cohabitation, not through thrift or husbandry, but by means of a different dimension:

. . . a completely uncerebrated rapport for the type and nature of male partner and situation, either the cold penuriousness of the fabled Vermont farmwife or the fantastic extravagance of the Broadway revue mistress as required, absolutely without regard for the intrinsic value of the medium which they saved or squandered and with little more regard or grief for the bauble which they bought or lacked, *using both the presence and absence of jewel or checking account* [my italics] as pawns in a chess game whose prize was not security at all but respectability within the milieu in which they lived.[19]

Then Faulkner zeroes in on Charlotte and her type, with a generalized swipe at all women:

> . . . It's not the romance of illicit love which draws them, not the passionate idea of two damned and doomed and isolated forever against the world and God and the irrevocable which draws men; it's because the idea of illicit love is a challenge to them, because they have an irresistible desire to (and an unshakable belief that they can, as they all believe they can successfully conduct a boarding house) take the illicit love and make it respectable, take Lothario himself and trim the very incorrigible bachelor's ringlets which snared them into the seemly decorum of Monday's hash and suburban trains.

Caught in the Venus's-flytrap, the man becomes impotent.

Faulkner was playing a double game: using Charlotte as the means of liberating Harry Wilbourne from his self-denying life, but then imprisoning him in a love nest of her own peculiar make. He may be Tannhauser falling to her Venus, the medieval knight enticed into the seductress's bower—but without salvation, without redemption. Charlotte is a fascinating type for Faulkner, in the way Helen Baird was, repeated in Laverne in *Pylon*, and before that, Margaret in *Soldiers' Pay*. Faulkner admires the ability of the woman, to whom we should add the recently created Drusilla of the *Unvanquished* stories, who can cross over; who possesses an epicene quality which, while making her desirable to certain kinds of men, also makes her dangerous and threatening, even fatal.

The two parts of the novel are uncannily linked. Although liberation for Harry and Charlotte means something quite different from what it comes to be for the convict on his part, nevertheless they repeatedly cross. The cold the lovers feel in the Utah mining camp, for example, is equated directly to the watery death the tall convict fears from the rampaging river. The use of pregnancies in both creates another obvious interweaving. Once liberation is effected, pregnancy brings both parties back to prison dimensions. Harry, the almost-doctor, is entrapped by fear that abortion is his fate; whereas the birth of the baby during the flood traps the convict into a family situation he never made.

Another large element linking the two segments is that of dissatisfaction, to the extent the quality becomes coexistent with emptiness. The empty vase or urn has been a common Faulkner image, and Harry is one such empty vessel. In one reading, it is possible to view the novel as an objective correlative of Faulkner's own emptiness at this time—the "heartbreak" he wrote and spoke about; but more than that, the man of forty testing out the waters. He had introduced Meta to Estelle as a way of breaking the mold, of walking the edge; and he had failed. His nerves or resolve had faltered. The novel now became the acting-out of what he could not personally do. His personal misery—and it was real, not just play-acting or posing—could be resolved only in the silence of the written word. The novel finds him toying with alternatives, and discovering they all lead back to the same thing. Harry does the cycle, as does the tall convict: liberation leads to anguish.

Both parts of the novel deal in spatial matters. Faulkner here presents the typical American theme of escape, running space as a means of liberating oneself. In "Old Man," there is the additional spatiality of the flooding river used to blur all distinctions of boundaries, state lines, limitations between town and country land. There is the shadow of *Huckleberry Finn* here, the river as an alternative to land. But Faulkner is an ironist, a mocker of pieties; and the river becomes more of a trap than the jail, not the road to freedom, but the roadway to a worse form of imprisonment. Similarly, as Harry and Charlotte run, they roam ever deeper into what will doom them; space provides temporary release, but ultimately leads to the grave. When we speak of Faulkner as a distinctly American novelist, we must cite how he cuts into all the traditional American themes; but at the same time, subverts them, shows how they fail. His "on the road" novel reveals all the self-destructiveness implicit in efforts to break out: a caveat we cannot help but apply to him personally.

Connected to the disappointments of space, as against its joys, is the idea of America as a dispossessed Eden, a pastoral gone bad. Here we have a constant in Faulkner, but intensified and anguished. The freeing-up of space ordinarily echoes an Edenic existence, the kind of contrast with one's present situation which recalls a golden age. Yet Faulkner does nothing of the sort. His pastoral is polluted, his Eden dispossessed (contaminated by man's doing): Eden in both parts seems to be "beyond" all boundaries, but when one arrives *there*, there is bondage. Harry says it himself, in his long speech to McCord, the journalist who helps the couple, at the end of *The Wild Palms*, section 3. He reveals that his effort to free himself with Charlotte has led him into another form of captivity: "They had used respectability on me and that it was harder to beat than money."[20] He feels he is doomed, and that is why he is afraid. His only hope is that ". . . maybe I can be the consort of a falcon, even if I am a sparrow."

Linked to his desire to find Eden, while discovering quite a different territory, is the theme of abandonment. We once again drift across Faulkner's personal life, in the sense that he has been abandoned, the emptying-out process he felt. Abandonment has two sides: one abandons others, one is oneself abandoned. It is the anxiety-ridden or fearful side of liberation. *The Wild Palms* is permeated by images of abandonment: Charlotte abandons her husband and children, Harry abandons his efforts to be a respectable doctor, both abandon one place after another, one job after another; they abandon hastily-made friends in order to make others, who in turn will be abandoned. By a certain point, they have abandoned whatever concept of themselves they may have had, as actuality catches up with them. In the "Old Man" segment, abandonment is equally forceful, and equally destructive. The two convicts are coupled together, paralleling the "coupling" of Harry and Charlotte, but one must abandon the other in order to fulfill his quest. The convicts are "married" to each other, chained, one tall and lean, one plump and short, a marriage which dissolves in their moment of liberation. Abandonment makes the tall convict nostalgic for jail; whereas Harry, in an overlapping sense, ponders his past before abandonment of everything had entered his mind. Images are of desolation, a watery wasteland, a frozen landscape, meaningless acts measured against the larger sense of things. In few other works has Faulkner seemed more a naturalistic writer, in the manner of Norris or Dreiser, working along the lines of a mechanical reciprocity against which human will is futile.

At forty Faulkner had put together a meaningful personal document, while attempting to resolve needs only words could deal with. A subtext of all the obvious imagery is the fear of drowning. But water is not necessary for that. The tall convict may actually fear drowning in the flood of Biblical intensity,* but Harry drowns otherwise. By the time he and Charlotte come to the beach cottage at the very beginning, a cottage facing out on the water, they have already gone under. The rhythms of interior monologue which take over the novel occasionally are part of an overall deliquescence: of people going under. Charlotte drowns in blood, Harry in the eventuation of his liberation. In prison, Harry smells the ocean or sea.

Drowning has another guise as well. Charlotte is willing to forsake her children and husband in order to achieve another level of experience: one which takes her out of herself into a kind of physical love, which in turn becomes spiritualized in its intensity. So inexorable is her pursuit she convinces Harry any other course of action is destructive. He realizes what is happening: ". . . it seemed to him that they both stood now, aligned, embattled and doomed and lost, before the entire female principle."[21] Later, Harry translates this pursuit of a doomed love into an attack on respectability; but his language is full of twists and turns suggesting something loathsome: ". . . I watched myself getting more and more tangled in it like a roach in a spider web; each morning, so that my wife could leave on time for her job . . . give us a little more time and we could have been dressing and undressing inside our kimonas in one another's presence and turning off all the lights before we made love."[22] He adds bitterly: "It's not avocation that elects our vocations, it's respectability that makes chiropractors and clerks and bill posters and motormen and pulp writers of us."

He is caught in the cycle of Charlotte's own bitter attack on family and work, her husband referred to as "Rat." But even as she mouths her assault on such values, she is moving toward them, and Harry, the reluctant partner at first, is now trying to swim in the destructive element, swim against the current. Convinced by her passion for love and romance, having abandoned the work ethic for sensation and experience, he has no tools

*The great flood of 1927 was the immediate source; but the legendary qualities of the description return to the Biblical flood, with the tall convict a kind of ironical Noah, breasting the waters created by an inscrutable God. The fact that the flood has banished all boundaries suggests its universal life, Old Man River seeping into everything and restoring a natural patriarchy. The flood may have started as the rampaging Mississippi, but now becomes all disasters, like the water rising in As I Lay Dying.

for coping with the new life thrust upon him. He has only his insight into what life can be, not the mechanism by which he can keep it going. He is in effect a swimmer who suffers a cramp at the beginning of the race and must either wait for rescue or go down. As Charlotte drowns in her blood from the abortion, he drowns from his inability to discover means of survival in a context bound to doom him.

What is also compelling is how Faulkner with this novel has moved into Hemingway territory, despite his desire to distance himself from his chief competitor. *The Wild Palms* segment often recalls *A Farewell to Arms;* but beyond that, there are Hemingway patterns and even characters. The newspaperman McCord is such a creation, the hard-drinking, helpful hanger-on from a dozen Hemingway stories. As the threesome mock the wealth of the Armour Meat Packing Company, McCord says, in pseudo-Joycean language: " 'Set, ye armourous sons, in a sea of hemingwaves.' " Nothing in the development of the novel calls for the Joycean language or the Hemingway references. Yet Harry is himself, perhaps, a mockery of Hemingway: the man who writes pulp fiction mechanically in order to earn a living. Even the bloody abortion recalls the early Hemingway story in which young Nick watches his father abort an Indian child. As if in some balletic relationship to each other, Hemingway would appear to imitate aspects of "Old Man" in his portrayal of the fisherman in *The Old Man and the Sea.* While the situations differ, the fisherman's dogged refusal to let go of the fish has echoes of the tall convict's refusal to go on without the state's boat: both characters define themselves by almost inhuman persistence. To maintain the lines of reciprocity, Faulkner received credit for the screenplay of Hemingway's *To Have and Have Not,* directed by Hawks and starring Bogart and Bacall.

We have already observed the abiding images of imprisonment, liberation, and drowning. But once the parallels become apparent, we see the interwoven stories are counterpointed, not blended.* While it is true each male protagonist has been "imprisoned," one by the work ethic, the other literally, each is made to respond differently. Harry chooses his destiny, although he chooses self-destruction; the tall convict has his thrust upon him by a natural disaster, a flood. It is as though Faulkner were measuring two earlier works: the Bundrens in *As I Lay Dying,* harassed by fire and flood, and the fliers of *Pylon,* who choose a destiny they cannot control or escape. The tall convict rides the waves of circumstance—first in the boat, then on land, working with the Cajun alligator hunter, and, finally, in being given an extended sentence for trying to escape. Nature's plan for a disaster has scooped him up, wrong man in wrong place at wrong time. Nature has no such plan for Harry; at each stage, he has a chance to choose.

*Both manuscript and typescript indicate that the section divisions fell generally at the points we find in the book version. The typescript setting copy reveals, however, that at one point the first "Old Man" segment and the second "Wild Palms" segment were considerably longer than in the book version, embracing in each instance the sections which succeed them. That is, the first and second sections of "Old Man" were run together, as were the second and third sections of "Wild Palms"; the rest was what we have in the book.

He is a man of destiny only in the broader sense everyone has a destiny to play out. This distinction cannot be simplified or ignored, for it generates two different ideologies. Like Faulkner himself, torn between the unhappy security of Rowan Oak and the precarious life he had experienced with Meta, the two male protagonists edge toward different experiences even while appearing to share the same ones.

Abortion is a key symbol or emblem in The Wild Palms, indicating danger, dislocation, exile. We seek significance in the working title of the manuscript: "If I Forget Thee, O Jerusalem." Deriving from Psalm 137, it gains its residue from its reference to the sorrowful ones exiled in Babylon. Sick with feelings of alienation, the exiles hang up their harps but are required to "sing Jehovah's song in a foreign land." But "If I forget thee, O Jerusalem, / Let my right hand forget her skill" and "Let my tongue cleave to the roof of my mouth." The conflict is between exile and art: as strangers in a foreign land, ordered to perform, they lose their art. Their hand and mouth skills are stilled. Creation is aborted. The emblems of abortion in the novel, if we follow the lines of the psalm, are opposed, somehow, to the possibility of creation. One way to read the novel, especially the Wild Palms segments, is as a conflict between life and art, a theme deeply personal for Faulkner and literarily one he was familiar with from Mann and Joyce.

The writing of the novel spanned ten months, from September 15, when he dated the first page of the holograph, to June, when he sent Random House the typescript. The drowning man had found some way to keep himself afloat, or else, to change the metaphor, the empty vessel had been filled with work. Despite pain with his back, he found time for quail shooting, and in family terms went through the dissolution of the marriage between Estelle's daughter, Victoria, and Claude Selby. She and her infant became another financial burden.

The relationship of Faulkner to his stepchildren is cloudy. There is little question he wished to do his best by them, to act as a surrogate father. But also from family reports, there is little question he showed considerable hostility, anger, even cruelty. He could be cutting, nasty, brutish. Although he spent time with Malcolm, he was unpleasant to the boy, who was himself none too stable. In fact, both Victoria and Malcolm were unsettled, with the young man taking to drink, and Victoria having an uncertain personal life. Members of the family emphasize Faulkner had a harsh, scathing tongue. Malcolm came to write a little book about growing up with Faulkner, really a hymn to nostalgia and happiness, but he called it Bitterweeds. Jill herself has put her feelings on record, revealing anger at her childhood and adolescent years. Her desire to remain isolated from the family remaining in Oxford, once she left for Virginia, is another indication of her need to put the growing-up years behind her.

With all the good will they could muster, the older Faulkners seemed incapable of moving beyond their own monumental needs to be attentive parents. With Estelle a chronic drinker, and Faulkner a binge drinker, there was little coherence to the home. Add to that the anger Estelle felt toward her husband, and the feelings of entrapment Faulkner felt toward his wife, and we have a home almost disintegrating. Take away servants, like Mammy Callie, and life at Rowan Oak would have exploded into incoherence.

As 1937 passed into 1938, the new year found Faulkner back into writing; working steadily on *The Wild Palms*, with its interwoven stories, and later in the year outlining an extended Snopes project. The year 1938, then, saw him involved in three book projects. On February 15, *The Unvanquished* was published, with the stories going back to 1934–36, with the addition of "An Odor of Verbena." That story, written for this volume, was his only published short fiction for 1938. *The Wild Palms* was completed by June and prepared for publication, on January 19 of 1939. Finally, he wrote a story called "Barn Burning," sent it to *Harper's* (June 1939), but, more importantly, used it as the beginning of his Snopes project, "The Peasants" (which became *The Hamlet*). With his work on "Barn Burning" and his recognition of future novels, he was readying himself for several years of sustained writing.

Late in the year he permitted an interview with Robert Cantwell, for a cover story *Time* was planning on him (January 23, 1939). He managed to stay away from Hollywood, although in 1939 the financial pinch was so great that even with newly won fame (*Time* cover and election to the National Institute of Arts and Letters), he tried to arrange a good contract. The Hollywood deal fell through, but his attempt to return under favorable circumstances indicates that financially he was undergoing extreme stress. And in that other area of stress, he remained married, although Meta was hardly out of his mind. In fact, when she returned from Europe and he found himself in New York—or manufactured reasons for going —he began to see her again. As she wrote, "The city conferred blessed anonymity upon him from the moment he arrived at Pennsylvania Station; he was far more relaxed in New York than in Hollywood. Only his few close friends, his agent, and his publisher knew that he was in the city."[23]

She indicates Faulkner spelled out to her his domestic situation. Estelle, according to him, was drinking as much as ever; but they had worked out a "kind of truce since all the unpleasantness in Hollywood." Meta tells Faulkner she loves her husband, and cherishes the moments she is in the center of New York musical life. She does complain of lacking money, and Faulkner offers to help her. Her report on 1938 and 1939: "He would suddenly appear at our door and it was as if he had never left and there would be riotous evenings together at the Bairds [Bill, the puppeteer] or with Bucky [Buckminster] Fuller and Jim Devine."

The early part of 1938 found Faulkner plunging ever deeper into anguish and doom—the doom of Harry, the martyrdom of Charlotte to a life of freedom, the alternating rhythms of the tall convict as he tastes freedom even while longing for the security of prison. The yo-yoing between liberation and imprisonment (or bourgeois life) intensified: Charlotte, bleeding at the beginning, will bleed through the novel. Whatever else she does to effect her and Harry's liberation, she is doomed by the seepage of blood established in the first section. Charlotte's blood, oozing, seeping, spurting, is a primary fact of the conception of the novel. The initial image is of a botched abortion, an emblem of the novel—and not one that the counter-ing emblem of release can disguise. In contrast, the tall convict's plight is witty—he, too, bleeds from one injury or another; but his is superficial, mainly his nose. We note the juxtaposition: the nose, which Freud's friend Fliess thought was the center of sexual response, bleeds profusely in his segment in rhythm to bleeding of a different kind in the other segment. The juxtaposition creates an amusing dimension to "Old Man," not other-wise notable for wit.

But even if the tall convict bleeds from a marginal area only, he comes to recognize another kind of doom. While the birth he helps occurs nor-mally, he nevertheless perceives he is in the hands of "the cosmic joker." This Hardyesque touch is not lost on him. Shortly after that perception, while working with the Cajan (Cajun) killing alligators for their skin, he has another revelation:

> . . . that though his life has been cast here, circumscribed by this environment, accepted by this environment and accepting it in turn (he had done well here—this quietly, soberly indeed, if he had been able to phrase it, think it instead of merely knowing it—better than he had ever done, who had not even known until now how good work, making money, could be) yet it was not his life, he still and would ever be no more than the water bug upon the surface of the pond, the plumbless and lurking depths of which he could never know.[24]

His role has been cast for him, and his only moment of actual life comes when he enters combat with the alligator and affirms his existence in that life-and-death struggle. He reminds us of a Hemingway matador: ". . . he accepted the gambit which he had not elected, entered the lashing radius of the armed tail and beat at the thrashing and hissing head with his lightwood club, or that failing, embraced without hesitation the armored body itself with the frail web of flesh and bone in which he walked and lived and sought the raging life with an eight-inch knife-blade."

Just before he performs the abortion on Charlotte, Harry has a momen-tary vision, one which Faulkner has used several times before, notably with Temple Drake: "Something is about to happen to me. Wait. Wait."[25] Premonition of doom is accompanied by loss of vital will. But more is at stake. As Faulkner proceeded with the interwoven parts, the very question of the will and its ability to function in a predetermined or doomed world is raised. Faulkner at forty has looked into the limitations of mortality. The two novels are an examination of an attitude toward life, a resignation of the will in the face of life massing to attack and smother. Harry is a failed artist with the knife; the tall convict a successful artist with his knife. One does not find the right spot and muffs the abortion; the other finds the heart of the alligator with his blade. Faulkner is measuring two very different acts of artistry; but both come with that context where grief is the measure of all things: ". . . between grief and nothing I will take grief,"[26] Harry muses as he stares out at the palms from prison.

Faulkner had had a bout with death in his imagination, and he had returned with a message that, withal, one was a water bug upon the surface of the water. With this revelation, we can better comprehend the terrible hostility to women the novel demonstrates. The hostility to Helen Baird is clear, and by indirection Meta; he kills the former, and by so doing gets at the latter. Harry tried to return to Jerusalem, but his right hand wavered. Faulkner's hostility is brutal: not only has he killed Helen, he has gotten her right in her center, in her most womanly part, and he has condemned her to an agonizing end. He has killed off a vital element of his own life in order to express himself as an artist—but in doing so, he has revealed to himself his own mortality, his own resignation to a loss which gave him great grief. For his part, the tall convict "gains" a woman, but someone else's and someone else's child. He becomes responsible for an extended family not his own, and his antagonism is intense. " 'Women ---t' " ends the novel—women shit, Faulkner means and says in the language of 1938.

Yet life took an upturn. Perhaps because it was not top-drawer work, *The Unvanquished*, published on February 15, immediately found a Hollywood buyer.* The day after publication Metro-Goldwyn-Mayer closed with Random House for $25,000, of which twenty percent went to the publisher. This infusion of money, another huge sum for 1938, came at an opportune time, since Faulkner was about to close with W. C. Bryant over Bailey's Woods and had already put down $200 for that deal. We see a familiar pattern—the infusion of large sums, the expenditure of that money on big purchases such as more land or an airplane, soon a working farm; then would follow the need for money, the inability to meet new levels of expenditure; that, in turn, would be followed by a frantic search for funds, from Hollywood or elsewhere. Starting in the mid-1930s, Faulkner's desire for property and worldly goods outpaced his ability to earn the money for them, and as a result he was forced to write with an eye on the marketplace. By 1938, after the publication of *Absalom*, he was no longer an author writing only for himself, but glancing nervously at

*The book satisfied some of those critics who found his earlier work difficult or impenetrable. This book was even called "cheerful." While Clifton Fadiman did not like this one, either, Kay Boyle did, comparing Faulkner to Poe: in their common "immunity to literary fashion, alike in their fanatical obsession with the unutterable depths of mankind's vice and even more with his divinity." Actually, Boyle's review applied more to other volumes. Alfred Kazin weighed in with a notice which took away more than it gave. He spoke of Faulkner as a willful child "in some gaseous world of his own, pouting in polysyllables, stringing truncated paragraphs together like dirty wash, howling, stumbling, losing himself in verbal murk"; but at the same time, insisting "on the dignity of loneliness and the joy in the compromises made with it" (O. B. Emerson, *Faulkner's Early Literary Reputation in America*).

sales, contracts, deals. Inevitably, whatever other forces in his life affected his talent, he was drawn into a somewhat different kind of fiction from what he had done before. The experimental, innovative mode tended to diminish, occurring only in segments, not as part of an overall conception.

Furthermore, his concentration on Snopes material, which had been the subject of only shorter work, indicated he chose to produce what publishers and editors requested from him. All through the early 1930s, once a few Snopes pieces emerged, editors asked for more. The Snopes trilogy occupied Faulkner for almost the next two decades, but admittedly, except for bursts here and there, the material is not his best, and in places misfires altogether. Yet Snopes pieces gave him sales, made Random House happy, and helped satisfy reviewers and critics who had missed his earlier greatness. Increasingly, he found himself drawn into the position of the old master in Matthew Arnold's "Growing Old," who hears the plaudits of the world even as he recognizes the slippage of his craft.

Then in a kind of farewell to Morton Goldman,[27] Faulkner renegotiated what his agent should receive. Goldman thought he should obtain an agent's fee on total sale price of the book, and Faulkner counter-offered ten percent of one seventh of the price MGM paid, on the assumption that meant only one story, "An Odor of Verbena." Faulkner felt that while Goldman handled stories, he, the author, handled all other rights. His offer came to $357.14. Goldman wanted five percent of the total, or $1250; but Faulkner said that after Random House got its share, he received only $20,000, and five percent of that was what he finally offered, $1,000. Faulkner took the blame, but also came back to Goldman shortly afterward: "I wish we had settled such a contingency such as this before hand, had had an understanding about it. It was my fault we didn't, as you brought up the matter of a contract between us and I declined, believing as I did that agents' equities in mss. did not extend to collections in volumes, etc. But that was my fault, and I am grateful for your offer to compromise, even though I do feel I have been screwed about 600.00 worth. But then, you probably feel you have been screwed 1,000.00, which is worse, I reckon." Whether intentionally or not, in anger or not, Faulkner failed to sign the letter; so that even this compromise agreement was not a contract.

With Goldman and Random House taken care of, he still would have $19,000, with which to buy more land. When Faulkner said he wanted a farm and needed Johncy to run it, the latter responded he knew nothing about how to do it. Faulkner admitted he didn't either, but they could learn. The farm was really a place to raise mules, and the grain to feed them. Johncy then started to look for a suitable spot, close enough to Oxford and yet far enough so they could purchase a big tract. In what was called Beat Two, seventeen miles northeast of Oxford, Johncy found a three-hundred-twenty-acre farm, and they bought it. Beat Two had the reputation of turning out the toughest people in northern Mississippi, hill people, bootleggers, men who policed their own territory and allowed no strangers to interfere. Government revenue agents entered on peril of never emerging, and violence and killing were not uncommon. The description of Frenchman's Bend at the beginning of *The Hamlet* gives a good idea of Beat Two, although Frenchman's Bend itself is located southeast, not northeast, of Jefferson:* In the middle of *The Wild Palms*, Faulkner worked out the financial details, borrowing money so that he did not have to expend his entire $19,000 from MGM. Some of the money he borrowed, $2,000 in all, came from the bank once owned by Joe Parks, and the farm had also once belonged to Parks. That name, familiar from earlier days, had dogged Murry Falkner, for Parks had purchased his home. For both brothers, this was retribution.[28]

Work on the farm went ahead while Faulkner was also working on the second half or so of *The Wild Palms*. It was another curious juxtaposition, in which his life and his work intertwined well below the surface of events. Even as he moved from Oxford into the expanse of a good-sized spread, into the pastoral dream he had harbored for some time, his characters were being carried ever more deeply into their narrowed-down fates. Although Faulkner showed no direct awareness of Nietzsche, he reached certain Nietzschean conclusions in his portrayal of the two protagonists. Nietzsche was, in one sense, the synthesizer of several nineteenth-century ideas that emphasized will (Arthur Schopenhauer, in particular) and the affinity of the body for magnetic forces (Friedrich Anton Mesmer and his followers). Nietzsche straddled questions of will: in his ironic vision, man must confront *amor fati*, or love of fate, which seemingly negates will. But love of fate does not mean that one embraces it—rather, one grapples with it. This is the mission only of the superior man, for the weak and pitiful succumb to the weight or demands of fate. Zarathustra speaks of dying "at the right time," for "He that consummates his life dies his death victoriously." Harry, at the end of Faulkner's book, forgoes suicide with the cyanide brought by Rittenmeyer. He has become in some way strengthened by his adversity, by his flirtation with the Faustian pact—and this fits precisely into a Nietzschean mold. The latter wrote that the best of us are not food for others, but those who ripen at their own pace and rot when they are ready. Some "rot already in the summer," but they have spent too much time on the tree—that is, they have died before they have lived.

*"Their descendants still planted cotton in the bottom land and corn along the edge of the hills and in the secret coves in the hills made whiskey of the corn and sold what they did not drink. Federal officers went into the country and vanished. Some garment which the missing man had worn might be seen—a felt hat, a broadcloth coat, a pair of city shoes or even his pistol—on a child or an old man or woman. County officers did not bother them at all save in the heel of election years. They supported their own churches and schools, they married and committed infrequent adulteries and more frequent homicides among themselves and were their own courts, judges and executioners. They were Protestants and Democrats and prolific; there was not one Negro landowner in the entire section. Strange Negroes would absolutely refuse to pass through it after dark" (*The Hamlet* [New York: Modern Library, n.d.], pp. 4–5).

Nietzsche's metaphors of food and the "tree of life" presuppose that death —whether of individual or God—is opportunity, not finality. Harry in particular had spent too much time on the tree; he had ripened in the summer and would die before he had lived. To escape this weight, he must make his Faustian pact with Charlotte, an avatar of Eve for this virginal Adam; and he must be thrust from his self-imposed Garden where he has confused life and death. Once expelled and torn by thorns, he recognizes that death exists, and this, in Nietzsche's terms, liberates him. In his misery, he has been strengthened—and so has the tall convict, whose course of action contains less self-conscious awareness. Both protagonists end up in Parchman for the remainder of their lives, but as different men from what they were; and that is all the Nietzschean vision asked for—not ultimate freedom, but awareness of magnetic forces, energies, subterranean elements.

Faulkner was grappling with these ideas, but they would have been impossible without the play of personal forces in his own life. He intuited the Nietzschean elements because he had located in himself the philosopher's ironic forces. And they play through him and his work even as he moves toward the farm, helping Johncy make the farmhouse livable for him and his family. Slowly, the farm had overtaken flying: as befitting his age, Faulkner had gone from one type of spatiality to another, from vertical to horizontal.

A photograph taken by J. R. Cofield—and part of the illustrious Cofield Collection—shows Faulkner in an entirely different role. The photograph is dated May 8 and shows Faulkner and Estelle dressed for a fox hunt with their majordomo, Uncle Ned Barnett, in the center, dressed to the teeth in old formal clothes. On each side is a child—to the left, a Negro girl named after Estelle, and on the right, Jill. All but Jill look straight into the camera, proud of their dress-up roles; but she looks downward, tight-lipped, somewhat pouting. She may be ashamed of the fuss, or else she is bewildered and shy. Whatever her precise feelings, she has taken herself out of the spirit of the event. The point of the affair was not only to dress up, but to enjoy a fox-hunt breakfast Estelle handled with the help of the house servants. A haunch of venison was the offering. It was a strange episode for Faulkner, given the profoundly depressing work he was engaged in; but it was also a release, and sign of his sense of fun. It also reveals his adherence to the glories of the old days, his desire to become ultra-respectable, to demonstrate his growing affluence.

By June 17, he could wire Random House that *The Wild Palms* was finished, although he was rewriting parts; he planned to send it on in a few days. He gave it to Estelle to read, and according to Blotner, she predictably did not like the Harry-Charlotte part. Did she see herself as part of the triangle, somehow identified with the cuckold Rittenmeyer, who allowed it all to happen? Faulkner sent the typescript off a week or so later, and then in a long revealing letter to Haas on July 8 discussed many aspects of the novel.

youthful amours, the city where he had written *Soldiers' Pay.* "[32] Her version of their rendezvous is, perforce, colored by *Gone With the Wind* atmospherics. The truth of the matter was that Faulkner sought sexual relief, that he indeed liked Meta, that the opportunity to break from Oxford was always welcomed. According to Meta, he offered to set her up in New Orleans—shades of Charles Bon and his wife—and he would come down to see her when he could. She was tempted, but went on to her family in Arizona, and in time returned to Rebner and marriage.

But Meta and tears were not Faulkner's only activities. He had brought along a short story "Barn Burning," to work on, which became his initial firm investment in a formal Snopes trilogy. He also formally agreed to "If I forget Thee, Jerusalem" becoming *The Wild Palms,* "* and did some flying out of Teterboro Airport in New Jersey. The largest development here was the alteration of title. Whereas the original was appropriate to the novel as a whole, the altered title was relevant only to the love story. Once the change was made, the book was free to be divided into two parts. Malcolm Cowley, in a move which brought Faulkner back into broader favor, did the book a disservice by printing *Old Man* alone, in his belief that Faulkner showed up best as a writer of long stories. After this, *Old Man* (or sometimes *The Old Man*) was published in separate editions, and the two segments of the novel intended to serve as counterpoint to each other became divided.

Back in Oxford, his ideas flowed. In the letter Haas received on December 15, Faulkner revealed a remarkable premonition of his future writing career. While some of it derives from *Father Abraham* and the Snopes material he had been writing, most of it comes from that massive block of material he seemed to carry around in his head, and from which he could, when ready, chip off the pieces that became novels and stories. "Barn Burning," meanwhile, was making the rounds, and by the time Faulkner wrote his long letter to Haas, it had been rejected by the *Saturday Evening Post*, probably by *Redbook*, then later by the *American Magazine, Country Gentleman*, and *Cosmopolitan*, before *Harper's* accepted it for $400 (June 1939).

The first volume, he wrote Haas, would be called "The Peasants" (*The Hamlet*, later), and would have to do with Flem Snopes's "beginning in the country, as he gradually consumes a small village until there is nothing left in it for him." He gains a foothold in Jefferson, and leaves country matters

*Thomas L. McHaney reports that in the spring of 1957, Saxe Commins told James Meriwether "about changing the title and the convict's last speech. It was done, he indicated, very much against Faulkner's wishes" (*The Wild Palms* [Jackson: University Press of Mississippi, 1975], p. xiii). Faulkner himself wrote Estelle that Haas had persuaded him to abandon the title. Haas later said "it would arouse anti-Semitic feeling" (Joseph Blotner, *Faulkner: A Biography*, 2 vols. [New York: Random House, 1974], vol. 2, p. 1002). The real reason had to do with saleability. The original title had the sound of a sermon or treatise on religion, and Random House surely wanted something which fitted more with Faulkner's market image as a racy writer. *The Wild Palms* has an ambiguous quality which lends itself to various sexual connotations. McHaney also reveals more than 650 changes between typescript and published book, suggesting Faulkner's visit to New York was for more than "play."

to his successive kinsmen. The second volume, later *The Town*, is "Rus in Urbe." "He begins to trade on his wife's infidelity, modest blackmail of her lover, rises from half owner of back street restaurant through various grades of city employment, filling each post he vacates with another Snopes from the country, until he is secure in the presidency of a bank, where he can even stop blackmailing his wife's lover." The third volume, what will become *The Mansion*, is called "Ilium Falling." "This is the gradual eating-up of Jefferson by Snopeses, who corrupt the local government with crooked politics, buy up all the colonial homes and tear them down and chop up the lots into subdivisions."[33]

But Faulkner had far more than merely a broad outline in mind. Details were there, many of them remaining as stated here, some of them altered as he wrote his way through over one thousand pages of Snopes material. Also, in what would become a problem, he forgot details as he worked, and there are several discrepancies in the final trilogy, although few on a major scale. The overall portrayal presented to Haas is of a gigantic invasion of locusts, who consume whatever is in their way. The image is of eating, consumption, digesting, regurgitating, then repeating the process with successive or lateral generations. The picture of the South Faulkner draws is not, as most critics have stated, the corruption and predatory quality of the Snopeses; for in many instances, they simply consume equally corrupt and predatory people already in charge. For every Snopes ready to corrupt someone, there is someone ready to be corrupted. But there is more at stake here than an exchange of one debased group for another. Faulkner has a vision of the future: that of a mass invasion. The older, settled, ingrown corrupt group had an individualization, the quality of some independence and distinction of self. The Snopeses, representing the new, the mass, are characterized by Flem's impotence, his willingness to take on someone's cast-off pregnant woman as a way of gaining leverage. Unlike Byron's feelings toward Lena Grove, there are no emotions except gain; therefore, the linkage to locusts—an instinctive need to consume.*

"Barn Burning" was rejected as too pessimistic, but the trilogy as outlined here to Haas would be hardly less gloomy. Although Faulkner planned humor, horseplay, boys-will-be-boys amusement, the overall thrust of the trilogy derives from a deeply pessimistic view of community, society, and state. Faulkner's Southern trilogy joins with Sinclair Lewis's and Dreiser's jejune view of American Midwest society,** and cuts heavily into Hemingway's by now familiar view that Eden has been so traduced one must seek renewal elsewhere, in war, in bullfighting, or on African

---

*Even in naming, Faulkner had a way of contrasting Snopeses from other predatory groups. Many of the latter (Compsons, Sartorises) have interlocking names, names repeated from generation to generation, Bayard and John, or Quentin and Jason. But the Snopeses do not repeat; each is distinct from the others.

**In *Look Homeward, Angel*, Wolfe "opened up" the nastiness and narrowness of a small Southern town, what Faulkner had already begun in *Soldiers' Pay*. The South now joined the Midwest of Anderson, Dreiser, and Lewis.

safari. The trilogy as a whole is a profound social and political statement about America, far more than a description of a particular region or even the South.

The Hamlet will be discussed later, when in 1939, Faulkner was further along. But it should be mentioned here he made several decisive choices, since for the first time he was writing not *a* novel but a trilogy. He needed a broader base of operations, and he had to create a setting which was both realistic and yet sufficiently "created" to make possible the various levels of individual and society. What we see in Faulkner's decisions about the first volume will influence how we read it and succeeding books. If we seek out only conventional areas, then, inevitably, there will be disappointment. But if we see Faulkner trying to write something different from a conventional novel and a novel sequence, we begin to perceive an experimental base to the trilogy. Faulkner was moving into a kind of fluidity, a new kind of novelistic structuring; his strategy, consciously or not, derived from painting, his own version of "action painting."

Faulkner had to alter "Barn Burning" and turn it into a broader introduction to the three volumes. Without forgoing the details of Ab Snopes's reputation for burning barns—he has burned at least Major de Spain's—Faulkner moved to a sweeping preparation for people and place.

Frenchman's Bend was a section of rich river-bottom country lying twenty miles southeast of Jefferson. Hill-cradled and remote, definite yet without boundaries, straddling into two counties and owning allegiance to neither, it had been the original grant and site of a tremendous pre–Civil War plantation, the ruins of which—the gutted shell of an enormous house with its fallen stables and slave quarters and overgrown gardens and brick terraces and promenades—were well known as the Old Frenchman's place, although the original boundaries now existed only on old faded records in the Chancery Clerk's office in the county courthouse in Jefferson, and even some of the once-fertile field had long since reverted to the cane-and-cypress jungle from which their first master had hewed them.[34]

The beginning recalls Sir Walter Scott and even Dickens, an adaptation of the opening city passages in *Bleak House*. What solidifies the resemblance is the attempt to be realistic and yet mysterious, detailed and yet legendary. The Faulkner passage is saturated with pastness even while representing the present. We are returned to before the war, to both its grandeur and its ruins. Decline will be Faulkner's focus, but the grand past, the historical element, must not be ignored. With this paragraph alone, he has provided sweep and mastery; after that will come the individual brush strokes. Even the change of the original Balzacian title, "The Peasants," to the title of the fourth segment, *The Hamlet*, indicates a more sweeping sense.

But as he worked on projects that would extend for the next several years, he also saw the publication on January 19, 1939, of *The Wild Palms*, his contrapuntal novel of ten alternating chapters.* With this, he gained a new kind of popularity, but not because the reviews were particularly strong. They were in fact rather poor. The daily *New York Times* found the book unpleasant and tortured, full of poor sentence structure. Clifton Fadiman in the *New Yorker* was ready with his annual assault, a review he could have written without reading the book. The Sunday *New York Times*, a bellwether for the East, saw it as not among Faulkner's best, but still "very good Faulkner," an example of his "sensational talent," even genius. Cowley, whose reviews of Faulkner so far showed a lack of understanding all out of keeping with his later important role in the author's revival, thought the juxtaposition of the two stories brought no literary reward. He preferred the "Old Man" segment, a sentiment which prevailed with most critics. It was definitely a disappointing haul, until *Time* appeared. There on the cover, in color, a man who could have been a farmer or small-town store owner peered out steadily at the reader. Faulkner had received the ultimate accolade of the growing Luce empire.**

*The year 1939 was also the beginning of serious Faulkner criticism, a kind of analysis very different from Robert Cantwell's superficial treatment in *Time*. Two pieces were very important beginnings: George Marion O'Donnell's "Faulkner's Mythology" (*Kenyon Review*, Summer 1939); and Conrad Aiken's "William Faulkner: The Novel as Form" (*Atlantic Monthly*, November 1939). Although brief, the two articles made it possible to see that Faulkner had joined the literary canon; that *Sanctuary* was not his only calling card.

**Also the accolade of the National Institute of Arts and Letters, to which he was elected on January 18, 1939. At the ceremony, Robert Frost received the Gold Medal of the Institute, while Faulkner was joined by a rather mixed group of William Beebe, Marjorie Kinnan Rawlings, John Steinbeck, and Charles A. Beard.

Chapter Nineteen

Midcareer

T HERE WERE SEVERAL indications as Faulkner began work on the Snopes trilogy, which would occupy him for years, that he was "arriving." He was the sole American novelist, except for Dos Passos in his *USA* trilogy (*The 42nd Parallel* in 1930, *1919* in 1932, *The Big Money* in 1936), to have assimilated the international style and yet remain a representative American. What Dos Passos achieved was a chorus of many voices moving polyphonically, although by necessity printed out sequentially. The aim was to assault the reader aurally, like Faulkner with his long winding sentences which read better aloud than on the printed page. Dos Passos's themes are also close to Faulkner's, especially in their common assumption that the individual is being crushed by the gears of a machine-oriented society, or else being propelled into a dubious, self-destructive success. Dos Passos did not have Snopes, but in his interpolated stories, he had other forms of American success—Ford, Morgan, Edison, *his* Snopes. Faulkner ultimately prevailed as having achieved the greater work because of the intensity which transformed region into country, whereas Dos Passos has, unjustly, come to be considered a period writer.

Progress reports to Haas continued, with one received on February 7, 1939, indicating 215 pages written. As Faulkner moved more deeply into his material, the earlier bases of the Snopes idea became less useful; he had to broaden and invent. Ratliff gave him an anchor in reason and decency, the

voice the novelist identified with as the teller. He is the talkative side of
Faulkner, moderate, balanced, witty, knowledgeable, a traveling historian
of the county. He balances out Flem Snopes, whose presence is pervasive.
One problem Faulkner had to grapple with was Flem's singularity. He
found it impossible to modulate Flem, and there is a one-dimensional
quality to his desire to get on. It is one of the book's strengths, and also
a major weakness.

Another area of mixed strength and weakness is Eula Varner, whom
Flem marries when she is pregnant by Hoake McCarron. In order to create
the range needed for the trilogy, in which Eula plays a significant role,
Faulkner had to expand upon what she was in *Father Abraham.* She is a
compelling creation, but she has, in this volume, only one string to her
bow. Faulkner must make this cowlike girl and young woman into a highly
charged, desirable creature who somehow embodies all female sexuality.
She is expected to play several roles in Faulkner's treatment, although she
seems singular: it is Faulkner working around her, rather than giving her
complexity. She comes at an interesting time in his life, when a fantasy
woman had to replace Meta as presently lost to him. Eula is everything
Estelle is not; she is the porno star of the male imagination, and Faulkner
does everything with her physically but undress her. But fantasy figure she
remains, far more desirable in the imagination than in actuality.

He needs, then, to give historical and mythical scope to her shaping: her
body becomes the sensual empty vessel which he must fill with men's
longing for her. She becomes Helen, and Semiramis, and a host of other
women, all based on Venus. She is, however, no goddess of love. Her
presence gives spice to the town, and creates a contrast with Flem's impotence, to be played off against him. She must, further, provide a magnet
for future action, when Gavin Stevens (who is coming alive in stories
which will eventually make up *Knight's Gambit*) lusts after her, and then
after her daughter, Linda.

Faulkner's descriptions of her stress her abundance: ". . . even at nine
and ten and eleven, there was too much—too much of breast, too much of
buttock, too much of mammalian female meat." He suggests there are two
Eulas: "There was one Eula Varner who supplied blood and nourishment
to the buttocks and legs and breasts; there was the other Eula Varner who
merely inhabited them, who went where they went because it was less
trouble to do so."[1] Yet even though there are two of her, she lives within
herself, seemingly disconnected from whatever passes around her. "She
had no playmates, no inseparable girl companion. She did not want them.
She never formed one of those violent, sometimes short-lived intimacies in
which two female children form embattled secret cabal against their masculine coevals and the mature world too. She did nothing. She might as
well have been a foetus. It was as if only half of her had been born, that
mentality and body had somehow become either completely separated or
hopelessly involved."

There is in these descriptions a reaching out for something which goes well beyond Eula. It is as though Faulkner were revaluating his entire conception of the female, trying to find out, as Freud suggested, exactly what she wanted. Eula becomes the female principle embodied, but somehow Faulkner cannot put her together. He sees her as halves, divided between mind and body. In the passage above, he conjectures that "either only one of them had ever emerged, or that one had emerged, itself not accompanied by, but rather pregnant with the other."[2] Clearly, there is a split in Faulkner's view of Eula. He apparently wants to envisage her as purely sensual, to reassert the sensual principle of the female; but to do that, he must comprehend what happened to the mental or thinking part of her. If it was born together with the body, where is it located, since she seems oblivious to all but her thickening body? He knows there must be more. The question is, where?

In his pursuit of meaning in Eula, Faulkner appears to be entering a new phase in his thinking about women: not forsaking his belief in their blind, driving, instinctual power, which makes them superior to men in this respect, but beginning to inquire about how this could be, what woman really is. It is conjectural but compelling to say that this revaluation has come hard upon his experience with the three women in his life: his courtship and marriage with Estelle; his portrayal of Charlotte Rittenmeyer, which sent him back to Helen Baird; and his now-broken-off affair with Meta. Not only Eula, but her relationship to the men in her life seems at stake in Faulkner's appraisal of himself: with Flem, who is impotent; with Major de Spain, an affair which Flem permits to his personal advantage; long before that, as the object of an obsessive love by the schoolteacher Labove; finally, in her offering herself to Gavin Stevens, and his need to be near her without possessing her.

As he finished with Eula and moved into material wrung from "Afternoon of a Cow," he encountered a personal problem which turned into two problems. The first concerned his insurance, which he had begun to carry when he made Hollywood money, but which he could no longer afford. "I found pretty soon that I was not a movie writer, yet I continued to carry the insurance as long as I drew money from Cal. I now believe that movies are done as far as I am concerned, unless they should buy my novels, etc."[3] In the same letter to Haas, he indicates he plans to drop one policy, which would become void anyway if he were killed flying. The letter, very frank for someone as reticent as Faulkner, mentions he has a big family to support, and he admits the farm will not be profitable enough to allow insurance premiums of $1,600 per year. "I have no other source save to borrow from publishers on work I have not written yet. I tried last month to put the novel aside and hammer out a pot-boiler story to meet this premium with, but I failed, either the novel is too hot in my mind or I failed to keep from stewing over having to make a home run in one lick to cook up a yarn."

The next letter, received at Random House five days later (March 22), was even more painful. "I have a friend here, I have known him all my life, never any question of mine and thine between us when either had it. His father died a few years ago, estate badly involved, is being sued on $7000.00 note, which will cause whole business to be sold up. He must have money in 3 weeks." They have to raise $6,000 (a huge sum in 1939), and Faulkner says he will sign any contracts or agreements. He offers to sell original manuscripts to supplement whatever Random House can give him and cancel his insurance policies. "If you will name what sum you can allow [Haas sent $1,200 by return mail], I will know then just what difference to try to raise. It will probably be hard to find anyone to buy mss. but that is best chance I see now. I would not want to sell any of it unless I was sure of getting what he must have."

Phil Stone was now almost completely dependent on what Faulkner could do for him. Unless his writing friend—whom he had slowly been denigrating over the years—could come up with this large sum, he would be sold up, his house gone. Arrangements were made, with an additional $3,000 from Haas, and with royalties to go directly to a bank if it intervened and saved Stone. Faulkner's letter of March 2 is full of strategies, turning in his annuity policy, forgoing premiums on other policies, consigning his royalties to a local bank. Intermixed with this is his "other," real life: he is eager to know what Haas thinks of the novel manuscript he is sending on, and he indicates he "may have enough short stories to make another volume"—the *Knight's Gambit* material. What resulted from all this was that Faulkner was writing for his life even more anxiously than earlier. Stone and his wife and child had now been added to his already large, extended family. There is a pattern here, in which Faulkner needed to take on as many responsibilities as he could as a way of reversing the view people once had of him. He began to support a good part of the Oxford population as a way of demonstrating the "town bum" had made good financially. It may have gone even deeper, into Faulkner's need to demonstrate to himself his writing was not only "literature," but commercially feasible.

Also involved was a form of control. We cannot simply repeat he was generous, helpful, supportive; he was these things, but he was also as a consequence of his help controlling many lives, pointing and guiding them —as with Johncy, as earlier with Dean, as with his domineering mother completely dependent on his financial support. Only Jack among immediate family moved outside this circle, with his own successful career as an FBI agent. If Murry had lived into the 1930s, it is very possible that he too would have been on his eldest son's payroll.

At first, Faulkner thought volume 1 would consist of only two (not four) books, as he indicates in a letter received April 24 at Random House. He put half of that, or thereabouts, into Haas's hands. Haas must have asked him to make the first parts more textured, for he indicates he has tightened up, "added some more here and there to give it density, make the people stand up."[4] His remarks and what we note of the manuscript indicate that he originally hoped to rely on stories—those already done as well as new ones—and to let them interconnect loosely to form a novel of stories. "The Hound" was another published short fiction he needed to incorporate, to join "Lizards in Jamshyd's Courtyard," "Fool About a Horse," and "Spotted Horses," which alone made up all of chapter 1 of book 4. Haas picked up that the connections of the material, deliberately loose in Faulkner's treatment, were too loose, too dependent on unabsorbed stories.

There is some question as to what extent Faulkner had been influenced by his film treatments—that is, to what extent his movement into this new kind of novel, based on stories, was the result of treating film properties, in which script elements could be loosely connected because the camera picked up continuity. One of Faulkner's difficulties in writing scripts and even treatments was his overwriting, his failure to take into account the camera as a narrative device. As he gradually became more adept, he found his scripts could be looser and less developed. Part of Faulkner's disenchantment with films came with his recognition that what he had mastered in one form, the written word, was secondary in the other. But even as he chafed against the restrictions imposed by film, he was sufficiently influenced to carry the technique over into his fiction.

In another inconclusive interview Faulkner gave, published in the "Carrier Edition" of the New Orleans *Item* (April 5, 1939), he mentioned his work on a three-volume novel that "he began in New Orleans 15 years ago." He said "he'd have finished it sooner, but for boiling the pot. It's about a poor white who comes to a little Southern town and teaches the populace corruption in government."[5] In the same interview, Faulkner mentions how he wrote *The Wild Palms*, using the two stories "like shuffling a deck of cards, only not so haphazardly."

Later in the year, in an interview for the *New York Post* (October 17), he seemed to create a different persona. The interviewer (Michael Mok) speaks of Faulkner as "the beardless Dostoyevsky of the canebrakes," and with this we know we are encountering media hype, not anything resembling the reality of Faulkner's life. The next paragraph exemplifies what "celebrity status" means. "You could have knocked The Post man over with the Sherman statue when he discovered that Mr. Faulkner, whom he had imagined as a light-shy, morose and misanthropic creature, was a jolly little man who likes nothing better than telling droll yarns between puffs of a well-seasoned pipe."[6] Mok must have seen Faulkner in a well-oiled moment, or else the writer was posing for the New York media. Mok describes him, with his "iron-gray hair, sly, dark-brown eyes, aquiline features, a ruddy complexion and a bristly little black mustache. In his rough herringbone tweeds there is about him something of the outdoor Englishman—until he talks." Then, Mok says, his accent is so heavily Southern, he must have difficulty in understanding himself.

Faulkner says he plans three or four volumes. He then tells of Montgomery Ward Snopes and his scheme to get rich on a collection of

French postcards. From the prominent part this story plays in the interview, we can conjecture Faulkner was playing a role for the media, offering a bit of scandal, Southern-fried, which he felt they wanted to hear, and embellishing it with some Southern politics with M. W.'s senator cousin. He completes this bit of homespun with another tall tale, this time of his New Orleans scriptwriting assignment with Tod Browning which brought him to a shrimp-fishing village. Faulkner was to write dialogue without knowing the story, and then was fired; after that the director went. It is precisely what Faulkner felt a New York interviewer wanted to hear.

In the meantime his plans for bailing out Stone had not worked. His assignment of royalties brought forth $1,700 from the local bank, and that meant he had to pump out some commercial stories. The additional pressure surely slowed "The Peasants"—Faulkner put it aside for two months—but he was so keyed into writing the book that painful interludes only geared him up to return. Another factor was also at play: on some of these commercial ventures, he developed ideas which became books at a later date. The story he wrote at this time, "Hands Upon the Waters," about Gavin Stevens, admittedly was not top drawer, nor was the volume in which it appeared, *Knight's Gambit*. But in the same time frame, he also wrote "The Old People" which, when revised, became the fourth section of *Go Down, Moses*. This was a pivotal piece, with his old cast of Sam Fathers, the hunting crowd of Ike McCaslin and Boon Hogganbeck, and an unnamed "father." The story indicates Faulkner's imagination, in conjuring up a potboiler, was actually moving at full speed. He had dipped as well into "A Justice" and moved aspects of that story forward to a new conception and a place in one of his most representative volumes.

Unlike Fitzgerald, who when he turned to the marketplace tended to repeat himself with lessening degrees of intensity, Faulkner approached commercial outlets now with some very meaningful material. In a letter to Haas (received May 3), he indicates a trip East when his crops are finished. The rest of the letter is financial, discussing the cashing in of the insurance policy "for enough to pay premiums on the other two, pay remaining income tax installments, and leave my remainder of $2,000.00 intact. God knows what I will do after it is gone. Maybe what I need is a bankruptcy, like a soldier needs delousing."

In a follow-up letter, probably dated in mid-August, Faulkner says he had no business coming to New York with money so low. If he can find a cheap hotel for a month's stay—he mentions $50 per month—he would then have enough to "buy liquor, and cadge grub from you all."[7] The plan sounds like a trumpet call for disaster: a grubby hotel, a good deal of private drinking, and indifferent eating, leading to malnourishment and possible hospitalization. Intermixed would be some work on "The Peasants" and perhaps time with Meta.

"The Old People," which the *Saturday Evening Post* rejected—and with that the plan for a fast $1,000—probed deeply into Faulkner's beliefs.* A marketplace story turned out to be a profound examination of what in large part he stood for. An innocent young boy is juxtaposed with Sam Fathers, the wise old hunter, the very spirit of the woods, son of Ikemotubbe, who called himself Doom. There is an echo in the boy's relationship to Fathers of Faulkner's to Phil Stone, the apprentice sitting worshipfully at the feet of the master. Sam Fathers is that Cooper-like Hawkeye creation, fearful of contacts with women, more at home with a male companion or the occasional male intruder into his forest domain. Fathers is the eternal bachelor, the man for whom women are a species beyond his comprehension or, possibly, taste. As part Indian, part white, and part black (from a quadroon slave woman who became his mother), he is the father of them all, the patriarchal figure of the forest, and, withal, a legendary god.

Although the revised version of this story is picked up again in *Go Down, Moses*—not only revised but thickened and given far greater texture—it should be mentioned here that Faulkner originally planned for it to be narrated by Quentin Compson. Quentin's name was removed after the magazine version; the narrator becomes unnamed. This is a critical change, since Quentin was already identified as a suicide in one novel and a young man crumbling under historical weight in another. Here Faulkner wanted someone fresh, whose experience with Sam Fathers will not allow him to turn morbid and self-destructive. The boy who is initiated with the "hot smoking blood" of the slain deer is not about to grow up to kill himself by drowning. It is Sam, in fact, who tells him of endurance, suffering, sustaining grief.

But there is another, more personal dimension to this story. As Faulkner moved more deeply into 1939 and pressures thickened rather than relented, a story like "The Old People" served personal needs. Having been initiated into the hunt, the boy takes his position awaiting the big legendary buck: "Then, as if it had waited for them to find their positions and become still, the wilderness breathed again. It seemed to lean inward above them, above himself and Sam and Walter and Boon in their separate lurking-places, tremendous, attentive, impartial and omniscient, the buck moving in it somewhere."[8] Here, it would seem, Faulkner found the perfect retreat—not his farm, which was loaded with debt, not Rowan Oak, where family pressures existed, not even various escapes in New York with Meta: but the big woods as an Edenic place.

*So unattractive was it for the marketplace it was rejected, in order, by the *Saturday Evening Post*, the *American Magazine*, *Collier's*, *Country Gentleman*, *Redbook*, *Cosmopolitan*, and *This Week*. Faulkner, apparently, sent it out on his own, shades of the earlier sending schedule. He finally asked Ober to send it elsewhere, *Harper's* taking it at a much lower payment, for the September 1940 issue.

That story's spatial fantasy is connected to a temporal one. It has the liquidity of Proustian time, in which memory and present become so interwoven the narrator cannot distinguish them: "And as he [Fathers] talked about those old times and those dead and vanished men of another race from either that I knew, gradually those old times would cease to be old times and would become the present, now, not only as if they had happened yesterday but as if they were still happening and some of them had not even happened yet but would occur to-morrow."*[9] So intense are these stories they seem to have taken place in a time and location before the unnamed narrator or his kin existed, in some legendary or mythical period only Sam Fathers could reach back to.

Along with the emphasis on the special space and the interwoven quality of time, there is the story's final warning, given in the early version by the narrator's father (and later by Ike McCaslin, the narrator in *Go Down, Moses*). Once the boy has seen the legendary buck, he needs to be told how that sight fits in with life itself: how the spirit of the woods can be translated into actuality. Ike speaks what we can assume to be Faulkner's hail and farewell, his desperate appeal to what has passed into time and been swallowed up in space:

All the blood hot and strong for living, pleasuring, that has soaked back into it [the earth]. For grieving and suffering too, of course, but still getting something out of it for all that, getting a lot out of it, because after all you dont have to continue to bear what you believe is suffering; you can always choose to stop that, put an end to that. And even suffering and grieving is better than nothing; there is only one thing worse than not being alive, and that's shame. But you can't be alive forever, and you always wear out life long before you have exhausted the possibilities of living.[10]

These words appear almost exactly in the earlier version, the only difference being a change of a word here and there. But the passage itself, deriving from 1939, remained steadily in Faulkner's mind, surfacing again in his Nobel Prize speech. It is full of everything he saw, even in 1939, slipping away from him—including youth.

In short order he returned to "The Peasants," realizing that he would never be able to hack it financially with stories or other strategies—that Hollywood was his sole salvation again. If he went West, the timing was

*For inclusion in *Go Down, Moses*, the passage becomes more abundant and textured: "And as he talked about those old times and those dead and vanished men of another race from either that the boy knew, gradually to the boy those old times would cease to be old times and would become a part of the boy's present, not only as if they had happened yesterday but as if they were still happening, the men who walked through them actually walking in breath and air and casting an actual shadow on the earth they had not quitted. And more: as if some of them had not happened yet but would occur tomorrow, until at last it would seem to the boy that he himself had not come into existence yet . . ." (*Go Down, Moses* [New York: Modern Library, n.d.], p. 171).

poor, since he was thoroughly immersed in ongoing work, while planning for future volumes as well. But screenwriting would not only break his continuity, it would wrench him from Meta, whom he hoped to see when he went North in the fall.* As it turned out, no one wanted him—neither Hawks nor Twentieth Century-Fox nor MGM. Even if Hawks had had work for him, it is doubtful if a large studio wanted him at his terms, $1,250 a week, for a set number of weeks. His reputation for heavy drinking and for writing unplayable dialogue had settled in.

While Faulkner was trying to make ends meet, although living well during the effort, George Marion O'Donnell spoke of the writer's exploration of a great myth. O'Donnell's critical point became very influential: that Faulkner saw the South as held together by a socioeconomic-ethical tradition, represented by the Sartoris clan; and that this "myth of the South" was being threatened by the incursions of the Snopes family. It is, accordingly, a bitter struggle between humanism and naturalism.

The O'Donnell equation, however, has only limited significance, and to locate the Faulkner "myth" in these terms is to ignore the far more problematical and intricate nature of his work. The Sartoris family does not represent an ideal for Faulkner; quite the contrary, he is very critical of it, and only seems to find it defensible in the face of the Snopes invasion. The great Faulkner myth, if we must single one out, has to do with the big woods—with "hut dreams," with escape into a different time and space where everything is possibility and the experience an echo of the Garden. The Sartoris clan, to the contrary, is associated with death, and not all the deaths are romantic. O'Donnell tries to make Faulkner into a contemporary Hawthorne, when in fact he is at least as close to Cooper as he is to Hawthorne.

Although intended as one of the potboilers, "A Point of Law," once revised, became part of chapter 1 of "The Fire and the Hearth," the second segment of *Go Down, Moses*. After the *Saturday Evening Post* rejected it, Faulkner found a publisher in *Collier's* (June 1940). Based on Lucas Beauchamp and the world of moonshining, it is not a distinguished piece of work. Lucas becomes caught in a triangular case with his daughter Nat and her boyfriend, George Wilkins. As a tenant of Roth Edmonds, the old man is prosecuted for having a still on the Edmonds property. But the prosecution falls through since no member of the family can be made to

---

*She writes she heard from him in mid-August, that he was coming North about October 15. "He protested that he didn't see me enough and that it was bad, physically, to live as he was now. He knew he should find a girl (a 'physical spittoon,' he phrased it), but although he had tried, he was unable to. 'I simply won't rise,' he wrote. 'That's strange, isn't it? After what I know and don't ever seem to stop remembering very long, all else is meat' " (Meta Carpenter Wilde and Orin Borsten, *A Loving Gentleman: The Love Story of William Faulkner and Meta Carpenter* [New York: Simon & Schuster, 1976], p. 244). The phrasing, if her report is to be trusted, is one we wish didn't derive from one of the world's great novelists; and also the sentiment, that physically he needed her because his wife has locked him out of her bed. The whole episode sounds adolescent, but we are of course dependent solely on this account of what was said and what transpired. One admires Meta's candor.

testify against another. The law has been confounded, and both George and Lucas return to moonshining with a new still. Once buried in *Go Down, Moses,* the feeble material does not appear so exposed as in short story form.

Intruding into this delicate operation was a brief visit to Washington, to testify at the plagiarism trial of one Robert H. Sheets, which came to nothing. Faulkner used the interlude as a way of paying his travel as far as Washington; after that, he headed for New York.

His stay was brief, and what occurred between him and Meta during this time is not unfolded in her book. Faulkner was back in Oxford within a week or so, and on October 24 made one of his few political gestures, the offer to donate the manuscript of *Absalom* to raise money for the Spanish Loyalists. His correspondent in this was Vincent Sheean, and Faulkner responded enthusiastically, agreeing to the statement prepared by the League of American Writers: "I most sincerely wish to go on record as being unalterably opposed to Franco and fascism, to all violations of the legal government and outrages against the people of Republican Spain."[11] He also offered other first-draft typescripts if Sheean wanted them. *Absalom* passed from Faulkner's hands into those of George Lazarus, who donated the funds to the Loyalists; then the manuscript went to the University of Texas, purchased from Lazarus. Faulkner's gesture was unusual for him since, as noted, his political interests were almost nil. Blotner reports he hated Roosevelt because of the latter's effort to move up the date of Thanksgiving. But this "hatred" was hardly political. Once the war started, however, he rallied behind the president, as did most other Roosevelt-haters.

As he continued to work over revisions of what was by now called *The Hamlet,* his letters (to Haas) are nearly all concerned with finances. In a letter received November 29, after a brief trip to New York, he expresses pleasure at winning the O. Henry Memorial Award for "Barn Burning," but wonders if there is a cash prize. The award, for the best short story published in an American magazine for 1939, carried a prize of $300; and it was also a considerable feat for a man who saw the shorter form as a potboiler. (We might add that 1939 was not a banner year for the short story.) In the same letter, he indicates he has no money and warns he must earn another $2,000 before January 1. ". . . I am trying to write short stories and earn it. If I can put bee on Sat Eve Post twice, I will get back at novel."[12] The *Saturday Evening Post,* however, found Faulkner writing too far from their market and showed no interest in any of his shorter works until "Tomorrow," which appeared on November 23, 1940. "Tomorrow," typically, was one of those potboilers, and turned up revised in *Knight's Gambit.*

In a follow-up letter, received on December 7, Faulkner ranged over a number of items, all of them still linked to finances. He mentions wasting his time writing two stories for the *Saturday Evening Post.* He reveals he was fully conscious that in his eagerness to cash in, he wrote mechanical pieces "in which I had no faith while my mind was still on the novel; hence a bust."[13] After enumerating his problems, including his return to the novel, he requests an additional $500, to be advanced against the next volume. He is uncertain, however, how he stands with the $2,000 advanced against the present one. He mentions he will take six months of 1940 to "try to write stuff that will make me a bank account for a little while, for the rest of the year anyway. If I have $500.00 from Random H. and the $300 prize [O. Henry Prize] and hang something on Post for $1000.00 by first of year, I will have a breather in which to invent salable stuff without having to haunt the post office for the check to pay coal and grocery bills with."

As 1939 ended, he was embattled. Financially, he was mortgaging his future to Random House, a kindly creditor, but a creditor nevertheless; and while his work went well, he seemed, in terms of security, little better off than five years before. He had of course spent freely. He owned a good deal of property, an airplane, a car, a working farm; he had renovated Rowan Oak into a distinguished residence, and he had achieved respectability. The money had gone into objects with visibility. But the farm was proving to be a losing proposition and the airplane was, admittedly, an indulgence. Another factor was his response to Phil Stone: that payment to keep his friend solvent was the extra which made his own situation so tight, even desperate.

As "The Peasants" went forward, Faulkner found solace in the fact he could incorporate "Lizards in Jamshyd's Courtyard" into the text of the last segment. This was after he had incorporated parts of "The Hound" and the idea of "Afternoon of a Cow." Now divided into four segments instead of the two divisions he originally intended, *The Hamlet* was probably in Saxe Commins's hands by early December. Since he had to return to Washington, it is probable he came up to New York for a brief time to work over the discrepancies in the manuscript/typescript.

When published on April 1, 1940, with the dedication to Stone, *The Hamlet* contained six stories incorporated into the text: the three mentioned to Haas ("Spotted Horses," going back to 1931; "Lizards in Jamshyd's Courtyard," from 1932; "Fool About a Horse," from 1936) plus "The Hound," from 1931; "Afternoon of a Cow," read to Coindreau in 1937; and "Barn Burning," from 1938. The use of material from almost a decade earlier and then extending along the 1930s reveals how Faulkner's imagination worked by a steady accretion and an attention to the details of the material. If anything demonstrated this accretive mode, *The Hamlet* did. Its strengths derive from its reliance on material simmering in Faulkner's mind, just as its weaknesses derive from the fact he let the original material run on too long, or else could not find sufficiently ingenious ways of incorporating the earlier fictions. But the other side of this view is that Faulkner's method is based on a loose series of stories which bleed out to the edges, like lines and masses of color in abstract expressionist painting.

632 | WILLIAM FAULKNER: AMERICAN WRITER

The year 1940 brought both turbulence and achievement. In his writing, Faulkner was moving along well, awaiting the publication of *The Hamlet*, working on what would become *Go Down, Moses,* planning several other books (such as *Intruder in the Dust* and *The Reivers*), publishing five stories (although not all written in 1940). The stories were "A Point of Law" (for $1,000, *Collier's,* June 22), which was incorporated in *Go Down, Moses* as chapter 1 of "The Fire and the Hearth"; "The Old People" (*Harper's,* September), which became part 4 of *Go Down, Moses;* "Pantaloon in Black" (*Harper's,* October), which, revised, became part 3 of *Go Down, Moses;* "Gold Is Not Always" (*Atlantic,* November), which became chapter 2 of "The Fire and the Hearth" in *Go Down, Moses;* and "Tomorrow" (*Saturday Evening Post,* November 23), which, revised, turned up as the fourth story in *Knight's Gambit.** The striking part about four of the stories is how they were becoming integrated in Faulkner's mind as segments of a larger work. Originally, *Go Down, Moses* would be titled "And Other Stories," but Faulkner for the second edition rightfully eliminated the stories aspect and made the volume appear as a novel, one based on interrelated shorter fictions.[14]

Meanwhile, his personal life was marred by disturbing elements, including his dissatisfaction with Random House, his overwhelming need for money to cover expenses, and his general depression as Europe appeared to be collapsing under Nazi onslaughts. The first of the personal griefs came with the death on January 31 at Rowan Oak of Caroline Barr, Mammy Callie. Although she was a servant, a woman of uncertain aptitudes and direction, and the source of many time-consuming searches when she disappeared for long stretches, she was, all in all (with the exception of Maud), possibly the person closest to Faulkner of anyone in the family. As a woman of sixty-two (her age was a sometime thing), Mammy Callie had come to the family in 1902, when Murry Falkner moved from Ripley to the "Big Place" in Oxford. She had interwoven her life with that of the Falkner boys, then with their children, especially Jill. Even though she lived in her own dwelling behind the house at Rowan Oak, she was a complete member of the household, beloved, respected, and a solid force in bringing up four wild boys. Faulkner felt nothing but love and admiration for this doughty woman, born a slave and devoted to the Falkners: Dilsey is based in part on her. She helped shape Faulkner's sense of loyalty and devotion, what he saw as an overarching integrity. To Haas, we catch the note of grief: "Sorry I am late with it [*Hamlet* galleys], but the old

---

*"Tomorrow" enjoyed an illustrious history—as noted, the *Saturday Evening Post* and then *Knight's Gambit,* followed by a CBS Playhouse 90 television production on March 7, 1960 (with Richard Boone, Kim Stanley, Beulah Bondi, and Charles Bickford), then by a film (like the TV production) written by Horton Foote and starring Robert Duvall, released in 1972. The story is itself typical of Faulkner's lesser works: a pastiche of the Lena Grove–Byron Bunch relationship in *Light in August;* an exercise in narration—Chick as primary narrator, plus two major interior ones; and an O. Henry surprise ending—in which the boy adopted by a country man turns out, now grown, to be the murder victim in a case on which the country man sits as juror. It works better on the screen, big and little, than on the page.

hundred-year-old matriarch who raised me died suddenly from a stroke last Saturday night, lingering until Wednesday, so I have had little of heart or time either for work. . . . The old lady was about 95. The old records were lost years ago, after she was freed, and we didn't know for certain. . . . She didn't suffer. She had a paralytic stroke in the kitchen just before supper, had lost consciousness within 30 minutes and never regained it, died Wednesday while my wife was sitting beside her bed. She couldn't have gone better, more happily."[15]

Mammy Callie was buried in St. Peter's Cemetery, in the segregated area reserved for Negroes. The stone reads:

Callie Barr
Clark
1840–1940
MAMMY
Her white children
bless her.

Faulkner dedicated *Go Down, Moses* to her: To MAMMY
CAROLINE BARR
Mississippi
[1840–1940]
Who was born in slavery and who
gave to my family a fidelity without
stint or calculation of recompense
and to my childhood an immeasurable devotion and love

Then in a follow-up letter to Haas two days later, Faulkner sent on his final words; they bear repeating:

Caroline has known me all her life. It was my privilege to see her out of hers. After my father's death, to Mammy I came to represent the head of that family to which she had given a half century of fidelity and devotion. But the relationship between us never became that of master and servant. She still remained one of my earliest recollections, not only as a person, but as a fount of authority over my conduct and of security for my physical welfare, and of active and constant affection and love. She was an active and constant precept for decent behavior. From her I learned to tell the truth, to refrain from waste, to be considerate of the weak and respectful to age. I saw fidelity to a family which was not hers, devotion and love for people she had not borne.

She was born in bondage and with a dark skin and most her early maturity was passed in a dark and tragic time for the land of her birth. She went through vicissitudes which she had not caused; she assumed cares and griefs which were not even her cares and griefs. She was paid wages for this, but pay is still just money. And she never received

634 | WILLIAM FAULKNER: AMERICAN WRITER

very much of that, so that she never laid up anything of this world's goods. Yet she accepted that too without cavil or calculation or complaint, so that by that very failure she earned the gratitude and affection of the family she had conferred the fidelity and devotion upon, and gained the grief and regret of the aliens who loved and lost her.

She was born and lived and served, and died and now is mourned; if there is a heaven, she has gone there.[16]

These remarks, somewhat revised, had appeared in the Memphis *Commercial Appeal*. We know Faulkner's feelings were genuine, and yet his relationship to Mammy Callie—and by inference the relationship of many white males to their Mammies—has several ambiguities in it. The same can be said of Faulkner's raising of Dilsey to heroic stature, or his later portrayal of Molly Beauchamp, the wife of Lucas. His response to Mammy Callie cuts deeply into race. Did Faulkner admire in the Negro—and especially in the Negro Mammy—that decency and integrity which came from people who knew their place and accepted it? Did he love Mammy Callie specifically because he observed and felt her wholehearted devotion to the Falkners? Did this mean that the Negro, represented by the Mammy, was to be revered because she/he stood and served? There was in Faulkner's reverence for this woman an emblem of those traditional relationships unchanged by the Civil War. While Mammy was not a slave and was free to go, she undertook the slave woman's role in the family, the household servant indispensable in nursing and raising the children. Mammy Callie was too old to nurse, but her taking on of the Falkner children as if her own, her dependence on this family's largesse, her assumption of their cares and griefs as if her own—all of this fixed a certain kind of Negro role in Faulkner's memory and imagination.

We can say without subverting his true feelings for her that Mammy Callie helped shape Faulkner's attitudes toward Negroes. He was kind, generous, willing to support, but he assumed well into his mature years that they were unable to fend for themselves; that except for a few individuals, they needed direction from whites; that left to themselves, they could not handle their lives, much less the business of life. Faulkner's fear of disorder and of subversion of the natural order of things, his emphasis on gradualism—especially in the 1950s, when matters started to come to a head—all derived from certain assumptions about Negroes Mammy Callie helped to reinforce. He saw Negroes as the salt of the earth, in many ways far superior to whites—but he saw them in their place, serving, childlike people waiting for guidance. He foresaw change, but did not figure on how many generations would have to pass, how many contemporary Negroes would have to be sacrificed in that transition. The suffering, grieving, loyal Negro was etched in his personal *and* literary imagination; it was his way of understanding.

Another area of turbulence, which we pick up in June of 1940, concerned his growing dissatisfaction with Random House over financial arrangements. In early June Faulkner decided he needed an additional $4,000 in advances, and Haas, on the basis of sales figures for *Absalom, The Unvanquished, The Wild Palms,* and *The Hamlet* to date, wrote he did not feel justified in offering additional monies. This left Faulkner free to go elsewhere for at least a collection of stories *(Knight's Gambit)* and a new novel idea *(Intruder in the Dust)*. Harold Guinzburg at Viking was still interested in acquiring Faulkner, and a break with Random House seemed imminent. Haas was away, but Cerf decided Faulkner was too valuable to let go and offered him an additional $2,000 to the $2,400 already advanced by Haas. This would mean an expenditure of $1,500, plus the monies already offered to Faulkner against royalties. Guinzburg then pulled out, wise in the short run—since Faulkner was clearly not earning back on sales—but of course foolish in the long run. This left Faulkner with Random House, but still financially in a hole. As a consequence, he returned to short stories with a renewed intensity. A good deal of his future career was predicated on this sustained drive to obtain ready cash, since much of his work from now on, *A Fable* excepted, has its origin in short story material. If he had earlier pioneered with a new kind of novel based loosely on short stories filling out the canvas, he was now, without desiring to, forced into writing just this kind of novel.

Short stories began to appear on Ober's desk with frequency. After the three stories which made up "The Fire and the Hearth" segment of *Go Down, Moses,* Ober, just past mid-March, received "Pantaloon in Black," which formed the third segment of *Go Down, Moses.* This attempt to penetrate into the thought processes of the Negro was surely given impetus by the recent death of Mammy Callie and Faulkner's genuine effort to understand how Negroes responded, despite the concealment of their feelings from whites. As we read these stories, we recognize Faulkner was chipping away at that large block of imaginative material he always had in readiness, but that no real integrative idea was available to make these shorter pieces cohere. Even when *Go Down, Moses* was brought forth in its second edition as a novel and not as a collection of short stories, that integrative coherence we expect in long fiction was missing. Financial pressures were affecting the imaginative thread.

When "Pantaloon in Black" was sent out, Faulkner told Ober he was being dunned for 1937 back taxes, and he was broke even before that. He had high expectations for *The Hamlet,* with its immersion in Snopes and his loving attention to Ratliff, plus his introduction of other amusing characters; but much depended on reviewers seeing his novel as something new. The six stories which went into its making, because not always fully integrated, created a sense of longueurs in the completed book. But everything else aside, a good deal depended on how sympathetic one was to Faulkner's aims before the book was even opened. Fadiman in the *New Yorker* weighed in with his usual incomprehension of any attempt at the new—in fact, congratulating himself that he has emerged from the reading, as if he had undertaken some dangerous journey which promised potential destruction. He reports that "the author apparently continues to enjoy as lively a case of the 'orrors as you are apt to find outside a Keeley-cure hostelry." Fadiman has apparently picked up information about Faulkner's binges and tosses it in as literary analysis.

The Sunday *Herald Tribune* called the experience of reading the book a "morbid absorption" in watching crawling things, like lizards; and the *New York Times*[17] described it as the best fiction of the year. The reviewer, Ralph Thompson, while not catching the whole sense of the novel, nevertheless noted that Faulkner had found an area of writing in which he was unsurpassed. He read the book as the "decay of the South" in postwar years, a somewhat thin way of seeing it; but the review was otherwise admirable and sympathetic. Malcolm Cowley, who in some of his reviews approached Fadiman, indicated he thought *The Hamlet* was Faulkner's best novel since *Sanctuary*. Although Cowley offered high praise, his predilection for this material led into his overevaluation of Snopes and Yoknapatawpha in his Viking *Portable* introduction and selections. By skipping over *Absalom*, and returning to *Sanctuary*, Cowley was beginning that distortion of Faulkner's career which only in later years straightened out. We have, then, a certain kind of reviewing, not at all uncommon, in which a lesser book is praised at the expense of far greater; in which a particular trend or tendency in a novelist becomes emphasized not because it is the writer at his best, but because it is simply the writer at his most accessible for that particular critic. Cowley reviewed the novel in the *New Republic*, when that magazine commanded serious attention. *Time* and *Newsweek*, for their part, continued their presentation of Faulkner as a bucolic Dostoyevsky—not without praise, but without real comprehension of either his ends or means.

The leading reviews were once again mixed. No clear direction appeared which could turn readers toward this book; there was nothing to generate that word of mouth which creates a pyramiding of sales. If Ober and Random House brought Faulkner up to date on the reviews, he could look forward to his usual early spurt of sales among those who followed him, and then the falling off; earning back less than his advances and leaving him financially no better off.

The Hamlet becomes more significant as a document in Faulkner's life than as a work of fiction. It is a curious book, since it seems quintessential Faulkner and certainly it and the rest of the Snopes trilogy have become his signature pieces. But unless we judge it in terms of rhythms, retellings, and overlappings, we may judge it harshly. Too many elements simply do not mesh: the death of Houston's wife by the stallion he has bought; the establishment of Houston himself—necessary so that Mink Snopes can kill him; the idiot Ike and the cow he is buggering, and its possible analogy to Eula and Major de Spain; the sudden emphasis on Ike and then Lump—peripheral figures; other like elements introduced so as to make use of the previously written stories. All of these do not cohere; these are discrepancies, incoherences, lack of continuity. Therefore, we feel the need to read the book differently because Faulkner has by this time educated us to read him differently; not to look for coherence, but for those lines, colors, and planes which bleed off to the edge of the canvas; not to insist on continuity in all places, but to find clusters and clumps which do not necessarily connect. Faulkner's characteristic telling and retelling, his use of recapitulation as the linchpin of the trilogy, all make it necessary to accept him on his terms. And yet even as we agree on this—that the subtext preempts the text—the first volume of the Snopes trilogy reveals a letting go, a relaxation. That superb authorial control exhibited in *Absalom* simply is not duplicated. So insistent was the pressure of financial matters, perhaps personal as well, that Faulkner had to reuse material without being able to assimilate it into his imagination. The "novel of stories"—except for *Go Down, Moses*—was for him a lesser thing than the novel.

The financial plaints began soon after publication of the book, and became a steady drone in his letters to Random House, chiefly to Robert Haas. He does not come to New York, he says, because he lacks railroad fare; and he has to arrange for deferment of tax payments for 1937—he now has until July 1. He needs another $500, which he can obtain by mortgaging some horses and mules at the bank. But if he mortgages, he cannot sell, and he finds it preferable to assign royalties directly to the bank, as of November 1. In the meanwhile, he asks for $1,000 on assignment as of that date. By doing this, he hopes to avoid drawing against royalties in advance, although his plan is simply that by another name. "I have got my account with you down under five hundred, not counting *The Hamlet,* and I want to keep it that way until it shows black again if possible. This alternative will come to the same thing, beside the interest, but at least it will be the bank's money and not the firm's." He concludes: "I'm a lug of the first water; what I should do (or any artist) is give all my income and property to the bloody govt. and go on WPA forever after."[18]

As his financial options narrowed, he even dusted off "With Caution and Dispatch," a 1932 story about John Sartoris, during his Royal Flying Corps days. Faulkner did considerable overhauling of this musty piece in 1939, probably during his feverish outpouring of short fiction, but Ober could not sell it, calling it outdated. The story remained unpublished and uncollected.

On April 28, as events began to narrow down only to money, Faulkner wrote Haas once more, and this time he upped the ante considerably. After repeating he needed $1,000 now to cover debts and current bills, he indicated he needed $9,000 more over the next two years, at the rate of $400 per month. He mentions his dire plight is the result of the *Saturday Evening Post* rejecting stories for which he expected to be paid $1,000 each; and without the *Saturday Evening Post,* the best he can hope for is $300 or $400 from *Harper's.* He laments he has wasted his time with potboilers which have not even sold. He says he has been mortgaging his mares and colts "to pay food and electricity and washing and such, and watching each mail train in hopes of a check."[19] He can raise the thousand on assignment to the bank, but he has run out of mules to mortgage. "And I will still have to keep trying to write trash stories which so far are not selling even fifty percent, because I am now like the gambler who simply has to double and pyramid, the poker player who can neither call nor throw in his hand but has got to raise." He indicates he has "a blood-and-thunder mystery story which should sell . . . But I dont dare devote six months to writing, haven't got six months to devote to it." This was, apparently, *Intruder in the Dust*, and when he did write it, it did sell; but that was eight years later, in 1948. He also mentions he has another book of stories like *The Unvanquished*, what would become *Go Down, Moses*; but since the stories already written for it haven't sold, he doesn't have the time to continue with it. His request for $400 at the beginning of the letter turns to an "even $300.00 a month in addition to first $1,000.00."

The letter did not mention his leaving Random House, but implicit in it was such a stressful financial need that if Haas could not come up with a new scheme of payment, he would be forced to look elsewhere. Such a break would be painful for both sides, since Random House proved to be a home away from home for the writer; and for Random House, which believed completely in him, Faulkner's name on their list was a mark of great prestige, like Hemingway's and Fitzgerald's at Scribner's. Also, for a new house like Random House, it was necessary to have great writers so as to draw other upcoming authors to their list.

Haas recognized all this, to which must be added his true personal regard for Faulkner, and responded with a new deal. After pointing out to the hard-pressed writer that his books did not earn out more than $3,000 each, at best, judging from *The Hamlet* sales, Haas did not see how Faulkner could ever get out of a hole with his new proposal. He countered with one of his own, a four-year contract, and then something still relatively new in publishing—a subsidy or stipend to the writer. Haas offered a three-book deal, with $1,000 down, another $2,000 for the following twelve months, and then for the next two years $250 per month. That met Faulkner's request for $9,000, but spread out over four years rather than the two he wanted. It was all in all a generous offer, and implied in it was the idea Faulkner should cut back on expenses. We never find Haas chastising Faulkner for living too high, or cautioning him to curtail this or that; rather, we find counteroffers to Faulkner's requests which are always under what the author says he needs.

Sensing that matters had reached a critical stage and that his career was as much at stake as his finances, Faulkner answered on May 3. It was a combination of seething rage and professional care of his career, and it is revealing as few Faulkner letters are:

Every so often, in spite of judgment and all else, I take these fits of sort of raging and impotent exasperation at this really quite alarming paradox which my life reveals: Beginning at the age of thirty I, an artist, a sincere one and of the first class, who should be free even of his own economic responsibilities and with no moral conscience at all, began to become the sole, principal and partial support—food, shelter, heat, clothes, medicine, kotex, school fees, toilet paper and picture shows—of my mother . . . [a] brother's widow and child, a wife of my own and two step children, my own child; I inherited my father's debts and his dependents, white and black without inheriting yet from anyone one inch of land or one stick of furniture or one cent of money; the only thing I ever got for nothing, after the first pair of long pants I received (cost: $7.50) was the $300.00 O. Henry prize last year. I bought without help from anyone the house I live in and all the furniture; I bought my farm the same way. I am 42 years old and I have already paid for four funerals and will certainly pay for one more and in all likelihood two more beside that, provided none of the people in mine or my wife's family my superior in age outlive me, before I ever come to my own.

Now and then, when pressed or worried about money, I begin to seethe and rage over this. It does no good, and I waste time when I might and should be writing. I still hope some day to break myself of it. What I need is some East Indian process to attain to the nigger attitude about debt. One of them is discussing the five dollars he must pay before sunset to his creditor, canvasses all possibilities, completes the circle back to the point of departure, where there is simply no way under heaven for him to get five dollars, says at last, "Well, anyway, he (the creditor) cant eat me." "How you know he cant?" the second says. "Maybe he wont want to," the first says.[20]

He offers some changes, which Haas agreed to. He recognizes he has received $500 on a novel which does not exist; he asks for $1,000 now to cover immediate bills and debts and permission to draw another $500 to pay July 1 deferred income tax from 1937. That adds up to the $2,000 Haas usually allowed as advance on new manuscripts. If this does not suffice, then he, Faulkner, will take up the arrangement of $200 per month. If the plan is workable, he will get started on a new novel, which develops, in 1951, into "Notes on a Horsethief," a short fiction which appears, revised, in *A Fable* (1954) and *The Reivers* (1961). The outline which follows in Faulkner's letter also has some marginal references to his detective novel, *Intruder in the Dust.*

It is a sort of Huck Finn—a normal boy of about twelve or thirteen, a big warm-hearted, courageous, honest, utterly unreliable white man with the mentality of a child, an old negro family servant, opinionated, querulous, selfish, fairly unscrupulous, and in his second childhood, and a prostitute not very young anymore and with a good deal of character and generosity and common sense, and a stolen race horse which none of them actually intended to steal. The story is how they travel for a thousand miles from hand to mouth trying to get away from the police long enough to return the horse. All of them save the white man think the police are after the horse. The white man knows the police have been put on his tail by his harridan of a wife whom he has fled from. Actually, the police are trying to return the boy to his parents to get the reward. The story lasts a matter of weeks. During that time the boy grows up, becomes man, and a good man, mostly because of the influence of the whore. He goes through in miniature all the experiences of youth which mold the man's character. They happen to be the very experiences which in his middle class parents' eyes stand for debauchery and degeneracy and actual criminality; through them he learned courage and honor and generosity and pride and pity.[21]

The outline ends with a renewed request for the $1,000 "at once." To sweeten the deal, Faulkner wrote to Haas less than three weeks later (May 22) that "Ober has four stories about niggers. I can build onto them, write some more, make a book like *The Unvanquished,* could get it together in six months perhaps." This became *Go Down, Moses.* Yet despite all these requests and Haas's considered response, the incoming money did not match outlay, and Faulkner would have to agree to a humiliating contract for work in Hollywood. With that, he entered a personal wasteland for several years in terms of serious production; the sole break being his early plans for what eventually became *A Fable* and the less than literarily successful *Intruder in the Dust.*

In Faulkner's letters to Random House and Haas in particular, there is his persistent use of the word "nigger." Sometimes he uses "Negro," but more often "nigger" is the preferred word, as in "four stories about niggers" or "nigger attitude about debt." By 1940 the word had become so beyond the pale in common usage one wonders why Faulkner did not recognize that Haas, a Northerner, a Jew, a man connected to a liberal publishing house, must have cringed at its usage. If Faulkner were working the farm and speaking to Johncy, who remained a segregationist and states's righter, we can understand that cultural contexts often dictate poor taste. But with Haas, the situation is quite different. This was not one Mississippian speaking to another in the common depreciatory idiom when referring to Negroes; but a sophisticated writer communicating with a sophisticated Northerner, who, he must have known, would not use the term himself. When speaking of Mammy Callie, Faulkner was all deference—she was not a "nigger," but a woman second only to his own mother. Was it out-and-out racism? Part of that intimidation which nearly all whites employed with Negroes? Was it Faulkner's way of making sure someone lower on the social and economic scale remained there, as a kind of scapegoat? Even though we know he consciously meant well for Negroes, it is difficult to assess his continued use of such a disparaging term when writing to Haas.

We can attempt to explain it away by saying the word was merely the baggage of childhood, so ingrained into the white Mississippian's vocabulary that it was simply without the poisonous connotations it now carries. But that is unacceptable, since by 1940 the word—like dago, kike, guinea, mickey, spic—was more than poor taste; it revealed a pathological mentality, the need to degrade others in order to maintain one's own position.[22] Was this part of Faulkner's equipment? For a man so alert to language and to nuances—in this respect, like Joyce or Eliot—it is inconceivable he did not know what he was doing or thought he was using the word neutrally. At its deepest levels, his continued use of the word indicates a racism so unconsciously insistent it becomes a force in his personal assessment of racial issues and racial justice. It would apparently nourish his desire for moderation and gradualism, although it would not permit him to ally himself with venomous elements who counseled caution as a way of avoiding issues altogether. Whatever weight we put upon his use of "nigger," it is disquieting.*

The follow-up letter to Haas on May 27 has another perspective altogether. While America was not yet at war, the draft had been put into effect, and the South was deeply affected. In terms of soldiering, the South had always provided a disproportionate number of soldiers and officers. Since the region was poor generally, the army and other services offered a way out, especially during the depression years. The white Southerner found in the army a home away from home, and since the services were segregated—in 1940, there were two Negro army officers, none in the navy —he found an accommodating cultural situation. Officers, in particular, as well as sergeants, tended to be from the South; and when the draft began, conscriptees found themselves being trained by a professional army heavy in men from Mississippi, Georgia, Alabama, and other Southern states.

The European war was going poorly, as German Panzers swept across Western Europe, trapping the British army and then allowing it to escape at Dunkirk—possibly one of the turning points in what was a one-way war. Yet despite selective service, America remained in policy isolationist: the vote to extend the draft in October passed Congress by only 203 to 202. Antiwar sentiment ran high, and most of it was planned to keep America free of European entanglements. Joseph Kennedy declared that the talk that Britain was fighting for democracy was bunk. John Foster Dulles proclaimed, "Only hysteria entertains the idea that Germany, Italy, or Japan contemplates war upon us." Senator Burton K. Wheeler, one of Roosevelt's favorites, said the triple-A plan was "to plow under every fourth American boy." Robert A. Taft, seeking the 1940 Republican nomination (which went to Wendell Willkie) opposed every measure which

---

*Some of the flavor of Mississippi racial wordplay could be heard in the well of the House; there Congressman John Rankin referred to a newspaperman as "a little kike." But this was small potatoes to Rankin's senatorial colleague, Theodore G. Bilbo, whose public statements went like the following: "We will tell our nigger-loving Yankee friends to go straight to hell." Bilbo insisted the "white man is the custodian of the gospel of Jesus Christ."

would aid Britain or create preparedness in this country. And the country itself, up to the time of the fall of France, was split evenly on conscription. When the draft was finally extended, sixteen million men registered —and Faulkner was one of those who thought of himself as a soldier.*

Even before that, in his letter to Haas of May 27, he indicated his readiness to serve, if the flesh were willing:

> What a hell of a time we are facing. I got my uniform out the other day. I can button it, even after twenty-two years; wings look as brave as they ever did. I swore then when I took it off in '19, that I would never wear another, nohow, nowhere, for no one. But now I dont know. Of course I could do no good, would last about two minutes in combat. But my feeling now is better so; that what will be left after this one will certainly not be worth living for.[23]

The feeling about combat indicates Faulkner was still harboring martial fantasies; and the uniform, which he had not earned, brought back to the man of forty-two the romance of more than two decades earlier. Faulkner imagines Immelmanns, loops, and other forms of aerial combat.

But the letter also turns very pessimistic, as he foresees, more than most, that the war would bring a new world, in which unknowns would wipe out the past. "But I can still write. That is, I haven't said at 42 all that is in the cards for me to say. And that wont do any good either, but surely it is still possible to scratch the face of the supreme Obliteration and leave a decipherable scar of some sort. Surely all these machines that can destroy a thousand lives or stamp out an entire car gassed and oiled and ready to run in two seconds, can preserve, even by blind mischance and a minute fault in gears or timing, some scrap here and there, provided it ever was worth preserving."[24] Then shocked back into immediate needs, Faulkner requests $500 and notes that the back income tax has now risen to $1,300; also, he needs a monthly stipend beginning July 1, or else he "might as well bust now as later."

Faulkner's despair at the coming situation can of course be attributed to a more general depression at his own condition at forty-two: ongoing financial problems, which seemed beyond solution; entering into what was then middle age; loss of Meta, as she and Rebner gave up their Riverdale digs and moved to Hollywood, where Rebner, now reconciled to a lesser career, would play background music in studio orchestras; the beginning of a slow period in his work, from a combination of the above factors and a general slowing of his creative powers; the depressing state of his home situation, in which the relationship with Estelle had stabilized but not

---

*A sampling of the Republican National Committee's radio spots: "When your boy is dying on some battlefield in Europe . . . and he's crying out, 'Mother! Mother!'—don't blame Franklin D. Roosevelt because he sent your boy to war—blame YOURSELF because you sent Franklin D. Roosevelt back to the White House." Willkie dissociated his campaign from this kind of talk, and actually such radio spots backfired.

appreciably improved. Nor had any of his responsibilities lessened. All his immersion in art could not disguise that he was mortal. If he had aligned himself early on with Keats that art conferred immortality, he could not, at forty-two, hold to a doctrine that rationalized youthful death. As he held up the uniform which had once been his, he felt life was passing him by. When he wrote Haas again, he did what many men of forty-two might do —he created a balance sheet: debts against credits, negatives against positives, minuses against pluses. It was the balance sheet of a man assessing the totality of his life; and in this frame of reference, while art may be long and life brief, life dominated.

In another letter to Haas four days later he began the assessment. He lists his tax indebtedness ($450 to federal government for 1937, $360 to the state in 1938), complicated by his friend's "trouble last summer." He also has present taxes to consider, and he repeats that $400 per month would see him through. He prefers the $400 for six months to $200 for twelve. But he would still accept $200 per month beginning July 1. He writes frankly: "I really meant what I said in my first letter. If you think this is a bad risk, say so. I have learned well what a goddam nuisance anyone becomes who, each time you see or hear him, you think, 'How much does he want now?' You and Don and Bennett have been my good friends for a long time, and I would hate to spoil it like this."²⁵ He indicates he cannot get a bite from Hollywood.

Faulkner recognized he was now at a critical juncture in his career. When he had entered a comparable period a decade earlier, his situation was dire and he responded with the sending schedule of short stories. But he was then thirty-two, not forty-two, and he had within him that large block of imaginative material he could tap and chip away at. Now he had diminished that treasure trove, and the toll of incessant labor, heavy drinking, and personal pressures was slowing him. He was correct in perceiving his situation as desperate, for beginning at this point he felt a gradual but steady decline, not only in production but in quality. It would be foolhardy to ascribe that falling-off to any one element; it must be understood in the light of everything which has gone before.

He recognized his rate of spending was too high—we note he had not mentioned the plane or car in his assets. He says his future rests on his ability to "write at least six commercial stories a year. I am still convinced that I can do it, despite the fact that I have not so far." He says he will liquidate assets, but then follows that with a statement indicating his profound need to be an important property owner. "I own a larger parcel of it than anybody else in town and nobody gave me any of it or loaned me a nickel to buy any of it with and all my relations and fellow townsmen, including the borrowers and frank sponges, all prophesied I'd never be more than a bum." Oxford measured success in visible property, not in books in the library or bookstore, not even in a *Time* cover story. Land was the thing, acres and acres of it, plus an estate, a car, a plane. These had replaced the uniform Faulkner had specifically designed for his return from the war; and it replaced as well those deceptive stories he told about his military service. Those tales faded away—when he became famous, he tried to bury them. Property now gave him his aura.

This letter then leads to what had hitherto been unmentionable, a possible departure by the firm's most prestigious author, at least for one book, the "collected story idea." His demands: ". . . besides the $3000 advance on the new unwritten novel, I need $4000 more by Jan. 1." He does not, however, want the Random House relationship to founder on this request, and he repeats how much their kindness and friendship have meant to him. But even as he says this, he mentions that many years ago, before he knew Random House, "a publisher [Guinzburg, of Viking] intimated to me that I could almost write my own ticket with him. This may not even hold now. But it is one thing more I can try before I decide to liquidate my property and savings." Faulkner even hoped, against realities, that the farm would turn a profit, although it lost at least $50 per month.

On June 10, 1940, Haas came back with his own list, the hard facts of book publishing during the depression years: *Absalom* had returned $3,037; *The Unvanquished*, $2,327; *The Wild Palms*, $5,360; and *The Hamlet*, so far, $2,700. Except for *The Wild Palms*, the figures did not warrant additional advances, and in effect he left Faulkner free to sign on with another publisher, if he could obtain his terms elsewhere. On June 12, in this crucial period, Faulkner responded, changing the terms somewhat. Since he needed $1,000 by January 1, he would probably have to contract for more than a volume of short stories, more likely for a novel as well. "Also, I may have to be able to give him [Guinzburg] a clean bill of health on me as far as any other future commitments on my writing go; in which case, I will have to be released from the unnamed future novel contract with Random House." But this will depend on the new arrangement: in fact, his new publisher may not even want the short story volume, only the novel. An additional factor, and here Faulkner protected his rear, the publisher may not agree to any of this, ". . . in which case I will take the additional 1,000.00 you offered in your recent letter, and try to write some salable short stories, then sell my mules etc. as I can."[26]

Events moved rapidly. Guinzburg made a good offer for a short story collection and novel for a total of $6,000. Faulkner cabled Random House: "RECEIVED CONTRACT FOR SHORT STORY BOOK AND A NOVEL. INFERENCE IS THAT I WILL BE PUBLISHED FROM NOW ON BY NEW FIRM. WOULD LIKE TO HAVE YOUR ACKNOWLEDGEMENT BEFORE CLOSING. WILL WAIT UNTIL NOON WEDNESDAY. WILL COME NEW YORK TO SETTLE DETAILS."[27] With this facing him, Cerf intervened and tried to make a deal Viking could not match. In all, he offered a package of $5,000—$1,000 still due Faulkner for the new novel, $2,000 advance for a volume of short stories, payable at $250 per month, plus the $2,000 already advanced. But Cerf added a sweetener. If by the end of 1940, Faulkner still needed money and had not produced the books fulfilling this agreement, Cerf would establish a general royalty account and Faulkner could draw on that. Cerf had additionally gotten Guinzburg to agree to withdraw if Random House equaled the Viking offer. He also told Guinzburg that if Faulkner left Random House, his new publisher would have to purchase the remaining unsold copies of *The Hamlet*. With that amount added on, the buyout would exceed $7,500. Cerf had come up with a detail which would discourage Guinzburg and Viking from the deal, although there was still plenty of dealing to go through. Beyond Cerf's loyalty to Faulkner, one must admire his business acumen.

On June 20, Faulkner wrote Cerf (Haas was away on military business) and ran through his predicament. He closes with both explanation and rationale for his behavior: "I must have that minimum sum, on my writing future if I can get it. I made the offer first to my present publishers, who declined. I made it to another publisher, who accepted, in the same good faith with which he must have believed I made him the offer. I cant play fast and loose with him this way. I cant use one publisher to blackjack another into advancing me money which that second publisher had otherwise declined to advance."[28]

This was the showdown. Faulkner had been perfectly honest; so had Random House and Viking. The publishing business at that time seems quaint, with Cerf and Guinzburg agreeing in gentlemanly fashion on a very valuable property, no one trying to sneak in and steal him away—and the author himself telling each side what the other was up to. The monies, while minimal by modern standards, were quite substantial for the time, when advances of $500 were not uncommon and authors felt pleased to be published at all during the last years of the depression. Cerf wrote Faulkner on June 24 and outlined his plan for Guinzburg to purchase all 2,801 copies of *The Hamlet*, regular and limited edition, including plates and stock, for a sum of $1,500. However, Faulkner did not receive Cerf's letter before he departed for New York to discuss terms directly with Guinzburg. After the talk, Guinzburg did not hang around, leaving town from that Tuesday (June 25) until the following Monday, when he spoke to Cerf. In between, in a miraculous state of mixed calm and agitation over his prospects, Faulkner worked over a short fiction called "Almost," which, when revised, became "Was" and part of *Go Down, Moses*. He sent it to Ober for the *Saturday Evening Post*, which rejected it. After having seen Guinzburg, Faulkner collected another $1,000 from Haas, now back at Random House after his stint establishing training camps for former officers. Guinzburg had told the writer he would inform him of the results of his talk with Cerf the following Monday, and from that, of the final outcome. Faulkner hung around in New York for a brief time, saw Ober, who, on the writer's advice, finally got rid of "The Old People," to *Harper's* for $400. By June 30, Faulkner had returned to Rowan Oak.

On July 3, it all began to come together. With his usual regard for the writer, Guinzburg wrote that advances plus plates added up to more than he could invest, but that he was prepared to listen to any future plans

Faulkner might have; it was a generous gesture on the part of a man who had lost. Cerf wrote five days later what Faulkner already knew, of Viking's withdrawal. Cerf reasserted his desire to do everything he could for Faulkner without injuring the firm, and reoffered his June 19 proposal. Faulkner waited almost three weeks (until July 28) to reply to Cerf. Other matters intervened, and when he wrote Cerf, he wasn't sure Guinzburg had clarified the situation to the Random House publisher.

Another dimension remains: was Faulkner piqued at Cerf for having introduced the deciding factor of the *Hamlet* plates? His letter demonstrates no hostile feeling. He assures Cerf he has no plans to approach another publisher, and that while Ober was holding his stories for the best prices he could obtain, he (Faulkner) suggested selling at whatever they could bring in such a poor market. If he cannot sell at least two stories, he speaks once again of mortgaging mules. Finally, he indicates that one more story ("The Bear") will "complete a mss. based on short stories . . . something like the UNVANQUISHED in composition."* He says: "This last story ["The Bear"] will be pretty long though, and I dont feel warranted in putting the time on it now, since I have got to write something short and quick to sell; this last story will be a novella, actually. Also, it might be best not to publish it, but to wait until I have time to write the Huck Finn novel which I described to Bob. It will be impossible to get at it though before next year at the earliest, unless lightning in some form strikes me a golden blow."[29] The twists, turns, and hesitations about what to write next indicate how deeply Faulkner's financial problems had made him stumble.

On July 24, four days before his latest plaint about finances, he got some hostilities off his chest to Cerf. The need to find some direction amidst so many unpleasant diversions—the war in Europe, the gradual preparation of America for entry, as well as his personal state—made him reevaluate himself against "the others." Using Walter Van Tilburg Clark's well-crafted *The Ox Bow Incident* as pretense, Faulkner let his feelings rip. After calling the Clark novel dull, he said it was little more than a short story, something Hemingway would have written in "about three thousand words, and in more distinguished and arresting prose."[30] But Clark was only the vehicle to other views. "What has happened to writing, anyway? Hemingway and Dos Passos and I are veterans now; we should be fighting tooth and toenail to hold our places against young writers. But there are no young writers worth a damn that I know of. I think of my day. There were Lewis and Dreiser and Sherwood Anderson and so forth, and we were crowding the hell out of them. But now there doesn't seem to be enough pressure behind us to keep Dos Passos and Hemingway writing

---

*Four days earlier, he wrote Ober he had completed "Go Down, Moses," the story which gave its name to the volume, and sent it directly to the *Post*. After rejection as unsuitable, *Collier's* took it for January 25, 1941. Faulkner then reworked it for inclusion in the volume of stories he later came to call a novel. He was now about halfway through the volume, lacking "The Bear" and "Delta Autumn."

even." In one sense, Faulkner was correct. The latter part of the 1930s, after the heavy political, ideological battles, had not resulted in a fresh generation of writers, although there was Richard Wright. By the end of the war, they would begin to appear in large numbers, but it is doubtful if Faulkner would find novelists like Bellow, Hawkes, and Mailer to his taste. His comments were probably ways of assessing his generation and concluding that they were giants—the critical remarks of a man trying to define his place in letters even as he was unsure of his future direction. "The Bear" was incubating, but he was not even sure he could write it; and yet "The Bear," as it found its place as the fifth segment in *Go Down, Moses*, would prove to be his most significant work for some time.

By then a number of things impinged on Faulkner's writing time. Johncy was no longer running the farm, but was working as an engineer on Oxford's WPA construction projects—another indication of his drifting. Other family matters intruded, but from a distance, when Estelle's once-divorced daughter, Victoria, remarried, this time in Shanghai to William Francis Fielden, employed by the British-American Tobacco Company. Unlike her mother, she planned to remain in the Far East, in Mukden, China. That left only Malcolm, who shortly headed into the military; and Faulkner, who vainly tried to contribute to the war effort.

The best he could do to get away from it all was to fly. But even that had lost some of its flavor, for now he felt flying was stealing time from grim necessity: writing to fulfill contracts, to keep up with outlay, to pay the tax man. When he found time, he read to Jill, selecting his favorites like *Moby-Dick*, regardless of what she understood. In the fall, he made two sales which brought him $1,300: "Gold Is Not Always," to the *Atlantic Monthly*, and "Go Down, Moses," to *Collier's* (for $1,000). In October he wrote Haas when Cerf remarried (he had been married to the actress, Sylvia Sidney): "My God, what a man. To have escaped once, and then daring fate again. If Bennett don't watch out, the gods are going to look around and see him some day."[31] It is fair to measure this as Faulkner's sense of marriage in 1940, having sampled it for eleven years.

The military was a fair seductress. In the same letter to Haas, who enjoyed temporary military duty while continuing at Random House, Faulkner spoke of his own uselessness, although he was an "advisor without portfolio" to the Civil Aeronautics Authority primary flying school attached to the university. He says he is doing some flying in a "low-wing monoplane" and is also trying to get a National Guard unit there, with a commission for himself. He laments he has not received a call from the RAF—although when things get worse they might call up aliens like himself. He adds he is doing no writing except potboilers.

I still have the novel in mind, may get at it, when bad weather stops farming and I become better adjusted mentally to the condition of the destruction-bent world. Saxon fighting Saxon, Latin against Latin, Mongol with a Slav ally fighting a Mongol who is the ally of a Saxon-

Latin ally of the first Slav; nigger fighting nigger at the behest of white men; one democracy trying to blow the other democracy's fleet off the seas. Anyway it will make nice watching when the axis people start gutting one another."[32]

Faulkner's response to this world turmoil and paradox was to fly more frequently and refresh himself on the Morse code. He was, in his way, moving toward what he hoped would be a commission, or even some informal role in the military or civilian arm of the military, like the CAA. While Faulkner's patriotism was real and unshakable, the war was also a form of salvation; with it he could, either literally or imaginatively, run away. With something of that in mind—that is, escape, impersonation, becoming a con artist—he wrote "An Error in Chemistry," hoping for a $1,000 Saturday Evening Post sale. The Saturday Evening Post rejected it, as did Collier's, another high-payer; it would be rejected until it appeared in Ellery Queen's Magazine, in June of 1946, for which Faulkner received $300. It then reappeared three years later in Knight's Gambit. These detective-type stories, in which Gavin Stevens plays problem-solver to Faulkner's conundrums, were indeed potboilers, not so poor of their kind as poor in relationship to the man writing them. Ellery Queen's Magazine maintained a high level of detective-fiction achievement, but it was not for a Faulkner. The best he could get out of this kind of production was a collection of stories, which by the time it appeared could not hurt him—he was already being hailed as one of the world's great novelists and was on the eve of the Nobel Prize. But the collection indicates he was, in his shorter fiction, falling well below the level of These 13 and Doctor Martino, which in themselves were uneven. His real proficiency in shorter fiction came only in what was now becoming much longer stories, the novella-length "The Bear" and the medium-length "Delta Autumn."

Johncy by now had his novel, Men Working, accepted at Harcourt, for which he received an advance of $500. He also agreed to change the spelling of his name, adding the "u," on the suggestion of Harcourt, Brace, which apparently hoped people would buy Johncy's book thinking it was by his brother. Although he had a mild success with Men Working, he never had a full career as a fiction writer. His work was inevitably compared with Faulkner's, but it lacked the spark of real imagination or real talent. It was solid and plodding, as the title indicates.

Then a situation developed for his elder brother, one of those circumstances in which he became completely dependent on others. As a periodic heavy drinker, Faulkner could moderate his intake when he was working hard, then suddenly go into a binge. Biologically derived or not, his drinking appeared to come at the juncture of several internal as well as external factors. He needed the right situation: a hotel room far from home, a party where he felt out of place, or a hunting camp. In the fall, Faulkner went to hunting camp, in the section of the Delta near Anguilla, almost in the corner where Mississippi, Louisiana, and Arkansas meet, due west of

Yazoo City. The area is now marked by the Delta National Forest to the south and the Yazoo National Wildlife Refuge to the north. The hunt was the annual affair, presided over by Bob Harkins, now on his forty-ninth consecutive trip; Faulkner, at forty-three, was one of the youngsters. By this time, he was not eager to kill deer, but came along for the male-bonding and for the return to a primitive life. This trip and future ones formed part of his resistance to civilization, to "progress," to the war raging in Rowan Oak and in the world beyond.

Early mornings (from 4:00 A.M.) were for hunting, or waiting at the deer stands, and evenings for eating the day's hunt, drinking, and storytelling. This, not Eastern literary cocktail parties, was Faulkner's world, and he could usually relax. But this time he carried to camp his heavy baggage of worries and anxieties, and he increased the tempo of drinking as the hunt went on. Soon, drinking preempted hunting. Faulkner was discovered unconscious one morning, and his condition seemed serious enough for the men to try to get him out of camp immediately.[33] Since they were deep in the wilderness, they needed time until a motorboat appeared—one of those rescuers which always seemed to save Faulkner from himself. Rushed to a hospital in Oxford, he was treated only a few hours before, as Dr. John Culley put it, it would have been too late. Both kidney failure and a perforated ulcer were feared, but Faulkner, with that extraordinary ability to recover, was fine in a few days, and flying.

When he wrote Cerf on December 15, he wished him a merry Christmas and a happy New Year, but did not indicate any difficulty. After asking for two copies of his latest books (*The Hamlet, The Unvanquished, The Wild Palms*) to give as Christmas gifts, he mentions having spent the last week in November in "the big woods after deer but never shot my rifle." He adds: "One nice thing about the woods: off there hunting, I dont fret and stew so much about Europe." No mention of nearly dying—information his publisher would not have been happy to hear, in any event. He ends: "But I'm only 43, I'm afraid I'm going to the damn thing yet."[34] Although men of forty-three did find positions in Washington or even in military units, Faulkner would not—and his heavy drinking seemed to work at cross-purposes, since it weakened him physically even as he hoped to be able enough to join up.

He did find time to write "Delta Autumn," a story about the hunt in the Delta, now observed by the "near seventy" ["near eighty" in the book revision] Ike McCaslin, both he and the hunt near the end of their lives. The story is very topical, full of the end of things, and in many ways a good indicator of Faulkner's state of mind in 1940, near the edge of America's entry into the war. As things beyond began to fall apart, Faulkner was genuinely fearful of the future of civilized life, and he writes about how man must be worthy of what nature has provided for him. It is not suffi-cient that the wilderness and "savage" life are *there*, man must rise to become worthy of them, or else their presence does not suffice. The rheto-ric becomes Biblical in its exhortatory quality: "I [the twelve-year-old boy who has just slain a buck] slew you [the buck]; my bearing must not shame your quitting life. My conduct forever onward must become your death." (Italicized in the revision.) Then for the book Faulkner added:

> ... marking him for that and for more than that: that day and himself and McCaslin juxtaposed not against the wilderness but against the tamed land, the old wrong and shame itself [slavery], in repudiation and denial at least of the land and the wrong and shame even if he couldn't cure the wrong and eradicate the shame, who at fourteen [twelve earlier] when he learned of it had believed he could do both when he became competent and when at twenty-one he became competent he knew he could do neither but at least he could repudiate the wrong and shame.[35]

The passage is so deeply felt that it becomes a valedictory. The boy will realize that despite Sam Fathers's tutelage, he has been expelled from the Garden, that the pastoral image in his mind cannot be matched by actuality. Like Sam, he foreknows the end. The woods and fields ravaged are the consequences of man's "crime and guilt, and his punishment."[36] Faulkner was reaching for the Keatsian urn, but could no longer fill it with his romantic longings; it was not the empty urn awaiting the artist, but one now overflowing with waste matter.

The wilderness itself was retreating, as if something with a soul which recognized its day had passed. In the revision, Ike is clairvoyant: ". . . he saw plain its ultimate doom, watching it retreat year by year before the onslaught of axe and saw and loglines and then dynamite and tractor plows, because it belonged to no man. It belonged to all; they had only to use it well, humbly and with pride."[37] He sees himself and the wilderness as two spans "running out together, not toward oblivion, nothingness, but into a dimension free of both time and space where once more the untreed land warped and wrung to mathematical squares of rank cotton for the frantic old-world people to turn into shells to shoot at one another, would find ample room for both."

With this, Faulkner became a great visionary American writer. Coequal with the meditations on the primitive wilderness are outbursts about race. The "nigger" references so common in Faulkner's letters have to be measured, now, against his sense of the terrible injustice done to the black race. "Delta Autumn" winds down with a vision of how the Delta has been traduced, the Garden newly dispossessed. Both original and revision are identical, except the former is italicized:

> *This land, which man has deswamped and denuded and derived in two generations so that white men can own plantations and commute every night to Memphis and black men can own plantations and even towns and keep their town houses in Chicago, where white men rent farms and live like niggers and niggers crop on shares and live like animals, where cotton is planted and grows*

man-tall in the very cracks in the sidewalks, where usury and mortgage and bankruptcy and measureless wealth, Chinese and African and Aryan and Jew, all breed and spawn together until no man has time to say which is which, or cares. . . . "No wonder the ruined woods I used to know don't cry for retribution," he thought. "The people who have destroyed it will accomplish its revenge."[38]

As Faulkner moved into 1941, he was entering a personal valley of death, somewhat on the analogy of the country, as a precursor of better times to come. As America's premier novelist, it was perhaps not presumptuous of him to find in his own life analogies to the country at large: its temporary loss of direction, its lack of initiative until pressed, then its recovery. America came out of the war as the world's greatest power, and Faulkner emerged from the postwar years as America's sole writer competitive with the great Europeans, the only one whose presence (not only influence) was acknowledged by other great writers.

Yet there is the question of how his financial troubles in the latter 1930s and early 1940s affected his whole emotional range, including sexual feelings. In some men, preoccupation with money sublimates sex or makes it impossible; with others, the identification with money-making might serve to speed up desire. In still others, there is little or no effect. Later on, when Faulkner was in his fifties, he seemed extremely eager for sexual intimacy —as we learn from Joan Williams, among others. But by that time, his finances had straightened out, he was then the great American man of letters, he had won the Nobel Prize in literature. Certainly, with his confidence reshaped in so many areas, he would feel that sexual relationships were part of the reward for achievement. Money, women, and power: these were the motivational forces, and Faulkner seems to have fitted well into this equation, if we define power as possessions and property. It is important, then, to see Faulkner's entrance into the valley, not of death itself, but of lesser achievement, as dependent on several factors: not only financial need, not only a gradual decline of creative ability, but also possibly a domestic situation in which he was only part of a man.*

Faulkner in 1941 looked to a year of uncertainties. His major project was *Go Down, Moses.* He would write what he had already referred to in his July 28 letter to Cerf as a novella, "The Bear," one of his strongest pieces of sustained writing. *Go Down, Moses* proved an extremely important statement for him, for well ahead of his society, he was willing to confront relationships "between white and negro races here."[39] A good deal of his writing time for 1941 was filled with revising stories already published, writing "The Bear," and then reshaping the material into the sequence he

---

*This has been mentioned before, but it bears repeating: Estelle is not to be blamed for this situation. If she appears to have failed as a wife, Faulkner failed as a husband. They came together out of free will, chose each other, and both admitted that early bonds forged a later link they could not ignore. They continued to present to Oxford society a façade of a married couple in control of their lives, however shakily. If, once the doors were closed, life was inharmonious, it was an arrangement they accepted, Faulkner as much as Estelle.

wanted for the volume. We can see how his production has slowed by the amount of time he needed to shape the volume, which was not published until May 11, 1942.

Before "The Tall Men" appeared (on May 31), Faulkner wrote Haas about the volume based on short stories, presented not as a novel but as stories: "The Fire and the Hearth," "Pantaloon in Black," "The Old People," "Delta Autumn," and "Go Down, Moses." Faulkner would add "Was" (once titled "Almost") and "The Bear," whose length of almost 150 pages turned this into a sizable volume, far longer than *The Unvanquished*, which he measured it by. But he was really asking Haas if it was worth his time to revise and shape the manuscript unless Random House was willing to publish such a book. In a follow-up letter after Haas indicated interest, Faulkner mentioned he was looking to Hollywood to keep him afloat. He was still far from a deal, but he offered up the name of William Herndon, an agent known to novelist Stephen Longstreet, now a scriptwriter. Faulkner's dealings with Herndon would prove nothing less than disastrous—financially, emotionally, psychologically.

"The Tall Men," written in March, was not one of his best—in fact, close to being one of his worst, it nevertheless targets a good many of his feelings as the depression began to pass into a wartime economy. It falls in easily with the ideas expressed in "Delta Autumn" and foreshadows "The Bear." Its chief thrust is the loss of Eden, the retreat of the pastoral ideal as an integrative force in men's lives, the government's trammeling of the Garden. The "tall men" of the title are not necessarily tall; they merely "stand tall," since they have refused to do the government's bidding. Faulkner is responding to economic changes affecting farmers in the 1930s, and turning these changes into an ideological and political statement indicating a stance well to the right of conservative.

An investigative agent of Selective Service has gone out to the McCallum farm with the local marshal. He plans to arrest the two McCallum twins for having failed to register for the draft. Before he arrives, he views people like the McCallums not only as draft dodgers, but as those who cheat the government on property, taxes, relief, and every other means at their disposal. When he arrives, the McCallum patriarch, Buddy, a hero of World War I, is about to have his leg amputated after an accident. Rejecting ether, he says whiskey will do. The marshal refuses to let the investigator leave until he educates him. What follows, after the twins drive off to enlist in Memphis, is Faulkner's Edenic view of Anglo-Saxon farmers, yeomen, proud, standing tall.

Having refused all government aid *not* to grow their cotton crop, the farmers quit raising cotton rather than comply with the federal plan to pay them for what they don't plant or gin. They do not ask for advice, and they continue to follow their own ways, until they have bales of unginned cotton they cannot sell, saying ". . . we can make out." Then follows the Faulkner ideology, essentially what he had said so much more eloquently in "Delta Autumn," given the difference of time and place:

Life has done got cheap, and life ain't cheap. Life's a pretty durn valuable thing. I don't mean just getting along from one WPA relief check to the next one, but honor and pride and discipline that make a man worth preserving, make him of any value. That's what we got to learn again. Maybe it takes trouble, bad trouble, to teach it back to us.[40]

These remarks reach back to *Pylon*, when Faulkner's response to government and officialdom became apparent, and ahead to the Nobel Prize speech with its emphasis on individual morality and ethics. The *Saturday Evening Post*, which liked this kind of homespun and staunch individualism, took the piece; it was also suitable for the *Reader's Digest*. The potboiler, it turned out, had been deeply felt, and it earned the author $1,000.

The name of William Herndon of Sunset Boulevard, Hollywood, begins to be repeated in Faulkner's letters to Haas, starting with his statement that Herndon wanted to sell some of his novels to the movies. This is followed by a request to send him *Soldiers' Pay*, if a copy can be found. By this time, Faulkner's books had been out of print so long some were collectors' items. Herndon was an extremely hard worker on behalf of his clients, but he promised far more than he could deliver, and had offered Faulkner a number of deals which fell through. One included a $500-per-week stint in Hollywood for twelve weeks; another was the *Soldiers' Pay* movie mentioned above, as well as a deal for *Go Down, Moses*. Foolishly, Faulkner dealt directly with Herndon, instead of letting Ober do it, although he did keep the latter informed.

The period during the late spring and summer of 1941 was a kind of holding pattern, as if Faulkner were tuned in to the country's attitudes: waiting for something to happen. Europe was capitulating to the Nazis, Britain was becoming isolated, and America was struggling against traditional isolationism. Faulkner, the doomsayer of civilization, was no isolationist, nor was he reassured by three thousand miles of ocean. He threw himself into civilian defense work, learning about the latest technical methods even while railing against rural electrification as a form of socialism. The staunch individualist was being swept up by a technological revolution which had arrived even in the deepest parts of the South; and now with the war effort gaining momentum he would have to learn the latest in aircraft spotting or else be a useless forty-three-year-old. Young men like Shelby Foote, from Greenville, North Carolina, came through Oxford. Foote, novelist and future historian of the Civil War, would have a distinguished service record. But for Faulkner the period was low-key, as he worked over *Go Down, Moses* stories, harbored plans to get into the coming conflict, and tried to meet his financial obligations.

By June 5, he had sent on to Haas the revision of "A Point of Law," which became chapter 1 of "The Fire and the Hearth" in the new volume. The revision emphasizes black-white relationships, particularly that of Lucas Beauchamp and Zack Edmonds, and how they "shared" for a time

Lucas's wife, Molly. As we shall see, the linkage of race by way of Molly signifies a new turn in Faulkner's thinking about race—not as exemplified in his public statements, but as demonstrated dramatically in his fiction. In a genealogical chart now at the University of Virginia Library, Faulkner had sketched in his version of the McCaslin and Beauchamp families, developing side by side in the sketch. Here he brought together black and white; "miscegenation" is in the chart, and then becomes even closer when Zack, his wife dead in childbirth, "borrows" Molly to nurse the white child. What else happens during the six months she is gone is not specified; but black and white potentially meet in Zack and Molly, literally in Molly and the white child (Carothers) and in the linkage of Zack and Lucas, both victimized in a sense by race.

The remainder of "The Fire and the Hearth," based on revised material, is concerned with racial relationships. "Gold Is Not Always" became chapter 2 of the extended version of this segment*; after which Faulkner took up an old, unsold story called "Absolution" (retitled "Apotheosis"). The new material was explosively racial in conception, intertwining black and white genealogically, until white repudiates black because of the South's social context. Lucas Beauchamp emerges as one of Faulkner's heroes: the man who, like Sam Fathers, has entered into a deeper truth, been strengthened by it, and refuses to budge from his principles even when death confronts him. He becomes, like the bear Faulkner was now writing about, an indomitable spirit, if not of the forest then of the black world where he is supposed to be deferential and compliant. In a great literary paradox of two Mississippi writers, Faulkner has his Lucas Beauchamp while Richard Wright has his Bigger Thomas.

As revisions continued and the book began to emerge from the stories, Faulkner replied on July 6 to a series of articles sent on by Warren Beck, a critic and fiction writer as well as university professor.** Faulkner's response fits well into the deeply felt positions he was taking in *Go Down, Moses*. His remarks show how *Go Down, Moses* anchors his midcareer as much as *The Sound and the Fury* his earlier career.

After telling Beck he had found implications which he, Faulkner, had missed, the novelist opened his feelings to the critic, a rare event. "I have

*"Gold Is Not Always" replays with Lucas Beauchamp a scenario already familiar from *The Hamlet*. In the novel Flem Snopes tricks Ratliff, among others, with hidden silver coins, the so-called salted-mine trick. In "Gold" Lucas becomes greedily fixed on finding buried money, gets Edmonds involved, and finally tricks a salesman who has a machine for divining buried money. The story takes the form of a lark, a tall tale; in the spirit of the stolen-horse episode as it will appear in *The Reivers*. But in the book, the following chapter (3) is quite somber, with Lucas's wife, Molly, serious about obtaining a divorce from a man who is totally caught up in greed. A very old lady now, Molly is the type of woman Faulkner felt comfortable with, especially with her distinct resemblance to Caroline Barr, Mammy Callie. Much of this foreshadows Lucas's later role in *Intruder in the Dust*.

**The Beck articles, later gathered together in *Faulkner: Essays by Warren Beck* (1976), were: "Faulkner and the South" (*Antioch Review*, March 1941); "Faulkner's Point of View" (*College English*, May 1941); and "William Faulkner's Style" (*American Prefaces*, Spring 1941). Like the O'Donnell and Aiken essays of 1939, the Beck pieces were the start of serious Faulkner criticism and evaluation.

been writing all the time about honor, truth, pity, consideration, the capacity to endure well grief and misfortune and injustice and then endure again, in terms of individuals who observed and adhered to them not for reward but for virtue's own sake, not even merely because they are admirable in themselves, but in order to live with oneself and die peacefully with oneself when the time comes."[41] He recognizes such a view does not mean liars and rogues will be snatched away by the devil; hypocrites and liars die peacefully in the odor of what they call sanctity. He feels such people with their own deceptive needs are beyond his reach. He is writing for others, who say it is preferable to be Ratliff than Flem Snopes.

Faulkner says he doubts if, as Beck suggests, balance of matter and manner exists for him. "I blame this partly on my refusal to accept formal schooling (I am an old 8th grade man), but most on the heat in which I wrote. I have written too fast, too much. I decided what seems to me now a long time ago that something worth saying knew better than I did how it needed to be said, and that it was better said poorly even than not said." He writes of preferring Shakespeare, bad puns and bad history withal, to Pater.

As the country moved toward a showdown struggle, in which all human values would be at stake, Faulkner found it incumbent upon himself to describe and redescribe the face of the South. If the South could organize its ideological priorities, then the country as a whole would be in better shape to confront the challenge from abroad. It is impossible to separate what Faulkner is saying here from the historical context of 1940–41: his material now was a type of history divorced from the tortured method of *Absalom*, a far greater but more ambiguous document. In a critical passage in "The Fire and the Hearth" segment, Faulkner presents the look of the South. Roth Edmonds peers at Lucas Beauchamp: "Now the white man leaned in the window, looking at the impenetrable face with its definite strain of white blood, the same blood which ran in his own veins, which had not only come to the negro through male descent while it had come to him from a woman, but had reached the negro a generation sooner."[42] This joins with a passage shortly after: "He [Roth] thought, and not for the first time: *I am not only looking at a face older than mine and which has seen and winnowed more, but at a man most of whose blood was pure ten thousand years when my own anonymous beginnings became mixed enough to produce me.*" The Beauchamp face is shaped "even in the expression in the pattern of his great-grandfather McCaslin's face."

Here Faulkner is moving well beyond the references to "nigger" cited in his letters. These words connect to passages a little later in the same segment, and we see that Faulkner, in the limbo between war and peace, is writing about the country, seeking some sense of what mixture means. Since the primary focus is race, then mixture, inheritance, and genes are the imponderables of the human race. Faulkner is pondering what creates a man, what creates a human being. The "surmise" or astonishment in Roth's view of Lucas is the wonder in Keats's and Balboa's prospect of the

Pacific, caught in stately cadences: "Then one day the old curse of his fathers, the old haughty ancestral pride based not on any value but on the accident of geography, stemmed not from courage and honor but from wrong and shame, descended on him. He did not recognise it then."[43] The subject is Carothers, Zack's son; and his response as it develops complements Huck Finn's as he sees in Jim not a slave, but a human being. Later the young Carothers and Lucas's son, Henry, as close as two boys can be, are separated by intangibles of race. "They did not hunt that morning. They never slept in the same room again and never again ate at the same table because he admitted to himself it was a shame now and he did not go to Henry's house and for a month he only saw Henry at a distance."

As the country moved toward a wartime footing, Faulkner was shaping his ideas to meet the racial challenge that was bound to come. With military segregation of the races (in actuality, if not in theory), Faulkner foresaw how injustice could subvert what the country stood for—and how his own region needed to be educated, not with bare statements but with dramatic presentation by way of fiction. As a sign of his frustration, he knew he was putting his most complex thoughts into fictions which would never be read by those who had power to effect change. Returning to "The Bear," he attempted a summa of sorts, perhaps his fullest statement since the decade of innovative work had ended. By July 25, the first part of "The Bear" was in Random House's hands.

Faulkner had reached page 206 in his typescript. Here he picked up an already published story, "Lion," which went back five years. By September 9, Haas had in his hands the second segment or chapter of the story. The material from "Lion" spilled over into the third segment, and arrived on November 9. The fourth part, one of the most complicated and important, engaged Faulkner well into December. He wrote Haas (December 2) that his promise to send on a completed manuscript by December 1 was already broken. "There is more meat in it than I thought, a section now that I am going to be proud of and which requires careful writing and rewriting to get it exactly right."[44] He suggests December 15 as a due date, and while coming close to that, he also finds he must rewrite "Delta Autumn" to get "matter into it pertinent to the story this mss. tells."[45]

One reason for delay was Ober told him the *Saturday Evening Post* wanted to see a story entitled "The Bear," if he could clarify it. He indicated he would rewrite from memory, and hoped the revision fitted. He implored Ober to sell it for anything, or almost anything. The *Saturday Evening Post* took it for its May 9, 1942, issue, paying $1,000. What the *Saturday Evening Post* received in this cut-down version was almost a travesty of the final novella.

In the *Saturday Evening Post* story, Faulkner has an unnamed ten-year-old boy go for the first time on the hunt for Old Ben, the wily, legendary bear that becomes for the growing boy the very embodiment of the wilderness. He then returns on the annual hunt, finally glimpses the bear, and has the opportunity to shoot. He does not, nor does Sam Fathers, his guide and the wise man of the woods. When his unnamed father asks the boy why he didn't shoot, the latter doesn't answer, but within him rages the response: "There was an old bear, fierce and ruthless, not merely just to stay alive, but the fierce pride of liberty and freedom, proud enough of that liberty and freedom to see it threatened without fear or even alarm; nay, who at times seemed deliberately to put that freedom and liberty in jeopardy in order to savor them, to remind his old strong bones and flesh to keep supple and quick to defend and preserve them."[46]

Yet even with all the sentiments stated forthrightly for the *Post* audience not to miss, the story retains mystery. There is in Faulkner's method a curious parallel to the artist seeking coherence; that the boy and his quest for understanding is analogous to the artist seeking among his materials for what can hold the pieces together. The boy's exploration of the woods —his ability to manage without even compass, stick, or watch—is the artist's exploration of his material without any tools but his imagination. The boy forsakes his gun because he knows, through Sam Fathers, that the bear will avoid him with an artifact present; if he wants to experience the bear, he must expose himself completely to the wilderness, without aids.* He must, in effect, make himself a rhythmic part of that experience as a way of getting close to the world of the bear, which is eternal and pure.

*In Norman Mailer's effective updating of "The Bear" in *Why Are We in Vietnam?* the protagonist D. J. and his friend head out into the Alaskan wilds without any weapons, pitting themselves nakedly against the land. To be completely on their own is the sole way they can compensate for the intrusions of D. J.'s father into the wilderness, which are tantamount to rape.

Chapter Twenty

Midcareer: At War

W ITH "THE BEAR," Faulkner had a metaphor for the writer, the artist, the man of imagination. In his wisdom, he saw creation, whether of the world or of the written word, as simple. Much as he loved and needed Keats, especially the poet of the Grecian urn, he recognized that poetic words complicate a simple linkage between the artist and his imagination. In 1941–42, years fateful for him and far more so for the country, Faulkner was trying to understand what eventuates, what prevails. As his own powers began to falter or become distracted, he sought renewal of strength in the boy's experience of the woods, in that magic meeting of wilderness and liquid. Both led into a supernal world—which was also the world of the writer seeking coherence. Even in a story crafted for a marketplace audience, Faulkner expressed himself. As things began to fall apart in 1941–42, he needed emblems of coherence.

In these hunting stories, Faulkner was a visionary and prophet, a man tuning in to the entire country, even as he seemed to be writing about himself. He was, like all major writers, transforming a private feeling into a general experience, an individual sense of things into the country's destiny. He welcomed the coming war since it provided a showdown between good and evil; but even as he met this condition with full conviction, he knew that Old Ben, wending his way through the woods, indifferent to those hunting him, represented something well beyond the struggle between good and evil. Other values went deeper, other equations had more profound meaning. It is striking that this story and the book which encapsulated it should become a kind of valedictory to that kind of world even as it becomes a valedictory for Faulkner working at his highest levels.

He had one compartment for profoundly serious work, another for a screen treatment. The film project turned out to be an interesting interlude. Writing to a man named Nathan at Warner Brothers on November 18, Faulkner describes at length a script sent to him by the studio, probably through the intervention of William Herndon, who wanted to be Faulkner's screen agent. The script was based on a novel by Harry C. Hervey, *The Damned Don't Cry* (1939). The protagonist is a poor white girl from Savannah, Georgia, named Zelda—no relationship to Zelda Fitzgerald or her story. The point of the novel is her effort to salvage her life amidst a series of misfortunes, an alcoholic father, a neurasthenic mother recalling Caroline Compson, and a troublesome brother. Her own unfortunate act is bearing a illegitimate child, which she tries to conceal but also refuses to surrender. The novel reads like a less-than-powerful Dreiser story, perhaps *Jennie Gerhardt.* Although it was material almost completely beyond Faulkner's competence to alter, he made a stab at it.

In his analysis and rearranging, he turns the protagonist into a neo-Faulknerian character. He tries to make her into a woman of character, although Hervey's protagonist is wishy-washy. She can barely keep her life going, whereas Faulkner wants her to make a moral gesture, such as (1) possibly publicizing her act and living with it; or (2) indicating she is hiding the birth because she fears for the child's future, not simply because society demands it. When the birth becomes evident, she might, under Faulkner's rearrangement, have "risen superior to the crisis and beaten it and so have gained admiration" or else "been completely beaten by it and so have gained pity."[1] But she is not a Faulknerian figure like (say) Caddy or Lena. She settles into shrieks and fainting until everything comes around, but not through her doing.

This is the script Faulkner toyed with at the time he was writing "The Bear," the novella. He prepared a treatment of nineteen pages (and found himself two and a half years later working on it again at Warner Brothers, when he was Herndon's and the studio's property more than he was his own). There seems to be no record of how much Faulkner received for his labor, perhaps because the treatment was not made into a film.

Ober asked in September if he wanted to redo his story, "An Error in Chemistry." The agent felt he could sell it if it were simplified. But Faulkner was hesitant about spending more time on it, and told Ober on October 27 he would revise it only if there was certainty of a sale.

Nothing came of it, and it ended up as the fifth story in *Knight's Gambit.* That volume was becoming a kind of refuse bin for second-rate material, published as a volume when Faulkner had little else to show for the 1940s.

Blotner tells us,[2] via Jill Faulkner, that she and her father went to many moving pictures together, and that Faulkner became a regular fan of films. If so, this was virtually the sole form of entertainment he pursued in the arts. With no inclination to listen to music on the radio, with an intense dislike of jukeboxes, with little sustained interest in the visual arts (that is, little desire when in New York or New Orleans to attend art shows or exhibitions), he was a man so completely of the word it is hard even to think of him attending an opening, listening to a concert, viewing a collection of paintings. Film, however, was something personally close as the result of his work, and also a good way to give Jill companionship. It is not clear how often Estelle went with them, since the Saturday night film venture seemed to be for father and daughter, or else Jill and her black companion, also called Estelle.

With the *Saturday Evening Post*'s acceptance of the story "The Bear" and $1,000 promised, Faulkner stretched out his work on the volume due Haas on December 1. It was just as well, since the material he wanted to include in the novella "The Bear" helped create its aura of a legendary tale and world, giving it the historical ballast he felt the story needed. "Delta Autumn" also required reworking. Faulkner took particular care in these days before sending on the finished work, as if sensing it would be his last serious fiction for some time to come. His flirtation with Hollywood in his nineteen-page treatment of *The Damned Don't Cry* indicated he knew that sooner or later Hollywood was his fate. In a rather ludicrous sale, Ober sent on the original version of "Delta Autumn" to *Story,* for $25. This was after its rejection by every high-paying magazine, including the *Post, Collier's,* and even *Harper's,* which had been taking Faulkner's stuff. *Story* published it in May–June of 1942, just at the time that *Go Down, Moses,* containing the heavily revised "Delta Autumn," appeared. It is possible that in its original stage (an eighteen-page typescript, far briefer than the final version) it was still too much of a sketch to be acceptable as a story.

In December, Faulkner steadily dispatched *Go Down, Moses* copy to Random House, where Saxe Commins had become his devoted editor. Part 4 of "The Bear" especially concerned him, and he wanted it to appear exactly as he sent it in, without capitals at the beginnings of paragraphs or end punctuation. The strategy was to create the sense of historical continuity, a stream of consciousness which recapitulated the past. The material about Ike McCaslin was to run on, so that the historical process became deliquescent. We observe Faulkner still using strategies from high modernism, especially Joyce and perhaps Woolf, with streamlike language recovering history. Part 5 swings back to

"Lion" and the woods with a more straightforward narrative method, in which Ike encounters Boon; and the final episode from "Lion" is reproduced, with the huge hunter hammering his gun barrel against the tree.

It was necessary for Faulkner to be rid of these stories, including the revisions of "Delta Autumn," so he could move into more financially rewarding work, such as those potboilers that became *Knight's Gambit*. But he also had to introduce "The Bear" into the typescript of the book version, then expand upon details in Ike's life, tying up references. But he was a man in a hurry, writing Commins that he had not proofread all the manuscript. "If anything sounds queer, send it back. Wish I had money to come up there and go through it with you. I think it's good stuff. But then I always do."³ He was right. It was not only good stuff, it was, quite possibly, the best stuff he would do for the rest of his career.

The book, with its dedication to Mammy Callie, reveals that Faulkner was becoming increasingly involved in racial matters, not only literarily and historically, as in *Absalom*, but more directly. He saw the American experiment in democracy seriously flawed by its treatment of the Negro, and he tried to infuse some common sense into Americans as America moved into war. For even as he was polishing *Go Down, Moses* for book publication, the Japanese had struck at Pearl Harbor. The limbo period ended and America, deeply wounded by the surprise attack, had to turn from a sleeping giant into a modernized, technological, machine-oriented marvel. Faulkner found himself in the anomalous position of defending every aspect of our technological recovery while lamenting what it meant to our individual lives. He was caught: while his vision was of the Garden, it was becoming inexorably a dispossessed, contaminated, polluted garden, with large parts of it uninhabitable for the likes of him. He had turned forty-four the previous September.

He would, in March of the next year, act on the war, hoping to obtain a commission with a pilot's rating. Like so much of his response to World War I, his response now was based on fantasy. His great writing career was insufficient; he needed a "male appearance," the uniform and wings of a hero. The year 1942 was another one of those divided experiences which seemed Faulkner's lot now. He would have a book this year —*Go Down, Moses*, published on May 11 as *Go Down, Moses and Other Stories;* not until the second edition did he challenge his own conception and turn it by way of the title into a novel. He would also write stories, two quick ones very early in the year. The first was "Knight's Gambit," which he hoped Ober could sell—"As always, I am broke."⁴ Ober could do nothing with the story, and it went into the later collection, giving that volume its title.

The other, "Two Soldiers," directly related to the December 7 Japanese attack on Pearl Harbor, was a piece of patriotic fluff which predictably the

Post took (for March 28), paying its customary $1,000. Knowing what the *Saturday Evening Post* wanted and being able to produce such copy was a form of literary prostitution, for the stories were not only inferior, they were turned out knowingly as inferior.* In 1942 Faulkner published two other stories, already written: "The Bear," already noted as accepted by the *Saturday Evening Post* (May 9), and "Delta Autumn" (May–June, *Story*). "Delta Autumn" would be used in four ways, as story, then revised in the new volume, eviscerated in *Big Woods* as part of the ending, and finally in *Collected Stories.*

By June he had written six stories, of which he had sold one, and was experiencing perhaps his worst financial crisis. Yet although he had no money, in March he applied for a commission. His career was splintered, for in July, his plans for a commission having come to nothing, he returned to Hollywood; in the meanwhile, his pleas for money were now arriving at Random House regularly, requesting $100 here or there. He was going from day to day, with no relief in sight except Hollywood.

Then, as we shall see, he fell into a hateful contractual agreement, working for only $300 per week, a fraction of what other writers were getting; but worse than that, he had entered into seven years of servitude, which Warner Brothers, pleased to get a top writer so cheaply, refused to let him break. The tale of this stint in Hollywood had near tragic dimensions; for, in effect, Faulkner could do little serious work for several years, and yet made only a relatively small amount of money. The sole gratification came from working on "The de Gaulle Story," which interested him, although after a huge script was written and rewritten, it was never produced. The year 1942 was dominated not by literary production, but by the war and his efforts to deal with his peonage in Hollywood. There were no real villains in the piece: Herndon was doing a job that made him a commission, and Faulkner failed to recognize the implications of what he was signing. It was a familiar story for the writer.

*What made "Two Soldiers" acceptable to the *Saturday Evening Post* was precisely what made the story so meretricious: every move and every scene aimed at a preconceived effect, characters suffocated, episodes evincing stereotypical responses. A young boy, almost nine, must face the departure of his elder brother for the war after Pearl Harbor is struck. The elder brother is himself barely seventeen, and the young boy sees them as "two soldiers," one fighting, the other backing him up with chopped wood and water to cook with. When the brother, Pete, leaves for Memphis to enlist, the boy waits one night and then sneaks out, and by using one trick or another manages to get to Memphis, by way of Jefferson. Once in the big city, he seeks the army enlistment office, finds it, and when thwarted by the soldiers there, draws his knife on one who attempts to throw him out. This is in effect his own little war, and he holds them at bay until his wish is granted: they locate Pete for him at the railroad station. Pete then reads him the law of the land: he must remain home and take care of the farm and their mother, while he, Pete, takes care of other matters. The story ends with a rich lady taking him home for dinner and then providing a chauffeured car for his trip back to Frenchman's Bend. The story fits precisely with Norman Rockwell's *Post* covers, arranging our responses in the same stereotypes.

The lack of direction was noticeable.* Faulkner's heavy drinking at this time could be a sign of his recognition that, at forty-four, he was going down the drain, that his best work was behind him, or else that he was without the financial freedom to test himself against what he was still capable of writing. In late June he wrote Ober a particularly bitter letter about his situation. It is the cry of a man who feels cornered, utterly frustrated by events. It was only a month before he would go to Hollywood in the shabbiest deal of his life.

I have been trying for about ten years to carry a load that no artist has any business attempting: oldest son to widowed mothers and inept brothers and nephews and wives and other female connections and their children, most of whom I dont like and with none of whom I have anything in common, even to make conversation about. I am either not brave enough or not scoundrel enough to take my hat and walk out: I dont know which. But if it's really beginning to hurt my work, I will choose pretty damn quick. I dont think that yet; it is only my earning capacity which is dulled; possibly because I have too little fun. But if I can get some money, I can get away for a while—either in service, or out of it. Incidentally, I believe I have discovered the reason inherent in human nature why warfare will never be abolished: it's the only condition under which a man who is not a scoundrel can escape for a while from his female kin. But now the formation of these Waacs and such gives a man to blink.[5]

Although this came on June 22, it well describes his state of mind in the earlier half of the year, as well as in 1941. He was frightened by the demands made upon him, and, primarily, by his inability to work seriously. His need for escape was overwhelming, and that need perhaps explained why he took such a poor Hollywood deal. It was not simply some financial return, but the itch to remove himself from Oxford, from the scene where nearly every familiar face meant a drain on his resources. But going well beyond all this was his tremendous hostility to relatives, including mother, brother(s), nieces, and nephews. He seems to have omitted Estelle, although the onslaught on females is so fierce she may have been the archetype of his disgruntlement.

All such fears and antagonisms eventually wound their way back to his stalled career. Except for the recent "The Bear," the stories coming from

---

*The story "Snow," intended to capitalize on hatred of Germans which swept America in the early 1940s, reveals only murkiness. The prologue-like first page gives the piece its topical reference, a news item that the Nazi governor of Czodnia was stabbed to death by his Frenchwoman companion. This part has almost no reference to what then becomes a first-person narration by a man like Don's companion in "Mistral" and "Evangeline." "Snow" has the writing and flavor of early Faulkner—the use, for example, of large chunks of descriptive prose which do little to advance the story. Description here is that of a young writer eager to get on paper his observations, and using up his material without regard for the narrative function of descriptive prose.

his desk and ending up on Ober's were clearly, to him, second- and third-rate. When he says that if the situation is "really beginning to hurt my work, I will choose pretty damn quick" about leaving, he was working through in his mind what he could not really do. It was fantasy, and that meant Hollywood, entrapment of another kind. When he was younger, he found he could work best when under such intense pressures; the stress and turmoil of the domestic situation somehow fueled him, gave him a sharper edge. But as he entered middle age and the material ceased to flow, he was no longer able to carry on with such heavy burdens. His imagination was not boiling over; his sole escape was in alcohol, and that only addled him further.

He confronted his mortality. He had only so much time left, and it was going up in support. He needed scapegoats; women—the nesters, the ones who prevented escape—filled that role. Mother, wife, daughter, sister-in-law, niece—he was surrounded mainly by women. Among men, only his brother Johncy presented a problem. Estelle's daughter Victoria and her husband were at Rowan Oak, and Faulkner could not have been happy about that—Victoria was not a favorite of his, nor did Bill Fielden make much impression. His feelings were an accumulation, not based on a single incident or person.

Preceding this accusatory letter was his fear the war would affect sales of *Go Down, Moses,* although he felt the book could pull its weight.* He tried two more stories, aimed at the *Saturday Evening Post.* One, "My Grandmother Millard and General Bedford Forrest and the Battle of Harrykin Creek," he thought was a "good funny story, with a message for the day: of gallant indomitability, of a willingness to pull up the pants and carry on, no matter with whom, let alone what."6 The *Saturday Evening Post* rejected it, and it ended up in *Story* (March–April 1943) for a pittance. Faulkner included it in his *Collected Stories.* The other, "Shall Not Perish," had a tortuous career as Faulkner wrote it for the *Post,* then rewrote it, saw it rejected by the *Post,* then rejected by several other magazines. It ended up in *Story* (July–August 1943) for $25. Even the pot-boilers were simmering down.

"Shall Not Perish" also appeared in *Collected Stories.* Faulkner here returned to the Grier family of "Two Soldiers," for more patriotic sentiments designed to make it attractive to the *Saturday Evening Post.* The story,

*Phil Stone's comment on the volume is full of misreading, deep resentment, and some acumen: "Several weeks ago, Faulkner gave me a copy of his last book of short stories 'Go Down Moses.' I think the best prose in it is in the dedication to Aunt Caroline. What Faulkner should do is to strike out on a new vein like 'The Hamlet.' If he ever completes the Snopes saga, it will be the best thing he has done yet. For several years, he has mainly been rewriting Faulkner at Faulkner's worst and I think he is all washed up unless he breaks the mold and starts over again. . . . I labored many years when Faulkner was under-rated as a writer and now for several years he [has] been overrated as a writer" (*Faulkner: A Comprehensive Guide to the Brodsky Collection, The Letters,* vol. 2, eds. Louis Daniel Brodsky and Robert W. Hamblin [Jackson: University Press of Mississippi, 1984], p. 24. Dated April 25, 1942, to Robert Daniel, who was seeking material for a Yale University exhibit of Faulkner materials, summer 1942).

however, is not narrative but sermon, a brief homily on what makes America great.

Later, in early June, Faulkner sent on, along with revisions of "Shall Not Perish," a new story: "A Courtship," which drew on a variety of earlier material, as well as Dave Hogganbeck (Boon's grandfather) from *Go Down, Moses*. It was part of a cycle of stories which in the *Collected Stories* was captioned "The Wilderness." It expressed Faulkner's admiration for the old ways when men held to their word and fought honestly over whatever they wanted. Ober could not sell it, but a little later, in July, Faulkner sent on still another story, "Shingles for the Lord," and with that Ober was successful, with the *Post* paying its customary $1,000.

Nothing came of his efforts to enlist, and he had the unpleasant sensation of seeing not only brother Jack in uniform, but a good many of the Random House staff, including Haas and Klopfer. Just at the time *Go Down, Moses* was published, he wrote Ober: "I am going before a board for a comm. in the Navy, a desk job in the Bureau of Aeronautics." He then asks Ober for an advance: "I'm the only writer I ever heard of who got advances from his agent; I wish to keep this distinction constant."[7] After the trip to Washington, D.C. he wrote Cerf (in early June) that the air force turned him down on application, which he attributes to age; but that he has a definite offer from the navy. He still wants an air force job, and wonders what inside track Klopfer had to get his commission in the Army Air Corps. "I was turned down after only about four weeks, so maybe there is some definite factor against me, like my age or lack of school degrees, or perhaps because I wrote my Senator and asked him to put in a word when I sent in the application. The Navy job is at a desk in the Bureau of Aeronautics in Washington. I want to stay out doors if possible, want to go to California. Incidentally, has Random House any job in California I could do?"[8]

The fantasy life continued in another letter to Ober, a follow-up to the plaint of June 22, where he saw physical escape as his only salvation. *Go Down, Moses and Other Stories* had appeared on May 11. It was a landmark volume for him. In it he had encapsulated his youth and at the same time distilled the wisdom of the middle-aged writer. Yet the reviews were not too favorable. The familiar charge of obscurity was hurled at him, as though obscurity defined his entire imaginative thrust. Passages *are* obscure; the prose can on occasion falter and move at a snail's pace. But to snatch at these elements—as reviewers in the Sunday New York *Herald Tribune* and the *Saturday Review* did—was to play at pettiness. Horace Gregory in the *New York Times*, however, heard Faulkner loud and clear, indicating that the stories were a book, not a collection, and that the author had matured into excellence. *Time*, since its cover story, now rated Faulkner as a modern master, speaking of him as a contemporary Twain and Melville. But it failed to see that in *Sound* and *Absalom* he had written books of such distinction he was certain of permanence not only in American literature but in world literature. *Go Down, Moses* did not fall far below that level, if at all.

Go Down, Moses brings to a head various aspects of Faulkner's development as a novelist. He had become a novelist of America, his subject "the matter of America." He tried to take on as much of America as Melville and Whitman did, and he accomplished as much. In several earlier works, he brought *his* America back to the incredibly divisive war fought less than four decades before his birth, and then he tried to bring *his* America forward from that war and its aftermath. He was the writer of mediation, his life falling almost precisely between the bad feeling after the war and the modernization of America. Like his entire generation—Hemingway, Cather, Fitzgerald, Dos Passos, Wolfe, Dreiser, Lewis—he was well situated; and while they took on significant portions of the country, he took on the entire nation.

When Faulkner was born, the battles had been won, but the war was still on; in the tales passed down to him, it was a living event in his family's history. Grant had decided to win the war by putting inexorable pressure on Lee's Army of Northern Virginia, and he finally forced capitulation. But the years afterward were somewhat like those final battles: years in which skirmishes replaced real victories, decades in which flank attacks on the laws and constitution of the country continued. The South won the aftermath, especially with the compromise of 1877 which brought Northern acquiescence to retreat from Reconstruction; but the South lost much in its effort to restore the status quo. Faulkner lived only sixty-four years, but he lived to see one hundred years of conflict. The civil rights battles of the 1950s were the extension of the pre- and post–Civil War battles of the 1860s and 1870s.

How he responded nourished his fiction. *Go Down, Moses* was his last great response to America of the last hundred years, the span of his novelistic life. When we speak of Faulkner's "imagination," we mean something more complicated than what we mean with nearly any other writer. His imagination—whatever was distinctly his and not part of his earlier borrowings—was steeped in history and the historical process, in ways not apparent in Hemingway or other contemporaries. They were social and political, but history was not their long card. Faulkner, quite simply, had been born into history—not only a community with values which he assimilated, but into a historical process he could both struggle against and assimilate. He is the most historical of our important writers: one who broke away from the past in his techniques even while the past meant so much to him.

Go Down, Moses, first a sequence of interrelated stories then novelistic in its interwoven patterns, is a mosaic of historical process. The Civil War, Reconstruction, the years after, small-town life in Yoknapatawpha and Jefferson split between white and black, between village and country people—all of these are as implicit in *Go Down, Moses* as is the wilderness, the idea of the pastoral, the sense of a dispossessed or a doomed, contaminated

Garden. History here *is* doom, as well as process and pressure. The Chick-asaw chief, Ikkemotubbe, is "Doom," the end of things implied in his name; and now the wilderness, in its splendor, is also doomed. The central story of *Moses* emphasizes Ike McCaslin's intense need to throw off history, to divest himself of the past so he can achieve liberation. His quest is for prehistory, even as he (and we, and Faulkner) know that history impinges at every turn. *The timelessness he envisages once he is freed from the past is an absolute that history itself will help defeat.* For even as he stops history within his beloved wilderness, history is all around, ready to invade: he has been expelled from the Garden, but does not know it or accept it.

Faulkner's imagination lies in *there:* in the interstices of the historical process where all the seams fail to come together. *Go Down, Moses* is para-digmatic: the stories range back from American prehistory into the 1900s. "The Bear" is pure prehistory, timeless, moments with no impingement from anything beyond itself—the perfect symbol of life Faulkner had assimilated from Keats's urn. Ike McCaslin exists only in the middle chapters, not having been born in the first, and being long dead in the last. He is, as Faulkner demonstrates, the embodiment of the historical process itself, taking into himself the conflicting elements of the American experi-ence. He is therefore the final vestige of liberation, symbolizing the man who lives from pre- to post-history—long enough to see that what he wishes to retain has become everything he wants to negate. He wishes to be liberated, and yet to be liberated means to be dispossessed. Here we have the Southern dilemma, and Faulkner has transformed it into the Ameri-can. Freedom and dispossession: liberation and expulsion. Faulkner found evidence of this conflict or contrast in every aspect of life, and his admoni-tion that one must endure turned outward as much as inward, from him-self to other individuals to the country.

Here is Faulkner's response to the radical division between the races, which is not only the immediate condition of the South, but the problem splitting the nation as well. Yearning for Eden and segregation of the Negro must clash. All history is contaminated by the condition of slavery. The Southern "way of life," and by implication the nation's, is corrupted by the slavery/segregation issue. The Civil War is alive and well, however diverted. Faulkner enters America through race.

Connected to race, perhaps integrally, is another contending force: the need for fathers. This has been a persistent quest in Faulkner's fiction—*Sound, As I Lay Dying, Absalom* are the most obvious examples—but *Go Down, Moses* is the quintessential search. Faulkner's choice of title, from the Negro spiritual, makes the father-quest central: Moses as the father of us all. *Go Down, Moses* and "The Bear" in particular are deeply autobiograph-ical, where autobiographical materials are deflected into symbolic or psy-chological forms: fears of weakness or the testing-out of oneself against daunting unknowns. Sons against fathers, the ultimate mystery.

While "The Bear" is chiefly concerned with fathers (and sons), it is like a shadowy presence or shadowy outline of elements Faulkner could not speak of directly—it is as though the wilderness in its great secrets could finally be penetrated if only one knew which clues to seek out. The "voices" of "The Bear" (and the book as a whole) speak to several constituencies: the hunting audience willing to grapple with the early genealogical difficulties in order to follow the trail of Old Ben; the overall Southern audience, with the second part a historical explanation of what the South was and has become; the American audience, in which the segments reveal the matter of America, our history (or paucity of it), our passage from one century to the next. Yet while all the above is of primary interest, another element obtrudes: the Faulknerian presence. And that voice is to transform all of the above factors into the quest for a father.

Faulkner used a twofold strategy: the use of multiracial figures as fathers, so that the paternal idea and race are never distant from each other, or the linkage between father-figures and death. With *Go Down, Moses*, Faulkner has passed into intimate revelations of his own mortality. This had been an ongoing theme in his work from his infatuation with Keats and the French symbolist poets through Housman and then on to his fictional handling of his own family. But from the late 1930s on, Faulkner was not only the artist writing about death but the man entering his forties contemplating mortality.

He had himself experienced a number of father-figures. The patriarch of the family was undeniably the overarching old colonel, William Clark Falkner, a combination of Jupiter and Moses—the Sutpen of the clan, but more polished and sophisticated. His son, the young colonel, somewhat diminished, was another patriarchal figure—successful in his enterprises, affluent, a supporter and reinforcer of the growing family, but not quite the inspiration and leader his father was. The country was itself less prepared for heroic types. His son, Murry C., Faulkner's father, was further diminished. He was in the eyes of the family a somewhat pathetic man, considered a loser by his wife; he came across to his sons as kind and amiable, but powerless. Whatever power he had—as at the dinner table, where he dictated silence—he held by physical force.

Faulkner's "fathers," then, came to him in degrees of dimunition. As the mantle passed to him as eldest son, he modeled himself on the old patriarchal colonel: the Rowan Oak estate, the steady acquisition of land, the establishment of himself as supporter of a large extended family. But with this came his assessment of himself as a father—no sons, a daughter, no real power except in the word. It was an extremely complicated process, intensified, of course, by his own negative response to *his* father and by his more positive response to ancestors: a grandfather he knew well and a great-grandfather who came to him as a legend.

He re-created that legend, or tried to. Sam Fathers in *Go Down, Moses* becomes Faulkner's patriarch. Only his paternalism is special: multiracial, he is divine by virtue of his mastery of the woods. Having assimilated all three American races, Sam "fathers" the boy who becomes his apprentice and student. It is astonishing to see Faulkner re-creating in new shapes the role Phil Stone once played; Stone himself as erst-while substitute for the father Faulkner missed having as as a teenager, when Murry became withdrawn and indifferent. Race-history-father/son relationships all come together, a compendium of Faulknerian motifs and concerns.

Another "father" is Lucas Beauchamp. Here too race and history are linked with paternalism. Lucas is not an instructor of the boy in *Go Down, Moses*, where he appears, but in *Intruder in the Dust*, Faulkner's next novel. There Lucas becomes the vicarious father, as Twain's Jim becomes the father of Huck. In Lucas and his taking on of a white boy, we experience another version of the racial theme in Faulkner, where racial linkage casts doubt on the purity of either black or white—that suggestion in Faulkner that the South is a single race of black and white, undifferentiated rather than demarked. Lucas is like Sam Fathers in at least one other major respect: he is like a god. The re-creation of fathers, Faulkner suggests, is the apotheosis of the paternal figure as larger than life. Thus Murry, the real father, is transcended as Faulkner reaches back to the earlier generations, specifically to the old colonel, to Abraham, the lawgiver (and -breaker). By leaping to the historical and legendary figure over the closer presence of the biological father, Faulkner is establishing not only a father, but a Father, and shaping not only a son, but a Son. As Edmonds says in *Go Down, Moses*: Lucas "is both heir and prototype simultaneously of all the geography and climate and biology which sired old Carothers and all the rest of us and our kind, myriad, countless, face-less."[9] The mythologizing is apparent.

Fathers and sons achieve God and Jesus dimensions, in a context of timelessness and spatiality. This need Faulkner had to reconstruct a god-like father or even a goddesslike mother (Mammy Callie transformed into Dilsey and Molly Beauchamp) is part of his quest for a heroic ideal and, on the personal level, his need to find some replacement figure for his own uncertain, obviously inadequate father. What is particularly striking is that none of these overarching paternal figures is an alcoholic or even a heavy drinker. Sam Fathers, in particular, is sexually neuter. Their pres-ence is sufficient for them to command, although in men like Sutpen they may be disreputable and obsessed. Their relationships to their sons can be problematic, to say the least, and even destructive. Henry Sutpen, for one, destroys his own life in order to preserve his father's grand design in which black blood must be excluded. Other sons are sacrificed to fatherly designs or conditions: the Compson children are destroyed by Mr. Comp-son's inability to cope with his life or to provide the guidance that sets standards.*

---

*Quentin's suicide, ostensibly over the loss of Caddy, is really equally traceable to his relationship to Mr. Compson. It is the father who makes Quentin passive and "feminized" (who castrates him) and who causes the son to die rather than confront the father. The Compsons, like the Falkners from the old colonel to Murry, are in descending order of importance from grandfather to grandson.

Faulkner's progression toward an obsession with fathers took a leap forward with *Absalom*. This coincided with the death of Dean and Faulkner's meeting with Meta in his 1936 stint in Hollywood. Before, there had been a preoccupation with the subject, and with sons—the Bundrens, Compsons, Sartorises, et al.—but after, a preoccupation became an obsession. This is attributable in part to his reaching forty, whereby the eldest son was becoming a father-figure; in part to delayed response to the death of his own father; another part to his having become an actual father. Most of all, the obsession with fathers, or alternately, fathers-and-sons, stems from his "desertion" of his family: his affair with Meta, in which he was of necessity the father-turned-lover with the much younger woman. Although she was not young enough to be his daughter, the age difference was quite a significant factor. And this appeared to trigger guilt or some reshaping of his sense of himself, revealed in his assessing father roles. Even as he becomes ever more insistently a father figure—with Meta, Jill, his extended family—he seeks the son's role in his work, where he is a less responsible player. The desire to be the child again becomes apparent.

"The Bear" becomes his greatest example of this intense father-and-son linkage, interlocked in intensity with the black-and-white racial motif. "The Bear" is also connected to another paternal theme, the hearth, one of the great symbols of *Go Down, Moses*. In the hearth, a little fire always burned, and this becomes an emblem of ongoing life, analogous to the lares and penates of the Romans. The hearth suggests what remains of the entire country after all the transgressions, after the country has been invaded, despoiled, stripped. Even more telling is the fact that the hearth burns in a Negro house and that Carothers (Roth) prefers the black to the white cabin. It is of further significance that Carothers does not know his own mother, that he has a white father and a black foster-mother: ". . . the strong warm negro smell,*[10] the night time hearth and the fire even in summer on it, which he still preferred to his own." Yet even that magical world of the hearth—so clearly linked to fathers and sons—must suffer from the "old curse of the fathers, the old haughty ancestral pride based not on any value but on an accident of geography, stemmed not from courage and honor but from wrong and shame."[11]

The image of hearth leads into "The Bear," so that through symbol and emblem we can see how stories are interpenetrated. For "The Bear" itself, the characters have been transformed into a kind of marginality, those who have, at least temporarily, forsaken the civilized world and sought the disorderly order of the wilderness.[12] Here the drama of fathers and sons will be played against a still intact but very fragile Garden. Once in the wilderness, Faulkner's hunters and father-figures identify with the "big

---

*Faulkner repeatedly associated Negroes with their "smell"—here, *Flags in the Dust*, *Light in August*, elsewhere—to such an extent we must connect it, somehow, with Negro sexuality. Not necessarily desirable, it is inescapable, part of the Negro "difference" which, nevertheless, attracts the white and links the races. In father-and-son terms, the Negro (Moses) possesses an olfactory presence which carries the white boy back to his beginnings with a mammy and other Negro servants.

woods," which gives them their credibility as parental figures, fathers of us all.

They can try to recover what was lost when Ikkemotubbe (Doom), by selling his wife and son into slavery, turned the land into a dispossessed Eden. What remains is only the wilderness, cut off from all the rest. Here fathers function. Ike divests himself of all properties in order to attract Ben, to be worthy of the bear. But the image Faulkner creates is gripping: Ike becomes "completely relinquished" to the wilderness, "a child alien and lost in the green and soaring gloom of the markless wilderness." The situation becomes a prototype of the Faulkner father-son link, as Ike *becomes son to Ben the father.* The bear: "It did not emerge, appear; it was just there . . . dimensionless against the dappled obscurity." "Then it was gone. It didn't walk into the woods. It faded, sank back into the wilderness without motion." Ben has apparitional, hallucinatory qualities: he is both real and unreal, both embodiment and fabulous, visible and invisible, comparable to Melville's great white whale. It is the ultimate parental figure: the mythical father who rises from the unknown or unseen, is briefly glimpsed, then blends with the shifting matter from which he has emerged.

If Ben is the ultimate father, then Ike, Sam Fathers, and others are avatars of the phenomenon: they are themselves great fathers, but also subservient to the still greater one. In a strange transformation, Ike becomes both father and son to himself. Part 2 of "The Bear" begins with a flashback to Ike at thirteen, after he has killed his buck and Sam Fathers had marked his face with the still-hot blood. The next November he kills his first bear. Through this method, he is, as it were, working his way toward fatherhood by moving up the rungs of sonhood. When he is ready —and Faulkner emphasizes how he moves toward ever-greater skill in woodsmanship—he has served his apprenticeship as a son and can be worthy of hunting, even killing, the father, Ben himself.

Once the bear is dead, Sam Fathers is afflicted, possibly by a stroke. He is fading, and it is not chance he declines even as Ben and the great dog Lion die. There is a close connection among them, father-figures all, since each in its way represents the wilderness and the passing of the glory. Sam Fathers: "He lay there—the copper-brown, almost hairless body, the old man's body, the old man, the wild man not even one generation from the woods, childless, kinless, peopleless—motionless . . . and only the boy knew that Sam too was going to die."[13] The doctor diagnoses exhaustion, shock maybe; but the real cause lies far deeper than Sam's physical condition. It lies in part in the nature of the country, the nature of the wilderness, and Sam's relationship to it. It lies primarily, however, in Sam's loss of paternal function over the woods, his lessening kinship with Ben, who shared with Sam the role of great father and keeper of the wilderness. With Ben gone and Lion dying, the absolutes of the woods have faded; and when they are gone, Sam knows he is a bit player in a debased comedy. For him to be a prince, a chief, a father, he needs the woods, or else he loses both power and voice.

One way to view various segments of *Go Down, Moses* is in terms of bondage, which fits well into the theme of fathers and sons and, of course, into race and history. Faulkner was as caught up with individual rights as he was with paternalism, and any prolonged assessment of the role of fathers must come to terms with the rights of the individual. Bondage leads us back into slavery, and then forward from slavery—Ike's family background—to the bondage civilization imposes.

The ultimate bondage—and, by implication, the ultimate sense of fathers and sons, of paternalism—is connected to what occurred to our concept of Ben. "Dispossessed of Eden. Dispossessed of Canaan, and those who dispossessed him dispossessed him dispossessed."[14] Columbus's founding of America opened up an opportunity for a land which "could be found in humility and pity and sufferance and pride of one to another." But Ike ponders that the land was "already accursed even as Ikkemotubbe and Ikkemotubbe's father old Issetibbiha's and old Issetibbiha's fathers too held it, already tainted even before any white man owned it by what Grandfather and his kind, his fathers, had brought into the new land." The corruption and taint go back into the deepest reaches of genealogy, into prehistory.

Faulkner's dwelling on taint inevitably bleeds over into the relationship of fathers and sons; it will lead eventually into *A Fable*, another intense statement of contaminated paternity. The taint is linked in Faulkner's mind to slavery, and before that to the impossibility of retrieving Eden. Even though the "big woods" afforded a glimpse of an earthly paradise, the vision was fading. But it had been a vision: ". . . even then I felt / Gleams like the flashing of a shield;—the earth / And common face of Nature spake to me / Rememberable things."

Cerf indicated good sales for the book, but warned that story collections do not do well in such times. That statement and the relatively slow sales may have prompted Faulkner to alter the title, so that the book became a novel. Before that rancorous letter of June 22 to Ober, Faulkner wrote Whit Burnett, who had asked him to choose one of his stories for *This Is My Best*, an anthology Burnett was editing. Faulkner's response in mid-June is in keeping with his airing of his situation to one and all. He tells Burnett to choose anything he wants: "I have become so damned frantic trying to make a living and keep my grocer etc. from putting me in bankruptcy for the last year that nothing I or any body ever wrote seems worth anything to me anymore. Sorry I couldn't have helped you and best wishes for anthology. I thought I had written you before to this effect, but I have been so worried lately with trying to write pot-boilers and haunting the back door of the post-office for checks that dont come to keep a creditor with a bill from catching me on the street, that I dont remember anything anymore."[15]

In the subsequent letter to Ober and follow-up correspondence with Ober and Cerf, there are more statements out of keeping with Faulkner's reticence. He is profoundly depressed as he continues with his litany of woes about money, his unhappiness, his loss of direction. One might pinpoint the bottom—Faulkner's personal death valley—at this time. Ironically, as the country rose to meet its foreign challenge and the depression lifted to accommodate a wartime economy, Faulkner found himself marginal, unable to work seriously, rejected by the military, as yet unable to catch on in Hollywood. The image of the writer "haunting the back door of the post-office" seeking checks to avoid further dunning notices is worse even than Conrad and his plaints about money and his creditors.

Faulkner will repeat all this to Cerf. He recognizes he has gone stale, that the stories he doesn't value highly are not selling. He would take even $100 per week in Hollywood, which, he says, is a good deal for a man with 60 cents in his pocket. He says he has given notes for debts, but he fears the notes will come due soon: "... and should I be sued, my whole house here will collapse: farm, property, everything."[16] He desperately needs a change of scene to freshen his mental condition. He also clearly needs an advance from Random House to pay the grocer before he leaves.

At the end of June, Faulkner began the negotiations leading to his long stint in Hollywood, followed by the equally long struggle to get away from Herndon, whose dealings brought him so little return. He'd had eight different contracts with Hollywood, starting with $250 to $600 per week in 1932–33, then rising to $1,000, retreating to $750, and ending with $1,000 in his latest, January to August 1937 stay. He feels if word gets out he wants $1,000, he will find nothing. To Ober: "I dont think I am or have been or will ever be worth that to movies. It just took them five years to find it out. I will take anything above $100.00. . . . I have borrowed a few dollars each week from my mother to pay the cook and laundry with. She has no income save what I have given to her."[17] He repeats what he told Haas and Cerf—that if anyone sued him, all his property except his home would go, and his daughter, wife, and mother would have nothing. He ends with this warning: "If a man with my experience and reputation has reached that point, there is something wrong and something had better be done. I think a change of scene is the answer."

The desperation of his situation explains how he got into the morass of the Hollywood contract that bound him for the next three years. Ober, true to his word and friendship, offered to help, and asked H. N. Swanson, a well-known Hollywood agent, to look for something for Faulkner. Ober, meanwhile, sent him another $100 to help him meet his most immediate expenses. Swanson did try to swing a deal with Warner Brothers, but Herndon, standing on the previous arrangement, balked at stepping aside. If any deal was to be made with Warner, Herndon would do it or else sue the author. Faulkner tried to disentangle what was becoming complicated by writing the head of the Warner story department, James J. Geller. He explains that since Herndon had not been in touch, he authorized Swanson to act for him. Then Herndon came back with an insulting telegram. With his back up, Faulkner told Geller that Swanson was his authorized agent.

In the same mail, he wrote Herndon, and the bad feeling between them is palpable. "You accused me of deliberate underhand dealing, which is not true, and inferred that I could be forced by threats into doing what is right, which I will take from no man."[18] He says he will give Herndon the benefit of the doubt (the old colonel would have shot him!).

Faulkner then goes into a long explanation, most of it based on what he does not know. Herndon had apparently made the necessary connections at Warner Brothers by getting first Geller, the writer, and then Robert Buckner, the producer, interested in Faulkner. He also got in touch with Jack Warner himself, the shaping force of the studio, and showed him Faulkner's treatment of "Turn About"; with Warner definitely interested and Geller and Buckner enthusiastic about working with Faulkner, a deal was struck, first for $200 per week, then for $300. Furthermore, the idea for the de Gaulle script that Warner was to produce was Herndon's. His job was not easy. Many important authors proved to be poor screenwriters —thus William Faulkner would join Aldous Huxley, Sinclair Lewis, and F. Scott Fitzgerald, among others. An additional factor was his reputation: Faulkner was known as a drinker and a disappearer, qualities which would have normally finished him in Hollywood. But Herndon showed the same persistence in hanging onto Faulkner that he showed in getting his client a deal.

At the point of a definite contract, Faulkner intended to bring in Swanson, and this is what made Herndon send his threatening telegram. But when Faulkner responded, he also tried an explanation that was beside the point. Near the end of his letter, Faulkner indicated that it would be impossible for them to work together and he has asked Ober to make "some equitable adjustment with you." Innocent of Herndon's tenacity, he went on:

> Then maybe we had better part company. Without being conscious of it, I must not have had enough confidence in your ability to sell me. I see now that in all my recent money troubles I never thought of writing you to try again. I suppose I took it for granted that you had done and were doing your best and had probably given me up at last as bad merchandise. And you didn't have enough confidence in me to believe I would be just and fair with you regarding any Hollywood matter you had anything to do with. If this is not satisfactory to you, then make good your threat and cause whatever trouble you wish.[19]

Faulkner was in the middle between the man who had gone ahead on their agreement and made the deal (Herndon) and the man who was ready to bring it to a definite contract (Swanson). Clearly he preferred Ober's agent to the threatening Herndon, but matters were becoming like one of the scams in his novels.

In the midst of this, he found time to finish a short story, "Shingles for the Lord," which Ober received on July 17, just before Faulkner wrote the letters to Geller and Herndon. "Shingles for the Lord" is still another return to the Grier family, known from "Two Soldiers" and "Shall Not Perish," themselves reminiscent of the Bundrens of *As I Lay Dying*. The story is by now formulaic for Faulkner. The problem from the beginning is that the Griers are not a compelling family, lacking the intensity of the Bundrens. The Griers, in fact, get lost in the ideological points Faulkner tries to establish in these pieces. The idea was not in the story but in the paycheck, and Ober got him $1,000 from the *Saturday Evening Post* (February 13, 1943).

Faulkner was now in the middle of his battle to stay alive. He admits to Ober that Herndon had brought him to the producer Buckner's attention. He indicates he wrote five "20–25 page story lines for various studios or individuals" under Buckner's directions, but nothing came of them. Then he expresses his real fear: "Also, if I go to Cal. to work, I would like to work in peace and not be heckled and bothered by him there. So please get me a clean slate with him."[20] He needed space for himself even in Hollywood, and Herndon was crowding him, occupying his thoughts, drawing out his attention. There is almost a sense of panic in this plea to Ober to buy Herndon off with his commission and be done with it.

He adds a somewhat sinister paragraph to Ober about having checks sent on to him. He wants any checks sent to California if he should go, not to Oxford. "I do not want checks to come here in my absence, as they will be misapplied." This is apparently the same trouble he'd had with Estelle when he inserted the notice that he was not responsible for her bills or charges. The misapplication he refers to can only mean she would spend regardless of their many debts, and he needed to control his finances completely. If this was the case, it must have been another source of worry and anxiety.

Continuing his barrage of letters to Ober and others about his contract, he wrote again to Ober on July 19. Faulkner admits he has made mistakes in dealing with Herndon and even grants the latter a measure of integrity:

> But I am certainly at fault in the fact that I did not get myself discharged with him before I undertook anything else. I simply did not once think about him while I was worrying about money. . . . Yet there is a certain sincerity in his letters, in all of them, a naivete almost. . . . At present I feel like throwing the whole thing up. But this will be funk, and you have done too much toward the deal for me to quit.[21]

During this exchange of letters Faulkner was futilely altering a rejected short story to make it marketable. On July 22, Ober received the revised version. But by this time, he and Swanson had withdrawn from the Hollywood deal, and Faulkner was counseled to deal with Warner Brothers through Herndon. Faulkner then wired Geller that he had accepted the deal made by Herndon, and on July 27 he was in Burbank.

It was the beginning of an ordeal—not forty days in the desert but seven years under options which made him one of the lowest-paid writers in Hollywood, while arguably the most renowned. On August 1, he wrote Ober a letter with ominous implications.

Although I was not aware of it when I left Oxford, I was committed to the contract which they offered me. It is a long series of options, 13–13–26–26, then a series of 52 week options. I thought it over for a day. Then feeling that I had committed myself, even though I was not aware that the deal included more than this one particular job, and on the strength of Geller's statement that, if I worked well, the contract would be voided by the studio, I decided to sign it.[22]

He had assurances from Buckner that the contract could be voided, and when that occurred he could make a new one. But Faulkner, even now, doubted this, as Warner Brothers would need to protect itself "against possibility of another studio working on me."

Faulkner's language reveals a deep fear that he may have been taken, as well as a fantasy that Warners will eventually let him go. What he failed to fully recognize was that he was the object of a business deal, and the studio as well as Herndon (who was not unfeeling) identified him as a pawn in money-making propositions. The author who was so shrewd with his Mississippi hill people was caught up in something which went well beyond his comprehension: the marketability of talent, with disregard for the person generating that talent. But there was also the question of his own situation: that he was so desperate financially he let himself be hoodwinked. The sum of $300 per week was paltry by Hollywood standards, but immense for someone who periodically requested $100 loans from Ober and Haas.

Faulkner slipped into Hollywood. In the 1940s Warner Brothers was noteworthy for its patriotic films supporting the Allied war effort. The studio was also an empire run with medieval (or modern) ruthlessness. It was headed by Harry, though his two brothers, Abe and Jack, somehow became the best known. The studio had a stable of well-known stars, from Bogart and Edward G. Robinson, to Errol Flynn and Jimmy Cagney, on to song-and-dance performers such as Dick Powell. Other stellar performers were Bette Davis and Paul Muni (although many, like Davis, Cagney, and Bogart, bought or fought their way out of contracts). Faulkner had entered a den of vipers, but he shared the plight of several actors and actresses who found themselves tied into long-term contracts with little chance of escape to another studio. Once tied up, performers either came through or found themselves without work until their contractual agreement ended. Withal, Warner Brothers was a distinguished studio, making classics such as Errol Flynn in *The Adventures of Robin Hood;* the powerful Paul Muni vehicle, *The Life of Emile Zola;* Edward G. Robinson in *Little Caesar,* along with a host of other groundbreaking gangster films, and many musicals which helped establish what was then still a novice genre.

As Blotner notes, the stable of writers Warners maintained was particularly strong. It included Stephen Longstreet, Faulkner's original connection with Herndon; younger men such as A. I. Bezzerides, who would become, along with Jo Pagano, close to Faulkner for many years; several of the later Hollywood Ten, including Dalton Trumbo, Alvah Bessie, and Albert Maltz, as well as Robert Rossen. It is especially ironic that the group who became known as the Hollywood Ten wrote some of the most patriotic films Warner Brothers produced during the war years. Faulkner, however, had nothing to do with them, and moved to the margins, although he and Bogart became drinking companions. He also had nothing to do with the large emigré population from Europe, including writers like Mann, whom he admired and considered "the foremost literary artist of his time."[23]

Faulkner moved into a small, clean, well-lighted room in the Highland Hotel at 1921 Highland Avenue, about three miles from the Burbank studios of Warner Brothers. Although in the next five years he worked intermittently on *A Fable*, he did not have an original novel publication until *Intruder in the Dust* in 1948. After that, except for collections of stories *(Knight's Gambit* and *Collected Stories)*, he had no book until *A Fable* in 1954. In effect, when he won the Nobel Prize for literature in 1949 (awarded in 1950), he was being rewarded for work he had completed by 1941–42, when he was forty-five. The explanation for this gap between 1942 and 1952 can be attributed to movie scripts, his need to write short stories for money, and possibly a decline in imaginative ability which might have come on even without movie work. But given Faulkner's rapid production of work, it is probable that he could have completed *A Fable* sooner if he had given his full attention to it; and with that novel out of his mind—it had become an obsession with him—he could have moved on. All this is conjectural. It can be asserted that Faulkner had in effect written himself out for several years—that he made a temporary comeback with *A Fable* and the final two volumes of the Snopes trilogy, and could do no more whatever conditions prevailed. Certainly, once his finances were relieved with the Nobel Prize money, he did not become the novelist he had been.

His immediate future, however, was "The de Gaulle Story," fortunately a sympathetic enterprise for his first assignment. Faulkner sent Geller of the story department an amusing interoffice memo:

GIRL AND 2 BOYS MEET FREE FRANCE
FINAL SCORE
GIRL 1 BOY UP & 1 TO CARRY
   1 BOY DOWN 2
1 BOY OUT
DE GAULLE 3 UP[24]

On August 3, Faulkner was given the important job of editing the script of "The de Gaulle Story." By September 19, he told Victoria (now Mrs. Fielden) he had the approval of de Gaulle's agent and the State Department to go ahead; all that remains is to "write in the dialogue."[25] He warns that this is confidential, although why he added that is unclear—unless the project was considered secret.

He tells "Moms" (Maud Falkner) on November 15 that he hopes to return in a month to spend Christmas with his family. His letter indicates his fears that if he presses the studio in any way, he may jeopardize a possible raise and even his position. The letter reveals the easy confidentiality he did not have with Estelle. In her battle to hold onto her sons no matter which women temporarily gained their affections, Maud had clearly won.

The producer for "The de Gaulle Story" was Robert Buckner, and the project was part of that wartime effort to praise and build up America's allies in the war against the Axis powers. Similar efforts would be made on films touching on the Soviet Union; when later purges came in Hollywood, it was forgotten how warm the studio feeling was for Stalin and his struggle. Faulkner read (or said he had read) de Gaulle's very important book on tank warfare. De Gaulle warned that the French Maginot Line would prove ineffective in a future war, and he predicted the Germans would go around this supposedly impregnable line. The German general staff was familiar with the thesis and totally in agreement. What de Gaulle predicted came true, and France was devastated.*

Faulkner's role went further than dialogue. He was responsible for the script, which meant not only dialogue, but narrative, treatment, point of view. Obviously, the viewpoint was to show de Gaulle in a heroic pose, while giving some sense of his career as a whole. From this, we can see why nothing ever came of the script. Whether the State Department stopped it or not, the material was itself intractable. De Gaulle's early career was not the stuff of movies, and the sole point of interest was his present stance as leader of the Free French. To put it mildly, he was not cinematic, and there was the additional great difficulty in finding someone to play the role. Edward G. Robinson would not do.

The de Gaulle assignment nevertheless fitted Faulkner's temperament and current need for heroes. Back in November 1942, in Hollywood, he was inspired by Captain Eddie Rickenbacker's ordeal of three weeks in a life raft in the Pacific. Rickenbacker was, of course, well known as America's greatest World War I ace (having destroyed twenty-six enemy aircraft); at fifty-two he was as tough as ever. Faulkner was inspired to write a three-page poem called "Old Ace," which he mailed to Ober on November 23,

---

*It was de Gaulle's contention that tanks made fixed positions untenable; that with tanks, the Maginot Line was a remnant of another war. The Germans, of course, used tanks and armored divisions to end-run the Line. De Gaulle's efforts to build a French tank corps to deal with what he saw was a new phase of ground warfare put him outside the tradition-bound military establishment. This part of the story appealed to Faulkner, as we can see from the first pages of his treatment.

sending a corrected version the following day. He took it seriously, indicating he wanted to make further corrections, but nothing came of it.

Still, in mid-August, we find Faulkner working smoothly, although a treatment was not his forte. He was much better suited to being a film doctor, touching up scenes which didn't work or adding bits of dialogue to bring a scene into focus. Hawks recognized this part of Faulkner's talent, a conceptualizing one within the larger framework of an already existing script; but Hawks as yet had no claim on him. At one point, in mid-August, something occurred in Faulkner's imagination which would occupy him for nearly a decade. He needed some balance to take the edge off de Gaulle's grandeur and grand design—he needed, as he did in his novels, some play from beneath, what Shakespeare used as comic scene. If de Gaulle were tragic France, then the people or a representative of the people (like Ratliff, for example) was necessary to keep the general in perspective. This figure, while an ordinary citizen, would be an important character, embodying the needs of the citizenry. In some shadowy way, this foreshadows *A Fable*, in which highly placed characters encounter the corporal: Romans confronting Jesus.

Blotner tell us Warners brought in another writer to step up the action, in effect to keep the reality principle going as Faulkner moved ever more deeply into symbolism. The writer was Frederick Faust, whose book credits numbered over one hundred, the best known being *Destry Rides Again*. Frederick Faust was unknown to American readers, but as Max Brand he was an enormously popular author of Westerns and adventure stories. Faulkner's father, who read Zane Grey, would definitely have approved of his son collaborating with Max Brand. Like Louis L'Amour or John Jakes in our own era, he had a formula for success: good detail surrounded by plenty of movement. He was the very opposite of the man he was teamed with, but he admired Faulkner tremendously. For most successful Hollywood screenwriters, in fact, Faulkner was the example of the man who took the high road and succeeded—"the writer" among the hacks. He was, however, paid only a fraction of what they were getting.

Faulkner and Brand got along well as drinking companions, although the latter, a huge man, was able to hold almost an unlimited amount. By mid-September of 1942, the collaboration had ended—Brand was killed later in Italy—and Faulkner was asked by Howard Hawks to work on another film, *Air Force*. This too was a story tailor-made for Faulkner—the account of a bomber crew, the death of the pilot, etc. He worked on the dramatization of incidents which were to occur just before the pilot dies. He then returned to "The de Gaulle Story," which was becoming increasingly expansive and intricate, and unacceptable to de Gaulle's agents in Washington on several grounds.

Faulkner defended his treatment in a way which is fully consistent with the abstract of the theme and plot he had submitted to Buckner in August. The actual development of the idea through story outline, story treatment, revised story treatment, first complete screenplay, and revised screenplay, reveal several factors at war in Faulkner. From the abstract:

This is the story of Free France, told in the simple terms of a Breton village: the collapse of France and the hopes and struggles for rejuvenation as seen through the eyes of villagers, told by means of village characters who are themselves the common denominator of France. The village is the strophe, with its passions and bafflements and divisions of brother against brother and blood against blood, that it may continue to exist as a symbol of home, security, happiness and peace which is man's heritage; France is the antistrophe, with its passions and bafflements and division of Frenchman against Frenchman in the national terms of a people struggling to survive and to keep alive their traditions and glory as a nation. It is a thesis that lust and greed and force can never conquer the human spirit.[26]

These comments suggest how profoundly Faulkner was immersed in his own novels. Implicit here is the Snopes trilogy; even the language, of village and villagers, refers to *The Hamlet* and ahead to *The Town* and *The Mansion*. There are also glimpses of what will become, eight years later, the Nobel Prize acceptance speech, not only in these intimations but in the screenplay, where the language is sometimes almost identical with the speech. And, of course, there is the even more immediate sense of *A Fable*. There is little question that Faulkner had not forsaken novel writing—he was simply doing it by means of another medium. As each studio came to recognize, Faulkner was not useful in crafting an entire screenplay; his strength lay in script doctoring, or in developing particular sequences, drawing them out, discovering their dramatic potential, inserting dialogue in a particular scene. Yet the film studio's loss is, in a sense, the gain for those with wider literary interests, for "The de Gaulle Story" affords uncanny insights into Faulkner's novelistic world even as he seems to have forsaken the writing of novels.

Throughout October, Faulkner kept adding to his screenplay, using material supplied by the Warner Brothers research team. Chronologies, names, place names, historical detail—all of these became more significant as Faulkner swept toward a complete screenplay. By October 30, the first screenplay was completed, numbering 153 typescript pages. As the editors of "The de Gaulle Story" estimated, about one thousand pages of typescript had gone into the work, if we count original manuscript, revisions, retyping, and supplementary materials. Faulkner worked as steadily on this script as he had on any novel, if not more intensely. But the fact remains he had come closer to a novel than to a film script, and de Gaulle's agents objected.

Nevertheless, like a good trooper obeying an officer's commands, Faulkner went back to the material. Infinitely adaptable, he moved to incorporate the French criticisms. He removed ambiguities and put in certainties. De Gaulle was referred to more often, and the entire script was tilted toward *la gloire*. By November 18, only nine days after receiving the criticisms, Faulkner had rewritten sixty-nine pages of the screenplay, an incredible display of energy and focused purpose. He was of course writing furiously so as to be able to return to Oxford for Christmas, as he wrote *Maud* on November 15. But in a sense, for lack of anything else to write, he was pouring himself out into this material. By November 19, Faulkner had revised the original screenplay and had produced what prints out to 122 pages (153 pages as submitted). In all, he had spent almost four months —from July 28 to November 19—on the outline, treatment, and screenplay, and their revisions. The film was then shelved for good. Faulkner had made about $5,000.

Why was the film never produced? Many answers come to mind: that Churchill and/or Roosevelt told Jack Warner to shelve it out of their own hostile feelings toward de Gaulle; that de Gaulle could not be cast, a real problem for a film with that title; that the Warner Brothers production of *Mission to Moscow* somehow befogged the air, and one controversial subject may have been enough for them. Another real problem, and perhaps the overriding one for shelving the production, was that the Faulkner script was not filmable. There is still a further point: possibly Buckner and his bosses felt that the Free French representatives would never be satisfied with the script, that rewritings could continue until the war ended, and that no film would ever be made. The material was in fact intractable, unless one made an epic like Abel Gance's *Napoleon* or Hans-Jürgen Syberberg's *Hitler*. Warners was organized around making well-shaped films, making them rapidly, getting them into theaters controlled by the studio, and moving on. This attempt at a heroic and grand film was turning into something experimental: Faulkner had moved it around to his way of doing it, and the studio, as the better part of discretion, simply shut it down.

For Faulkner, "The de Gaulle Story" was by no means a wasted experience. If we look deeply enough into several of his movie-making projects, we find him thinking about his own material, working things out through a script, coming upon matters he will later expropriate. One speech in particular comes to mind, spoken by a priest in one of the original segments. He starts by saying the land is constant:

> . . . it will remain. Earthquake and flood and drought come and pass as this man [Hitler] will pass, and there is still the land. Oppression and suffering come upon mankind and even destroy him as individuals. But they cannot destroy his immortal spirit. That endures. It is more than the simple will to freedom and contentment. It is his immortality, his hope and belief that out of his suffering and his resistance to tyranny and evil and oppression he finds himself.[27]

In another place, the priest says: "We must endure. . . . To remain France, it will have to endure. If it still is France, it will endure." He adds: "But somewhere in the long annals of human suffering our suffering will remain, fixed: one little rock at least in the foundation of our children's security and peace."[28]

Language, image, forward thrust of rhythmic prose all foreshadow the Nobel Prize acceptance speech; but more than that, the words reflect Faulkner's Jeffersonian ideology. Strikingly, the priest says this, suggesting how Faulkner was working his way into a religious parable of sorts, which was forthcoming in *A Fable*. In any assessment of Faulkner's career in the early 1940s, we must not glide over the Hollywood scripts as only meaningless busywork. Of course, some of the time was wasted. A good deal of energy that might have gone into books went into anxiety and being at war with himself. But that is not the whole story. For as we have observed many times, Faulkner needed that break with Oxford to recharge himself.

How did he live, beyond his stint at the studio, where he averaged twenty-five pages a week (although capable of far more)? His aim was to hang on, and toward that end he had to appear sober each working day, despite some very hard drinking. He sent a good part of his money to Oxford—not to Estelle, but to pay off bills. He owed money all around town, debts he could not possibly repay from $300 after deducting his own living expenses. At the current rate, he would need years in Hollywood. His days were spent writing at the studio, then drinking in the evening with younger, lesser writers. He saw Ruth Ford occasionally—he knew her from Ole Miss, and she would play a large part in his later life when she took *Requiem for a Nun* on the road, in a role written specifically for her. As "The de Gaulle Story" wound down, he was not moving rapidly; often he had nothing to do, and certainly on weekends if he didn't drink by himself, there was little else he cared to do. It was a strange and possibly fearful time, a war of sorts.

What helped was the presence of Meta. Although she had returned to Rebner and they had gone to Hollywood for work, the relationship was not working. Possibly because of her memories of Faulkner, Rebner became such an overbearing presence in her life she had to divorce him. Rebner—his serious intentions compromised, forced to do negligible work, unable to hang on except by demeaning his wife, emotionally incapable of dealing with American realities—was a deeply troubled man. Having failed in his professional life, he became intolerable in private, and Meta decided to divorce him. That this made her available to Faulkner when and if he came to Hollywood was, of course, another dimension to this strange triangle. Incidentally, Faulkner and Rebner remained cordial, even friendly, after Rebner knew of his ex-wife's affair with the writer.

Before Faulkner arrived at Warners, Meta had arrived at the Burbank studio as script clerk, a position she handled very competently. At Warner

Brothers, the stars were exceptional: in addition to Robinson, Flynn, Davis, Bogart, Cagney, etc., there were Ann Sheridan, Pat O'Brien, Ronald Reagan, Jane Wyman (whom the future president married), John Garfield, Ida Lupino, Olivia de Haviland, Alexis Smith, Barbara Stanwyck, Jack Carson, Wayne Morris, and scores of others almost as luminous. Directors included John Huston, Michael Curtiz, William Wyler, Anatole Litvak, and Raoul Walsh; among producers were Jerry Wald, Hal B. Wallis, Mark Hellinger, and Buckner, who became Faulkner's link to the de Gaulle project.

As she awaited Faulkner's possible arrival in Hollywood in the early 1940s, Meta began to recall not only the good times but the frustrating ones: "He was not a sadistic man, but his unwillingness to communicate his moods, and his drinking were in themselves a kind of cruelty."[29] She measured her memories, more fond than bitter, against her present state with Rebner, who needed her maternal care while he railed against fate. The juxtaposition was compelling: with the younger man, she was the protector, with the older one protected. But the flaw in the latter was that he withheld himself. Faulkner could give only so much: he offered courtesy, sexual ardor (not always), consideration; but in the critical area of real exchange he simply was not there. He had not given to Estelle, although they were destiny's partners, and he would not give to anyone else, however desperate he was for companionship. Starved for affection and sexual satisfaction, he was nevertheless so deeply immersed in his own world, whether that piece of Yoknapatawpha or elsewhere, that he had to abstract himself.

As Meta's career once again picked up, Faulkner's letters to her indicate his poor state of mind and his disastrous financial position. When she went to New York briefly, she suggested they meet for a few days, but Faulkner replied he did not have the fare. By this time Meta was writing directly to Oxford, for Estelle knew of the relationship and apparently accepted it. Her unrelenting drinking was surely connected in part to Faulkner's "desertion" of her; but then their life together had so broken down, the sole thing which could hold the marriage together was alternate forms of experience, whether mutual dependence on each other through heavy drinking, or else Faulkner's affairs with other women. In one respect he and Estelle had made their peace by establishing the terms of the war. While they complemented each other as drinkers and he was free to pursue his younger women, she maintained her position as the lady of Rowan Oak, the custodian of Jill, the accepted matron of Oxford. To the uncritical eye, they maintained a respectable front.

Meta also discovered why Faulkner was having so much difficulty in landing a Hollywood job—and why, later, Warner Brothers got him so cheaply. He was quite simply being blackballed or blacklisted. His reputation as a heavy drinker and his rudeness—his refusal to play the game according to the unstated rules—had made him persona non grata in most studios. The drinking especially had done him in with such heads of studio as Zanuck, Zukor, Louis B. Mayer, and the Warner brothers. These producers saw Faulkner, despite his reputation as America's greatest writer, as self-destructive and, therefore, unemployable. Howard Hawks, however, remained staunchly loyal to Faulkner and was not particularly disturbed by the drinking as long as the writer could get the job done.

In the period just before Faulkner managed this present Hollywood deal, he wrote Meta (according to her) a sequence of erotic letters. If what she reveals is true, in this area at least he was able to "let go" and open himself up. Although puritanical in his dislike of openly sexual talk and forbidding in his manner when women were around, he could apparently be reached. "The letters during this period of high expectancy," she says, "were unabashedly erotic, the outpourings of a man too long denied carnal love. Bowen [D. H. Lawrence's 'John Henry'], asserting himself, was uncontrollable. At night, Bill found it difficult to sleep; Bowen was trying to take him over completely, and since Bowen couldn't write, though he did what he was designed to do competently enough, that would be unfortunate."[30] Faulkner indicated, according to Meta, that he wanted to press his 129 pounds on her, and penetrate her: " 'and as much in you as I can can can can must must will will shall." Auxiliary verbs here express a deep longing, and we have a kind of metonymy, in which Faulkner's outlet was language, which stood in for thwarted sexual satisfaction. It is both an amusing and a depressing passage.

Then, unexpectedly, Faulkner showed up in front of Meta's apartment, luggage stacked on the steps. This began a long on-and-off-again relationship, and it was run mainly on his terms. His life in Oxford, he said, called him back, and he cited Jill especially as a means of convincing Meta he could not desert his extended family for her. This was a constant irritant in their affair, inasmuch as (according to her) she gave everything and received only a partial offering in return. Her remarks spare neither him nor herself. In the summer of 1942—when Faulkner was just beginning on the de Gaulle project, writing about Free French heroism and the legendary general exhorting his forces from London—America's greatest living novelist was caught in a kind of exile in Hollywood, a hostage to his creditors back in Mississippi, carrying on a heated affair with a younger woman, missing his daughter back in Oxford, letting his work lie fallow for a seemingly unlimited period of time. The dissonance of elements demonstrates how this man with "that old guarded eagle look,"[31] as Meta put it, had become fragmented, his life a series of discontinuous elements.

Running through this period of the relationship, Meta sensed how Faulkner missed his regular writing routine, how he feared he was going down the drain. We know from the suggestions in the de Gaulle project that his imagination was indeed working toward future fiction; but he could not be certain. Whatever good spirits he transferred into the movie script can be ascribed to Meta's presence, but overall his general attitude was depressive and anxiety-ridden, creating the circumstances in which he drank heavily and steadily. At this point, his life had become so complicated, so diffuse, so lacking the continuity he depended upon as a writer, that alcohol and sexual relief were his only response.

Meta raised the question of living together so Faulkner could save money from his salary to pay off creditors, but he felt it would be "a grievous error." She wondered if he meant because of Estelle; but Faulkner answered that " 'She couldn't say a word this time,' "[32] presumably because they had ceased sexual relations. Meta sensed the puritanical streak in him, what he jestingly called his "Southern rectitude." What the younger woman failed to recognize, however, was that Faulkner would not make the commitment living together enforces. He may have been miserable in Oxford with Estelle, and he may have needed the periodic release in order to reshape himself literarily and emotionally, but he was desperate for continuity. The wild-drinking man was deeply conservative, profoundly tied to his past and to his home base. He could not break from his own historical background by living with this woman as husband and wife while still married; and he did not want a divorce. One begins to understand that emotionally he needed this unsatisfactory marriage, its unfortunate sexual consequences, the outbursts of self-pity, the financial disaster looming ahead—that he needed all this as some way of prodding himself. He also needed what was slowly cooking him, the steady dosage of booze; he was, in a sense, as addicted to it as Estelle to her Seconal and alcohol. Meta could never hope to intrude permanently into the Oxford symbiosis which entrapped Faulkner like the coils crushing Laocoön.

She noticed Faulkner's fastidiousness, something apparent in his handwriting: an obsessive neatness, a desire to maintain absolute control, the need to give nothing of himself away, a penchant for hiding. His holograph style changed the language to something personal: the omission of letters, the use of a single letter to stand for brief words, the reshaping of letter forms as part of the creative act of reshaping itself. The handwriting reveals an anal-retentive personality, withholding everything—even though as a writer, he was disclosing and opening up. In his personal tidiness, Meta noted, he bathed whenever they made love, he ran the water when using the john, he coughed or sneezed into a handkerchief. The fastidiousness suggests some uneasiness about his body and his bodily functions, perhaps a corollary of the early years when he was rejected by women and began to form a poor image of himself as a man. But probably the attitudes went deeper, into his conception of himself as a person so withdrawn and recessive even bodily odor had to be disguised. Much of this fitted well with a puritanical nature. What is remarkable is that the sexual drive remained so strong when working against what seemed to be a dislike of the body, and continued to function when alcohol should have rendered him impotent.

The fastidiousness extended further, to his distaste of abusive or coarse language when women were present. Much of this quality has been attributed to Faulkner as a traditional Southern male, and even Meta's title of her book, *A Loving Gentleman,* suggests she accepts this explanation. But his own nature dictated his responses, not regional qualities. Faulkner defined himself in so many ways outside of Southern manners that it is incorrect to say he was reacting solely as a Southern gentleman: he was responding as someone shaped by his own experiences in a particular context.

Sensing that he was falling apart, he insisted on returning to Oxford for Christmas, and began petitioning the studio for permission. Although he had Meta and some money, he was slipping away, not only from her, but from himself. The drinking was suicidal. At his desk, at the studio, where he knew one mistake could finish him, he dared the bosses to discover him. "Pages from the screenplay he was working on [the de Gaulle material] were scattered over the room and there was a bottle of whiskey, one-third full, tipped over on its side near his typewriter. His ashen skin, when I lifted his head, struck alarm in me. It was as if some terrible dysfunction had hit him with paralyzing force."[33] Meta and his new friend, Buzz Bezzerides, managed to carry Faulkner, as if he had suddenly become ill, from the studio to a place at Yucca to be dried out. That he dared the studio in this way—when his salary was to be raised an additional $50 a week and he hoped for a new contract—indicates how he feared he was losing his prowess as a writer. As he admitted to Meta, " 'Sometimes I think if I do one more treatment or screenplay, I'll lose whatever power I have as a writer.' "[34]

The incredibly heavy drinking continued. Meta says that on one occasion he drank nine or ten double bourbons, this for a man who weighed about 130 pounds. She caught in his look "the visage of the drowned man." Each bout meant he had to be sobered to make the studio the next day; if he began to miss days, the bosses would know why. She attributed his depression to the fact that lesser writers like Bezzerides and Jo Pagano were making far more money than he, although Bezzerides was an excellent scriptwriter and deserved his money. She was misjudging in failing to see that his misery was not based solely on money but on a variety of elements; it was doubtful that even if all his problems had solutions, he could have stopped drinking. It was too much part of his life: the need to come close to death, and then to be saved. Maud had surely created some of this scenario with her domination of husband, sons, household; and now Faulkner was turning to one friend after another, male or female, to save him as he got in deeper.*

Faulkner went home for the Christmas of 1942 after having been shifted around to several films once the de Gaulle project was shelved. His first

---

*Another way to view the material is to see Faulkner was seeking love in a disguised way; that, having missed it from his mother—jostled out of position by succeeding siblings—he went chasing after it wherever and whoever. But the record seems to have too much rather than too little, and his need was not to make up but to regain what he had lost.

new assignment was on "Liberator Story" (the B-24 bomber which became the backbone of the air force bomber command), or "Life and Death of a Bomber." Then, after only three or four days, he was shifted again, to a film based on Eric Ambler's *Uncommon Danger,* retitled "Background to Danger," with George Raft. Here he worked with the director, Raoul Walsh, on a script already crafted by W. R. Burnett. Faulkner's cowriter was Daniel Fuchs. But this too fell through after two weeks, although Faulkner's work as script doctor was highly praised by Jerry Wald. He was then summarily reassigned to "Liberator Story," which he was permitted to work on at Rowan Oak, a concession Jack Warner made to the best writer in America, whom he had obtained for only $300 per week. The script was to Faulkner's liking, since it dealt with an airplane and was directly related to the war effort. He was given a definite schedule, a draft by Christmas. He was to return on January 14, after a month's leave, finally home after five months in Burbank.

It was during this time that the studio picked up his option, and Faulkner earned $350 per week, about a third of what he had once been paid. Even the lowest hacks were getting twice or three times that; but by January 16, he was back. Meta says he returned "happy and loquacious," without any mention of Estelle. Her description of Faulkner's return to Oxford has something of the sanitized idealism with which she surrounded him. She envisaged him as "lord of the whole damned manor," blacks, his dead brother's wife and daughter, and so on. What she failed to see, or perhaps chose not to mention, was the level of hostility existing in that extended family. Johncy had become a well-received novelist with his second novel, *Dollar Cotton.* But he held deep resentment against his more famous brother, not only for Faulkner's success in the larger world but because he had depended on him for support. It was far more complicated than that, for Maud had established her eldest son as her favorite, and there was the vying for placement in the pecking order. Further, while Maud resented all her daughters-in-law and disliked them to the point of not permitting them to enter her home, she relented somewhat with Estelle. Johncy and Jack's wives fared less well. But hostilities and resentment went further. Estelle was herself a wounded creature: still alcoholic, undependable, making Faulkner uncertain about leaving Jill with her; and she, of course, harbored resentment of her husband taking up again with Meta, living in Hollywood, moving in the larger world. Jill also began to show signs of the internalized anger she felt toward a discontinuous family life —an uncertain existence in which she had an absent father (uncommon in those days, unless he was away for military service), an alcoholic mother, a great deal of tension, some competition with a cousin (Dean's daughter) of nearly her own age, and an unsure sense of herself. It was not a happy place Faulkner was so eager to return to, though Meta was deceived into thinking it was a real home. It was, instead, a place where Faulkner needed to touch down to regain strength, like Antaeus; but unlike that unfortunate creature, Faulkner could afford to leave his home base, or earth, in order to strengthen himself.

The year 1943 is notable not for any profound changes in Faulkner's life, but for the firming up of his ideas for *A Fable*. That novel, one should be cautioned, is not an integrated, fully wrought work. It lacks the probe and dimensionality of *Go Down, Moses*. But it was Faulkner's most ambitious project of his last twenty years, and he poured into it everything he knew, including craft and language.

Faulkner published three stories in 1943, all written in prior years: "Shingles for the Lord" (*Saturday Evening Post*, February 13), reprinted in *Collected Stories;* "My Grandmother Millard and General Bedford Forrest and the Battle of Harrykin Creek" (*Story*, March–April), reprinted in *Collected Stories;* and "Shall Not Perish" (*Story*, July–August), reprinted in *Collected Stories*. As he well knew, none was particularly distinguished. The major part of the year was spent working on film treatments, scripts, and doctoring. His major script work, on Hemingway's *To Have and Have Not* with Bogart and Bacall, did not come until after a long vacation from Hollywood, which lasted to mid-February of 1944. He continued to see Meta during his extended stay in Burbank.

The vicissitudes of screenwriting were brought home to him as he was shifted around like a writing puppet. Once he finished with the "Liberator Story" (by January 23)*, he was reassigned, this time to "Northern Pursuit" (variously titled "To the Last Man" and "Five Thousand Trojan Horses"). At least the alternate titles were amusing. The script having taken on great difficulties, Faulkner was called in as doctor. The basic story was of a group of Nazi infiltrators in Canada who were to get hold of a plane and bomb the Sault St. Marie Canal. This seemingly innocuous act would prove mightily disruptive to the American war effort. It was an archetypal war story, with that archetypal hero, Errol Flynn. Faulkner only tinkered with the script before he was removed for another assignment. Not all projects would be of this sort. In "Battle Cry," which Faulkner crafted in the summer, he had novelistic materials, and his work warrants attention. And then in *To Have and Have Not*, which he worked on in 1944, he had another script worthy of his skills.

Faulkner moved from "Northern Pursuit" to "Deep Valley." By this time, he thought he might be able to make ends meet, and he still spoke of joining up, in his forty-sixth year. In his January 25 letter to Ober, he had written of trying for the ferry command or some other war work. But if that fell through, he wanted to return home to look after his farm. Yet he feared he might jeopardize his position with the studio if he sought a leave of absence "and must resign myself to being a part-time script writer

---

*Although the main message of "The Life and Death of a Bomber" is that the home front must not permit selfish interests to let down its fighting men, also of interest is Faulkner's conception of a bomber with its own energies, will, purpose.

at least."³⁵ He then decided to postpone requesting a leave. "As soon as
. . . [my] debts [are] paid, money put aside for my family, I will broach the
subject." "Deep Valley," where his work was buried under successive
rewritings, had a kind of Faulknerian literary treatment. The script links
a bank president who has run off and a convict labor camp; running
parallel to this Snopes-like action is the president's daughter and a convict.
The latter wishes to serve in the war and petitions the governor for his
freedom. His aim is to ship out on the Murmansk supply run. The script
was evidently part of the love affair Warner Brothers, under government
request, was having with America's wartime ally, the Soviet Union. And
Faulkner, who was so firmly anticommunist, was assigned to give life to
a script where the distant hero is Russia in its valiant struggle to survive
against the Nazi invasion.*

On March 15 he wrote Ober he was interested in adapting F. Scott
Fitzgerald's "The Curious Case of Benjamin Button" (later collected in
Tales of the Jazz Age) into a play, its method based loosely on Thornton
Wilder's *The Skin of Our Teeth*, which he called "By the Skin of His Teeth."
"If, for Mrs Fitzgerald's sake, you cant refuse a money offer for the rights,
can you include in the sale something stipulating that only I can use the
story? I wish I could buy the option myself now. I would make the play
first, then sell it to the movies."³⁶ Faulkner followed this up with another
letter on April 26, an indication of his continuing interest. Part of the
difficulty in getting hold of the option, however, was connected to Herndon. "I am not supposed, have signed to that effect, to write anything of
my own while drawing a studio's pay, and I am pretty busy at studio work
also. So I dont think I will try anything else until this option is finished
and I can take leave, or be fired, which will probably happen. Then I will
try the play."³⁷

The desire to write a play foreshadows his intense work on *Requiem for
a Nun*, cast as both a novel and play. Disgust with Herndon and his
contract which tied Faulkner to script work was building. So was his
distaste for Hollywood while the war was raging and young men and even
women (such as Haas's daughter) were serving; his growing recognition
he was not going anywhere—that Hollywood seemed his fate and doom;
that whatever ideas he had would have to be cleared with Herndon, whose
intentions he no longer knew; that returning to Oxford was still distant
and his future in Hollywood uncertain. There was still Meta, and his
desire to be with her had not cooled. She tells of how new faces began to
appear at Musso's, where she and Faulkner often met: John Steinbeck,
Sinclair Lewis, Carl Sandburg, Arthur Miller, Clifford Odets, Raymond

---

*Also as part of this Yoknapatawpha revival in Hollywood, he was moved into "Country
Lawyer," loosely based on the chronicle of that name by Bellamy Partridge. In his adaptation,
Faulkner moved it from New York state to Jefferson, Mississippi, and, reminiscent of *Go
Down, Moses*, filled it with racial and generational conflicts. He worked on it briefly in March,
but like so much else that he touched it was stillborn.

Chandler, Mary McCarthy, among many others. Most of them received more than Faulkner, who was still tied to $350 per week and unable to break out because of Herndon.

The frustration or dullness ("a damned dull life," he told Ober) brought him down. He responded to all the pressures, both the apparent ones and the more silent ones, by falling ill. As he told Cho-Cho, on April 3, he had a terrible cold, lumbago, earache. "I am a rachitic old man in the last stages of loco-motor ataxia." As he describes his ills, we recognize how little illness he suffered as an adult; whenever he was down, it was drink-related. His physical well-being was remarkable, considering the abuse his body absorbed. Later, that abuse would also come from horses—falls, broken bones, bruises and sprains. Yet except for these—and the burned back, the result of a binge—he seemed in perfect health, with even his appearance failing to take on the qualities of a man pickling himself in alcohol.

At this time, he wrote a letter to Jimmy Falkner, Johncy's son, then serving in the air force, in which he cautioned him about fear and attention to detail when flying. The forty-five-year-old writer is in a sense presenting a mirror image: looking at himself in the eighteen-year-old nephew and going through all the stages of his own military career, complete with the embroidery of heroic actions he never experienced. The letter shows Faulkner at his most revealing—truly worried about Jimmy and yet using the occasion as a way of bidding farewell to a part of his life he had himself constructed. In a short time, he began to downplay the deceptions he had perpetrated in order to reshape his life for outsiders, and insisted on a version closer to the truth—as he told Malcolm Cowley, he had just served in the air force. Yet with Jimmy, he could relive the romance of war, a man's world even more dramatic than deer camp, and, more significantly, the way in which a man entered history.

Four days after this, on April 7, he began preliminary work on "Battle Cry." In Faulkner's hands it became a wartime epic, and his treatment involved all the resources of the novelist. As before, he refused to see only with the camera eye. He wrote 140 pages within two weeks, only to have Hawks ask him to rewrite from the beginning. His homesickness is apparent in letters to Victoria's husband, William Fielden, and to Jill. To Fielden: "I too like my town, my land, my people, my life, am unhappy away from it even though I must quit it to earn money to keep it going to come back to. Can you unravel that sentence?"[38] He refers to Estelle as "Big Miss" and indicates she seems to be doing fine without him. This was quite different from what he was telling Meta: that Estelle was drinking steadily and he did not trust her with Jill. He speaks of his option being picked up at the end of July, or else being fired. He would like a leave, which he did get later in the year, until mid-February of 1944.

To Jill, he wrote on May 16 that he has heard how nice she looks with her hair cut. He tells her of his routine: rising at seven, going down to the Musso-Frank restaurant, reading his paper, and eating a typical Southern breakfast of orange juice, sausages, marmalade, and toast; then he goes to

the studio with Bezzerides and Tom Job, in their car. And if he is fortunate, there will be on his desk a letter from "Mama and my Jill. That makes
me feel just fine."[39] He mentions he is writing a movie for Howard Hawks,
a long one lasting about three hours, costing three and one-half million,
with three or four directors and all the big stars—he is referring to "Battle
Cry." He sends his love and promises to send on two Victory Bonds. He
also wrote his stepson, Malcolm, in mid-May, as the young man was
heading off for the army. Faulkner's address to him (as "Buddy, my dear
son") shows he was demonstrably touched by all the young men who were
leaving for military service. *His* duty consisted of writing "Battle Cry,"
which became not only his "novel" for the period but also his contribution
to the war effort.

Chapter Twenty-one

Midcareer:
The Hollywood War

FAULKNER ATTEMPTED TO bring to the script of "Battle Cry" what he had experienced as a novelist.[1] More than that, he tried to transform a visual medium into something which owed a great deal to a more purely verbal one; and reciprocally, he attempted to extend the possibilities of the novel into film. We would be mistaken to see his efforts as only turning film into novel; he also turned novel into film. The residue of his script-writing was not only concern with ethical and moral issues, but scenic formulations, strategies of montage, panning. *A Fable* was the recipient of much of this filmic influence.

"Battle Cry" was an immensely ambitious effort. It was to utilize scenes showing the Allies as they fought, got pushed back, died, and triumphed in their holy war against the fascists. The project was to film a kind of "united nations" in action on the battlefield and just behind the action. It would cut through race, class, caste, national identification, personal identity itself as a means of revealing the deep and abiding solidarity among those opposing the Axis. It consisted of a large number of scenes, cutting back and forth between them, with some secondary elements involving love affairs and other personal matters, but all subsumed to the needs of the war effort. It was, in brief, a great cry of patriotism.

But there was more. "Battle Cry" gave Faulkner the opportunity to introduce Lincoln, history, themes from the Civil War; it allowed him to relate the Eliotic point: that all wars are interconnected, and that this one was merely more critical, but not more important, than the American Civil War. It also gave him the opportunity to look again at the Negro: the Negro, like America, badly wounded but still indomitable, foreshadows Lucas Beauchamp of *Intruder in the Dust.* Calling him "America" is itself a huge step for this man from Oxford, Mississippi, involving a new role for the Negro now that the war began to open up society.

"Battle Cry" was an extended film treatment of a subject Faulkner had already tried to put together for "The Life and Death of a Bomber." That film concerned civilians who were working to build American bombers. Although it took place on the home front, it had war potential. A labor dispute at the plant, along with a love triangle, results in a defective bomber being sent overseas. The message was clear: that national unity and patriotic sense of purpose had to override personal needs, or else a defective bomber brings disaster to its crew. Although on a vastly different scale from "Battle Cry," the underlying motif is the same: whether civilians or military of various nations, only one goal exists; to wipe out the fascist threat to world order.

The treatment of "Battle Cry"—Faulkner did the expanded story treatment, as well as the second temporary screenplay—was to use battle scenes, scenes behind the lines, acts of individual patriotism, a love interest, all against a background of a musical cantata, with music by Earl Robinson and libretto by Millard Lampell, called "Abe Lincoln Comes Home." The death of Lincoln served as the inspiration for America to pull together, a symbol for the world to link itself in triumph. But other properties were involved and had to be worked in: "Diary of a Red Army Woman," developed by Violet Atkins and William Bacher; "Ma-Ma Mosquito," a news feature by Dean S. Jennings. This was a true story based on the exploits of Madame Chao Yu-tang, who at sixty-five led an army of guerrillas against the Japanese. Also included were story ideas by Hawks about American soldiers in North Africa and an American war correspondent in Malta. To these elements were added stories depicting French and Greek resistance, as well as several others discarded along the way. The film, if produced, would have run well over three hours, with distinct links to saga or epic films of a later generation like *The Sorrow and the Pity* and *Hitler.*

Faulkner's immense undertaking was to create coherence of these disparate elements, to pull them together into a consistent and compelling narrative, using the musical background of the Lincoln cantata. Although he had considerable collaborative help on the enterprise, the "Second Temporary Screenplay" is acknowledged as his work. It follows in many of its major outlines his "Expanded Story Treatment." In his treatment, Faulkner depicts a young recruit being seen off by his grandfather, in the Springfield, Illinois, railway terminal. In the screenplay, the Springfield backdrop is given full treatment with the Lincoln cantata, voiceovers, and then Paul Robeson singing. The beginning is inspirational, concluding with an appeal to buy war bonds (a pan shot to a sign on the wall). Then comes the scene of the young recruit (named Fonda) and his grandfather.*

Then in a montagelike scene, Fonda (in the treatment) is seen in the North African desert as a member of a platoon doomed by its mission to hold off a German attack. Reagan, who seems retarded, is now in command, a sergeant who must control the survivors as well as a German and an Italian prisoner. Two members of another platoon are caught up with him, one a black called America, the other a white Southerner named Akers. America is wounded badly, with a bullet in his spine, paralyzed from the waist down, and Akers is the tough white Southerner who nurses and mothers America. Faulkner was clearly living through a fantasy of a racially neutral South, virtually a single-race South—what we have already seen as his fantasy in *Absalom.* America, the symbolic country, is embraced by Akers who, once he is liberated from his home territory, can show his true "love" for America. They become, among other things, father and son, or mother/nurse and son; what passes between them is nothing less than love, the homoeroticism of black and white. There is still some condescension in Faulkner's arrangement, since Akers must care for America: somehow, the white is the black's "keeper." But while this is an undeniable by-product of the arrangement (perhaps its very theme), the depiction also shows the kinship of white and black Faulkner envisioned after the war.

This kinship is solidified in the cutting away from the North African episode to the cantata. Here we have the quintessential American message: that although Lincoln is dead, the "fight for freedom's just begun." In a sense, Lincoln lives on in the hearts and minds of "Lincoln's people." We are all, in this respect, Lincoln's people. The words of the cantata bring blushes to the reader's cheek; but with the surging music, the backdrop of the war, the overwhelming desire for unity of races and nationalities, the verbiage becomes more acceptable. In any event, Faulkner did not write the libretto—his job was to integrate it into the rapidly shifting scenes.

The message of the cantata is, in reality, the message of the movie which the various scenes exemplify. The movie is too long and varied for us to follow each scene, but what is of paramount importance is how Faulkner was able to integrate such disparate and often conflicting material—clear preparation for his massive job of "enfolding" in *A Fable.* The key is integration of elements, and for this Faulkner developed a sliding, montagelike technique, which recalls his own fiction: one can find here the four distinct and yet overlapping sequences of *Sound,* or the interweaving of story elements in *Light in August.* To that can be added some of the "slid-

*Since Fonda becomes "Flynn" in certain scenes, it is possible Faulkner was using actors' names as ways of visualizing the role through visualization of the actual person. Errol Flynn was of course known to him on the Warners lot. There was, also, Reagan, as we shall see— although whether he had Ronald Reagan in mind we cannot tell. The future president in a film written by William Faulkner would have defied credibility (when released with Ronald Reagan and Alexis Smith, "Stallion Road" was no longer Faulkner's work, but Stephen Longstreet's).

ing" technique associated with *As I Lay Dying.* The effort to integrate "Battle Cry," although unsuccessful in the long run, reveals Faulkner's still working well within modernist techniques, only here applying them to film.

Hawks tried to find a formula that worked. Obviously, this farrago of material would not cohere. But screen tests were made, including one of Lauren Bacall. A large factor was that this could turn out to be the most expensive film ever made, so expensive, in fact, it should have been made part of the defense budget. Faulkner did not consider costs—he simply wrote in scenes requiring armies of thousands and waves of planes. Some filming took place, on one day, July 28, and that was that. While Faulkner worked well into July on the script, it was doomed—by finances, by its own unworkability, by the lack of control which let each writer run off by himself.

Faulkner had been sick since April and the war was taking its toll. As his early July letters to Haas and to Malcolm demonstrate, he could barely tolerate the idea of young men going off to die while he did nothing. The need to become personally useful was palpable; and his inability, at his age and in his condition, to find anything in the military was taking him lower and lower. For a period of time, he was spending amounts close to his salary to cover his medical expenses. The cycle was completed. He was in Burbank for money he needed; being there at that time created such tension that he drank to excess, even for him; as a result of binging, he spent the money he was earning, thus necessitating that he remain in Hollywood to earn more. America's finest novelist was trapped.

Writing to Ober, Faulkner mentioned he felt the studio would pick up his option on August 1, which it did, to the tune of $400 per week, but he was unable to break his connection with Herndon. Somewhat desperately, he asked Ober if Swanson, Ober's West Coast representative, would take him up; he was willing to pay Herndon his commission if he could be rid of him. Meanwhile, Steve Fisher, who had success with *Destination Tokyo,* and Faulkner* worked rapidly on "Battle Cry," with the younger man doing the Russian segment and Faulkner the Red Chinese. He also wrote the French sequence and revised another segment.

Then he heard that one of the first young men to enlist, Haas's son Robert, had been lost in action in North Africa. Robert Haas, Jr., was a carrier-based pilot, on torpedo-bombers, where losses were extremely high. Faulkner wrote Bob Haas, as if his own son had been lost:

My nephew, 18, is about to be posted to carrier training. He will get it too. Then who knows? the blood of your fathers and the blood of

---

*Blotner repeats a fine interchange between Steve Fisher and Howard Hawks. Fisher had no idea who Faulkner was, nor did he care, and he treated the man almost twenty years his senior condescendingly. Hawks asked Fisher who his favorite author was, and the writer answered that Hemingway was. " 'Well,' Hawks said, 'Faulkner is *Ernest's* favorite writer' " (Joseph Blotner, *Faulkner: A Biography,* vol. 2, p. 1145). After that, the young man changed his attitude.

mine side by side at the same long table in Valhalla, talking of glory and heroes, draining the cup and banging the empty pewter on the long board to fill again, holding two places for us maybe, not because we were heroes or not heroes, but because we loved them.[2]

Faulkner's choice of imagery is compelling: the mixed blood of Gentile and Jew in Valhalla, a mixed image if one ever existed; and yet it was consistent with his sense of racial mixture, one people; America becoming, against all prohibitions and prejudices, a single-race society, black-and-white, Jew-and-Gentile. The words suggest a vision.

Then to Malcolm, on July 4, Faulkner wrote out of concern, bitterness, and reconciliation. It was to become the turning point in his attitude toward Jews, as earlier *Absalom* had become a pivotal period for him concerning Negroes and their role in a white-dominated society. Never virulent, never dominantly anti-Semitic like Hemingway or Wolfe, Faulkner had used Jews in stereotypical ways, making them responsible for the kind of civilization he found unacceptable. The letter deserves to be quoted in full, because this is the Faulkner everyone wants to believe in—except that with Negroes, he waffled and hedged.

Mr. Robert Haas is vice president of Random House. They publish my books. During the times when I would be broke, year after year sometimes, I had only to write him and he would send me money— no hope to get it back, unless I wrote another book. He's a Jew.

He had an only son, and a daughter. In '40, the son withdrew from Yale and became a Navy pilot. In '41, the girl about 20, joined that Women's Ferry Squadron, is now flying aeroplanes from factories to bases. The boy was flying torpedo planes off carriers (what Jim is training for) in Pacific. He was killed last week. The girl is still flying. All Jews. I just hope I dont run into some hundred percent American Legionnaire until I feel better.

There is a squadron of negro pilots. They finally got congress to allow them to learn how to risk their lives in the air. They are in Africa now, under their own negro Lt. Colonel, did well at Pantelleria, on the same day a mob of white men and white policemen killed 20 negroes in Detroit. Suppose you and me and a few others of us lived in the Congo, freed seventy-seven years ago by ukase; of course we cant live in the same apartment hut with black folks, nor always ride in the same car nor eat in the same restaurant, but we are free because the Great Black Father says so. Then the Congo is engaged in War with the Cameroon. At last we persuade the Great Black Father to let us fight too. You and Jim say are flyers. You have just spent the day trying to live long enough to learn how to do your part in saving the Congo. Then you come back down and are told that 20 of your people have just been killed by a mixed mob of civilians and cops at Little Poo Poo. What would you think?

A change will come out of this war. If it doesn't, if the politicians and the people who run this country are not forced to make good the shibboleth they glibly talk about freedom, liberty, human rights, then you young men who lived through it will have wasted your precious time, and those who dont live through it will have died in vain.[3]

The feelings expressed here support the contention Faulkner was desperately depressed about his uselessness, and this was surely a large contributor to his excessive drinking. If we examine the drinking not from its possible genetic derivation but from its place in Faulkner's situation, we must conclude he had ample reason for desiring a form of oblivion. With alcohol, he had found the middle ground or perfect balance between life and death. Suicide by direct means was out, but suicide through drinking was a way of dealing with life, especially now when he sensed all lack of continuity.

The problem was familiar. He tried this or that, but it always came back to the same thing: he was laboring for far too little; his talent was buried; and when he did expend himself on a script, it was shelved. By August 13, it was clear his role on "Battle Cry" had ended. Hawks and Warners were feuding, but even under better circumstances, Faulkner's role in the script was over. Production had in fact closed down by August 8. By August 13, Faulkner was off the film, and "Battle Cry" was a ghostly presence on the Warner Brothers shelf.

Faulkner felt the time was right to get out. He was doing neither himself nor the studio much good, and he requested a six-months leave. He understood that whatever length of time he stayed away would be tacked on to the end of his option years: he was not escaping, merely postponing. Then there occurred one of those chance occasions which activate an idea, from intimation to actuality. He had already formed the kernel of *A Fable* in scripting "The de Gaulle Story," and now he met producer William Bacher, who, with director Henry Hathaway, was interested in doing a film based on the Unknown Soldier. Hathaway presented the idea with the notion that the Unknown Soldier was Jesus Christ, something he had picked up from a writer. This was of course Faulkner's own intimation, only partially formed in his mind, but there. Warner Brothers had meanwhile granted him a leave without pay from mid-August until November 15. In his October 30 letter to Ober, he enclosed fifty-one pages of what was originally a story, not a novel, idea. Faulkner had gone ahead with it, sweetened by a $1,000 advance from Bacher. The three, Faulkner, Bacher, and Hathaway, were to make the film, and then share in the profits. They would, of course, need an angel. Faulkner, however, was entrapped by another catch in his contract. He could not work on a movie script for anyone else, and if he did, Warner Brothers would drop him—and he could also expect to be blacklisted. "So," he told Ober, "to kill two birds with one stone, I am writing this story in an elaborated, detailed, explicit synopsis form, from which I can write a script later when my status with Warner is cleared, and which I can try to turn into a play now, or rewrite as a novelette-fable, either or both of which, under my leave of absence from Warner which reserved me the right to write anything but moving pictures while off salary, I can do."[4]

He wants Ober to show it around, for a sale or even a reasonably definite commitment. "This is about half of it [it proved to about about one-tenth]. It continues on through the Three Temptations, the Crucifixion, the Resurrection. The epilogue is an Armistice Day ceremony at the tomb of the Unknown Soldier." He repeats that he sees it as a magazine story, and even as a play. In developing it, he assures Ober he will smooth out the "primer-like biblical references and explanations" but retain the "Christ-analogy through understatement." This moves Faulkner ahead to November 17. One thing was clear in his mind: that the Unknown Soldier buried under the Arc de Triomphe in Paris was somehow linked to another sacrificial figure, the Jesus of Christian belief, both of them reincarnations of value systems man must pay attention to. Faulkner's interest in the reincarnated Jesus Christ was not a sudden religious fervor on his part, but a natural development of his sense of the war years, when young men all over the world were being sacrificed. He perceived these young men in this war were linked to all young men sacrificed; and they, in turn, connected to the greatest sacrifice of them all in the Christian myth.

In mid-August, Faulkner was back in Oxford. Money was already a worry, since with the leave of absence there was no income. The farm involved not only expenses but endless details with horses, feed, picking cotton, and help. But inside the man supervising these chores was a story percolating, the kernel of *A Fable*, the Unknown Soldier as Jesus Christ.* On October 30 he told Ober he was "working on a thing now," coming to about ten to fifteen thousand words. "It is a fable," he wrote, "an indictment of war perhaps, and for that reason may not be acceptable now. I am writing it out in a sort of synopsis. I'll send it to you in that form; if anyone wants it, I'll rewrite and clean it up."[5]

Then in the letter already cited, Faulkner told Ober he was sending on fifty-one pages of the story; that letter (on November 17) gives the origin of the idea. His plan at this stage was for Ober to show it around to generate some income. So far he had only the $1,000 from Bacher. Ober found it exceptionally well done thus far, but asked Faulkner to bring the story forward closer to reality and reshape it less along Biblical lines before he showed it to magazines. Even in this initial response, when Faulkner was still struggling with form, Ober showed considerable insight. For one of the problems with *A Fable* as it developed was that Faulkner mixed styles, from realistic to mythical, with his language straining to capture

---

*The completed novel was dedicated to William Bacher and Henry Hathaway "who had the basic idea from which this book grew into its present form," as well as to James Street, in whose work *Look Away* Faulkner read the story of the hanged man and the bird, and to Hodding Carter and Ben Wasson of the Levee Press, for the publication in a limited edition of the story of the stolen racehorse.

each mode, and that not always compellingly. But Ober nevertheless caught the ambitious, outreaching nature of the work.

What Faulkner was straining for was no less than a mixture of Job, Jesus, suffering, martyrdom, repentance—the entire Christian experience grafted onto a war story, so that war becomes a timeless experience which can be associated with man's greatest sacrifice, the crucifixion. Faulkner was not writing as a believer, but as a man of faith in certain unchanging principles of behavior. In some ways, *A Fable* is a rewriting of "The Bear," different though the materials of each piece are. That long development of father-figures and their sons which had begun in the mid-1930s and which became accentuated in "The Bear" (and more generally in *Go Down, Moses*) found focus in this long-developing work. He was seeking some way of comprehending what man was like in situations of extreme stress. The nature of the material reinforces our belief that Faulkner, now forty-six, envisaged this novel as a capstone, a kind of valedictory. We must approach it as his epitaph.

Even as America and its allies began to turn the war against the fascists, Faulkner was writing steadily of another war, which becomes for him, like the Civil War, an archetypal conflict. *A Fable* was his attempt to create a visionary novel that brought together past and present, myth and actuality. These qualities bring it close to "The Bear," which had created in the smaller world of the big woods a kinship with a passing era—and which now, in the war story, was enlarging that theme of man's need to find principles by which he could live, endure, survive. The *myth* of war—as, in the earlier work, the myth of the hunt, the myth of the hunter—was the focus of the vision. By returning to the earlier conflict, Faulkner could write a philosophical novel, transforming the war/combat novel into socio-historical fiction or into complex political statement.*

Even in its earliest stages, Faulkner was interweaving a complex series of themes: a generational struggle that is also a political struggle (worked through in class and caste terms) and that is, in turn, a religious struggle (between Jesus and God, son and father). All that is played out in the conflict between Allied and German armies on the western front, where the ultimate is life and death. Here, a corporal who organizes the mutiny of a regiment of three thousand men on the French front is a Christ-like figure in a struggle against a general and a marshal (his father, the supreme commander) and politicians, who demand that the war continue. Like the big woods, the war purifies if one plays it according to certain rules; but if one allows the outside world to intrude, then every dimension of the war becomes corruptive.

Further connecting *A Fable* to "The Bear" as idea and performance is a rhetorical manner, which in its way is as important as what the words

---

*In a curious parallel, John Hawkes in *The Cannibal* (1949)—which slides from one war to another—tries on a smaller scale to do the same. Like Faulkner, Hawkes eschewed the action novel, going against the grain of Mailer, Jones, Burns, and others, heading instead for conceptualization, a frame of reference for war—the phenomenology of war, so to speak.

actually mean. Faulkner needed a language for the novel, and what he attempted was a variation on his own rhetoric in *Absalom*. But by this time, whether it was the result of aging or too much alcohol or the bad habits formed in scriptwriting, Faulkner had lost touch with the grandeur of his mid-thirties rhetoric.* It is often ill-advised, unnecessarily clogged and difficult, or else straining for effects which Faulkner miscalculated. The following is not unrepresentative: "That you were chosen by destiny out of the paradox of your background, to be a paradox to your past in order to be free of human past is to be the one out of all earth to be free of the compulsions of fear and weakness and doubt which render the rest of us incapable of what you were competent for."[6]

Language strains for Biblical significance, but does not find a level. It misses as voice. Faulkner writes of "not even the crashing ejaculation of salute this time." The juxtaposition of a sexual image with saluting is a grand rhetorical gesture, but as language seems almost amateurish. Sometimes the same rhetoric clicks into place: "the vast cumbrous machinery of war grinding to its clumsy halt in order to reverse itself to grind and rumble in a new direction—the proprietorless wave of victory exhausted by its own ebb and returned by its own concomitant flux, spent not by its own faded momentum but as though bogged down in the refuse of its own success." The prose is on the edge, almost a parody of itself, a Max Beerbohm burlesque of Faulkner; and then redeemed in that final image, where language and vision of war encounter each other. He was wobbling between very high and very low levels of achievement.

Very possibly some of the wobble or uncertainty in the text resulted from Faulkner's intense immersion in family potentialities. For *A Fable* encapsulates a significant number of his by-now-familiar family relationships. The key family is that of the corporal, characterized by an absent father (the marshal, who has deserted the corporal's pregnant mother) and a strong self-willed mother; plus an equally strong-willed sister in Marthe, a mother substitute. The corporal becomes in his sexual life one of Faulkner's losers, with peripheral linkage to Quentin and Henry Sutpen, among others.** It is possible to see the many family ramifications of *A Fable* as a shadowy presentation of intimate elements in Faulkner's life; with that as our perception, we can better understand his effort to weave in so much material and, at the same time, his worrying of the manuscript to "make you see."

*Yet Malcolm Cowley quotes Faulkner: " 'I am writing and rewriting, weighing every word which I never did before. I used to hang it on like an apprentice paper hanger and never look back' " (Malcolm Cowley, *The Faulkner–Cowley File: Letters and Memories, 1944–1962* [New York: Viking, 1966], p. 128).

**As one critic comments, parenting is a dismal affair. "Three of the major male characters in *A Fable* are orphans, all are fatherless for most of their lives, nearly all are wifeless and childless, and over and over again men in *A Fable* respond to the present reality of World War I in the terms of their problematic relationships with their parents: over and over again soldiers, even—and in particular, the old marshal—are described as, are treated like, or act like children" (Noel Polk, "Woman and the Feminine in *A Fable*," in *Faulkner and Women*, eds. Doreen Dowler and Ann J. Abadie [Jackson: University Press of Mississippi, 1986], p. 182).

At the structural level, Faulkner worked daringly, unfolding his tale of mutiny through flashback and parallelism of event, revealing small segments at a time, so that anyone who hopes to grapple with events must reread, not read. Many of the strategies here are prefigured by Faulkner's work on film scripts. "Battle Cry" is a particularly good example of how he interwove seemingly disparate elements, created flashbacks within flashbacks, used temporal sequencing adventurously, as he would do in *A Fable*. Not all of his innovative filmic devices remain in the final two versions which we know are his; several segments were dropped along the way.[7] But if we review those sequences, often just a brief scene, we can see how the film script becomes his way of shaping and reshaping his material for the novel. Faulkner worked on disguises and shields, dribbling out information of the regiment's mutiny, the corporal, the general in charge (Gragnon), and the supreme commander, the marshal who arranges the façade. Since the mutiny must be buried so that the soldiers do not end the war themselves, Faulkner could come at his material as though from the narrow end of a funnel. As he burrows toward divulgations, we begin to perceive the political-religious-social patterns.

The basic story is of the corporal who becomes the Unknown Soldier, and is himself identified with the Christ-figure, during Passion Week. The corporal, who seems ubiquitous, is, at thirty-three, destined for martyrdom, especially after rejecting escape from punishment. As a rebel against authority—and Faulkner's ingrained Jeffersonian individualism can be seen here—he may well be France's Unknown Soldier after his death, as well as its savior. He also has intimations of Jeanne d'Arc, given the fact he has grown up in a village called Vienne-la-Pucelle, a kind of harbinger of the virgin or Joan coming to save France. When he dies, he gains a crown of thorns of barbed wire, so that religion and war extend themselves to touch. War is, Faulkner repeats, all wars, the Civil War as archetypal. And if war is all wars, temporality is eternal presentness. The German general who flies in to agree to the arrangement by which the mutiny can be disguised from the rest of the army speaks of the next war and tells the British they will not even prepare for it. In the German general's words, material from the de Gaulle script, and the Frenchman's ignored warnings, surface. Faulkner turns the German's words into a kind of battle cry for the way democracies, unlike totalitarian societies, operate:

You will wait until an enemy is actually beating at your front gate. Then you will turn out to repel him exactly like a village being turned out cursing and swearing on a winter night to salvage a burning hayrick—gather up your gutter-sweepings, the scum of your slums and stables and paddocks; they will not even be dressed to look like soldiers, but in the garments of ploughmen and ditchers and carters; your officers look like a house party going out to the cutts for a pheasant drive.[8]

The weak efforts of democracy are, of course, their strength; the author intends the German's speech to be a kind of litotes. In "Battle Cry" Faulkner had already suggested this response, in his efforts to bring together all the elements comprising a democratically composed army, its ragtag elements which finally cohere into a fighting force. This is Jefferson's farmer working his fields until called to duty, the Roman Cincinnatus.

We must account for the terrible grip this material had on Faulkner: in the uncertainties of the coming decade, including his winning of the Nobel Prize, he was caught, utterly, by his story. He was offering up nothing less than an American view of the great war, the way in which an American can salvage both honor and victory. The German foresees that the future belongs to those who can mobilize force, not moral suasion—it is his fatal flaw. Through his presence and speech, Faulkner extends his "fable" forward, just as by means of the Christ-like corporal he extends it backward. At the heart of the struggle, on all levels of the novel, is the split between man's endurance as measured by his power and man's endurance by virtue of his spirit. The supreme commander is victimized by political power and intrigue, whereas his son is a sacrifice to elements marshaled by spiritual, moral, and ethical considerations. This ideological division defines the structure of the novel and is part of Faulkner's heritage from his film work.

Faulkner's Nobel Prize acceptance speech is echoed in the novel, in that man endures "not because he is immortal but [is] immortal because he endures. He may endure from several points of view, even rapacity; but ultimately man cannot fail man, or else he ceases." Every life experienced intensely and with comprehension of all the stakes is a form of endurance, and by extension a form of immortality. We see Faulkner building a bridge between Jeffersonian individualism and the responsibility one has to state or government—a tenuous linkage, but one which each man must attempt. The frequent contemporary references in "Battle Cry" to the rights of Negroes and the injustices perpetrated upon them, as well as his comments in his letter to his stepson, are part of this rethinking and regrouping.

As Faulkner developed the ideas shaping *A Fable*, his emphasis on ethical considerations would put him at odds with many other novels of the 1940s and 1950s. For even as he stressed such imperatives, other writers were "opening up" human experience, so that ethics themselves became problematic, subservient to individual need. What he told Cowley in 1948 was fully consistent with what he had written Ober in 1943 about the Three Temptations, the Crucifixion, the Resurrection. To Cowley he said he had finished five hundred pages: "It is about Christ in the French army, a corporal with a squad of twelve men—and a general who is Antichrist and takes him upon a hill and offers him the world. Symbolic and unreal, except for 300 wild pages about a three-legged racehorse in Tennessee. Mary Magdalene and the other two Marys."[9] From Faulkner's point of view, Christ will be crucified each time he appears—an idea he may have picked up from reading the "Grand Inquisitor" scene in *The Brothers*

Karamazov. But Faulkner did not need the Russian writer to understand that a fallen, dispossessed America, now caught in the coils of a great conflict, needed sacrifice, crucifixion, repentance.

His development of *A Fable* confirms the validity of his remark that the writer must have the courage to risk "bad taste, clumsiness, mawkishness, dullness."* Faulkner had decided at some point as he reshaped *A Fable* from story to long novel to risk it all, *even though* his linguistic ability had slackened. The largeness of the vision, he felt, preempted other considerations. As for his verbal failure, some of that may be attributed to his work on film scripts, although this is difficult to prove. Film dialogue is so problematic and so apt to be rewritten several times over there is a built-in carelessness or disregard for precision. In most instances, whatever Faulkner wrote was blue- or red-penciled. Under such circumstances, the writer is encouraged to produce broadly, on the assumption that whatever he does will not end up as his. How far this "spoiled" his use of language, or whether his gradual decline in this area was the result of other causes, can never be determined.

It is also interesting that Faulkner saw the original fifty-one-page segment submitted to Ober (received November 17) as a possible play. There had always been a theatrical, dramatic appeal to his work, and many scenes in his greatest novels lend themselves to readings or even dramatic presentations. At the annual Faulkner conferences in Oxford, Mississippi, dramatic readings from Faulkner's major works reveal how theatrically he conceived his material. Particularly illuminating is how he was able to modulate different voices, something that becomes apparent only when he is read aloud: not only black against white, but variations and modulations within each racial community. Further, his work on film scripts led him into forms of theater, in which the spoken word takes on resonances one does not find in the word intended to be read.

As November of 1943 advanced, it became clear Faulkner did not intend to return to Hollywood within the original three-month leave of absence. He had worked sufficiently so that with royalties dribbling in and Hollywood monies, he had earned well over $11,000 for the year, minus agents' fees. Under normal conditions, a family could live on that in Oxford quite well, but he had a long list of creditors, plus he had to support dual (triple, with Maud's) residences for much of 1943. As the year wound down, he was a little further along than in the previous year, in that he had an idea for a book that was shaping itself in his head as it moved from story or play

*In giving his rating of novelists, Faulkner ranked Hemingway, Wolfe, Dos Passos, Caldwell, and then added: "That Wolfe made the best failure because he had the most courage . . . to shoot the works win or lose and damn the torpedoes. That Dos Passos was next since he sacrificed some of the courage to style. That Hemingway was next since he did not have the courage to get out on a limb . . . to risk bad taste, overwriting, dullness, etc." Faulkner had made the remarks in an Ole Miss class, and his comments were carried in the May 11, 1947, New York *Herald Tribune.* Hemingway was deeply wounded and asked his pal Brig. Gen. C. T. Lanham to respond; Faulkner's elucidation of what he said occurs in his letter to Lanham, later (June 28, 1947, to Brig. Gen. C. T. Lanham; *Selected Letters of William Faulkner,* ed. Joseph Blotner [New York: Vintage Books, 1978], p. 251).

form to novel. For Christmas of 1943, he was one of the few adult males of the family in attendance at Rowan Oak; everyone else was spread across the map of the United States or abroad. It was a muted celebration, with Victoria and her husband; Dean's widow, Louise; and Dean's daughter, Dean, as well as, of course, Estelle and Jill.

Work on *A Fable*, which at first Faulkner still thought of as story or play material, gave the year 1944 some continuity. It also brought him back to Hollywood, with his return to work on February 15. This time around, Estelle and Jill joined him for two and one-half months. Hollywood became a little less depressing, since he worked on *To Have and Have Not* and became friendly with Bogart and Bacall. He was also working for Howard Hawks once again, with Meta as script clerk. Faulkner than moved from *To Have and Have Not* to Raymond Chandler's *The Big Sleep*, an assignment which had its rewards as he admired both Chandler and Dashiell Hammett.

Another area, a fateful one for the writer, was his growing involvement with Malcolm Cowley. Cowley would, in a sense, lead into a great Faulkner revival with the publication of his *Portable Faulkner* in 1946; but earlier on he was interested in writing an article on the writer. This article, published on October 29, presaged Cowley's work of resurrection in the *Portable*. Faulkner remained in Hollywood until December of 1944, then returned to Oxford to work on *A Fable*, or early forms of it. He did not return to California until June of 1945.

It was not a distinguished year: no short stories or books published, no plans except those for the fable material, and that still inchoate. Early in the year, on January 8, he told Ober he had finished the first draft of the fable story and had started to rewrite it. He mentions he has to return to Hollywood on February 10, but hopes to complete the rewrite by then. This indicates how still unformed the idea was. Yet when he wrote Haas on January 15, the outline seems to have emerged more clearly. His book is a fable about men who want to stop not only *that* war, but all war. He mentions he will send on fifty to sixty pages of the final draft. What he needs, however, if they like the idea, is an advance from Random House, although money would not be forthcoming for almost another year.

Then, with the fable idea percolating, Faulkner returned to Hollywood, where he joined Hawks on the Hemingway film. With "Battle Cry" shelved, he was fortunate in the way his Hollywood career had gone, although his low salary and the extension of his option to January 22, 1945, were sources of rancor. Resentment built even as he began to work in a hospitable situation with an old friend on a sympathetic project. What was foremost was his continuing fear that his talent was draining away—that with the war, his intense work on film scripts, his need to bring in money to cover his debts, he was ignoring the one part of himself he deemed the most important. In a revealing letter to Ober which covers the period of his life from his return to Hollywood in February to April 22, he runs through his schedule and then reflects upon it. After telling Ober that he has gone slack with *A Fable*, he says Hawks asked for him, threw a script away and told him to start the rewrite. Then he, Faulkner, had the difficult chore of keeping ahead of Hawks as he began to shoot before the script was completed. It was, in its way, like writing a novel as it was being serialized, forced to stay ahead by a week or so, but even more difficult, since a film script was so frequently altered as the shooting proceeded. As we shall see, Faulkner's progression on the Hemingway was not smooth.

This April 22 letter to Ober is full of foreboding:

I dont know when I shall get back at it [*Fable*], maybe then. War is bad for writing, though why I should tell you. This sublimation and glorification of all the cave instincts which man had hopes that he had lived down, dragged back into daylight, usurping pre-empting a place, all the room in fact, in the reality and constancy and solidity of art, writing. Something must give way; let it be the writing, art, it has happened before, will happen again. It's too bad I lived now though. Still too young to be unmoved by the old insidious succubae of trumpets, too old either to make one among them or to be impervious, and therefore too old to write, to have the remaining time to spend waiting for the trumpets and the lightning strokes of glory to have done.

His concluding sentiment is even more dire: "I have a considerable talent, perhaps as good as any coeval. But I am 46 now. So what I will mean soon by 'have' is 'had.' "[10]

His doubts about himself are paralleled by his fears the written word itself may be passé. He observed in the growth of motion pictures and in the temper of the times a disregard for written words, books, the old-fashioned means of communication. This deeply conservative man had to confront what he suspected was a major shift in man's attention span. "After being present for a while at the frantic striving of motion pictures to justify their existence in a time of strife and terror, I have about come to the conclusion which they dare not admit: that the printed word and all its ramifications and photographications is nihil nisi fui [nothing was yet final]; in a word, a dollar mark striving frantically not to DISSOLVE into the symbol 1 A."[11]

This moves Faulkner ahead to a relatively tranquil period when he was focused on *To Have and Have Not*, although at the beginning it was not so smooth. As part of the mysterious ways in which studios acted, he was removed from the Hemingway project only three days after starting on it and shifted to *God Is My Co-Pilot*, an immensely successful book by Colonel Robert Lee Scott combining great adventure episodes with inspirational material. Faulkner realized when he read the existing script that there was a split between the adventure elements and the attempt to use action as a means of revealing God's intervention in man's activities. But his perception of what was wrong meant an almost complete rewrite to introduce a sin or crime which could justify divine intervention. This kind of script doctoring was not in any sense meaningful work. The brief work here coincided with Faulkner's moving in with Bezzerides and his wife and two children, so as to save rent and to be sure of having a ride to the studio. (Estelle and Jill had not yet arrived.) Bezzerides lived just outside Santa Monica, at 621 N. Saltair.

Faulkner was unhappy with *God Is My Co-Pilot* and wanted out, as he told Hal Wallis. He was refused permission to work at home, and he felt so frustrated that the usual pattern began: heavy drinking, indifference, frustration. He was, however, removed from this unattractive project and placed back on the Hemingway with Hawks. He would shortly enter a strange period in his life, as Cowley, intent on "resurrecting" Faulkner, asked him to delve into himself and his earlier work, particularly the great period around *Sound:* past met uncertain present and even more uncertain future. Cowley was returning to vintage Faulkner, while the writer was himself stalled and mired.

Some pluses on the set, besides Hawks, were, of course, Meta and Bogart, also Bacall and Hoagy Carmichael, all of whom he liked. Faulkner's cowriter on the script was a professional, Jules Furthman, who commanded a salary six or seven times his own. Furthman knew films; Faulkner did not. One provided know-how, the experience which shaped a scene; Faulkner supplied words. The method was improvisation, writing to the moment, as it were, as the cameras rolled.

In crafting the film, Faulkner left Hemingway well behind, except for catching some of the atmosphere, and altered the characters so they reflected Bogart and Bacall. Hemingway's Harry Morgan was not the kind of American a studio wished to present to a wartime audience, and he was rewritten to become politically and morally acceptable. Carrying over some of the esprit de corps from his de Gaulle script, Faulkner made the villains into Vichyites collaborating with the Germans, and turned Morgan into an American caught up in his country's fight for survival. Bacall became "Slim," a distinctly American type combining toughness and sentiment. But in a script frequently rewritten as it was being filmed, it is difficult to distinguish Faulkner's contribution from Furthman's. Both received film credits for the screenplay.

Meta by then was contemplating Estelle's arrival with loathing. Faulkner of course foresaw Meta's resentment and anger, and tells her nothing has to change. " 'We can go on as we have.' " But she explains Jill is almost a teenager and Estelle knows about them; everything *has* changed. Meta perceives herself as mistress, while the wife and child come first. Faulkner seems blind to her humiliation, while she misjudges his need for stability even when it involves the tension of living with his wife. His and Meta's relationship was permanently altered by this new move, and although they resumed it after a brief period of coolness, it was winding down. They stayed away from each other during the family's time in

Hollywood (from June 24 to September 7), and then got together again after they left. Of course, Faulkner needed to drink heavily to get through this period, although he held up at the studio.

It was all in all a fallow period, in which he marked time by drinking steadily at Musso-Frank's, eschewing more celebrated invitations from Hawks, Bogart, and others. He preferred drinking with familiar faces like Jo Pagano, or by himself, the solitary man from Yoknapatawpha on a mission to a strange territory. In the cosmopolitan atmosphere of the studio, where men of such different backgrounds had come together to write and shoot films, Faulkner felt himself receding into worlds within worlds, getting ever further from his base where his imagination could shape *his* material, not Hemingway's or Chandler's, not the co-pilot's or God's. He had skewered himself. The only way to deal with it was apparently to settle back with nonthreatening people and drink away the hours. What he especially wanted to avoid was anyone who tried to talk to him about his work. And while some of this reticence derived from his being a private man, part of it also came from his embarrassment that he was not producing anything at the present time. During this period, when *To Have and Have Not* was winding down, he wrote Ober about feeling useless, fearing the printed word itself was indistinguishable from the dollar mark.

Faulkner worked on the Hemingway script until May 13, although his main bout of writing was completed by the first of the month. In all he produced 118 pages of a revised script, and the film was released on October 11, 1944. Treatment was listed as being by Howard Hawks and Ernest Hemingway; screenplay by William Faulkner and Jules Furthman; revisions by Faulkner, Furthman, Hawks, and "Stuttering Sam." The cast of Bogart, Bacall, and Carmichael was enhanced by Walter Brennan and Marcel Dalio.

Then on May 7, 1944, Faulkner wrote a letter to Cowley which proved very important to his career. All Faulkner lacked to lift him from his present situation was the recognition of his past achievement, something that went beyond reviews of his work. Up to this point, there had been insightful pieces on him, but nothing that brought together the entire body of his work. He needed recognition that carried beyond the seriatim notices of his books as they appeared—something that created a continuity of recognition and an authorial presence on the cultural scene. It had long since happened with Hemingway and Fitzgerald; but he had proven more intractable, perhaps because of the insensitivity of professional staff reviewers and the difficulties his more innovative novels created. He demanded a good deal more of his readers than did any of his major contemporaries, and he antagonized many reviewers who were unwilling or unable to learn how to read him.

Cowley wanted to provide a corrective. In February of 1944 he had written Faulkner about his plan to assess his career in an extended essay. At that time, Cowley was putting together *The Portable Hemingway*, and his subsequent work on Faulkner led to *The Portable Faulkner,* which helped to invest the writer's individual works with the sense of a coherent career. At this time—and it seems difficult to believe—Faulkner's works were hardly obtainable, and even the largest libraries did not carry him. Cowley reports that the New York Public Library had copies of only *A Green Bough* and *The Hamlet.* Others might be found in secondhand bookstores, but not readily, and then only in New York or other large cities. Outside urban areas, Faulkner had barely penetrated. Cowley himself had not been exactly a supporter, but had blown hot and cold in his reviews of Faulkner's books as they came out, and rarely gave the writer his due. While a more intelligent reader than Fadiman or the reviewers who controlled the front page of the *New York Times Book Review,* Cowley had not perceived Faulkner's overwhelming talent and great accomplishment.

He set out to change this. As was his way, Faulkner put aside Cowley's letter received in February until May 7, probably because it did not contain any return postage—these letters Faulkner opened to get the stamps and then dumped the missives in a drawer. Incidentally, he continued this habit after he had received the Nobel Prize, a sign perhaps of contempt for all correspondents, or else an obsessive parsimony. After some persiflage in which he informed Cowley that people write him either to request money or to tell him he has no talent, he gets to the point. "I would like very much to have the piece done. I think (at 46) that I have worked too hard at my (elected or doomed, I dont know which) trade, with pride, but I believe not vanity, with plenty of ego but with humility too (being a poet, of course I give no fart for glory) to leave no better mark on this our pointless chronicle than I seem to be about to leave."[12] He mentions he is working in the salt mines, but Cowley is welcome to come and share his cubbyhole of an apartment until June 1, when he expected Estelle and Jill. He indicates he would like the piece, "except the biography part." It was at this point Faulkner began to back away from his deceptive war stories, and started to move closer to the record—that he was in the Royal Air Force in Canada, and that was it.

"You are welcome to it [biography] privately, of course. But I think that if what one has thought and hoped and endeavored and failed at is not enough, if it must be explained and excused by what he has experienced, done or suffered, while he was not being an artist, then he and the one making the evaluation have both failed." It was, all in all, a warm reception. Cowley responded on July 22 at great length, busy though he was with *The Portable Hemingway.* He says he would like to meet Faulkner, although it would be possible to go ahead with the article without a personal encounter; and the biographical data, he agrees, are not essential, although such material would make him feel more secure. Cowley then provides a rather brutal accounting of Faulkner's standing in the New York literary market. His letter is worth quoting at some length since it offers a good glimpse into Faulkner's reputation just six years before he received the Nobel Prize.

"It's about what I suggested in my other letter—very funny, and a great credit to you, but bad for your pocketbook. First, in publishing circles your name is mud. They are all convinced that your books won't ever sell, and it's a pity, isn't it? they say with a sort of pleased look on their faces. . . . the bright boys among the critics did a swell job of incomprehending and unselling you, Fadiman especially." But now, Cowley said, things are different.*

You hear almost nothing but admiration, and the better the writer the greater the admiration is likely to be. Conrad Aiken, for example, puts you at the top of the heap. The funny thing is the academic and near-academic critics and the way they misunderstand and misstate your work. You probably haven't read Maxwell Geismar's book, *Writers in Crisis*, but he's not so dumb for a professor [Geismar was not, although some of his criticism qualified him to be a professor at the University of Mars] and does a very good job on Hemingway, but when he comes to Faulkner you might as well have written your novels in Minian or Hittite for all the sense he makes of them.[13]

Cowley then indicates that if he can overcome indolence, he will write something. But first he wants to find out about Faulkner's use of symbolism, and he quotes Cleanth Brooks's analysis of the symbolism of *Sanctuary*. It was not Brooks, however, but George Marion O'Donnell, and he had said that Temple Drake was the South, raped by modern industry (Popeye), which, because of its sterility, needed a substitute. Cowley doesn't indicate what the corncob might mean within this industrial rape of the Old South; but he does recognize such interpretations of symbolism as reductive and simplistic. He wonders how much of the symbolism is deliberate, how much unconscious. Faulkner did not respond to this July 22 letter until early November, three and a half months later.

*Cowley felt even Random House was not working hard enough to put Faulkner across, and that the writer might consider another house. He thought of Scribner's, where the reigning monarch was Maxwell Perkins, a myth in his time and matched perhaps only by Robert Giroux in a later era. Perkins, earlier, had considered bidding for Faulkner's books —he had read *Sanctuary* and considered it a horrible novel by a very talented writer. Perkins thought he could bring Faulkner to Scribner's rather easily, since none of his books except *Sanctuary* had sold. The story was that the renowned editor feared Hemingway's wrath if he brought Faulkner in. Hemingway could tolerate Fitzgerald and Wolfe, but Faulkner was a different kind of competition, perhaps someone better; and what Hemingway wanted, Scribner's did. Later, when Cowley thought the time was ripe for Scribner's to acquire a distinguished author, he went to Perkins—by now, Faulkner had published over a dozen works of fiction, nearly all out of print, and with six houses. But on this occasion, Perkins was not interested and pronounced Faulkner as finished. He perhaps felt that Faulkner's future production was uncertain, although in the mid-1940s, this was not easy to judge. The real problem for Perkins was that for all his dedication to the craft of editing and to publishing fine books, he was not happy with an innovator or with a difficult writer. One way to view his editing of Wolfe was as a regularizer, making Wolfe more traditional than his stream-writing suggested. Also, Perkins was losing his edge—so that dealing with Faulkner and with his reputation as a demanding, querulous author was too much. Cowley came away empty-handed.

In the meanwhile, he was not worried about symbolism in his work. He was worried about a number of other things: assignments to new movies when *To Have and Have Not* wound down; the arrival of his family; his ongoing affair with Meta; the uncertain future of his career; his still-inadequate finances, even with Hollywood money. There was a new man in his life, Jerry Wald, a kind of Sammy Glick–figure who spun off so many ideas some were bound to be workable. Blotner reports a few, and they suggest a great sense of humor: a remake of *Anna Karenina* with Vronsky as a test pilot; a movie based on *For Whom the Bell Tolls*, in which the Spanish antigovernment forces become a band of outlaws in Wyoming; and a movie version of Joyce's *Ulysses*. All three ended up on film, but not quite in the way Wald indicated.

Faulkner told Ober about his new project, *The Damned Don't Cry*. "It is one of the usual turkeys (a novel, good title but little else) which (God know why) studios pay 40,000 dollars for." He adds: "I told Wald I thought it was napoo. He said all right, throw it away [it had already passed through three writers], that what we wanted was some 'Faulkner' in a picture. He said he wanted the story of a southern girl born on wrong side of tracks, trying to raise herself." Faulkner recalled he had invented that very character in his own short story, "The Brooch" (which appeared in *Scribner's* in 1936, not 1938, as Faulkner remembers it). He had also worked over this same film property earlier, when the script of *The Damned Don't Cry* was sent to him at Oxford for doctoring. Then, Faulkner found the material intractable, for the story met few expectations, and the woman with an illegitimate child is neither heroic nor practical. But Faulkner's interest now, in May of 1944, went further; he thought Wald should reimburse him for the use of the story. "If the studio paid a lot of money for the novel, and invested more money in three failed screen plays, they should pay something more to get some of the investment back."[14] He wanted Ober to act as his agent for the sale.

Wald, however, was having no part of that. With shrewd insight into Faulkner's predicament, he told the writer not to get the studio stirred up or angry. Instead, Faulkner should complete the treatment (he had seventy-nine pages by early June), submit the treatment with "The Brooch," and then let the studio decide whether to throw the entire project away or accept it. At that stage, bring in the agent. Faulkner agreed, although he was, of course, being finessed. He was charged to *The Damned Don't Cry* from May 15 to June 10. His treatment was not used.*

Within two days of completing his assignment on that treatment, he moved over to *The Adventures of Don Juan* with Wald, who despite his reputation as a cutthroat treated Faulkner with considerable respect. Here Faulkner's job was to revise a screenplay by Herbert Dalmas, although Faulkner's own work was overridden by George Oppenheimer and Harry

---

*The Damned Don't Cry was finally released in April of 1950, with screen credits going to Harold Medford and Jerome Weidman; directed by Jerry Wald and starring Joan Crawford. In the original treatment—the discarded one—Faulkner was aided by Gertrude Walker.

Kurnitz. Wald directed, and the movie, released in December of 1945, starred Errol Flynn and Viveca Lindfors. It was a time of some tension for Faulkner, for his work on this dismal project coincided with the eventual arrival of Estelle and Jill. In the meantime, he approved Ober's sale of his story "Two Soldiers" for a radio series. In the line provided Whit Burnett as to why he liked the story, Faulkner said because it portrays a "type which I admire. . . . an independent creature with courage and bottom and heart—a creature which is not vanishing, even though every articulate medium we have—radio, moving pictures, magazines—is busy night and day telling us that it has vanished, has become a sentimental and bragging liar."[15] He still looked forward to a deal on "The Brooch" property.

But the tension was palpable: his family arrived more than three weeks after he had planned, on June 24, not the first. He had entered an estranged period with Meta, already cited. His work on movie scripts was not rewarding—he was being used as a common laborer, tinkering here, writing pages there, but generating little of value to him or, apparently, to the studio. His own work lay in abeyance—*A Fable* was still a fragmentary idea. He could see little end to his present circumstances.

Yet another factor lay deep below the surface. It was something which profoundly affected his work after *Go Down, Moses*. He was changing as a writer as a consequence of his movie writing. One of Faulkner's most concentrated periods of film treatment and scripting came in the war period, and as a result he had been writing materials which demanded to be moralistic, sermonistic, educational. He had been caught up in the patriotic fervor of Hollywood, particularly at Warner Brothers, where Jack Warner was sensitive to what the government needed. Much of Faulkner's most important work on treatments and scripts had come with "The de Gaulle Story" and "Battle Cry." Sermonizing was explicit in nearly every scene of "Battle Cry" and in much of the de Gaulle material. Whether he recognized it or not, Faulkner was being drawn into a different kind of mental activity from what he had experienced in his work in the 1930s.

He was also getting older, and with that, more conservative, literarily. But along with aging was the need to turn out lines and scenes which directed the audience to particular ends. The open-endedness of fiction, *his* fiction, was being sacrificed to a predetermined, patriotic end. It was inevitably to lead to changes in Faulkner's own imagination. He was profoundly touched by the work he was doing, even when the work was itself the source of considerable resentment. He flattened out, he directed sentiments, his work became heuristic, reductive. Even his work on *A Fable*, a book undeserving of simplification, demonstrates how the war years in Hollywood penetrated his imagination and drove him toward moralizing. Faulkner felt he could separate himself into his Hollywood half and his professional writing half; but that proved to be an illusion. In fact, much against his conscious will, he was interpenetrated by Hollywood. Not only *A Fable* but *Intruder in the Dust* and the last two parts of the Snopes trilogy suggest how dependent he became on attitudes formed during scriptwriting. The bottom line for him had become not only the money he earned in Hollywood, but the nature of the experience.

There was another even more subtle result of the Hollywood years that is difficult to measure, but impossible to ignore. Because so many of the treatments and scripts he worked on were not used—either discarded or else reworked so that his contribution was buried—he was being conditioned to failure or wastage. It was a bizarre situation for a writer, and perhaps the reason why Hollywood experiences generally proved unfruitful. As Faulkner was shifted from job to job, he became accustomed to doing a segment here and there, doctoring someone else's script, providing a lengthy treatment and watching it shelved or being moved on to the next writer. Unlike his work on novels, there was little sense of continuity or completion, little sense of that sustained effort which sees something through. What he may have gained in craft, he lost in conditioning to failure, to waste, to studio indecision about what the public wanted. This was poor conditioning for the novelist, for Faulkner had always crafted his novels from within, from what *he* wanted. Now it was a question of what an amorphous audience wanted, and what the studio, as a supplier of dreams, could offer. All this was psychologically and emotionally wearing. Unable to help himself or to counter it, Faulkner was increasingly keyed into sermonizing or audience expectations.

Estelle and Jill arrived and settled into his small apartment near the Cedars of Lebanon Hospital off Sunset Boulevard. Faulkner's primary function as father to Jill seemed to center on his arrangements for her to ride horses at Jack House's Glendale stables. During their visit, which lasted until September 7, Faulkner worked on *Fog over London,* a remake of *The Amazing Dr. Clitterhouse,* a 1938 film with Edward G. Robinson, screenplay by John Huston and John Wexley. In the original, Dr. Clitterhouse researched the ways personality changed as the result of commission of crimes; he finally decided to become a criminal to test out his own theories. Faulkner altered him into a psychiatrist—already a chimerical change given the writer's antipathy to such procedures—whose split personality derives from a need to remedy injustice. Two treatments of the original material were made, one in July and another in August.

This dismal undertaking did not last long, and Faulkner moved on to another project on July 12, a remake of *The Petrified Forest.* The original movie, based on a play by Robert Sherwood, had been released in 1936. When Faulkner and Bezzerides worked on the remake, it was called "Strangers in Our Midst," but when that remake was released, it was called *Escape in the Desert* (May 1945), with no mention of Faulkner or Bezzerides, Thomas Job getting the credit. The first *Petrified* had a sensational cast—Bogart and Leslie Howard, among others—and concerned criminals escaping to a desert hotel. In the remake, the war intruded, and the desert hotel of the original was now the refuge of Nazis fleeing from an internment camp. Faulkner looked on this assignment with nothing but contempt, and he and his friend wrote scenes which were unusable. While the matter with Cowley and his essay was being worked out in the distance, Faulkner flitted from movie to movie. Cowley produced part of his piece, "William Faulkner's Human Comedy," with its bow to Balzac, for the *New York Times Book Review*, October 29. None of this made any difference, however, in the summer of 1944, when Faulkner was shifted around like a pawn, for the time being a hack writer. By early August, he was off *The Petrified Forest*. His personal life had been complicated by Estelle's arrival, and it is not altogether clear to what extent he continued to see Meta secretly. With Estelle, he entered into some of the party routine, something he possibly had to do to entertain her and to show her the famous, celebrated side of the colony. Jack Warner gave huge parties, and the Faulkners attended these as well as small dinner engagements, with the Gary Coopers and others.

In August he returned to *God Is My Co-Pilot*. He tinkered for a brief while with the treatment of the Scott autobiography and was soon moved on to another project, probably *The Big Sleep*, although *The Southerner* fell across this general period. But the latter film was an independent action on Faulkner's part, outside of a studio, and his work on it is not precisely clear. *God Is My Co-Pilot* did not take much of his time. It was released in March of 1945, produced by Buckner, with a script credited to Peter Milne, starring Dennis Morgan, Raymond Massey, Alan Hale, and Dane Clark.

Faulkner was drinking heavily, evidence he had withdrawn and become unreachable. Although he genuinely liked having his family with him, even with the tensions, his working conditions up to *The Big Sleep* were unbearable. As his salary rose in multiples of $50 per week, the work itself seemed to be getting worse. *The Big Sleep*, however, provided a respite. Not only was he with Hawks and a congenial cast, he saw Meta, who was present as script clerk. But before he appeared on this scene, he returned once more to *Fog over London*, the Clitterhouse project, for the second treatment. This lasted only two weeks, and finally he had a congenial assignment in the scripting of the Chandler novel. Faulkner worked on the screenplay in August and September, through the remainder of Estelle and Jill's stay. When they left, he moved back in with Bezzerides.

After *The Big Sleep* passed from his hands in late October, Faulkner moved on to *Mildred Pierce*, to carve a movie from James M. Cain's novel. Faulkner's work on this screenplay—his was the second one attempted—was eventually buried, and he received no credits. But at the very moment he was moving on to an uncongenial piece of hackwork, Cowley published the first part of his longer piece on Faulkner. Cowley sent on a passage from the essay, about *Absalom*:

First of all he was writing a story, and one that affected him deeply, but he was also brooding over a social situation. More or less unconsciously, the incidents in the story came to represent the forces and elements in the social situation, since the mind naturally works in terms of symbols and parallels. In Faulkner's case, this form of parallelism is not confined to Absalom, Absalom! It can be found in the whole fictional framework that he has been elaborating in novel after novel, until his work has become a myth or legend of the South.[16]

Here was criticism, appearing in a prominent and influential newspaper, which set Faulkner in time and place with a generous assessment of his accomplishment. As Cowley worked his way into the larger piece of criticism, he fixed Faulkner, for good or ill, for future generations. The writer answered the critic at considerable length in early November. He suggested that Cowley seemed to be doing all right and did not need his prereading of the piece. Faulkner went on to agree with the idea that he is telling a story, but that that is incidental to his real function:

> ... taking my output (the course of it) as a whole I am telling the same story over and over, which is myself and the world. . . . This I think accounts for what people call the obscurity, the involved formless "style," endless sentences. I'm trying to say it all in one sentence, between one Cap and one period. . . . I'm inclined to think that my material, the South, is not very important to me. I just happen to know it, and dont have time in one life to learn another one and write at the same time. Though the one I know is probably as good as another, life is a phenomenon but not a novelty, the same frantic steeplechase toward nothing everywhere and man stinks the same stink no matter where in time.[17]

He adds he is trying to go a step further than even Thomas Wolfe, whose insistent "I" attempts to embrace the world.

In *Absalom,* he says, "I think Quentin, not Faulkner, is the correct yardstick here, I was writing the story, but he not I was brooding over a situation. . . . He grieved and regretted the passing of an order the dispossessor of which he was not tough enough to understand. But more he grieved the fact (because he hated and feared the portentous symbol) that a man like Sutpen, who to Quentin was trash, originless, could not only have dreamed so high but have the force and strength to have failed so grandly." Faulkner generalizes: "Art is simpler than people think because there is so little to write about. All the moving things are eternal in man's history and have been written before, and if a man writes hard enough, sincerely enough, humbly enough, and, with the unalterable determination never never never to be quite satisfied with it he will repeat them, because art like poverty takes care of its own, shares its bread."

He notes that beginning in December he will be free of Hollywood for six months, but must return because of a seven-year contract with Warners. He mentions an offer from Doubleday for a nonfiction book about the Mississippi River, which he rejects for the time being. (Later in his career, he wrote for *Holiday* a long essay on the Mississippi.) He is optimistic he can do without the fee ($5,000 advance) and compartmentalize his Hollywood work and his serious writing—six months for one, six months for the other. "I'm like the old mare who has been bred and dropped foals 15–16 times, and she has a feeling that she had only 3 or 4 more in her, and cant afford to spend one on something from outside." He indicates he is working on something now, the fable piece for Bacher and Hathaway, with seventy pages sent on to Random House.

The interchange with Cowley went on hold for several months. Cowley had not mentioned that he had been urging Viking to do a *Portable Faulkner* and had been met with tepid responses. Viking (which had once tried to acquire Faulkner) felt his audience was too limited and his literary standing too dubious; that such an enterprise would have no sale. Cowley then began to publish parts of his long essay, first in the *New York Times Book Review*, then in the *Saturday Review* (where Harrison Smith presided) and the *Southern Review* (edited by Allen Tate). With that, sufficient interest was generated so that Viking asked Cowley to go ahead. As far as Faulkner was concerned, this was future news: Cowley did not tell him until August 9, 1945, that there would be a *Portable*. He said not to expect much of a sale.

The entire episode with Cowley had a certain ironic side. For even as the literary critic was starting to establish Faulkner's reputation as one of his country's truly great writers, Faulkner was rewriting the original script of *Mildred Pierce*. He felt more than ever indentured to an unjust contract. Michael Curtiz made suggestions on the script; Faulkner listened in silence, then got up and walked out. His solution was to drink himself into oblivion, and only the intervention of Pagano and another writer, Tom Reed, saved him from being discovered and dropped. Faulkner's hatred of Herndon increased, and he told Bezzerides he wanted to carve him up. Bezzerides was more upset by the drinking than possible murder, fearful Faulkner would drink himself beyond the point of return and seriously damage himself. What he did not know was that Faulkner was a physical marvel, with organs so resistant to damage he could last this way for another eighteen years. At that point, his heart, probably damaged by the excesses of fifty years of alcohol, gave way.

But Faulkner did need outside help. For all his devotion, Bezzerides, often aided by Pagano, could not handle the situation. Trips to the sanitarium were in order, at least two in which Faulkner had become so weakened and malnourished he needed intense medical attention. The familiar cycle was there: the inability to resolve his degradation at the hands of someone like Curtiz or Warner Brothers; his sinking into oblivion as a way of gaining strength for a new foray; and his utter dependence on friends to be there when he needed them for salvation from real damage and even death. It was the "mother syndrome," Bezzerides, Pagano, and Reed coming to the rescue, handling him like a small child, providing nourishment and medical attention.

The assignment to *Mildred Pierce* fortunately ended by December 2, and Faulkner returned to *The Big Sleep*, rewriting and counting the days until he could leave for Oxford. His release came on December 13, without pay. He also had to say goodbye to Meta. His words to her, if she is accurate, were signs of his real fear: "I'll never get it [the new novel] written in this town. Sometimes I think if I do one more treatment or screenplay, I'll lose whatever power I have as a writer.' "[18] But his fear had already become something of a reality, for his work in Hollywood left a mark on everything he wrote henceforth.

After assuring her he would miss her at every moment, Faulkner parted from her until the following June, when he returned for what became his final long stint. She tells of his letters, mainly filled with tales of Estelle: she was tippling, drunk by nightfall, becoming slovenly. It was a familiar pattern of the older male gaining pity for his unhappy marriage, solidifying a relationship with the younger woman by stressing his dependence on her love and compassion as against his wife's indifference or even hostility. In point of fact, Estelle was out of control; he had his writing, whereas she had nothing except buried lost causes, whatever they were.

On December 12, Faulkner took the train to Oxford, working on the script of *The Big Sleep* as the train headed east. He sent back twelve pages, rewritten and retyped in Oxford; that ended his involvement with Hollywood for the time being. He accompanied the pages with a laconic note, thanking the studio "for the cheerful and crowded day coach which alone saved him from wasting his time in dull and profitless rest and sleep."[19] Oxford, however, did not mean salvation. All the familiar tensions were there: not only Estelle, but countless bills, obligations, duties, chores, interruptions. The war was winding down, and there was less anxiety on that account, although several huge, wasting struggles were still to come. But the opening of the second front in June of 1944, and the rapid advance of the Allied armies across Europe, indicated the fascists were on the run.

It was with his personal problems in mind that Faulkner wrote to Ober about Doubleday's generous offer to bail him out, offering $5,000 (a large advance for the day) for a nonfiction book on the Mississippi River, a kind of reprise of Twain's *Life on the Mississippi*. But the project found Faulkner uncertain, grateful for the offer, but fearful his real talent would dry up while he pursued something outside his mainstream career.

> . . . I am grateful to the blokes who thought of it, very pleased and comforted that such men exist, not just on my account but for the sake of writing, art, and artists, in America and the world. . . . [But] I have never done a book of that sort, never had the notion to do one, and so I don't know exactly where to begin. So in a sense that means to learn a new trade at age of 47 . . . starting 'cold,' without that speck of fire, that coal, from which a book or a picture should burst almost of its own accord. I am 47. I have 3 more books of my own I want to write. I am like an aging mare, who has say three more gestations in

her before her time is over, and doesn't want to spend one of them breeding what she considers (wrongly perhaps) a mule.[20]

Faulkner says he must think about it a little longer, get Hollywood out of his system. "I would not insult the men who made the offer possible by taking the money for anything less than my best; if I did that, the whole purpose of the offer would be exploded, as I would be morally and spiritually in Hollywood." With this thought, and uncertainty about his future, he closed out 1944. In the next year, he felt cheered that the new book was percolating to such an extent; he felt excitement; he was coming into something new.

Chapter Twenty-two

Postbellum

F OR FAULKNER, 1945 was a curious year; it was as if his career were somehow paralleling what was occurring in the country at large. The year saw the end of military hostilities with Germany and Japan: the savage fighting in Europe, the destruction of a good part of Germany's cities, the devastation of Japan in the dropping of two atomic bombs. While America celebrated the ending of the war, the dropping of the bombs, especially the second one on Nagasaki, left the country with mixed feelings —that perhaps a different means to end the war might have been attempted. For most, however, what counted was its termination. Yet even as the war ended and millions of refugees started to crisscross Europe, the seeds for future conflict were being planted: another kind of war for which blame would be assigned and reassigned. By analogy, Faulkner saw the end of his own conflict—he had returned from Hollywood and was ready to resume his serious career. But in Oxford he found all the seeds of his discontent, of a different kind and degree. In Hollywood, he had been free but professionally thwarted; in Oxford, he was tied down but professionally liberated. He had, like the country, exchanged one circumstance for another, one sequence of events for a different level of experience.

He needed money, and Random House agreed to advance what he needed. *To Have and Have Not,* one of his most successful screenplay ventures, was released, and he received credits. He did significant work on

A Fable, but foresaw a long incubating and developmental period—it was not to be one of his relatively quick jobs, such as he once gloried in. In June he returned to Hollywood at $500 per week—not an insignificant amount, but still far less than what others received. He would return to Oxford by October 18 and complete what came to be known as the "Compson Appendix," one of his most significant pieces of writing since *Go Down, Moses.* He attempted to break the Warners contract, but the studio insisted on the letter of the law: that it owned all he wrote since he signed the contract. He corresponded at length with Cowley about the upcoming *Portable Faulkner* and seemed to recognize that it would change the course of his life. He published no books or stories in this year; stories would be few and far between in the coming years.

Faulkner began 1945 with a revealing letter to Cerf and Haas at Random House, charting his development up to this point. He states that what he is writing and thinking about is "pretty good." "Unless I am wrong about it, have reached that time of an artist's increasing years when he no longer can judge what he is doing. I have grown up at last. All my writing life I have been a poet without education, who possessed only instinct and a fierce conviction and belief in the worth and truth of what he was doing, and an illimitable courage for rhetoric (personal pleasure in it too! I admit it) and who knew and cared for little else."[1] He adds a thought already noted: "Well, I'm doing something different now, so different that I am writing and rewriting, weighing every word, which I never did before; I used to bang it on like an apprentice paper hanger and never look back." He knows this project will take longer than he had thought, and he is running out of money. He has six months to take care of before his next stint in Hollywood: six months off, six months on. He asks for two or three thousand, if he needs it, about March—a request Haas immediately agrees to. He still sees the new project as connected to William Bacher's idea (for which he was advanced $1,000) and he still sees it as a play. On a carbon of the same letter, Faulkner asks Ober whether, in the event Random House rejects his request for an advance, he could get him some money on the strength of forty to fifty pages.

With the "fable" material pressing, it was predictable that Faulkner would reject the Mississippi River book, which he did in a letter to Ober on January 24. He hedged somewhat, in case of a real need for the money, but the entire drift of his thought was to follow his talent before he returned to Hollywood. He was, in fact, incubating a novel for the first time in ten years—in one respect or another, everything since *Absalom* had been "stories," whether the long ones of *The Wild Palms,* the briefer ones of *The Unvanquished,* or the complicated, intertwined ones of *The Hamlet* and *Go Down, Moses.*

It is unclear if Faulkner understood fully what was happening to him. He knew the years were flying away, that he was in danger of losing his grip; but there is little direct indication that he recognized how profoundly Hollywood had reshaped his imagination and made its indelible impression on his future work. His remarks indicate he thought he could still divide and subdivide himself: so much for Hollywood, so much for Faulkner, so much for long, intricate novels, so much for other books. He seemed to forget, in his need to put Hollywood behind him, the cardinal rule of a serious writer: the need for continuity in that which he does best; not interruptions for other kinds of work, not relaxation, but that intensive work which leads either to burnout or to mature development. European authors had always been better than Americans at maintaining this intensity. If Faulkner needed any indication of what could happen, he had Hemingway and Fitzgerald as prize exhibits.

He settled down to a manuscript that was perhaps the most critical of his life. He was going to invest a good part of his mature life in one book —as it turned out the entire stretch of his middle to later career was carried in *A Fable*. It was a daunting experience for this man for whom facility had been a trademark—facility in both original composition and in revision. If this book failed, or failed to satisfy him, then he had frittered away a good part of the time remaining to him. This was the personal burden under which he attacked the almost intractable material of *A Fable*. This was possibly the book which would catch the eye of the Nobel Prize committee—although as it turned out he won the prize four years before the novel finally appeared.

Refreshed by his ability to tackle with intensity an ongoing long project, Faulkner began to feel the shadow of another Hollywood stint. In mid-March—he would have to return in June—he rehashed to his understanding agent how he had been trapped by Herndon. It was an explanation he had given several times before; but Geller had indicated in December that perhaps one more long run would fulfill the contract. Yet Faulkner feared they might force him to sign another seven-year contract at more money, when, in fact, he wanted a one-year commitment only. He refused to mortgage his future "any longer than the expiration of this one." "If they had any judgment of people, they would have realised before now they would get a damn sight more out of me by throwing away any damned written belly-clutching contract and let us work together on simple good faith and decency, like with you and Random House."[2] He then commented on his ongoing book. "It may be my epic poem. Good story: the crucifixion and the resurrection. I had about 100,000 words, rewrote them down to about 15,000 now. I had my usual vague foundationless dream of getting enough money to live on out of it while I wrote and finished it. But I ought to know now I dont sell and never will earn enough outside of pictures to stay out of debt." Bitterness, frustration, uncertainty about his future were all implicit in these relatively mild words to Ober, who had become the repository of his deepest feelings.

When Whit Burnett asked for "Two Soldiers" for his anthology, *Time To Be Young,* but wanted certain words vetted ("hell" and "nigger"*), Faulkner agreed. He demanded, caustically, an asterisk at each point of alteration, and asked for $50, not the $25 proffered. He supplied no photograph, no comment, nothing—his usual practice. Burnett printed the story as it was originally written. Meanwhile Cowley was publishing another segment of his long essay, which Harrison Smith ran in the *Saturday Review* for April. It caught Faulkner's life at a crossroads. He was of course interested in what Cowley was doing for him, but he was also coming more and more to the realization that his work in Hollywood and his indentured position with Herndon had to terminate. He was like a man being periodically choked and then freed to be given the opportunity to start breathing again. A legal technicality was destroying the quality of his life. This all surfaced on July 25 when he told Herndon he was finished paying him any commission as of August 18, 1945.

Meanwhile, Cowley had moved Faulkner into ethereal company, comparing him with such classic American authors as Hawthorne.[3] Cowley was not all reverence; he found fault in Faulkner's style, and some rhetoric bothered him. But he did not dwell on these matters. Instead, he set Faulkner in a context of mythmaking, of writing a poetic form of fiction, and of creating a literary version of the Southern legend. It was, for the time, a solid piece of criticism—even-handed and yet catching some of Faulkner's reach. Where it faltered was in Cowley's failure to see how Faulkner had shifted the whole nature of American modernism; how he and almost he alone had absorbed European literary lessons and transformed such methods into distinctly American forms. Cowley also failed to see how Faulkner's use of memory and technical strategies were interlinked with his sense of history, so that in his major works the historical sense comes to us as a unique version of our past. As a traditional critic, Cowley was not drawn to technical virtuosity—but Faulkner, by 1945, could not be discussed without regard for his use of strategies no other American writer was utilizing. Cowley tended to capture Faulkner's literary uniqueness in his linkage to the South, rather than in his broader relationship to modern life.

Nevertheless, the essay was hugely welcome as an enhancement of Faulkner's reputation. Cowley wrote him on August 9 about what he planned to do in the *Portable;* by that time the critic had received a letter from Phil Stone. The latter was monitoring Faulkner's career from the

---

*Despite the derogatory usage, Faulkner—as a forerunner of how he would later help individual Negroes—assisted a local black named Joe C. Brown. They had met, and Faulkner invited the young man out to Rowan Oak to discuss his poetry. In a letter of January 25, the writer sent on his telephone number and in the second letter (January 29?) (both letters are in typescript at the Alderman Library, University of Virginia), he made some changes in a poem Brown had written about black aspirations for freedom. Faulkner warned that passion had become rhetoric, feeling had turned into sermon—an ironical comment given his own penchant for this in his 1940s and 1950s work.

vantage of his law practice in Mississippi, as though fearful someone might steal *his* Faulkner; he seemed certain that anyone else who tried to understand the writer was an interloper, if not a complete fool. Stone admitted the article was the best he'd seen on Faulkner, but that was faint praise. His major point was that Faulkner often introduced material (such as the story of the cow) without any regard for a "comprehensive sense of design." Stone, of course, read Faulkner literally, disallowing the stylistic rhythms which privileged interruptions. But his chief criticism was utterly damning: that Faulkner was only rewriting *Sanctuary* with every novel. He condemned the characters by saying they all talk like William Faulkner. Stone was pursuing his own demon, using Cowley's essay as a way of trying to retrieve what he now saw as a golden age when the young and callow Billy depended on only one person, Phil Stone.[4]

Faulkner never replied directly to Stone's ill-advised attacks on him, attacks that went to the heart of his greatest works and simply ignored achievement in favor of weakness. By May, he was looking ahead with dread to returning to Hollywood in early June. What awaited him there was the usual hack work, although he would pick up again with Meta. But even that relationship, so important to him and to her, would take on the quality of final things. After his six-month stay in Oxford, Faulkner renewed the affair with great ardor, but found he couldn't hang on; and Meta felt betrayed when he decided after a few months to pull up stakes permanently. Meta had misread her love, for even now she believed that once Jill was old enough to face her parents' separation, Faulkner would divorce Estelle and marry her. Jill was twelve, and Meta felt the time was right; but Faulkner was too conservative, too uncertain about everything in his life, too symbiotically attached to Estelle to make any such break. Meta resolved that all was over. In December 1945, she remarried Rebner, a remarriage that proved as unsatisfactory as the original one. The marriage came apart, and when Faulkner later returned briefly to Hollywood (at $2,000 per week), he and Meta met for the final times; the writer was then in his mid-fifties, world-renowned, still hanging on to Meta but unwilling to abandon Estelle. Afterwards, they corresponded, and that was all.

Estelle's father, Lem Oldham, died on May 6. She deeply mourned him, but the Faulkners as a family disliked the Oldhams intensely, and Major Oldham was himself a fallen man in his later years—unwilling to work, living off snippets from Estelle, sitting on his laurels as one of Oxford's aristocrats. Faulkner wrote consolingly to Mrs. Oldham in June from Hollywood, but mainly about flowers and gardens. There was no love lost between him and Estelle's family, certainly not after their rejection of him. The big event for the writer was his return to Warner Brothers on June 7. He told Ober (May 25) he would return on a new option and expected $450 (which turned out to be $500) when the option was renewed on June 16. If the original seven-year contract was adhered to, Faulkner, because of his annual releases from the studio, could have spent almost the rest of his life fulfilling the deal. Each time he left, the time remaining on the contract was tacked on to the end; the Biblical seven slowly stretched closer to Jacob's fourteen.

In the same letter to Ober, he mentions that the fable material is a novel now, no longer "just a lot of rhetoric."⁵ He wants the original portions back from Haas so he can retype along new lines. With $500 per week, Faulkner had risen from the $300 originally contracted for, but the amount was the same MGM had paid him thirteen years earlier. Allowing for inflation and the buying power of the dollar, he had lost considerable ground since 1932, when $500 per week was an enormous amount.

Faulkner's new assignment was based on Stephen Longstreet's novel *Stallion Road.* He was to do the treatment, seventeen pages by June 12. The novel concerned a ranch owner in California—a gambler, veterinarian, and all-around charmer. The role was played by Ronald Reagan, costarring with Alexis Smith and Zachary Scott (the husband of Faulkner's good friend, Ruth Ford). Faulkner produced a temporary screenplay and a second one (in all 285 pages), but the third and final one was by Longstreet, who received screen credits. The film was released in April of 1947, with no mention of Faulkner's 17-, 134-, and 151-page versions.

In a clandestine operation, he was also involved in another movie Warners did not know of. How he found time to write parts of *A Fable* is difficult to determine; but Bezzerides said the writer arose at 4:00 A.M. to put in four hours at his desk before heading for the studio. Faulkner became involved with Jean Renoir when the latter was adapting Hugo Butler's treatment of George Sessions Perry's "Hold Autumn in Your Hand"—released as *The Southerner.* Renoir was possibly the greatest of the directors Faulkner worked with, and their admiration for each other was mutual. Both Renoir and Nunnally Johnson had worked on the screenplay, but were dissatisfied. Renoir asked for Faulkner. Most of what Faulkner added to the script proved unusable—he began to shift the direction of the narrative and to emphasize elements that had been marginal. Renoir took credit for the script when *The Southerner* was released, starring Zachary Scott, Beulah Bondi, J. Carrol Naish, and Betty Field.

In late July, with his letter to Herndon terminating their contract as of August 18, Faulkner attempted to put his life in order. He followed the letter to Herndon with one to Ober on July 26. There he revealed that if Herndon offered to compromise, he was willing to "pay him 10 weeks' commission ($500.00) as a termination, instead of the 4 ($200) which I have offered. I have not told him so yet." Faulkner did not expect his adversary to go down without fighting back. "His next step will be to attach and put in escrow or whatever you call it, my salary. The moment he does that I'm going to pack my toothbrush and return to Mississippi. . . . if he does not behave, if at any time before I begin to pay him the $200.00 offered or at any time during that period he starts refusing and delivering warnings to and threats to me, I will stop paying him then and he will not even get the $200."⁶

As expected, Herndon did not go silently into the dark, but told Faulkner if he discontinued the agent's fee, he, Herndon, would file suit through his attorneys. He gave the writer a week to think it over. The studio lawyer, R. J. Obringer, told Faulkner that Herndon could deduct ten percent of each salary check and have it held in escrow by the sheriff pending a suit. Faulkner was trapped. If he could break the Warners contract, then he might be able to break the one with Herndon, which related only to that studio. But if he could not put pressure on Warners to release him, then Herndon, because of the exchange of letters and telegrams between him and Faulkner, had a rightful agent's commission. Obringer told Faulkner that Herndon's position was strong, but he should sit tight and see what the agent did. Finally, on August 8, Herndon informed Faulkner that his total commissions for the remainder of the contract (about five years, allowing for Faulkner's frequent vacations) came to $21,320. He offered to take $10,000, at the rate of $100 per week, until the total was paid. Even this was not final, simply a rough figuring.

Although Herndon comes through as a bloodsucker, legally Faulkner had gotten himself into this position through his own negligence. In his letter to Ober of July 30, where he passes on Obringer's advice to sit tight, Faulkner goes through the whole matter again, as though Ober had not comprehended what a trap he was in. He seems to feel that he did not contract for a seven-year deal, but only for the de Gaulle picture. If this is true, then Herndon was owed only for the time Faulkner spent on that production. "When I reached California, I went to work at once on the de Gaulle job, with a guarantee of 13 weeks, and that any contract presented to me would cover only this one job."[7] After two weeks, Herndon, according to Faulkner, told him he had to sign a seven-year contract; but the writer refused. Herndon then announced he was already committed to it, that he was drawing salary on it. But whatever was said or not said was superseded by subsequent events. Faulkner continued to work under the Warner Brothers contract and continued with Herndon drawing ten percent on his slowly rising weekly salary. Faulkner had indeed acquiesced to the whole deal, and now was trying to escape it. As he realizes, he does not have much of a case in court. "So I will think my best 'out' is to clear out of here as soon as he makes the first legal move. The studio will suspend me, but it may be worth it to my peace of mind."

Yet when he wrote to Estelle on July 26—the same day as one of his desperate letters to Ober—he makes little mention of his inner turmoil over the contracts and Herndon. Addressed to "Dear Miss E.," his letter is in part lighthearted and with enough gossip to make her think he was busy with something besides Meta. He mentions having written 145 pages on *Stallion Road*. He adds he has spent two weeks working at night and on weekends "fixing up a picture for Ginger Rogers." He also has written a fifty-page story with Bezzerides which they hope to sell to Hawks, a treatment based on Faulkner's "Barn Burning." (Nothing came of it.) He does say he is trying to make enough money "to get the hell out of this place and come back home and fix Missy's [Jill's] room and paint the house and do the other things we need."[8] Only at the end does he indicate his battle to rid himself of Herndon and to pry more salary from the studio. With the Herndon matter on hold—the trap around him as tight as ever —he heard from Cowley. As his Hollywood situation deteriorated, his reputation at large was about to improve. Cowley had gotten the go-ahead from Viking to do the *Portable;* in addition, he had published the third segment of his essay in the *Sewanee Review.* Cowley wrote Faulkner on August 9 that he hoped his project would be "a bayonet prick in the ass of Random House to reprint" Faulkner's other books. Cowley's plan was ingenious. Instead of selecting the "best" of the writer, as in a typical anthology, he would choose short and long stories and passages from novels, all of which form part of Faulkner's Yoknapatawpha County series; thereby the reader would gain a sense of the writer's whole achievement. The major problem with this—and Cowley stressed he had only six hundred pages, about two hundred thousand words—was the need to omit a work like *Sound,* and include nothing from *Absalom* except "Wash," a story whose characters overlap with those of the novel.

If he included an entire novel, it would have to be *As I Lay Dying,* since it is short. He also would omit *Light in August,* which did not fit any of the categories.* Cowley defended his method: ". . . I think that a better picture of your work as a whole could be given in this fashion. You know my theory, expressed somewhere in the essay—that you are at your best on two levels, either in long stories that can be written in one burst of energy, like "The Bear" and "Spotted Horses" and "Old Man," or (and) in the Yocknapatawpha [sic] cycle as a whole. The advantage of a book on the system I have in mind is that it would give you at both these levels, in the stories and in the big cycle."[9]

Cowley assured Faulkner that his Mississippi work is an "entire creation" and "there is nothing like it in American literature." He closed his letter with a considerable accolade, the words of Jean-Paul Sartre ("a little man with bad teeth"): "Pour les jeunes en France, Faulkner c'est un dieu" (for the youth of France, Faulkner is a god). "Roll that over on your tongue."[10] Faulkner was apparently touched, for he answered almost immediately, on August 16. As his position in Hollywood worsened, he recognized that he had to grasp at any form of salvation, and Cowley was throwing him a lifeline to the real world. He says a meeting is out of the question, but answers Cowley's points carefully. "By all means let us make a Golden Book of my apocryphal county. I have thought of spending my old age doing something of that nature: an alphabetical rambling genealogy of the people, father to son to son."[11] Faulkner did something of this

*Cowley did manage to include the Percy Grimm segment from *Light in August,* as well as the Dilsey section of part 4 of *Sound.* The "novel" turned out to be the "Old Man" half of *The Wild Palms,* not *As I Lay Dying. Absalom* was even represented in the original *Portable* by chapter 2, "Wedding in the Rain." It was later replaced by an excerpt from *Requiem for a Nun,* "The Courthouse (A Name for the City)." And Cowley added, at the end of the revised *Portable,* "The Jail (Nor Even Yet Quite Relinquished)," also from *Requiem.*

in his appendix on the Compsons, which then appeared in later editions of *Sound*. Reviewing his career, Faulkner is impressed: he got it all done, and now it would appear with some sense of order close to his own idea.

Yet Cowley's brilliant scheme—and we cannot overpraise his attempt to present Faulkner in the best possible light as a unique novelist and short-story writer—also distorted the writer's career. By stressing the "saga" quality of Faulkner, a word he himself repeated, Cowley detracted from the brilliant quality of works which do not fit into the saga: those very novels which had to be more or less neglected—*Absalom, Sound, As I Lay Dying, Light in August*. Faulkner as a brilliant and original novelist was somehow bypassed in favor of a regionalist who wrote magnificent segments. His reputation as a Southern writer was enhanced, but his Americanism was limited because of the emphasis on the Yoknapatawpha designation. Thus, Faulkner was perceived as a writer of brilliant short bursts, a regionalist rather than a full-scale American author, a novelist whose novels somehow are not representative of the entire nation. Not that Cowley intended this, but it was an inevitable by-product of his selective process. An anthology is almost always a distortion, and in this instance, the distortion took the reader away from what was the real achievement.

But at this stage, Faulkner was not concerned with distortion. His life was divided into parts which did not cohere: Cowley in the Northeast, Herndon and Warners in California. In a confessional letter to Ober on August 20, he poured out his bitterness and grief. Circumstance is the enemy. "Apart from this Herndon matter, I think I have had about all of Hollywood I can stand. I feel bad, depressed, dreadful sense of wasting time, I imagine most of the symptoms of some kind of blow-up or collapse. I may be able to come back later, but I think I will finish this present job [on *Stallion Road*, where his treatment and two screenplays were submerged in Longstreet's final draft]. Feeling as I do, I am actually afraid to stay here much longer."[12]

The fear he expresses is that he will soon drink suicidally. He recognizes all the familiar signposts: frustration, irresolvable circumstances, loneliness, dislike of work he is doing, sense of his serious career dissipating itself in meaningless tasks. "For some time I have expected, at a certain age, to reach that period (in the early fifties) which most artists seem to reach where they admit at last that there is no solution to life and that it is not, and perhaps never was, worth the living." This is a deeply hopeless note and clashes with later sentiments of man's endurance in the face of adversity, or with statements in his screenplays whereby duty, discipline, and the job before one demand perseverance and even hope.

He asks Ober, now his closest confidant, if there is any work he can do for some income. He says he will scrounge around in Hollywood to see if he can take work home with him. But then comes the note of self-pity: "My books have never sold, are out of print; the labor (the creation of my apocryphal country) of my life, even if I have a few things yet to add to it, will never make a living for me. I dont have enough sure judgment about trash to be able to write it with 50% success." He says he may do some editorial work or hack-writing at home, where expenses will be less. "I think mainly though that I am not well physically, have lost weight, etc., though nothing serious that I know of or anticipate. Only, if I pull out of here now, I may leave myself in such bad odor that it will be hard to come back, even to Warner's who of course will put me under suspension, unless something can be done about this contract, from which they have declined to release me."[13] Faulkner enclosed Herndon's counteroffer, that he would release the writer if he paid back $10,000 at the rate of $100 per week. He then has another idea: to pay off Herndon and use Swanson (Ober's West Coast representative) to get him a better contract. If he could draw, for example, $1,000 per week, he could pay Herndon his $100 and Swanson another $50 or so and still come out ahead. But he does not say how he would feel about staying on for another year or two, so as to build up sufficient money for a return home. His expenses would be enormous— the double payoff for agents' commissions, plus living in Hollywood, while he supported a large extended family in Oxford.

The plan to evade Herndon as of August 19 fell through. The prospect was daunting: to remain another four years after his current contract period ended, on the assumption that since he was so poorly paid Warners would continue to pick up his option. Eventually, his salary would rise another $100, then $250 more in the final three years. But he would barely be keeping up with inflation, and pay would still be far less than other writers were receiving. Ober tried to pull him back from a binge, indicating that Swanson might work out an arrangement to end the contract and that the Doubleday offer for the Mississippi book still stood. Ober wondered if Faulkner could undertake that project and still work on the fable material, then possibly return to Hollywood under better conditions. It all sounded hopeful, but there was nothing solid in Ober's response except that life would go on and Faulkner could survive if he kept faith in himself. Faulkner's imagery in his letters is of a man being strangled by coils, whereas Ober countered with projects.

On a note of desperation, he wrote Estelle (August 25) that while he was back at the hospitable Bezzerideses', he could not intrude on them indefinitely. Yet he couldn't find a hotel room and had to eat in restaurants so as not to deplete the Bezzerideses' ration points. He felt little but homesickness; his only solace (which he did not mention to Estelle) was Meta. Through all this, Faulkner had been laboring on *Stallion Road*, the movie made from Longstreet's novel, and he had reached 151 pages. But the script was discarded as unfilmable. Like "Battle Cry" it had qualities which characterized a much later period in films, when story line, narrative, even characterization were composed of fragments or of montagelike scenes, everything either oblique or broken up. Faulkner's failure in many of his extended scripts can be attributed to his effort to bring modernistic techniques into a traditional form of filmmaking. Warner Brothers was one of the most conventional studios in this respect, introducing innovative ideas, but using very traditional forms of storytelling and characterization.

In an interesting letter to Richard Wright (which developed out of Faulkner helping Wright's friend Joe C. Brown), the white Mississippian supports the black Mississippian. Faulkner indicates he preferred *Native Son* to *Black Boy (A Record of Childhood and Youth)*. "You said it well, as well as it could have been said in this form. Because I think you said it much better in *Native Son*. I hope you will keep on saying it, but I hope you will say it as an artist, as in *Native Son*. I think you will agree that the good lasting stuff comes out of one's individual imagination and sensitivity to and comprehension of the suffering of Everyman, Anyman, not out of the memory of his own grief."[14] This is the same advice, more or less, Faulkner had given Joe Brown. But Faulkner's assessment of Wright's work is problematic. *Native Son* has greater power, but it is seriously flawed as a work of fiction; it demonstrates less artistic control than *Black Boy*, which is almost perfect of its kind. What Faulkner probably had in the back of his mind—and what possibly made him overrate Wolfe—was that an imperfect imaginative re-creation of experience is preferable to an almost perfect nonfictional creation: novels are better than "records." By October 18, he was back at Rowan Oak.

In order to make his departure possible, Faulkner had to obtain a six-month leave of absence from the studio. Warner Brothers, however, insisted it had the right to purchase whatever novel Faulkner completed when he left; since he had already sold that right to Bacher, for *A Fable*, he could not agree. It was still another instance of how his original errors led to legal complications, not to mention promises made without precise legal standing. His trap was now three-sided—he was caught up in a Warners contract, which made him work for several more years; the Herndon deal, still not being discussed in realistic terms; and the deal with Bacher and Hathaway, which foreclosed any release from the studio.

Faulkner wrote Ober on September 17 about the Doubleday deal for $5,000, but despite his poor situation, resisted the idea of writing something halfheartedly. "I'll sell myself here to do what I am not sure I can do, but I have too much respect for my ancient and honorable trade (books) to take someone's money without knowing neither of us will be ashamed of the result."[15] He asked Ober to keep the Doubleday offer on hold, in the event his situation worsened. The following day, having already told Herndon all bets were off and having been informed in turn that his agent would sue, Faulkner left the studio for the final time. His sole connection to the real world now was Cowley.

The critic wrote on September 17, full of excitement at being able to go ahead full blast, but also running into problems, which he itemized. Yet Cowley was on track. He recognized that the more he read Faulkner, the more compelling he seemed. Faulkner wrote to be reread, as Gide indicated. Cowley then tells a story calculated to lift his recipient's spirits.

These remarks would bring a candid, perhaps unexpected rejoinder from Faulkner. Cowley writes:

> Did I tell you about the story I heard from Sartre, about Hemingway drunk in Paris insisting that Faulkner was better than he was? Hemingway wrote me a long, rambling, lonely letter complaining that writing was a lonely trade and there was no one to talk to about it. He said about you, "Faulkner has the most talent of anybody but hard to depend on because he goes on writing after he is tired and seems as though he never threw away the worthless. I would have been happy just to have managed him."[16]

Cowley says Hemingway feels so lonely and unhappy it might be a good idea for Faulkner to write to him at Finca Figia, his farm-estate in Cuba.

Faulkner's reply, which Cowley deleted when he produced Faulkner's letter in his *File,* was a blazer:

> I'll write to Hemingway. Poor bloke, to have to marry three times to find out that marriage is a failure, and the only way to get any peace out of it is (if you are fool enough to marry at all) keep the first one and stay as far away from her as much as you can, with the hope of some day outliving her. At least you will be safe then from any other one marrying you—which is bound to happen if you ever divorce her. Apparently man can be cured of drugs, drink, gambling, biting his nails and picking his nose, but not of marrying.[17]

The wittiness of the lines cannot disguise his fears of returning to Estelle even as he is desperate to return to Oxford. Although these lines come unexpectedly in 1945, as Faulkner is reaching his forty-eighth birthday, they reinforce what he has been saying all along, or demonstrating in much of his fiction. Marriage was part of the entrapment. The woman was not at fault, for the man also falls into the traps. But because of a combination of forces, the man—from Faulkner's perspective—cannot do his proper work or live his proper life once married; and yet, as Faulkner realized, there is no way to escape it. Marrying three times, as Hemingway did, seemed to Faulkner to mean having to deal with three Estelles. Hemingway had of course thrown away, in his first marriage, precisely the woman he should have stayed with, providing she could have tolerated a long marriage with him.

When Faulkner left Hollywood, he took Jill's favorite horse, Lady, with him in a trailer, with Newt House at the wheel, and House's wife accompanying them. The night before, at a party, he had found himself worshiped by three men, listening intently to everything he said: Christopher Isherwood; the French surrealist, Jean Hélion; and an unidentified third man. "I'll have to admit though that I felt more like a decrepit gaffer telling stories than like an old master producing jewels for three junior co-laborers."[18] Faulkner sounds put upon, but it is hard to believe, given his years of frustration in Hollywood, that he was not pleased at the homage paid to him—as he was pleased at the respect with which Sartre and Hemingway received his work.

Faulkner and his entourage, including the horse, arrived at Oxford in the middle of the night—as the twenty-third of September turned into the twenty-fourth. The following day was Faulkner's birthday, and to celebrate he had not only returned, he had given Jill a marvelous surprise. He had left behind one unresolved problem after another, as his letter to Jack Warner on October 15 indicates.

Faulkner is quite frank in the letter, although he leavens his hatred of his Hollywood work with some exaggerated praise for Warner Brothers. He emphasizes that he should not sign the leave-suspension agreement, which commits him to unacceptable terms. He wants to sever all studio connections. "I feel that I have made a bust at moving picture writing and therefore have mis-spent and will continue to mis-spend time which at my age I cannot afford. During my three years (including leave-suspensions) at Warner's, I did the best work I knew on 5 or 6 scripts. Only two were made and I feel that I received credit on these not on the value of the work I did but partly through the friendship of Director Howard Hawks."[19] The two for which he received credits—*To Have and Have Not* and *The Big Sleep*—were satisfactory enough, but were based on others' work: Hemingway and Chandler. And even there, he shared credits, in the Hemingway with one other writer, in the Chandler with two others.

He continues:

For that reason, I am unhappy in studio work. Not at Warner's studio; my connection with the studio and all the people I worked with could not have been pleasanter. But with the type of work. So I repeat the request this time not so much to the head of the studio, as to that same fairness which you have shown before in such situations, two of which I have specific knowledge of since friends of mine were involved. So I know my request will receive fair consideration, and I hope favorable.[20]

Faulkner appealed in the name of decency, but the studio head knew only business considerations. Before he relented, he had come under a barrage of other petitions, from Cerf and others; and he had also taken a look at the "fable" material and rejected it. Once the business potentialities of Faulkner were exhausted, Warner let him go—but not in the way Faulkner hoped for. He remained on a string for another six months, and was in fact in danger of having to return to Hollywood under the terms of the original contract. To keep him jumping, on October 22 Obringer told him he would have to sign the leave agreement, so that while he sat in Oxford he was back where he had started—everything unresolved, with Jack Warner adamant he would not let this low-salaried star slip away.

Faulkner became increasingly involved with Cowley, as both men recognized they were on to a major project—something very important not only for author and critic, but for American literature. Faulkner wrote out the Compson genealogy, the Compson appendix, which showed that he had not lost his mastery. He sent this on in his letter of October 18, along with ways in which to handle the discrepancies. "I think this is all right, it took me about a week to get Hollywood out of my lungs, but I am still writing all right, I believe."

The Cowley project started to become a collaboration, since Faulkner's complicated presentation of the material with resulting discrepancies meant Cowley had to make critical decisions. The latter did not seem to recognize at the time what a miraculous piece of work the Compson appendix (1699–1945) was, how it both tied together *Sound* and also brought to light new ways of reading the material. But their collaboration was connected mainly to getting the record straight: shouldn't "du homme" be "de l'homme," which is correct? Faulkner claims poetic license: ". . . it seemed righter to me that Ikke., knowing little of French or English either, should have an easy transition to the apt name he gave himself in English, than that the French should be consistent."[21] He clarifies Jason's assertion on how much was stolen from him by Quentin, Caddy's daughter*; and in a subsequent letter (November 7), he tries to clarify the genealogy of the Indian stories.

The period between early November and the new year of 1946 was curiously calm. Faulkner seems to have gone almost entirely on hold, caught up as he was in Cowley's project and still unable to get a firm grip on his own affairs. He went hunting, often with his stepson, and he appears to have made some peace with his life at Rowan Oak. Blotner tells how Sinclair Lewis turned up one day at the door, but Faulkner was gone and it was left to Estelle to give him lunch. This says something about Faulkner's reputation with other writers, inasmuch as Lewis, so different as a writer, came to pay homage. Cowley asked for a map of Yoknapatawpha, and Faulkner drew it and sent it off. He wrote to Haas on November 2, repeating how he is trapped by Warner's intransigence. He mentions that the legal department told him he could not release his present work until the California situation is clarified. He expects to return to the novel, but the specter of going back to Hollywood is always present. He feels Warner intends to starve him into fulfilling the contract. He hopes to make "enough stink through publicity over it to free myself."[22]

---

*In the text, Jason reports $3,000 stolen; in the Appendix, $7,000. In the novel, the implication is that all the money in the box was stolen from Quentin; in the appendix, $2,840.50 was saved by Jason from change. Even more problematic is the fact that the Jason of the Appendix, while not sympathetic, is a more favorable creature than the repellent man of the novel; like Henry Armstid, he seems to have acquired a different self.

On November 2, Cowley kept up the barrage, in earnest of his effort to get things right. He was cutting up his own books in order to put together the printer's copy of *The Portable Faulkner*, what is known as a pasteup. In some instances, he was destroying valuable editions, and he particularly did not want to ruin his copy of *Sound*; so he hired a typist to copy out the passage of part 4 that he was using. Cowley's remarks give a good idea of how in 1945 Faulkner's novels were unavailable in this country, even as the French were worshiping him as a god. When charges are made that the South failed to hail him, that in his own town he was disregarded, it must be added that the entire country, except for a few critics and readers, barely knew of his existence. The man of the hour was Hemingway or else Steinbeck, not Faulkner. While Random House is to be commended for its financial support of Faulkner during his worst times, as well as for the loyal support of Haas, Cerf, and Commins,* nevertheless Random House did not keep his books in print very long and made little effort to spread his name. Consciously or not, they made Faulkner completely dependent on their largesse. By restricting the spread of his books (and forsaking the longer view), they made him come back for advances. But with small sales, the advances had to be kept relatively small. Even in this best of worlds, with Random House Faulkner was caught inside a publishing trap. What finally got him out was less his own effort than a series of circumstances made possible by great work now several years in the past.

In a long letter on November 2, Cowley complained that separate pieces of Faulkner's work often did not make sense without character names, which were either delayed in the text or hardly given. Cowley was questioning one of Faulkner's trademark habits, which was to throw names and pronouns into confusion. "A Justice" was typical, and since it began the volume, Cowley added Compson, Candace, and other names for clarification. Yet so much of Faulkner depended on omission of the expected, or withholding the ordinary. In particular, his pronominal omissions are critical to his way of relating a story, so that it comes down to a tale between the people who are *there*, not between author and audience. For the same reason, Faulkner often modulated tenses, using the present when another author might use the past, to eliminate the reader and create a different response. This disturbed Cowley personally and aroused fears that a volume full of this could miserably fail. It is necessary to say that even as Cowley made a huge contribution in this volume, he distorted and reduced Faulkner as he attempted to turn him into a more accessible writer.

---

*None of this questions Random's loyalty. Not only did they court Faulkner as an author, they did great service for him as a man. Haas, in particular, was drawn to him, and ran errands, bought him a watch (as a personal gift), sent him tobacco. And, in some instances, everyone covered for him when he came North and found some woman to his liking.

The critic plowed on, his work gaining something of the saga Faulkner himself referred to in his letter of December 8. This letter has other interesting features as well, but here is Faulkner's suggestion for the front:

> . . . saga of . . . county . . . A chronological picture of Faulkner's apocryphal Mississippi county, selected from his published works, novel and stories, with a heretofore unpublished genealogy of one of its principal families.
> Edited by M. Cowley*

Later in December Cowley tried to cheer his correspondent. "The book is getting along to the point where I think it's looking fine—Godamighty it's wonderful; and I wonder whether the reviewers will really *read* you this time instead of judging by their preconceived ideas and their memories of what Clifton Fadiman said in the days when he was writing for the New Yorker."[23] Also, he follows up his earlier suggestion to Random House about printing a *Collected Stories*, and Robert Linscott, a senior editor there, agreed for a year down the road. (It appeared in 1950.) Cowley suggests that the map of Yoknapatawpha County printed at the end of *Absalom* be reproduced in *The Portable Faulkner;* even better, he wondered if Faulkner could redraw it to include the Compson domain. Faulkner said he could "log in 'Compson' on the old map—if I had it."

Finally, Cowley needed biographical information, and found little to use in *Who's Who,* except date of birth and titles of books. Even Faulkner's name had not been updated, lacking the "u." The writer answered Cowley's inquiry with a good deal of both information and misinformation. The latter is of particular interest. He has his great-grandfather, the old colonel, die in a duel, a romantic way of evading the fact he was shot. He gives a long explanation of why he added the "u," making it appear he changed the spelling to make pronunciation easier, or he did not want to "ride on grandfather's [great-grandfather's] coat-tails, and so accepted the 'u,' was glad of such an easy way to strike out for myself."[24] But Faulkner's change of name came with his enlistment in the RAF, and it was far more complicated psychologically than he suggests.

Continuing with his background, Faulkner does not repeat the deceptions about his military service, but says simply that he "went to RAF, returned home," and mentions it no more. He hopes Cowley will use

---

*What survived was this, on the book's front cover: "The saga of Yoknapatawpha county, 1820–1945,/Being the first chronological picture of / Faulkner's mythical county in Mississippi. . . . / In effect a new work, though selected from / His best published novels and stories; with / His own account of one of the principal / Families, written especially for this volume. Edited with an introduction by Malcolm Cowley." The published description was obviously more promotional than Faulkner's original suggestion.

only public facts; the private ones are "my own business." He says he more or less grew up in his father's livery stable, and as the eldest escaped his mother's influence "pretty easy;" which was hardly the case. After detailing some of his wandering jobs (house painter, serving as fourth-class postmaster), he indicates he worked for a New Orleans bootlegger, was also a deckhand on freighters, was a hand on a Gulf of Mexico shrimp trawler. These activities, which may have been briefly true, are presented as part of a romanticized past, the writer soaking up experience, riding the freights, shipping out like Conrad and O'Neill. Even his "barnstormed an aeroplane out of cow pastures" has a whiff of Eden.

We find in his assessment of his past a replacement of romantic tales on one level for those on another. He deleted the RAF exploits, the limp, plate in the head, crash, combat over France, but substituted exploits more difficult to pinpoint because they may have been briefly true and cannot be disproved.* He ends his panoply of role-playing with the fact he was a scoutmaster before being "fired for moral reasons." Cowley footnotes this "because he was the author of *Sanctuary;*"[25] but the cause was more prosaic—excessive drinking.

During the discussions over his military service, Faulkner probes deeply into the psyche of the South, and we see him moving back into memory when he first wanted to be a poet and how difficult it was given the region and its expectations of a man. He says oratory was the "first art; Confederate generals would hold up attacks while they made speeches to their troops. Apart from that, 'art' was really no manly business. It was a polite painting of china by gentlewomen. When they entered its domain through the doors of their libraries, it was to read somebody else's speeches, or politics, or the classics of the faintly school, and even these were men who, if they had been writing men, would have written still more orations." Negroes invented song, but this was not a written art. Faulkner says there was no literate middle class to produce a literature. The battle on the land concerned not letters but economics, middle class against slaveholder and slave. When anyone emerged, it was not as a middle class, but as a Sutpen—men who willed to become barons. Eventually, after the war, the baron idea died out, the planter was replaced slowly, and a middle class emerged. Losing the war gave the South something to write about, something to read. Faulkner then gets into difficulties when he tries to explain why the North has not produced a literature out of the war—because, he says, it has become enslaved by machines. Here his hatred of modern technology has interrupted any kind of coherent discussion. He ends this part of his argument with a

---

*Faulkner's sensitivity to his RAF exploits is brought home in a letter he wrote to Cowley in early January of 1946: "If you mention military experience at all (which is not necessary, as I could have invented a few failed RAF airmen as easily as I did Confeds) say 'belonged to RAF in 1918' " (Yale Typescript; *Selected Letters of William Faulkner,* ed. Joseph Blotner [New York: Vintage Books, 1978], p. 215).

visionary point about Southern abolitionists invading the North to destroy machines, "followed by a vast influx of Tennessee and Mississippi and Virginia carpetbaggers, and then the North will have a war to write about."[26] With this, he enters the world of his own tall tales, although a personal truth underlies the hyperbole.

The correspondence with Cowley over the wartime experience bled over into the new year, which was almost a replay of much of 1945. Like the previous year, the new one was part of a holding pattern, although some of Faulkner's deeper problems were solved. He published only one short story, "An Error of Chemistry." In addition, the story "Honor" was reprinted in the *American Mercury* (October), having originally appeared in July of 1930. This time the *Mercury* paid Faulkner $500 and noted it was proud to have been the first national periodical of its class to print his fiction. He was cheered by Random House's plan to reissue *Sound* and *As I Lay Dying* in a single volume,* with the Compson appendix coming first, although it was not intended as a foreword. But even more cheering was news Warner Brothers would not pursue him further, that he could complete his novel without worrying whether the studio had rights to it. The studio told him he could return to the coast and fulfill his contract when the novel was finished—which, as they well knew, he would never do. This also completed his deal with Herndon, who had no claim on Faulkner now that the Warners arrangement was broken. Random House gave him maintenance money, and he spent four weeks on a script, for $3,500.

He received his copy of *The Portable Faulkner* on April 23, 1946, and saw it published six days later. With some peace of mind, he returned to full-time work on *A Fable*. Ober, meanwhile, was working well for his client, selling "Death Drag" and "Honor" to the movies for $6,600. *The Big Sleep* also premiered, with Faulkner receiving cocredits for the screenplay (along with Leigh Brackett and Jules Furthman). The year 1946 was marked not so much by a resurgence within Faulkner as a resurgence in the world beyond him. Simply being there and having produced those great books led to attention. There is little question Cowley's work and the publication of *The Portable Faulkner* helped, with Random House beginning to reissue older books and other properties becoming valuable. And there was notice in Europe, particularly in France but also in Sweden, where the Nobel Prize Committee was stirring.

Yet at the beginning of 1946 (January 5), Faulkner complained to Ober of the lack of attention. He had steadily believed in himself, but events

*Although these Modern Library editions of Faulkner were faulty—poorly edited, poorly proofread, somewhat misleading in their descriptions—withal, they were the means by which many of us first came upon the writer. Returning from the service and entering college, many of us could afford books for the first time, and we purchased Faulkner. In those days, *Sound* and *As I Lay Dying* seemed absolutely wedded, as if they, and not the two halves of *The Wild Palms*, were part of one novel.

of the past few years, especially in his dealings with Herndon and Warners, had made even his iron resolve waver. After running through his baleful situation, he thanks Ober for an Ellery Queen check ($250) for second prize in its contest. "What a commentary. In France I am the father of a literary movement. In Europe, I am considered the best modern American and among the first of all writers. In America, I eke out a hack's motion picture wages by winning second prize in a manufactured mystery story contest."[27] He accepted the $250, nevertheless. He mentions to Ober his good feeling about Cowley, who has done "a fine job in Spoonrivering my apocryphal county, to be a Viking Portable, they call them." There is good humor here, aimed at himself: comparing himself to Edgar Lee Masters, and then finding fun in the Viking *Portable Faulkner*—all those great books brought down to a portable. It was distinctly American and egalitarian, since the equivalent in France was something very exalted, the Pléiade, which published an author entire, not in fragments.

Although money was not pouring in, it was slowly becoming more abundant through Random House's help, Ober's work on Faulkner's behalf, and occasional sales or prizes. But still in Faulkner's mind (and Cowley's) were the comments in his introduction about his military service, old ghosts surfacing. On January 21, as *The Portable Faulkner* headed for the presses, Faulkner wrote, more concerned than ever that something had to be done. "You're going to bugger up a fine dignified distinguished book with that war business. The only point a war reference or anecdote could serve would be to reveal me a hero, or (2) to account for the whereabouts of a male of my age on Nov. 11, 1918 in case this were a biography." Simply say: "Was a member of the RAF in 1918." He adds: "I'll pay for any resetting of type, plates, alterations, etc." Finally: "I'm really concerned about the war reference. As I said last, I'm going to be proud of this book. I wouldn't put in anything at all about the war or any other personal matter."[28]

By return mail, Cowley agreed to delete the statement that Faulkner's plane had been "damaged in combat," but could not make more extensive alterations at this stage. Faulkner replied promptly on February 1: "I dont like the paragraph because it makes me out more of a hero than I was, and I am going to be proud of your book. The mishap was caused not by combat but by (euphoneously) 'Cockpit trouble' i.e., my own foolishness; the injury I suffered I still feel I got at bargain rates." He tries to excuse his dissembling:

A lot of that sort of thing happened in those days, the culprit unravelling himself from the subsequent unauthorised crash incapable of any explanation as far as advancing the war went, and grasping at any frantic straw before someone in authority would want to know what became of the aeroplane, would hurry to the office and enter it in the squadron records as 'practice flight.' As compared with men I knew, friends I had and lost, I deserve no more than the sentence I suggested before: 'served in (or belonged to) RAF.'[29]

But even here Faulkner was maintaining his dissembling act, a kind of sleight of hand in which he was injured in an unauthorized use of an airplane. The likelihood of this occurring was very slight, in fact nonexistent; and his injuries, such as they were, seemed to have disappeared with time. He did not walk with a limp after an initial period, and the plate in his head was never noticed by any medical examiner when he was drying out or going through an examination. Now that this had been clarified, Faulkner moved to the reissue of *Sound*, either alone (with the Compson appendix) or with *As I Lay Dying*. Linscott, Random House's new senior editor, had asked Faulkner for an introduction, but he had no idea how to write one, even for the $250 he wanted.

Like *The Portable Faulkner*, slated for April publication, the reissue of these two works was a significant development in the publicizing of Faulkner's career. For years he had seemed dead; doubly so, since Warner Brothers had treated him like a minor hack-writer. But now, in the prestigious Portable series and with a reissue of two of his greatest novels, he was resurfacing. Faulkner wrote to Linscott specifically about the reissue, on February 4. He wanted the Compson appendix published with the novel and noted how it clarified all four segments. He definitely wanted it first. He gives his dates for the sections, April 5 (Benjy), June 2, 1910 (Quentin), April 6 (Jason), April 7 (the author). The final dating was April 7, 1928; June 2, 1910; April 6, 1928; April 8, 1928; putting it more solidly in Holy Week, Holy Saturday, Good Friday, and Easter Sunday. He then mentions that while he does not know what an introduction should be—he recalls his efforts to introduce a special edition of *Sound* marked in different colors— he may be interested in order to get hold of the $250. "But I will do a lot for $250," even subcontract for it. He asks for hints from Linscott, some idea which would be quicker than his doing a "course in introduction reading."[30]

Faulkner clearly had Cowley in mind as the subcontractor, with a split of the $250. The critic commented on this to Linscott a week after hearing from Faulkner.* After some amusing give-and-take about how copies of Faulkner's books are unavailable and the available ones are being loaned back and forth, he warns against letting the writer do an introduction. Cowley points out, shrewdly, that Faulkner's introduction to *Sanctuary* poisoned him with the critics: they looked foolish praising a novel the author then announces he wrote only for money. Temperamentally,

---

*"What about doing it yourself?" Faulkner wrote on February 18, "or would that be too much Cowley plus F? let me know about it. I will then write Linscott and ask for someone to do it. I dont want to read TSAF again" (to Cowley, February 18, 1946, Yale Typescript; *Selected Letters of William Faulkner*, ed. Joseph Blotner [New York: Vintage Books, 1978], p. 222).

Faulkner was unsuited for an introduction, and Cowley mentions several others capable of writing a brief one: Conrad Aiken, for one; Kay Boyle; Hemingway—an interesting choice, given the competitive nature of the two writers; and Cowley's own choice, Jean-Paul Sartre, which is a magnificent suggestion, but one, Cowley says, sure to be turned down. Cowley also displays some of his own, then limited, taste—*As I Lay Dying*, he says, may not be a good novel to reissue, since he (Cowley) does not consider it top-drawer Faulkner. "Too much shifting about from one stream of consciousness to another. Not enough contrast with TSATF, both being stream-of-consciousness novels." He suggests *The Wild Palms* instead—not the whole novel, just that half.

Cowley later changed his mind about *As I Lay Dying*. He was also concerned with Random House's plan to reissue *The Wild Palms* in the fall, feeling there would be a conflict with *The Portable*, where "Old Man" was appearing. Cowley correctly argues that Viking was putting a good deal of money and effort into this *Portable*, and it would lead eventually to a renewed interest in Faulkner. Then and only then should Random House reissue. He feels that cooperation, not rivalry, should characterize the re-publication of Faulkner's books. All of his advice went amiss: *Sound* and *As I Lay Dying* were reissued, without Sartre's planned introduction but with a somewhat revised appendix to clear up more discrepancies. As for Cowley's dislike of putting *Sound* and *As I Lay Dying* together, he was plain wrong. They fit because they demonstrate key strategies in Faulkner's literary technique, each the obverse of the other. Separate reissue would have been better, of course, but if two books had to be bracketed, Random House made the correct choice. *Sound* and *The Wild Palms* would make little sense.

Faulkner's definitive statement on discrepancies came in his February 18 letter to Cowley. ". . . I dont care much for facts, am not much interested in them, you cant stand a fact up, you've got to prop it up, and when you move to one side a little and look at it from that angle, it's not thick enough to cast a shadow in that direction.* But in truth, though maybe what I mean by truth is humility and maybe what I think is humility is really immitigable pride. I would have preferred nothing at all prior to the instant I began to write, as though Faulkner and Typewriter were concomitant, coadjutant and without past on the moment they first faced each other at the suitable (nameless) table." As if to exemplify his point about facts, Faulkner says he would prefer to let the appendix stand with inconsistencies, because

the inconsistencies in the appendix prove that to me the book is still alive after 15 years, and being still alive is growing, changing; the

*As we read these words, written more than forty years ago, in the 1980s, we see how Faulkner created such joy for generations of great Latin-American novelists. That "disregard" for fact gave him weight and standing, since idea, conception, strategy were all. García Márquez, Fuentes, Vargas Llosa, Donoso, and, before them all, Borges, could create their invented worlds out of Faulkner's "I dont care much for facts."

appendix was done at same heat as the book, even though 15 years later, and so it is the book itself which is inconsistent, not the appendix. That is, at the age of 30 I did not know these people as at 45 I now do; that I was even wrong now and then in the very conclusions I drew from watching them, and the information in which I once believed.[31]

Faulkner has been quite consistent with himself. From early on, even in his poetry, he tried to manipulate reality—most of all in his stream-of-consciousness strategies of those early novels. He was very close to what Henri Bergson had said about the matter of the world: that it was an aggregate of images. By images, Bergson meant something between what the idealists call a representation and what the realists call a thing. Matter, then, exists somewhere in the seams of that dissociation which idealism and realism have wrought—an intermediary between existence and its appearance. For Bergson, as for Faulkner in his best work, memory relates matter and spirit, and, accordingly, we cannot experience the simple perception of an object. Yet while memory is all we have, Faulkner undercuts it with the alternative that memory distorts and makes of matter something we can never perceive. Like Bergson, Faulkner was eager to subvert the notion that matter exists alone.

Faulkner also believed, like the French philosopher, that the logical mind creates continuity where none really exists; that this logical mind shapes mechanistic theories of existence because it has no other way of dealing with life; and that, besides this mechanistic impulse, there is another which tries to understand vital phenomena. Faulkner's distaste for fact fits into this tradition; and although his words are lost on Cowley, he is arguing for an artistic strategy which falls outside of what the critics will embrace. For Bergson, vital phenomena can be understood only by intuition, that voiding of objects which makes Faulkner at times seem a realist, at other times a surrealist. Both philosopher and novelist agree that art rests on "becoming," something which emanates from the unconscious and which Bergson attributed to intuition. One must view matter not as a thing, not as a fact, but as becoming—which is precisely what Faulkner says to Cowley about his book coming alive fifteen years later. The enemy here is mechanism or associationism, which brings together elements without regard for their becoming. As against associationism, we have duration—that sense of the real, concrete, live present which lies between past and future. Energy lies in becoming; matter is the death of energy. These ideas, in very different forms, became the basis of Einstein's early work and are a foundation stone of modernism. Faulkner explains his role in this movement in his comments about fact.

But Faulkner's linkage to Bergson's ideas goes further. It was as though the Southern writer, despite his brief education, had reached back and touched the mind of the French philosopher. What happened was that Faulkner through his early homage to French symbolists and to Mallarmé in particular had picked up what was Bergsonian in their practices; he had done so unconsciously, perhaps, so that these ideas became assimilated to him as strategies indistinguishable from his own. Bergson spoke of our body occupying the center of matter, and in this center we must deal with past and present; the way we handle the past is through memory. But the problem is that *pastness differs from memory;* and this difference or distinction will have a considerable impact on language, literary methods and strategies, on our way of thinking about thought. Bergson argues—and we see how Faulkner follows—that once we actualize the past, turning it into "image," it has contaminated pure memory. We have turned pastness into a present state, so that its sole share in the past is the memory which was its vehicle. Pastness distorts memory.

True consciousness is continuity of existence in which pastness is not actualized, but made part of a flow or stream. If you actualize the past into memory images, Bergson says, you "are compelled to extend to the totality of the states of the material world that complete and independent survival of the past, which you have just refused to psychical states." The nature of man lies in process and flux, which is what Faulkner is conveying to Cowley and which underlies his conception of *Sound* and *As I Lay Dying.* Cowley's distress at the use of stream-of-consciousness is beside the point; without it, the novels do not exist. Memory (telling and retelling) is so significant in Faulkner because it bypasses mere pastness and re-creates a truer form of history; actualization would be a betrayal.

Meanwhile,* near the end of February, while the world awaited the Viking *Portable Faulkner,* Faulkner bombarded Ober and Haas about his situation, and indicated to both he would have to return to California in March if nothing else came his way. This was the drumbeat by which he seemed now to march, and it was insistent, even as he drank to forget it. To Ober: "I now have only about 500$ cash. Am writing the studio today I will be there about Mar[ch] 15 if they will find me a place to live."**32 To Haas, now his father confessor, he laid out the situation in greater detail. He mentioned that he had hung on Geller's promise that once he, Faulkner, received a credit, the present contract would be torn up and a new one drawn; but Geller had been summarily fired last year. Faulkner told Haas he had lost or misplaced his contract and, therefore, did not know what rights he had. But despite all his missteps, Faulkner was

---

*In France, Maurice Coindreau's translation of "Afternoon of a Cow" was to appear in *Fontaine* (June–July 1943), as the almost Mallarméan "L'Après-midi d'une Vache." *Furioso* published it in America in the summer of 1947.

**On March 4, Finlay McDermid of the studio story staff wrote Faulkner he had had success in finding him a place. Within ten minutes walking distance of the studio, one of the Warners secretaries would be glad to rent him a room and semibath in her apartment. This was hardly the kind of accommodation Faulkner had in mind; nor could the secretary have known much about him to have made the offer. In other pieces of correspondence, McDermid, whatever his gaffe here, seems like an intelligent person honestly trying to help Faulkner with a residence and with his contractual difficulties.

right on target when he told Haas how he thought it would have to work out. His friends in Hollywood "all say my only hope is to get the contract abrogated, get myself fired somehow, that legally I am helpless, that the contract, and Herndon's arrangement, which is based on the contract and is automatically a part of it, will stand in court, and the only way I can get out of the contract is by means of someone who can say privately to Warner: 'Let this guy go today, and I'll scratch your back tomorrow.' "³³

But he was slowly edging toward a resolution. In March and April, his prospects looked up, part of that familiar cycle of alternating depression and gloom followed by some break. On March 2 he was visited by Thorsten Jonsson, a Swedish journalist who, with his wife, Else, would play a significant role in Faulkner's life. Jonsson's visit, first to Moon Mullen at his *Eagle* office and then to Rowan Oak, was not happenstance. He brought a message to Faulkner that one day he would win the Nobel Prize. The committee had already been considering him—and when Faulkner did win the award, it was for work well in the past, so that in 1946, he was as eligible as he would be three years later. As it turned out, the winners, beginning in 1945 and extending to Faulkner's own prize, had been solid, not the usual unknowns or Scandinavians the committee seemed to favor: Gabriela Mistral in 1945, Hermann Hesse in 1946, André Gide in 1947, T. S. Eliot in 1948, Faulkner in 1949 (received in 1950). He could have little argument there, but at the time of Jonsson's visit, about the only attractive part of the prize, if it did come, was the handsome bundle of cash it conferred.

Haas then told him to postpone his departure for Hollywood. It was possible, Haas said, that he, Ober, and their agents could work something out with Warner so as to release him from servitude. Bennett Cerf also entered into it, as a friend of Jack Warner. Together, the pincers movement worked: Jack Warner was not interested in *A Fable* (it was unfilmable) and agreed to a further suspension agreement between Faulkner and Warners, which was in effect a termination agreement.* Ober told Faulkner all this, and the further good news that Random House wanted the novel.

He wrote Haas: "I feel fine, am happy now, thanks to Harold and you."³⁴ But money problems remained, more pressing than ever; he needed an advance and an additional $400 per month. He was asking Random House for terms very similar to those Joseph Conrad gained from his agent, Pinker, a fixed sum for living expenses and additional monies for unexpected expenditures (medical bills, taxes, etc.). Once again, as if thrust back

---

*There seemed, however, to be a mix-up at Warners, for while Obringer wrote Faulkner on April 2 that he was released for the time being but would have to return after completing the novel, McDermid wrote Ober Faulkner should sign the original agreement which gave Warners first refusal of the novel as a film property. The nagging went on until it became clear that, except in the fine print, he was free.

ten years or more, he was writing against advances: attempting to work at his highest pitch while dependent on money he had not earned, and he was approaching his forty-ninth birthday.

He had moved from one form of servitude to another. He was also still concerned with the Random House reissue. He insisted to one and all that the appendix appear at the beginning; that a foreword or introduction was unnecessary, and that the appendix could serve as an introduction, "with perhaps a paragraph over my name explaining how it came about: that I should have written this when I wrote the book, and failed to see its needs or perhaps at that time I too didn't know my own characters as well as their creator should, that perhaps the characters themselves grew up after they escaped the nest, as human beings do— that sort of thing."[35]

He touches on an interesting aesthetic question here. When Faulkner wrote *Sound,* he was deeply gripped by the terms of modernism. The novel was written with a full sense of the difficulties modernism presented for the reader: in fact, the exclusion of the reader, so that only the words on the page had meaning. By excluding the reader, modernism in effect established its own terms for significance, as far from realism as it was possible to go. Even without Eliot or Joyce, Faulkner needed only Mallarmé early on as an example of the poet who wrote without regard for the practical or realistic needs of the reader: for him, the poem was a system of language the reader penetrated to the best of his abilities. This too was Faulkner's stance, and the greatness of his novel was its insistence on its own terms of meaning.

When he returned to it under the tutelage of Cowley, he was moving away from modernism; he was becoming more realistic in nearly everything he wrote or would write, with the possible exception of *A Fable.* Cowley was himself not a strong advocate of the leading edge of modernism, his remarks on the stream indicating how he tended to prefer a more realistic mode. He was a man tuned in to Hemingway and Fitzgerald, not to those who upended reality by putting it into a matrix of language. The appendix, then, derives from a more conservative tendency in Faulkner, and also to the prodding of Cowley that the writer necessarily must find his audience. As well, Faulkner's own need for the larger audience which would bring him sales cannot be disregarded in any analysis of how his literary methods proceeded. His insistence on the appendix appearing where it did, then his words about its earlier need, in 1928–29, all suggest he was wavering in his literary strategies—trying to see where he went wrong in not garnering a larger audience. The appendix, fine as it is, is just such a transitional document.

He told Ober, meanwhile, that his current project is "going to be a lot of book, something new for me, really not a novel. It may go slow at times; it may take me two years to get it right. I shant release it until it is right. In which case, I may have to go back on studio salary about next Sept."[36] All of this was still connected to studio byplay.

On April 23, Faulkner received his copy of the Viking *Portable*. He immediately wrote Cowley that it was a splendid job. "Damn you to hell anyway. But even if I had beat you to the idea, mine wouldn't have been this good. By God, I didn't know myself what I had tried to do, and how much I had succeeded."*[37] Cowley's arrangement of the material became extremely important, for it showed readers how to approach Faulkner; in effect, it "educated" his audience in a way Faulkner had failed to do. That was both the glory and the disadvantage of *The Portable*. It really did enable one to "see" the writer almost whole. Yet at the same time it became reductive of his achievement, for it made him appear as the author of small pieces, of the brief episode—when in fact he was master of the longer work, of the unexpected, the obscure, and the entangled. After Cowley's introduction and the Compson appendix, *The Portable* was arranged as follows:

I. The Old People
    1820. "A Justice" (from *These 13*)
    1833. "Wedding in the Rain" (chapter 2 of *Absalom, Absalom!*)
    18—. "Red Leaves" (from *These 13*)
    1859. "Was" (from *Go Down, Moses*)
II. The Unvanquished
    1864. "Raid" (from *The Unvanquished*)
    1869. "Wash" (from *Doctor Martino*)
    1874. "An Odor of Verbena" (from *The Unvanquished*)
III. The Last Wilderness
    1883. "The Bear" (from *Go Down, Moses*, including chapter 4)
IV. The Peasants
    1900. "Spotted Horses" (from *The Hamlet*, chapter 4, part I)
V. The End of an Order
    1902. "That Evening Sun" (from *These 13*)
    1918. "Ad Astra" (from *These 13*)
    1924. "A Rose for Emily" (from *These 13*)
    1928. "Dilsey" (from section 4 of *The Sound and the Fury*)
VI. Mississippi Flood
    1927. "Old Man" (one of the sections of *The Wild Palms*)
VII. Modern Times
    1928. "Death Drag" (from *Doctor Martino*)
    1929. "Uncle Bud and the Three Madams" (chapter 25 of *Sanctuary*)
    1930. "Percy Grimm" (from chapter 19 of *Light in August*)
    1940. "Delta Autumn" (from *Go Down, Moses*)

*Faulkner did not inscribe *The Portable Faulkner* directly to Cowley, but used a copy of *Sound* which the latter had sent him, and there he wrote the inscription intended for *The Portable Faulkner:* "To Malcolm Cowley—who beat me to what was to have been the leisurely pleasure of my old age." In time, Faulkner inscribed two copies to Cowley, one of which has ended up in the Brodsky Collection.

An anthology is, of course, under the best of circumstances an artificial enterprise. It regularizes what has been cast out as a vision, a fantasy, or an apocryphal element; it brings to the rational mind what was revealed as imaginative and created. The unfortunate thing is that critics and reviewers for many years did not see past this arrangement and formalization of Faulkner to the writer himself: that would take almost another generation.

Cowley feared that this *Portable*, like others, would be passed over. But the moment was perfect. There were people waiting for just this publication to say what should have been said years before. Caroline Gordon reviewed it on the front page of the *New York Times Book Review*, and while that was gratifying, the review which pumped energy into the Faulkner revival was Robert Penn Warren's in the *New Republic*. Gordon called Faulkner a major novelist and said he had "compassion for all created things." But Warren really made the assessment that led toward the Nobel Prize: an assessment which perceived that Faulkner was not a regionalist, or even a wider Southern novelist, but a writer concerned with the issues of the modern world. His material was the human situation.

The study of Faulkner is the most challenging single task in contemporary American literature for criticism to undertake. Here is a novelist who, in mass of work, in scope of material, in range of effect, in repertorial accuracy and symbolic subtlety, in philosophical weight, can be put beside the masters of our own past literature. Yet this accomplishment has been effected in what almost amounts to critical isolation and silence, and when the silence has been broken it has usually been broken by someone (sometimes one of our better critics) whose reading has been hasty, whose analysis unscholarly and whose judgments superficial.[38]

He adds that Cowley's book "is especially valuable at this time. Perhaps it can mark a turning point in Faulkner's reputation. That will be of slight service to Faulkner, who, as much as any writer of our place and time, can rest in confidence. He can afford to wait. But can we?"

As much as Faulkner suspected academics and academic critics, or even the whole idea of the university as a privileged, enclosed place, his future lay in the hands of professors and professional critics. It was the academic community which picked him up, and by assigning his work to students, gave him the broadening audience that enabled him to catch on. In the later 1940s, the reigning gods of English and American literature were Henry James, T. S. Eliot (then writing plays), and Herman Melville; Yeats was making his way into this pantheon, and interest in Joyce had quickened. In a way, these academic favorites served Faulkner well, since they all required close reading, the explication of text which made up the New Criticism. But he was also hurt by new critical exclusivity: the application of standards which held that only the text mattered and that historical and cultural considerations were unnecessary baggage, at best secondary. But even in this hieratic view of literature, Faulkner offered language which could be evaluated and analyzed as one would work over a poet, an Eliot or a Yeats. Warren had struck exactly the right note: the time was ripe for a revival.

Not that lightning struck. Faulkner was still moving along on *A Fable* and worried about money. On May 5 he sent Haas a batch of manuscript. The accompanying letter cautions that the book is growing, and that he is anxious because Random House may not want to finance him through such a long enterprise. In a reckless assessment of his chances, he says he may get through it in four months. But as he begins to "see the whole plan of it . . . it looms too big in size to be finished in that time."[39] Speaking before a freshman English class at Ole Miss at the invitation of the teacher, Margaret Parker, Faulkner reiterates his favorite authors, the greatest influences on him—the Old Testament, Melville, Dostoyevsky, and Conrad, the latter perhaps most of all. Of his contemporaries—Wolfe, Dos Passos, Steinbeck, Hemingway, and Caldwell—he indicates that Wolfe came closest to success. He had made similar pronouncements before; but it is difficult to understand how he saw Wolfe as the most successful of the five.*

His attitudes toward visitors had not changed. He said he would receive Ilya Ehrenburg, the well-known Russian writer, for an hour and no more, which was sufficient to turn him away from a visit. In the meanwhile, Random House found Faulkner's old introduction to *Sound*, written for a special edition which was never published. Linscott suggested Faulkner add a postscript to it, and offered a revision. But Faulkner was wary of writing an introduction, even a revised one, pleading he was "hot" on his new book. That introduction, written in 1933, was published in the *Southern Review* (Autumn 1972).**

At about the same time or a little later, Faulkner wrote back he couldn't do an introduction and suggested Caroline Gordon for the task. He further suggested that they print the appendix, then follow with *Sound*, and then after that *As I Lay Dying*, which, he says, is not obscure and needs no further explanation. He adds that the title for the appendix should not be *The* Compsons, as Viking had it, but

---

*Usually, his lists included Willa Cather, the one female contemporary he regarded highly, mentioning her (in Nagano) as one of the five greatest American novelists up to the end of the nineteenth century. The chronology is off, but not the sentiment. Other female novelists whom he was aware of but without any specific impact on him were Evelyn Scott (the early admirer of *Sound*), Djuna Barnes, Anita Loos, Ellen Glasgow, Elinor Wylie, and Elizabeth Madox Roberts. The latter's work includes names we find in Faulkner, among them Burden, Horace, and Gowan.

**So many revisions and drafts, partial or "complete," exist that the *Southern Review* publication is only one possible version. A longer one appeared in James B. Meriwether's *A Faulkner Miscellany* (1974) and may be a later revision of the 1933 introduction.

COMPSON
1699 1945

It's an obituary, he says, not a segregation.

The tone of the letters has picked up; Faulkner, now that he is writing again, seems to be feeling better about his position. The major problem, however, was he could see no clear way to a solution of his expenditures. He had cut deeply into Random House's graces with advance money, and he was writing slowly, too slowly to make up the difference. There was as yet nothing in his working mind which could salvage his situation except a return to Hollywood at $500–600 per week; but that meant a stalemate on the novel, which he now owed to Random House.

Faulkner took time out to read an advance copy of Robert Penn Warren's *All the King's Men*, at about the time Warren was preparing to review the Viking *Portable* for the *New Republic*. Faulkner's reading of the novel is illuminating, less for what it says about Warren than for what it suggests about Faulkner in 1946, at the age of forty-nine. *All the King's Men* is a compelling fictional achievement, with Willie Stark's political career clearly based on Huey Long's in Louisiana. Yet the moral pivot of the novel is not Stark but the narrator Jack Burden. Warren's strategy is to perceive Stark's unfolding through Burden's eyes. The latter is a historian by training, having gone through all the work on the Ph.D. except the final stages of his dissertation, a study of the pre–Civil War figure Cass Mastern. In a life that straddled small events, all of them involving moral decisions and moral courage, Mastern struggled to be decent in an amoral world, and ended up a sacrifice to a Union bullet. His is a "small life," but from Burden's point of view, it proves instructive; it parallels the crisis in his own life as he drifts increasingly from moral to atavistic choices.

Faulkner latched on the Cass Mastern story as a "beautiful and moving piece" in and of itself. He felt that it *was* the novel: Warren should have taken that material and made a book of it. "The rest of it I would throw away. The Starke [sic] thing is good solid sound writing but for my money Starke and the rest of them are second rate. . . . As I read him, he wanted neither power for the sake of his pride nor revenge for the sake of his brevity; he wanted neither to purify the earth by obliterating some of the population from it nor did he aim to give every hillbilly and redneck a pair of shoes. He was neither big enough nor bad enough."[40] Except for *A Fable*, all of Faulkner's work henceforth was in the "Cass Mastern pattern."

By mid-August, Faulkner had sent 199 pages of *A Fable* on to Random House. One of the problems with the novel was his need to erase the screen-treatment aspect of it and to turn it into a novel. That is, he had conceived of the novel in dramatic terms and had written it in synoptic form. Now he had to turn synopsis back into novel, with the addition of narrative, dialogue, and character development through words as well as images. Part of the difficulties with his development of the book, apart from interruptions, was his need to get back into novelistic patterns, to slough off his Hollywood habits. Another factor in his slowness was the urgency of harvesting the Greenfield Farm crop, which would take him two and a half months, to November. It was a curious alternation of activities: working the farm and writing *A Fable* at Rowan Oak.

None of this pickup activity is an indication that Faulkner had made final peace with himself. As he told Haas, he was eager to come up to New York. "I've been buried six years now."*⁴¹ Perhaps his sense of being buried was exacerbated by brother Jack's proximity, assigned to FBI headquarters in New Orleans with his second wife, the French Suzanne. Faulkner appeared to like her, but Maud did not, and Suzanne was added to the list of daughters-in-law who were not permitted into the older Falkner's home.

As Faulkner moved toward a money-making proposition—editing a film script without leaving Oxford, for the lordly sum of $3,500—he was being lauded in France by Jean-Paul Sartre. Sartre's article appeared in the *Atlantic Monthly* and concerned itself with the intense impact that American fiction—especially that of Faulkner and Dos Passos—had made upon French life. Sartre particularly emphasized literary techniques, recognizing that these two were the only Americans writing in the modernist tradition. "American Novelists in French Eyes," he called his piece. He claimed that while Faulkner and Dos Passos were neglected in America, in France it was quite different—that Faulkner and to some extent Hemingway were men of the hour. *Sanctuary* is cited as one of the major works for the French: ironic for the writer who had written greater novels and who had himself depreciated it as a potboiler.

Faulkner's life during this period was a mosaic of events aimed at keeping himself within bounds. He did a good deal of riding, and it began to be characterized by foolhardiness and abandon. Often he could not completely control his horse, and in time, accidents piled up. The riding of large, powerful horses until they threw him, indeed broke his bones, was part of a large scheme in which he moved to the edge, indulging the same suicidal impulse which characterized his binge drinking. Horses, planes, drinking are all part of his need to destroy, sacrifice, repent, so as to become manly and unique—and at the same time become the recipient of the ministrations of others when he fell, crashed, or became oblivious.

He wrote Cowley about a hunting trip he took, and repeated almost the same description to Haas. These trips, which Faulkner continued to make

*Or as he told Cowley in December, it was a dull life; and then in a passage Cowley deleted for publication: "I need some new people, above all probably a new young woman" (Yale typescript, *Selected Letters of William Faulkner*, ed. Joseph Blotner [New York: Vintage Books, 1978], p. 245). His fiftieth birthday was looming.

even after he was awarded the Nobel Prize, took on the qualities of a profound ritual in which nearly every stage was regularized as it had been done for the previous fifty-two years. Within the seeming disorder of the camp he created a perfect order, a kind of formalized activity which would have fitted well into Lévi-Strauss's structuralist view of a subsociety establishing very clear and unambiguous terms for its existence. At one time the ritual had been played out at the Stone camp, which was close by; but now, with the encroachment of civilization, the adult Faulkner and his companions had to drive deep into the Delta where the big woods had remained untouched. They went to a camp due west of Yazoo City, almost in northeastern Louisiana, near Rolling Fork. The present-day Delta National Forest was directly to the south, and Panther Swamp National Wildlife Refuge was close by.

In his words to Haas, then repeated to Cowley, Faulkner tried to capture some of the excitement of this ritual: ". . . lived in a tent, shot a small buck, missed a magnificent stag twice ['had what you call 6 points and we here 12, since we count both horns and antlers,' he told Cowley]. He was a beautiful creature, broke out of a thicket 100 yards away running like a horse, perfectly flat, not jumping at all, doing about 30 mph, ran in full view for 75 yards, I picked two perfect openings in trees and shot twice. I left my customary 30–30 carbine at home for my boy to use and was shooting a .270 bolt action. I think the first bullet hit a twig and blew up. The second one missed him clean, over or maybe behind him; he was just running too fast. He was a beautiful sight. I'm glad now he got away from me though I would have liked his head."[42]

This taste for blood sports—which Faulkner rejected later, when he went on the hunt but refused to kill—is connected to that male bonding which involved living under uncomfortable circumstances, eating a monotonous diet of game (or coon), staying damp most of the time, drinking heavily after the day's hunt, rising early into chill and wet, standing still for several hours at a deer stand, occasionally getting a shot, but more often than not seeing nothing worth bringing down. The "big woods" experience, whatever its discomforts, was like renewal—not only for a complicated man like Faulkner but for the other hunters, whose own feelings were allayed by this temporary life within a life. But it was not only the hunt; it was the anticipation that preceded it, and then the stories which evolved afterwards around the campsite. This encapsulates some of the Faulknerian mode, telling and retelling: here past and memory are as significant as anything that occurs during any particular year. Once the day has closed, dark has settled in, the fire has been lit, food is being prepared, whiskey is available—when that setting is created, men without women, the stories can flow; and Faulkner had learned from and contributed to this process. It was a mode which entered deeply into his work. What may sound dull or discomforting to the outsider had the completion of a society, of a community. The beauty of it was that it occurred outside civilization—it was as though the men had found an island separated by moat and drawbridge from everyone else. No wives, children, girlfriends, no debits and credits—the men established the terms on which they would be invited back, and that was all. Rifle in hand, they had each other—and it was a profound need in Faulkner to know he was welcome on these annual trips.

Part V

Fame, Fortune, and Fear

Chapter Twenty-three

Post-Portable

B Y EARLY 1947 Faulkner had 251 pages of the novel, but he felt it was not right. Getting it right was his task for most of the year. It was on the surface an uneventful year, except that he turned fifty. He wrote steadily, with four hundred pages by July, and then feeling that that was only a start, projected a novel of one thousand pages. His sole short story published in 1947 was "Afternoon of a Cow," already translated by Coindreau into French; now it appeared in *Furioso*, edited by Reed Whittemore. This weak, flabby piece had been incorporated into *The Hamlet* (part 2 of chapter 3), but would not appear in *Collected Stories*. He almost sold a piece of *A Fable* to *Partisan Review* for $1,000, but that deal fell through when the segment in question, on the stolen racehorse, proved too long for the magazine.* The year appears to be a consolidating process for Faulkner, and although little seems to have occurred, he was trying to get away from film habits formed in past years and move back into novelistic ones. He needed to rediscover his basic tools. He had to unlearn as well as relearn. When he put aside *A Fable* early in 1948, he raced through *Intruder in the Dust* in three months of furious activity; but that novel, despite the ease and rapidity with which he wrote it, owed a great deal to his Hollywood years. It was in part the bad seed of those several unproductive years, a negative influence of considerable significance.

*Excerpts from "Notes on a Horsethief," however, were published, in 1954, in *Vogue* and *Perspectives USA*.

To detail 1947: Faulkner tentatively agreed to sell "Afternoon of a Cow" to *Furioso* for $5 per page, although he suffered some misgivings at seeing it in print. He finally leaves it up to Ober to decide whether to use it. Then in a follow-up note to Ober, he repeats that many people thought it in bad taste, but he tells him to sell it now (February 25). The real question is not whether it transgresses good taste—many fine works do—but a question of whether someone of Faulkner's stature wanted to be represented by such an inferior piece of writing, something done as a lark. There is, possibly, a darker side to all this, that Faulkner harbored such resentment against the Jiggitts-Lester parody of a quarter of a century before (what they called "Une Ballade d'une Vache Perdue") that he decided to make a little money out of their suggestion. Faulkner rarely forgot, almost never forgave, and with this he may have arced back to the earliest days of his writing career: gaining a form of revenge by turning a penny on his tormentors.

A Fable was gradually taking over Faulkner's life. He asked Ober to return twenty-three pages (229–251) as they were "not right." In the third week of March, he wrote Ober that this "book is going to be a book."[1] He is thinking, he says, of coming up to New York so as to tell both his agent and publisher what he is up against. He will need money as he is clearing up debts (a note on the Greenfield Farm), giving his mother $1,000, and feels he should justify what Random House had laid out and will have to continue to advance. If written, his explanation would take a twenty-five-page letter. He admits he cannot write as fast as he once could, and he projects another year or two for completion. On the same day he writes Haas a more detailed letter about his theme and subject. He indicates he has about three hundred pages and knows where the rest is going. He suggests coming up to New York, perhaps in April, and his reasoning is subtle. It "has to do with the locale and the matter [of the novel]. If the book can be accepted as a fable, which it is to me, the locale and contents wont matter. Perhaps they wont anyway. But then you might not want to publish it. I may be wrong about this, probably am. . . . So the best thing is for me to come up, take a whole evening and tell you all the story, get your reaction, and then plan between us about advance for me for some specific time ahead—say a whole year, maybe more."[2] He indicates that by "locale and contents" he means that the villain, historically, is the French army or all of the Allied armies of 1918; and the principal ones (fabulous, imaginary, as well as historically) are Ferdinand Foch, Douglas Haig, and John Joseph Pershing.

The subtle point is that Faulkner saw the book from its earliest conception, even before he had the title, as a "fable" and *not* as a novel. Yet with few exceptions, the reception of the book has been based on its measurement as a novel. Many of the episodes do not in fact need the realistic or probablistic underpinning associated with the novel. The fable allows far more leeway in fantasy and possibility—it is connected to the magical and fabulous, and can be read as a prose poem. Faulkner was educating Haas how to read the novel; and yet he would fail to reach his critics, who perceived *A Fable* as a failed *novel.* *

One side of Faulkner's long-time effort on *A Fable* was connected to his brooding about the nature of democracy. The book is linked profoundly to questions of egalitarianism, and with the ways Western democracies deal with issues of rebellion, justice, caste, and power in societies at war. These questions go back to the Civil War when Lincoln, the great egalitarian, suspended habeas corpus and moved around other civil rights issues in order to promote Union successes. A related question is to what extent constitutional rights should be suspended during a national emergency, and, by extension, in a wartime situation of an army abroad at war. Some of this brooding about democracy and egalitarianism bled over into *Intruder in the Dust*, where emphasis on race reveals several ideas extrapolated from the early development of *A Fable*. Faulkner the moralist —the man attempting to be just in a society permeated by injustice, hypocrisy, and deception—became in these works his own Redeemer, his message that of Jesus' Sermon on the Mount.

Yet we must remember that in matters of justice and race Faulkner was not a free man; that whatever he said could bring contumely upon him; that as a respectable Oxford citizen with considerable landholdings in the town and outside, he was expected to maintain a certain level of cohesive behavior. The people he bucked might be his banker, his lawyer, the holder of his note on the Greenfield Farm, as well as most members of his family. He would live to see how the Citizens Councils, formed after the *Brown* vs. *Board of Education* Supreme Court decision in 1954, put pressure on even moderates to go along with racially repugnant policies in order to survive. Repeatedly, a few virulent racists could line up support for their segregationist policies by way of threat and intimidation. It should also be remembered that Oxford, because of its proximity to the university, while not racially liberal, was atypical of small Mississippi towns. More representative were Philadelphia, Tunica, Tupelo, and other towns in that northern belt, where fanatical racism lay just below the surface.** When Faulkner took a stand, as he increasingly did in the late 1940s and 1950s, he was defying more than elements in moderate Oxford; outside that town, he was

---

*Including this writer. When I wrote about *A Fable* in *American Fictions: 1940–1980*, I considered it a noble failure as a novel. Trying to see the book as part of an old master's work reaching into a new generation of writers, I gave it little of the leeway a fable should have over a novel. None of this implies that *A Fable* is necessarily a better book as a fable; but it should be read within its genre, as more of an imaginative prose poem than as a realistic depiction of war and historical events. Nevertheless, several historical events, some recounted in books, lie behind the mutiny in *A Fable*, most notably Humphrey Cobb's *Paths of Glory*, but others which Faulkner may have known. See Cleanth Brooks, *William Faulkner: Toward Yoknapatawpha and Beyond* (New Haven: Yale University Press, 1978), p. 414ff.

**When James Meredith attempted to integrate Ole Miss in 1962, the large influx of racists on the campus attempting to stop him from registering came mainly from outlying districts. The sole input of Oxford residents appeared to be university fraternity students, who, brought up on racism, continued to practice its more virulent aspects in their fraternities. But among nonstudent elements, the hills and towns outside Oxford supplied the brutality.

anathema, virtually in fear of his life as he expressed increasingly independent views. None of this is intended to excuse or reason away his more
intemperate outbursts; but whatever weight we put on his statements, we
must recognize he was not popular.

A Fable was a testing-out of Faulkner's sense of egalitarian democracy,
his idea of a just society, and he had the opportunity to put some theory
into practice when a memorial plaque was planned for the courthouse
yard. The Veterans' Club of Oxford was behind the movement, for Oxford
had sent hundreds of young men off to war and seen more than a fair share
killed. The South in particular, of all the regions of the nation, had contributed its young to the war, and the listing of names became a sacred duty.
But which names? Should Negro dead be intermixed with white? In the
local cemetery, where the Falkners were buried or planned to be, a separate area was allocated to the Negro dead, including Mammy Callie. And
now the plaque: should the war dead, like the other dead, follow segregationist rules? Tempers flared; those opposed to the blending of names were
far more active than those who saw the hypocrisy of separation. For the
opposition, any such recognition of Negro rights would be a step toward
integration. Faulkner told Moon Mullen, the *Eagle* editor, that the plaque
should contain names of both races: "The only time they're not niggers is
when they're dead." But it is unclear if he favored blending or simply
listing of both races. In any event, the monument contained the names of
fifty-three whites and, below and separated, seven designated "Of the
Negro Race." The plaque was itself devised by Faulkner.

AFRICA   ALASKA   ASIA
EUROPE   THE PACIFIC
Dec. 7, 1941   Sept. 9, 1945
THEY HELD NOT THEIRS BUT ALL MEN'S LIBERTY
THIS FAR FROM HOME, TO THIS LAST SACRIFICE

Of course the fight over the plaque and the question of blending makes
the message on it ludicrous—"They held not theirs but all men's liberty"
—when it came to members of the Negro race. Faulkner was apparently
satisfied by the inclusion of the seven Negro names; but his real response
to the question of injustice only came with *Intruder in the Dust.* Not that
this novel becomes a clear-cut denunciation of segregation; but it does
demonstrate in no uncertain terms Deep South injustice to the Negro.

Just as we can trace Faulkner's movement from mild anti-Semitism to
even philo-Semitism on the occasion of Haas's son's death, so we can trace
a significant alteration in his personal view of Negro injustice to his early
work on *A Fable.* The importance of that novel, apart from reasons already
cited, was that it enabled Faulkner to think through who and what he was
ideologically, so that the book had equally important justification as a
biographical or literary event. And possibly because the finished product

becomes such a catchall, it is ultimately unsatisfactory aesthetically, whether one considers it as novel or fable.

Letters from now on touch upon how he was writing with a "serious bug," the old ease gone. He tells Haas he has realized lately "how much trash and junk writing for movies corrupted into my writing." He asks (in the spring) for part of the manuscript so that the first 250 pages can be made "all right." It is now a "slow thing compared to the speed I had once. I am a little stale."[3] He complains about the Penguin edition of *Soldiers' Pay*, introduced by Richard Hughes, because of "biographical stuff and literary opinions," also objecting to "more and more seeing my name and picture in print." He was well past 250 pages, up to three hundred by March 24 or so. He was also entering into spring planting at the farm, while telling Haas he foresaw another year of writing and necessitating a return to the $500 monthly stipend against royalties. He keeps repeating to both Ober and Haas that he would like to come up to New York, sending out feelers for Random House to fund the trip. Part of this desire was linked to his need to get away, to reject everything he was working to support; part to his wish to do some binging away from Oxford and any family constraints; part to his need for a "new young woman" who would make him feel a little less than fifty. Working along on *A Fable*, however literarily exciting the problems, was personally boring. Dying of tedium, he was trying to make a go of his life.

Jill had turned into a teenager. Faulkner meant well, but had no idea what she was thinking and feeling; no idea of the effect of who and what he was on her young life as she tried to be accepted; no idea what his and Estelle's drinking meant to a daughter who wanted to bring friends home and could not for fear of what she might find. The nuclear Faulkner household was composed of two individuals so deeply set into their own pattern of need they had little time for understanding others. Since his and Estelle's lot was set, the hardest part of this fell on the child growing up, trying to grapple with a famous father who was a part-time alcoholic, an embittered alcoholic mother who also subsisted on Seconal, and a household which lacked coherence or pattern. And there were occasions when both binged, or fought physically, or when Faulkner became oblivious and fell downstairs, and the servants fled until the moment blew over. Faulkner was conscious of how much he had to get away from all this.

Boredom was so overwhelming he agreed to something he would have rejected if life had been more intense. For the sum of $250, he agreed to lecture to classes at the University of Mississippi English department from April 14 to 17. Having been assured no notes would be taken, no faculty present, he was to appear in six classes: the novel, modern literature, creative writing, American literature, and Shakespeare—quite a round of material for a man who considered himself the country's oldest sixth-grader. There was, as he might have foreseen, a good deal of fallout, but in unexpected areas.

As it turned out there *were* notes, taken by a student named R. M. Allen, and these were both corroborated and disputed by a graduate student named Margaret (Peggy) Parker. As a consequence, a record of the lectures was made, albeit a debatable one. Allen's notes, whatever their accuracy, were to become the basis of the English department's publicity of the four-day event. The controversy came when Faulkner was asked whom he considered the five most important contemporaries. He ranked them: Wolfe, Dos Passos, Hemingway, Cather (someone thought he most likely meant Caldwell), Steinbeck. When pushed to be less modest, he redid the list: "1. Thomas Wolfe—he had much courage, wrote as if he didn't have long to live. 2. William Faulkner. 3. Dos Passos. 4. Hemingway—he has no courage, has never climbed out on a limb. He has never used a word where the reader might check his usage by a dictionary. 5. Steinbeck—I had great hopes for him at one time. Now I don't know."[4]

Other views were less controversial. He agreed that Joyce was the father of modern literature, ducked the question of whether the great American novel had been written (asserting that while *Huck Finn* will be read for a long time, it is not really a novel), stated that Sherwood Anderson was a better talker than writer. The memorable part of course came with his basically unfair assessment of Hemingway. The early stories of Hemingway show tremendous flair and daring, a writer going to the very edge of language. Faulkner's own sense of the word and his reliance on a very different mode of rhetoric prejudiced him to Hemingway's equally adventurous foray into literature.

The university's director of public relations, Marvin M. Black, prepared a release on the sessions. He sent it to the *Eagle*, which featured it prominently. But Black, hoping for greater publicity, also dispatched it to Harrison Smith at the *Saturday Review of Literature*. Black planned to expand the release into a full-scale article-essay. Faulkner was, of course, upset, and in an exchange with the department chairman, W. Alton Bryant, asked that such releases be stopped; after Bryant squelched Black over the publicity, he agreed that the English department could use a corrected version of the material. But Faulkner took that occasion, in a letter to Bryant on May 12, to compose a diatribe—an almost incoherent attack—on publicity and the American penchant for commercializing everything:

> I just hate like hell to be jumbled head over heels into the high-pressure bally-hoo which even universities now believe they must employ: the damned eternal American BUY! BUY!! BUY!!! 'Try us first, our campus covers ONE WHOLE SQUARE MILE, you can see our water tank from twelve miles away, our football team almost beat A. & M., we have WM FAULKNER at 6 (count them: 6) English classes.' That sort of thing I will resist with my last breath. But if the English department, not the publicity dept., uses the material, I shall have no qualms and fears.[5]

Hatred of the publicity mills is palpable, and yet from now on nearly everything Faulkner said or did was newsworthy. One of the media gods, Walter Winchell, had already mentioned him as having undergone treatment in a New York sanitarium.

Such a publicity release did not die easily. The New York *Herald Tribune* picked up excerpts from Black's release, and this started a round-robin of bad feelings and letters, some merely started, some sent. It pitted the two giants of American fiction against each other. Hemingway, deeply hurt, decided not to write Faulkner directly, but asked his friend General ("Buck") Lanham to respond. Lanham pulled out all the stops, stressing Hemingway's heroism under fire as a war correspondent, his responsibility to the military and to truth under dangerous conditions—all calculated to get at Faulkner, who had seen no action in any capacity. Faulkner answered Lanham at length,[6] sent a copy to Hemingway, and wrote the latter briefly as well. He corrects Lanham, saying that his statement made no reference to Hemingway the man, only Hemingway the writer. In a passage already cited above, Faulkner says that when pressed he gave rankings; but he meant "failure" in the sense they were all failures, since they lacked the stature of Dickens, Balzac, Dostoyevsky, and other giants. Within that context of failure, Wolfe failed least because he had the most courage. He risked clumsiness, bad taste, mawkishness, dullness. Dos Passos sacrificed some courage to style, but Hemingway was faulted because he did not courageously go out on a limb, did not risk bad taste, dullness. Faulkner excuses himself by saying he spoke extemporaneously, without notes, informally, not for publication.

It was, all in all, a curious episode because it illuminated a side of Faulkner we might not have suspected: his egoism, his need for personal aggrandizement, his depreciation of the man competing with him for the Nobel Prize. If we read behind the lines—and Faulkner did not explain why he had made the rankings nor did he pull back from their "veracity" —we see a writer desperate for attention and fame, even while fighting against the release of publicity materials. The rankings alone, whatever his specific comments on the courage of his contemporaries, demonstrate how he was measuring himself; and by putting his own achievement second to Wolfe's, he was revealing he was second only to a writer safely dead. The remarks are part brooding, part a lament for being so far from the centers of power, part compensation for financial troubles even at fifty (Hemingway commanded huge advances and large sums for articles, all the while living on a grand scale).

But other factors are at work, and with some conjecture one can find a sexual etiology. As far as we know, as long as Faulkner remained in Oxford, at Rowan Oak, he was sexually inactive. It is possible but unlikely that he had sexual liaisons with local women, or that at this stage he could sneak away to Memphis brothels. Hemingway may have been remarrying and gaining Faulkner's scorn for that, but he was, at least in the public eye, accessible to fawning women, even to new wives. Faulkner did not know of Hemingway's sexual problems, of his impotence or fear of it; what he derived from the news was the public Hemingway—his success at the desk, in the field, and, apparently, in bed. While condemning Hemingway's style of life, Faulkner could not have helped contrasting it with his own: an asexual relationship with Estelle, a tension-filled household, financial burdens only periodically relieved, utter and complete boredom while he wrestled with an implacable project. Hemingway sailed the seas, hunted on safari, gathered in women, ran with the bulls; he was the world's adventurer. Faulkner was unaware of the despair, the fears and anxieties, the early deterioration, the suicidal impulses—Hemingway kept that out of the publicity mills. What he revealed was the male version of the American dream: power, achievement, money, women, seemingly unlimited sex and booze, intensely male pursuits including disposable wives and children. Cooped up in the house of his own making, Faulkner was writing about Jesus Christ, while Hemingway was living like a modern Don Juan.

Work on *A Fable* was apparently his only link with the greater reality; in the immediate world, he complained bitterly that he was occupied with household chores which once fell to Negro servants. As a result of the war, a large rerouting of easily available help had taken place, and Negroes were leaving farms and households of the Deep South in record numbers. Only the most loyal, infirm, or elderly stayed on—for the young Negro, the future lay elsewhere, since the war had not brought to Mississippi any appreciable leavening of the racial situation. As a consequence, Faulkner found himself only with Uncle Ned, now in his eighties, and a young boy of twelve. With Estelle unable to be counted on—except that she was a fine cook—Faulkner himself did many of the chores.

Nevertheless, he wrote Ober during the Hemingway controversy that the manuscript was going well, although he could not afford twenty-five cents a page for retyping of corrected pages. He wanted a completely retyped manuscript, but jokes that it would be better for him to stop writing and do the typing himself than to pay anyone else. He was pleased: "It's getting right now. It was a tragedy of ideas, morals, before; now it's getting to be a tragedy of people."[7] On July 13, with the Hemingway affair over, he told Ober he was in the middle of an entirely new section, following page 120 of the manuscript. He originally thought it would run short, but now finds it to be about fifty to seventy-five pages. This is the one-hundred-page chapter about the racehorse, the episode that he published separately as *Notes on a Horsethief* (1951) and of course incorporated in *A Fable* three years later.

I am now in the middle of a hundred page new chapter which itself is a good story, a complete novelette, about a white man and an old Negro preacher and the preacher's 14 year old grandson who stole a crippled racehorse and healed its broken leg and spent a year dodging from one little back country track to the next racing the horse before the police ever caught them, then the white man shot the horse. They did it not to win money but because (the horse was a valuable champion) its owner would have retired it to stud because of its ruined leg while the thieves knew that what the horse wanted to do was to run races: a champion: a giant among horses.[8]

Faulkner's excitement in relating this episode is surely the result of his return to home territory. He knew the ground on which this horse would run, whereas the rest of the book, the "fable" part, fell on unfamiliar territory. There is also another factor at work: not only familiarity, but the opportunity to get back to a kind of America which was passing, an America which he assimilated at the feet of Sherwood Anderson. There is here some of the Anderson of "I'm a Fool" and also the Al Jackson stories the two swapped more than twenty years before. The stolen racehorse recaptures a Mark Twain–like America, before war, commercialization, publicity—it is Faulkner at his most nostalgic, when he could be a believer.

In a follow-up letter to Haas, he further describes the section as a flashback—"It describes what caused a man to do or be capable of doing one single act which carries on the story of the mss. itself. The reason may be 1. This is perhaps the last book I'll write [he means, probably, of this intricate a narrative] and I am putting all the rest of it into it, or 2. It may contain the germs of several more books."[9] He sees no chance of completing it this year and suggests a fall visit to Random House. But by two and a half weeks later, he has changed his mind. He wants to remain to work on the manuscript; but the farm is making its usual demands. He says he will require more money to cover corn and hay crop damage, the result of drought and heat following a flood. The money will go for feed, not food. Taxes are also a problem—back taxes as well as estimated taxes for 1947. Withal, he says he wants to buy another horse before he becomes too stiff in the joints for anything but old man's riding. Yet he insists he doesn't want the money from Random House—although he knows they will send it—and he speaks of another hitch in Hollywood. He states he is negotiating with Ober about striking a deal with Warners for his return for perhaps a full year at least.

The inconclusiveness of this letter—demonstrating the indecision which kept Faulkner working in a kind of limbo between Oxford and Hollywood—is followed by one with more certainty. He raises several points which will have considerable influence upon his future career. The entire year of 1947 was characterized by this in-and-out quality. He generated a good many pages—by October 3, he told Haas he had five hundred. He was not wasting his time, and we must grant that the complications of the theme demanded a great deal of narrative skill. This was Faulkner's most narratively involved novel since *Absalom*, his book of the 1930s and his thirties. He was not writing simplistic books like Hemingway's *Across the River and into the Trees*, or the later *The Old Man and the Sea*, or even the earlier *To Have and Have Not.* He was writing, he felt, great literature: a summa, something to match his idols, Dostoyevsky, Tolstoy, Dickens, or Conrad. And yet he was not fully involved in it: that suspension linking him to two places gave him little firmness. With his purpose divided his concentration was diluted.

The idea of Hollywood, moving between the back and the front of his mind, had more effect on him than he acknowledged. It was not only Hollywood money he coveted, but a certain freedom from Oxford and Rowan Oak. He might rail at the artificiality and tinsel of the place, but it did allow him movement. There were, of course, women: not Meta anymore, but others, available. There was also the sense of contact with the larger world. Yet even as he wanted to break out, he knew his future lay at his desk at Rowan Oak. The entire year was one in which he did a kind of balancing or pivoting act, weighing his future against his personal needs, trying to find direction. In the eyes of the literary world—critics, scholars, serious readers—he was a magnificent success, author of half a dozen masterpieces; but in his own eyes all that counted was the book he was writing, the career he was trying to plot, the deterioration he was attempting to postpone.

He knew he was quite far from completion, although he did not estimate another five years. He found himself in the unusual situation of having his publisher show more confidence in him than he felt in himself. His concept of self-reliance and independence had been taking a beating, and he kept dipping in and out of plans. While *Partisan Review* showed interest in the racehorse segment, or some part of it, and was willing to pay $1,000, he needed far more. He was becoming desperately worried about himself and his powers, perhaps fearful that all the years of drinking were turning his brain soft. Meta had noted memory lapses and some fuzziness. He worried also about being so close to the book, standing next to something so large he couldn't see it anymore.

Feeling stale, tired, anxious, he wondered why he was fretting and stewing when Haas told him years ago not to worry about the money. He suspected he was being kept as Random House's mistress, although everyone had been unfailingly kind and understanding. Ober had done everything a considerate agent can do. He had had nothing but generosity, and he believed he had not repaid it—nor could he foresee when he could. Hollywood was always there as a nagging presence. He even spoke of writing a short story to make some money, a potboiler; but he was out of practice for that, and with his slowness now, it seemed an unlikely prospect. All he could do as he wrote his way in and out of every scenario was to reject them all and push along on the novel. Even the racehorse segment was too long by far for the high-paying magazines, and he took up *Partisan Review*'s request to see it, with an offer of $1,000 on acceptance. But the editors said that unless Faulkner made alterations amounting to sharp cuts, they would reject it. He thought *Partisan Review* could make the cuts, as long as the editors didn't rewrite anything. But *Partisan Review* felt it was still too long, perhaps sixty pages in print, even if Faulkner wrote a brief introduction which could slice out a good deal. And then it was, finally, rejected, even as a fragment. All this worked out in late November and early December, and it was disheartening; not only for the loss of the $1,000 but for the rejection of something he had put all his energy and belief into. It weakened his resolve about the novel, and also it foreshadowed what the reception for *A Fable* would be—magnificent fragments, flabby whole.

All through late October and into the first half of November, Faulkner labored to get the long story right, gnawed by financial needs. For the first time, he mentioned to Ober (October 30) his fear that he might be broke in his old age, like so many artists (perhaps he had Fitzgerald in mind). Faulkner lived well, but even if he had saved, he would not have been able to put aside very much. Now that he was fifty, it was a depressing possibility that he would scrape along until his death. He became so eager to make magazine money on the story he agreed to a synopsis or summary, which earlier had been anathema. The blow that *Partisan Review* was wavering came when he returned from hunting camp in the Delta. His disappointment was intense. As he wrote Ober: "Did PR give a reason for turning the piece down? I would like to know. I have a notion they were disappointed in it. Did they find it dull as written?"[10] Not only did they find it dull, they found it unrealized—first-draft stuff, as Philip Rahv put it. Ober softened the real blow by stating length as the reason for rejection. Yet Faulkner suspected strongly he was losing his stuff. "What is your opinion of this section in question? Dull? Too prolix? Diffuse?"

He tries a defense of himself, before returning to the underlying suspicion of his value.

> I have an idea that this may have been PR's reason [diffuse, prolix]: The world has been so beat and battered about the head during the last few years that man is in a state of spiritual cowardice: all his bottom, reserve, strength has to go into physical stamina and there is nothing left to be very concerned with art. That that magazines does not exist now which would have printed sections from *Ulysses* as in the 1920s [*The Little Review*]. And that the man crouching in a Mississippi hole trying to shape into some form of art his summation and conception of the human heart and spirit in terms of the cerebral, the simple imagination is as out of place and in the way as a man trying to make the Egyptian water wheel in the middle of the Bessemer Foundry would be.[11]

What Faulkner neglects is execution, so intent is he on intent; and his execution was off target, prolix, too ripe for *Partisan*'s more stringent policies. He returns to the questions: "Will anybody read it in the next say 25 years? Are Random House by taking me on absolute faith as they have, wasting their money on it?" He cannot believe it is all a waste: "My own time doesn't count. I dont believe I am wasting it or I would have stopped before now. There is nothing wrong with the book as it will be, only it may be 50 years before the world can stop to read it. It's too long, too deliberate."

Besides the shock of being rejected at this stage with what he considered to be his summa work, there are other considerations, artistic and personal. It is very possible that with this rejection, he was discouraged sufficiently to put the project aside; he had second thoughts, and with that he turned to another kind of work within a little more than a month, the writing of *Intruder in the Dust.* The work went rapidly and restored his confidence in his ability to produce copy without blockage or anxiety. Yet his remarks indicate he feels the world has so altered that someone like himself is an anachronism. He refused to meet the modern world and its needs on its terms—his dislike of radio music, of jukeboxes, of any kind of beamed-in sound was only one part of this rejection. At fifty he suspected he was writing for a world which no longer existed, an audience which had shifted because of the war.

In a real sense, he was correct. The war had changed the rules of the game. And even as he became America's most honored writer in the 1950s (besides the Nobel, he garnered Pulitzers, the National Book Award, the Howells Medal), he was being replaced by a younger generation of writers: John Hawkes, Norman Mailer, J.D. Salinger, William Styron, Saul Bellow, and others. He became celebrated, a classic—but was relegated to an earlier time, set in a historical frame of reference. Even as he influenced many in that next generation, he was someone who had to be replaced. Flannery O'Connor put it well: "I braved the Faulkner," she wrote John Hawkes, "without tragic results. Probably the real reason I don't read him is because he makes me feel that with my one-cylinder syntax I should quit writing and raise chickens altogether."[12] Or: "It's [*Light in August*] a real sick-making book but I guess a classic. I read it a long time ago and only once so I'm in no position to say. I keep clear of Faulkner so my own little boat won't get swamped."[13] Faulkner is now a historical figure even for (or particularly for) such a strong writer as Flannery O'Connor.

Faulkner's immediate response was a crisis of nerve. The prolixity which marked the racehorse segment carried over into *Intruder.* Like the pitcher throwing what he believes is his best stuff and getting hit, Faulkner had lost his rhetorical touch, mixing superb passages with some which clot and clog. He still worked hard at his desk, he still suffered insomnia, which meant he could put in a day's writing before the day really began, and he still believed he had something to offer morally and ethically. But the revelation had struck. He was writing now to live, whereas earlier he had lived to write: a trite message, perhaps, but one that in this particular case went very deep.

As Faulkner turned the new year, 1947 to 1948, he was a man caught up deeply in fears of aging, in revelations of failure, in financial worries—turning old without sufficient resources; with, still, a mother dependent on him, a wife, daughter, niece, and all the rest. His personal life lay in ruins, a matter of intermittent peace between outbursts; he was drinking heavily, or else thinking of it, sexually dissatisfied, lacking the female companionship he yearned for. He saw quite clearly that, with his own needs preempting the paternal role, he could be a poor father and husband; and he was living parasitically off the largesse of a New York publishing house. Further, he was immersed in a difficult, cumbersome, intricate manuscript which did not easily provide solace. It was scratched over, interlarded and interpolated, with flashbacks within flashbacks. It was a manuscript lacking in coherence, organization, even plan at several stages. It was far from completed, and in fact might need radical overhaul to bring it around. Narrative was lost in extensive emendation; passages were written which went nowhere; he had exhausted numerals and needed to use letters of the alphabet to keep track of cancellations, insertions, interpolations. Discouragement faced him in nearly every segment of the manuscript; nearly every page reflected indecision, uncertainties.

When 1948 began, Faulkner shelved *A Fable* and moved on to other matters. He wrote *Intruder in the Dust* in about three months (published September 27). It made his fortune, since he gleaned $40,000 of the $50,000 purchase price MGM paid for it. One short story, "A Courtship," appeared in 1948 in the *Sewanee Review* (Autumn) and was reprinted in *Collected Stories.** In addition, Random House decided to go ahead with a new collection, which became *Collected Stories,* one of the landmarks in the making of his reputation. On November 24, he was elected to the American Academy of Arts and Letters. The year 1948 proved ambiguous: he gained some financial independence with MGM's purchase, but remained stalled on *A Fable. Intruder* did not advance his career but assimilated what he had done; and even the first planning for a collection of his stories was based on already published material, a memorial to the past. Yet on the whole 1948 was an improvement. He proved to himself he could still write, even if not at his highest pitch.

He told Ober (on February 1, 1948) that he had put aside the "big mss" and now had sixty pages on "an approximate 120 pages short novel, set in my apocryphal Jefferson." Although the narrative is cast as a mystery/murder, it is not Raymond Chandler stuff. Instead, it is more the relationship between Negro and white, "specifically or rather the premise being that the white people in the south, before the North or the govt. or anyone else, owe and must pay a responsibility to the Negro." But he insists it is a story, that nobody preaches in it—which of course is not true: it is sermonistic almost from the start: ". . . a Negro in jail accused of murder and waiting for the white folks to drag him out and pour

---

Sewanee paid $200 for "A Courtship," but Faulkner picked up an additional $300 when the story won first prize in the O. Henry short story awards. "A Courtship" went back to 1942, and was not enthusiastically received by Ober when Faulkner submitted it for publication. The story of the struggle between Ikkemotubbe and David Hogganbeck for Herman Basket's daughter was not one of Faulkner's most compelling; but after *The Portable Faulkner,* he was able to pull it from the drawer, sell it, and even win an award.

gasoline over him and set him on fire, is the detective, solves the crime because he goddam has to keep from being lynched, by asking people to go somewhere and looking at something and then come back and tell him what they found."*[14] By February 1, he felt he might be finished in three weeks, and by February 22 (?), he told Haas he had a first draft. "Am rewriting it now, a little more of a book than I thought at first so the rewrite will actually be the writing of it, which will take some time yet. I wont set a date; I'll just work at it."[15]

As Faulkner moved along the story of *Intruder*, his ideas about the relationship between Negro and white were once again undergoing revaluation. In *Absalom*, he had gone to the edge and suggested, in a shadowy way, that the South was really the embodiment of a single race —that racial purity was a myth. The South was black-and-white. But he had backed off from that. Then, in "Battle Cry," he had created the Negro as "America." There was no need for this particular touch, even in a patriotic movie, unless Faulkner sensed that the moment was right: that the white race and the nation owed something to the Negro to redress past injustice and present inequality and intimidation. Faulkner was moving toward his progressive statements of the 1950s, when ideas he had shadow-boxed with in his fictions became national realities.

Intruder is an outgrowth of his personal feelings rather than a reflection of his novelistic art. Although it has superficial linkage to ideas in *Light in August* and *Absalom*, it is really in its own category: a book which met the needs of the person rather than those of the artist. In such a work as *Intruder*, Faulkner withdrew into himself from being an American novelist to being a regionalist. He was directing his story at his own people, specifically at Mississippians. But even more than this, he was speaking to himself. He wrote the novel out of some need (besides financial, which is not to be neglected) to purge himself of quasi-racist feelings, to express his sympathy for the Negro and his equally strong need to define a role for the region. He felt the South had little time in which to work itself out, to pull itself together, for the Negro would show patience only a little longer. Lucas is his weapon: the Negro who refuses to act like one, or who, when he does, leaves whites bitter.

One element of interest in the novel is how Faulkner's views on race have become intertwined with his ideas about marriage, sex, and paternalism. Fathers and sons in this novel compete for attention with husbands and wives, marriage rights, adultery between Negro and white. Suffering in marriage is somehow linked to Negro suffering in general; there is no escaping either. The sensitivity to marriage and to adultery must be par-

*On June 7, 1940, Faulkner had written Haas about a short story he was planning. One of them was a murder mystery, "original in that the solver is a negro, himself in jail for the murder and is about to be lynched, solves murder in self defense." The story was never written, but Faulkner did not forget his plan and revived it fully seven and a half years later. Originally, the story was to become part of a sequence of short fictions which he would string together like the pieces in *The Unvanquished*. That idea too came to fruition with *Knight's Gambit* in 1949.

tially connected to Faulkner's own adulterous behavior—and even more to his revaluation of marriage itself and the value of long-time relationships, such as Lucas and Molly's, or his and Estelle's. But factored into this are fathers and sons—chiefly, the way in which Lucas takes on the paternal role with Chick, whose own father remains backgrounded, a gadfly, not a component. Gavin Stevens is also a kind of father figure, the close uncle, but one who fails. Fathers and sons here become part of a familiar Faulkner subspecies: the surrogate father becomes the real one, while the blood father steps aside.

Part of the difficulty Faulkner had in handling the material, besides the arrangement of his own feelings, was his use of the external narrator who also plays a significant role in the action. Faulkner was laying a tremendous burden on the narrator; as a sixteen-year-old, he not only observes and acts, he must also "overnight become a man," as Faulkner put it. His original impulse had been to write directly about Lucas, but as his point of view shifted, Faulkner located his post of observation outside himself, using Chick as he had done with others, going back to *Sound* and *As I Lay Dying*. The technique here was curious; when he first used this manner of observation, he had resorted to the stream-of-consciousness method to combine observation and personal experience. Now he wanted a more accessible means of narrating the story, and yet he also wanted to employ the benefits of the stream: an impersonal mode of expression. Using flashback, a modified stream coming from just beyond Chick's preconscious, Faulkner located himself outside the material and yet not distant from it.

While Random House was reading the manuscript and hoping for a more popular audience, Faulkner was thinking of magazine sales. He wanted a big killing with *Intruder,* perhaps a serial. He asked Haas to set a publication date which would make such a sale possible, and Haas wrote to say how much they all liked the manuscript. Meanwhile, Faulkner was back at the farm, involved in spring planting—not able to get back to *A Fable* until about July 4, he says. But in his eagerness to locate a magazine sale for *Intruder,* he tells Ober how to make it more palatable for serialization. By eliminating chapter 9—which contains a good deal of commentary on the South and on black-white relationships—Faulkner says he can offer a simpler story. Even chapter 11 might be deleted or pared down "to its essential story matter, which is to show that the sheriff and Lucas were successful, Lucas vindicated, murderer caught, etc."[16] Worried the manuscript might be too complicated for popular consumption, Faulkner uncharacteristically was willing to make concessions, with cutting, adapting, reconnecting. He reveals a slackening of aesthetic control, not only a desire for income. Not since *Sanctuary* had he made such a concession to a wider audience in one of his serious works (apart from his deliberately written potboilers).

Unknown to Faulkner, Cerf had been working behind the scenes to get a movie sale for *Intruder.* It was an astute move on his part, since he saw in the manuscript a film possibility, garnering money not only for the hard-pressed author but for the firm as intermediary in any transaction. Both Warner Brothers and Cagney Productions were interested. Faulkner wrote (May 18) that he favored Warners, and his reasoning is quite calm considering the agonies he had suffered because of Jack Warner's recalcitrance. "Warner agreed to hold no claim on what I did while on leave, but my relations have been amicable with them, about getting time away when I insisted, no great fuss about it. And since they did not become stuffy about relinquishing claim to movie rights on what I do while off their pay, I would like to give them the refusal, then let Cagney see it." The letter indicates, implicitly, that Faulkner recognized he had made a legal deal with Warners, and that, given the legality of the agreement, the studio had given him considerable leeway.

Neither Warners nor Cagney Productions bought film rights to *Intruder;* MGM did. Faulkner would make only a passing contribution to the screenplay, looking over Ben Maddow's work and offering slight alterations. He received no film credit, nor apparently did he want to have much to do with the production. All in all, MGM made a movie that was quite faithful to the spirit of the book, and even caught by means of careful camera work and a shimmering, scrimlike shooting of scenes some of Faulkner's sharp cutting, his introspection, his depth of narrative. Faulkner was very pleased with the sale—$40,000 to him, $10,000 to Random House. Now his way was clear to come up to New York without further borrowing from his publisher.

One powerful element in *Intruder,* which Cowley caught in his review for the *New Republic,* was something no film version could include. Faulkner was moving into a period wherein he became increasingly the public champion of Negro rights, a supporter of racial justice, a critic of Southern mores. But at the same time, Faulkner was profoundly a man of his state and the South: he needed the idea of community and of the South as independent of what the North felt was best for it. He was too much the great-grandson of the old colonel to be otherwise, too much the recipient of those stories of honor and courage. Yet, as he would see to some extent in *Intruder,* the two parts would not cohere or resolve themselves: Negro justice, if it came, would have to arrive with federal insistence. Faulkner believed in the good auspices of the region, but he was deceived by his own conservatism, his fear of radical change, and even by the fact that Oxford was less racially hateful than other areas.*

Even as he wanted the two parts to come together—fairness to the Negro and the South's independence—he suspected it could not occur; his comments through Gavin Stevens or through Chick's observations show

---

*When John Falkner wrote about the attempt of James Meredith to integrate Ole Miss in 1962, an effort met by mob violence, Faulkner's brother insisted that *all* of the violence and hatred derived from those outside Oxford. What he neglected to add was that a good deal of it was also generated by Ole Miss fraternities, supposedly the educated sons of the more enlightened part of the state.

the need to keep the Negro in his place. As long as he remembers he is inferior, the Negro can gain property and advance. While Cowley felt Faulkner was trapped in an equation of his own making, there is good reason to believe he recognized the impasse. It was the impasse of the South: to remain its own master and yet to throw off, finally, the heritage of slavery. The shrillness of many of Faulkner's statements in the 1950s, as he came to grips with these terrible dilemmas, can be explained in part by his realization that not he, but the South, was trapped by its own rhetoric. He had tried to put some of this into *Intruder,* and he suffered the backlash. He was accused repeatedly of having sold out his birthright in order to gain the coin of the realm; he who had scorned Jews as interested only in seeking profit was bracketed with them.

On August 16, Faulkner re-signed the necessary legal papers for the movie sale of *Intruder,* having already signed and then mixed up the papers. Taxes were still an annoyance, but he was able to settle with the government for less than was demanded, and he had the movie money to count on. Besides the possibility of a *Life* profile by Cowley, if he agreed, the *New Yorker* wanted a profile, to be done by an old Faulkner friend from New Orleans, Hamilton Basso. He rejected that, saying he wanted to remain a private person, "the last private individual on earth."*[17]

But something else was looming: a rather pleasant enterprise, the volume of his short stories. From the beginning he treated it seriously, knowing that, like Cowley's *Portable,* it was to be a monument. He also recognized he was not capable anymore of that kind of work; short stories were part of that insane burst of creativity which had overpowered him in his early thirties. Now moving toward fifty-one, he could hope only to turn out the occasional novel, consolidate what he had, and reappear packaged attractively in this volume and in the reissue of his earlier books.

His exchange over the volume came with his request to Haas to send on a list—he had mislaid the original one—and to give him a chance to mull it over. He wanted to "give this volume an integrated form of its own, like the Moses [*Go Down, Moses*] book if possible, or at least These 13."[18] He mentions the big book, *A Fable,* but fears he will not return to it until the winter of 1949. He feels now that he is free of money worries for at least four years, he can get a lot done on it. He reveals he "got thrown for a loss last month with an ulcer which still bothers" him a little. But he sounds optimistic and hopes to come up next month for a week or so.

By then Faulkner was beginning to receive *Intruder* reviews and backlash. Many Southern reviewers were upset that he seemed to have gone

---

*It was also at about this time Carvel Collins visited Rowan Oak, through the intercession of a common friend. That fall Collins was going to teach the first full Faulkner course at an American university, at Harvard. His early work on Faulkner, continuing into the present decade, began the first serious sustained research on the writer. Entering Faulkner's life as he did, in the late 1940s, Collins was able to interview scores of people who had died by the time the next generation of Faulknerians started to gather information. Little of this material, however, has been made accessible.

over to the enemy. One in the Memphis *Commercial Appeal,* however, felt that the book was full of artistic skill. The *New Yorker* had finally gotten away from Fadiman and his jejune reviews of Faulkner, Edmund Wilson replacing him with a different dimension of commentary. But Wilson giveth and Wilson taketh away. Missing how Faulkner gained strength from his isolation in Oxford, from its language and community values, he felt that the writer owed his careless and extravagant rhetoric to provinciality. On the other hand, Wilson found the rhetoric and method to work well on occasions, giving perhaps an accurate appraisal of winds of change in the South. He perceived in the novel Faulkner's response to civil-rights legislation, asserting that Gavin Stevens was Faulkner's spokesman in his rejection of outside interference. Little of the review gets into questions of art. Eudora Welty, in a December 15 letter to the *New Yorker* (published January 1, 1949, in its "Department of Amplification"), defended Faulkner against what she felt was Wilson's condescension and pretension. Other reviewers took issue with the problem of provinciality which Wilson focused upon, arguing quite differently. Cowley saw in Faulkner two contrary drives, the desire for Negro equality along with the equally forceful need to maintain Southern white hegemony. Very few reviewers tried to treat the novel generically, as a fiction within the detective-mystery mold; most attempted to find in it social and political content.

By the time of publication in 1948, a growing issue in the Deep South and the nation was the rise of the Dixiecrat party (the States' Rights Democrats). After Harry Truman was nominated by the Democratic party as its presidential candidate, the Dixiecrats met in Birmingham and ran their own candidates: Strom Thurmond, governor of South Carolina, for president and Fielding L. Wright, governor of Mississippi, for vice-president. The issue was, of course, race, specifically the civil rights plank in the Democrats' platform. The Dixiecrats were to offer the Deep South and the nation an alternative: status quo, no relenting on racial issues, not even moderation. This was a party formed on values described in *I'll Take My Stand* almost two decades before: America as a white Eden which must be kept racially pure. The party gained thirty-eight electoral votes, with a thirty-ninth coming later when an elector defected, and carried Mississippi and three other states. While Truman swept to a broad victory (304, later 303, electoral votes to 189 for Dewey), the solid South was broken; and the racial problem, far from moving toward Faulkner's idea of moderate resolution, was severely exacerbated. The South was in turmoil over the split, since many senior Southern Democrats (like Richard Russell of Georgia and Harry Byrd of Virginia), while sympathetic to the Dixiecrats, did not bolt the main party for fear of losing their seniority. What in effect occurred was that these powerful committee chairmen used their positions to further the aims of the Dixiecrats without forgoing their Democratic party allegiance. The consequence was a Congress superficially more liberal than the one before (both Senate and House went heavily Democratic),* but in actuality controlled by committee heads who agreed almost down the line with Thurmond and Wright.

Into this came *Intruder in the Dust,* which from the resolutely white Southern point of view was little more than a sellout to Yankee values. It is necessary to view the Faulkner of *Intruder* from two perspectives—first against an agitated, immoderate, defiant Mississippi and South in general, where any flexibility on race made one a scalawag (a Southerner who favored the Union during the Civil War); second as a man who deeply feared change and who hung on to moderation in race and everything else long after the battle for moderation was lost. Faulkner was always involved in a balancing act: the desire for human equality and decency coming to the surface, but then the pullback from what might be needed to effect that change. In 1877, with Reconstruction in effect finished, the South had reestablished states' rights: it continued to treat the Negro in slave terms even with slavery banned, and the Negro, until he began to migrate in great numbers, had little alternative but to go along. This was the ground to which Faulkner was inclined to retreat.

Faulkner played on every chord in this dismal symphony. He knew every note, every sharp and flat, every modulation. And he had his own temperament to deal with—something the reviewers could not know. That fear of rapid change, of any alteration in the rhythms and paces of Southern life, filled him with horror. Beneath the often daring content and the innovative fictional methods was a man not at all bohemian or avant-garde, but deeply traditional. The tensions of all this were palpable, especially after 1948, when Mississippi seemed to be heading on its own course outside the reach of the federal government. What the Dixiecrat movement meant in reality was a form of secession, nothing less.

Intruder was not only a troublesome book for Faulkner's fellow Oxonians** to accept; it is a difficult book to locate in his canon. One problem is that it is an earnest but ambiguous avowal of where he stood on one of the most significant issues for him and the South, race. Another problem is that he used Lucas Beauchamp's story as a catchall for what he believed about modern society—an extension of ideas already laid out in *Go Down, Moses.* A third area of difficulty comes in his effort to graft onto Lucas, a Negro, what he believed generally about man's independence of spirit and ability to endure. Yet at the same time Faulkner does not view Lucas as representative, but solely as an individual. A fourth problem comes with his effort to link a faulty detective-story plot to issues of great moment: race, culture, caste, modern society, individual rights. The consequence of

*Such liberals as Paul Douglas, Hubert Humphrey, Estes Kefauver, and Lyndon Johnson became elected to the Senate for the first time. In governor seats, we find Adlai Stevenson, Chester Bowles, and G. Mennen Williams. Yet despite their liberal racial sympathies and their desire for change, they would be bottled up until the mid-1960s by Southern Democrats who fought to maintain status quo racial politics.

**Copies were available in Oxford toward the end of September, and the Oxford *Eagle,* not always Faulkner's greatest fan, now featured him as "Oxford's great novelist."

so much packed into a relatively brief book—Horace Gregory called it a long short story—is that vital issues are discussed, not acted out. The resolution of all these problematical areas comes as sermon, lacking the texture and intricacy the problems themselves demand.

There is a serious ambiguity in Lucas: his loyalty to his part-white past, and thus to his line of descent, and his loyalty to the Negro as a race. Gavin Stevens directs most of his comments on Lucas to Lucas as a Negro, but little to Lucas defending his descent from the McCaslins. Cleanth Brooks has made this point, and it is one that deserves attention, although there is a flaw in Brooks's argument. He separates the two matters: Lucas as Negro and Lucas as eager to defend his proud heritage derived from Carothers McCaslin. The two, however, are inseparable in Lucas, but separable in Gavin Stevens's view. The problem lies not in Lucas's identification, for he is both Negro and McCaslin, but in Stevens, who sees only the racial, but not the familial, question.

Another problematic area, besides the absurdities of the plot mechanism and its working out, is Faulkner's inability to turn his educated lawyer into more than a windbag. Faulkner gains an audience for Gavin by keeping Chick close to him; only a courteous young nephew would pay attention. Yet Gavin's interminable statements contain a good deal of the racial moderation Faulkner himself propounded in the 1950s. In fact, Gavin defends a mode of life which is clearly not working for the benefit of the man whom he says he wants to benefit. " 'I'm defending Lucas Beauchamp. I'm defending Sambo from the North and East and West—the outlanders who will fling him decades back not merely into injustice but into grief and agony and violence too by forcing on us laws based on the idea that man's injustice to man can be abolished overnight by police."[19] It is unclear what weight Faulkner is placing on these remarks, inasmuch as the South since 1877, when Reconstruction ended, had not provided any accommodation for the Negro. On what basis does he have Gavin make this statement, when by 1948 the Negro was little better off than he had been seventy-five years earlier?

The novel becomes ruptured on many grounds. What is perhaps most successfully done is the slow shaming and transformation of Chick faced by the realities of Yoknapatawpha life. Like most Southern boys, Chick was filled with Civil War lore, with Southern victories, with Pickett's charge at Gettysburg as a kind of valorous last hurrah in a war already lost. It is this world of memory and legend which is threatened by Lucas and what he seems to stand for: his refusal to be intimidated, his insistence on his own proud heritage. Chick must absorb this bifurcation between a valorous past and a Negro who refuses to hold his place, and he must resolve these conflicting impulses. How he deals with this becomes part of the novel's major meaning, and it should be the deciding factor. But Faulkner does not leave that alone. He must drag in a great deal of other baggage which is only peripherally meaningful to Chick, and much of that in the "false" education Gavin tries to impose on him. Gavin speaks of community values, and yet it is these very values Chick observes to be deteriorating in the face of reality.

But whatever the ideological difficulties of the novel, Faulkner was planning his trip to New York, telling Haas he would come from October 15 to 20, "soon as squirrel and dove shooting is over." He promises to bring some of the "big mss. and give Random House a chance to see what goes."[20] Faulkner actually came to New York on October 18, and Random House gave him a full menu of activities. The results of this were predictable—he simply could not take this kind of schedule without letting go, by binging himself close to death. He also had another form of release in mind. Her name was Ruth Ford, an actress he had met before, and who had appeared in Sartre's *No Exit*. Faulkner tried to advance himself with her, although whether anything took place is unclear; but Ruth played a large role in Faulkner's future when he structured *Requiem for a Nun* in its dramatic version around her. Blotner quotes Faulkner's words to her, as she reported them later: " 'Ruth,' he said, 'I've been your gentleman friend for quite a while now. Ain't it time I was promoted?' Ruth laughed. 'Oh, Bill!' she said."[21]

On the nineteenth, a Tuesday, Haas threw a party to celebrate Faulkner's book and his appearance in New York. At this lavish Fifth Avenue gathering, with two butlers hired for the occasion, Faulkner met Cowley and his wife for the first time, and saw his old publishing friends Harrison Smith, Cerf and his wife, Klopfer and his wife, and Jim Devine, who had saved him when he fell unconscious against the radiator at the Algonquin. The presence of Devine meant Faulkner would not settle for the party, but would continue on when the Haas celebration ended. Cowley was interested in Faulkner's appearance at fifty-one: estimated at 5' 5" tall (weight 148), slim and muscular—although at that height and weight, slim does not seem quite right. Faulkner was becoming stocky, although Cowley stresses the slimness of his waist. He also emphasizes the shapeliness of Faulkner's hands. Cowley characterizes his expression as being like Poe's in photographs, "crooked and melancholy."

Cowley: "His forehead is low, his nose Roman, and his gray hair forms a low wreath around his forehead," giving the impression of a Roman emperor. Tracing Faulkner's features through photographs from youth to middle age, one observes his rather undefined facial structure becoming quite strong and distinctive. An uncertain chin had taken more shape as the rest of the face took on the look of the man. Faulkner was an example of a man whose appearance improves greatly as he ages because the look comes from within; not simply from aging, but from what the man feels about himself. He was quite a commanding-looking man at this time, as Cowley noted: "Bush eyebrows; eyes deeply set and with a droop at the corners; a bristly mustache."[22] Faulkner carried himself well, which helped to compensate for his small stature. Although short by midcentury standards (about three or three and a half inches under the white-male average), he did not give the impression of insignificance or wispiness; he had presence, the appearance factor one finds in many actors (like Raft, Robinson, Cagney) who are surprisingly short. Faulkner's deep, often difficult to comprehend Mississippi accent intensified his sense of dignity. He was clearly a personage.

They discussed, according to Cowley, his idea of arranging a collection of short stories by subject matter and then printing it in one big volume. Faulkner also told him about his new novel and revealed for the first time his plan to put a cross design on the jacket. Cowley observed that if Faulkner's real intention had been carried out, the title would have been THE CROSS: A FABLE, in the form of a rebus, whereby a sign or symbol suggests the word(s). They also discussed the proposed *Life* profile, and when Cowley assured Faulkner he wouldn't intrude into his personal life, the writer reluctantly agreed with "a sigh of resigned assent."[23] They ranged widely and in some detail over the writer's life, but Cowley waited for him to leave for home (on October 26) before setting it down. Most of the details Faulkner provided (or Cowley dug out) are fairly accurate and include a few remarks about racial relationships. Faulkner felt Gavin Stevens was speaking for the "best type of liberal Southerners," and that if the race problem "were just left to the children they'd be solved soon enough. It's the grown-ups and especially the women who keep the prejudice alive." Cowley seems to accept this, although Gavin Stevens in context represents futile talk, not progressive racial ideas; and when Faulkner mentions women as obstacles, he omits how economic conditions imposed by an almost solely male world help to keep Negroes as an underpaid underclass, a pool of cheap labor.

What Cowley omitted in his *Faulkner-Cowley File* was how Faulkner behaved when he was still in New York, and what ensued from that. The trigger was a *New York Times* interview with Ralph Thompson, which, turning literary, sent him into a panic. He said whatever came to mind, as he would later do on questions of race. He bad-mouthed Oxford, saying that now he had made money townspeople came around to borrow; or else, they downgraded his achievements and denied he had accomplished anything. He figured he was better off when he had "one pair of pants, one pair of shoes, and an old trench coat with a pocket big enough for a whiskey bottle."[24] Now he gets letters asking for personal details, or critiques "about curves and linear discreteness." The latter was a response to Thompson's asking him about Richard Chase's quite perceptive article, in which Chase saw Faulkner imagery in terms of curves, lines, planes. Such a question was bound to receive a venomous response.

It also set off the deeper panic button: what Faulkner had been building up to had arrived. He was ready to let go, and the interview was probably only the catalyst; anything would have done—the press of people, the ambiguity he felt toward New York, the kindness of friends he had to test further by turning them into maternal figures, the need to release whatever had been bottled up, emotionally, sexually, physiologically. At such times—and October 20 was one of them—he was driven by demonic energies of destruction. He set out drinking suicidally. Starting on Wednesday, the twentieth, and continuing through the twenty-second, he drank steadily in his Algonquin room, not coming out, not accepting any invitations (not even from Ruth Ford on the twentieth and twenty-first), avoiding Harvey Breit of the *New York Times*, whom he genuinely liked, evading Cowley, who had planned a luncheon appointment. The latter went to the room, entered, accepted a drink, and left. Later that day, Ruth and Breit tried the room, were let in by the manager, and saw a desperately drunk and ill Faulkner, halfway between unconsciousness and death. Cowley and others arranged for immediate medical care, at the Fieldstone Sanitarium. The diagnosis was the usual: severe alcoholism, malnourishment, exhaustion of the entire system. But he was still a fast recuperator and by the next day was ready to leave, demanding to be let out, whereas the doctor recommended keeping him for several days. Two such different points of view were resolved when Cowley agreed to take him in, in his home in Sherman, Connecticut, from the twenty-third to the twenty-sixth.

For those three days, Cowley and his wife, Muriel, became nurses and benefactors to the man who would be recommended for the Nobel Prize the next year. They got him to withdraw slowly by giving him watered-down drinks, and they gently forced him to eat nourishing food. Faulkner was in full withdrawal: attacks of nerves, chills, sweating, pacing up and down like a caged animal, finally breaking down and requesting a drink. A good deal of the information Cowley reveals in his *File* about Faulkner's background was communicated during this time, when Faulkner talked so as to relieve his withdrawal, a kind of psychiatrist and patient session. By the second day, Monday, he was well enough for a long drive on a lovely fall day, and on Tuesday he felt ready to return to Oxford. He had withstood another severe binge—and had gotten what he wanted, in that he had turned admirers into nurses, and had found his form of release from what had been tensing him for months.

Back in New York he saw Ruth at a dinner party, and drank, but in moderation. He saw Saxe Commins, also Cowley; by the thirtieth he was on his way, having taken time to thank the Cowleys, and particularly Muriel, with a dozen long-stemmed roses. By October 31, he was back in harness in Oxford, with plans for the six categories of *Collected Stories.* He also suggests that instead of "Wasteland," "Desert" or "Barren" would suffice, but he preferred the first choice, which stood. On November 1 he wrote Cowley to set out the essential terms of the volume. He insisted that it be unified, that parts interrelate, and he quoted by heart (although inaccurately) from *Pan Michael* by the Polish writer who deeply influenced the young Joseph Conrad, Henryk Sinkiewicz.* Faulkner recalled: "This

*Sinkiewicz won the Nobel Prize for Literature in 1905, and the part Faulkner comes closest to remembering is the Polish writer's statement of purpose as to why he writes: "for the strengthening of men's hearts." In his Nobel Prize acceptance speech, Faulkner brought together both Conrad and Sinkiewicz for their words about the function of literature and a delineation of man's purpose on earth; but they had already come together earlier in Conrad's own dependence on some of Sinkiewicz's writing and his admiration of him as a man.

book written in . . . travail (he may have said even agony and sacrifice) for the uplifting of men's hearts." He stresses that even a collection of short stories must be integrated, "an entity of its own, single, set for one pitch, contrapuntal in integration, toward one end, one finale."[25]

Other matters arose, and they seemed about of equal importance in Faulkner's mind. He told Haas on November 11 that he was working on the big manuscript, but not too hard "as our deer hunting camp opens next week and due to the deaths this past year of the two senior members, most of the work—getting the dogs and horses sent up, cook, tents, feed etc., has fallen to my lot."[26] Then two weeks later, on about November 24, he wrote Saxe Commins about something he had already mentioned: he had been thinking of another volume of stories, before they got on with *Collected Stories*. He had in mind *Knight's Gambit*. "I am thinking," he wrote, "of a 'Gavin Stevens' volume, more or less detective stories. I have four or five short pieces, averaging 20 pages, in which Stevens solves or prevents crime to protect the weak, right injustice, or punish evil. There is one more which no one has bought ["Knight's Gambit"]. The reason is, it is a novel which I tried to compress into short story length. It is a love story, in which Stevens prevents a crime (murder) not for justice but to gain (he is now fifty-plus) the childhood sweetheart which he lost twenty years ago. It will probably run about 150 pages, which should make it a volume as big as INTRUDER."[27] The volume ran considerably shorter than *Intruder* and consisted of six stories, of which the last, "Knight's Gambit," is more a novella than a story, itself printing out to little less than half the volume. He thinks it can be ready for fall publication in 1949—it appeared in November. He was also thinking of reprints—the time was right, and he wanted to be sure *Absalom* was in print again.

At about the time he was writing this letter, Faulkner received the highest honor an American writer can be granted: he was elected to the American Academy of Arts and Letters on November 24, when he was already in deer camp. He had been a member of the National Institute of Arts and Letters since 1939, but the Academy was a body of fifty within the much larger (250) membership of the Institute. It was a signal honor which, typically, Faulkner ignored. He wrote to the president of the American Academy on the last day of the year that the letter of appointment had been mislaid, that he had been in deer-hunting camp, and that by responding to their follow-up letter he was taking this opportunity "to express my awareness of the honor." He was now in a position to move on to other, international honors.

In another development on a completely different front, MGM was planning on filming *Intruder in the Dust* in Oxford. The town seemed receptive to the prospect and told the location manager it could handle the crew and cast, about 125. Mullen of the *Eagle* encouraged the shooting of the film in its authentic setting, and, although no advocate of racial equality, defended Faulkner against Dixiecrat opposition. Mullen's argument, which carried the day, was an appeal to the money that would pour in as the result of a large group of outsiders; a welcome infusion of funds into an economy none too strong, despite the general economic recovery in the country.

For Faulkner, it was the beginning of a heady time. Although he seemed so laid back he appeared oblivious to the honors accruing to him, he was in fact quite aware, and in a sense rejuvenated. The Hollywood of Warners' terms was behind him; he had money in the kitty, living expenses, a long novel on the drawing board, a volume of short stories for the immediate future, his *Collected Stories* the next year; and he had already projected a follow-up to *The Hamlet*, the books in the Snopes trilogy. At fifty-one, he was not finished. And if he looked at his chief competitor, Hemingway, he saw a man who had published nothing since *For Whom the Bell Tolls* in 1940, a man who seemed played out, too much the great man of letters to find time or energy to write seriously.*

*Over the years Hemingway had not spared Faulkner, taking pot-shots at him on several occasions, so that Faulkner's relatively low ranking of Papa for lacking courage in his writing was not an isolated judgment. In attempting to establish his own hegemony in American letters, Hemingway had tried to floor everyone with his blows. Aware that he and Faulkner had published together in the New Orleans *Double Dealer*, he said that his contribution, "Ultimately," was poor enough to fit in a collection of Faulkner's "early shit." In *Death in the Afternoon*, well before Faulkner warmed up his rankings, he had written: "You can't go wrong on Faulkner. He's prolific too. By the time you get them ordered there'll be new ones out." By 1936 he recognized, or so he said, Faulkner was a better writer than he, but he told Cowley in 1945 that Faulkner, like Fitzgerald, "just needs a sort of conscience that isn't there." Jeffrey Meyers reports that Hemingway referred to his rival as "Corncob." When Faulkner won the Nobel Prize (Hemingway won it five years later, in 1955), he told Cowley that the Southern writer lacked moral fiber, and was as much of a prick as Edgar Allan Poe. He envied Faulkner the prize, and then when he won it himself, criticized Faulkner for having sold out to Hollywood and for being an alcoholic. What particularly rankled Hemingway, if we can believe his condemnation, was that Faulkner wrote the screenplay of *To Have and Have Not* and improved on the novel, along the way revealing all of the novel's worst flaws. He considered *A Fable* as worse than shit, comparing it to the night soil of Chungking, a nightmarish memory of his reporting days in China. And in 1959, as Meyers shows, when both were old and alcoholic, he said: "[I] built him up about as high as he could go because he never had a break then and he was good then. So now whenever he has a few shots, he'll tell students what's wrong with me. . . . He cons himself sometimes pretty bad. That may be just the sauce. But for quite a while when he hits the sauce toward the end of the book, it shows bad" (Jeffrey Meyers, *Hemingway: A Biography* [New York: Harper & Row, 1985], pp. 431–33). What Hemingway could not accept was that when the sweepstakes ended, Faulkner, sauce and all, held the field.

The Prize

I N 1949 FAULKNER reached for a new life. There was to be a major film based on one of his novels, and the recommendation would come from the Nobel Prize Committee that he be awarded the prize in literature. The committee vote, however, was not unanimous, as required, with three members holding out. By the time it became unanimous, it was too late for the award, and it was held over to the following year. Still, by the end of 1949 it was known that Faulkner would receive it, this year or another. *Knight's Gambit* appeared on November 27, not one of his stronger efforts by any means, but a book he had managed to squeeze out. He published no short stories this year, but he did see the reissue of *The Wild Palms, The Hamlet,* and *Go Down, Moses*; the latter in a second edition was presented as a novel. There was further consideration of *Collected Stories.*

Looming over Faulkner as the year began was the possibility of Cowley doing a *Life* profile. For the writer, *Life* represented nearly everything he detested about American culture: the promotion and self-promotion, the use of publicity to cloud real issues of literary value, the photographs revealing private lives, the intrusion into personal, even intimate, affairs to titillate an ignorant public, the use of captions to simplify and reduce meaning. Along with *Time,* whose cover Faulkner had graced on January 23, 1939, *Life* represented that whole patina of pseudo-sophistication which characterized the New York–Los Angeles scene. He opened the year on January 5 by writing Cowley how he felt. He starts by confusing *Life* and *Time*, and says that ten years ago he had told the magazine he didn't want a piece about him; he had repeated the same message to *Vogue* two years ago. "I still dont want it, I mean, me as a private individual, my past, my family, my house. I would prefer nothing about the books, but they are in the public domain, and I was paid for that right. The only plan I can accept is one giving me the privilege of editing the result. Which means I will want to blue pencil everything which even intimates that something breathing and moving sat behind the typewriter which produced the books."[1]

Although Cowley would have done a careful, discreet job on the profile, what happened once it passed through the *Life* editors was something else. When Faulkner later saw the Hemingway profile, he was repelled—not only by *Life* but by Hemingway. Part of their career-long clash resulted from two such different personalities. Hemingway ate up the camera, mugging for it, opening up his private life to gossip columnists, providing copy for a nation of journalists. *Life* revealed Hemingway at breakfast, half naked at the table eating an egg, Hemingway as a child, the warrior wounded in the first war, Hemingway drinking from a bottle in the Spanish civil war, Hemingway as an aviator flying a mission over enemy lines in the second war, and, to Faulkner's everlasting chagrin, Hemingway's four wives, all of whom were decidedly good-looking women. Faulkner saw such a display as obscene.

Faulkner tells Cowley that *Life* has no intention of paying its money to talk about someone's "mere output," since "I imagine they dont care two whoops in the bad place about art but only about what they would call 'personalities.'" Then he thinks of Cowley's need and says he would like to come up with some approach so that the critic "can collect on it."[2] He tells Cowley to write again to see what they might be able to work out. Nothing, however, came of the enterprise with Cowley, and *Life* assigned another reporter to the job, Robert Coughlan, who focused on Yoknapatawpha and came at Faulkner through anecdotes and speculations, inasmuch as the writer refused to cooperate.

Cowley did not give up, though, and told Faulkner he wanted to do a piece on his "mythical empire," emphasizing the work, not the author. He planned photographs not of the author but of the places in his novels, like the Old Frenchman's Place; of a black man plowing, of a church set amidst pines and hills, of a crossroads store on Saturday afternoon.* There would be little infringement on Faulkner's privacy. But the Hemingway profile, which had appeared by the time Cowley wrote (on January 11), contradicted everything the critic was saying. It poked and probed and revealed, the very kind of obscene document Faulkner feared about himself. Cowley admits the pictures and captions "are pretty God-awful,"[3] but

*As far as I know, only one photographer has ever caught Faulkner's world in this way. Eva Miller of Memphis has assembled hundreds of magnificent color photos of Faulkner's "world": places, things, people in his novels; so that she has a record on slides of Faulkner's creation, something close to what Cowley (naively) thought *Life* would do.

blames the editors. Yet that package of photos and text was what *Life* was all about, a gossip mill with great photographs.

Meanwhile, Faulkner was occupied with setting up the text for *Knight's Gambit*. He doesn't have personal copies of the stories, he tells Commins, and he can't remember one of them at all ("Monk," which had appeared in *Scribner's* in May 1937). His haziness about his own stories did not speak well for the volume, into which he shoveled whatever fitted, a Gavin Stevens catchall. This would also be Cowley's criticism of the projected *Collected Stories*—that it included material which should have remained unknown. From Cowley's point of view, that involved all the early work reprinted in the "Beyond" segment which closed the volume. The critic felt such a segment created a false impression of Faulkner—but Cowley was of course assuming people read the volume straight through. In any event, he took Faulkner on his own terms, assuming the volume had a coherence beyond an anthology of stories, and then finding the volume wanting because of Faulkner's desire to include what should have been omitted.

When Haas mentioned the reissuing of *Go Down, Moses* (along with *The Hamlet* and *The Wild Palms*), Faulkner insisted on publishing it as distinctly a novel: "Do you think it necessary to number these stories like chapters? Why not reprint exactly, but change the title from GO DOWN, MOSES, and other stories, to simply: GO DOWN, MOSES, with whatever change is necessary in the jacket description." He adds: "We did THE UNVAN-QUISHED in this manner, without either confusion or anticipation of such; and, for that matter, THE WILD PALMS had two completely unrelated stories in it [not what Faulkner said about it earlier]. Yet nobody thought it should be titled THE WILD PALMS and another story. Indeed, if you will permit me to say so at this late date, nobody but Random House seemed to labor under the impression that GO DOWN, MOSES should be titled 'and other stories.' I remember the shock (mild) I got when I saw the printed title page. I say, reprint it, call it simply GO DOWN, MOSES, which was the way I sent it to you 8 years ago."[4]

Faulkner's insistence on the integration of elements to make the book a novel and eliminate its standing as a volume of stories goes beyond the aesthetic appeal into something deeply personal. He had not published a novel in some time. *The Unvanquished*, which he cites, was a series of stories, yet became in his mind part of the story/novel mode. *The Wild Palms* was two *related* long stories or novellas. *The Hamlet*, while more strictly a novel than the others, was composed of several story elements, tacked into the longer fiction. Faulkner needed *Go Down, Moses* to reestablish himself as a novelist. A related disturbance was his recognition that whatever he had published since *Absalom* had not had the intricate interworkings of that novel—so that the wrestling with *A Fable* was an effort not only to smooth out that book's problems but to move back to firm novelistic ground.

By February 11, he had had time to read Cowley's piece on Hemingway, and his response to the hyped *Life* treatment of the text was predictable:

he asserted that he did not read it, but assumed it was all right because Cowley put his name to it. Whether or not he read the text, he was profoundly repelled by photographs and text creating a circuslike atmosphere in the *Life* format: ". . . I hope that it will profit him [Hemingway] —if there is any profit or increase or increment that a brave man and an artist can lack or need or want." Then comes the blast at the entire enterprise of modern public relations and self-aggrandizement:

> But I am more convinced and determined than ever that this is not for me. I will protest to the last: no photographs, no recorded documents. It is my ambition to be, as a private individual, abolished and voided from history, leaving it markless, no refuse save the printed books; I wish I had had enough sense to see ahead thirty years ago and, like some of the Elizabethans, not signed them. It is my aim, and every effort bent, that the sum and history of my life, which in the same sentence is my obit and epitaph too, shall be them both: He made the books and he died.[5]

This intense desire to withdraw behind his books was part of Faulkner's obsessive need to control every aspect of his life, to conserve and reveal only what he chose to exhibit. There is almost a physical squeamishness here—as though he were afraid of being caught nude or sitting on the toilet. Despite his public persona of seeming indifference, his lady friends have called attention to his fastidiousness, his showering and scrubbing himself off before he would have sexual relations, and the dandylike way in which he presented himself, even when in old clothes. He looked brushed and scrubbed and coiffed. It was all part of the same personality trait: not to let anyone penetrate the façade. The handwriting, of course, reinforces this view. With its personal codes, its tiny, minuscule letters, its crowded appearance on the page, it is the handiwork of someone who cannot let go, or who fears divulgation of self. Faulkner also typed most of his own manuscripts, another example of his need to control and resist external intrusion. Such qualities worked well for him: they fueled his ideas and supported his social and political positions. By temperament, he should have been a states' righter, a right-wing extremist who saw his country going down the drain because of progressiveness and excessive liberty. His world was really the past, not present or future; but his imagination had thrust him into modernism as a technique and a movement, and he had absorbed its lessons early in his career. Yet avant-garde modernism was not congenial to a temperament which eschewed anarchy, disorder, subversion. Faulkner practiced a precarious literary act, and one reason he could not hang on fully after the early 1940s was the sheer teetering nature of it.

Cowley warned Faulkner that some reporter or other would try to get the story for *Life* and that whoever he was, he'd do it unscrupulously. He had greater insight into what happens to a celebrity than anything

Faulkner could have contemplated, for the critic had just finished with Hemingway, a figure in whom promotion and self-promotion crossed. *Life* was already planning to photograph scenes of the Oxford countryside when *Intruder* was being filmed. Cowley reported that the "Faulkner boom" was continuing, that some professors and librarians indicated Faulkner's work was being paid more attention in the colleges than that of "any other living American author."*[6]

Faulkner was now more occupied with *Knight's Gambit* than he was with *A Fable*. He was working on the long story which closes the volume and gives its name to the collection, a story he now sees must be not a short fiction but a novella. He asks Ober (February 19) to recall the present version from Whit Burnett (editor of *Story* magazine) so that he can rewrite it at greater length. In its new form, it will be the single unpublished piece in the volume and will become almost half the book. He hopes this will create sales. Writing to Saxe Commins (March 5), Faulkner seems to be working full blast on the collection and suggests the final order: "Smoke" (from *Doctor Martino*), "Monk" (*Scribner's*, May 1937), "Hand upon the Waters" (*Post*, November 4, 1939), "Tomorrow" (*Post*, November 23, 1940), "An Error in Chemistry" (*Ellery Queen's Mystery Magazine*, June 1946), and "Knight's Gambit." He hopes, he says, to have the final story in by May 15, and is looking forward to some kind of legal title, "some play on the word *res*, like *res in justici* or *Ad Justici.*"[7]

He does not mention to Commins or Ober that the excitement from the filming of *Intruder* had already begun. An advance crew hit Oxford in early February to scout for locations and to see about housing the crew of more than a hundred. The big problem was what to do with the Negro performers, especially the lead, who was not a Negro but a dark Hispanic, Juano Hernandez. Elements in the town were already opposed to a film about lynching, but on the whole there was cooperation, although the Negro issue remained a sore point. The director, Clarence Brown, himself a Southerner, tried to soothe everyone's feelings, and by following strict segregationist policies—the whites having the run of the town, the Negroes in Negro homes, where they ate and slept—he received chamber of commerce support. Oxford merchants were particularly eager to see this enterprise as a success. The *Eagle* featured a full-page ad: "We are Proud to be the Stage for Mr. William Faulkner's Great Story, Intruder in the Dust." Photographs showed scenes from the square, the jail, surrounding areas, with one of Faulkner at the "quicksand scene" location.

Faulkner had only himself to blame for some of the publicity, since he agreed to take Brown around; and while this was going on, the camera crew was not inactive. In a sneaking way, while protesting all the way, he

---

*This is not quite accurate. The late 1940s and early 1950s was a time of considerable resurgence of interest in Melville and James; and while of living authors Faulkner gained a good deal of attention, in comparison with these two dead authors, he was still a relatively small study in college classes. Among scholars, however, a small army was poised ready to do battle.

appeared to enjoy the uproar: it was a kind of final satisfaction, Oxford's bum becoming a Hollywood celebrity with his own town as studio backdrop. As he wrote Eric Devine: "Much excitement here. . . . It's too bad I'm no longer young enough to cope with all the local girls who are ready and eager to glide into camera focus on their backs."[8] Faulkner apparently took to Brown, who was a regular guy, like Howard Hawks, and able to communicate with the writer in nonliterary areas. Although there are no records to substantiate what Faulkner did with the script, Blotner says he read it over and made a few suggestions. The screenplay seems to have been tight and acceptable, for he apparently made suggestions only for the final scene. Blotner feels there is no record because Faulkner had to hide from Warners any work for MGM, even on his own book. Jack Warner still held an option on him, although one he would never exercise.

Intermixed with pride of achievement was some tension and anxiety. In one sense, it was a time of ultimate triumph over those who had marked him for failure; in another sense, it brought home to him that he was part of the publicity mill, the hoopla which only a film could bring.

Nor was Faulkner let off the hook by those who saw him as no better than Judas selling out his town and region for the Yankee dollar. Most of the contumely came from outside, from the Jackson *Daily News*, a virulent journal of white supremacy.

By May 1 film work was completed, the first crew having left in late April. The filming had turned out well, and was celebrated in a party at Rowan Oak hosted by Faulkner, Estelle, and his Aunt 'Bama. Then came one of those decisive moments in which Faulkner might have shown grace under pressure, to use his rival's standard of a man's courage. The role of Lucas in this film about the need for justice to the Negro was taken by a dark-skinned Puerto Rican. There is little question Juano Hernandez was a dignified, proud man, and he had infused his own sense of purpose into the role. The figure of Lucas fills the screen and becomes a haunting presence. Yet the question at the party hosted by the man who authored the book was how to handle a dark-skinned man who had resided throughout with the local Negro undertaker, G. W. Bankhead. The decision was to hold the party, but exclude the actor of Lucas Beauchamp: Hernandez was not invited because it might have meant extending the invitation to the Bankheads.

The omission was nothing short of morally horrendous. Oxford social prohibitions forbade inviting a Negro through the front door—if a Negro had business, he went to the back or side. Yet at a film party—with dozens of outsiders, many of them Yankees and Westerners—Faulkner could have broken the social code with impunity. Those who opposed him and his book, together with the film, would have complained; others would have felt Faulkner did the wrong thing, but without verbalizing it; and many others would have accepted it, since it was not a private party but a big, open affair. The film historically loses much of its flavor once one knows the story. Equally incomprehensible is why the director and his film crew, people who worked daily with Hernandez, permitted a party to take place which excluded the male lead, *when the very point of the story is to give dignity to that man.* Against Faulkner's words about justice and equality that were bound to come if only the North allowed the South to proceed at its own pace, this one episode stands. It belies all talk of compliance by slow methods, since slowness and due process of law meant exclusion, humiliation, the moral demeaning of all language.

Faulkner left no record of this episode or his feelings about it. By May 18 or so, he considered the manuscript of *Knight's Gambit* finished, but tells Commins he is not satisfied with parts. Apparently he made and submitted his revisions within a week or so, because Commins reported reading the title story by June 2. Expenses were mounting, probably for *The Ring Dove,* a sailboat he bought that spring: Faulkner requested about $5,000 from Random House, drawn on his film money. But now sailing competed with decisions about *Knight's Gambit* and "Knight's Gambit." For the story, Faulkner worked out a chess analogy, but also probed into his own life, shadowing his marriage to Estelle. The play is on "knight": the knight's gambit involves a jump (the story is full of horses, mares, a stallion) along with a choice of alternatives, either up or down, or left or right—that is, horizontal and vertical. It is a good metaphor for Faulkner's sense of life at fifty-one going on fifty-two: one can jump, move two squares on the life board, and have a decision at the end. There is choice, chance, and adventure; and the knight is Gavin Stevens, forced to make decisions about his own life.

The chess imagery playing through almost the entire story is clearly critical. Gavin Stevens's immersion in chess gives him opportunities at a rational life his own personal life has not afforded him. On the board, with pawns, rooks, castles, queen, and king, he can plot his strategies; in his own life, he has faltered. He can win on the board what was lost in life—always going after the queen, who has eluded him in his first fifty years. That sense of elusiveness of what might have made him contented is part of the biographical freight of the novel. The novel flows outward into detective and mystery elements from this broad personal involvement. Educated to futile pursuits, Gavin is full of sound and fury, transferring into talk what he cannot manage personally. He is at the other end from Ratliff, another man who became a voice for Faulkner. One is settled into contentment, deep within his center; the other, the highly educated one with the Heidelberg Ph.D., has worked the margins of experience and remained unfulfilled. His scholarly project, to render "the Old Testament back into the classic Greek into which it had been translated from its best Hebrew infancy," reveals the kind of meaninglessness characteristic of his life. Trying to be a knight, Gavin is a pawn. The other central image of the story, linked to the chess image, is the horse. Horses appear as blind, as killer stallion, as centaur; and they comment on the men who would be knights. Only the Argentinian Gualdres comes close, and he is an outsider, whose sense of honor supersedes all else, and who disdains a life without his utter commitment to self. In Gualdres, Faulkner has lifted a Hemingway character from one of the latter's fictions—perhaps a matador, or white hunter, or all-around sport. Withal, the story is weak as Faulkner was unable to blend characters and events into that inevitability which makes detective-mystery fiction meaningful.

By early June Faulkner was free of all responsibilities for the volume, and if he wished he could return to the big manuscript. On June 3, the setting copy arrived at the printer's. If his letter of July 5 to Haas is any indication, he postponed returning to *A Fable* while he tried out *The Ring Dove.* * Financial independence from Hollywood money made him less compulsive about returning to serious work and more prone to relaxation. It was a period of leisure but also of family tensions, since the boat became something of a family affair, often including at least Jill. As he aged, Faulkner became increasingly a patriarchal figure, insisting on certain prerogatives. Having a particular view of what a genteel young woman should be, he tried to turn Jill into his ideal. He insisted on a dress code —she was to wear a dress on Oxford streets (and he would ignore her if she didn't), not shorts, certainly not pants (although he himself cultivated a studied indifference to how he appeared in public). Often, even on the eve of the Nobel Prize, he still looked the town bum, with a rope for a belt, hacked-off trousers, the garb of thirty years before. Jill, however, was to be a model of decorum.

In other areas as well, there were mixed signals. His abhorrence of radio or jukebox music was well known, and Jill grew up deprived of a radio and phonograph in her home. Now that television was becoming available, that was another enemy. Faulkner liked absolute quiet; Jill wanted what her schoolmates and friends had—a normal pipeline to the outside world through, at least, radio. He finally relented when, as Blotner tells the story, Bill Fielden (Victoria's husband) warned the writer that if he didn't permit a radio, Jill would have her fun outside the home. He permitted a phonograph.

But the mixed messages he and Estelle sent were more intense. He maintained his image of what Jill should be—studious, a reader, someone who shared in his work as copyeditor, a young woman who presented charm and gentility to the outside world. He wanted classiness, elegance, and achievement within what was suitable for a Southern lady—all as part of his fantasy of Jill, rather than what the real young woman desired or hoped for. Yet his own example was abysmal. Faulkner may have been the great writer to the outside world, but to Jill he was *also* an embarrassing, shameful drunk. Along with Estelle, Faulkner might be lying unconscious on the floor when Jill came in; if she wanted to bring friends home, she could never be sure what condition her parents would be in. The drinking was constant and incessant. Blotner tells of a recurring dream Jill de-

*On one such occasion, he had as his guest Eudora Welty; she arrived in Oxford as a guest of Ella Somerville, Estelle's good friend, and Faulkner invited her first to Rowan Oak and then on *The Ring Dove.*

scribed to him: "In twenty-four hours her legs were going to give out, or be cut off. She would never walk again, and she had to decide how she would spend those hours, with her father or with her mother. They both stood looking down at her, and she realized, as she tried to decide, that neither of them really cared."[9]

It is a dream of many layers, but key is her sense of abandonment. While she received messages of love, she perceived that in the environment of their own needs, her parents had forgotten her existence. They were not deliberately cruel—although Faulkner's verbal thrusts could be—but in their desperate search to escape each other and themselves, they quite simply abandoned her. This had created a kind of maiming, her loss of legs, and a sense of guilt that time was running out when she could regain their affection. Her inability to walk was somehow transferred into her willingness to sacrifice, if she could only gain recognition; but even in the light of that sacrificial move, they remained untouched. She was in one respect being smothered by a life which, while stifling independence and release, insisted on a certain code of behavior no one else in the house lived up to.

Enter Joan Williams, at twenty-one only five years older than Jill. She came to Oxford to visit her cousin, the wife of John Reed Holly, who knew Faulkner and had access to Rowan Oak. She was a beginning writing student, having attended three colleges in three years, and a winner of *Mademoiselle*'s short story contest. She was now a student at Bard, entering her senior year. One of her writing heroes was Faulkner, and her purpose in coming to Oxford was to see the now-famous writer. Holly arranged a meeting at Rowan Oak, and the initial encounter went well: Faulkner seemed surprised to see a young woman both attractive and obviously intelligent.* She was, in one respect, a replay of Meta, only younger. Joan Williams must have noted in Faulkner's demeanor or behavior that he was interested, because she followed up the visit with a letter telling him who she was, what aspirations she had as a writer, asserting that for her he stood at the center of writing. She mentioned she had a number of questions to ask him, and in his response to her (August 31), he told her to ask and he would answer when he found time.

Write she did, and answer he did, in words that were already measuring her as more than student. He told her that her questions were the wrong ones: "A woman must ask these of a man while they are lying in bed together," after sexual intercourse, when they are at peace or lying quietly on the edge of sleep; "so you'll have to wait, even to ask them."[10] Some of the advice was more paternal, telling her not to grieve over her problems, which were of several kinds. Her family had bourgeois aspirations for her and were unsettled by her choice of profession; her father drank—although that meant she would not mind Faulkner's binging; she needed guidance from someone who could understand her. Her approach to

*Their second meeting took place in the Memphis bus terminal in January of 1950. In 1952–53, he asked Joan to marry him.

Faulkner seems on the surface innocent; but she was twenty-one and, unless very shielded, must have recognized that a man of fifty-two with an alcoholic wife was very vulnerable; his initial response, while reassuring in a way, had brought them to the edge of something different from paternalism. She was entering into a relationship which was indeed a quid pro quo: to take on his literary knowledge, she would have to take him.

In 1971, Joan Williams published a novel, *The Wintering,* which describes her relationship to Faulkner; he is called Jeffrey Almoner and she is Amy Howard. Joan presents Jeffrey as particularly forceful in bringing about an affair, although once it is a fact, she enters deeply into it. In reality, Joan was rather reluctant, not only because of the thirty-year age difference but because of the breach of proprieties. By this time, Estelle had accepted Faulkner's infidelities—although she so drowned herself in drink it's difficult to know what a sober woman would have done. In the Williams novel, Estelle (Inga) is a pitiful, frail lady "as light and defenseless as a bird"; Amy feels sorry for her even as she is stealing her husband. The two women lunch together, Inga trying to hold on, Amy trying to sort out her own feelings. Jeffrey tells Amy he is the father she always wanted, that they've committed incest—and that act (and knowledge) will always hold them together. Joan was a devoted reader of *Sound,* and her own fictional treatment has in it the typical Faulkner theme. Nevertheless, his growing involvement with a young woman not much older than his daughter and her response to him as writer and father-figure suggest she was close to the target.

Meanwhile, another kind of excitement was brewing. The film of *Intruder* was previewed in Memphis, and Faulkner attended. But the true premiere was to take place in Oxford on October 9, and this news was the banner headline in the *Eagle.* The buildup in town was enormous, and yet Faulkner seemed inclined to stay away. Estelle apparently could not force him, so she got in touch with Aunt 'Bama in Memphis, who called Faulkner and told him to be ready to escort her. By the time the film began at the Lyric Theater, he appeared, clean-shaven, with jacket and tie. At the theater, he was introduced to the audience along with members of the cast, and he acknowledged loud applause. At the end of the well-received film, he slipped out with his family and friends.

An aunt he could not say no to had overcome his reluctance to attend, but his initial impulse not to go was part of a persona he had structured for himself. It is difficult to know where Faulkner ended and the persona began, or, conversely, where the persona ended and Faulkner began. Although so unlike Hemingway, in this one area they were alike: both worked along the lines of an image of themselves which they sustained as they became more famous. Faulkner retreated behind his image of the withdrawn, solitary artist, shy of publicity and hateful of the world it derived from. This same reluctance to emerge from behind the structured self came in his refusal, at first, to attend the Nobel Prize ceremonies in Stockholm. Yet the desire for privacy went beyond a real desire to avoid the publicity mills, into an even more desperate need to fulfill the persona he had created. Earlier, that persona had included the deceptions and outright lies about his military service in World War I. With that image no longer functional, in fact biographically dangerous, he moved into another one: not a new one, but one more intense and functional as he gained fame. The new one was indifference to fame itself: insisting on the farmer and barely literate author behind the books and film(s) which made him a national figure. By struggling against publicity, he became more mysterious, more desirable, *in direct proportion to his inaccessibility.* *

His continuation of his deer-camp activities was, of course, deeply connected to an abiding sense of value in the big woods. It was, in his view, an alternative existence, clearly superior to the civilized life of the town. But in another sense, the deer camp helped Faulkner sustain that persona he had so carefully structured. Besides providing an alternate set of values, it gave him an identity which fitted perfectly with the image he cultivated and presented to the outside world: of a dropout from the world's success, of the man who preferred hunting or farming to literature, of the laid-back, still shiftless Oxford citizen. Faulkner was really quite different, with a strong bourgeois streak, a desire for position and respectability, a man very careful of the figure he cut. He was always "presenting" himself: on one hand, the estate at Rowan Oak and the surrounding park, the daughter who behaved like a Southern princess, the moneyed success which was beginning to become apparent; but on the other, the man who eschewed everything except being his own person, insisting on privacy and an inviolable self. He found himself divided into at least two, perhaps more, selves. When Hemingway went public and became "Papa," writer to the world, there is little if any indication he ever sought complete privacy, that he hoped to retreat back to an Arcadian Oak Park self. But with Faulkner, there were persistent conflicts: the insistence on retreat, which was part of a structured image, in conflict with the equally insistent need to appear successful, to have the accoutrements of the antebellum planter class.

He was not writing, but he was hearing about earlier work. Film rights were being negotiated for Valerie Bettis's ballet of *As I Lay Dying,* and Virgil Thompson requested permission to base an opera on *The Wild Palms.* Faulkner referred the suggestions to Ober,** along with his comments on the film of *Intruder:* "It is a good picture, I think."[11] Most of his time was

---

*A contemporary version of this, far more sustained than with Faulkner, comes with Thomas Pynchon. Here, elusiveness and withdrawal from all publicity have created their own kind of celebrity.

**It was still unclear how Ober would be repaid for certain pieces like the revised version of "Knight's Gambit." Toward that end, he and Haas worked out an agreement whereby they would divide certain rights. Ober retained the right to handle and receive commissions on Faulkner's short stories, essays, and serial rights to novels; but film versions of Random House properties remained in the publisher's hands. Ober apparently did not receive any commission on the rewritten "Knight's Gambit." He was in this, as in every other way, the most unobtrusive of agents.

taken up with arrangements for deer camp, for he was now club secretary. On November 19, just nine days before the publication of *Knight's Gambit*, he set out for Rolling Fork. He would be gone until deer season ended on December 1. In writing Haas, he mentions perhaps coming up to New York for a week or so in early December, although he hopes to stay within his budget. He says he wants to talk about setting up an annuity with his remaining film money, and also he would like a few days in town with his old friends. He was in fact gearing up for another breakout.

While all of this was occurring—just before deer camp, and while advance copies of *Knight's Gambit* were being sent to reviewers—Faulkner's earlier career was the subject of intense scrutiny. What was disquieting in this examination was that Faulkner was being considered for the Nobel Prize in literature on the basis of work which went back at least a decade, and earlier. The body of work which gave him international stature was fiction clustered in the period essentially from *Sound* in 1929 through *Absalom* in 1936, and, possibly, through 1942, with *The Wild Palms*, *The Hamlet*, and *Go Down, Moses*.

The competition for the prize on a world scale was bitter. Not only Faulkner among Americans, but Steinbeck and Hemingway were being considered; elsewhere, Camus, Mauriac, Pasternak, Sholokhov, Churchill, Lagerkvist, and several others of equal or greater renown were in the running. But it was clear at the end of 1949 that Faulkner was the overwhelming choice for the 1949 award, which would be decided upon and granted in 1950. He wrote to Joan Williams that he had been hearing rumors for three years, "have been a little fearful. It's not the sort of thing to decline; a gratuitous insult to do so but I dont want it." He reasons: "I have rather to be in the same pigeon hole with Dreiser and Sherwood Anderson, than with Sinclair Lewis and Mrs. Chinahand Buck."[12]

Faulkner was being somewhat harsh on himself and on others. Although the award to Pearl Buck in 1938 is inexplicable, Lewis surely deserved it in 1930, especially since most of the giants of early modernism who did not receive the prize (Kafka, Conrad, Proust, Rilke, Lawrence) were dead. But by 1938, when Buck received it, Joyce and Woolf were still alive. As for refusing it, there was no way Faulkner would reject the huge cash award that came with the prize; his desire for privacy did not extend to turning down the money that would become the cornerstone of his financial independence.

Threading through this intermixed scene of deer camp, publication of *Knight's Gambit*, and rumors of the Nobel Prize was the shadow of Joan Williams. She kept up with Faulkner by mail from Bard College and indicated she wanted to see him. He was definitely interested, but fearful of domestic consequences—he had never pursued someone in his own area. He suggested she drive to Oxford and they would have an outing on the *Minmagary*, Faulkner's new boating toy. This was really the beginning of their strange relationship, wherein he took her under his wing in much the same way Phil Stone had taken him, with the obvious difference that he was physically attracted to her. The relationship was not too different from ones he had seen in Hollywood, when young starlets attached themselves to older actors or to directors in order to learn their craft and to enhance their chances of finding a role. Joan was intent on finding her place in the literary world, and she had a double problem: she needed technical help (she was not precocious) and she felt pressure from her family to shape up as a typical Southern young woman. Faulkner knew a good deal about the demands of the artistic life as well as about art.

Estelle appeared friendly and generous when the young woman came to Oxford on January 3, 1950—perhaps she saw that this relationship, still in its early stages, would stabilize her own marriage. By this time she seemed to have accepted Faulkner's philandering, although how she felt about it occurring in her own back yard we cannot tell. But it seems difficult to deny that Estelle, observing an attractive young woman as she had seen Meta before, missed her husband's interest. They spent the day picnicking on the boat, and whatever transpired, Faulkner was beginning to declare what he really had in mind besides artistic lore. Through it all, he did help her, shoring her up against her family's wishes and trying to get her to feel and observe more deeply. No matter what he privately felt about the material she showed him, he encouraged her in what she was doing. He did not, however, write or rewrite her material. Then he had an idea, which revealed that Jill had disappointed him: he suggested to Joan, as he had once suggested to his daughter, that they collaborate—as a way of drawing out of her what she was capable of doing.

In what appears a daring move, he called at the Williams' home in Memphis, spoke to Joan's mother, and carried back with him her story "Rain Later," which had won a *Mademoiselle* prize. He then wrote her about what he thought, though he was writing more about himself than her, infusing her work with his own sense of isolation and solitude:

> It is moving and true, made me want to cry a little for all the sad frustration of solitude, isolation, aloneness in which every human being lives, who for all the blood kinship and everything else, cant really communicate, touch. It's all right, moving and true; the force, the passion, the controlled heat, will come in time. Worry because it's —you think—slow; you've got to worry; that's part of it: the suffering and the working, most of all the working, the being willing and ready to sacrifice everything for it—peace, money, duty too, if you are so unlucky. Only quite often, if you are really willing to sacrifice any and everything for it, everything will not be required, demanded by the gods.[13]

The letter was a form of seduction, the language literary, the sentiments romantic. It was designed to establish the terms on which their relationship could proceed: literary on the surface, but unorthodox and socially unacceptable beneath. He would be Pygmalion, she would be his love; and out of their relationship would come not only a literary product (a play, as it developed), but her commitment to the life of art. He had his apprentice, someone who could add considerable excitement (and pathos) to his current life.

The year 1950 proved to be extraordinary. He began to work with Joan on the idea, already suggested in his earlier fiction and comments on what would become *Requiem for a Nun*. This deeply flawed work in dramatic form proved immensely popular abroad, and particularly captured the imagination of postwar French intellectuals. What started out as a play, however, eventually became a novel—or rather a novel enclosing the play, and then later the play itself. At the same time, not purely coincidentally, Faulkner began to comment publicly on racial matters, with a letter to the Memphis *Commercial Appeal* concerning the sentencing of a white man to a simple prison term for the slaying of three black children. His work on *Requiem for a Nun* contains a good deal of direct commentary on race—it becomes a follow-up to *Intruder* as public matters enter more directly into his literary works.

Although he published no short stories in 1950, he saw the reissue of the Modern Library edition of *Light in August*, one of his favorites, and also the publication of his *Collected Stories*. The latter was an uneven volume, containing forty-two of the forty-six stories he had placed in magazines going back to 1930, but also a monument: the kind of memorializing necessary for a writer entering literary history. It was perfectly timed for the news on November 10 that he and Bertrand Russell were corecipients of the Nobel Prize in literature. (Faulkner was considered the 1949 winner, Russell the 1950.)

But the thread in his life now was Joan, and she became intertwined in a project which played an important part in his later career. Checking into the Algonquin in New York on February 2, he arranged with Joan to come down from Bard for a few days. What had already passed between them had made it clear his intentions extended beyond literary advice. He told her now of his idea for a play which would resurrect the black servant Nancy who had appeared in "That Evening Sun Go Down" ("That Evening Sun" as it appeared in *These 13* and *Collected Stories*). The idea went back to October 1933, when he wrote to Harrison Smith about "Requiem for a Nun," a story about "a nigger woman. It will be a little on the esoteric side, like *As I Lay Dying*."[14] This Nancy—Faulkner projected her into an incomplete short story, dated December 17, 1933—worked as a servant for the Compsons, had been a prostitute and a cocaine addict, and was involved in a deadly relationship with a man who eventually cut her throat. This is the property he wanted to collaborate on with Joan: this relatively sheltered, white, Southern young lady still in college.

During the visit, Faulkner made a sincere effort to find her a position on a magazine. He was also interested in Bard College for Jill, who was nearing the completion of high school. The juxtaposition of Joan and Jill —even the name alliteration—shows how Faulkner was becoming the incestuous father. He had already commented to Joan that she wanted a father and he would play that role. The shadowy father-daughter incest suggested by brother-sister-father incest in his fiction is here worked through in a deflected way. Once Faulkner gains one young woman from Bard, he will send on another (although Jill actually went elsewhere). Joan came to the Haas party on February 7 as his protégée. There was the usual Random House crowd, editors almost as famous as their authors: Albert Erskine, Saxe Commins, Robert Linscott, Harrison Smith, as well as Irita van Doren and Ruth Ford, with whom Faulkner had tried to be romantically involved and who would make her reputation with Requiem for a Nun.

He drank heavily on this trip, but seemed more in control. There was considerable excitement, all heightened by the presence of a young woman: for a man of his age and his recent poverty of sexual experience, it was a momentous time. He accompanied the Haases to the Wildenstein Gallery and genuinely seemed to enjoy the exhibition of great European paintings. For a man of such strong visual sensibility—the observer who missed nothing—Faulkner had been peculiarly indifferent to formal viewing at museums since his 1925 trip to Europe; but once guided through the gallery, he brought to it the same intensity of observation he brought to all visual experiences. He went on to other parties, some arranged by Ruth Ford. He explained to several people his ambivalence about New York: that if he had to live anywhere else than in the country, it would be New York; but in the next breath, he maligned the city as inhuman, asserting that no one seemed to be behind the windows.

Blotner reports one amusing incident in which Faulkner came to Hemingway's defense. Riding in a taxi with Truman Capote, he heard the elfish young man deride Hemingway's latest novel, Across the River and into the Trees. Capote was having a waspish field day at Papa's expense when Faulkner broke in: "Young man, I haven't read this new one. And though it may not be the best thing Hemingway ever wrote, I know it will be carefully done, and it will have quality."[15] Capote was silenced, but the book's critical reception bore out his estimation.

Faulkner left New York by train on February 12 and almost immediately sketched out notes for the beginning of Requiem, cast as a play. The Negro Nancy Mannigoe now worked for Temple Drake and Gowan Stevens, all familiar figures from his earlier work and part of what he considered to be his working stable of characters.* He sent on his jottings to Joan, along with a summary of what was very close to a final version:

> You can begin to work here. This act begins to tell who Nancy is, and what she has done. She is a "nigger" woman, a known drunkard and dope user, a whore with a jail record in the little town, always in trouble. Some time back she seemed to have reformed, got a job as

*In many respects, Faulkner's recycling of characters from earlier work recalls Balzac's fiction and the latter's use of the same characters in his cycle of novels; or else Zola's, where characters recur in a long cycle of fictions.

nurse to a child in the home of a prominent young couple. Then one day suddenly and for no reason, she murdered a child. And now she doesn't even seem sorry. She seems to be making it almost impossible for the lawyer [Gavin Stevens] to save her.[16]

Faulkner agrees she deserves to hang, and that even Stevens agrees with that.

What he intended Joan Williams, at twenty-one, to do with this intractable material is difficult to imagine. His follow-up letter a few days later was equally inconclusive:

Anything we do on this first draft may have no connection at all with the finished one. Let it change itself in either your hands or mine while we are getting it on paper; we expect that. So herewith is not only a few pages of play, but (as I see it now) a kind of synopsis of it. I wont remind you of your school work again; I'll just leave it with you to work—think—on the play when you feel you can. Rewrite that first scene if you want to, write any of the rest of it; this is just *first* draft; all we want is to get something on paper to pull apart and save what is good and right.[17]

Faulkner sounds as though he has just handed a toy to a child and told her to play good and true with it; or else he was a schoolmaster handing out a homework assignment to a pupil. And yet behind this amusing game of collaboration with Joan, there was the full germ of an idea. But why would Faulkner turn to such seemingly intractable material at this time? Part of it surely was that his signature work was still *Sanctuary:* no matter what he wrote, he was firmly associated in the public's mind with that book. In fact, when he received the Nobel Prize at the end of the year, many of the remarks criticizing the award remind us Faulkner was the author of a perverse work, with rape, incest, and murder his trademark, Hemingway's "Corncob."

Furthermore, Temple Drake was in one way his prototypical but perverse young Southern girl, and she had established herself in his imagination. Here would be a sequel, in which she could partially redeem herself for her damning testimony in *Sanctuary* and at the same time interact with a Negro woman, so that Faulkner's own growing sense of interracial themes could be developed in dramatic form. Nancy becomes, in some zigzagging way, a female working through what Faulkner had started with Lucas Beauchamp: a very different sort of person, but a commanding figure nevertheless. Although we have the Negro woman in one of her typically demeaning roles—as servant, as deferential wife or mistress, as drunkard and drug addict, as faithful family retainer subservient to wayward employers—Nancy is not passive, nor does she turn the other cheek. She commits a horrible crime, but does it as a kind of moral act. We cannot dismiss her as simply another one of Faulkner's Negro submissives.

There is also another dimension to this project: the promise of financial gain. A straight play could be mounted for relatively little in those days, and if it had a respectable run, it could bring considerable return to the author. Faulkner had as example his friend Stephen Longstreet, who wrote the book for the musical *High Button Shoes* and watched the royalties pour in. Of course, much of this is the dream of the gold miner seeking a rich lode. Most plays end in the dustheap, and even if produced make little for the writer.

The play also put Joan on a string. She could not dismiss Faulkner's interest in her career if he asked her to collaborate with him. He was rumored to be the next Nobel Prize laureate; thirty-one years' difference in age could be wiped out by that consideration. In the letter in which he announces he would rather not be bracketed with "Mrs. Chinahand Buck," he tells Joan to get on with her undergraduate thesis while he moves along. He says he has the first act laid out in a rough draft of about twelve pages. Eight days later (March 2), he assures her that "the play is yours too. If you refuse to accept it, I will throw it away too. I would not have thought of writing one if I hadn't known you." He was offering bait which he knew she couldn't resist. He tells her that her notes are "all right, so all right there is no need to comment on them." He says the important thing now is to get everything down on paper, then clean it up later. He is insistent, as he may sense she is slipping away into her thesis, into her own young life so different from his, or else into confusion under the barrage of his tempting offers. "You will help," he writes, "you will do your own work too of course; that should come first; you do that, and I will keep on at the play until you can take up on it; no hurry."[18]

The next letter suggests he is battling a fish he must not allow to get away. His insistence has a pathetic tone to it, and yet there is an underlying sense of adventure. He notes she will be home from April 5 or 6 to the following Tuesday, which would be the eleventh. "We should be able to meet twice, anyway. Your family will want most of your time probably, but maybe you could come down here one day, and I will come up one day. That is, we will do one or the other as soon as you are home. Talk, lay out work, then you can work, telephone me when you need, until the last day of visit, then we will meet again and plan how to carry on when you are back at school."[19] He is taking over, directing her life, as well as tilting his own.

One of the problems Faulkner faced with *Requiem* was that he lacked the stage awareness which makes a dramatic work come alive. The same problem had arisen in his film scripts—written to be read, not to be produced and seen. Also, the material was indeed intractable. A good deal of the difficulty lay in the conception. The viewer's knowledge of *Sanctuary* was necessary, or else part of the play had to be a reprise of what Temple Drake had done in that novel which now cried out for redemption. To compound the difficulty, Temple was not really the focus of *Requiem*—Nancy was. Faulkner was caught in a crossfire of conflicting elements: those which necessitated recovering the past of Temple, and those which needed to make Nancy's terrible crime of child-murder meaningful. There were further problems, in that Faulkner did not feel comfortable with Temple whatever she did, whereas he had entered deeply into Nancy's predicament with a good deal of sympathy. His two major female characters not only pulled apart, they were distinctly separated in the author's own imagination: one was worth saving, one was not.

Blotner cites an actual case which he feels helped to give impetus to Faulkner's tale of Nancy; but the differences are so great no clear parallel or presence should be drawn. The case, already mentioned, has an interest of its own, however, since it drew Faulkner's attention and ire. To the south of Oxford, a white man was convicted of murdering three black children. The state asked for the death penalty, but the jury balked, and in the ensuing disagreement the murderer was given a life sentence with the chance of parole in perhaps ten or fifteen years. Faulkner wrote an irate letter to the Memphis *Commercial Appeal.* He said he felt pride that a jury convicted a white man, but great concern that the sentence was no more than what he would have received if he had not murdered three children but robbed three banks or stolen three automobiles. He was worried also that Mississippians were sending a message to the rest of the country, that justice for whites and blacks was vastly different—as, of course, it was. It was in fact a courageous state prosecutor who recommended the death penalty. Faulkner wrote:

> And those of us who were born in Mississippi and have lived all our lives in it, who have continued to live in it forty and fifty and sixty years at some cost and sacrifice simply because we love Mississippi and its ways and customs and soil and people; who because of that love have been ready and willing at all times to defend our ways and habits and customs from attack by the outlanders who we believed did not understand them, we had better be afraid too,—afraid that we have been wrong; that what we had loved and defended not only didn't want the defense and the love, but was not worthy of the one and indefensible to the other.[20]

Yet Faulkner was not finished, and he saved his best stroke for the end. He hoped, he said, that the jurors would sleep without nightmares, considering that the murderer, Turner, would be paroled in ten or fifteen years, and will murder another child. This child "who it is to be hoped—and with grief and despair one says it—will this time at least be of his own color." Faulkner saw execution of Turner as giving him the same kind of justice given Negroes who had committed far lesser crimes, since the death penalty was the law of the state. But he was not finished. The leading newspaper of the state, the Jackson *Daily News,* was discriminatory, segregationist, and, while not opposed to the death penalty in general, opposed the death penalty for Turner. Besides the newspapers, others attacked Faulkner, saying he betrayed the state of Mississippi by holding it up to outside ridicule. Two weeks after his initial letter, Faulkner responded in words so anguished his syntax is tortured and twisted.

> It seems to me that the ones who injected race issues into this tragedy were whoever permitted or created a situation furnishing free-gratis-for-nothing to all our Northern critics, the opportunity to have made this same statement and protest but with a hundred times the savagery and a thousand times the unfairness and ten thousand times less the understanding of our problems and grief for our mistakes—except that I, a native of our land and a sharer in our errors, just happened to be on the spot in time to say it first. This should be some satisfaction to a Southerner.[21]

Such comments were quite in keeping with Faulkner's new phase, in which a high moral tone enters into his work, constricting to some extent the play of aesthetic dimensions while directing itself to social and racial injustices. It is part of a long line of development which can be traced back to his extensive stays in Hollywood, where his film work had revealed a moralistic frame of reference, as in "Battle Cry" or even "The de Gaulle Story." What had begun as studio work had overtaken his imagination. Aging also had something to do with it, along with a growing sense of a Christian mission. His long work on A Fable both reinforced his sense of divinity and led to the constriction of purely aesthetic questions. He becomes increasingly a "spokesman," forgoing the role of the novelist who was satisfied with negative capability: that ability the artist has to hold himself open to diverse possibilities. As racial issues became the dominant factor in Mississippi politics, as Mississippi tried its own form of secession with the Dixiecrat party, as town after town formed itself into opposition —prefiguring the white Citizens' Councils after the 1954 Supreme Court decision—Faulkner found himself caught in a situation akin to a form of civil war against the federal government. Under the leadership of hypocritical politicians in the governor's house and in the Congress, Mississippi was girding itself for a fight which relived the Civil War: the enemy was not its own racial injustice but the Yankee. What exacerbated it even more was the return of Negroes who had served in the armed forces, who had seen life elsewhere, who had absorbed both foreign and Northern values, and who were not the same men who had gone away. As racial matters headed toward Armageddon—Faulkner's language is full of final things, of imminent disaster—he turned his work increasingly to a "moral solution." And while this was good for the man, it was limiting for his work; but it was inevitable, now part of him, something he would be unable to struggle against.

The result of such moralistic statements both in his fiction and in his public utterances was to create a pariah. Mississippi did not feel that much for a Nobel Prize winner. It wanted a solid front and felt cursed by its most famous citizen, who seemed to desert the ship when it needed his voice most. In time—later in the decade—Faulkner found Virginia a more friendly host, although Virginia was certainly no oasis of race relationships, either. But he increasingly found it impossible to remain in his home state, and the eventual decision to move to Virginia had its origin here in the late 1940s and early 1950s. Faulkner's anguish turned to self-destruction: alcohol, binging, obliteration of the situation. Not even a letter from Mark Van Doren informing Faulkner he had been selected to receive the prestigious Howells Medal, conferred by the American Academy, could cheer him. The Howells Medal was conferred every five years for distinguished work in American fiction, and in previous years it had gone to writers Faulkner hardly admired wholeheartedly: Pearl Buck, Ellen Glasgow, Willa Cather, and Booth Tarkington. Since its inception in 1921 to honor William Dean Howells, it had appeared to him to be a "woman's prize." No Dreiser, no Sherwood Anderson, not even Sinclair Lewis had won it —Faulkner was not tempted to go up to New York to receive it.

He wrote disingenuously to Van Doren, indicating first his appreciation of the honor: ". . . nothing makes a man feel better than for his fellow craftsmen publicly and concretely to depose that his work is all right." Then he gives his excuse: "I am a farmer this time of year; up until he sells crops, no Mississippi farmer has the time or money either to travel anywhere on. Also, I doubt if I know anything worth talking two minutes about." He tells Van Doren not to wait upon his final decision, but to accept it now that he will not be able to come in May, signing off "in great pride for the honor and gratitude for the letter."[22]

He followed this with a more formal letter in the spring, addressed to the secretary of the Academy; it was full of ambiguities. It reveals Faulkner, on the eve of one of his greatest honors, as a deeply troubled man, pulled in several directions by conflicts he could resolve only in obliteration. He was undergoing a turbulent sea change—had in fact been experiencing it for some time. And his enjoyment of certain things in life was diminished by a profound depression he was able to alleviate partially through drinking and through a kind of plodding work. In many ways— and the comparison has its ironies—he and Hemingway were undergoing the classic American response to fame and success: deep depression, the need to seek oblivion, undertaking a kind of life which was half living and half suicidal impulses. Hemingway utterly destroyed his health, and Faulkner appeared to rule out any pleasurable response to what was the culmination of all his endeavors.

He told the secretary that while he was honored to be so judged by his peers he was unsure of the value of his work—he could not tell if he had succeeded or failed. He thought that at fifty he would be able to judge; but he is now as confused as ever. "Then one day I was fifty and I looked back at it, and I decided that it was all pretty good—and then in the same instant I realised that that was the worst of all since that meant only that a little nearer now was the moment, instant, night: dark, sleep: when I would put it all away forever that I anguished and sweated over, and it would never trouble me anymore."[23]

This is a desperately sad letter full of a sense of final things: a man's consciousness of mortality. But even more: a wished-for oblivion. It was an unusual letter to send to the secretary of the most prestigious artistic organization in America after it has conferred its highest award. The deep depression was personal, of course, as well as literary: he wanted to solidify his relationship with Joan; he found little or no satisfaction at home; and he recognized—as Matthew Arnold had put it in his poem "Growing Old" —that as he diminished in his powers, the world was applauding his past work as if he were already a memory.

His work on *Requiem* could be only partially satisfactory. It had, after all, little of the knotty, intricate quality of his best work, and it was, with all its virtues, a parasitical work, living off his own past and his own characters. It was not a novelty but a reprise of sorts; and he had stalled completely on the work he had put so much faith in, *A Fable*. Unable to work on that or to concentrate on its intense working-through of the Christian legend in modern times, he labored on something which would keep Joan interested and close. Personal needs had overtaken him to a far greater degree than he wished to admit; and inability to confront what was happening to him led to depression and oblivion.

His progress on *Requiem* was so deeply interwoven with his desire to hang on to Joan that we have a curious paralleling of young women: the destructive, youthful Temple Drake, amoral, evil; and the salvation he expected from Joan, who would brighten a sad personal life. As he moved into act 2, he flashed back to Temple's misdeeds, creating the picture of a fully perverse girl, who then hoped to redeem or purge the past by bringing Nancy into her household when she is married and has children. When Faulkner sent on these pages to Joan, they served a double, even triple function. They gave some reason for two such unlikely people to see each other; they kept alive in Faulkner's mind the saving qualities (for him) of Joan as against the destructive, sinking qualities of the young Temple; and finally they gave him further opportunity to comment on the Negro at a time when he felt a moral stance was necessary. It would be a huge mistake to see this profoundly flawed work as simplistic or reductive, since it came at a crossroads in Faulkner's career and provided, along with *Intruder*, a kind of bridge between early and later work.

As she wrote later, Joan felt somewhat recalcitrant. Faulkner was drawing her more deeply into his life by way of a piece of work she had little intention of rewriting. He had told her she had to break with the middle-class values of her family if she hoped to liberate herself to be an artist. His words to her are a signature statement about himself, not only as a youth, but now: ". . . you have to fight your family for every inch of art you gain —at the very time when the whole tribe of them are hanging like so many buzzards over every penny you earn by it."[24] The deep hostility to his own family surfaces in his advice to a young woman who, besides being attractive, gives him this opportunity to vent his feelings. He can pour into her situation whatever he has felt in his own: that a small army of relatives has used him for their own gain. The advice is melancholy stuff, directed at a student just finished with her thesis and who has displayed as yet only a modicum of talent. In another sense, Faulkner is building her up so that she can be worthy of him, spending time on her in thought and fantasy.

In mid-May, he told Haas he was unable to write a play, but that it might be a novel. If a play, it would have to be rewritten by someone else, possibly Joan, if she can. Perhaps, he suggests, they should print it first as a book. He wonders if Haas can find something to give Joan a foothold in New York. As in so many of his other "adventures," Faulkner dragged in Haas and Random House. Ever devoted, Haas responded that the daughter of Harry Scherman, head of the Book-of-the-Month Club, would try to find her a position when she was ready to come to New York. With that, Faulkner wrote his protégée to communicate with Mrs. Rosin at once. He then formulates strategy for how she can manipulate her family's opposition to her course of action:

> You will have two "clubs" to hold over your Memphis ties now: Mrs. Rosin, and what Haas will be able to do. You could come home, acquiesce to what extent, and pull out after your people are more reconciled. While you are at home in Memphis, you can work on the play. If it comes off, it will be enough to get you back east. If it doesn't then you can use Bob or Mrs Rosin.[25]

He works out alternatives. She can go directly to Haas and Mrs. Rosin without testing the waters at home, in the event her family opposes her leaving. "They can't keep you in Memphis when you really want to get out. Remember that. Dont take my advice too hard. There may be more in your background than I know about; all I can answer is that you write to me." He mentions he is finished with his version of the third act, but it is not a play. It will have to be rewritten into a play; it is now some kind of novel. But they will make no commitment, he says, until after they decide together: ". . . we'll just finish it and hold until we get together on it."

Faulkner was playing an extremely dangerous game, and his disclaimer that there may be more in her background than he knows is a signal he was aware how dangerous it was. For he was assuming the Pygmalion role, shaping a young woman into the daughter he wanted and yet with the ulterior motive of setting up an extended affair. At the same time, he was creating a wedge between her and her family, a division which already existed but which he was exacerbating by holding out to her the joys of release. He is, no less, playing god with her, and he recognizes how deeply involved he is in what must have started out as a lark. We can only explain his immersion here by way of the desperation he felt in his personal life: he had been thwarted for so long he felt he had the right to find liberation where he could. Joan was halfway interested in becoming a writer and yet partly pulled back by those alleged bourgeois tendencies Faulkner attributed to her family. But he had heavy guns.

The Collected Stories was being prepared for publication, and Commins asked Faulkner about issuing it in August (it appeared August 21). The latter feared that two volumes of stories so close together might be poor business, but agreed because he found the collection standing up "amazingly well after a few years."[26] He also told Haas he had finished the first draft of the "story, the play," and was now "writing the three introductory chapters which hold the 3 acts together."[27] He feels no hurry, since he does not want a quick printing, not until fall at the earliest.* Then a week later (May 22), he wrote Haas of still firmer plans. With the first draft of the play finished, he will rewrite it, but enfolded within a novel as seven play scenes, running to about two hundred typed double-spaced pages. "This summer I will set Joan at it, see if she can lift the play scenes and condense the long speeches into a workable play script. Then get some advice from some playwright who knows how to do it. Mine will print as a book, will be—to me—an interesting experiment in form."[28]

The printed (as opposed to the acting) version was an experiment in keeping with his earlier experiments to create "novels" from interrelated short stories and novellas. This sense of experimentation—finding alternate ways of structuring a novel—goes back to The Unvanquished, The Hamlet, and Go Down, Moses, and continues through Knight's Gambit, where it works far less well. We see it in A Fable when the horsethief episode is introduced. In Requiem the effort is to combine two contrasting modes, drama and fictional prose; what results is not a novel but a demonstration of how intractable certain generic experiments can prove. Part of the problem is not only generic but linked to Faulkner's use of his materials. As already suggested, his attempt to extend the meanings of Sanctuary through Temple Drake involved a method which clashed with his effort to establish Nancy Mannigoe as the moral center of the novel, the one who activates Temple toward redemption. When this unfocused material is connected to the three introductory prose pieces, which he intended to hold it all together, we have a clash of modes. The prose sections are overly rhetorical, and the so-called dramatic segments are not sufficiently theatrical: they read, but do not play.

Haas, for his part, could not have been thrilled by the idea of having a twenty-one-year-old apprentice writer working over Faulkner's play, even rewriting him. Since the older man seemed infatuated with the young woman, it was very possible he would accept changes that otherwise he would dismiss, or at the least, from Haas's point of view, encourage her in directions which did not work. The chances of her satisfying both

---

*He did draw an additional $5,000, ostensibly to buy a new tractor to replace a fifteen-year-old one. Faulkner was rapidly depleting his MGM money, much more rapidly than he had foreseen; and therefore it is idle to think of his rejecting the Nobel Prize and its large cash award.

Faulkner and his publisher were of course possible but given the nature of her inexperience and Faulkner's enthrallment, slight.

Faulkner spent some time on the sloop, *The Ring Dove*, and found himself in a squall, where he lost his toolbox and his pants with his wallet and cash in the pocket. He liked to go sailing with Jill, but when she wasn't available he took along Johncy to manage the tiller. And often he went alone, as he did the time the squall struck. He also wanted to do some painting with the tubes of paint he brought back from New York, but hadn't found the time. Both Maud and Estelle were amateur painters, and Faulkner had occasionally tried his hand, though without sustained interest. It was a curiously lackadaisical existence for a man on the eve of a great event in his life, but he simply did not have the peace of mind to return to the immense complexities of *A Fable*.

On July 1 he sent Ober the segment of prose called "A Name for the City" as a by-product of his play. He hoped for a *Post* sale (and payment), but settled for $500 from *Harper's* (in October 1950). This segment became in time the prologue to act 1, with the title "The Courthouse (A Name for the City)." There was an evident need for money at this time, but when Ober offered a project proposal to him, he tentatively rejected it on the grounds that he only wanted to do such things in his free time. He was afraid to associate his name with trash, and he wanted to continue on *Requiem*, which was his link with Joan.

This was the surface of his life. In the background, Phil Stone was arranging his own version. As we read his letters to Carvel Collins,[29] in April and May, we see not so much a countering life being put forth (although that would come later) but a life according to Stone. In his letter of April 20, Stone tells Collins that all biographical information he has gotten should be submitted to him, Stone, before submission to the publisher. He will verify it. He says Faulkner has not been feeling well, and he recommended the clinic—Faulkner was drinking heavily; but he says, derisively, that the Faulkners all think they can defy the laws of nature.

Although Faulkner had not gotten on with the successors to *The Hamlet*, he returned to that material through the three prose segments of *Requiem*. He also returned to the world of *Go Down, Moses* by charting how the land has gone from wilderness to highway, from big woods to settled communities, and how in the process not only land but man was lost. Faulkner is no Wordsworthian romantic who finds in noncity living the best and brightest of life; but he does find in the give-and-take of an older society, with all its flaws, something missing now in the rush toward technology and progress. Like Jefferson, he thought that the land contained something of man's soul, whereas cities, even towns and villages, chewed up that soul, corrupted it not with crime but with the sloth of modern life. He came very close to the assumptions of those who wrote the manifesto, *I'll Take My Stand*, perhaps siding with them more firmly in his later years than in his younger. As he moved from his involvement in European modernism to his more distinctly American phase after *Absalom*, he became more than ever convinced that progress was tantamount to subversion of the human spirit.

Almost his sole sense of excitement came from his relationship with Joan. While it will never be known precisely what she meant to him, it can be said with certainty that he had little else and therefore counted more on her than he would have had his cup been full. Professional honors like the Howells Medal—and even the Nobel Prize—did not seem to lift him into better spirits: only alcohol and Joan helped. A letter to her, dated September 29, indicates how deeply committed he had become to this apprentice writer. He has an idea for a short story, which he tells her to write objectively, from the outside, in the third person. It is the story of their relationship, with one difference:

> . . . a young woman, senior at school, a man of fifty, famous—could be artist, soldier, whatever seems best. He has come up to spend the day with her. She does not know why, until after he has gone. They talk, about everything, anything, whatever you like. She is more than just flattered that a man of fame has come up to see her; she likes him, feels drawn to an understanding, make it wisdom, of her, of people, man, a sympathy for her in particular; maybe he will of a sudden talk of love to her. But she will know that is still not it, not what he came for; she is puzzled a little; when he gets on the train, she is sad, probably worried; she does not know why, is uncomfortable because she is troubled. There is something inconclusive, yet she cannot imagine what conclusion there could be between the two of them. But she knows he came for some reason, and she failed to get it, whether he thought she would or not or is disappointed that she didn't. Then she finds why he came, what he wanted, and that he got it. She knows it the next day; she receives a telegram that he is dead, heart; she realises that he knew it was going to happen, and that what he wanted was to walk in April again for a day, an hour.[30]

A mark of Faulkner's depression, or else his melodramatic sense, is his death in this scenario, or, possibly, as Blotner suggests, he got the idea from Hemingway's *Across the River and into the Trees,* where Colonel Cantwell loves the young Renata as he awaits a sudden death from a weakened heart. Wherever the idea comes from, it possesses Faulkner's insight into Joan's dilemma about him and at the same time contrasts sharply with the kind of story he himself could write. What it reveals is that he can see the material from a female point of view—not only how he feels but how she responds to his mixed messages. The letter also reveals how deeply involved Faulkner had become, and his fear that her understanding of him might come too late.

The meetings were no longer secret. Faulkner could not have expected he could enter Memphis unseen. He felt, however, that Estelle had dealt with his affair with Meta and he could continue here, discreetly. In fact,

Estelle had toughened and was less passive in these matters, forcing the issue by opening Joan's letters or else, as she claimed, coming upon them after they were opened by her son, Malcolm. In the meanwhile, on August 21, Faulkner's *Collected Stories* was published.* It included none of the stories which had appeared in *The Hamlet* or in novel-like collections of stories, *The Unvanquished, Go Down, Moses,* and *Knight's Gambit.* With those exceptions, he omitted only four of the forty-six stories which had had magazine publication. The volume was well publicized, with the Book-of-the-Month Club taking it as an alternate fiction selection for September, and the reviews were strong.

As suggested, the collection was put together in an effort to create a novelistic effect. The stories were so arranged that, with some exceptions, they moved along as a coherent, rather than a discrete, portrayal of Faulkner's world. (The one mistake in this was the final segment, "Beyond," which several contemporary reviewers also found weak and unintegrated into the volume.) Reading along from story to story, one recognizes the coherence of Faulkner's imagination and returns to that image of a mass packed away in his head which he could chip away at, gaining novels and stories as he wished. He was not a writer who gained his material from steady or developing experience; he had assimilated it all at once and then drew upon it. Conrad was also that kind of writer once he turned from the sea; Hemingway quite the opposite, and that is perhaps one reason he spent himself so rapidly.

The *New York Times Book Review* made several points about the collection in Faulkner's favor, one of them quite astute. The reviewer, Harry Sylvester, called him superior to all American writers since James and possibly since Melville, saying he knew so much more than the others. The "ranking" of Faulkner was long in coming. It should have been obvious, if critics and reviewers had not been so sunk into 1930s naturalism and realism, that with *Absalom* such an overarching talent had appeared that all other writers, in comparison, looked miniature. The Sunday New York *Herald Tribune* reviewer, Horace Gregory, who had not always been favorable to Faulkner's work, now saw him as the master of his generation. "He is more distinctly the master of a style than any writer of fiction living in America today."[31] This was indeed the perfect volume for a man to publish who is about to receive a Nobel Prize. Only Hemingway could match him with this high quality of story, but he did not have Faulkner's astonishing range.

Yet while he was being toasted in New York, his main theater of activity centered on Oxford and Memphis. Joan was hesitating, not only from fear of disclosure of their meetings and correspondence but out of anxiety about her family. Her career still seemed the most important thing for her, and that meant linking herself to Faulkner; but she recognized he was pressing for a deeper relationship—or it had already begun—and she

---

*In Britain, Chatto & Windus published the stories in three separate volumes: *These Thirteen, Doctor Martino and Other Stories,* and *Uncle Willy and Other Stories.*

doubted if that was what she wanted. The explosions with Estelle came later, in 1952, and Faulkner's publisher was dragged into it. Random House was of course necessary for him to carry on his affairs, since his editors arranged meeting places and gave him cover. All of them were aware of his activities and willing to help him, since he figured so large in their plans —and Estelle was the wife whom Faulkner frequently bad-mouthed as an alcoholic, helpless, an unfit mother when he was not around. How much they believed we do not know; we do know that they felt Faulkner had to be protected.

On one of her trips to Oxford, under the eyes of Estelle, Faulkner presented Joan with the manuscript of *Sound*. It was as if, under different circumstances, he had given her an engagement or wedding ring. He was in effect offering the deepest part of himself—not just a manuscript of considerable value but something derived from his deepest reaches. He had written it when barely ten years older than she, and it carried him back to the time when it would have been appropriate for him to court a woman of twenty-two. It also coincided with his marriage to Estelle. She could not compete with this kind of gesture; she was caught, and very possibly she wanted to be caught. He tried every means to continue to meet Joan, whether in Oxford or in Memphis, where her family disapproved, or even in Jackson, where he had some business.

It was during this kind of intense activity that we find Faulkner writing to Saxe Commins fully two years later. It is his version of what occurred —Estelle's came in 1954, also to Commins. Faulkner (October 25, 1952):

> Hell's to pay here now. While I was hors de combat [having fallen down the staircase at Rowan Oak while drunk] E. opened and read Joan Williams's letters to me. Now E. is drunk, and I am trying to nurse her before Malcolm sends her to a hospital, which costs like fury and does no good unless you make an effort yourself. I cant really blame her, certainly I cant criticise her, I am even sorry for her, even if people who will open and read another's private and personal letters, do deserve exactly what they get.[32]

He then moves into his general situation, and his revelations of his domestic situation are devastating. What is clear is that behind the bourgeois façade he had erected at Rowan Oak, with all the markings of success in property and propriety, there was an ongoing war not too different from Scott and Zelda's. Estelle was sane but alcoholic and driven to fury by Faulkner's disregard of her, his acts of contempt, his savage verbal thrusts; and he was so frustrated by a marriage doomed from the start he responded often with cruelty and abandonment. The failure of the marriage to produce any sexual satisfaction, for either, had made all communication faulty, and had resulted in each pursuing his and her own private demons. When we speak of a falling-off in Faulkner's work by the early 1940s, we must keep the domestic situation in mind. So much of Faulkner's energies were going into *countering* his married state, in trying to carve out an area of happiness or something to sustain himself with, that he was constantly diverted. His work may well have fallen off for other reasons —financial needs, too much soaking in alcohol, the natural expenditure of his original body of material—but there is little question his home life was part of that deterioration. He would have binged under any conditions, but the intervals between drunken bouts might have been more spread out, the bouts themselves less intense, the desire for oblivion less immediate. Faulkner:

> . . . this is a terrible situation; never can I remember ever being so unhappy and downhearted and despaired. I have done no work in a year, am living on my fat, will begin soon to worry about money, and I do not believe I can work here. I must get away. I want to come up to Princeton, per your invitation, and finish the big book [*The Fable*]. Yet I cant leave E. drunk here, and if I came anywhere in the neighborhood of N.Y. city, nothing would ever convince her that it was not only to be near Joan, since she (E.) has never had any regard or respect for my work, has always looked on it as a hobby, like collecting stamps.

He then recycles the argument he had used several years before with Meta Carpenter, that to leave Estelle was to abandon Jill, not now as a child with a drunken mother, but to scandal and opprobrium, given his fame.

> Of course, I could come anyway, regardless. But I am fearful about Jill. I mean, to disrupt her in the middle of her senior year at her school [Pine Manor Junior College]. I am afraid that, if I came up, E. would insist on some public formal separation and so forth, so that every time Jill entered a class room or the dining room, she would think: *All these people know that my parents have separated*, and it would ruin her year, even if she herself did not do something in desperation. So I dont see much hope until after she graduates, though I dont see either how I can go on like this; particularly have I got to get back to work, not only for the money, but to get the book finished.[33]

Beyond the words and obvious anguish is something else, the nature of his symbiotic relationship to Estelle. We have noted she often preferred Faulkner drunk, so she had some role in his life; but for his part, her alcoholism gave him a role in the household which he might otherwise have abdicated. And he held on to that role, as he held on to Estelle. He needed her as intensely as she needed him: the bond formed so early in their lives superseded all other considerations, however unhappy they made each other. Whenever Faulkner was faced with the abyss of separation and/or divorce, he retreated behind the need to protect Jill. It was a real need, and he evidently wanted to shield his daughter from scandal; but it was his need as well. He also, perhaps, could not face the awareness of failure; some of this need to stick could be face-saving, whatever the misery. For all his affairs and expressions of distaste for his domestic situation, he was a man of marriage. Faulkner was enmired in something he desperately wanted, as much as he wanted to break out. His response to his marriage is like his response to Oxford and the South: an intense need to maintain his ties, and an equally intense desire to reject it all, to liberate himself. We recall Quentin's plaint at the end of *Absalom.*

By fall, while spending time with Jill as well as with Dean (his niece) and Vicki, Cho-Cho's daughter, Faulkner started to hear more than rumors about the Nobel Prize. An Associated Press statement from Stockholm in early November announced that of the fifty or so candidates for the prize in literature, William Faulkner's name was near the top for the 1949 prize which had not been awarded. Sentiment had been for Faulkner, and the Swedish Academy was led by a man, Gustaf Hellström, who enthusiastically supported his candidacy. What might have hurt Faulkner during the 1949 voting was the paucity of his works in Swedish. That country had fallen behind France, Italy, Germany, and even Japan in this regard.* A few books had been translated: *Light in August* (1944), *As I Lay Dying* (1948), *The Unvanquished* (1948), and *The Wild Palms* (1949), and *Intruder in the Dust* was to follow in 1950. After the prize was awarded, several other books appeared: *Sanctuary, The Town, Sartoris, Requiem for a Nun,* and "The Bear." But now there seemed little doubt Faulkner was the leading candidate.

On November 10, the Swedish Academy issued the statement that William Faulkner was the recipient of the Nobel Prize in literature for 1949, with a money prize of $30,171, for his "powerful and independent artistic contribution in America's new literature of the novel." Faulkner received word in an early-morning call from Sven Ahman, New York correspondent of *Dagens Nyheter,* and was asked to express his feelings. He said he was impressed and flattered that his work "had been considered worthy of this distinction." When asked about Stockholm, the writer said he wouldn't be able to get away, since he was a farmer and it was too far away. He followed this with a letter to Ahman on November 16, indicating he had told the secretary of the Academy he was unable to attend. He then explains:

> . . . I hold that the award was made not to me, but to my works—crown to thirty years of the agony and sweat of a human spirit, to make something which was not here before me, to lift up or maybe comfort or anyway at least entertain, in its turn, man's heart. That took thirty years. I am past fifty now; there is probably not much more in the

*One says "even Japan" with the full knowledge that Faulkner, after his visit to Japan in 1955, became almost a cult figure in that country, and much valuable scholarship on Faulkner's work has been done by Japanese scholars. At the time of the Nobel Prize, however, Japan was still recovering from the war, not translating Faulkner.

tank. I feel that what remains after the thirty years of work is not worth carrying from Mississippi to Sweden, just as I feel that what remains does not deserve to expend the prize on himself, so that it is my hope to find an aim for the money high enough to be commensurate with the purpose and significance of its origin.*[34]

He tells Ahman he is free to print this letter, subject only to the authority of the Academy. With that, he prepared for his annual deer hunt in the Delta.

According to Blotner, Faulkner told no one about the call and started the day in his usual way—driving Jill and Vicki to school. Apparently he feared an avalanche of inquiries, interviews, reporters—everything which sent him into a panic.** Not telling even Estelle, however, had another dimension. If she had taken, as he asserted, no interest in his work, had viewed it as no better than stamp collecting, then he would not share the momentous news. It does fit—that he had almost no one to inform, so isolated had he made himself; or else, in the circuitry of self, he felt the news had little meaning to anyone but himself.

The outcome of such monumental news was predictable. The award, the ensuing celebrity, the influx of well-wishers and reporters, the conflict of whether to go to Stockholm or not all created an unresolvable series of dilemmas. His routine and desire for withdrawal within that routine were shattered. He had no way to handle it except through drinking, heavily. That came when he headed on November 16 for hunting camp. He still had to get through the intervening days, however—in his mind six days of labor. Estelle took the brunt of reporters' questions, as Faulkner went into his usual funk when anyone tried to penetrate his shield. He did repeat that he had no plans to go to Stockholm to receive the Nobel Prize in person; and he gave away almost nothing to the barrage of questions and questioners. Congratulations came in even from old enemies in the press, except for the racist Jackson *Daily News*, which called him a "propagandist of degradation" who "properly belongs in the privy school of literature." But Mullen in the *Eagle* pulled out all stops and even quoted from a number of cronies: Ike Roberts from deer camp, Mac Reed on their long friendship, Phil Stone on the early years of discouragement. Stone was particularly charming, saying that someone who knows Faulkner as well

*Faulkner's negative response to the Stockholm trip was possibly linked to a self-assessment: that he felt ashamed to accept in person a grand award for work he could no longer do. Under such circumstances, he believed too large a gap between present and past work existed for him to accept an honor for past fiction, the best of it almost twenty years ago.

**He was right. Moon Mullen got word and insisted Faulkner see him. The editor of the *Eagle* had been a sometime friend and supporter, tending to help Faulkner when the town criticized him, but himself critical. Now he wanted a photo and a personal story. He obtained them, and Faulkner even added that while he was a member of the RAF, he did not see any service. Having read the story through, he approved it, and Mullen telephoned it in to the Associated Press in Jackson. Mac Reed, another old friend and supporter, came by, followed by Memphis reporters in the afternoon.

as he can say "he is even greater as a man than he is as a writer."[35] Stone seemed genuinely gratified at the award to his friend, speaking of Faulkner as a friend who could always be counted upon.

In the world outside, however, the reception was mixed. Although Faulkner had clearly emerged as the most significant American novelist of this century (if we assign James to an earlier era), the newspapers were begrudging in their acceptance of his award, arguing that he was too grim in a darkening world, or else unrepresentative of American life, where incest and rape are uncommon. Perhaps they failed to read their own newspapers. Even at his moment of glory, Faulkner's critics continued.

It is fitting to put here a Frenchman's response to the critical reception Faulkner received in America. Maurice Coindreau was appalled that the man was still without honor in his own country. His words are indicative of foreign responses, as contrasted with American.

> I admit that one of the reasons which determined me to write today about the author of *Sanctuary* is the extreme reserve—not to put it more strongly—with which the American press seems to have received the news that William Faulkner has been awarded the Nobel Prize. I expected the critics for all the important newspapers to pay him due homage immediately, if only in a few paragraphs. I thought I would see his portrait, in black and white or in color, on the covers of literary or news weeklies, as on the most insignificant occasions one sees the portraits of politicians, generals, boxers, and film stars. Of course, I do not read all the periodicals, but I must say that until this moment I feel like Sister Anne: I wait but nothing of importance happens. A small notice, a small photograph at the bottom of a page —not much more. I do not believe I am going too far in asserting that there has been a stronger reaction in France, and I presume that pens and typewriters were not idle there the day after November 10. More precisely, I can affirm that M. Jean-Paul Sartre, with the speed of a reflex, is already preparing to publish in the next numbers of his journal *Les Temps Modernes* one of the two parts that make up *The Wild Palms*. Several works—notably *Absalom, Absalom!*—are in preparation.[36]

Sartre had already written a piece called "Time in the Work of Faulkner." He had gained his interest in the American writer from Simone de Beauvoir, who read Faulkner almost from his earliest days, from the late 1920s. She read English, Sartre did not; and she would repeat aloud long passages and pages, translating to Sartre as she read. When Faulkner started to become available in French, Sartre read him and rushed into print. De Beauvoir did not publish on Faulkner, whereas Sartre, through her interest in the American, became known as an early spokesman in France for Faulkner's work.

At the very end of 1949 (December 30), Phil Stone weighed in with one of his appraisals of Faulkner's work. Writing to Glenn O. Carey, who had recently completed a master's thesis on humor in the fiction of William Faulkner, Stone made one of his typically depreciating remarks about his friend's work: "I am glad that someone had finally decided to write on the humor in Faulkner's work. I have tried to get a dozen people to do it without success. For a number of years I have had the opinion that Faulkner's future as a writer lay in the possibility of him becoming a great American Humorist."[37] With these remarks, Stone could bypass the Faulkner of *Absalom*, hardly a humorous novel, rather one that dissects the blackness of the whale.*

But by 1951 Faulkner was beginning to notice a considerable increase in criticism and scholarship about his work. In that year the first full-length book of criticism appeared, Harry Campbell and Ruel F. Foster's *William Faulkner: A Critical Appraisal*. In the meanwhile, Professor Dayton Kohler of the Virginia Polytechnic Institute had written on Faulkner and the social conscience in the widely circulated and influential *College English* (December 1949). Faulkner responded (January 10) that he agreed with the piece. "You and Cowley have both seen it [his aim] along with Prof. [Warren] Beck of Wisconsin and one twenty-one-year-old Tennessee school girl." The reference to Joan indicates to what extent she had entered his imagination: a schoolgirl, Warren Beck, Malcolm Cowley, and Professor Kohler.

Meanwhile the world was trying to mobilize its forces so as to bring Faulkner to Stockholm against his wishes. According to Blotner,[38] who reconstructed the strategies used to entice the laureate to make the trip, the first step came with the American ambassador to Sweden. W. Walton Butterworth got in touch with the State Department, pointing out there was considerable consternation that Faulkner had let down his supporters for the prize by declining to come. Only his appearance could justify their devoted commitment to their cause. Many writers were especially supportive, not simply academics and bureaucrats, several of whom originally opposed Faulkner as too depressing or as unrepresentative of the Nobel positive ideal. The most effective workers on behalf of the Swedes were, however, friends, relatives and immediate family. One telling argument as it emanated from Washington to Mississippi, through the poet, Muna Lee, was that Thorsten Jonsson, now dead, the man who had visited Faulkner in 1946, had been responsible for the writer's high reputation in Sweden. Faulkner at least owed it to Jonsson's memory to accept the award in person. But while persuasive, that would not be the telling argument.

*Stone took credit for Faulkner's humor: "I get credit for a lot that Faulkner has accomplished but as far as his actual writing is concerned I helped him very little except with the humor, but I actually made his humor for him. At the beginning he was a very humorless person." One hangs on to "made his humor for him" (Faulkner: *A Comprehensive Guide to the Brodsky Collection, the Letters*, eds. Louis Daniel Brodsky and Robert W. Hamblin, vol. 2 [Jackson: University Press of Mississippi, 1984], p. 47).

Muna Lee, who was from Washington, moved closer to Faulkner by getting in touch with Mrs. Joseph M. Howorth, a lawyer in Cleveland, Mississippi, and the sister of Ella Somerville, Estelle's long-time friend. Stone was ruled out as a possible intermediary because it was known he was on occasion bad-mouthing Faulkner and might spoil everything. Colonel Hugh Evans, a friend of Faulkner's, was to be the intermediary, and he tried to persuade the recalcitrant writer when he returned from hunting camp on November 27, albeit in very poor shape. Binging had done its usual damage, and additionally he suffered from a severe cold close to pneumonia. Under these conditions, he was not ready to listen to anyone from outside the family; and it was Estelle, pleading that Jill wanted to make the trip, who turned his decision around. According to Blotner, Jill was not at all eager to go, but the argument held, and Faulkner relented. They would travel together, without Estelle.

Faulkner's connection with the Swedish government was Erik Boheman, the ambassador, who wrote him in carefully chosen words: that as a farmer himself he would understand Faulkner's reluctance to make such a long trip; but that such a trip, which would delight his Swedish admirers, would take him from his farm for only a few days. It was a perfect finesse of Faulkner, appealing in exactly the right way, and the writer telegraphed on November 27 that he would "be pleased to journey to Stockholm."[39] The Swedish end of this saga was complete, with Boheman offering to make all travel arrangements; but on Faulkner's end there was much to be done. The job of the immediate family and friends was to keep him in shape for the departure on December 6 for New York. He planned to drink up until the evening of December 4, the Monday before the Wednesday departure. He was now a very sick man and looked it, needing all his powers of recovery to return from the kind of binge which really required drying out. He began to withdraw on more widely spaced drinks, while nourishment was coaxed into him. The situation was an exact duplication of ones he had created before. While he was the center of attention in the world at large, he had managed to so enfeeble himself that he was a small child fed, watched over, coaxed, doctored. The family needed to get him well not to send him to school but to Stockholm; and they had to do it by subterfuge, setting the calendar ahead so that he thought December 4, the Monday of the final drink, was closer than it was. Even when he penetrated the subterfuge, they ministered to him. It was, incidentally, impossible to stop him, since he refused all nourishment unless it was accompanied by some dose of alcohol. The alcoholic Estelle found her mission, and in such situations was devoted and committed to his welfare.

Preparations continued in the few days before departure: photos, passports, and the acquisition of a dress suit, that job falling to Saxe Commins, who received Faulkner's measurements by telephone and then went to a rental store. Everyone in the Faulkner orbit was working to bring him around and to make him presentable. He had also begun to sketch in his speech, that brief speech that has become more famous than any other delivered by an American (or perhaps world) writer. He began with the idea the award was not made to him as a man, but to his work; and it was, in effect, to be held in trust for all writers. As we shall see when he delivered the finished speech before the assembled dignitaries and other Nobel Prize winners, he mined ideas he had already worked over in *A Fable*. Dignified, even elegant as they were, they were ideas from Faulkner the moralist—the man seeking a philosophy by which to live—rather than from Faulkner the complex, arcane, experimental author of an earlier time. The Nobel speech became a fine human document, but as a revelation of the writer, it showed a reductive Faulkner making his peace more with the world than with his craft. Its enthusiastic reception was part of the ironies of writer and world: the latter likes nothing better than a positive statement from the man it is honoring, even when his art is compromised or even contradicted.*

On Wednesday morning, December 6, his drinking having tailed off but the heavy cold continuing, he departed for New York—with a very wary and often withering press attacking his selection as the Nobel laureate. For many Americans, and for the press in particular, he had never lived down the notoriety of *Sanctuary;* and for that group its abiding literary qualities were secondary to its sensationalism. As articles on his selection increased, so did references to "Mr. Corncob," a denigrating tag for the author of three or four of the finest novels in contemporary American literature.

Although he made the flight from Memphis to New York, there was still the touchy question of keeping him sober and getting him on the plane to Stockholm. Faulkner was shifted from one set of keepers to another. He saw himself as the prisoner of the situation, as reporters and other interviewers tore at him, awaiting him in airports or at other stops. Those who had seen him off into the hands of American Airlines personnel were in turn replaced by the Haases, who met him at La Guardia Airport in New York. The Haases were not only to guide him through the New York stopover but to nurse him, for he was still a sick man and looked it. Once they settled him and Jill at the Algonquin, Merle Haas began to dose him with the antibiotic Aureomycin, which should not be taken with alcohol. Faulkner drank steadily while under medication, and from what we know now, he could have been struck down by the combination. At the dinner party that night, all his old friends from publishing were present once again—Harrison Smith, Bennett Cerf and his wife, the Klopfers, Maurice Coindreau, and Malcolm Cowley. This was a favorable situation for Faulkner to drink in, because virtually everyone there was a potential nurse: he would be well guarded and cared for if he collapsed. He drank.

---

*In this spirit, Faulkner insisted he would give the money away, that it should not be wasted on a middle-aged man to buy him comforts. Faulkner's discomfort with the monetary reward is clear in his desire to divest himself of what he feels belongs to many. With some of the money, he did establish scholarships for educationally deserving Negroes, among other charities.

Malcolm Cowley observed him carefully and left a description which compares the writer with soldiers ready to face death as they went over the top:

Faulkner was polite but abstracted that evening, as if reserving his strength for a supreme ordeal. I thought he had the look to be found on the faces of British Tommies at Ypres, in photographs taken a moment before they went over the top. His eyes lighted only when he looked at Jill, who, shyly polite and self-possessed, was radiating the pleased excitement that her father might have been expected to feel.[40]

The image is appropriate: Faulkner carried himself like a man preparing to face a firing squad at dawn, collecting his forces, but not quite succeeding. By the next morning, the inevitable occurred: fever, chills, a severe grippe. A doctor ordered him to bed until his flight to Stockholm. But he had remarkable recuperative powers, and that night he was at Cerf's for another party.

In his desire to be considered more important than he was as a force in contemporary American fiction, John O'Hara had the unpleasant habit of celebrating those he deemed to be in the forefront: first Fitzgerald, and then recently in an absurdly enthusiastic *New York Times* review of Hemingway's *Across the River and into the Trees*. A very heavy drinker himself, O'Hara may have been under the weather when he approached Faulkner and began to butter him up. Only two months before, he had called Hemingway the outstanding author "out of the millions who have lived since 1616." To Faulkner, none of this meant anything, unless pushed, and then he could become cruel. O'Hara approached him and said they were "running neck and neck" as authors until Faulkner began to pull away, leaving him, O'Hara, behind. Literature had become a horse race. Faulkner was quiet and then murmured agreement. O'Hara became carried away when he did not receive the answer he had fished for, and produced from his pocket a cigarette lighter which he said once belonged to his father. He gave it to Faulkner, and waited for a word of praise or recognition. Faulkner thanked him, and that was it, pocketing it, and O'Hara was left holding his vanity. Faulkner told Blotner later he was "cooked either way." So ended the O'Hara-Faulkner encounter, somehow indicative of everything Faulkner feared and tried to avoid.

On Friday, December 8, Faulkner and Jill left for Stockholm on Scandinavian Airlines, and he began to sketch in his Nobel Prize address. The brief speech of about six hundred words went through many alterations, deletions, and shifts of emphasis. At first, in an act of generosity, he wanted to pay homage to some of his contemporaries as the children of Sherwood Anderson—Hemingway, Dos Passos, Wolfe, and Caldwell. This was in keeping with his original impulse that the award had been given to him as a trust to keep for all American novelists who deserved it as much as he. In this he intended to interweave his sermonistic belief that man was immortal, that whatever occurred, man would survive. Here he is moving well into his own *Fable*, still inchoate in manuscript, and his understanding of Conrad, whose presence throughout the entire speech proved enormous. In rooting around for the right images and tones for his talk, Faulkner fell heavily on the Conrad of his more positive and simplistic phases, not the author of *Heart of Darkness* or *Nostromo*, where the message counters wholeness and integrity.*

Numerous personal references in the first drafts of the address are deleted from the final version. Faulkner retained the fear of being blown up in an atomic war, but eliminated all references to his Hollywood experience, where his words had been extremely derisive. In the draft, he wrote of a soulless place, where no one was interested in either personal or universal truth, but in getting the story right, coming in at the right angle —his locale was Hollywood, and he clearly had in mind Warner Brothers. Probably there was the desire for revenge in putting matters this way when the world was listening; but his better judgment was to omit such intimate detail in favor of the more overarching point about personal and universal truths. He also attacked in this early version the younger generation of writers who write not from the heart but from the glands, as if they were unconcernedly observing the end of man. He quieted this sentiment considerably in the revision, and turned it into something much more positive. In its original formulation, it was unfair, since the work of the younger generation when Faulkner wrote this—writers such as Bellow and Mailer—was very much concerned with the dictates of the heart and soul.

As he worked his way toward his final version, he reached back to ideas set forth in "Battle Cry" and continued through Gavin Stevens's long speeches in *Intruder*. From the ashes comes man's voice. What comes through (and this has not been noticed) is a reprise of Conrad's preface to *The Nigger of the "Narcissus,"* adapted to fit Faulkner's theme of man prevailing and enduring, whereas Conrad focused on the kind of art and artist which would endure. The cadences, sentiments, tones appear analogous, and Conrad's intensity and moralism are there. Faulkner concluded: "The poet's voice need not merely be the record of man, it can be one of the props, the pillars to help him endure and prevail." Conrad wrote, in 1897, that the artist speaks "to the subtle but invincible conviction of solidarity that knits together the loneliness of innumerable hearts, to the solidarity in dreams, in joy, in sorrow, in aspirations, in illusions, in hope, in fear, which binds men to each other, which binds together all humanity—the dead to the living and the living to the unborn." Before his final line,

---

*Blotner cites a striking passage in Conrad's essay on Henry James ("Henry James: An Appreciation") which Faulkner may have plundered. "When the last aqueduct shall have crumbled to pieces, the last airship fallen to the ground, the last blade of grass have died upon a dying earth, man, indomitable by his training in resistance to misery and pain, shall set this undiminished light of his eyes against the feeble glow of the sun" (Conrad's *Notes on Life and Letters*).

Faulkner said that the poet's privilege is "to help man endure by lifting his heart, by reminding him of the courage and honor and hope and pride and compassion and pity and sacrifice which have been the glory of his past."

Once he landed in Stockholm, still suffering from his cold and not completely recovered from his recent binge, Faulkner was caught up by welcoming parties, interviews, photographers, journalists, receptions. To his hosts, he appeared tentative and fatigued, anxious and somewhat distracted. Unknown to them, he was teetering, but supported by a circle of people eager to care for him, including an English butler who served as his valet. Faulkner was interviewed at the official embassy press conference, and Jill also answered questions put to her, diplomatically and fearlessly. A formal dinner was next, at the Bonnier villa, the home of Faulkner's Swedish publisher. It was at this formal gathering—a dinner party with heavy Ingmar Bergman overtones of a straitlaced society trying to have fun—that Faulkner met the attractive and intelligent widow of Thorsten Jonsson, Else. Fluent in English and a knowledgeable one-time resident of New York's Greenwich Village, she and Faulkner struck it off, and he was put at ease in surroundings that otherwise might have driven him to flee. They forged a friendship on the spot: the woman recently widowed, her late husband a man who had admired Faulkner, and the writer himself, personally miserable in his domestic life and now feeling alone and isolated in this formal gathering.

Faulkner decided to remain sober, although as the time of his speech approached, he grew visibly nervous.*[41] He dressed in his evening clothes but refused to shave the stubble which up close made him look old and bummy. Photographs taken of him, however, do not catch the skin, and the overall effect is impressive: slim, slightly roguish, but elegant. Bertrand Russell, the 1950 laureate in literature honored at the same celebration, left some memories of Faulkner, whom he unsuccessfully tried to engage in conversation. Russell was an old hand at such ceremonies and functions; but Faulkner, as the philosopher put it, seemed completely out of place "in the atmosphere of Royalty, trumpets and general grandeur." Faulkner remained too shy and reticent for any meaningful exchange; and one receives the impression that beyond shyness lay real fear at his role in the ceremonies. Three other Americans (including Ralph Bunche, receiving the Peace Prize) were also present, but Faulkner had few words for them either. When he was called, he went up to receive the Nobel diploma and medal; his address came later, after the great formal dinner for all the laureates.

That part of the ceremony over, Faulkner had to prepare himself for the worst part of all, his address. As many have commented, he stood

*Blotner reports a humorous incident, reminiscent of Faulkner's days as postmaster. He tossed all of his mail into a wastebasket, including his invitation to the king's dinner, where the valet discovered it. One projects a scenario in which Faulkner, the laureate in literature, shows up for the dinner and is turned away for lack of an invitation.

too far from the microphone, his voice was too low, and he slurred and speeded up his speech. This, added to his deep Southern accent, made the address unintelligible. But the next day, when his speech was printed, it created a tremendous impression, and some thought it might be the best Nobel acceptance speech ever given. For those who seemed surprised at the positive nature of the speech, *Intruder,* in fact, had already said it all. There Faulkner spoke of the Negro's ability to "wait and endure and survive" until the white Southerner gives him his just rights economically and politically. In the speech, he took up this theme and brought to it a more universal application. For his sense of man's survival, he clearly had the Southern Negro as his model. As we see Faulkner position himself in race relations in Mississippi and the South, for him the ability to prevail and endure belongs to the Negro—and in his Nobel speech, the Negro is at the center of his mind, at the center of the universe.

What is most remarkable about the speech, however, is not its sentiments, but its pacing and rhythms. Faulkner took time with it, shaped it, and then brought it to its economical pitch. He started by disclaiming the award as being made to him as a man. It was his craft, his "life's work in the agony and sweat of the human spirit," that was being rewarded. This sentiment astutely moved the center of gravity away from the often seediness and nastiness of his themes, to the spirit of art itself. He appeals to those "already dedicated to the same anguish and travail, among whom is already that one who will some day stand here where I am standing."

With that out of the way, Faulkner proceeds to the main body of his argument, which will take only three paragraphs. He says the main question of the day appears to be not problems of the spirit, but when we will all be blown up. The potential of the bomb creates an urgency which has made the present generation of writers forget "the problems of the human heart in conflict with itself which alone can make good writing because only that is worth writing about, worth the agony and the sweat." The reasoning here is quite specious, and, as indicated, quite unfair to those young writers who were indeed grappling with life under the shadow of the bomb.

In the extension of this argument, Faulkner becomes heuristic. Man must recognize that he is afraid, and then, without forgetting that, leave no room in his workshop for anything but the "old verities and truths of the heart." If he fails to do this, he labors under a curse. He must incorporate love, not lust; values, even in defeat; pity and compassion, even in victory. He must leave scars, or else he "writes not of the heart but of the glands." With this impressive rhetoric, based on sermonlike repetition and on the image of waves rolling in a little further each time, Faulkner is ready for his full statement and summation.

The finale is a grand piece of rhetoric which disguises the dubiety of the statement. He declines, quite simply, to accept the end of man.

. . . it is easy enough to say that man is immortal simply because he will endure: that when the last ding-dong of doom has clanged and faded from the last worthless rock hanging tideless in the last red and dying evening, that even then there will still be one more sound: that of his puny inexhaustible voice, still talking. I refuse to accept this. I believe that man will not merely endure: he will prevail.

Faulkner becomes mystical as he prepares his audience not only for his impressive and orotund statement, but for his labors on *A Fable.* Unlike the younger generation, what he is writing comes right from the heart, and it assumes man's soul. He, man,

is immortal, not because he alone among creatures has an inexhaustible voice, but because he has a soul, a spirit capable of compassion and sacrifice and endurance. The poet's, the writer's duty is to write about these things. It is his privilege to help man endure by lifting his heart, by reminding him of the courage and honor and hope and pride and compassion and pity and sacrifice which have been the glory of his past. The poet's voice need not merely be the record of man, it can be one of the props, the pillars to help him endure and prevail.

The cadences are superb. But one reason the speech became so immediately famous once it was printed was that it touched upon a world that had gone very sour. Faulkner's timing was miraculous. His sense of time and place, his insight into how people felt was perfect. After the few years of optimism at the end of the war, the world saw one conflict in the West and another in the East that threatened peace. In the West, the need developed in Berlin to fly in supplies to keep the city from succumbing to the Soviet blockade; the airlift had ended only the previous year. In the East, the Korean War created an equally delicate situation. In retrospect, that war seems like a skirmish, savage at the time, but contained. But while it was occurring, it had tremendous potential for expansion, and it took an enormous toll in casualties. It was in all ways a disillusioning experience, since the United States depended on a corrupt and hated South Korean leader, and the North Koreans were doing the bidding of the Soviets.

While Stockholm in traditionally neutral Sweden seemed distant, Faulkner's speech skewered the sense of defeat which cold and hot war had brought to mankind only a few years after the most devastating war in history. We cannot explain the power and thrust of his brief talk without acknowledging its appeal to the very political elements the world was wondering about. It became, then, a document: not only expertly put together, but touching on man's needs. Descriptions of the talk emphasize that Faulkner made a deep impression despite the fact his voice was pitched too low and his accent too thick for most listeners. He created, whatever the vocal liabilities, a dramatic appearance, for despite his small physical stature, he possessed tremendous presence.

Additionally, for Faulkner, *his* document was aimed at reshaping how we should look at him. He turned his novels and shorter fictions into moral, human documents by way of his speech—or would have us do it. In one respect *he made himself more mainstream than his major work was;* and in a very guileful way, he prepared the listener (or reader) for the kind of fiction he was now writing. In that regard, for all its glory as rhetoric, the Nobel Prize acceptance speech misdirects us. In some ways, it is an outgrowth of Cowley's presentation of Faulkner in *The Portable Faulkner,* and it fits the taste of those critics who never accepted Faulkner at his most difficult and recalitrant.

With the ordeal of the presentation over, the ceremonies moved on to another phase: an outing, and then a dinner on Monday. Faulkner's companion, whenever possible, was Else Jonsson. He also started to drink, although containing himself. He was touched by Stockholm, with its profusion of lakes, and he indicated a desire to return. The Swedish hosts, and especially Else Jonsson, made the country particularly pleasant for him. According to Blotner, the American embassy reported that the three most attractive figures at the ceremonies had been Faulkner, Bertrand Russell, and Ralph Bunche. And in later years, the embassy recalled this when the government began to use Faulkner as a highly successful ambassador of literary culture to the world.

Faulkner and Jill went on to Paris, where he had been exactly twenty-five years earlier. They arrived on December 12, Jill sick with flu, and then went on to London on December 15. They spent one day in London, which Jill was too indisposed to enjoy, and were back in New York for one night. By December 18, ten days after leaving, Faulkner and his daughter returned to Oxford, to be greeted by the local high-school band. Faulkner wrote Erik Boheman, the Swedish ambassador (on December 27) expressing his thanks "for your kindness in making even more pleasant my daughter's and my most pleasant visit to your country in December."[42] He adds that he hopes his conduct and his daughter's left as high an opinion of Americans in Sweden as the regard for Sweden they brought away.*

By January 1, Faulkner was back at his desk. He still had unfinished work, some of it nearing completion *(Requiem),* some of it still inchoate and intractable *(A Fable).* He indicated he was pleased with his Nobel speech, although he thought he might have said it better with more time to compose it. He mentions the "big work," *A Fable,* which, as he knew, needed "some cleaning up"—in fact, it needed considerable reworking and rewriting. But his main enterprise was finishing *Requiem.* He says he has farm work to look to, and with that and *Requiem,* he expects to be busy until March. When the book is finished, he says, he would like Robert Sherwood

---

*He also wrote Mrs. Haas he did not regret going to Stockholm. "I realise it was the only thing to do; you can commit mistakes and only feel regret, but when you commit bad taste, what you feel is shame. Anyway, I went, and did the best I knew to behave like a Swedish gentleman, and leave the best taste possible on the Swedish palate for Americans and Random House" (December 27, 1950, *Selected Letters of William Faulkner,* ed. Joseph Blotner [New York: Vintage Books, 1978; orig. publ. 1977], p. 311).

to look at it, to tell him if it is a play or not. By 1950, Sherwood had written a number of successes which also won Pulitzer Prizes—*Idiot's Delight, Abe Lincoln in Illinois,* and *There Shall Be No Night*—plus several other plays of considerable fame, including *The Petrified Forest, Reunion in Vienna,* and *Waterloo Bridge.* Whatever Sherwood decides, however, Faulkner tells Random to print *Requiem* as a novel next fall. He asks Haas for $10,000 from his account, while he decides what to do with the bulk of his Nobel award of $31,000.

Chapter Twenty-five

After the Prize

THE PRIZE CHANGED Faulkner's life, and he had to come to terms with the differences. The events of 1951 show that adaptation had both its positive and negative aspects. As a celebrity, the laureate found all kinds of incursions on his desk time; but at the same time, many of these incursions proved pleasant diversions. In February the Levee Press (of Ben Wasson and Hodding Carter) published *Notes on a Horsethief,* a seventy-one-page chunk of *A Fable,* in a limited signed edition of 975 copies. It was, like some of Joyce, a "work in progress." He spent a little over a month of 1951 in Hollywood, but now on his terms, at $2,000 per week, working on the script of *The Left Hand of God* for Twentieth Century-Fox. This reunited him with Humphrey Bogart, who played the lead, plus an illustrious cast of Gene Tierney, Lee J. Cobb, Agnes Moorehead, and E. G. Marshall.

The Hollywood visit also reunited him with Meta, whose marriage to Rebner was now shattered. As he resumed his affair with Meta, Faulkner was in effect seeing three women: Meta Carpenter in Hollywood, Joan Williams whenever they could get together, and Else Jonsson, who joined him in Paris in April. By this time, he had come to terms with Ruth Ford, and their relationship settled down to friendship and mutual admiration for each other's talents. In March, after his stint in Hollywood, he received the National Book Award for *Collected Stories.* By early April, he was sending on *Requiem* material, including the prologue and act 2. In mid-

April he left for Europe, stopping off in London and then spending two gratifying weeks with the Gallimards and Monique Salomon (later Lange), where Else joined them.

In May he received the prestigious Legion of Honor from President Auriol of France. By mid-June, *Requiem for a Nun* was being typeset, and would be published as a novel in September. Ruth Ford told him a producer was interested in it as a play, and Faulkner assured her it was her property—that the play was written for her. There were to be unforeseen difficulties, and in time Faulkner had to give the property to Ober to handle professionally. He was in and out of Oxford for the remainder of the year: in New York in July, mainly for *Requiem;* in Wellesley, Massachusetts, for Jill's enrollment at Pine Manor Junior College;* in Cambridge in October for work on the adaptation of *Requiem* for Ruth Ford and her company; in New Orleans in later October to receive the Legion of Honor bestowed the previous May; back in Cambridge for further work on the *Requiem* script; then back on familiar ground in November for the annual hunt with his friends.

The year found Faulkner treated as a personage. He had of course gained considerable clout, and *Requiem* was one beneficiary of his new influence. Had it been written by an unknown author, it is doubtful that such material would have been received with such fanfare. Despite rewriting and tinkering, the moral center of the play remains ambiguous, as does the motivation Faulkner provides for the murder of the child. In novel form, *Requiem* can get away with a looseness which dramatic form simply will not allow. The dramatist has some two hours to pull it all together; the novelist is given far greater play of time and space. Also, the prologues (of course deleted from the drama) helped keep the reader of the novel off balance, working as a kind of counterpoint or contrast. In adjusting to the innovative form of this novel play, the reader does not expect the coherence a theater audience demands.

As he became more of a public person, Faulkner's depression seemed to lift. Of course he still protected his privacy, but he was willing to break up his work schedule to fly now and then. He also appeared to come to terms with his relationship to Joan. If anything, the disproportion between them had intensified; there was not only age, but now his celebrity and reputation, and she a struggling twenty-two-year-old writer. But Faulkner was understanding, especially after he had met Else Jonsson and found her companionship attractive. Nevertheless, he continued to bombard Joan

---

*The choice of college for Jill is interesting. Faulkner had considered more demanding institutions of learning, but had rejected them, although Jill was intelligent and learned easily. Part of it was the image of his daughter he wished to present: of someone who went to college, but was not too well educated to frighten off a suitor, and not educated beyond her status as an upper-middle-class Southern woman. In a sense, he was preparing her for nothing, as Estelle had been prepared for nothing. Estelle apparently acquiesced in these decisions, and may have been, for all we know, a directing force in convincing Jill to attend a finishing school rather than a demanding Ivy League women's college. In family matters, Faulkner's traditionalism was apparent.

with advice about her writing, telling her in a letter on January 28, 1951, that she some day will write. "Maybe now you haven't anything to say. You have to have something burning your very entrails to be said; you dont have that yet but dont worry about it; it is not important whether you write or not; writing is important only when you want to do it, and nothing nothing else but writing will suffice, give you peace."[1] The advice is amusing, coming from a man who had disciplined himself to write whether his entrails were burning or not—and who was writing now without any burning sensation. In the same letter, he sent on "our" act 3 section, the scene in the jail. He asks her to look it over and return it to him in California. Mail from Joan to Oxford was becoming dangerous; telephone calls were also out, since Estelle often called Memphis to get hold of Joan directly. Faulkner told Joan he was leaving for California on Thursday, February 1.

Arriving in Hollywood on that day, Faulkner stayed this time not in a small apartment, but in the posh Beverly-Carlton. He renewed his friendship with Bezzerides; but Faulkner was a man in a hurry. If he finished the script of *The Left Hand of God* within four weeks, he would receive a bonus. He had gone out to help Howard Hawks on the script, but in time, Hawks was removed from the film and Edward Dmytryck became the director of record. While Faulkner's letters to Joan sound cheerful, he was not really happy—and he drank, but not to excess. Joan mailed parts of *Requiem*, which he tinkered with in whatever spare time he found between the studio and trying to keep himself together.

He had suggested she accompany him to the West Coast, which would have publicized the relationship. As he expected, she refused, and he took up again with Meta. According to her, Faulkner had written in the period preceding his Hollywood trip that they must get together. She was still married, but, as she put it, her marriage was "a twisted wreckage." She agreed immediately to meet Faulkner when he called, and they resumed their affair. He was now five years older, and she noticed less ardor but a still-sweet presence. For both of them it was a relief. In nearly every way, they were the married couple, while Estelle and Rebner were extraneous. Had Faulkner not hesitated over the divorce earlier—and over Jill's predicament in particular—there is little question the intervening years would have been happier for him. He was a man with great loyalty to the women in his life, and the long affair with Meta was in some respects an alternate marriage without benefit of clergy. The two were old pals as well as lovers, and Faulkner talked freely of Jill and Estelle. He told her Estelle suffered from cataracts, that her vision was badly impaired; and he seemed to feel sympathy for her even after the years of misery together. By March 4, he was gone from Hollywood, and while he and Meta corresponded extensively, they were unable to meet again.

In the ensuing years, Faulkner wrote frankly to Meta of his family, of how the clarity of his mind was sometimes clouded, that he had had three spells of what he termed "almost amnesia."[2] He feared something had happened to his brain from a blood clot, perhaps the result of a fall from a horse; or else from his heavy drinking; or even, we can conjecture, from an incipient Alzheimer's disease syndrome. He told her of how Estelle had to give up drinking because of her liver and the destruction to her esophagus. She had hemorrhaged and needed nine transfusions, followed by two weeks of hospitalization. All this indicated to Meta that his attachment to Estelle went beyond how they got along, into some deeper strata of linkage. She was trying to change her habits through Alcoholics Anonymous. Faulkner loaned money to Meta, who was down on her luck, but when she tried to repay it, he returned the check torn into pieces. Faulkner eventually moved on to Else Jonsson, to a young Japanese woman, to Jean Stein —a succession of women, all of them as young as Joan, except for Else.

Faulkner's letters on this Hollywood experience are less depressing than usual and on occasion contain some humor directed at himself and the place. As he completed his stint, however (for $12,000, including bonus), he told Joan, "This is a nice town full of very rich middle class people who have not yet discovered the cerebrum, or at best the soul. Beautiful damned monotonous weather, and I am getting quite tired of it, will be glad to farm again."[3] During his stay in March, his National Book Award for *Collected Stories* was accepted by Saxe Commins, in lieu of an author too occupied with a Hollywood film and a big book on his drawing board.

Returning to Oxford, he had plenty to occupy him.* He wanted to complete *Requiem* before taking up *A Fable*, although that incomplete manuscript nagged at him. His indecision here did not bode well for the novel. It became the recipient of too many starts and stops, too many stylistic mannerisms from an author coming to it from different directions. After seven years of developing the initial idea, he still found the material intractable; and his decision to get on with *Requiem* first indicates his hesitation

---

*Blotner reminds us of the Willie McGee case in Laurel, Mississippi, itself a reprise of "Dry September." McGee was accused of raping a white woman and was condemned to death, without proof of violence or force on McGee's part. Faulkner took up the case and argued that since force and violence had not been used, McGee should not be executed. Yet even here his views were ambiguous. For while he undeniably showed courage in opposing the execution for the crime of all crimes for white Mississippians, he warned that a delegation of women from the Civil Rights Congress (which itself opposed the sentence) should not be heeded. He argued that the execution of McGee would only serve their cause—that is, further leftist causes. He told Mullen, now of the *Commercial Appeal*, that since he didn't believe in McGee's guilt, he was accused by District Attorney Swartfager of having aligned himself with the communists. Such were not only Mississippi politics in the 1950s, but American politics; and Faulkner, for all his sensitivity, was not immune.

Faulkner's protest about Willie McGee's execution did not sit well with J. Edgar Hoover's FBI, and Faulkner ended up in their files. His specific transgression was linked to the Civil Rights Congress, which worked on behalf of McGee (executed anyway) and which the FBI deemed a communist or communist-front organization. The FBI seemed less interested in Faulkner's support of the Spanish Nationalists during the Spanish civil war. In 1961, Robert Kennedy, as Attorney General under his brother, did a name check on Faulkner, an action which originated with Richard Goodwin, a liberal member of the White House staff. Faulkner's name was among several supplied to Kennedy, perhaps to ascertain his purity before he was invited to any White House functions. In comparison with his contemporaries, major and minor, Faulkner's FBI file is slight and contains little more than the Willie McGee connection.

about the "big work." In this mixing of energies, he sent Haas in late March his prologue and act 2 of *Requiem*, the segment called "THE GOLDEN DOME (Beginning Was the Word)," which arrived at Random House on April 2. He tried out some Greek (incorrectly), paraphrasing Eliot's "Mr. Eliot's Sunday Morning Service," as a way of presenting "In the Beginning," followed by Greek for "the word." He later dropped this affectation.

Meanwhile, having sent Saxe Commins the first part of *Requiem* at the end of January before heading for Hollywood, he had written his editor again, possibly in mid-February, about a most confidential project. "This is in complete confidence. The principal reason is, I dont want my family in Oxford to learn about it until I decide to tell them myself. If it works out that, I will let them think that I am merely in New York finishing my play-novel." His plan was to fly to Paris on about April 15, for two weeks, in Betty Haas's (Bob Haas's daughter's) plane, using her flight over and back, April 15–30. If she was not scheduled then on her regular run, he asked Commins to book him on BOAC. He also wanted Eliot Paul's address—Paul was best known for his immensely successful memoir, *The Last Time I Saw Paris* (1942). He insists that all should be kept "under Random House's hat until I explain."[4]

Before departing for Hollywood, Faulkner also wanted his will redrawn, and Phil Stone carried this out on February 1. On the twelfth, he gave Faulkner some details,[5] including wording he further redrew. He advised his client to take up his tax position with an expert to see what the consequences of the will were, especially with regard to a trust agreement of $25,000 Faulkner had established with Nobel Prize money. He asked him if he would like to have him, Stone, lend out some money at five percent from the interest on the trust, in real estate, which could make both of them some money. Before departing for Europe, Faulkner continued on the theme of the will by telling Haas that in the event of his death, Random House was to continue as publisher of his past work as well as of any work still unpublished; that Commins had full authority over all material issued after his death. He should also act in an advisory role concerning any Faulkner manuscripts sold or donated to museums and libraries. Commins was to become his literary executor and editor, for all past and future literary work. (Commins died in 1958, however, four years before Faulkner.)

Plans went ahead for his European trip, with tickets purchased on BOAC, from April 15 to 29. In late March, in a letter to Commins, Faulkner's excitement is evident: the trip to Europe, the tour of old 1918 battlefields, the liaison with Else (not mentioned in the letter), the completion of the second section of *Requiem*, and the feeling he will return to the "big book" soon. He follows this up with another letter in early April, again to Commins, who was now his private secretary as well as editor, asking him to engage a room in Paris (at the Lutetia on the Boulevard Raspail) and at Brown's on Dover Street in London. He indicates the coming intrigue by telling Commins to find another hotel, "more obscure if anything, so I wont be too well known." He adds: "You can see by now what all this is leading to; of course, I will tell you as much more as you want to know."[6] He says that if Eliot Paul can't help on another hotel, then Commins should reserve two rooms at the Lutetia (Faulkner spells it Leutitia). Continuing to prod Commins, who had not yet made the arrangements, Faulkner said at least one room at the Lutetia should be reserved on the seventeenth.* He announces that France has awarded him the Legion of Honor, to be conferred on him in New Orleans on October 26.

With his head full of *Requiem* (both novel and play versions) and *A Fable*, Faulkner flew to New York on April 12. As his prose in the second segment of the *Requiem* prologue reveals, he was caught up in the romantic grandeur of the past as it clashed, in memory and in architecture, with the mechanistic, less colorful present. It was his usual theme, presented now with great urgency. But his mind was also moving ahead to the Legion of Honor, certainly an award which pleased him; and the thought of a reunion with Else Jonsson, who seemed the perfect companion—attractive, intelligent, understanding, widow of a man who believed in him. Furthermore, he was beginning to feel some rapport with his major work, reactivated with visits to battlefields and the completion of *Requiem*. He saw this as a valedictory—he wrote in May to Else that after the big one, he would break the pencil and throw it away, thirty years of anguishing and sweating over for him.

In New York Faulkner met a wide variety of people, but his withdrawal technique was still working, especially around literary critics such as Lionel Trilling. He also met Henry Green, the English novelist; while Green did all the talking, Faulkner remained sunk into silence. He also spoke briefly about farming to Anthony West, the novelist and son of H. G. Wells and Rebecca West. The Page One Award of the Newspaper Guild of New York honored him, along with his old friend Tallulah Bankhead and,

---

*While Faulkner was trying to slip out of New York for his Paris tryst, other events were playing in the background. His "paper" had suddenly become sought after and valuable. While Yale was shrewdly building a Faulkner Collection under librarian James Babb, William Wisdom was also collecting first editions, letters, some manuscripts—what would eventually become the valuable William Wisdom Collection at Tulane University in New Orleans. Writing to Stone, Wisdom renews acquaintance and wonders if he can get some response to his letters to Faulkner. Stone's April 23 reply is amusing. He implies Faulkner is an ingrate who accepts favors and then will not answer anyone's letters—Wisdom should not feel he is being singled out. "Please don't get the idea, as some people do, that this is just one of the peculiarities of genius. It is nothing but that damn Faulkner in him. If you had known four generations of them as I have you would understand." He agrees with Wisdom that the Nobel Prize speech "is the best thing he has ever written." Stone then has a go at John Faulkner, whose *Men Working* had been praised highly. "We think," Stone wrote, "John can't write at all and it amuses us that he can get the stuff published at all. Don't repeat this because we are very fond of both John and Lucille and John's success just pleases us beyond words. I think he is really the nicest one of all the Falkners, personally" (*Faulkner: A Comprehensive Guide to the Brodsky Collection, the Letters*, eds. Louis Daniel Brodsky and Robert W. Hamblin, vol. 2 [Jackson: University Press of Mississippi, 1984], p. 68). At this point, in 1951, it is difficult to know where Stone's hostility will land.

among others, Joe DiMaggio; but he refused to attend, sending Saxe Commins in his place. Faulkner and DiMaggio would have been a classic moment: a battle over who could say the fewest words, reminiscent of Joyce and Proust meeting in a taxi. At the Haases, he saw the old Random House crowd, now like family. He stayed relatively sober, since this was a pleasure trip and he wanted it to go well. After a stopover for one night in London, where he saw his British publishers, Chatto & Windus, he entered into the hospitable milieu provided by Gallimard, his French publisher, now recovered from its wartime collaboration with the German occupation. Gallimard assigned to him someone they hoped he would like, a young editor named Monique Salomon; once Faulkner saw she was not threatening, he became extremely friendly with her and her husband. Despite all this, he began to drink steadily and heavily. At some point, he and Else were reunited, and they resumed (or began) an affair of two people well suited for each other. Faulkner genuinely liked her as a person, and she admired and respected him; as a mature woman, she tolerated his drinking and depressions and brought him along until he recovered. All those in touch with him in France—the Salomons and Else, as well as the people around Gallimard—found him a sympathetic, though troubled, person.

He left Paris behind for several days while he toured the battlefields of Verdun, where over 400,000 soldiers were buried, and where several more hundreds of thousands were wounded. If anything could influence one to see war as, in Wilfred Owen's words, legitimizing the old killing off the young, then Verdun was the place. Observing the area of such meaningless carnage, imagining the waves of young men who rose out of the trenches to meet inevitable death from German machine guns, trying to penetrate to their thoughts, fears, and bravery in those final moments before they went over the top, obeying their officers in a final gesture, Faulkner found himself revived.* He gathered together maps of the area and of the offensives, as well as a medal of the city of Verdun. He was deeply moved. What he could not imagine of the war, he could revive through stories and reading of the Civil War battles, where an almost comparable carnage had destroyed an entire generation.

Paris proved exactly what he had wanted: he had sneaked in, been handled beautifully by Gallimard and the Salomons, not gotten too drunk, renewed his relationship with Else, and by April 29 was ready to depart for New York. Once back in the States, he managed a brief trip to see Joan at Bard. Then it was on to Oxford, further work on *Requiem*, and attention to his family and farm. As he sent on material for *Requiem* to Commins, the editor was surprisingly forbearing with a manuscript which fitted into no previous pattern known to Random House. The strange combination

---

*On May 23, he wrote Else that his manuscript was going well, meaning *Requiem*. But then: "I have one more to do, the big one (Verdun) and then I have a feeling that I shall be through" (*Selected Letters of William Faulkner*, ed. Joseph Blotner [New York: Vintage Books, 1978; orig. publ. 1977] p. 314. Following quotation, p. 315).

of interspersed prose prologues and dramatic acts suggested a form which would make marketing difficult. Furthermore, the prologues were not models of lucidity. On the contrary, they manifested Faulkner at his most prickly—long, interminable sentences, parenthetical material set within already lengthy sequences, Latinate punctuation. The prologues, which were quite important for Faulkner, are veritable thickets of prose. Yet Commins accepted the work, fully knowing that Faulkner would accept very little editing except for obvious faulty places. As he proceeded, he began to move *Requiem* and *Sanctuary* even closer; they had always been linked by Temple and by other considerations; but now he saw them as the obverse of each other.

In June Ruth Ford told Faulkner a young producer, Lemuel Ayers, was interested in producing *Requiem for a Nun*. Ayers was already highly successful as the producer of the musical *Kiss Me Kate*. In his June 18 letter to Ford, Faulkner is full of news, plans, a schedule which will bring him to New York in later June or in July. The play, he says, goes directly to her, although Commins wanted to see any contract he agreed to. Ober was also getting nervous since these unorthodox arrangements had already gotten Faulkner into considerable trouble, contractually and financially. Faulkner seemed genuinely exhilarated that he had written a play, despite his concession to his friend that the second act needs to be rewritten, and possibly the third as well. He denies being "playwright enough to do it." He mentions some farm work, also the imminent arrival of Cho-Cho, her husband, and child. He promises to come up after this visit. Then the part about Ruth which made Random House and Ober turn color: "Tell your man (I was so excited that I didn't remember his name) not to bother about sending me a contract, the play part, was written for you, so no contract is needed until we have talked and decided if anything can come of the matter."[7] The farmer Faulkner was striking a theatrical deal as though he were selling a horse and shaking hands on it."[*] He adds he is pleased with the title, "one of my best."

On the same day he wrote Joan about his projected trip to New York to help in the production of "our play, even though you have repudiated it."[8] He plans to see her. Four days later he wrote Else that if all goes well he hopes to be in Europe in 1952 at the latest, and perhaps before then—if he can find some workable reason for going. Ruth Ford, Joan Williams, Else Jonsson—Faulkner was making sure he had female company as he made plans to leave Oxford.

Arriving in New York at the beginning of July, he stayed at the Algonquin for two weeks, returning to Oxford by the nineteenth. In New York Faulkner kept busy, first writing brief synopses of each act and trying to

---

*Nevertheless, Faulkner's idyllic arrangement could not stand, and on September 25, he told Random House he authorized Harold Ober to act as his agent in all matters concerning *Requiem*, although this in no way altered Random's participation in his earnings from dramatic, film, and other rights as stipulated in the contract between Random House and himself.

create more dramatic coherence. Part of the problem was pacing in dramatic terms, since as a novelist—and an increasingly didactic one—Faulkner was more concerned with exposition than with dramatization of character and motive. With all his recently developed expertise as a detective-mystery writer, he tended toward prose overkill, and it was this quality Ayers wanted to lessen. In fact, Ayers had a very different conception of the play, which involved the rethinking of the entire forward movement of the narrative. The producer wanted Nancy's innocence or guilt to remain problematical, not to be announced at the start; and this meant Faulkner's strategy had to be completely overhauled. He was in effect writing a new play, one that fitted the dramatic necessities of the commercial stage, whereas Faulkner's original conception had been more philosophical than dramatic, more moralistic than viable as narrative. With such radical changes in mind, Ayers was putting Faulkner to work on a script which, like those he tinkered with in Hollywood, had to be realigned and rewritten.

The rest of Faulkner's summer was placid. His descriptions of the beginning of harvest[9] to Else has within it Tolstoyan qualities of contentment with hard work on the land. In speaking of his help, Faulkner uses "Negro" with Else, whereas with Haas he uses "nigger." The distinction is interesting. Faulkner assumed Haas shared his world-view, although as a liberal Northern Jew, Haas was probably very uncomfortable with the word; but with Else, a foreigner, Faulkner was far more careful, assuming that the pejorative and demeaning "nigger" would identify him as a racist, or sympathetic to racists. The distinction gains in importance as he works on *Requiem;* for while Nancy would be in any other context a "nigger" for Faulkner, in the context of his play, she takes on distinctive qualities as a "Negro." This aside, Faulkner's letter is full of the cycle of nature: what to cut, what to leave, how to figure the rain, where to plow, what to leave fallow, how heavy to seed. And then there are the cattle to be vaccinated, inoculated, nursed, until November when work will shift to harvesting the corn, and another cycle. Whatever his domestic tensions, there is little question farming gave Faulkner pleasure. His expenditures on the farm would never be recouped, but having an agricultural role—a "Garden" role, one could say—gave him that Edenic glimpse he needed for personal balance.

In the middle of this, Robert Coughlan from *Life* arrived, full of good intentions to write well about a writer he admired. Faulkner was forewarned, and he was adamant: no interview; indeed, try to head Coughlan off at the pass. Coughlan was a decent young man, and he certainly deferred to Faulkner as a great literary genius, but his employer was *Life* magazine, representing everything Faulkner detested. Everyone and everything came through the *Life* editorial wringer sounding conservative, patriotic, homogenized. Hemingway got his kicks from this kind of publicity, in many ways disguising his failure as a writer; but for Faulkner, who had not given up, the prospect was that of accepting an invitation to hell.

At first, he told Coughlan to leave, refusing even to say a few words to him. But in a spurt of his own form of genius, the young man said he admired Faulkner's work and was pleased just to say hello. At this, Faulkner was touched and did not want to destroy the young man's career; he invited him in and spoke. In fact, Faulkner offered to put Coughlan in touch with people who could answer questions, like Moon Mullen, who introduced him to Phil and Emily Stone; Ike Roberts and Red Brite, of the hunting expeditions; relatives and even close members of the family. With that, Faulkner cast Coughlan adrift, refusing even to acknowledge him when they met in town.

Faulkner was now in the middle of a strange period, not at all like the years in the 1940s when he seemed to be moving nowhere. But there was a sense that events, rather than his own intense inner direction, were pushing and pulling him. Part of it was the fame garnered through the Nobel Prize and the reissue of many of his books: he was reaching more readers, and especially in colleges and universities. But even more than this, a certain kind of pressure was put on him which counterbalanced or even outweighed his own sense of direction. The effort to please the producer of *Requiem* was just such an example. Here he was roughly back into the days of doctoring scripts, although now it was his script. He told Joan he was the magnetic force which draws unhappiness—although we cannot tell if that was a pose he took to make her feel sorry for this aging eagle, or the actual truth. But if there was a high degree of unhappiness or uncertainty, it came from his recognition that the urgency to write now derived in part from outside him, not from within, where it had always been located.

He was clearly off balance literarily. That inability to pull together *A Fable* reveals a good deal. Much of his time was taken up with coming and going.[10] One such venture involved getting Jill registered at Pine Manor in Wellesley, a trip he took with Estelle, reaching Massachusetts on September 19. But as he told Else, he was everywhere. He left Oxford on September 12 for the North; then returned for farm work; then back to Boston on October 2 for the rewriting of his play, which opened at the Brattle Street Theater in Cambridge; remaining in Boston until October 15; then on to New Orleans to receive formally the Legion of Honor from the French consul general; then back to Boston for the play. What all this did was to create the circumstances by which he could avoid *A Fable*. In the old days, none of these interruptions kept him from working seriously; now the interruptions were part of a carefully contrived shield which separated him from his writing.

Depositing Jill at Pine Manor released a lot of tension. One can only see the household as emptying out one source of conflict, not created, of course, by the child, but generated by the atmosphere in which she moved. By the end of September, however, Faulkner had another source of interest: *Requiem for a Nun* was published. Since it was such a hybrid, its reception was interesting; and that reception, in turn, affected what happened to the play distilled from the novel and revised into more dramatic shape. Few of the reviewers (Irving Howe, Harvey Breit, Harrison Smith, Anthony West, among others) took on the novel on its own terms as a hybrid, experimental work, perhaps leading toward an innovative form of literary expression or the shaping of a new genre. Even when the praise was high, it shunted aside what Faulkner was attempting to do, whether or not successfully. Instead, piecemeal, reviewers went after his prose in the prologue material—praising it; or they found the dramatic content lacking readability, but suggested that it might be workable on the stage; or they found weaknesses in each part. Assessments of the whole work, however, were not forthcoming.

Admittedly, *Requiem* is one of Faulkner's problematical works. But after more than twenty years of having educated reviewers and critics on how to read him, he could have expected a more sophisticated reception than he received.* A work which crosses generic lines always presents problems; but then Faulkner had been creating these problems for more than two decades. Surely *Sound,* which began the reputation which led to the Nobel Prize, was problematic; it was far more difficult to absorb than *Requiem,* and it came at a time when modernism had barely penetrated into America. Surely *As I Lay Dying* stretched the notion of what a novel is; and surely, beyond Faulkner, the idea of the novel as a genre had undergone sufficient stretching to include many works which broke with traditional forms. *Requiem* must be viewed as falling within that category, although, once so defined, it seems less than successful.

While the large prose segments may have created problems in generic terms for those expecting a play, the real problem of the book is lack of focus. One can argue that the focal point of the morality play is Nancy Mannigoe, the whorish, drug-addicted servant who kills Temple Drake's baby by Gowan Stevens. Others, however, have argued nobly that the center is Temple, and that the focus is not on her redemption but on her crucifixion. This argument carries further to say that Gavin Stevens, her lawyer, is not out to save her, but to destroy her. If the moral center *is* Temple, then Nancy is a moral monster, not at all the saint portrayed by those who see *her,* not Temple, as holding center stage.

A third way of looking at *Requiem* is to see the ambiguity in the very title —as a question of which woman is the nun, Temple or Nancy. Faulkner had Ford in mind for the role of Temple Drake and gave her several opportunities for virtuoso acting; her role is seemingly the center, because of the linkage to Ford. But the moral center in the subtext of the play belongs to Nancy, in her inchoate, almost incoherent way. The result is a bifurcation of purpose and an unfocused execution: the main lines may belong to Temple, but the moral decisions, the creation of the dramatic moment, belong to Nancy.

---

*James B. Meriwether described it as "a novel in the form of a three-act play with a narrative prologue in each act," his way of bibliographically categorizing it (*The Literary Career of William Faulkner,* p. 36).

But that is only part of the problem. Another crucial aspect of the play is the enormous chance Faulkner took in creating a sympathetic black woman who has admitted to the commission of a heinous crime, the murder of an infant in her care. The enormity of the crime must somehow be weighed against the nobility of purpose for which the crime was committed. This is Dostoyevsky territory, and it is doubtful if even the Russian writer could have made such a situation dramatically meaningful on the stage. In print it is possible, as Dostoyevsky demonstrated with Raskolnikov, to sway people's feelings, because the characters are shaped by words, not by physical definition. On stage, with Nancy's presence recalling the fact she has murdered an infant, there is no audience which can be convinced of the moral conviction of the play. Yet, withal, Nancy utters the lines which are expected to change Temple permanently: the key one uttered on the eve of her execution, " 'Believe.' " It is her final piece of advice, her final word in the play, and it supposedly represents what she represents. On other occasions, she says, " 'I believes.' " Faulkner has carried us into some supernal world, where belief somehow wipes away terrible sin; but the word cannot carry the dramatic momentum of the play, and its utterance, however sincerely felt, only reveals the wobble in the dramatic structure.

There is still another problem, and that lies in Gavin Stevens. Like the Gavin of *Intruder,* the over-educated Oxonian here talks too much, and his speeches sound like sermons. He is more than august, he is the town bore. Yet he also carries a good deal of weight in the moral structuring of the play. The problem rests in the role Faulkner wanted for him. Gavin seems present at times as a catalyst for Temple's movement toward ultimate redemption, and toward her recognition that Nancy was trying to help her morally and ethically. But in leading Temple toward this state of being, he harangues and tortures her: his intention at times seems sadistic, not redemptive, more satanic than Christian—on one occasion ripping her apart with the truth, on another trying to help her understand her own immoral (or amoral) history.

Faulkner was unclear about what he wanted to accomplish in either the book as a whole or the play element of it. The idea went back to 1933, when he wrote Harrison Smith about the title, which he held to, and the subject matter: "It will be about a nigger woman." Yet *Requiem* also seemed to derive from *Sanctuary* in this early, still inchoate form. The Rowan Oak papers (manuscript pages discovered in a hidden spot at Rowan Oak) contain three manuscript pages which relate to this process of welding *Sanctuary* and *Requiem* and also help us to understand how Faulkner fell between two stools in creating the latter work. A two-page segment of the Rowan Oak papers has more references to *Sanctuary* than to *Requiem;* it features Gavin Stevens's questioning of a Negro man and woman, the latter having had her neck slashed with a razor. This obviously refers to the scene in *Sanctuary* wherein a Negro slashed his wife so that her head was almost off its stem. It also looks ahead to Joe Christmas's murder of

Joanna Burden in *Light in August*, so that her head points in a different direction from her body.

It is unclear from the fragment whether the Negro woman whose throat has been slashed is the prototype of Nancy Mannigoe; but the play element of *Requiem* seems to point in this direction, even as the incident returns us to *Sanctuary*. In the other fragment, one page of text, the focus is on the jailhouse—the prose part that, enlarged, becomes the third segment of *Requiem*. The evidence we have for the early formation of what Faulkner called *Requiem for a Nun* in his letter to Harrison Smith shows several dispersed areas of development, a lack of clarity which carried over into the final work.

There are additional problems. In 1932, and possibly before that, Faulkner contemplated an unusual project, a series of biographical sketches to be called "The Golden Book of Jefferson & Yoknapatawpha County in Mississippi as compiled by William Faulkner of Rowanoak, Rowanoak, MCMXXXII." In his 1956 interview with Jean Stein, he incidentally referred to this enterprise by saying, "My last book will be the Doomsday Book, the Golden Book, of Yoknapatawpha County." With that, he told her, he would break the pencil and stop writing. The original Golden Book—which was not at all a Doomsday Book—was to list his characters, the main players in his Yoknapatawpha cycle, a kind of dramatis personae. Faulkner abandoned the project after a few pages; but then for Cowley's edition of *The Portable Faulkner* he provided the "Compson Appendix," which in several respects approximates for the Compson family what he had intended for all his characters in the "Golden Book." To this can be added the chronology and genealogy supplied for *Absalom* which also has relevance to the "Golden Book" earlier and to the idea of a "Doomsday Book" later.

All of these prose segments—the Golden Book notations, the Compson appendix, the chronology and genealogy for *Absalom*—are early starts on the prose parts of *Requiem*. But they all serve different functions: they were not simply historical tableaux, but deeply integrated parts of his work. In *Requiem* Faulkner followed through on such prose segments, yet it is unclear what specific role they play as they move with and/or against the play elements. Faulkner's experiment can be seen as a noble one—intermixing genres toward a supreme fiction; but while we defer to the intention, we pause at the accomplishment. One way to argue for the efficacy of the method is to see the play as enforcing history and the past, and in that way blending in with the historical prose of courthouse, state capital, and jail; as such, the prose elements support the method of the play, based on recall, on telling and retelling. This is possibly part of Faulkner's plan: to use *Requiem* as both a historical notice and a moral statement, with both parts fused.

That process has holes in it. The historical material is concerned repeatedly with one theme: the replacement of an independent and individualistically-based society with one given over to homogenization and technological development. The motifs are familiar. In the second section, "The Golden Dome," we find Faulkner reaching back into "The Bear":

> Obsolete too: still felling the two-hundred-year-old tree when the bear and the wild honey were gone and there was nothing in it any more but a raccoon or a possum whose hide was worth at the most two dollars, turning the earth into a howling waste from which he would be the first to vanish, not even on the heels but synchronous with the slightly darker wild men whom he had dispossessed, because, like them, only the wilderness could feed and nourish him.[11]

The prose segments are about loss, waste, decline, and diminishment, even as life settles, civilizes, improves. Improvement, however, is a chimera, bringing with it loss of individualism.

This is an old Faulkner story, and a valid one for anyone writing in the late 1940s. Government was run by Snopeses. But what connection does this salient point about individualism have to do with the *play* element of *Requiem?* There is no such element there, nor of state activity which leads to loss. In the play Faulkner has taken the high ground of repentance and redemption—material which seems an outgrowth of *A Fable,* on which he worked during his development of the final version of *Requiem.* The prose parts, historically based, work in one direction, the play in another. It is unclear where or how Faulkner thought they could play off or with each other.

How much of this ambiguity of purpose and divisiveness of achievement can be attributed to the collaboration with Joan? There was still another collaboration, that with Ayers, Ruth Ford, and Albert Marre (the director) in the summer of 1951, but that collaboration produced changes in the text of the playing version, not in the text of the novel. There is no evidence his collaborative effort with his young protégée led to any changes in *Requiem* which were not his idea. From this we must conclude *Requiem* was Faulkner's work and that its ambiguities were those he could not work through. And while we certainly applaud his audacity in trying to create a hybrid genre at this late stage in his career, we must perceive the hybrid as pointing in too many disparate directions to provide an integrated, or even coherent, book.

The stay in Cambridge, where Faulkner went in October to work on the play and stayed to get drunk, ended when he left for New Orleans to receive the Legion of Honor from the French consul, an event which took place on October 26. Faulkner was leaving loose ends everywhere: his ability to conclude a project within a given time frame was gone. Although his Nobel Prize speech can be seen as his exhortation to himself to hang on, not to succumb, he was having difficulty. He had two projects now which, while very different from each other, were creating comparable problems. He wanted to become a playwright, but did not have the ingredients for it; and he wanted to write a supreme fiction about morality and ethics, but he no longer had the technical grasp or strategies to accomplish it. In both instances, the craft had deserted him—which is another way of saying his literary intellect was faltering.

The New Orleans ceremony was preceded by a heavy bout of drinking, which necessitated Faulkner's being hospitalized in Baptist Hospital in that city, where he had planned to be with the Lymans, Helen (Baird) and Guy. The breakdown was inevitable, given the Cambridge experience and the fact he could not confront his own loose ends. After treatment, he returned to Oxford, and then went back to New Orleans for the ceremony. Characteristically, Faulkner received the award—one he coveted—dressed in casual clothes, clothes he might have gone hunting in. As old friends from his early days came up—Flo Field, Albert Goldstein, and others—he seemed to freeze. It was not out of lordliness, but out of fear his protective shield might be penetrated—by nostalgia? memories? the past itself? Such ceremonies, including the one for the Nobel Prize, brought out his moat-and-drawbridge defenses.

On November 5, in this tour of the United States (as he put it to Else), he returned to Cambridge for more work with Marre. Their collaboration brought little in the way of results, although they did hit on a method which worked better than others. Marre wrote lines, Faulkner doctored them, and the play moved forward slightly. Meanwhile, the *Harvard Advocate* devoted an issue to Faulkner, with contributions from several writers who had reviewed his work, or else were simply admirers: Alfred Kazin, Carvel Collins, Cleanth Brooks, with signs of admiration from Camus and Mann. Faulkner was, however, drinking steadily. His intake was prodigious, considering his size and age. He could handle a fifth of whiskey or bourbon and still function; and he was seen at parties downing fifteen or more martinis, which even his system could not resist. He was not the kind of alcoholic who became drunk on one or two drinks; his capacity remained enormous, and his recuperative powers even in middle age were still amazing. Part of what kept him drinking so heavily was that he paid so lightly for his indulgence. He appeared to suffer few hangovers, or if he did he recovered rapidly; and his physical condition did not manifest this steady abuse. He did not gain excessive weight, his waist remained that of a youth, and his liver seemed unaffected. His ulcer seemed to pass, and his brain still functioned, albeit at a slower pace than when he was younger. For a man who had so abused his system, he was a physical marvel.

By November 17, he was back in Oxford again, preparing for hunting camp. He spent six days, until the twenty-third, at Anguilla, without sighting a deer. On the twenty-fourth he returned to New Orleans to sponsor a local professor who was raised from chevalier to officer of the Legion of Honor; then he returned to Oxford on the twenty-seventh to do some farming. He later went back to Boston to work on what he called "the damned play again, of which I am quite sick now."[12] On November 18 he wrote to Joan from Oxford, part of his plan to maintain the relationship, however shadowy it had become. With a fictional idea in mind as a way of keeping her dependent on him, he says he will have to tell it to her: "It's not a short story anyway but a short novel really; you will have to work at it. Do you want to? Dont decide now; I will have to see you and tell you first." He adds that it is a good idea, with a line and a plot. "This is a reversal, isn't it? I failed to persuade you to help me write a play; now I seem determined to help you write a novel whether you want to or not."[13] In a follow-up letter the next month (December 20), he advises her about a short story she has sent on, in which there is no movement. Even a static character, he says, must be described in motion; "man in motion" was a quality of his own technique he was trying to graft on to her work. Although it did permit him to maintain the connection, his help was sincere; and when *Harper's* announced a novel contest with a first prize of $10,000, he told her he wanted her to win it. With his help, of course.

With this and the usual Christmas celebration at Rowan Oak, a year ended for Faulkner which brought him further great renown, and a considerable sum of money from his Hollywood stint. Yet it was a year which was most problematical in his own sense of himself. He was for the time being standing still. He had published *Requiem*, but was unable to craft a play; he still had *A Fable*, unfinished, on his desk. And he did not seem highly motivated. Did he feel, like T. S. Eliot, that the Nobel Prize was a step toward one's funeral, the end of any future work of value? He was going through the motions, traveling here and there without much purpose, acting out the role of the famous man receiving the crowd's plaudits when he knew he was well past his prime.

The year 1952 saw Faulkner return to *A Fable*. But it was not the work in a long, sweeping period of time which had characterized his efforts on previous complex novels. Instead, it became tucked in, a month or two here and there. The novel does reveal such a lack of steady, continuous work which might have resolved the difficult strategical problems of the text. Developments with *Requiem* brought Marre to Oxford, with an eye toward a May 30 Paris production; he also wanted to discuss problems with financing the play, which only Faulkner could solve. The Paris connections took Faulkner back there to attend a festival organized by the French Congress for the Liberty of Culture; he renewed his relationship with Else Jonsson, and was briefly hospitalized for a back problem and drinking. He visited Oslo with Else, spending ten days there, mainly resting. At home by mid-June, he worked sporadically on *A Fable*, drawing a synopsis of the novel on the walls of his Rowan Oak office. He had free time from mid-June through the first week in September for the novel, but did not make satisfactory headway. September and October found him hospitalized for back pain, after falling on the stairway at Rowan Oak, all of it alcohol-related. After the fall, he was humiliated by the need for a steel backbrace. Having renewed his relationship with Joan in mid-June, after returning from Oslo, a man of fifty-four did not want to present a steel brace to a young woman of twenty-three. November and December became months of diversions, neither satisfactory as relaxation nor fulfillment as work. In December he needed electric-shock treatment for his back condition, and spent part of the month in Princeton and New York.

There were no stories or books published in 1952. There was still the after-glory of the prize: awards, ceremonies, invitations trailing him and making him anxious and withdrawn. Alcoholism was becoming acute, whereas before it had been chronic with acute episodes.* He seemed to be pursuing a self-destructive course, and at least part of it can be attributed to his frustration with *A Fable*, his inability to craft *Requiem* as a play. He was not spinning off new ideas, nor was he able to handle the material on his desk. With the drinking, which alarmed even those accustomed to it, he hoped to alleviate the back pain; but it made serious work difficult or impossible.

The first big disappointment in 1952 came with the dramatic version of *Requiem*. Faulkner originally had been promised a May 30 premiere in Paris, after a series of promises for a January 10, then a February 20, opening in Cambridge. But when Marre visited Faulkner in Oxford, he told him Ayers was unable to raise sufficient money. His backers claimed that the publication of the book had taken the edge off the play, but he planned to open it nevertheless in September. In the meanwhile, Marre, with the support of Ford, was going ahead with a Paris production to coincide with a spring festival of concerts, plays, operas, and a writers' conference. The French sponsors offered $7,000 to help fund the play, but needed an additional $15,000 to cover salaries, royalties, and rehearsals for a week's run. Pavel Tchelitchew, the surrealist, was to design the sets. Marre felt that if the play ran for a week, the sponsors would return the earnings, perhaps $10,000–12,000. Then Marre would go on to a London production, and from there to one in America.

Faulkner told Commins[14] he was inclined to risk it, since he liked Tchelitchew's idea of going back to the original version of the script, before all the rewriting. Besides this, he felt his commitment to Ford obliged him to go ahead, since this seemed her chance to become a top actress. He says he doesn't mind losing the money, but doesn't want to pay the huge tax he will owe the government if he draws this sum; he asks Commins if perhaps he can amortize the amount. He is evidently excited, for he feels the French sponsors, covering theater and stagehand costs, have offered a good deal. Great excitement, in fact, runs through the entire letter, that of a middle-aged man chasing after a chimera. That Faulkner would become involved in such a poorly-structured financial arrangement—

---

*Joan Williams, who saw Faulkner during this time and observed him carefully—she understood alcoholism from her own father—says the writer was not an alcoholic. She asserted that Seconal and alcohol did him in on binges, but he could desist. Still, the binges were now coming so frequently that his system was becoming alcohol-poisoned and saturated. She expressed her views almost thirty years after the event (in "Twenty Will Not Come Again"; *Atlantic* [May 1980], pp. 58–65).

when he finally had the money he needed to handle his large expenses—is evidence of a need to break out of boredom. America-Paris-London, a play running, box office receipts flowing in, a favorite, Ford, in the lead role—all of this would provide some reinforcement.

Random House of course thought it was a foolish venture, and as far as we can tell, Faulkner did not ask Ober's advice (he would have been equally horror-stricken at his client's prodigal nature). Faulkner and Marre spent several days examining angles, and when Faulkner finally offered $2,000, not $15,000, the project went on hold while Marre scouted around for further backers. He continued to correspond with Joan, and this back-and-forth eventuated in the terrible event in October, when he told Commins of Estelle's action in opening his letters, if that is indeed what she did. He also wrote to Else, always assuring her he was working on the big book as well as farming. He mentions another fall from a horse, telling her that years ago he got used to falling off horses. He also announces to her, without any firm commitment from the Paris sponsors, that his play will open in Paris. In mid-March he was invited to the Festival "Oeuvres du XXe Siècle," organized by the French Congress for the Liberty of Culture.

When he finally did write to Ober on March 28, he indicated he was holding the revised contracts, since he didn't know whether to sign with Ayers or not. Inasmuch as he didn't know what the contract was for, whether for Paris (with Ford and Marre) or elsewhere, he was being cautious. The entire episode has an amusing side. With contracts needing his signature, Faulkner had little sense of what he was signing or signing away. His final paragraph to Ober catches some of the unintentional humor: "I have heard nothing from Marre since my wire promising 2 thousand. I assume this is not enough, but I don't know, dont want to botch his and Ford's plan by signing too quick. Marre said, if we produced ourselves, in Paris, we would own all rights to it." At one time, Faulkner would have plunged ahead, but now Ober made him more cautious.*

He accepted the invitation to the Paris festival, telling Else, whom he planned to see there, that he declined being a delegate. He says the words "delegate" and "freedom" in the same sentence sound incongruous and terrifying. "I will not accept any commitment. I will pay my own way, give that time to the festival which will meet my conscience."[15] If he had chosen not to be a free agent, as he put it, the French would have paid his way. But there was also the dilemma of when to arrive. The festival was scheduled for the last two weeks in May, but if *Requiem* went into production, he would be needed by late April. He made tentative plans to be in Paris from May 18 to June 10, if nothing further happened with the play.

*Similarly, when the president of Tulane University in New Orleans invited him to receive a Doctor of Letters degree in May, he responded that for someone who did not even graduate from grammar school to accept an honorary degree "would debase and nullify the whole aim of learning" (to Rufus C. Harris, April 11, 1952, Tulane typescript; *Selected Letters of William Faulkner*, ed. Joseph Blotner [New York: Vintage Books, 1978; orig. publ. 1977], p. 329).

He also approved a Ford Foundation documentary on his work, offering to cooperate. Besides some farming, he found time to accompany Shelby Foote, the novelist and later great Civil War historian, to Corinth, to celebrate the ninetieth anniversary of the battle of Shiloh.

He was writing regularly to Joan now, encouraging her in her work, trying to pull her out of a stagnant period, giving her information about his upcoming Paris trip. One thing he hammers at is her inability, in his view, to agonize and sweat sufficiently with her stories. She is, he feels, too easily satisfied. She must dig down into suffering and anguish, and then express it, rewrite it, revise, until the right shape is there. She must also learn to be economical, surprising advice from a writer who was becoming, as he aged, more prolix and abundant, unable to turn it off. But by economy, he does not mean only language, but the lean way by which a story is established and told. Furthermore, he says, she needs an approach, so that she learns where the fulcrum of her story lies and does not digress. His own life, he says, is purely physical: farming, training a colt, working with a jumping horse over hurdles; and he admits he is forgetting how to put words together, "as though I had forgotten that form of anguishment."[16] He sees that as an encouraging sign, that he is perhaps storing up his material, getting it ready for an explosion. He also announces he is going to speak before the Delta Cotton Council in Cleveland, Mississippi, on May 15. He had hoped to be in Paris, but when the production of *Requiem* fell through, he went ahead with his speech commitment.[17]

It was a curious situation. Faulkner looked like a poor white farmer in contrast to the sleekly dressed, successful planters and buyers who were part of the Cotton Council. Hosting the event were the governor of Mississippi, Hugh White, and James F. Byrnes, then governor of South Carolina. It became a typical Faulkner performance, conceding little to the audience, and full of the rhetoric which filled *Requiem* and his Nobel Prize address. It was a plea for independent man, yet directed at men who waxed rich on federal farm subsidies and who accepted federal welfare programs while attacking the government for creeping socialism. In his talk, Faulkner revealed the hypocrisy of those who assaulted government interference but welcomed government subsidies of their own enterprises. As he had done with Temple Drake's speeches in *Requiem*, Faulkner stressed every person's responsibility for his own acts, which is the true meaning of liberty and the core of duty. Without individual responsibility, the Declaration of Independence means little or nothing. Faulkner lavished rhetoric, in his soft, drawling voice, on the Jeffersonian vision of man: the farmer who depends on no one besides himself. It was a secular view of society, giving nothing to God and expecting nothing in return.

As he moved toward the present condition, Faulkner saw welfare programs as subverting this Jeffersonian ideal. His words were precise in identifying the enemy: he feels secure "beneath the eagle-perched domes of our capitols and from behind the alphabetical splatters on the doors of welfare and other bureaus of economic or industrial regimentation." The enemy's artillery "is a debased and respectless currency which has emasculated the initiative for independence by robbing initiative of the only mutual scale it knew to measure independence by." The language has some mixed metaphors: currency does not really emasculate, although the sharp edge of the economy may; but the intent is clear—an all-out indictment of how our tough old ancestors have been traduced. Those who form these laws in Washington do not believe in man; they disbelieve his independence and responsibility by subverting his courage and endurance.

What Faulkner wanted, he forcefully emphasized in the final segment of his talk, was a return to the tough old farmer of past times. Speaking as an incurable romantic in this respect, he hoped to see the return of yeomanry. Implied here is some sense of justice for the Negro, some defense of his rights, although the subject remains shadowy. Yet these very men who gave Faulkner an ovation when he finished became the backbone of the white Citizens' Councils formed when the Supreme Court decision enforced school integration. They were also Dixiecrats, a good many of them, who had bolted from the Democratic party and represented everything Faulkner detested. Despite his links with the federal government, Governor Byrnes spoke of the need for a new party, and when he finished, according to Blotner,[18] Ben Wasson leaned over to Faulkner and called him a Snopes, which Faulkner agreed with. What made the entire proceeding so curious was that Faulkner struck a responsive note in those he hated, and they roared their approval of someone who was and would become even more, for them, the enemy.

The speech reveals for us, as noted above in other circumstances, how intent Faulkner was on heuristic principles of language: words now must insist on moral and ethical consequences. His Nobel speech seems to have coalesced ideas which he feels compelled to pronounce; yet what was good for his image was poor for his fiction.

Faulkner left Oxford on May 16, planning a direct flight to Paris from New York. This time, instead of the Algonquin, he stayed at the Weston Hotel, where he was close to Random House. *Requiem* was the topic of conversation, but just when it appeared the money was available, the actors in place (Ford as Temple, her husband, Zachary Scott, as Gavin Stevens), the deal fell through in controversy about script and sets. In Paris, he saw Else, who came from Sweden, and he was entertained by Gallimard.* Mainly Faulkner experienced the kind of drift in his life which could be filled only by heavy drinking: the condition was a familiar one, in which he emptied himself out so that he could pour in large

---

*Like many French publishers, the Gallimard war record was a mixed one. To keep the business going, Gaston Gallimard published under German censorship, banned Jews and other writers expressing anti-German feeling, and allowed the fascist Drieu la Rochelle to take over the editorship of *La Nouvelle Revue Française*. But many authors, including Camus, Sartre, and Malraux, expressed support for Gallimard's house as a safe house for antifascists and testified he had not directly collaborated. What saved the owner was the loyalty of his authors, and the fact that some, like Malraux, considered Drieu a friend despite (or because of!) the latter's anti-Semitism and admiration for German theories of racial superiority.

volumes of liquid. He had a painful back, which only alcohol seemed to help. He stayed a good deal of the time in his hotel room drinking, although he did attend the congress and gave a very brief speech.* The presence of Malraux, a true wartime hero, helped carry him through an excruciating experience. Finally, as his condition worsened (back and alcohol), he checked into the Clinique Remy de Gourmont, and there X-rays found several fractures in his vertebrae, the result of falls from horses. The sole solution after the diagnosis—bones grating together, muscle spasms, bones growing together incorrectly—was corrective surgery, fusion of the vertebrae. Faulkner, of course, refused, preferring a few days of rest and his own home cure, alcohol, to deaden the pain.

He flew out of Paris at the end of May and spent a little time in London, where he visited Chatto & Windus. As his back pain continued, even worsened, he decided not to return to Paris, but to fly to Oslo, where he could recuperate under Else's care. It was an ideal solution: a mature, understanding admirer, an attractive, intelligent woman to boot, and someone who catered to his needs. A masseur recommended by Else proved helpful, and Faulkner was able to function socially. He liked the Norwegians he met, and of course they deferred to his great reputation. Faulkner flew from Oslo to New York on June 14. On his return, he almost immediately wrote to Monique and Jean-Jacques Salomon, toward both of whom he felt gratitude and friendship. Their care of him in Paris had been exemplary, and he sent on to them an unused airline ticket which, when redeemed, would become his gift for their child, his goddaughter.

Considering the details of the trip to Paris, we see that Faulkner was in no shape for work on anything. His state of mind had brought him close to abulia, a condition of will-lessness. Having seen Else in Paris, still corresponding regularly with Joan, whom he visited in Memphis en route home, he now sat in Oxford and the full thrust of his domestic situation hit him. His plaint is to Saxe Commins, Random House's resident "psychiatrist." "I am completely bored, fed up, my days are being wasted. It is just

---

*In a letter from Ward Miner to Phil Stone (November 29) about the writer's appearance at the Paris festival, we see what the Faulkner mystique had become.

The hall was packed and it was quite evident that they were there for one person—Faulkner—even though people such as Malraux, Auden, etc. were also on the platform. When Faulkner stood up there was a tremendous ovation for several minutes. Unfortunately, his talk was rather feeble, and so the applause was not nearly as great at the conclusion. But it was apparent to anybody that Faulkner the novelist was looked up to with awe even though Faulkner the speaker was not (*Faulkner: A Comprehensive Guide to the Brodsky Collection, the Letters*, eds. Louis Daniel Brodsky and Robert W. Hamblin, vol. 2 [Jackson: University Press of Mississippi, 1984], p. 101).

Miner continues: "What is amusing to an American is to find French novelists trying to imitate Faulkner's mannerisms of writing, and the result is usually so bad as to be really funny. The prestige of Faulkner is still greater in France than in the States. The three books they like best are *Sanctuary, Light in August,* and *The Sound and the Fury. Hamlet* and *Absalom* they have not read, since they have not as yet been translated" (*Faulkner: A Comprehensive Guide to the Brodsky Collection, the Letters*, eds. Louis Daniel Brodsky and Robert W. Hamblin, vol. 2 [Jackson: University Press of Mississippi, 1984], p. 101).

possible that I shall do something quite drastic about the matter before long. I have done no work in a year, do not want to, yet I have work which I must do." His "release" in Paris, the beckoning of a more satisfactory relationship without the secrecy, plus the tremendous pressure of a long work to which he cannot devote himself—all brought back the old ideas of freeing himself, as he had once confessed to Meta. He writes:

> We talked some of my giving myself six months of absence, getting completely away from here and all my familiar life. I think now it will take more than that. I think now I may, to save my soul, something of peace, contentment, save the work at least, quit the whole thing, give it all to them, leave and be done with it. I can earn enough to live on, I think. I am really sick, I think. Cant sleep too well, nervous, idle, have to make an effort not to let the farm go to pot, look forward only with boredom to the next sunrise. I dont like it. Maybe I will have to get away, for at least a year, almost vanish. Then maybe I will get to work again, and get well again.[19]

The real dilemma is how to escape his marriage, his responsibilities with house and farm, and reestablish himself in another relationship, what he glimpsed with Else and, to a lesser extent but no less attractively, with Joan, to whom at some point he proposed.* He emphasizes he doesn't have enough time to waste it like this. ". . . I will want what I have always wanted: to be free; probably until now I have still believed that somehow, in some way, someday I would be free again [by outliving his wife, which he said was every married man's hope]; now at last I have begun to realise that perhaps I will not, I have waited, hoped too long, done nothing about it; and so now I must, or—in spirit—die."[20] He foresees the scorn and opprobrium which will fall on him once he separates from his wife of over twenty years, but, he adds, "perhaps I have already sacrificed too much already to try to be a good artist, to boggle at a little more in order to still try to be one."

The meeting with Joan, we can suppose, started this run of profound despair. As he dined with the young woman, he recognized the potentialities of freedom from Rowan Oak, to come and go freely without subterfuge, deception, or need for Random House shielding. The correspondence with Joan remained heavy throughout the summer, ostensibly to encourage and correct her writing, but also apparently to maintain the connection with someone who had entered deeply into his life. All those early rejections in his late teens and early twenties were now counterbalanced by almost infinite possibilities with women; and he who had been rejected by one woman in particular was tied to her, with, he felt, only a few years remaining to him.

*She indicated that had he been free, she would have married him. (From Joan Williams.)

The summer of 1952 was a time of aimless activity, not of the kind which allows the simmering of ideas leading to a large work. There is now little mention of the big book, not even the plan to return to it fitfully. We know Faulkner tinkered with the novel, but lacked the will or direction to get on with its multifold problems. He tried to get away to Memphis as often as possible to see Joan at her home. They worked on a television script together—something Faulkner would never have ordinarily done—and came up with a brief work called "The Graduation Dress." He sent it to James Geller, who sold it for $500.* Joan was working on a short story which later became the title of her first novel, *The Morning and the Evening*. Faulkner sent her lengthy advice on how to handle her main character, Jake, whom Faulkner labels an idiot. His suggestions about alternating sections for different characters recall how he handled *Sound*. His comments indicate she has it all wrong, at least from his point of view, and he even dislikes the title. He stays on top of every aspect of it: reducing her paragraphs to single sentences, retitling it, revising the opening; advising her even how to send it on. He did not, however, rewrite her prose, and at no time in their "collaboration" did he do any writing for her.

He was seeing Joan in Memphis, and Estelle even suggested they work together at Rowan Oak, perhaps the better to keep them under observation. But Estelle herself was in poor condition, requiring hospitalization, the first in a series of collapses and breakdowns which would force her to stop drinking in order to live. During this time, late July and early August, Faulkner was at the end of a rope held by Joan, whose own inconclusive situation was no happier than his own. He held on to her as his link with some Edenic vision which had evaded him, and she stuck to him out of a mixture of respect and need for guidance. He feared she lacked the right mix for a serious writer, not only that she could not bear the anguish but that she would make a conventional marriage. Then he would back off from his remarks, reminding himself he was remaking her in his own image. He asked people he knew to help her, although if she left the area, they would be more or less finished. He wrote to *Harper's*[21] on July 14 saying the enclosed story was written by his student, the first one he had seen which warranted a covering letter. He asks for a careful reading, even a double reading, if necessary. This leads him to ask Joan if they couldn't start a cottage industry, whereby she sends on stories under his name in order to get the higher price; but little came of this scheme since *Harper's* rejected the piece.

In a curious turn, the role of impresario brought Faulkner back to his own work. Even as he began to use this young lady more than thirty years

---

*Geller, who had been supportive of Faulkner at Warners, was now a television executive and seeking ideas and plots for scripts, although not the finished work. Faulkner conceived of this script idea and sent it in under his name, but hoped to be able to slip in Joan as a television writer or rewriter (July 11, 1952; *Selected Letters of William Faulkner*, ed. Joseph Blotner [New York: Vintage Books, 1978; orig. publ. 1977], p. 336).

his junior as the recipient of his most intimate thoughts, he began to find himself engaged. He and Joan apparently decided to break up this phase of their affair, sometime in late July or early August, at the time Faulkner wrote his despairing letter to Commins about the need to break away, even to separate from Estelle permanently. This somehow energized him. He tells Joan he wrote *The Wild Palms* to stave off what he then thought was heartbreak. His heart didn't break then, and he assures her it won't break now. His advice to her now, about "The Morning and the Evening," which she planned to revise, is like D. H. Lawrence admonishing a disciple for writing from the mind only.

> You have to feel Jake from inside, as you did. To write him properly, you must have no instruction nor criticism, but imagination, which you had to have to invent him, and observation and experience. . . . You have to be capable of anything, everything, accepting them I mean, not as experimentals, clinical, to see what it does to the mind, like with drugs or dead outside things, but because the heart and the body are big enough to accept all the world, all human agony and passion.[22]

He adds:

> You ran from your heart and your body, back into your mind, which is dead matter, nothing, since only the heart, the body, the nerves, are capable of feeling fire, anguish, passion, exultation, happiness, hope. No wonder your mind walled your heart and body in, once it got them, since the mind is afraid of fire.[23]

This argument in favor of body and nerves was good advice for a writer, even better advice for the man trying to keep an affair going.

Apparently Faulkner was willing to keep up the friendship even if the rest was missing. Even with his stated return to the manuscript of *A Fable*, there is here still such a loss of direction we sense he was doing whatever came to hand as a way of relieving boredom, nervousness, anguish, severe anxiety, even conjecturing money troubles as a sign that he might have to return to Hollywood. As he moved toward his fifty-fifth birthday, he was not anchored in anything able to hold his attention. The farm no longer seemed to interest him; he did not speak of books, or of any period of reading; his personal life was shredded and fragmentary. None of it added up, and he knew it. He told Ober a dark tale of a writer who was past his prime, like a prizefighter who wants to enter the ring when he knows his skills are diminished. But before writing Ober, he had told Else an even darker tale, full of resentment, self-hatred, hostilities which simmered within him, and made him incapable of acting. The dirge sounds like severe alcoholic depression or even a mental malfunctioning brought on by excessive intake. He complains of back trouble, although he has forsaken horses for the time being; but he attributes it to psychological causes:

"... probably the great trouble is unhappiness now, stupid existence seeing what remains of life going to support parasites who do not even have the grace to be sycophants. Am tired, I suppose. Should either command myself to feel better, or change life itself, which I may do; if you hear harsh things of me, dont believe all of them."[24]

Had he been able to control his life, he would have separated from Estelle and left her Rowan Oak and an income; none of which would have surprised Jill, who had viewed too much domestic instability to be disturbed by anything more. And he could have worked out a relationship with Else, a mature companion with mutual admiration on both sides. But he was apparently not ready to give up Rowan Oak; nor was he willing to get into the financial difficulty separation involved. There was within some factor he was not admitting to himself: that he and Estelle were linked for life. In terms of the pact or bond they had forged when teenagers, it made little difference whether the marriage worked or not.

With the above plaint to Ober, he enclosed Joan's story, although his comments indicate he knows the story doesn't work. Then he comes into his own problems, which are massive. He feels the pressure of money and says he doesn't want to return to Hollywood. He says he is committed to Hawks if he should return, not to Warner Brothers, which still might pick up the old option:

> But I will have to do hack work of some sort soon, or be broke and a nuisance to my friends again. I have the POST in mind still, but nothing of it yet. Maybe I shall have to cut completely away from my present life, at least for a time. I seem to have lost heart for working. I can't find anything to work, write, *for*. I failed to form the habit of letting money be sufficient, or even a factor, and I am not likely to earn any more glory at 55, and that doesn't leave much.[25]

Behind Faulkner's despair is his awareness, now indisputably clear, that in such a situation he will binge and seek a kind of alcoholic suicide.

Of greatest significance is his knowledge that the one thing holding his life together, his writing, has somehow come apart. The great thread which, Ariadne-like, had led him through his life was frayed and breaking. Without his work, everything was subterfuge, self-deception, shielding. Even his affairs, while supportive of certain feelings, were inadequate because of their secret and incomplete nature. Except for Meta, his extramarital affairs were experienced on the run. He had once achieved a balance between farming and writing; yet even this plan fell through by the 1950s. The farm had been an idea as much as a place, and he had poured money into it; but it was now perceived as a drain on him, like the legions of relatives and servants he was supporting. It was as though everything that had served as a partial shield for many years was suddenly removed, and Faulkner saw himself clearly. If his writing had held up, he could have maintained the pretense that the rest of his life had some order. But now with final order gone, he was experiencing what Wallace Stevens, his great contemporary in poetry, described as the houses haunted "by white night-gowns," the body inhabited by visions of death.

A shrewd observer as well as a loyal friend, Saxe Commins noted the decline. Estelle had summoned him to handle Faulkner, who was acutely alcoholic and in need of medical attention, which he resisted. Commins assessed the man in a letter written in Oxford on October 8:

> I found Bill completely deteriorated in mind and body. He mumbles incoherently and is totally incapable of controlling his bodily functions. He pleads piteously for beer all the time and mumbles deliriously. Every twenty minutes or so through the night I had to carry him virtually to the bathroom. His body is bloated and bruised from his many falls and bears even worse marks. . . . The disintegration of a man is tragic to witness."[26]

Commins concludes Faulkner desperately needs professional care so he can regain his bodily functions, at least; and he assures his wife, Dorothy, that in no case will he bring him back North. "This is more than a case of acute alcoholism. It is a complete disintegration of a man." What Commins failed to reckon with was Faulkner's remarkable recuperative powers —even now, in his physical decline, he returned not only to the living but to his desk. He still had several novels in him.

An amusing sidelight in this grim context derives from Commins's view of the house, which, he admits, may have been influenced by the shock of what he saw on his arrival. He found Rowan Oak "rather distasteful." "It is a rambling Southern mansion, deteriorated like its owner, built in 1838 and not much improved since. Ours is a heavenly mansion in comparison, if very much smaller. The rooms are bare and what they do contain is rickety, tasteless, ordinary. There is none of the charm and orderliness and comfort that you give to a home." He adds: "I tell you this is a ghastly business and I don't let myself think how it can be straightened out."[27] This was Faulkner's beloved Rowan Oak, one reason why he remained with Estelle!

Commins somehow found time to write a long letter to Cerf and Haas, detailing the condition of their Nobel Prize author. He says that for six weeks before he came, Faulkner was drinking himself into this condition. He describes the ordeal of carrying the battered and bruised author to the bathroom. The bruises and contusions were not only facial but covered his body—from falls, stumbling, slamming into objects, a disregard for all safety precautions. Commins describes a man bent on suicide, but who depends on those who will save him, especially those "parasites" like Estelle, Malcolm, and Malcolm's wife, Gloria, who were helping out. Commins finds it all disagreeable, but also pathetic. "The fact is," he writes, "that Bill has deteriorated shockingly both in body and mind. He can neither take care of himself in the most elementary way or think with any coherence at all. This may be only evidence of his condition in a state of acute alcoholism. But I believe it goes much deeper and is a real disintegration.[28] He was in desperate need of professional care, and yet to move him even to Memphis was unthinkable. The local hospital was also out of the question, because his case was too difficult. Commins says that Estelle is "really desperate," and that Malcolm, who had taken so much abuse, is "a very fine fellow"—but, as we know, himself an alcoholic.

Commins feels the burden of taking on all the decisions. Estelle and Malcolm are dependent on his judgment, and he tells Cerf and Haas they must also trust his decisions. But there is little he can do except prevent Faulkner from doing further injury to himself. Withal, Commins is glad he came, as it was the least he could do for a friend; but he longs to return to New York "and the amenities of publishing." In a gracious and grateful letter, postmarked two days later, Estelle wrote the Comminses that Faulkner was coming around and it was because of Commins's trip that the writer was saved. He was now hospitalized, under a nurse's care, sedated, and gradually recovering from alcohol poisoning. Estelle had wired earlier that she wanted Faulkner's whereabouts kept confidential.[29] Since everyone in Oxford knew about his alcoholism, it was probably to prevent Joan from visiting, or even inquiring.

Behind the scenes, like a groundhog periodically emerging, Phil Stone was still constructing his own view of Faulkner's life, becoming the chief resource for those writing about him in a scholarly and/or popular way. Corresponding with Ward Miner, who had just published his *The World of William Faulkner,* one of the earliest holistic studies, Stone starts to cut through the Faulkner myths. He says he is disturbed about such critiques because they perpetuate myths and ignore truths. They stress elements which were "entirely unintentional" on Faulkner's part, a comment which utterly ignores that as an artist Faulkner went well beyond "intention." Stone settles in and gives his assessment:

> Another thing is that such critiques make me a little sad because they seem to be in the nature of literary obituaries. After all, the Nobel Prize was for work he did between 1928 and 1940 and he has done very little since then of the same stature as the work of that period. I think now that he never will and I think that his great success and the adulation that has followed it has really been a misfortune.[30]

Before the acute alcoholic poisoning which brought Commins to Oxford on October 8, Faulkner had been taken, on September 18, to the Gartly-Ramsay Hospital in Memphis. He was desperately ill with alcohol intermixed with Seconal in his system, plus large quantities of beer, which he drank also as a sedative.* The Seconal was plentiful in the household, as Estelle also took it. In explaining his back trouble,

---

*Seconal taken with alcohol creates intense depression and helps explain Faulkner's dismal psychological state; chemicals were altering him.

Faulkner went through his experience in wartime of a plane crash (a chimera) followed by falls from horses. Whatever the etiology, his back was in spasms, and X-rays showed vertebrae fractures and compressed fractures, with a good deal of improper healing. The consequences of such a mixture of compression and healing led to an arthritic condition; and only corrective surgery could help. The back condition was quite real, not merely an excuse for alcohol and sedation; and it could not be treated with psychiatric therapy, although the latter may have possibly helped Faulkner's attitude toward it. The doctors weaned him from the alcohol and Seconal, but the back condition, while temporarily responding to massage and heat, was incurable except by radical means, and that Faulkner balked at. As soon as the spasms relented, he insisted on leaving the hospital, after eight days, when he should have remained for at least another week or two.

Once back in Oxford, Faulkner returned to his cycle of pain, alcohol, and Seconal, until he was in worse shape than during his visit to Gartly-Ramsay in Memphis. He fell down the staircase at Rowan Oak, and with this Estelle called Saxe Commins, as related above. Once he was deemed in shape to travel the seventy-five miles to Memphis, he was brought back to Gartly-Ramsay on October 9, where he stayed until the twenty-first. He was, as Commins remarked to his wife, and then to Cerf and Haas, in terrible shape: malnourished, exhausted, poisoned from alcohol and medication. He was given paraldehyde, an anticonvulsant which controlled delirium tremens, but was kept on Seconal and Pantopon to make sure he slept. Since he refused surgery, he had to accept a back brace, what was called a Taylor spinal brace, which was extremely uncomfortable and unwieldy, and hardly the piece of equipment an older man interested in younger women would choose to wear.

The inner man was anguished, the outer man a tremendous success. *Life*, *Holiday*, the Ford Foundation seeking a film—all were part of the success syndrome in the wake of the prize. While his chief literary rival was an open book, a publicity man's dream, Faulkner intrigued observers because he was such a closed fist, a publicity man's nightmare. But because of his enforced privacy, he had created a legendary figure quite different from the accessible, always-talking, always-moving Hemingway. Yet strikingly, behind the masks each devised for himself, there was the terrible desperation of lost powers, alcoholic fogs, deep and impenetrable anguish. Outer success was a parodic shield. On his return to Oxford on October 21, Faulkner had few options. He sensed his mortality while in the hospital, and while he still courted his own form of suicide, he did so more circumspectly than did Hemingway, who went after it with gusto. Faulkner's "suicide efforts" were acts of regression by a man who, while acting responsibly in his financial support of a small tribe, was nevertheless still a boy emotionally in his need for others' help. Phil Stone, who felt he knew everything about his friend, in reality knew little.

His sole emotional support became Joan. But it was during his stay in the Memphis hospital that Estelle—according to Faulkner—began to open his letters. Estelle disclaimed this accusation. She insisted (in her own letter to Commins at the end of February 1954) that Faulkner asked Malcolm to open and read the letters to him; Malcolm, disturbed at the contents, showed the already opened letters to Estelle, who professed not to have known before how deeply involved Joan and Faulkner were. It is difficult to determine who is dissembling here, Faulkner or Estelle, and it is also difficult to understand how Estelle was unaware of the depth of the relationship, especially since she and Faulkner had not had sexual relations for some twenty years.

At the beginning of November, the Ford Foundation film crew came to Oxford to shoot the script on which Moon Mullen had acted as adviser. Mullen showed it to Faulkner beforehand, and he approved it. The filming went well, with Faulkner cooperating as actor in various reenactments of high points in his life. Shooting lasted until mid-November, when elections were over and Eisenhower had received a huge vote of confidence from the electorate.* By the time the shooting ended, Faulkner was on his way to Princeton to stay with Dorothy and Saxe Commins and then at the Princeton Inn. He wrote the Comminses he needed to watch his money, and they could also work on unraveling the manuscript. *A Fable* was back in his mind for the first time in many months, although he emphasizes how slow and difficult the writing process is. He assures them his judgment is still good. He also stresses he must have peace—this following Estelle's outburst concerning his correspondence with Joan.

In all his other communications about his condition, he tells people he hurt his back and has been recovering, making no mention of the way he treated the pain. Once in Princeton and settled at the inn, Faulkner gave an interview to a French graduate student studying political science at Princeton, Loïc Bouvard. It was unusually full and revealed Faulkner intellectually as possibly no other interview besides the one with Jean Stein ever did. Coming to Faulkner as a true French intellectual, Bouvard demanded of his subject significant responses, and obtained them. The interview took place at the inn on November 30, only a month after he had been incoherent and unable to control his mental or physical functions.

Bouvard started by saying Faulkner contributed greatly in France to an understanding of man, the implication being that the French existentialists saw in his treatment of the human condition a model which fitted into their own world-view of man. When questioned about the contemporary

---

*Blotner indicates Faulkner voted for Eisenhower over Adlai Stevenson because he, Faulkner, felt that with another "president on the left," Joe McCarthy would become the next president. From Oxford, Stevenson looked like a leftist; from New York, too conservative. Like the Oldhams, Faulkner found himself voting Republican.

French attitude toward God—the idea of replacing Him by man—
Faulkner indicated that one can never eliminate God or morality, although
by God he means the symbol of perfection which mankind can aspire to,
or someone who becomes "the most complete expression of mankind."[31]
Such a God *is*, whether one believes in him or has faith. He is depersonal-
ized and represents a striving. After a brief discussion of Bergsonian time,
Faulkner expressed his agreement: "There isn't any time. . . . only the
present moment, in which I include both the past and the future, and that
is eternity. In my opinion time can be shaped quite a bit by the artist; after
all, man is never time's slave." At his best, Faulkner had striven for a
seamless, continuous temporal scheme: an eternity of the present. Yet the
very ideas he was expressing now in the interview were ideas he could no
longer structure fictionally.

Bouvard then swung the interview around to what he really wanted to
discuss—Faulkner's sense of man. What emerges is a kind of Jeffersonianism which sounds temptingly at moments like contemporary French exis-
tentialism. Faulkner insisted man is free and responsible. He emphasizes
man's tragedy is his inability to communicate, but man keeps on trying to
express himself, to "make contact with other human beings." Faulkner
says he does not hold with the myth of Sisyphus—but in reality, he expressed in his Nobel speech, patterns of thought which fit well into the
modern interpretation of the Sisyphean myth of man striving and not
quite reaching attainment, and then starting all over again. What Faulkner
may have rejected in the myth is the sense of hopelessness; but in the
Camus interpretation, Sisyphus and his strivings are an affirmation, not a
denial, of man's endurance, a view very close to Faulkner's.

Faulkner apparently spoke very fervently about his faith in God, but
Bouvard did not pick up his peculiar way of looking at God until Faulkner
came to his sense of the artist. Then the writer returned to his earliest
ideas, of how the artist achieves his highest function as a kind of seer, a
Rimbaud-like clairvoyant:

> Art is not only man's most supreme expression; it is also the salva-
> tion of mankind. . . . the artist is the one who is able to communicate
> his message. In doing this, he has no intention of saving mankind. On
> the contrary, the artist speaks only for himself. Personally I find it
> impossible to communicate with the outside world. Maybe I will end
> up in some kind of self-communion—a silence—faced with the cer-
> tainty that I can no longer be understood. The artist must create his
> own language. This is not only his right but his duty. Sometimes I
> think of doing what Rimbaud did—yet, I will certainly keep on writ-
> ing as long as I live.[32]

This statement contains the essential Faulkner. But unfortunately it
refers to a conception of the artist to which he could no longer adhere.

That "silence" and the need to forge one's own language of expression were precisely his weapons in his best work. Rimbaud had spoken of himself as "an other." ("Je est un autre," stretching French grammar to express his sense of "I" and "other.") With this, Rimbaud identified the archetypal author with Prometheus—a Prometheus of the mind who penetrates reality as we know it and ravishes celestial fire. As such, the writer passes his season in hell—communes only with himself and forges his own language. In doing this, the writer or poet remakes the art form in each endeavor; he becomes a one-man movement, eschewing all schools and groups. He does not rise above anything, but always works against. Only new language(s) will suggest the impossibility of reality; and a shadowy reality will emerge only because language has approached the impossible. The key to structure or shape in this new language is correspondence, or associations—precisely the way Faulkner moved in his work from *Sound* through *Absalom*. What he denies in this vision, however, is its nihilism: its need to destroy and negate in order to rebuild and reshape. Here the American, with his roots in region and community, balks.

Faulkner also emphasized how arduous artistic creation is—what he had been telling Joan and what he feared was missing from her conception of the writer's mission. Hard work, striving, almost dying in order to create, while romantic concepts, were connected to Faulkner's need to defend his craft within a context where writing was considered effeminate, not man's work. He sees it as work he can justify to his hunting companions, to townspeople, to his father when Murry was alive. Inspiration was insufficient. He speaks of how he loves France, its people, its spirit—the subject of his current big work; but he fears French reliance on mind, its tendency to see man in the abstract, as he puts it. He says Flaubert played a role in his work, also Balzac; Bergson, obviously. He finds himself very close to Proust: "After I read *A la Recherche du Temps Perdu* I said 'This is it'—and I wished I had written it myself. I know Malraux because I have read his latest books on the psychology of art. On the other hand, I know neither Sartre nor Camus."[33]

Finally, they spoke of the South and how it entered into Faulkner's consciousness, although his comments could as well apply more generally: "It's the only really authentic region in the United States because a deep indestructible bond still exists between man and his environment. In the South, above all, there is still a common acceptance of the world, a common view of life, and a common morality."[34] Yet what he is saying applies just as well to small-town or village life as to the South—his remarks are clearly directed *against* large cities and the Northeast; they could also apply to the Midwest, the northern tier of farming states, and the Northwest. Faulkner is revealing his sense of a Jeffersonian America, rather than a definitive South. He omits entirely that there is the South of the Negro; the South as he explains it to Bouvard is a white man's region. Only *there* is a community, a common and shared feeling. That "morality," which he repeated, is very much the artist's sense of his mission, not that of the people he is describing.*

The stay in Princeton afforded Faulkner the opportunity to see Joan unencumbered by secrecy and deception. She came to the inn and spent Thanksgiving with Faulkner at the Commins'. They discussed his insistent point, that she must choose, that the craft of fiction required unending application. But even though conditions were perfect for his work, and he did tinker with *A Fable,* Faulkner began to go under once again. He was, most likely, in a deep phase of alcoholism, unable to define himself for any length of time now except as drunk or near drunk. The drinking was not solely a physical need, however, or so we can conjecture; it seemed to be part of a deep depression he could not shake. In numerous letters in preceding years, he had defined it, and it somehow appeared linked to his having achieved everything he had striven for. With nothing left to achieve, he felt life itself slipping away. Or else he was caught in a reciprocity: depression led to drinking, drinking led to deeper depression, which could only be temporarily relieved by more drinking. The cycle was claiming his life, if we consider his life to be his ability to pull himself together in order to write.

His condition during his Princeton stay worsened to such an extent he required hospitalization at the Westill Sanitarium in Riverdale, the Bronx. This time a more radical treatment was attempted, a series of electroshock episodes—something similar to what Hemingway would undergo later at the Mayo Clinic. In this treatment, which was quite in vogue at the time, the patient was tied down and electrodes were positioned at his temples, a rubber bit placed in his mouth (to prevent him from biting his tongue), and electricity applied until the patient became unconscious. The patient's body became convulsed; this violent response was a way of reordering the

---

*The intensity of this interview should be contrasted with the fluffy one in the *New Yorker* the following year (February 28, 1953). The latter, done by Lillian Ross, is close to parody, with an effort to reproduce Faulkner's deep Mississippi accent as he tells of his falls from horses and the story of the mare he bought for Jill in Hollywood. The picture is of a man hunched over his typewriter in the middle of Random House activity, oblivious to people coming and going. He appears insistent on accruing words for *A Fable,* which he now estimates at about 500,000, counting discards. He coughs, and when Commins asks if he has a cold, Faulkner responds that he has nothing whiskey won't cure. The parodic nature of the "interview" looks forward to the more famous one Ross did with Hemingway, also in the *New Yorker.* Ross followed Hemingway around on his brief visit to the city and recorded every outrageous moment. The "interview" with Faulkner is located differently. It tries to capture him at a moment of his workday at Random House, but in its dealing with trifles, it ignores the salient fact that this is Faulkner, not some eccentric third-rate hack. It trivializes the writer into an old codger, with his gray suspenders, tweed trousers, his trench coat and green felt hat, clearly not Brooks Brothers or Press. Even the language is arch: ". . . we retreated to a corner of the office and watched the sole owner and proprietor of Yoknapatawpha County bring forth prose. He typed very, *very* slowly, mostly with the middle finger of his right hand, but with an occasional assist from the index finger of his left" (*Lion in the Garden: Interviews with William Faulkner,* eds. James B. Meriwether and Michael Millgate [Lincoln: University of Nebraska Press, 1968], p. 75). This is what celebrity had come to! The author lost, the *New Yorker* style won.

patient's mind-set, with the hope of bringing about a recovery. The theory and practice, of course, left many unanswered questions; but the procedure seemed to work in many instances—as though the instigation of a gigantic trauma were sufficient to move the patient from depression into another view of himself. Faulkner came out of each treatment very gentle, even affectionate, almost a child. The psychoanalyst, Eric P. Mosse, offered to care for the writer, feed and nurse him. The situation, which was as pitiful as it sounds, reduced Faulkner to a childlike condition, somewhat akin to his regression while drinking, making himself helpless so he could be saved by those who loved him.

He was well enough after this series of treatments to be discharged, and he went on to New York, where Saxe Commins (across the street at Random House from Faulkner's New Weston Hotel) served him as resident "psychiatrist." But even with Commins in attendance, ready to minister to his client's needs, Faulkner was unable to produce much. At the end of December, he told Joan he had run dry. He indicated it began three days before, on December 28, when he could not get right what he put down on paper. He blamed it on Oxford, saying he would not work there, even after the momentum New York provided. In the past, Rowan Oak was the perfect setting for his work; his office provided him with everything he needed, a desk, an old typewriter, and the incredible rush of words for which he had to devise a shorthand code in order to get them down before they evaporated.

The delayed production of *Requiem* arose once again near the end of 1952, as a kind of mockery of the hopes with which the year began. Ober told Faulkner that Lemuel Ayers had said the play could not be produced successfully as long as Ford remained the lead. Although she was likable, she was not the actress to play Temple Drake; the play could only succeed with a great actress. Ayers decided to bow out, although he would return if Ford left the production. Ober tried to be understanding. He wondered what Faulkner had in mind, since no one seriously considered producing the play with the lead stipulated. He suggested that she be given a reasonable period of time in which to sell the play with herself as lead, and if she could not, then Faulkner was free to offer the play without her. Faulkner replied quite simply and with the stubborn support he showed for women with whom he was involved: the play was written for her and was hers. That ended any potential deals.

Finances also were uppermost in Faulkner's mind, since now that he had recovered from his debilitating binging, he saw his chance for freedom lay not in legal separation, but in travel. Estelle made it clear that whatever he did and no matter how miserable they might be together, she did not intend to dissolve the marriage. As she wrote to Commins in 1954, "*Nothing* can alter my love and devotion—nor upset my faith in Bill's actual love for me—although right now, he swears he doesn't care. . . . All I want is Billy's good—and to prove it, I'll do *anything* that is best—The only thing that I shudder at and might try to evade, is a divorce—and *that,* only on Jill's account."[35] For Faulkner money was the overriding issue, to get enough of it so as to be free: ". . . money is what I am going to need to extricate myself and still live in the state of creature comfort that I have let myself get used to. I should have stayed the tramp with one shirt, which I was born to be."[36] He was writing to Commins from Oxford, with Jill home from college for the Christmas vacation—the period when he had written Joan Williams he had run dry; but he indicated here he was trying to maintain a daily stint on the manuscript. Yet he suspected the blowup was coming, once Jill departed: "Things are calm here, due to Jill's presence. But it will probably blow up as soon as she is gone; already, after a few drinks in her [Estelle], the lightning flicks a little. Hope to God I can keep J out of it, but dont know of course." The major issues, the usual ones: probably Joan, Faulkner's increasing absences, and the fact that Rowan Oak imprisoned two alcoholics.

Chapter Twenty-six

Walking the Edge

T HE YEAR 1953 started badly with another hospitalization in New York, and the pattern for the year was set. Faulkner's chronic alcoholism had become acute, in a spiral of depression, drinking, deepening depression, more frantic drinking, until collapse. In his fifty-sixth year, his system had become alcohol-clogged; and while his organs remained basically sound, he was slowly wearing himself down. He needed psychiatric care, but he refused to cooperate when a psychiatrist tried to explore his relationship with his mother. That particular area was ripe for picking, although in precisely what ways we can only speculate. The year also saw a further physical deterioration in Estelle, who hemorrhaged and had some heart difficulty following the operation for cataracts in January. He who needed nursing found himself caring for his wife.

Through all this, Faulkner managed to work along on *A Fable;* by November he had finished the segment of the "Three Temptations." He also helped with the preparation of *A Faulkner Reader,* an anthology of his work* quite unlike the *Portable* edited by Cowley. In the fall, *Life* finally published its two-part article on Faulkner, which he considered an insidi-

---

*Foreword, Nobel Prize address, *The Sound and the Fury,* "The Bear," "Old Man" (from *The Wild Palms*), "Spotted Horses" (from *The Hamlet*), "A Rose for Emily," "Barn Burning," "Dry September," "That Evening Sun," "Turnabout," "Shingles for the Lord," "A Justice," "Wash," "An Odor of Verbena," "Percy Grimm" (from *Light in August*), "The Court-House" (from *Requiem for a Nun*).

ous invasion of his privacy. The completion of *A Fable* coincided more or less with the ending of his affair with Joan, sporadic though it had been; but he quickly met someone else—the attractive, intelligent, and very affluent Jean Stein. He also spent time in Stockholm with Else, but before that flew to Egypt to work with Howard Hawks on *Land of the Pharaohs.* The year saw one short story ("Mr. Acarius"), not published in his lifetime, and found Faulkner bringing *A Fable* to a close, short of final revisions.

The next year saw the publication of both the long-awaited novel and the anthology, creating the impression he was working at feverish pitch; in fact, he was struggling to keep afloat personally and professionally. As per his plan, he spent a good deal of time away from Oxford, so that in effect he and Estelle were separated while remaining married. The pattern would intensify in 1954, with his spending most of that year (as opposed to half of the previous one) well outside the Oxford circle, more or less with people he came to know after the prize. One exception was Hawks, whom he saw in Cairo. Except for work on *A Fable,* we sense considerable drift and loss of purpose in 1953, a kind of burnout. Faulkner appeared to value personal peace over professional obligations to himself. He did not spell this out specifically, but the way his life moved zigzaggingly indicated he had either lost control or made a conscious decision to let personal needs supersede literary excellence.

Early in January 1953, he asked Commins for another $5,000. His letter indicated that he was working daily on the manuscript, but the "initial momentum ran out, and it is getting more and more difficult, a matter of deliberate will power, concentration, which can be deadly after a while."[1] He emphasized that he had to get away soon. To Joan, he wrote in such a way as to leave it up to her to continue the liaison, saying that any woman who received letters such as the ones Faulkner wrote, expressing love and desire, should know what to do. The tone sounded commanding, but in actuality it was a form of pleading: in his depression, which was by this time constant, he could not tolerate rejection.

The farm was also a matter of concern. Faulkner decided to let his nephew, Jimmy, Johncy's son, have his cattle, and then rent the farm to the people living on it, who could care for it and pay the taxes. He emphasized to one and all that his work was very hard to do in Oxford and was coming along slowly. When Estelle's operation for cataracts was successful, Faulkner was freed for another trip North, originally scheduled for January 15 but postponed to January 31. On December 28 the CBS *Omnibus* show had televised its documentary on Faulkner, but he seemed unaware of it, and it did not serve, as it might have, as a temporary pickup in morale. It brought him to a much wider audience than his reception of the Nobel Prize had done, and would complement the *Life* articles on September 28 and October 5. But all his mental energies seemed focused on getting away from Oxford and Rowan Oak: another migration and rejection even as, later in the decade, he swung back to his Yoknapatawpha material, in that oscillation of rejection and need which characterized so much of his career. His quarters when he arrived in New York were splendid: Harrison Smith's apartment at 9 East Sixty-third Street in Manhattan. With Smith on vacation, the conditions were perfect for work—and also perfect for a binge, since Faulkner had carried away from Oxford all his physical and emotional problems. He saw Joan, but even she could not pick up his spirits; and she was herself full of uncertainties about her personal life and career. She rarely felt comfortable in their liaison, recognizing more clearly than he the desperate nature of it, judging her role in it as a vicarious journey through youth for the writer who could not reconcile himself to aging. Their depression became reciprocal: he needed to be with her, and yet subsequent meetings only revealed she was making decisions which would permanently separate them. Unlike Meta, she rejected marriage with him; the liaison had nowhere to go on any level. Given the situation, Faulkner regressed into helplessness. The back pain had not abated—it is doubtful if he regularly wore the prescribed back brace—and his cure was a bout of heavy drinking. Within a few days of his arrival in New York, he required care, which is probably what he was seeking—friends in New York to rush to his aid as he became increasingly helpless.

He attended the National Book Award ceremonies where Ralph Ellison received the award for *Invisible Man*. With that book, the new generation had arrived, a generation which relegated Faulkner to classic status (Melville, Hawthorne, Twain, James, and Faulkner as America's "great tradition"), but then moved on from him as a relic of the past. The *New Yorker* reporter, the wag known as Stanley, wrote that Faulkner was the center of attraction. The legend was working well, and his reticence and withdrawal from such scenes had given him a charismatic quality. He spoke of his new work as a "magnum opus," which was true; and he posed for a photograph with Commins and William O. Douglas, the speaker at the ceremonies. Incidentally, Faulkner and Douglas would have gotten on well; ideologically, they were quite close in their fervent support of the individual against the state. He left the proceedings, however, not with the Supreme Court justice but with an attractive (female) reporter.

This kind of event put him under enormous strain, and he responded by drinking himself into a spell of forgetting. He needed professional treatment, and the spells of amnesia were particularly frightening to those around him. Joan, Robert Linscott of Random House, and Harrison Smith found him care at the Charles B. Townes private sanitarium on Central Park West. Just as the biographer of Faulkner has to become acquainted with several branches of medicine and medication, so did his friends have to become knowledgeable about treatment centers, and signs that he needed professional help. Even Joan had now entered that aspect of Faulkner's life in which he required maternal care.

He wrote to Malcolm Franklin and his wife, Gloria, to assure them he was all right, although he attributed his last three bouts of amnesia to a fall from his horse the last March, when he hit his back hard and possibly his head. "Tell Mamma [Estelle] I am all right, since I have an idea what the trouble might be, I will take better care of myself. I want you to be fond of me always, but I dont want you to worry, to let worry over me interfere with your work. *Dont worry.* I am earning money again, first time in two years almost now, and have every reason to keep on at a gait which wont give anyone reason to worry."[2] He warns Malcolm not to inform Estelle, since "Mr. Saxe" is taking good care of him. Haas found a good doctor, Commins was in attendance, Smith helped him get into the hospital on Central Park West, Joan was solicitous about his amnesia: a hovering group of Florence Nightingales. He also assures his stepson he is working on his commencement address for Jill's June graduation from Pine Manor.

With these bouts of amnesia and a kind of hallucinatory memory of events when he was supposed to be unconscious or semiconscious, Faulkner's mental responses appear part of a general brain deterioration. The medical equipment of the day could not pinpoint exactly what was occurring, but it seems clearer in retrospect that alcohol was causing malfunction, although as yet only slight. Despite his strong system, the acute drinking bouts were getting, not to his liver or stomach and intestines, but to his brain. When he had been brought to various hospitals in New York or Memphis, he experienced delirum tremens, which paraldehyde relieved.

Yet, withal, he wrote Else a list of his projects, including the short story "Mr. Acarius." He thought the *New Yorker* would take it, but that magazine was not keyed in to Faulkner, major or minor, and the story did not appear until after his death, when the *Saturday Evening Post* took it for its October 9, 1965, issue. Not only the *New Yorker* but two other magazines rejected the Nobel Prize–winner's work. He tells his Swedish friend of four other projects: continuing attention to *A Fable,* a foreword for Sherwood Anderson's letters (which ended up not as part of the book but in the *Atlantic* for June), and that piece on Mississippi, an autobiographical memoir in the shape of a historical walk through Mississippi and Faulkner family history.

The fourth project was a television script based on his story "Weekend Revisited," which became "Mr. Acarius" after its rejection by three magazines.* As he told Else at the end of March, he was now writing television scripts since the key to his future was the acquisition of money. He also needed money for his medical expenses, which skyrocketed with repeated hospitalizations. He revealed that a doctor told him a part of his brain was

---

*Besides the *New Yorker, Collier's* and *Esquire* rejected it. It is noteworthy that the *Post,* which had earlier rejected so many of his better submissions, finally took it. Faulkner had surely misread Lillian Ross's interest in it and him when he had Ober submit it to William Shawn on her recommendation. Ross's parodic "interview" with Faulkner indicated she was looking for "angles," not for serious moments.

hypersensitive to alcohol, and recommended that he stop drinking for three or four months and be retested. But the doctor did not forbid him alcohol, a fuzzy diagnosis. The doctor said the brain was still normal, but near the borderline of abnormality. Faulkner said he already knew that from his strange behavior. He told his friend all this straightforwardly, but he knew something serious was occurring—he told Malcolm that if anything drastic happened to him Saxe Commins would not lie about it.

The recognition was growing slowly that at fifty-five he had started a downward spiral which could not be turned around. The story he wrote, "Weekend Revisited," has unpleasant reverberations in his own life, since its outlines are clearly autobiographical, however twisted the finale. It is a "snake pit" experience, based, as Blotner surmises, on Charles Jackson's *The Lost Weekend,* but founded even more intensely on his own needs as an alcoholic.

"Mr. Acarius" demonstrates that Faulkner was wise to discontinue the writing of short fiction. The prose is weak, the shaping of scene flabby, the reverberations of the piece except for the personal element are thin. If anyone else had signed it, it would not have been a publishable story. In its ultimate publication, the *Saturday Evening Post* was cashing in on a hallowed name. The tone of the story is all wrong. Mr. Acarius is trying to fathom nuclear destruction and planning to drink himself into oblivion so that he can plumb human suffering. After making all arrangements for a sanitarium stay, he drinks until he must be hospitalized; once ensconced in a room, he hopes to experience a wide range of despair, a personal sense of the bomb. Before going in, he and his doctor have an exchange on marriage in vintage-Faulkner terms. Acarius says he wants to experience the human race, and his doctor tells him to find a mistress. The former says that doesn't work, what he wants is debasement. The doctor, accordingly, suggests marriage. "What better way than that to run the whole gamut from garret to cellar and back again, not just once, but over again every day."[3]

Acarius chooses drink. Once in the sanitarium, he finds a festival atmosphere. Having entered to seek suffering, he finds men planning only how to get hold of liquor. While Acarius is trying to figure out the role of someone like himself, "another cypher in the abacus of mankind," the other men scramble for bottles, all attempting to outwit the staff. Acarius's serious ideas run into farce. When he finally gets out, he destroys all the liquor in his cabinet. The story ends with his smashing bottle after bottle against the bathtub.

The story is a curious document, since it so clearly tries to say something about Faulkner's own condition—but then when it comes close, he distances himself with farcical behavior. The story shows a divisive ambiguity in the writer's relationship to his own condition, an ambiguity reinforced by the uncertainty of tone. Acarius apparently wants to reveal all about himself, and tries to level with the doctor; but the more he attempts to enter into his condition, the more the author of the story distances himself from any revelation. Character and author pull against each other. Acarius hopes to open up, to gain understanding of his situation, whereas Faulkner is concerned with disguising. The destruction of the liquor at the end is not a resolution, since what led Acarius into his original choice has not been addressed. Faulkner here splits himself and evades. Part of the evasion, however, is the uncertainty of his artistry as much as it is the ambiguity of his self-revelation. It is compelling in a sad respect because it illuminates Faulkner's own retreat from illumination.

Faulkner's career in television has not received much attention. Although he was active in only two adaptations and one original script, ten others adapted from his work appeared on the screen. In March he wrote "The Brooch" for broadcast on April 2 on Lux Video Theatre. On February 11 of the following year, "Shall Not Perish" was telecast on CBS Video Theatre. Both were adaptations of his own stories. "The Graduation Dress" was telecast on October 30, 1960, the result of a collaboration with Joan Williams, and was an original work. His work adapted by others includes "Smoke" (Gore Vidal as adaptor); "Barn Burning" (Vidal); "An Error in Chemistry"; "Wild Stallion" (adapted from "Knight's Gambit"); *The Sound and the Fury* (Frank W. Durkee, Jr.); *As I Lay Dying* (John McGiffert); "Ad Astra"; "The Tall Men"; "Old Man" (Horton Foote); and "Tomorrow" (Foote). The productions were often lavish and the casts included many famous Broadway and Hollywood stars: Paul Henreid, Franchot Tone, Mary Astor, Evelyn Keyes, Mildred Dunnock, E. G. Marshall, Pat Hingle, Edmund O'Brien, Ethel Waters, Lillian Gish, Sterling Hayden, Geraldine Page, Richard Boone, Kim Stanley, and Charles Bickford. While the adaptations made by others were sources of easy money, the fact that Faulkner would bring himself to work on two of his own in 1953 and 1954 indicates how he saw income as a means of escaping his old life.

February and March of 1953 were filled with projects, but they were also times of continued medical attention. He underwent examinations, and he also sank back into heavy drinking, which required the ministrations of Commins; yet as soon as he felt better, he started up again and had to be admitted to Doctors Hospital. Further tests, X-ray and electroencephalogram (for any brain damage), proved negative, as did a test of his liver. It was after this series of tests that he told Else the doctor thought he should abstain for three or four months and then retest. His back was still troubling him—he suffered from arthritis—but was otherwise mended. A psychiatrist was called in, although this avenue of treatment was doomed to failure. Dr. S. Bernard Wortis of the New York University medical school started to probe, and the area he went for almost immediately was the pattern of infantile regression which Faulkner revealed in his binging. Dr. Wortis focused on his relationship to Maud, and hypothesized he had not received sufficient love from her. This fact, according to Wortis, made Faulkner particularly sensitive to others' problems and as a consequence of this sensitivity he drank heavily to narcotize himself.

The psychiatric intervention was doomed for other reasons. Although he was modest and least given to boasting or vaunting his achievements, Faulkner had the self-absorption of a man who had spent untold hours picking away at his own imagination. That withdrawn quality we have noted so frequently was part of the self-absorption, and any intrusion into his private world threw him off balance. Further, as a drinker, he was a loner, not a man who sought parties or bars to raise his elbow with the boys. His preferred binge was to stock up on bourbon or whiskey in a hotel room, and there drink himself into oblivion. This is the depressive's true journey toward death. Withal, the pattern was not one that a psychiatrist could penetrate in a few sessions with an uncommunicative patient who disbelieved in the practice anyway. Faulkner would later complain bitterly about Wortis's charges, $50 per hour, a standard figure for those days.

Through all this, Faulkner nevertheless wrote. He finished the brief foreword to Anderson's correspondence, which Ober sold to the *Atlantic* for $300. Faulkner described his former mentor as a giant in a land populated by pygmies, although admittedly Anderson was at his peak in only two or three works. It was a just evaluation, with a fondness for memories which had somehow become twisted. Also in March, now living on West Sixteenth Street, he finished the *Holiday* piece on Mississippi—one of his most compelling pieces of prose. This piece uses something of the dramatic method employed in *Requiem,* which was still very much in his mind. The opening pages were taken up with background history, which then passed into personal history of the Falkner clan, with large roles assigned to servants Mammy Callie and Ned. He also covered contemporary issues, including justice to Negroes and the hideousness of lynching; then he moved into his feelings as a native, loving the state, the place, even while hating some of it—an updated Quentin Compson.

As part of this surge of writing—all of which proved distraction from the still incomplete *Fable*—Faulkner began to sketch out his own television adaptation of the "Old Man" segment of *The Wild Palms.* He had a long synopsis and was moving toward a working script, when he suddenly had to stop. On April 18 Estelle hemorrhaged, and both he and Jill rushed to Oxford. Estelle was close to death, needing steady transfusions of blood to carry her through, possibly from an ulcer which suddenly became acute. A team of doctors was working over her at Oxford Hospital. Faulkner was uncertain now about his plans because even after she was out of danger he couldn't tell if she could be left. Two days later, he told Commins things were looking better as she was able to take food. The plan was to keep her at home until she built up sufficient strength to undertake the trip to Memphis, where medical facilities were more sophisticated. Although Estelle had surely not planned to bring herself close to death, she had found a way of bringing Faulkner home. She also made him dependent on her recovery, making herself the center of a faltering household and even bringing Jill home from college only two months before her graduation.

By April 29, with Estelle still recovering in Oxford, Faulkner wrote Joan a revealing letter, in which a superbly talented author looks back into memory and recognizes what an extraordinary journey he has taken.

I know now—believe now—that this may be the last major, ambitious work; there will be short things, of course. I know now that I am getting toward the end, the bottom of the barrel. The stuff is still good, but I know now there is not very much more of it, a little trash comes up constantly now, which must be sifted out. . . . And now I realise for the first time what an amazing gift I had: uneducated in every formal sense, without even very literate, let alone literary, companions, yet to have made the things I made. I don't know where it came from. I don't know why God or gods or whoever it was, selected me to be the vessel.[4]

He was, as he often commented, an empty vessel which his "amazing gift" filled; and now with the vessel full, he was unsure of himself. *A Fable* would be the test of what was still left.

Estelle having been tested and found to be recovering, Faulkner left for New York on May 9, sharing Harrison Smith's apartment for the time being. He announced he was writing a full-length motion picture for the actress Julie Harris, based on one of his books, although nothing came of the project. He also saw Joan again as their affair was winding down. Faulkner attended a Dylan Thomas reading at the East Side YMHA, and the two met afterward. Thomas admired Faulkner, and the latter had found the reading compelling. But in the din of two such celebrities meeting, there was almost no interchange. Thomas wanted another meeting, but in a short time he was dead from acute alcoholism. Shortly afterward, Faulkner returned to Oxford; then in early June he and Estelle left to attend Jill's graduation, where Faulkner was the featured speaker. His talk later appeared in the *Atlantic* (August) as "Faith or Fear."

His speech was cloned from his address at the Cotton Council in the Delta, emphasizing the need for individuality, free will, and man's capacity for decision. Whatever peace and security were attainable could be achieved only through individual acts, not through group or state action. He deplored mass mentality, comparing it to a drove of sheep. The heuristic function was clear: to tell the graduating class its destiny was Jeffersonian, not Hamiltonian. The enemy, implicitly, was the state and its welfare programs, which turned people into wards; salvation lay in individual initiative, even with all the attendant mistakes. In a related point, he perceived the role of the artist as revealing those aspects of life—love, fidelity, respect—which somehow carried out God's plan. There was a pattern to existence which the writer, the artist, could reveal; the artist, as though a French existentialist, reminds man he is capable of revolt and change. Faulkner attacked racism as a narrow view of life, saying it had to be superseded if man was to complete his job. It was, in all, a splendid piece of rhetoric for a graduating class of young people, despite its sermonistic quality. Faulkner unfortunately could not quite draw the line between these forcefully stated sentiments in recent talks and his attitude toward fiction; the latter was becoming enclosed by the former. The *Atlantic* took the graduation talk for $250.

Faulkner's address was on June 8. Jill had done well: valedictorian of her class, president of the student body, an attractive and intelligent young woman just approaching twenty. It was a fine personal moment, and one of the few Faulkner could be proud of: his daughter stood for everything parents hoped for and his address was well received. But there were memories in Jill no achievement could erase; and it was these memories which led her away from Oxford and made her resistant to returning home to the fights, the drinking, the incoherence of the household. Within less than a year, she expressed the wish to marry.

It was back to Oxford for the Faulkners. He wrote a cautionary letter to Joan, warning her not to be afraid of anything, certainly not to be fearful about money. "That is death to an artist."[5] There were successive letters, on June 18 and July 3, mainly about the craft of fiction. Even as he wrote her about writing, he was himself writing, so that his advice, while somewhat reductive, was nevertheless advice to himself as he moved along on *A Fable.* He speaks of how she has not maintained a consistent point of view, so that her fiction "tells" what should be dramatized. He feels she has not done her best work, is capable of more:

> Where you didn't work hard enough was in using the time I was with you to learn from me the best point of view to approach a story from, to milk it dry. Not style: I dont want you to learn my style anymore than you want to, nor do I want to help you with criticism forever anymore than you want me to. I just want you to learn, in the simplest and quickest way, to save yourself from the nervous wear and tear and emotional exhaustion of doing work that is not quite right, how to approach a story to tell it in the manner that will be closest to right that you can do.[6]

He tells her he learned from other writers and she should do the same. But her problem is quite different from Faulkner's because she feels her stories are no longer hers after he has worked them over—that not only is she learning, she is being overwritten by him. Putting down a story on paper, he repeats, is a craft; what she can do if she feels too heavily indebted to his revisions is to destroy that story and use the learning process on another. He compares the craft of writing to the craft of carpentry, where each learns by doing. The analogy, however, makes little sense, since carpentry creates tangible and measurable results; writing remains subjective, personal, sensitive to whim. He keeps up the pressure on her, in helping her with her first novel. He tells her to show it to Ober, to see if it is salable as it is.

In a subsequent letter (July 3), he mentioned that he was working at the big book, but, as expected, it ran dry after only two days. He kept at it, nevertheless, though the result was not good and he destroyed every night what he had written that day: "very bad two weeks." He was pursuing *A Fable*, but unlike the old days, he could not easily find the right rhetoric; as so often happens with "language writers," including Hemingway, he had lost his way with words. He finds his work lacking the resonances and reverberations his earlier prose had gloried in. But he keeps at Joan, especially concerning point of view: "The story is there, but it is told too gently."[7] Although he was advising her on angle of attack and tone, his own problem was language. Her story, he repeated, was not coming through because she has not established the terms in which it could be "seen."

Although there is no mention of domestic problems in his letters, Faulkner was eager to get away. Estelle told the Comminses that while she puttered around the house, putting up jellies, etc., Faulkner was working hard; but both she and Jill will be "relieved and glad when he decides to 'take off' again." She says people have been sending in malicious letters telling her about her husband's activities "that could be disturbing."[8] But she says she is keeping a stiff upper lip. She is correct, of course, in her assessment, for Faulkner was planning his next escape. It came from an unforeseen source, Howard Hawks. On July 10, the director telephoned him from Paris to say he, along with Gary Cooper, had a movie project that they wanted Faulkner to write for them. This would become *Land of the Pharaohs*. It meant a trip abroad in the near future, and Faulkner's excited response indicates how he wished to be liberated from his domestic situation. The project did not come around for some time, for Cooper needed surgery, but for Faulkner it was a perfect getaway plan. He saw it as a way of traveling with Joan, and in the interim before that scheme worked out, he suggested Mexico. They never made that trip.

The reprinting of Faulkner's books was now an ongoing industry, and New American Library offered to reissue in paper *Sanctuary* and *Requiem* in one volume, *The Wild Palms* and "Old Man" in another. The rub was that for the latter volume, NAL did not want the interleaving of stories, but each one intact, with *The Wild Palms* followed by "Old Man." After telling Commins, who recommended accepting the deal, that it would destroy the integrity of *The Wild Palms*, Faulkner agreed. He agreed because he did not want any interruption on *A Fable*, whose "Three Temptations" scene he finished the following day, on August 4. As he tells his editor and friend, "It is either nothing and I am blind in my dotage, or it is the best of my time. Damn it, I did have genius, Saxe. It just took me 55 years to find it out."[9] He promises the manuscript in the near future, about seven hundred typed pages. The "three temptations," closely paralleling the scene in the life of Jesus, is extremely important to the novel, and is one of Faulkner's most compelling segments. It is structured quite closely not only on the New Testament story, but on the Grand Inquisitor scene in Dostoyevsky's *The Brothers Karamazov.* The general, who represents Lucifer, offers the Jesus-like corporal his life, his freedom, and the earth, all of which the corporal must resist. While the scene is effective, it is also moralistic, full of Nobel Prize sentiments and lacking the brutal irony which makes the Dostoyevsky scene so morally devastating.

Random House had other plans as well, the aforementioned *Faulkner Reader,* an anthology consisting of entire works, long and short, as well as excerpts. It was Random House's answer to the Viking *Portable,* but a less shaped and directed anthology than Cowley's. It had little of the latter's use of Faulkner as an integrated author—but by now times had changed. Cowley published his book when the writer was neglected; now Faulkner was salable and Random House wanted to cash in, considering how much money it had advanced on *A Fable.* The *Reader* was to contain the entire *Sound,* plus the long pieces "The Bear," "Old Man," and "Spotted Horses." There were also eight stories from *Collected Stories,* and selections from *Light in August, The Unvanquished,* and *Requiem for a Nun,* along with the "Nobel Prize Acceptance Speech." An elegant volume, it turned out to be well suited for the college and university courses in Faulkner which were being developed across the country.* Faulkner wrote the foreword in November, and the book was published on April 1, 1954.

Meanwhile, he asked Commins for $10,000—$2,500 to invest in a business, but also funds to give Estelle and Jill. His daughter planned to enroll in the University of Mexico for the fall semester, and Estelle was accompanying her as duenna. There is in his alacrity to let his wife draw on his account the desire to have Rowan Oak for himself. He would then have a clear run at *A Fable,* and also enjoy his personal freedom. Yet all was not well, even after his wife and daughter left on August 25. Joan was away, and an even bigger blow came in Saxe Commins's suffering a heart attack. Faulkner had turned Commins into brother, father, confessor, resident psychiatrist; and now he telegraphed, with his own form of irony: "Glad to hear it. Begged you last spring to rest and let joint explode. Maybe you will now. Love to Dorothy."[10] This attack was unfortunate not only for Commins, of course, but for Faulkner, who now found himself with a monstrously complicated book, on which he had worked almost a decade, and no editor.

The consequences were clear, as the spiral of depression returned, abetted by several factors. The near completion of *A Fable* removed one of the supports from his life; he had counted on it even when he could not bring himself to work on it. Estelle was away—for the first time, *she* had escaped; and however tense their married life, there was linkage that seemed necessary for both. On a lessening scale, Joan was pulling away from him. Public figure and international celebrity though he was, he could not gather her in; she resisted his age, his influence, his mere presence. She felt trapped in the hands of a man much stronger than she, a figure whose fame made

*In a further effort to capture the college market, Random House reissued in 1958 a small book of novellas called *Three Famous Short Novels* ("Spotted Horses," "The Bear," "Old Man").

her defer to his wishes. Blotner reports that Faulkner wrote her a letter full of self-humiliation, in which he abases himself before her youth, displaying his fear she will throw him over for a young man:

One of the nicest conveniences a woman can have is someone she can pick up when she needs or wants him; then when she doesn't, she can drop him and know that he will still be right there when she does need or want him again. Only she should remember this. Sometimes when she drops him, he might break. Sometimes, when she reaches down for him, he might not be there.[11]

Yet in his need for someone, preferably young, he was not being completely fair. He knew she leaned on him for advice and influence with the New York publishing world, and he was himself carrying on a discreet liaison with Else Jonsson. Also, as it turned out, she could be replaced by other attractive, bright young women, as he found when he met Jean Stein. While he speaks here of his feelings and abases himself, he neglects to recognize that he "used" her, not badly, but not always well. At the moment, each meant a great deal in the life of the other, but for such different reasons that the affair was doomed.

Everything Faulkner did had a legendary dimension. The record of the corporal's Passion Week which he had sketched out on his office walls at Rowan Oak became the source of interest, for example. The calendar was photographed: each day, with its notations beneath, last supper, execution, burial—the pattern established by the Passion of Jesus Christ. The record still remains on Faulkner's walls and has in itself become a tourist attraction. Yet even as he moved toward final shaping of the novel, he went back on his old anodyne of alcohol and Seconal, ostensibly to relieve his back pain, but equally to contain his depression. Depression now was acute and did not appear to depend on any particular event. In the midst of what seemed happy occasions, meetings with friends (as now with Ben Wasson) or plaudits from the world at large, the depression was there. He needed treatment, and through the auspices of Malcolm and his wife he ended up again in the Gartly-Ramsay Hospital in Memphis.

The usual treatment ensued, including Paraldehyde, which as an anticonvulsant allayed the delirium tremens. Faulkner thought the Paraldehyde would wean him from alcohol, but it really did not function that way. It settled him. His back, also, was bothering him, as well it should have, given the nature of what the X-rays revealed. And he suffered abdominal pain, an incipient ulcer perhaps, or the beginning of an inflamed liver. Yet within two days he got himself together and skipped from the hospital, forgoing the recuperative period. What he needed was an extensive rest, relief from the acute phase of his binging, and then release. A good pickup followed shortly—another call from Howard Hawks, saying plans for *Land of the Pharaohs* were going ahead, and he wanted Faulkner in the fall, which meant an extended stay in Egypt. He jumped at the idea.

Then on September 28, Robert Coughlan's long essay in *Life* appeared: "The Private World of William Faulkner," followed on October 5 by "The Man behind the Faulkner Myth." Even the headings were sufficient to turn Faulkner's stomach, since they catered to gossip: "private" and "man behind." The two articles were obviously full of veneration; but they also said things which disturbed not only the Faulkner family but even Mullen. The latter assured Faulkner he had not supplied the personal details. Phil Stone wrote Coughlan that the first article has the town stewing, and that he looks for "a terrific feud in the Faulkner family because they surely can't blame those family photographs on me."[12] The effect was as Stone thought. Coughlan had struck everyone's nerves. He said that Faulkner, because he had created books which belong to America, does not belong entirely to himself. He went into the writer's drinking, calling him not an alcoholic but "an alcoholic refugee." As Blotner says, Coughlan actually toned down some of the things he had heard, not the least from Phil Stone. Stone bad-mouthed his friend on grounds of poor grammar, having a turncoat temperament, and tastelessness, a constant in Stone criticism. The latter thought that because Faulkner could not write with precision, he devised strategies and subterfuges to disguise his inability.

Just after the second segment appeared, Faulkner wrote Mullen, telling him his mother had canceled her subscription in a fury. "What a commentary, Sweden gave me the Nobel Prize. France gave me the Legion d'Honneur. All my native land did for me was to invade my privacy over my protest and my plea. No wonder people in the rest of the world dont like us, since we seem to have neither taste nor courtesy, and know and believe in nothing but money and it doesn't much matter how you get it."[13] He was particularly upset that Maud Falkner's photo was used when she had specifically requested no photo be printed. *Life* dragged out a photo of her from 1941, when a crew had come to Oxford to interview John Falkner.* Yet the Coughlan article did catch one thing well, despite historical and biographical errors. He described Faulkner accurately, capturing that mixture of easy manner with self-possession, which made him "courteous, speculative, and deadly." With his pipe at his lips, a drink in his hand, "he is like a somnolent cat who still in the wink of an eye could kill a mouse." He adds: "He acts like a farmer who had studied Plato and looks like a river gambler."[14] He describes the face as evidencing "melancholy, calculation and humor" variously reflected. What Coughlan misses entirely is the presence of demons. Since *Life* was a family magazine, he perhaps did not

---

*Just before he wrote this letter and the second *Life* segment appeared, Faulkner was in Byhalia, not sight-seeing but hospitalized in Wright's sanitarium for that cycle of depression and binging which had also brought his father to Byhalia. The ironies are all present: as *Life* was splashing his biography and photos all over America, the subject had withdrawn as far as he could go, into a sanitarium bed while he fought against delirium tremens, malnourishment, and alcohol poisoning.

look too deeply, for fear of what he would discover; and surely he did not want to probe the etiology of the near-alcoholism he mentions. Coughlan catches the certainties but misses the uncertainties, the suicidal impulses, the wish for oblivion.

Once again in the background of Faulkner's life, the articles proved exciting for Stone. He was now gaining considerable publicity as the man behind the great figure and as the impeccable source for Faulkneriana. What the critics failed to comprehend was Stone's peculiar slant, his mis-judgments of Faulkner's work, and the hostilities which underlay nearly every assessment. Stone wrote often to Coughlan, repeating that the arti-cles had everyone in a boil; then again, that nearly all of Oxford's grand ladies think his articles are fair and accurate. One point is both amusing and instructive. The second segment was called "The Man Behind the Faulkner Myth," and Stone says many people[15] in Oxford think Coughlan was referring to him, not Faulkner. To the editors of *Life,* Stone offers a correction about his own family, the name of the grandfather who rode with General Forrest. In other ways, Stone was helpful, getting Estelle out of a scrape with the Mississippi Department of Public Safety after she had her driver's license revoked for not reporting an accident she was in. But overall, Stone was less Faulkner's lawyer than he was the writer's historian and, in some personal way, conscience.

While all this was brewing, and Oxford was assessing and reassessing its most famous native son, Faulkner was driving with Joan to New York. His letters from mid-October on seem more excited, especially as he saw the end of *A Fable.* Although he had predicted and even announced the end on several occasions, he still had work to do on the novel. He rented an apartment suite at One Fifth Avenue off Washington Square and New York University, around the corner from where Henry James had lived. He saw Joan a good deal, and was drinking moderately. Publicity hounds like Earl Wilson, who wrote a famous column, pursued him, all the more eager to draw him from his lair because of his reputation for elusiveness. The Hawks deal was still pending, and Faulkner, while definitely inter-ested in joining his old friend and benefactor, wanted to complete the novel first. Also, the Book-of-the-Month Club had chosen *The Faulkner Reader* as its main selection, which made Faulkner eager to do a good job of editing. On October 17, when he wrote Malcolm, he seemed to have a sequence of activities: stay in New York until December 1 to finish the book and edit it with Commins; edit the *Reader;* and then on the first leave for Paris to work with Hawks. He expected to be finished by February 1. As he wrote his mother, the offer of $15,000 and expenses was too good to reject.*

---

*Coughlan got to meet Faulkner while the latter was in New York, and to discuss with him his two articles, which Faulkner insisted he had not read. The latter did show interest in Coughlan doing a book, and even agreed to take such a manuscript with him when he left, although he never spoke to Coughlan about it again. A particularly volatile situation had been resolved by Faulkner remaining neutral and letting Coughlan talk himself out.

As the novel wound down, Commins, recovering at home, conveyed some of his excitement to Klopfer: "With this letter Bill is bringing the final, complete, ready-for-the-printer manuscript of *A Fable*. Both of us feel, in the excitement and lift of working so steadily and to such wonderful purpose, that the script is as near perfection as we can make it. . . . I don't have to tell you how I feel about it as a work of art."[16] Haas had just before that (October 26) commented to Commins that he thought Faulkner's new book was "simply tremendous. To my mind it's one of the greatest novels that I've ever read, and I use the word 'greatest' advisedly."[17] Haas goes on to say he finds some passages obscure, that the structures and sequences are sometimes more difficult to follow than seems necessary, and the horse segment is too long. Klopfer wrote to Commins (October 30) that the book is "great." He indicates Faulkner has agreed to provide a two-page summary of what he was trying to do, something to clarify story line, symbolism, meaning of characters, and related items. There was clearly among all the kudos some concern about the darker, obfuscating portions of the novel which appeared to resist even intelligent readings.

Meanwhile, Faulkner worked with Commins on providing a final copy. The book needed a coherent sequencing of events, which meant bringing in passages from many parts of the long manuscript and finding the right location for them. The sorting out had to be done by page and number, but the passage also had to find its right slot; a long manuscript, which could have used computerization, had to be taken apart and then put together again.* When some order was achieved, Commins told Klopfer in the same November 5 letter that the appearance of the novel had to be very carefully planned. These arrangements were worked out fully with Faulkner, and it is significant that the writer took such interest in the book's appearance, as though it were his monument. The presence of a cross on the front jacket, one on the back, but none on the spine suggests a burial place not only for Jesus but for Faulkner. If anything, the jacket replicates the idea of a funeral setting; and the cover itself repeats this motif, with three crosses, one top, one bottom, one to the right. Faulkner also stipulated how acknowledgments should appear: to William Bacher and Henry Hathaway of Beverly Hills, California, to James Street, author of *Look Away*, and to Ben Wasson and Hodding Carter, publishers of the original version of the story of the stolen racehorse; as well as dedication: "To My Daughter, Jill." Commins comments:

*The process may superficially recall what Maxwell Perkins and then, later, Edward C. Aswell did with the Thomas Wolfe manuscripts. But Perkins performed a line-by-line editing and Aswell actually did rewriting as well as rearranging, which was hardly the case with Commins and Faulkner. Nevertheless, the "final" *Fable* is, as the Alderman Library holograph, ribbon typescript, carbon typescript, and interlineated separate typescript leaves indicate, a somewhat arbitrary affair. That is, material excluded as well as included could have been revised further, since so much lies in revisions, shifting around, loose pieces of paper, texts written on pages belonging to other manuscripts. The sorting of *Fable* texts awaits the hand of a magician. Even the now-famous plotting of the novel on the walls at Rowan Oak may have had another version.

This is terribly important. We must avoid the use of denomina-
tional crosses and want simple, the simpler the better, wooden crosses
throughout. Where the crosses appear at the opening of each of the
ten parts, they must be quite large and so placed as to give the opening
chapter page a great deal of sinkage. Where we indicate three little
crosses to make a lapse of time or change of scene we want the crosses
to be no larger than the upper case of the regular type measure used
for text, no larger than an ordinary asterisk.[18]

The final version came out this way.

It was done: the composition of *A Fable* was noted as from "December
1944 Oxford to New York Princeton November 1953." If we count the time
when the idea first came to Faulkner, the span was closer to a decade. The
book memorialized almost one-fifth of Faulkner's life, and if we count only
his writing life, almost one-third of that. Inevitably, he was cheerless and
depressed. During this general period of recovery from the intense, long
haul, he wrote the foreword to *The Faulkner Reader,* and there he attempted
to find reasons for man holding on, not succumbing. Even as he felt himself
going under, he grabbed Henryk Sinkiewicz for support, the Polish novelist who had also meant a good deal to Conrad, and whose twin affirmations
he had drawn upon in his Nobel Prize address. The import of the foreword
was to say no to death; as if the novel just completed were indeed a form
of death, replete with burial crosses. The letdown for Faulkner was more
than that cyclical turning on and off which occurs when a writer completes
a book. It went far deeper, into a novel which recapitulated his feelings
about the war whose tag end he had caught, and which recapped his
attitudes toward morality, justice, corruption, and deception.

But even deeper than this was his growing fear he might have lost it all;
that even if he believed in this, he was finished for the future. He saw Joan
drifting away; Dylan Thomas died suddenly, on November 9, from complications derived from alcohol poisoning; and he became aware of his age,
his distance from the generation of Jill, and of Joan, as she moved toward
men closer to her own age. Blotner mentions Faulkner quoting from
Housman, lines of Poem XLVIII from *A Shropshire Lad,* to the effect the
poet ponders "When shall I sleep again?" The affirmative talk in his public
speeches and letters only underscores his pessimism, his need for verbal
props. The demons were always at work, and even as he fancied himself
free of Rowan Oak and liberated from the novel, he was nervous and
anxiety-ridden, without any clear focus. His self-absorption was almost a
form of autism. At the Comminses, he met Einstein and his sister, but had
nothing to say to the physicist, himself a shy man. They seemed to like each
other without exchanging more than pleasantries. He was withdrawing so
deeply into himself only a radical change of scenery could pull him out,
or else his fate was alcoholic oblivion.

Living on the edge of his nerves, he moved beyond any rational assessment of what bothered him into his own kind of shadowed area. He used

Joan as a prop on which to hang his fears, and she was smart to withdraw from what he tried to make a Laocoön embrace. On November 27, as the liaison was winding down, he wrote her that the people she knows are sophomores, irresponsible parasites. "They go through the motions of art —talking about what they are going to do over drinks, even defacing paper and canvas when necessary, in order to escape the responsibility of living."[19] There is a note of Svengali in this, as his fear of losing her to some young man makes him use art as a means of making her feel guilty. It was an argument which made little rational sense, inasmuch as she was not an artist of his order, nor did she seem prepared to martyr herself. Uncertain about his own direction, and with Jill outside his realm, he tried to make and remake her, even using Random House as an agent when he was away.

On November 30, he flew to join Hawks. Now fifty-six, he was embarking, this year and afterward, on a series of journeys which kept him busy, which he seemed to enjoy, and which papered over his depression. He arrived on December 1 in Geneva, while Hawks and his friend, the photographer Robert Capa, waited for Faulkner at Orly outside Paris. It was a comedy of errors, perhaps not surprising Hawks, who recalled how he had covered up for the writer in Hollywood. Faulkner set out by train for Paris; by the time he was brought together with Hawks he was dead drunk, his head gashed, and accompanied by two sympathetic policemen who had noticed the Legion of Honor emblem in his buttonhole. Otherwise, he would have gone into the slammer as a common drunk. Thus Hawks saw his writer. It was like old times.

In the background, there was movement on *Requiem for a Nun*. Camus, a fervent Faulkner admirer, had asked for permission to adapt the play for the French stage. Faulkner liked the idea, but referred all queries to Ford, to whom he remained loyal. On December 4, he and Hawks were settled into Stresa, on the Italian side of Lake Maggiore and overlooking some of the most spectacular scenery in Europe. They stayed, Faulkner bragged to his mother,[20] in a "palace" belonging to an Egyptian millionaire, with three servants to help them. "Elegant" was his comment. Hawks was a good influence, and Faulkner began to work on a story outline with the director and the veteran screenwriter, Harry Kurnitz. The plan was to spend about two weeks in Stresa, then move on to St. Moritz; Hawks promised Faulkner a piece of *Pharaohs*, which he estimated at about $60,000, as well as a share in two more films to be made in Egypt, one on Solomon, the other on Ruth. Faulkner revealed a certain excitement at the prospect of being rich at last. When he arrived at St. Moritz, where he stayed at the Suvretta House, he wrote Maud that the place was chock-full of famous people, including Farouk of Egypt (not for long!) and Gregory Peck.

He did not mention to his mother that he had met an attractive, bright, and very rich young American woman named Jean Stein shortly after arriving in St. Moritz. He also went ahead with plans to spend Christmas in Stockholm with Else. He may have grieved over Joan—and he continued to write to her during this jaunt—but he was not inactive. He also could not fail to contrast his stay in northern Italy and Switzerland with his journey through almost thirty years before. Then, in youthful poverty, but with everything opening up before him, he had enjoyed northern Italy but disliked the bandbox of a country, Switzerland. Now he was surrounded by wealth and was himself a great celebrity; in Stockholm, he was sought after by reporters and "gangs of schoolchildren."[21] It was heady stuff, and he appears to have been carried along by it, not fighting people as he had done in the past.

While Faulkner remained Faulkner in most respects, he was slowly becoming more of a public man—enjoying the lifestyle of the rich and famous, being intrigued by the women he could meet in this circumstance,* and getting accustomed to the unsettled quality of life this dictated. One reason he could adjust better to it was that he had completed *A Fable* and was no longer under its massive burden; but also he had few other pressing or burning ideas. There were still several books to come, including the rest of the Snopes trilogy, but the anguish and pain to get these books out seemed less intense. He had begun to accept what he had done, what he was, the ways in which the world responded to him. He returned to St. Moritz until New Year's Day, and then flew to London and traveled down to Kent. By January 6, he was back at the Suvretta House, having spent the holiday almost exactly like the rich and famous.

The year 1954 might seem to be the fulfillment of everything a writer dreams of. At fifty-six, Faulkner appeared to have it all in his grasp. With the Nobel Prize and celebrity, he moved in circles that were exciting, intelligent, and luxurious; he had worked out a liaison with Jean in St. Moritz and Paris, and he was still on very friendly terms with Else in Stockholm. He was comfortably distant from Estelle, Jill seemed ready to make her own plunge into life, and with the prospect of considerable income he did not have any serious money problems. On April 1, *The Faulkner Reader* appeared, the anthology being of the kind only a great writer sees during his lifetime. Also in April, his long piece on Mississippi appeared in *Holiday,* and he knew he had done a solid piece of writing there. With *A Fable* being prepared for publication in early August, he was still full of it and told Commins he intended a small revision. *A Fable* was published on August 2, and with the reception admiring and respectful, he received the National Book Award for it in 1955. The State Department invited him to São Paulo, Brazil, to attend an international writers' conference in August, and he accepted. He saw his daughter married on August 21 to Paul D. Summers, Jr., then in the army, a West Point graduate. He

---

*For example, Jean Stein, whom Faulkner met at a Christmas Eve party, was the daughter of Jules Stein, founder of the Music Corporation of America. Now nineteen, Stein had been in part educated abroad, was accustomed to a lavish lifestyle, and knew her way around places like St. Moritz. Shy, intelligent, admiring of Faulkner, she was more than willing to pair off with him.

got together with Jean on and off during the year, although conflicting schedules often kept them apart. He published one short story, "Sepulture South: Gaslight" (*Harper's Bazaar*, December).

In all, it was a time of reaping the rewards of achievement. And yet Faulkner barely managed to get through much of it. He was hospitalized in Paris, and was deeply depressed. He was away from Rowan Oak, and yet missed it. He had a lovely young lady as companion, but still wrote to Joan. He had a mature woman friend in Stockholm, and yet was drawn back to Estelle, with whom he had little but domestic discomfort. He was universally hailed, and still felt only doubts, the awareness that he was winding down as a writer. He was vigorous, and yet felt himself aging. He was caught in the usual spiral of coping with life at one level while fighting off his self-destructive impulses on another. He depended deeply on friends coming to his support when he became helpless; and he managed to become helpless frequently enough so that he needed the friends to survive. There was, to the observer, one Faulkner, but to those close to him, another Faulkner, with little chance the dueling halves would ever resolve their struggle.*

After a short stay with an English admirer, Harold Raymond, at his Kent home, Faulkner returned to St. Moritz and Jean Stein for the remainder of the Christmas (1953) holiday season. He even managed to fit in some work—he went over *Fable* galleys and he signed five hundred sheets of *The Faulkner Reader* for the limited edition. But he was wistful about his old life, and fearful his insides were disturbed. They were finally rebelling against the alcohol he had been pouring in for thirty-five years. He made a brief trip to Paris, accompanied, apparently, by Jean, where he saw his young friends Monique and Jean-Jacques Salomon. Then he headed out on January 19 for Rome, to stay at the Ambassador on the Via Veneto.

The glamorous existence continued in full force, as he reencountered Humphrey Bogart and Lauren Bacall; but he was drinking, most of the time alone, not socially. He wrote Joan, saying he was enjoying Rome, and he followed Hemingway's latest page-one episode: his near-fatal crashes in

---

*There is always the possibility (probability) Faulkner was distressed at his sexual performance. Meta Carpenter, the only one to comment upon it, indicated that his youthful ardor was gone, and this was to be expected. But now as he sought younger and younger women, he perhaps could not meet his expectations, or felt he did not meet theirs. Brought up in a frontierlike society, Faulkner would have seen any breakdown in his sexuality as a loss of manhood. The drinking, as with Hemingway, disguised a good deal, including the fact that if he were drunk, little sexuality could be expected of him; but there was also the reciprocal effect—the more he drank, the more his sexual performance was lessened. As we survey the "big three" of American fiction, Faulkner, Fitzgerald, and Hemingway, we see a similar pattern: the need to present a masculine façade, undercut by compulsive drinking which made sexual performance weak or impossible. Fitzgerald in the eyes of others enjoyed a dubious masculinity, and his drinking was one way to prove what a man he was. Hemingway was constantly testing himself as a man, and while there seem no homosexual experiences, he felt a psychological need to prove himself that was excessive. Faulkner was not quite the same, but his frontierlike childhood, the presence of a beefy paternal figure, the need to compensate for his having taken up a less than masculine pursuit like writing—all of this required overcompensation, and drinking fulfilled that. But it also probably undercut his bedroom athletics.

two planes in Africa. Faulkner was amused and, according to Blotner, told Jean his literary colleague really wanted to die by a bull-goring. It was a remark made in persiflage, but with a good deal of hostility behind it. Meanwhile, as he moved from one elegant place in Switzerland to another, then to Paris, Stockholm, and now Rome, family life at Rowan Oak was far more prosaic, and Phil Stone continued to undermine his reputation. At Rowan Oak, Estelle was extremely upset at the illness of her mother; Jill was working as a saleslady in an Oxford dress shop; and Faulkner in two weeks had not sent on any word. With Christmas coming on, Estelle put a good face on spending it alone except for Jill and a young woman from the university. On the Stone front, however, there was little but vitriol. Stone heard that Carvel Collins was putting together a slim volume of Faulkner's early New Orleans sketches, which are now recognized as an important part of the writer's career. Stone thought otherwise, telling Collins: "They are certainly not worth publishing." He then takes credit for having gotten the work for Faulkner, at $5 apiece for the sketches. Then comes the full blast, about Faulkner going to Egypt to soak up atmosphere for the script he was writing. "I don't think it will be necessary for him to go to Egypt in order to write the script because any Faulkner can tell you everything about Egypt even though he has never been there. Strictly between us and completely off the record, I am just about fed up with Bill and as far as I am concerned I don't care if he never comes back."[22]

Still in the background, Faulkner had asked Commins to transfer $2,500 to his account at the First National Bank in Oxford, but *not to notify anyone at Oxford*. Estelle, meanwhile, was being dunned by Levy's department store in Memphis for back bills, a "threat," she called it, and yet she was not authorized to write checks on Faulkner's account. She tells this to Commins, who knows that $2,500 is sitting in the Faulkner account in Oxford. Estelle says she sent on unpaid bills in care of Gallimard in Paris, a "frightening pile" of them,[23] she says. She indicates their allowance is sufficient, but the unpaid bills, which they cannot take care of, go back to 1952.

Before the film crew departed for Cairo on February 11, Faulkner moved ahead on the script. He hated to leave Rome, and he really did not want to go to Egypt, which held no wonders for him. In January he also had to work out arrangements with Chatto & Windus for a one-volume anthology of his work, to be called *Faulkner's County*, consisting of one novel, some short stories, excerpts from longer works, and, of course, the Nobel Prize speech. Another matter arose which demonstrated Faulkner's intense loyalty—a conflict over the motion-picture rights to *A Fable*. Bennett Cerf was afraid William Bacher, who had given Faulkner the basic idea for the novel, would claim them as his rightful property. Once Bacher was acknowledged at the front of the novel, Cerf felt he could move in and stake out his claim. Faulkner said the acknowledgment must remain, that Bacher not only gave him the idea but advanced $1,000 on the project. Then he adds: "But to me, none of this is a binding in any legal sense, nearly as strong as the moral one which I feel and assume and, of course, will defend."[24] He tells Commins to inform Cerf of the agreement, and that a release must come from Bacher himself.

He points out that after ten years of his life spent on the book, he does not want any dust left on his tongue. He says there can be no other way: Bacher, Ober, and Random House all advanced him money, and no one can be cut out from the film side, if that eventuates. "Let it be so that no man alive will be sorry of the book, have any bad taste in the mouth because of it." The solution was out of proportion to the problem, however, since *A Fable* was hardly movie material, although someone might have adapted it as a kind of more complex *Paths of Glory*. Cerf acceded, the acknowledgment remained, and Faulkner's loyalties held fast.

While this was occurring in the foreground of his life, Commins was receiving letters of quite a different order from Estelle. Commins responded to her dunning notices from Levy's in Memphis by informing her he could not pay off the due account without Faulkner's approval. She apologizes for even suggesting this, and says she has saved $200 from household expenses for an immediate payment on the threat. Faulkner, she adds,[25] was fully aware before he left that she and Jill had an account at Levy's; but, we can surmise, as with his earlier advertisement refusing to pay for her debts, he was hesitant to give Estelle her way with money. Estelle also mentions that Jill now had an editorial job with the Oxford *Eagle* and is studying shorthand, history, and conversational French and Spanish at Ole Miss.

But these letters are nothing compared with the two that followed to Commins, the first on February 11, the other misdated February 29, and already referred to as the "letter-opening" episode. In the first, Estelle was preparing a bombshell: nothing less than that she was on the verge of writing Faulkner she was suing him for divorce; that it was the only wise thing to do, for him, for her, and for Jill. Her words sound desperate, for obviously she is still very attached and in love either with him or the idea of him. "Bill has been home very little during the past four years, and a good bit of that time spent here, has been a nightmare of drunkenness— He must be very unhappy—so the only cure I know of is to help him get free—legally—Heaven only knows he has been free in every other sense." She says she and Jill are also *"more at ease"* when he is away. "Since his unfortunate disclosure to Jill about his current affair [with Joan Williams] —she hasn't felt too secure around him—As for me—I'd do anything for peace—and my own sense of *doing the right thing.*"[26] Commins discouraged this course of action, and Estelle indicated she would wait for his further advice.

The second letter involved Estelle's reputed opening of Faulkner's mail, a kind of skirmish in their ongoing war. This was mail from Joan, which Estelle insists she did not open, but which she learned about from Malcolm, who was following his stepfather's request to open such letters and read them aloud on the telephone. The Joan news, however, was old stuff, something Estelle had known about for some time, although she claims not to have known the seriousness of it. Yet ironically, Joan was now in the past, and Faulkner was with another young woman about whom Estelle knew nothing. Commins, the middleman here, would host Faulkner and Jean at the end of the year; and, of course, he knew the full details of his author's liaison with Joan. The conclusion one can draw from all these unfortunate episodes and disclosures is that in some way Faulkner wanted Estelle to know, whether to disturb her or not, or else to make it clear he still had the appetites of a healthy male.

During this period and subsequently, both Estelle and Faulkner unraveled their thoughts and, in some instances, their lives for this man who had become the assigned therapist at the Random House hospital for insulted and injured authors and their wives. March brought both coming at Commins from different sides. Estelle complained[27] that Faulkner's letters since he has been away have numbered only three and have all been about business matters, "just plain statements and instructions." She reads the situation as one in which he is driving her to make a break. "I'd rather not be driven—still it's hard to be completely indifferent and ignore him—I am far from callous—worse luck." If she goes to her lawyer and claims incompatibility as grounds for divorce, she feels foolish doing this after twenty-five years. She attempts to understand Faulkner and Joan, indicating that if she had herself been an aspiring young writer and an elderly celebrity had fallen in love with her, she "would have accepted him the way Joan did." Estelle's perception here is of Joan, not of Faulkner. She ignores his susceptibility, but also in the venting of what are deeply felt emotions without "personal animosity," Estelle cannot know of Joan's struggle to stay free of Faulkner while serving an apprenticeship under this "elderly celebrity." She says she knows Faulkner is in a mess, and she foresees an even worse time for him. She tells Commins her one thought is to get herself, Jill, and her husband "out of a tragic—and in some ways —comic—situation, in as dignified a manner as possible." She emphasizes once more she will follow Commins's advice, and then mentions having seen "Mississippi," which convinces her there are "two Bills. He is so definitely dual I think—Perhaps artists must needs be."

Absorbed in her own problems and her physical condition, Estelle nevertheless reveals a largeness of spirit. In a related letter, she comments on Joan Williams's marriage to Ezra Bowen on March 6. She indicates, however, that Joan's marriage does not change the situation of the immediate family, although she and Jill get along fine without Faulkner's presence— she hears he may go from Egypt to India with Hawks.

From Egypt, where he had been deposited by Hawks and Kurnitz in an ambulance, Faulkner wrote Commins, also commenting on Joan's marriage. But his approach is quite different: she married because she lacked the right stuff to be an artist. "We knew a year ago that her life was not right, she was not demon-driven enough for art, writing to suffice, too much middle-class background staying home, marriage, children. I was not free to marry her, even if I had not been too old [she would have, if he had been free].* So I—we—expected this. This was my trouble last winter 1953: the art should have been enough. But it was not."²⁸ He consoles himself that Joan has informed him herself, although he gets the date (April) wrong, inasmuch as she married in March. The letter has a hungover or still-drunk quality to it; Faulkner had been binging ever since he received the definite news.

But he glides over to his new friend, Jean. "She came to me in St. Moritz almost exactly as Joan did in Oxford. But she has none of the emotional conventional confusion which poor Joan had. This one is so uninhibited that she frightens me a little." He says she was supposed to return to the Sorbonne for school, but remained in St. Moritz to see Faulkner on his return from England for New Year's. Ordered back to Paris by her mother, she accompanied Faulkner to Rome, until once more ordered back to Paris. He expects her to turn up in Cairo. "She is charming, delightful, completely transparent, completely trustful. I will not hurt her for any price. She doesn't want anything of me—only to love me, be in love."²⁹ He ends by saying that except for this the Williams affair would have hurt. The two affairs, however, were completely different in nature. Jean came to Faulkner unencumbered, whereas the affair with Joan was interwoven with Faulkner's Pygmalion-like need to create someone like young Billy out of the writer. The Williams affair brought pastness into present and was, for Faulkner, quite a different level of engagement.

Estelle's final letter to Commins in March is full of social news, including her entertaining Supreme Court Justice Felix Frankfurter, who was lecturing at the Ole Miss law school. In the letter she indicates she has kept in touch with Judge Franklin, her ex-husband, and comments on how Franklin lives near the "gnome," Commins's quaint name for Frankfurter. She ends by expressing pleasure that Faulkner will be away at least until June.³⁰

As for Faulkner, when Hawks and Kurnitz left for Cairo in early March, he stayed on in Italy and then flew to Paris before joining them in Egypt. On March 12 he arrived, but an ambulance stretcher, as noted, had to take him off the plane. He had been drinking since he left Orly Airport, and he needed not a hotel but a hospital. At Cairo's Anglo-American Hospital he recovered slowly, once he could wean himself from hard liquor to beer, but he remained out of sorts, testy, and impatient with himself and others. Kurnitz proved the perfect companion; he admired the writer so much he could forgive the failings. Faulkner passed on material to Kurnitz which was unsuitable, aimed more at Mississippi frontier people than a pharaoh and his aides. After a while, with Kurnitz as shield, he began to feel his way into the material, although he demonstrated little desire for the usual tourist sites, not even for the pyramids. What Faulkner was revealing, even at this late date, was an avoidance of anything—music, historical sites,

*He also proposed to Jean Stein, but however much she admired and respected him, the age difference, for her, was far too great.

museums—which did not fit into his own view or plan. Deprivation, however, did not mean narrowness, but intensity.

On March 22, Jill wrote her father she had met the young man she was going to marry, Paul Dilwyn Summers, Jr., a man about as different from Faulkner as a person could be. Summers was a West Point graduate and a Korean War hero. He had trained with the legendary Eighty-second Airborne Division (the one offering "nuts" at Bastogne in World War II), then fought with the Fortieth Infantry Division in some of the most brutal soldiering of that brutal war, including the famous Pork Chop Hill. Jill met him at Fort Bragg, and, according to Blotner, when she was introduced as the daughter of William Faulkner, Summers asked, "Who's he?" Hearing this, Jill decided, "He's for me."[31] She asked Faulkner to return home. There is little question Jill was eager to marry not only because she had met a young man she liked, but because the domestic situation was one she no longer cared to confront.

Faulkner left Egypt for Paris on March 29, making his way home through a city he had come to find very congenial. Hawks had found he was getting very little of use from Faulkner—that, in fact, the writer needed caring for. There was no problem in stretching the terms of the contract to permit him to leave, even as Nasser began to take over Egyptian political life and make it interesting for foreigners. At the start of his stay in Paris, *The Faulkner Reader* appeared (April 1), and in a short time, Faulkner was in the American Hospital, taken there by Monique Salomon and Else, who had come from Stockholm to see him. Although they hospitalized him as part of his general orders, he was so testy about staying that he demanded to leave after a day. And true to his powers of recuperation, he was back in action by April 12, when he cabled Commins about a possible revision of *A Fable:* "FORGOT JUDAS MISERY DESIRE REWRITE ONE SECTION PLAN ARRIVE 20 APRIL OR WILL CABLE TO SEND SECTION HERE." While in Paris he also saw Jean, but held to his plan to return on April 20 to New York. He had Commins handle all his New York–Oxford business preparatory to the return; he asked Monique Salomon to manage all loose ends in Paris for him. Hawks, meanwhile, did not require his services, and, one suspects, was quite pleased to be rid of him.

Once back in New York, Faulkner planned a preface to *A Fable* to explain his intentions. The preface never appeared (it lies in the Random House files), and may have been written before this April date. The first paragraph is didactic, like his Nobel Prize speech, and reductive of the novel. Faulkner was outspoken against war, although clearly he was not in favor of pacifism either. His point, stressed and restressed, is that man must invent something more powerful than war and the thirst for power. War destroys those who wage it as well as those who, opposing it, use warlike methods. What must succeed is a different orientation. The second paragraph refers directly to the symbolism of three characters in *A Fable* —Levine, the French quartermaster general, and the British battalion runner. Each one is a third of the "trinity of man's conscience"—Levine is the nihilistic third; the quartermaster general is the passive; and the battalion runner is the active. Levine chooses nothing: "Between nothing and evil, I will take nothing." The quartermaster general perceives evil all around and weeps for it. Only the battalion runner, disfigured at the end, offers a resolution: he refuses to die before he does something about the evil in the world.

The preface was attuned to several elements: the senselessness and brutality of the Korean War; the heating up of the cold war, in which confrontation seemed possible, exacerbated by the Soviet Union's joining the nuclear club; the lack of morality on the domestic front as Joseph McCarthy, whom Faulkner detested,*[32] was having his way with a president who would not squash him; and, more generally, his long-felt sense that war showed man not at his most heroic, but at his most abysmal. Fortunately, the preface was filed away, since the book didn't need explanation but steady and careful reading.

On April 28 Faulkner was back in Oxford facing a domestic situation which had not improved during his six-month absence, and yet he felt a need to paper it over for the sake of Jill. She planned the traditional Southern engagement and marriage, and Faulkner would have to play the paternal role. He was, for the time being, the family man. The engagement party took place in Rockville, Maryland, on June 10, in affluent and conservative surroundings—the kind of country-club money Faulkner later associated with when he fox-hunted in Virginia. With that in mind, his remarks to Commins about the event are amusing. After asking for a "ghastly amount" of money, $5,000 at present, what he called "quite a piece of jack," he offered his assessment of the crowd his daughter was marrying into: ". . . damndest collection of prosperous concerned stuff-shirt republican senators and military brass hats and their beupholstered and becoiffed beldames as you ever saw. Fortunately hardly any of them ever heard of me, so I was let alone."[33] It is unlikely they had not heard of him; more likely, they were uninterested. Paul Summers, for his part, was leaving the army and entering the University of Virginia law school, where he and Jill planned to make their home.

In rapid order, events intruded in Faulkner's life, as *Time* became interested in doing another cover story on him. He told Commins, and then Klopfer, that he was fiercely against it. His words here anticipate an article called "On Privacy—the American Dream: what happened to it?" that he published in *Harper's* (July 1955). Citing the intrusion into his privacy of the previous *Time* and *Life* stories, he said that even if he is news, at least his family should be protected against such indignities. He

*Jill's fiancé, Paul Summers, came from a right-wing political tradition, and at the engagement party which his uncle and aunt threw for him, some of the most reactionary, pro-McCarthy political figures were there: among them, Senators Mundt, Welker, and Hickenlooper. These men on domestic issues were to the right of McCarthy, in fact, as well as being red-baiters in the same class. Faulkner told a reporter he felt shame at the Army-McCarthy hearings, which featured Mundt as one of the Wisconsin Senator's defenders.

doesn't blame the journalists, saying they are all right as individuals—but they are also victims of the system. There was, incidentally, a good deal Faulkner did not want publicized; parts of his private life read like a soap opera and reverberated to no one's credit. If *Time* had really activated its bloodhounds, it could have sniffed out drunkenness, binges, domestic difficulties, affairs, possibly divorce proceedings or intentions. That would be for starters. It could have uncovered alcoholism further along in the family, a good deal of parasitism, and, withal, a private life that did not fit the public view of a Nobel Prize winner. Faulkner: "One individual can protect himself from another individual's freedom, but when vast monied organizations such as the press or religion or political groups begin to federate under moral catchwords like democracy and freedom, in the structure of which the individual members or practitioners are absolved of all individual moral restraint, God help us all."[34] As a last resort, Faulkner described himself as defender of his privacy "to the last bullet."

After pressure from Cerf, the project was canceled.* But *Newsweek* came after him via Mullen. That magazine finally put Faulkner on its cover, although he refused to cooperate. There was, however, no invasion of privacy in this instance, since the cover story (for August 2) included only a word-picture and a review of *A Fable;* the *Newsweek* piece appeared on the same day as the novel. The physical description of Faulkner is interesting: "his face covered with stubble, bare-chested and wearing slightly ragged shorts. . . . the impression of a surprisingly chunky, small man with small sharp eyes, a pointed chin, and the airs of an ancient regime."[35] There is considerable wit in these lines, especially the latter remark, and some indication that Faulkner might have enjoyed the company of the interviewer, William Emerson.

Yet even Faulkner's hunting-camp manner to Emerson could not conceal that he was excited about *A Fable.* With all the self-admitted faltering of his powers, with his succession of physical, emotional, and psychological ailments, he was still able to write a novel that was daring, challenging, difficult, and complex.** Although in retrospect we may see *Absalom* as the apex of Faulkner's art, he himself approached *A Fable* as his fullest expression. There are several reasons why this novel would reveal his deepest needs. It was begun as a way of overriding his dismal Hollywood experience with Warner Brothers. It concerned war, when the present war was

---

*Before discouraging the project, Cerf made a futile effort to convince Faulkner of the value that would accrue to *A Fable* from a *Time* cover story. Faulkner sent back a telegram, to the effect he should be allowed to write the books, someone else to collect the publicity. He tells Cerf to estimate how much Random House thinks it is losing on sales, and he will reimburse them (June 24, 1954; *Selected Letters of William Faulkner*, ed. Joseph Blotner [New York: Vintage Books, 1978; orig. publ. 1977], p. 366).

**Some, like Keen Butterworth, view the horsethief episode as part of the contrapuntal structure of the novel, the way "Old Man" complements *The Wild Palms;* a neat argument that dissipates somewhat even in the most sympathetic readings of *A Fable (A Critical and Textual Study of Faulkner's A Fable* [Ann Arbor: UMI Research Press, 1983; orig. publ. 1971]).

itself only beginning to go well. It opened up the possibility of a deep moral and ethical statement when Faulkner was being influenced by the heuristic quality of movies he was working on. Most important, *A Fable* reflected his growing disenchantment with how the world was going—so that the Christian heroism of the corporal, his parallelism to the story of Jesus, his resistance to temptation, became for Faulkner needed symbols for a world he wanted to encapsulate; his own Garden, so to speak. Put another way, he needed a transformational idea; something to redeem modern man's baseness.

One way to do this was to retell the Christian story and graft it onto the war, so that Jesus and a soldier—a man who serves others by corporaling —become intertwined: man's greatest story. The profound depression out of which the novel arises cannot be ignored. Although it appears to reflect a triumphant event, in which the corporal passes through the story of Jesus in order to become, possibly, France's unknown soldier, the novel is itself a revelation of Faulkner's depression over his own aging and the parlous state of the world in war. Because of his depression, we must view the novel as a personal statement, even though at another level it seems to be one of his most historically based fictions.

Although shaped as a novel, unlike *Go Down, Moses* or *The Unvanquished, A Fable* shares some of their structural uncertainty. For if we see it as a series of stories, most notably in the long racehorse insertion,* but also in the way individual segments are virtually complete in themselves, we can understand that Faulkner was experimenting with fiction, as he had in the other two books. Instead of viewing it as a novel, as Faulkner seemed to insist, we can perceive a series of set pieces welded together to create one long fiction. Begun in 1943, with a synopsis and fifty-one pages of manuscript, it grew for a decade. But he also saw it at first not as a novel primarily, but rather as a magazine story, then to be collected in a book of Random House published stories—like those in *Go Down, Moses;* and finally to be redone as a play. All this he spelled out to Ober, adding that he would remove the primerlike Biblical references and let the "story reveal its Christ-analogy through understatement."[36] Although this original plan underwent revision, the basic structure of the novel still reveals the idea. He rather quickly came to see the material as book-length, although he did not foresee how it would grasp his imagination and make it almost impossible for him to work seriously on anything else.

*In that background world Phil Stone was structuring around his friend, we have something rather different. Stone used, as he usually did, questions from Coughlan, who was shaping his *Life* articles into a brief book on Faulkner. Coughlan's book, *The Private World of William Faulkner*, would in fact elicit from the writer his article on "Privacy," which *Harper's* published the following spring. Stone subverts Faulkner's claims (in "Mississippi") that he had become master of the hunt as nonsense. He denies that Faulkner ever sailed on any trawler on the Gulf (also from "Mississippi"). He says that the writer lied about speaking to General Longstreet, for that episode belonged to him, Stone. Then he repeats his feeling that Faulkner will never write anything of value again (*Faulkner: A Comprehensive Guide to the Brodsky Collection, the Letters*, eds. Louis Daniel Brodsky and Robert W. Hamblin, vol. 2 [Jackson: University Press of Mississippi, 1984], p. 141ff).

A Fable, moreover, gave Faulkner his final opportunity to take on the ideas of European modernism and transfer them to the American novel. Since by virtue of its title Faulkner was warning the reader of a visionary performance, he could assemble his segments in a temporal scheme which disrupted realistic expectations. He is less interested in war than the myth of war; less concerned with actuality than with the representation or reflection of it. *A Fable* is one of his books about how to put together a novel, as much as it is a novel: his "vision" of a final fiction. One cannot overestimate how much of himself Faulkner put into this work, a matter apart from its ultimate success or failure as fiction. Temporally, his ambition is exemplary—he has tried interruption, interpolation, time looping, temporal suspension, temporal speeding up—all in the service of trying to capture the "idea of war," a disjointed, unreal experience. The closest approximation we can find, quite suitable to ideas of the fabulous, is of dream: here is not war as his contemporaries perceived it, but the dream of war, perhaps the nightmare.

In one major area, the book is an obvious retelling of the Christian myth, using the final week of the life of Jesus as its example, ending with Jesus' resurrection and the possibility he is, through accident, France's unknown soldier. But the sequence is by no means linear; on the contrary, Faulkner does whatever he can to disrupt lineality, to achieve a kind of looping suitable for ideas of dream or fantasy or vision. Material moves backward and forward as he roves through the book, the author as ultimate director and arbiter. Just as we feel, moreover, that the book is moving forward, Faulkner interrupts with the three-legged racehorse story; but even before that, he has moved back from Wednesday to Tuesday, then on to Wednesday and Wednesday night; before that, from Wednesday to Tuesday; and before that from Tuesday night to Monday. In the first half or so, before the racehorse interruption (or counterpoint), the novel seems to be losing ground as rapidly as it is moving along; although that should not surprise us, since after the first segment, Wednesday, we go to the second, which is labeled Monday, Monday night. The purpose is multifold.

Faulkner obviously hoped to impart a great complexity of vision—a generational struggle that is also a political conflict (worked through in class and caste terms, the Snopes theme transferred to a broader canvas); a religious struggle (between Jesus and God; and all that played out in the conflict between Allied and German armies on the western front, where the ultimate is life and death. Here, a corporal who organizes the mutiny of a regiment of three thousand men on the French front is a Christ-like figure in struggle against generals (his father, the supreme commander) and politicians, who demand that the war continue. This particular material, we can see, is continuous with *Go Down, Moses,* and especially with "The Bear." The corporal, who becomes a martyr to peace, reminds one of Sam Fathers, who remains inviolate in his vision of the woods; or else he recalls aspects of Ike McCaslin, who forsakes his heritage because of its taint. The supreme commander (to maintain the status quo) is the ultimate despoiler: the man whose mission is so clear he will destroy all in his wake, analogous to those who in the name of progress are pushing back the woods until even the mythical frontier vanishes.

The links with "The Bear" and *Go Down, Moses* are there as part of a commonality of feeling for what should be universal about men and which has been traduced and betrayed. Just as Sam Fathers resists betrayal by those who do not understand his heritage, so the corporal resists surrendering his trust, a commonality with all men, even at the expense of his young life. Reading back from the corporal and from the spirit of redemption in *A Fable*, there is the sense in Faulkner's earlier career of a strong spiritual bond that may have been missed or minimized. Sam Fathers's trust in the woods is akin to a form of conversion to a spiritualized existence, what Mircea Eliade refers to as a sacralized world, much as the corporal insists on his transformed, sacralized sense of things. In both figures can be found that mysterious element the artist and shaman share: both are specialists in the human soul. Shamans are separated, Eliade points out, "from the rest of the community by the intensity of their own religious experience," a distinction which lies close to Faulkner's sense of both Sam Fathers and the corporal. In another respect, when the corporal is paralleled to Jesus Christ, he undergoes an experience in which he must respond to his stay in the wilderness, a wilderness somewhat different from Sam Fathers's, but analogous. Both must assimilate the wilderness as transformational and redemptive; when they return to civilization or what passes for it, they are unfitted for that. Outside their milieu, they are renegades; within, they are revelatory of man's spiritual quest for Eden, for absolutes.

A Fable is a summa in another sense. Faulkner's effort at a vast novel of war and peace links him to many contemporary war novels (Humphrey Cobb's and Erich Maria Remarque's in the recent past, Mailer's and Burns's in the 1940s); more aptly, it provides a thread of continuity with another difficult work, Thomas Pynchon's *Gravity's Rainbow* in the 1970s. What links Faulkner and Pynchon, apart from their common attempt to collect the things of the world into one book, is an inclusive rhetorical manner. Faulkner needed a language for the novel, and what he attempted was a variation on his own rhetoric in *Absalom* and "The Bear," just as later Pynchon was to try out a linguistic exploration of ways in which visions could be verbalized. Unfortunately, the visionary quality of Faulkner's novel is often badly served by language, undermined by excessive and indulgent passages which confuse rather than excite.

Linguistically, then, the book is an indulgence, as the following passages suggest: ". . . couldn't forget you because you were why we were where we were." "That you were chosen by destiny out of the paradox of your background, to be a paradox to your past in order to be free of human past to be the one out of all earth to be free of the compulsions of fear and weakness and doubt which render the rest of us incapable of what you were competent for." Language strains for Biblical significance, but it does not find a level and it misses one's ear. Faulkner writes of "not even the crashing ejaculation of salute this time." Yet he wrote Cowley that he was writing and rewriting, "weighing every word which I never did before." Sometimes, as noted, the same rhetoric clicks into place: "the vast cumbrous machinery of war grinding to its clumsy halt in order to reverse itself to grind and rumble in a new direction—the proprietorless wave of victory exhausted by its own ebb and returned by its own concomitant flux, spent not by its own faded momentum but as though bogged down in the refuse of its own success."[37] Prose is on the edge, and then redeemed in that final image, where language and vision of war encounter each other.

At the structural level, Faulkner has worked with his usual mastery of concealment and withholding of vital information. Flashback, parallelism of event, withholding or suspending time, revealing small segments through withdrawal—all of these characterize the novel, so that the reader must not simply read, but reread. Faulkner has worked on disguises, dribbling out information of the regiment's mutiny, the corporal, the general in charge (Gragnon), and the supreme commander who arranges the façade. Since the mutiny must be disguised so that the soldiers do not end the war themselves, Faulkner can come at his material as if from the narrow end of a funnel. As he burrows toward divulgation, we begin to perceive the political-religious-social patterns. The military is arranged like Yoknapatawpha and Jefferson, Gragnon and the supreme commander replacing Will Varner, Flem Snopes, and Major de Spain; and the group of thirteen soldiers who mutiny, not the apostles but those townspeople who move through Jefferson. Faulkner sees the military as a malignant community, but with most of the class and caste characteristics ascribed to his mythical Mississippi county. The difference is that in *A Fable* people will die—and it is a "fable," a fantasy of what may happen under certain circumstances, a vision of unending doom except for those who reach for redemption.

Faulkner was not at all times clear in his plans. As he worked through fifty or more pages, his sense of the whole began to shape itself. He envisioned it as a *War and Peace* for our times, but for American ears, as he told Robert Haas. It became, like his script for "Battle Cry," a crusade for freedom. The mutiny, as he worked into it, is arranged by a corporal who seems ubiquitous, who, at thirty-three, is destined for martyrdom, and who refuses the role of dutiful son when the supreme commander offers him escape. As the plan developed, Faulkner saw that the corporal, as played off against the runner and the sentry, must be France's savior, as well as possibly its unknown soldier. The sentry is the moneylender in the temple, and the runner is only interested in making a statement against authority. The corporal's idealism is more flexible, and when he dies, he gains a crown of thorns of barbed wire, war and religion touching now as spirit and battlefield crisscross. War is all wars. A far younger contemporary of Faulkner's, John Hawkes, was coming to the same conclusion in his compact but explosive book *The Cannibal*.

The German general who flies in to agree to the arrangement by which the mutiny can be disguised from the rest of the army—and who shoots his pilot in the face to keep the mission secret—speaks of the next war and tells the British they will not even prepare for it. Faulkner evidently had Britain on the eve of World War II in mind. As noted:

You will wait until an enemy is actually beating at your front gate. Then you will turn out to repel him exactly like a village being turned out cursing and swearing on a winter night to salvage a burning hayrick—gather up your guttersweepings, the scum of your slums and stables and paddocks; they will not even be dressed to look like soldiers, but in the garments of ploughmen and ditchers and carters; your officers look like a country-house party going out to the cutts for a pheasant drive.[38]

The German foresees that the future belongs to those who can mobilize force, not moral persuasion; and by means of his presence and speech, Faulkner has extended his fable forward, just as by means of the Christ-like corporal he has extended it backward. At the heart of the struggle, on all levels of the novel, is the split between man's endurance as measured by his power, and man's endurance by virtue of his spirit. Archetypically, the supreme commander is indicative of political power and intrigue, whereas his son is a sacrifice to the elements marshaled by spiritual, moral, and ethical considerations. This ideological division defines the structure of the novel, much as the political discussions between Cummings and Hearn define the ideological setting of Mailer's *The Naked and the Dead*, the difference being that Hearn is a weak idealist, whereas the corporal is a strong one.

Faulkner's Nobel Prize speech is echoed in the novel *The Fable* in that man endures "not because he is immortal but [is] immortal because he endures." He may endure from several points of view, even rapacity (the sentry); but ultimately man cannot fail man, or else he ceases. Every life experienced intensely and with comprehension of all the stakes is a form of endurance, and by extension a form of immortality.

There is an ethical imperative in the Faulkner novel that is considerably at odds with many other novels of the 1950s, where the drive was to achieve liberation from moral positions, exemplified by parts of Bellow's *The Adventures of Augie March* and *Henderson the Rain King*, Barth's early fiction, and William Gaddis's *The Recognitions*. Faulkner's own concern is retold by Cowley in *The Faulkner-Cowley File*: "Then he told me [October 25, 1948] about his new novel, of which he has written 500 pages. It is about Christ in the French army, a corporal with a squad of 12 men—and a general who is Antichrist and takes him upon a hill and offers him the world. Symbolic and unreal except for three hundred wild pages about a three-legged race-horse in Tennessee. Mary Magdalene and the other two Marys." Faulkner saw the Biblical dimension as early as 1943, when he wrote Ober: "It continues on, through the Three Temptations, the Crucifixion, the Resurrection," this being at a time when he had half or less of an earlier draft of an inchoate manuscript. The ethical dimension is emphasized in a follow-up letter to Haas (January 15, 1944), in which he comments that when Christ reappeared he was recrucified: i.e., "we are in the midst of war again." Christ will be crucified each time he appears.

Faulkner wanted to grasp it all, more so than most of his younger contemporaries in the 1940s and early 1950s, except perhaps for Gaddis and, to a lesser extent, Mailer. Even Bellow in *Augie March*, his most far-reaching novel, attempted less. Yet withal the ambitious scale, the part revealing most assurance is the long insertion on the lame racehorse, whose story Faulkner had suggested previously in many shapes and forms. It was his signature story. The resoluteness of the horse to run and win despite handicaps is analogous to the same quality in the corporal and those who choose to die rather than sacrifice their ethical imperatives. As the narrator says: "We had to save it until it could die still not knowing nothing and not wanting nothing but just to run out in front of everything else." Where we find Faulkner weakening, despite his interest in the experimental nature of the narrative, is in that roving back and forth which makes up the main body of the novel.

Wednesday night is focal. As the middle of the week, it becomes the key player in the roving mechanism. Although the inevitable movement is toward the agony of Jesus on the cross in Holy Week, Wednesday plays a greater part in *A Fable* than any other day. The novel begins with Wednesday, and some of the longest sections are given over to that day. After its first introduction, the next segments on Wednesday convey much significant information. And in the fourth mention of Wednesday (after a brief Tuesday episode still shielding facts), we obtain the following: how the regiment had been "led, cajoled, betrayed into revolt by a single squad of twelve soldiers and their corporal; that the entire three thousand men had been corrupted into capital crime and through it, right up into the shadow of the rifles which would be its punishment, by thirteen men, four of whom, including the corporal-leader, were not only not Frenchmen by birth, but three of them were not even naturalised Frenchmen. In fact, only one of the four—the corporal—could even speak French."[39] Shortly afterward, Faulkner points out the obscure origin of the corporal leading them—giving him the kind of anonymous, dark beginnings we associate with the mythological hero. He is an enigma, historyless, pastless; this gives him the cachet of a savior or hero, the man who, having flourished in darkness, suddenly emerges to illuminate the present situation.

It is also in a Wednesday segment that we learn that Gragnon, the division commander, has been put under arrest because of the rebellion of his regiment. He too can be executed for countenancing or permitting mutiny. After the interruption for the Tuesday racehorse elements, Wednesday returns, with Wednesday night as an exceptionally long section.[40] Here we find one of the key stories, that of Marthe, part of the group of three women who have men in the regiment. There are three women (the three Marys), three flags, three supreme generals—the tripartite dimension of the novel is evident, and it is one more parallel to the Holy Trinity which hovers over the western front. Faulkner was nothing here if not ambitious. Yet the insistence on Christian symbolism is suitable, since the war had become far more than men facing men. It had come to mean the testing of a Christian world; in its killing fields a real subversion of the very idea of God and His Son, that Christian framework within which the war was ostensibly being fought. Faulkner struggled desperately to get it right.

The more one ponders the dominance of the Wednesday material, the more one balks at the inclusion of the crippled-racehorse section, however much that segment parallels in the horse's courage and endurance comparable qualities in the corporal and his activities. Faulkner was much taken with the horse story, as we can see from his letter to Haas: "I am now in the middle of a hundred page new chapter which itself is a good story, a complete novelette, about a white man and an old Negro preacher and the preacher's 14 year old grandson who stole a crippled racehorse and healed its broken leg and spent a year dodging from one little back country track to the next racing the horse before the police ever caught them, then the white man shot the horse."[41] Faulkner worked mightily to integrate this basically separate piece ("a complete novelette") into the novel, making the white man part of the western front action and attempting to link white man, Negro, and grandson. But he was trapped in his own recent writing habits: that inability to work through what a novel demanded, and that attempt to create novels from shorter materials. This inability to work through a novel as such was to dog him in the entire second half of his career; so one way to view the later career is that of the man writing short stories who is trying to become, once again, a novelist.

Even the interpolated story *in itself* was not quite right. What could not stand alone—*Partisan* was not happy with it even if edited—was now introduced into *A Fable* and kept there. Faulkner asked Ober and Haas if the section was too prolix, perhaps dull. Even as the novel was being prepared for publication, Faulkner showed how tentative he was about what he had written, for he planned originally to append a preface to the published novel explaining why it was not a pacifist book. He feared to be misunderstood because he suspected he had not created an artistic entity. He wrote two paragraphs, which Random House scrubbed. But Faulkner was not finished with justifying his purpose in writing *A Fable*. He also intended to explain details. When Estelle, a solid and intelligent reader, read portions, she complained she could not understand them. Faulkner explained in this second paragraph about the "thirds": Levine the nihilist, the old quartermaster general as passive, the corporal as activist. Although the preface intended to explain the novel, and Random House felt Faulkner should have stood by the fiction alone, there is some reason to think an explanation was not an entirely poor idea. However moralistic and fervent, the preface would have spelled out for early readers and reviewers many elements only murkily worked out in the novel; and such an explanation may have provided that outline of major characters which would have made reading less arduous. Even after all these years, *A Fable* is still a somewhat obscure novel.

There is little question that all of this held such personal meaning for Faulkner that he could not let go. The preface, in another respect, suggests he could not surrender the novel even when it was moving into Random House's publication schedule. Blotner calls attention to a letter from Jean Stein to himself (February 8, 1969), in which she says Faulkner identified with the runner and told her his usual World War I stories, including the one of crashing in a plane. "One day the plane crashed. I was pulled out of the wreck, laid on the ground and declared dead. I knew I wasn't dead. They couldn't kill me."[42] These words, spoken to Jean only shortly after *A Fable* was published, parallel the runner's assertion that he was never going to die. Especially compelling is how intertwined Faulkner became with the runner that he re-created an untrue story about himself so that he could fit himself even more conclusively into the fictional character. He had to fantasize his own life so as to reinforce his sense of a created fictional character. What this suggests so far is that *A Fable* was no longer for Faulkner a "fiction," but a central document in his life; autobiographical in intention and execution. His overwhelming need to say "no to death" found expression as an antidote to World War II, where he saw an apocalyptic end to everything. His novel would balance things. One reason he took nearly a decade to write *A Fable* was that he saw it not only as a personal document, but as a final statement, the way Nietzsche saw some of his philosophical works as superseding even their personal import to become apocalyptic messages.

The weakest parts of the novel, unfortunately, concern what was closest to Faulkner's heart—the linkage between the men on the front and the religious significance of their activities. Particularly significant, of course, is the association between the corporal and Jesus Christ, the three women and the three Marys, the supreme commander and his son as emblems of God and Jesus, and the placement of Magda as the Virgin Mary, who becomes the mother of Jesus-corporal. The linkages are forced, and they make Faulkner stop everything, in the Wednesday night segment just past the center of the novel, in order to provide connections. When he puts the German general into this section as well, we find it so packed with various strands the novel begins to disperse itself. What should in fact become more intense becomes more diffuse.

Faulkner was apparently counting on the establishment of different coordinates of time for the novel, some kind of temporal withholding or suspension in which he could pack several levels of disparate materials. Through this use of time, he apparently felt he could make linkages which ordinarily could not be made; he could leap from realistic narrative structures to structures more in keeping with fable, vision, fantasy, apocalypse.

He was using "fable" in the apocalyptic sense of nonrealistic, even antirealistic, almost surrealistic. Thus he could double back, look, interpolate, interrupt, intercede, move in and out of his narrative as though he were disconnected or suspended from its own movement. Time is not only suspended, it is extended, looped.* The sentry hits the runner with his rifle (on page 85) on Tuesday night; then again, on Thursday, the sentry (the groom of the crippled-racehorse segment) is present when the "runner struck the guard between the ear and the rim of the helmet" (page 315). Faulkner is intent on doubling incidents, even while altering them sufficiently so that they are not congruent.

Only about halfway through the very long segment of Wednesday night devoted to the women does Faulkner begin to move the narrative forward. Before that, he has provided nearly two hundred pages of interwoven material which does not justify its difficulties. Part of the problem could well be that having written it over a period of nine years or so, Faulkner himself lost sight of reader problems in grappling with the early sections and could not find ways of justifying the obstacles. Connected to their opaqueness is Faulkner's insistence here, more than in any other work except perhaps *Absalom*, on withholding information; then on telling and retelling until the vision opens up. But what is strategic for the novel becomes self-defeating. The diffusiveness of narrative, added to the faltering prose, does not allow the reader in. One may marvel at Faulkner's fervor and even at his daring strategical intent, but also confess that the language blocks, negates, frustrates, ultimately bores. For all its ambitious aims and significance in Faulkner's life, the novel leaves little impact except in isolated passages. His effort at a *Gesamtkunstwerk*—a totality of word, scene, decor—stumbled.

Reviews were mixed, as they had been for Faulkner's more impressive novels. Having taken Clifton Fadiman off the battlefield, the *New Yorker* put Brendan Gill on the book, and he, predictably, called it a "calamity." The *Atlantic* reviewer, Charles Rolo, found it inaccessible; Cowley in the New York *Herald Tribune* cited it as imperfect and unfinished but still standing above everything else on the contemporary scene. Leslie Fiedler in the *New Republic* trashed the novel at nearly every point, finding nothing to praise and everything to condemn. Except for Cowley, this crowd, joined later by a more praiseworthy one, failed to come to grips with Faulkner's daring. Certain novels like *A Fable* or Gaddis's *The Recognitions* the following year do not lend themselves to newspaper and magazine

---

*Michael Millgate notes that when Faulkner originally submitted *Notes on a Horsethief* to Hodding Carter at the Levee Press, it was called "A Dangling Participle [he means 'Clause'] from Work in Progress." From this, Millgate theorizes that such a "dangling participle" is indicative of temporal matters as a whole, as a matter of "time-suspension" (Michael Millgate, *The Achievement of William Faulkner* [Lincoln: University of Nebraska Press, 1978, orig. publ. 1966], p. 230). Several Faulkner titles or near titles have this "dangling" quality, a temporal suspension: *As I Lay Dying* and "If I Forget Thee, O Jerusalem" (*The Wild Palms*) among the novels; the stories: "Once aboard the Lugger," "With Caution and Dispatch," "Barn Burning," and "Shall Not Perish."

reviewing. One need only look to the reception of *Absalom* to see what fools staff reviewers made of themselves. *A Fable* needed time to percolate, so its virtues could be perceived as clearly as its more obvious flaws.* Whatever its drawbacks, Faulkner's "summa" continues to resonate.

With this novel, his long essay "Mississippi," and a modest prose piece called "Sepulture South: Gaslight," Faulkner demonstrated he could still put on a show. *A Fable* wobbles, but the article is right on target, and the short story so archly named is a triumph of how language can evoke a period and place. If we speak of decline in Faulkner's later career, we must distinguish clearly among various works; surely these three, widely different though they are, do not fit a seriatim decline theory. *A Fable* won the National Book Award the following year, at a time when the award meant something, as well as the Pulitzer Prize for fiction. By then, 1955, he was competing against an entirely new generation of writers. This generation had loosely formed mainly right after the war. It included a considerable array of talent, including those, like William Styron, who imitated Faulkner in their early work. But there were several others: Salinger, Mailer, Hawkes, Ellison, Gaddis, Bellow, Malamud; and a little later, O'Connor, Roth, and Updike. They were prolific, and in those early days of their careers, careful writers. The competition for awards and recognition was immense. Faulkner was like a relict of another era, associated with Wright (still alive), Hemingway (the 1954 winner of the Nobel Prize, but written out), Steinbeck (a surprise future winner of the Nobel, in 1962), and Fitzgerald and Wolfe, both long dead. His appearance in 1954 with his "big book" suggested that his generation could not be dismissed; that the younger generation had not only an influence and a presence to deal with, they had a novelist, whatever the warts.

During the excitement over *A Fable*, Faulkner was involved in what would be the first of his many missions for the State Department. This one

---

*The biographer of Robert Frost, Lawrence Thompson, wrote Saxe Commins an extremely long assessment of *A Fable*, denigrating it in Faulkner's canon to the level of *Across the River and into the Trees* in Hemingway's. Thompson forgot that the book is called "A Fable" and that much of what occurs will therefore be fabulous, surreal, fantastic. He kept repeating that Faulkner was working within the allegorical mode, and with that assumption, he tarred everything that did not fit generically: characterization, narrative, situation, analogues to the Christ story, et al. "His task, as artist, was to make us *feel* the significance of those analogies, rather than to make us go groping and searching for the significance." Thompson concludes ruefully that the allegorical element, as he calls it, is "merely decorative, and not functional. It approaches the slap-happy decorative mode of the bastard-baroque. . . . The analogy is clear, but it is laid on from without, and it is quite meaningless. . . . You must remember that I am a rabid Faulkner admirer, and I consider him a great artist. But Faulkner is nowhere near his best, in *A Fable*. No wonder that he spent nine years trying to make this book jell, because he himself must have realized, repeatedly, that he had not succeeded in making it jell" (July 2 or 9, 1954; *Faulkner: A Comprehensive Guide to the Brodsky Collection, the Letters*, eds. Louis Daniel Brodsky and Robert W. Hamblin, vol. 2 [Jackson: University Press of Mississippi, 1984], pp. 149–51). A lot of hard truth here, but too narrow. In contrast, Delmore Schwartz's review was so laudatory as to give the novel a stature it does not achieve. Calling *A Fable* "a masterpiece," Schwartz says it was inspired by the "tormented hope and tragic recognition of a man obsessed with the atomic age" (reprinted in *Selected Essays of Delmore Schwartz*, eds. Donald A. Dike and David H. Zucker [Chicago: University of Chicago Press, 1985], p. 304. The review appeared originally in *Perspectives USA*, 1955).

was to São Paulo, Brazil, for an international writers' conference, August 9–21. Faulkner spent a good deal of time and energy moving around the world under State Department auspices, and it is possible to perceive his activity as implicit admission he had little left to write. Yet it is equally possible to see this activity as something keeping him from that self-destructive withdrawal which occurred when he was left to himself. Although he often drank heavily on these trips—and State Department personnel were usually prepped beforehand on treatment of alcoholism— he did manage to meet his obligations. The jaunts overseas were not wastes of time; on the contrary, they seemed, like drink itself, to allow him to go on, eventually to get his work done. Faulkner's decision to accept the Brazil assignment, even though it stood for nearly everything he disliked and feared, was part of his sense of what was right for him. He needed to get away, he needed to deal somehow with Jill's marriage, which he did not completely favor, and he needed to regain his balance after being awash in family matters.

The State Department shrewdly put a Southern poet named Muna Lee on the phone, the right person to win Faulkner over. She tried to tempt him with Robert Frost, who had also agreed to go, but Faulkner cared not at all for the poet, and had his own reasons for accepting.* The request came in June, the conference to take him to Brazil during August 7–16, in plenty of time for his return for Jill's wedding on August 21. It removed him from the house when final preparations were going on, a time when someone like Faulkner felt suffocated. His letter to Muna Lee demonstrating interest and querying her about what his role would be was followed by one to Commins concerned almost solely with clothes. He needed dress clothes and special shoes—English shoes by Church—in a rather dainty size, six and one-half B or C, but definitely not pumps. This sudden veering toward sartorial splendor is a new turn for this period, quite different from the bare-chested, stubble-faced writer who confronted the *Newsweek* staffman.

The trip was on, and it became the kind of high comedy filled with achievement which characterized many of his future journeys for the State Department. There was, of course, no way in which he could undertake such a trip and meet so many new people without getting overwhelmingly depressed; and that kind of depression could be allayed only by excessive drinking. He left Memphis on August 6, arriving in Lima, Peru, on the following day, for what proved to be an eight-day stay in South America, with departure on the fifteenth, return to Oxford on the sixteenth. He appeared fresh for his first press conference, but an afternoon cocktail party, where he was the center of attention, proved too much. With food

*But he firmly rejected the offer from PEN (poets, playwrights, editors, essayists, and novelists) to attend its big conference in September. Commins told PEN that Faulkner would not do anything of the sort until he wrote the final volumes of his trilogy. Faulkner told Commins he was busy with horses (June 12, 1954, *Faulkner: A Comprehensive Guide to the Brodsky Collection, the Letters*, eds. Louis Daniel Brodsky and Robert W. Hamblin, vol. 2 [Jackson: University Press of Mississippi, 1984], p. 146).

distant—South Americans favored very late evening dining—Faulkner began to pour an almost endless succession of drinks. The State Department people apparently had not been briefed—on future trips they would be. The next day, as he flew to São Paulo, there was more of the same— drinking brandy on the flight and then moving on to vodka, eating little or nothing. Predictably, he collapsed; but within two days he was back on his feet prepared to meet the press and his literary colleagues. Also, the State Department people were a little wiser.

Faulkner recovered and made a brief talk on equality and justice in race, which he saw as the world's chief problem. He answered an endless stream of questions about his tastes, including musical ones—he said he preferred Beethoven, Mozart, and Prokofiev, although he listened to very little music. He made trips to various showplaces: plantations, etc. He missed meeting Frost. The latter part of his trip seemed to pick him up, and he said all the obligatory things, indicating on a stopover in Venezuela that the energetic youth of South America had impressed him, that he planned to study Hispanic literature when he returned. He also indicated he would like another visit, to Peru, Bolivia, and Brazil, to learn more about what makes an American.

While the remarks seem perfunctory and even amusing, given the half-light in which Faulkner operated, nevertheless he was perceptive of the problems he encountered. Writing to Harold Howland[43] of the State Department on his return on August 16, he thanked the department for the courtesy and efficiency which expedited his trip. He mentions that tact and dignity are necessary in dealing with Latin America, but he is too inexperienced to assess what his visit accomplished. He hopes the State Department will let him know when reports come in.

If we can believe the State Department report sent to Saxe Commins (on September 15), Faulkner made an excellent impression. Particularly cited was his two-hour interview with Peruvian writers, artists, and press. His delicacy in not offending anyone was emphasized—Phil Stone should have received a copy of this letter! The visit to São Paulo was also deemed a success. The report recapitulates Faulkner's pronouncements, his musical tastes, his dislike of Eliot's *The Family Reunion*, his liking for Fry's *The Lady's Not for Burning;* that he considers *A Fable* a good work, but weak in spots; that his favorite books are *Don Quixote* and the Bible. He also insisted he was a farmer, not a writer, although his Nobel Prize was not in agriculture. And he advised all young Brazilian writers to write the truth—although in many South American countries that would mean their disappearance. He stressed that all men are equal, in that all suffer the same anguish and pain; the only solution for mankind is solidarity, for men of all creeds, colors, and social conditions. If McCarthy had heard of this, Faulkner might have been accused of softness on communism.

What the State Department liked was the upbeat nature of Faulkner's responses, although his attitude had little to do with reality, or with American policy, which was to shore up ostensibly anticommunist regimes which hardly pressed for justice, equality, or solidarity. Faulkner's reductive policies, a Jeffersonian farmer's view of men and the world, fitted well into the State Department's plans; he became, after this, an emissary who said all the right things. Overall, reports from Brazil indicated that Faulkner's and Frost's visits "had established a new level of distinction in inter-American cultural relations; and are immensely valuable, among other things, in counteracting international communist propaganda attempts to depict the United States as not only lacking culture but inimical to it." The department was quoting Carlos Dávila, an important Chilean writer and political figure, but it obviously agreed intensely with Dávila. In the final analysis, we can say Faulkner's visit did not hurt, that it may have helped by touching South American youth; but there is no denying that he was being used by the State Department for its own purposes and apparently without his recognition. He returned to South America, to Venezuela, in April of 1961.

Rowan Oak meant the wedding. After the ceremony Jill moved to Charlottesville, Virginia with Paul Summers, but she was evidently concerned about her mother. She had felt for a long time that Faulkner was mistreating Estelle, was even responsible for his wife's poor condition. Once settled in an apartment near the University of Virginia law school, Jill wrote Faulkner reminding him of his word to open an account for Estelle at the Oxford bank. She emphasized that she wanted his help in "making Mamma happy." She repeated: "Please, Pappy, I'm depending on you to do everything possible to give Mama happiness. I'm afraid she feels I'm more or less lost to her." Estelle was planning to visit Victoria and Bill Fielden in Manila, and would, of course, need funds. We can assume that when Faulkner returned from South America, one of the topics which came up repeatedly with Jill was his relationship with Estelle, as they both approached sixty.

Faulkner tried to stay out of the way, working with a colt, which kicked him and hurt his back again. He walked around the growing festivities dressed like the town tramp, now and then helping with outdoor decorations. The wedding itself took place at St. Peter's Episcopal Church, and it went smoothly. But there were hitches to come. Faulkner had forbidden the press, but a woman reporter and her photographer from the Memphis *Commercial Appeal* sneaked in with Estelle's permission. Faulkner was less irate than usual, but he was beginning to fade. Once the wedding couple departed, he started to let go; he tried to engage guests to stay and drink their way through the night. Ben Wasson had come, as had the Comminses. He and Estelle began to go after the hard stuff, and, according to reports, the two became messily drunk. It was the old Rowan Oak scene, only now without Jill in attendance. She had escaped into a marriage that produced three sons in rapid succession (by 1961), but which also proved less than satisfactory. Like Estelle and Cornell Franklin, or Estelle and her father, she and her husband grew apart.

Faulkner then left Oxford for New York, where he checked into the Algonquin Hotel. He came North for several reasons. He could not, of course, stand to remain at Rowan Oak with just Estelle—they had moved past that; he needed an influx of money to compensate for the extraordinary expenses of the wedding, well in excess of $5,000; he wanted to see Jean; and he hoped to do some writing—short stories, television adaptations, or even originals. CBS broadcasted "An Error in Chemistry" from *Knight's Gambit,* and he managed to write a story which he published in the *Saturday Evening Post* in 1955, "Race at Morning," receiving $2,500.

We do know he had the Snopes material in mind again, although he had not yet established a schedule for completing the trilogy. In October of 1954, he wrote a story called "By the People" and reintroduced many of the old cast—Ratliff, Gavin Stevens, perhaps Chick Mallison (an unidentified war veteran), Will Varner, and the Snopeses. This entire period, in late 1954, was productive. "Race at Morning," one of four hunting stories which ended up in *Big Woods,* * fitted Faulkner's sense of summing-up his life. The major event is a nonevent. After tracking a big buck, the boy-narrator and Mr. Ernest, as a part of a larger hunting party, let the buck go. Ernest has purposely not loaded his rifle. As he explains to the boy, his ward, it is better to know the buck will be available next year for hunting than to have its "bloody head and hide on the kitchen floor yonder and half his meat in a pickup truck."[44] The need to preserve the Edenic dream of buck hunting in the big woods indicates that the experience itself was ending. If the buck, like Ben in "The Bear," could be shot, that meant there was still an ongoing experience. By letting the buck survive, Ernest and the boy prolong what is ending. They will try again next year, but with another kind of knowledge, of final things.

The story is suffused with the end of things. Even the boy is going to be transformed, from the farmer and hunter he wants to be into someone literate. Because the world around him is changing, he must go to school. School is not something positive, but the only possible extension of the changing world—not a good in itself, but a necessity. Farming for eleven months, the woods for the twelfth are insufficient. But there is other loss. The boy is a ward, his mother having run off with a "Vicksburg roadhouse feller," and then his father having disappeared as well. Just as the big woods experience is collapsing, so is family. Ernest, his benefactor, a hunter, is going out of style as well. Life is a series of diminishments, and school is perceived not as enlargement but as the inevitable response to loss.

*"Race at Morning," except for a dozen or so new lines added to it, appeared intact in *Big Woods.* Other parts underwent greater alteration. For "The Bear," Faulkner deleted part 4, which is an essential element, the part on Ike's heritage, the historical dimension. Without this, the story becomes an adventure piece—a commercialization of the inner tale. "A Bear Hunt," however, remained intact; the sole change the introduction of Boon Hogganbeck's son Lucius.

The story, not one of Faulkner's strongest, is nevertheless full of his 1950s pessimism. "The Bear" was filled with affirmation, for the hunt was a successful venture. Getting Ben was a mission accomplished, with some loss of brave blood. In the later story, there is the forsaking of the mission just when it could be successful so as to give it at least another year. Faulkner saw it all falling apart; if the big woods was his metaphor for America or American life, then the dream was indeed shattered, the vision lost.

"By the People" (which *Mademoiselle* took for October 1955) involves Gavin Stevens and Ratliff lined up against a demagogue named Homer X. Yarbry. Yarbry is precisely the type of political candidate who played on the basest Mississippi instincts and controlled the political life of the state and its representatives in Congress. He supports the Klan, but speaks against it; he deceives, lies, becomes the ultimate hypocrite. To defeat him, Ratliff devises a scheme; he will wipe Yarbry's trouser legs with switches from a dog thicket. As he attempts to speak, dogs try to piss on him, and he is forced to make a rapid exit. Ratliff tells Will Varner that if he withdraws the candidate, he will keep the incident quiet; that ends Yarbry. The typescript name of Yarbry was altered to Clarence Eggleston Snopes, to bring the story into line with Faulkner's view of the Snopeses in politics. Faulkner has clearly defined the division: Ratliff and Stevens, as voices of moderate decency, against Snopes, the same Clarence who had appeared as the seedy politico in *Sanctuary*. Needless to say, Ober had difficulty selling a story which depended on dogs urinating on a politician; it may have been what readers wanted to hear, but it could not appear in any family magazine. The *Saturday Evening Post, Journal,* and other leading magazines rejected it. *Mademoiselle,* far down on the list, took it; but the story reveals little of Faulkner's skill. It depends on a backwoods trick, without providing any textured sense of political life in the deep South.

"Hog Pawn," also written in this period, was improved when it was integrated into *The Mansion.* As an independent story, it has most of the weaknesses of the Gavin Stevens pieces in *Knight's Gambit.* Viewed from the outside by the twenty-eight-year-old war veteran, Chick Mallison, but narrated by the omniscient author, "Hog Pawn" desperately needs a context to become meaningful. Crusty and violent old Meadowfill, his daughter, her eventual suitor, McKinley Smith, recently returned from the Korean War, plus an unnamed Snopes are characters seeking an idea or theme. Faulkner involves them in a mystery (shades of *Knight's Gambit*) which is insufficiently mysterious because there are too few complications. The situation involves efforts of Meadowfill to outwit a Snopes and of a Snopes to outwit a Meadowfill, with a piece of land coveted by an oil company as the bait. In the middle is Gavin Stevens, who works out an equitable solution when Snopes tries to arrange to have McKinley Smith kill Meadowfill. The eventual beneficiary of it all is the mousy Essie Meadowfill, who comes into valuable property and gains a husband. The tale has some of the quality of a medieval morality tale, in which the weak dominate the strong, while the latter take their lumps. But for this, Faulkner was reaching deeply into the drawer.

In this general period of September–October, Faulkner wrote still another brief piece of prose. All four, crafted within a short time of each other, recall the early 1930s, when Faulkner made a run at short fiction and flooded the market with considerable success. Now, as a kind of left-handed effort, he returned to this mode; but we see work derivative in nature, some of it well-crafted but lacking in daring. Not that one should expect another "Bear." Rather, Faulkner was writing well but not significantly, reaching back, playing safe, doing what he knew he could do well. Responding to a photograph of a cemetery made by Walker Evans and shown to him by Anthony West, the novelist, Faulkner wrote a piece of fine prose. Not really a story, not an essay, but one of his intermediate forms, he called it "Sepulture South: Gaslight." One fragmentary text inserts an "in" before Gaslight in the title, but Faulkner went with the other, which appeared in *Harper's Bazaar* in December.

He reached back into both his own life and his work: the death of a grandfather recalling the young colonel's death, but the remainder of the family appearing to derive from Faulkner's work, with some distant linkage to people in his personal history. The piece is a meditation on final things. It is also a portrait of a small town as it responds to a death in the family. The smooth surface of the town is broken by the event, although no one appears to grieve very deeply. But the perspective is that of a boy, who is moved by the gravity of the situation, the finality of death, the quality of ceremony in a community itself passing away. The boy, now fourteen, had once vowed, when four, he would never die. But now he meditates on the experience of death, the cemetery tombs:

> And now we could already see them, gigantic and white, taller on their marble pedestals than the rose-and-honeysuckle-choked fence looming into the very trees themselves, the magnolias and cedars and elms, gazing forever eastward with their empty marble eyes—not symbols: not angels of mercy or winged seraphim or lambs or shepherds, but effigies of the actual people themselves as they had been in life, in marble now, durable, impervious, heroic in size, towering above their dust in the implacable tradition of our strong, uncompromising, grimly ebullient Baptist-Methodist Protestantism, carved in Italian stone by expensive Italian craftsmen and shipped the long costly way by sea back to become one more among the invincible sentinels guarding the temple of our Southern mores.[45]

As the observer proceeds, now grown, now moving back and forth in time, he visualizes the passing of mortality into the eternality of cemetery and marble. What makes this such a durable piece of prose—although derivative from earlier Faulkner works—is its vision of mortality, its sense of the cycles of existence. It is an extremely wise piece of language, for which Faulkner's long, almost ceaseless, rolling sentences are the perfect medium of ebb and flow. The piece becomes a prose equivalent of Arnold's "Dover Beach," also concerned with ebb and flow since Sophocles' time. Faulkner's grandfather is, for the American writer, an analogue to Sophocles. At the end, the observer rounds off his vision of mortality as it passes into eternity.

And three or four times a year I would come back, I would not know why, alone to look at them, not just at Grandfather and Grandmother but at all of them looming among the lush green of summer and the regal blaze of fall and the rain and ruin of winter before spring would bloom again, stained now, a little darkened by time and weather and endurance but still serene, impervious, remote, gazing at nothing, not like sentinels, not defending the living from the dead by means of their vast ton-measured weight and mass, but rather the dead from the living; shielding instead the vacant and dissolving bones, the harmless and defenseless dust, from the anguish and grief and unhumanity of mankind.[46]

Faulkner wrote an essay at this time on the inviolability of the individual —it was ostensibly a response to Coughlan's *The Private World of William Faulkner*, but it also addressed the whole range of what *Life, Time,* and *Newsweek* had come to stand for: parasitism on the body of the individual. Coughlan's book in particular enraged him, since it was so clearly part of that contamination of individual rights carried out in the name of freedom of the press. Faulkner drafted a segment, called "Freedom of the Press," and sent it to Commins, then asked for its return, revised it, and retitled it "On Privacy: The American Dream: What Happened to It?" (which *Harper's* took for July 1955). He told Commins it was not to be considered an article but a lecture, part of a symposium which might have five or six parts, on THE AMERICAN DREAM: WHAT HAS HAPPENED TO IT? He says he has had several offers to lecture, that his price is $1,000, and he may use this as the first of a series, later to be gathered into a book on what has happened to the American dream to which the world once aspired.[47]

While Faulkner was writing again, all was not well on the domestic front. Writing to Commins on (probably) October 26, just before Estelle's departure for Manila, Faulkner says: "E. leaves for Manila Friday [October 29], still says she does not want to go, but ticket bought, trunk shipped, and apparently she is. Nice to be able to spend 3000 bucks doing something you constantly remind the owner of the 3000 bucks you dont really want to do."[48] Estelle is spending *his* money, with little awareness it might be considered *their* money, a shared matter. *He* scrounged for it, brought it in by means of his sacrifice; *she* spends it, and idly at that. He also informs Commins he has received the Caedmon record he had cut on September 10, "Faulkner Reads from His Works."*

With Estelle leaving for several months, this gave him a clear run, which in the main meant getting together with Jean whenever their schedules permitted. It also meant he could indulge himself without recriminations as he headed for the annual deer hunt in the last week in November. He tells Jean he has inherited the headship of the club, but even so, he does not intend to shoot a deer. He alludes to "Race at Morning," where it is preferable to maintain the idea of the buck for the following year than to mount the head and cure the skin: ". . . every time I see anything tameless and passionate with motion, speed, life, being alive, I see a young passionate beautiful living shape."⁴⁹ He was developing a marvelous way with young women.

Gloria Franklin, Malcolm's wife, wrote amusingly to the Comminses that everyone was relieved when Estelle got off, but she is worried how Faulkner will manage with no one to cook for him. She wishes he would leave for New York until Estelle returns in March. Yet, withal, she thinks that having Estelle leave him, instead of the other way around, will do him good. The letter from Gloria indicates how much Commins and his wife had become intimates of the family, recipients even of complaints from Faulkner's stepdaughter-in-law.

Hunting camp did not appear to lift him from his gloom—one gets the impression that even that hallowed event had begun to seem like an obligation: "I don't particularly want to go," he wrote Jean. He was being overtaken by the kind of depression, new with him, which was making all activity appear futile. Even his explanation to Jean that he would not shoot a deer anymore, which was good news for the deer and for conservationists, indicated less a respect for life than the fact old ways no longer gave pleasure. By implicitly comparing the tameless deer with Jean, he was praising her, but closing out a meaningful piece of the past. He was settling

---

*In the background, Phil Stone was still preoccupied with Faulkner's reputation. He tells Coughlan that Clifton Fadiman "is stupid about writing" in reference to Faulkner. In his review of *Absalom*, Fadiman had condemned his method as "anti-narrative," devices used to withhold the story. Stone here attacks Fadiman, saying Faulkner is best at withholding information, like the detective-story writer. But in a letter to Fadiman in April 1956, Stone reversed himself and agreed that his old friend "does not have a style," that, as Fadiman has said all along, "the emperor does not have on any clothes" (*Faulkner: A Comprehensive Guide to the Brodsky Collection, the Letters*, eds. Louis Daniel Brodsky and Robert W. Hamblin, vol. 2 [Jackson: University Press of Mississippi, 1984], p 191). In another letter (November 6) Stone told Osmar Pimentel that Carvel Collins, although a real authority on the writer, overestimates Faulkner. In a March 1955 letter to Dave Womack, he says that Faulkner may be a writing man, but his "ignorance on so many subjects is so profound that it would shock you. I have been puzzled and perturbed the last few years at his habit of writing to the editors concerning subjects [i.e., the Negro] about which I know that he knows practically nothing" (March 28, 1955; *Faulkner: A Comprehensive Guide to the Brodsky Collection, the Letters*, eds. Louis Daniel Brodsky and Robert W. Hamblin, vol. 2 [Jackson: University Press of Mississippi, 1984], p. 179,).

into gloom. And even the Christmas he spent with Commins, accompanied by Jean, did not help.

Also, in a strange way—and we don't know precisely how this affected him—he had been squeezed out of family life. Was it wish or circumstance? His stepson, Malcolm, who had not had an easy time of it, had just fathered a baby with Gloria. Jill and Paul Summers were settling down in Charlottesville, she entering very much into her own domestic life. The Comminses were themselves expecting a grandchild and very excited about that. Estelle was with her daughter and son-in-law, quite distant in Manila. Phil Stone was no longer an attractive companion, although he remained, in his way, a friend. He too was wrapped up in family, work, as well as resentment. The hunting crowd was slowly dying off, or losing its excitement, as the hunt had to move ever further from Oxford to find big woods. Many of the old hunters had become enfeebled, or had passed on. They too had been family.

The country itself was becoming an alien place, with Snopeses in Faulkner's eyes creating the values by which the nation lived and thrived. That Faulkner turned to the Snopes material, later, cannot be removed from the historical evidence, eight years of Eisenhower in which Snopesism dominated. When we put it all together, we see Faulkner squeezed to the margins of all his own subcultures, unhappy in Rowan Oak, which now echoed all the battles and scenes of the past, its own Civil War battleground. Oxford was itself not supportive: he could no longer hide there, away from Northeastern publicity hounds; and the townspeople, while honoring him, had never really taken to him or his books. As Christmas of 1954 approached, Faulkner, now fifty-seven, had only Jean—a young lady thirty-five years his junior—to hang on to. It was a strange situation, in which one of the world's most sought-after celebrities had only one home situation left: Random House and its personnel.

Approaching a
Sixty-Year-Old Smiling Man

I N 1955 FAULKNER tried to deal with depression and despair by
becoming a man in motion. He spent one-quarter of the year abroad,
including the trip that became the most famous of them all, to Nagano,
Japan. Although a year of considerable activity, it was also mainly consolidation. Near the end of the year he started another Snopes novel,
volume 2 in the proposed trilogy. It was also the year in which he became
totally immersed in the racial problems following the *Brown v. Board of
Education* Supreme Court decision desegregating the American public
school system.

This decision had a much more radical effect on the South than on
segregated schools in the North, where segregation was by neighborhood.
There, as Negroes moved into a district, whites moved out, leaving inner-
city schools overwhelmingly black. In many instances, even with busing,
there were an insufficient number of white students to go around to create
an integrated school. The South responded with Citizens' Councils and
private academies, which drained off white students, leaving the public
schools in many larger towns and cities all black. But gradually the South
came around, not out of willingness to abide by federal law, but out of fear
of losing federal subsidies. It was "reconstruction" of a new sort. Faulkner
was now caught in the trap of his thinking. He wanted equality and justice
for the Negro; he hated the local Citizens' Councils, which acted as a kind
of inquisition, but he also hated federal intervention. Yet it was federal

intimidation, with the prospect of withholding of federal funds, which broke the back of much Southern segregation. In this contest, Faulkner found he had almost no place to go; for while he had moral arguments on his side, the physical argument he rejected—and yet it proved the sole one to work. The consequence was that whatever he said exacerbated the situation, for himself, but also for his family, friends, and townspeople. If he had felt an outcast before, he was clearly one now: the voice of one, whose own position made only contradictory sense.

Writing, however, was not completely forgotten. He published two short stories in 1955, written a few months earlier: "Race at Morning," in the *Saturday Evening Post* (March 5), which with some minor additions became part of *Big Woods;* and "By the People," in *Mademoiselle* (October), after many rejections from other magazines. The latter became part of *The Mansion,* but "Race at Morning," he feared, would remain uncollected and unused. He began to put together a new collection of four hunting stories, along with five brief prose narratives before, after, and between the stories to give the volume coherence. It was called *Big Woods,* published October 14. He granted Albert Camus permission to adapt *Requiem for a Nun,* a shrewd move inasmuch as Camus helped to make the work well known. He saw the publication of the Modern Library edition of *Go Down, Moses* as a novel, not as a collection of stories. On March 20, he started a group of four letters, caustically written, to the Memphis *Commercial Appeal,* arguing the case for school desegregation. These letters embroiled him in controversy that extended into his own family, which favored traditional segregation. John Faulkner, in particular, was upset by his elder brother's views, and aired his own, which were kindly toward Negroes, but patronizing and condescending.

On August 1, Faulkner arrived in Tokyo on what was to be the most important foreign journey of his life. His stay in Nagano produced some of his most memorable interviews and public statements (collected in *Lion in the Garden*). On the return from Japan, he visited for three days in Manila, and then moved on to Italy. He gave additional interviews and participated in seminars in Rome, Naples, and Milan, where he was accompanied by Jean Stein. He went on from Italy to Munich (where *Requiem* was playing) to Paris, then headed for London, finally going to Iceland for conferences and interviews, before returning to Oxford. In November his appearance at the Southern Historical Association meeting in Memphis, where he condemned segregation, added to the notoriety he had now gathered around himself. He was condemned from all sides, while his supporters, although firm, were few. He was accused of nothing less than betrayal of the South, of having sold out for Yankee dollars—the same charge which accrued after *Sanctuary* appeared. He was also subjected to death threats, anonymous poison calls, hate letters, and ostracization by members of his own family. And since his position was hardly radical or extreme, he was attacked by Northern liberals as not going far enough, as being the typical Southern apologist. He had entered a no-win territory, of course, but he continued to pursue his course. From the distance of thirty or more years, he seems, with his moderation, a kindly but outdated figure; but given the nature of the South's violent feelings, what he voiced at the time was nothing less than courageous. However moderate his statements seem for the Northern liberal, he was going against every facet of his tradition, history, and personal family background. He was indeed "betraying" the South for what he saw as higher moral and ethical principles.

On December 2, he told Jean he was writing the second Snopes volume, *The Town*—and this too cannot be read outside the context of a turbulent, violent, unhappy South riven by choices it cannot make decently and justly. Wherever Faulkner turned, the year 1955 marked his entrance into public debate, suggesting that his reliance on his novels and stories was insufficient in the face of what he perceived as another civil war.

He was also looking for diversion. He began to attend events as a reporter for *Sports Illustrated*, activities he would not have considered before: a hockey game between the Montreal Canadiens and the New York Rangers; later, the Kentucky Derby. Even there, he was disappointed. Team sports seemed to him a loss of individual initiative, whereas hunting, fishing, and trapping were the acme of sporting pursuits. With team sports, he foresaw another closing-off of the frontier, just as in "The Bear" and in his own annual hunting trips, he saw the restrictive roof of civilization. But probably equally disappointing was that he was himself becoming an observer; in team sports, he saw something of his own physical decline, his role not as participant but as note-taker of others' activity. He was slowly moving to the sidelines. We could argue that his insistent entrance into political and racial issues was linked to his desire to remain part of the process. He entered a fray where he could not win, perhaps as a way of rejecting "nothing" and embracing "grief" as the better part of wisdom.*

With the contract for *Big Woods* signed on January 14, Faulkner had a volume which he could look forward to, even if it did not include much original work. All the large materials had been published, and the only new writing was introductory and for linkage. The main pieces were "The Bear," "The Old People," "A Bear Hunt," and "Race at Morning." The

---

*In the background, Estelle wrote Commins on January 4 of her experience of the holidays (*Faulkner: A Comprehensive Guide to the Brodsky Collection, the Letters*, eds. Louis Daniel Brodsky and Robert W. Hamblin, vol. 2 [Jackson: University Press of Mississippi, 1984], p. 176). Jill had written her that Faulkner was spending them with the Comminses in Princeton, but omitted the presence of Jean Stein. Estelle sounds much improved now, for she depicts as something past to how "blue" she felt before leaving. Her plans include possible travel to Siam (Thailand) and Cambodia, then on to Rome, Switzerland, France, and home. She expects to stay in Manila another month. Only shortly after her letter arrived, Faulkner, Jean, and Commins attended the National Book Awards presentation in New York, where he was honored for *A Fable*. But even as Estelle seemed picked up by the Far East trip, she was worried about Malcolm, who was drinking and clearly unhappy with his situation. The round-robin does not end there, for Faulkner revealed his distaste at the way his step-granddaughter (also called Vicki) had turned out.

linkages were what he called "interrupted catalysts," and were concerned in large part with final things. Illustrations were to be by Edward Shenton, who had also done the drawings for *The Unvanquished*. Like the stories which Faulkner had written near the end of 1954, this volume was a farewell, not an opening up.

On January 25, he made his way to the National Book Awards ceremony. Cowley's assessment had proven correct: while *A Fable* was not comparable to Faulkner's best, it was the best of 1954. His fellow co-winner was Wallace Stevens for poetry. Also present, actually presiding over a group interview of Faulkner (who apparently gave no indication of having heard of the critic), was Fadiman. Faulkner seemed uncomfortable, depressed, and miserable—not at Fadiman or anything in particular, but at the celebrity-hopping which went on. He was once again the center of attention, and the questions, many of them inane, came like buckshot. He gave different answers to the same question: telling one he had not been in combat in World War I, telling another he had been at the front. It really made no difference, since what he said was secondary to the fact he could be quoted saying anything; the ultimate celebrity ride. Faulkner could not bear this, and his attitude became increasingly remote, depressed, and withdrawn. After Fadiman read the citation—ironies in the publishing world never cease—Faulkner read his prepared paper[1] at a gallop. He viewed the artist as the conscience of his day, although never fully succeeding in achieving his vision of what he wanted to do. He also said that the artist has little or no influence in America, being treated more like a hobby than a meaningful enterprise, because the engines running America are the practical people, not the visionaries. He harked back to something very close to him, the meaning of success and the ease with which it can be gained in America—too easily gained at the loss of privacy.

He was on the edge of morbidity. Although his speech contained bitter sentiments, he was aware of how little it all meant: whether one was a serious artist or a cultural pimp really meant little in America. He had tried to define the distinction between those who produced art because they had a vision and those who were in the art and book business because they needed to earn a living. He had not recognized Fadiman, but his remarks applied. And there were people at the ceremony who agreed with him, many of them serious artists, like Conrad Aiken or Lillian Hellman, for whom ideas, wherever they led, did mean something. But Faulkner felt easy with none of them.

People were grabbing at him from every direction. Chatto & Windus was going ahead with its anthology, *Faulkner's Country*, with *As I Lay Dying* as the centerpiece. Hollywood was interested in buying his properties, offering options for *Requiem* and *The Wild Palms*, as well as for *Pylon, Sound,* and *Soldiers' Pay* (the latter three from Jerry Wald). ABC television asked him to craft a half-hour show with a McCarthy tie-in, but after he submitted a synopsis he dropped out of the project when ABC insisted on several restrictive contractual arrangements. He was involved in *Big Woods* material—text, illustrations, his own additional comments. He fought off another attempt to invade his privacy, a photographer from Camera Clix, working for *Cosmopolitan* magazine. In his long letter to Commins (February 17 and 18?), he commented on Shenton's illustrations, wondering why the illustrator made Sam Fathers so clearly an Indian, but otherwise showing agreement. He mentions to Else Jonsson the following day that he has another book in mind (which is probably *The Town*). He says he does not feel the gap which he expected once *A Fable* was finished. He suffered, however, from a stomach ailment, a bug he said which he picked up in Egypt; but it could have been that his gut was wearing thin from alcohol. His back pain seems to have subsided. When he was hospitalized in March for the stomach pain, tests proved negative; which meant, possibly, that there was only a slow wearing down of his health, not anything acute.

But other activities were piling up. On the positive side, in addition to Albert Camus's gaining permission to adapt and stage *Requiem* in France, at the end of February. On March 11 *Go Down, Moses* was published in the Modern Library edition, as part of that recovery of Faulkner's past which Random House was undertaking. In Hollywood, Jerry Wald was pressing for film rights, in particular *Sound* and *Soldiers' Pay*, with Faulkner possibly providing the film scripts. But the biggest event, on March 20, was the first of the series of four letters to the Memphis *Commercial Appeal*. Concerned as they were with the question of school segregation and desegregation, and while they argued for human decency and justice for the Negro, they meant the parting of the ways between Faulkner and most other Deep Southerners. As subsequent events revealed, he was isolating himself to such an extent that when the opportunity arose to go to Virginia, he took it. Oxford became for him hostile territory. The first letter on March 20 was followed by those on April 3, 10, and 17.

Before getting to the substance, we can see in Faulkner's letter to Else his desperation about the situation:

> . . . there are many people in Mississippi who will go to any length, even violence, to prevent that [desegregation of schools, voting rights for Negroes], I am afraid. I am doing what I can. I can see the possible time when I shall have to leave my native state, something as the Jew had to flee from Germany during Hitler. I hope that wont happen of course. But at times I think that nothing but a disaster, a military defeat even perhaps, will wake America up and enable us to save ourselves, or what is left. This is a depressing letter, I know. But human beings are terrible. One must believe well in man to endure him, wait out his folly and savagery and inhumanity.[2]

The moment had arrived when Faulkner felt he had to step forward. His was a famous voice which people listened to; and even if he was to be ostracized, he knew he could not live with himself in silence. The conflict within was enormous, for this most private of men was going public. The pivot had been, as noted, the 1954 Supreme Court decision striking down separate but equal schools for whites and Negroes. The dual school system, which had never been equal, was ordered to be dismantled and replaced by a unified one. Faulkner argued that the best students left the state, that Mississippi lost the very part of its black population which it should retain. It also lost some of its best white students, who wanted schooling beyond turmoil and intimidation. Faulkner's remarks do not suggest integration now. At the moment of one of his most radical stands he was trying to be conciliatory. He pressed against human waste and folly, the pursuit of a course of action, opposition, which would destroy the state. He argued not only the justice of equal education for Negroes, but the fact that existing schools were not nearly up to mark. The state's schools were so poor, he said, that if Negro education were raised up to the level of white education, both would be miseducated, instead of solely whites now.[3]

Faulkner's position was centrist, looking toward some movement which would ameliorate a century of injustice. Yet the vituperation began almost immediately. His critics never took up his argument, but rather pointed to the need to keep a poor Negro population to maintain the farm economy. Of course, once machinery began to replace cheap labor, this argument failed, and only resistance for its own sake obtained. Faulkner failed to take into account that, rationally or not, for many white Southerners the Civil War situation was being repeated. Even in the Faulkner household, both John and Jack opposed their brother's public letters, John actively, Jack behind the scenes. What they failed to recognize, or didn't care about, was that these outbursts from Faulkner were not anomalies but part of his 1950s outlook on the individual, justice, and the rights of privacy. They were part of the vision he had expressed sermonistically in the Nobel Prize acceptance speech and very much part of his sense of an American and an American writer. We have found these ideas rooted in Jeffersonian individualism, and supported strongly by the kind of men he found in hunting camp, although they were, for the most part, diehard segregationists.

In a letter (to a Mr. Green) on another matter—the expulsion from the United States of the Metropolitan of the Russian Orthodox Church—Faulkner once more took up the argument against the state, here the federal government. He says it is more important to "keep people talking about freedom in communist countries" than it is "to keep people talking communism out of this one."[4] He adds that he has dealt with enough members of the State Department to know their problems come not from the foreign countries they are sent to, "but from their Washington headquarters." Here, Faulkner sounds like a Northern liberal at the height of the McCarthy pollution.

Yet the main thrust of his argument was not about communism, but Mississippi segregationists and political hypocrisy. Faulkner foresaw a lock developing which could not be broken, and he observed both sides hardening. As someone who abhorred rapid or radical change, feared it as much as he feared for the future of the country under continued segregation, he was, for even his gradualist approach, labeled a communist, a red sympathizer, a traitor. He did not even argue for a fully integrated school system; but he did emphasize that if Mississippi did run a two-track system, it should be equal for all. He also advocated a two-tier setup, the first tier academic, the second trade and craft. But whatever shape they took, these schools must be accessible to whoever can achieve in them. Color was not a viable exclusionary principle. These points he argued in his two April papers of the third and tenth. On the seventeenth, he was encouraged by a white student who wrote him that he was willing to accept change; but at the same time he foresaw the federal government at loggerheads with the Mississippi state government, and violence not distant.

But despite his despair at what was shaping up, he was now a man on the move. At the University of Oregon, then at the University of Montana, he delivered a speech, "Freedom American Style," which when published in *Harper's* in July became "On Privacy (The American Dream: What Happened to It?)." There was a follow-up paper on a related subject in 1956, called "On Fear," which with the above was to form a small book on public issues (never written). The Oregon talk took place on April 14, the Montana one on April 17, and by May 7 he was reporting on the Kentucky Derby for *Sports Illustrated* for $2,000 plus expenses. On April 20, he took time to send a telegram to Commins on Einstein's death—Faulkner had met the physicist at the Comminses: ". . . one of the wisest of men and one of the gentlest of men. Who can replace him in either let alone in both."

When he returned to Oxford after the Derby, Faulkner entered into a series of steps which affected him profoundly. He found at Rowan Oak the letter, already two months old, from Harold Howland of the State Department inviting him to attend an August seminar for Japanese professors of English and American literature, to be convened in Nagano, Japan. His activities would be multifold, but mainly to meet with fifty or so Japanese professors on a regular afternoon and/or evening basis. In addition, there would be press conferences, airport interviews, private gatherings with various notables. It was the complete menu of events which normally drove him into a need for hospitalization. But he had a sympathetic female guide, and he was obviously touched by the sincere Japanese interest in his work. He was also the ultimate "lion in the garden" in this country: idolized, pursued, respected, deferred to. He obviously enjoyed the attention of courteous and well-mannered people, who at times reminded him of the South at its best; but he also enjoyed the Japanese "difference," the cultural disparities between him and his hosts. At first, when he wrote Howland, he indicated he preferred Europe, or at least some follow-up to the Nagano trip with a continuation in Europe. The latter meant Else, also Jean, and other old friends. But he emphasized he was ready to perform any tasks within his capacity.

But even as he embarked on these new commitments, he was still deep in Mississippi affairs, political and personal. We have already cited from his anguished letter to Else the passage in which he says he may have to leave the state, as Jews left Germany; and we have noted, in the background, Phil Stone's sardonic commentary on Faulkner's interest in desegregation. Stone now commented[5] that very likely Faulkner would come forward with a plan to perfect the entire school system; that any Faulkner could bring forth a reorganization of heaven itself. The less they know, he adds, the more they are willing to voice their opinions. But Faulkner was truly anguished, as he saw the country ripped up by racial matters—most of all his own state, which was responding irrationally to a national tragedy. On another front, he asked Commins to send on another $5,000 for several purposes: to send his dead brother Dean's daughter, Dean, to school, and to provide allowances for Estelle and Maud. He planned to be away for some time, and although he and Estelle were not officially separated, they were and would be separated for long periods of time. He indicates considerable pleasure at the forthcoming publication of *Big Woods* (October 14), and regrets he will not be home on publication day. There was also the question of arranging for an option on *Soldiers' Pay*, for a ten percent advance on a sale price of $22,500. Faulkner tells Ober that if the amount seems right to go ahead, so he, Faulkner, can repay his debt to Geller, who often protected him at Warner Brothers. Geller and Jerry Wald were trying to get hold of the film property, but nothing came of this venture.

In a revealing presentation of himself to Howland (July 8), Faulkner tries to clarify what he is and what could be expected of him. ". . . I am not a lecturer, no practice at it, and I am not a true 'literary' man, being a countryman who simply likes books, not authors, nor the establishment of writing and criticism and judging books. So if I go anywhere as simply a literary man or an expert on literature, American or otherwise, I will be a bust." Then he defines his strengths: "I will do better as a simple private individual, occupation unimportant, who is interested in and believes in people, humanity, and has some concern about man's condition and his future, if he is not careful."[6] He is also concerned about copyright, indicating he has in progress a book composed of chapters on the subject of what has happened to the American Dream. He presented one chapter at the University of Oregon and published it in *Harper's;* but the book, as we have noted, never got written.

Land of the Pharaohs, for which Faulkner was credited with the screenplay, along with Hawks, Harry Kurnitz, and Harry Jack Bloom, previewed in Memphis and was released on July 2.* Before leaving on July 29 for Japan, Faulkner tied up loose ends: *Big Woods* galleys, final financial arrangements for Estelle and his extended family, workouts with his horses, while trying to avoid serious injury. What he was leaving behind was a mixed sense of life: no real improvement with Estelle, although by this time they had, tacitly or explicitly, decided to stick the course, despite

*A final screenplay, with some revisions, cited only Hawks and Kurnitz as writers, but Faulkner's name remained as having worked on an earlier script.

his marriage proposal to Jean. Estelle was herself moving toward temperance, the result of serious stomach trouble, an ulcer which acted up, and a run-down physical condition generally. She had more or less accepted her husband's philandering, and decided that the marriage was preferable to divorce. Faulkner's finances were in reasonably good shape, since he gathered in an additional $3,500 from Jerry Wald and Columbia Pictures for an option on *Sound,* ten percent down on an ultimate payment of $35,000 if the option were picked up (as it was).

But while certain areas were cleared, the demons could not be stilled. He was upset and anguished over the racial question, his writing (the second volume of the Snopes trilogy), the desert of his love life. Dissatisfied and unfulfilled, inevitably he began to drink. Even the prospect of an interesting trip took on a different dimension when he was confronted with the reality: he feared all the interviews and conferences. And Japan, unlike Europe, was unknown. His attitude was one of conflict at every level except financial. The local Oxford doctor, Chester McLarty, put him under his care. Faulkner had to be monitored carefully if he were to make his flight on the twenty-ninth. He made it, twenty-four hours of plane time, from Memphis to Tokyo, via Fort Worth and Los Angeles.

When he arrived in Tokyo on August 1, Faulkner carried with him all these internal problems. He had been drinking steadily, and he was malnourished. When he was met by a crowd of reporters—the buildup had been considerable, with the State Department hoping to make a killing with this event—his first reaction was to clam up and withdraw into a binging situation. As observers reported, this Nobel Prize winner feared most of all that he would be unable to meet the expectations of the Japanese; that in the situation he was a fraud, a country man with a vivid imagination. Faulkner always underestimated his intellectual abilities, carrying with him throughout his life his perception of himself as a school dropout, not as a man who compensated for lack of schooling with broad reading. We see emerging in this harried situation his sense of inferiority when he was with educated people, or those he thought would have intellectual expectations of him. As he emerged from the plane and was asked for a statement, it was as though he had walked into a gigantic cocktail party where everyone suddenly turned to him. Every instinct and feeling made him want to withdraw. He managed, finally, a somewhat incoherent statement about his interest in Japanese culture, and his desire to speak in Nagano about problems common to all mankind. The initial statement did not add up to anything in particular, but it was sufficient that he had responded.

The three-week party was on its way. One problem which occurred to Dr. Leon Picon, who was in charge of the embassy's book program, was to make sure Faulkner was supervised at every moment. His schedule was packed with one event after another, with little regard for the age of the subject or his physical response to the grind. Faulkner was taken to International House at Azabu, Tokyo, given lunch, taken to see a Japanese rehearsal of *The Teahouse of the August Moon*, put before reporters at a press conference later in the afternoon. By the end of this conference, which was in itself grueling, he still had eaten little, but was drinking and spiraling into one of his conditions. The consequence would be inability to continue, collapse, hospitalization. The hyped-up external situation met the internal depression and will to withdraw. With this, deep in struggle, he collapsed inwardly, and only alcohol relieved the pain.

At the press conference, he tried gallantly to provide what was expected of him. He tells the interviewers he wants to see Japan behind the tourist version: "how people live, what they do, and I would like to know if possible what they think." He wanted to see the countryside, the farmer. When asked if he was currently working on a novel (a question which had no relationship to anything which came before), he deflected it, and went off on his desire to perceive the Japanese soul, what makes all men human beings. Asked about Hemingway, whose ghost trailed him everywhere, Faulkner repeated his well-known position, that Hemingway "never did try to get outside the boundary of what he really could do and risk failure. He did what he really could do marvelously well, first rate, but to me that is not success but failure . . . failure to me is the best."[7] Even *The Old Man and the Sea*, which he labeled a first-rate job, was not enough, not a sufficient challenge.

Then the questions zeroed in on Faulkner's basic ideas, and he was asked if he considered human life basically a tragedy. His answer was not only pure Faulkner but pure Conrad: ". . . man's immortality is that he is faced with a tragedy which he can't beat and he still tries to do something with it"; reminiscent of Stein's advice to Jim to immerse himself in the destructive element. With his philosophy based on potential doom, his sense of personal demons, and his awareness of political disaster, Faulkner found this a congenial resting place. His long-term criticism of Hemingway can be found here, that the writer cheapened the tragic sense of life with his dependence on forms of heroic action. Hemingway did this well, but he reduced experience to what heroism could resolve. Faulkner felt he knew otherwise: that life had its own coordinates.

The Japanese asked Faulkner if he believed man could achieve perfection. He said yes, but it would be at the expense of being a man. He believed in his kind of man who strives, works, does not accept easy forms of progress, who tries to improve himself—he may fail, but the effort is what makes him a man. This line inevitably moves to the question of the Negro in America. Faulkner responded with his usual concern, but also with his philosophy of moderation which meant little in the way events were going. "I think," he said, "if the Negro himself has enough sense, tolerance, wisdom, to be still for a short time, there will be complete equality in America. His black skin will make no difference."[8] He understands the white man is fearful that if the Negro advances socially, his economic status will change; and the cotton crop, for one, depends on cheap Negro labor. But in asking Negroes to "be still," Faulkner was thinking mainly of the older Negroes, those he knew from town and on the farm, or his own house servants; he had little sense of the younger Negroes, those who were students in the Negro colleges, as well as those who had served in the war and were not ready to accept the dictates and intimidations of a white world.

He stressed that the plight of the Negro was economic—but even here, he was simplifying racial hatred that went well beyond the Negro as cheap labor. There was fear, social and sexual as well as economic. If he absorbed the broadsides coming from the various Citizens' Councils around the state, he would know it was *Birth of a Nation* reborn—the free, unintimidated Negro would pillage and rape. Once restraints were off, this version went, the Negro would revert to his animal heritage, an ape out of Africa. Faulkner either failed to hear this message or ignored it out of fear of the politicization that was taking place. He agreed the Supreme Court decision on segregation in the schools is "right, it's just." He sees it as an enforcement problem, and that is why he thinks the Negro must be patient and sensible, must wait for, perhaps, three hundred years—his figure.

In running through literary matters once more, he assigned Wolfe as the finest failure, then himself, followed by Dos Passos, Hemingway taking up the rear. No mention of Fitzgerald. Asked about Steinbeck, he says he is just a reporter, "a newspaperman, not really a writer." With a nonsequitur typical of interviews, this bleeds over into more on the Negro. He tells of white people in Mississippi—he perhaps had in mind Silver of the University of Mississippi history department—who supported desegregated schools and suffer ostracism, even violence, for their opinions. Asked about Hodding Carter, he says he is a fine man, thought by some to be wishy-washy, but a man who must live in the region he criticizes. Asked, in another nonsequitur, which of his books he thinks are most successful, Faulkner cites *Sound* as his "finest failure" and, therefore, his best book. He repeats the story of writing *Sanctuary* because he needed money. At the other end of the spectrum, he indicates he wrote *A Fable*, not for money, but because he had something important to say. He admits it was not "good enough," but suggests that he will try to say it again next year. Asked about what phases of Japanese culture he was interested in, he says its "culture of intellect." By that, he meant the rules by which men can live with courtesy, politeness, courage—what he assumes is close to the samurai tradition: not to be brave for its own sake, but at the right time; perilously close to Hemingway's grace under pressure. He transforms, at least here, the samurai tradition into a Southern one.

That was day one. The next day Dr. Leon Picon recognized Faulkner was in no shape to appear before a large group of foreign correspondents and guests at the Foreign Correspondents Club. The writer said his back hurt, for which he had been drinking. Picon went ahead alone and tried to explain that Faulkner was under the weather (i.e., affected by the heat), but the savvier correspondents knew otherwise and took "under the weather" less metaphorically. An afternoon reception, with the American ambassador present, deteriorated; Faulkner came, but did little but drink steadily.* The ambassador, John M. Allison, wanted Faulkner out before he made a mess of things, and he wrote a memo to Lew Schmidt to that effect. Schmidt, Picon, and Don Ranard, all junior officers in charge of getting Faulkner around, decided to put their own necks on the line and offered to resign if they could not pull the writer together and make a success of things. It was apparently the one thing which made Faulkner come around, even as he was on the edge of collapse. He was touched by the young men who had jeopardized their own careers for him, and their act raised in the writer all of his hostility to authority, located in the ambassador. With his egalitarian sympathies alerted, he decided not only to go on, but to make the young men proud of him.

The interviews came on in waves. Meeting six Japanese authors at the PEN Club, Faulkner spoke a lot of malarkey about his closeness to land which had been handed down to him by his forefathers; apparently thinking that the traditional Japanese would like the idea of continuity and historical backgrounding. None of this was true for the writer, however —he had started as a "new man," with only memories and stories of the past, no land, no money, nothing passed down. The Japanese themselves felt mixed about his statements, since they were attempting to cope with that very postwar interruption and destruction of tradition Faulkner made to seem so important. Yet they liked him—his silences, his impassivity, his lack of forwardness; they took this to mean good manners, perhaps an antidote to their preconception of the loud, pushy American. They praised him as a paternal figure in the Japanese mold, and once they accepted him personally, it did not really matter what he said. During the stay, he said a lot of things which made little sense, either generally or for him in particular—although commentators and Faulknerians have taken his words as if scripture. But for the most part, he tried to be honest, and in some circumstances we do get insights into his way of thinking and what was important for him.

A good example of the gibberish he proclaimed came with the August 4 interviews, the day before he left Tokyo for Nagano City, about one hundred miles northwest of the capital. The conditions of the interviews —one series of questions after another, four separate interviews, running on for three hours—probably had something to do with Faulkner's responses. By the middle and end, Faulkner was just talking, without regard for sense or consistency. Early on, he repeated his dictum from the Nobel Prize speech that man is more important than his environment, his laws, than even the sorry things he does as a nation or race. He added that he uses violence, not for itself (has he forgotten *Sanctuary*?), but "to tell some truth which you think is important."[9] With Nancy Mannigoe from *Requiem* in mind, he says man must often commit evil in order to correct or

---

*Including spilling his drink on the dress of the ambassador's wife.

change it. The writer must try to leave the world a little better than he found it, to help get rid of war, injustice, inequality. To do this, he must often sink to the level of the elements he is attempting to alter.

Then came an inevitable question: Gide had commented that ". . . there is not one of Faulkner's characters who properly speaking has a soul." Gide said this apparently without reference to Quentin Compson, Joanna Burden, Joe Christmas (who could compete with Gide's own Lafcadio for "soul"), some Bundrens, and Gavin Stevens. Faulkner answered dutifully, that the fault lay in him. "To me they had souls, and I was doing the best I could to show man's soul in conflict with his evil nature or his environment. Now if I didn't do that, then the fault is not the character's, but mine." He adds that he thinks Gide has "good talent, very intelligent talent"—a kind of Hemingwayesque parody.

Then a question on literary influences. Faulkner mentions Anderson and Dreiser but rejects Poe, Hawthorne, and Longfellow because "they were easterners, they were really Europeans." The Japanese accept this and slide off to Oscar Wilde, another European, along with Swinburne and the transplanted Poe. Then he is asked about T. S. Eliot, and Faulkner answers that while Poe dealt in prose, Eliot deals in poetry, which is so universal it doesn't matter whether he's English, American, or Japanese. They accept this also and move on to Dreiser and social realism, followed by Eliot and the new humanism. The question had neither historical nor critical significance—it didn't even make sense—but to this Faulkner gave a lengthy reply. He says that Dreiser wrote in a kind of isolation, but with Eliot "so much has happened in the world." He adds that in his, Faulkner's time, even more has occurred. As a result, tradition—and he cites the Japanese example as well—loses its continuity and must become "humanitarian or conscious of sociological changes whether it wants to or not."[10] Faulkner ended this particular marathon with his statement, now his signature piece, that one must believe in man, "that man will prevail, that there's no suffering, no anguish, that man is not suitable to changing, if he wants to, then to work hard."

With their discontinuous questions and Faulkner's responses off the top of his head, these interviews set the pace for the remainder of the trip. As long as Faulkner showed up, stayed reasonably sober, and poured out a requisite number of words, it really didn't matter what he said. The Japanese liked him. Not only courteous and polite, he was even small enough in stature so they did not feel physically intimidated. Also, nearing sixty, he was old enough to be venerated for age as well as accomplishment—a fatherly and grandfatherly figure in Japan, someone over the hill in America. The smiling sixty-year-old man had only to stay reasonably sober and set his face to meet the faces.

On the morning of August 5, Faulkner traveled to Nagano, a vacation spa, where he stayed at the Gomeikan Hotel for the next twelve days. Fifty Japanese professors and four American faculty advisers awaited the writer, and this news, plus the change of venue, only made him more anguished. The location was a lovely Japanese *ryokan* as residence, functional and stark in its clear lines. First came another interview with the press. When asked about his admiration for Japanese culture, Faulkner answered that it is "so much longer than our American tradition." The Japanese have had thousands of years in which to train themselves in culture and in intelligence, "which we don't have, and any American will of course have an admiration for that." He indicates he does know a little Japanese poetry through Ezra Pound. Then he was asked one of those ludicrous questions which could drive even a sober man to drink. "Do you anticipate that oriental culture will create something different from Western culture?" It drove Faulkner to an equal idiocy in his response. "Not really different— its manifestation will be different, but the culture I think is the same. The oriental culture is much older than the Western culture, so in that way it is different."[11]

He apparently felt that if he continued to repeat "culture" he could work his way back into reason. Luckily, there was no follow-up, and the topic shifted to Japanese authors he had met, to which he responded they were much more intelligent than he. He was asked if *A Fable*, with its tale of a resurrection of a soldier, was a new trend in his work, perhaps a new militarism. Faulkner said it was simply an old story in Western culture which people can understand and believe. And when prodded if he was a believing Christian, he gave his standard response: that while Christianity "gets pretty debased," he does believe in God, by which he means man has a soul that aspires toward God. He says Christianity remains untried, although it might prove useful one day. And, finally, the inevitable question about his feelings about the South. His response is Quentin Compson's at the conclusion of *Absalom*—"Well, I love it and hate it.[12] Some of the things there I don't like at all, but I was born there, and that's my home, and I will still defend it even if I hate it." Faulkner omitted the fact that shortly after making *his* statement of ambiguous feelings, Quentin committed suicide.

With that under his belt, he moved to the Nagano Seminar Colloquies, which proved trying. One of the problems was something endemic to the pecking order of academic life: although the younger professors were interested in ideas, they held back because, in Japan, the older ones had to speak first; yet the latter were already encased in stone. Faulkner read a brief statement about how American writers were less interested in ideas than in the universal truths of men's hearts. With that, he became silent, the professors remained silent, and after one or two desultory questions the session ended. Finally, through Leon Picon's aid, he was able to work out a modus operandi, with the help of the older professors as well; and he also turned his meals into seminars. He was particularly struck with Kyoko Sakairi, a member of Picon's staff, and later with Midori Sasaki, whom he decided to send back to the United States with a scholarship. A Hiroshiman of twenty-four, Midori Sasaki called up his liking for quiet, reticent, deferential young women. It is not clear at precisely what stage in his trip Faulkner suggested that they become intimate.

Once these arrangements were made and the question period became less formalized, Faulkner appeared to expand, and even the questions put to him seemed less arch. They were now coming to him, in the main, from people trained in literature. Faulkner's responses run to the size of a small book, and they become, despite a good deal of wastage, a kind of loose, discontinuous autobiographical statement. While he does not make any startling revelations, he is candid about himself and he does demonstrate his tremendous commitment to art as the highest form of human expression. One gets the impression he feels that without art man would regress to even greater bestiality than he has already manifested. "To me, a proof of man's immortality . . . that the idea of a God is valuable, is in the fact that he writes the books and composes the music and paints the pictures. They are the firmament of mankind. They are the proof that if there is a God and he wants us to see something that proves to him that mankind exists, that would be proof."[13]

In Faulkner's remarks here and later, in response to questions about civilization and progress, he reveals a startling linkage to Nietzschean ideas. Without assigning any formal connection between the Southern novelist and the German philologist-philosopher, we can see Faulkner operating in comparable areas, especially in his sharp sense of human bankruptcy. The dominant society which drew Nietzsche's venom stressed very real values of progress, technology, and scientific discovery. Man was beginning to enjoy a better life, especially as medical advances (anesthesia, sanitation, hygiene, pasteurization, discovery of antibodies for killer diseases) decreased infant mortality and prolonged adult life. Statistically, one could measure progress, not simply profess it. What was true in Nietzsche's day was equally true of Faulkner's, although the level and intensity of progress were somewhat different. Yet all of this activity was, for the German, physical energy having little to do with true energy, which was psychological and psychical. Nietzsche understood and insisted upon the "other life," where physical energy is transformed into psychical energy. That energy within was the source of a reality that, like a Platonic ideal, lay beyond physical dimensions and could be released as drives, impulses, and forces.

Progress untransformed into such inner energy was a form of death; desire for such empty truths was a deformation of human need. For all its benefits, civilization meant a dilution of a life. For Nietzsche, all acts of suicide, displays of suffering, manifestations of illness were forms of dying which led to transformation; not final acts, but parts of a process through which man could save himself. Faulkner, for his part, had always insisted on the need for ambitious failure over easy success; and his sense of failure as a means of estimating man's achievement fitted well into Nietzsche's formulation that "Man is something that must be overcome." A good deal of this sounded familiar, also, from Conrad.

Nietzsche had to deal with the paradoxes in his own theories, as would Faulkner. To emphasize transformation, to argue that man must often seek success through failure, that even that failure can be a degree of achievement—to argue thus is to tamper with the idea of history and historical process. Both Nietzsche and Faulkner supported modernism and avant-gardes, with all their implications of breaking with traditional modes, in fact destroying them in the process of rebuilding something new or different. As we know, Faulkner moved at his best within a strong historical context; as a sensitive Southerner, he could do no less. Yet the paradox is that the historical process is inhibited by the emphasis on avant-gardes, which must clash with continuities. Put another way, if history is not to become ossified, it becomes dependent on renewal; otherwise it declines into pastness, not vital historical process. Yet every act of renewal threatens history, just as the historical process threatens to swallow up what renews it, whether a new generic mutation or a novel idea. The paradox remains of each canceling out the other, and that is why Nietzsche, ever alert to contradictions, called one essay "Of the Use and Misuse of History for Life."

Faulkner never theoretically worked his way through this paradox, although in *Absalom* he met it head-on as a fictive process, where he does have to deal with the clash of history and method. In that novel, in fact, as in no other, he demonstrates how the two seemingly conflicting elements can encounter each other literarily, whereas in theory they cannot. Yet the problem nagged at Faulkner, although not in the theoretical, philosophical manner of a Nietzsche—rather in his efforts by which he could continue to perceive tradition and yet not become tradition-bound. His comments on art as the transcendental expression of man's linkage to God is one such form of expression.

Furthermore, there was the question of how much historical process could still be honored when Faulkner's South was being riven by racial issues, which turned tradition and custom into enemies of justice and decency. In this environment—which he insisted "shaped culture rather than culture treated environment"[14]—we have the disruption of the old in the name of the new. This was still another dimension of the problem Faulkner had to deal with. Although not a systematic thinker, he had absorbed into himself the terrible dilemmas that lay in wait for any serious artist in the twentieth century. What makes the Nagano seminars valuable, despite many inane encounters, is how they reveal his assimilation of these dilemmas, his effort to grapple with them, his withdrawal in the face of what cannot be sustained.

He is harsh on the younger American generation, calling it confused and nihilistic. Although basically sound, young Americans walk away from problems—one of which involves keeping the Negro down so as to sustain an agricultural economy. When asked if America had economic equality, Faulkner responded with exceptional force.

> Actually, in my country, I think there's a desire everywhere that it [racial prejudice and consequent economic inequality] be got rid of, that such a condition is in itself a sickness, that there are—a minority —other people whose economy depends on that sickness, and they will drown themselves to the fact that no nation can live very long sick, it has got to suffer the operation which will remove this sickness, this cancer. In time, that cancer will be removed. It's—I prefer—to think that this is the only practical way to do it—that people must be calm.

Then he repeats his dictum: the victims of injustice must be patient.

Given the readiness of Faulkner to answer openly and fully, it would have been interesting if the Japanese interviewers had pressed him on his conception of victims' patience while the majority formed Citizens' Councils to evade the Supreme Court decision. And it would have been doubly interesting if the interviewers had also asked him about Northern forms of evasion. But the interviewers put no pressure on the subject, practiced no follow-through. He had himself mentioned that the Japanese were free of prejudice against "the color of skin"; but he passed up the chance to point out the Japanese distrust of outsiders, their inhuman treatment of the Chinese during their occupation of China, their denigration of Koreans based on class and caste during their occupation of Korea, their poor treatment of the Taiwanese during their occupation of Formosa. He could have reminded his hosts that while racial prejudice, accompanied by class- and caste hatred, was a blight in Mississippi, in its broader sense it also infected Japan. Many such moments went by, with the Japanese unwilling to press their famous visitor, and Faulkner, for his part, willing to forgive the Japanese all. There is in his delicate comments not only a desire to be courteous—we can expect that—but somehow a need to compensate for the bomb.

What followed (in the third session of the seminars) was a long segment on "The Bear," and especially on whether the wilderness was a metaphor for the whole of modern civilization. Faulkner responded eagerly. Denying that the wilderness represented the whole modern scene, he made a distinction. "The wilderness to me was the past, which could be the old evils, the old forces, which were by their own standards right and correct, ruthless, but they loved and died by their own code—they asked nothing. . . . The bear was a symbol of the old forces, not evil forces, but the old forces which in man's youth were not evil, but that they were in man's blood, his inheritance, his [instinctive] impulses came from that old or ruthless malevolence, which was nature."

Once the attraction of being center-stage began to wear thin, Faulkner became, as expected, distracted, nervous, anxiety-ridden. A crisis was developing which had to be avoided. He was drinking, as yet moderately, but he told Picon, whom he regarded highly, that he could not go on without alcohol. Picon reminded him of his obligations and, like a good student, Faulkner braced himself for the next session. There was clearly something torturous about the proceedings as this most private of men was picked clean by professors who in reality knew little about him or his work. It was in this context that the introduction of some female loveliness and companionship became essential: Kyoko Sakairi and Midori Sasaki helped keep him going.

Faulkner promised to compare his impressions of Japan—polite, courteous, full of beautiful scenery—with the American South. This was tricky, but he attempted to find an analogy between Southern planter aristocracy and the Japanese samurai tradition, a rather severe bending of two different cultures. He also compared Southern peasantry with Japanese peasants, another jolting analogy. But this was a hurdle he had to overcome. He stressed once again the injustice done to Indians and Negroes, based on skin color. His answers here are standard, more likely to help him escape than to elucidate highly complex scenarios. He was more at home when asked about Mark Twain, and he gives Hemingway's response: that Twain was the father of us all, "the first truly American writer, and all of us since are his heirs."[15] Whitman, he says, cannot be forgotten, but Twain grew up believing there could be an American literature and set out to write it. Then came another batch of questions on Hemingway, who, along with Faulkner, was considered a master of contemporary American fiction. Faulkner got through this, and found something he felt more comfortable with, horses, discussing the five he owned. He adds that it was from horses that he learned to have sympathy for creatures not as wise as man, and to have pity for physically weak things.

Déjà vu and exhaustion were setting in as the questioner, now on the trail of animals in Faulkner, focused once again on "The Bear," after a swipe at "Spotted Horses." Faulkner made his little talk on symbolism, on the old ways, on the bear representing not evil but obsolescent ways. As he describes the piece, reducing and simplifying it, it sounds increasingly like a rerun of *Huckleberry Finn*, with its boy's initiation into life and nature. Twain is of course present in the Faulkner story, but not to the degree a reductive explanation of "The Bear" suggests. He would appear more insistently in *The Reivers: A Reminiscence*.

With this, Faulkner moved on to what had been promised as the final session, the sixth plenary meeting. He read from what was to become his new book, on questions of privacy and how its loss was subverting the American dream*; and then he spoke of segregation, of how it was based

---

*In later form, this segment became part of the chapter called "On Fear: The South in Labor," reprinted as "On Fear: Deep South in Labor: Mississippi" (1956).

on the fear that the Southern economy depended on cheap Negro labor. He foresaw America's survival in dramatic terms: as either giving justice to all or perishing against the propaganda onslaughts of the totalitarian nations. Urged on by his perception of real external threat, he affirmed the American spirit to create a just society, his tone suggesting America might have little time left to rectify its injustices. Yet we must also consider his audience, for he was telling the Japanese, who only ten years before were a militaristic, totalitarian partner of Hitler's Germany, that democratic ways are the only salvation for a country. The Japanese were apparently deeply moved by his fervor. Faulkner was doing what he believed in and also precisely what the American State Department desired.

The Japanese admitted that they too had racial problems, citing their relationship with Koreans. But Faulkner insisted America's were on a broader base, and that racism "is a blot not only on the American face but it's on the face of all humanity." He detested, he says, the hypocrisy of those who don't come out and say the inequality must continue for economic reasons; arguing instead that the Bible says the Negro must not be our equal, "that if the Lord wanted him to be our equal, the Lord would have made him white," that a "different kind of blood runs in the Negro's veins from the white man's veins."[16] Faulkner was upset not only at the injustice but at the subversion of language, at words being used to shield the truth.

He was being drawn in fully, and consequently we have some of his most anguished efforts at dealing with the racial situation in the Deep South. His questioners finally follow up. They ask him about gradualism, especially in New Orleans, which one of the interrogators is familiar with. Faulkner insists, as before, that because the situation is not only moral but economic, that it cannot be changed overnight. But here his argument falls into a gray area, because while progress depends on good will, he is unable to demonstrate where the broad base for good will can come from. Faulkner tries to deal with what he senses is unresolved by distinguishing between man's instincts and his conscience. His instincts tell him to hang on to everything he has at any price, but his conscience tells him to relent, to be more flexible. Man is only base, Faulkner feels, when he takes a high moral tone while pretending his motives are other than those we know he has. Faulkner says each man must seek truth in himself, or else writhe with doubt and shame at night; but he also knows appeals to conscience are meaningless given the nature of Mississippi politics—its corruption of ideas and language.

Once again, he was not pressed further than this—he has by now made his set speech on the subject, which reverberates with good will but a sense of impotence. Once more, the turn is toward his fiction, specifically to *Sound* and its inception, especially the first section. In remarks already quoted, Faulkner indicates it began as a short story, with some children being sent away from the house during their grandmother's funeral. Although we have heard this explanation before, we still marvel at how Faulkner put together this novel with so much mature comprehension of the needs of his craft, himself barely out of his twenties. He insists it was not a deliberate tour de force, but that it just grew. His questioner wonders how he could have written without notes, but Faulkner does not answer this; he says he wanted to use colors to indicate speaker, thinker, time, even discrete moments in time. He is asked about drinking, and says he considers it "a normal instinct, not a hobby. A normal and healthy instinct."[17] No one pursues. Asked why *A Fable* took nine years to write, he says it would be comforting to think it was that the theme required such a long gestation period; but he thinks he wasn't ready to write it, and perhaps his powers had failed as he got older.

Faulkner visited the Zenkoji Temple. He had also begun to form impressions of Japan, as he got to know Midori Sasaki better, and compared her and her type to others, observing farmers, priests in the temple, common people on the street. The temple, he says, impressed him with its age-old qualities, its sense of tradition; but he could not grapple with what it meant to a Japanese. He also responded to other impressions: he sees water, he says, as part of the intimate life of the Japanese, not just to drink, but integrated as if totemic.

With Leon Picon prodding him, he began to write up his impressions, and Picon himself kept a journal of events. On August 14, Faulkner went sailing on Lake Nojiri. It turned out to be one of those magical days in which he was back in his milieu, sailing with Picon, getting stuck, helping release the boat from a mudflat, paddling and using sail as needed. His impressions were very much on the Japanese interviewers' minds, as though by forcing *him* into comments *they* could build up their own sense of the country, only ten years beyond unconditional surrender. If Faulkner desperately needed their support during this long stay, they needed him to give them a sense of their own worth. They pressed with queries about mountains, people, their racial characteristics (were they too serious? too intellectual?), even their songs. Faulkner responds that his impressions come from faces. ". . . I saw the face and when I had the pencil and paper I found out what I thought when I saw that face."[18]

On the eve of his departure from Nagano, Faulkner gave a document of his impressions to the moderator and then offered something as a postscript. He thanked his hosts for their warmth. "They say to part is to die a little—not to die, but to leave something, perhaps. So when I go I will have left something in Japan and in its place I'll take something back with me to my country, something of the courtesy and the warmth of the Japanese people."[19] Despite some early difficulties, the Nagano seminars had proved to be a lovefest. The American ambassador who wanted to ship Faulkner back home had little understanding of the writer or his response to the new situation. Leon Picon and his staff had saved the day, and it proved to be the best kind of thing: rewarding to Faulkner personally, and rewarding to American-Japanese relations, which is what the State Department had wanted in the first place. His going-away gift from the students was a kimono, fitted with a pipe pocket.

Faulkner's relationship with Midori Sasaki had become much closer. Blotner describes her appearance, as he got it from Picon:

> . . . small, petite, and intensely feminine. She had black hair, black eyes, and a beautifully clear complexion which she protected from the sun with a dainty parasol. She also carried a folding fan, which she would use to conceal the quick and genuine blushes that signaled her frequent shy embarrassment at the attention Faulkner sometimes showed her in the presence of elder and much more prominent Japanese. . . . When she ventured to speak, her high-pitched voice was little more than a whisper. Raised within the traditional Japanese concept of the place of woman, she spoke with a hesitancy which stemmed partly from genuine modesty and partly from custom.[20]

Faulkner pursued this young woman, whose deference and shy manner fitted well into the type of Southern young lady he favored. He honored her with a page of his writing, which he asked her to translate into Japanese; but she said it was too difficult and shared pieces of the page with her friends. Faulkner decided to send her to the United States on a scholarship, an example of his quid pro quo relationships with young women, recalling his mentor-student liaison with Joan.

Before the stay in Tokyo, which ended his trip, Faulkner headed for Kyoto, perhaps the most beautiful of Japanese cities. When the United States first planned to use the atomic bomb on Japan, Kyoto was one of the original targets, along with Hiroshima and Nagasaki. But Kyoto was finally rejected, turned into an "open city" because of its artwork. South of Nagano, Kyoto was Faulkner's "home" for four days, a city of Buddhist temples, formal gardens, and elegant private homes. The entire city, not just its museums, was a museum. Kyoto proved as arduous in terms of interviews, press conferences, and meeting of new people, but the questions stayed the same, so that Faulkner rarely felt pushed. He called on various Japanese dignitaries, including a Nobel Prize winner in physics, Hideki Yukawa; he had less to say to him than he had to Einstein. The press conferences were the most demanding, as nearly five hundred scholars, newsmen, teachers, intellectuals of various stripes, and professionals from all fields converged to ask questions which he had already answered elsewhere.

Returning via Kyoto, he stayed three days in Tokyo and then to head for Manila to see his stepdaughter, Victoria, and her husband. He was also looking ahead to Europe and to seeing Jean in Rome. His mood was turning taciturn and uncertain, his attitude depressed. There was, of course, the letdown, the feeling that momentary glory could not hide the problems which remained: he was not writing, and Rowan Oak awaited him whenever he chose to return. He was in effect postponing his real life, while the transitory, fairy-tale existence continued. He was not even drinking heavily, just steadily, to keep him on course, functional. He depended on his State Department "family" to support him, and yet even they were insufficient. Perhaps it was the surging interviews and press conferences he had to give which depressed him. Blotner suggests[21] that Faulkner felt that somehow he had let down the youth of the country; that they had problems and conflicts he had not addressed. But their conflicts lay deep within Japanese culture, with that sharp clash of old and new which resulted from the American occupation and MacArthur's imposition of a democratic constitution on the country. As the psychiatrist Robert Jay Lifton has written, the Japanese were compelled to make shifts in their attitudes and ideas so rapidly they either adapted or else became marginal, suicidal, depressed, unable to cope with their new lives. The youth of a certain age were caught in this spiral: remaking Japan and themselves, or else falling away useless. Faulkner had no way of dealing with any of this, although it reminded him dramatically of what was occurring in his own Deep South.

There was a long meeting at the Tokyo American Cultural Center, an extremely important part of Faulkner's visit, although it came at the conclusion. Asked about Negro writers, Faulkner cited Richard Wright as one who "had a great deal of talent. . . . He wrote one good book and then he went astray, he got too concerned in the difference between the Negro man and the white man and he stopped being a writer and became a Negro."[22] Faulkner continued: "Another one named Ellison has talent and so far he has managed to stay away from being first a Negro, he is still first a writer." He says those two have the talent that both Hemingway and Fitzgerald had as young men. Faulkner's assessment that "being a Negro" will destroy a Negro writer on the face of it seems bizarre, if not perverse. But what he has in mind is some grand, sweeping sense that a writer overcomes what he is—black, white, male, female—in order to be a writer, that somehow the act of writing preempts all other considerations. Yet he recognizes the burden this puts on the Negro, who must dissociate himself from what he is in order to become a writer. He also recognizes that the white writer does not have this pressure on him "to remind him of what he is by the color of his skin, by social condition, by status."

With that, he was ready for the next stage of his Far East journey, covering ground Estelle had covered before him, visiting the Philippines, where he remained for forty-eight hours.* Arriving on August 24, he was met by Victoria, Bill Fielden, and their daughter Vicki. The plan was to intersperse interviews and press conferences with some family visiting and relaxation. Since Faulkner was not fond of either Victoria or her daughter, there must have been some level of tension, although in such a short visit it probably remained muted.

---

*Faulkner's sessions in Manila were taped and collected in a pamphlet called "Faulkner on Truth and Freedom," published by the Philippine Writers Association in 1956.

On Saturday, August 27, Faulkner put Manila behind him. His time with the Fieldens was necessarily brief, as he was taken up with ceremonial activities. But he left behind nothing but good will. He had been drinking, but moderately; travel seemed to have kept him on an even keel, although not without sharp dips into depression. What did Faulkner gain from the long stay in Japan and the Philippines? Apart from an enlargement of his sense of cultural possibilities and a good feeling resulting from his admiring reception, not much. Questions by their very nature led him into simplifications of himself, his work, and his ideas. He had not probed any of his assumptions, nor in explaining his views of segregation and discrimination had he enlarged earlier ideas. Hitting at the same points, he disregarded unresolvables in his argument. Although he was present at a particularly exciting time in Japan, when old and new confronted each other, he simply assimilated what he saw into what he already knew. The Japanese experiment became buried in the Southern experience.

Rome with Jean Stein and old ruins was a welcome respite. Not so welcome was a reception given by Ambassador Clare Booth Luce, whose invitees, besides Faulkner, included the cream of the Italian literary world, among them Alberto Moravia and Ignazio Silone. Every part of this enterprise was a mistake. Luce was the kind of person Faulkner disliked on sight; and he had no interest in literary discussion, although Silone, at least, could have proven a sympathetic figure to him. He mumbled and withdrew, and everyone considered him rude, which he was in this type of situation.

Faulkner traveled to other Italian cities—Naples and Milan as part of this itinerary, with Rome as his base, and visited with his Italian publisher, Mondadori. The interviews and conferences planned for him followed the same procedures as in the Far East, and he was tiring. But he was not too tired to issue a broadside in the Emmett Till case. A fourteen-year-old Negro from Chicago, Till had been accused of "leering," some said "whistling," at a white woman near Greenwood, Mississippi. He vanished, and two men, relatives of the woman's husband, were charged with kidnapping and murdering him. On September 6, the United States Information Service issued a four-hundred-word statement from Faulkner embodying such moral outrage, such detestation of the politics of race, such a revulsion that America should be caught in this kind of child-murder that we must see the statement as something of a shift in his sensibility. No other issue —he did not live to see James Meredith's effort to desegregate Ole Miss— had ever touched him with this intensity of moral revulsion.

Faulkner cast his statement in terms of America's survival:

Perhaps the purpose of this sorry and tragic error in my native Mississippi by two white adults on an afflicted Negro child is to prove to us whether or not we deserve to survive. Because if we in America have reached that point in our desperate culture when we must murder children, no matter for what reason or what color, we don't deserve to survive and probably won't.[23]

He was concerned not only with the survival of America, but with that of the white race, which was only one-fourth of the world's population. How can whites speak of freedom and justice when such words do not apply to people of another color? There is almost hysteria in this statement, since the kidnapping and murder occurred so close to Oxford. But despite its impact, it did not alter his larger view of how racial justice could be achieved. Although the majority of Mississippians were repelled by such a murder, the murderers themselves must have felt they had the support of the community. Faulkner had only a minuscule audience for what he was saying, and an even smaller one of those who would stand up for justice, men like James Silver, Hodding Carter, and, later, Evans Harrington of the university's English department.

Faulkner answered questions from Romans, Milanese, and Neopolitans; and those answers that come down to us demonstrate he was by now formulaic. All peasants are the same; all people want the same things; people are similar once you get past superficial distinctions. It was reductionism at its worst. Blotner provides[24] some of the reviews of his stay. The United States Information Service (USIS) found his visit the "cultural event" of the summer, although Clare Boothe Luce might have felt otherwise. The Catholic press decried his lack of interest in religion, and the Communist press called him a "myth," whatever that meant. What it all added up to was what each group predetermined to hear. Americans heard success, religionists found no religion, and communists thought he was decadent and degenerate (translation of "myth" into English). Faulkner himself, with Jean at his elbow, seemed to like it well enough. In any event, it was better than Rowan Oak in the heat of the summer.

He went briefly to Munich to attend a performance of *Requiem,* but his dislike of Germany and Germans went back to World War I and he stayed only one day. He moved on to Paris, where, through Jean, he came into contact with a number of interesting people, including the French communist author, Louis Aragon. Monique Salomon (as Monique Lange, her maiden name) turned up, now separated from her husband. Also, fellow Mississippian Tennessee Williams came, and when the latter questioned Faulkner about race in the South, the novelist clammed up—but whether the silence derived from a disinclination to discuss race or from an antagonism to a homosexual cannot be determined. Blotner reports that Faulkner referred to the playwright as one of Monique's "queers." An old friend, Anita Loos, showed up, the two not having met since 1926 in New Orleans. A lavish party was held at Gallimard, with a splashy guest list including Camus, Françoise Sagan, and other members of the glittering Gallimard entourage. The meeting between Camus and Faulkner came to nothing, as the latter went into retreat, refused to speak, and looked steadily ahead, as though he had caught sight of one of his demons. He was polite, even courteous, but noncommittal.

The French author and journalist Madeleine Chapsal left a good account of the Gallimard affair, where Faulkner was the prey and most of the guests the hunters. When he first arrived, the writer was besieged by journalists and a photographer—everything calculated, in his expression, to tree him like a coon. He answered yes or no, feeling that if he were not rescued, he would not survive. Chapsal said that after these besiegers left, Faulkner, accompanied by a young woman, felt better. Shrewdly, she comments that he likes women because he feels they are not going to pick his brain or probe his inner feelings. Then she says "the hunt was on." Amidst this glittering group, there was little question who the celebrity was. Faulkner started to retreat, seeking refuge in the garden, his back against a wrought-iron barrier—literally caged. When people came at him, he put up his shield and, like Bartleby, refused. "Nothing," she writes, "is more pathetic than the tired indifference with which he lets people stare at him so that they can go home and say, 'What a head! What wonderful hair.' "[25] Like a suddenly freed animal, he fled.

Before leaving Paris for London, Faulkner gave still another interview, published in French, but full of errors, indicating he had spent a year abroad in 1923, when it was the latter half of 1925; also agreeing that André Malraux was a translator of his. Faulkner had four days in London, then five days (October 12–17), in Reykjavík, Iceland, where he read from "The American Dream" and gave several interviews. This part of the trip seemed quite pleasant, inasmuch as the Icelanders did not press him, and he liked the feel of the place. His only controversial moment came when he responded to questions about American soldiers on Icelandic soil. He justified their presence, pointing out they were there under the auspices of NATO, in the name of freedom, not like Soviet troops who were in the Baltic states in the name of repression. Faulkner was playing the American emissary in every respect, but we sense that his intense patriotism—despite his intense suspicion of government in general—was sincere. He felt —and Jean Stein confirms this—that the country was going to tear itself apart, in a reprise of the pre–Civil War situation, and that in the face of this conflict, America, a wounded giant, would become fair picking for the Soviets.

On October 14, a publication appeared that pleased Faulkner immensely, his volume of four previously published hunting stories. *Big Woods* is a handsome volume, with Edward Shenton illustrations, well-written, brief, narrative introductory pieces which hold the stories together, and a fine coda. The stories are a valedictory, for the "big woods" are no longer so big and have receded even further. The pleasure of the volume is counter-weighted by Faulkner's knowledge that the Snopeses have won. The introductory material is drawn from previous work—from *Requiem*, "Red Leaves," "A Justice," "Mississippi," and "Delta Autumn." The volume is dedicated "To Saxe Commins. From the author / to the editor we have never seen eye to eye / but we have always looked / toward the same thing." The book's appearance was a pleasant moment, and from New York he wrote to Else that he was well, "still working, there is a new book which I will send you." He mentions he must return to Mississippi—he left New York on October 23—for Estelle was ill, with acute alcoholism, and Maud Falkner, at eighty-four, had suffered a cerebral hemorrhage.

Estelle's condition had become increasingly precarious, with alcohol the major consideration, although she had now joined Alcoholics Anonymous. In time, she managed to conquer her addiction to liquor and stabilized her health. Maud's hemorrhage, probably the result of a stroke, eventually also stabilized. She lived until 1960, almost to her eighty-ninth year.

With Estelle settled and Maud stable, Faulkner began to reenter the racial dilemma. He was preparing to appear in Memphis to address the Southern Historical Association in the Peabody Hotel, before a racially mixed audience. James W. Silver, the liberal professor of history at Ole Miss and a friend of Faulkner's, had arranged for the writer to attend. It was a talk filled with anguish, regret, personal ambiguities, and revelations. Faulkner needed considerable courage to appear, for the Peabody did not want Negroes to attend, and his own family, particularly Johncy, was disgusted with him. Faulkner spoke after Benjamin Mays, the Negro president of Morehouse College in Atlanta, one of the most distinguished of Negro colleges.* The speech foreshadowed Faulkner's worst fears, which turned to real terror in early 1956 when it seemed as though Authorine Lucy would try to integrate the University of Alabama. Faulkner's anguish should not be minimized, for with his novelistic perceptions, he saw a South preparing to secede; in fact, with the Dixiecrat party in 1948, the region had, in effect, attempted a secession. Witnesses say the Lucy case had him crazed, with his fear she would be killed (like Emmett Till, whose killers had been exonerated) and his even greater fear some form of civil war was in the making.

An apt image sets the tone: "To live anywhere in the world of A. D. 1955 and be against equality because of race or color, is like living in Alaska and being against snow."[26] He immediately draws a historical analogy, between America and the communist countries, pointing out that if we do not support liberty and equality we have lost our chief weapon. He establishes that equality is both an absolute good and a weapon against our enemies. He says we must, if we can, win the minds and hearts of nonwhites all over the world, although even at the time he was saying this, America had not influenced the newly liberated countries of Africa and Asia. He believes our nonwhite population fervently believes in freedom; what we need to do is to permit them to exercise it.

The reverberations from this and subsequent comments were extensive, nearly all vituperative. Letters to the *Commercial Appeal* were overwhelm-

*The speeches of Faulkner, Mays, and Cecil Sims (on November 10, 1955) were rejected for publication by the *Journal of Southern History* as being too crusading and propagandistic (i.e., racially unacceptable).

ingly opposed to Faulkner's position and favored continued segregation. The main thrust of the remarks was the need to keep the race pure, although a war had just been fought over, among other issues, racial purity and the proponents of that view had seen their country destroyed. John Faulkner stopped speaking to his brother, although if we read his *My Brother Bill*, we find only minor disagreements on issues; in point of fact, John was ready to settle it with fists (at least not pistols, in the old colonel's manner). Neighbors felt there was a sellout, a betrayal; and late-night calls and hate mail suggested there was a traitor in their midst. The real showdown would come, shortly after the writer's death, when James Meredith with the support of the American army integrated the University of Mississippi. Faulkner's belief in state action never had a chance.

He and Jean Stein made a tour of Mississippi sites, starting with a visit to Hodding Carter and Ben Wasson in Greenville; then they went on to New Orleans and down the coast to Pascagoula. There they ran into Helen Baird, now widowed. It may have been at this time Faulkner proposed to Jean, or a little later. Certainly his showing of his most cherished places to her revealed on his part a deep affection and a desire for something more permanent. But his mind was also moving in other directions, and he was almost ready to begin on the second volume of the Snopes trilogy. Despite numerous interruptions and continued anguish over racial issues, he finished it by the following August, and by November 1956 began the final volume of the trilogy, *The Mansion*. Part of the reason for his rapid work on *The Town* was his ability to incorporate into it material already used as short stories. Part of the slackness of the trilogy can in fact be attributed to Faulkner's desire (or need?) to use previous episodes, not to waste anything; and that, in turn, linked to the fact he was tiring, unable to work through a new novel.

The year 1955, one filled with a tremendous range of activities, but little serious writing, did not wind down without controversy.* One element, in fact, continued right into early 1956: race. A rerun of the Emmett Till case came along, with the shooting of a black filling-station attendant by

---

*Money, however, was not a consideration, since it was pouring in: $2,250 for an option on *Soldiers' Pay;* $3,000 from NBC for a telecast of the Dilsey episode in *Sound;* another $3,500 of option money for that novel; a possible option for $3,500 on *Pylon,* toward a purchase price of $35,000—which turned into a $50,000 sale to Universal International when Jerry Wald hesitated. *Pylon,* retitled *The Tarnished Angels,* was directed by Douglas Sirk in 1957, but the film was undercut from the start by the miscasting of Dorothy Malone in the role of Laverne. Malone was a fine actress, but the quality of Laverne could perhaps only be caught by someone with an outlaw dimension, like Joan Crawford or Barbara Stanwyck. Sirk also turned the story around to fit the Hollywood image. The sense of doom, the pursuit of glory, the nihilism of the novel are all turned into an internal love story between Laverne and the reporter, who saves her from prostitution. The screenwriter, George Zuckerman, had not only turned Faulkner's novel on its ear, he made it into a dozen other Hollywood films. It was to be in the mold of tough-guy romances—Malone had previously played in Faulkner's and Hawks's adaptation of *The Big Sleep.*

But there was far more than film money. Faulkner's books were back in print, and with the paperback revolution, they were selling well, as was *Big Woods*. He was becoming a rich man, and he could not have missed the irony: with no more *Absalom* volumes in him, he could sell nearly anything.

a white cotton-gin manager named Elmer Kimbell. Faulkner read of how the Lions Club of Glendora condemned the shooting. Such was his haste in responding to this latest outrage that he wrote on the verso of page 40 of *The Town* typescript. However, his protest veiled a serious retreat. These remarks appealed to almost no one, since they undercut the Negro and at the same time pleaded for justice for him. Faulkner starts by telling of a letter he had from a Memphis Negro, unsigned, in which she said she was against complete integration, which only kept "the bad ones in her race stirred up." What Negroes really want, according to her, "is to be let alone in segregation as it is, that the Negroes are against NAACP."[27]

Faulkner agrees that the "best" Negroes no more want integration with white people than do the "best" white people. He defines his position, and we must note how he has shifted it from the talk a little earlier: ". . . since there is much pressure today from outside our country to advance the Negro, let us here give the Negro a chance to prove whether he is or is not competent for educational and economic and political equality, before the Federal Government crams it down ours and the Negro's throat too." Here justice and equality for the Negro as an absolute value no longer obtains; what matters is taking the best possible position because of outside pressure. He adds he feels the Negro simply wants justice—to be left alone by the NAACP and by whites threatening violence. Negroes who do not wish integration must join with white people like the club members who oppose injustice and violence. In that meeting of minds, the South could tell the federal government to keep out of its affairs. To reach this position, Faulkner has twisted himself out of all recognizable positions.

He picked up this theme in the new year, when he warned the NAACP to go slow, while deploring also the Citizens' Councils. The year 1956 was, like 1955, a period without the integrated qualities of his much earlier times, when all his resources were mobilized for writing. He was indeed working steadily on *The Town*, but his mind and energies were so dispersed the novel became something of a marginal activity. Authorine Lucy preoccupied him, and in letters and interviews he tried to clarify his position and prove himself a centrist; but his efforts only muddied the waters and forced him into denials and charges of misquotation. His position at times became so untenable in trying to placate whites while attempting to clear space for Negroes that the august W. E. B. Du Bois, one of the founders of the NAACP, now eighty-eight, offered to debate him on integration. He suggested that the place of the debate be the courthouse steps in Sumner, Mississippi, where the murderers of Emmett Till were tried and exonerated.

Personal matters, good and bad, entered into his life. His first grandson was born on March 26, but a few days before, on March 18, he needed to be hospitalized. His physical deterioration was a compound of several elements: the drinking had caught up with him, but it was intermixed with the emotional pain and anguish he was experiencing and whatever old internal injuries remained. He had been riding and jumping, and falling.

He coughed blood, fell unconscious, and was hospitalized for the next nine days. With his usual remarkable powers, he recuperated and was able to accept a position, while still in the hospital, as writer-in-residence at the University of Virginia at Charlottesville for periods of eight to ten weeks every year. One advantage was that it brought him close to Jill and his grandson and gave him the opportunity to remove himself from an increasingly antagonistic Oxford. The large family he had supported for so many years was not the least of his reasons for wishing a removal; some he helped the most turned on him.

Meanwhile he also continued his involvement in "emissary" matters, becoming part of a group dedicated to promoting American culture behind the Iron Curtain, called the "People-to-People Program." Late in the year, he wrote letters indicating his interest in foreign affairs, this time related to the intervention of England, France, and Israel in the Suez Canal. Late in the year he began *The Mansion* and became interested in the Camus production of *Requiem* in Paris. There were no short stories. Quite the contrary, previous stories were being consumed by the two volumes of the Snopes trilogy. It was a curious reversal of energies: what he had written earlier was now being rewritten and reused to sustain novels.

Remaking the Past, Retelling the Story

THE YEAR 1956 was one of stark contrasts for Faulkner. As he entered deeply into the Snopes material for his books, he was using his position as a public figure to try to turn back the political consequences of people like the Snopeses: those rednecks who backed the Citizens' Councils for fear of Negro economic gains. Not only had the Snopes phenomenon triumphed in Faulkner's fiction, he was spending a good deal of time trying to roll back its economic and political consequences even while writing about its successes. Meanwhile, as his properties became sought after by both television and Hollywood, the money rolled in. Jean Stein was reading his new Snopes material and apparently liked it. He says he feels he may have written himself out, but since the material pleases her, he will have to go on. "I want to believe I am wrong you see."[1] The advantages of having a young friend are multifold. At about this time, early in the year, Faulkner granted Stein the interview which has become a classic of its kind, for the spring issue of the *Paris Review.* Much of that interview has already appeared in these pages, but it is instructive to see how Faulkner could go well beyond the Japanese remarks when he felt less harassed.

At her Sutton Place apartment in New York City, Faulkner presented his young interviewer with a sense of his vision, a kind of mission in which the writer seeks perfection, but measures himself to the degree he can cite a "splendid failure." The artist, he says, hopes that each time he comes to his work, he will find that perfect combination—hoping "to bring it off." But he cannot, and he should be glad, because if he did, all that remains is suicide. The good novelist needs ninety-nine percent talent, ninety-nine percent discipline, ninety-nine percent work; which is another way of saying his task never ends, he must always keep reaching beyond himself to be "better than yourself." He adds: "An artist is a creature driven by demons." Although this has something in it of the Faustian pact for the artist, it is the bedrock of Faulkner's belief in himself. It winds back to his awe that he has been able to fill that "amazing vessel," that in some way he was selected by a special edict to do the job. He stresses that the true artist, like the drug addict and alcoholic, will commit any crime in order to "get the work done." In this respect, the artist is amoral, and his sole responsibility is to his art. If that calls for ruthlessness, he must be ruthless. But Faulkner shifts the moral implications of this—which he confronted near the end of the year in the Ezra Pound case—by adding that the artist has a dream which must be exorcised: ". . . the *Ode on a Grecian Urn* is worth any number of old ladies."[2] We can assume that includes Maud Falkner.

Stein pursues this point well, not pulling back as other questioners had. She asks about the best environment for the writer, and Faulkner responds there is none. The point is important, for the question leads to the place of Yoknapatawpha in Faulkner's imagination, and his response is that the true artist creates the necessary environment; it can be anything which permits peace, solitude, stability. The argument comes close to Henry James's in "The Art of Fiction," where he says the artist finds experience as an "immense sensibility, a kind of huge spiderweb of the finest silken threads suspended in the chamber of consciousness, and catching every airborne particle in its tissue." Such a mind "takes to itself the faintest hints of life, it converts the very pulses of the air into revelations."[3]

Faulkner insists on the intangibles of experience, for the ultimate meeting place of materials occurs in the artist's purpose and imagination, not in any specific details. He says he needs only paper, tobacco, food, and a little whiskey, bourbon preferably, but scotch will do. He is also insistent the artist cannot be diverted from his task; not even the movies injured him, he says. What he omits is how much he was influenced by movie writing, certainly in his post-1940s work. He then rerelates that legendary experience, when he went home and continued to work for MGM on a film by Tod Browning, the director of *Freaks*. Instead of telegrams indicating "Faulkner is fired," followed by one "Browning is fired," he heard from Sam Marx in quite cordial terms; but it is the legend he wants to perpetuate.

Moving from Hollywood, where Faulkner's answers are set pieces, the interviewer shifts to his "techniques" or strategies. Here he is very firm, repeating that no serious writer has a technique or method. Theory is for fools, or surgeons, or bricklayers. The writer learns by writing, although there is validity to having a technique for that particular work in hand. Faulkner uses *As I Lay Dying* as an example of a work in which technique took over, but before that happened all the material was at his command. Faulkner is grappling with a mixture of imaginative processes worked over by some conscious decisions; but withal, imagination preempts the rational ("technical") impulse. He certainly did not adhere to what the Dadaists proclaimed: that the work is the product of some unconscious process working through the medium of the artist and his materials. But he also rejected any academic analysis of writing as somehow the product of method. The serious writer for him has reached the point of knowing himself so well the material is only coherent when it encounters the correct method in which it can be presented.

Faulkner's emphasis on morality recurs in his insistence on the individual's code, which is what he means by Christianity. He makes it clear the label has little to do with organized religion, but with character building, the way by which man "makes himself a better human being than his nature wants to be."[4] This concern, as we have noted, is a later expression in his thought. He admits that Christian allegory and symbolism are necessary for *A Fable*, but denies their centrality in *Sound*. The aim of Christianity is not to know God or to achieve faith and a state of grace; rather, it shows man "how to discover himself, evolve for himself a moral code . . . by giving him a matchless example of suffering and sacrifice and the promise of hope."

The remarks here blend well with Faulkner's plea for racial equality in America. His letters, speeches, and public comments were all intended to reach toward the best in man—and yet had he forgotten he had spent the best part of his writing life noting the worst; or if not quite the worst, then the delicate balance between good and evil. Stein asks him about the preponderance of violence in his work, and he responds that is "like saying the carpenter is obsessed with his hammer."[5] It is tempting, of course, to read back through Faulkner's comments here and see violence, incest, massive evil as part of that image of "holy innocence" made known to him through his imagination and his reading in Dostoyevsky. The evil deed, as in Joe Christmas's murderous act or Temple Drake's amorality, is a testing of limits which somehow sanctifies the individual. Purification can come only after this individual experiences the worst act of which he or she is capable. We usually associate such "holy innocence" with deep believers—Dostoyevsky, most obviously, O'Connor, Graham Greene, François Mauriac—not with such a lukewarm Christian as Faulkner. But his use of Christianity does persist, against his denials, and it does seem to involve a cauldron of experience, whether murder, incest, or deviance. The only real murderer who seems beyond the reach of Christian forgiveness or redemption is Popeye in *Sanctuary;* and yet, when O'Connor wrote her great story "A Good Man Is Hard to Find," her Misfit seems patterned on Popeye, and *he* is saved in ways the good people are not. Such perversity of character-building would appear to fit Faulkner's ironic imagination; and we should not accept his denials of his own way of working.

On writers: Faulkner reiterates that Sherwood Anderson was the father of his, Faulkner's, generation of writers. Dreiser, he says, is his "older brother" and Mark Twain "the father of them both": as for the Europeans, there are Joyce and Mann. He repeats that he does not read his contemporaries (although we know he was familiar with J. D. Salinger, Ralph Ellison, James Baldwin) and denies he has ever read Freud. But then, he says, neither did Shakespeare, Melville, or Moby-Dick. This is Faulkner at his most obdurate, sounding like the typical hard-boiled American writer who feels Freud is for women: tough guys don't read Freud. His favorite characters: Sarah Gamp, Falstaff, Prince Hal, Don Quixote, Lady Macbeth, Sancho Panza, Huck Finn and Jim, Tom Sawyer, and Sut Lovingood, from a novel by George Harris in the mid-nineteenth century.

The same antagonism to Freud or Freudian analysis recurs when he says his work has to please him and there is no need to talk about it. "I am not a literary man but only a writer. I don't get any pleasure from talking shop."[6] Then Stein, in one of her best questions, asks what he means by motion in relation to the artist. Faulkner replies that the "aim of every artist is to arrest motion, which is life, by artificial means and hold it fixed so that 100 years later when a stranger looks at it, it moves again since it is life." We note the absolute hold that Keats's "Ode on a Grecian Urn" has on his imagination: the aesthetic of Keats's urn and its sense of history and presentness. Linked to that is his agreement with Joyce over the dominance of the epiphany, and the need for an art which is static—the argument Stephen presents in *A Portrait of the Artist as a Young Man*. That static art, left for future generations, is man's sole way to achieve immortality. Faulkner comes full circle, for this is the doctrine he believed in from the first, almost forty years ago when he began to write seriously.

Commenting on his characters in the age group from twenty to forty, Faulkner agrees with Cowley that they are not sympathetic. He says that people of that age create most of the world's anguish, whether the killers of Emmett Till, Negro rapists of white women, or monsters like Hitler. The interview ends with Faulkner at his most fluent, explaining why he began to write his Yoknapatawpha saga. The passage is famous, and although it has been cited before, it could serve as an epitaph:

> With *Soldiers' Pay* I found out writing was fun. But I found out after that not only each book had to have a design but the whole output or sum of an artist's work had to have a design. With *Soldiers' Pay* and *Mosquitoes* I wrote for the sake of writing because it was fun. Beginning with *Sartoris* I discovered that my own little postage stamp of native soil was worth writing about and that I would never live long

enough to exhaust it, and by sublimating the actual into apocryphal I would have complete liberty to use whatever talent I might have to its absolute top. It opened up a gold mine of other peoples, so I created a cosmos of my own. I can move these people around like God, not only in space but in time too. The fact that I have moved my characters around in time successfully, at least in my own estimation, proves to me my own theory that time is a fluid condition which has no existence except in the momentary avatars of individual people. There is no such thing as *was*—only *is*. If *was* existed there would be no grief or sorrow. I like to think of the world I created as being a kind of keystone in the Universe; that, as small as that keystone is, if it were ever taken away, the universe itself would collapse. My last book will be the Doomsday Book, the Golden Book, of Yoknapatawpha County. Then I shall break the pencil and I'll have to stop.[7]

Although a kind of valedictory, that final passage did not silence Faulkner. His public career, as of 1956, was robust; but it also enervated him. The affair over Authorine Lucy at the University of Alabama became for him a test case of whether America was mad or sane. Stein, who was with him during this period, says he was on the edge of madness and breakdown over what he felt were the consequences of Lucy's effort to integrate the university. He felt her life was in real danger, as it was; but, more important, he thought it would tear the country apart. He sent Ober his piece called "On Fear: the South in Labor" for publication, he hoped, in *Harper's*, which had already published his "On Privacy." He was like a man possessed, as we can see in his letter to Ober telling him not to market the article in the slicks *(Life, Look)*, "since on the subject, segregation, in the South here, the slick ones are automatically attaint. That is, here too often we have come to believe they are biased, and so doubt as propaganda anything they print."[8] He says the *Saturday Evening Post* is a possible outlet, but he wants the piece printed with headlines, pictures, and fanfare. "This is a serious piece, to help, I hope, my native country in a dilemma whose seriousness the rest of this country seems incapable not only of understanding but even of believing that to us it is serious."

The urgency of this has the same concentration and fire in it that Faulkner's more private writing once had. That writing of novels and stories no longer had the same meaning for him is clear in his immersion in a public matter. While his concern for terrible social and political circumstances is admirable, we must also see the other side; his expenditure of time and effort here would never have occurred had his creative imagination remained more active, his writing energies been more agile. In a January letter to Commins, he reveals what he knows about himself:

The Snopes mss. is going pretty good. I still have the feeling that I am written out though, and all remaining is the craftsmanship, no fire, force. My judgment might be extinct also, so I will go on with this until I know it is no good. I may finish it without knowing it is bad, or admitting it at least.[9]

Harper's published "On Fear" in June, a lapse of time which put it well beyond the Lucy episode. By the time of publication, Faulkner was immersed in another bitter controversy over remarks which he made in an interview with the London Sunday Times correspondent Russell W. Howe. "On Fear" is an attempt to provide a reasoned argument for sanity in racial matters. Faulkner points out that when Brown v. Board of Education was decided, instead of seeking ways to improve existing white schools, the state was trying to raise taxes to establish another system for Negroes. Simply put, Mississippi schools were not good enough, he says, for anyone, and the best students leave the state and do not return. He cites a letter he received addressed to "Weeping Willie Faulkner," followed by another sneering at his Nobel Prize and calling him a traitor. Yet Faulkner was not interested in responding, but in examining the problem: that the federal government asked for absolute equality in education, and Mississippi insists white and Negro pupils shall never sit in the same classroom. Behind it all, Faulkner repeats, is the fear that Negroes, bettered as a class, will prove an economic threat to whites, and that the real opposition is not racial, but economic.

Faulkner does some historical analysis of the present predicament, along the way castigating Mississippi's Senator James O. Eastland who was not following the oath of office he took; but most of all, he asks, where is the voice of the church? He brings up the Emmett Till case, which has haunted him as a true act of evil. He tries to grapple with the roots of the white fear that every Negro, once he gets his foot in the door, will want to marry "our daughter and she will immediately accept him?"[10] Where does this fear derive from? He mentions his travels and cautions that if the white world does not make common bond with nonwhites, then we can forget the latter, since they will go over to the communists. He pleads for the Negro who, while producing a Ralph Bunche and George Washington Carver, has "yet to produce a Fuchs or Rosenberg or Gold or Burgess or McLean or Hiss, and where for every Robeson there are a thousand white ones."[*][11] This latter reasoning was quite specious, and the reference to Robeson (then in the Soviet Union) was patently unfair.

Events picked up as Faulkner got into the infamous interview with Russell Howe at the Random House offices,[**] and then became involved

*Robeson's name was repeated from his speech to the Southern Historical Association. A negative comment on Richard Wright was deleted for fear of libel: "for every Robeson or Richard Wright."

**On February 21, 1956, in Saxe Commins's office. The interview appeared on March 4 in the London Sunday Times and in a revised, longer version in the Reporter on March 22. Faulkner wrote to both the Reporter and the New York Times (which had taken up the notorious part) and denied having said what Howe reported. In the April 19 issue of the Reporter, Howe's rejoinder about the correctness of his transcript was printed along with Faulkner's repudiation of it.

in the Lucy Alabama case. The notorious part of the Howe interview—whose validity the British journalist insisted on—is revealed when Faulkner said: "But if it came to fighting I'd fight for Mississippi against the United States even if it meant going out into the street and shooting Negroes. After all, I'm not going out to shoot Mississippians [meaning whites]."[12] If Faulkner did say this—Howe insisted he did and there are two separate printed versions of the interview—it is reprehensible beyond belief. But there may have been a context which, while it could not excuse the comment, would make it seem less like the ravings of a white Mississippian. It is possible that Faulkner had been drinking heavily and the interview took place when he was out of his mind with anguish and alcohol. Further, the Howe interview has an edge of antagonism, goading, and hostility, as though the Englishman were seeking to provoke his subject. This note of hostility drove Faulkner crazy and created the context for his reply—to say something off the wall which Howe could then use to support what he thought all along: that every white Southerner, including Faulkner, was a racist at heart.

Yet our belief in Faulkner's ideas is further undermined when we read his reply to a W. C. Neill, the one who had attacked him as "Weeping Willie." Neill had sent on a copy of his letter to Faulkner, also another copy to Congresswoman Edith Green of Oregon. Faulkner replied (January 12, 1956): "Thank you for it, but I doubt if we can afford to waste even on Congress, let alone on one another, that wit which we will sorely need when again, for the second time in a hundred years, we Southerners will have destroyed our native land just because of niggers."[13] Faulkner's choice of label here may be his way of showing Neill, from North Carrollton, Mississippi, that they speak the same language; or else it could be a sarcastic play on Neill's racism; or, the worst scenario, Faulkner's way of speaking without regard for the degrading nature of "nigger."

We must conjecture that Faulkner was drunk, provoked, at the end of his tether, and Howe pushed him over the edge. For the major part of the interview does not lead up to shooting Negroes in the streets. Quite the contrary. Howe was correct, however, in questioning the writer's go-slow policy after Faulkner had indicated that while it was a lot to ask of the Negro, it was the only way to avoid another Civil War. The writer's tone is one of near hysteria—"another Civil War," the South "whipped again," "high emotions" among the people.[14] Faulkner was so on edge he suggested that in another three hundred years the Negro race will vanish through intermarriage: a reprise of his fictional vision of a black-and-white society, one race. He warns of the liberals, particularly the NAACP effort to integrate the University of Alabama, suggesting instead test cases in Georgia, South Carolina, and Mississippi, until people get tired of fighting back and let the admissions happen. He raises the specter of guns and ammunition being stored against a future civil war.

Howe asks what Faulkner's strategy would be, since he attacks liberals for going too fast and suggests that the Negro keep patient. Even given Faulkner's own deeply felt need for racial justice, his response makes little sense. He says everyone should hold back, so that the opposition can see how foolish and laughable it is being. If that happens, then the South will not go to war. He indicates that conditions are improving: "Only six Negroes were killed by whites in Mississippi last year, according to the police figures."[15] Statistics are, as we know, funny things. He adds that the Supreme Court decree came one hundred years too late; in 1863, it would have been a victory. In 1954 "it was a tragedy." Howe then asks what advice Faulkner would give to an ambitious Negro—should he get out? The writer says no, he should stay and be patient, since he has a right to equality. He agrees that the Montgomery bus boycott is a good thing, as a form of passive re‹istance—but he fears it could become inflammatory. He opposes enforced integration as much as he opposes enforced segregation. Then comes the infamous statement about taking sides, if necessary, and shooting Negroes in the streets.*

There was consistency in Faulkner's position only if we recognize that *more than anything else,* including equality and justice, he feared violence and loss of life. The man who introduced such extreme violence and degradation into the American novel, so that his reputation remained "Mr. Corncob," was against any kind of violence in his home state and in America generally. That distaste for violence cut very deep, involving his fear of change, his sympathy for traditional ways, and his belief in the continuity of history. Within this context, he can speak of maintaining traditional values even while moving toward racial equality; however unacceptable his rhetoric and solutions are to those suffering threats, intimidation, inferior education, and few job opportunities. All of Mississippi's governmental processes, at both state and federal level, were arraigned against the Negro; and only a handful in the state, like Hodding Carter, James Silver, and Faulkner himself, were concerned. Faulkner indicates that most Negroes were themselves fearful of change: "Ninety per cent of the Negroes are on one side with the whites against a handful like me who believe that equality is important."[16] Whatever the accuracy of the percentages, it is a regrettable truism that those who are down are fearful of any change which might make their position worse.

*Another way of looking at Faulkner's comments here and elsewhere is suggested by Thadious M. Davis. She says his view "is, in a convoluted way, developed at least partially around (and out of) the white man's reaction to socially established images of the Negro, as opposed to contextually determined conditions involving individuals who happen to be black" (Thadious M. Davis, *Faulkner's Negro: Art and the Southern Context* [Baton Rouge, Louisiana State University Press, 1983], p. 195). According to this, to Faulkner the black was "the Negro," a social rather than a racial concept. This means of characterizing Faulkner and Negroes works better in his public statements than in his fiction, where the contexts are more complex.

With his infamous statement on the record, Faulkner was in an untenable position. Like Camus in France over the Algerian issue, he had become a pariah. The Authorine Lucy case comes up again, and Faulkner says the Negroes are right—"make sure you've got that—they're right." But then he retreats: "I've always been on their side, but if there's no middle ground, if people like me have got to choose, then I'm on the side of Mississippi."[17] Strikingly, Faulkner's immersion in racial issues coincided with the publication of *A Fable*, and yet in that novel he emphasized the need of a small group of men to confront the group. He argues there for Christian martyrs, for the supreme sacrifice which duplicates the sacrifice made by Jesus. He had in that novel a kind of wartime foreshadowing of the moral decisions necessary in Mississippi's racial battles; but whereas in the novel he argued for extremism in defense of a moral position, when it came to his own choice he could only go part of the way. Yet he repeats to Howe that the white Southerner is wrong, his position untenable. He cites Robert E. Lee, who opposed slavery and yet fought against the invasion of his land; he also brings in his grandfather (he means his great-grandfather) who owned slaves, but fought not to preserve slavery, rather to defend against Yankee interference.

Although he continues to emphasize that Negro peonage is at the heart of a cotton economy, by 1956 this was simply not true. Mechanized means were rapidly replacing Negro labor, and in fact Negroes were migrating North in successive waves. The cotton crop no longer needed them, and, as a farmer, Faulkner must have known that. Of course, mechanization favored the large, not small, farmer, but that is another matter. The interview peters out with Faulkner's praise of the Negro as calmer, wiser, and more stable than the white man; he has the ability to rise above his anger. The Negro, he says, can also get more done within limitations than the white man; and whatever vices he has have been created by the white man's treatment of him. Invoking his Nobel Prize address, Faulkner says there is no such thing as an Anglo-Saxon heritage or an African heritage: "There is the heritage of man."[18] All races are capable of bravery and toughness when the age demands it.

When the interview appeared in the *Reporter* and created an uproar, Faulkner, in a letter, stated he was misquoted, and ended his comments:

The statement that I or anyone else would choose any one state against the whole remaining Union of States, down to the ultimate price of shooting other human beings in the streets, is not only foolish but dangerous. Foolish because no sane man is going to choose one state against the Union today. A hundred years ago, yes. But not in 1956. And dangerous because the idea can further inflame those few people in the South who might still believe such a situation possible.[19]

In his brief rejoinder, Howe stated he set down what Faulkner said. As a follow-up to these remarks, Faulkner released for sale to *Life* his "Letter to the North" (retitled "Letter to a Northern Editor"), for which he received $1,500. It appeared on March 5. He felt that *Life* would provide him with a larger audience than one of the more select magazines. He was becoming insistent on his sense of an apocalyptic future. While deploring compulsory segregation, he warns the NAACP to go slowly—the power, he says, has shifted to them, and they should use it judiciously. He tells the rest of America that it knows nothing about the South. "The rest of the United States assumes that this condition [of a Southern people "decadent and even obsolete through inbreeding and illiteracy"] in the South is so simple and so uncomplex that it can be changed tomorrow by the simple will of the national majority backed by legal edict."[20] Faulkner tries to justify his quandary, that Negroes have also implored him to be quiet and to stop doing them harm. Yet, he says, he cannot accept their opposition to equality; that peace cannot be preferred to racial justice. The South should be left to work out its problems and will not accept enforced integration from the outside. Southern obsolescence is only something the South itself can cure; peace can come when both a moral and a physical condition is changed. Once again, Faulkner has located himself in a no-man's-land, that middle which was unsatisfactory to Negro activists and traitorous to those who saw in the making another wave of carpetbagging.

On March 8, just three days after the piece in *Life* appeared, Faulkner wrote to David Kirk, who had begun an interracial dialogue among students at the University of Alabama, where the Lucy case was still volatile. Extensive rioting had already occurred, and the issue had not vanished. Education was apparently the answer—education of the students. Faulkner's reasoning, however, is tortuous. He believes segregation is going; but if relief comes from the South, the Negro will be grateful, whereas if it derives from the outside by compulsion, he will be "the winner against opposition." He adds: "And no tyrant is more ruthless than he who was only yesterday the oppressed, the slave." That, he says, is the expediency of it, not the morality. He also fears we must have 17 million people on our side, on the side of freedom, not on the Russian side. He tells Kirk to get in touch with the student newspaper at the University of North Carolina, where the matter has been handled well, for the creation of an interstate university organization. Then all the Southern schools could stand together, this based on Faulkner's belief that young people will act differently from their parents. He warns Kirk that when he meets individuals in opposition he will be meeting cowards: "Most segregationists are afraid of something."[21] To Jean Stein, he indicated relief the NAACP did not press the Lucy affair.

But Faulkner's activities were not all political. He had been riding Tempy, his jumper, and he had fallen, injuring a rib; his back bothered him as well. This episode would be repeated in the next few years: Faulkner attempting to handle horses for which he was unfitted, or horses simply too strong for him to control. Tempy and he were involved in some kind of showdown, the powerful horse refusing his handler, Faulkner insisting. With the Lucy matter over, he could drift back into life at Oxford, get back into a routine, continue writing *The Town*.

But there was a penalty to pay. Whatever specifically set it off—the fall from Tempy, the drinking, the pent-up emotions over the Lucy case, his sense that his writing was moving along solely on craftsmanship, even the death of Mrs. Oldham—he fell violently ill. He coughed blood, became unconscious, and may have been near death when he was hospitalized at the Baptist Hospital in Memphis on March 18. Other contributing factors may have been the harsh reception his remarks in *Life* received in Oxford, although he was praised in other quarters for his "middle program."* In Oxford, all he heard was vituperation. His brother John said that if a Negro went to school with one of his family, he would be out shooting. Maud Falkner was upset at his stirring up people. Townspeople stopped him to say he was "a nigger-lover." Everything was building toward a collapse; back and rib pain, plus emotional anguish, could be stayed only by liquor. Drink he did, until he needed intravenous nourishment and even blood transfusions. He also needed rest. The immediate diagnosis was an ulcer which led to hemorrhaging. But there was no ulcer. Warned not to drink—warned by his brother Jack, who had stopped—he did not, and whatever the condition was it did not kill him. He did agree to stay off alcohol for three months, abstain from coffee, live on soft, easily digestible foods—rather than the usual Mississippi diet of fried, greasy, oversalted food. In four days, he was on his way to recovery. Nine days after collapsing, he was up and around, and preparing to return to Rowan Oak.

Shortly after his return to Rowan Oak—recovered but still troubled by stomach pain, his back acting up, and depression settling deep upon him —he and Estelle went to Charlottesville for the birth of Jill's first child (Paul D., III, on April 15). But Faulkner did not remain for more than a few days, and headed for New York, to see Jean Stein. He had been challenged at this time by the aged Negro leader William E. B. Du Bois to a debate on Faulkner's recent statements. But the latter declined, saying he agreed with Du Bois, that the latter's moral, legal, and ethical position was right; that if it was not clear now that his, Faulkner's, own position of moderation and patience was not right practically, then "we will both waste our breath in debate."[22] In a sense, he was exhausted by events and wanted to retreat into less demanding activities.

He tried to help Jean gain wider circulation for the *Paris Review,* where she was an editor. He wrote to Harold Raymond at Chatto & Windus

---

*Walter Lippmann, for one, applauded this program, similar to his own, but foresaw that it had nothing concrete in it and would prove impractical.

asking for the names of some well-known English people to whom she could send copies of the *Paris Review*. He says she hopes to use the May number with his interview as a "come-on." He was terribly depressed in the days before the birth of Jill's son, and he saw a doctor, Ben Gilbert, who had treated him before. The encounters were social as well as professional, although as Gilbert found out, Faulkner had no intention of staying on his soft-food diet ("baby food," he called it) and keeping away from whiskey. The only way a doctor could gain his confidence was to let him run his course.

While at Jill's place, Fox Haven Farm, he was approached by Floyd Stovall,[23] the chairman of the University of Virginia English department, and Frederick Gwynn, an associate professor, to see if he would be interested in becoming part of their writer-in-residence program. Emily Clark Balch had left the money for such a program, and while it was not much for such a distinguished guest (perhaps $2,000), it would enable him to be near Jill and to escape periodically from Oxford. Faulkner immediately liked the idea, did not care about the money (he was doing very well from other sources), and agreed to come in 1957 for a period of eight to ten weeks in late winter and early spring. His duties were to meet some classes and to make himself available to students. But Faulkner's eager acceptance did not settle the matter. As Stovall discovered, the president of the university, Colgate W. Darden, was not at all eager; in fact, he did not want Faulkner, fearing the writer's drinking habits and disregard of protocol. Darden was himself all protocol, winding down a distinguished career as former governor; besides, he had married into Du Pont money and was representative of that crusty, elitist Virginia manner which penetrated deeply into the university. Faulkner was indeed somewhat uncouth for this aristocrat; the writer, despite his Nobel Prize, was a kind of Snopes. Darden preferred manner to matter, but agreed to recommend the appointment to the responsible body, the Board of Visitors.

As Faulkner drifted away from Charlottesville in late April, returning to New York and then going back to Oxford on May 8, his life was emptying out rather than filling. He was a deeply unhappy, deeply depressed man. He had worked out a modus vivendi with Estelle, by which he could (and did) have his affairs as well as his family; but there wasn't too much consolation there. His repeated comments on his work indicate one source of depression. But in personal matters, he felt things slipping away. Although he was still with Jean, that relationship, which had brought him considerable comfort, would soon begin to thin out. His health was not good; he was unable to eat what he liked, and he was worried about the effects of his drinking. There may also have been concern about his sexual performance. But his true sickness was a malaise, "just dull." His back did not permit him to work Tempy, and his other project, *The Town*, was, he feared, possibly "trash"—as he told Saxe Commins when he sent on one third of the typescript in June. At times he could write, but his general disposition was one of drift, in work and personal life.

Fame, reputation, even money had not filled the "empty vase." The true thread of his life had snapped, as he felt his writing was mechanical, his imagination used up, his talent a matter of craftsmanship. He who had always denied the efficacy of inspiration found himself lacking the elusive quality. Despite certain personal comforts, the main thrust of his post-prize years had been depression, which cut much deeper than mere aging. There is the question of how seriously alcohol had damaged his brain, or brought him down physically, so that his mental outlook was affected. We can speculate that Faulkner was suffering not so much from specifics as from a general deterioration of his system, perhaps even some brain damage.

The only solution was to keep going. *The Town* was one product of that desire to endure and prevail. But that novel, as we shall see when the book was published in May 1957, had become a crazy quilt of earlier material, much of it recalled in retrospect by Ratliff. Blotner speculates that Faulkner was drawing on so much other material from previous books because he feared this might be his last novel. More likely, he was drawing on early material because that was the sole way he could proceed, given the patchwork way he was now writing and thinking. The argument goes that once his ability to craft a novel fully was lost, he had little choice but to draw on memory-material and to use history as a way of filling in. In one respect, this is a given of any trilogy, in which succeeding volumes must be related to predecessors. But it was a more intense experience for Faulkner, who found he could use the mechanics of the trilogy as a way of telling and retelling his own career as a writer. It was both shrewd and necessary.

Another possible dimension of his method, which was to skip around among several narrators (Ratliff, Gavin, Chick), was that he was using narration as a smoke screen for paucity of imaginatively created material. This explains his remark to Commins that it may be "trash" except for certain parts, although he thought it was funny. A by-product of all this, as he found out, was a series of inconsistencies, chronological and otherwise, among the three volumes; and this was something he would have to deal with before *The Mansion* was published in 1959.

But other business interfered, and one cannot believe he would have responded as he did unless he was so utterly bored or depressed that he sought any outlet. Dwight Eisenhower had asked for the formation of a people-to-people program which would be made up of leaders in various professions; their function was to deal with comparable citizens of other countries as a way of preventing the cold war from culturally isolating the United States. The chief area of work would be behind the iron curtain. This matter came up in September, and Faulkner agreed to attend a meeting in Washington, D.C., on September 11. Present and speaking on that occasion were Eisenhower, Vice-President Nixon, and Secretary of State John Foster Dulles. It was fitting this meeting should take place as Faulkner was immersed in his Snopes material. But well before that meeting, Faulkner had been asked to head up a section on bettering relationships between American and foreign writers.* Although not an administrator, he agreed. He told Commins that the committee business was taking up time, but he hoped to have the novel by December 1, if not sooner. (He made the deadline with time to spare.)

But before that august event, he stepped back into the integration battle. He became involved with some liberal members of the University of Mississippi faculty (among them, James Silver) to form a moderate group which could serve as a sane grounding in the coming struggle. Out of this came a satirical publication—it lasted for one issue—which made fun of Senator Eastland and all those who asserted they derived from a Scotch-Irish background. The issue, called the *Southern Reposure*, headlined: "Eastland Elected by NAACP as Outstanding Man of the Year." But like all efforts to deal wittily or sanely with racial matters, it fizzled. In another related area, Faulkner came into touch with an editor of *Ebony*, who wanted some clarification of the writer's *Reporter* remarks. Faulkner responded with an essay called "If I Were a Negro" (later known as "A Letter to the Leaders in the Negro Race"), which *Ebony* bought for $250 for its September issue.

It was, all in all, a terrible mistake, so terrible as to suggest a masochistic intent. Faulkner put himself in a no-win situation; what he said outraged segregationists and integrationists. It made him appear as an enemy of the Negro people, when in fact his brand of gradualism was more a miscalculation on his part than an outgrowth of racism. Unconsciously, of course, he could be perceived as a racist shielded by moderate talk; but given the courage it took for him to speak out at all, it is difficult to view him as such. Had he been less distinguished, he, a white man, might have been done violence in Oxford—his house burned, his property vandalized—for his views.

Since this was one of Faulkner's final efforts to state and restate his position, even though it repeats much of what we already know, it deserves attention. Now he was addressing directly a Negro audience, one mainly in the North and one fairly affluent. *Ebony* was directed at upwardly mobile Negroes who knew what their rights were and insisted on them. Faulkner miscalculated his audience. First he began with his clarification

*Eisenhower wrote: "In accepting this appointment [as chairman for writers' activities], you will be undertaking an assignment demanding of some time and effort on your part to make it successful. But it is patriotic work and work which I am convinced is of vital importance to our national interest. I seek your help confident that you will be able to impress this fact upon leading authors throughout the country and convince them that by taking part in creating understanding abroad they will contribute to lessening world tensions and to helping solve our problems" (June 1956; *Faulkner: A Comprehensive Guide to the Brodsky Collection, the Letters*, eds. Louis Daniel Brodsky and Robert W. Hamblin, vol. 2 [Jackson: University Press of Mississippi, 1984], p. 195). The blandness of the language already dooms the endeavor.

of his statement to Howe about shooting Negroes in the streets, repeating it was a statement no sober man would make, no sane man would believe. His language suggests he was drunk, although that was small consolation for those on the receiving end of violence. He then heads toward another part of his argument, that directed at the NAACP, to go slow, stop for a moment, let events catch up to the rhetoric. He miscalculates here, too, by saying the NAACP had the white man off balance, had made him the underdog; this was hardly the case, since the white South held all the economic, social, and political cards. The NAACP had little but dedication, its cases argued mainly by Jewish lawyers, its support mainly from Jewish money, with a vanguard of courageous Negroes who took chances by belonging to the organization.

He does a reprise of the Lucy case, telling of his fear that if she had been sent back to register, she would have been killed. He asks for Negro leaders and organizations to be flexible and adaptable; to send a freshly dressed and courteous student each day to a school, and if refused, to send another individual the next day. He says this was Gandhi's way. He would be a member of the NAACP, he says, if he were a Negro, but only under certain conditions: that it recognize flexibility of response. "The watchword of our flexibility must be decency, quietness, courtesy, dignity; if violence and unreason come, it must not be from us."[24] These adjectives imply a form of racism, since they suggest that the Negro must fit standards the white man does not; but the reverse of that, for Faulkner, was that the Negro must win his case and that he can do so only by being better. The racism here is more latent or unconscious, since it seems based on Faulkner's belief that Negroes are better people than whites. Any broad generalization, even if benevolent, contains latent racial stereotyping.

Halfway through, Faulkner recognized how presumptuous it was of him to say, "If I were a Negro, I would do this or that"—it is impossible, he says, for a white man to imagine himself anything else. Nevertheless, he tries, and the message continues for moderation. He recalls Booker T. Washington and his ability to work with both races, but he fails to recognize that Washington, for this new, younger generation of Negroes, was a sellout. He says the Negro should tell his leaders: "We must learn to deserve equality so that we can hold and keep it after we get it." Yet the white man does not have to learn to deserve equality; it is his by law. As though he were addressing a child, Faulkner adds that the Negro must learn responsibility. The real decency of several of his observations is negated by condescending passages; it is as if Negroes had to earn what the Constitution has given them as citizens. He speaks of the responsibilities of "physical cleanliness and of moral rectitude, of a conscience capable of choosing between right and wrong"[25]—qualities lacking in most of the white characters in Faulkner's fiction. He was destroying his credibility with the very people he wished to sway. But he was also laying out a program or path Martin Luther King, Jr., himself profoundly influenced by Gandhi, would take with his forceful passive resistance, his efforts to educate Negroes as to their rights and to the ways they could achieve them. King, however, put his body and life on the line; Faulkner was a white man giving advice which, whether latently racist or not, was patronizing and condescending.

He was so eager to get this into print he told Ober that although *Ebony* might wish to pay for it, he would prefer to have it in the Negro magazine at no price if they printed it intact, unedited. Yet whatever he hoped for from it was, of course, lost. Negro activists would not accept condescension from a white man, even such a distinguished one; and for white segregationists in the South, he was clearly a "nigger-lover," a traitor, a scalawag. He failed to recognize that by 1956 there was no middle ground, that confrontation was inevitable and one had to choose sides. The further argument which Faulkner failed to acknowledge was that Negroes had waited with patience and courtesy since 1865, and while many did not want integration (for whatever reasons), they surely wanted an end to intimidation, threats, and taxation without representation.*

As defeated as ever on this critical issue, Faulkner went back to writing *The Town*. Saying he wanted to work on his book, he rejected a $5,000 offer from *Look* to do a picture story on him. He had become immersed in his characters, especially in Eula Varner and her daughter, Linda. From the sexual clown she had been in *The Hamlet*, Eula had grown into a tragic figure. Gavin also came in for greater complexity as he turned from Eula to Linda, almost incestuously, although he is unrelated to the young girl. Paternal and avuncular, he also pursues her romantically. How much this was connected with Faulkner's own pursuit of much younger women, where the age difference was thirty-five years or so, we cannot pinpoint; but Gavin's sliding away from mother to daughter has within it something of a Faulknerian personal drama. Gavin shapes Linda's mind, much as Faulkner helped to shape Joan's; and he hopes to turn her into a more sophisticated person, as Faulkner tried to do with his protégées. As he moved into August, he headed toward completion of *The Town*, telling Jean it was "going splendidly, too easy. Each time I begin to hope I am written out and can quit, I discover I am not at all cured and the sickness will probably kill me."[26] Twenty days later, he tells her he's finishing the book, with one scene (Eula's suicide) breaking his heart. He sees now that it is not just a funny book, and there is little question that despite all the interruptions he has presented an exceptionally well-realized portrait of the older Eula, trapped in the tragic circumstances of her life and unable to break through.

The book would be completed in early fall (late September or early

*With Faulkner, however, there was nearly always another side of the coin. In this instance, while he cautioned moderation, he was or would be drawing on his own money to pay tuition for two young Negroes at Alcorn A & M and Morehouse College, respectively: Ernest McEwen at the former, Norfleet Strother at the latter.

October), by which time Faulkner was immersed in the State Department program to better relationships among writers. He wrote to Harvey Breit, an editor of the *New York Times Book Review*, on September 13, that he would like him to do most of the preliminary work, using Random House as a command post. Faulkner became quite the supervisor, speaking of the need for an executive committee of perhaps a dozen or so to do the actual work. He sent Breit some mimeographed letters which were to go out over Faulkner's signature. The mimeograph, which brought answers from over thirty writers, is quite amusing—and the signature, which purports to be Faulkner's, was, incidentally, hand-copied. Eisenhower would have done better choosing John Marquand for the job. Among other things, Faulkner enclosed some of his own ideas. He explained first that the president had asked him to see what he could do to give "a true picture of our country to other people." Faulkner suggested:

1. Anesthetize, for one year, American vocal cords.
2. Abolish, for one year, American passports.
3. Commandeer every American automobile. Secrete Johnson grass seed in the cushions and every other available place. Fill the tanks with gasoline. Leave the switch key in the switch and push the car across the iron curtain.[27]

For the fourth point, he suggests bringing ten thousand communists between eighteen and thirty to this country. "Let them see it, buy them an automobile, if they want it, find them jobs, let them enjoy the right to say whatever they wish, have them go to the corner drugstore for ice cream. After a year, they must return home, and all their instalment cars and gadgets would be impounded. If they decide to return, they can have everything back, or equity in newer models. Each year, bring in another 10,000 people."

Enclosed with these suggestions was Eisenhower's description of the project. The work was then dumped into the lap of Harvey Breit. Faulkner entered physically into the process when he journeyed on September 11 to Washington, D.C., to hear Eisenhower, Nixon, and Dulles tell of the need to provide favorable views of America behind the iron curtain. The efforts of Faulkner's group would be part of American foreign policy, behind the scenes, their function nothing less than to show that a free country was a better one. That was the opening-day pitch. After that, the larger group was broken down into study sessions, with Faulkner's own group a motley collection of writers and artists along with an assortment of medical, religious, and handicapped people. Since Faulkner assumed the sole way to get anything working was to do it on an individual, not a group, basis, all of this was off-putting. Harvey Breit's role was to solicit ideas, and then to deal with them not through committee but through individual action. Once replies started to come in, there was to be a New York meeting—

in all, twenty writers accepted; and from that, a steering committee was formed of Faulkner, Donald Hall (poet), and John Steinbeck.

Faulkner, however, by now paid only scant attention to this enterprise —he withdrew from it before the end of the year—and was eager to complete *The Town*. With the end in sight, he worked rapidly, finishing the typescript of 478 pages in time for the setting copy to be at the printer's by October 22. One problem in a work arriving so many years after its predecessor was discrepancies, and to help work these out, Saxe Commins brought in James B. Meriwether, who was also involved in putting together a Faulkner exhibition at Princeton. The Washington connection was becoming farcical, as writers' replies, scattered in dozens of directions, came in.

His personal life was still uncertain. Jean Stein would start to drift away soon. Money, however, was pouring in, as Hollywood was taking him up, and the Paris *Requiem* (opened September 20) meant royalties. Also, his books were back in print and selling. Offers came in which he could reject because he did not need money. When in Oxford, he worked with Tempy, jumping the horse, trying to handle an animal too powerful for him. His life apparently had broken up into a series of small parts, as episodic as his latest novel; and there was really no coherence. In the winter of 1957, he went to Charlottesville for his stint at the University of Virginia, Estelle accompanying him—but that too was a holding action. If he took care of himself, considering his remarkable recuperative powers, there was reason to believe he could live another fifteen or twenty years, taking after the long-lived Maud. Yet as he went past his fifty-ninth year, it was not clear what he had in mind for such a long spread of time. His work with Tempy (with falls, bruises, et al.) and his drinking surely indicated he did not intend to stretch out his life: that he was willing to let it take its course without any help from himself.

The replies to his letter and Eisenhower's statement of mission began to come in. Predictably, some, like Lionel Trilling, indicated that such a mission was for state departments, not writers. This was probably close to Faulkner's point, especially after he attended the Eisenhower-Nixon-Dulles meeting. William Carlos Williams, who hated Ezra Pound's politics and anti-Semitic utterances on Italian television, responded that the committee should work for the poet's release from St. Elizabeth's Hospital. This suggestion reached "resolution" stage. Hemingway then came into the act, as did Eliot, Auden, Berryman, and several others. Aiken agreed with Faulkner that American vocal cords should be anesthetized, that the entire plan was unworkable. Allen Tate, however, favored interchanges of ideas at the level of small groups. Edmund Wilson wondered why Faulkner had gotten involved in such a project—perhaps not giving boredom sufficient place in a writer's motives, or else missing Faulkner's patriotism when called to duty by his government. Archibald MacLeish, an important voice in all official functions, disapproved of the effort, suggesting instead that American writers should speak to Americans. Faulkner could have agreed with that, although his "speaking out" on racial issues did not seem to reach many receptive ears. Steinbeck liked the idea, but wanted to wait for elections, perhaps hoping, like Faulkner (in 1956), that he would be working for Adlai Stevenson rather than Eisenhower, Nixon, and Dulles. Faulkner himself commented that Stevenson had three strikes against him: "wit, urbanity, and erudition."

With Breit and Jean Ennis of Random House's publicity department doing all the work, a meeting was held in New York where a draft of proposals, written by Commins, would eventually appear. One proposal was that the best thing was to elect Stevenson as president. Faulkner then headed back to Oxford for a month and a half before his duties (in 1957) at Virginia began. His appointment had been approved, with an honorarium of $2,000, which for the time he was there factored out to about what he had received in Hollywood from Warner Brothers. His duties in the English department would be far less onerous, however, and the prestige higher.

In Oxford he worked on touching up *The Town* and planned ahead for the final novel of the trilogy. Through the support of Alcoholics Anonymous in Memphis, Estelle had stopped drinking, admitting to Commins that she was, as she says, "a most unpleasant, unpredictable alcoholic. . . . Especially, when I got upset over unfortunate occurrences etc—drink seemed to me an ideal escape . . ."[28] In the same letter (November 5), now well after the event, she tells Commins that last March, when Faulkner drank himself into a collapse, he told her about Jean as they drove out to Sardis Lake, about twenty miles from Oxford. Estelle says she has accepted this news, as well as other equally disturbing news, without forgoing her pledge to stop drinking. "I haven't had one drink and feel capable of dealing with whatever comes with some poise and dignity . . ." She explains Faulkner: "I know, as you must, that Bill feels some sort of compulsion to be attached to some young woman at all times—it's Bill—At long last I am sensible enough to concede him the right to do as he pleases, and without recrimination—It is not that I don't care—(I wish it were not so) —but all of a sudden [I] feel sorry for him—wish he could know without words between us, that it's not very important after all . . ." She fears, however, that Jill, whom she calls "a puritanical little monogamist" does not understand and was hurt by the Stein affair. "I pray Bill will think of that and be discreet this time . . ." She says she and Faulkner have never lived more amicably than now, which she attributes to her changed values or to her acceptance of the "Miss Stein affair."[29]

This behind-the-scenes expression of feeling has several dimensions to it. It is inexplicable why Faulkner told Estelle directly—although we have only her word he did. Also, her fear Jill would be hurt or upset was not borne out; their daughter, too, seemed to accept it, given her effort to distance herself from her parents' mode of life. But what comes through is Estelle's new strength—she has grown in control of her life, narrow though it was, even as Faulkner increasingly felt his was moving beyond his ability to shape it. As for her innocence of why Faulkner felt compelled to attach himself to young women, she is being disingenuous. Home life at Rowan Oak was not harmonious; their sex life ended when he was still young, and both had made a marriage based on earlier commitments rather than on present compatibility. She found her outlet in alcohol and various drugs, he in binging and younger women. Each lived off the other's dependency: she could handle him as long as he drank, and he could control her as long she remained addicted to one thing or another. The affairs were tolerated even when they were not described in detail. It was, all in all, the way they had arranged their marriage. It was not a "compulsion" on Faulkner's part but a natural outgrowth, a need to relieve his depression, and part of the way he survived the Hollywood scene. Despite her present display of calm, Estelle had her own forms of rebellion from the marriage. Hostilities, in fact, remained and would surface again shortly.

Faulkner's work on the People-to-People's Committee was reaching its climax, and soon wound down. When replies to the questionnaires had been tabulated—thirty filled out and in all forty-one replies—they were hardly a sufficiently large sampling on which to base any conclusions. What Eisenhower's request had led to was a recognition of how the American artist was so independent he or she could not agree on anything. Replies finally fell into three categories: a large group in which suggestions came from everywhere, including the "free Ezra Pound" group; those in favor of exchanges; those favoring the opening up of governments to further contacts. Exchanges were to be of books, periodicals, and people. Relaxation of controls meant in areas of the McCarran Act (still on the books at this writing), and passport and visa regulations (still used to exclude those unsympathetic to American policies). Except for the freeing of Pound, which came a little later from another direction, none of the recommendations meant anything.

In a real effort to get something off the ground before he left the committee and its enterprises, Faulkner suggested to all concerned a meeting at Breit's on East Sixty-fourth Street in Manhattan. Yet even as he requested the meeting, Faulkner was not happy with it—it was the kind of get-together he could not absorb without plenty of fortification. Present were three Random House people, fourteen writers, and two State Department officials. What was curious was that here an effort was being made to create greater understanding of America and Americans in iron curtain countries, while America had on its books acts excluding those who might have had an impact. The McCarran Act kept out those whose ideas differed, and other visa restrictions were aimed at keeping America purified of conflicting interests. There was a basic contradiction between government policy and Eisenhower's directive. Faulkner stressed the need to bring "the enemy" over to see what made America go. Saul Bellow, however, angrily wondered what would happen to such people when they returned. Faulkner agreed it was a consideration, but felt such things could work themselves out. There is a kind of Alice-in-Wonderland quality to the passions of the people involved. For Faulkner was speaking of people who might not be allowed out of their countries to begin with, who might not be admitted to this country because of their political views; while Bellow was getting exercised that such people—who might not be let out, who might not be let in—would run into difficulty on their return. Bellow left in a huff, while Faulkner simply kept going at the glass in his hand.

There was a good deal of sympathy for Hungarian refugees, and someone suggested an airlift. Hungary had recently risen against Soviet forces and had been crushed, leaving tens of thousands who wanted to emigrate to America. But the committee was not supposed to be concerned with such matters; that had not been its directive. Furthermore, many of those Hungarian refugees, now enemies of the Soviet Union, had only shortly before been enemies of America, when they fought on the side of the Nazis or were Nazi sympathizers. Many refugees slipped in who had Nazi records and had committed war crimes, and were the very people who could slide by the McCarran Act; whereas those who had fought against the Nazis for the Soviet Union were denied visas because of present-day Soviet sympathies or hostility to American policies. The crazy quilt of political patterns is apparent; and while Faulkner may not have been aware of some of this—although it was Snopesism at a high level—he did know the committee suggestions were bound by State Department regulations, not by humanitarian considerations. The Eisenhower directive had been a futile effort chased by a chimera.

Everyone was beginning to see the futility of the arguments and proposals. It was also clear that American labor, led by the plumber George Meany, had no intention of letting in hordes of iron curtain people who would take jobs from Americans. Everything Faulkner feared about America in his fiction had come true: lines had hardened, there was no flexibility, frontiers everywhere were closed. The committee began to fragment into bickering and individual comments so unacceptable to the State Department that its two representatives became uneasy. As he saw the entire enterprise disintegrating, Faulkner tried to strike some rational course. He felt that the State Department was not free, since it was beholden to the elected members of Congress; that Congress itself had to follow what it felt the people wanted. And since the people had bought some or all of McCarthy's line, there was pressure to keep out anyone who did not accept true-blue Americanism.

It was in the midst of this, while some still argued for an American airlift of Hungarian refugees, that William Carlos Williams used the opportunity to plead, not for Hungarians, but for Ezra Pound, many of whose opinions had been shared by those Hungarians attempting to leave their country. The entire perspective of the committee shifted, as Williams on one hand and Robert Hillyer on the other began to go toe to toe. Behind this particu-

lar verbal bout was a struggle of extreme complication. For Hillyer, opposed to modernism and its various works, saw in the Pound issue a way
of striking at modernism in poetry, which he detested and which threatened his traditional forms. Williams, however, while sensitive to Pound's
incorrigible behavior and his anti-Semitism, thought Pound had been sufficiently punished; and as being himself part of that modern movement
aided and abetted by Pound, Williams favored freeing him from St. Elizabeth's Hospital.

By now, the committee had wandered over the face of the twentieth
century, and while the issues were clearly political, the solutions were
trying to be person-to-person. Every single proposal or idea came up
against political realities. Steinbeck thought that a Sears & Roebuck catalogue would best describe America to other countries; although he failed
to see that such a venture would probably best benefit the post office
department and those renting cargo planes. By now feeling the refilled
glass which never left his hand, Faulkner agreed to everything: free Ezra
Pound, let in the Hungarians, disseminate free books, try to deal with the
labor unions over refugee labor. Having settled some proposals along these
lines, Faulkner, Donald Hall, and Steinbeck met in Commins's office,
where the editor with the help of Jean Ennis drafted their statement. They
agreed on the Hungarian refugees and on disseminating books, but on
little else. Over Steinbeck's objections, Faulkner insisted on the Pound
suggestion, saying: "The government of Sweden gives the chairman of this
committee its greatest award and the government of the United States
keeps its best poet in jail."[30] Steinbeck, who was not against freeing Pound,
thought that was good and removed his objection. Faulkner's fervent support of the poet involves many possibilities. The salient point was that for
him the work of the creative person preempted all other considerations,
even when Pound had committed what were clearly traitorous acts during
the war with his broadcasts attempting to undermine American resolve.
His assumption, which went back to his days under the sway of the French
symbolists, was that a man of imagination has complete freedom to express
himself, even when the expression is vile and inhuman.

That was, except for loose edges, the end of Faulkner's involvement.
When Commins sent on a draft of his report, Faulkner responded that once
the replies were in, he would dispatch it to the president as the sum and
substance of their proposals.

Estelle and Faulkner celebrated Christmas of 1956 at Rowan Oak.
Maud had recovered sufficiently to come over for dinner; the other
guests included the close family, Dean, her mother, Louise, Estelle's sister, Dot Oldham, also friends like Phil Stone and Faye Mullen. We note
the absence of Johncy and his family, since the two brothers, despite
Johncy's comments to the contrary, were barely speaking to one another;
and Jack and Faulkner were not on the best of terms, either. Before the
end of the year, he had read galleys of The Town—by December 28, he
indicates he has returned them to Commins, along with 450 signed pages.

He also tells Commins something is still wrong with him, that he may have to return to "last spring's baby pap diet again." What was wrong was surely not helped by his drinking; and what was bothering him was not a discernible ulcer, but a preulcerous condition exacerbated by alcohol. There was in these words the dingdong of slow physical deterioration taking effect.*

The year 1957 had a fullness to it that previous years lacked. This fullness was not simply the result of numerous activities—previous years had plenty of moving around. The plenitude resulted from Faulkner's immersion once more in serious writing. He saw the publication of *The Town* on May 1, with its dedication (like that of *The Hamlet*) to Phil Stone. He was also able to sell the final segment of that novel, called "The Waifs," to the *Saturday Evening Post* for $3,000, which brought him up to what Fitzgerald had much earlier been receiving. While he did not write any more self-contained short stories, he did work on *The Mansion,* to complete the Snopes trilogy.

Other activities were equally literary. From February to June, he assumed his duties at the University of Virginia as writer-in-residence. Out of his give-and-take with students and other groups came an important publication, *Faulkner in the University,* edited by Frederick L. Gwynn and Joseph L. Blotner. While little new comes from these questions and responses, the sessions nevertheless reveal Faulkner speaking openly about his work in a congenial setting, and some of his comments illuminate well-worn topics.

Faulkner's residence at Virginia was not continuous. He broke it in March for a trip to Greece, where he received the Silver Medal of the Athens Academy. He returned to Virginia in April, and also found himself the recipient of a contract to film *The Hamlet,* which became known as *The Long Hot Summer,* with Orson Welles, Joanne Woodward, and Paul Newman. Beginning in May, Princeton exhibited "The Literary Career of William Faulkner," which James Meriwether turned into a significant document cataloguing the convoluted record of Faulkner manuscripts and typescripts. On May 22, he gave a brief talk before the American Academy of Arts and Letters in New York, which presented its Gold Medal to John

*If we move behind the scenes once again to letters crossing and crisscrossing about Faulkner, we see that the collection of his work had and would become a large cottage industry. While still an undergraduate at Yale, in the early 1960s, Louis Daniel Brodsky had started to collect. Linton Massey was working on his collection, which upon his death ended up at the University of Virginia. Massey started his collection in 1931, the earliest of all, and he had by 1956, as he told James Silver, twenty-five shelf feet of Faulkneriana. The Princeton University exhibition of his manuscript and typescripts from May 10 through August 30, 1957 (memorialized by James B. Meriwether as "The Literary Career of William Faulkner"), helped solidify the importance of Faulkner collections. Others who became involved include Carl Peterson and Toby Holtzman, not to speak of the public holdings at Virginia, the Berg Collection of the New York Public Library, the William Wisdom Collection at Tulane University, the Yale and Princeton collections, and the holdings of the Humanities Research Center at the University of Texas at Austin.

Dos Passos. He returned to Charlottesville for the remainder of the term, and then left for Oxford.

On November 13, he was back in Charlottesville, and in December sent a warmly-felt telegram to Camus on the latter's receipt of the Nobel Prize, at the age of forty-four. In more personal terms, his life began to empty out as the relationship with Jean wound down, for he had no one to replace her. She fitted very well into Faulkner's life, as we glean from a dinner in which he, she, and Thornton Wilder came together at Voisin, at that time one of New York's most elegant and expensive French restaurants. Faulkner remained quiet during the entire dinner, while Wilder and Stein talked. Wilder found her "beautiful and intelligent and charming." Faulkner did not take to Wilder, and there was no way he would enter into discussions; but with Stein present, he kept his own counsel and let her speak for him. However, she was interested in people her own age, not in the sixty-year-olds who were Faulkner's contemporaries. The break was inevitable, especially since he had offered a permanent relationship which she rejected.

The year 1957 found him moving in and out of Rowan Oak, apparently unable to bear Estelle, and yet unable to make the break. His anger at his situation boiled over in drinking and then verbally when he found women impossible to deal with. On a later occasion, when he bitterly maligned women as fit only for the kitchen, he was, however unconsciously, offering up Maud Falkner as his ideal: children and kitchen, as the Germans say, and for that Maud fitted. Implicit here is a further bitterness that Estelle and he never had sons, a speculation which is reinforced by Faulkner's kindness to Jimmy, Johncy's son, whom he often treated as his own boy. His treatment of the older Malcolm was something else—not kind, not sympathetic, but deeply critical and ultimately very damaging. But Malcolm was a reminder of Estelle's betrayal.

January found Faulkner reaping some of the poisonous atmosphere generated by his succession of young women. The People-to-People's Program was winding down, with a final meeting of group chairmen called for February 4 in New York; convened by General Electric's Charles E. Wilson (*not* the Charles E. Wilson who reputedly said "what's good for General Motors is good for the country"), who was chairing the project. This left Faulkner, before his move to Charlottesville, some loose time, which he spent in Oxford with Estelle. There and at the February 4 meeting in New York antagonisms were exacerbated by drinking, and the latter ended Faulkner's participation in a program for which he was, perhaps, the most unlikely man in the country.

Scurrilous calls were bringing Estelle to the breaking point. She poured out her emotions to Dorothy and Saxe Commins. First she thanked Saxe for once again being a nurse to Faulkner, who had binged for three days, February 5–8, at the Hotel Berkshire in New York. She senses Faulkner cannot bear her any longer and is at the breaking point; she indicates she has offered him a divorce—this was the basis, probably, of his proposal to

Jean. Estelle and Faulkner were now back in Charlottesville, and apparently they had been at each other's throats, since she feels Faulkner will agree to a divorce "after our stay here." But he did not want to speak of divorce, although he had offered marriage to Jean.

Estelle repeats that she still loves Bill, that for her love is forever; but she seeks escape "from the utterly false, undignified position I've occupied the past six years." She says: "I am tired of being the poor deceived wife in the background—to his loves, that is—Actually Bill has told me, in his cups, about his affairs, and I've tried very hard to rationalize my reactions and see *his* way as a *necessity*—and forget it all . . ."[31] She says Joan Williams was a difficult time, since Faulkner brought her into the home and flaunted the affair; but with Jean Stein it was different, since he seemed discreet, until the telephone calls started to come in. Now she recognizes that probably all of New York knows about the couple, that it is no longer an abstraction. She says she must try not to assuage a hurt heart, but to deal with an affront "to that little dignity I've been able to salvage." She says she is sick of it and will welcome a decisive end. Estelle indicates she desperately needs advice, and only Commins knows them both well enough—earlier he had dissuaded her from seeking a divorce.

Then came the breakdown, despite good news from Ober about the sale of "The Waifs" (Faulkner wanted to call it "Them Indians") to the *Saturday Evening Post*, where it appeared on May 4, for the largest amount by far he had ever received from a magazine, $3,000. As Faulkner's misery intensified, his coffers filled. *Sound* was up for imminent sale, and other properties were beginning to move, with large sales in the future. But faced by his duties in Virginia, the events in Oxford with Estelle, and driven by his own private demons acknowledging the need for self-destruction, Faulkner became comatose. Commins came to the rescue, along with a team of doctors; and on February 9, the writer was cooped up and sent on to Charlottesville.

Under different circumstances—Faulkner arrived drunk—the Virginia assignment could have been delightful, and even in his personal misery he seemed to gain something from the pleasant surroundings, with eager faculty members, like Blotner and Frederick Gwynn, ready to help him get oriented. The campus of the university is idyllic. The inner core, which remains, was designed by Thomas Jefferson, and there has been a real effort to keep the outlying buildings in proportion to the core campus. As one looks back and forth from the rotunda at one end to the campus stretched out before it, there is a symmetry which becomes a form of peace and resolution. In another dimension, Virginia is lush and rolling, as against the clay hill country of northern Mississippi. While the latter has its own charms, it looks rough and raw compared with the almost Scottish beauty of the Virginia setting in Charlottesville and its environs.

After suitable photographs and other matters of protocol, Faulkner was put on view for students. He did not lecture in any of the classes where he appeared, but answered questions, beginning on February 15 with Gwynn's graduate course in American fiction. Characterizing Faulkner's responses to questions heard repeatedly wherever he went was his equitable manner and tone. What book should one begin with? (*The Unvanquished*). How did *Sound* evolve, and why did Caddy have no segment of her own? Some questions were more compelling, such as one suggesting that his "great book" could encompass the entire pageant of his county from Indians to early settlers. The interrogator must have had in mind a historical book of the kind Faulkner never wrote. Faulkner slipped around answering it. Another question which indicated close observation concerned the change in Narcissa Benbow between *Sartoris*, where she is almost acceptable, to *Sanctuary*, where she is vicious. Faulkner slides by, saying that a character must fulfill certain qualities for that particular role.

The first day of student questions was followed by a press conference, and then he was free for the next five days, except for time spent in his office puffing on his pipe and reading the newspaper. Undergraduate sessions followed, with one on the twenty-fifth of March, following one on the twentieth. These were literature as well as writing courses. In early March he appeared before the English Club. Asked about "Spotted Horses," he reminisced about his father, saying he was a big man, "but mentally he was about ten years old too," Faulkner's age at the time they attended an auction together. He then moved on to give an excellent description of Thomas Sutpen, saying he "wanted to establish the fact that man is immortal, that man, if he is man, cannot be inferior to another man through artificial standards or circumstances."[32] Sutpen's experience as a boy—being turned away at the big house—was decisive, and we can perceive in Faulkner's explanation how he had come to understand the Negro and *his* being turned away, as he had suggested earlier in the story "Pantaloon in Black." But he goes on to agree that Sutpen never achieved his respectability, and, as in Greek tragedy, he was destroyed; he wanted a son, got too many sons, and a son destroyed him. There is in this something of a parable, the Absalom tale updated to suggest Faulkner's fears that Negro insistence on "equality now" may go too fast and bring on another version of that tragedy. Faulkner used the notion of tragedy to underline his own conservatism and fear of change, his advocacy of gradualism and moderation. He appears to be attacking respectability, but he is in actuality warning that one's drive to achieve it must come in stages, not suddenly; Sutpen brought everything down on him because of his headlong dash to possess it all.

Before an undergraduate class in contemporary literature (March 9), Faulkner asserts that Percy Grimm, the grim avenger of white women's purity in *Light in August*, is a storm trooper before he, Faulkner, ever heard of such a phenomenon. But he says Grimm lives on in the white Citizens' Councils, probably more so there than anywhere else in the South, although he is everywhere. Two more sessions followed before the same group, on March 11 and 13. With those out of his way, he was free for a month, and he made a two-week trip to Greece. While he was still "on duty," as he put it, he entered into some of the social events, and became increasingly interested in fox-hunting, for which Albermarle County was famous. He also spoke with local residents, like Linton Massey, the collector of Faulkner material, as well as several others unconnected to literature. Riding, hunting, and fishing were his favorite topics, and he tolerated cocktail parties, at which Estelle played the grand lady, as long as no one delved into literary matters.

For the outside observer, he had an ideal life.* Jill lived nearby, and Estelle and Faulkner located a pleasant Georgian-style house on Rugby Road, itself a lovely, bosky area. From there he could walk to his classes in Cabell Hall, entering the campus off a tree-lined road. His time was relatively free, since his duties were spread out, and he spent increasing amounts of time on a horse farm situated at what was once the Dixie Flying Field, where he had formerly landed. He began to ride, although his back was poor and he needed a polo belt to hold his limbs tightly together. He was, at sixty, a man looking for an accident, but instead of discouraging him, disaster only goaded him on. He was intent on learning how to jump large and powerful horses over various hazards, although such horses were really for larger and stronger men. It was like mastering flying earlier—only now he was twenty-five years older and showing his age.

There were inevitable falls, one in which he probably seriously damaged or even broke some ribs. He loved the openness, the danger, the power of the large animal between his legs, and his ability to control it. Even if only temporarily, it returned him to an America which his fiction revealed as no longer existing. George Washington had himself jumped horses in this area. Yet all this seeming pleasure was only superficial. He still felt the demons, and when the chance came to represent the State Department in Greece, he jumped at the opportunity.

On March 17, he arrived at Athens, his journey sweetened by the fact that a Greek production of *Requiem* was underway at Athens's Kotopouli Theatre. When he arrived, the carefully briefed foreign service officers disregarded warnings and introduced Faulkner to the bar at the Grande Brétagne. But he came through the first day, and even gave the kind of interview the State Department wanted. He told the Greeks, who had just been the recipients of considerable American aid in order to help defeat the communists, that their country was the "cradle of civilized man." They already knew this but it was pleasant hearing it from a distinguished American, even if he was part of the State Department propaganda program. Faulkner meant what he said, evidently recalling the reading he had done in Greek classics under Phil Stone's direction. He added: "Your

---

*Money continued to pour in. An option on *Sound* brought Faulkner $2,835 after the deduction for Random House; the Paris production of *Requiem* brought $2,973, and the option on *The Hamlet* another $2,835. Ober also told Commins that if Faulkner agreed he could sell television rights to "A Rose for Emily" for $4,000. He refused that particular deal.

ancestors are the mothers and fathers of civilization, and of human liberty. What more do you want from me, an American farmer?"[33]

As the receptions piled up—at the Kotopouli Theatre in Faulkner's honor, another given by the Association of Traffic Police of Athens, followed by a performance that evening of *Requiem*, with a curtain speech by the author—Faulkner was beginning to crack. He met the cast, including the sensational Voula Zoumboulaki as Temple Drake, and her husband, Dimitri Myrat, as Gavin Stevens (Myrat was also the producer). By this time, Faulkner had been drinking and was fading rapidly when the evening finally ended at the reception following the performance. It was all heady stuff, and he could not help but be pleased at the high caliber of the people involved in his play; but he was not being kept on a close enough rein by the State Department people. His chief cultural officer, Duncan Emrich, was not being as cautious as Leon Picon had been in Nagano.

For the next two days, Faulkner escaped the madding crowd of eager sympathizers and admirers and went sailing, while drinking the national liqueur of Greece, ouzo, which, while seemingly innocent, is quite potent. The "sail" became a jaunt on a magnificent yacht, a drinker's paradise, stocked with champagne and all the thirst-makers, like caviar and smoked salmon. As the yacht plied the small islands outside Athens and then stopped at Mycenae, the two days were idyllic. When Faulkner got back to Charlottesville he told a group of engineering students (on May 8) of his experience, and it was quite moving. He says the scenery looked exactly like what his reading and background had made him expect—the "Hellenic light," Homer's "wine-dark sea," a place where the past fitted. He contrasted that with how the past in other parts of the Old World seemed Gothic and somewhat terrifying. "The people," he said,

> seem to function against that past that for all its remoteness in time it was still inherent in the light, the resurgence of spring, you didn't expect to see the ghost of the old Greeks, or expect to see the actual figures of the gods, but you had a sense that they were near and they were still powerful, not inimical, just powerful.

He interprets this as something magical in which the gods are free of man's problems, that "they at last had the time to watch what man did without having to be involved in it."[34]

What is remarkable about Faulkner's comments, apart from the sensitivity of his response, is how he was grafting onto the Greek experience his own sense of America. Although he was drinking steadily when he saw Mycenae and other Aegean sites, he perceived them in Edenic terms, so that the "cradle of civilized man" had within it the same kind of innocence of land which he had once located in America. But now that it was gone in America, he could not accept it had passed entirely from the world; and here in Greece, at the very beginning of things, he assured himself that if he traveled far enough he could confront what was only a gleam in his own country. In those sites of ancient ruins, magnificent seas, solid, independent people, Faulkner for the moment was returned to beginnings and frontiers. Memories, history, and language were revived, if only for a time.

The cultural officer, Emrich, somehow had to arrange for Faulkner to prepare an acceptance speech for his Silver Medal, to be awarded by the Athens Academy when they returned. The Gold Medal was to go to the people of Cyprus. But Faulkner was not easily dissuaded from the ouzo. Also, even with moderate doses of the liqueur, he had moved into a kind of oblivion: the extravagant yacht, the fairy-tale quality of the scenery, the remoteness of location, the memories flooding back from his reading, all of this was akin to a form of drunkenness. Faulkner was in another dimension when Emrich insisted he must write his acceptance speech. He preferred to remain on deck, drinking, getting his back massaged, dreaming backward in time. When pressed, he began to write somewhat incoherently, and then stopped.

Faulkner conveyed an idea, a few words, and Emrich completed it. The finished product was characteristic of Faulkner's talks—brief, over before the audience could adjust to his accent. But as the weather worsened and threatened to swamp or overturn the yacht, the captain decided to return to Siros, and they remained trapped there, with the Academy ceremony looming on March 28. The sole way to get back was by way of a large steamer which journeyed from island to island, a ship with none of the comforts of the yacht. Faulkner drank, was unaffected by the wild weather, and was ready to go in the morning. At sixty, his recuperative powers were still amazing.

That evening a large reception was arranged, with representatives from several countries, including the United States and Israel. On the next day followed a series of events, including a meeting with Greek students of American literature. Faulkner went through the motions, apparently on his way into a stupor, but still able to function. Ouzo had become his closest companion, although he did remark on the attractiveness of Greek women. The Academy affair took place that afternoon, with Faulkner scheduled to speak before an audience of 440 members and guests. His talk lasted less than ten minutes. Using his somewhat scattered beginning on the yacht, he found a way to relate it to the main theme of his talk: how "the sun of Pericles" cast a shadow which curved back on America, so that an American like him walks "the shadow back to the source of the light which cast the shadow."[35] It was a lovely image, and he had his idea. But his development was so brief it lacked final substance.

The next morning, Faulkner left—two weeks after his arrival—on a flight back to New York. His trip had proved to be a great success. Despite his periodic withdrawals, he had impressed the Greeks with his own deep impressions of their country and with his courtliness, which came through whether he was drunk or sober. He regretted having spent only two weeks there. But he had started into a curve of his own, not the curve into the shadow that brought one back to the cradle of civilized life, but into that curve which would end up in a hospital in Virginia. At the same time, his stepson, Malcolm, was also suffering from too much alcohol, and in complete collapse. But Faulkner had time to recuperate before his first class met at the university on April 13.

In the uproar of his departure from Athens, Faulkner had misplaced or lost, or allowed to be stolen, his Silver Medal, and wrote Emrich to try to find a replacement. Emrich did, especially since Faulkner insisted he wanted the medal to be exhibited with his other medals and decorations at Princeton in May. He sent his "sincerest respects" to all those who got him through—Emrich's wife, Sally, Mr. and Mrs. Gebelt, and George, the racetrack tout and handicapper.

Just after he resumed his duties at the university, he wrote Joan Williams Bowen that he hadn't got over her yet, and that she knows it: "Women are usually quite aware of the men who love them, so I thought maybe you were dodging me."[36] Earlier in the year, on January 12, he had written at greater length why he had ignored her letter, pleading the Authorine Lucy case, his own collapse, his going on the Tex and Jinx show, and his general anguish which kept him from responding. How deeply he still felt for Joan is debatable; he may have missed her even more intensely now that he had no one, really, to turn to.

A letter (dated April 23) from Estelle to Dorothy Commins[37] reveals what Charlottesville had become while Faulkner was away and then on his return: it was a world which presented one face, respectability, while real, far more intense activity occurred just below the surface. Faulkner lived in those two worlds: that of great achievement and recognition but also that in which demons operated, creating anguish and torture. Malcolm was part of that demonic world, and had been for some time. Estelle recognized her son was in "a desperate state, mentally and physically," and that he could not remain in Oxford. So she brought him to Charlottesville. Malcolm had been deteriorating badly for some time, and although the precise reasons remain hazy, we can conjecture a few discernible causes. On the surface, he had grown up in a real home, after the disruption of Estelle's divorce, but his position in it was ambiguous—especially if he was not the son of Cornell Franklin.[38] Further, living in the shadow of a great man was especially difficult for him as the other male figure in the household. While superficially Faulkner seemed to pay attention to Malcolm, he could also treat him harshly, if not with contempt. Malcolm's mother was herself so caught up in her own problems, her own alcoholism and drug-taking, that, although living in the house, she was frequently "absent." His drift began shortly after his return from military service, with alcoholism the norm at Rowan Oak, breakdown and collapse an integral part of it.

Estelle finally convinced Faulkner that Malcolm needed medical aid fast, since his alcoholism had led to a complete collapse, what used to be identified as a nervous breakdown. He needed more than the drying-out which was endemic in the family, and was brought to a sanitarium in Richmond. The problem was exacerbated by the fact that Faulkner was himself out of control: what had begun in Greece as a means of confronting the situation had snowballed into a full-blown binge and a subsequent collapse. That meant Malcolm's collapse was intertwined with Faulkner's, although Faulkner's was physical, not mental.

Faulkner recovered sufficiently to help Malcolm. First, Estelle had to get her husband to a hospital, check him out, and then solicit his help in getting Malcolm to the sanitarium in Richmond. After ten days there, he seemed much better—although there was no complete cure. For the rest of his life, Malcolm drifted this way and that, drinking heavily, suicidally, unable to find any direction, uncertain what he wanted to do and could do. Jill had gotten out—even Victoria had made something of a life for herself—but Malcolm was the sacrifice.

Estelle felt victimized, wondering if she'd ever lead "a sane, normal life —Doubt it—involved as I am . . ." She deeply resents that Joan "is bombarding Bill with her manuscripts once more—and most likely he'll rewrite them for her [not so]," but she says, without believing it, she will not bother about that. She feels besmirched: "I would still feel cleaner—rid of it all—Bill included . . ."[39] It is unclear what her deeper feelings are, for she is writing to Dorothy right after the passions of a terrible situation, her son and husband drifting into ever murkier territory.

In a follow-up letter which carries Estelle to May 10, she complains to the Comminses that Malcolm's troubles are still bad, that when they go to see him, he wants to leave the hospital. She says only Faulkner's "marvelous control" keeps him there. The prognosis is that his mental and physical condition were so bad he needed several more months of treatment. Estelle indicates that Judge Franklin, Malcolm's father, was useless in the matter. Faulkner paid the bills, which were considerable.

Meanwhile, despite all this on the domestic front, Faulkner continued to meet his classes and, according to Blotner, even became interested in track (men, not horses). The day before his first formal session with students in both American fiction and the novel, he greeted Dos Passos, who had come to the university to address the law school and the Jefferson Society. Although he had little to say to Dos Passos, Faulkner felt it was necessary to pay homage to one of the real American men of letters in the 1930s and 1940s. Of course, by the time Dos Passos came, in 1957, his current work ranged from superficial to contemptible, as he intruded a reductive political ideology into his fiction and sacrificed what had once been a subtle and imaginative attitude. As it turned out, neither had anything to say to the other, although in May, as mentioned, Faulkner agreed to give a brief speech before the American Academy of Arts and Letters when Dos Passos received the Gold Medal for fiction.

By now, student questions had become more sophisticated, and Faulkner was apparently pleased with how closely his readers were dealing with his works. In 1957, the "new criticism," with its close readings and its effort to see the work as self-enclosed, reigned. Many questions focused on images and symbols, and whether they were conscious or otherwise—

motive being a negative word in the new critical vocabulary. Faulkner denied conscious intentions in any number of symbols, such as the yellow smoke coming from Joanna Burden's cabin or the naming of Hightower. Students were also interested in narrative design, and wondered how much of *Absalom* was conjecture, how much objective truth, inquiring further how the reader could distinguish inasmuch as the story is reconstructed by Quentin and Shreve. Faulkner's response is shrewd: that if Quentin had been alone and told the story, it would have been unreal; Shreve was the necessary solvent. Faulkner suggested that since everything was real as a form of perception, objective truth could not be distinguished from conjecture. In certain narrative forms like *Absalom*, speculation may be equated to "objective truth." It is a fine discrimination, and it helps us to see how Faulkner had consciously assimilated a modernist strategy of point of view and its linkage to narrative method.

The sessions were well spaced, going from April 13 to April 15, then the twenty-fifth, the twenty-seventh, and the thirtieth. Faulkner had sufficient opportunity to work on *The Mansion*, even while awaiting publication of *The Town;* and he had time to improve his jumping. Groups changed, not only students from the university, but visitors from other colleges, the Jefferson Society, and others. The questions, while sophisticated when coming from students, were often less insightful when deriving from other groups. The students had been well schooled in reading a text; but others wandered all over the territory, asking Faulkner why he satirized the South, whether he really had any feeling for the region, and the like. Such questions ignored his work and made him defend himself. Nothing can be more annoying to a writer, but he held up his part of the deal and answered evenly. The final question of the session was: "Mr. Faulkner, do you always write one story at a time, and finish that before you go on to the other one?"[40]

In a combined graduate and undergraduate meeting, he was asked why, since there was so much violence in his work which seemed to parallel Ku Klux Klan violence, he never mentioned it directly. Faulkner said that burning sticks in one's yard is "pretty prevalent in Mississippi, but not all Mississippians wear the sheet and burn the sticks." He says that while only a few do the burning, and are looked upon with contempt by the majority, that majority has "the same spirit, the same impulse," in them, "but they are going to use a different method from wearing a night-shirt and burning sticks."[41] He adds that the Klan is too dreary, too much a minority, for him to use them in a story, the implication being he went after the majority, who reviled the Klan but found other means to accomplish the same purpose. It suggests such a distaste for the views of most Mississippians— obviously he has in mind the Citizens' Councils and other organizations using intimidation—that we can understand his desire to live less and less in the state. But when questions swing back to his feelings about the state, he professes his deep attachment to the region and to Mississippi—once again, Quentin Compson's dilemma.

Meanwhile, Faulkner awaited the publication of *The Town* on May 1, with its dedication to Phil Stone: "He did half of the laughing for thirty years." *The Hamlet* had also been dedicated to Stone, as would be *The Mansion*, but without any further comment. The trilogy was very much in his mind, because on many occasions before the questions began he did readings from "The Waifs" and "Spotted Horses" and was additionally nibbling at *The Mansion*.

The response to *The Town* at first seemed favorable, but then negative reviews overwhelmed the good notices. The consensus was that while there were flashes of the old Faulkner here and there, he was tired, enervated, mining an exhausted lode. Kazin in the *New York Times Book Review:* "Tired, drummed-up, boring, often merely frivolous," but also an "unflaggingly passionate mind." Others found it dull, or *(Time)* confused and magnificent in turn. Still others thought he was tired of writing and, most of all, tired of Yoknapatawpha County. This came up in a question in one of his classes. Faulkner answered at length, trying to be honest with the questioner and with himself.

> . . . it's probably not tiredness, it's the fact that you shouldn't put off too long writing something which you think is worth writing, and this I have had in mind for thirty years now. So maybe it could be a little stale to me, though I don't think that's true, either. It was not a novel. . . . This is really a chronicle that seemed to me amusing enough or true enough to be put down no matter what rules of integrity it had to violate, so that in that sense it's not a novel, it's a chronicle, and I don't think fatigue had anything to do with it—that is, fatigue with the county, the background.[42]

What Faulkner might have pointed to—and few of the reviewers noted this—was the carefulness of arrangement. And he might also have pointed to the fact that a trilogy by definition requires recapitulation, repetition, replaying similar matters to create a sense of unity. As for the arrangement, *The Town* has something of the quality of *As I Lay Dying*, with each chapter or segment connected to a speaker. This speaker serves as surrogate for the novelist, so that there is constant smooth transition from exterior to interior, and back again. The arrangement is twenty-four books or chapters, the Homeric twenty-four; and the constant recapitulation also has epic proportions. What reviewers in the main missed was the grandeur of the scheme, the size of the enterprise, the attempt—however far it falls short—to write the epic not only of Yoknapatawpha but of the South.

What strikes us is how Faulkner in 1957 had not completely forsaken the adventurousness of his earlier work. The technical dimensions of *The Town* are a reprise of those in *As I Lay Dying*—daring in 1929 and still daring today. The difference, of course, is that the sharp, mordant cutting of the earlier novel has given way to a far more discursive manner; so that shifting back and forth to different voices and narrators lacks the starkness and drama of *Dying*. Nevertheless, Faulkner was attempting a great deal; for the voices not only move the Snopes material along, they also serve to retrieve memory and history, so essential to Faulkner's career as a writer. What admittedly does subvert the grand plan is a sentimentalization of the material, perhaps inevitable given Faulkner's age and the fact that this material, beginning thirty years ago with *Father Abraham*, had become so familiar it appeared to the writer as part of his own life. Unfortunately, the Civil War is turned into nostalgia, along with other matters; before, the war lay before us as the great historical tragedy, the war of wars, truly Homeric in its epic sweep. Now it is the source of deeds, allowing the sentimentalization of those who fought in it. The war is "present," not as tragic intervention in the life of the South but as a valiant effort, the opportunity for heroic acts.

A good deal depends, however, on how we choose to read *The Town*. Faulkner suggested it as a chronicle, but we might shift the terms somewhat and call it a chronicle of place; or else an "as I lay dying" of a region as it disintegrates morally and physically. In another respect, *The Town* gobbles up enormous portions of Faulkner's own life, not only historically but in terms of present-day feelings and activities. There was for him decline, wastage, exhaustion, not the least of these his courtship of Joan: that mixture of books, writing, education, and sexual interest carried over into Gavin's "courtship" of Linda Snopes in lieu of her mother. But the primary focus is "place," with a heavy dosage of growing up in the shape of Chick Mallison, a registering of consciousness at twelve years old. *The Town* is at once several kinds of book, and indications are that Faulkner was balking at generic needs and attempting to break through into a sprawling, overlapping, epical prose narrative. To call it a "novel" is to place generic restraints on it. At sixty, Faulkner was prepared to extend the sense of the novel beyond his own earlier definition of the genre, which was itself an extension of traditional novel lines.

The other side of this view of the novel as sprawl is that Faulkner, unable to shape or control his material, made a virtue of necessity. Lacking the tools to write a strategically shaped prose narrative, according to this argument, he settled for sprawl and tried to redefine his work as "chronicle" as a means of disguising his failings. Both arguments are correct. In the negative sense, the novel acquires longueurs which the sprawl and chronicle dimension breed; on the positive side, we see Faulkner attempting to breathe life into material, coming at it from angles and shaking it repeatedly before acknowledging he has squeezed everything from it. It is very much an older writer's work—not only in its wisdom, but in its effort to include; not only in its attempt to recapitulate a career, but in its misjudgments.

Whatever else we say, *The Town* is a splendid reprise of Faulkner's method of telling and retelling the story, remaking the past: squeezing narrative until all that remains is place. But the design was also social and economic, if not political: ". . . the chain unbroken, every Snopes in

Frenchman's Bend moving up one step, leaving that last slot at the bottom open for the next Snopes to appear from nowhere and fill, which without doubt he had already done though Ratliff had not yet had time to go out there and see."[43] Yet the Snopeses are not the only examples of the new element in society; Major de Spain is too, despite the fact that his father had been a major in the Confederate cavalry. De Spain, a West Pointer who, like Donald Mahon in *Soldiers' Pay*, has suffered a hideous facial scar, his in the Spanish-American War, brings into town the "first real automobile." To make room for the car (a red EMF roadster), he has torn out his horse stalls and tack room and established the first garage and automobile agency in Jefferson. De Spain's action is, of course, of the type which made Murry Falkner's livery business untenable. In this regard, the major creates an elite of sorts, part of that movement toward the new represented in another stage by the creeping-in of Snopeses.

The centerpiece and a triumph of Faulkner's maturity is his presentation of a new Eula, a woman who belies charges he could not develop in his views of women (as Linda later shows in *The Mansion*). In most instances, Eula remains a pronoun, unnamed—because she is always present. She is now far more than a Venus's-flytrap. She has become a tragic figure, caught in a trap of immense proportions, with only Gavin present to help; and he fails, incapable of taking action. There is in this inner core of the novel—these interior players whom Chick, the innocent twelve-year-old, from his exterior post of observation can never understand—the working-out of a small-town fate. Rarely has Faulkner shown his indebtedness, as he does here, to Sherwood Anderson and the *Winesburg, Ohio* stories.

Faulkner has provided a two-tiered development: the exterior novel as viewed through the eyes of the narrators, with Chick the least aware; and the interior novel, where a society is being transformed through the personal needs of the major players. Flem Snopes is at one end (although not all Snopeses are like him) and de Spain at the other, both pulling the town down. Eula is the bait, and Gavin a kind of moral conscience, however unaware he may be of his motives. Ratliff is the most aware of the observers, the town chorus, recalling Greek tragedy. Playing through the narrative is the perfidy of Flem, the effort of Eula to deal with a diminishing situation, the sexual desire of Gavin which runs up against his inhibitions; and, overall, the moral confusion which reigns when events outrun principle. Upward mobility, Flem's desire to get hold of the presidency of the Sartoris bank, signals only greed, deception, and conspiracy. Faulkner replayed much of what happened to his grandfather, the young colonel, when he lost his bank, his house, and his position in town. People from the past recur, real and imagined: a lawyer Stone, Jason Compson, and others.

But more is at stake than a "summing up." There was the need, not really fulfilled, to provide a panorama of change, what was transforming the South into an adjunct of the North. One by one, the amenities disappear, the older order passes; and even as he is sorrowful at its demise,

Faulkner cannot defend the old order. Near the center of the book, Ratliff has his voice, and he speaks one line only: "Because he missed it. He missed it completely."[44] The brief interlude may be little, or it may be everything. It both centers and decenters the novel, because we are never quite certain what Ratliff means by "missed." It closes down and it opens up. It decenters because it suggests that what we think is the main thrust, Flem's rapacity, could be the failure of an entire society, willing its own crash. There is a doomsday quality to the novel, as if Faulkner, who spoke at Virginia of his desire to write his Doomsday Book, was already doing so. We can speak of the humor of *The Town*, as we can of the entire trilogy —not wit, not irony any more, but humor. But like all good humor, it serves a larger function; it is rarely the humor which serves as counterpoint. Instead, it is humor which integrates with the tragic sense of life passing before the Jefferson residents without their even being aware of it. Flem may be a comic character, recalling Molière, but the quality of his life belies comedy. Ratliff's next appearance, his fourth, has only three lines; but his refrain is that "still he missed it." We observe that "missed it" takes the comedy out of the antics of the novel and transforms its terms into "loss," which is not comic but tragic. Loss has always been Faulkner's great theme, and, flawed though it is in language and execution, *The Town* comes out four square for loss.

Before leaving for New York to make his speech before the American Academy, Faulkner had several Virginia engagements. On May 15, he was interviewed before university and community audiences, and on May 16, before the law school wives.

On race, he did not defer to his audience, which wanted to hear that the South could work through its own racial problems without violence. He says no nation can endure with 17 million second-class citizens; "it's an outrageous, anomalous condition that simply cannot continue."[45] Despite opposition, the Negro must be given equality in economics and education. He says not all Americans believe like McCarthy, and, by analogy, not all Americans feel like Huey Long. The minority of racists intimidates the majority of people, and the latter remain silent; but if they spoke up, the minority could be silenced. The "hard fierce light of publicity" destroyed McCarthy and Long and can destroy those who threaten violence to the majority if they act on their beliefs. With all his knowledge of Southern life, Faulkner let his optimism about people mislead him about how much people can change when faced with change. He had only to look at his own family, more sophisticated and educated than most, to see how resistant to change the Deep South could be: Maud, a college graduate; Jack, a lawman with a law degree; Johncy, an engineering graduate; Estelle, a college graduate. If they opposed his views on gradualism, on whom could he count?

While Faulkner was conducting his seminars in Charlottesville on life and literature, he was being honored in another way in Princeton. At the

Princeton University Library on May 10, an exhibition opened called "The Literary Career of William Faulkner." Truly a banner event for Faulkner, it was also a great moment for American literature. Assembled by James Meriwether, with the university librarian, William S. Dix, and the ever-attentive Saxe Commins, the exhibition turned Faulkner into a classic. The importance of the exhibition and the Meriwether book growing from it (also called *The Literary Career of William Faulkner*) was that it established first and subsequent editions for future scholars to work from, and also provided an organization of materials for Faulkner biography. In several ways, it served as a corrective for articles that had biographical pretensions, and was the first in-depth examination of the life by way of the work. Further, it drew out of Faulkner his own considerable manuscript collection, which he lent to Princeton for the occasion, and drew forth from Linton Massey some significant parts of his sizable collection. Two years later, in June 1959, the Faulkner manuscripts became part of the holdings of Virginia's Alderman Library, where, through the acquiescence of Jill Faulkner Summers, they remain available to scholars, readers, and interested tourists.

This was not the sole event of note in May, which also included Faulkner's appearance at the American Academy of Arts and Science in New York on its presentation of the gold medal for fiction to Dos Passos. For the occasion, Faulkner prepared a brief speech of three paragraphs, only the last of which he delivered: "It is my honor . . ." The other two paragraphs are on familiar ground: the need of the artist for humility in the face of his craft, the fact that the artist has no more place in today's American culture than in the economy; and that since this is the case, it is perhaps a good thing. This keeps him humble and makes him work through his oblivion until he achieves the moment, as Dos Passos has, when he is recognized and honored. Like Baudelaire's albatross, he, the artist, is reviled; but despite his ugliness and ungainliness, he persists to maintain his dignity and position.

The entire proceeding turned Faulkner into a wreck, and he drank steadily to get through it. Such a ceremony meant a good deal of verbal obeisance to other members of the Academy, now deceased, and a formal dinner which he could barely get through. In his way, he became less and less accessible, so that when Lillian Hellman appealed to him on behalf of Dashiell Hammett, jailed for refusing to testify before the House Un-American Activities Committee, Faulkner snubbed her. According to Blotner, he simply remarked that Hammett drank too much, and let it go at that, as though he barely knew either the writer or Hellman. She had come upon Faulkner at the worst possible time.

By May 30, he was back to questions from a university and community audience. After the usual queries about his writing habits (disorderly, without a regular schedule) and his use of pen or typewriter (longhand first, then rewritten on the typewriter), questions focused on his work. He explains that Eula Varner Snopes commits suicide to protect her child, and his words here almost perfectly describe what he had said to Meta about himself nearly two decades before: ". . . she had reached an impasse where her lover would have demanded that she leave her husband and then that child would have found out that it had grown up in a broken home."[46] Better a suicide for a mother than a runaway! He indicates his next book will be about the daughter, Linda Snopes. But we are drawn to Faulkner's way of adjusting his fiction to the facts of his own life; a pivotal point in *The Town*, Eula's suicide can be explained not so much in anything that has come before in her life, but what has preceded in Faulkner's. Another and equally powerful reason for Eula's suicide would be that her life added up to little, that marriage to Flem had been so humiliating she had already died before she killed herself. Major de Spain was himself only suitable because of what she was married to, not someone to run off with. And even with this, her suicide is not completely satisfactory—it appears more a plot necessity than a derivative from what the character has been. On *Light in August*, he affirms that the title has to do with a certain slant of light at that time of year, "a luminous quality to the light, as though it came not from just today but from back in the old classic times," the times of fauns and satyrs and gods. He says it lasts only a day or two, and he associates it with Lena Grove, something of a pagan quality.

One final session before the same group on June 5 ended Faulkner's first year at the university. Asked about female authors he has liked, he named Brontë (one? or all?), Glasgow, Cather—several others, he says. He is careful to add that when he uses "he" for an author, he does not mean only males, but both sexes. Asked about his Christian humanism, he says Christianity has never harmed him and he hopes he has not harmed it. He says he thinks that in his way he is a good Christian, but doesn't know if it would meet anyone else's standard.[47] On the question of heroism in his work—as, for example, in Sutpen or Colonel Sartoris—he feels there is still room for the heroic in man; the man and the hour must meet, however, and when that occurs the heroic can still emerge. He finds that when man "didn't find his chance to be what he could have been and might have been," he becomes tragic.

Remarkably, Faulkner kept his commitments, did not excuse himself or become indisposed, and lucidly answered questions, however banal. He was scrupulous about keeping his office hours, even when it was apparent that few students or faculty would drop by. As his semester wound down, Blotner, a junior member of the English department, paid tribute to the man who was becoming his close friend. He indicated how meticulous Faulkner had been about his duties, meeting on twenty-four different occasions, counseling perhaps 150 students who had come by. We know how heavily he had been drinking, how divisive his domestic situation was, how torn apart his relationship with Estelle was as she contemplated divorce—and yet he maintained the surface of his life and did not let down those who had pushed for his appointment against a disbelieving president.

Before leaving Virginia for Rowan Oak, Faulkner gave a brief interview to Betty Beale of the Washington *Evening Star*, [48] the second of his interviews with this reporter. In the first, he had charmed her; in the second, he was at his most boorish. It was all a put-down of her, of the press, of how reporters never get at the truth, of how freedom eluded those who do not write fiction. Although she saw that Faulkner was inaccessible, she persisted, and received predictably rude answers. What did he think of criticism of *The Town?*—he said he never read criticisms. Who was his favorite author?—he doesn't read anything but the books from his childhood. How about Thomas Wolfe?—Wolfe bores him. Did he plan to return for another semester?—No. He said there was no need for someone like him; he answered questions, he indicated, which could be answered by a priest or veterinarian. He ended by saying he never told the truth to reporters. In all, the brief interview was one he chose to control by mocking the reporter. That she was a woman catching him on the lip of an abyss was possibly his motive.

Part VI

There We Are

Chapter Twenty-nine

Inhabiting the Mansion

O N JUNE 26, 1957, Faulkner left Charlottesville for Oxford, where Dot Oldham had been taking care of Rowan Oak in his and Estelle's absence. He found little to deal with, although he was concerned his farm had suffered seriously and needed attention. He had numerous expenses, as evidenced by his drawing $20,000 from his Random House account on September 14. He funded Dean's year abroad, as well as tuition costs for his Japanese friend, Midori Sasaki, who was at Chapel Hill. He paid off Rowan Oak and farm expenses, and he took care of Maud Falkner's medical, tax, and other expenses. He was flush with money from film options, book sales, and other sources; but he was also like a bank, paying out endless streams of money to his extended family.* Work on *The Mansion* was proceeding slowly, if at all—as of April 14, 1958, he told Else he was about one-third through. There was, here, a kind of autumnal quality to Faulkner's life, a settling in to what was to be his lifestyle until his death.

Racial matters surfaced again, especially when federal troops were called out to keep the peace at the enforced integration of Central High School in Little Rock, Arkansas—a forerunner of what would happen at Ole Miss shortly after Faulkner's death. Phil Stone interpreted Faulkner's involve-

*Jill Faulkner Summers commented: "Pappy had no sense of money at all—never did. And he was the easiest touch. He always had several families completely dependent on him. Anyone could come to him with a hard luck story . . ." (*William Faulkner: A Life on Paper*, p. 84).

ment in this latest incident as his need "to do something to attract some publicity since he has not been getting publicity lately."[1] In a letter to the Memphis *Commercial Appeal*, Faulkner reiterated that as long as we tax the Negro and expect him to serve in the military, we cannot offer him second-class citizenship. If the South persists in this, then very soon a bill far worse than *Brown* v. *Board of Education* will be passed by Congress—the Civil Rights Act of 1965 was the kind of bill Faulkner feared.

To the *New York Times* (published October 13), he wrote that it was now clear from the Little Rock tragedy that white and black do not like each other. But, he says, out of this may come some agreement, since it removes a white fear that Negroes want full integration, including intermarriage. He says we must recognize the problem if we are to survive as a nation. His solution is pure Jefferson: "Against that principle which by physical force compels man to relinquish his individuality into the monolithic mass of a state dedicated to the premise that the state alone shall prevail, we, because of the lucky accident of our geography, may have to represent that last community of unified people dedicated to that opposed premise that man can be free by the very act of voluntarily merging and relinquishing his liberty into the liberty of all individual men who want to be free."[2] That is a beautifully composed statement disdaining federal force, but only if the South voluntarily gives freedom to all.

But preceding this submission of two letters, Faulkner had to respond on still another front, this time to an unlikely source, Norman Mailer. It was a brief, but amusing exchange. At his most Reichian while thinking through his ideas for "The White Negro" essay, Mailer illuminated why whites resisted Negro integration. It appeared in the *Independent*, and Mailer's statement was sent to Faulkner by Lyle Stuart, its owner. Mailer felt that white resistance was sexual: the white feared Negro sexuality and therefore kept him in thrall to balance out the Negro's superior potency. Accordingly, the Negro has his sexual supremacy, the white his white supremacy. One wonders if Mailer, even during this uproarious time for him, recognized the racism implicit in his argument, and how it played into the hands of the very elements he disdained. Faulkner decided on a witty response, to Stuart: "I have heard this idea expressed several times during the last twenty years, though not before by a man. The others were ladies, northern or middle western ladies, usually around 40 or 50 years of age. I don't know what a psychiatrist would find in this."[3] Clearly outraged, Mailer tried to establish a dialogue, but Faulkner would not respond further.

At about the same time, he received an invitation to return to Virginia in 1958, and he was clearly pleased to be "THE writer-in-residence of the University." But other matters were intruding, mainly his farm, which would need more attention in 1958 than it had received in 1957. He asked for a split schedule, giving him four or five weeks at Oxford in early spring. He would spend, in all, eight to ten or eleven weeks at Virginia. The university agreed to his terms, for the grand sum of $1,600, plus free rent.

Except for his two letters carefully written and rewritten on racial integration—in which he stated what *he* felt the Negro wanted—the fall of 1957 was given over to farming. There may have been continuing but sporadic work on *The Mansion*, since by the early part of 1958, he was typing parts of the manuscript. Also, he was looking forward to speaking out even further on racial matters, although for the time being he was concerned with his cotton crop. In Hollywood Jerry Wald was filming a segment of *The Hamlet*, almost unrecognizably. His only immediate plans called for him to rejoin Estelle in Charlottesville for the fox-hunting season.

Having received the Nobel Prize at fifty-three, Faulkner was not necessarily exhausted as a writer; fifty-three for many European authors was the middle of the journey, not the beginning of the end. Further, he had a strong, long-drawn novel on the desk, one that had been percolating in the deepest reaches of his imagination. The close Faulkner-watcher had reason to believe the prize would prove an impetus, not an inhibitor.

But Faulkner's sense of himself at fifty-three was considerably different. He was beginning to feel that he had little left, except for that one big novel of Jesus and the Unknown Soldier. His assessment of his potentialities was quite realistic. And if the close reader had looked carefully at the career, he would have recognized that Faulkner had received the Nobel for work he had done by forty-three, not fifty-three. On that score, Phil Stone was correct. For the last twenty years of his life, while he did not coast, he also did not work at the level that the reader, hoping to see a continuous career, could applaud.

The consequence is that the devoted follower of Faulkner's career has expectations for him that he could not fulfill. There is the x-variable: the damage years of heavy drinking had done, not to his body, which seemed to recover, but to his brain, to those mental processes nourishing his imagination. This remains an unstable element in any equation of Faulkner+Nobel Prize=waning of writing ability. The reader may be disturbed by Faulkner riding off to hounds and by his neglect of writing in order to work his farm—or all along by the farm—but Faulkner had put such concentration into his early and middle career he needed a respite. Further, there is little question affluence accompanied by age had changed his outlook. He enjoyed the fruits of affluence, and had been, all along, divided between serious writing and a desire for the good things of the world. A strong bourgeois streak accompanied the romantic sense of the struggling artist. None of this fits into "selling out." What it does fit is the coming together of a number of factors usually ignored by those who see only a writer's "decline."

Still another factor was at work, a delicate matter and purely speculative. Faulkner did not have any coherent world-view which could be sustained by an intellectual approach; he lacked the ability to draw on reading and broad ideas in the manner of European novelists. He had instead the kind of great, intuitive intellect which he shared with many other American writers. Unlike their European contemporaries, they had not broadened their knowledge—to philosophy as well as literature and the other arts—so that they tended to have brief careers when the original talent was exhausted. With that played out, there was little or nothing to draw upon, and the tendency was to repeat or reduce. There is considerable irony here. While Faulkner had had a far more significant career than Sherwood Anderson, the very criticism he had leveled against the older man could return to haunt him. Anderson had started to repeat himself early on, even by the time Faulkner met the writer in the 1920s. Faulkner had gently mocked Anderson in his "Creole" comments; but he was even harsher on him in his less public statements; all concerned with how a considerable talent had exhausted itself, forcing the writer to remake the same book. Faulkner was now in the same position, having of course found far more to mine than Anderson did.

Faulkner tried desperately to have fun. In Charlottesville he had the devoted attention of young faculty, like Blotner and Gwynn, and he had entered into activities, including attendance at football games.* But drinking also had its attractions, especially when he fell ill from a strep throat infection which did not respond to his usual home remedies. He drank himself into a Richmond private hospital after attempting to quench the fire in his throat with firewater. As was usual with him, he recuperated within a short time, but was not ready for the traditional Thanksgiving Day fox hunt. Having changed his plans earlier in November for a visit to Princeton and the Comminses, so that he could be in Charlottesville for the hunt, he now found that strep throat and alcohol left him too weak to ride to hounds. He and Estelle returned to Oxford, with Faulkner interested in recovering his stride more through drinking than through taking his medicine.

In the background was the usual domestic turmoil, which appeared to accompany him everywhere. Writing to Commins, probably in mid- to late October, Faulkner took account of Malcolm's deteriorating condition. An alcoholic with severe emotional problems, Malcolm had not really recovered from an earlier siege. Faulkner reported that his stepson "does nothing at all," stays in bed all day until Estelle forces him to get up, and then he sits around "in a sullen, surly, moody way, saying nothing for days." Furthermore, he refused all medical attention, would not go to a hospital or see a psychiatrist. He sounds like a close pupil of his stepfather. "I personally think he has quit, given up, will never be any better."[4] He sees no resolution of this, in a man of thirty-four. Estelle would have to care for Malcolm even if she went to Charlottesville while he, Faulkner, was in Princeton. Malcolm's problems were diagnosed correctly as emotional/psychological, but as he drifted into anomie and indifference, he sank into a condition not too different from Benjy's in *Sound*: virtually the same age, not an idiot, of course, but incapable of taking care of himself, requiring a nurse or keeper, a mental and emotional burden for the entire family.

---

*He also apparently found another woman friend, whom he saw during his trips to Princeton, although little came of it.

This incident fits well into an entire series which reveals further aspects of family pathology. A dreadful situation was developing involving Malcolm and Gloria Franklin's divorce from him. During this time, he was particularly difficult, as he saw whatever shreds of his life still remaining now falling away. He drank steadily, to obliteration. Johnette Tracy and her husband, close friends of Malcolm, had tried to steady him, and had taken an interest in his new situation as a divorced man. Mrs. Tracy felt deeply that Malcolm's condition was a direct outgrowth of his treatment by the Faulkner family; and apparently she held Faulkner to blame as much as anyone.

What precipitated a real crisis in Malcolm and the family was a letter, unsigned, which went out to him, in which he was told to act like a man when Gloria, newly divorced, remarried without informing him. The letter, which condemned Gloria and implicitly told Malcolm he was a weasel, was inflammatory, and it brought an already troubled young man close to murder. He actually telephoned Gloria's new husband, Lamar, and challenged him to a duel with pistols—shades of the old colonel and his shenanigans. The letter in actuality had been written by Estelle's sister, Dot Oldham, who was known for her interference in family matters—she had at one time told Faulkner himself in regard to Estelle to put up or shut up, and had forced the marriage. Now she had written the letter, shown it to Estelle and to Faulkner, gotten their approval, and even had Estelle add a postscript. But she had failed to sign the letter before sending it to Malcolm, who, out of his mind with drink and grief, thought Faulkner had written it. This was for him the ultimate betrayal.

Faulkner had had nothing to do with the composition of the letter, which tried to make Malcolm "act like a man" in the situation, but he approved it and felt it would do good. As he wrote Johnette Tracy in early December,[5] he thought Dot had "every right to blow her top. I also think in the end it will help Malcolm. He has been babied too much in his life. That's why he got himself into the mess he did." Faulkner shows no comprehension of Malcolm's real illness, which could not be dealt with by way of a sharp letter telling him to measure up. Since everyone seemed unaware of the depth of Malcolm's illness, his feelings of impotence, his need for self-destruction, Johnette Tracy intervened directly. Malcolm told her Faulkner had written him a letter saying terrible things, and read it to her. The letter, which has not surfaced, apparently told him to settle matters with Gloria's new husband—that was the Faulkner way. Tracy shrewdly saw that the letter was written by Dot Oldham and informed Malcolm of this, asking him to show her the letter so she could authenticate the handwriting. But he refused, for he felt that even if Faulkner had not actually written the missive, he had approved of it, especially since Estelle had added a postscript. Malcolm proceeded to call Lamar and Gloria, and threw down a challenge with pistols. Nothing came of that, and he felt more like a fool than ever, becoming hysterical, but now promising to show Tracy the letter.

She felt he was "absolutely *non compos,*" and feared he might destroy himself. Her long explanation[6] of this episode (in a letter to James W. Silver) contains veiled references to a huge fire Malcolm had started the previous spring, from which Gloria was lucky to escape. He now spoke of ambushing Lamar, committing the perfect crime; he claimed that Gloria had driven him crazy. Tracy sees this as paranoia and understands that Malcolm must be treated, not asked to be a man. She manages to calm down his obsession with murder; but her position is undermined by the fact he would not stay sober, that he had been drinking for days at a time. Tracy consulted a doctor, for she was afraid Malcolm would do harm to Lamar or Gloria, and she asked him to get medical help, but he refused. Meanwhile, he was showing up later and later for his job and letting his life slip away in paranoiac fantasies that he was everyone's favorite target.

Tracy felt the Faulkner family had to be informed. She wrote to Estelle and Faulkner, who had returned to Charlottesville, describing the letter and indicating she had no idea where it had derived from. She told Silver that "the great man" said that Dot Oldham had written the original letter, but he was surprised Malcolm did not know who wrote it, although it was unsigned. Malcolm wanted to believe Faulkner was not the writer, but could not be convinced—he was, as ever, caught in the coils of that pattern of alternating acceptance and rejection which characterized his home life. He deeply desired to be accepted by Faulkner, truly admired and respected him, and yet had found himself repeatedly rejected, reviled, demeaned. He had not measured up—which is precisely the implication of Dot Oldham's letter. Tracy characterized this entire episode as "terrible, monstrous, and a few other choice adjectives," words which she used directly with the family. She wondered if the Faulkners would ever speak to her again on the Oxford streets. But Malcolm was calmed by the proof Faulkner was not the culprit, and Tracy succeeded in talking him out of revenge on Gloria's new husband. He even cut down on his drinking, and for a while he appeared to Tracy to be in much better shape. But in her remarks, she put her finger on one present problem, the family's habit of blaming Gloria for everything, while babying Malcolm—apparently his marriage had been a large topic, and everyone had felt free to comment.

Tracy says that what he needed was "a little honest love and affection, and he's just blooming like the rose." Of course, this was temporary. In a sense, Faulkner had abstracted himself from family problems, some of which he had surely contributed to by his treatment of his stepchildren. The family situation comes very close to pathological, in which all interactions send members deeply into depression and defeat, which can be relieved only by either drugs or alcohol, with the latter here the favorite nostrum. No wonder once his situation made it possible, Faulkner sipped away as much as he could.

Upon returning to Charlottesville, Faulkner settled in and did some riding. He also found time to work, but slowly and with little of the early energy. He kept referring to himself as more or less burned out, giving up after his next effort. The spark was almost extinguished, and his life now, as he saw it, was mainly drift, filled not with promise but with moments of pleasure. Riding had become consuming, replacing flying in the 1930s, and for him not less dangerous. One of his last acts in 1957 was to send a congratulatory telegram to Camus, who had just been announced as the winner of the Nobel Prize in literature. "ON SALUT L'AME QUI CON-STAMMENT SE CHERCHE ET SE DEMANDE." ("We salute the spirit that constantly seeks out and questions [or makes demands upon] itself.") In a way, Faulkner's words were almost precisely those he could no longer follow himself.

The year 1957 ended with a kind of passing of the guard in Nobel Prize terms. Camus, only forty-four, represented another generation. But more than his young age, he stood for another kind of fiction, in several ways deeply indebted to Faulkner, but in others, a step away from Faulkner's immersion in a time and place. Camus, particularly with *The Fall*, began that invasion of imaginary territories—what Italo Calvino would call "invisible cities," such as the later Macondo of Gabriel García Márquez's great novel, *One Hundred Years of Solitude*, and other supernal places of the imagination. Influenced as many of these ideas are by Faulkner's Yoknapatawpha, they depart from his kind of realism into fantasy, magic, problems of time and place, indeterminacy of people and motivation. *The Fall* is itself located in the Mexico City bar (heights) in Amsterdam (depths, below sea level), and the novel moves in fogs, watery scenes, mists—place is subverted, a geography of the mind substituted. Imaginative uncertainties, inventions, a vacuuming-out of reality have displaced Faulkner's certainties.

The year 1958 was singularly lacking in dramatic events, although it did find Faulkner solidly immersed in his Snopes trilogy. He was working along on *The Mansion* (finished in early March 1959, for publication on November 13). But he was also involved with Albert Erskine at Random House over the numerous inconsistencies and discrepancies which had accrued in a trilogy that took him twenty years to finish. Such problems fell into several categories: chronology, detail, description. The problem was intensified by the fact that Random House liked the idea of a unified edition of the three novels, perhaps boxed, or else in one volume. But this meant altering the individual novels to conform with one another, and Faulkner resisted. He saw his work as "living literature" and as such subject to the flaws which creep into something in motion, change, evolving. He didn't want to create the impression that what he wrote in 1958 was "better" than his work in 1938; and alterations meant he was correcting with twenty years of hindsight. In fact, he pulled back so vociferously from the notion of change that we might suspect he did not want comparison with 1938 for very different reasons: the earlier work might show up the later, rather than the later "correcting" the earlier. He did agree to some cosmetic changes, but larger discrepancies remained.

When not working on *The Mansion* or dealing with the Snopes trilogy overall, Faulkner made his planned appearances at the University of Virginia, but was refused permanent membership in the English department. The reasons for this were several, but two in particular stand out—his reputation as a heavy and at times uncontrollable drinker; and, more important, his controversial position on racial integration. Virginia took no second place to Mississippi in its resistance to school integration and either established alternate schools or closed down the public school system to avoid implementation of the Supreme Court decision. Faulkner's class sessions were far briefer in number and content, although he did offer two important "papers" in this series. He was on the move, back and forth to Princeton, then Oxford, then Charlottesville; his three places now well defined. On July 17, he sincerely mourned the passing of Saxe Commins, who stood for him in his later years what Phil Stone had done in his earlier.

His social-political-educational role was no less insistent this year than in the past. He agreed to be interviewed on the school situation in Little Rock where Governor Faubus, to insure his own reelection, opposed integration until federal troops had to be called out. In many senses, the Faubus position in Little Rock foreshadowed the Ole Miss situation, when Governor Barnett opposed its integration and federal troops had to be called in. The political aspect of Faulkner's later views came when he refused an invitation to the Soviet Union, calling it a police state, saying his Russia—of Dostoyevsky, Tolstoy, and Chekhov—was no longer there. He felt that his presence in the Soviet Union would be a betrayal of those writers and their aspirations, perhaps forgetting that Dostoyevsky fervently supported a Czarist government as repressive, narrow, and prejudicial as the then-current Soviet regime. Faulkner's position seemed consistent with his growing patriotism, even while he opposed Eisenhower's administration and the men appointed to run it. Cold-war chauvinism had penetrated. In fact, Faulkner's brand of individualism and its application to the artist as a free spirit would have been precisely what the Soviet writers needed to hear: not to change them or their regime, but to repeat what America at its best could stand for.

By June, he had completed and typed chapter 6 of *The Mansion*. In the fall, he met briefly with students at Princeton University, and was, by mid-November, beginning chapter 13. His main love now was fox hunting, riding to the hounds in Virginia—the "big woods" having given way to dressing up with wealthy riders and chasing a fox on a powerful mount. It gave Faulkner great joy, but it would also provide him with a new series of injuries, some of them serious.

Early in the year Faulkner was pleased by Carvel Collins's well-edited volume which brought together the New Orleans sketches and portraits. He agreed with William Sloane that the volume does "scholarly credit and literary justice to the whole enterprise."[7] In the background of his own slow movement on *The Mansion* was almost an avalanche of interest in his earlier work. A film based on *Pylon*, directed by Douglas Sirk and called

The Tarnished Angels, premiered in January. Faulkner's portrait of the fliers and their entourage had been of interest because he saw them, like writers and other artists, as clearly lying outside society. In their disregard for their lives, they lived for the moment; and in their disregard for society at large, they demonstrated solidarity with each other, however roughly. Sirk's film, however, subverted everything compelling in *Pylon* and turned it into a Hollywood love story with a message: love of those close to one should preempt dreams of glory.

But despite the inability of anyone to make a meaningful film of Faulkner's novels, there was still plenty of interest. *Light in August* and *As I Lay Dying* were being sought for dramatic rights. Peter Glenville was interested in taking an option on *Absalom,* [8] as was Jerry Wald, who had himself purchased *Sound* and *The Hamlet.* Wald would, of course, pay far more than Glenville; but with the latter, the book had a better chance. Glenville was also interested in *Light in August,* for which he offered between $35,000 and $50,000, with ten percent down and a nine-month option. Ober, who was literarily sophisticated, knew that the film of *Pylon,* as he put it, "was terrible," that the two Wald properties "will be poor ones."[9] He felt Glenville would do far better and recommended him to Commins. Whatever the outcome as art, all this meant a steady influx of money, in addition to book monies.*

In February Faulkner began again at the University of Virginia. A week before he gave an important speech on race before the Raven, Jefferson, and ODK Societies, however, Faulkner was denied a permanent position in the English department by President Colgate W. Darden. Darden's ostensible argument was that other writers who entered under the Balch Program would also request permanence if Faulkner received it. But the real reason, Blotner and Gwynn felt, was the potential embarrassment the writer's racial views would have on the state legislature when Darden went for university funds. At this time, Virginia was involved in a program of "massive resistance" to the court decision, and the resistance was led by the governor—including the closing of many schools in Charlottesville and in Albermarle County as a whole. Virginia was taking the lead in "seceding," as it had in the period prior to the outbreak of the Civil War. A state Faulkner had assumed would be a leader in his vision of a gradually changing America was for political reasons proving recalcitrant. The result was Faulkner's outspoken talk on February 20, "A Word to Virginians."

*Less heartening was the steady deterioration of relations between Faulkner and Phil Stone. The writer visited Stone's law office off the square and sat there waiting for the lawyer to emerge. But Stone did not, claiming he was too busy. Then Faulkner would leave and return another time. Some reasons are clear: Stone owed Faulkner money, a debt that went back many years; also, Stone could hardly face the man he was bad-mouthing in nearly every letter to literary critics, saying that since Faulkner had won the Nobel Prize he was suffering from attacks of Nobelitis. A further reason was, possibly, that Stone could not bear his friend's success, whereas he toiled in relative obscurity; and, besides, the lawyer was beginning to go under, in that deterioration which saw him institutionalized near the end of his life.

Faulkner started by saying he admired Virginia and Virginians (the people he rode to hounds with were the backbone of the resistance to integration), and he was speaking as a private citizen from another state. He cites Lincoln's statement that this nation cannot endure half slave and half free, and amends it to say no nation can endure where ten percent of its population holds second-class citizenship. It can only exist if everyone is first class or everyone second class. In what would rightly inflame Negro leaders, he says that perhaps Negroes are not capable of anything more; but nevertheless the problem exists. Even if the Negro accepted his situation as inferior, it would not solve anything: the nation would remain divided and be operating at only ninety percent of its power. He says if he were a Northerner, he would blame the South; for it has the power to solve the problem, but has not. Let us agree, he insists, that the Negro is not ready for equality—although he does not ask if white sharecroppers in Mississippi's northern hills were ready for equality—but if we do, we must bring him into equality through education: "take him in hand and teach him that responsibility."[10] This would not be the first time, he says, when moral and practical considerations are identical. Much of this sounds familiar, but there is a renewed urgency, since Virginia clearly has disappointed Faulkner—he had expected results different from his own state's. Implicit in these remarks is his awareness, growing gradually, that his moderate approach had turned to ashes, and that it was as unacceptable to the South, deep or otherwise, as was any other scheme which seated black and white together.

He admits that whites and Negroes may never like each other; but that is not the important point. The significant element is to bring Negroes into the mainstream of American life. He stresses that the white man can never understand the Negro because he, the white man, has insisted the Negro be a Negro, who cannot dare to be open and let the white man know what he thinks. He says knowledge is possible only in individual cases. Then in words which make us cringe now, but which were daring then, he says the Negro must be taught "the responsibility of personal morality and rectitude"; either by taking him into white schools or putting white teachers into his schools, who can then teach Negro teachers how to teach Negroes. The thought process here is so lacking in the understanding of another race—and yet simultaneously so outrageous to most of the white population—that Faulkner was becoming a pariah to both races. He asks Virginia to lead in this.

An excellent question began that portion of the session. The questioner wonders whether white people can teach Negroes anything, since they have been irresponsible in that respect; wouldn't it be better "to educate the white people to accept the Negro?"[11] This turns Faulkner's twisted perception into a more logical procedure, and he agrees, but insists the Negro is not going to wait around while the white man educates himself. The Negro wants something now, deserves it now. Another question suggests idiocy, picking up Faulkner's metaphor of bridling wild horses as a way of handling Negroes and saying that would result in a lot of half-wild horses. The questioner fits the metaphor. Another person asks if Faulkner thinks that other Southerners would lose respect for Virginians if they led the way to integration. He feels that that would not be the case at all, that there is a middle run of people in all states who are seeking leadership, who know that a new situation has developed which cannot be dealt with by the Klan or its more respectable brothers, the Citizens' Councils. Virginia could provide just this leadership—at a time when the state was leading a massive resistance. He repeats what he has been saying for years, however, that whites really fear Negro resurgence economically.

Faulkner also repeats what is by now familiar—that within five hundred years (it once was three hundred), the Negro will vanish through intermarriage, and anyone who wants to join the DAR then will "have to prove that she's got somewhere a strain of Negro blood."[12] Asked about implementation in education, Faulkner says the first step is to raise the standard of all schools, and he approves of federal aid if the aim is improvement. Open to all races, however, schools should be a privilege, and anyone not measuring up should find another outlet—trade school, army, whatever. Faulkner now had shifted his ground from Negro education to education in America, and, revealing his respect for formal schooling, insists it is not for everyone—putting him in opposition to those egalitarian critics who felt education must be available to all regardless of ability. He repeats that the North is also going to have to learn because increasingly Negroes are moving north, including 4,800 from his county alone. He correctly predicts that when the Northern cities have to absorb large numbers of Negroes, they will change their tune about integration. He was quite prophetic, since the major issue for most large cities shifted to busing.

". . . the Negro can be equal without having to come in and sleep with you,"[13] he says. When someone points out that every civilization has had its second-class citizens, Faulkner repudiates that as irrelevant to the South, saying that in no civilization did skin color dictate lower social level: people gravitated to racism on their own. And when ancient Egypt is mentioned as having had hundreds of thousands in slavery, Faulkner wittily mentions Moses leading "a big gang of them out himself." He is, however, dubious about giving everyone the vote, saying education must come first, although he does not question that illiterate hill farmers from northern Mississippi took the franchise for themselves for granted. He does agree that many white people don't have any business voting, but he has no plan to take it away from them. What he fears is a large bloc of Negro votes, deriving from people who don't know what or whom they are voting for.

Faulkner takes a jejune view of the Northern handling of integration. He feels that Northerners "love the Negro in theory, but they don't want much to do with him. I've noticed that the Southerner, he don't love the

Negro in quantities, but he will defend some particular Negro." Such views take him quite distant from a moral stance, which does not take into account what people like or do not like. There is in Faulkner's answers a bending with the questions, so that he seems reasonable and will not alarm anyone; but underneath is his own ambiguity, unquestionably hoping for the best for the Negro, but torn by his own "betrayal" of what the South more generally feels. He recognizes, as he says, that the majority in the South let the minority lead them because they do not want any unpleasantness. Questioners wonder how, if the worst elements (Klan, etc.) are in control in the Deep South, any action from Virginia can penetrate into that psyche? Faulkner's sole response is that there is a responsible leadership in such places which would respond to signs of liberality in other states. Faulkner knows that the Klan comes from poor whites who fear Negro progress, and yet these poor whites, because of skin color, command allegiance from those who would not themselves use the same methods, but acquiesce out of solidarity. In that joining of Klan and white Citizens' Councils, we find much cutting across class lines: well-to-do professionals and commercial interests acquiescing to the methods of a lower class, often a different caste. What Faulkner could not accept was that a Civil War mentality gripped his region.

A quite inflammatory question leads Faulkner into a statement he really does not accept, but which part of him believes; and it is damning. The questioner says that since the Negro has mores detrimental to our society, wouldn't it be better to educate him and raise his economic standard but keep him segregated? Faulkner bites, and says that is precisely his idea:

> I agree with you, that's what I'd like to do. I would like to give him such good schools that he wouldn't want to go to the white schools. I would like to give him so much equality in his own race and responsibility for it and make him have to spend so much time being responsible for his own equality that he wouldn't have time to bother with the white man's.[14]

Here Faulkner turns his own argument into nonsense; as though Negroes once they have improved educationally and economically will forgo the larger society in order to hang together in their own. And what has happened to the moral issue, which, in Faulkner's own terms, condemns segregation as an absolute wrong?

Faulkner closed this very dense questioning with his reiterated point that assimilation of the Negro was not the issue, equality was. He repeats the fact, which is unanswerable, that the Negro is drafted into the military and expected to sacrifice his life if need be, but has no compensatory rights in exchange. For Faulkner, the "compensation" will be equality, so that the Negro "don't have to pay any more for the Cadillac that he dreams of owning some day than the white man has to pay for it." With this, Faulkner made his last long plea for racial equality, except for a March interview with the *New York Times* over the Little Rock impasse over school integration.*

Before leaving for Princeton, at the invitation of Whitney J. Oates, the distinguished classicist and chairman of the Interdepartmental Committee of the Council of the Humanities, Faulkner met a class at Virginia. Blotner tells the story of an amusing exchange with a student. Student: "Mr. Faulkner, I have read all your books and short stories, and I want to know, is there one character that is saved by grace?" Faulkner: "Well, I have always thought of God as being in the wholesale rather than the retail business."[15] On March 1, he left for Princeton, for two weeks of eight group sessions for $500. He stayed with the Comminses and seemed to behave himself. But he was withdrawn, obviously unhappy, even severely distressed, and Commins did not know what to make of it. The periods of depression and blackness came on in circumstances which did not seem threatening; surely by this time Faulkner had become accustomed to the questions. But the presence of a faculty and an academic setting, the threat of discussing literature and writing with his peers—any or all of these could set him off.

One of the things Faulkner wanted to discuss with his Random House friends and agent as they gathered in Commins's home was the possibility of his purchase of a Virginia farm property. Money did not seem a problem, although he would be extended, having Rowan Oak and the Greenfield farm, as well as a large Virginia farm, presumably stocked with horses. As before, his lifestyle was always ahead of income. But Ruth Ford's London production of *Requiem* in later 1957 earned him good royalties, and film money was coming in. He was much encouraged, and although he returned to Charlottesville only briefly on his way back to Oxford, this idea was planted as his next real estate venture. It was also his way of avoiding Oxford, where he knew his views on race had made him unacceptable to most. Even this late in his life, he had a need to reject what was close to him, even as he worked on *The Mansion,* based so deeply on Yoknapatawpha.

Work on that book, as he told Else (on April 14) was about one-third finished. That brought him to the end of part 1, called "Mink." The

---

*Phil Stone also commented on the issue. No member of the Klan, Stone was another one of Faulkner's "moderates" who opposed every move for racial equality. Writing to Maud Falkner over the Little Rock plan for integration, he says he agrees thoroughly with her. "It sounds like Alice in Wonderland when you consider that the taxpayers have had to pay out over $800,000 apiece to keep nine negro children in a school when they, the negro children, have a brand-new million-dollar school just a few blocks away which is a better school than the one they are now in." He adds: "I don't think we are going to have any integrated schools in Mississippi any time soon, and it is my own feeling that the NAACP is breaking its own neck and that everybody is getting tired of it" (February 14, 1958; *Faulkner: A Comprehensive Guide to the Brodsky Collection, the Letters,* eds. Louis Daniel Brodsky and Robert W. Hamblin, vol. 2 [Jackson: University Press of Mississippi, 1984], p. 232).

scummy Mink Snopes had become more significant in Faulkner's thinking as he turned into an avenging figure, with something of the grandeur, in his hatred, that we associate with more tragic characters. Faulkner's evident plan was to use Mink and his desire for revenge on Flem Snopes as a means of giving some human dimension to the Snopes clan; in so doing, he turned Mink into an individualized portrait of a man without anything who still makes a claim upon life. While it is difficult to forget the earlier, scummier Mink and his murder of Houston, nevertheless Faulkner is also making a claim on the reader.

On his return to Charlottesville, Faulkner addressed the English Club on April 24 with a message called "A Word to Young Writers." Speaking about the younger generation of writers, Faulkner suggests that the latter (presumably, Salinger, Bellow, Mailer, Styron) must function "in a kind of vacuum of the human race. Their characters do not function, live, breathe, struggle, in that moil and seethe of simple humanity as did those of our predecessors who were the masters from whom we learned our craft: Dickens, Fielding, Thackeray, Conrad, Twain, Smollett, Hawthorne, Melville, James."[16] For such writers, characters were "an affirmation of an incurable and indomitable optimism—men and women like themselves, understandable and comprehensive even when antipathetical, even in the very moment while they were murdering or robbing or betraying you."

The contrast with today is clear; for now, the writer's characters move in isolation, and they cannot pursue "the anguishes and hopes of all human hearts in a world of a few simple comprehensible truths and moral principles," but must exist "alone inside a vacuum of facts which he did not choose and cannot cope with and cannot escape from like a fly inside an inverted tumbler." He cites *Catcher in the Rye*, which he considers "the best one," and says Holden's problem is not that he is insufficiently tough to enter the human race, but that when he tries "there was no human race there. There was nothing for him to do save buzz, frantic and inviolate, inside the glass walls of his tumbler until he either gave up or was himself, by his own frantic buzzing, destroyed."

Faulkner concludes:

That is the young writer's dilemma as I see it. Not just his, but all our problems, is to save mankind from being desouled as the stallion or boar or bull is gelded; to save the individual from anonymity before it is too late and humanity has vanished from the animal called man. And who better to save man's humanity than the writer, the poet, the artist, since who should fear the loss more since the humanity of man is the artist's life blood.[17]

This is, in a sense, a last hurrah, Faulkner eloquently trying to see the artist in his traditional role, refusing to accept that the artist can no longer find the human race because it has divided itself into so many subspecies. He is trying verbally to stand off the worst ravages of modernism, with its loss of human values (i.e., Pound's nihilism): that very modernism he had explored and exploited in his best work. He had come close to achieving what he was asking young writers to do: not to abdicate their roles as artists, but to graft onto their technical and strategical methods the human values which are the sole justification of art. We note in Faulkner's words his recognition that the time has passed, and that his words, while well received, cannot be assimilated into practice. He perceives that in Holden Caulfield, Salinger had captured something very close to the bone of the culture: an extremely sensitive young man who had become an anachronism; trying, as Faulkner says, "to cope with a struggle with the present-day world which he was not fitted for . . . he just wanted to find man and wanted something to love, and he couldn't."[18]

This talk was a last hurrah in another sense, for except for a few more appearances in April and May, this was his valedictory statement. He gave way to Katherine Anne Porter the following year. One session, on May 7, warrants attention, since in it Faulkner answered questions from the department of psychiatry, an event calculated to bring out the worst in him. Clearly, the psychiatrists and the writer are moving on different levels and speaking different languages. One doctor asks if he would say a few words about "irrational human behavior." Faulkner then went off on the unpredictability of all human behavior, which is not what the psychiatrist had in mind. He was seeking some pathological etiology, whereas Faulkner was responding in terms of literary characters and their breadth of difference. He states that human behavior is such because the universe is not a rational one, emphasizing that the writer does not attempt to better man's condition but to present its multiplicity, beyond judgment. He even admits that, possibly, "the writer has no concept of morality at all, only an integrity to hold always to what he believes to be the facts and truths of human behavior."[19]

The next questioner agreed that the psychiatrist also does not make judgments, or likes to think he doesn't (although, in reality, he does). He wonders how the writer can avoid personal judgments. Faulkner says it is possible the writer as writer has a split personality: that he "is one thing when he is a writer and he is something else while he is a denizen of the world." But this is not really what Faulkner means, since in other places he has spoken of the writer's need to use his integrity of purpose for human progress; and not to accept the division of the man and writer into separate entities. What occurred in this session was that both sides were sparring and saying things they did not mean. When asked where he learned psychology, Faulkner says he picked it up from listening to people: "Freud I'm not familiar with." The psychiatrists then went into a series of questions which sound more sophomoric than those from undergraduates: do you believe in extrasensory perception? do you have any ideas on the trend toward conformity? why do you, Faulkner, not want to belong to anything? how do you rate people as first- and second-rate? The answers became as ludicrous as the questions, but the session ended without anyone going over the edge.

Despite the end of his Balch visiting writer-in-residence position, the Faulkners were still interested in buying a place in Virginia. Estelle confided in Dorothy Commins: "We've found an ideal home and grounds that I already feel at home, in and on, but of course I realize how serious a move it will be for Billy—and say little—I've trained myself to be reasonably satisfied anywhere—but to be near Jill and her little family means a great deal . . ."[20] As Faulkner was finishing up with his usual pronouncements, this time at Washington and Lee University, saying that Joyce and Mann were the greatest writers of his time, he was preparing to return to Oxford. About the same time, by May 31, he declined the State Department's invitation to visit the Soviet Union.

He indicates that now at sixty, and having "possibly done all the good work I am capable of," he would go if he thought he could rescue an *Anna Karenina* or *Cherry Orchard*. But it would be a lie for him to go to a country which has driven underground "the heirs of the old giants of the Russian spirit"; he would feel a betrayal of the very idea of literary endeavor. "If I, who have had freedom all my life in which to write truth exactly as I saw it, visited Russia now, the fact of even the outward appearance of condoning the condition which the present Russian government has established, would be a betrayal, not of the giants; nothing can harm them, but of their spiritual heirs who risk their lives with every page they write; and a lie in that it would condone the shame of them who might have been their heirs who have lost more than life; who have had their souls destroyed for the privilege of writing in public."

Faulkner's motives might have been intermixed with other ideas. He was proceeding on *The Mansion*, often in a hit-or-miss manner. He was writing the novel and then typing it on scraps of paper; even the above letter to Colwell of the State Department had on the verso of its first page a page of his new novel. While still in Charlottesville, he had given one-third of it to Blotner to read and had received suitable encouragement. He was now, at the end of May, beginning chapter 6, "Linda," the second segment, one of his most interesting fictional conceptions of women. After the amoral Temple Drake, the elusive Caddy, the resolute Laverne, the possessed Charlotte, now in Linda he had a woman of many parts. She is, more than any of the others, a modern woman. Daughter of Eula Varner Snopes, she has thrown off the restraints of a small town, thrown off the shackles of what a woman is expected to do, married a Jewish Greenwich Village sculptor, gone to Spain to support the forces fighting Franco, returned deaf, with a desire to help Negroes, and refuses to conform to what is still expected of her. Further, she plots Flem Snopes's death with a fine strategy that is Snopesism at its best (or worst).

On July 16 and 17, respectively, Faulkner went through two difficult experiences. The first, on the seventeenth, was Saxe Commins's death of a heart attack at sixty-six, bringing him considerable grief. Estelle sent the first telegram, indicating how shocked and heartbroken everyone was, indicating that she or Faulkner would come immediately if Dorothy needed them. Faulkner sent his telegram on July 18: "The finest epitaph everyone who ever knew Saxe will have to subscribe to whether he will or not quote he love me unquote."[21] He followed up in a letter about how they all missed Commins; he shortly after moved to Donald Klopfer, although the nature of the relationship never became so intimate.

The matter of July 16, the day before Commins's sudden death, was less grief than annoyance. Maud Brown, whose daughter had been the recipient of *The Wishing Tree* in 1928, wrote Faulkner asking if she could sell her presentation copy. Faulkner, we recall, had written the brief children's book in 1927 and presented it to Mrs. Brown's daughter, Margaret, who, afflicted, died a few years afterward. But that presentation copy was in reality the second copy, since the original manuscript had gone to Victoria, his stepdaughter. Mrs. Brown's request went unanswered. James Silver, the Ole Miss historian, was drawn into it as intermediary, and he counseled not to push Faulkner, but to wait until September. This relatively minor matter developed into an entire campaign; it touched upon a gray area, since Faulkner did not write the story for publication and was now being importuned for a purpose contravening his original intention. Silver concedes that Faulkner's purpose had been humanitarian, and that there was now a commercial aspect to Mrs. Brown's desire to sell the manuscript. Whatever Silver did or did not do, Mrs. Brown wrote Faulkner again on December 1, repeating her earlier request and adding she felt such a charming story should be made available to all children. Faulkner never responded to this letter either, and the matter remained there until Random House published *The Wishing Tree* posthumously.*

---

*But he did respond to Ober (on February 4, 1959) that he had given the story to Mrs. Brown's daughter as an act of compassion for a doomed child (dying of cancer). He says he felt quite shocked when she wrote "that she even considered getting money from it. To tell the truth, I didn't believe her. When I told her the story (after the child's death) belonged to her, to do as she wanted with it, it never occurred to me that she would want to commercialise it, since it was, as I said, a gesture of pity and compassion." He indicates that if Mrs. Brown wants money so badly, he will not stand in her way; but he assumed she wanted to sell it to a collector, not *Life*. Then from this seemingly innocuous episode pours a good deal of rancor, and his hostility to Phil Stone is illuminated.

By now I should certainly have got used to the fact that most of my erstwhile friends and acquaintances here believe I am rich from sheer blind chance, and are determined to have a little of it. I learned last week (he didn't tell me himself) that another one [Phil Stone] gathered up all the odds and ends of mine he had in his possession, and sold it to a Texan university [at Austin]; he needed money too evidently. So do I—the $6000.00 of my cancelled life insurance which paid a mortgage on his property 20 years ago and which I'll never see again" (Alderman Library; *Selected Letters of William Faulkner*, ed. Joseph Blotner [New York: Vintage Books, 1978; orig. publ. 1977], p. 421).

Rankles went both ways.

Faulkner's failure to respond directly was clearly intentional. He felt that what was given as a gift should not enter the marketplace. The magazine interested in publishing it was *Life*, on whose behalf Ralph Graves became involved in the Brown-Silver connection. But *Life* was high on Faulkner's list of magazines he interpreted as destructive of individual privacy. Silver wrote once more to Graves, on December 22, and suggested the latter get in touch with Ober—the historian recognized defeat and knew Faulkner's failure to respond was an implicit answer.

Back in Oxford, Faulkner pursued his horsemanship. With Tempy, it was a battle of wills, each winning a little but Faulkner losing most. While preparing Tempy for a night horse show, he tried to force the horse to face the lights and crowd. The consequence was a torn ligament in his groin, so that his leg was "rainbow-colored, red, purple, green, yellow, down to the knee, besides breaking the bridle and flinging the groom into a ditch before we got her into a stall immobilised."[22] But Faulkner persevered and endured, and he was soon back in the saddle again, spurred for further combat by a worthy opponent.

Still, Oxford, despite Tempy, was boring him: "I have got a belly full of Oxford." He was finding it difficult to keep tourists from rubbernecking in his front yard. Also, his usual complaint recurred: he couldn't eat anywhere without being forced to listen to a jukebox. He tells Ober (August 11) that he plans to buy a place in Virginia on credit and a mortgage. He even contemplates mortgaging a year in Hollywood for $75,000. Offered a speaking engagement at Purdue, he rejects it, saying his only universities are Virginia and Princeton; and what he needs is not $1,000, but $100,000. He was accumulating small sums from television rights on "Old Man" ($7,500) from *Playhouse 90*, another $1,000 from *Esquire* for the Nagano material, royalties from *Requiem*, and, of course, from renewed interest in his books. He also had the invested remainder of the Nobel money. He was well fixed, but if he purchased the Virginia property without selling Rowan Oak—which he did not contemplate—he would be as overly extended as he had been when he took on Rowan Oak in 1930.

What is curious as Faulkner worked his way into the "Linda" segment of *The Mansion* in the fall of 1958 is how closely he located the young woman in his own social and racial position. On October 13, Faulkner commented to the *New York Times* on the Little Rock situation, his final public statement on racial issues. We have noted how he felt Little Rock might be salutary, for it revealed what everyone already knew, that "white people and Negroes do not like and trust each other, and perhaps never can."[23] But his main point was to get beyond that attitude and move toward some response to a national crisis. In Linda Snopes Kohl, now returned to Jefferson as a card-carrying communist, deafened from a bomb bursting near her in the Spanish civil war, we have a person intent on establishing Faulkner's terms for racial reconciliation. Since Linda advocates helping Negroes educationally she is branded "a nigger-lover," but she is hardly a radical even there. Her plan, already suggested by Faulkner in his "A Word to Virginians" delivered at Charlottesville, is to weed out top Negro students from the mass and have them taught by white teachers for a week. In its mixture of the impossible and the condescending, the ploy is itself cockeyed. In *The Mansion* Linda advocates the plan for such a competition among Negroes, but the Negro principal insists to Gavin Stevens that it cannot work. The principal himself argues Faulkner's unique position—calculated to drive Negroes to anger and to create little but opposition among whites—that the Negro must make the white man need him. When that occurs, the white man will acquiesce to certain Negro rights. This was in effect Faulkner's valedictory to the situation.

By the time Faulkner had written this, he had been back to Charlottesville to await the birth of Jill's second son. During his stay—Estelle remained until delivery—Faulkner and his wife lived with Jill and her husband in a cottage on the grounds of Linton Massey's estate. By this time, Massey had accumulated an incomparable Faulkner collection of manuscripts, typescripts, letters, and memorabilia. Back in Oxford, Faulkner could look forward to the wedding of his niece, Dean, to Jon Mallard, a career army officer, a marriage which produced three children before dissolving. Between preparations and Dean's wedding, Faulkner bruised a few ribs in a fall from his horse; but managed to get through the party, and used the occasion, after the couple left, to celebrate for himself.

As he worked along slowly on *The Mansion*, reaching in those fall days the third and final section, "Flem," he was preparing to leave Oxford again, this time for Charlottesville and Princeton. At Princeton, he would complete his duties for the Council on Humanities, making himself available for nonteaching duties. Large sums of money were suddenly becoming available, including an offer from Twentieth Century-Fox of $135,000 for film rights to *Requiem for a Nun*, of which Faulkner would receive $81,000, sufficient to cover purchase of a good Virginia property. The movement back and forth between Oxford and Virginia, between Charlottesville and Princeton, the splitting of himself into little pieces—all indicated a lack of concentration, which in turn helped explain the discrepancies in the trilogy. With more concentration, he would have reread the first two books and made a greater effort to align details among the three novels. Instead, he chose to explain[24] to Albert Erskine at Random House that since his trilogy was living literature, it could reflect "motion, change, constant alteration," all of which equals evolution, and that, in turn, improvement. The question of discrepancies began well before *The Mansion* was submitted, but heated up in the spring of 1959, when Random House was confronted with what seemed an insoluble problem: details which contradicted each other, and an author who saw the differences as a creative act.*

By the time he arrived in Princeton for his light duties, he was well along on chapter 13, part 3, of *The Mansion*. On November 16, he settled in, seeing students for six days. The visit also gave him the opportunity to see Dorothy Commins and Maurice Coindreau, his French translator. Commins invited luminaries from the Institute for Advanced Study to a party honoring Faulkner, but his mind was elsewhere—on riding and on shoes, especially on chasing the elusive fox. The evening with Institute people was a typical Faulkner fiasco, and he made an impression which went beyond boorishness, revealing a disquieting side no amount of explanation can allay. When J. Robert Oppenheimer, a man Faulkner admired, commented that he saw the writer's story "The Brooch" on television, and enjoyed it, Faulkner responded: "Television is for niggers."[25] Yet Faulkner himself watched television, particularly sports events and even some comedy series. Dorothy Commins tried to explain it by saying he thought the medium was for a mass audience; and Blotner says, in apology, Faulkner felt pushed to the wall, not wanting to be at the party, not feeling up to the august company. Yet no explanation obtains except that he fell into the white man's most obvious retreat, using the Negro as someone so much lower in caste that the retort becomes unanswerable.

Such a spontaneous remark makes suspect much of Faulkner's hard-earned opposition to Deep South racism; it makes one perceive that his positioning of himself was less a matter of racial justice than of a fear injustice could lead to federal interference and Southern violence. There is, however, a third view—that is Faulkner represented both elements, containing within himself the potentiality of advocacy of racial justice and the traditional attitudes which can result in such a remark.

Which Faulkner do we identify? The Faulkner who seems to perceive terrible injustice? The Faulkner who says he will fight in the streets to preserve a white society? The Faulkner who so feared disorder that he frantically advocates racial justice? The Faulkner who is himself unable to take a position, and who falls back on racial stereotyping? Finally, the Faulkner who harbors all of the Deep South's attitudes toward the Negro

---

*For starters: whatever happened to the other fourteen children of Varner? Jody and Eula appear to be the only survivors in *The Mansion*, his sole heirs. Perhaps those older than Jody had died—he was the ninth child—but how about all those younger than he? In *The Mansion*, Mink has words for the dying Houston, whereas in *The Hamlet*, Houston is shot dead, no longer receptive to Mink's taunts. In *The Town*, Houston marries Letty Bookwright; in *The Hamlet*, she is Lucy Pate. In *The Mansion* she goes unnamed, becoming "the wife." As we can see, none of these amounts to much. But the trilogy was not alone in revealing discrepancies. As Cleanth Brooks points out, in *Requiem for a Nun*, Temple Drake is seventeen at the time of her rape, losing a year of age from *Sanctuary*, where she is eighteen. Also, in *Requiem*, Temple recalls getting off the train in *Sanctuary* five years before, but Gavin states it as eight. As with the above, the slips were not momentous. The dating of the events of *Requiem*, then, becomes either 1937 or 1934, inasmuch as *Sanctuary* clearly takes place in 1929. For the reader seeking still further discrepancies and inconsistencies, check the chronology and genealogy in the Modern Library edition of *Absalom* against the text, especially for Ellen Coldfield, Charles Bon, and Judith Sutpen.

and yet who fights to establish a more just society? If the latter is the "real" Faulkner, as one suspects, then such a remark as he made to Oppenheimer lies just below the surface. It hovers there waiting for the moment when, unable to handle his circumstances, he must lash out—and in that, the denigration of the Negro becomes his commonplace comment.

The yo-yoing continued for the remainder of the year. Faulkner went up to New York at the end of November, having completed his stint in Princeton (his final stint at any American university, in fact). Then he made his way back to Charlottesville for the fox hunting, as part of the activities of the Keswick Hunt Club. Still without permanent digs of their own, he and Estelle were renting in Farmington. Life among the fox hunters was a form of acceptance for Faulkner into the higher reaches of American society. It was intensely "breed" conscious, not only of its mounts but of its riders and their wives. There were money, position, background, and family lines; and the group favored plenty of whiskey along with the riding. Most of all, there was tradition. Faulkner loved to put on the full regalia, which made him look like a dapper Mississippi riverboat gambler. He equally embraced the formalities: the prehunt breakfast, the coming together of men and women who loved their horses, the posthunt parties, and the hard drinking which accompanied everything. He also admired the daring, the taking of obstacles on a big horse which required a timing and strength which were just beyond him. Being "just behind" the needs of the situation drove him to excel. Horses, jumping, traps, and obstacles gave a danger to his life; he apparently needed that physical goad to stir himself, even at the expense of broken limbs. The hunt for fox replaced the hunt for deer; only now, he had moved up socially, and he had taken on the danger of a powerful horse between his thighs.*

On December 2, Jill's second son was born and named, in honor of her father, William Cuthbert Faulkner Summers, carrying the given name down from the old colonel to the illustrious great-grandson, to still another grandson. He had some further good news—publication by Random House of the "play" segment of *Requiem*. There were some problems, nevertheless, even in this relatively simple procedure, for Ford had adapted Faulkner's play episodes in order to create a working acting version. Random House subtitled the publication "A Play from the novel by William Faulkner adapted to the stage by Ruth Ford." Faulkner suggested adding "as adapted to the stage by Ruth Ford by means of altered or additional dialogue and movement."[26] He indicates he doesn't believe Ford wants to state that the play was written originally by anyone else but Faulkner, or that she wanted her name on it as a joint work.

---

*His daughter agrees: "I think one reason he liked fox hunting, not only for the dress-up part, was the element of risk. It appealed to him. I think it appealed to him in everything" (to Ober, December 12, 1958, Alderman Library; *Selected Letters of William Faulkner*, ed. Joseph Blotner [New York: Vintage Books, 1978; orig. publ. 1977], p. 417). We should not, however, underestimate the need for transformation: Jay Gatz became Jay Gatsby, and William Falkner, the Oxford town bum, became part of the Virginia horsey set.

The Mansion was inching along, but we get some idea of its progress from the fact that Faulkner's own "wishing well" of imaginative material was running dry and he was picking up odds and ends to incorporate into the novel. Blotner tells of how his own experience in a German prisoner-of-war camp (after being shot down over Cologne) was used for Chick Mallison's experience in Germany, in chapter 13. Faulkner also used his own discarded material, the story "By the People," which many magazines had rejected as too raunchy: the tale of how dogs had peed on Clarence Snopes and ruined his candidacy for office. Such use of material is a little like the novelist combing newspaper columns for bits he can include in his fiction, without giving it any opportunity to be digested and reshaped. It is a little too raw for fictional comfort and suggests a novelist dredging his memory futilely. As a consequence, *The Mansion* may seem less than the total of its parts.

Faulkner began 1959, appropriately enough, with letters concerning his riding, and the still open chance of buying a Virginia property. The year was almost a duplicate of the previous one, the chief difference being publication of *The Mansion* on November 13 with the subtitle, as in *The Town*, "A Novel of the Snopes Family," and dedicated to Phil Stone. The manuscript was itself completed by January 23. The remainder of the year also brought a recapitulation of Faulkner's career—the transfer of his manuscripts and typescripts from Princeton to Virginia's Alderman Library; the exhibition of Linton Massey's huge collection at the Alderman Library; an exhibit at the University of Texas's Humanities Research Center. These are all retrospectives, suggesting the end of things, the career being exhibited because the current life is considered complete. Other final things were occurring: the death of Estelle's former husband, Cornell Franklin, who also lived in Albermarle County, Virginia, where Faulkner hoped to settle; and the more significant death, to him, of Harold Ober. Ober had been, along with Commins, a man most devoted to Faulkner's interests, and a perfect foil, in his calm and patience, to Faulkner's somewhat riotous way of doing business. The writer finally bought a Virginia property, on Rugby Road in Charlottesville; not a horse farm but a residence which put him in the center of things—a brief walk from the university campus, and accessible to riding country surrounding the campus.

Two publications suggested his growing stature as a classic. In 1958, Carvel Collins put together, edited, and introduced *New Orleans Sketches*, making available in a republication these early pieces. In 1959 *Faulkner in the University: Class Conferences at the University of Virginia, 1957–1958* appeared, a valuable collection of his remarks, from which we have quoted extensively. From the Virginia exhibition of his manuscripts and typescripts would later come Linton Massey's *Man Working, 1919–1962: A Catalogue of William Faulkner Collections at the University of Virginia*, and Joan St. C. Crane and Anne E. H. Freudenberg's compilation *Man Collecting the*

Works of William Faulkner: An Exhibition in the University of Virginia Library Honoring Linton Reynolds Massey (1900–1974), the first in 1968, the latter 1975.

As 1959 began, Faulkner was competing against his reputation. That use of old material was, in one respect, fitting, since *The Mansion* was a retrospective, a filling in of the past, as though he were seeking a suitable summation. The final two books of the trilogy should be read as having heavy personal freight: not only as a completion of the Snopes saga, but as a touching up of the white spaces still remaining in his own personal canvas of Yoknapatawpha. He was to continue the analogue, like a painter returning to a canvas after many years and, finding a good deal of space remaining, taking out his brush and paint to fill in, until he can "break the pencil."

The novel was in Faulkner's mind in 1959; he could telegraph Estelle on January 23 that the first draft was completed; and just before that he told Klopfer he would need only an additional month or so to clean it up. He was writing and working steadily, but there seemed little more than the desire to get on with it and done. He was, one suspects, losing interest in Jefferson and Yoknapatawpha even as he was exploring it in a final summation; he had exhausted that "little postage stamp" of territory within his imagination.

In the background, Ober and the lawyer, Arnold Weissberger, were trying to work out a film sale of *Requiem* to Twentieth Century-Fox before the play opened in New York. Tony Richardson's production with Ruth Ford and Zachary Scott had received remarkable notices in London; it would also receive excellent notices in its New Haven and Boston productions. The deal was struck, although the movie would combine details from both *Sanctuary* and *Requiem*.*

Requiem for a Nun finally came to a major New York theater when the production opened on January 30 at the Golden. Faulkner turned down the opportunity to attend, preferring bird shooting in Mississippi, saying he had already seen it in German and Greek. Yet even the repetition of the

---

*It was a curious hybrid (see Bruce F. Kawin, *Faulkner and Film*, p. 35ff), not only in the casting of Yves Montand as "Candyman" (an amalgam of Popeye, Red, and Red's brother), but in the way the sequence of events is assimilated from one work to another. The other casting was inspired: Lee Remick as Temple, Bradford Dillman as Gowan Stevens, and Odetta, the gospel- and folksinger, as Nancy. The decision to collapse Popeye, Red, and his brother into one character, the Cajun called Candyman, makes the character somewhat more sympathetic than he would be as Popeye, and there is no Goodwin killing, although Temple is raped. In the *Requiem* part of the film, Temple, after marrying Gowan, has taken Nancy home; but Candyman turns up, and the two plan to run away. To bring Temple back to her senses, Nancy kills the child. The film stresses a mutual redemption: Nancy in her cell awaiting execution, and Temple and Gowan attempting a new start. They have all discovered a "temple" or sanctuary worthy of its name in a kind of mutual morality, black and white, lower class and bourgeoisie. The strength of this aspect of the film version is that it demonstrates Faulkner's purpose quite well. But the film nevertheless loses much of the force of *Sanctuary*, whose elements suffer more than *Requiem*'s. Without the murder, Temple does not have that much to repent; and without Ruby Goodwin (collapsed into Nancy), we do not have Horace's edgy legal support of her husband. Dramatic force gives way to sleeker lines. Further, Popeye is changed radically, with Montand bringing too much masculine command to the role. The film sanitizes a much nastier novel and its sequel.

London-styled play could not bring it sufficiently alive for most New York critics. Although Brooks Atkinson in the *Times* lauded it, most found it leaden. It is hard to dispute their contention that there was little drama in this drama. However much the play had undergone considerable stream-lining and highlighting to distinguish it from its original appearance as a novel-play, it still carried the novelistic weight of narration, rather than dramatization. Weissberger and Ober agreed it was good they had insisted on consummating the film agreement before the New York reviews appeared. After forty-three performances, *Requiem* closed, at the end of February. A long run would have brought Faulkner large royalties, but he was more disappointed for Ford, who had single-mindedly devoted so much of her professional life to the play.

Faulkner found himself occupied on other more directly personal matters. We have already noted his refusal to respond to the sale of *The Wishing Tree* by Mrs. Brown, and his answer to Ober on February 4 indicating his disappointment she would sell something given as a gift. The latter part of that letter contained a bitter reference to Phil Stone and his nonpayment of the $6,000 loan even while he was selling his Faulkneriana to the University of Texas. James B. Meriwether was the intermediary in this business transaction, and he offered to get Faulkner the same amount Stone was receiving, $2,000. Faulkner rejected this offer, but continued to burn with hostility at Stone's underhanded manner. The materials Texas picked up so cheaply were fragments of early Faulkner manuscripts and typescripts, including the poetry which Judith Sensibar later made the basis of her study, *The Origins of Faulkner's Art.* Stone had saved these fragments, and when he decided to sell them, he went about it deceptively —since he obviously did not wish to redeem the note for $6,000 owed to Faulkner. It must be added he had not built up a sufficiently successful legal practice to both support himself and his family and pay off the debt. As Blotner indicates, he sold off a good deal of Stone property—becoming in this and other respects like Mr. Compson. He was sliding, and sinking into mental confusion, perhaps suffering from what we now identify as Alzheimer's disease. Even after granting his former friend and mentor all possible considerations, Faulkner was wildly angry, since at the time that $6,000 had meant a great sacrifice for him and the endangerment of his family's security.

The other matter was also one which would not go away. Even well before *The Mansion* was delivered to Random House, Faulkner's publisher was disturbed by discrepancies in the trilogy, and the writer had had correspondence over this in 1958. Now with the submission of the "Monk" segment of *The Mansion* and the rest being readied for delivery, Albert Erskine confronted the author with some real problems. Erskine, who after Commins's death was responsible for Faulkner's submissions, wrote, on February 6, that "Mink," the opening segment, had arrived safely. Faulkner had included a letter with the manuscript, indicating that one day would suffice to go over the text to make necessary changes. Erskine foresaw far more than one day, and led Faulkner gently into understanding that a considerable chore lay ahead. He asks the writer "how much editor" he wants, or "will put up with," Faulkner's reputation for anger at editorial interference being well known in Random House offices. He assures the writer that no matter what the decision on changes, he has "never been given an assignment that gave . . . [him] more pleasure."[27]

That aside, Erskine says he has reread *The Hamlet* and *The Town*, taking notes in anticipation of the submission of *The Mansion*, and he was alarmed at the discrepancies in the first two volumes even before he read "Mink." Discrepancies included those of matters of fact, event, names of characters, elements which are doubled and redoubled. Erskine is treading warily because he does not know directly how Faulkner feels about such matters, but he does know from James Meriwether, who had it from the writer, that discrepancies in the trilogy and between the trilogy and other Yoknapatawpha novels and stories should be clarified. Meriwether offered his assistance in such clarification, as he had offered his help to Saxe Commins over *The Town*.

As Erskine's letter indicates, matters went further than whether Faulkner had forgotten this or that detail or changed something from one book to another. Erskine was entering into the very difficult area of the author's way of perceiving. For as noted very early in his life, Faulkner was uninterested in detail, more concerned with matters of style, coherence, overall balance and rhythms of writing. Carrying over these early concerns to his later writing, he perceived his works as "inventions" which did not need mooring in matters of fact. As a writer who was growing and developing (his own words), he did not concern himself with whether he had contradicted himself or not. Each book came at a different time, had its own rationale, its own dependence on the circumstances of that particular work. Yet even as Faulkner held to this notion and so informed Erskine, he was worried about obvious slips in books written over a twenty-year period.

Erskine promises to send along separately a "Memorandum on Discrepancies," with a copy going to Meriwether. He assures Faulkner he is not trying to make difficulties, and Faulkner, in his response, is quite humble and agreeable. He does attempt to blur what he can, saying, "If we know the discrepancy, maybe, if to change the present to fit the past injures the present, we will not come right out and state the contravention, we will try to, you might say, de-clutch past it somehow." He will, despite his fuzziness, attempt his own list, while welcoming outside aid. With that, he promises to send on "Linda" before leaving for Charlottesville and the Hunt Club. In early March, chapters 12 through 16 were submitted, with the final two promised shortly by personal submission. Faulkner, however, mailed them to Erskine, and promised to come up to New York for a conference with Meriwether. He was now quite willing to have someone else do the work, apparently, since he did not wish to lose time on the hunt. He felt, as he thought Erskine did, that this volume should be the definitive one, and "others can be edited in subsequent editions to conform. Unless of course the discrepancy is paradoxical and outrageous."[28] On March 14, just two days after this letter, he fell with his horse at the Farmington Hunter Trials and suffered a fractured collarbone. With most men, a fractured collarbone, while extremely painful, in time heals; but with Faulkner, there were the usual complications—his inability to be a good patient, some infection, and the inevitable drinking to relieve both pain and boredom. No trip to New York was possible.

Meanwhile, as Faulkner recuperated, he was being bombarded with deals for his works. He approved Ruth Ford's plan to film *Light in August*, with an advance of $5,000 on a purchase price of $50,000 in four installments. Further, *Old Man* was repeated on *Playhouse 90*, for an additional $7,500. The Jerry Wald *Sound and the Fury* was being premiered in Jackson, Mississippi, but Faulkner refused to have anything to do with it—refused to see it, refused to be interviewed by Edward R. Murrow on *Person to Person* as a publicity device. Wald requested appearances and comments, which would publicize the film; but Faulkner, getting more and more testy, turned down everything. At Virginia, as a sign of respect, he was given a writing area at the Alderman Library and made a nonpaid consultant on contemporary literature, so that he would have some connection to both library and university. It was there that he labored over the final segments of "Flem."

The impression is that Faulkner's main interest had shifted from writing desk to hunting field. He was hooked on fox hunting, as much a part of him now as flying earlier and, before that, the annual deer camp. Fox hunting fed many of his needs, besides its dangers. Being accepted by prestigious clubs meant the early rejections by Oldhams and others in Oxford found more than adequate compensation. Paramount was Faulkner's sense he had entered a new role where his friends accepted him because he could compete on their terms; that once a man mounted and rode off behind the hounds, his other achievements counted for little; and yet behind that was the fact no man was accepted unless he had achieved and achieved well. Also, with the crowd a hard-drinking one, Faulkner's excesses were not anomalous; and even the dressing-up brought with it a kind of acting out.

Before the hunt when he fractured his collarbone, he had injured his eye with a twig. But on March 14, riding his huge mount, Powerhouse, he fell from the horse while making a turning maneuver and broke his clavicle. Yet even this did not prevent him from enjoying his day; for by later afternoon, his shoulder bandaged, his right arm in a sling, he was back riding. He made light of it, telling Dr. Nicoll, who treated him in Charlottesville, that his strength was returning.

He took over his own doctoring, which meant he disregarded the medication prescribed for him and diagnosed his case as he usually did: whiskey would prove his salvation, ridding him of pain and providing the calm which enabled him to weather the disability. But now at sixty-one and a half, Faulkner was not the physical specimen he had been when he could "cure" his ailments with alcohol. His body was deteriorating, although still remarkable for a man who had so abused himself.

Erskine and Meriwether had planned a discussion in Charlottesville, to clarify editorial decisions which could not be accomplished by mail. But Faulkner was heading into heavy difficulty. Having developed an upper respiratory ailment, he tried dousing it, but without success. The collarbone was not healing as well as expected, but there was little cause for alarm there. Other areas, however, were showing trouble signs. A urinary tract infection needed medication, and that, too, was no real sign of future difficulty since sulfa drugs could clear it up. But Faulkner was suffering (although not seriously as yet) a series of what could prove to be life-threatening ailments: an enlarged prostate, an enlarged heart, and an enlarged liver—although liver X-rays revealed no abnormality. The clear diagnosis: nothing that was in itself terminal if he regulated his life. Abstinence was called for, especially as a way of reversing any liver damage; a decent diet to control the various infections, and a regimen of medication. Given the nature of the patient, the doctor sensed that his advice would be ignored.

On April 6, Faulkner left for Oxford, with Estelle and a driver. He could afford luxuries and ease, since he had just received another huge check, $14,000 for the film rights to *Requiem*. But even back in Oxford, and under treatment of a good doctor (F. E. Lindner, a neighbor), he did not recover easily. He was forbidden to ride for two months, but even with that prohibition, he did not heal and suffered a possible pressure of the broken area on a nerve. He had planned to use the time to write another book, but although the pain was proving unbearable, he refused all medication and continued with his own remedy.

Beginning here, we find Faulkner in a series of medical confrontations with himself at a time when his body simply could not recuperate the way it had earlier. His repeated phrase, about "breaking the pencil," comes back ominously, as though he were preparing himself for the end, but in his own way. There is little question that something of a death wish, or flirtation with death, lies just below the surface; for his failure to heed medical advice and his disregard for certain signs of deterioration are indications of a submission to final things. We conjecture that with the winding down of his writing—only *The Reivers* remains—Faulkner had begun to lose the central core of his life. And while riding, drinking, hobnobbing with the horsey set all provided gratification, they could not compensate for what was being lost. An indication of his submission comes in his acceptance of Erskine and Meriwether, stalwart and worthy although both were, to make revisions in work that went back to his best days twenty years ago. A healthy, forward-looking Faulkner would never have agreed. Whatever his name was attached to would have had to incorporate his, not another's, work.

In early May he sent off to Erskine a little of the old spirit, but he was incapable of backing it up with an attention to detail. In a charged paragraph, he says he is a "veteran member of a living literature. In my synonymity 'living' equals 'motion, change, constant alteration,' equals 'evolution,' which in my optimistic synonymity equals 'improvement.' So if what I write in 1958 aint better than what I wrote in 1938, I should have stopped writing twenty years ago; or since 'being alive' equals 'motion,' I should be 20 years in the grave."[29]

Faulkner responded to a desperate-sounding letter from Erskine wondering how the discrepancies could be handled; he was ready to admit they were so widespread that if one changed an early volume, then a later one would provide difficulties, and vice versa. The real solution, which Erskine was afraid to present to Faulkner, was a rewriting of large portions of all three volumes prior to publication of *The Mansion*, which would then become part of a single-volume Snopes trilogy with all problems clarified. The original volumes would then become collectors' items, and there would be that one definitive volume. But Faulkner's letter about being in "motion" put that idea to rest. The remainder of his reply was equally discouraging; he simply did not feel the need to get involved in the dreary rewriting of what he had once written. He admits (in a May 7 letter) that using the same device of misfired guns in killing both Houston and Flem is "too much coincidence." He feels that "the more moving truth"—as apart from fact itself—belongs to Flem's murder. That means *The Hamlet* would have to change, while *The Mansion* remained as is; but since the fact of the murder of Houston has nothing to do with "truth," he wouldn't bother to change *The Hamlet*. He had talked himself into doing nothing.

He also notes how Houston was called Ernest Cotton in a story called "The Hound," a 1931 publication. But since this change of name hasn't "outraged too many academic gumshoes [like Meriwether, presumably]" he doubts if this is a major problematical area. The result of all this was a move toward a disclaimer to appear at the beginning of *The Mansion*, explaining the discrepancies as part of the creative process. In this war, Faulkner won all the main battles. The "warning" appeared:

This book is the final chapter of, and the summation of, a work conceived and begun in 1925 [*Father Abraham*]. Since the author likes to believe, hopes that his entire life's work is a part of a living literature, and since "living" is motion, and "motion" is change and alteration and therefore the only alternative to motion is un-motion, stasis, death, there will be found discrepancies and contradictions in the thirty-four year progress of this particular chronicle; the purpose of this note is simply to notify the reader that the author has found more discrepancies and contradictions than he hopes the reader will—contradictions and discrepancies due to the fact that the author has learned, he believes, more about the human heart and its dilemma than he knew thirty-four years ago; and is sure that, having lived with them that long time, he knows the characters in this chronicle better than he did then.

By this disclaimer, Faulkner has turned his contradictions into assets; seeing change as deepening of vision, and by repeating his idea of motion, suggesting that literature is a living organism. His resolution of the problem was more artistic than practical.

As he endeavored to recover, he was unable to stay still. Rowan Oak was its usual reassuring but boring place, and he needed diversion. By the middle of May, he was, still unhealed, back in the saddle, pursuing his demons. This time Faulkner was saved, providentially, by having his accident take place right near Dr. Lindner's house. His horse shied, and he fell backward on the pavement. The fall created several internal injuries, leading to hemorrhaging, and if the accident had occurred in the woods without quick intervention, he might have died. But with rapid attention to his injuries, by Lindner, he was up and around in a short time. But such injuries no longer vanished after a spell of pain; these lingered, and subsequent X-rays revealed another vertebra break, as bad as the earlier ones which had created such discomfort. Walking, no less riding, became a chore, and Faulkner needed crutches. He also needed painkillers, inasmuch as back and leg pain was severe.[30]

In these accidents, which were not finished, that persistent pattern of dependence and helplessness recurs. The small child seeking his mother's attention, or taking it for granted, was being repeated in the sixty-one-year-old man, whose mother, now eighty-eight, was still alive, but herself unable to help.* Faulkner sought a succession of mothers and helpers elsewhere. He had doctors in Oxford and Charlottesville, editors at Random House, the publisher himself (Cerf), and others who coveted his properties—for interviews, use of his name, purchase of stories, adaptation of works to television and screen, even for purchase of earlier, unpublished work (like the offer from the *Texas Quarterly* of $500 for "With Caution and Dispatch"). He was cocooned—agents, editors, publishers, purchasers, doctors, wife, directors all working to keep him alive; while he dared them all with his effort to be a bad boy.

*Maud's presence in his life was a long shadow, both presence and influence. She, not Murry, represented the "Law," as Lacan calls the authority figure, normally associated with the father. But she also represented an Edenic vision—the ultimate place he could go for comfort and support. No other woman (or man) could fill this need. He drank not to displease her, but perhaps to test her indulgence, the reach of her forgiveness. Jill confirmed this, in her late 1970s statement: "I think that probably Pappy's idea of women—ladies—always revolved a great deal around Granny. She was just a very determined, tiny old lady that Pappy adored. Pappy admired that so much in Granny and he didn't find it in my mother and I don't think he ever found it in anybody. I think that maybe all of these including my mother were just second place" (*William Faulkner: A Life on Paper*, p. 105).

Among the purchasers and seekers after a piece of Faulkner, we find even the august Modern Language Association seeking to use his name as a fellow of MLA—he declined; the aforementioned effort by *Texas Quarterly* to buy the story—rejected for the time being; the request by NBC to have a taped interview with him for $1,000, also rejected, on the assumption he had nothing to say; another request, later, from MGM, to use his name in a film called "The Voice at the Back Door," rejected out of hand as too dreary even to warrant a reply; the pending request from Muna Lee of the State Department for him to speak at a UNESCO function in September. He accepted reluctantly, in a reply that seemed to negate the whole function of the conference, entitled "Cultures of the Americas: Achievements in Education, Science, and the Arts." By this time, he knew that conferences, talks, interchanges were minor affairs; that they made no impression on large events; and that the world was heading toward doom because of decisions made far from conference tables.

In June Faulkner and Estelle were back in Charlottesville, having purchased a Georgian brick house on Rugby Road. They had gone north to attend the christening of Jill's second son. From there Faulkner went on to New York for a week of editorial conferences. With a cane for support, he headed for the Algonquin, to settle matters with Random House over the trilogy. We know his "resolution" came in the passage preceding the novel, explaining how matters change over a thirty-four-year passage of time. But before reaching that point, he decided to contradict his previous conclusion that *The Mansion* should be the final arbiter. Instead, he planned to alter that novel to fit *The Hamlet,* in the killing of Houston, both murders (Houston and Flem Snopes) from misfiring. In other changes, Faulkner was amenable to Erskine's careful editorial proceedings, and even acquiesced to stylistic changes, even involving pronouns.

After signing the contract for filming *Light in August* (the novel was not filmed), with $4,500 as the initial installment, Faulkner returned to Virginia. In Charlottesville, under the title "William Faulkner [Man Working] 1919–1959," Linton Massey, meanwhile, had been assembling his sizable collection of Faulkner materials. To this, the writer added his own, from the Princeton Library; and Random House sent on further items. For Faulkner, it was a pleasant moment, for he could view in one place the enormous amount of work he had accomplished. The title of the collection and exhibition was chosen by Faulkner, who on June 17 was now back in Charlottesville. Although they could not move as yet into the house on Rugby Road, since the closing did not take place until August, Faulkner and Estelle spent long hours with Jill and her two sons, until the June 27 christening. After that, they returned to Oxford.

What he could look forward to was the acquisition of another home in two months, without relinquishing Rowan Oak; the exhibition "Man Working" at the Alderman Library, from October 1 through December 23; and the publication of *The Mansion* on November 13. In addition he saw the publication of the careful transcriptions of his class comments, in *Faulkner in the University*. He was, all in all, being memorialized in every possible way an American writer can, although his hometown and its state university were slow in recognizing his value. Nearly all of the acclaim had come from other areas of America or from abroad, as had the awards and prizes. Mississippi was uneasy, at best, with its most famous son; and there were those who still harked back to Stark Young, not Faulkner, as the more representative and fitting author.*

Because Ober wanted to publish pieces of it before the book appeared, *Faulkner in the University* created some difficulty. Faulkner recalled that Saxe Commins opposed its publication altogether, since it had first been offered to Random House. Commins feared it would eventually be taken as the definitive word of Faulkner on Faulkner, replacing the fiction as his central voice. But Commins had agreed that if the book were published elsewhere, Random House wanted commercial rights, which it took up in the Vintage edition of 1965. Faulkner felt, rightly, that his remarks there would not preempt his novels and stories. Except for specialists, the book has rarely entered into discussions of Faulkner; nor have his more forceful remarks reprinted in *Essays, Speeches, and Public Letters* (except perhaps for the passage about shooting Negroes in the streets if Mississippi were threatened).

Whatever else, Faulkner's desire for money had not mellowed, but increased. He was seeking to scrape every cent he could from his vast literary properties, and he told Ober to go after it. He was now owner of three large properties, including the farm, and he purchased a new car, an inexpensive Rambler station wagon, to replace the seven-year-old Plymouth which Malcolm wrecked, nearly killing himself, Estelle, and Dot Oldham. He felt his earning days were almost over, and he wanted Random House to postpone publication of *The Mansion* so he could collect $2,500 from *Esquire* for the first chapter, called "Mink Snopes" (December 1959). In actuality, the story appeared shortly after the novel, but with distribution taken into account, the two came out at about the same time. Faulkner's words to Ober are ominous, for they speak of final things. "Having, with THE MANSION, finished the last of my planned labors, and, at 62, having to anticipate that moment when I shall have scraped the last miniscule from the bottom of the F. barrel; and having undertaken a home in Virginia where I can break my neck least expensively fox hunting, I am interested in $2500.00 or for that matter, in $25.00."[31]

He speaks of avoiding inheritance taxes—more final things; so that on her twenty-first birthday, Jill was deeded all his Mississippi property. He

---

*Mississippi was not the only hesitant admirer. Critics cast in stone like Arthur Hobson Quinn (the "dean" of Americanists) felt the Nobel Prize had been misguided, the work of foreigners ignorant of America; and Howard Mumford Jones, as well known as Quinn, spoke of Faulkner's besmirching his, Jones's, America. Edmund Wilson himself was uncertain about Faulkner's literary quality, and Faulkner-bashing by other reputable critics and academics ran concurrently with the honors heaped upon him.

also intends to deed the Virginia house to her—which he purchased for $43,750; and to give $14,000, now with a Wall Street broker, to her children. He asks Ober to evaluate all the manuscripts, so he can give those to her as well. Estelle would, of course, be taken care of during her lifetime; but when Estelle died, all would pass to Jill and her children. At almost sixty-two, Faulkner was planning for the end. With these matters in hand, we can perceive that he was using the Virginia experience to obtain final pleasure from a life riven by demons; and his desire to continue horseback riding, while suicidal for someone in his condition, was also a means to the excitement he no longer obtained from writing, or from his personal life.

Another matter arose, however, which he did not find pleasurable, which, in fact, created some heat; a matter deeply involving him and his work. A hunter companion of Faulkner's, John B. Cullen, completed a manuscript which was to be titled *Old Times in the Faulkner Country*, and it told stories of Faulkner in his setting. Although respectful of the writer, Cullen does present a portrait with several warts; the drinking episodes are not neglected, and they are not flattering. Cullen, whose name has so far remained anonymous, received help from Floyd Watkins, who taught American literature at Emory University, and it was Watkins who asked Erskine about publishing it. Erskine then brought the matter to Faulkner, who answered in anger.

Faulkner saw in this the worst possible outcome of what was occurring: that everyone with a piece of gossip was ready to turn it to profit, if the subject were celebrated enough. His private life now meant nothing, and anyone who entered into his setting could, uncontrolled, reproduce a version of it. *Life* and its epigoni had reached into every aspect of American life, a gigantic stain.

At just about the time Faulkner and Estelle moved into their Rugby Road house in Charlottesville, he had to leave for the UNESCO meeting in Denver, called the National Conference of the U. S. National Commission, the seventh such meeting. Filled with considerable apprehension, Faulkner went as a consultant. He foresaw that such conferences were doomed by the very terms they were couched in, this one being on achievements in education, science, and the arts in the Americas (i.e., the Western Hemisphere). To begin with, the topic was far too broad for a four-day meeting (from September 29 through October 2); and, secondly, it was clearly not an open conference, but a propaganda move for the American State Department.

On October 31, he heard that Harold Ober had died. Ober had suffered from a series of heart attacks, but had remained at his post almost until the end, an extremely loyal friend as well as agent. Faulkner told Haas that Ober would be missed by the people who, he hoped, would also miss him. The note of final things is once again unmistakable. Commins, Ober, and then Faulkner: he foresaw it. As he awaited publication of *The Mansion*, on the thirteenth, he saw in the Memphis *Commercial Appeal* a photograph of

"The Flying Faulkners," It included three of the four brothers (Jack was missing) and Johncy's son Jimmy, who had flown in the war. It was, like *The Mansion* coming along shortly, a tribute to the past. In the present, as he told Haas, he had "a tremendous big strong hunter, 16–3 [hands] and [would] need another horse, since on alternate days I must depend on borrowing someone else's."[32]

He was still in touch with Joan Williams Bowen, to whom he had promised the manuscript of *Sound,* now on exhibit at Virginia. But she refused it, accepting instead some pages, which, once thought missing, were rewritten by Faulkner. "The ones enclosed here are inscribed as having been re-written for you, so they may not be what you want to frame on your wall. But here they are. When this show is over, I can send the rest of the mss. to you. Let me hear from you where to send mss. I want to be sure you get the mss."[33] The manuscript remained at the University of Virginia.

The Mansion appeared to the kind of reviews Faulkner had been receiving since *Go Down, Moses.* Sections of the novel were considered praiseworthy—especially the "Mink" segment—but the novel as a whole was deemed uncertain, weak, rambling, lacking creative power. *Time* granted him a "personal poetry," despite sloppiness of writing and construction. True to its savaging of so much of Faulkner's far greater work, the *New Yorker* was consistent, with Anthony West calling the novel "appalling." Several other reviewers tried to soften their view of the individual novel by speaking of Faulkner's career as a whole, although Cowley in the *New York Times Book Review* was favorable. Once the heat of publication was over, critics replaced reviewers, and the trilogy, when evaluated as a whole, was viewed progressively against the body of Faulkner's work. *The Mansion* does lose in isolation. But if seen intertextually, as part of a larger design, a figure in the carpet, it achieves more. Reviewers spoke quite often of Faulkner's mythical county, but when they came to discuss individual works, they lost sight of design and pattern.

Inhabiting *The Mansion,* Faulkner touches on nearly every matter of intimate concern to him. The book is more than the capstone of the trilogy; it provides a psychological and emotional capstone for the author himself. It reeks of the need of the aging writer to reveal himself, even to expose his secrets. It is a deeply personal book; less a projected fiction than a filming of his own life. And perhaps because it is so personal, Faulkner could not control it better artistically, although in several parts it reveals the writer at his strength.

One dimension which made it impressive in parts is Faulkner's ability to work both inside and outside. In the segment "Mink," for example, he gets inside this minimalist creature and, at the same time, views him within his social context. Whatever the weaknesses, they are not of the method, but of the material itself. What comes through in the entire book, unfortunately, is the authorial need to draw it out; not only the retelling and recapping necessary for a trilogy, but the sluggishness of the material itself, and then repetition of what has already been established. It is in these areas that we see Faulkner succumbing to age and loss of control: in his inability to make each paragraph and page a living element, with longueurs replacing movement.

Faulkner needed *The Mansion*, whatever its flaws, for his final word on the Snopeses.* Here more than any other place, he sees they are not to be triumphant; that their particular kind of social anomie harbors a deep sense of self-destruction. The novel is concerned with Flem's long wait for Mink's revenge, what he knows to be inevitable, despite all his strategies to postpone it. The inevitability, Mink's murder of Flem, overlies the entire conception of Faulkner's Snopes material: the man who outsmarted the town of Jefferson as well as the cagey Ratliff and Jason Compson, is finally brought down by his own kinfolk. Only a Snopes could kill the predominant Snopes; and with that, Faulkner could ring down the red-neck epic.

Mink's journey to kill Flem has personal overtones for Faulkner which cannot be ignored: not in the murder itself, but in the passage of time, which takes Mink in his own life through many of the ideological phases we associate with Faulkner's. The changes in America during Mink's thirty-eight years in Parchman represent, for the writer, the passage of time from a "big woods" atmosphere to one of urban values. Mink notes the changes, and they are all part of the author's historical imagination. This illiterate dirt farmer, this subsistent, minimal human being, virtually a field rat, takes on the burden of Faulkner's sense of the past, his sense of time. Mink is Faulkner's bridge between past and present. What began with *Father Abraham* in 1926 is completed in *The Mansion* in 1959; thirty-three, not thirty-eight, years, but memorialized as a passage of time and an accumulation of history.

Juxtaposed with this theme is modern life, involving Linda Snopes and Gavin Stevens. Even though Linda has no Snopes blood, she is part of that

---

*Not only Snopeses (including Ab and Wallstreet Panic) but several kinds of incorporation: two stories, "By the People" and "Hog Pawn," plus a recounting of Mink's murder of Houston and Eula's affair with Hoke McCarron; also, Narcissa Benbow, Lucius Binford, Captain McLendon, even Compsons, with Jason tricked by Flem. This is only a partial listing. As a reiteration, *The Mansion*, as noted above, must be read as part of the trilogy, not alone. While I think Warren Beck overestimates the trilogy (calling it "the very crown of Faulkner's creativity"), he is correct in assessing its parts as an entity. "To see it steadily . . . requires attention not just to its main narrative continuity and over-all design, but also to its intricate continuous counterpointing, those recurrences of detail which are never merely repetitious if considered from the altering angle of new context and with something of Faulkner's own willingness to take a second look for a possible refinement and enlargement of awareness." He continues: "What the trilogy *Snopes* realizes, therefore, is the illumined sustained embodiment of an epically conceived legend, populous, circumstanced, and relevantly projected through all its intricate recapitulations and extensions. The creative vision gathers up its actors' retrospection, immediate experience, intent musings and deeply intuitive apprehensions into the swirling nebula of the work of art, not just a continuum but the present as a presence, multiple-dimensioned, multi-relevant" (*Man in Motion: Faulkner's Trilogy* [Madison: The University of Wisconsin Press, 1963], pp. 5–6).

self-destruction which occurs in the clan; deafened, turned inward, blunted, as it were. This "present" scene involves a modern world which points up impotence, on Gavin Stevens's part, which in turn reflects aspects of Flem's impotence. Gavin's hesitation is a modern illness, part of his Prufrockian inability to commit himself: first with Eula, now with Linda. A man who will marry only when all the danger and edginess have worn off, he withdraws from Linda because he fears the physical commitment.

Even politically and socially, Faulkner caught an earlier sense of the region, when the redneck began to become a political force in the state. While not much more than a swamp rat, Mink has a certain logic on his side when he considers how hard he had worked and still has nothing:

People of his kind never had owned even temporarily the land which they believed they had rented between one New Year's and the next one. It was the land itself which owned them, and not just from a planting to a harvest but in perpetuity; not the owner, the landlord who evacuated them from one worthless rental in November, onto the public roads to seek desperately another similar worthless one two miles or ten miles or two counties or ten counties away before time to seed the next crop in March, but the land, the earth itself passing their doomed indigence and poverty from holding to holding of its thralldom as a family or a clan does a hopelessly bankrupt tenth cousin.[34]

All those like Mink take on a quality in which they must strike back. They are held in thrall as much as the postslavery Negro; and their only recourse —which Mink does not even have—is to scapegoat the Negro. Faulkner understands their political and social desperation, in this capstone volume, while not accepting it; arguing its destructive and self-destructive quality.

It is necessary to read *The Mansion* not only as a finale, but as an emblem of the South during Faulkner's lifetime. The positioning of Mink as part of the hopeless proletariat and then as an avenging force which splits the family apart has a good deal of that "divided house" quality Faulkner perceived in the state and in the region, even in the nation. The state had remade itself, to some extent, in the image of the Snopeses, appealing to the redneck and lower middle class, and its aspirations for power. Faulkner saw Mississippi split open by such divisiveness, and we must read *The Mansion* as a reflection of this.

The novel, further, is generational. It is concerned not only with Gavin Stevens's puppy love for first Eula and then for Linda, but with two generations of Snopes women. Although Linda is not a Snopes by birth, she carries herself in their shadow. And her energies once she returns from Spain are directed toward two areas anathema to Snopes welfare: the attention to Negro education and the desire to see Flem killed by Mink. Her mother had been used by Flem to further his ambitions—she had become his whore, he her pimp, and de Spain her "John"; and the result had been that Flem's fortunes waxed. Linda now, as a kind of avenging Orestes-Electra, will kill not the mother as in the original drama, but the father, whose actions led to the suicide of the mother. Clearly, Faulkner had in mind something quite resonant, with reverberations for the entire South. A divided house has become the scene of a Greek tragedy, overseen not by traditional rulers or princes of the realm, but by those who have moved up in political importance because of their rebellion against the past.

Gavin Stevens is the cementing element here: his impotence in the face of first Eula and then Linda serving the purpose of highlighting the generational struggle. The woman assumes the role of Maenad, the avenger; and that is proper, since it must not be someone of Gavin's generation, but the new one. Much is made of the fact Linda has married a Jew. When Chick Mallison makes a somewhat disparaging remark about Jews usually changing their names, Gavin chides him for not having learned to wash the anti-Semitism of his background from his system while at Harvard. " 'You didn't find that in Cambridge, you might not even recognise it again when you came back to Mississippi.' "[35] Chick says he is sorry and ashamed. But the point of the exchange is not to emphasize Gavin's racial tolerance but to demonstrate Linda's generational daring in freeing herself of provincial constraints: making an exogamous marriage to a Jew, a sculptor (an artist, not a working man), a Greenwich Village free spirit, and a communist, who gets killed in the Spanish civil war. The break is so complete, further finalized when she returns to help Negro educational facilities, that the novel jumps from personal matters to a symbolic representation of generational change.

These generational shifts are linked to temporal shifts: the roving back and forth between past and present in *The Mansion* can be justified not solely as strategies for "catching up" past action, but as ways of perceiving the material. Those changes from a rural to a more urbanized society (cars, roads, housing clusters) are not just matters of time passing, but ideological changes. Faulkner sees, by the end of his life, that such shifts require new thought; that Mink's desire for revenge, while pure and uncluttered, is taking place within a vastly more complicated world, part of that change effected by young women like Linda, who have broken from the mold.

The portrait of Linda, a mixture of energy and misdirected feeling, is sympathetic; and yet unusual in terms of Faulkner's own predilection for compliant, more traditional women. But we recall his advice to Joan, to be more daring, to break away; and we see in Linda, perhaps, what he had hoped for Joan. Certainly, she has reshaped her life to provide the greatest possible danger. She is so "far out" we might suspect Faulkner intended a parody of the liberated woman, but such is not the case.* He is extending the possibilities for a woman, just as he had begun that extension earlier with Eula, although within a more traditional frame of reference.

The Mansion is full of alternative possibilities. The tendency is to view it as a summing-up of Faulkner, when, in fact, it is a revelation of his many contradictory positions. He has a go at virtually everything in his personal and professional life. Gavin's pursuit of Linda is only the beginning. Faulkner discloses sharp feelings about marriage (dismal), political developments in Mississippi (dismal), the making of the modern world (dismal), human endurance and perseverance (unshakable), toleration of unpopular ideas (more open than before), anguish and despair (abiding). He comments, indirectly, on his feelings about Dean Falkner, his brother killed in a plane Faulkner gave him, in Chick's reverie about Bayard Sartoris and his twin, John. He even shows a glimmer of sympathy for someone like Flem, who had to "tear and scrabble" both money and respectability out of hard, enduring rock. As with Mink earlier, he recognizes the possibility of forms of existence anathema to him personally, but valid in terms of individual need. *The Mansion,* not *The Reivers,* is his true farewell.

Now that the book was out of mind, Faulkner was intent on riding his "tremendous mount," Powerhouse, and inevitably suffered several more falls, including one in which the 1200-pound horse had him pinned to the ground. But he suffered no severe injuries, merely bruises and cuts; until, one day, he was thrown badly by another horse, Quilter, and smashed into the rails on his weakest spots: ribs and lower back. But this did not discourage him, and he kept going on Powerhouse, until he acquired another horse, Tiffany, for $1,500. What he liked about Powerhouse was his intractability, his fierce will and determination, which Faulkner gentled along, not wanting to break the horse's spirit. The writer's very insistence on qualities which he praised in people he carried over to his favorite horse, and Powerhouse repaid him loyally by throwing him whenever the opportunity arose. Faulkner was simply not strong enough to control so much horse, and his seat, as several remarked, was not tight enough to give him full thigh control over the animal.

Blotner tells of how Faulkner offered full support when the former was coming up for promotion and tenure at the University of Virginia. The writer said that if Blotner goes, so does Faulkner—and Blotner was told repeatedly he could let that word get around. Blotner did not take that route, and in time received his promotion, but Faulkner remained loyal throughout the episode, an exceptionally trying time for a faculty member. He considered the Virginia assistant professor and Vandevender as his

*Linda, in fact, has a distinct predecessor in her political ideology, going back to Faulkner's work at MGM in 1933, on the unproduced script of "Mythical Latin-American Kingdom Story." In that script, so heavily indebted to Conrad's *Nostromo,* the character Maria Rojas has the same revolutionary, independent, and unsentimental qualities Linda reveals. Maria is more of a political manipulator than Linda, but both show the ability to manage men for their own ends: Maria to get hold of the gold for revolutionary purposes, Linda to bring down her stepfather Flem.

best friends in the area. As holiday season arrived, Faulkner suffered from another respiratory ailment, at first thought to be pleurisy and then diagnosed as pneumonia. This time he took medication and was cured. But the recurrence of upper respiratory problems should have alerted his doctors to more serious troubles, especially with his heart. Although Dr. Falk asked the writer to take a full physical, Faulkner refused as soon as he found his immediate ailment clearing. With parties, hunting, and riding, the year 1959 was closed out.

Chapter Thirty

From Oxford to Eternity

THE YEAR 1960 was one of shuttling back and forth between Oxford and Charlottesville, with little thought of writing. Maud Falkner, now eighty-eight, was ailing, and Faulkner visited her regularly, until her death on October 16. Commins, Ober, then Maud Falkner—the roll call was continuing. Faulkner's great-aunt 'Bama, however, was still going strong, living until 1968, although she had been born only nine years after the Civil War ended.

Early in January (the third) Faulkner left Charlottesville alone for Oxford. His visit was ostensibly to help with his mother's care and to make sure he did not spend more than half the year in Virginia, or else he would become liable for that state's income tax. He was back only a short time, having done some hunting, when he became ill again with an upper respiratory ailment, possibly a recurrence of the pleurisy or pneumonia he'd had in Charlottesville only weeks earlier. While being treated with penicillin, he also began his own course of treatment. What happened he related to Estelle, in which his illness and recovery take on qualities of a saga, the legend of a Faulkner blowout. Starting on Monday morning, Faulkner was ill and initiated both medication and his own cure. By Wednesday, he was left alone until his brother John drove up in an ambulance, and then Faulkner ceased to recall what happened. On Friday, he woke up in Wright's Byhalia sanitarium. Both brothers needed help. After telling Estelle the details, Faulkner closes: "Evidently John has sold another book or something, and is going to be a nuisance and a menace until he has drunk it up."[1]

It was an amusing escapade, but for a man of sixty-two a little drawn-out in its search for fun, unless the man is terribly bored. There was little to do, except visit his ailing mother, who remained as irascible as ever; and engage in some hunting with his nephew Jimmy. He did contribute a brief piece to *La Nouvelle Revue Française*, in its special issue "Homage à Albert Camus." Camus had died in a car crash, and Faulkner was touched not only by his youth (he was forty-seven) but by Camus's devotion to *Requiem*. He tried to make sense of Camus's early end, just as Camus had himself tried to make sense of human life in what he considered to be an absurd universe. Faulkner understood the dilemma of the writer who, seeing all life as contingent, as lacking in overall pattern, is, nevertheless, stalwart about finding meaning in that pattern through individual will and determination. One aspect of Faulkner's great popularity in France, in fact, can be attributed to the French perceiving in the American kindred fears. The French made Faulkner into perhaps more of an existentialist than he was, but in his tribute to Camus the American reveals his own kinship with Camus: that search for answers within a patternless world right up to the moment the car hit the tree. As for the French writer's youth, Faulkner said he was not taken before he could complete his work; he had done it: ". . . it is not *How long*, it is not *How much*; it is simply *What*. When the door shut for him, he had already written on this side of it that which every artist who also carries through life with him that one same foreknowledge and hatred of death, is hoping to do: *I was here*. He was doing that, and perhaps in that bright second he even knew he had succeeded. What more could he want?"[2] When Ober's office asked him about publication, he said he wrote it as a tribute without thought of commercial publication: "a private salute and farewell from one bloke to another doomed in the same anguish."[3]

In another exchange, this time with Paul Pollard, who had formerly worked for the Faulkners in Charlottesville, Faulkner revealed how his racial views had hardened; how what he had to say now was so insulting to Negroes he could not possibly be said to speak in their interest. Now living in Connecticut, Pollard asked Faulkner to subscribe for him a lifetime membership in the NAACP. The request was unusual, but Faulkner's response, while respectful of Pollard and his request, was no; indicating that while he once thought the NAACP was the sole organization to offer Negroes hope, he now felt it was involved in actions doing Pollard's people harm. Such harm was caused by the organization taking stands and actions which would, he said, force moderate people to choose either for or against their own people. What the NAACP was doing was testing out in the American courts case after case, trying to establish black rights already protected by the Constitution.

Then Faulkner moved into the main part of his argument, which was to use Booker T. Washington and George Washington Carver as valid spokesmen for contemporary Negro rights. Citing them, Faulkner agrees that any social justice and equality imposed only by law and police force will "vanish as soon as the police force is removed, unless the individual members of your race have earned the right to it. As I see it, your people must earn by being individually responsible to bear it, the freedom and equality they want and should have."[4] He states that years ago, with his Nobel Prize money, he set aside funds "which I am using, and will continue to use, in education, to teach the people of your race to *earn* the right to equality, and to show the white people that they are and will be responsible to keep it." He then zeroes in on the crux of his later thought, much hardened over what he said earlier, although the theme remains similar: "As I see it, if the people of your race are to have equality and justice, as human beings in our culture, the majority of them have got to be changed completely from the way they now act. Since they are a minority, they must behave better than white people. They must be *more* responsible, more honest, more moral, more industrious, more literate and educated. They, not the law, have got to compel the white people to say, Please come and be equal with us." He fears that if the individual Negro does not do this, through education, responsibility, and morality, there will be more trouble between the races.

Besides the insulting nature of the remarks, there is, in 1960, the inappropriateness of Faulkner's advice. His entire attitude, however well meant, had proven ineffective, since it drew on a fantasy of racial relationships, rather than realities. As noted above, if he had simply taken account of the feelings among his immediate family, he would have observed that no amount of Negro education, responsibility, and morality—to use his triumvirate of qualities—could have won over his brothers, mother, or Estelle. Yet they were educated, enlightened, far more perceptive than most. Where, then, could he expect acceptance to come from? If he followed Mississippi politics on both state and national levels, he could observe that racial politics were the sure way of getting elected, as governor, senator, and representative, not to speak of the local level. Moderates like himself were becoming increasingly marginal, as Citizens' Councils, intimidation, separate white schools or academies were making certain no Negro achieved education, responsibility, or morality. There were few indications, except among a few stalwarts like James Silver and Hodding Carter, that World War II or any other advances in democracy could change the perception people had of the Negro. If Faulkner had wanted to see what happened when a Negro sought "education" by admission to Ole Miss, he should have lived to observe James Meredith, who enrolled with the aid of the United States Army, while white fraternities rioted to keep him out. We assume these young men came from families which were educated, enlightened, responsible; and it was these students who led the fight to keep Meredith out.

For anyone who follows Faulkner's career, to end on this note in an area as important to him as race, is sad. For in his novels and stories, he had presented quite a different picture. Even though his portraits of individual Negroes were not always admirable, his theory of race in *Absalom, Light in August,* and other works indicated a complex, textured sense of Negro potentiality if only white injustice and prejudice were alleviated. But further than that, he had perceived race as a form of damnation, with the white Southerner dooming himself as much as he had doomed the Negro. And going even further than that, he had played with forbidden ideas, one of them being a uni-race, in which black and white separation gave way to black-and-white. Here was indeed a forbidden subject, but it forms a dimension of his racial thought. When we arrive at these late, hardened positions, in which Negroes in a democratic country must "earn" equality, we recognize how powerful the pull of custom and history are; so powerful that Faulkner has become one of the people whom Faulkner, with all his literary and public rhetoric, has been unable to convince.

On a lighter note, he responded to Joan Williams Bowen's manuscript of what became *The Morning and the Evening,* her first novel, published in 1961. Since he had helped her with a short story which became the germ of the novel, he was especially interested, even though she had long been lost to his life. He praises the work, but in the shadows of his praise is a recognition that she did not work through her literary problems sufficiently well to achieve something fully creditable. "It is a good first book but it will be a bad last one. . . . Go on, write another. Not only because this one will not be good enough for your last book, but because the more you write the more you will learn to correct the faults, all minor in my opinion, in this one."[5] He continues: "Next time, if you keep your sights high, you will do it better since the more you write, the more you will learn how to express, milk dry, the love and hatred you have to feel, not for man in his behavior, but for man in his condition." Then he focuses on a real criticism he could make of many young writers, not simply his former protégée: ". . . your people do the right, the inevitable, things, but you yourself dont always seem to know why, or at least to tell me why they did them. That's minor though. . . . it is all right, PROVIDED, you dont become satisfied and stop there." Then in a handwritten postscript (the body of the letter is typed), he adds: "You still wont quite let yourself go. What are you trying to save? for what? Every time you give all, there is always plenty more." The postscript sounds less like literary criticism than a harking back to the relationship.

As Oxford headed toward spring, Maud Falkner was sinking. Like so many elderly people, she had fallen, though without severe damage except on one occasion; but now there was general deterioration. After finding supervision for her—and with Dot Oldham caretaking Rowan Oak—Estelle and Faulkner headed, once more, for Charlottesville, early in May, eager not to miss the excitement of show time. Faulkner read "The Old People" to the English Club, and the Charlottesville *Daily Progress* (May 26) reported some off-the-cuff remarks on race. He was now speaking in sadness at how all his ideas had failed, and he remarked how sickening it was that some Southern libraries closed rather than integrate. This was, for him, a terrible blow—preventing the Negro his access to books which are held in a public trust and supported by public funds. Faulkner identifies himself as someone feeling the old inherited prejudices, but also as someone who recognizes that when those "old inherited prejudices" drive a man to do certain things, then he thinks "the whole black race is laughing at him."

Propositions continued to flow in. *Life* offered him $5,000 for an article for its Civil War centennial series, at the rate of $1.00 per word. But he responded: "Even when I was young and 'hot,' I was never much of a 'to order' writer, so I had better not undertake this one."[6] By June he was back in Oxford, where he visited his mother nearly every day, either at her home or at the hospital. Blotner relates a story Faulkner told him about his mother, apocryphal or not. He says he created a fairy tale for her. " 'I would tell her about Heaven, and what it was going to be like, how nice it was going to be and how she would like it.' She said, 'Will I have to see your father there?' 'No,' I said, 'not if you don't want to.' 'That's good,' she said, 'I never did like him.' "[7]

In the meanwhile, Faulkner was offered a Balch Lectureship in American literature, at Virginia, on a one-year basis, renewable, for which he would receive $250. His duties were minimal, one public reading and a few classroom appearances. He responded by saying he would do it for free. On August 22, Muna Lee, of the State Department, came back to Faulkner for another tour, this time to Venezuela. To this, he also agreed, offering October as best time, so he wouldn't miss fox hunting season, or after February 15, 1961.*

One senses boredom in Faulkner's perfunctory replies to letters, one about credit and payment for "The Graduation Dress," which he had started with Joan Williams many years before, another about deferring payment on film rights to *Light in August,* because Ruth Ford could not arrange a production. He had reached the stage in life when little seemed

---

*In the background, the ever-busy Phil Stone was correcting what he thought were errors, this time in James B. Meriwether's "The Literary Career of William Faulkner: Catalogue of an Exhibition in the Princeton University Library," which had just appeared in the *Princeton University Library Chronicle* (Spring 1960). Stone is less keenly on the attack, possibly because the third dedication to him, of *The Mansion,* had relieved some of the resentment in him, at least temporarily. Correcting Meriwether on Murry Falkner's university position in 1919, Stone was himself incorrect. Murry was Assistant Secretary then, not Business Manager. On the river boundaries of Lafayette County, he is correct. But his most interesting comment comes on *The Sound and the Fury.* Faulkner told Stone he didn't know why he kept on writing, that he probably did it to keep from having to work. Stone encouraged his friend, although, he says, he didn't believe it at the time. "So I told him to go ahead and write what he damned pleased, just like he damn pleased, and see whether they took it or not, that even if he could not make money out of it he would probably get some literary recognition which might help" (to James B. Meriwether, July 7, 1960; *Faulkner: A Comprehensive Guide to the Brodsky Collection, the Letters,* eds. Louis Daniel Brodsky and Robert W. Hamblin, vol. 2 [Jackson: University Press of Mississippi, 1984], p. 278). He says he had an experience which "no other human being has ever had or ever will have" when Faulkner read aloud to him from *Sound.* Stone further says that Faulkner's *Green Bough* poems were written under the influence of Housman, whose work Stone introduced him to, especially to the use of single-syllable words.

to hold out pleasure, except perhaps that moment of danger as he eased a powerful mount over the rails and dared it to throw or fall on him. He has, we sense, recognized that the achievement of all his goals led to this, a sixty-three-year-old man who felt himself coming down toward the end with a worldwide reputation, all the honors and prizes literature begets, and yet without any current of warmth in his life—except, perhaps, from Blotner. His mother was dying, he and Estelle had made a truce of sorts, Jill was established in her own life, Victoria was away, and Malcolm was sinking. He had the love and respect of Dean, his niece, and her mother, Louise Meadow, but he was, by nature of his own temperament, a man who demonstrated little feeling; who sank himself into alcohol whenever he felt people or events coming too close. What made Faulkner so fascinating as a person to much of the world was the very quality which isolated him from others and from himself: that inner demon which only he heard and which disallowed warmth.

Most major American writers die alone—not only because they have carved out their own space, but because their need to assert themselves in America has cut them off from what might be personally authentic. *They become part of the film, not the reality.* Faulkner was not in the position of Hemingway, who had lost contact with whatever he was because he had confused person and persona. Hemingway was doomed, as Faulkner recognized when his contemporary and competitor killed himself in 1961. Faulkner's aloneness was not like that, but it did involve his having so embedded himself in an individual talent, without reinforcement from without or from intellectual contacts, that when the talent began to wane, he found himself cut off from himself. It is the problem of the American writer: the enormous talent quarried out relatively young, leaving the writer out of touch and unable to find sustenance elsewhere. If we need any American paradigm for Faulkner, it would be Melville, a more extreme case; but among his contemporaries, we can also cite Fitzgerald, Hemingway, Dos Passos.

On October 16, with the death of Maud, Faulkner lost not warmth, but support. At eighty-eight, she died of a cerebral hemorrhage, after she had advised the family not to keep her alive on support systems. After six days of sitting by her bedside, the family saw her slip deeper into a coma and die. Yet if Faulkner grieved, he did so without too much display. Within a week, he and Estelle were preparing to return to Charlottesville. Once there, he was hit by a familiar problem: with Random House's plans to publish *The Town* in paperback, the question of discrepancies was reopened. If Faulkner went along with the disclaimer printed at the front of *The Mansion*, then he could let the contradictions stand; but since he had made changes already in *The Town*, then those changes and the disclaimer were working at cross-purposes. Erskine felt they had to deal with that, and left it up to the writer to decide which course to follow. Faulkner told his editor he would get to the corrections "between fox hunting, and then in Miss. [where he intended to return before Christmas]," clearly more concerned with fox hunting than with writing. "Fox hunting is fine here, country is beautiful. I have been awarded a pink coat, a splendor worthy of being photographed in."[8] Writing to Jimmy Faulkner, he requests that his boots be sent, and specifies which ones he wants, and that they are to be taken to Howard Duvall for sending. He promises a photograph, and as done it is resplendent, Faulkner the tramp-poet now transformed into an elegant country gentleman, to the manor born.

The Stone letter to James Meriwether, cited above, suggests some toning down of hostility, but in a somewhat later letter to a student at Tulane, Kraig Klosson, he is acerbic and dismissive. Yet even he felt he may have gone too far, because he wrote to Klosson's professor, Richard P. Adams, to mediate his own remarks. To Adams, he indicated he thinks Faulkner "is grand" and has "many beautiful talents in writing and he is still the best of the present crop in the United States."[9] But then he says the present crop "is not so good and second, I get peeved because with all the ability Bill has he could have been a greater writer if he had really bothered to try." But to the student, Stone lets go, moving from peevish (at the funeral of Maud Falkner) to outright hostile in his assessments. "I don't think he will stay in Virginia because, frankly, I think he stayed there so long that the Virginians found out he didn't know as much as they thought he knew. . . . There is a good deal of symbolism in what Bill has written, but a lot of it they think is there is not there at all. This is another thing that is due to their tendency to overrate Bill as a novelist. Subconsciously he may have picked up something. The vital thing for you to remember, as my wife has said, is that Bill is an empirical writer. He has no theory and, like all authors, he is a jackdaw picking up things here and there."[10] Stone adds that he is not criticizing, that it is "perfectly legitimate." That Stone wrote like this to a student suggests that, despite his calmer remarks elsewhere, he was working up a storm; taking out on Faulkner what had proven so disappointing in his own life.

Also in the background and beyond Faulkner's immediate reach was the continuing saga of Ruth Ford and Zachary Scott in their pursuit of the writer's properties. As a loyal and devoted follower of Faulkner's work, not to speak of a once-close friendship, Ford seems to have become a rather sad case. She appears trapped by her acquaintanceship with the writer, unable to get beyond him even when the work is intractable for her and her husband. She now indicates to Ivan Von Auw, Jr., of the Ober Agency,[11] that there is no chance to make an art film at present. She mentions that Scott wanted to play either Christmas or Hightower, and she "Lizzie," by whom she may have meant either Lena Grove or Joanna Hightower. Her unsuitability for Lena is so evident one cannot see a film cast this way. One of the problems with this devoted following of Faulkner was the general unsuitability of roles for Ford and Scott, even given their talent to transform themselves on stage or screen. Faulkner simply had a different style, and it is perhaps fortunate Ford and Scott did not make *Light in August.*

Faulkner returned to Charlottesville to pick up his duties as Balch lecturer. For the rest, he drifted—seeing his grandchildren, riding, watching others ride, even while telling Erskine he would get to the contradictions in the trilogy. Although the editor wanted quick action, Faulkner did not reply until August 1961. What did interest him was the Keswick Hunt, mounted on Powerhouse. His health had returned, and while he ached from his various bone ailments, he felt at home as a country squire. What was also at stake was his refusal to go out with a whimper. Now in his sixty-fourth year, he needed the riding as a sign of manhood. This was not simply a new role for him, not an extension of farmer; but a throwback to his desire to be a war hero, an aviator, now a horseman on a powerful mount. Even the naming of his horse, Powerhouse, is relevant. All of these gave him the image of command, ultimately of manliness. We cannot underestimate how important this image had been for him, from the start: small in a family of large men, the eldest and looked up to, a writer in a society where writing was deemed womanly, a man without a regular stake in the economy or job market. Given these coordinates for his youth and manhood, Faulkner adopted attitudes which disproved or disguised what he was. As hunter and farmer, he became one of the boys; as flier, he was on the boundaries of the new; as alleged wounded pilot, he had fought for his country. Now as horseman, he was completing the cycle of masculine activities. Add to this the manly drinking, and we have a "created self" which existed alongside the other self which went into his writing. In his sixties, Faulkner was quite consistent with the younger man.

As 1960 ended, he changed his will with a codicil, bequeathing to the William Faulkner Foundation his manuscripts "and other tangible property at the Alderman Library." The creation of the foundation was aimed at avoiding death taxes, but it also had another purpose. One such area was the establishment of funds for the education of outstanding Mississippi Negroes. Faulkner was following through on all his statements of the past decade, that the Negro must be educated to take his place in America; and no matter how patronizing or condescending the attitude was, it did benefit several individual Negroes. What Faulkner neglected to foresee, however, was that as soon as an individual Negro was well educated, he left the state; since, contrary to what the writer thought, rural white Mississippi was not prepared to accept an educated Negro in the professions.*

Faulkner held Christmas of 1960 at Rowan Oak, and as the year changed, he posed in his full hunting regalia for Cofield, the photographer on the square. The photographer caught Faulkner in poses which recalled those of George Washington, straight-backed, coiled whip in hand, a man for all

---

*When this writer lived in Mississippi in 1986, Negroes who had been educated at state colleges were still leaving the state: lawyers, doctors, engineers felt they had little future in Mississippi, even though federal mandates had changed many attitudes in schooling and housing patterns.

seasons. For Faulkner, this was a moment of considerable pleasure; dressing-up afforded him that role-playing so important throughout his career. As the writing waned, the dressing-up played a significant vicarious role: he was now, as he posed with aristocratic disdain, a character of his own invention, having shaped and reshaped himself. The town drifter and drunk, as others saw him, had taken on an impeccable persona and pedigree. It was all there, in the series of photographs Cofield shot, the writer as *arriviste*.

The year 1961 brought Faulkner back to writing, as he worked steadily on his final novel, *The Reivers*, for publication on June 4, 1962. But the rest of the year continued the kind of wandering which characterized his previous decade. Early in the year he accepted an invitation, from Superintendent General Westmoreland, to visit West Point and read to the young officers in training. The year passed languidly, with offers of large sums of money for his properties. He saw his tribute to Camus published in the *Transatlantic Review*. The *New York Times* announced the formation of the William Faulkner Foundation and the fact that it would encourage Latin American writers and support Negro education in Mississippi. By very early August, he had completed the first third of *The Reivers*, in which he used the pseudonym Ernest V. Trueblood. Within three weeks, he completed the novel, dating the typescript August 21. He spent the summer in Oxford, and returned to Charlottesville in October, then went on to New York in late November. There, he worked with Erskine over the discrepancies (still) in the Snopes trilogy, and made some changes in *The Reivers* typescript.

The aging writer indulged his eccentricities. If he was eating and anyone turned on a jukebox, he got up and left immediately. He still culled his correspondence for return postage and saved the stamps—gaining considerable satisfaction from the fact that, rich though he was, he was using other people's postage for his own use. He was, somehow, beating the government. He rarely read his correspondence, examining incoming envelopes for checks or stamps, then discarding them. He alternated, as Blotner tells us, between dressing up in hunting pink or in a sweaty, ragged jacket or sweater: the clothes, in one, his reshaped persona; in the other, his trade as a writer. He made extraordinary pronouncements on race, saying that the Negro had outendured the Indian and would survive the white, who one day will be "a small minority group among equally educated black and yellow people." He predicted the Chinese, then, will be the bosses. He continued to live in Mississippi, but increasingly as an intruder in the dust, not as a native son. Blotner writes of how David Yalden-Thomson, a professor at the university and now an excellent friend of Faulkner, told him that "he always thought of Faulkner as himself . . . a Highlander living in exile in Mississippi. This attitude gave him, I think, an objectivity and a detachment about Mississippi, about the United States, which was one of the hallmarks of his conversation."[12]

The remark seems sound, but does neglect how Faulkner needed what at bottom he also had to renounce. That posing in hunter pink did take him back to his Scottish forebears (McAlpine, Cameron, Murray, and Falconer), but that, too, had to be rejected. To achieve himself as a writer, Faulkner carved out for himself a middle space: part Oxonian and Mississippian, part not; part native son, part exile. That fluctuation from one to the other afforded him a center of gravity. He paid a price for his achievement, which was that he was not at home anywhere; even though he made his home in Oxford, Charlottesville, and, to some extent, in the Hotel Algonquin and the Random House offices.

By mid-February, he wrote Auw at the Ober Agency that he was committed to the Venezuela visit. He had been judged by Venezuelans as their unanimous choice, far more than Hemingway, who was physically and mentally incapable of making the trip anyway. Hemingway would kill himself within a few months. But at the same time he had to look ahead to the trip, which he hesitated to make, he received an offer from Raoul Levy, the French director, to coauthor a screenplay for $50,000. Since the sum of money was considerable, Faulkner was tempted, but warned Auw: "I may not have enough power left to cope with someone else's story at all: it's been two years now since I've done anything much but ride and hunt foxes."[13] He agrees to read the story, saying he would like to return to France and hoped to live long enough to need $50,000. But his words indicate he knew nothing could come of this. He simply did not have the energy or inclination to undertake the job, although the offer may have triggered in his mind the idea of writing another book.

Money, nevertheless, nagged at him. Jill and her husband were planning to move outside Charlottesville, on Owensville Road, to a thirty-acre piece of land, with a house and an outlying cottage. The property needed renovation, but its attraction was the cottage, where Faulkner and Estelle could stay—separated from Jill's house, but with access to horses and riding trails. All this required large sums of money, including the building of stables, renovation of the main house, redoing of the cottage. It was to remain a dream of sorts. The upcoming trip to Venezuela, scheduled for April, however, was no dream; it was taking on qualities of a nightmare. Faulkner told Muna Lee he wished he did not have to fly. "As I get older, I get more and more frightened of aeroplanes. But I reckon I have to fly, not?"[14] No surer sign of rapid aging than that admission. He was also worried about where he would live, saying that while Victoria and William Fielden lived in Caracas, "they stay up too late at night for me. I'd prefer a hotel. In fact, I insist, not with them. I have enough kinfolk at home."

Succeeding letters indicate Faulkner's hesitancy about making the trip. It was as though he'd had a premonition of disaster, and while seeking ways to avoid it was forcing himself to go through with it. He told Muna Lee he did not consider this a pleasure trip but a job during which he hoped to serve the ends of the North American Association. But "I am still afraid I am the wrong bloke for this. Even while I was still writing, I was merely a writer and never at all a literary man; since I ran dry three years ago, I am not even interested in writing anymore: only in reading for pleasure in the old books [Dickens, for example] I discovered when I was eighteen years old." He says he wants to avoid autographs for Anglo-Americans, since that is something he gets paid for; but he will sign "any and all from Venezuelans and other Latin-Americans who ask."[15]

Plans to return to Charlottesville were postponed because of Estelle's illness, an old kidney ailment going back to her drinking days. Faulkner told William Fielden about their change of plans, but most of his letter is full of hesitation and withdrawal. "I have never had any confidence in this visit. As I read it, it is a group of North Americans who found they could make more net money living in Venezuela than anywhere else, who wish to keep on making more net money there even to the desperate length of paying the expenses for a two-week visit of a man like me who is neither interested in visiting Venezuela nor in money either."[16] He declined it, he said, until the Bureau of Inter-American Affairs of the State Department began to get after him to make the trip. He considers it "two deadhead weeks with my North American kinfolks and their circle." Faulkner's hostility is both particularized, aimed at tax dodgers and exiles, and general, part of a jejune view of things. With Estelle too ill to travel, Faulkner went alone.

The trip turned out to be a pleasant surprise, perhaps because he lived through its worst features in advance. What made the venture so problematical was that the very intellectuals, leaders, and other officials who would be welcoming Faulkner were vociferously anti-American. Like most South American intellectuals, Venezuelan writers could not understand America's support of repressive regimes, and also recalled the long years of American colonialism through the United Fruit Company and similar enterprises. Further, South American intellectuals were beginning their romance with the third-world, in which they winked at third-world repression and authoritarianism while condemning American failures of policy and practice. There was, just beyond Faulkner, a kind of fantasy world inhabited by some of Venezuela's finest writers, like Rómulo Gallegos and Juan Bosch, who condemned America while embracing repressive and dictatorial regimes. Whereas they judged America as an amoral capitalist predator, they perceived the Soviet Union as a supporter of third-world aspirations.

Further, as a white Mississippian, Faulkner could expect a good many barbed questions on racial issues, especially since Venezuela was a mixed-color society. What intensified all this as a fantasy situation was that while intellectuals rightly condemned American racial policies, they closed their eyes to extreme racism in third-world countries, or in the Soviet Union itself. Faulkner would have to deal with the double standard, part of which had developed because America, which had once been an ideal, failed those who expected so much. Yet Faulkner represented to these intellectuals and writers an America of tremendous interest, not on race but on matters pertaining to literary technique, devotion to craft, creation of a mythical kingdom. Faulkner's influence on succeeding generations of Latin-American writers—Gabriel García Márquez, Carlos Fuentes, Mario Vargas Llosa, José Donoso, and others—had already begun; but his visit helped solidify an enduring popularity and admiration.

The racial issue was, of course, a mine field. Faulkner, however, refused to become ruffled, and offered up his own assessment: that Negroes, confronting terrible handicaps, had advanced significantly even under these circumstances. He made a virtue of their handicap, saying that despite severe disadvantages and opposition they had progressed far in America —turning it into a tribute for his country. By refusing to retreat before hostile questions, by contrasting American Negroes with blacks elsewhere, for example, Faulkner made his point stick: that while conditions were still momentously difficult for Negroes, they were on the march. This is not, of course, precisely what he had said in other recent public statements, in which he had been more hesitant and cautious. But he did win over a tough, demanding audience.

Venezuela was enjoying a period of democracy under Rómulo Betancourt, who was expansive in his handling of Faulkner. The trip began to descend into a huge cocktail party given by the North American Association, and Faulkner felt himself sinking under the weight of trivial attention. But he carried on, with calls back to Mississippi to check on Estelle —she needed a kidney removed and was now hospitalized in Jackson, at the University of Mississippi Medical Center. Faulkner continued to win people over, with his efforts to say a few phrases in Spanish and his modest manner with reporters, intellectuals, and even Americans, whom he had dreaded meeting. At the Ministry of Education, he was awarded the Order of Andrés Bello, a civilian honor which carried with it a broad sash. Reading from a prepared text, Faulkner offered up some usual fare, that man achieves immortality only through art—a remarkable consistency in that this was what he had said forty years ago in his talks with Sherwood Anderson. Faulkner read his speech in Spanish translation, and what it lacked in finesse it made up for with sincerity. He spoke of "truth," which he equated to immortality: the Keatsian message coming through even in his strange accent, Mississippi softness overlaid with a Spanish he could not enunciate clearly.

As Venezuelans took him to heart, honors poured in. Official luncheons were followed by a Sunday evening concert in his honor by the Venezuelan Symphony Orchestra. At the Museo de Bellas Artes, he made a brief speech; and at many of these functions, he entered spiritedly into a question-and-answer period. He saw Victoria and William Fielden, and even visited the latter's factory outside Caracas. He made other visits to Valencia and Maracaibo, answered student questions, was met with enthusiasm. After a return trip to Caracas for a farewell cocktail party given by the American embassy, he flew out on April 16, exactly two weeks after having arrived. The feedback to Muna Lee at the State Department was all good, in fact enthusiastic, and Faulkner was lauded as a patriot. His own response, in a letter to his interpreter, Hugh Jencks, written in Spanish, shows the writer deeply touched by his reception, especially since he has learned that the trip "was not a fiasco, but a little success."

Faulkner's foundation set up a competition among participating Latin-American countries to help select a worthy novel which had been published but not translated into English. The selection of this novel, by three judges, would be honored with the William Faulkner Foundation Plaque, and their influence used to have it translated and published in the United States. Meanwhile, in America, John Knowles's *A Separate Peace* had received the Faulkner award for the year's best first novel, an award which continues to the present time and has seen many distinguished novels so honored. What had occurred, clearly, was that Faulkner had transformed his early career as an innovator and avant-garde modernist into an international reputation in which he was completely accepted by those otherwise alien to his sensibility. He had influenced writers much earlier, especially in France, but his popularity now in other areas, particularly Latin-America and Japan, indicated how his experimental type of fiction was considered the measure of the novel. As Faulkner's production shifted and began to decline in intensity and effectiveness—as his language became less electric—his pre-1940 reputation resurged. What had occurred with him was what had happened with Hemingway, except that Faulkner had a much larger body of work to demonstrate. Yet both had done their best work early, Hemingway barely out of his apprenticeship, and then watched as their reputations stretched to fit the world. The difference was that Faulkner had produced not only a larger body of major work, but had brought American fiction into alignment with efforts overseas. Instituted by his late 1920s and 1930s novels, American modernism became the major fiction of the postwar era; even though reviewers and centrist critics continued to praise novelists who were imitational and derivative. While conditions and other influences (including Kafka and Joyce) were also instrumental in this remaking of contemporary American fiction, Faulkner played a huge role here. And as invitations came in from other countries requesting his presence, not as speaker or lecturer, but just as William Faulkner, he was recognized as having become the outstanding figure in American literature.

As he assumed his role as Balch Lecturer in American Literature late in May, he was also concerned with another aspect of "final things," the tombstone for his mother. Writing not to his brothers but to Jimmy Faulkner, Johncy's son, Faulkner suggests using "Maud Butler, wife of M. C. Falkner," only there is the question of which M. C., since there are three. It was preferable to say: "Maud Butler 1871–1960 Wife of M. C. Falkner with his dates added, then there can be no misunderstanding."[17] But he adds he will agree to whatever the majority want. He relates his routine, and while speaking of horses makes no mention of work on *The*

Reivers. He says he gets up at daylight and rides until about 10 A.M., that he is looking at other horses because he needs at least three, for jumping and hunting. He announces he is now a member of the Longreen Hunt of Germantown, Tennessee.

During this period, a Mississippian, Elliott Chaze, interrupted Faulkner's rounds on Rugby Road, and insinuated himself into the household to gain an interview. It was everything the writer detested, and one reason he had left Oxford. Chaze even interrupted Faulkner while typing; but the latter gave him an interview of sorts, full of hostility and animosity. Chaze's tastes, as Blotner reports them, are odd: "Two Soldiers" and "Mule in the Yard," hardly works one would praise on a visit to Faulkner. The interview-article ended up in *Life* (July 14, 1961), a publication that accepted anything on Faulkner it could get hold of. Chaze's observations are bizarre, calling the writer "a tiny man," as if five feet five inches qualified him as a dwarf, and calling attention to his "hooded eyes," as though Faulkner were a predatory animal or bird. Chaze really got nothing, not even a look at Faulkner's typewriter; but *Life* apparently did not care if it published a non-interview.

Faulkner was aging and declining. But Hemingway killed himself, the news coming to Charlottesville on July 2. Faulkner was quite upset, and in his response there is little question he saw reference to himself. He told Blotner[18] he considered it unmanly—suggesting, perhaps, that he had weighed it for himself. He added such an end indicates a man has chosen death over living with his current wife—suggesting, even more strongly, the possibility he had contemplated suicide as a way out of a bond with Estelle which went deeper than life or death. He knew that Hemingway was ill, but also felt that beneath the Hemingway persona there was another being who was neither tough nor virile. As soon as he heard of the death, he suspected it was suicide, and felt Hemingway had constructed a fierce male exterior to shield him from whatever he was. It was a wall or shield Faulkner could understand well. Illness/manliness/wife-shielding oneself: all of these came to his mind, all linked to himself. Also, at close to sixty-four, the death of a figure like Hemingway at close to sixty-two, when the two of them had been bracketed for years, was deeply disturbing.

Faulkner idled away some of the summer, spending time with his two grandchildren, in attendance at the birth of his third (on May 30), but also working. Sometime in June, he put together three chapters of "The Horse Stealers: A Reminiscence," which became *The Reivers: A Reminiscence.* By August 2, he told Albert Erskine he had about one-third; and on the twenty-eighth, he announced completion of the first draft. He expected a clean copy by the end of September, and suggested a blurb for the jacket: "An extremely important message. . . . eminently qualified to become / the Western World's bible of free will and private enterprise," signed Ernest V. Trueblood, / Literary & Dramatic Critic, / Oxford, (Miss.) Eagle." Ernest Trueblood, an old pseudonym, had turned up in "Afternoon of a Cow," in 1937, the story then brought back for an encore in *The Hamlet,* with Ike Snopes's love for Jack Houston's cow. The story appeared in *Furioso* (Summer 1947) under Trueblood's name. Intermixed with this fun-making was Faulkner's desire to help Erskine, finally, do something definitive about the discrepancies in the trilogy. He says he recollects having done all this, including typing of corrected passages, rewrites, etc., and sending them back to Random House; but in actuality he had post-poned the job. He tells his editor it was too hot: "It's 64 years I have said I'll never spend another summer in Miss."[19]

"The Horse Stealers" in reality goes back to another idea Faulkner presented to Haas in a letter of May 3, 1940. He was trying to justify a $5,000 advance from the firm and promised a Huck Finn–type of novel. "A normal boy of about twelve or thirteen, a big, warmhearted, courageous, honest, utterly reliable white man with the mentality of a child, an old Negro family servant, opinionated, querulous, selfish, fairly unscrupulous, and in his second childhood, and a prostitute not very young anymore and with a great deal of character and generosity and common sense, and a stolen race horse which none of them actually intended to steal." As we read Faulkner's 1940 plan, we see how this material, with the prostitute part deleted, fits *Intruder in the Dust* as well, especially when he says: "During that time the boy grows up, becomes a man, and a good man, most because of the influence of the whore. He goes through in miniature all the experiences of youth which mold a man's character. . . . through them he learned courage and honor and generosity and pride and pity."[20]

But even further than its similarities to other novels, stories, and plans, "The Horse Stealers" indicates how intertwined Faulkner's Yoknapataw-pha County pieces had become with his own family; for with the narrator (a grandfather), Faulkner was telling his family story by way of the Priest family. In the early parts, we meet the narrator who has worked for his father, Maury, in a livery stable, has three younger brothers, a Negro helper called Mammy Callie, someone resembling the servant Ned Bar-nett; and intermixed with them are the characters from Faulkner's mythi-cal kingdom, Boon Hogganbeck, a McCaslin, and others. As the novel continues, it plays in and out of incidents and stories about his own family as easily as it scoops up previous Faulkner work. It reinforces the sense we had earlier, that the material for his fiction was an undifferentiated mass in his imagination, which he could draw on, mingling fact and fancy as the case may be. With *The Reivers*, we sense that consciously he has reached the end of his material, but there is no telling how much more remained buried, ore from an endless lode.

Obviously, his new novel should be concerned with horses, since his life was taken up by riding and even a trip to Oklahoma to purchase two horses. He told Albert Erskine, on August 28, that he had finished the first draft, about how "an eleven-year-old McCaslin and a Negro (McCaslin) groom stole an automobile and swapped it for a race horse."[21] Deeper in the background of Faulkner's life, however, the matter was not horses, but manuscripts. By 1961 Faulkner material had suddenly become valuable, and several collectors were vying for whatever was in private hands. The episode over *The Wishing Tree* continued, but another item was available, James Silver's manuscript of Faulkner's speech before the 1955 meeting of the Southern Historical Association. Since he was strapped for tuition money for his two children, Silver was willing to sell it to John Cook Wyllie, and he accompanied the manuscript with an explanatory letter. But first he asked Wyllie, who was buying for Virginia's Alderman Library, not to tell Faulkner or Jill about the sale since Silver had avoided cashing in on their friendship and he felt ashamed of what he was doing.

The matter of *The Wishing Tree* was not over, despite the displeasure Faulkner had shown about Mrs. Brown's desire to sell her copy for publication. She had always thought she had the original, but in actuality Victoria, Faulkner's stepdaughter, had that, dated on the front flyleaf February 5, 1927. Silver has incorrect information about Mrs. Brown owning the original. But the point is not who has the more valuable piece, but the industry which had grown up while Faulkner was still alive, the dealing in his manuscripts and first editions as though he were a dead classic. Furthermore, this cross-reference of buying and selling, hardly restricted to Silver, joins another cottage industry: the writing of books, articles, dissertations, all as if Faulkner were safely interred.

In writing to Linton Massey, Silver comments[22] on the just published *Old Times in the Faulkner Country,* the Cullen and Watkins collaboration. Silver speaks of how Watkins, who lived in the history professor's house one summer while interviewing people, believed a lot of what people said, when Silver knew they were unreliable. Stone, for one, is cited for knowing a good deal, but "he is unreliable." John Faulkner, "as big an unconscious liar as he may be," was another source of misinformation. Silver believes all information, misleading and otherwise, should be gathered before people die, and then perhaps it can be sifted for the truth, an early form of oral history. Some of this was being done, but not systematically, as dissertation students were getting in touch with Phil Stone for his biased and unreliable recollections.

Massey removed any of Silver's equivocations about Faulkner's greatness and the need to gather information. Silver had said that as a historian he did not know Faulkner's worth as a writer. Massey was unequivocal:

> He has written many memorable books that will live in our literature; at least four of them will endure as long as our culture survives, and maybe longer. That he is an enigmatic figure in Oxford I am well aware, but in the long run this estimate of him will become, I am convinced, a puzzle to later generations. He is in some ways a writer's writer. He is often obscure. He is more frequently, profound. Anything about that will explain his work without intruding upon him as an individual I am determined to fasten upon. . . . Unselfish and devoted friends such as you can help pursue a similar course; and the more you can do to dispel the myths, the falsehoods, the distortions,

and the misrepresentations surrounding William Faulkner the better. Every creative artist makes more enemies than friends.[23]

On the Stone front, Richard P. Adams,[24] who was exploring in detail Faulkner's early career, presented the lawyer with a sequence of searching questions. His primary purpose was to see what influence T. S. Eliot had on Faulkner, and how the writer's acquaintanceship with Eliot's work came about. Stone says Faulkner had access to *Poetry* and *The Little Review* through him, although all these early copies burned when Stone's house caught fire in 1942. Adams was moving toward establishing that Eliot's influence on the younger Faulkner was "the most important." Yet we know several other elements were involved: chiefly, Swinburne, then the French symbolists, Keats, and Housman, to some extent Aiken.[25] Adams was searching Faulkner's career for clues—he, in fact, refers to himself in legal terms, as a cross-examiner. He was also interested in the effect of *The Golden Bough* on Faulkner, to which Stone responded that the writer read a few paragraphs here and there, but not the entire book, and surely not related studies by Jessie Weston, Cornford, Jane Harrison, or Lord Raglan. As for Bergson, Stone recalled that Faulkner read a good deal of *Creative Evolution*. Adams had spotted as early as *Soldiers' Pay* some ideas on time and concreteness which derived from Bergson. In all of his responses, Stone emphasized, mockingly, that Faulkner read very selectively.

The background revealed this continuing battle over what Faulkner said or what Faulkner read; the foreground, the writer completing his novel and telling Erskine on September 19 that he can send along the finished manuscript in a few days. He has switched the title from "The Horse Stealers" to "The Reavers," whose spelling he prefers as *The Reivers*, the Scottish form. The novel was slated for 1962 publication, along with a Modern Library volume of *Selected Short Stories of William Faulkner*. Once the book was sent off, Faulkner assured Erskine he had found *The Hamlet* and the editor's notes, that he planned a trip North to work on the contradictions. But he was also facing back-tax problems, to the tune of $30,000, and he needed to know what royalties had accrued, since he was afraid he would have to pay interest on underestimated taxes. His letter to Erskine about this matter indicates how, now that anxiety over having enough money has passed, he has let financial matters slide.

By October 22, he was back in Charlottesville, living with Estelle in a rented house at 2027 Minor Road, while their cottage on Jill's property was being readied. The Rugby Road house, now up for sale, had been broken into while they were away, but what was taken was negligible. Faulkner made light of it when he wrote Erskine, telling him he could be in New York on November 6 for an editorial conference. He also indicated changes of names in *The Reivers*: Bullock to Buffaloe, Mink to Son Thomas, Butch Lovelass to Butch Lovemaiden, Cerebus (a horse) to Acheron. He liked the play of pronunciation Acheron would cause: the whites saying Acheron, the Negroes saying Akron, and Ned saying Akrum. Some of the other changes were made to avoid names of Oxonians who might not take kindly to his mockery. Almost by return mail, he learned from Cerf that *The Reivers* had been made a Book-of-the-Month Club selection.

Yet even as everything he touched now turned to gold, Faulkner knew this was his final novel—he had broken the pencil and thrown it away. At sixty-four, he was not old, and literary history is filled with writers who did fine work at this age or older, but they were not Americans. By sixty-four, most of Faulkner's contemporaries were dead, or else, like Dos Passos, trivializing their careers. A Mann or a Gide working well into their seventies was not the American mode. Faulkner felt rightly that he had earned relaxation, although in his earlier days, writing *was* his life and he needed no respite. What is difficult to measure, and we have stressed this throughout, is the degree to which the intake of alcohol had broken down his resolve. *The Reivers* demonstrated he could still write effectively in spurts, but missing was that degree of daring which is a dimension of imagination. Yet he did not give up entirely, or else he wrote the following simply for Bennett Cerf's consumption: "I am not working on anything at all now, busy with horses, fox hunting. I wont work until I get hot on something; too many writing blokes think they have got to show something on book stalls. I will wait until the stuff is ready, until I can follow instead of trying to drive it."[26]

By the end of October, Estelle and Faulkner had left their rented property and were installed at the Knole Farm cottage. Estelle was ill on and off, catching colds, influenza, bronchitis; and Faulkner arranged much of his life without her—his horses, his planned trip to New York, his hunting companions. The marriage was now firm because they had worked through hostilities not by resolving differences, but by mutually agreeing to walk away from them. His interest in young women appeared to have passed from the active stage; and Estelle was now hanging on to her own frail health, having remained sober for several years and controlled her drug intake. As Faulkner moved into his late fifties and early sixties, his looks waxed, whereas hers waned, as she became rail thin, almost anorexic.* She looked like a wasted female from one of her husband's stories, although in actuality she had proven stalwart, tough, a survivor of two difficult marriages.

Instead of November 6 as the date for the New York trip, Faulkner arrived fully three weeks later, checking into the Algonquin, the scene of so many of his personal combats. There was work to do on *The Reivers* as well as the Snopes trilogy. But before he left, there were the continuing problems with Malcolm, who would never be right. Estelle told James Silvers that Malcolm was fearful of change, of doctors, hospital, treatment: ". . . in fact Mac hasn't been the same since they moved the medical school—That disrupted his tight little world. God! I do worry so—not

---

*Thinness had once been her allure, as Phil Stone's wife, Emily, observed: "Well, the boys were just crazy about Estelle. She just looked like skin and bones, a walking skeleton, but she had whatever it takes" (*William Faulkner: A Life on Paper*, p. 44).

knowing what to do—except to treat him as a child, and simply take care of him . . ."²⁷ We do know that Faulkner did take an interest in Malcolm's condition, but at this point whatever wounds his stepson had suffered psychologically or emotionally could not be cured. He had let go, and was now, as Estelle indicated, helpless.

The Reivers had become a valuable property. Besides the sale to the Book-of-the-Month Club, it was excerpted in the *Saturday Evening Post* ("Hell Creek Crossing") and in *Esquire* ("Education of Lucius Priest"). Faulkner made further changes of names and other matters. Lucius gained a year, to eleven; van Grafe became van Tosch; Valden Priest, Lucius's mother, became Allison Priest. The main arena, however, was the Snopes trilogy, not *The Reivers*. Faulkner spent a generally relaxing time in New York, catered to by Random House, which had supported him when he was poor and relatively unknown, but was now delighted to have a celebrated author who made them a good deal of money. He was, however, walking through his life as though he were an invented character: playing the role of the famous author, retaining his famous eccentricities, using his silences and withdrawals as need be, walling himself in, then giving as he felt the need to do so. He had cleared sufficient space around him so that he could be whatever he chose; and if he expanded with some friends (like Ben and Anne Gilbert),* he withdrew from others, especially in crowded circles. There is something unreal about this Faulkner, something puppet-like; perhaps because he was no longer defining himself by work.

His life had become routinized—even the binges were predictable, especially after he suffered a severe fall in early December back in Charlottesville. By then, Estelle was back in the hospital, her ulcer having acted up. But as soon as she seemed to recover, Faulkner went down—how much of this was a kind of one-upmanship, using illness or injury as a form of attack, we cannot tell. But his fall led to heavy drinking, since he was bored, and then complications set in, with another respiratory ailment—one in a series which should have alerted doctors to growing difficulty. Even Jill was not immune to this cycle of illness, having contracted hepatitis. Although they were all living somewhat apart, there is a replay of pathology in this drama of sickness, as if only a family epidemic could carry them through their new closeness. Faulkner was discharged sooner than he should have been, the familiar procedure, and he suffered a relapse, with his medication for the upper respiratory ailment meeting his large alcoholic intake, and all that compounded by his back pain. Although it was not diagnosed as such, Faulkner was entering a final stage of decline. He recovered from this bout, but with each successive attack, he was sinking lower. The local doctors insisted he be taken to the Tucker Neurological and Psychiatric Hospital in Richmond. What they had on their hands was a man almost as suicidal as Hemingway: not ready to blow his head off, but prepared to bring himself to the edge of death.

*Dr. Benjamin Gilbert, who attended Faulkner on several occasions.

His constitution had been exemplary, low blood pressure, a liver which resisted the ravages of alcohol, a gut of iron, and even a back which took such a heavy pounding from falls. What was remarkable, however, was the failure to note anything wrong with his heart or lungs when he had repeated respiratory attacks; and, in fact, the medical report from Dr. Shield at the Richmond Hospital was of normal heart and lung action. There was, in effect, nothing wrong with this man who was visibly declining. Treatment was mild: nourishment, of course, since Faulkner stopped eating when he drank heavily; sedation, rest. The back came around with heat packs. In all, home remedies—chicken soup and a heating pad.

But Faulkner was not finished with the job of self-demolition he had begun several years before. He had decided to live by horses and now, it seemed, die by them. Having missed Christmas with his family (by design?), he could not bear the hospital, and by December 29 was back at Knole Farm. By the beginning of the new year he was out riding, with his back still tender and not right from the previous fall. Fenceman stepped into a hole, and Faulkner was thrown to the ground. This time he developed a whole series of ailments which signaled that something was seriously wrong. He needed sedation for the back pain (Demerol), but then the upper respiratory ailment returned, badly. He had bruises and a painful hemorrhaging in one eye—from the impact with the ground. The bruise on his forehead suggested a concussion, and he suffered some amnesia. By now, January 8, he could not be treated at home and was back at Tucker Hospital in Richmond.

The various conditions were, once again, treated in much the same way: nourishment, rest, no alcohol, liquids. But this time he did not respond, and he reported chest pains accompanied by a rise in temperature. His lungs were examined, with pneumonia or pleurisy suspected; and his heart indicated some speeding up in one area. Yet it was not considered abnormal, and an electrocardiogram showed no problems; in fact, a good rhythm. What came out of extensive examinations at Richard Hospital by Dr. Paul Camp was that once the respiratory ailment was cleared up by antibiotics, Faulkner was not really a sick man. We find he had the finest medical treatment—Dr. Camp had been a student of Paul Dudley White, Eisenhower's heart specialist, and heart specialist to the nation—and had been declared fit, once his immediate problems passed. Yet there was little question he was sinking with each fall. It had taken the last fall to set off this set of circumstances, but the ailments were there, somehow beyond the reach of medical diagnosis and medication. Once he began to regain strength and was renourished, Faulkner could leave the hospital on January 15, considered remarkably well for a man of sixty-four. Yet he was seven months from death.

The year 1962, truncated by Faulkner's death on July 6, in Byhalia, Mississippi, was one of continued honors. His brief stay at West Point was a high point, with a volume called *Faulkner at West Point* to follow, in 1964. He was invited by John F. Kennedy to attend a White House dinner, but refused with a statement which would become famous. He gave two more interviews, including one to a professor from the University of Belgrade. On May 24, he received the Gold Medal for fiction from the American Academy of Arts and Letters, and delivered a brief address. On June 4, *The Reivers* was published, dedicated to Victoria (his stepdaughter's daughter), Mark (Malcolm's son), and Jill's three sons, Paul, his namesake William, and Burke.

The year had started poorly enough, with the fall and hospitalization; but it proved to be seven months of considerable activity and traveling. He also was gratified to see that Joan Williams's first novel, written and then rewritten with Faulkner's support, was awarded the John P. Marquand First Novel Award, with a prize of $10,000. The award was bestowed by the Book-of-the-Month Club, and that in turn heavily infiltrated by Random House personnel. Such matters brought her one-time mentor pleasure, as did the continuing viability of *Requiem*, now being prepared for a Polish production in Camus's version. In a letter to Auw, Faulkner gave his permission for it to go ahead, indicating his indebtedness to Camus for his adaptation. Other properties were moving as well, including the Modern Library edition of *Sanctuary*, for which Faulkner omitted the controversial preface written for the first edition. When Ford gave up on *Light in August* for a filming, Elliot Kastner took up the option. Auw asked Faulkner if her advance money ($5,000) should be returned to her, although there was no legal basis for that. Faulkner immediately agreed to the return, as soon as a sale was made. She also told Auw that Ober, before his death, had arranged for her to have rights of first refusal for *As I Lay Dying*, *Absalom*, and "The Bear," although her only "proof" was a telephone conversation. Auw questioned the validity of this, but Faulkner responded that "if Miss Ford says he [Ober] did do so, I suggest we take her word on it."[28] Faulkner's only stipulation was that if any other offer was received, she respond yes or no within twenty-four hours.

In a curious attempt at interviewing, an English schoolboy at the Cate School in California approached Faulkner, in Oxford. The writer agreed on March 23, and the interview later appeared in the *Cate Review*, June 1962. Simon Claxton's introductory remarks give some indication of how townspeople viewed Faulkner, as "something between awe and fear. One man in a filling station pointed up the road and wished me luck in a threatening chuckle, as if he never expected to see me come out alive."[29] The famous Faulkner silences and withdrawals had left their mark. He walked within a space of his own making, and people left him alone. It was with some trepidation, "amused audacity," that the young man walked up the road to Rowan Oak: ". . . just as I was about to move forward, I noticed an old man in a wicker chair, about 25 yards down the verandah in the shade. It was Faulkner." After a few tense moments, the English boy found

Faulkner more receptive, although the writer said he had not received his letter presenting himself and his request for an interview. "I was overwhelmed by this reception, for I had half been expecting a fire-breathing ogre." Even though he had no idea who was intruding into his life, Faulkner turned gentle and pleasant. Claxton's sense of the physical Faulkner is interesting, if we take into account this is a very young person, completely awed by his subject. He notes Faulkner's shortness, but especially his "tiny feet." But he observes a person of enormous inner strength. "His face has a set, serious expression, which many would call hard and cruel. He rarely smiles." Claxton emphasized the dignity and strength the writer radiates: "You can feel it in the air." Claxton says Faulkner does not talk much, is very passive, and although his clothes were good, they were scruffy and dirty. He finds the hooded eyes mesmerizing, inescapable, alternately friendly and cruel. "A withered old face . . . glittering hooded eyes."

Faulkner gave Claxton mainly single-word answers, to questions which were generally off the mark or lacking in interest. The latter asks about his forthcoming story in the *Saturday Evening Post,* but even that draws little interest. The boy then tries another tack and indicates that Faulkner's novels are disliked by many Southerners because he draws such a depressing picture of the region. Faulkner answers that it doesn't worry him, he doesn't read reviews. He says he "couldn't care what other people say about him, that it wouldn't affect him."[30] He reiterates that he writes to tell a story: "Thus I stack and lie at times, all for the purposes of the story —to entertain." Of course, such an explanation fails to deal with *Sound* and *Absalom,* which are hardly "entertaining." Faulkner at his best did not "tell a story," but *prevented* the story from being told, quite a different process.

He then goes into his Nobel Prize stance, as though it were a ready response awaiting the right question. He says he introduces comic and tragic elements to "illustrate Man in his dilemma—facing his environment." He denies he seeks "truth." Rather, he "wants to create a story, with his imagination and facts helping of course."[31] When Claxton asks the writer about final things, like the future of mankind, Faulkner gives his set Nobel answer that man will "outlive all other things, even the wheel and the A-bomb, just as he has outlived the dinosaur." He even denies Oxford is the Jefferson prototype, although he admits all these local towns add to Jefferson. Asked about what advice he would give to a young writer, Faulkner becomes talkative. His first counsel is to read a lot—everything, fiction, biography, history, law. He says he read all the law and medical books of his father and grandfather. He indicates that all this reading will give the writer a feel for man, who "becomes the victim of the writer's will." His next piece of advice is not to worry about the reception given one's books. He stresses, however, that a novel must give pleasure, that it must be enjoyed. His repetition of this point seems more to justify *The Reivers* than the larger body of his major work.

The interview over, Faulkner walked the boy toward the gate, asking about England and how he was enjoying America. Claxton indicates that the writer lingered, as though now that he had become engaged, he hated to have a pleasant moment pass. He had genuinely liked Claxton: his manner, style, accent, country of origin. Also, we must not forget, Faulkner has mellowed.

In the final interview of his life, with Vida Marković, chairperson of the English department at Belgrade University, on May 6, in Charlottesville, Faulkner went directly to talk about animals and farms. He spoke of the intelligence of horses, dogs, and rats; of his farm, growing cotton and wheat, although he told Claxton he no longer participated in it actively. He says he does not like cars and buses, and wishes he could ride horseback everywhere, even to the movies. Marković wonders if he is not interested in what is happening in towns and cities, in what has changed in life and people. Faulkner gives his standard answer, that people do not change even under industrialization; youth does not alter its ways. He adds that when he was young, he liked a restless life, but now he prefers the quiet of Rowan Oak. We hear the words of an Odysseus who has returned home, weary; not ready, like Dante's and Tennyson's old warrior, to venture out again on new exploits. This Odysseus has returned to stay, finding the outside world, which he has experienced, somehow forbidding. Faulkner speaks of everyone rushing into towns, while the land decays—his vision of America now frozen into the conflicted agony he conveyed in his "big woods" stories. The interview generates its own momentum, but Faulkner seems weary—congenial out of good manners, but without anything within to draw upon. Only three months from his death, but apparently still in good health, he has wound down in his own mind, refusing to answer questions about where his subjects come from or who his models are. Part of his weariness may be he hears the echo of these questions ringing down the chambers of past interviews and also hears the boring repetitive echo of his own answers; and now he simply wants to get past another standard interview without hurting the interrogator.

Faulkner was asked to West Point, for April 19–20, under the invitation of General William C. Westmoreland, superintendent before his appointment to lead American forces in Vietnam. The air force sent a plane for the Faulkners, who were the immediate guests of Major Joseph L. Fant. Fant and Robert Ashley would put together a book, *Faulkner at West Point*, based on the visit. The treatment of the writer was that afforded a visiting dignitary or head of state: private plane, presidential suite at the local Hotel Thayer, consideration for his every need. Estelle, writing later to James Silver, described the trip to the Point: "They sent an air-force plane up from Georgia with a crew of Jews to cart Bill, Jill, Paul, and me to West Point last week."[32] In the same letter, she refers to President Kennedy's invitation to Faulkner, to be part of a dinner celebration at the White House, made up of Nobel Prize winners and other celebrities. Faulkner made his now famous response that "he wouldn't go to Washington just to eat." Estelle says she would like to go.

Faulkner's remark has become so famous* that his perception of the dinner party may be lost. All along, he knew that artistic accomplishment and politics do not mix. Kennedy was "using" the Nobel Prize dinner party as a means of aggrandizing not them, not their accomplishments, but his own administration. Where little or none existed, he was endeavoring to give a patina of culture. While witty and charming, the president had only low-level cultural tastes, and the dinner lacked cultural resonance; it was all political, good newspaper copy. Faulkner refused to become party to such a "bread and circus" circumstance.

West Point, however, was somewhat different, for here he was center stage, and the main event was not military or political, but his reading of a segment of *The Reivers*, the amusing passage about the horse race. The moment was enlivened by the photographs of Henri Cartier-Bresson. The stay was celebratory, and the reading itself went well, bringing forth a standing ovation. The next day in the class meetings Faulkner spoke of his admiration for aspects of the military, its sense of valor and courage, but attacked war and especially those old generals who decide the fate of young men without jeopardizing themselves. At mess, he was given "thunderous applause." Having apparently become weary of the whole thing and uninterested in a sight-seeing tour of the Point, Faulkner was now ready to leave.

His next "duty" was to head for New York, give a brief speech, and accept the Gold Medal for Fiction from Eudora Welty on behalf of the American Academy of Arts and Letters, the same kind of celebration in which he had presented it to Dos Passos. This was precisely the kind of circumstance which made him nervous and jumpy, almost unable to function. Perhaps he felt that "terror" which his old friend Bezzerides ascribed to him when events or people came too close. He asked Blotner to draft his speech for him, and his future biographer received as reward Faulkner's revised copy, plus the original draft. In the interim, before the actual presentation on May 24, Faulkner and his immediate family attended the Virginia Gold Cup running, for which he and Estelle were listed as patrons. Then the Gold Medal day arrived, more like a doomsday for him, despite the prestige of the event.

He checked into the Algonquin, his favorite New York shelter. At the institute, Cowley tried to make things easier for him, and also Aiken, whose poetry Faulkner recalled well from earlier times. At the luncheon, Muriel Cowley sat on one side, Kenneth Burke on the other, but Faulkner sank back into silence, that "terror" of social involvement upon him. Only

---

*His actual words, when *Newsweek* called to see why he had turned down the illustrious dinner, were: "Tell them, 'At my age, I'm too old to go that far to eat with strangers.' " He altered that to "I'm too old at my age to travel that far to eat with strangers" (Joseph Blotner, *Faulkner: A Biography*, vol. 2 [New York: Random House, 1974], p. 1821). Many magazines and newspapers picked up the quotation, and it entered history: the old eagle of a writer and the young, wily president, both edging toward their deaths.

during small talk of family and Virginia countryside did he open up, saying he was looking forward to a granddaughter. Cowley describes him as "glowing with health," bronzed face under white hair. Then came the proceedings.

Eudora Welty made a plain but eloquent statement, full of her own pleasure in bestowing the medal on a fellow Mississippian. Faulkner spoke, using the outline and even lines of Blotner's draft. In his final public statement, he compared his medal to those bestowed at country fairs in Europe or St. Louis, suggesting that his "product" was of the same order as those products. He sees these ribbons given for "a piece of tatting or an apple pie" as more than the record of a victory; rather, as part of that premise there are no degrees of what is best; that one may be best in any number of areas. From this, he draws his point:

> We should keep that quantity, more than ever now, when roads get shorter and easier between aim and gain and goals become less demanding and more easily attained, and there is less and less space between elbows and more and more pressure on the individual to relinquish into one faceless serration like a mouthful of teeth, simply in order to find room to breathe.[33]

He added: "Let the past abolish the past when—and if—it can substitute something better; not us to abolish the past simply because it was."

After the talk, according to Cowley, Faulkner retreated into silence, drawing around him that self-made wall behind which he could protect himself from faces and voices.* Recalling how trying the Gold Medal Award for Dos Passos had been when Faulkner made the presentation, Cowley had arranged as brief a program as possible. Even with foreshortened activities, Faulkner barely got through, beginning in retirement and ending in that abstraction of himself which had become his signature. Afterward, Donald Klopfer picked Faulkner up for dinner, and on the following day he had lunch with Jean Stein, now married to the politician, William van den Heuvel. By the next day, he was back in Charlottesville. Now only weeks before his death, he was thinking of buying Red Acres, a farm property he had set his heart on. He asked Linton Massey for $50,000 on demand against "any part of the mss. you want."[34] If his offer for Red Acres is accepted, he will be broke, and he says he will have to write a book or books. Further, he says he can earn about $10,000 or more any year from lectures. "I will do this, write books or lecture, to own Red Acres, but I dont want to have to guarantee to." Klopfer did not think it was a good idea, but Massey agreed to the guarantee of the sum, which meant Faulkner did not have to auction off his future with books or lectures. To support the writer's pastoral dream, Massey was proving as true a friend as the Random House people.

*Even the presence of Joan Williams did not help.

What remains remarkable as his life was nearing its end was how full of plans Faulkner was, and how good his health, except for aches and pains, appeared to be. He and Estelle maintained a social schedule in Charlottesville, and there were those plans for the purchase of another property. Yet there was some sense of an ending, for when he left Charlottesville with Estelle at the end of May to return to Oxford, he said goodbye as if for the final time. He returned to reviews of *The Reivers*, if he paid them any attention. They too were a kind of farewell, full of the misunderstanding that had often characterized the reception of his work. But this time, it was different: the important critics lambasted the book or deemed it lukewarm; whereas the knuckleheads (Orville Prescott of the *New York Times* and Fadiman of the *Book-of-the-Month Club News*, having moved on from the *New Yorker*) praised it highly. Prescott read it as a moral book, Fadiman as a book concerned with "virtue." But the reviewers who had read him more sympathetically in his major phases deemed it everything from a minor work done successfully to a calamity (Fiedler). Those who liked it compared it to Twain, which it is not at all like; and those who disliked it contrasted it with his more important work, which some of them hadn't liked much anyway. Whether in America or in Europe, it is difficult to find a major writer, except perhaps Dreiser, who consistently received such poor or warped reviews as Faulkner did, and who was eventually redeemed by those who took the longer view. From 1929 on, those who chose to review him almost willfully misunderstood his work, damning the major fiction, praising the minor, or waffling about where they stood. If reviewing is haphazard and on occasion dishonest, Faulkner drew the worst possible combinations; and it was just as well he ignored what they were saying about him.

Whatever the reviewers claimed for the book, with *The Reivers: A Reminiscence*, Faulkner wrote a slightly off-centered *Saturday Evening Post* cover story, or a Hallmark greeting card message. Although there is still some bite, he is folksy, the old codger; not Prospero with his magic wand, as he may have wished, but an updated Joel Chandler Harris and his Uncle Remus. The novel picks up a good deal of earlier Faulkner, but at a far lower level of density and intensity. And it carves up America into only two discordant elements, whereas, before, his America had been made up not of two but of innumerable sectors crossing and crisscrossing each other. He still hopes to recover Eden; only now he simplifies the possibility.

Faulkner sets the narrative in 1905, when Lucius Priest is eleven, when he was himself eight; an Edenic time, just before he started school (Maud held the boys out until they were eight). It was, also, in retrospect, a simpler time for America, just before the automobile definitively began to replace the horse, when livery stables held priority over garages. Not only was it a boy's Eden, it seemed so for the country: the huge conflict of 1914 still distant and unshaped, the Civil War well behind, the romance of the victorious Spanish-American War still wafting in from the turn of the century. It was like the Garden itself, held in suspension, magical, even sacred. Lucius Priest, a priest, sets forth into his initiation. He is not Huck Finn with an evil father whom he must evade, but a boy trembling before an adventure. Lucius's father, Maury, like Murry, runs a livery stable— and Faulkner is off and running, like the horse which will dominate the inner text.

By chapter 2, Boon Hogganbeck is resurrected as a mythical figure, a man of great strength, with a background that goes back into a true American Eden, the world of Chickasaws. "He was tough, faithful, brave and completely unreliable," with the bulk of a tank and "the mentality of a child."[35] He is observed in retrospect by "grandfather," and the entire narrative takes place as a reminiscence of the older man about the young boy, Lucius, who is experiencing the events even as he is speaking about them from the distance of time. It is a familiar temporal collapsing; older man and young boy of eleven, after and before the Fall. It is Faulkner roving in and out of his life and work: dedicating the novel to his grand-children, peering down from the throne of time, speaking of himself and his three brothers and their father, and his livery stable. It was a trip of sorts, alternately funny and sentimental; full of general pokes at women,* not the least in the affirmation of the reformed whore, Corrie, full of nostalgia for a time when a certain kind of innocence obtained, loaded with dislike for whatever we have become.

Amidst all the funny doings, we should not neglect to see that while this novel affirms something of the human spirit, it negates the modern age, disdains contemporary life, has nothing positive to say about the way we are now. Faulkner has, in effect, turned his back, as if some Nietzschean avenging spirit. Even as he immersed himself in the Virginia horsey set (itself politically conservative, antidesegregationist, supportive of Citizens' Councils and rigidly enforced separate but unequal schools) which was hell-bent on making money, obtaining the good things, piling up posses-sions, establishing class and caste lines, Faulkner extrapolated the horses, woods, and chase from their enterprises and ignored the rest.** We find him in a series of contradictions—not in the novel itself, but in the man writing a novel of this kind.

The novel's generally good press suggests that Faulkner had tapped a nerve in those who wanted to get away from 1961–62, in the way that many people looked to John F. Kennedy as someone who would lead them back into Eden, neglecting the fact he had achieved the presidency on the tainted money of the elder Kennedy. Faulkner had to ignore the contami-

---

*"In those days females didn't run in and out of gentlemen's rooms in hotels as, I am told, they do now, even wearing, I am told, what the advertisements call the shorts or scanties capable of giving women the freedom they need in their fight for freedom . . ." (*The Reivers* [New York: Random House, 1962], p. 196).

**He was not, however, fooled by their politics, if we consider this: ". . . a Republican is a man who made his money; a Liberal is a man who inherited his; a Democrat is a barefooted Liberal in a cross-country race; a Conservative is a Republican who has learned to read and write" (*The Reivers* [New York: Random House, 1962], p. 109).

nation and dispossession of his Eden. For his idyll, he stepped back to 1905, but even here some of the Garden variety is compromised by the presence of an automobile; but the auto can be retrieved only through the heroics of a horse—so Faulkner met his compromise with a triumph. Other "triumphs" also work to cancel the tilt toward mechanization. A good woman appears in Corrie (the Everbe Corinthia of "The Leg," Faulkner's early story), her life transformed from warmhearted whore in Miss Reba's establishment in Memphis to a woman who insists on her rights and dignity. But the main "transformation" occurs in the nondescript Lucius, the eleven-year-old, turning into a knowledgeable preteen; an initiation not through the loss of innocence, as many have read his adventure, but as a deeper investigation of what true innocence is. One of the mainstays of the novel is not "loss of," but exploration. Lucius deepens his knowledge of what it is to be eleven—this not only through Faulkner's transforming humor but through his own understanding of race and sex as they interplay in acts of transmutation.

One means by which Faulkner achieved this transformation is through his familiar means of the journey. What the journey achieves is that exposure of the individual, here the boy, to a life beyond the home; where the dictates of "the Law," whether mother or father, are replaced by the problems of the situation and one's response to it. This is, in a humorous turn, a replay of *As I Lay Dying*. Even the episode at Hell Creek bottom has within it something of the need to "get through" which the earlier novel evinced, with water once more providing the obstacle. Water as transformation for Faulkner remained constant: one came through water, or went under; a Conradian pattern he adapted from early on. But other kinds of transformation take place. As suggested above, Lucius must adapt to a woman (Corrie) quite different from any he has been in contact with before; and with a Negro, Ned, who represents a shrewdness and worldliness he has never before experienced. These, too, are aspects of the journey, if we see it as encompassing that movement out into new experiences, that intensification of knowledge, though without loss of innocence. Faulkner, of course, mutes evil in this world. It is easily defeatable because it has few ramifications beyond power plays, not even the high-toned Mr. Binford or the low-toned deputy-sheriff, Butch. Opposition is clearly defined and, as befitting a humorous work, exists to be surmounted easily.

The pieces are there to fall into place—none of the early tragedy, not even the disasters of *As I Lay Dying*, surely none of *Old Man* or *The Wild Palms*, other journey novels. *The Reivers* has something of the quality of *Intruder in the Dust*—which leads one to observe that Faulkner linked Negroes and children: Ned as a version of Lucas, Lucius as Charles Mallison. With *Huckleberry Finn* as analogue, the juxtaposition of Negro and young boy removed Faulkner from the tragic world of race into the world of innocence, even when, as in *Intruder*, the context is grim. Lucius must preserve his innocence, and the Negro, Ned here, despite his shrewdness, operates also within that innocent world. This is of some biographical interest, since it brings Faulkner full circle: well past the troublesome 1950s, when racial issues became so problematic, to a time when they were simple and clear, when the Negro could be associated with "the child" or the boy.

The nostalgia here has a cutting edge, and it does not represent Faulkner at his finest. For it implies his desire to return not only to a pastoral idyll, but to a racial idyll when house servants and field workers were stratified in the community. It was, for Faulkner, the by now critical question of order versus disorder; and the 1905 scene, despite the rushing to and fro, was ordered. The alternative was the disorder of the present. Faulkner's farewell statement, if we view it as that, was to carry us outside contemporary events, and their intense urgency, into a mythical-magical world where black and white harmonized because each knew his/her place. Lucius's exploration of himself is as much a quest for order, or reorder. Once he sees that a new kind of order lies beyond the disorder of his four-day quest, then he glimpses adolescence and boyhood. He must, paradoxically, absorb and assimilate experience without losing innocence. Once that is effected, he has moved beyond the whipping he expects from both father and grandfather into the nature of his own mystery.*

The Negro characters, whom many critics, including Brooks, have praised, are stereotypical, an earnest of Faulkner's later need to relocate the Negro back into an ordered world which was clearly disintegrating around him. Ned reveals all the stereotypes, the echo of the Negro, not the reality: wily under his deferential manner; sexually loose, without morality, a tomcat; full of strategies and schemes for bending the system. Uncle Parsham is a male Dilsey, a high-toned churchman, devout and ethical. These Negroes fit easily into white society, sliding around problems of race, class, and caste; and since they are presented in a humorous, folksy light, all threat has been removed. They are "safe Negroes." How desperately Faulkner required this prospect as the troublesome 1950s passed into the even more troublesome 1960s we can only tell by his deliberately stereotypical portraiture.

Race bleeds off into views of women. Boon hits Everbe, and Ned approves, saying that hitting a woman doesn't hurt her; she just bides her time, and when your back is turned she'll have a go at you with flatiron or butcher knife: ". . . what better sign than a black eye or a cut mouf can a woman want from a man that he got her on his mind?"[36] Put in the mouth

---

*Cleanth Brooks (in *William Faulkner: The Yoknapatawpha Country*) sees the novel as a "courtesy book," a harking back to those Elizabethan books of instruction on how to behave like a gentleman. Here, he says, the analogue is to seek a code by which one can live. But Brooks is himself nostalgic for some kind of earlier life associated with codes, order, gentlemen. Faulkner is testing out codes, not to display them, but to illuminate how they can be broken without loss of innocence.

of a sympathetic character, such a "humorous" remark, supported by the sympathetic Boon hitting his woman, locates Faulkner in hunting camp, where such comments were comic.* All of these remarks and gestures are cautionary: *The Reivers* may present itself as a reminiscence about reaving or plundering, it may seem full of humor and nostalgia for a lost world; but it is, also, a revelation of the author who has given up on the complexities, the layering, the dimensions. If that is a farewell, it is a sad one, because it ignores all the elements he once confronted; which, now, he loops away from.

Faulkner's main preoccupation in Oxford was waiting. He worked his horses, especially one called Stonewall, which had replaced Powerhouse in difficulty. Even as he moved toward his sixty-fifth birthday, he felt the challenge in the horse and rose to meet it. The inevitable occurred. On June 17, while they were riding through Bailey's Woods, the horse became skittish or frightened and threw Faulkner hard, on his already weak back. As attentive to one of his wounded as the general he was named after had been, Stonewall tried to help the fallen rider with a nuzzle, and then wandered home when Faulkner was too badly injured to grasp the reins. He finally got up and limped home, grabbed Stonewall, mounted, and rode him over the jumps in the paddock; an act of willfulness tantamount to an injured flier going back up right after a crash. Faulkner refused to admit the horse had won.

Although the injury was not in itself serious—more a groin pull than any further back damage—it seemed to be the trauma that set off Faulkner's final decline. There may have been internal bleeding which could not be picked up on existing equipment or through the usual soundings. In any event, Faulkner needed a cane, carrying him back to the days after World War I when he also walked with a cane; but now it was necessary, not part of a scheme to heroize himself. The fall, however, did more than strain his groin; it aggravated the existing back condition, as he discovered several days later. If the pain could not be relieved, the real fear was he would try his own remedy; and although Chester McLarty, his personal physician in Oxford, recommended clinic treatment (at the Memphis Campbell Clinic) and painkillers, Faulkner was now no better a patient than he had been before.

Blotner tells of when Faulkner saw Dr. Felix Lindner on a social call and expressed what was clearly on his mind, what he had been looking into for some time: his coming death. He told Lindner: "I don't want to die."[37]

---

*Or else not so comically, it parallels something Faulkner did with Estelle. Marc Connelly, the playwright, recalled in the early 1930s a very strange situation: "His wife was a very nervous girl who occasionally had some kind of slips of mental processes, of thinking, and so on. And I don't know what she did, but it was something with which Bill was obviously familiar. And quite objectively, without a bit of reproachment in it, he looked at his wife and reached out and slapped her face very hard which, undoubtedly, was physically painful to her. She went right back to completely normal conduct, and Bill, without any apologies or anything else, continued whatever he had been talking about" (*William Faulkner: A Life on Paper*, p. 68). No one else appears to have noticed this, or else it was so embarrassing no one reported it.

Lindner, a retired orthopedist, offered to give Faulkner some painkillers, but the writer said that was not what he had in mind; not pain, death. Although we cannot draw too much from one remark, and that second-hand, Faulkner's comment seems not some chance remark, but the buildup of what he had been feeling. Better than anyone else, he knew his body and recognized that, despite reports of good health, he was deteriorating: not only his hearing and coordination, not only memory, but something he could not identify. Too much had passed before him as final things; too many voices. The fact he had lost his desire to write, that he had finally broken the pencil, was an indication for a writer the end was near. Also, it is difficult to calculate what Hemingway's suicide the previous year had meant to him. Frost said all old men know when an old man dies. Faulkner saw something ominous in Hemingway's death, since the two had become famous together, the twins of American fiction from 1930 to 1950 or so. Even their novels were almost back-to-back. For Faulkner, Hemingway had a divine talent, which he permitted to miscarry; and Faulkner also knew Hemingway revered him. The two were intertwined, and it may not be too conjectural to assert that Faulkner saw in the other's death something of his own. It was not only the death of Hemingway, however, but the end of an era in American writing: the few great ones had passed. Faulkner felt there was no one to replace them.

Inasmuch as he refused treatment which might have relieved pressure on his back, he had to live with his discomfort. As he had indicated, he had his mind set on Red Acres, with a price tag of $200,000, but containing what he needed in facilities for horses, as well as the usual amenities and a fine view of the Virginia countryside. Yet even as his health was entering its final decline, in late June and early July of 1962, Faulkner became interested in the case of James Meredith, who was attempting to become the first Negro to matriculate at the University of Mississippi. The writer indicated that if Meredith had trouble, it would come from Beat Two people, the area known for its white supremacy views, those rednecks Faulkner felt were also responsible for electing the Snopes-like Ross Barnett as governor. He expressed these views on July 2, when he went on a boat outing with Aubrey Seay, owner of a local restaurant. Just four days before he died, Faulkner was moving around fairly well, complaining of little except some back pain, enjoying the outing on Lake Enid near Oxford, drinking, and going to dinner with Estelle. It was a leisurely, seemingly relaxed time.

The next day, however, Faulkner found he was losing his sense of taste differentiation. Eating filet mignon and bread at the mansion with Estelle, he indicated he could not distinguish between them. Either a breakdown of functions was developing rapidly, or else he started to drink his way into a condition, or both. By the next day, he was drinking heavily, as well as taking painkillers—Demerol, Darvon, Seconal, among others. His back pain had gone from chronic to acute, and he was in agony; but also his attempt to accommodate the pain with that mixture of alcohol and painkillers was putting an enormous strain on his heart and other organs. With the matter getting out of hand, Chester McLarty came by; but as so often before, Faulkner's bodily functions indicated nothing abnormal—regular heartbeat, low blood pressure. Everyone was talking Byhalia, for a typical drying-out.

It must be stressed that the family (primarily Estelle and Jimmy Faulkner) was not unduly alarmed and was treating this episode as merely another one requiring a drying-out. Faulkner had created the circumstances whereby what was now proving to be a fatal attack was viewed as simply another in a series of the same old thing. Byhalia was hardly the place to send a man in need of support systems; it was the old family homestead for alcoholism and little else. Faulkner himself seemed eager to go, whereas on other occasions he had resisted. Also, the cycle of drinking was still in its early phases. Faulkner's eagerness to be treated, however, indicated that like so much else which he sensed, he felt something was "happening to me"—that phrase which he had used so often with his characters, especially Temple Drake and Joe Christmas. He was taken by car to Wright's Sanitarium, where he was admitted on July 5, at 6:00 P.M. He underwent medical examination, especially for vital signs, which all proved normal. Although he was now complaining of chest pain, there was no indication of irregularities. He was within hours of death, and all his organs checked out as normal, some of them in remarkable shape for a man of his age who had so abused himself. The prescribed treatment was for the usual drying-out—nourishment, weaning away from alcohol, rest, Benadryl; no particular medication for any ailment, since none was indicated. It was an eerie moment, since no sign revealed anything more serious than usual was at stake, and Dr. Wright himself, who attended Faulkner on his admission, did not seem perturbed by his patient.

At 1:30 A.M. on July 6, just seven-and-one-half hours after admission to Wright's Sanitarium, William Faulkner died. Everything simply stopped —heart, pulse, and all the other organs which had checked out as normal only a brief time before. According to reports, he sat up, groaned, and died, before anyone could reach him. Dr. Wright appeared within minutes and applied external chest massage, as well as mouth-to-mouth resuscitation, but to no avail. The diagnosis was coronary occlusion, which had remained undetected; there is no indication Faulkner underwent an electrocardiogram in that earlier medical examination. But even if he had, it is not certain he could have been saved at this late stage. Had his heart been thoroughly examined earlier and had medical techniques been more advanced, it is possible that a bypass might have worked; but that was out of the question in 1962. A nagging question remains in that the Byhalia facility was simply not prepared for this kind of case, and one wonders if in a more advanced facility, Faulkner might have received treatment which could have prolonged his life. A clinic for alcohol poisoning was not the place to go for a serious heart condition. The diagnosis was definitely coronary thrombosis, in which a bit of fat that has formed on the vein wall breaks away and blocks the passage of blood in the vein; the result, loss of blood flow, heart stoppage, almost immediate death. Given Faulkner's poor diet of fats and grease, his incessant smoking, the continued ravages of alcohol, and that combination of liquor and drugs near the end, the condition of his veins in an otherwise healthy body was determining the outcome.

Faulkner had always indicated he wanted a simple ceremony, as quiet as Maud's. The body was returned to Rowan Oak, where he lay in a plain casket which Dot Oldham—always one to interfere in family matters—changed to a more expensive and fancy one, cypress with silver handles and a rich felt interior. Faulkner was getting the burial Dot Oldham wanted, possibly for social reasons, rather than the one he had requested. Friends and relatives gathered, part of a sequence of deaths. Faulkner's Uncle John (J.W.T., Jr.) had died just earlier that year; Brother Johncy would die the next year, at sixty-one. Of the brothers, only Jack enjoyed a long life (d. 1975).* The press also came, with its endless questions about the death. Jack Falkner took over and insisted that no photographs or interviews could be taken at the residence. The plan was to get Faulkner buried, and then to permit interviews and questions. The world did pay attention—even condolences from President Kennedy, himself only a little more than a year from death. Random House was well represented, with Cerf and Klopfer; Cerf for the first time in Oxford. John Williams Bowen came in for the funeral, as did the Masseys, Ben Wasson, and Shelby Foote, whom Faulkner had particularly liked and admired.

The service was read by Duncan Gray, Estelle's minister, a typical Protestant ceremony in its simplicity: readings from the *Book of Common Prayer*, then Psalm 46, next from Paul's *Epistle to the Romans*, ending with the Lord's Prayer. It was tasteful, perhaps a little more than what Faulkner would have wanted, but it satisfied Estelle that her husband was gathered up by the church at his death, a church which had formally meant little or nothing to him in life. Led by a police car, the hearse was then taken to St. Peter's Cemetery, where the Falkners, except for the old colonel, were buried. Malcolm was there, at the graveside with his mother and his uncles. Blotner was one of those who handled the coffin at the cemetery, the sole non–family member, but from Faulkner's point of view, as close to a son as he would ever have. Duncan Gray intoned final prayers. Whitman speaks to eternity:

> The spotted hawk swoops by and accuses me, he complains of my
>   gab and my loitering.
> I too am not a bit tamed, I too am untranslatable,
> I sound my barbaric yawp over the roofs of the world.

*Estelle died in 1972, at seventy-six; Victoria in 1975, at fifty-six; Malcolm in 1977, at fifty-three; Dot Oldham in 1968, at sixty-three. Of all the Falkners, Oldhams, and Franklins, only Maud, Jack, and Estelle had long lives.

The last scud of day holds back for me,
It flings my likeness after the rest and true as any on the
  shadow'd wilds,
It coaxes me to the vapor and the dusk.
I depart as air, I shake my white locks, at the runaway sun,
I effuse my flesh in eddies, and drift it in lacy jags.
I bequeath myself to the dirt to grow from the grass I love,
If you want me again look for me under your boot-soles.
You will hardly know who I am or what I mean,
But I shall be good health to you nevertheless,
And filter and fibre your blood.
Failing to fetch me at first keep encouraged,
Missing me one place search another,
I stop somewhere waiting for you.

Selected Bibliography

1. William Faulkner—Novels, Stories, Poetry:
   The Marble Faun, 1924 (reissued along with *A Green Bough* in 1965).
   Soldiers' Pay, 1926.
   Mosquitoes, 1927.
   Sartoris, 1929.
   The Sound and the Fury, 1929.
   As I Lay Dying, 1930.
   Sanctuary, 1931.
   Idyll in the Desert, 1931.
   These 13, 1931.
   Miss Zilphia Gant, 1932.
   Light in August, 1932.
   A Green Bough, 1933.
   Doctor Martino and Other Stories, 1934.
   Pylon, 1935.
   Absalom, Absalom!, 1936.
   The Unvanquished, 1938.
   The Wild Palms (with *Old Man*), 1939.
   The Hamlet, 1940.
   Go Down, Moses, 1942.
   Intruder in the Dust, 1948.

Knight's Gambit, 1949.
Collected Stories, 1950.
Notes on a Horsethief, 1950.
Requiem for a Nun, 1951.
A Fable, 1954.
The Faulkner Reader, 1954.
Big Woods, 1955.
The Town, 1957.
The Mansion, 1959.
The Reivers, 1962.

2. Also (posthumous publication):
The Wishing Tree, 1966 [1927].
Flags in the Dust, 1973 [1927–1929].
The Marionettes: A Play in One Act, 1977 [1920].
Mayday, 1977 [1926].
Helen: A Courtship and *Mississippi Poems*, 1981 [1925–26, 1924, respectively].
Father Abraham, 1983 [1926?].
Elmer, 1987 [1925].

3. Letters and Collected Fugitive Pieces:
Blotner, Joseph, ed. *Selected Letters of William Faulkner*, 1977.
Cowley, Malcolm, ed. *The Faulkner-Cowley File: Letters and Memories, 1944–1962*, 1966.
Meriwether, James B., ed. "Faulkner's Correspondence with the *Saturday Evening Post*," 1977 (in the *Mississippi Quarterly*, Summer).
————. "Faulkner's Correspondence with *Scribner's Magazine*," 1973 (in *Proof*, 3).
Collins, Carvel, ed. *William Faulkner: Early Prose and Poetry*, 1962.
————. *William Faulkner: New Orleans Sketches*, 1968.

4. Speeches, Public Letters, Interviews, and Incidentals:
Fant, Joseph L. and Robert Ashley, eds. *Faulkner at West Point*, 1964.
Gwynn, Frederick L. and Joseph Blotner, eds. *Faulkner in the University: Class Conferences at the University of Virginia, 1957–1958*, 1959.
Jelliffe, Robert A., ed. *Faulkner at Nagano*, 1956.
Meriwether, James B., ed. *A Faulkner Miscellany*, 1974.
————., ed. *Essays, Speeches & Public Letters*, 1966.
———— and Michael Millgate, eds. *Lion in the Garden: Interviews with William Faulkner, 1926–1962* (including the Nagano interviews), 1968.

5. Faulkner and Other Hands:
Faulkner: A Comprehensive Guide to the Brodsky Collection
Volume II: *The Letters*, 1984.
Volume III: *The de Gaulle Story*, 1984.
Volume IV: *Battle Cry*, 1985.
(all edited by Louis Daniel Brodsky and Robert W. Hamblin)
Country Lawyer and Other Stories for the Screen, 1987 (eds. Brodsky and Hamblin).

Faulkner's MGM Screenplays (Manservant, The College Widow, Absolution, Flying the Mail, Turn About/Today We Live, War Birds/A Ghost Story, Honor, Mythical Latin-American Kingdom Story, Louisiana Lou/Lazy River, 1982 (ed. Bruce F. Kawin).
Road to Glory, 1981.
Tomorrow & Tomorrow & Tomorrow, 1985 (eds. David G. Yellin and Marie Connors).
6. *Checklists:*
Blotner, Joseph. *William Faulkner's Library: A Catalogue,* 1964.
Brodsky, Louis Daniel and Hamblin, Robert W., eds. *Faulkner: A Comprehensive Guide to the Brodsky Collection.* Volume I: *The Bibliography,* 1982.
Butterworth, Keen. "A Census of Manuscripts and Typescripts of William Faulkner's Poetry," 1973 (in *Mississippi Quarterly,* Summer, reprinted in *A Faulkner Miscellany,* cited above in 4).
Hayhoe, George F. "Faulkner in Hollywood: A Checklist of His Film Scripts at the University of Virginia," 1978 (in *Mississippi Quarterly,* Summer).
Kawin, Bruce F. *Faulkner and Film,* 1977 (checklist at end).
Massey, Linton R. *"Man Working," 1919–1962, William Faulkner: A Catalogue of the William Faulkner Collections at the University of Virginia,* 1968.
Meriwether, James B. 4 items: *The Literary Career of William Faulkner: A Bibliographical Study,* 1961; "The Short Fiction of William Faulkner: A Bibliography," 1971 (in *Proof,* 1); "William Faulkner: A Check List," 1957 (in *Princeton University Library Chronicle,* Spring); *William Faulkner: An Exhibit of Manuscripts,* 1959 (at the University of Texas Humanities Research Center in Austin).
Peterson, Carl, *Each in Its Ordered Place: A Faulkner Collector's Notebook,* 1975.

Chronology

1825, July 6.   Birth of William Clark Falkner (the old colonel) in Tennessee, son of Joseph Falkner and Caroline Word.

1840.   William Clark Falkner arrives in Mississippi, first at Pontotoc, then at Ripley.

1847, July 9.   William Clark Falkner marries Holland Pearce in Knoxville, Tennessee.

1848, September 2.   Birth of John Wesley Thompson Falkner (the young colonel), only child of William Clark Falkner and Holland Pearce, in Ripley.

1849, Spring.   William Clark Falkner kills Robert Hindman (acquitted on grounds of self-defense); May 31, death of Holland Pearce.

1850, October 14.   Birth of future wife of John W. T. Falkner, Sallie McAlpine Murry.

1851, October 12.   William Clark Falkner remarries, to Elizabeth Houston Vance, who bears him eight children; he publishes *The Siege of Monterrey*.

1861, May. William Clark Falkner is elected colonel of the Magnolia Rifles, participates in the battles of Manassas; 1863, ousted as commander of his regiment, he forms the Partisan Rangers.

1869, September 2. John W. T. Falkner marries Sallie McAlpine Murry; they settle in Ripley.

1870, August 17. Birth of Murry Cuthbert Falkner (William Faulkner's father), first child of John W. T. Falkner and Sallie Murry.

1871, November 27. Birth of Maud Butler (William Faulkner's mother), daughter of Charles Butler and Lelia Dean Swift ("Damuddy").

1881, June. Book publication of William Clark Falkner's *The White Rose of Memphis*.

1885. John W. T. Falkner (William Faulkner's grandfather) moves to Oxford.

1889, November 6. Death of William Clark Falkner, after being shot on November 5 by Richard Jackson Thurmond, in Ripley.

1896, February 19. Birth of Lida Estelle Oldham, future wife of William Faulkner, to Lemuel Earl Oldham and Lida Allen.

November 8. Marriage of Murry C. Falkner and Maud Butler.

1897, September 25. Birth of William Cuthbert Falkner (Faulkner) in New Albany, Mississippi.

1898, December. Murry C. Falkner is appointed treasurer of the railroad built by his grandfather; the family, with William, moves to Ripley, Mississippi.

1899, June 26. Birth of Murry Charles, Jr. ("Jack"), to Murry and Maud Falkner.

1901, September 24. Birth of third son, John Wesley Thompson III ("Johncy"), to Murry and Maud Falkner.

1902, September 22. Murry and Maud Falkner, with three sons, move to "The Big Place" in Oxford.

1905, September 25. Falkner enters first grade at age eight. Skips second grade the next year.

1907, August 15. Birth of Dean Swift Falkner to Murry and Maud Falkner.

1910, October 4. John W. T. Falkner establishes the First National Bank of Oxford.

1911, September. Faulkner enters eighth grade; becomes increasingly distracted at school and begins to avoid it.

1914, June. Faulkner, now writing poetry, begins friendship with Phil Stone. In September he enters the eleventh grade, from which he drops out in December. He re-enters school to play football, leaves in fall of 1915.

1915. He and Estelle become a "couple."

1916, Winter. Faulkner works briefly at his grandfather's bank as an assistant bookkeeper. He continues to write poetry, often showing his work to Estelle.

1917. First work of Faulkner appears, a drawing in *Ole Miss*, the university annual.

1918, Early Spring. Faulkner is rejected by the air corps as physically too slight; leaves for New Haven and begins to work as clerk in the Winchester Repeating Arms Company. On April 18, Estelle Oldham marries Cornell Franklin.

——, July 9. Faulkner arrives in Toronto as a recruit in the Royal Air Force.

——, December. Faulkner is discharged from the RAF and returns to Oxford. On December 1, his father, Murry, is appointed assistant secretary at the University of Mississippi.

1919, Spring. Faulkner writes poems which will later appear in *The Marble Faun;* publishes first poem, "L'Apres-Midi d'une Faune," in the *New Republic,* August 6.

——, September 19. Faulkner enrolls as a special student at the university in French, Spanish, and second-year literature. In subsequent months he publishes several poems and a prose sketch in the *Mississippian,* the student newspaper.

1920, Autumn. Faulkner, once again a special student at the university, cofounds "The Marionettes," a dramatic club, for whom he writes *The Marionettes,* a one-act play with strong *fin de siècle* overtones.

1921, Summer. Faulkner completes *Vision in Spring*, a collection of love poems, which he presents to Estelle during one of her returns from the Far East. She is now a mother (Victoria, born February 8, 1919).

———, Autumn. Faulkner accepts a position as a bookstore assistant in New York; returns in December to Oxford to become fourth-class postmaster at the university, a position he holds from spring of 1922 to October 31, 1924.

1922, March 10. Faulkner publishes "The Hill" in the *Mississippian*, with intimations of Yoknapatawpha.

———, March 13. Death of John W. T. Falkner, the writer's grandfather.

1923. Faulkner makes intense effort to have his work published in book form, with the Four Seas Company of Boston, but cannot come up with the necessary subvention. He writes steadily, poetry and short fictional pieces, "Adolescence" and "Love."

1924, May. Four Seas Company agrees to publish *The Marble Faun*, a volume of Faulkner's poetry. That summer he is dismissed from his scoutmaster's post for drinking.

———, November. Having resigned his postmaster's position (under threat of legal proceedings), Faulkner goes to New Orleans, where he meets Sherwood Anderson. Presents *Mississippi Poems* to Myrtle Ramey in October or November.

———, December 15. Publication of *The Marble Faun*, dedicated to Maud Falkner, with a preface by Phil Stone.

1925, January 4. Faulkner returns to New Orleans; in January–February, publishes in the *Double Dealer*, and in February in the *Times-Picayune*. He begins work on *Soldiers' Pay*, his first novel.

———, June. Faulkner writes poems which he will complete and collect the following year as *Helen: A Courtship*, dedicated to Helen Baird.

———, July 7. With William Spratling, Faulkner sails for Genoa on the *West Ivis*. He visits Milan, Stresa, Rapallo, and other places in Italy, then heads for Paris. Liveright has advanced him $200 for *Soldiers' Pay*.

———, Summer–Autumn. Faulkner works on a novel, "Elmer," incomplete and unpublished in his lifetime. He visits England briefly, travels through the northern parts of France. He returns to America on December 19, is back in Oxford on the twenty-fifth.

1926, January 27. *Mayday*, a brief allegory, is dedicated to Helen Baird.

———, February 25. Publication of *Soldiers' Pay*.

———, September 1. Having completed *Helen: A Courtship* and abandoned "Elmer," Faulkner finishes the typescript of *Mosquitoes*.

———, December. Faulkner collaborates with William Spratling on *Sherwood Anderson and Other Famous Creoles*, caricatures of several New Orleans figures, including Faulkner's of Anderson.

ca. late 1926–early 1927. Faulkner writes a story, "Father Abraham," which foreshadows his Snopes trilogy.

———, February 5. *The Wishing Tree*, a fairy tale written for his future stepdaughter, Victoria. Published posthumously.

———, April 30. Publication of *Mosquitoes*. Faulkner is writing *Flags in the Dust*, which Liveright rejects on November 25.

1928, Spring. Faulkner begins to write *The Sound and the Fury*, with *Flags* on hold. Later, Harcourt agrees to publish the latter if cut; Ben Wasson makes the revisions.

1929, January 31. Publication of *Sartoris*, the revised *Flags in the Dust*.

———, April 29. Estelle and Cornell Franklin divorce (along with Victoria, she is also the mother of Malcolm, born December 3, 1923).

——, May 25.   With *Sound* completed but rejected by Harcourt, Faulkner finishes the typescript of *Sanctuary.*

——, June 20.   Faulkner marries Estelle Oldham Franklin in the College Hill Presbyterian Church; they honeymoon in Pascagoula, where Estelle attempts suicide by drowning.

——, October 7.   Publication of *Sound* by the firm of Cape and Smith.

——, October 25–December 11.   Dating of manuscript of *As I Lay Dying.*

1930, January 25.   Faulkner starts his "sending schedule," his listing of short stories, dates, and magazines to which they were submitted, accepted, or rejected.

——, April 12.   Faulkner and Estelle buy Rowan Oak, an antebellum home dating to 1844.

——, April 30.   *Forum* publishes "A Rose for Emily," Faulkner's first short story in a national magazine.

——, October 6.   Publication of *As I Lay Dying* by Cape and Smith; ongoing revisions of *Sanctuary* to make it suitable for publication.

1931, January 11.   Birth of Faulkner's and Estelle's first child, Alabama, who dies after nine days.

——, February 9.   Publication of the revised *Sanctuary* by Cape and Smith.

——, September 21.   Publication of *These 13*, Faulkner's first collection of short stories, dedicated to Estelle and Alabama; *Light in August* having been begun the previous month.

——, October 23–24.   Faulkner attends the Southern Writers' Conference in Charlottesville, Va., moving on to New York until December 10, when Random House publishes a limited edition of the story, *Idyll in the Desert.*

1932, March.   Publication of the Modern Library edition of *Sanctuary* with Faulkner's "notorious" introduction.

——, May 7.   Faulkner's first trip to Hollywood, to Culver City (Metro-Goldwyn-Mayer), returning to Oxford when his father dies on August 7. In Hollywood he makes the important connection to Howard Hawks.

——, October 6.   Publication of *Light in August*, Faulkner having returned to Culver City on October 3.

1933, February 2.   Faulkner takes up flying, eventually gaining his pilot's license and owning his own plane. (Received wings on December 14.)

——, April 28.   *Today We Live* (based on Faulkner's "Turn About") is generally released (premiered in Memphis on April 12), with Faulkner given a credit.

——, June 24.   Birth of Jill Faulkner, Faulkner's only surviving child.

1934 (early).   Faulkner has an idea called "Dark House," which will develop into *Absalom, Absalom!*

——, February 15.   Faulkner is in New Orleans for the dedication of Shushan Airport, material he transformed into *Pylon*.

——, April 16.   Publication of *Doctor Martino and Other Stories*. Shortly after he begins a series of Civil War stories, which will make up *The Unvanquished*.

——, July 1.   Faulkner is at Universal Studios in Hollywood until July 24, for $1,000 per week. Through rest of 1934, he submits five Civil War stories and writes the seven chapters of *Pylon*.

1935, March 25.   Publication of *Pylon*. Faulkner is moving along on *Absalom*.

——, November 10.   Dean Faulkner is killed in an airplane crash, leaving a pregnant widow, for whom Faulkner assumes responsibility.

——, December 10.   Faulkner returns to Hollywood, to Twentieth Century-Fox, under Howard Hawks. Meets Hawks's script clerk, Meta Carpenter, beginning a long and troubled relationship.

1936, January 31. Completion of manuscript of *Absalom.* Total breakdown, followed by recovery in Byhalia, Mississippi, nursing home. Smith and Haas, Faulkner's publishers, become part of Random House, with Cerf and Klopfer.

——, February 26, July 15. Two more stints in Hollywood, the latter with Estelle and Jill.

——, October 26. Publication of *Absalom.*

1937, Winter. Continued work in Hollywood on *Gunga Din, Drums Along the Mohawk,* and others, but without credit.

——, September 15. Back at Rowan Oak, Faulkner begins *The Wild Palms.*

——, Mid-October. Faulkner spends three and a half weeks in New York, suffers third-degree back burn from a steam pipe when drunk.

1938, February 15. Publication of *The Unvanquished,* seven Civil War stories revised into "novelistic" form. Continued work on *The Wild Palms* (and "Old Man"). By late February, he buys land which he names Greenfield Farm.

——, November 7. First work on *The Hamlet;* project is described on December 15 as "The Peasants," "Rus in Urbe," "Ilium Falling," the Snopes trilogy which became *The Hamlet, The Town, The Mansion.*

1939, January 18. Faulkner is elected to the National Institute of Arts and Letters.

——, January 19. Publication of *The Wild Palms.* While work continues on *The Hamlet,* Faulkner seeks work in Hollywood as his financial obligations increase.

1940, January 4. Faulkner sends Ober "A Point of Law," the foreshadowing of *Go Down, Moses.*

——, January 31. Death of Caroline Barr ("Mammy Callie"), to whom *Go Down, Moses* will be dedicated.

——, April 1. Publication of *The Hamlet,* the first part of the Snopes trilogy. Ongoing work on the stories which will make up *Go Down, Moses.*

——, June. Faulkner is considering leaving Random House for Viking Press, but Bennett Cerf offers counter-terms to keep him.

1941, Spring–Summer. Faulkner continues work on stories for *Go Down, Moses,* including the writing of the shorter version of "The Bear."

1942, May 11. Publication of *Go Down, Moses and Other Stories* (the second edition will drop "and Other Stories").

——, July 27. Faulkner arrives in Burbank, California, to work for Warner Brothers in what proves to be a seven-year contract, at only $300 per week. Works on "The de Gaulle Story," which is never produced.

1943, January 13. Faulkner is back in Hollywood for a seven-month stint. Works on several scripts, including *Northern Pursuit* (starring Errol Flynn) and "Battle Cry" with Hawks. He is then assigned to *To Have and Have Not,* based on the Hemingway novel, for which he receives a credit.

——, October 30. He indicates to Ober he is working on "a fable," which he sees as a short fiction of ten to fifteen thousand words. It will occupy him for almost the next ten years.

1944, February 14. Faulkner returns to Hollywood after a stay in Oxford.

——, August 28. After spending two months on *To Have and Have Not,* Faulkner, working with Hawks, begins to adapt *The Big Sleep* as part of his continuing Warner contract.

1945, June 7. Faulkner is back in Hollywood for what will prove to be his last (his eleventh) stay. Extensive work with Jean Renoir on *The Southerner,* although he does not receive a credit.

1946, April 29.   Publication by Viking Press of Malcolm Cowley's edition of *The Portable Faulkner*, which creates new interest in him and helps to bring his books back into print.

——, December 20.   Publication of the one-volume Modern Library edition of *Sound* and *As I Lay Dying* with the "Compson Appendix."

1947.   Work continues on *A Fable*.

——, April 14–17.   Faulkner meets some classes at the University of Mississippi, where in an interview he ranks Thomas Wolfe as his most important contemporary (Wolfe had been dead for almost ten years).

1948, July 11.   MGM pays $50,000 for screen rights to *Intruder in the Dust*, published on September 27.

——, November 24.   While Faulkner is deer hunting, he is elected to the American Academy of Arts and Letters.

1949, Spring.   *Intruder* is filmed in Oxford, with some aid from Faulkner.

——, August.   Joan Williams, a young student and aspiring author, visits at Rowan Oak, beginning an important relationship with Faulkner.

——, November 27.   Publication of *Knight's Gambit*, a collection of detective stories with Gavin Stevens at their center. Faulkner almost wins the Nobel Prize in 1949, but falls three votes short of the required unanimous vote; by the time of a revote, it is too late for the award.

1950, early February.   Faulkner is in New York, seeing both Joan Williams and Ruth Ford. He is beginning work on *Requiem*, which he sees as a collaboration with Williams.

——, May.   Faulkner receives the Howells Medal for distinguished fiction from the American Academy of Arts and Letters.

——, August 21.   Publication of *Collected Stories*, forty-two stories, his third and final volume of short fiction.

——, November 10.   Faulkner is awarded the 1949 Nobel Prize in literature.

——, December 10.   Faulkner delivers his acceptance speech before the Swedish Academy in Stockholm. He meets Else Jonsson, whom he continues to see through the 1950s. By December 18, he is back in Oxford.

1951, February 10.   Publication of *Notes on a Horsethief,* a segment of *A Fable.*

——, February 1–March 4.   Returns to Hollywood, under Hawks, now at $2,000 per week. Renews relationship with Meta Carpenter, who has been married and separated.

——, March.   Receives National Book Award for *Collected Stories.*

——, September 27.   Publication of *Requiem.* Problems of financing the play derived from it by Ruth Ford, and producing it, will occupy several months.

——, October 26.   Faulkner receives the Legion of Honor from the French consul in New Orleans.

1952, May 16.   Faulkner leaves on a one-month trip to Europe, chiefly Paris and Oslo (for a stay with Else Jonsson), also to address the French Congress for the Liberty of Culture.

——, November 15.   Faulkner spends one month in New York and Princeton, working on *A Fable* and seeing Joan Williams.

1953, January 31.   Faulkner stays in New York on and off until October; hospitalized for alcoholism and neurological disorders, brief attempt with psychiatry.

——, June 8.   Addresses Jill's graduating class at Pine Manor Junior College. Finishing touches on *A Fable,* with November 1953 as final date on the manuscript.

——, December 1.   Faulkner arrives in Geneva en route to Egypt, to work with Hawks on *Land of the Pharaohs;* they go on to Italy.

——, Christmas Eve. Faulkner meets Jean Stein, a young American, in St. Moritz, and forms a relationship with her; the affair with Joan Williams all but over.

1954, January 1. Beginning of travels to England, France, Italy, then to Cairo, where he must be nursed.

——, April 1. Publication of *The Faulkner Reader*.

——, April. A long autobiographical essay, "Mississippi," appears in *Holiday*; Faulkner hospitalized in Paris. Back in Oxford by the end of the month.

——, August 2. Publication of *A Fable*. Trip to Lima and São Paulo for a week.

——, August 21. Marriage of Jill Faulkner and Paul D. Summers, Jr., a West Point man.

1955, January 25. Accepts in person the National Book Award for *A Fable*, which also receives the Pulitzer Prize in fiction.

——, March 20. Faulkner releases the first of four letters to the Memphis *Commercial Appeal* on racial injustice in America, part of his general concern in the 1950s with racial relations; his views upset blacks, white liberals, and segregationists alike.

——, July 29. Faulkner leaves for a three-week trip to Japan under State Department auspices; he is enormously popular and sought after. He spends two days in Manila with his stepdaughter, Victoria, and her husband.

——, October 14. Publication of *Big Woods*, five narrative pieces connecting four previously published hunting stories.

1956. Early in the year, Faulkner is increasingly agitated over Authorine Lucy's attempt to integrate the University of Alabama; his efforts at reconciliation only fan the flames.

——, Winter–Fall. Faulkner moves steadily from Oxford to New York and back again, with stops in Charlottesville, where Jill has her first child, a son. He is caught in racial controversy, with his infamous statement about "going out into the street and shooting Negroes."

——, early. Faulkner's interview with Jean Stein for the *Paris Review*. Writing of *The Town* ongoing.

——, September. Faulkner becomes involved in the "People-to-People Program" of the Eisenhower administration, an effort to promote American culture in iron curtain countries.

1957, mid-February–June. Faulkner is writer-in-residence at the University of Virginia chiefly for question-and-answer sessions.

——, March 17. Faulkner goes to Greece on a two-week trip for the State Department; receives the Silver Medal of the Athens Academy.

——, May 1. Publication of *The Town*, volume 2 in the Snopes trilogy.

——, May 10–August 30. Princeton University Library presents an exhibition, "The Literary Career of William Faulkner," arranged by James B. Meriwether.

——, May 22. In New York Faulkner addresses the American Academy of Arts and Letters at its presentation of the Gold Medal for Fiction to John Dos Passos.

1958, January 30. Faulkner returns for his second semester as writer-in-residence at the University of Virginia, but is refused a permanent position by the president apparently because of his moderate racial views. Work on *The Mansion*. Moves back and forth between Charlottesville and Princeton (for two weeks with the Council on Humanities), then between Charlottesville and Oxford. Declines an invitation to attend a writers' conference in the Soviet Union.

1959, January 30. American premiere of *Requiem* in New York.

——, Winter–Spring. Faulkner spends more and more time in Virginia, in June transferring his manuscripts from Princeton to the Alderman Library at the University of Virginia, and in August purchasing a house in Charlottesville.

1960, August. Faulkner accepts an appointment at the University of Virginia which requires few duties.

——, October 16. Death of Maud, Faulkner's mother. At the end of the year, Faulkner wills all his manuscripts to the William Faulkner Foundation.

1961, April 2. Faulkner arrives in Caracas, Venezuela, on a two-week State Department trip. Later, begins work on *The Reivers*, his final novel.

1962, January. Another injury in a fall from a horse, one of many such accidents; Faulkner hospitalized.

——, April 19. Visit to West Point with Estelle, Jill, and his son-in-law; he reads a passage from the now-completed *The Reivers*.

——, May 24. Eudora Welty presents Faulkner with the Gold Medal for Fiction awarded by the American Academy of Arts and Letters.

——, June 4. Publication of *The Reivers*. Further accidents with horses.

——, July 5. He enters hospital in Byhalia, Miss.

——, July 6. Faulkner dies of a heart attack, is buried on July 7 in St. Peter's Cemetery in Oxford. Jill Faulkner Summers is his literary executrix, with his possessions left to Estelle.

Notes

PART I: *HISTORY, MEMORIES, LANGUAGE*

Chapter One: Overview

1. April 29, 1953; *Selected Letters of William Faulkner*, ed. Joseph Blotner (New York: Vintage Books, 1978; orig. publ. 1977), p. 348.

2. For some of my remarks, I am indebted to suggestions made by Louise J. Kaplan in *Adolescence: The Farewell to Childhood* (New York: Simon & Schuster, 1984).

3. Except for *Gone With the Wind*, which denied the historical context in favor of a hoopskirt view.

4. April 9, 1918; also, the following quote.

Chapter Two: Backgrounds

1. December 8, 1945; Malcolm Cowley, *The Faulkner-Cowley File: Letters and Memories, 1944–1962* (New York: Viking, 1966), p. 66.

2. *The Portable Faulkner*, ed. Malcolm Cowley (New York: Viking, 1946; revised, 1967), p. vii.

3. *Faulkner-Cowley File*, p. 75.

4. Ibid., p. 77.

5. The most useful sources for Faulkner family background are: Donald Duclos, *Son of Sorrow: The Life, Works and Influence of Colonel William C. Falkner, 1825–1889* (Ann Arbor, Mich.: University Microfilms, 1962); Joseph Blotner, *Faulkner: A*

Biography, 2 vols. (New York: Random House, 1974); one-volume edition, 1984; Faulkner's own long essay "Mississippi"; and court and county records.

6. In the Alderman Library of the University of Virginia.

7. Ripley *Advertiser*, May 1, 1886; also Duclos, *Son of Sorrow*.

8. *Absalom, Absalom!* (New York: Vintage Books, 1986), (the Corrected Text), p. 471.

9. Blotner, *Faulkner*, vol. 1, p. 30. Blotner reports this part of the campaign in some detail.

10. The succeeding events come from Duclos, *Son of Sorrow*, p. 319ff. Blotner's note (vol. 1, p. 27) fleshes out the sources.

11. *Sartoris* (New York: New American Library, 1983), p. 299.

12. Blotner, vol. 1, pp. 53–54.

13. Blotner, vol. 1, p. 64, for these details.

14. In September 1902.

15. Murry (Jack) C. Falkner, *The Falkners of Mississippi* (Baton Rouge: Louisiana State University Press, 1967), p. 16.

16. Some useful studies: Richard Lingeman, *Small Town America* (New York: Putnam, 1980); John Dollard, *Caste and Class in a Southern Town* (New York: Harper's, 1937, reissued as Anchor Book, 1957); W. J. Cash, *The Mind of the South* (New York: Knopf, 1941; reissued as Anchor Book, 1969); Frank L. Owsley, *Plain Folk of the Old South* (Baton Rouge: Louisiana State University Press, 1949); Pete Daniel, *Standing at the Crossroads: Southern Life in the Twentieth Century* (New York: Hill and Wang, 1986); Eugene Genovese, *The Political Economy of Slavery* (New York: Vintage Books, 1967); Eugene Genovese, *The World the Slaveholders Made* (New York: Vintage Books, 1971); perhaps the most useful of all, Thomas D. Clark's *Pills, Petticoats, and Plows* (Indianapolis: University of Indiana Press, 1944); John B. Cullen, with Floyd C. Watkins, *Old Times in the Faulkner Country* (Chapel Hill: University of North Carolina Press, 1961).

17. Blotner, vol. 1, p. 80.

18. Blotner, vol. 1, p. 85.

Chapter Three: The Beginnings of Imagination

1. *Faulkner in the University*, eds. Frederick L. Gwynn and Joseph L. Blotner (Charlottesville: University Press of Virginia, 1959, reprinted 1977), pp. 29–30.

2. Blotner, vol. 1, p. 120.

3. *The Reivers: A Reminiscence* (New York: Random House, 1962), p. 46.

4. John Falkner, *My Brother Bill: An Affectionate Reminiscence* (New York: Trident Press, 1963), pp. 78–80, 121–122.

5. Lingeman, *Small Town America*, p. 261.

6. Ibid., p. 389ff.

7. Interview with Jean Stein, *Writers at Work: The Paris Review Interviews*, ed. Malcolm Cowley (New York: Viking Compass Books, 1959), p. 141.

Chapter Four: Estelle, Phil, and War

1. Details from Blotner, vol. 1, p. 142.

2. *Lion in the Garden: Interviews with William Faulkner*, eds. James B. Meriwether and Michael Millgate (Lincoln: University of Nebraska Press, 1968), p. 112.

3. Blotner, vol. 1, p. 146.

4. See *The Falkners of Mississippi*, passim.

5. Details from Blotner, vol. 1, pp. 154–155.

6. Beginning with the January 1915 Oxford *Eagle*, one picks up a running history of Falkner, Stone, Oldham, and more general Mississippi politics. For the latter, see in particular July 29, 1915; August 5 and 12, 1915.

7. Phil Stone, "William Faulkner: The Man and His Work," *Oxford Magazine*, 1 (1934).

8. "Verse Old and Nascent: A Pilgrimage," in *William Faulkner: Early Prose and Poetry*, ed. Carvel Collins (Boston: Little, Brown, 1962), p. 116. The essay appeared originally in *Double Dealer* 7 (April 1925); "proselyting" is Faulkner's usage.

9. Some of these stories, apocryphal or not, appear in Marshall J. Smith's "Faulkner of Mississippi," *Bookman* (December 1931).

10. Ben Wasson, *Count No 'Count* (Jackson: University Press of Mississippi, 1983), p. 25. Although there is no reason to doubt Wasson's physical description of Faulkner, his other evaluations are often suspect.

11. Poem No. XIII.

12. By his first novels, Faulkner surely knew *A Portrait of the Artist as a Young Man* and, most probably, *Ulysses*, either as a whole or in its parts, supplied him by Phil Stone.

13. *Light in August* (Library of America, 1985), p. 632.

14. Much of the following derives from Michael Millgate's "William Faulkner, Cadet," *University of Toronto Quarterly* (January 1966). Still other information comes from Carvel Collins's talk at the 1966 MLA meeting, "Faulkner's War Service and His Fiction," as reported by Blotner, vol. 1. Other related pieces are Millgate's "Faulkner and the Air: The Background of *Pylon*," *Michigan Quarterly Review* (Fall 1964) and "Faulkner in Toronto: A Further Note," *University of Toronto Quarterly* (January 1968).

15. Blotner, vol. 1, p. 215.

16. Falkner, *The Falkners of Mississippi*, pp. 90–91.

17. Blotner, vol. 1, p. 226.

PART II: *THE NEW MAN*

Chapter Five: William Faulkner of Oxford

1. *My Brother Bill*, p. 139.

2. January 10, 1945, Ober-Faulkner Collection, Alderman Library of the University of Virginia.

3. August 3, 1951, Alderman Library.

4. Blotner, vol. 1, p. 235. Some of Blotner's sources were Dorothy Conkling, Phil Stone, Emily Stone (his wife), and Dot Wilcox.

5. *Southern Review* (Spring 1985), pp. 376–403.

6. Ibid., p. 395.

7. Blotner, vol. 1, pp. 236–237.

8. *The Falkners of Mississippi*, p. 125; following quote, ibid.

9. Faulkner's borrowings from other poets were legion, sometimes to the exact wording. Many of these came later from Housman, *A Shropshire Lad* and *Last Poems*, earlier from Keats, Shakespeare, Tennyson, and Swinburne. But the list extends to Eliot (extensive, especially "The Love Song of J. Alfred Prufrock" and *The Waste Land*), Cummings, FitzGerald's *Rubàiyàt*, the Bible (Job, Matthew), and others. Faulkner borrowed not only for his poetry but for his fiction. Eliot, in particular, became a model for both Faulkner's poetry and fiction ("Portrait of Elmer," *Soldiers' Pay, Pylon, The Wild Palms, A Fable*). For more detailed discussions of the parallels between Faulkner and other writers, see Richard P. Adams's "The Apprenticeship of William Faulkner," *Tulane Studies in English* (12, 1962), pp. 113–156; Cleanth Brooks's *William Faulkner: Toward Yoknapatawpha and Beyond* (New Haven: Yale University Press, 1978), pp. 345–354.

10. Blotner, vol. 1, p. 247.

11. Ibid., p. 251.

12. Ibid., p. 251.

13. Alderman Library.

14. Blotner, vol. 1, p. 255.

15. The dates, respectively, for this group of poems are: January 28, 1920; February 4, 1920; February 25, 1920; March 3, 1920; April 14, 1920, all in the *Mississippian*.

16. Blotner, vol. 1, p. 267.

17. Blotner, vol. 1, p. 270.

18. *Selected Letters of William Faulkner*, ed. Joseph Blotner (New York: Vintage Books, 1978; orig. publ. 1977), pp. 13–14.

19. Ibid., p. 17.

20. Ibid., p. 20.

21. Alderman Library.

22. Joan Williams, *The Wintering* (New York: Harcourt, Brace, 1971), p. 132.

23. Blotner, vol. 1, p. 275.

Chapter Six: Where To?

1. With Oxford's population under 2,000, fraternity life for the university student was socially important. Even now, in the late 1980s, with Oxford's population over 10,000, fraternities are the centerpiece of the university's social activities.

2. Blotner, vol. 1, p. 289.

3. The *Mississippian*, February 16, 1921, p. 5. Reprinted in *Early Prose and Poetry*, ed. Collins, pp. 74–76.

4. Collins, ibid., p. 75.

5. Ibid., p. 75; following quote, p. 76.

6. *Big Woods* (New York: Random House, 1955), p. 224.

7. *Faulkner-Cowley File*, p. 108.

8. *Early Prose and Poetry*, p. 75.

9. *Vision in Spring*, introduction by Judith Sensibar (Austin: University of Texas Press, 1984), p. 55. Following quotations from this edition, p. 58, pp. 63–64.

10. *Vision in Spring,* p. 38.

11. Ibid., p. 5.

12. Ibid., p. 12, from "The World and Pierrot: A Nocturne."

13. Ibid., p. 10ff., for remaining quotations.

14. "A Symphony" (VII), p. 40; "Love Song," p. 55; "The Dancer," p. 65.

15. All quotations from *A Green Bough* (New York: Harrison Smith and Robert Haas, 1933; facsimile), p. 12ff.

16. Available as *Helen: A Courtship* and *Mississippi Poems,* introductory essays by Carvel Collins and Joseph Blotner (published jointly by Oxford: Yoknapataw-pha Press, and New Orleans: Tulane University, 1981).

17. From Young's *The Pavilion: Of People and Times Remembered, of Stories and Places* (1951), quoted by Blotner, vol. 1, p. 315.

18. Blotner, vol. 1, p. 318.

19. Ibid., pp. 321–322.

20. *Uncollected Stories of William Faulkner,* ed. Joseph Blotner (New York: Vintage Books, 1981; orig. publ. 1979), p. 503. Earlier quotations from p. 495, p. 496.

21. Blotner, vol. 1, pp. 324–325.

Chapter Seven: The Center of Indifference

1. *Early Prose and Poetry,* p. 91.

2. Ibid., p. 94.

3. Ibid., p. 94.

4. *Uncollected Stories,* p. 473.

5. Ibid., p. 463.

6. *Early Prose and Poetry,* p. 101.

7. *The Faulkner Reader* (New York: Random House, 1954), p. viii.

8. Alderman Library.

9. Ibid.

10. See Judith Sensibar, *The Origins of Faulkner's Art* (Austin: University of Texas Press, 1984), p. 224, n. 7; p. 225, n. 12.

11. Preface, *The Marble Faun* (Boston: Four Seas, 1924), p. 7.

12. *My Brother Bill,* pp. 144–145.

13. Alderman Library. Details on the photographing from Blotner, vol. 1, p. 361.

14. *The Portable Anderson,* ed. Horace Gregory (New York: Viking, 1949; Penguin Books, 1979), p. 44.

15. Ibid., p. 45.

16. Blotner, vol. 1, p. 329.

17. Ibid., p. 330.

18. *Faulkner in the University,* p. 230.

19. Ibid., p. 231.

20. Ibid., p. 232.

21. *The Portable Anderson,* p. 7.

22. Ibid., p. 398.

23. Ibid., p. 402.
24. *Early Prose and Poetry*, p. 110.
25. *William Faulkner: New Orleans Sketches*, ed. Carvel Collins (New York: Random House, 1958), p. 3.
26. Ibid., p. 4; also following quotation.
27. *New Orleans Sketches*, pp. xvi–xvii of Collins's introduction.
28. Ibid., p. 126.
29. Ibid., p. 85.
30. Ibid., p. 87.

Chapter Eight: The Wasteland

1. The William B. Wisdom Collection, Tulane University Library.
2. Sensibar, *The Origins of Faulkner's Art*, p. xvi.
3. *Early Prose and Poetry*, p. 116ff.; essay dated April 1925.
4. Blotner, vol. 1, p. 379.
5. *The Faulkner Reader*, p. viii.
6. *Uncollected Stories*, p. 476.
7. *Essays, Speeches & Public Letters by William Faulkner*, ed. James B. Meriwether (New York: Random House, 1965), p. 7.
8. *The History of Southern Literature*, eds. Louis D. Rubin, Jr., Blyden Jackson, Rayburn S. Moore, Lewis P. Simpson, and Thomas Daniel Young (Baton Rouge: Louisiana State University Press, 1985), p. 420.
9. *Soldiers' Pay* (New York: Boni & Liveright, 1926; reissued 1954), p. 225.
10. Ibid., p. 31.
11. Ibid., p. 231.
12. Hong = fragrant, as in Hong Kong; Li can mean nearly anything.
13. Anderson's remarks are directed generally at Faulkner, without particular reference to *Soldiers' Pay*. See *Essays, Speeches & Public Letters*, pp. 8–9.
14. Ibid., p. 20.
15. Blotner, vol. 1, p. 438.

Chapter Nine: Into the Den

1. Postmarked September 10, 1925; Alderman Library.
2. Ibid.
3. *Selected Letters*, p. 13. Successive references to pp. 14, 15, 17.
4. Ibid., p. 17.
5. Ibid., p. 22.
6. Introduction by Carvel Collins to *Mayday* (Notre Dame: University of Notre Dame Press, 1978), p. 27ff.
7. *Selected Letters*, p. 24. Following quotation from p. 25.
8. October 9, 1925; ibid., p. 30.
9. All references to "Elmer" come from materials at the Alderman Library of the University of Virginia, along with some brief material in the Rowan Oak Papers at the University of Mississippi (including a missing section from the Alderman material, pp. 34–43). The Alderman typescript has been reproduced

in the Garland edition of "Elmer," ed. Thomas L. McHaney (New York, 1987). Also, note *Mississippi Quarterly* (Summer 1983) for the "Elmer" typescript, arranged and edited by Dianne L. Cox and James B. Meriwether.

10. *Mosquitoes* (New York: Washington Square Press, 1985), p. 265.

11. McHaney, for example.

12. See McHaney *(Mississippi Quarterly,* Summer 1973).

13. *Uncollected Stories,* p. 616. Following quotation from p. 621.

14. Blotner, vol. 1, p. 471. (See his note for p. 467, line 14, p. 69 of Notes.)

15. *My Brother Bill,* p. 155.

16. Ibid.

17. *Letters of Sherwood Anderson,* p. 155.

18. Blotner, in correspondence with me, does not believe Estelle had Malcolm out of wedlock and cites a resemblance between Malcolm and Cornell Franklin in photographs.

19. In his 1962 Vanderbilt University dissertation, later published, O. B. Emerson collected many early reviews, for which this writer is indebted.

20. The typescript of *Mosquitoes,* with several holograph emendations and revisions, is at the Alderman Library of the University of Virginia. The manuscript does not appear to exist. Among the people Faulkner caught from his New Orleans days: Patricia Robyn=Helen Baird; her brother=Helen's brother, Peter; the Semitic man=Julius Weis Friend; Gordon=Sprȧtling; Mrs. Eva Weisman=Julius's sister, Mrs. Lillian Friend Marcus; Dawson Fairchild=Sherwood Anderson (but not consistently); Mark Frost=Samuel Louis Gilmore; Major Ayers=Colonel Charles Glenn Collins. Jenny plays in and out of young women who rejected Faulkner. Faulkner himself appears as Faulkner, once. (See Brooks, *Toward Yoknapatawpha and Beyond,* p. 378.)

21. *Faulkner at West Point,* eds. Joseph L. Fant III and Robert Ashley (New York: Random House, 1964), p. 57.

22. Berg Collection of the New York Public Library.

23. *Mosquitoes,* p. 207.

24. Ibid., p. 266. Following quotations, p. 267.

25. Ibid., p. 267.

26. Ibid., p. 152.

27. Ibid., pp. 172–73.

28. *Mosquitoes* TS, Alderman Library.

29. *Mosquitoes,* p. 264.

30. Ibid., p. 289.

Chapter Ten: Perceiving Himself

1. Blotner writes me that Estelle asserted she destroyed the manuscript.

2. *The Wishing Tree* (New York: Random House, 1964), p. 81.

3. Blotner, vol. 1, p. 543.

4. February 1927, typescript, Harvard; *Selected Letters,* p. 35.

5. *Flags in the Dust* (New York: Vintage Books, 1974), p. 181.

6. Several writers have generated considerable heat over whether Faulkner's imaginary Jefferson town and Lafayette County were, respectively, Oxford town and Lafayette County; or whether both town and county represented a cross-section of places (Holly Springs or Memphis Junction in *The Mansion*, Ripley, New Albany, Pontotoc, and Batesville, Mississippi). Since the geographical descriptions in Faulkner's fiction more or less fit Oxford, we can assume that his own town and county were the basis of his metaphorical re-creations. The two maps he drew, for *Absalom, Absalom!* and *The Portable Faulkner*, bear out that Oxford was his point of reference, although the maps differ in details and mileage from one place to another. See Calvin S. Brown's rebuttal in "Faulkner's Geography and Topography" (PMLA, December 1962) to G. T. Buckley's "Is Oxford the Original of Jefferson in William Faulkner's Novels?" (PMLA, September 1961).

7. Beinecke MS. Blotner, *Faulkner*, has a fuller description of the document, vol. I, pp. 531-32.

8. Stone quoted by James B. Meriwether in "Sartoris and Snopes: An Early Notice," *The Library Chronicle of the University of Texas* (Summer 1962), pp. 36-39.

PART III: *THE TRANSFORMATION OF WILLIAM FAULKNER*

Chapter Eleven: The Sound and the Fury

1. Alderman Library.

2. November 30, 1927; Alderman Library.

3. Alderman Library.

4. Alderman Library.

5. Alderman Library.

6. Alderman Library. Blotner dates this letter October (1928), although it could be later.

7. See Blotner, vol. I (p. 82 of notes for p. 566, line 2) for a long discussion of the writing and dating of these stories within this period of time.

8. *Lion in the Garden*, p. 146.

9. Faulkner's introduction for a Random House edition of *The Sound and the Fury* exists in several forms, as manuscript and typescript fragments, from the summer of 1933. See *A Faulkner Miscellany*, p. 159.

10. *Lion in the Garden*, p. 146. Following quotations from same page.

11. Maurice Coindreau's preface to *The Sound and the Fury*, *The Time of William Faulkner* (Columbia: University of South Carolina Press, 1971), (trans. George McMillan Reeves), p. 41; originally in *Mississippi Quarterly* (Summer 1966).

12. *A Faulkner Miscellany*, p. 159 (from his introduction to *The Sound and the Fury*).

13. Ibid., pp. 159-160.

14. Blotner, vol. I, p. 570. Faulkner repeated these sentiments almost word for word in his introduction to *The Sound and the Fury*, cited above.

15. *Lion in the Garden*, p. 147.

16. Alderman Library.

17. p. 157

18. Last sentence from Blotner, vol. 1, p. 577; earlier quotations from draft of introduction to *The Sound and the Fury*, reprinted in *A Faulkner Miscellany*, p. 161.

19. Carvel Collins, *A Faulkner Miscellany*, p. 161. See his persuasive argument in "The Pairing of 'The Sound and Fury' " and " 'As I Lay Dying,' " *Princeton University Library Chronicle* (Spring 1957): pp. 114–123; also "William Faulkner: *The Sound and the Fury*," in *The American Novel from James Fenimore Cooper to William Faulkner*, ed. Wallace Stegner (New York: Basic Books, 1965), pp. 219–228.

20. Coindreau, p. 42.

21. There is the obvious temptation to compare Faulkner's "twilight imagination" with Dostoyevsky's: to see him as the Russian's "American heir" (André Bleikasten, *The Most Splendid Failure: Faulkner's The Sound and the Fury* (Bloomington: Indiana University Press, 1976), p. 222. One argument is that the polyphony of voices in Faulkner (what Mikhail Bakhtin calls *dialogism*) helps create an analogue. But ideologically Faulkner and Dostoyevsky are far removed. The Russian's desire for spiritual redemption, his adherence to Mother Russia as savior, his fervent belief in the Messianic qualities of Jesus, his worship of the City of God are hardly Faulknerian qualities. Much of the polyphony Faulkner could have garnered from Eliot and Joyce.

22. *Lion in the Garden*, p. 146. Following quotation from same page.

23. *Paris Review Interviews*, p. 130.

24. *The Sound and the Fury* (the Corrected Text), p. 144.

25. Ibid., p. 154. Following quotation from p. 156, then p. 168.

26. Ibid., p. 182.

27. Following quotation from p. 194.

28. Ibid., p. 197.

29. *Literary and Philosophical Essays*, trans. Annette Michelson (London: Rider, 1955), p. 85.

30. *The Sound and the Fury*, p. 105.

31. Ibid., p. 147.

Chapter Twelve: The Depths of Yoknapatawpha

1. Blotner, vol. 1, p. 591.

2. Private source.

3. Answered December 22, 1928; Princeton typescript; *Selected Letters*, p. 42.

4. From the "infamous" 1932 introduction to the Modern Library edition of *Sanctuary*. Text in Library of America *Faulkner*, eds. Joseph Blotner and Noel Polk, pp. 1029–30.

5. Alderman Library; *Selected Letters*, p. 45.

6. Alderman Library, letter cited above as early summer of 1929. Following quotation from same source; *Selected Letters*, p. 45.

7. From 1932 introduction to Modern Library *Sanctuary*, cited above. (Also in the Library of America; *Faulkner*, pp. 1029–30.)

8. Rowan Oak Papers of the University of Mississippi; previous quotation from same source.

9. Ibid.

10. In his valuable afterword to the original *Sanctuary* (New York: Random House, 1981), Noel Polk suggests that Faulkner attempted to rescue some of the material deleted from *Flags*; not so much in terms of plot and incident, of course, but in matters of ambience and atmospherics.

11. Ibid., p. 156.

12. Ibid., p. 266.

13. Ibid., p. 145. Following quotation, p. 146.

14. Ibid., p. 220.

15. *Macbeth*, Act V, 5, line 27.

16. Original *Sanctuary*, p. 231; revised text (New York: Penguin, 1947), pp. 139–40.

17. Revised text, p. 52.

18. *Selected Letters*, p. 43.

19. Cited above, from the 1932 Faulkner introduction to the Modern Library *Sanctuary*.

20. Dated in late May or so; Berg Collection of the New York Public Library.

21. Blotner, *One-Volume Edition*, p. 245.

22. Blotner, vol. 1, p. 626.

23. From O. B. Emerson.

24. James B. Meriwether, "Faulkner: Lost and Found," *New York Times Book Review* (November 5, 1972).

25. Michael Millgate, *The Achievement of William Faulkner* (Lincoln: University of Nebraska Press, 1978; orig. publ. 1966), p. 111. The Millgate book remains an excellent introduction to the survey of Faulkner's career as novelist and short story writer.

26. *As I Lay Dying*, Library of America, pp. 15–16.

27. Ibid., p. 34.

28. Ibid., p. 67.

29. Ibid., p. 68.

30. Ibid., p. 17.

31. Ibid., p. 116.

32. Ibid., p. 117.

33. Ibid., p. 119.

34. Ibid., p. 69.

35. Ibid.

36. Ibid., pp. 136–37.

37. Ibid., p. 97.

38. Ibid., p. 97.

Chapter Thirteen: *Annus Mirabilis* and Thereafter

1. *I'll Take My Stand: The South and the Agrarian Tradition* (Baton Rouge: Louisiana State University, 1983; a reissue with introduction by Louis D. Rubin, Jr.), p. xxxviii.

2. Ibid., p. xxxix.

3. Ibid., p. xlii.

4. Ibid.

5. Princeton Manuscripts; *Selected Letters*, pp. 46–47.

6. *Selected Letters*, p. 47.

7. *I'll Take My Stand*, p. 47.

8. All quotations from *I'll Take My Stand*, p. xlvi.

9. See Blotner, vol. I, p. 638.

10. December 30, 1930; Alderman Library.

11. Nobel Prize address.

12. Cleanth Brooks detects the influence of Irvin S. Cobb on this story, more generally on Faulkner. See Brooks's *William Faulkner: Toward Yoknapatawpha and Beyond*, pp. 375–76.

13. *Collected Stories* (New York: Random House, 1950), p. 169.

14. Ibid., p. 511.

15. Ibid., p. 531.

16. Ibid., p. 481.

17. Ibid., p. 495.

18. From "The End of the World."

19. From "Anthem for Doomed Youth."

20. Both in the Rowan Oak Papers of the University of Mississippi.

21. *Collected Stories*, p. 360.

22. Ibid., p. 736.

23. Blotner, vol. I, p. 668.

24. Ibid., p. 537.

25. *Collected Stories*, p. 665.

26. Ibid., p. 359.

27. Ibid. All three quotations from page 187.

Chapter Fourteen: Into the Mouth of Cannon

1. Blotner, vol. I, p. 678.

2. Alderman Library.

3. Blotner, *One-Volume Edition*, p. 275.

4. Ibid., p. 627.

5. *Collected Stories*, p. 799.

6. To Ben Wasson, Alderman Library; *Selected Letters*, pp. 71–72.

7. *Collected Stories*, op. cit., p. 792.

8. *Uncollected Stories*, p. 593.

9. Ibid., p. 595. Following quotations from pp. 595 and 598.

10. Ibid., p. 600.

11. Ibid., p. 606. Following quotation from p. 608.

12. *Faulkner in the University*, p. 74.

13. *Faulkner in the University*, p. 199. Many foreign translations—see, for example, the Dutch—went along with the pregnancy interpretation of the title and used

the foreign word for "lightening" oneself of a burden. In still another class discussion, Faulkner repeated, on May 30, 1957, that "somewhere about the middle of the month [in Mississippi] when suddenly there's a foretaste of fall, it's cool, there's a lambence, a luminous quality to the light, as though it came not from just today but from back in the old classic times. It might have fauns and satyrs and the gods and—from Greece, from Olympus in it somewhere" *(Faulkner in the University,* p. 199). Some of this very language appeared in the published novel, in reference to the Reverend Hightower. Michael Millgate sees the opening of *Light in August* as suggestive of Thomas Hardy's *The Mayor of Casterbridge,* but the overall conception of the novel, once we move past the beginning, is not Hardy's.

14. Library of America, *Light in August,* p. 543.

15. Ibid., p. 585.

16. Ibid., p. 586. Two following quotations from same page.

17. Perhaps Hightower's uncertainty about his identity is linked to the question of what happens to him. Some readers feel he dies, although Faulkner said he did not. Because of his head injury, he is confused and mad, or else undergoing a mixture of madness and sanity toward some final realization.

18. Library of America, *Light in August,* p. 446.

19. In chapter 4.

20. September 24, 1931; Alderman Library.

21. October 22, 1931; *Selected Letters,* p. 52.

22. *Lion in the Garden,* pp. 17–18.

23. Ibid., p. 18.

24. Both quotations from *Selected Letters,* pp. 52–53.

25. Ibid., p. 53. Following quotation from same page.

26. Blotner, vol. 1, p. 735.

27. *Lion in the Garden,* p. 20, for all quotations.

28. Ibid., p. 21.

29. Ibid., p. 24.

30. Blotner, vol. 1, p. 739.

31. Library of America, *Light in August,* p. 561. Following quotation from same page.

32. Ibid., p. 563.

33. Ibid., p. 565.

34. Ibid., pp. 482–83.

35. Ibid., p. 487.

36. Both in chapter 5, the first time while listening to Brown's (Lucas's) breathing, the second time as he moves toward Joanna's house.

Chapter Fifteen: Anti-Eden

1. Blotner, vol. 1, p. 751.

2. Alderman Library; *Selected Letters,* pp. 54–55.

3. Library of America, *Light in August,* p. 559.

4. Alderman Library; *Selected Letters,* pp. 56–77.

5. Mid-January 1932, Alderman Library; *Selected Letters*, p. 58. Following quotation from Alderman Library, received January 26, 1932; *Selected Letters*, p. 59.

6. Alderman Library, Winter 1932; *Selected Letters*, p. 60. Following quotation from same source and page.

7. *Lion in the Garden*, p. 29.

8. Ibid., p. 32. Following quotation from same page.

9. *Selected Letters*, p. 61.

10. Library of America, *Light in August*, p. 585. Following quotation from same page.

11. Ibid., p. 590.

12. Blotner, vol. 1, p. 767.

13. Ibid., p. 772, and Notes.

14. Ibid., p. 775.

15. "Turn About" became transformed into *Today We Live*, the original distorted almost beyond recognition by the need to give Joan Crawford a role. The studio (MGM) publicity: "William Faulkner is named as being, with Ernest Hemingway, author of 'Farewell to Arms,' the greatest literary discovery of the decade." From Bruce F. Kawin, *Faulkner's MGM Screenplays* (Knoxville: University of Tennessee Press, 1982), p. 109.

16. Blotner, vol. 1, p. 782.

17. Library of America, *Light in August*, pp. 623–24.

18. Emerson, *Faulkner's Early Literary Reputation in America*, p. 24.

19. November (?) 1932, Alderman Library; *Selected Letters*, p. 68.

20. Library of America, *Light in August*, p. 582.

21. *Selected Letters* (Christmas 1932), p. 69.

22. Alderman Library; *Selected Letters*, p. 70.

23. Ibid., p. 762.

Chapter Sixteen: Air and Airless

1. Alderman Library typescript; *Selected Letters*, p. 71.

2. See Kawin, *Faulkner's MGM Screenplays*, for a discussion of the script, followed by the script itself, p. 429ff.

3. *Lion in the Garden*, part of the apocryphal story he repeated to Jean Stein in that *Paris Review* interview.

4. Alderman Library; *Selected Letters*, p. 71. Following letter and quotation from same source; *Selected Letters*, p. 72.

5. *Selected Letters*, July 19, 1933, p. 73.

6. Alderman Library, summer of 1933; *Selected Letters*, p. 73.

7. *A Faulkner Miscellany*, p. 157.

8. Alderman Library, mid-August 1933; *Selected Letters*, p. 74.

9. October (?) 1933; *Selected Letters*, p. 75.

10. *Collected Stories*, p. 539.

11. Ibid., pp. 548–49. Following quotation from p. 547.

12. Ibid., p. 550. Following quotation from p. 539.

13. Ibid., p. 64.

14. To Morton Goldman, March–April 1934, Alderman Library; *Selected Letters,* p. 79.

15. Alderman Library; *Selected Letters,* p. 78, for both quotations.

16. Alderman Library, February 1934; *Selected Letters,* pp. 78–79.

17. Alderman Library, already cited for March–April 1934; *Selected Letters,* p. 79.

18. Alderman Library, late spring–early summer 1934; *Selected Letters,* pp. 80–81.

19. Alderman Library; *Selected Letters,* p. 83. Following quotation from same source.

20. Alderman Library; *Selected Letters,* pp. 83–84.

21. Alderman Library; *Selected Letters,* p. 87.

22. March 7, 1957; *Faulkner in the University,* p. 36. Following quotation from same source.

23. Blotner, vol. i, p. 839.

24. *Oxford Magazine:* pp. 13–14. Following quotation from same source.

25. *The Unvanquished* (New York: Signet, 1952; orig. publ. 1938), p. 126.

26. Blotner, vol. i, p. 857ff.

27. October 18, 1934, Alderman Library; *Selected Letters,* p. 85.

28. Late December 1934, Alderman Library; *Selected Letters,* p. 87. Following quotation from same source, p. 86.

29. Library of America, *Pylon,* p. 788, for all three quotations.

30. Ibid., p. 787.

31. Ibid., p. 790.

32. Ibid., p. 970.

Chapter Seventeen: The Death of Absalom

1. Scene 5, lines 9–13. Following quotation from lines 19–28.

2. January 21, 1935, Alderman Library; *Selected Letters,* p. 88.

3. Ibid., p. 721.

4. To Smith, early February (?) 1935, Alderman Library; *Selected Letters,* p. 88. Following quotations from Alderman Library and p. 89 (to Goldman, February 18, 1935).

5. Alderman Library; *Selected Letters,* p. 90.

6. March (?) 1935, Alderman Library; *Selected Letters,* p. 90. Following quotation from Alderman Library and *Selected Letters,* p. 91.

7. *Collected Stories,* pp. 184–85. Following quotations from pp. 186, 190, 192 of *Collected Stories.*

8. Ibid., p. 199.

9. See *Uncollected Stories,* pp. 684–85, note.

10. Oxford *Eagle,* April 4, 1935.

· 11. *Faulkner in the University*, p. 76. Following quotation from same source, p. 75.

12. Ibid., p. 35.

13. *Absalom, Absalom!* (the Corrected Text, New York: Vintage Books, 1987), p. 118.

14. Ibid., p. 119.

15. Ibid., p. 148.

16. Late July 1935, Alderman Library; *Selected Letters*, p. 92.

17. *Selected Letters*, p. 92. Following quotation from same source and page.

18. Blotner, vol. 1, p. 903.

19. Alderman Library; *Selected Letters*, p. 93. Following quotation from same source, p. 94.

20. Meta Carpenter Wilde and Orin Borsten, *A Loving Gentleman: The Love Story of William Faulkner and Meta Carpenter* (New York: Simon & Schuster, 1976), p. 16. Following quotation from same source, p. 27.

21. Ibid., pp. 323–24.

22. Blotner, vol. 2, p. 927.

23. *Selected Letters*, pp. 94–95.

24. Alderman Library typescript; *Selected Letters*, p. 95. Following quotation from same source, p. 96.

25. Blotner, vol. 2, p. 938.

26. Blotner, vol. 2, p. 939.

27. September 4, 1936, Alderman Library typescript; *Selected Letters*, p. 96.

28. Wilde and Borsten, *A Loving Gentleman*, p. 172. Following quotation from same source, p. 173.

29. Ibid., p. 173. Following quotation from same source, pp. 174–75.

30. Ibid., p. 46 for both quotations.

31. Ibid., p. 183.

32. Blotner, vol. 2, p. 945.

33. Rainer Maria Rilke, *Letters on Cézanne*, trans. Joel Agee (New York: Fromm), p. 64.

34. December 28, 1936, Alderman Library; *Selected Letters*, p. 97.

Chapter Eighteen: Anguish

1. February 26, 1937; *Selected Letters*, p. 99.

2. Wilde and Borsten, *A Loving Gentleman*, p. 186. Three following quotations from same source, pp. 187–88.

3. Ibid., p. 194. Following quotation from p. 195.

4. Blotner, vol. 2, p. 956.

5. *Uncollected Stories*, p. 434.

6. *The Unvanquished*, p. 146.

7. Received January 27, 1947, Alderman Library; *Selected Letters*, p. 245. Following quotation from same source, p. 245.

8. Postmarked July 28, 1937; *Selected Letters*, p. 101.

9. Blotner, vol. 2, p. 971.

10. *Knight's Gambit* (New York: Vintage Books, 1978), pp. 50–51.

11. *Memoirs* (Chapel Hill: University of North Carolina Press, 1969), p. 466.

12. *Essays, Speeches & Public Letters,* p. 10.

13. *Lion in the Garden,* pp. 33–34 for all quotations.

14. *Selected Letters,* p. 101.

15. August 8, 1952, Alderman Library; *Selected Letters,* p. 338.

16. *Lion in the Garden,* pp. 247–48.

17. *Selected Letters,* op. cit., p. 102.

18. December 28, 1937; ibid., p. 103.

19. *The Wild Palms* (New York: Vintage Books, n.d.), pp. 81–82. Following quotation from same source, p. 82.

20. Ibid., p. 140. Following quotation from same source, p. 141.

21. Ibid., p. 57.

22. Ibid., p. 135. Following quotation from same source and page.

23. Wilde and Borsten, *A Loving Gentleman,* p. 228.

24. *The Wild Palms,* p. 266. Following quotations from same source and page.

25. Ibid., p. 204.

26. Ibid., p. 324.

27. Letters of February 19 and 28, 1938, Alderman Library; *Selected Letters,* pp. 104–5.

28. *My Brother Bill,* p. 177.

29. *Selected Letters,* p. 106. Following three quotations from same source, p. 106.

30. *My Brother Bill,* p. 195.

31. *A Loving Gentleman,* p. 237.

32. Ibid., pp. 241–42.

33. December 15, 1938; *Selected Letters,* pp. 107–8.

34. *The Hamlet,* p. 3.

Chapter Nineteen: Midcareer

1. *The Hamlet,* p. 100 for both quotations. Following quotation, p. 96.

2. Ibid., pp. 96–97.

3. Ibid., p. 111.

4. Ibid., p. 113.

5. *Lion in the Garden,* p. 37. Following quotation, p. 36.

6. Ibid., p. 38. Following quotation, p. 39.

7. *Selected Letters,* p. 114.

8. *Go Down, Moses* (New York: Modern Library, n.d.), p. 181.

9. "The Old People," *Uncollected Stories,* p. 204.

10. Ibid., p. 186.

11. Blotner, vol. 2, p. 1030.

12. *Selected Letters,* p. 116.

13. Ibid. Following quotation from same source, p. 116.

14. In another dimension of interrelatedness, Faulkner at first overlapped the story "Go Down, Moses" with aspects of *Absalom, Absalom!* In the fourteen-page typescript of the story, the character who becomes Samuel Worsham Beauchamp in the book version is named Henry Coldfield Sutpen. Faulkner's decision at first to use Sutpen is another example of the "intertextuality" of his own imagination.

15. February 5, 1940; *Selected Letters*, p. 117.

16. February 7, 1940; *Selected Letters*, pp. 118–19.

17. Monday, April 1. The Fadiman review in the *New Yorker* appeared April 6.

18. To Robert Haas, April 18, 1940; *Selected Letters*, p. 121.

19. Ibid., p. 122. Following two quotations from same source, p. 122.

20. Ibid., pp. 122–23.

21. Ibid., pp. 123–24.

22. That "sage of Baltimore" and occasional drinking companion of Faulkner's did not think too highly of the writer, saying there was no more sense in Faulkner "than in the wop boob, Dante." (Quoted by Charles A. Fecher in *Mencken: A Study of His Thought* [New York: Knopf, 1978], p. 251.) Stark Young put his distaste of his friend's work differently: "I am an old friend and appreciator of William Faulkner but not a raging admirer." (In *Stark Young: A Life in the Arts: Letters 1900–1962*, ed. John Pilkington [Baton Rouge: Louisiana State University Press], 1975, p. 1408.)

23. *Selected Letters*, p. 125.

24. Ibid.

25. June 1, 1940; ibid., p. 126.

26. Ibid., pp. 129–30.

27. June 18, 1940; ibid., p. 130.

28. Ibid., p. 132.

29. Ibid., p. 135 for both quotations.

30. Ibid., p. 134.

31. October 5, 1940; ibid., p. 136.

32. Ibid., pp. 136–37.

33. Recalling John B. Cullen's comment, in *Old Times in the Faulkner Country*, about how Faulkner's eyeballs rolled back and his kidneys locked (p. 16).

34. *Selected Letters*, p. 138.

35. *Uncollected Stories*, pp. 273–74.

36. *Go Down, Moses*, p. 349.

37. Ibid., p. 354. Following quotation, p. 354.

38. *Uncollected Stories*, pp. 279–80.

39. To Robert Haas, May 1, 1941; *Selected Letters*, p. 139.

40. Ibid., p. 60.

41. *Selected Letters*, p. 142.

42. *Go Down, Moses*, p. 70.

43. Ibid., p. 111. Following quotation, p. 112.

44. *Selected Letters*, p. 146.

45. To Saxe Commins, December 7 (?), 1941; ibid., p. 147.

46. *Uncollected Stories,* p. 294.

Chapter Twenty: Midcareer: At War

1. To Nathan, November 18, 1941; *Selected Letters,* p. 145.

2. Blotner, vol. 2, p. 1087.

3. Mid-December 1941; *Selected Letters,* p. 147.

4. January 19, 1942, Alderman Library; *Selected Letters,* p. 148.

5. June 22, 1942, Alderman Library; *Selected Letters,* p. 153.

6. To Ober, received March 30, 1942, Alderman Library; *Selected Letters,* p. 150.

7. March 30, 1942, Alderman Library; *Selected Letters,* p. 150.

8. June 6 (?), 1942; *Selected Letters,* p. 152.

9. *Go Down, Moses,* p. 118.

10. Ibid., pp. 110–11.

11. Ibid., p. 111.

12. Ibid., p. 208. Following quotations, p. 209 for both.

13. Ibid., p. 246.

14. Ibid., p. 258. Following quotations, pp. 258, 258–59.

15. Mid-June (?) 1942, Princeton typescript; *Selected Letters,* p. 152.

16. *Selected Letters,* p. 155.

17. June 28, 1942, Alderman Library; *Selected Letters,* p. 155. Following quotation from same source, p. 156.

18. July 18, 1942, Alderman Library; *Selected Letters,* p. 157.

19. Ibid., to Herndon.

20. Received July 20, 1942, Alderman Library; *Selected Letters,* p. 159. Following quotation, p. 159.

21. Alderman Library; *Selected Letters,* p. 160.

22. Ibid., p. 162. Following quotation, p. 162.

23. To Haas, early August (?) 1942; *Selected Letters,* p. 163.

24. Mid-September (?) 1942; *Selected Letters,* p. 163.

25. *Selected Letters,* p. 163.

26. Ibid., p. 335.

27. Ibid., p. xxxiii.

28. Ibid., p. 110. Anyone interested in this phase of Faulkner's professional life finds himself indebted to this volume in the Brodsky Collection. It was produced through the continuing support of the Center for the Study of Southern Culture, directed by William Ferris.

29. Wilde and Borsten, *A Loving Gentleman,* p. 252.

30. Ibid., p. 264.

31. Ibid., p. 277.

32. Ibid., p. 279.

33. Ibid., p. 286.

34. Ibid., p. 309.

35. Alderman Library; *Selected Letters,* p. 167. Following quotation, p. 167.

36. Ibid., p. 169.

37. Ibid., p. 172.

38. April 27, 1943; *Selected Letters,* p. 172.

39. Ibid., p. 173.

Chapter Twenty-one: Midcareer: The Hollywood War

1. For the consolidation of "Battle Cry" details, I am indebted to Louis Daniel Brodsky and Robert W. Hamblin for their meticulous edition of *Battle Cry: A Screenplay by William Faulkner;* vol. 4, of *Faulkner: A Comprehensive Guide to the Brodsky Collection.*

2. July 1, 1943; *Selected Letters,* p. 175.

3. *Selected Letters,* pp. 175–76.

4. November 17, 1943, Alderman Library; *Selected Letters,* p. 179. Following quotations, p. 179.

5. *Selected Letters,* p. 178.

6. *A Fable* (New York: Random House, 1954), p. 328.

7. See "Battle Cry," pp. xlv–xlviii.

8. *A Fable,* p. 305.

9. *Faulkner-Cowley File,* dated October 25, 1943.

10. Alderman Library; *Selected Letters,* p. 181.

11. Ibid., p. 181.

12. May 7, 1944, Yale typescript; *Selected Letters,* p. 182. Following quotation, p. 182.

13. *Faulkner-Cowley File,* pp. 9–10.

14. May 18, 1944, Alderman Library; *Selected Letters,* p. 183.

15. To Ober, May 29, 1944, Alderman Library; *Selected Letters,* p. 184.

16. *Faulkner-Cowley File,* p. 13.

17. To Cowley, Yale typescript; *Selected Letters,* p. 185. Following quotations from same letter, pp. 185, 185–86, 186.

18. Wilde and Borsten, *A Loving Gentleman,* p. 309.

19. To James J. Geller, mid-December 1944; *Selected Letters,* p. 187.

20. To Ober, December 20, 1944, Alderman Library; *Selected Letters,* p. 187. Following quotation, p. 187.

Chapter Twenty-two: Postbellum

1. January 10, 1945, Alderman Library; *Selected Letters,* p. 188.

2. To Ober, March 19, 1945, Alderman Library; *Selected Letters,* pp. 190–91. Following quotation, p. 191.

3. "William Faulkner Revisited," *Saturday Review* (April 14, 1945).

4. Details from Stone's letter to Cowley; Blotner, vol. 2, pp. 1181–82.

5. May 25, 1945, Alderman Library; *Selected Letters,* p. 192.

6. Alderman Library; *Selected Letters*, p. 194.

7. Alderman Library; *Selected Letters*, p. 196. Following quotation, p. 196.

8. *Selected Letters*, p. 194.

9. *Faulkner-Cowley File*, p. 23.

10. Ibid., p. 24.

11. Yale typescript; *Selected Letters*, p. 197. Following quotation, p. 197.

12. Alderman Library; *Selected Letters*, p. 199. Following quotation, p. 199.

13. Ibid., pp. 199–200.

14. September 11 (?), 1945; *Selected Letters*, p. 201.

15. Alderman Library; *Selected Letters*, p. 202.

16. *Faulkner-Cowley File*, p. 29. Following quotation, p. 30.

17. Ibid., p. 203.

18. To Cowley, October 5, 1945, Yale typescript; *Selected Letters*, pp. 203–204.

19. *Selected Letters*, p. 204.

20. Ibid., p. 205.

21. To Cowley, October 27, 1945, Yale typescript; *Selected Letters*, p. 206.

22. *Selected Letters*, p. 209.

23. *Faulkner-Cowley File*, p. 60. Following quotation, p. 61.

24. To Cowley, December 8, 1945, Yale typescript; *Selected Letters*, p. 212. Following quotation, p. 213.

25. *Faulkner-Cowley File*, p. 68.

26. Ibid., p. 217.

27. To Ober, January 5, 1946, Alderman Library; *Selected Letters*, p. 218.

28. To Cowley, Yale typescript; *Selected Letters*, p. 219.

29. Yale typescript; *Selected Letters*, pp. 219–20.

30. To Robert N. Linscott; *Selected Letters*, p. 221.

31. Yale typescript; *Selected Letters*, pp. 222–23.

32. To Haas; *Selected Letters*, p. 225.

33. Ibid., p. 226.

34. March 30, 1946; *Selected Letters*, p. 232.

35. Ibid.

36. Received April 18, 1946, Alderman Library; *Selected Letters*, p. 233.

37. April 23, 1946, Yale typescript; *Selected Letters*, p. 233. During this pleasant time with the *Portable*, in the background there was considerable studio byplay. See vol. 2 of the Brodsky Collection, *The Letters*, pp. 38–41. Although some of these letters or memos reached Faulkner's ears, he was clear of the infighting.

38. *Faulkner-Cowley File*, p. 93. Following quotation, p. 94.

39. To Haas, May 5, 1946; *Selected Letters*, p. 234.

40. To Lambert Davis, Warren's editor, July 25, 1946, Yale typescript; *Selected Letters*, p. 239.

41. Mid-August (?) 1946; *Selected Letters,* p. 241.

42. To Haas, December 8, 1946; *Selected Letters,* p. 244.

PART V: *FAME, FORTUNE, AND FEAR*

Chapter Twenty-three: Post-Portable

1. Received March 24, 1947, Alderman Library; *Selected Letters,* p. 246.

2. March 24 (?), 1947; *Selected Letters,* p. 247.

3. Spring 1947; *Selected Letters,* pp. 248–49. Following quotation, p. 248.

4. *Lion in the Garden,* p. 58.

5. *Selected Letters,* p. 249.

6. June 28, 1947; *Selected Letters,* p. 251.

7. Received June 9, 1947, Alderman Library; *Selected Letters,* p. 250.

8. To Haas, August 24, 1947; *Selected Letters,* pp. 253–54.

9. Received September 4, 1947; *Selected Letters,* pp. 254–55.

10. December 5, 1947, Alderman Library; *Selected Letters,* p. 261. Following quotation, p. 261.

11. Ibid. Following quotation, p. 262.

12. July 27, 1958; *Letters of Flannery O'Connor: The Habit of Being,* ed. Sally Fitzgerald (New York: Farrar, Straus & Giroux, 1979), p. 291.

13. March 20, 1958, to "A"; *Letters,* p. 273.

14. To Ober, Alderman Library; *Selected Letters,* p. 262.

15. February 22 (?), 1948; *Selected Letters,* p. 263.

16. To Ober, April 27 (?), 1948, Alderman Library; *Selected Letters,* p. 267.

17. Blotner, vol. 2, p. 1261; *Selected Letters,* p. 276.

18. To Haas, September 18, 1948; *Selected Letters,* p. 273.

19. Ibid., p. 155.

20. September 28, 1948; *Selected Letters,* p. 276.

21. Blotner, vol. 2, p. 1265. Faulkner apparently tried on other occasions as well.

22. *Faulkner-Cowley File,* p. 104.

23. Ibid., p. 107. Following quotation, p. 11.

24. Blotner, vol. 2, p. 1266.

25. To Cowley, November 1, 1948, Yale typescript; *Selected Letters,* p. 278.

26. *Selected Letters,* p. 280.

27. Ibid., p. 280.

Chapter Twenty-four: The Prize

1. Yale typescript; *Selected Letters,* p. 282.

2. Ibid.

3. *Faulkner-Cowley File,* p. 123.

4. January 26, 1949; *Selected Letters,* pp. 24–85.

5. To Cowley, February 11, 1949, Yale typescript; *Selected Letters*, p. 285.

6. *Faulkner-Cowley File*, p. 128.

7. *Selected Letters*, p. 287.

8. February 23, 1949; ibid., p. 286. Devine was the friend who broke into Faulkner's room at the Algonquin and found him unconscious, a steam pipe cooking his back.

9. Blotner, vol. 2, p. 1291.

10. Blotner, *One-Volume Edition*, p. 507.

11. To Ober, October 14, 1949, Alderman Library; *Selected Letters*, p. 294.

12. February 22, 1950, Alderman Library; *Selected Letters*, p. 299.

13. Postmarked January 13, 1950, Alderman Library; *Selected Letters*, pp. 297–98.

14. *Selected Letters*, p. 75.

15. Blotner, vol. 2, p. 1308.

16. February 13, 1950, Alderman Library; *Selected Letters*, p. 298.

17. February 17 (?), 1950, Alderman Library; *Selected Letters*, p. 299.

18. Alderman Library; *Selected Letters*, p. 299.

19. March 22, 1950, Alderman Library; *Selected Letters*, pp. 300–301.

20. *Essays, Speeches & Public Letters*, pp. 203–204.

21. Ibid., p. 205.

22. April 1, 1950; *Selected Letters*, p. 302.

23. June 12, 1950; *Essays, Speeches & Public Letters*, p. 206.

24. Blotner, *One-Volume Edition*, p. 518.

25. May 19, 1950, Alderman Library; *Selected Letters*, pp. 303–4. Following quotation, pp. 303–4.

26. Mid-May 1950; *Selected Letters*, p. 304.

27. Mid-May 1950; ibid., p. 305.

28. Ibid., p. 305.

29. *Faulkner, The Letters*, vol. 2.

30. Alderman Library; *Selected Letters*, p. 307. Blotner cites Hemingway's *Across the River and into the Trees* as a parallel fiction; *Selected Letters*, p. 307, n. 1.

31. Blotner, vol. 2, p. 1329.

32. Ibid., p. 94.

33. Ibid.

34. *Selected Letters*, p. 309.

35. Blotner, vol. 2, p. 1344.

36. "William Faulkner's Art," in Maurice Coindreau, *The Time of William Faulkner* (Columbia: University of South Carolina Press, 1971), pp. 67–68. (Originally published as "L'Art du William Faulkner," *France-Amérique*, December 3, 1950.)

37. Brodsky, vol. 2, p. 47.

38. Ibid., p. 1347ff.

39. *Selected Letters*, p. 309.

40. *Faulkner-Cowley File,* p. 129.

41. Several details from Blotner's description of the Stockholm trip. Faulkner's Nobel Prize acceptance speech is available in *Essays, Speeches & Public Letters.*

42. *Selected Letters,* p. 310.

Chapter Twenty-five: After the Prize

1. Alderman Library; *Selected Letters,* p. 312.

2. Wilde and Borsten, *A Loving Gentleman,* p. 324.

3. March 4, 1951, Alderman Library; *Selected Letters,* p. 313.

4. Faulkner, *The Letters,* vol. 2, p. 62.

5. Ibid., p. 60.

6. Ibid., p. 66.

7. Ibid., p. 318.

8. June 18, 1951, Alderman Library; *Selected Letters,* p. 317.

9. To Else Jonsson, August 27, 1951; ibid., p. 321.

10. To Else Jonsson, September 30, 1951; ibid., p. 322. "I am all over the U. S. at present, or half of it."

11. *Requiem for a Nun,* p. 90.

12. To Else Jonsson, November 30, 1951; *Selected Letters,* p. 323.

13. November 18, 1951, Alderman Library; *Selected Letters,* p. 322.

14. January (?) 1952; *Selected Letters,* p. 326.

15. To Else Jonsson, April 19, 1952; ibid., pp. 330–31.

16. May 7, 1952, Alderman Library; *Selected Letters,* p. 331.

17. *Essays, Speeches & Public Letters,* pp. 126–34.

18. Blotner, vol. 2, p. 1417.

19. Postmarked July 30; ibid., p. 80.

20. To Commins, ibid. Following quotation, p. 80.

21. Alderman Library; *Selected Letters,* p. 337.

22. August 12, 1952, Alderman Library; *Selected Letters,* p. 338.

23. Blotner, vol. 2, p. 1432.

24. August 19, 1952; *Selected Letters,* p. 339.

25. August 20, 1952, Alderman Library; *Selected Letters,* p. 339.

26. Faulkner, *The Letters,* vol. 2. Following quotation, p. 89.

27. Ibid., p. 90.

28. October 8, 1952; ibid., p. 91.

29. Ibid., p. 92.

30. September 29, 1952; ibid., p. 84.

31. *Lion in the Garden,* p. 70. Following quotations, pp. 70–71.

32. Ibid., p. 71.

33. Ibid., p. 72.

34. Ibid.

35. February 29 (sic); *Faulkner, The Letters*, vol. 2, p. 135.

36. To Commins, December 24, 1952 (?); ibid., p. 103. Following quotation, p. 104.

Chapter Twenty-six: Walking the Edge

1. January 5, 1953; *Selected Letters*, p. 345.

2. February 16, 1953; *Selected Letters*, p. 346.

3. *Uncollected Stories*, p. 436.

4. April 29, 1953; *Selected Letters*, p. 348.

5. June 16 (?), 1953, Alderman Library; *Selected Letters*, p. 349.

6. June 18, 1953, Alderman Library; *Selected Letters*, p. 350.

7. Ibid., p. 351.

8. *Faulkner, The Letters*, vol. 2, p. 117. (Postmarked July 31, 1953.)

9. Early August 1953; *Selected Letters*, p. 352.

10. August 29, 1953; ibid., p. 353.

11. September 4, 1953; Blotner, vol. 2, p. 1463.

12. October 1, 1953; *Faulkner, The Letters*, vol. 2, p. 120.

13. October 7, 1953; *Selected Letters*, p. 154.

14. "The Private World of William Faulkner," *Life* (September 28, 1953), pp. 118–36. This became the title of Coughlan's book in 1954.

15. October 5, 1953; *Faulkner, The Letters*, vol. 2, p. 121.

16. Dorothy Commins, *What Is An Editor: Saxe Commins at Work* (Chicago: University of Chicago Press, 1978), p. 200.

17. *Faulkner, The Letters*, vol. 2, p. 122.

18. Commins, *What Is An Editor*, p. 200.

19. Alderman Library; *Selected Letters*, p. 357.

20. December 12, 1953; *Selected Letters*, p. 357.

21. To Joan Williams, January 11, 1954, Alderman Library; *Selected Letters*, p. 358.

22. December 14, 1953; *Faulkner, The Letters*, vol. 2, p. 130.

23. January 29 (?), 1954; ibid., p. 132.

24. To Commins, February 4, 1954; *Selected Letters*, p. 351. Following quotation, p. 362.

25. Postmarked February 6, 1954; *Faulkner, The Letters*, vol. 2, p. 132.

26. Ibid., p. 134.

27. March 1954; ibid., p. 136, for all quotations.

28. Postmarked March 14, 1954; ibid., p. 138.

29. Ibid.

30. In a lengthy letter to Robert Coughlan on a variety of matters, Phil Stone indicates that Faulkner will never return to Oxford, first because he meets only idolaters in New York, and, second, because "he is permanently getting rid of Estelle" (April 15, 1954; ibid., p. 143).

31. Blotner, vol. 2, p. 1491.

32. To Jean Stein, April 22, 1954; *Selected Letters*, p. 363.

33. June 18, 1954; ibid., p. 365.

34. To Klopfer, June 19, 1954; ibid., p. 366.

35. *Newsweek* (August 2, 1954).

36. To Ober, received November 17, 1943, Alderman Library; *Selected Letters*, p. 179.

37. *A Fable*, quotations from pp. 295, 328, 13, 71–72, respectively.

38. Ibid., p. 305.

39. Ibid., p. 126.

40. *A Fable*, beginning p. 212.

41. August 24, 1947; *Selected Letters*, pp. 253–54.

42. *Faulkner, The Letters*, vol. 2, p. 189 notes.

43. August 15 (actually 16), 1954; *Selected Letters*, p. 369.

44. *Uncollected Stories*, p. 310.

45. Ibid., pp. 453–54.

46. Ibid., p. 455.

47. Mid- or late October, 1954; *Selected Letters*, p. 372.

48. *Faulkner, The Letters*, vol. 2, p. 169.

49. Mid-November, 1954; *Selected Letters*, p. 372.

Chapter Twenty-seven: Approaching a Sixty-Year-Old Smiling Man

1. *Essays, Speeches & Public Letters*, pp. 143–45.

2. June 12, 1955; *Selected Letters*, p. 382.

3. *Essays, Speeches & Public Letters*, pp. 215–16.

4. April 4, 1955, Alderman Library; *Selected Letters*, pp. 379–80. Following quotation, p. 380.

5. To Mississippi state representative Dave Womack, March 28, 1955; *Faulkner, The Letters*, vol. 2, p. 180.

6. *Selected Letters*, p. 384.

7. *Lion in the Garden*, p. 88.

8. Ibid., p. 89. Following quotation, p. 90.

9. Ibid., p. 94. Following quotation, p. 94.

10. Ibid., p. 96. Following quotation, p. 97.

11. Ibid., p. 98.

12. Ibid., p. 101. At the end of his essay "Mississippi" (*Holiday*, April 1954), Faulkner had expressed similar sentiments: the subject is Mississippi. "Loving all of it even while he had to hate some of it because he knows now that you don't love because: you love despite; not for the virtues, but despite the faults." In part 4 of "The Bear," Ike feels a comparable conflict.

13. Ibid., p. 103.

14. Ibid., p. 105.

15. Ibid., p. 137.

16. Ibid., p. 143.

17. Ibid., p. 149.

18. Ibid., p. 159. Following quotation, p. 159.

19. Ibid., p. 163.

20. *Faulkner, The Letters,* vol. 2, p. 1558 (from communication with Picon, who also kept a diary or journal).

21. Ibid., p. 1564.

22. *Lion in the Garden,* p. 185. Following quotation, pp. 185–86.

23. *Essays, Speeches & Public Letters,* pp. 222–23.

24. *Faulkner, The Letters,* vol. 2, p. 1573.

25. *Lion in the Garden,* p. 230.

26. *Essays, Speeches & Public Letters,* p. 146.

27. To Bob Flautt, president of the Lions Club of Glendora, December 8, 1955, Alderman Library; *Selected Letters,* p. 389. Following quotation, p. 389.

Chapter Twenty-eight: Remaking the Past, Retelling the Story

1. January 13, 1956; *Selected Letters,* p. 391.

2. *Lion in the Garden,* pp. 23, 39 for the quotations.

3. *Partial Portrait* (Ann Arbor: University of Michigan Press, n.d.), p. 388.

4. *Lion in the Garden,* p. 247.

5. Ibid., p. 248.

6. Ibid., p. 252. Following quotation, p. 253.

7. Ibid., p. 255.

8. To Ober, January 18, 1956, Alderman Library; *Selected Letters,* p. 392. Following quotation, p. 392.

9. *Faulkner, The Letters,* vol. 2, pp. 189–90.

10. *Essays, Speeches & Public Letters,* p. 100.

11. Ibid., p. 104.

12. *Lion in the Garden,* p. 261.

13. Alderman Library; *Selected Letters,* p. 391.

14. *Lion in the Garden,* p. 258.

15. Ibid., p. 260.

16. Ibid., p. 261.

17. Ibid., p. 262.

18. *Lion in the Garden,* p. 264.

19. Ibid., p. 265.

20. *Essays, Speeches & Public Letters,* p. 88.

21. *Selected Letters,* pp. 395–96.

22. April 17, 1956; ibid., p. 398.

23. Details from *Faulkner, The Letters,* vol. 2, p. 1605ff.

24. *Essays, Speeches & Public Letters,* vol. 2, p. 110.

25. Ibid., p. 112.

26. August 12, 1956; *Selected Letters,* p. 402.

27. *Faulkner, The Letters,* vol. 2, p. 196.

28. Ibid., p. 199.

29. Ibid., p. 200.

30. Blotner, vol. 2, p. 1625.

31. *Faulkner, The Letters*, vol. 2, p. 206, for both quotations.

32. *Faulkner in the University*, p. 35. First quotation, p. 29.

33. Details from Blotner, vol. 2, pp. 1645–46.

34. Ibid., notes, pp. 129–30.

35. *Essays, Speeches & Public Letters*, p. 152.

36. Postmarked April 17, 1957; *Faulkner, The Letters*, vol. 2, p. 213.

37. April 24, 1957; ibid., p. 214.

38. From a private source.

39. *Faulkner, The Letters*, vol. 2, pp. 214–15.

40. *Faulkner in the University*, p. 88.

41. Ibid., p. 94.

42. Ibid., p. 107.

43. *The Town* (New York: Random House, 1957), p. 9.

44. Ibid., p. 153.

45. *Faulkner in the University*, p. 162.

46. Ibid., p. 195.

47. Ibid., p. 203.

48. Appeared June 12, 1957; included in *Essays, Speeches & Public Letters*.

PART VI: *THERE WE ARE*

Chapter Twenty-nine: Inhabiting the Mansion

1. September 16, 1957, to James B. Meriwether; *Faulkner, The Letters*, vol. 2, p. 219.

2. *Essays, Speeches & Public Letters*, p. 231.

3. In Mailer's *Advertisements for Myself*; *Selected Letters*, p. 411. It was unsigned.

4. *Faulkner, The Letters*, vol. 2, p. 222.

5. Ibid., p. 223.

6. December 13, 1957; ibid., p. 224. Following quotations, pp. 224–25.

7. William Sloane to Saxe Commins, January 14, 1958; ibid., p. 229.

8. Ibid., pp. 229–30.

9. To Saxe Commins, February 5, 1958; ibid., p. 23.

10. *Faulkner in the University*, p. 210.

11. Ibid., p. 212.

12. Ibid., p. 215.

13. Ibid., p. 218. Following quotations, pp. 219–20.

14. Ibid., p. 225. Following quotation, p. 227.

15. Blotner, vol. 2, p. 1689.

16. Ibid., p. 243. Following quotations, pp. 243, 244.

17. Ibid., p. 245.

18. Ibid., pp. 246–47.

19. Ibid., p. 267. Following quotations, p. 268.

20. May 2, 1958; *Faulkner, The Letters*, vol. 2, p. 240.

21. Ibid., p. 241.

22. To Ober, August 7, 1958, Alderman Library; *Selected Letters*, p. 414.

23. *Essays, Speeches & Public Letters*, p. 230.

24. May 7, 1959; *Selected Letters*, p. 429.

25. *William Faulkner: A Life on Paper*, p. 119.

26. To Ober, December 12, 1958, Alderman Library; *Selected Letters*, p. 417.

27. Erskine to Faulkner, February 6, 1959; *Faulkner, The Letters*, vol. 2, p. 250.

28. Received March 12, 1959; *Selected Letters*, p. 426.

29. May 7 (?), 1959; ibid., p. 429.

30. Faulkner, *My Brother Bill*, p. 258.

31. To Ober, July 26, 1959, Alderman Library; *Selected Letters*, p. 433.

32. November 4, 1959; *Selected Letters*, p. 438.

33. To Joan Williams, November 6, 1959, Alderman Library; *Selected Letters*, p. 438.

34. *The Mansion* (New York: Random House, 1959), p. 91.

35. Ibid., p. 110.

Chapter Thirty: From Oxford to Eternity

1. January 20, 1960; *Selected Letters*, p. 442.

2. *Essays, Speeches & Public Letters*, pp. 113–14.

3. To Anne Louise Davis (an Ober employee), February 8, 1960, Alderman Library; *Selected Letters*, p. 443.

4. February 24, 1960; *Selected Letters*, p. 444. Following quotation, p. 444. The *New York Times* for August 3, 1967, printed the letter, during an intense part of the civil rights movement.

5. January 4, 1960; *Faulkner, The Letters*, vol. 2, p. 269. Following quotation, p. 269.

6. To Dorothy Olding, received June 23, 1960, Alderman Library; *Selected Letters*, p. 445.

7. *Faulkner, The Letters*, vol. 2, pp. 1761–62.

8. Late October or November 1960; *Selected Letters*, p. 450.

9. October 31, 1960; *Faulkner, The Letters*, vol. 2, p. 285.

10. To Kraig Klosson, October 21, 1960; ibid., p. 284.

11. October 18, 1960; ibid., pp. 282–83.

12. Blotner, vol. 2, p. 1777.

13. February 14, 1961, Alderman Library; *Selected Letters*, p. 451.

14. March 2, 1961; *Selected Letters*, p. 452. Following quotation, p. 452.

15. Ibid.

16. March 21, 1961; ibid., p. 453.

17. May or June 1961; ibid., p. 454.

18. Blotner, vol. 2, p. 1790.

19. To Erskine, August 2, 1961; *Selected Letters*, p. 455.

20. Cited above, *Selected Letters*, pp. 123–24.

21. Ibid., p. 455.

22. September 3, 1961; *Faulkner, The Letters,* vol. 2, p. 293. See also the Silver letter of September 1, 1961, p. 291.

23. To James W. Silver, September 10, 1961; ibid., p. 294.

24. Best known for his *Faulkner: Myth and Motion* (Princeton: Princeton University Press, 1968).

25. Stone emphasizes Aiken, to Adams, October 4, 1961; *Faulkner, The Letters,* vol. 2, p. 296. Stone: "Eliot had a big influence on Bill, but Conrad Aiken had almost as much or more. . . ."

26. November 3, 1961; *Selected Letters,* p. 458.

27. November 22, 1961; *Faulkner, The Letters,* vol. 2, p. 298.

28. Received April 10, 1962, Alderman Library; *Selected Letters,* p. 460.

29. *Lion in the Garden,* p. 270. Following three quotations, pp. 271, 272, 273.

30. Ibid., p. 277. Following two quotations, p. 277.

31. Ibid., pp. 277–78. Following quotations, pp. 278, 280.

32. April 23, 1962; *Faulkner, The Letters,* vol. 2, p. 300. Following quotation, p. 301. The dinner was on Sunday, April 28.

33. *Faulkner-Cowley File,* pp. 149–50.

34. June 20, 1962; *Selected Letters,* p. 461.

35. *The Reivers* (New York: Random House, 1962), p. 19.

36. Ibid., p. 263.

37. Blotner, vol. 2, p. 1829.

Index

About the Author

Frederick R. Karl is the author of numerous works of literary criticism and biography, including *The Adversary Literature, American Fictions: 1940–1980, Modern and Modernism: The Sovereignty of the Artist 1885–1925,* and the acclaimed *Joseph Conrad: The Three Lives.* He is general editor and volume coeditor of Joseph Conrad's *Collected Letters,* which will reach eight volumes. In preparing this biography, he has been visiting scholar at the University of Virginia in Charlottesville, the repository of the major Faulkner collection, and visiting professor at the University of Mississippi in Oxford.

Professor of English and American literature at New York University, Dr. Karl lives with his wife in New York City and East Hampton, Long Island.